How Does Psychology Apply to YOUR Everyday Life? This text is full of hundreds of applications of psychology's fascinating findings. Our student reviewers helped us select their 50 favorites, shown here, and continued on the inside of the back cover. ◎ How do biological, psychological, and social-cultural factors contribute to psychological disorders? (Chapter 13) ◎ How are near-death experiences similar to LSD "trips"? (p. 387) ◎ How many college students have experienced depression in the last year? (p. 390) ◎ How does heredity affect the risk of bipolar disorder? depression? anxiety? schizophrenia? anorexia? (pp. 394–395) ◎ How can we alter our thinking in stressful situations so that we feel less anxious? (p. 418) ◎ What should a person look for when selecting a therapist? (p. 424) ◎ How, by adopting a healthier lifestyle, might people find some relief from depression? (pp. 430–431) ◎ What may help prevent psychological disorders? (pp. 431–432) ◎ What psychological factors affect our feelings of hunger? (pp. 260–261) ◎ How do sleep, friends, and genetics affect weight? (pp. 261–262) ◎ Why does it feel so painful to be excluded, ignored, or shunned? (pp. 263–266)

What are the social and emotional effects of all of our online social networking? (pp. 266–268) How do women and men differ at reading others' nonverbal emotions? (p. 275) How do our facial expressions and movements affect the way we feel? (pp. 277–278) How does the stress of life changes (leaving home, divorcing, death in the family, etc.) affect our health? (pp. 284–285) What are some appropriate ways of coping with stress? (p. 291) How is our health affected by social support? (pp. 294–296) Does aerobic exercise work as a therapy for depression and anxiety? (p. 297) What are some predictors of happiness? (p. 305) Are there personality differences among dogs? (p. 323) What is the best predictor of a person's future behavior? (p. 328) Is it true that most of us have a self-serving bias? (pp. 330–331) What are some tips for becoming happier? (p. 306) Would a toddler peering over a steep cliff perceive the dangerous drop-off and draw back? (pp. 146–147) Could we adjust if special glasses turned our world upside down and backwards? (pp. 150–151) In what ways can we control pain? (pp. 155–157)

PSYCHOLOGY
IN EVERYDAY LIFE

PSYCHOLOGY
IN EVERYDAY LIFE
THIRD EDITION

David G. Myers
Hope College
Holland, Michigan

C. Nathan DeWall
University of Kentucky
Lexington, Kentucky

WORTH PUBLISHERS

A Macmillan Higher Education Company

Vice President, Editing, Design, and Media Production:
    Catherine Woods
Publisher: Kevin Feyen
Executive Marketing Manager: Katherine Nurre
Development Editors: Christine Brune, Nancy Fleming
Assistant Editor: Nadina Persaud
Media Editor: Anthony Casciano
Supplements Editor: Betty Probert
Photo Editor: Robin Fadool
Photo Researcher: Donna Ranieri
Art Director: Barbara Reingold
Cover Designer: Lyndall Culbertson
Chapter Opener Designer, Interior and Layout Designer:
    Charles Yuen
Cover Photo: Geri Lavrov/ Photographer's Choice/Getty Images
Cover Illustration: Celia Johnson
Director of Print and Digital Development: Tracey Kuehn
Managing Editor: Lisa Kinne
Senior Project Editor: Jane O'Neill
Illustration Coordinator: Matt McAdams
Illustrations: Shawn Barber, Keith Kasnot, Matt McAdams,
    Evelyn Pence, Don Stewart, TSI Graphics
Production Manager: Sarah Segal
Composition: TSI Graphics
Printing and Binding: RR Donnelley

Library of Congress Control Number: 2013957984

ISBN-13: 978-1-4641-0936-2
ISBN-10: 1-4641-0936-2

Printed in the United States of America

First Printing

David Myers' royalties from the sale of this book are assigned to the
David and Carol Myers Foundation, which exists to receive and distribute funds to other charitable organizations.

Worth Publishers
41 Madison Avenue
New York, NY 10010
www.worthpublishers.com

Permission has been secured to reprint the following photos at the
beginnings of chapters and in the table of contents:

pp. x top left, xlviii, Fotosearch/SuperStock; p. 1 top, Lane Oatey/Getty
Images; p. 1 bottom, Maciej Oleksy/Shutterstock; pp. x top right, 28
center, RubberBall/SuperStock; p. 28 top, © Anna63/Dreamstime.
com; p. 29, © Yuri Arcurs/INSADCO Photography/Alamy; pp. x bottom
right, 66 bottom, Clover/SuperStock; pp. xi left, 66 top left, Image
Source/Getty Images; p. 66 top center, Oliver Rossi/Corbis; p. 66 top
right, © Jose Luis Pelaez Inc/Blend Images/Corbis; p. 67 top, Juice
Images/JupiterImages; p. 67 bottom, Andersen Ross/Blend Images/
Alamy; p. 106, Image Source/SuperStock; p. 107 top, Petrenko Andriy/
Shutterstock; p. 107 bottom, MGP/Getty Images; pp. xi right, 132 center,
Trinette Reed/Blend Images/Getty Images; p. 132 top, Lauren Burke/
Digital Vision/Getty Images; p. 133 top, Rubberball/Mike Kemp/
Getty Images; p. 133 bottom, Eric Isselée/Shutterstock; pp. xii top
left, 166, BLOOMimage/Getty Images; p. 167 top right, Eric Isselée/
Shutterstock; p. 167 top left, Mike Kemp/Rubberball/Getty Images;
p. 167 bottom, Stanislav Solntsev/Digital Vision/Getty Images; pp. xii
bottom left (both images), 192 center, RubberBall/SuperStock; p. 192 top,
© D. Hurst/Alamy; p. 193, © Sigrid Olsson/PhotoAlto/Corbis; pp. xii
right, 218 center, RubberBall/SuperStock; p. 218 top, Lars Christensen/
Shutterstock; p. 219 top, Jaimie Duplass/Shutterstock; p. 219 center,
Johan Swanepoel/Alamy; p. 219 bottom, Life on white/Alamy; pp. xii
left, 254, Don Bayley/Getty Images; p. 255 top, Thomas Northcut/Getty
Images; p. 255 center, Photodisc/Getty; p. 255 bottom, lina aidukaite/
Flickr RF/Getty Images; pp. xiii top right, 282 center, Ann Marie Kurtz/
E+/Getty Images; p. 282 top, Rubberball/Mark Andersen/Getty Images;
p. 283 top, © PhotosIndia.com LLC/Alamy; p. 283 center, © PhotoSpin,
Inc/Alamy; p. 283 bottom, © D. Hurst/Alamy; pp. xiii bottom right, 310
center, Aurora Open/SuperStock; p. 310 top, © VStock/Alamy; p. 310
bottom, Image Source/Getty Images; p. 311 left, Craig Greenhill/
Newspix/Getty Images; p. 311 right, Timothy Large/Shutterstock;
Trinity Mirror/Mirrorpix/Alamy; pp. xiv left, 336, Ryan McVay/
Photodisc/Getty Images; p. 337, © Hero Images/Corbis; pp. xiv right,
370 center, alberto gagna/E+/Getty Images; p. 370 top, © mikeledray/
Shutterstock; p. 370 bottom, Hemera Technologies/Jupiterimages/
Getty; p. 371, Martin Harvey/Jupiterimages; pp. xv, 408 bottom, Colin
Hawkins/Cultura/Getty images; p. 408 top, jaroon/iStockphoto; p. 408
center, Tetra Images/Getty Images; p. 409 left, William Britten/iStock;
p. 409 right, Rubberball/Nicole Hill/Jupiterimages

For Alexandra Corinne Myers,
beloved granddaughter

For my mother, Beverly DeWall (1950–2011),
an educator who provided love, support, and inspiration

About the Authors

Hope College Public Relations

David Myers received his psychology Ph.D. from the University of Iowa. He has spent his career at Hope College, Michigan, where he has taught dozens of introductory psychology sections. Hope College students have invited him to be their commencement speaker and voted him "outstanding professor."

His research and writings have been recognized by the Gordon Allport Intergroup Relations Prize, by a 2010 Honored Scientist award from the Federation of Associations in Behavioral & Brain Sciences, by a 2010 Award for Service on Behalf of Personality and Social Psychology, by a 2013 Presidential Citation from APA Division 2, and by three honorary doctorates.

With support from National Science Foundation grants, Myers' scientific articles have appeared in three dozen scientific periodicals, including *Science, American Scientist, Psychological Science,* and the *American Psychologist.* In addition to his scholarly writing and his textbooks for introductory and social psychology, he also digests psychological science for the general public. His writings have appeared in four dozen magazines, from *Today's Education* to *Scientific American.* He also has authored five general audience books, including *The Pursuit of Happiness* and *Intuition: Its Powers and Perils.*

David Myers has chaired his city's Human Relations Commission, helped found a thriving assistance center for families in poverty, and spoken to hundreds of college and community groups. Drawing on his experience, he also has written articles and a book (*A Quiet World*) about hearing loss, and he is advocating a transformation in American assistive listening technology (see www.hearingloop.org). For his leadership, he received an American Academy of Audiology Presidential Award in 2011, and the Hear-

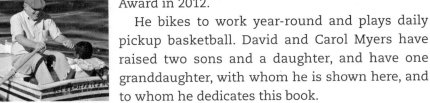

Kathleen Paulsson

ing Loss Association of America Walter T. Ridder Award in 2012.

He bikes to work year-round and plays daily pickup basketball. David and Carol Myers have raised two sons and a daughter, and have one granddaughter, with whom he is shown here, and to whom he dedicates this book.

Nathan DeWall is professor of psychology and director of the Social Psychology Lab at the University of Kentucky. He received his bachelor's degree from St. Olaf College, a master's degree in social science from the University of Chicago, and a master's degree and Ph.D. in social psychology from Florida State University. DeWall received the 2011 College of Arts and Sciences Outstanding Teaching Award, which recognizes excellence in undergraduate and graduate teaching. In 2011, the Association for Psychological Science identified DeWall as a "Rising Star" for "making significant contributions to the field of psychological science."

Brian Connors Manke

DeWall conducts research on close relationships, self-control, and aggression. With funding from the National Institutes of Health and the National Science Foundation, he has published over 120 scientific articles and chapters. DeWall's research awards include the SAGE Young Scholars Award from the Foundation for Personality and Social Psychology, the Young Investigator Award from the International Society for Research on Aggression, and the Early Career Award from the International Society for Self and Identity. His research has been covered by numerous media outlets, including *Good Morning America, Newsweek, Atlantic Monthly, New York Times, Los Angeles Times, Harvard Business Review,* and National Public Radio. DeWall blogs for *Psychology Today.* He has lectured nationally and internationally, including in Hong Kong, China, the Netherlands, England, Greece, Hungary, and Australia.

Nathan is happily married to Alice DeWall. He enjoys playing with his two golden retrievers, Finnegan and Atticus. In his spare time, he writes novels, watches sports, and runs and runs and runs—including in 2013 a half marathon, two marathons, three 50-mile ultramarathons, and one 100-mile ultramarathon.

Alice DeWall

Brief Contents

Contents

CHAPTER **4**
Gender and Sexuality 107

CHAPTER **5**
Sensation and Perception 133

Preface

PSYCHOLOGY IS FASCINATING, and so relevant to our everyday lives. Psychology's insights enable us to be better students, more tuned-in friends and partners, more effective co-workers, and wiser parents. With this new edition, we hope to captivate students with what psychologists are learning about our human nature, to help them think more like psychological scientists, and, as the title implies, to help them relate psychology to their own lives—their thoughts, feelings, and behaviors.

For those of you familiar with other Myers introductory psychology texts, you may be surprised at how very different this text is. We have created this uniquely student-friendly book with the help of input from thousands of instructors and students (by way of surveys, focus groups, content and design reviews, and class testing).

New Co-Author

For this new edition I [DM] welcome my new co-author, University of Kentucky professor Nathan DeWall. (For more information and videos that introduce Nathan DeWall and our collaboration, see www.worthpublishers.com/myersdewall.) Nathan is not only one of psychology's "rising stars" (as the Association for Psychological Science rightly said in 2011), he also is an award-winning teacher and someone who shares my passion for writing—and for communicating psychological science through writing. Although I continue as lead author, Nathan's fresh insights and contributions are already enriching this book, especially for this third edition, through his leading the revision of Chapters 4, 10, 11, and 14. But my fingerprints are also on those chapter revisions, even as his are on the other chapters. With support from our wonderful editors, this is a team project. In addition to our work together on the textbook, Nathan and I enjoy co-authoring the Teaching Current Directions in Psychological Science column in the APS *Observer*.

What Else Is New in the Third Edition?

In addition to the long, chapter-by-chapter list of Content Changes that follows this preface, other significant changes have been made to the overall format and presentation of this new third edition.

NEW Study System Follows Best Practices From Learning and Memory Research

The new learning system harnesses the *testing effect,* which documents the benefits of actively retrieving information through self-testing (FIGURE 1). Thus, each chapter now offers 12 to 15 new **Retrieve + Remember** questions interspersed throughout (FIGURE 2). Creating these *desirable difficulties* for students along the way optimizes the testing effect, as does *immediate feedback* (via inverted answers beneath each question).

In addition, each main section of text begins with numbered questions that establish **learning objectives** and direct student reading. The Chapter Review section repeats these questions as a further self-testing opportunity (with answers in the Complete Chapter Reviews appendix). The Chapter Review section also offers a page-referenced list of **Terms and Concepts to Remember,** and new **Chapter Test** questions in multiple formats to promote optimal retention.

Each chapter closes with **In Your Everyday Life** questions, designed to help students make the concepts more personally meaningful, and therefore more memorable. These questions are also

FIGURE 1 Testing effect For suggestions of how students may apply the testing effect to their own learning, watch this 5-minute YouTube animation: www.tinyurl.com/HowToRemember

RETRIEVE + REMEMBER

- What are the three requirements that a psychological test must meet in order to be widely accepted? Explain.

ANSWER: A psychological test must be *standardized* (pretested on a similar group of people), *reliable* (yielding consistent results), and *valid* (measuring or predicting what it is supposed to measure or predict).

FIGURE 2 Sample of Retrieve + Remember feature

designed to function as excellent group discussion topics. The text offers hundreds of interesting **applications** to help students see just how applicable psychology's concepts are to everyday life.

These new features enhance the Survey-Question-Read-Retrieve-Review (SQ3R) format. Chapter outlines allow students to *survey* what's to come. Main sections begin with a learning objective *question* (now more carefully directed and appearing more frequently) that encourages students to *read* actively. Periodic Retrieve + Remember sections and the Chapter Review (with repeated Learning Objective Questions, Key Terms list, and complete Chapter Test) encourage students to test themselves by *retrieving* what they know and *reviewing* what they don't. (See Figure 2 for a Retrieve + Remember sample.)

Reorganized Chapters and More Than 600 New Research Citations

Thousands of instructors and students have helped guide our creation of *Psychology in Everyday Life,* as have our reading and correspondence. The result is a unique text, now thoroughly revised in this third edition, which includes more than 600 new citations. Some of the most exciting recent research has happened in the area of biological psychology, including cognitive neuroscience, dual processing, and epigenetics. See p. xxxiii for a chapter-by-chapter list of significant **Content Changes.** In addition to the new study aids and updated coverage, we've introduced the following organizational changes:

- Chapter 1 concludes with a new section, "Improve Your Retention—and Your Grades." This guide will help students replace ineffective and inefficient old habits with new habits that increase retention and success.

- Chapter 3, Developing Through the Life Span, has been shortened by moving the Aging and Intelligence coverage to Chapter 8, Thinking, Language, and Intelligence.

Scattered throughout this book, students will find interesting and informative review notes and quotes from researchers and others that will encourage them to be active learners and to apply their new knowledge to everyday life.

- Chapter 7, Memory, follows a new format, and more clearly explains how different brain networks process and retain memories. We worked closely with Janie Wilson, Professor of Psychology at Georgia Southern University and Vice President for Programming of the Society for the Teaching of Psychology, on this chapter's revision.

- Chapter 10, Stress, Health, and Human Flourishing, now includes a discussion of happiness and subjective well-being, moved here from the Motivation and Emotion chapter.

- Chapter 11, Personality, offers more complete coverage of clinical perspectives, including improved coverage of modern-day psychodynamic approaches, which are now more clearly distinguished from their historical Freudian roots.

- The Social Psychology chapter now follows the Personality chapter.

- Chapter 13, Psychological Disorders, now includes coverage of eating disorders, previously in the Motivation and Emotion chapter. This chapter has also been reorganized to reflect changes to psychiatry's latest edition of its diagnostic manual—the **DSM-5.**

- There are two new text appendices: Statistical Reasoning in Everyday Life, and Subfields of Psychology.

More Design Innovations

With help from student and instructor design reviewers, the new third edition retains the best of the easy-to-read three-column design but with a cleaner new look that makes navigation easier thanks to fewer color-distinguished features, a softer color palette, and closer connection between narrative coverage and its associated visuals.

Our three-column format is rich with visual support. It responds to students' expectations, based on what they have told us about their reading, both online and in print. The narrow column width eliminates the strain of reading across a wide page. Illustrations appear near or within the pertinent text column, which helps students see them in the appropriate context. Key terms are defined near where they are introduced.

key terms Look for complete definitions of each important term in a page corner near the term's introduction in the narrative.

In written reviews, students compared our three-column design with a traditional one-column design (without knowing which was ours). They unanimously preferred the three-column design. It was, they said, "less intimidating" and "less overwhelming" and it "motivated" them to read on.

In this edition, we've also adjusted the font used for research citations. In psychology's journals and textbooks, parenthetical citations appropriately assign credit and direct readers to sources. But they can also form a visual hurdle. An instructor using the second edition of *Psychology in Every-*

day Life suggested a new, less intrusive style, which has been encouraged by most of our reviewers. We've honored APA reference style with parenthetical citations (rather than, say, end notes), yet we've eased readability by reducing the strength of the citation font. The first instance of a citation is called out in Chapter 1 and explained to students who may be unfamiliar with the APA style for sourcing.

Dedicated Versions of Next-Generation Media

This third edition is accompanied by the new **LaunchPad,** with carefully crafted, prebuilt assignments, **LearningCurve** formative assessment activities, and **Assess Your Strengths** projects. This system also incorporates the full range of Worth's psychology media products. (For details, see p. xxiv.)

What Continues in the Third Edition?

Eight Guiding Principles

Despite all the exciting changes, this new edition retains its predecessors' voice, as well as much of the content and organization. It also retains the goals—the guiding principles—that have animated all of the Myers texts:

Facilitating the Learning Experience

1. **To teach critical thinking** By presenting research as intellectual detective work, we illustrate an inquiring, analytical mind-set. Whether students are studying development, cognition, or social behavior, they will become involved in, and see the rewards of, critical reasoning. Moreover, they will discover how an empirical approach can help them evaluate competing ideas and claims for highly publicized phenomena—ranging from ESP and alternative therapies to hypnosis and repressed and recovered memories.

2. **To integrate principles and applications** Throughout—by means of anecdotes, case histories, and the posing of hypothetical situations—we relate the findings of basic research to their applications and implications. Where psychology can illuminate pressing human issues—be they racism and sexism, health and happiness, or violence and war—we have not hesitated to shine its light.

3. **To reinforce learning at every step** Everyday examples and rhetorical questions encourage students to process the material actively. Concepts presented earlier are frequently applied, and reinforced, in later chapters. For instance, in Chapter 1, students learn that much of our information processing occurs outside of our conscious awareness. Ensuing chapters drive home this concept. Numbered Learning Objective Questions at the beginning of each main section, Retrieve + Remember self-tests throughout each chapter, a marginal glossary, and Chapter Review key terms lists and self-tests help students learn and retain important concepts and terminology.

Demonstrating the Science of Psychology

4. **To exemplify the process of inquiry** We strive to show students not just the outcome of research, but how the research process works. Throughout, the book tries to excite the reader's curiosity. It invites readers to imagine themselves as participants in classic experiments. Several chapters introduce research stories as mysteries that progressively unravel as one clue after another falls into place.

5. **To be as up-to-date as possible** Few things dampen students' interest as quickly as the sense that they are reading stale news. While retaining psychology's classic studies and concepts, we also present the discipline's most important recent developments. In this edition, 250 references are dated 2011–2013. Likewise, the new photos and everyday examples are drawn from today's world.

6. **To put facts in the service of concepts** Our intention is not to fill students' intellectual file drawers with facts, but to reveal psychology's major concepts—to teach students how to think, and to offer psychological ideas worth thinking about. In each chapter, we place emphasis on those concepts we hope students will carry with them long after they complete the course. Always, we try to follow Albert Einstein's purported dictum that "everything should be made as simple as possible, but not simpler." Learning Objective Questions and Retrieve + Remember questions throughout each chapter help students focus on the most important concepts.

Promoting Big Ideas and Broadened Horizons

7. **To enhance comprehension by providing continuity** Many chapters have a significant issue or theme that links subtopics, forming a thread that ties the chapter together. The Learning chapter conveys the idea that bold thinkers can serve as intellectual pioneers. The Thinking, Language, and Intelligence chapter raises the issue of human rationality and irrationality. The Psychological Disorders chapter conveys empathy for, and understanding of, troubled lives. Other threads, such as cognitive neuroscience, dual processing, and cultural and gender diversity, weave throughout the whole book, and students hear a consistent voice.

8. **To convey respect for human unity and diversity** Throughout the book, readers will see evidence of our human kinship—our shared biological heritage, our common mechanisms of seeing and learning, hungering and feeling, loving and hating. They will also better understand the dimensions of our diversity—our individual diversity in development and aptitudes, temperament and personality, and disorder and health; and our cultural diversity in attitudes and expressive styles, child raising and care for the elderly, and life priorities.

The Writing

As with the second edition, we've written this book to be optimally accessible. The vocabulary is sensitive to students' widely varying reading levels and backgrounds. And this book is briefer than many texts on the market, making it easier to fit into one-term courses. *Psychology in Everyday Life* offers a complete survey of the field, but it is a more manageable survey. We strove to select the most humanly significant concepts. We continually asked ourselves while working, "Would an educated person need to know this? Would this help students live better lives?"

Culture and Gender—No Assumptions

Even more than in other Myers texts, we have written *Psychology in Everyday Life* with the diversity of student readers in mind.

- *Gender:* Extensive coverage of gender roles and gender identity and the increasing diversity of choices men and women can make.
- *Culture:* No assumptions about readers' cultural backgrounds or experiences.
- *Economics:* No references to back yards, summer camp, vacations.

- *Education:* No assumptions about past or current learning environments; writing is accessible to all.
- *Physical Abilities:* No assumptions about full vision, hearing, movement.
- *Life Experiences:* Examples are included from urban, suburban, and rural/outdoor settings.
- *Family Status:* Examples and ideas are made relevant for all students, whether they have children or are still living at home, are married or cohabiting or single; no assumptions about sexual orientation.

Four Big Ideas

In the general psychology course, it can be a struggle to weave psychology's disparate parts into a cohesive whole for students, and for students to make sense of all the pieces. In *Psychology in Everyday Life,* we have introduced four of psychology's big ideas as one possible way to make connections among all the concepts. These ideas are presented in Chapter 1 and gently integrated throughout the text.

1. Critical Thinking Is Smart Thinking

We love to write in a way that gets students thinking and keeps them active as they read. Students will see how the science of psychology can help them evaluate competing ideas and highly publicized claims—ranging from intuition, subliminal persuasion, and ESP to left-brained/right-brained, alternative therapies, and repressed and recovered memories.

In *Psychology in Everyday Life,* students have many opportunities to learn or practice their critical thinking skills:

- *Chapter 1 takes a unique, critical thinking approach to introducing students to psychology's research methods.* Understanding the weak points of our everyday intuition and common sense helps students see the need for

psychological science. Critical thinking is introduced as a key term in this chapter (page 6).

- *"Thinking Critically About . . ." boxes* are found throughout the book. This feature models for students a critical approach to some key issues in psychology. For example, see "Thinking Critically About: The Stigma of Introversion" (Chapter 11) or "Thinking Critically About: Do Video Games Teach, or Release, Violence?" (Chapter 12). "Close-Up" boxes encourage application of the new concepts. For example, see "Close-Up: Waist Management" in Chapter 9, or "Close-Up: Pets Are Friends, Too" in Chapter 10.
- *Detective-style stories* throughout the text get students thinking critically about psychology's key research questions. In Chapter 8, for example, we present as a puzzle the history of discoveries about where and how language happens in the brain. We guide students through the puzzle, showing them how researchers put all the pieces together.
- *"Try this" and "think about it"* style discussions and side notes keep students active in their study of each chapter. We often encourage students to imagine themselves as participants in experiments. In Chapter 12, for example, students take the perspective of participants in a Solomon Asch conformity experiment and, later, in one of Stanley Milgram's obedience experiments. We've also asked students to join the fun by taking part in activities they can try along the way. Here are a few examples: In Chapter 5, they try out a quick sensory adaptation activity. In Chapter 9, they try matching expressions to faces and test the effects of different facial expressions on themselves. Throughout Chapter 11, students are asked to apply what they're learning to the construction of a questionnaire for an Internet dating service.

- *Critical examinations of pop psychology* spark interest and provide important lessons in thinking critically about everyday topics. For example, Chapter 5 includes a close examination of ESP, and Chapter 7 addresses the controversial topic of repression of painful memories.

See **TABLE 1** for a complete list of this text's coverage of critical thinking topics.

2. Behavior Is a Biopsychosocial Event

Students will learn that we can best understand human behavior if we view it from three levels—the biological, psychological, and social-cultural. This concept is introduced in Chapter 1 and revisited throughout the text. Readers will see evidence of our human kinship. Yet they will also better understand the dimensions of our diversity—our *individual* diversity, our *gender* diversity, and our *cultural* diversity. **TABLE 2** provides a list of integrated coverage of the cross-cultural perspective on psychology. **TABLE 3** (turn the page) lists the coverage of the psychology of women and men. Significant gender and cross-cultural examples and research are presented within the narrative. In addition, an abundance of photos showcases the diversity of cultures within North America and across the globe. These photos and their informative captions bring the pages to life, broadening students' perspectives in applying psychological science to their own world and to the worlds across the globe.

3. We Operate With a Two-Track Mind (Dual Processing)

Today's psychological science explores our *dual-processing* capacity. Our perception, thinking, memory, and attitudes all operate on two levels: the level of fully aware, conscious processing, and the behind-the-scenes level of unconscious processing. Students may be surprised to learn how much information we process outside of our awareness. Discussions of sleep (Chapter 2), perception (Chapter 5), cognition and emotion (Chapter 9), and attitudes and prejudice (Chapter 12) provide some particularly compelling examples of what goes on in our mind's downstairs.

TABLE 1   Critical Thinking

Critical thinking coverage may be found on the following pages:

A scientific model for studying psychology, p. 172

Are intelligence tests biased?, pp. 249–250

Are personality tests able to predict behavior?, p. 325

Are there parts of the brain we don't use?, p. 46

Attachment style, development of, pp. 81–84

Attention-deficit/hyperactivity disorder (ADHD), p. 371

Causation and the violence-viewing effect, p. 188

Classifying psychological disorders, pp. 374–375

Confirmation bias, p. 221

Continuity vs. stage theories of development, pp. 93–94

Correlation and causation, pp. 16–17, 84, 90

Critical thinking defined, p. 7

Critiquing the evolutionary perspective on sexuality, pp. 127–128

Discovery of hypothalamus reward centers, pp. 41–42

Do animals think and have language?, pp. 228–229

Do lie detectors lie?, p. 274

Do other species think and have language?, pp. 234–235

Do video games teach, or release, violence?, pp. 358–359

Does meditation enhance immunity?, pp. 298–299

Effectiveness of "alternative" therapies, p. 422

Emotion and the brain, pp. 40–42

Emotional intelligence, p. 238

Evolutionary science and human origins, p. 129

Extrasensory perception, pp. 161–162

Fear of flying vs. probabilities, pp. 224–225

Freud's contributions, p. 318

Genetic and environmental influences on schizophrenia, pp. 398–400

Group differences in intelligence, pp. 246–249

Hindsight bias, pp. 9–10

Hindsight explanations, pp. 127–128

How do nature and nurture shape prenatal development?, pp. 69–71

How do twin and adoption studies help us understand the effects of nature and nurture?, p. 72

How does the brain process language?, pp. 232–233

How much is gender socially constructed vs. biologically influenced?, pp. 110–115

How valid is the Rorschach ink-blot test?, pp. 316–317

Human curiosity, pp. 1–2

Humanistic perspective, evaluating, p. 321

Hypnosis: dissociation or social influence?, pp. 156–157

Importance of checking fears against facts, pp. 224–225

Interaction of nature and nurture in overall development, pp. 85–86, 91

Is dissociative identity disorder a real disorder?, pp. 402–403

Is psychotherapy effective?, pp. 420–421

Is repression a myth?, p. 318

Limits of case studies, naturalistic observation, and surveys, pp. 14–15

Limits of intuition, p. 9

Nature, nurture, and perceptual ability, p. 150

Overconfidence, pp. 10, 223

Posttraumatic stress disorder (PTSD), pp. 378–379

Powers and perils of intuition, pp. 225–226

Problem-solving strategies, pp. 220–221

Psychic phenomena, p. 12

Psychology: a discipline for critical thought, pp. 3–4, 9–12

Religious involvement and longevity, pp. 299–301

Scientific method, pp. 12–13

Sexual desire and ovulation, p. 115

Similarities and differences in social power between men and women, p. 109

Stress and cancer, pp. 288–289

Suggestive powers of subliminal messages, p. 136

The divided brain, pp. 47–49

The powers and limits of parental involvement on development, p. 91

Using psychology to debunk popular beliefs, p. 6

Values and psychology, pp. 22–23

What does selective attention teach us about consciousness?, pp. 51–52

What factors influence sexual orientation?, pp. 121–125

What is the connection between the brain and the mind?, p. 37

Wording effects, pp. 15

TABLE 2 Culture and Multicultural Experience

Coverage of culture and multicultural experience may be found on the following pages:

Academic achievement, pp. 247–249, 294
Achievement motivation, p. B-4
Adolescence, onset and end of, p. 92
Aggression, p. 356
Animal learning, p. 229
Animal research, views on, pp. 21–22
Beauty ideals, pp. 360–361
Biopsychosocial approach, pp. 6–7, 85–86, 110–115, 374, 389
Body image, p. 401
Cluster migration, p. 265
Cognitive development of children, p. 80
Collectivism, pp. 331–333, 338, 342, 343
Contraceptive use among teens, p. 118
Crime and stress hormone levels, p. 404
Cultural values
  child-raising and, p. 85
  morality and, p. 88
  psychotherapy and, p. 423
Culture
  defined, p. 7
  emotional expression and, pp. 276–277
  intelligence test bias and, pp. 249–250
  the self and, pp. 331–333
Deindividuation, p. 348
Depression
  and heart disease, p. 290
  and suicide, p. 392
  risk of, p. 393

Developmental similarities across cultures, pp. 85–86
Discrimination, pp. 350–351
Dissociative identity disorder, p. 402
Division of labor, p. 113
Divorce rate, p. 98
Dysfunctional behavior diagnoses, p. 372
Eating disorders, p. 374
Enemy perceptions, p. 365
Exercise, p. 262
Expressions of grief, p. 101
Family environment, p. 90
Family self, sense of, p. 85
Father's presence
  pregnancy and, p. 119
  violence and, p. 356
Flow, p. B-2
Foot-in-the-door phenomenon, p. 340
Framing, and organ donation, p. 224
Fundamental attribution error, p. 338
Gender roles, pp. 113, 128
Gender
  aggression and, p. 109
  communication and, pp. 109–110
  sex drive and, pp. 125–126
General adaptation syndrome, p. 285
Happiness, pp. 303–304, 305
HIV/AIDS, pp. 117, 288
Homosexuality, attitudes toward, p. 121
Identity formation, pp. 89–90
Individualism, pp. 331–333, 338, 343

ingroup bias, p. 352
  moral development and, p. 88
Intelligence, pp. 235–236
  group differences in, pp. 246–250
Intelligence testing, p. 239
Interracial dating, p. 350
Job satisfaction, p. B-4
Just-world phenomenon, p. 352
Language development, pp. 231–232
Leadership, pp. B-6–B-7
Life satisfaction, p. 99
Male-to-female violence, p. 356
Mating preferences, pp. 126–127
Mental disorders and stress, p. 374
Mere exposure effect, p. 359
Motivation, pp. 256–258
Naturalistic observation, p. 14
Need to belong, pp. 264–265
Obedience, p. 345
Obesity and sleep loss, p. 262
Optimism, p. 294
Ostracism, p. 265
Parent-teen relations, p. 90
Partner selection, p. 360
Peer influence, p. 86
  on language development, p. 90
Personal control, p. 292
Personality traits, pp. 322–323
Phobias, p. 381
Physical attractiveness, pp. 360–361
Poverty, explanations of, p. 339
Power differences between men and women, p. 109
Prejudice, pp. 352–353
  automatic, pp. 351–352
  contact, cooperation, and, p. 366

forming categories, p. 353
group polarization and, p. 348
racial, p. 340
subtle versus overt, pp. 350–351
Prosocial behavior, p. 186
Psychoactive drugs, pp. 381–382
Psychological disorders, pp. 371, 374
Racial similarities, pp. 248–249
Religious involvement and longevity, p. 299
Resilience, p. 432
Risk assessment, p. 225
Scapegoat theory, p. 352
Schizophrenia, p. 398
Self-esteem, p. 305
Self-serving bias, p. 330
Separation anxiety, p. 83
Serial position effect, p. 205
Social clock variation, p. 99
Social influence, pp. 343, 345–346
Social loafing, p. 347
Social networking, p. 266
Social trust, p. 84
Social-cultural psychology, pp. 4, 6
Stereotype threat, pp. 249–250
Stereotypes, pp. 350, 352
Stranger anxiety, p. 81
Substance abuse, p. 389
Substance abuse/addiction rates, p. 389
Susto, p. 374
Taijin-kyofusho, p. 374
Taste preference, pp. 260–261
Terrorism, pp. 224–225, 393, 339, 352, 354, 393
Trauma, pp. 318, 421
Universal expressions, p. 7
Weight, p. 262

4. Psychology Explores Human Strengths as Well as Challenges

Students will learn about the many troublesome behaviors and emotions psychologists study, as well as the ways in which psychologists work with those who need help. Yet students will also learn about the *beneficial* emotions and traits that psychologists study, and the ways psychologists (some as part of the new *positive psychology* movement—turn the page to see TABLE 4) attempt to nurture those traits in others. After study-

ing with this text, students may find themselves living improved day-to-day lives. See, for example, tips for better sleep in Chapter 2, parenting suggestions throughout Chapter 3, information to help with romantic relationships in Chapters 3, 4, 12, and elsewhere, and "Close-Up: Want to Be Happier?" in Chapter 10. Students may also find themselves doing better in their courses. See, for example, following this preface, "Time Management: Or, How to Be a Great Student and Still Have a Life"; "Improve Your Retention—and Your Grades" at the end of Chapter 1; "Improving Memory"

in Chapter 7; and the helpful new study tools throughout the text based on the documented testing effect.

Enhanced Clinical Psychology Coverage, Including Thorough DSM-5 Updating

Compared with other Myers texts, *Psychology in Everyday Life* has proportionately more coverage of clinical topics and a greater sensitivity to clinical issues throughout the text. For example,

TABLE 3 Psychology of Women and Men

Coverage of the *psychology of women and men* may be found on the following pages:

Age and decreased fertility, pp. 94–95
Aggression, pp. 108–109, 354
  testosterone and, p. 354
Alcohol use and sexual assault, p. 382
Alcohol use disorder, p. 383
Alcohol, women's greater physical vulnerability, p. 383
Attraction, pp. 358–363
Beauty ideals, pp. 360–361
Bipolar disorder, p. 392
Body image, p. 401
Depression, p. 393
  among girls, pp. 89–90
  higher vulnerability of women, p. 395
  seasonal patterns, p. 391
Eating disorders, p. 401
  sexualization of girls and, p. 120
Emotional expressiveness, pp. 275–276
Emotion-detecting ability, p. 275
Empathy, p. 276
Father's presence
  pregnancy rates and, p. 119
  lower sexual activity and, p. 119
Freud's views on gender identity development, p. 314
Gender, pp. 6–7

anxiety and, p. 377
biological influences on, pp. 110–112
changes in society's thinking about, pp. 107, 113, 128, 350
social-cultural influences on, pp. 6–7, 113–115
widowhood and, p. 100
Gender differences, pp. 6–7, 108–110
  rumination and, p. 395
  evolutionary perspectives on, pp. 125–128
  intelligence and, pp. 246–247
  sexuality and, pp. 125–126
Gender discrimination, pp. 350–351
Gender identity, development of, pp. 113–115
  mismatch in transgendered individuals, p. 114
Gender roles, p. 113
Gender schema theory, p. 114
Gender similarities, pp. 108–110
Gender typing, p. 114
HIV/AIDS, women's vulnerability to, p. 117
Hormones and sexual behavior, pp. 115–116
Human sexuality, pp. 115–121
Leadership styles, p. 109

Learned helplessness, p. 395
Life expectancy, p. 108
Love
  companionate, pp. 362–363
  passionate, pp. 361–362
Marriage, pp. 97–98
Mating preferences, pp. 126–127
Maturation, pp. 86–87, 94
Menarche, pp. 86, 92
Menopause, p. 95
Obedience, p. 344
Physical attractiveness, pp. 359–360
Posttraumatic stress disorder, p. 379
Puberty, p. 86
  early onset of, p. 92
Relationship equity, p. 362
Responses to stress, p. 286
Schizophrenia, p. 398
Sex, pp. 6, 115–117
Sex and gender, p. 110
Sex chromosomes, p. 111
Sex drive, gender differences, pp. 118, 125
Sex hormones, p. 110
Sex-reassignment, p. 112
Sexual activity and aging, p. 96
Sexual activity, teen girls' regret, p. 119
Sexual arousal, gender and gay-straight differences, p. 123

Sexual intercourse among teens, p. 117
Sexual orientation, pp. 121–125
Sexual response cycle, pp. 116–117
Sexual response, alcohol-related expectation and, p. 384
Sexual scripts, p. 357
Sexuality, natural selection and, pp. 125–127
Sexualization of girls, p. 120
Sexually explicit media, pp. 119, 357
Sexually transmitted infections, pp. 117–118
Similarities and differences between men and women, pp. 108–110
Social clock, p. 99
Social connectedness, pp. 109–110
Social power, p. 109
Spirituality and longevity, p. 299
Substance use disorder and the brain, p. 383
Teen pregnancy, pp. 118–119
Violent crime, pp. 108–109
Vulnerability to psychological disorders, p. 108
Weight loss, p. 263
Women in psychology, pp. 2–3

Chapter 13, Psychological Disorders, includes lengthy coverage of substance-related disorders, with guidelines for determining substance use disorder. The discussion of psychoactive drugs includes a special focus on alcohol and nicotine use. Clinical references, explanations, and examples throughout the text have been carefully updated to reflect DSM-5 changes. Chapter 13 includes an explanation of how disorders are now diagnosed, with illustrative examples throughout. See **TABLE 5** for a listing of coverage of clinical psychology concepts and issues throughout the text.

Everyday Life Applications

Throughout this text, as its title suggests, we relate the findings of psychology's research to the real world. This edition includes:

- chapter-ending "In Your Everyday Life" questions, helping students make the concepts more meaningful (and memorable).

- fun notes and quotes in small boxes throughout the text, applying psychology's findings to sports, literature, world religions, and music.

- "Assess Your Strengths" personal self-assessments online in LaunchPad, allowing students to actively apply key principles to their own experiences.

- an emphasis throughout the text on critical thinking in everyday life, including the "Statistical Reasoning in Everyday Life" appendix, helping students to become more informed consumers and everyday thinkers.

See inside the front and back covers for a listing of students' favorite 50 of this text's applications to everyday life.

APA Assessment Tools

In 2011, the American Psychological Association (APA) approved the new **Principles for Quality Undergraduate Education in Psychology.** These broad-based principles and their associated recommendations were designed to "produce psychologically literate citizens who apply the principles of psychological science at work and at home." (See www.apa.org/education/undergrad/principles.aspx.)

TABLE 4   Examples of Positive Psychology

Coverage of *positive psychology* topics can be found in the following chapters:

Topic	Chapter
Altruism/compassion	3, 8, 11, 12, 14
Coping	10
Courage	12
Creativity	7, 11, 12
Emotional intelligence	8, 12
Empathy	3, 6, 10, 12, 14
Flow	App B
Gratitude	9, 10, 12
Happiness/life satisfaction	3, 9, 10
Humility	12
Humor	10, 12
Justice	12
Leadership	9, 11, 12, App B
Love	3, 4, 9, 10, 11, 12, 13, 14
Morality	3
Optimism	10, 11
Personal control	10
Resilience	3, 10, 12, 14
Self-discipline	3, 9, 11
Self-efficacy	10, 11
Self-esteem	9, 11
Spirituality	10, 12
Toughness (grit)	8, 9
Wisdom	2, 3, 8, 11, 12

TABLE 5   Clinical Psychology

Coverage of *clinical psychology* may be found on the following pages:

Abused children, risk of psychological disorder among, p. 172
Alcohol use and aggression, pp. 354–355
Alzheimer's disease, pp. 33, 245, 262
Anxiety disorders, pp. 376–381
Autism spectrum disorder, pp. 78–79, 108, 236
Aversive conditioning, pp. 415–416
Behavior modification, p. 416
Behavior therapies, pp. 414–417
Bipolar disorder, pp. 391–392
Brain damage and memory loss, p. 206
Brain scans, p. 38
Brain stimulation therapies, pp. 427–429
Childhood trauma, effect on mental health, pp. 83–84
Client-analyst relationship in psychoanalysis, p. 411
Client-centered therapy, p. 413
Client-therapist relationship, p. 320
Clinical psychologists, p. 5
Cognitive therapies, pp. 396, 417–419
eating disorders and, p. 417
Culture and values in psychotherapy, pp. 423–424
Depression:
adolescence and, p. 89
heart disease and, p. 290
homosexuality and, p. 122
mood-memory connection and, p. 205
outlook and, pp. 395–396
self-esteem and, pp. 16–17, 89, 90–91, 178
sexualization of girls and, p. 120
social exclusion and, pp. 90–91
unexpected loss and, pp. 100–101

Dissociative and personality disorders, pp. 401–403
Dissociative identity disorder, therapist's role, p. 402
Drug therapies, pp. 18, 424–427
Drug treatment, p. 173
DSM-5, pp. 374–375
Eating disorders, pp. 389, 400–401
Emotional intelligence, p. 238
Evidence-based clinical decision making, p. 422
Exercise, therapeutic effects of, pp. 296–297, 426, 430
Exposure therapies, pp. 414–415
Generalized anxiety disorder, p. 377
Grief therapy, p. 101
Group and family therapies, pp. 419–420
Historical treatment of mental illness, pp. 372, 410
Humanistic therapies, pp. 412–414
Hypnosis and pain relief, pp. 156–157
Intelligence scales and stroke rehabilitation, p. 240
Lifestyle change, therapeutic effects of, pp. 430–431
Loss of a child, psychiatric hospitalization and, p. 101
Major depressive disorder, pp. 390–391
Medical model of mental disorders, pp. 373–374
Mood disorders, pp. 390–396
Neurotransmitter imbalances and related disorders, p. 33
Nurturing strengths, p. 320
Obsessive-compulsive disorder, p. 378
Operant conditioning, pp. 416–417
Ostracism, pp. 265–266
Panic disorder, p. 377
Personality inventories, p. 324

Personality testing, pp. 316–317
Phobias, pp. 377–378
Physical and psychological treatment of pain, pp. 155–156
Posttraumatic stress disorder, pp. 378–379
Psychiatric labels and bias, p. 375
Psychoactive drugs, types of, pp. 424–427
Psychoanalysis, pp. 410–412
Psychodynamic theory, pp. 315–316
Psychodynamic therapy, p. 412
Psychological disorders, pp. 371–404
are those with disorders dangerous?, p. 376
classification of, pp. 374–375
gender differences in, p. 108
preventing, and building resilience, pp. 431–432
Psychotherapy, pp. 410–424
effectiveness of, pp. 420–423
Rorschach inkblot test, p. 316
Savant syndrome, p. 236
Schizophrenia, pp. 397–400
parent-blaming and, p. 91
risk of, pp. 399–400
Self-actualization, p. 319
Self-injury, pp. 392–393
Sex reassignment surgery, p. 112
Sleep disorders, pp. 58–60, 374
Spanked children, risk for aggression and depression among, p. 178
Substance use and addictive disorders, pp. 381–390
Suicide, pp. 392–393
Testosterone replacement therapy, pp. 115–116
Tolerance, withdrawal, and addiction, p. 382

APA's more specific **2013 Learning Goals and Outcomes,** from their *Guidelines for the Undergraduate Psychology Major,* Version 2.0, were designed to gauge progress in students graduating with psychology majors. (See www.apa.org/ed/precollege/about/psymajor-guidelines.pdf.) Many psychology departments use these goals and outcomes to help establish their own benchmarks for departmental assessment purposes.

Some instructors are eager to know whether a given text for the introductory course helps students get a good start at achieving these APA benchmarks. TABLE 6 on the next page offers a sample, using the first Principle, to illustrate how nicely *Psychology in Everyday Life,* Third Edition, corresponds to the 2011 APA Principles. (For a complete correlation guide to all five of the 2011 APA Principles, see http://tinyurl.com/m62dr95.) Turn the page to see TABLE 7, which outlines the way *Psychology in Everyday Life,* Third Edition, could help you to address the 2013 APA Learning Goals and Outcomes in your department.

In addition, an APA working group in 2013 drafted guidelines for **Strengthening the Common Core of the Introductory Psychology Course** (http://tinyurl.com/14dsdx5). Their goals are to "strike a nuanced balance providing flexibility yet guidance." The group noted that "a

TABLE 6 Sample Correlation: *Psychology in Everyday Life*, Third Edition, Corresponds to the 2011 APA Principles for Quality Undergraduate Education in Psychology

Quality Principle 1: Students are responsible for monitoring and enhancing their own learning.

APA Recommendations	Relevant Coverage or Feature From *Psychology in Everyday Life*, Third Edition
1. Students know how to learn. 2. Students assume increasing responsibility for their own learning. 3. Students take advantage of the rich diversity that exists in educational institutions and learn from individuals who are different from them. 4. Students are responsible for seeking advice for academic tasks, such as selecting courses in the approved sequence that satisfy the institution's requirements for the major and general education. They are also responsible for seeking advice about planning for a career that is realistic and tailored to their individual talents, aspirations, and situations. 5. Students strive to become psychologically literate citizens.	• LaunchPad course management, with the acclaimed LearningCurve self-testing, guides students toward effective self-monitoring with personalized study plans. • Time Management preface helps students learn to maximize their reading, studying, and exam preparation efforts. (p. xli) • Powerful new study system adopts best practices from learning and memory research. Includes numbered Learning Objective Questions, periodic Retrieve + Remember questions, and Chapter Review self-tests including In Your Everyday Life questions. • Improve Your Retention—and Your Grades section at the end of Chapter 1 teaches students how to apply the science of learning to their own studies. • Improving Memory section at the end of Chapter 7 teaches students how to use memory research findings to do better in this course and others. • LaunchPad's Assess Your Strengths feature allows students to apply psychology's principles to their own lives and experiences, and nurture key strengths in themselves. • The importance of understanding and respecting a diversity of people and perspectives is introduced in Chapter 1 and integrated throughout the text. (See also Tables 2 and 3 on pp. xxi and xxii for an overview of coverage.) • Appendix C introduces psychology's main subfields so that students may begin to consider realistic career options. Regularly updated Careers in Psychology information may be found at www.worthpublishers.com/MyersPEL3e. • Chapter 1 and Appendix A introduce the scientific attitude and the research methodology that students will need to understand to become psychologically literate. The importance of becoming psychologically literate is emphasized throughout the text and LaunchPad activities and quizzes.

mature science should be able to agree upon and communicate its unifying core while embracing diversity."

MCAT Will Include Psychology Starting in 2015

Beginning in 2015, the Medical College Admission Test (MCAT) is devoting 25 percent of its questions to the "Psychological, Social, and Biological Foundations of Behavior," with most of those questions coming from the psychological science taught in introductory psychology courses. From 1977 to 2014, the MCAT focused on biology, chemistry, and physics. Hereafter, reports the new *Preview Guide for MCAT 2015,* the

exam will also recognize "the importance of socio-cultural and behavioral determinants of health and health outcomes." The exam's new psychology section covers the breadth of topics in this text. For example, turn the page to see **TABLE 8,** which outlines the precise correlation between the topics in this text's Sensation and Perception chapter and the corresponding portion of the MCAT exam. For a complete pairing of the new MCAT psychology topics with this book's contents, see www.worthpublishers.com/MyersPEL3e.

Next-Generation Multimedia

Psychology in Everyday Life, Third Edition, boasts impressive multimedia options. For more information about any of these

choices, visit Worth Publishers' online catalog at www.worthpublishers.com.

LaunchPad With LearningCurve Quizzing and Assess Your Strengths Activities

LaunchPad offers a set of prebuilt assignments, carefully crafted by a group of instructional designers and instructors with an abundance of teaching experience as well as deep familiarity with Worth content. Each LaunchPad unit contains videos, activities, and formative assessment pieces to build student understanding for each topic, culminating with a randomized summative quiz to hold students accountable for the unit. Assign units in just a few clicks, and find scores in your gradebook upon submission. LaunchPad appeals not only to instructors who have been interested in adding an online component to their

TABLE 7 *Psychology in Everyday Life*, Third Edition, Corresponds to 2013 APA Learning Goals

Relevant Feature from *Psychology in Everyday Life*, Third Edition	Knowledge Base in Psychology	Scientific Inquiry and Critical Thinking	Ethical and Social Responsibility in a Diverse World	Communication	Professional Development
Text content	•	•	•	•	•
Four Big Ideas in Psychology as integrating themes	•	•	•		•
Thinking Critically boxes	•	•	•		•
Close-Up boxes	•		•		•
Learning Objective Questions previewing main sections	•	•		•	
Retrieve + Remember sections	•	•	•	•	•
In Your Everyday Life questions	•	•	•	•	•
"Try this"-style activities integrated throughout	•	•		•	•
Chapter Tests	•	•		•	
Statistics appendix		•		•	•
Psychology at Work appendix	•	•	•	•	•
Subfields of Psychology appendix, with Careers in Psychology online appendix	•		•		•
LaunchPad with LearningCurve formative quizzing	•	•		•	
Assess Your Strengths feature in LaunchPad	•	•	•	•	•
Book Companion Site	•	•	•	•	•

course but haven't been able to invest the time, but also to experienced online instructors curious to see how other colleagues might scaffold a series of online activities. Customize units as you wish, adding and dropping content to fit your course. (See **FIGURE 3**.)

LearningCurve combines adaptive question selection, personalized study plans, immediate and valuable feedback, and state-of-the-art question analysis reports. Based on the latest findings from learning and memory research, LearningCurve's game-like nature keeps students engaged while helping them learn and *remember* key concepts.

With **Assess Your Strengths** activities, students may take inventories and questionnaires developed by researchers across psychological science. These

FIGURE 3 Sample from LaunchPad

TABLE 8 Sample MCAT Correlation With *Psychology in Everyday Life*, Third Edition

MCAT 2015	Myers, *Psychology in Everyday Life*, Third Edition, Correlations	
Sample Content Category 6e: Sensing the environment		Page Number
Sensory Processing	Sensation and Perception	132–165
Sensation	Basic Principles of Sensation and Perception	134–139
Thresholds	Thresholds	135–137
Signal detection theory	*Difference Thresholds*	136
Sensory adaptation	Sensory Adaptation	137–138
Sensory receptors transduce stimulus energy and transmit signals to the central nervous system.	From Outer Energy to Inner Brain Activity (*transduction* key term)	134–135
Sensory pathways	Vision	139–142
	Hearing	151–154
	Understanding Pain	154–155
	Taste	157–158
	Smell	158–159
	Body Position and Movement	159–160
Types of sensory receptors	The Eye	141–142
	Decoding Sound Waves	152–153
	Understanding Pain	154–155
	Taste	157–158
	Smell	158–158
	Body Position and Movement	159–160
	Table 5.3, Summarizing the Senses	160
The cerebral cortex controls voluntary movement and cognitive functions.	Functions of the Cortex	43–47
Information processing in the cerebral cortex	The Cerebral Cortex	42–47
	Our Divided Brain	47–50
Vision	Vision	139–151
Structure and function of the eye	The Eye	140–142
Visual processing	Visual Information Processing	142–143
Visual pathways in the brain	*Figure 5.15, Pathway from the eyes to the visual cortex*	143
Parallel processing	*Parallel processing*	143
Feature detection	*Feature detection*	142–143
Hearing	Hearing	151–154
Auditory processing	Hearing	151–154
Auditory pathways in the brain	*Sound Waves: From the Environment Into the Brain*	151–152
Perceiving loudness and pitch	*Sound Waves: From the Environment Into the Brain*	151–152
	Figure 5.10, The physical properties of waves	140
Locating sounds	*How Do We Locate Sounds?*	153–154
Sensory reception by hair cells	*Decoding Sound Waves*	152–153
	Table 5.3, Summarizing the Senses	160

TABLE 8   Sample MCAT Correlation With *Psychology in Everyday Life*, Third Edition *(continued)*

MCAT 2015	Myers, *Psychology in Everyday Life*, Third Edition, Correlations	
Sample Content Category 6e: Sensing the environment		Page Number
Other Senses	Touch, Taste, Smell, Body Position and Movement	154–160
Somatosensation	Touch	154–157
Sensory systems in the skin	Sensory Functions (of the cortex)	45
	Touch	154
Tactile pathways in the brain	*Somatosensory cortex*	44, 45
	Table 5.3, Summarizing the Senses	160
Types of pain	Pain	154–155
Factors that influence pain	*Understanding Pain*	154–155
	Controlling Pain	155–156
	Hypnosis and Pain Relief	156–157
Taste	Taste	157–158
Taste buds/chemoreceptors that detect specific chemicals in the environment	Taste	157–158
	Table 5.3, Summarizing the Senses	160
Gustatory pathways in the brain	*Figure 5.29, Taste, Smell, and Memory*	158
Smell	Smell	158–159
Olfactory cells/chemoreceptors that detect specific chemicals in the environment	Smell	158–159
	Table 5.3, Summarizing the Senses	160
Pheromones	*Smell of sex-related hormones*	123–125
Olfactory paths in the brain	*Figure 5.29, Taste, Smell, and Memory*	158
Role of smell in perception of taste	Sensory Interaction	160–161
Perception	Sensation and Perception	132–165
Bottom-up/Top-down processing	Basic Principles of Sensation and Perception (*bottom-up* and *top-down processing* key terms)	134
Perceptual organization (i.e., depth, form, motion, constancy)	Visual Organization: Form Perception, Depth Perception (including Relative Motion), Perceptual Constancy	145–150
	Figure 5.16, Parallel processing (of motion, form, depth, color)	143
Gestalt principles	Visual Organization: Form Perception (*gestalt* key term)	145–146

self-assessments allow students to apply psychology's principles to their own lives and experiences. After taking each self-assessment, students will find additional information about the strength being tested (for example, personal growth initiative, sleep quality, empathizing/systemizing, intrinsic/extrinsic motivation, mindfulness, self-control, and hope), as well as tips for nurturing that strength more effectively in their own lives.

Faculty Support and Student Resources

- Faculty Lounge—http://psych.facultylounge.worthpublishers.com—(see **FIGURE 4** on the next page) is an online gathering place to find and share favorite teaching ideas and materials, including videos, animations, images, PowerPoint® slides and lectures, news stories, articles, web links, and lecture activities. Includes publisher-as well as peer-provided resources—all faculty-reviewed for accuracy and quality.

- Instructor's Media Guide for Introductory Psychology

- Enhanced Course Management Solutions (including course cartridges)

- e-Book in various available formats, with embedded Concepts in Action

- Book Companion Site

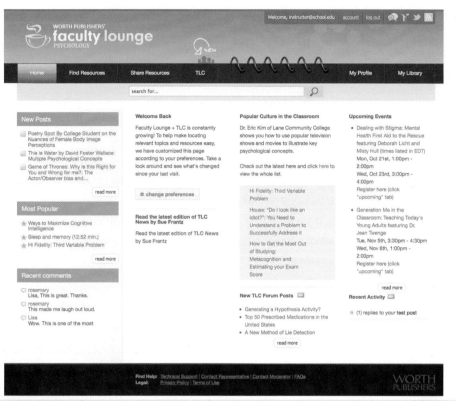

FIGURE 4 Sample from our Faculty Lounge site (http://psych.facultylounge.worthpublishers.com)

Video and Presentation

- **The Worth Video Anthology for Introductory Psychology** is a complete collection, all in one place, of all of our video clips. The set is accompanied by its own Faculty Guide.

- **Interactive Presentation Slides for Introductory Psychology** is an extraordinary series of PowerPoint® lectures. This is a dynamic, yet easy-to-use way to engage students during classroom presentations of core psychology topics. This collection provides opportunities for discussion and interaction, and includes an unprecedented number of embedded video clips and animations.

Assessment

- **LearningCurve** summative quizzing
- Printed Test Banks
- Diploma Computerized Test Banks
- Online Quizzing
- i•clicker Radio Frequency Classroom Response System

Print

- Instructor's Resources
- Lecture Guides
- Study Guide
- *Pursuing Human Strengths: A Positive Psychology Guide*
- *Critical Thinking Companion,* Second Edition

- *Psychology and the Real World: Essays Illustrating Fundamental Contributions to Society.* This project of the FABBS Foundation brought together a virtual "Who's Who" of contemporary psychological scientists to describe—in clear, captivating ways—the research they have passionately pursued and what it means to the "real world." Each contribution is an original essay written for this project.

In Appreciation

Aided by input from thousands of instructors and students over the years, this has become a better, more effective, more accurate book than two authors alone (these authors at least) could write. Our indebtedness continues to the innumerable researchers who have been so willing to share their time and talent to help us accurately report their research.

For this edition, we especially appreciated Jim Foley's (Wooster, Ohio) detailed consulting review of the clinical materials, primarily for the purpose of updating for the DSM-5.

Our gratitude extends to the colleagues who contributed criticism, corrections, and creative ideas related to the content, pedagogy, and format of this new edition and its two predecessors. For their expertise and encouragement, and the gift of their time to the teaching of psychology, we thank the reviewers and consultants listed here.

First and Second Edition Reviewers

Tricia Alexander, *Long Beach City College*

Pamela Ansburg, *Metropolitan State College of Denver*

Randy Arnau, *University of Southern Mississippi*

Stacy Bacigalupi, *Mount San Antonio College*

Kimberly Bays-Brown, *Ball State University*

Alan Beauchamp, *Northern Michigan University*

Richard Bernstein, *Broward College—South Campus*

Diane Bogdan, *CUNY: Hunter College*

Robert Boroff, *Modesto Junior College*

Christia Brown, *University of Kentucky*

Alison Buchanan, *Henry Ford Community College*

Norma Caltagirone, *Hillsborough Community College—Ybor City*

Nicole Judice Campbell, *University of Oklahoma*

David Carlston, *Midwestern State University*

Kimberly Christopherson, *Morningside College*

Diana Ciesko, *Valencia Community College*

TaMetryce Collins, *Hillsborough Community College*

Patricia Crowe, *Hawkeye College*

Jennifer Dale, *Community College of Aurora*

David Devonis, *Graceland University*

George Diekhoff, *Midwestern State University*

Michael Drissman, *Macomb Community College*

Laura Duvall, *Heartland Community College*

Jennifer Dyck, *SUNY College at Fredonia*

Laura Engleman, *Pikes Peak Community College*

Warren Fass, *University of Pittsburgh*

Vivian Ferry, *Community College of Rhode Island*

Elizabeth Freeman-Young, *Bentley College*

Ann Fresoli, *Lehigh Carbon Community College*

Ruth Frickle, *Highline Community College*

Lenore Frigo, *Shasta College*

Gary Gargano, *Merced College*

Jo Anne Geron, *Antioch University*

Stephanie Grant, *Southern Nazarene University*

Raymond Green, *The Honors College of Texas*

Sandy Grossman, *Clackamas Community College*

Lisa Gunderson, *Sacramento City College*

Rob Guttentag, *University of North Carolina—Greensboro*

Gordon Hammerle, *Adrian College*

Mark Hartlaub, *Texas A&M University*

Sheryl Hartman, *Miami Dade College*

Brett Heintz, *Delgado Community College*

Suzy Horton, *Mesa Community College*

Alishia Huntoon, *Oregon Institute of Technology*

Cindy Hutman, *Elgin Community College*

Laurene Jones, *Mercer County Community College*

Charles "Ed" Joubert, *University of North Alabama*

Deana Julka, *University of Portland*

Richard Kandus, *Mount San Jacinto College, Menifree*

Elizabeth Kennedy, *University of Akron*

Norm Kinney, *Southeast Missouri University*

Gary Klatsky, *SUNY Oswego State University*

Dan Klaus, *Community College of Beaver County*

Laurel Krautwurst, *Blue Ridge Community College*

Juliana Leding, *University of North Florida*

Gary Lewandowski, *Monmouth University*

Alicia Limke, *University of Central Oklahoma*

Leslie Linder, *Bridgewater State College*

Chris Long, *Ouachita Baptist University*

Martha Low, *Winston-Salem State University*

Mark Ludorf, *Stephen F. Austin State University*

Brian MacKenna-Rice, *Middlesex Community College*

Vince Markowski, *University of Southern Maine*

Dawn McBride, *Illinois State University*

Marcia McKinley, *Mount St. Mary's University*

Tammy Menzel, *Mott Community College*

Leslie Minor-Evans, *Central Oregon Community College*

Ronald Mossler, *Los Angeles Valley College*

Maria Navarro, *Valencia Community College*

Daniel Nelson, *North Central University*

David Neufeldt, *Hutchinson Community College*

Peggy Norwood, *Community College of Aurora*

Fabian Novello, *Clark State Community College*

Fawn Oates, *Red Rocks Community College*

Ginger Osborne, *Santa Ana College*

Randall Osborne, *Texas State University—San Marcos*

Carola Pedreschi, *Miami-Dade College, North Campus*

Jim Previte, *Victor Valley College*

Sean Reilley, *Morehead State University*

Tanya Renner, *Kapi'olani Community College*

Vicki Ritts, *St. Louis Community College—Meramec*

Dave Rudek, *Aurora University*

R. Steven Schiavo, *Wellesley College*

Cynthia Selby, *California State University—Chico*

Jennifer Siciliani, *University of Missouri—St. Louis*

Barry Silber, *Hillsborough Community College*

Madhu Singh, *Tougaloo College*

Alice Skeens, *University of Toledo*

Jason Spiegelman, *Towson University & Community College of Baltimore County*

Anna-Marie Spinos, *Aurora University*

Betsy Stern, *Milwaukee Area Technical College*

Ruth Thibodeau, *Fitchburg State College*

Eloise Thomas, *Ozarks Technical Community College*

Susan Troy, *Northeast Iowa Community College*

Michael Verro, *Empire State College*

Jacqueline Wall, *University of Indianapolis*

Marc Wayner, *Hocking College*

Diane Webber, *Curry College*

Richard Wedemeyer, *Rose State College*

Peter Wooldridge, *Durham Technical Community College*

John Wright, *Washington State University*

Gabriel Ybarra, *University of North Florida*

Third Edition Reviewers

Diane Agresta, *Washtenaw Community College*

Barb Angleberger, *Frederick Community College*

Cheryl Armstrong , *Fitchburg State College*

Jamie Arnold, *Letourneau University*

Sandra Arntz, *Carroll College*

Grace Austin, *Sacramento City College*

Stephen Balzac, *Wentworth Institute of Technology*

Chip (Charles) Barker, *Olympic College*

Elaine Barry, *Pennsylvania State University—Fayette Campus*

Karen Beale, *Maryville College*

Michael Bogue, *Mohave Community College—Bullhead*

Karen Brakke, *Spellman College*

Christina Bresner, *Champlain College, Lennoxville*

Carrie Bulger, *Quinnipiac University*

Sarah Calabrese, *Yale University*

Jennifer Colman, *Champlain College*

Victoria Cooke, *Erie Community College*

Daniel Dickman, *Ivy Tech Community College—Evansville*

Kevin Dooley, *Grossmont College*

Mimi Dumville, *Raritan Valley Community College*

Julie Ehrhardt, *Bristol Community College—Bedford Campus*

Traci Elliott, *Alvin Community College*

Mark Evans, *Tarrant County College—Northwest*

Brian Follick, *California State University—Fullerton*

Paula Frioli-Peters, *Truckee Meadows Community College*

Deborah Garfin, *Georgia State University*

Karla Gingerich, *Colorado State University*

Darah E. Granger, *Florida State College at Jacksonville—Kent*

Carrie Hall, *Miami University*

Christina Hawala, *DeVry University*

John Haworth, *Chattanooga State Technical Community College*

Toni Henderson, *Langara College*

Mary Horton, *Mesa Community College*

Bernadette Jacobs, *Santa Fe Community College*

Joan Jensen, *Central Piedmont Community College*

Patricia Johnson, *Craven Community College—Havelock Campus*

Lynnel Kiely, *City Colleges of Chicago—Harry S. Truman College*

Jennifer Klebaur, *Central Piedmont Community College—North Campus*

Sarah Kranz, *Letourneau University*

Michael Lantz, *Kent State University at Trumbull*

Mary Livingston, *Louisiana Tech University*

Donald Lucas, *Northwest Vista College*

Molly Lynch, *Northern Virginia Community College*

Brian MacKenna-Rice, *Middlesex Community College*

Cheree Madison, *Lanier Technical College*

Robert Martinez, *Northwest Vista College*

David McAllister, *Salem State College*

Gerald McKeegan, *Bridgewater College*

Michelle Merwin, *University of Tennessee—Martin*

Shelly Metz, *Central New Mexico Community College*

Erin Miller, *Bridgewater College*

Barbara Modisette, *Letourneau University*

Maria A. Murphy, *Florida State College at Jacksonville—North*

Jake Musgrove, *Broward College—Central Campus*

Robin Musselman, *Lehigh Carbon Community College*

Dana Narter, *The University of Arizona*

Robert Nelson, *Montgomery Community College*

Caroline Olko, *Nassau Community College*

Maria Ortega, *Washtenaw Community College*

Lee Osterhout, *University of Washington*

Terry Pettijohn, *Ohio State University—Marion Campus*

Frieda Rector, *Yosemite University*

Rebecca Regeth, *California University of Pennsylvania*

Miranda Richmond, *Northwest Vista College*

Hugh Riley, *Baylor University*

Craig Rogers, *Campbellsville University*

Nicholas Schmitt, *Heartland Community College*

Christine Shea-Hunt, *Kirkwood Community College*

Brenda Shook, *National University*

David Simpson, *Carroll University*

Starlette Sinclair, *Columbus State University*

Gregory Smith, *University of Kentucky*

Eric Stephens, *University of the Cumberlands*

Colleen Sullivan, *Worcester State University*

Melissa Terlecki, *Cabrini College*

Lawrence Voight, *Washtenaw Community College*

Benjamin Wallace, *Cleveland State University*

David Williams, *Spartanburg Community College*

Melissa (Liz) Wright, *Northwest Vista College*

We were pleased to be supported by a 2012/2013 Content Advisory Board, which helped guide the development of this new edition of *Psychology in Everyday Life* as well as our other introductory psychology titles. For their helpful input and support, we thank

Barbara Angleberger, *Frederick Community College*

Chip (Charles) Barker, *Olympic College*

Mimi Dumville, *Raritan Valley Community College*

Paula Frioli-Peters, *Truckee Meadows Community College*

Deborah Garfin, *Georgia State University*

Karla Gingerich, *Colorado State University*

Toni Henderson, *Langara College*

Bernadette Jacobs, *Santa Fe Community College*

Mary Livingston, *Louisiana Tech University*

Molly Lynch, *Northern Virginia Community College*

Shelly Metz, *Central New Mexico Community College*

Jake Musgrove, *Broward College—Central Campus*

Robin Musselman, *Lehigh Carbon Community College*

Dana Narter, *The University of Arizona*

Lee Osterhout, *University of Washington*

Nicholas Schmitt, *Heartland Community College*

Christine Shea-Hunt, *Kirkwood Community College*

Brenda Shook, *National University*

Starlette Sinclair, *Columbus State University*

David Williams, *Spartanburg Community College*

Melissa (Liz) Wright, *Northwest Vista College*

We are also grateful for the instructors and students who took the time to offer feedback over the phone, in an online survey, or at one of our face-to-face focus groups. Over 1000 instructors responded to surveys related to depth of coverage and concept difficulty levels.

Seventeen instructors offered helpful and detailed feedback on our design:

Sandra Arntz, *Carroll University*

Christine Browning, *Victory University*

Christina Calayag, *North Central University*

Tametryce Collins, *Hillsborough Community College—Brandon Campus*

Traci Elliott, *Alvin Community College*

Betsy Ingram-Diver, *Lake Superior College*

Bernadette Jacobs, *Santa Fe Community College*

Patricia Johnson, *Craven Community College—Havelock Campus*

Todd Joseph Allen, *Hillsborough Community College*

Donald Lucas, *Northwest Vista College*

Susie Moerschbacher, *Polk State College*

Marcia Seddon, *Indian Hills Community College*

Christine Shea-Hunt, *Kirkwood Community College*

Brenda Shook, *National University*

Beth Smith, *Hillsborough Community College—Brandon Campus*

Heather Thompson, *College of Western Idaho*

Melissa (Liz) Wright, *Northwest Vista College*

Nine instructors coordinated input from 131 of their students about our text design:

Sandra Arntz, *Carroll University*

Christina Calayag, *North Central University*

Tametryce Collins, *Hillsborough Community College—Brandon Campus*

Traci Elliott, *Alvin Community College*

Patricia Johnson, *Craven Community College—Havelock Campus*

Marcia Seddon, *Indian Hills Community College*

Christine Shea-Hunt, *Kirkwood Community College*

Heather Thompson, *College of Western Idaho*

Melissa (Liz) Wright, *Northwest Vista College*

We consulted with eight instructors by phone for lengthy conversations about key features:

Christina Calayag, *North Central University*

Tametryce Collins, *Hillsborough Community College*

Patricia Johnson, *Craven Community College—Havelock Campus*

Todd Allen Joseph, *Hillsborough Community College*

Lynne Kennette, *Wayne State University*

Christine Shea-Hunt, *Kirkwood Community College*

Heather Thompson, *College of Western Idaho*

Melissa (Liz) Wright, *Northwest Vista College*

We gathered extensive written input about the text and its features from 38 students at North Central College (thanks to the coordinating efforts of Christina Calayag). We hosted three student focus groups at the College of Western Idaho (coordinated by Heather Thompson), Hillsborough Community College (coordinated by Todd Allen Joseph), and Kirkwood Community College (coordinated by Christine Shea-Hunt).

We also involved students in a survey to determine level of difficulty of key concepts. A total of 277 students from the following schools participated:

Brevard Community College

Community College of Baltimore County

Florida International University

Millsaps College

Salt Lake Community College

And we involved a group of helpful students in reviewing the application questions for this new edition:

Bianca Arias, *City College of New York*

Brigitte Black, *College of St. Benedict*

Antonia Brune, *Service High School*

Gabriella Brune, *College of St. Benedict*

Peter Casale, *Hofstra University*

Alex Coumbis, *Fordham University*

Julia Elliott, *Hofstra University*

Megan Lynn Garrett, *Ramapo College*

Curran Kelly, *University of Houston Downtown*

Stephanie Kroll, *SUNY Geneseo*

Aaron Mehlenbacher, *SUNY Geneseo*

Brendan Morrow, *Hofstra University*

Kristina Persaud, *Colgate University*

Steven Pignato, *St. John's University*

Ryan Sakhichand, *ITT Tech Institute*

Carlisle Sargent, *Clemson University*

Josh Saunders, *The College of New Jersey*

At Worth Publishers a host of people played key roles in creating this third edition.

Although the information gathering is never ending, the formal planning began as the author-publisher team gathered for a two-day retreat. This happy and creative gathering included John Brink, Thomas Ludwig, Richard Straub, and me [DM] from the author team, along with my assistants Kathryn Brownson and Sara Neevel. We were joined by Worth Publishers executives Tom Scotty, Elizabeth Widdicombe, Catherine Woods, and Craig Bleyer; editors Christine Brune, Kevin Feyen, Nancy Fleming, Tracey Kuehn, Betty Probert, and Trish Morgan; artistic director Babs Reingold; sales and marketing colleagues Tom Kling, Carlise Stembridge, John Britch, Lindsay Johnson, Cindi Weiss, Kari Ewalt, Mike How-ard, and Matt Ours; and special guests Amy Himsel (El Camino Community College), Jennifer Peluso (Florida Atlantic University), Charlotte vanOyen Witvliet (Hope College), and Jennifer Zwolinski (University of San Diego). The input and brainstorming during this meeting of minds gave birth, among other things, to the study aids in this edition, the carefully revised clinical coverage, the revised organization, and the refreshing new design.

Publisher Kevin Feyen is a valued team leader, thanks to his dedication, creativity, and sensitivity. Catherine Woods, Vice President, Editing, Design, and Media, helped construct and execute the plan for this text and its supplements. Elizabeth Block, Anthony Casciano, and Nadina Persaud coordinated production of the huge media and print supplements package for this edition. Betty Probert efficiently edited and produced the print supplements and, in the process, also helped fine-tune the whole book. Nadina also provided invaluable support in commissioning and organizing the multitude of reviews, mailing information to professors, and handling numerous other daily tasks related to the book's development and production. Charles Yuen did a splendid job of laying out each page. Robin Fadool, Bianca Moscatelli, and Donna Ranieri worked together to locate the myriad photos.

Tracey Kuehn, Director of Print and Digital Development, displayed tireless tenacity, commitment, and impressive organization in leading Worth's gifted artistic production team and coordinating editorial input throughout the production process. Senior Project Editor Jane O'Neill and Production Manager Sarah Segal masterfully kept the book to its tight schedule, and Art Director Barbara Reingold skillfully directed creation of the beautiful new design and art program. Production Manager Stacey Alexander, along with Supplements Production Editor Edgar Bonilla, did their usual excellent work of producing the many supplements.

As you can see, although this book has two authors it is a *team* effort. A special salute is due our two book development editors, who have invested so much in creating *Psychology in Everyday Life*. My [DM] longtime editor Christine Brune saw the need for a very short, accessible, student-friendly introductory psychology text, and she energized and guided the rest of us in bringing her vision to reality. Development editor Nancy Fleming is one of those rare editors who is gifted at "thinking big" about a chapter while also applying her sensitive, graceful, line-by-line touches. Her painstaking, deft editing was a key part of achieving the hoped-for brevity and accessibility. In addition, Trish Morgan joined our editorial team for both the planning and late-stage editorial work, and once again amazed me with her meticulous eye, impressive knowledge, and deft editing. And Deborah Heimann did an excellent job with the copyediting.

To achieve our goal of supporting the teaching of psychology, this teaching package not only must be authored, reviewed, edited, and produced, but also made available to teachers of psychology. For their exceptional success in doing that, our author team is grateful to Worth Publishers' professional sales and marketing team. We are especially grateful to Executive Marketing Manager Kate Nurre, Marketing Manager Lindsay Johnson, and National Psychology and Economics Consultant Tom Kling, both for their tireless efforts to inform our teaching colleagues of our efforts to assist their teaching, and for the joy of working with them.

At Hope College, the supporting team members for this edition included Kathryn Brownson, who researched countless bits of information and proofed hundreds of pages. Kathryn has become a knowledgeable and sensitive adviser on many matters, and Sara Neevel has become our high-tech manuscript developer, par excellence.

Again, I [DM] gratefully acknowledge the influence and editing assistance of my writing coach, poet Jack Ridl, whose influence resides in the voice you will be hearing in the pages that follow. He, more than anyone, cultivated my delight in dancing with the language, and taught me to approach writing as a craft that shades into art.

After hearing countless dozens of people say that this book's supplements have taken their teaching to a new level, we reflect on how fortunate we are to be a part of a team in which everyone has produced on-time work marked by the highest professional standards. For their remarkable talents, their long-term dedication, and their friendship, we thank John Brink, Thomas Ludwig, Richard Straub, and Jennifer Peluso.

Finally, our gratitude extends to the many students and instructors who have written to offer suggestions, or just an encouraging word. It is for them, and those about to begin their study of psychology, that we have done our best to introduce the field we love.

*   *   *

The day this book went to press was the day we started gathering information and ideas for the next edition. Your input will influence how this book continues to evolve. So, please, do share your thoughts.

Hope College
Holland, Michigan 49422-9000 USA
www.davidmyers.org

University of Kentucky
Lexington, Kentucky 40506-0044 USA
www.NathanDeWall.com

Content Changes

Psychology in Everyday Life, Third Edition, includes more than 600 new research citations, a new study system that reflects the latest in cognitive psychology research on retention, a revised chapter organization, a fresh new design, and many fun new photos and cartoons. In addition, you will find the following, significant content changes in this new third edition.

CHAPTER 1
Psychology's Roots, Big Ideas, and Critical Thinking Tools

- New illustration introduces *biopsychosocial perspective* more effectively.

- Chapter organization lightly modified and improved. (For example, naturalistic observation is now covered before surveys rather than after, and illusory correlations coverage removed.)

- Now introduces *basic research/applied research* distinction.

- Now introduces *health psychologists;* and new *forensic psychology* example and photo.

- Now includes discussion of Perceiving Order in Random Events, with World Cup photo example.

- New current event examples incorporated.

- New research support for *hindsight bias.*

- Scientific method now illustrated with theory about sleep's value for effective learning.

- New case study photo example of Freud's work with Little Hans.

- New survey data examples.

- New pornography experimental versus correlational study example.

- New research examples of the placebo effect in athletes and others.

- U.S. health insurance controversy used as new example of effect of wording on survey results.

- Now includes discussion of *confounding variables.*

- Discussion of experimental ethics expanded; new key terms *informed consent* and *debriefing.*

- Now closes with new section titled Improve Your Retention—And Your Grades detailing the *testing effect* and how to apply it effectively to learning with this text.

CHAPTER 2
The Biology of Mind and Consciousness

- New chapter introduction tells the story of a brain tumor changing a man's sexual behavior.

- New coverage of *glial cells.*

- New illustration of serotonin pathways in the brain.

- Expanded illustration of the functional divisions of the nervous system.

- Clarified discussion of *reflexes.* New research example of reflex speed and size of organism.

- New coverage of *oxytocin's* effects on physical and social responses.

- New example of woman with destroyed amygdala experiencing no fear.

- New neuroscience research suggesting that there is no one "God spot" in the brain that is activated during religious experiences.

- New photo series shows neural prosthetic in action.

- New research demonstrates the role of dopamine in pleasant experiences and memories.

- Coverage of language in the brain moved to Chapter 8.

- New coverage of brain plasticity in those who are blind or deaf.

- Brain plasticity and music therapy demonstrated with example of Gabrielle Giffords.

- Expanded coverage of conscious awareness, with several new research examples.

- *Selective attention* discussion expanded, with new research examples related to cell phones and driving.

- Additional research support for some level of awareness—via brain response—in noncommunicative patients.

- *Change blindness* is now a key term, with additional narrative coverage.

- This chapter adopts the new American Academy of Sleep Medicine classification of sleep stages (REM, NREM-1, NREM-2, and NREM-3).

- New art illustrates sleep times of various animals.

- New coverage of effects of sleep deprivation—reducing memory, athletic performance, driving safety, immune system functioning, and longevity, and increasing depression rates (in adolescents and adults) and cyberloafing.

- New, improved art for Stages in a Typical Night's Sleep, with new graphs comparing sleep among older and younger adults.

- Improved, expanded sleep tips.
- New anatomical art shows physiological effects of sleep deprivation (in the brain, immune system, and stomach and reflected in blood pressure and weight).
- New table compares dream theories.

CHAPTER 3
Developing Through the Life Span

- David Myers' personal story now opens the chapter.
- New discussion of *epigenetics*, with new art, elaborates gene-environment interaction.
- Infant sensory abilities expanded with new research on smell, and long-term learned preferences.
- New discussion of *assimilation* and *accommodation*.
- Autism spectrum disorder discussion significantly revised to match DSM-5 update, with new research.
- Expanded discussion of value of the Harlow experiments.
- New research stories of devastating effects on children of Romanian and other poorly run orphanages, but value from quality orphanages in some communities, with new photo.
- Now includes epigenetics of child abuse effects.
- New coverage suggests trauma may boost *resilience*.
- Parenting Styles expanded with new cross-cultural research.
- New research explains emotional stability and agreeableness changes in late adolescence, and gender differences in adolescent challenges.

- New coverage of *moral intuition* and automatic moral responses.
- New research expands Emerging Adulthood discussion.
- New social networking research updates peer relationship discussion.
- New research on sexuality in middle adulthood.
- Aging and Intelligence moved to Chapter 8.
- New research explores many older adults' reluctance to embrace new technologies.
- New subsection on Sustaining Mental Abilities.
- New discussion of what maintains (exercise) and what wears down (aging, smoking, obesity, stress) the *telomeres*.
- New research, with new graph, suggests well-being relates to time spent socializing, for all ages.
- Dementia is now *neurocognitive disorder* (DSM-5 update).
- New research explains neuroscience of age-related moderating of emotional experiences, and overall more positive interpretations with age.
- Includes discussion of new research on persistence of personality traits throughout life, the link between self-control and less trouble later, and the connection between smiling school photos and later marriage success (with new illustrations).

CHAPTER 4
Gender and Sexuality

- New co-author Nathan DeWall led the revision of this chapter for the third edition.
- Revised introduction includes new gender diversity story.
- Gender and Social Power expanded and improved with new research

throughout, including gender inequality in advanced career positions.

- New research on gender differences in aggression, with *relational aggression* now a key term.
- New research on gender differences in size of social network.
- New key term *spermarche*.
- New research updates discussion of earlier puberty.
- Gender Development expanded with new research on evolution of pink and blue gender colors, and the discussion of *transgender*.
- New research details gender similarities in self-esteem.
- Gender and Social Connections includes new research on gender differences in texting behavior, on differences in vocational interests, and on changing gender-related attitudes for parents.
- The Nature of Gender updated with new research throughout, including relationship between prenatal testosterone exposure and later male-typical play and athletic success. Includes new section on Variations on Sexual Development.
- New research expands discussion of Hormones and Sexual Behavior.
- New research updates and expands discussion of changing gender roles in U.S. academia, and cross-cultural perspectives on women at work.
- Psychology of Sex updated with new research.
- New section on Sexual Dysfunctions and Paraphilias with DSM-5 updates; includes enhanced discussion of sexual disorders in women.
- Discussion of Sexually Transmitted Infections updated with new information about oral sex.
- Sexual Orientation statistics updated with new research.
- Biology and Sexual Orientation updated with new research.

- New research enhances coverage of Sex and Human Values.
- New research updates Natural Selection and Mating Preferences.

CHAPTER 5
Sensation and Perception

- Now includes explanation of *bottom-up* and *top-down processing* with new photo example.
- New coverage of the adaptation of emotion perception, with "try this" photo example.
- New research describes effects of motivation and emotion on our perceptions.
- New coverage of face recognition in the brain, with new anatomical art.
- Now includes complete coverage of color vision.
- New coverage of the experience of hearing loss; includes *sensorineural* and *conduction hearing loss* and new coverage of *cochlear implants*, with new art.
- New research on recent increased hearing loss among teens.
- New research-based discussion of gender, genetic, and environmental effects on experience of pain.
- Two new sports examples of the powerful effect of distraction on the experience of pain.
- New research on the effects of various smells on our attitudes and behaviors.
- New cognitive neuroscience research helps explain smell-cognition connection.
- Expanded coverage of Sensory Interaction is now its own section (previously mentioned within Taste) and now includes *embodied cognition*.

- New research expands discussion of gender differences in sensory experiences.
- New research on effects of action video games developing spatial skills.

CHAPTER 6
Learning

- New art illustrates operant conditioning.
- Now includes discussion of Thorndike's *law of effect*, with new photos and graph.
- New research on subtle effects of learned associations.
- New research demonstrates process of learning healthy habits, and how long it takes to learn a habit.
- New research example suggests we generalize our dislike based on learned facial features.
- Now includes information on what happened to "Little Albert."
- New research example of extinguishing a learned fear of flying.
- Improved table compares Ways to Decrease Behavior.
- Now includes coverage, with new neuroscience research, on *vicarious reinforcement* and *vicarious punishment* via observed models.
- New neuroscience research suggests we unconsciously synchronize behaviors with those we are observing; leads to cravings for smokers observing others' smoking.
- New research suggests that observing risk-taking increases real-life risk-taking.
- New research examples update media violence viewing/violent behavior discussion.

CHAPTER 7
Memory

- Follows a new format, and more clearly explains how different brain networks process and retain memories. David Myers worked closely with Janie Wilson, Professor of Psychology at Georgia Southern University and Vice President for Programming of the Society for the Teaching of Psychology, in this chapter's revision.
- New music recognition research example.
- Now includes separate section on memory in the brain, with new research and more detail on brain locations where memories are processed and retained.
- New research on persistence of emotion even in brain-damaged patients who cannot form new conscious memories.
- Atkinson-Shiffrin's three-stage model de-emphasized in favor of more current theories.
- Levels of Processing reconceptualized and improved.
- Memory subsystems clarified and simplified as automatic versus effortful, with implicit/explicit differences presented within that simpler organization; details provided about brain areas for these differing memory functions.
- New section presents Measures of Retention.
- Coverage of *working memory* updated and expanded with new research and new art; includes new research on effects of multitasking at various ages.
- New discussion with new research on the *testing effect* and other study tips, including best times to study and effects of spacing on memory

over time. With link to Myers' explanatory YouTube animation.

- New research shows that learning increases synaptic number as well as efficiency, with new application examples.

- New research describes tunnel-vision memory, and our better memories of personal best experiences.

- New research example expands discussion of emotions and memory.

- Updated coverage of Henry Molaison's case, including new photo of those studying and preserving his brain.

- New discussion, with new research, of inaccurate autobiographical memories.

- Memory construction now demonstrated with Myers' personal experience at Loftus presentation.

- New coverage of effects of *priming* on negative and positive behaviors.

- New research and examples expand discussion of *misinformation effect* and its influence on attitudes and behaviors.

CHAPTER 8
Thinking, Language, and Intelligence

- Updated and improved discussion of why we fear the wrong things, with new research and new illustrations.

- New research and examples improve *framing* discussion.

- New research suggests value of employing *intuition* for complex decisions.

- Now includes more information about the development of creative traits in girls.

- New research suggests ways to develop creativity, including value of creativity-fostering environments.

- Animal cognition now covered at end of Thinking—separate from animal language. New photo examples and new research on animals' cognitive feats.

- Discussion of language development in the brain updated with new neuroscience research and moved here (from Chapter 2).

- New research updates discussion of *g* factor and cognitive abilities predicting later accomplishments.

- New research compares animal and human intelligence peaking in mid-life.

- New research suggests mastery (for example, of chess) requires 3,000–11,000 practice hours.

- New research suggests influence of intelligence on creativity.

- Narrative examples and explanation have been updated to 2008 version of the WAIS.

- New research updates SAT prediction strength.

- Aging and Intelligence moved here from Chapter 3, with *cross-sectional* and *longitudinal studies* as new key terms (repeated in Appendix A). New research supports strength of intelligence stability over time and explains resistance to new technologies in those with cognitive decline.

- New research suggests those with higher intelligence live healthier and longer.

- New research graph shows how word power changes with age.

- Grade inflation effects now included, with new research.

- New discussion, with new research, outlines interaction of schooling, intelligence, and motivation.

- Now includes coverage of the extremes of intelligence, including *intellectual disability*.

- New research updates discussion of twin studies and heritability of intelligence.

- New cross-cultural research supports impact of gender expectations on academic flourishing.

- New research suggests importance of establishing a *growth mind-set* for academic success.

- Gender differences in intelligence and vocation choices updated with new research.

- New research expands discussion of intelligence variation due to racial, ethnic, and socioeconomic differences.

- *Stereotype threat* discussion updated with new research and new explanations.

CHAPTER 9
Motivation and Emotion

- *Hunger Games* example now illustrates Maslow's hierarchy.

- Psychology of Hunger updated with new research.

- Eating Disorders moved to Chapter 13.

- Obesity section updated with new research on negative social, health, and memory effects; increased risk for late-life cognitive decline; and increasing rates worldwide.

- New section on *ecology of eating* covers effects of social factors, serving size, and food variety.

- New research on changing workplace, with most modern jobs not requiring physical activity.

- Now includes research suggesting value of joining a support group for weight loss.

- Benefits of Belonging updated with new research, including on value of *chain migration* for immigrants.

- The Pain of Being Shut Out updated with new research, including on prison suicides in solitary confinement, love as a natural painkiller, and effects of Tylenol on relieving social pain. New example from *Survivor* TV show.

- Social Networking section thoroughly updated.

- Theories of Emotion reorganized, consolidated, and improved.

- New coverage, with new anatomical art, of our two-track mind pathways for emotional reactions in the brain.

- New neuroscience research expands discussion of emotional experience, including gender differences.

- New research suggests no one except some police professionals are able to beat chance in accurately detecting deceiving expressions.

- New research on using brain scans for lie detection.

- Now includes coverage of importance of context for accurate detection of facial expressions, with new illustrations.

- Anger is no longer a separate section; coverage has been streamlined and integrated within other discussions.

- New facial feedback research updates discussion of Botox slowing others' interpretation of emotional expressions.

CHAPTER 10
Stress, Health, and Human Flourishing

- New co-author Nathan DeWall led the revision of this chapter for the third edition.

- Revised organization; now includes happiness and subjective well-being, moved here from Chapter 9.

- *Resilience* is now a key term here (as well as in Chapter 14).

- New research supports men's tendency to socially withdraw under stress, and women's tendency to *tend and befriend*.

- New research examples related to work and to pregnancy update discussion of harmful effects of stress, and new research supports value of low stress for effectiveness of vaccinations.

- New research updates stress reports in college students.

- New research expands coverage of oxytocin effects in relationships.

- New research updates Stress and AIDS.

- Stress and Heart Disease revised and updated with new explanation of role of *inflammation*. Now includes *Type D* personality (as well as *Type A* and *Type B*, with new research supporting *Type A*/heart disease link).

- New cross-cultural research suggests greater heart attack risk with work stress.

- Personal Control section revised and expanded with new research and photo examples.

- New research revises and expands discussion of *optimism/pessimism*.

- Social Support revised and updated with new research and new examples, including effect of friend clusters on promoting positive or negative health behaviors going out to three degrees of separation.

- Finding Meaning expanded with new research and explanations.

- More new research supports effects of exercise on preventing or reducing depression and anxiety, and new cross-cultural research supports exercise/life satisfaction link.

- Relaxation and Meditation section revised and updated with new research and examples, showing decrease in depression and anxiety due to meditation.

- New subsection on meditation and mindfulness; includes explanation of neurological changes prompted by practicing mindfulness.

- New research supports longevity/religiosity link, with new information about possible contributions of self-control, smoking, and other behaviors.

- Huge new Facebook study tracks positive versus negative posts across days of the week.

- New research shows higher happiness levels when buying shared experiences rather than stuff.

- New research suggests happiness value of meaningful conversations over small talk, and of having an income that is *comparatively* high.

- New research argues for considering psychological well-being when debating policies and planning neighborhoods.

- New research supports protective health benefits of happiness.

- New research suggests happiness levels affect marital success, and that we feel happier after spending money on others rather than ourselves.

CHAPTER 11
Personality

- New co-author Nathan DeWall led the revision of this chapter for the third edition.

- Compelling new chapter introduction.

- Improved coverage of modern-day psychodynamic approaches, now

- more clearly distinguished from historical Freudian roots.

- Freud's work now presented in context of Victorian era.

- New research expands discussion of *modern unconscious mind*.

- New research supports value of humanistic psychology's positive regard.

- More detailed introduction to Trait Theories.

- New critical thinking box on the Stigma of Introversion (replaces Astrology box).

- New section on Biology and Personality covers personality-related brain activity variation, and personality differences in animals.

- Big Five discussion expanded and updated with new research, including cultural changes over time, relation to brain structure/function, and actual prediction of behavior.

- New research suggests communication preferences vary with personality traits.

- New research shows music preferences, bedrooms, and offices give clues to personality traits.

- Social-Cognitive Theories revised and updated with new research; *self-efficacy* now a key term; expanded to include *heredity-environment interaction*.

- New subsections on Assessing Behavior in Situations, and Evaluating Social-Cognitive Theories.

- New table compares major perspectives on personality, including assumptions, assessment methods, and key proponents.

- New research outlines importance of positive goal-setting in considering *possible selves*.

- The Benefits of Self-Esteem and Self-Serving Bias subsections updated with new research.

- New research explains increase in U.S. *individualism,* including increase in distinctive baby names with new graph.

- New discussion of *collectivist* attitudes and elder respect.

CHAPTER 12
Social Psychology

- This chapter now follows Personality (rather than following Therapy, as in previous edition).

- New research shows power of priming in how attitudes affect actions.

- New research expands group pressure and conformity discussion, including Iraq and Afghanistan War research on factors that contribute to conformity.

- New research on use of classroom clickers to discuss controversial topics.

- New research in online communities supports *deindividuation* findings, with new photo example of 2011 British riots.

- New data, with new graph, on increased acceptance of interracial dating.

- New research and coverage of persisting subtle prejudice, including *implicit prejudice*.

- New research examples of *ingroup bias* in political partisanship.

- Forming categories discussion enhanced with new research on categorizing mixed-race people by their minority identity, with visuals from the research.

- New research updates Biology of Aggression section.

- Psychology of Aggression updated with new research and new explanations.

- Observing Models of Aggression updated with new research data and examples, including new research linking nonviolent pornography with aggression.

- New research updates discussion of Media Models for Violence.

- New graph tracks prejudice over time in various age groups.

- New research on contributors to aggression, including more information on alcohol consumption, external temperature, and prior provocation, with new graph of baseball research example.

- Discussion of effects of video games on violence updated with new research on prosocial effects of playing positive games, on violent video games increasing players' aggression and decreasing their compassion and altruism, and on increased game playing leading to more trouble at school.

- Expanded box on Online Matchmaking and Speed-Dating.

- Attraction section updated with new evolutionary psychology research, and research on beneficial effects of mutual self-disclosure.

- New biochemical research supports forming of companionate love.

- New research suggests emotional response to witnessing altruism; includes new research example demonstrating *reciprocity norm*; also new research showing link between religiosity and volunteer work and charitable giving.

- New research demonstrates positive effects of *contact* for heterosexuals' attitudes toward gay people.

CHAPTER 13
Psychological Disorders

- Reorganized and thoroughly updated to reflect changes to psychiatry's latest edition of its diagnostic manual—the **DSM-5**. Includes integration of psychiatric diagnoses into mainstream medical practice, redefinition of disorders, new disorder categories, changes in labels, and new definition of *psychological disorder*.

- New, careful explanation of how care providers use DSM-5 criteria and codes for diagnosis and treatment, using insomnia disorder as illustrative example.

- New critical thinking box on ADHD, including controversies about diagnosis, and concerns about those seeking the "good-grade pills."

- New mentions of controversial changes in the DSM-5 throughout the chapter, including the new disruptive mood dysregulation disorder, removal of the bereavement exception for depression, and loosened criteria for adult ADHD.

- New results of *field trials* on clinician agreement with DSM-5 for certain categories of disorder.

- New Close-Up box: Are People With Psychological Disorders Dangerous?

- New research updates PTSD statistics.

- Learning perspective on anxiety disorders, OCD, and PTSD updated with expanded coverage of observational learning; new subsection on cognitive learning includes role of *hypervigilance* and intrusive thoughts.

- New table outlines When Is Drug Use a Disorder?

- Updated *addiction* discussion now includes gambling and hoarding disorders, with mention of Internet gaming

disorder "for further study"; new definitions for *addiction* and *withdrawal*.

- New research on success of smoking cessation attempts.

- New research highlights how depression can have adaptive value.

- Suicide rates discussion updated to reflect higher fatal attempts in U.S. states with more gun ownership.

- New research updates discussion of depression, including statistics from college student populations, effects of natural disasters on rates, gender differences research (with updated graph), and new information on typical long-term prognosis.

- New coverage of *dysthymia*.

- Suicide section expanded with new research and explanations; now also covers *nonsuicidal self-injury*.

- New discussion of *seasonal pattern* for depression and bipolar disorder.

- Detailed new table, Diagnosing Major Depressive Disorder.

- New graph illustrates heritability of various psychiatric disorders.

- Now includes *epigenetic effect* on experience of depression.

- New research emphasizes dangers of relentless, self-focused rumination.

- Understanding Mood Disorders updated with new research studies exploring genetic, biochemical, cognitive, and behavioral predictors.

- New research updates discussion of cognitive symptoms of schizophrenia; offers more information on typical prognosis.

- Now includes discussion of epigenetic factors in schizophrenia onset, with new genetics research updates.

- New cross-cultural and other research updates Eating Disorders (moved here from Chapter 9).

- Discussion of antisocial personality disorder updated and improved with new social psychological, develop-

mental, learning, biological, and genetics research.

CHAPTER 14
Therapy

- New co-author Nathan DeWall led the revision of this chapter for the third edition.

- New research updates Psychodynamic Therapy.

- Now includes key term *insight therapies*.

- Cognitive-behavioral therapy discussion updated with new research and information, including on Internet therapy; new research on importance of homework for client with new examples.

- New research suggests that certain psychotherapies work best for specific disorders.

- New table details Selected Cognitive Therapy Techniques.

- New explanation of personal differences for what we find rewarding, and how that affects cognitive therapy.

- Beck's Therapy for Depression has a new introduction and now includes concept of *catastrophizing*.

- Biomedical Therapy explains that primary care providers now do most prescription writing.

- New emphasis on importance of cultural match for therapeutic alliance, and APA efforts to achieve this.

- New case study example of successful use of *antipsychotics*.

- Clarified and updated explanation of *antidepressants*, with revised key term definition; includes idea that many professionals prefer the term *SSRIs* given their multiple treatment uses (not just for depression).

- New research explores placebo effect in ECT treatment.

- Psychosurgery updated with new research on value of micro-scale surgery in extreme cases.
- Therapeutic Lifestyle Change updated with new research suggesting value of time spent outdoors.
- New table compares psychotherapies and biomedical therapies by the way they understand the problems, their aims, and their techniques.
- New research suggests value of *deep-brain stimulation* for treating bipolar disorder and substance use disorders.
- New research supports concept of higher *resilience* in certain groups.
- New research suggests importance of *finding meaning* to foster posttraumatic growth after tragedy, and as a preventive mental health strategy.
- Now includes a brief conclusion to the text.

APPENDIX A
Statistical Reasoning in Everyday Life

- New appendix covers descriptive and inferential statistics.
- Includes measures of central tendency *(mean, median, mode)*, measures of variation *(range, standard deviation, normal curve)*, details on correlation *(correlation coefficient, scatterplot)*, regression toward the mean, and reliability and significance of observed differences.

- Design methodology focuses on *cross-sectional* and *longitudinal studies* as key example of importance of understanding which method was used in a study.

APPENDIX B
Psychology at Work

- New research suggests busier, focused people are happier.
- New *grit* research on danger of getting "stuck in the middle" of projects (easy to start, hard to finish).
- New research explores success–morale relationship for employees.
- Expanded discussion of successful goal-setting from effective leaders, and value of *collective intelligence*.
- New research links feelings of empowerment at work with creativity.
- New example of employee-owned company and benefits of that level of employee engagement.

APPENDIX C
Subfields of Psychology

- New appendix focuses on educational requirements, type of work, and likely places to work for each of psychology's main subfields.

APPENDIX D
Complete Chapter Reviews

- In an effort to encourage students to self-test, the Chapter Review section at the end of each chapter includes only a list of the Learning Objective Questions—repeated from within the chapter. "Answers" to those questions form the complete chapter review, which may be found here in Appendix D for students to check their answers or review the material.

APPENDIX E
Answers to the Chapter Test Questions

- Students may check their answers here for the new multiple-format questions found in a self-test at the end of each chapter and the first two appendices.

Time Management

OR, HOW TO BE A GREAT STUDENT AND STILL HAVE A LIFE

Richard O. Straub, University of Michigan, Dearborn

Desislava Draganova/Alamy

OVERVIEW

How Are You Using Your Time Now?

Design a Better Schedule

Plan the Term

Plan Your Week

CLOSE-UP: More Tips for Effective Scheduling

Make Every Minute of Your Study Time Count

Take Useful Class Notes

Create a Study Space That Helps You Learn

Set Specific, Realistic Daily Goals

Use SQ3R to Help You Master This Text

Don't Forget About Rewards!

Do You Need to Revise Your New Schedule?

Are You Doing Well in Some Courses But Not in Others?

Have You Received a Poor Grade on a Test?

Are You Trying to Study Regularly for the First Time and Feeling Overwhelmed?

We all face challenges in our schedules. Some of you may be taking midnight courses, others squeezing in an online course between jobs or after putting children to bed at night. Some of you may be veterans using military benefits to jump-start a new life. Just making the standard transition from high school to college can be challenging enough.

How can you balance all of your life's demands and be successful? Time management. Manage the time you have so that you can find the time you need.

In this section, I will outline a simple, four-step process for improving the way you make use of your time.

1. Keep a time-use diary to understand how you are using your time. You may be surprised at how much time you're wasting.

2. Design a new schedule for using your time more effectively.

3. Make the most of your study time so that your new schedule will work for you.

4. If necessary, refine your new schedule, based on what you've learned.

MGP/Getty images

How Are You Using Your Time Now?

Although everyone gets 24 hours in the day and seven days in the week, we fill those hours and days with different obligations and interests. If you are like most people, you probably use your time wisely in some ways, and not so wisely in others. Answering the questions in **TABLE 1** can help you find trouble spots—and hopefully more time for the things that matter most to you.

The next thing you need to know is how you *actually* spend your time. To find out, record your activities in a *time-use diary* for one week. Be realistic. Take notes on how much time you spend attending class, studying, working, commuting, meeting personal and family needs, fixing and eating meals, socializing (don't forget texting, Facebooking, and gaming), exercising, and anything else that occupies your time, including life's small practical tasks, which can take up plenty of your 24/7. As you record your activities, take notes on how you are feeling at various times of the day. When does your energy slump, and when do you feel most energetic?

Design a Better Schedule

Take a good look at your time-use diary. Where do you think you may be wasting time? Do you spend a lot of time commuting, for example? If so, could you use that time more productively? If you take public transportation, commuting is a great time to read and test yourself for review.

Did you remember to include time for meals, personal care, work schedules, family commitments, and other fixed activities?

How much time do you sleep? In the battle to meet all of life's daily commitments and interests, we tend to treat sleep as optional. Do your best to manage your life so that you can get enough sleep to feel rested. You will feel better and be healthier, and you will also do better academically and in relationships with your family and friends. (You will read more about this in Chapter 2.)

Are you dedicating enough time for focused study? Take a last look at your notes to see if any other patterns pop out. Now it's time to create a new and more efficient schedule.

Plan the Term

Before you draw up your new schedule, think ahead. Use your phone's calendar feature, or buy a portable calendar that covers the entire school term, with a writing space for each day. Using the course outlines provided by your instructors, enter the dates of all exams, term-paper deadlines, and other important assignments. Also be sure to enter your own long-range personal plans (work and family commitments, etc.). Keep your calendar up-to-date, refer to it often, and change it as needed. Through this process, you will develop a regular schedule that will help you achieve success.

Plan Your Week

To pass those exams, meet those deadlines, and keep up with your life outside of class, you will need to convert your long-term goals into a daily schedule. Be realistic—you will be living with this routine for the entire school term. Here are some more things to add to your calendar.

1. Enter your class times, work hours, and any other fixed obligations. Be thorough. Allow plenty of time for such things as commuting, meals, and laundry.

TABLE 1 Study Habits Survey

Answer the following questions, writing Yes or No for each line.

1. Do you usually set up a schedule to budget your time for studying, work, recreation, and other activities?

2. Do you often put off studying until time pressures force you to cram?

3. Do other students seem to study less than you do, but get better grades?

4. Do you usually spend hours at a time studying one subject, rather than dividing that time among several subjects?

5. Do you often have trouble remembering what you have just read in a textbook?

6. Before reading a chapter in a textbook, do you skim through it and read the section headings?

7. Do you try to predict test questions from your class notes and reading?

8. Do you usually try to summarize in your own words what you have just finished reading?

9. Do you find it difficult to concentrate for very long when you study?

10. Do you often feel that you studied the wrong material for a test?

Thousands of students have participated in similar surveys. Students who are fully realizing their academic potential usually respond as follows: (1) yes, (2) no, (3) no, (4) no, (5) no, (6) yes, (7) yes, (8) yes, (9) no, (10) no. Do your responses fit that pattern? If not, you could benefit from improving your time management and study habits.

2. Set up a study schedule for each course. Remember what you learned about yourself in the study habits survey (Table 1) and your time-use diary. Close-Up: More Tips for Effective Scheduling offers some detailed guidance drawn from psychology's research.

3. After you have budgeted time for studying, fill in slots for other obligations, exercise, fun, and relaxation.

Make Every Minute of Your Study Time Count

How do you study from a textbook? Many students simply read and reread in a passive manner. As a result, they remember the wrong things—the catchy stories but not the main points that show up later in test questions. To make things worse, many students take poor notes during class. Here are some tips that will help you get the most from your class and your text.

Take Useful Class Notes

Good notes will boost your understanding and retention. Are yours thorough? Do they form a sensible outline of each lecture? If not, you may need to make some changes.

More Tips for Effective Scheduling

There are a few other things you will want to keep in mind when you set up your schedule.

Spaced study is more effective than massed study. If you need 3 hours to study one subject, for example, it's best to divide that into shorter periods spaced over several days.

Alternate subjects, but avoid interference. Alternating the subjects you study in any given session will keep you fresh and will, surprisingly, increase your ability to remember what you're learning in each different area. Studying similar topics back-to-back, however, such as two different foreign languages, could lead to interference in your learning. (You will hear more about this in Chapter 7.)

Determine the amount of study time you need to do well in each course. The time you need depends on the difficulty of your courses and the effectiveness of your study methods. Ideally, you would spend at least 1 to 2 hours studying for each hour spent in class. Increase your study time slowly by setting weekly goals that will gradually bring you up to the desired level.

Create a schedule that makes sense. Tailor your schedule to meet the demands of each course. For the course that emphasizes lecture notes, plan a daily review of your notes soon after each class. If you are evaluated for class participation (for example, in a language course), allow time for a review just before the class meets. Schedule study time for your most difficult (or least motivating) courses during hours when you are the most alert and distractions are fewest.

Schedule open study time. Life can be unpredictable. Emergencies and new obligations can throw off your schedule. Or you may simply need some extra time for a project or for review in one of your courses. Try to allow for some flexibility in your schedule each week.

Following these guidelines will help you find a schedule that works for you!

© Hero Images/Corbis

Keep Each Course's Notes Separate and Organized

Keeping all your notes for a course in one location will allow you to flip back and forth easily to find answers to questions. Three options are (1) separate notebooks for each course, (2) clearly marked sections in a shared ring binder, or (3) carefully organized folders if you opt to take notes electronically. For the print options, removable pages will allow you to add new information and weed out past mistakes. Choosing notebook pages with lots of space, or using mark-up options in electronic files, will allow you to add comments when you review and revise your notes after class.

Use an Outline Format

Use roman numerals for major points, letters for supporting arguments, and so on. (See **FIGURE 1** for a sample.) In some courses, taking notes will be easy, but some instructors may be less organized, and you will have to work harder to form your outline.

Clean Up Your Notes After Class

Try to reorganize your notes soon after class. Expand or clarify your comments and clean up any hard-to-read scribbles while the material is fresh in your mind. Write important questions in the margin, or by using an electronic markup feature, next to notes that answer them. (For example: "What are the sleep stages?") This will help you when you review your notes before a test.

Create a Study Space That Helps You Learn

It's easier to study effectively if your work area is well designed.

Organize Your Space

Work at a desk or table, not on your bed or a comfy chair that will tempt you to nap.

Minimize Distractions

Turn the TV off, turn off your phone, and close Facebook and other distracting windows on your computer. If you must listen to music to mask outside noise, play soft instrumentals, not vocal selections that will draw your mind to the lyrics.

Ask Others to Honor Your Quiet Time

Tell roommates, family, and friends about your new schedule. Try to find a study place where you are least likely to be disturbed.

Set Specific, Realistic Daily Goals

The simple note "7–8 P.M.: Study Psychology" is too broad to be useful. Instead, break your studying into manageable tasks. For example, you will want to subdivide large reading assignments. If you aren't used to studying for long periods, start with relatively short periods of concentrated study, with breaks in between. In this text, for example, you might decide to read one major section before each break. Limit your breaks to 5 or 10 minutes to stretch or move around a bit.

Your attention span is a good indicator of whether you are pacing yourself successfully. At this early stage, it's important to remember that you're in training. If your attention begins to wander, get up immediately and take a short break. It is better to study effectively for 15

Sleep (Chapter 2)

When is my daily peak in circadian arousal? Study hardest subject then!

I. Biological Rhythms

   A. Circadian Rhythm (circa-about; diem-day)—24-hour cycle.

      1. Ups and downs throughout day/night.

         Dip in afternoon (siesta time).

      2. Melatonin—hormone that makes us sleepy. Produced by pineal gland in brain. Bright light shuts down production of melatonin. (Dim the lights at night to get sleepy.)

   B. FOUR Sleep Stages, cycle through every 90 minutes all night! Aserinsky discovered—his son—REM sleep (dreams, rapid eye movement, muscles paralyzed but brain super active). EEG measurements showed sleep stages.

      1. NREM-1 (non-Rapid Eye Movement sleep; brief, images like hallucinations; hypnagogic jerks)

      2. NREM-2 (harder to waken, sleep spindles)

      3. NREM-3 (DEEP sleep—hard to wake up! Long slow waves on EEG; bedwetting, night terrors, sleepwalking occurs here; asleep but not dead—can still hear, smell, etc. Will wake up for baby.)

      4. REM Sleep (Dreams…)

FIGURE 1 Sample class notes in outline form Here is a sample from a student's notes taken in outline form from a lecture on sleep.

minutes and then take a break than to fritter away 45 minutes out of your study hour. As your endurance develops, you can increase the length of study periods.

Use SQ3R to Help You Master This Text

David Myers and Nathan DeWall organized this text by using a system called SQ3R (Survey, Question, Read, Retrieve, Review). Using SQ3R can help you to understand what you read, and to retain that information longer.

Applying SQ3R may feel at first as though it's taking more time and effort to "read" a chapter, but with practice, these steps will become automatic.

Survey

Before you read a chapter, survey its key parts. Scan the chapter outline. Note that main sections have numbered Learning Objective Questions to help you focus. Pay attention to headings, which indicate important subtopics, and to words set in bold type.

Surveying gives you the big picture of a chapter's content and organization. Understanding the chapter's logical sections will help you break your work into manageable pieces in your study sessions.

You will hear more about SQ3R in Chapter 1.

Question

As you survey, don't limit yourself to the numbered Learning Objective Questions that appear throughout the chapter. Jotting down additional questions of your own will cause you to look at the material in a new way. (You might, for example, scan this section's headings and ask "What does 'SQ3R' mean?") Information becomes easier to remember when you make it personally meaningful. Trying to answer your questions while reading will keep you in an active learning mode.

Read

As you read, keep your questions in mind and actively search for the answers. If you come to material that seems to answer an important question that you haven't jotted down, stop and write down that new question.

Be sure to read everything. Don't skip photo or art captions, graphs, boxes, tables, or quotes. An idea that seems vague when you read about it may become clear when you see it in a graph or table. Keep in mind that instructors sometimes base their test questions on figures and tables.

Retrieve

When you have found the answer to one of your questions, close your eyes and mentally recite the question and its answer. Then write the answer next to the question in your own words. Trying to explain something in your own words will help you figure out where there are gaps in your understanding. These kinds of opportunities to practice *retrieving* develop the skills you will need when you are taking exams. If you study without ever putting your book and notes aside, you may develop false confidence about what you know. With the material available, you may be able to recognize the correct answer to your questions. But will you be able to recall it later, when you take an exam without having your mental props in sight?

Test your understanding as often as you can. Testing yourself is part of successful learning, because the act of testing forces your brain to work at remembering, thus establishing the memory more permanently (so you can find it later for the exam!). Use the self-testing opportunities throughout each chapter, including the periodic Retrieve + Remember items. Also take advantage of the self-testing that is available through LaunchPad (www.worthpublishers.com/launchpad/pel3e).

Review

After working your way through the chapter, read over your questions and your written answers. Take an extra few minutes to create a brief written summary covering all of your questions and answers. At the end of the chapter, you should take advantage of three important opportunities for self-testing and review—a list of the chapter's Learning Objective Questions for you to try answering before checking Appendix D (Complete Chapter Reviews), a list of the chapter's key terms for you to try to define before checking the referenced page, and a final self-test that covers all of the key chapter concepts (with answers in Appendix E).

Don't Forget About Rewards!

If you have trouble studying regularly, giving yourself a reward may help. What kind of reward works best? That depends on what you enjoy. You might start by making a list of 5 or 10 things that put a smile on your face. Spending time with a loved one, taking a walk or going for a bike ride, relaxing with a magazine or novel, or watching a favorite show can provide immediate rewards for achieving short-term study goals.

To motivate yourself when you're having trouble sticking to your schedule, allow yourself an immediate reward for completing a specific task. If running makes you smile, change your shoes, grab a friend, and head out the door! You deserve a reward for a job well done.

Do You Need to Revise Your New Schedule?

What if you've lived with your schedule for a few weeks, but you aren't making progress toward your academic and personal goals? What if your studying hasn't paid off in better grades? Don't despair and abandon your program, but do take a little time to figure out what's gone wrong.

Are You Doing Well in Some Courses But Not in Others?

Perhaps you need to shift your priorities a bit. You may need to allow more study time for chemistry, for example, and less time for some other course.

Have You Received a Poor Grade on a Test?

Did your grade fail to reflect the effort you spent preparing for the test? This can happen to even the hardest-working student, often on a first test with a new instructor. This common experience can be upsetting. "What do I have to do to get an A?" "The test was unfair!" "I studied the wrong material!"

Try to figure out what went wrong. Analyze the questions you missed, dividing them into two categories: class-based questions and text-based questions. How many questions did you miss in each category? If you find far more errors in one category than in the other, you'll have some clues to help you revise your schedule. Depending on the pattern you've found, you can add extra study time to review of class notes, or to studying the text.

Are You Trying to Study Regularly for the First Time and Feeling Overwhelmed?

Perhaps you've set your initial goals too high. Remember, the point of time management is to identify a regular schedule that will help you achieve success. Like any skill, time management takes practice. Accept your limitations and revise your schedule to work slowly up to where you know you need to be—perhaps adding 15 minutes of study time per day.

* * *

I hope that these suggestions help make you more successful academically, and that they enhance the quality of your life in general. Having the necessary skills makes any job a lot easier and more pleasant. Let me repeat my warning not to attempt to make too drastic a change in your lifestyle immediately. Good habits require time and self-discipline to develop. Once established, they can last a lifetime.

REVIEW

Time Management: Or, How to Be a Great Student and Still Have a Life

1. How Are You Using Your Time Now?

- Identify your areas of weakness.
- Keep a time-use diary.
- Record the time you actually spend on activities.
- Record your energy levels to find your most productive times.

2. Design a Better Schedule

- Decide on your goals for the term and for each week.
- Enter class times, work times, social times (for family and friends), and time needed for other obligations and for practical activities.
- Tailor study times to avoid interference and to meet each course's needs.

3. Make Every Minute of Your Study Time Count

- Take careful class notes (in outline form) that will help you recall and rehearse material covered in lectures.
- Try to eliminate distractions to your study time, and ask friends and family to help you focus on your work.
- Set specific, realistic daily goals to help you focus on each day's tasks.
- Use the SQ3R system (survey, question, read, retrieve, review) to master material covered in your text.
- When you achieve your daily goals, reward yourself with something that you value.

4. Do You Need to Revise Your New Schedule?

- Allocate extra study time for courses that are more difficult, and a little less time for courses that are easy for you.
- Study your test results to help determine a more effective balance in your schedule.
- Make sure your schedule is not too ambitious. Gradually establish a schedule that will be effective for the long term.

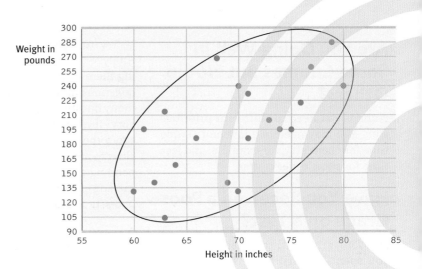

1 Psychology's Roots, Big Ideas, and Critical Thinking Tools

A note to our readers: I am delighted to welcome Nathan DeWall as co-author for this edition of Psychology in Everyday Life. He led our shared revision work for Chapters 4, 10, 11, and 14.

Hoping to understand themselves and others, millions turn to psychology, as you now do. What do psychologists really know? "What's it like being married to a psychologist?" people have occasionally asked my wife. "Does he use his psychology on you?"

"So, does your Dad, like, analyze you?" my children were asked many times by friends.

"What do you think of me?" asked one barber, hoping for an instant personality analysis after learning that I am a psychologist.

For these questioners, as for most people whose ideas about psychology come from the Internet and popular shows, psychologists analyze personality, examine crime scenes, and testify in court. They offer counseling and dispense ideas about parenting, the path to love and happiness, and even the meaning of dreams. Yet psychologists do much more. Psychology's roots are broad, its ideas are big, and its investigations are scientific. Consider some of the questions psychologists study that you may also wonder about:

- Have you ever found yourself reacting to something as one of your biological parents would—perhaps in a way you vowed you never would—and then wondered how much of your personality you inherited? *How much are we shaped by our genes, and how much by our home and community environments?*

- Have you ever worried about how to act among people of a different culture, race, gender, or sexual orientation? *In what ways are we alike as members of the human family? How do we differ?*

- Have you ever awakened from a nightmare and, with a wave of relief, wondered why you had such a crazy dream? *How often, and why, do we dream?*

- Have you ever played peekaboo with a 6-month-old and wondered why the baby finds the game so delightful? The infant seems to think you actually disappear, only to reappear again like magic. *What do babies actually perceive and think?*

- What do you think leads to success in life? *Are some people just born smarter? Can we make it on intelligence alone? What about creativity and emotional intelligence? How about self-control?*

- Are people affected by the changing ways we communicate? *How do today's electronic media influence how we think and how we relate to each other?*

1

- Have you ever become depressed or anxious and wondered whether you'll ever feel "normal"? *What triggers our bad moods—and our good ones? What's the line between a normal mood swing and a psychological disorder for which someone should seek help?*

As you will see, psychological science has produced some fascinating and sometimes surprising answers to these questions.

Psychology's Roots

◎ Once upon a time, on a planet in your neighborhood of the universe, there came to be people. These creatures became intensely interested in themselves and one another. They wondered, "Who are we? Why do we think and feel and act as we do? And how are we to understand—and to manage—those around us?"

To be human is to be curious about ourselves and the world around us. The ancient Greek naturalist and philosopher Aristotle (384–322 B.C.E.) wondered about learning and memory, motivation and emotion, perception and personality. We may chuckle at some of his guesses, like his suggestion that a meal makes us sleepy by causing gas and heat to collect around the source of our personality, the heart. But credit Aristotle with asking the right questions.

Today, psychology asks similar questions. But with its roots reaching back into philosophy and biology, and its branches spreading out across the world, psychology gathers its answers by scientifically studying how we act, think, and feel.

Psychological Science Is Born

1-1 How has psychology's focus changed over time?[1]

Psychology as we know it was born on a December day in 1879, in a small, third-floor room at a German university. There, Wilhelm Wundt and his assistants created a machine to measure how long it took people to press a telegraph key

---

1 Throughout this book you will find numbered questions that preview main sections and suggest your learning goal, or objective. Keep the question in mind as you read the section to make sure that you are following the main point of the discussion. These learning objective questions are repeated at the end of each chapter as a self-test, and answered in Appendix D, Complete Chapter Reviews, at the end of this book.

after hearing a ball hit a platform (Hunt, 1993).[2] (Most hit the key in about one-tenth of a second.) Wundt's attempt to measure "atoms of the mind"—the fastest and simplest mental processes—was psychology's first experiment. And that modest third-floor room took its place in history as the first psychological laboratory.

Psychology's earliest pioneers—"Magellans of the mind," Morton Hunt called them (1993)—came from many disciplines and countries. Wundt was both a philosopher and a physiologist. Charles Darwin, who proposed evolutionary psychology, was an English naturalist. Ivan Pavlov, who taught us much about learning, was a Russian physiologist. Sigmund Freud, a famous personality theorist and therapist, was an Austrian physician. Jean Piaget, who explored children's developing minds, was a Swiss biologist. William James, who shared his love of psychology in his 1890 textbook, was an American philosopher.

Few of psychology's early pioneers were women. In the late 1800s, psychology, like most fields, was a man's world. William James helped break that mold when he accepted Mary Whiton Calkins

---

2 This book's information sources are cited in parentheses, with name and date. Every citation can be found in the end-of-book References, with complete documentation.

WILHELM WUNDT Wundt established the first psychology laboratory at the University of Leipzig, Germany.

WILLIAM JAMES AND MARY WHITON CALKINS William James was a legendary teacher-writer of psychology. Among his students was Mary Whiton Calkins, who became famous for her memory research and for being the first woman president of the American Psychological Association.

MARGARET FLOY WASHBURN After Harvard refused to grant Calkins the degree she had earned, Washburn became the first woman to receive a psychology Ph.D. She focused on animal behavior research in *The Animal Mind*.

as his student. Although Calkins went on to outscore all the male students on the Ph.D. exams, Harvard University denied her a degree. In its place, she was told, she could have a degree from Radcliffe College, Harvard's "sister" school for women. Calkins resisted the unequal treatment and turned down the offer. But she continued her research on memory, which her colleagues honored by electing her the first female president of the American Psychological Association (APA). Animal behavior researcher Margaret Floy Washburn became the first woman to receive a psychology Ph.D. and the second, in 1921, to become an APA president.

The rest of the story of psychology—the story told by this book—develops at many levels, in the hands of many people, with interests ranging from therapy to the study of nerve cell activity. As you might expect, agreeing on a definition of psychology has not been easy.

For the early pioneers, *psychology* was defined as "the science of mental life." And so it continued until the 1920s, when the first of two larger-than-life American psychologists dismissed this idea. John B. Watson, and later B. F. Skinner, insisted that *psychology* must be "the scientific study of observable *behavior.*" What you cannot observe and measure, they said, you cannot scientifically study. You cannot observe a sensation, a feeling, or a thought, but you *can* observe and record people's *behavior* as they respond to and learn in different situations. Many agreed, and these **behaviorists**[3] and their colleagues were one of psychology's two major forces well into the 1960s.

The other major force was *Freudian psychology,* which emphasized our unconscious thought processes and our emotional responses to childhood experiences. Some students wonder: Is psychology mainly about Freud's teachings on unconscious sexual conflicts and the mind's defenses against its own wishes and impulses? *No.* Psychology is much more, though Freudian psychology did have an impact. (In chapters to come, we'll look more closely at Freud and others mentioned here.)

As the behaviorists had rejected the early 1900s definition of *psychology,* two other groups in the 1960s rejected the behaviorists' definition. The first group, the **humanistic psychologists,** led by Carl Rogers and Abraham Maslow, found both Freudian psychology and behaviorism too limiting. Rather than focusing on childhood memories or learned behaviors, Rogers and Maslow stressed the growth potential of healthy people.

They drew attention to ways that an environment can help or hinder our personal growth, and to our needs for love and acceptance.

The second group searching for a new path in psychology pioneered the cognitive revolution, which led the field back to its early interest in mental processes. *Cognitive psychology* scientifically explores how we perceive, process, and remember information, and even why we can become anxious or depressed. **Cognitive neuroscience,** with researchers in many disciplines, explores the brain activity underlying mental activity.

To include psychology's concern with observable behavior *and* with inner thoughts and feelings, today we define **psychology** as the *science of behavior and mental processes.*

---

3 Throughout the text, important concepts are boldfaced. As you study, you can find these terms defined in a boxed section nearby, and in the Glossary at the end of the book.

---

behaviorism the view that psychology (1) should be an objective science that (2) studies behavior without reference to mental processes. Most psychologists today agree with (1) but not with (2).

humanistic psychology emphasized the growth potential of healthy people.

cognitive neuroscience the interdisciplinary study of the brain activity linked with mental activity (including perception, thinking, memory, and language).

psychology the science of behavior and mental processes.

JOHN B. WATSON AND ROSALIE RAYNER Working with Rayner, Watson championed psychology as the scientific study of behavior. He and Rayner showed that fear could be learned, in experiments on a baby who became famous as "Little Albert." (More about Watson's controversial study in Chapter 6.)

B. F. SKINNER This leading behaviorist rejected the idea of studying inner thoughts and feelings. He studied how consequences shape behavior.

SIGMUND FREUD The controversial ideas of this famous personality theorist and therapist influenced twentieth-century psychology and culture.

Let's unpack this definition. *Behavior* is anything a human or nonhuman animal *does*—any action we can observe and record. Yelling, smiling, blinking, sweating, talking, and questionnaire marking are all observable behaviors. *Mental processes* are the internal states we *infer* from behavior—such as thoughts, beliefs, and feelings. For example, I may say that "I feel your pain," but in fact I *infer* it from the hints you give me—crying out, clutching your side, and gasping.

The key word in psychology's definition is *science*. Psychology, as I will stress again and again, is less a set of findings than a way of asking and answering questions. My aim, then, is not merely to report results but also to show you how psychologists play their game, weighing opinions and ideas. I hope you, too, will learn how to play the game—to think smarter when explaining events and making choices in your own life. ■

AP Photo/Paul Sakuma, File

ONE PSYCHOLOGY MAJOR'S CAREER Psychology students, such as Facebook CEO Mark Zuckerberg (who majored in psychology and computer science while at Harvard), end up in varied careers.

4 Study Tip: Memory research reveals a *testing effect*. We retain information much better if we actively retrieve it by self-testing and rehearsing. To boost your learning and memory, take advantage of the Retrieve + Remember self-tests you will find throughout this text.

Contemporary Psychology

1-2 What are psychology's current perspectives, and what are some of its subfields?

Psychologists' widely ranging interests make it hard to picture a psychologist at work. You might start by imagining a neuroscientist probing an animal's brain, an intelligence researcher studying how quickly infants become bored with a familiar scene, or a therapist listening closely to a client's depressed thoughts. Psychologists examine behavior and mental processes from many viewpoints, which are described in

TABLE 1.1   Psychology's Current Perspectives

Perspective	Focus	Sample Questions	Examples of Subfields Using This Perspective
Neuro-science	How the body and brain enable emotions, memories, and sensory experiences	How do pain messages travel from the hand to the brain? How is blood chemistry linked with moods and motives?	Biological; cognitive; clinical
Evolutionary	How the natural selection of traits passed down from one generation to the next has promoted the survival of genes	How has our evolutionary past influenced our modern-day mating preferences? Why do humans learn some fears so much more easily than others?	Biological; developmental; social
Behavior genetics	How our genes and our environment influence our individual differences	To what extent are psychological traits such as intelligence, personality, sexual orientation, and optimism products of our genes? Of our environment?	Personality; developmental; legal/forensic
Psycho-dynamic	How behavior springs from unconscious drives and conflicts	How can someone's personality traits and disorders be explained in terms of their childhood relationships?	Clinical; counseling; personality
Behavioral	How we learn observable responses	How do we learn to fear particular objects or situations? What is the most effective way to alter our behavior, say, to lose weight or stop smoking?	Clinical; counseling; industrial-organizational
Cognitive	How we encode, process, store, and retrieve information	How do we use information in remembering? Reasoning? Solving problems?	Cognitive neuroscience; clinical; counseling; industrial-organizational
Social-cultural	How behavior and thinking vary across situations and cultures	How are we alike as members of one human family? How do we differ as products of our environment?	Developmental; social psychology; clinical; counseling

TABLE 1.1. These perspectives range from the biological to the social-cultural, and their settings range from the laboratory to the clinic. But all share a common goal: *describing and explaining behavior and the mind underlying it.*

Psychology also relates to many other fields. You'll find psychologists teaching not only in psychology departments but also in medical schools, law schools, business schools, and theological seminaries. You'll see them working in hospitals, factories, and corporate offices. In this course, you will hear about

- *biological psychologists* exploring the links between brain and mind.
- *developmental psychologists* studying our changing abilities from womb to tomb.
- *cognitive psychologists* experimenting with how we perceive, think, and solve problems.
- *personality psychologists* investigating our persistent traits.
- *social psychologists* exploring how we view and affect one another.
- *counseling psychologists* helping people cope with personal and career challenges by recognizing their strengths and resources.
- *health psychologists* investigating the psychological, biological, and behavioral factors that promote or impair our health.
- *clinical psychologists* assessing and treating mental, emotional, and behavior disorders. (By contrast, *psychiatrists* are medical doctors who also prescribe drugs when treating psychological disorders.)
- *industrial-organizational psychologists* studying and advising on behavior in the workplace.

Ted Fitzgerald, Pool/AP Photo

Image Source/Punchstock

PSYCHOLOGY IN COURT Forensic psychologists apply psychology's principles and methods in the criminal justice system. They may consult on witnesses, or testify about a defendant's state of mind and future risk.

Psychology is both a science and a profession. Some of its members conduct *basic research,* to build the field's knowledge base. Others conduct *applied research,* tackling practical problems. Many do both. (Want to learn more? See Appendix C, Subfields of Psychology, at the end of this book, and go to the regularly updated **Careers in Psychology** at www.yourpsychportal.com/myers for more on the many interesting psychology careers available.)

Psychology also influences modern culture. Knowledge transforms us. After learning about psychology's findings, people less often judge psychological disorders as moral failures. They less often regard women as men's inferiors. They less often view children as ignorant, willful beasts in need of taming. And as thinking changes, so do actions. "In each case," noted Hunt (1990, p. 206), "knowledge has modified attitudes, and, through them, behavior." Once aware of psychology's well-researched ideas—about how body and mind connect, how we construct our perceptions, how a child's mind grows, how people across the world differ (and are alike)—your own mind may never again be quite the same. ■

RETRIEVE + REMEMBER

- The _____ perspective in psychology focuses on how behavior and thought differ from situation to situation and from culture to culture.

  ANSWER: social-cultural

- The _____ perspective emphasizes how we learn observable responses.

  ANSWER: behavioral

Four Big Ideas in Psychology

1-3 What four big ideas run throughout this book?

◎ I have used four of psychology's big ideas to organize material in this book.

1. *Critical thinking* Science supports thinking that examines assumptions, uncovers hidden values, weighs evidence, and tests conclusions. Science-aided thinking is smart thinking.

2. *The biopsychosocial approach* We can view human behavior from three levels—the biological, psychological, and social-cultural. We share a biologically rooted human nature. Yet cultural and psychological influences fine-tune our assumptions, values, and behaviors.

3. *The two-track mind* Today's psychological science explores our *dual-processing* capacity. Our perception, thinking, memory, and attitudes all operate on two levels: a conscious, aware track, and an unconscious, automatic, unaware track. It has been a surprise to learn how much information processing happens without our awareness.

4. *Exploring human strengths* Psychology today focuses not only on understanding and offering relief from

troublesome behaviors and emotions, but also on understanding and building the emotions and traits that help us to thrive.

Let's consider these four big ideas, one by one.

Big Idea 1: Critical Thinking Is Smart Thinking

Whether reading a news report or swapping ideas with others, **critical thinkers** ask questions. *How do we know that? Who benefits from this? Is the conclusion based on guesswork and gut feelings, or on evidence? How do we know one event caused the other? How else could we explain things?*

In psychology, critical thinking has led to some surprising findings. Believe it or not . . .

- massive losses of brain tissue early in life may have few long-term effects (see Chapter 2).
- within days, newborns can recognize their mother's odor (Chapter 3).
- some people with brain damage can learn new skills, yet at the mind's conscious level be unaware that they have these skills (Chapter 7).
- most of us—male and female, young and old, wealthy and not wealthy, with and without disabilities—report roughly the same levels of personal happiness (Chapter 10).
- an electric shock delivered to the brain (electroconvulsive therapy) may relieve severe depression when all else has failed (Chapter 14).

This same critical thinking has also debunked some popular beliefs. When we let the evidence speak for itself, we learn that . . .

- sleepwalkers are not acting out their dreams (Chapter 2).
- our past is *not* precisely recorded in our brain. Neither brain stimulation nor hypnosis will let us push "play"

and relive long-buried memories (Chapter 7).

- most of us do *not* suffer from low self-esteem, and high self-esteem is not all good (Chapter 11).
- opposites do not generally attract (Chapter 12).

In later chapters, you'll see many more examples of research in which critical thinking has challenged our beliefs and triggered new ways of thinking.

Big Idea 2: Behavior Is a Biopsychosocial Event

Each of us is part of a larger social system—a family, a group, a society. But each of us is also made up of smaller systems, such as our nervous system and body organs, which are composed of still smaller systems—cells, molecules, and atoms.

If we study this complexity with simple tools, we may end up with partial answers. Consider: Why do grizzly bears hibernate? Is it because hibernation helped their ancestors to survive and reproduce? Because their biology drives them to do so? Because cold cli-

mates hinder food gathering during winter? Each of these is a partial truth, but none is a full answer. For the best possible view, we need to use many *levels of analysis*. The **biopsychosocial approach** integrates three levels: biological, psychological, and social-cultural (**FIGURE 1.1**). Each level's viewpoint gives us a valuable insight into a behavior or mental process, and together they offer us the most complete picture.

Suppose we wanted to study gender differences in a group of men and women. *Gender* is not the same as *sex*. *Gender* refers to the traits and behaviors we *expect* in a man or a woman. *Sex*

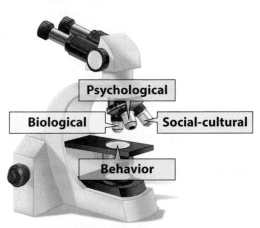

Biological influences:
- genetic predispositions (genetically influenced traits)
- genetic mutations
- natural selection of adaptive traits and behaviors passed down through generations
- genes responding to the environment

Psychological influences:
- learned fears and other learned expectations
- emotional responses
- cognitive processing and perceptual interpretations

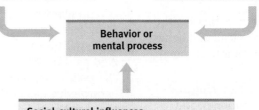

Social-cultural influences:
- presence of others
- cultural, societal, and family expectations
- peer and other group influences
- compelling models (such as in the media)

FIGURE 1.1 Biopsychosocial approach: Three paths to understanding Studying events from many viewpoints gives us a more complete picture than any one perspective could offer.

refers to the biological characteristics people inherit, thanks to their genes. To study gender differences, we would want to know as much as possible about biological influences. But we would also want to understand how the group's **culture**—the shared ideas and behaviors that one generation passes on to the next—defines *male* and *female*. Even with this much information, our view would be incomplete. We would also need some understanding of how the *individuals* in the group differ from one another because of their personal abilities and learning.

Studying all these influences, researchers have found some gender differences—in what we dream, in how we express and detect emotion, and in our risk for substance abuse, depression, and eating disorders. Psychologically as well as biologically, women and men differ. But the research shows we are also alike. Whether female or male, we learn to walk at about the same age. We experience the same sensations of light and sound. We feel the same pangs of hunger, desire, and fear. We exhibit similar overall intelligence and well-being.

A SMILE IS A SMILE THE WORLD AROUND Throughout this book, you will see examples not only of our cultural and gender diversity but also of the similarities that define our shared human nature. People in different cultures vary in when and how often they smile, but a naturally happy smile *means* the same thing anywhere in the world.

Psychologists have used the biopsychosocial approach to study many of the field's big questions. One of the biggest and most persistent is the **nature–nurture issue:** How do we judge the contributions of *nature* (biology) and *nurture* (experience)? Today's psychologists explore this age-old question by asking, for example:

- How are differences in intelligence, personality, and psychological disorders influenced by heredity and by environment?

- Is our *sexual orientation* written in our genes or learned through our experiences?

- Can life experiences affect the activity of our heredity (our genes)?

- Should we treat depression as a disorder of the brain or a disorder of thought—or both?

A NATURE-MADE NATURE–NURTURE EXPERIMENT Identical twins (left) have the same genes. This makes them ideal participants in studies designed to shed light on hereditary and environmental influences on personality, intelligence, and other traits. Fraternal twins (right) have different genes but often share the same environment. Twin studies provide a wealth of findings—described in later chapters—showing the importance of both nature and nurture.

critical thinking thinking that does not blindly accept arguments and conclusions. Rather, it examines assumptions, uncovers hidden values, weighs evidence, and assesses conclusions.

biopsychosocial approach an approach that integrates different but complementary views from biological, psychological, and social-cultural viewpoints.

culture the enduring behaviors, ideas, attitudes, values, and traditions shared by a group of people and handed down from one generation to the next.

nature–nurture issue the age-old controversy over the relative influence of genes and experience in the development of psychological traits and behaviors. Today's psychological science sees traits and behaviors arising from the interaction of nature and nurture.

In most cases, *nurture works on what nature provides.* Our species has been graced with a great biological gift: an enormous ability to learn and adapt. Moreover (and you will read this over and over in the pages that follow), every psychological event—every thought, every emotion—is also a biological event.

Big Idea 3: We Operate With a Two-Track Mind (Dual Processing)

Mountains of new research reveal that our brain works on two tracks. Our conscious mind *feels* like our body's chief executive, and in fact we do process much information on our brain's conscious track, with full awareness. But at the same time, a surprisingly large unconscious, automatic track is processing information outside of our awareness. Thinking, memory, perception, language, and attitudes all operate on these two tracks. Today's researchers call it **dual processing.** We know more than we know we know. As a fascinating scientific story illustrates, the truth sometimes turns out to be stranger than fiction.

During my time spent at Scotland's University of St. Andrews, I came to know research psychologists Melvyn Goodale and David Milner (2004, 2006). A local woman, whom they call D. F., was overcome by carbon monoxide one day while showering. The resulting brain damage left her unable to consciously perceive objects. Yet she *acted* as if she *could* see them. Asked to slip a postcard into a mail slot, she could do so without error. And although she could not report the width of a block in front of her, she could grasp it with just the right finger-thumb distance.

How could this be? How could a woman who is perceptually blind grasp objects accurately? Goodale and Milner knew from animal research that the eye sends information to different brain areas, each of which has a different task. Sure enough, a scan of D. F.'s brain activity revealed normal activity

in the area concerned with reaching for and grasping objects, but not in the area concerned with consciously recognizing objects. So, would the reverse damage lead to the opposite symptoms? Indeed, there are a few such patients. They can see and recognize objects, but they have difficulty pointing toward or grasping them.

We think of our vision as one system: We look, we see, we respond to what we see. Actually, vision is a great example of our dual processing. A *visual perception track* enables us to think about the world—to recognize things and to plan future actions. A *visual action track* guides our moment-to-moment actions.

This big idea—that much of our everyday thinking, feeling, sensing, and acting operates outside our awareness—may be a weird new idea for you. It was for me. I long believed that my own intentions and deliberate choices ruled my life. In many ways they do. But in the mind's downstairs, as you will see in later chapters, there is much, much more to being human.

Big Idea 4: Psychology Explores Human Strengths as Well as Challenges

Psychology's first hundred years focused on understanding and treating troubles, such as abuse and anxiety, depression and disease, prejudice and poverty. Much of today's psychology continues the exploration of such challenges. Without slighting the need to repair damage and cure disease, Martin Seligman and others (2002, 2005, 2011) have called for more research on *human flourishing.* These psychologists call their approach **positive psychology.** They believe that happiness is a by-product of a pleasant, engaged, and meaningful life. Thus, positive psychology focuses on building a "good life" that engages our skills, and a "meaningful life" that points beyond ourselves. Positive psychology uses scientific methods to explore

MARTIN E. P. SELIGMAN "The main purpose of a positive psychology is to measure, understand, and then build the human strengths and the civic virtues." (Seligman, 2002)

- *positive emotions,* such as satisfaction with the past, happiness with the present, and optimism about the future.

- *positive character traits,* such as creativity, courage, compassion, integrity, self-control, leadership, wisdom, and spirituality. Current research examines the roots and fruits of such qualities, sometimes by studying the lives of individuals who offer striking examples.

- *positive institutions,* such as healthy families, supportive neighborhoods, effective schools, and socially responsible media.

Will psychology have a more positive mission in this century? Can it help us all to flourish? An increasing number of scientists worldwide believe it can. ■

RETRIEVE + REMEMBER

- What advantage do we gain by using the biopsychosocial approach in studying psychological events?

  ANSWER: By considering different levels of analysis, the biopsychosocial approach can provide a more complete view than any one perspective could offer.

- What is contemporary psychology's position on the nature–nurture debate?

  ANSWER: Psychological events often stem from the interaction of nature and nurture, rather than from either of them acting alone.

Why Do Psychology?

Many people feel guided by their *intuition*—by what they feel in their gut. "Buried deep within each and every one of us, there is an instinctive, heartfelt awareness that provides—if we allow it to—the most reliable guide," offered Britain's Prince Charles (2000).

The Limits of Intuition and Common Sense

1-4 How does our everyday thinking sometimes lead us to the wrong conclusion?

Prince Charles has much company, judging from the long list of pop psychology books on "intuitive managing," "intuitive trading," and "intuitive healing." Intuition is indeed important. Research shows that, more than we realize, our thinking, memory, and attitudes operate automatically, off screen. Like jumbo jets, we fly mostly on autopilot.

But intuition can lead us astray. Our gut feelings may tell us that lie detectors work and that eyewitnesses recall events accurately. But as you will see in chapters to come, hundreds of findings challenge these beliefs.

Hunches are a good starting point, even for smart thinkers. But thinking critically means checking assumptions, weighing evidence, inviting criticism, and testing conclusions. Does the death penalty prevent murders? Whether your gut tells you *Yes* or *No*, you need more evidence. You might ask, *Do states with a death penalty have lower homicide rates? After states pass death-penalty laws, do their homicide rates drop? Do homicide rates rise in states that abandon the death penalty?* If we ignore the answers to such questions (which the evidence sug-

> "The first principle, is that you must not fool yourself—and you are the easiest person to fool."
> Richard Feynman (1997)

gests are *No*, *No*, and *No*), our intuition may steer us down the wrong path.

With its standards for gathering and sifting evidence, psychological science helps us avoid errors and think smarter. Before moving on to our study of how psychologists use psychology's methods in their research, let's look more closely at three common flaws in intuitive thinking—*hindsight bias, overconfidence,* and *perceiving patterns in random events.*

Did We Know It All Along? Hindsight Bias

Some people think psychology merely proves what we already know and then dresses it in jargon: "So what else is new—you get paid for using fancy methods to tell me what my grandmother knew?" But consider how easy it is to draw the bull's eye after the arrow strikes. After the football game, we credit the coach if a "gutsy play" wins the game and fault the coach for the "stupid play" if it doesn't. After a war or an election, its outcome usually seems obvious. Although history may therefore seem like a series of predictable events, the actual future is seldom foreseen. No one's diary recorded, "Today the Hundred Years War began."

This **hindsight bias** (also called the *I-knew-it-all-along phenomenon*) is easy to demonstrate. Give half the members of a group a true psychological finding, and give the other half an opposite result. Tell the first group, "Psychologists have found that separation weakens romantic attraction. As the saying goes, 'Out of sight, out of mind.'" Ask them to imagine why this might be true. Most people can, and nearly all will then view this true finding as unsurprising—just common sense.

Tell the second group the opposite, "Psychologists have found that separation strengthens romantic attraction. As the saying goes, 'Absence makes the heart grow fonder.'" People given this false statement can also easily explain it, and most will also see it as unsurprising. When two opposite findings

HINDSIGHT BIAS When drilling the Deepwater Horizon oil well in 2010, oil industry employees took some shortcuts and ignored some warning signs, without intending to harm the environment or their companies' reputations. *After* the resulting Gulf oil spill, with the benefit of 20/20 hindsight, the foolishness of those judgments became obvious.

REUTERS/U.S. Coast Guard/Handout

dual processing the principle that, at the same time, our mind processes information on separate conscious and unconscious tracks.

positive psychology the scientific study of human functioning, with the goals of discovering and promoting strengths and virtues that help individuals and communities to thrive.

hindsight bias the tendency to believe, after learning an outcome, that we could have predicted it. (Also known as the *I-knew-it-all-along phenomenon.*)

both seem like common sense, we have a problem!

More than 800 scholarly papers have shown hindsight bias in people young and old from across the world (Roese & Vohs, 2012). Hindsight errors in what we recall and how we explain it show why we need psychological research. Just asking people how and why they felt or acted as they did can be misleading. Why? Not because common sense is usually wrong, but because common sense more easily describes what *has* happened than what *will* happen.

Nevertheless, Grandma's intuition is often right. As baseball great Yogi Berra once said, "You can observe a lot by watching." (We have Berra to thank for other gems, such as "Nobody ever comes here—it's too crowded," and "If the people don't want to come out to the ballpark, nobody's gonna stop 'em.") We're all behavior watchers, and sometimes we get it right. Many people believe that love breeds happiness, and it does. (We have what Chapter 9 calls a deep "need to belong.") But sometimes Grandmother's intuition, informed by countless casual observations, gets it wrong. Psychological research has overturned many popular ideas—that familiarity breeds contempt, that dreams predict the future, and that most of us use only 10 percent of our brain. Research has also surprised us with discoveries we had not predicted—that the brain's chemical messengers control our moods and memories, that other species can pass along their learned habits, that stress affects our ability to fight disease.

> Fun anagram solutions from Wordsmith (www. wordsmith.org):
>
> Snooze alarms = Alas! No more z's
>
> Dormitory = dirty room
>
> Slot machines = cash lost in 'em

Overconfidence

We humans also tend to be *overconfident*—we think we know more than we do. Consider these three word puzzles (called anagrams), which people like you were asked to unscramble in one study (Goranson, 1978).

WREAT → WATER

ETRYN → ENTRY

GRABE → BARGE

About how many seconds do you think it would have taken you to unscramble each anagram? Knowing the answer makes us overconfident. Surely the solution would take only 10 seconds or so? In reality, the average problem solver spends 3 minutes, as you also might, given a similar puzzle without the solution: OCHSA. (When you're ready, check your answer against the footnote below.[5])

Are we any better at predicting our social behavior? At the beginning of the school year, one study had students predict their own behavior (Vallone et al., 1990). Would they drop a course, vote in an upcoming election, call their parents regularly (and so forth)? On average, the students felt 84 percent sure of their self-predictions. But later quizzes about their actual behavior showed their predictions were correct only 71 percent of the time. Even when they were 100 percent sure of themselves, their self-predictions were wrong 15 percent of the time.

Perceiving Order in Random Events

In our natural eagerness to make sense of our world we often perceive patterns. People see a face on the Moon, hear Satanic messages in music, or perceive the Virgin Mary's image on a grilled cheese sandwich. Even in random, unrelated data we often find order, because *random sequences often don't look random* (Falk et al., 2009; Nickerson, 2002, 2005). In actual random sequences, patterns and streaks (such as repeating numbers) occur more often than people expect (Oskarsson et al., 2009). To demonstrate, I flipped a coin for heads or tails 51 times, with these results:

5 The solution to the OCHSA anagram is CHAOS.

Maciej Oleksy /Shutterstock

1. H	11. T	21. T	31. T	41. H	51. T
2. T	12. H	22. T	32. T	42. H	
3. T	13. H	23. H	33. T	43. H	
4. T	14. T	24. T	34. T	44. H	
5. H	15. T	25. T	35. T	45. T	
6. H	16. H	26. T	36. H	46. H	
7. H	17. T	27. H	37. T	47. H	
8. T	18. T	28. T	38. T	48. T	
9. T	19. H	29. H	39. H	49. T	
10. T	20. H	30. T	40. T	50. T	

Looking over the sequence, it's hard not to see what appear to be patterns. Tosses 10 to 22 provided an almost perfect pattern of pairs of tails followed by pairs of heads. On tosses 30 to 38 I had a "cold hand," with only one head in nine tosses. But my fortunes imme-

BIZARRE SEQUENCE OF COMPUTER-GENERATED RANDOM NUMBERS

ScienceCartoonsPlus.com

Bizarre looking, perhaps. But actually no more unlikely than any other number sequence.

diately reversed with a "hot hand"—seven heads out of the next nine tosses. Similar streaks happen—about as often as one would expect in random sequences—in basketball shooting and baseball hitting (Gilovich et al., 1985; Malkiel, 2007; Myers, 2002). These sequences are random but don't look it, so we misread them as being meaningful ("When you're hot, you're hot!")

What explains these streaky patterns? Was I exercising some sort of magical control over my coin? Did I snap out of my tails funk and get in a heads groove? Actually, these are the sort of streaks found in any random data. Comparing each toss to the next, 23 of the 50 comparisons yielded a changed result—just the sort of near 50-50 result we expect from coin tossing. Despite seeming patterns, the outcome of one toss gives no clue to the outcome of the next.

However, some happenings seem so amazing that we struggle to believe they are due to chance. The media often report on unlikely events, and statisticians (who collect and study facts and figures) help to explain them. When Evelyn Marie Adams won the New Jersey lottery *twice*, newspapers reported the odds of her feat as 1 in 17 trillion. Bizarre? Actually, 1 in 17 trillion are indeed the odds that a given person who buys a single ticket for each of two New Jersey lotteries will win both times. And given the millions of people who buy U.S. State lottery tickets, statisticians reported, it was "practically a sure thing" that someday, someone would hit a state jackpot twice (Samuels & McCabe, 1989). Indeed, offered another statistician team, "with a large enough

> *"The really unusual day would be one where nothing unusual happens."*
> Statistician Persi Diaconis (2002)

sample, any outrageous thing is likely to happen" (Diaconis & Mosteller, 1989). An event that happens to but 1 in 1 billion people every day occurs about 7 times a day, over 2500 times a year.

The point to remember: We trust our intuition more than we should. Our intuitive thinking is flawed by three powerful tendencies—hindsight bias, overconfidence, and perceiving patterns in random events. But scientific thinking can help us sift reality from illusion. ■

The Scientific Attitude: Curious, Skeptical, and Humble

1-5 What are the three key elements of the scientific attitude, and how do they support scientific inquiry?

What makes scientific inquiry so useful for detecting truth? The answer lies in three basic attitudes: *curiosity, skepticism,* and *humility.*

Underlying all science is, first, a hard-headed *curiosity,* a passion to explore and understand without misleading or being misled. Some questions (*Is there life after death?*) are beyond science. Answering them in any way requires a leap of faith. With many other questions (*Can some people read minds?*), the proof is in the pudding. No matter how crazy an idea sounds, the scientist asks, *Does it work?* When put to the test, can its predictions be confirmed?

Magician James Randi has used the scientific approach when testing those

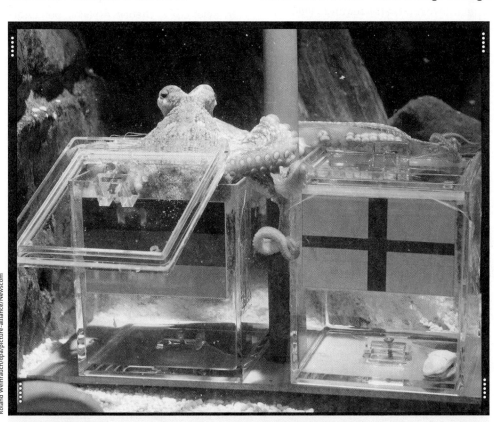

Roland Weihrauch/dpa/picture-alliance/Newscom

GIVEN ENOUGH RANDOM EVENTS, SOME WEIRD-SEEMING STREAKS WILL OCCUR During the 2010 World Cup, a German octopus, Paul, was offered two boxes, each with mussels and a national flag. Paul selected the right box eight out of eight times in predicting the outcome of Germany's seven matches and Spain's triumph in the final.

AP Photo/Alan Diaz

THE AMAZING RANDI Magician and skeptic James Randi has tested and debunked supposed psychic phenomena.

claiming to see glowing auras around people's bodies:

Randi: *Do you see an aura around my head?*

Aura seer: *Yes, indeed.*

Randi: *Can you still see the aura if I put this magazine in front of my face?*

Aura seer: *Of course.*

Randi: *Then if I were to step behind a wall barely taller than I am, you could determine my location from the aura visible above my head, right?*

Randi told me that no aura seer has agreed to take this simple test.

When subjected to scientific tests, crazy-sounding ideas sometimes find support. More often, they become part of the mountain of forgotten claims of palm reading, miracle cancer cures, and out-of-body travels. For a lot of bad ideas, science serves as society's garbage disposal.

Sifting reality from fantasy, sense from nonsense, also requires us to be

skeptical—not cynical, but also not gullible. "To believe with certainty," says a Polish proverb, "we must begin by doubting." As scientists, psychologists greet statements about behavior and mental processes by asking two questions: *What do you mean?* and *How do you know?*

When ideas compete, skeptical testing can reveal which ones best match the facts. Do parental behaviors determine children's sexual orientation? Can astrologers predict your future based on the position of the planets at your birth? As you will see in later chapters, putting these two claims to the test has led most psychologists to doubt them.

A scientific attitude is more than curiosity and skepticism, however. It also requires *humility*—an awareness that we can make mistakes, and a willingness to be surprised and follow new roads. In the end, what matters is not my opinion or yours, but the truths nature reveals in response to our questioning. If people or other animals don't behave as our ideas predict, then so much the worse for our ideas. This humble attitude was expressed in one of psychology's early mottos: "The rat is always right."

Historians of science tell us that these attitudes—curiosity, skepticism, and humility—helped make modern science possible. ■

◎ Psychologists transform their scientific attitude into practice by using the *scientific method*. They observe events, form theories, and then refine their theories in the light of new observations.

The Scientific Method

1-6 How do psychological theories guide scientific research?

Chatting with friends and family, we often use *theory* to mean "mere hunch." In science, a **theory** *explains* behaviors or events by offering ideas that *organize* what we have observed. By organizing isolated facts, a theory simplifies. There are too many facts about behavior to remember them all. By linking facts to underlying principles, a theory connects many small dots and offers a useful summary so that a clear picture emerges.

A theory about the effects of sleep on memory, for example, helps us organize countless sleep-related observations into a short list of principles. Imagine that we observe over and over that people with good sleep habits tend to answer questions correctly in class, and they do well at test time. We might therefore theorize that sleep improves memory. So far so good: Our principle neatly summarizes a list of facts about the effects of a good night's sleep on memory.

Yet no matter how reasonable a theory may sound—and it does seem reasonable to suggest that sleep could improve memory—we must put it to the test. A good theory produces testable *predictions*, called **hypotheses**. Such predictions specify what results (what behaviors or events) would support the theory and what results would cast doubt on the theory. To test our theory about the effects of sleep on memory, our hypothesis might be that when sleep deprived, people will remember less from the day before. To test that hypothesis, we might assess how well people remember course materials they studied before a good night's sleep, or before a shortened night's sleep (FIGURE 1.2). The results will either support our theory or lead us to revise or reject it.

Our theories can bias our observations. Having theorized that better memory springs from more sleep, we may see what we expect: We may perceive sleepy people's comments as less insightful.

As a check on their biases, psychologists use **operational definitions** when they report their studies. "Sleep deprived," for example, may be defined as "2 or more hours less" than the person's natural sleep. These exact descriptions will allow anyone to **replicate** (repeat) the research. Other people can then re-create the study with different participants and in different situations. If they get similar results, we can be confident that the findings are reliable.

Let's summarize. A good theory:

- effectively *organizes* a range of self-reports and observations.

- leads to clear *predictions* that anyone can use to check the theory.

- often stimulates research that leads to a revised theory which better organizes and predicts what we know. Or, our research may be replicated and supported by similar findings. (This has been the case for sleep and memory studies, as you will see in Chapter 2.)

We can test our hypotheses and refine our theories in several ways.

- *Descriptive* methods describe behaviors, often by using (as we will see) case studies, naturalistic observations, or surveys.

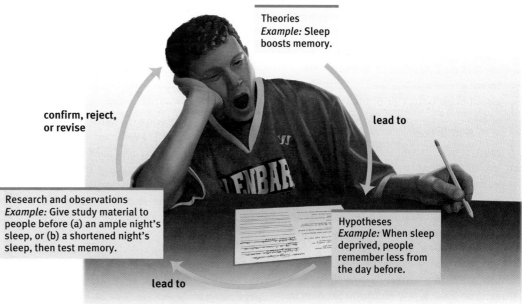

FIGURE 1.2 The scientific method A self-correcting process for asking questions and observing nature's answer.

- *Correlational* methods associate different factors. (You'll see the word *factor* often in descriptions of research. It refers to anything that contributes to a result.)

- *Experimental* methods manipulate, or vary, factors to discover their effects.

To think critically about popular psychology claims, we need to understand the strengths and weaknesses of these methods. (For more information about some of the statistical methods that psychological scientists use in their work, see Appendix A, Statistical Reasoning in Everyday Life.) ▇

Description

1-7 How do psychologists use case studies, naturalistic observations, and surveys to observe and describe behavior, and why is random sampling important?

In daily life, we all observe and describe other people, trying to understand why they behave as they do. Professional psychologists do much the same, though more objectively and systematically, using

- *case studies* (in-depth analyses of special individuals).

theory an explanation using principles that organize observations and predict behaviors or events.

hypothesis a testable prediction, often implied by a theory.

operational definition a carefully worded statement of the exact procedures (operations) used in a research study. For example, *human intelligence* may be operationally defined as what an intelligence test measures.

replication repeating the essence of a research study, usually with different participants in different situations, to see whether the basic finding extends to other participants and circumstances.

- *naturalistic observations* (watching and recording individuals' behavior in a natural setting).

- *surveys* and interviews (self-reports in which people answer questions about their behavior or attitudes).

The Case Study

A **case study** examines one individual or group in great depth, in the hope of revealing things true of us all. Some examples: Medical case studies of people who lost specific abilities after damage to certain brain regions gave us much of our early knowledge about the brain. Jean Piaget, the pioneer researcher on children's thinking, carefully watched and questioned just a few children. Studies of only a few chimpanzees jarred our beliefs about what other species can understand and communicate.

Intensive case studies are sometimes very revealing. They often suggest directions for further study, and they show us what *can* happen. But individual

FREUD AND LITTLE HANS Sigmund Freud's case study of 5-year-old Hans' extreme fear of horses led Freud to his theory of childhood sexuality. Freud believed Hans' intense fear of being bitten by a horse had its roots in the boy's unconscious desire for his mother and his fear of being castrated by his rival father. As Chapter 11 will explain, today's psychological science does not support Freud's theory of childhood sexuality. It does, however, agree that the human mind processes much information outside our conscious awareness.

cases may also mislead us. The individual being studied may be *atypical* (not like those in the larger group). Viewing such cases as general truths can lead to false conclusions. Indeed, anytime a researcher mentions a finding (*Smokers die younger: 95 percent of men over 85 are nonsmokers*), someone is sure to offer an exception. (*Well, I have an uncle who smoked two packs a day and lived to be 89.*) These vivid stories, dramatic tales, personal experiences, even psychological case examples—often command attention and are easily remembered. Stories move us, but stories can mislead. As psychologist Gordon Allport (1954, p. 9) said, "Given a thimbleful of [dramatic] facts we rush to make generalizations as large as a tub."

The point to remember: Individual cases can suggest fruitful ideas. What is true of all of us can be seen in any one of us. But just because something is true of one of us (the atypical uncle), we should not assume it is true of all of us (most long-term smokers suffer ill health and early deaths). We look to methods beyond the case study to uncover general truths. ■

Naturalistic Observation

A second descriptive method records behavior in a natural environment. These **naturalistic observations** may describe parenting practices in different cultures, students' self-seating patterns in American lunchrooms, or chimpanzee family structures in the wild. New smartphone apps and body-worn sensors hold promise of expanding naturalistic observation. Using such tools, researchers might track willing volunteers—their location, activities, opinions, and even

AN EAR FOR NATURALISTIC OBSERVATION Researchers have used electronically activated recorders (EARs) to sample naturally occurring slices of daily life.

some physical factors—without interfering with the person's activity. One evolutionary psychologist (Miller, 2012) notes, for example, that GPS data "could reveal whether peak-fertility women go out more often to areas with bars and clubs, and Bluetooth scans could reveal whether they go out more often to places with a lot of people."

In one study, researchers had 52 introductory psychology students don hip-worn tape recorders (Mehl & Pennebaker, 2003). For up to four days, the electronically activated recorders (EARs) captured 30-second snippets of the students' waking hours, turning on every 12.5 minutes. By the end of the study, researchers had eavesdropped on more than 10,000 half-minute life slices. What percentage of the time did these researchers find students talking with someone? What percentage captured students at a computer? The answers: 28 and 9 percent. (What percentage of *your* waking hours are spent in these activities?)

Like the case study method, naturalistic observation does not *explain* behavior. It *describes* it. Nevertheless, descriptions can be revealing. ■

- What are the advantages and disadvantages of naturalistic observation, such as the EARs study?

ANSWER: In the EARs study, researchers were able to carefully record and describe naturally occurring behaviors outside the artificial environment of the lab. However, they were not able to explain all the behaviors because they could not control all the factors that may have influenced them.

The Survey

A **survey** looks at many cases in less depth, asking people to report their behavior or opinions. Questions about everything from sexual practices to political opinions are put to the public. In recent surveys,

- half of all Americans reported experiencing more happiness and enjoyment than worry and stress on the previous day (Gallup, 2010).

- 1 in 5 people across 22 countries reported believing that alien beings have come to Earth and now walk among us disguised as humans (Ipsos, 2010b).

- 68 percent of all humans—some 4.6 billion people—say that religion is important in their daily lives (from Gallup World Poll data analyzed by Diener et al., 2011).

But asking questions is tricky, and the answers often depend on the way you word your questions and on who answers them.

WORDING EFFECTS Even subtle changes in the order or wording of questions can have major effects. Should violence be allowed to appear in children's television programs? People are much more likely to approve "not allowing" such things than "forbidding" or "censoring" them. In one national survey, only 27 percent of Americans approved of "government censorship" of media sex and violence, though 66 percent approved of "more restrictions on what

is shown on television" (Lacayo, 1995). People are much more approving of "aid to the needy" than of "welfare," and of "revenue enhancers" than of "taxes."

Consider two national surveys taken in 2009. In one, 3 in 4 Americans approved of giving people "a choice" of public (government-run) health insurance or private health insurance. Yet in the other survey, most Americans were *not* in favor of "creating a public health care plan administered by the federal government that would compete directly with private health insurance companies" (Stein, 2009). Wording is a delicate matter. In this case, *choice* is a word that triggers support. Critical thinkers will reflect on how a question's phrasing might affect the opinions people express.

RANDOM SAMPLING For an accurate picture of a group's experiences and attitudes, there's only one game in town— a *representative sample*—a smaller group that accurately reflects the larger **population** you want to study and describe.

So in a survey, how do you obtain a representative sample of, say, the total student population at your school? You would choose a **random sample,** in which every person in the entire group has an equal chance of being picked. You would not want to ask for volunteers, because those extra-nice students who step forward to help would not necessarily be a random sample of all the students. But you could assign each student a number, and then use a random number generator to select a sample.

Time and money will affect the size of your sample, but you would try to involve as many people as possible. Why? Because large representative samples are better than small ones. (But a small representative sample of 100 is better than an unrepresentative sample of 500.)

> With very large samples, estimates become quite reliable. *E* is estimated to represent 12.7 percent of the letters in written English. *E*, in fact, is 12.3 percent of the 925,141 letters in Melville's *Moby-Dick*, 12.4 percent of the 586,747 letters in Dickens' *A Tale of Two Cities*, and 12.1 percent of the 3,901,021 letters in 12 of Mark Twain's works (*Chance News*, 1997).

Political pollsters sample voters in national election surveys just this way. Using only 1500 randomly sampled people, drawn from all areas of a country, they can provide a remarkably accurate snapshot of the nation's opinions. Without random sampling, large samples— including call-in phone samples and TV or website polls—often merely give misleading results.

The point to remember: Before accepting survey findings, think critically. Consider the question's wording and the sample. The best basis for generalizing is from a random sample of a population. ■

- What is an unrepresentative sample, and how do researchers avoid it?

ANSWER: An unrepresentative sample is a survey group that does not represent the population being studied. *Random sampling* helps researchers form a representative sample because each member of the population has an equal chance of being included.

case study a descriptive technique in which one individual or group is studied in depth in the hope of revealing universal principles.

naturalistic observation a descriptive technique of observing and recording behavior in naturally occurring situations without trying to change or control the situation.

survey a descriptive technique for obtaining the self-reported attitudes or behaviors of a group, usually by questioning a representative, random sample of that group.

population all those in a group being studied, from which samples may be drawn. (*Note:* Except for national studies, this does not refer to a country's whole population.)

random sample a sample that fairly represents a population because each member has an equal chance of inclusion.

Correlation

1-8 What are positive and negative correlations, and how can they lead to prediction but not cause-effect explanation?

Describing behavior is a first step toward predicting it. Naturalistic observations and surveys often show us that one trait or behavior is related to another. In such cases, we say the two **correlate**. A statistical measure (the *correlation coefficient*) helps us figure how closely two things vary together, and thus how well either one *predicts* the other. Displaying data in a **scatterplot** (FIGURE 1.3) can help us see correlations.

- A *positive correlation* (between 0 and +1.00) indicates a *direct* relationship, meaning that two things increase together or decrease together. Across people, height correlates positively with weight. The data in Figure 1.3 are positively correlated, because they are generally both rising (moving up and right) together.

- A *negative correlation* (between 0 and –1.00) indicates an inverse relationship: As one thing increases, the other decreases. The number of hours spent watching TV and playing video games each week correlates negatively with grades. Negative correlations can go as low as –1.00. This means that, like children on opposite ends of a teeter-totter, one set of scores goes down precisely as the other goes up.

- A coefficient near zero is a weak correlation, indicating little or no relationship.

The point to remember: A correlation coefficient helps us see the world more clearly by revealing the extent to which two things relate. ■

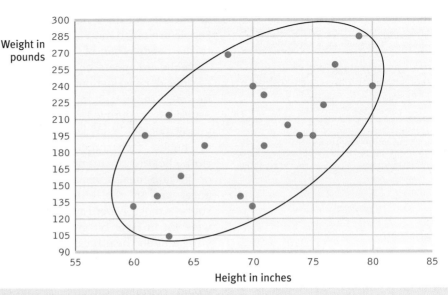

FIGURE 1.3 Scatterplot for height and weight This graph displays data from 20 imagined people, each represented by a data point. The scattered points reveal an upward slope, indicating a positive correlation.

Correlation and Causation

Correlations help us predict. Here's an example: Self-esteem correlates negatively with (and therefore predicts) depression. (The lower people's self-esteem, the more they are at risk for depression.) But does that mean low self-esteem *causes* depression? If you think the answer is *Yes,* you are not alone. We all find it hard to resist thinking that associations prove causation. But no matter how strong the relationship, they do not!

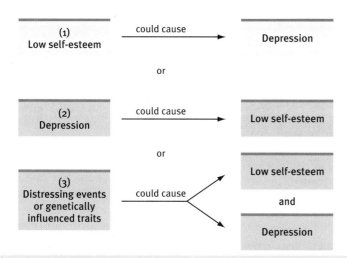

| (1) Low self-esteem | could cause → | Depression |

or

| (2) Depression | could cause → | Low self-esteem |

or

| (3) Distressing events or genetically influenced traits | could cause ⟨ | Low self-esteem and Depression |

FIGURE 1.4 Three possible cause-effect relationships People low in self-esteem are more likely to report depression than are those high in self-esteem. One possible explanation of this negative correlation is that a bad self-image causes depressed feelings. But, as the diagram indicates, other cause-effect relationships are possible.

Random Assignment: Minimizing Differences

Researchers have compared infants who are breast-fed with those who are bottle-fed with formula. Several studies show that children's intelligence test scores are somewhat higher if they were breast-fed (Kramer et al., 2008). Moreover, the longer they were breast-fed, the higher their later scores (Jedrychowski et al., 2012). So we can say that mother's milk correlates modestly but positively with later intelligence. But what does this mean? Do smarter mothers (who in modern countries more often breast-feed) have smarter children? Or do the nutrients in mother's milk contribute to brain development?

Lane Oatey / Getty Images

How else might we explain the negative correlation between self-esteem and depression? As **FIGURE 1.4** suggests, we'd get the same correlation between low self-esteem and depression if depression caused people to be down on themselves. And we'd also get that correlation if something else—a third factor such as heredity or some awful event—caused *both* low self-esteem and depression.

This point is so important—so basic to thinking smarter with psychology—that it merits one more example, this one from a survey of over 12,000 adolescents. The more those teens felt loved by their parents, the less likely they were to behave in unhealthy ways—having early sex, smoking, abusing alcohol and drugs, behaving violently (Resnick et al., 1997). "Adults have a powerful effect on their children's behavior right through the high school years," gushed an Associated Press (AP) news report on the study. But no correlation has a built-in cause-effect arrow. Thus, the AP could as well have said, "Well-behaved teens feel their parents' love and approval; out-of-bounds teens more often describe their parents as disapproving."

The point to remember (turn up the volume here): *Correlation indicates the possibility of a cause-effect relationship, but it does not prove causation.* Knowing that two events are associated does not tell us anything about which causes the other. Remember this principle and you will be wiser as you read and hear news of scientific studies. ■

Experimentation

1-9 How do experiments clarify or reveal cause-effect relationships?

Descriptions don't prove causation. Correlations don't prove causation. To isolate cause and effect, psychologists have to simplify the world. In our everyday lives, many things affect our actions and influence our thoughts. Psychologists sort out this complexity by using **experiments.** With experiments, researchers can focus on the possible effects of one or more factors by

- *manipulating the factors of interest.*
- *holding constant ("controlling") other factors.*

Let's consider a few experiments to see how this works.

correlation a measure of the extent to which two events vary together, and thus of how well either one predicts the other. The *correlation coefficient* is the mathematical expression of the relationship, ranging from −1.00 to +1.00, with 0 indicating no relationship.

scatterplot a graphed cluster of dots, each of which represents the values of two factors. The slope of the dots suggests the direction of the relationship between the two factors. How much the dots are scattered suggests the strength of the correlation (with little scatter indicating high correlation).

experiment a method in which researchers vary one or more factors (independent variables) to observe the effect on some behavior or mental process (the dependent variable).

To find the answer, we would have to isolate the effects of mother's milk from the effects of other factors, such as mother's age, education, and intelligence. How might we do that? By experimenting. With parental permission, one British research team **randomly assigned** 424 hospital premature infants either to formula feedings or to breast-milk feedings (Lucas et al., 1992). By doing this, they created two otherwise similar groups:

- an **experimental group,** in which babies received the treatment (breast milk).
- a **control group** without the treatment.

Random assignment (by flipping a coin, for example) minimizes any pre-existing differences between the experimental group and the control group. If one-third of the volunteers for an experiment can wiggle their ears, then about one-third of the people in each group will be ear wigglers. So, too, with mother's age, intelligence, and other characteristics, which will be similar in the experimental and control groups. Thus, if the groups differ at the experiment's end, we can assume that the treatment had an effect.

The British experiment found that breast milk is indeed best for developing intelligence (at least for premature infants). On intelligence tests taken at age 8, those nourished with breast milk scored significantly higher than those formula-fed.

The point to remember: Unlike correlational studies, which uncover *naturally occurring* relationships, an experiment *manipulates* (varies) a factor to determine its effect.

Sometimes correlational and experimental studies are used in combination. In one such case, a research team explored the association between pornography use and romantic commitment (Lambert et al., 2012). In one set of studies, the researchers found three correlations. Higher rates of pornography use were associated with (and predicted):

- lower commitment to a partner.
- greater online flirting with others.
- greater infidelity.

A follow-up *experiment* studied men and women who were in a relationship and reported more than monthly pornography use. Half were randomly assigned to a control group, and they were instructed to "abstain from eating your favorite food or treat for the next three weeks." The other half (the experimental group) were instructed to abstain from "sexually explicit materials of any kind for the next three weeks." At the experiment's end, 30 percent of those in the control group predicted they would still be with their romantic partner a year or more into the future, as did 63 percent in the experimental group. "Our research suggests that there is a relationship cost associated with pornography [use]," the researchers concluded.

The Double-Blind Procedure: Eliminating Bias

Thinking back to the breast-milk experiment, we can see how the researchers were lucky—babies don't have expectations that can affect the experiment's outcome. Adults do.

"If I don't think it's going to work, will it still work?"

Consider: Three days into a cold, many of us start taking vitamin C tablets. If we find our cold symptoms lessening, we may credit the pills. But after a few days, most colds are naturally on their way out. Was the vitamin C cure truly effective? To find out, we could experiment.

And that is precisely what investigators do to judge whether new drug treatments and new methods of psychotherapy are effective (Chapter 14). Often, the people who take part in these studies are *blind* (uninformed) about which treatment, if any, they are receiving. The experimental group receives the treatment. The control group receives a **placebo** (an inactive substance—perhaps a look-alike pill with no drug in it).

Many studies use a **double-blind procedure**—neither those in the study nor those collecting the data know which group is receiving the treatment. In such studies, researchers can check a treatment's actual effects apart from the participants' belief in its healing powers and the staff's enthusiasm for its potential. Just *thinking* you are getting a treatment can boost your spirits, relax your body, and relieve your symptoms. This **placebo effect** is well documented in reducing pain, depression, and anxiety (Kirsch, 2010). Athletes have run faster when given a fake performance-enhancing drug (McClung & Collins, 2007). Drinking decaf coffee has boosted vigor and alertness—for those who thought it had caffeine in it (Dawkins et al., 2011). People have felt better after receiving a phony mood-enhancing drug (Michael et al., 2012). And the more expensive the placebo, the more "real" it seems—a fake pill that costs $2.50 works better than one costing 10 cents (Waber et al., 2008). To know how effective a therapy really is, researchers must control for a possible placebo effect. ∎

- What measures do researchers use to prevent the *placebo effect* from confusing their results?

ANSWER: Research designed to prevent the placebo effect randomly assigns participants to an experimental group (which receives the real treatment) or to a *control group* (which receives a placebo). A comparison of the results will demonstrate whether the real treatment produces better results than *belief* in that treatment.

Independent and Dependent Variables

Here is an even more potent drug-study example: The drug Viagra was approved for use after 21 clinical trials. One trial was an experiment in which researchers randomly assigned 329 men with erectile disorder to either an experimental group (Viagra takers) or a control group (placebo takers). It was a double-blind procedure—neither the men nor the person who gave them the pills knew which drug they received. The result: Viagra worked. At peak doses, 69 percent of Viagra-assisted attempts at intercourse were successful, compared with 22 percent for men receiving the placebo (Goldstein et al., 1998).

This simple experiment manipulated just one factor—the drug Viagra. We call the manipulated factor an **independent variable:** We can vary it *independently* of other factors, such as the men's age, weight, and personality. These other factors, which could influence the experiment's results, are called **confounding variables.** Thanks to random assignment, those factors should be roughly equal in both groups.

Note the distinction between random sampling (discussed earlier in relation to surveys) and random assignment (depicted in Figure 1.5). Through random sampling, we may represent a population effectively, because each member of that population has an equal chance of being selected (sampled) for participation in our research. Random assignment ensures accurate representation among the research groups, because each participant has an equal chance of being placed in (assigned to) any of the groups. This helps control outside influences so that we can determine cause and effect.

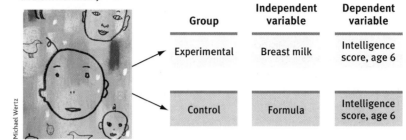

Random assignment (controlling for other variables such as parental intelligence and environment)

Group	Independent variable	Dependent variable
Experimental	Breast milk	Intelligence score, age 6
Control	Formula	Intelligence score, age 6

Michael Wertz

FIGURE 1.5 Experimentation To study cause-effect, psychologists may randomly assign some participants to an experimental group, others to a control group. Measuring the dependent variable (intelligence score in later childhood) will determine the effect of the independent variable (type of milk).

Experiments examine the effect of one or more independent variables on some behavior or mental process that can be measured. We call this kind of affected behavior the **dependent variable** because it can vary *depending* on what takes place during the experiment. Experimenters give both variables precise *operational definitions.* They specify exactly how they are manipulating the independent variable (in this study, the precise drug dosage and timing) and how they are measuring the dependent variable (the questions that assessed the men's responses). These definitions answer the "What do you mean?" question with a level of precision that enables others to repeat the study.

Let's see how this works with the breast-milk experiment (**FIGURE 1.5**). A *variable* is anything that can vary (infant nutrition, intelligence). Experiments aim to *manipulate* an *independent* variable (infant nutrition), *measure* the *dependent* variable (intelligence), and control *confounding variables.* An experiment has at least two different groups: an *experimental group* (infants who received breast milk) and a *comparison* or *control group* (infants who did not receive breast milk). *Random assignment* works to control all

random assignment assigning participants to experimental and control groups by chance, thus minimizing any differences between the groups.

experimental group in an experiment, the group exposed to the treatment, that is, to one version of the independent variable.

control group in an experiment, the group *not* exposed to the treatment; the control group serves as a comparison with the experimental group for judging the effect of the treatment.

placebo [pluh-SEE-bo; Latin for "I shall please"] an inactive substance or condition that is sometimes given to those in a control group in place of the treatment given to the experimental group.

double-blind procedure a procedure in which participants and research staff are ignorant (blind) about who has received the treatment or a placebo.

placebo effect results caused by expectations alone.

independent variable in an experiment, the factor that is manipulated; the variable whose effect is being studied.

confounding variable in an experiment, a factor other than the independent variable that might produce an effect.

dependent variable in an experiant, the factor that is measured; the variable that may change when the independent variable is manipulated.

TABLE 1.2 Comparing Research Methods

Research Method	Basic Purpose	How Conducted	What Is Manipulated	Weaknesses
Descriptive	To observe and record behavior	Do case studies, naturalistic observations, or surveys	Nothing	No control of variables; single cases may be misleading.
Correlational	To detect naturally occurring relationships; to assess how well one variable predicts another	Collect data on two or more variables; no manipulation	Nothing	Does not specify cause-effect.
Experimental	To explore cause-effect	Manipulate one or more factors; use random variable(s) assignment	The independent variable(s)	Sometimes not possible for practical or ethical reasons.

other (confounding) variables by equating the groups before any manipulation begins. In this way, an experiment tests the effect of at least one independent variable (what we manipulate) on at least one dependent variable (the outcome we measure).

Let's pause to check your understanding using another experiment. Psychologists tested whether landlords' perceptions of an applicant's ethnicity would influence the availability of rental housing. The researchers sent identically worded e-mails to 1115 Los Angeles–area landlords (Carpusor & Loges, 2006). They varied the sender's name to imply different ethnic groups: "Patrick McDougall,"

"Said Al-Rahman," and "Tyrell Jackson." Then they tracked the percentage of positive replies. How many e-mails triggered invitations to view the apartment? For McDougall, 89 percent; for Al-Rahman, 66 percent; and for Jackson, 56 percent.

* * *

Each of psychology's research methods has strengths and weaknesses (TABLE 1.2). Experiments show cause-effect relationships, but some experiments would not be ethical or practical. (To test the effects of parenting, we're just not going to take newborns and randomly assign them either to their biological parents or to orphanages.) ∎

RETRIEVE + REMEMBER

- In the rental housing experiment, what was the independent variable? The dependent variable?

  ANSWER: The independent variable, which the researchers manipulated, was the set of ethnically distinct names. The dependent variable, which they measured, was the positive response rate.

- Match the term on the left with the description on the right.

  1. double-blind procedure
  2. random sampling
  3. random assignment

  a. helps researchers generalize from a small set of survey responses to a larger population

  b. helps minimize preexisting differences between experimental and control groups

  c. controls for the placebo effect; neither researchers nor participants know who receives the real treatment

  ANSWERS: 1. c, 2. a, 3. b

- Why, when testing a new drug to control blood pressure, would we learn more about its effectiveness from giving it to half the participants in a group of 1000 than to all 1000 participants?

  ANSWER: We learn more about the drug's effectiveness when we can compare the results of those who took the drug (the experimental group) with the results of those who did not (the control group). If we gave the drug to all 1000 participants, we would have no way of knowing whether the drug is serving as a placebo or is actually medically effective.

Frequently Asked Questions About Psychology

◎ We have reflected on how a scientific approach can restrain, or limit, biases. We have seen how case studies, naturalistic observations, and surveys help us describe behavior. We have also noted that correlational studies assess the association between two factors, showing how well one predicts the other. We have examined the logic underlying experiments, which use controls and random assignment to isolate the effects of independent variables on dependent variables.

Hopefully, you are now prepared to understand what lies ahead and to think critically about psychological matters. Before we plunge in, let's address some frequently asked questions about psychology.

1-10 How do simplified laboratory conditions help us understand general principles of behavior?

Do you ever wonder whether people's behavior in a research laboratory will predict their behavior in real life? For example, does detecting the blink of a faint red light in a dark room have anything useful to say about flying a plane at night? Or, after viewing a violent, sexually explicit film, does an aroused man's increased willingness to deliver what he thinks are electrical shocks to a woman help us learn whether violent pornography makes a man more likely to abuse a woman?

Before you answer, consider this. The experimenter *intends* to simplify reality—to create a mini-environment that imitates and controls important features of everyday life. Just as a wind tunnel lets airplane designers re-create airflow forces under controlled conditions, a laboratory experiment lets psychologists re-create psychological forces under controlled conditions.

An experiment's purpose is not to re-create the exact behaviors of everyday life but to test *theoretical principles* (Mook, 1983). In aggression studies, deciding whether to push a button that delivers a shock may not be the same as slapping someone in the face, but the principle is the same. *It is the resulting principles—not the specific findings—that help explain everyday behaviors.* Many investigations have shown that principles derived in the laboratory do typically generalize to the everyday world (Anderson et al., 1999).

The point to remember: Psychologists are less interested in particular behaviors than in the general principles that help explain many behaviors.

1-11 Why do psychologists study animals, and what ethical guidelines safeguard human and animal research participants?

Many psychologists study animals because they find them fascinating. They want to understand how different species learn, think, and behave. Psychologists also study animals to learn about people. We humans are not *like* animals; we *are* animals, sharing a common biology. Animal experiments have therefore led to treatments for human diseases—insulin for diabetes, vaccines to prevent polio and rabies, transplants to replace defective organs.

> "Rats are very similar to humans except that they are not stupid enough to purchase lottery tickets."
>
> Dave Barry, July 2, 2002

ANIMAL RESEARCH BENEFITING ANIMALS Thanks partly to research on the benefits of novelty, control, and stimulation, these gorillas have enjoyed an improved quality of life in New York's Bronx Zoo.

Mary Altaffer/AP Photo

Humans are more complex. But the same processes by which we learn are present in rats, monkeys, and even sea slugs. The simplicity of the sea slug's nervous system is precisely what makes it so revealing of the neural mechanisms of learning.

Sharing such similarities, should we respect rather than experiment on our animal relatives? The animal protection movement protests the use of animals in psychological, biological, and medical research.

Out of this heated debate, two issues emerge. The basic one is whether it is right to place the well-being of humans above that of other animals. In experiments on stress and cancer, is it right that mice get tumors in the hope that people might not? Should some monkeys be exposed to an HIV-like virus in the search for an AIDS vaccine?

Is our use and consumption of other animals as natural as the behavior of carnivorous hawks, cats, and whales? The answers to such questions vary by culture. In Gallup surveys in Canada and the United States, about 60 percent of adults have said that medical testing on animals is "morally acceptable." In Britain, only 37 percent have (Mason, 2003).

If we give human life first priority, what safeguards should protect the well-being of animals in research? One survey asked animal researchers if they supported government regulations protecting research animals. Ninety-eight percent supported such protection for primates, dogs, and cats. And 74 percent backed regulations providing for the humane care of rats and mice (Plous & Herzog, 2000). Many professional associations and funding agencies already have such guidelines. British Psychological Society guidelines call for housing animals under reasonably natural living conditions, with companions for social animals (Lea, 2000). American Psychological Association (APA) guidelines state that researchers must ensure the "comfort, health, and humane treatment" of animals and minimize "infection, illness, and pain" (APA, 2002). The European Parliament has set standards for animal care and housing (Vogel, 2010).

Animals have themselves benefited from animal research. One Ohio team of research psychologists measured stress hormone levels in samples of millions of dogs brought each year to animal shelters. They devised handling and stroking methods to reduce stress and ease the dogs' move to adoptive homes (Tuber et al., 1999). Other studies have helped improve care and management in animals' natural habitats. Experiments have revealed our behavioral kinship with animals and the remarkable intelligence of chimpanzees, gorillas, and other animals. Experiments have also led to increased empathy and protection for other species. At its best, a psychology concerned for humans and sensitive to animals serves the welfare of both.

What about human participants? Does the image of white-coated scientists delivering electric shocks trouble you? If so, you'll be relieved to know that most psychological studies are free of such stress. With people, blinking lights, flashing words, and pleasant social interactions are more common. Moreover, psychology's experiments are mild compared with the stress and humiliation often inflicted by reality TV shows. In one episode of *The Bachelor*, a man dumped his new fiancée—on camera, at the producers' request—for the woman who earlier had finished second (Collins, 2009).

Occasionally, though, researchers do temporarily stress or deceive people. This happens only when they believe it is unavoidable. Some experiments, such as those about understanding and controlling violent behavior or studying mood swings, won't work if participants

know everything beforehand. (Wanting to be helpful, they might try to confirm the researcher's predictions.)

The APA ethics code urges researchers to

- obtain the participants' **informed consent.**
- protect them from harm and discomfort.
- keep information about individual participants confidential.
- fully **debrief** participants (explain the research afterward).

Moreover, most universities now have ethics committees that screen research proposals and safeguard participants' well-being.

1-12 How do personal values influence psychologists' research and application? Does psychology aim to manipulate people?

Psychology is definitely not value free. Values affect what we study, how we study it, and how we interpret results. Consider: Researchers' values influence their choice of topics. Should we study worker productivity or worker morale? Sex discrimination or gender differences? Conformity or independence? Our values can also color "the facts." As noted earlier, what we want or expect to

see can bias our observations and interpretations (**FIGURE 1.6**).

Even the words we use to describe something can reflect our values. Are the sex acts we do not practice *perversions* or *sexual variations*? Labels describe and labels evaluate. One person's *rigidity* is another's *consistency*. One person's *faith* is another's *fanaticism*. One country's *enhanced interrogation techniques,* such as cold-water immersion, become *torture* when practiced by its enemies. Our words—*firm* or *stubborn, careful* or *picky, discreet* or *secretive*—reveal our attitudes.

Applied psychology also contains hidden values. If you defer to "professional" guidance—on raising children, achieving self-fulfillment, coping with sexual feelings, getting ahead at work—you are accepting value-laden advice. A science of behavior and mental processes can certainly help us reach our goals, but it cannot decide what those goals should be.

Some have a different concern: They worry that psychology is becoming dangerously powerful. Is it an accident that astronomy is the oldest science and psychology the youngest? To these questioners, exploring the external universe seems far safer than exploring our own inner universe.

Might psychology, they ask, be used to manipulate people? Knowledge, like all power, can be used for good or evil. Nuclear power has been used to light up cities—and to demolish them. Persuasive

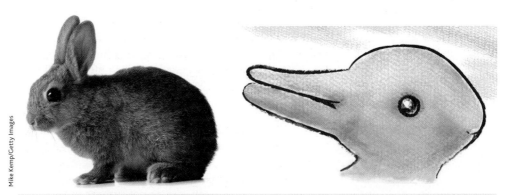

FIGURE 1.6 What do you see in the image on the right? Our expectations influence what we perceive. Did you see a duck or a rabbit? Show some friends this image with the rabbit on the left covered up and see if they are more likely to perceive a duck instead. (Shepard, 1990.)

Mike Kemp/Getty Images

power has been used to educate people—and to deceive them. Although psychology does indeed have the power to deceive, its purpose is to enlighten. Every day, psychologists are exploring ways to enhance learning, creativity, and compassion. Psychology speaks to many of our world's great problems—war, climate change, prejudice, family crises, crime—all of which involve attitudes and behaviors. Psychology also speaks to our deepest longings—for nourishment, for love, for happiness. And, as you have seen, one of the new developments in this field—positive psychology—has as its goal exploring and promoting human strengths. Many of life's questions are beyond psychology, but even a first psychology course can shine a bright light on some very important ones. ■

arabianEYE/Getty Images

RETRIEVE + REMEMBER

- How are human research participants protected?

ANSWER: Researchers using human participants should obtain *informed consent*, protect them from harm and discomfort, treat personal information confidentially, and fully *debrief* them after their participation. Ethical principles have been developed by international psychological organizations, and most universities also have ethics committees that safeguard participants' well-being.

Improve Your Retention—and Your Grades

1-13 How can psychological principles help you learn and remember?

Most students assume that the way to cement new learning is to reread. Do you? If so, you may be surprised to hear that repeated self-testing and rehearsal of previously studied material helps even more. Memory research-

ers call this the **testing effect** (Roediger & Karpicke, 2006). (This is also known as the *retrieval practice effect* or as *test-enhanced learning*.) In one study, students learned 40 Swahili words. Those who had been tested repeatedly later recalled the words' meaning much better than others who had spent the same time restudying the 40 words (Karpicke & Roediger, 2008). Researchers have found that "trying and failing to retrieve the answer is actually helpful to learning" (Roediger & Finn, 2010).

I have designed this book to help you benefit from the testing effect and other memory research findings. As you will see in Chapter 7, to master information you must *actively process* it. Your mind is not like your stomach, something to be filled passively. Your mind is more like a muscle that grows stronger with exercise. Research shows that people learn and remember best when they put material in their own words, rehearse it, and then retrieve and review it again.

The **SQ3R** study method converts these principles into practice (McDaniel et al., 2009; Robinson, 1970). SQ3R is an acronym—an abbreviation formed from the first letter of each of its five steps: Survey, Question, Read, Retrieve,[6] Review.

6 Also sometimes called "Recite."

To study a chapter, first *survey*, taking a bird's-eye view. Scan the headings, and notice how the chapter is organized.

Before you read each main section, try to answer its numbered Learning Objective *Question* (for this section: "How can psychological principles help you learn and remember?"). By testing your understanding *before* you read the section, you will discover what you don't yet know.

Then *read*, actively searching for the answer to the question. At each sitting, read only as much of the chapter (usually a single main section) as you can absorb without tiring. Read actively and think critically. Ask your own questions. Take notes. Relate the ideas to your

informed consent giving people enough information about a study to enable them to decide whether they wish to participate.

debriefing after an experiment ends, explaining to participants the study's purpose and any deceptions researchers used.

testing effect enhanced memory after retrieving, rather than simply rereading, information. Also sometimes called the *retrieval practice effect* or *test-enhanced learning*.

SQ3R a study method incorporating five steps: *Survey, Question, Read, Retrieve, Review.*

personal experiences and to your own life. Does the idea support or challenge your assumptions? How convincing is the evidence?

Having read a section, *retrieve* its main ideas. Test yourself—even better, test yourself repeatedly. To get you started, I offer periodic Retrieve + Remember questions throughout each chapter (see, for example, the two at the end of this section). After trying to answer these questions, check the answers (printed upside-down beneath the questions), and reread the material as needed. Testing yourself will make you aware of what you don't know. And it will help you learn and retain the information more effectively.

Finally, *review*: Read over any notes you have taken, again with an eye on the chapter's organization, and quickly review the whole chapter. Write or say what a concept is before rereading the material to check your understanding.

Survey, question, read, retrieve, review. I have organized this book's chapters to help you use the SQ3R study system. Each chapter begins with an outline that aids your *survey*. Headings and Learning Objective *Questions* suggest issues and concepts you should consider as you read the section. The length of the sections is controlled so you can easily *read* them. The Retrieve + Remember questions will challenge you to *retrieve* what you have learned, and thus better remember it. The end-of-chapter *Review* includes the collected Learning Objective Questions and key terms for self-testing. A complete Chapter Test focuses on key concepts, and In Your Everyday Life questions help make the chapter's concepts more meaningful, and therefore more memorable.

Four additional study tips may further boost your learning:

Distribute your study time. One of psychology's oldest findings is that *if you want to retain information, spaced practice is better than massed practice.* So space your practice time over several study periods—perhaps one hour a day, six days a week—rather than cramming it into one long study blitz. You'll remember material better if you read just one main section (not the whole chapter) in a single sitting. Then turn to something else.

Spacing your study sessions requires discipline and knowing how to manage your time. (Richard O. Straub explains time management in a helpful preface at the beginning of this text.)

Learn to think critically. Whether you are reading or listening to class discussions, think smart. Try to spot people's assumptions and values. Can you detect a bias underlying an argument? Weigh the evidence. Is it a personal story that might not represent the whole group? Or is it scientific evidence based on sound experiments? Assess conclusions. Are other explanations possible?

Process class information actively. Listen for a lecture's main ideas and sub-ideas. *Write them down.* Ask questions during and after class. In class, as in your own study, process the information actively and you will understand and retain it better. How can you make the information your own? Take notes in your own words. Make connections between what you read and what you already know. Tell someone else about it. (As any teacher will confirm, to teach is to remember.)

Overlearn. Psychology tells us that we tend to be overconfident—we overestimate how much we know. You may understand a chapter as you read it, but that feeling of familiarity can trick you. Overlearning helps you retain new information. By using the Retrieve + Remember opportunities, you'll devote extra study time to testing your knowledge.

Memory experts Elizabeth Bjork and Robert Bjork (2011, p. 63) offer the bottom line for how to improve your retention and your grades:

> Spend less time on the input side and more time on the output side, such as summarizing what you have read from memory or getting together with friends and asking each other questions. Any activities that involve testing yourself—that is, activities that require you to retrieve or generate information, rather than just representing information to yourself—will make your learning both more durable and flexible. ■

RETRIEVE + REMEMBER

- The _____ _____ describes the improved memory that results from repeated retrieval (as in self-testing) rather than from simple rereading of new information.

  ANSWER: testing effect

- What does SQ3R mean?

  ANSWER: SQ3R is an acronym—an abbreviation formed by the first letters in five words: Survey, Question, Read, Retrieve, and Review.

CHAPTER REVIEW

Psychology's Roots, Big Ideas, and Critical Thinking Tools

Test yourself by taking a moment to answer each of these Learning Objective Questions (repeated here from within the chapter). Then turn to Appendix D, Complete Chapter Reviews, to check your answers. Research suggests that trying to answer these questions on your own will improve your long-term memory of the concepts (McDaniel et al., 2009).

Psychology's Roots

1-1: How has psychology's focus changed over time?

1-2: What are psychology's current perspectives, and what are some of its subfields?

Four Big Ideas in Psychology

1-3: What four big ideas run throughout this book?

Why Do Psychology?

1-4: How does our everyday thinking sometimes lead us to the wrong conclusion?

1-5: What are the three key elements of the scientific attitude, and how do they support scientific inquiry?

How Do Psychologists Ask and Answer Questions?

1-6: How do psychological theories guide scientific research?

1-7: How do psychologists use case studies, naturalistic observations, and surveys to observe and describe behavior, and why is random sampling important?

1-8: What are positive and negative correlations, and how can they lead to prediction but not cause-effect explanation?

1-9: How do experiments clarify or reveal cause-effect relationships?

Frequently Asked Questions About Psychology

1-10: How do simplified laboratory conditions help us understand general principles of behavior?

1-11: Why do psychologists study animals, and what ethical guidelines safeguard human and animal research participants?

1-12: How do personal values influence psychologists' research and application? Does psychology aim to manipulate people?

Improve Your Retention—and Your Grades

1-13: How can psychological principles help you learn and remember?

TERMS AND CONCEPTS TO REMEMBER

Test yourself on these terms by trying to write down the definition in your own words before flipping back to the referenced page to check your answer.

behaviorism, p. 3	dual processing, p. 8	naturalistic observation, p. 14	double-blind procedure, p. 18
humanistic psychology, p. 3	positive psychology, p. 8	survey, p. 15	placebo effect, p. 18
cognitive neuroscience, p. 3	hindsight bias, p. 9	population, p. 15	independent variable, p. 19
psychology, p. 3	theory, p. 12	random sample, p. 15	confounding variable, p. 19
critical thinking, p. 6	hypothesis, p. 12	correlation, p. 16	dependent variable, p. 19
biopsychosocial approach, p. 6	operational definition, p. 13	scatterplot, p. 16	informed consent, p. 22
culture, p. 7	replication, p. 13	experiment, p. 17	debriefing, p. 22
nature–nurture issue, p. 7	case study, p. 14	random assignment, p. 18	testing effect, p. 23
		experimental group, p. 18	SQ3R, p. 23
		control group, p. 18	
		placebo [pluh-SEE-bo], p. 18	

CHAPTER TEST

Test yourself repeatedly throughout your studies. This will not only help you figure out what you know and don't know; the testing itself will help you learn and remember the information more effectively thanks to the *testing effect*.

1. In 1879, in psychology's first experiment, _William Wundt_ and his students measured the time lag between hearing a ball hit a platform and pressing a key.

2. In the early twentieth century, _____ redefined psychology as "the science of observable behavior."
   a. John B. Watson *and later B.F. Skinner*
   b. Abraham Maslow
   c. William James
   d. Sigmund Freud

3. A psychologist treating emotionally troubled adolescents at a local mental health agency is most likely to be a(n)
   a. research psychologist.
   b. psychiatrist.
   c. industrial-organizational psychologist.
   d. clinical psychologist.

4. A mental health professional with a medical degree who can prescribe medication is a _psychiatrist_.

5. A psychologist doing research from the _____ perspective might be interested in how our blood chemistry affects our moods and motives.
   a. psychodynamic
   b. behavioral
   c. neuroscience
   d. social-cultural

6. How can critical thinking help you evaluate claims in the media, even if you're not a scientific expert on the issue?

7. Nature is to nurture as
   a. personality is to intelligence.
   b. biology is to experience.
   c. intelligence is to biology.
   d. psychological traits are to behaviors.

8. "Nurture works on what nature endows." Describe what this means, using your own words.

9. ___Dual processing___ is the principle that our mind processes information on two tracks simultaneously—one with our full awareness and the other outside of our awareness.

10. Positive psychology uses scientific methods to explore positive _emotions_, positive _intuition_, and positive _character traits_.

11. ___Hindsight bias___ refers to our tendency to perceive events as obvious or inevitable after the fact.

12. As scientists, psychologists
    a. approach research with a negative cynicism.
    b. assume that an article published in a leading scientific journal must be true.
    c. believe that every important human question can be studied scientifically.
    d. put competing ideas to the test and collect evidence.

13. Theory-based predictions are called _hypotheses_.

14. Which of the following is NOT one of the DESCRIPTIVE methods psychologists use to study behavior?
    a. A case study
    b. Naturalistic observation
    c. Correlational research
    d. A phone survey

15. You wish to survey a group of people who truly represent the country's adult population. Therefore, you need to ensure that you question a _random_ sample of the population.

16. A study finds that the more childbirth training classes women attend, the less pain medication they require during childbirth. This finding can be stated as a _negative_ (positive/negative) correlation.

17. Knowing that two events are correlated provides
    a. a basis for prediction.
    b. an explanation of why the events are related.
    c. proof that as one increases, the other also increases.
    d. an indication that an underlying third factor is at work.

18. Here are some recently reported correlations, with interpretations drawn by journalists. Knowing just these correlations, can you come up with other possible explanations for each of these?
    a. Alcohol use is associated with violence. (One interpretation: Drinking causes, or triggers, aggressive behavior.)
    b. Educated people live longer, on average, than less-educated people. (One interpretation: Education lengthens life and improves health.)
    c. Teens engaged in team sports are less likely to use drugs, smoke, have sex, carry weapons, and eat junk food than are teens who do not engage in team sports. (One interpretation: Team sports encourage healthy living.)
    d. Adolescents who frequently see smoking in movies are more likely to smoke. (One interpretation: Movie stars' behavior influences teens.)

19. To explain behaviors and clarify cause and effect, psychologists use *experiments*

20. To test the effect of a new drug on depression, researchers randomly assign people to control and experimental groups. People in the control group take a pill that contains no medication. This is a *placebo* .

21. In a double-blind procedure,

    a. only the participants know whether they are in the control group or the experimental group.

    b. experimental and control group members will be carefully matched for age, sex, income, and education level.

    c. neither the participants nor the researchers know who is in the experimental group or control group.

    d. someone separate from the researcher will ask people to volunteer for the experimental group or the control group.

22. A researcher wants to know whether noise level affects workers' blood pressure. In one group, she varies the level of noise in the environment and records participants' blood pressure. In this experiment, the level of noise is the *independent variable* .

23. The laboratory environment is designed to

    a. exactly re-create the events of everyday life.

    b. re-create psychological forces under controlled conditions.

    c. provide a safe place.

    d. reduce the number of animals and humans used in psychological research.

24. In defending their experimental research with animals, psychologists have noted that

    a. animals' biology and behavior can tell us much about our own.

    b. advancing the well-being of humans justifies using animals in research.

    c. animal experiments sometimes help animals as well as humans.

    d. all of these statements are correct.

    Find answers to these questions in Appendix E, in the back of the book.

IN YOUR EVERYDAY LIFE

Answering these questions will help you make these concepts more personally meaningful, and therefore more memorable.

1. How would you have defined *psychology* before taking this class?

2. Imagine that someone claims she can interpret your dreams or can speak to the dead. How could critical thinking help you check her claims?

3. Which of the four big ideas is most interesting to you? What was it that attracted your attention to that idea?

4. What about psychology has surprised you the most so far?

5. If you could conduct a study on any psychological question, which would you choose? How would you do it?

6. What other questions or concerns do you have about psychology?

experience
more of the
testing
effect

Multiple-format self-tests and more may be found at www.worthpublishers.com/myers.

The Biology of Mind and Consciousness

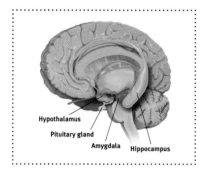

Hypothalamus
Pituitary gland
Amygdala   Hippocampus

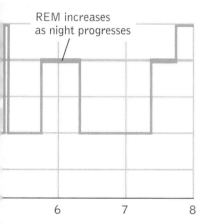

REM increases
as night progresses

6   7   8

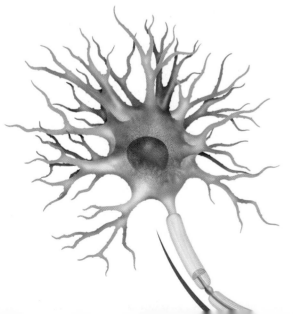

I n 2000, a Virginia teacher started collecting sex magazines and visiting child pornography websites. When he began making subtle advances on his young stepdaughter, his wife called the police. He was arrested and later convicted of child molestation. Though put into a sexual addiction rehabilitation program, he still felt overwhelmed by his sexual urges. The day before being sentenced to prison, he went to his local emergency room complaining of a headache and thoughts of suicide. He was also upset about his uncontrollable impulses, which led him to proposition nurses.

A brain scan located the problem—in his mind's biology. Behind his right temple was an egg-sized brain tumor. After surgeons removed the tumor, his lewd impulses faded and he returned home to his wife and stepdaughter. Alas, a year later the tumor partially grew back, and with it the sexual urges. A second tumor removal again lessened the urges (Burns & Swerdlow, 2003).

This case illustrates what you likely believe: that you reside in your head. If surgeons transplanted all your organs below your neck, and even your skin and limbs, you would (*Yes?*) still be you. Someone I know received a new heart from a woman who, in a rare operation, needed a matched heart-lung transplant. When the two chanced to meet in their hospital ward, she introduced herself: "I think you have my heart." But only her heart. She, like most of us, was assuming that her mind—her very self—dwells inside her skull, a creation of her brain.

Biology and Behavior

2-1 Why are psychologists concerned with human biology?

No principle is more central to today's psychology, or to this book, than this: *Everything psychological—every idea, every mood, every urge—is biological.* We may talk separately of biological influences and psychological influences, but they are two sides of the same coin. To think, feel, or act without a body would be like running without legs. Without our bodies, we would be nobodies.

Biological psychologists study the links between our biology and our behavior. These links are a key part of the biopsychosocial approach, which is one of the Four Big Ideas that appear throughout this text. In later chapters, we'll look at some of the ways our thinking and emotions can influence our brain and our health. In this chapter, our exploration of the biology of the mind starts small and builds from nerve cells to the brain. We'll also see how our brain states form the waking and sleeping mind.

"You're certainly a lot less fun since the operation."

Neural Communication

The human body is complexity built from simpler components. Part of this complexity is our amazing internal communication system. Around the world, researchers are unlocking the mysteries of how our brain uses electrical and chemical processes to take in, organize, interpret, store, and use information. The story begins with the nervous system's basic building block, the *neuron,* or nerve cell. We'll look first at its structure, and then at how neurons work together.

A Neuron's Structure

2-2 What are the parts of a neuron?

Neurons differ, but each consists of a *cell body* and its branching fibers (**FIGURE 2.1**). The neuron's bushy **dendrite** fibers receive messages and conduct them toward the cell body. From there, the cell's **axon** fiber sends out messages to other neurons or to muscles or glands. Dendrites listen. Axons speak.

The messages that neurons carry are nerve impulses called **action potentials.** These electrical signals travel down axons at different speeds. Messages travel faster along axons that are covered in a layer of fatty tissue called a *myelin sheath.* Supporting our billions of nerve cells are nine times as many spidery **glial cells** ("glue cells"). Neurons are like queen bees; on their own they cannot feed or sheathe themselves. Glial cells

> *"All information processing in the brain involves neurons 'talking to' each other at synapses."*
> Neuroscientist Solomon H. Snyder, 1984

are worker bees. They provide nutrients and insulating myelin. They guide neural connections and clean up after neurons send messages to one another. Glia may also play a role in information transmission, thinking, learning, and memory (Fields, 2009; Miller, 2005).

Researchers have tracked some action potentials trudging along at a sluggish 2 miles per hour, and others racing along at 200 or more miles per hour. Can you guess which reacts faster, a human brain or a high-speed computer? The computer wins every time. Even our brain's top speed is 3 million times slower than electricity zipping through a wire. Thus, unlike the nearly instant reactions of a computer, your "quick" reaction to a sudden event, such as a child darting in front of your car, may take a quarter-second or more. Your brain is vastly more complex than a computer, but slower at executing simple responses. And your reflexes would be slower yet if you were an elephant. The round-trip time for a message that begins with a yank on an elephant's tail and then travels to its brain and back to the tail is 100 times longer than in the body of a tiny shrew (More, 2010).

Neurons interweave so tightly that even with a microscope you would have trouble seeing where one ends and another begins. But end they do, at meeting places called **synapses.** At these points, two neurons are separated by a tiny gap less than a millionth of an inch wide. "Like elegant ladies air-kissing so as not to muss their makeup, dendrites and axons don't quite touch," noted poet Diane Ackerman (2004). How then does a neuron send information across the tiny *synaptic gap?* The answer is one of the important scientific discoveries of our age. ■

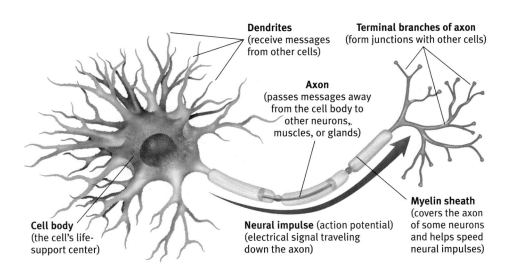

Dendrites
(receive messages
from other cells)

Terminal branches of axon
(form junctions with other cells)

Axon
(passes messages away
from the cell body to
other neurons,
muscles, or glands)

Cell body
(the cell's life-
support center)

Neural impulse (action potential)
(electrical signal traveling
down the axon)

Myelin sheath
(covers the axon
of some neurons
and helps speed
neural impulses)

FIGURE 2.1 A motor neuron

sites on the receiving neuron, as neatly as keys fitting into locks. They act as excitatory or inhibitory signals, and the process begins again in this new cell. In a final step, called *reuptake,* the sending neuron absorbs any leftover neurotransmitters in the synapse. ■

How Neurons Communicate

2-3 How do neurons communicate?

Each neuron is itself a miniature decision-making device, reacting to signals it receives from hundreds, even thousands, of other neurons. Most of these signals are *excitatory,* somewhat like pushing a neuron's gas pedal. Others are *inhibitory,* more like pushing its brake.

If the excitatory signals exceed the inhibitory signals by a minimum intensity, or **threshold,** the combined signals trigger an action potential. (Think of it this way: If the excitatory party animals outvote the inhibitory party poopers, the party's on.) The neuron then fires, sending an impulse down its axon, carrying information to another cell.

A neuron's firing doesn't vary in intensity. The neuron's reaction is an **all-or-none response.** Like guns, neurons either fire or they don't. How, then, do we distinguish a big hug from a gentle touch? A strong stimulus (the hug) can trigger *more* neurons to fire, and to fire more often. But it does not affect the action potential's strength or speed. Squeezing a trigger harder won't make a bullet bigger or faster.

When the action potential reaches the axon's end, your body performs an amazing trick. Your neural system converts an *electrical* impulse into a *chemical* message. At the synapse, the impulse triggers the release of **neurotransmitter** molecules, chemical messengers that can cross the synaptic gap (**FIGURE 2.2,** on the next page). Within one 10,000th of a second, these molecules bind to receptor

biological psychology a branch of psychology concerned with the links between biology and behavior.

neuron a nerve cell; the basic building block of the nervous system.

dendrites neuron extensions that receive messages and conduct them toward the cell body.

axon neuron extension that sends messages to other neurons or cells.

action potential a nerve impulse.

glial cells (glia) cells in the nervous system that support, nourish, and protect neurons; they may also play a role in learning, thinking, and memory.

synapse [SIN-aps] junction between the axon tip of a sending neuron and the dendrite or cell body of a receiving neuron.

threshold level of stimulation required to trigger a neural impulse.

all-or-none response a neuron's reaction of either firing (with a full-strength response) or not firing.

neurotransmitters neuron-produced chemicals that cross synapses to carry messages to other neurons or cells.

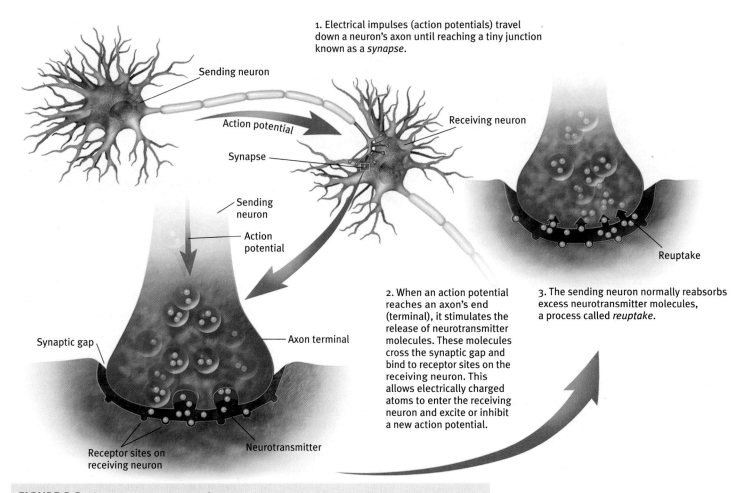

1. Electrical impulses (action potentials) travel down a neuron's axon until reaching a tiny junction known as a *synapse*.

Sending neuron

Action potential

Receiving neuron

Synapse

Sending neuron

Action potential

Reuptake

Synaptic gap

Axon terminal

Receptor sites on receiving neuron

Neurotransmitter

2. When an action potential reaches an axon's end (terminal), it stimulates the release of neurotransmitter molecules. These molecules cross the synaptic gap and bind to receptor sites on the receiving neuron. This allows electrically charged atoms to enter the receiving neuron and excite or inhibit a new action potential.

3. The sending neuron normally reabsorbs excess neurotransmitter molecules, a process called *reuptake*.

FIGURE 2.2 How neurons communicate

How Neurotransmitters Influence Us

2-4 How do neurotransmitters affect our mood and behavior?

Dozens of different neurotransmitters have their own pathways in the brain. As they travel along these paths, they carry specific but different messages that influence our behavior and emotions. *Serotonin* levels, for example, can make us more or less moody, hungry, sleepy, or aroused. *Dopamine* levels influence our movement, learning, attention, and emotions. **TABLE 2.1** outlines the effects of these and other neurotransmitters.

In Chapter 1, I promised to show you how psychologists play their game. Here's an example. An exciting neu-rotransmitter discovery emerged when researchers attached a radioactive tracer[1] to morphine, an **opiate** drug that elevates mood and eases pain (Pert & Snyder, 1973). They noticed that the morphine was binding to receptors in brain areas linked with mood and pain sensations. Why would these natural "opiate receptors" exist in the brain? Why would the brain have these chemical locks, unless our body produced some natural key to open them? Could the brain have its own built-in painkillers?

Further work revealed the answer. The brain does indeed produce its own natural opiates. Pain and vigorous exer-cise trigger the release of several types of neurotransmitter molecules similar to morphine. These **endorphins** (short for *endogenous* [produced within] *morphine*), as we now call them, help explain why we sometimes seem unaware of pain following extreme injuries. They also explain good feelings, such as the "run-ner's high" and the painkilling effects of acupuncture.

If our natural endorphins lessen pain and boost mood, why not achieve these ends by flooding the brain with artifi-cial opiates? One problem is that when flooded with artificial opiates, such as heroin and morphine, the brain may shut down its own "feel-good" chem-istry. If the drugs are then withdrawn, the brain will be deprived of any form of relief. Nature charges a price for sup-pressing the body's own neurotransmit-ter production.

---

1 A *radioactive tracer* sends out harmless but detectable energy as it passes through the body. This allows researchers to track its every movement.

TABLE 2.1 Some Neurotransmitters and Their Functions

Neurotransmitter	Function	Examples of Imbalances
Serotonin	Affects mood, hunger, sleep, and arousal.	Undersupply linked to depression. Some drugs that raise serotonin levels are used to treat depression.
Dopamine	Influences movement, learning, attention, and emotion.	Oversupply linked to schizophrenia. Undersupply linked to tremors and loss of motor control in Parkinson's disease.
Acetylcholine (ACh)	Enables muscle action, learning, and memory	With Alzheimer's disease, ACh-producing neurons break down.
Norepinephrine	Helps control alertness and arousal.	Undersupply can depress mood.
GABA (gamma-aminobutyric acid)	A major inhibitory neurotransmitter.	Undersupply linked to seizures, tremors, and insomnia.
Glutamate	A major excitatory neurotransmitter; involved in memory.	Oversupply can overstimulate brain, producing migraines or seizures (which is why some people avoid MSG, monosodium glutamate, in food).
Endorphins	Neurotransmitters that influence the perception of pain and pleasure.	Oversupply with opiate drugs can suppress the body's natural endorphin supply.

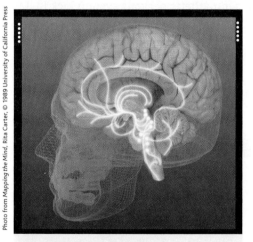

Photo from *Mapping the Mind*, Rita Carter, © 1989 University of California Press

SEROTONIN PATHWAYS

The biology-of-mind story is woven throughout this book. You will hear more about neurotransmitters in later chapters. ■

The Nervous System

2-5 What are the two major divisions of the nervous system, and what are their basic functions?

◎ To live is to take in information from the world and the body's tissues, to make decisions, and to send back information and orders to the body's tissues. All this happens thanks to your body's **nervous system** (FIGURE 2.3, on the next page). Your brain and spinal cord form the **central nervous system (CNS),** your body's decision maker. Your **peripheral nervous system (PNS)** gathers information from other body parts and transmits CNS decisions to the rest of your body.

Nerves are electrical cables formed of bundles of axons. They link your central nervous system with your body's sensory receptors, muscles, and glands. Your optic nerve, for example, bundles a million axons into a single cable carrying the messages each eye sends to your brain (Mason & Kandel, 1991).

Information travels in your nervous system through three types of neurons.

● **Sensory neurons** carry messages from your body's tissues and sensory receptors inward to your spinal cord and brain for processing.

● **Motor neurons** carry instructions from your central nervous system out to your body's muscles and glands.

● **Interneurons** within your brain and spinal cord communicate with one another and process information between the sensory input and motor output.

Your complexity resides mostly in your interneuron systems. Your nervous system has a few million sensory neurons, a few million motor neurons, and billions and billions of interneurons.

opiate chemical, such as opium, morphine, or heroin, that depresses neural activity, temporarily lessening pain and anxiety.

endorphins [en-DOR-fins] "morphine within"—natural, opiate-like neurotransmitters linked to pain control and to pleasure.

nervous system the body's speedy, electrochemical communication network, consisting of all the nerve cells of the central and peripheral nervous systems.

central nervous system (CNS) the brain and spinal cord.

peripheral nervous system (PNS) the sensory and motor neurons connecting the central nervous system to the rest of the body.

nerves bundled axons that form neural cables connecting the central nervous system with muscles, glands, and sense organs.

sensory neuron neuron that carries incoming information from the sensory receptors to the central nervous system.

motor neuron neuron that carries outgoing information from the central nervous system to the muscles and glands.

interneuron neurons within the brain and spinal cord; communicate internally and process information between sensory inputs and motor outputs.

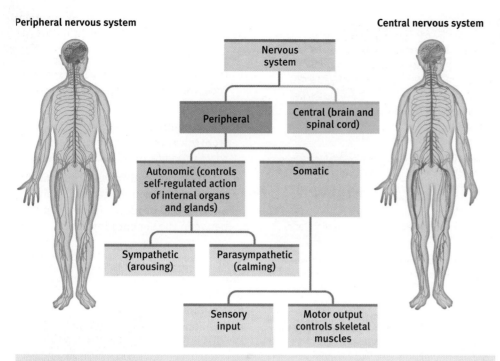

Peripheral nervous system

Central nervous system

FIGURE 2.3 The functional divisions of the human nervous system

The Peripheral Nervous System

The peripheral nervous system has two parts—somatic and autonomic. Your **somatic nervous system** monitors sensory input and triggers motor output, controlling your skeletal muscles (which is why it is also called the *skeletal nervous system*). As you reach the end of this page, your somatic nervous system will report the information to your brain and trigger your hand to turn the page. Your **autonomic nervous system** (ANS) controls your glands and the muscles of your internal organs, including those of your heart and digestive system. Like an automatic pilot, this system may be consciously overridden, but usually it operates on its own (autonomously).

The two subdivisions of your autonomic nervous system help you cope with challenges (**FIGURE 2.4**). If something alarms or challenges you (perhaps giving a speech or presentation), your **sympathetic nervous system** will arouse you, making you more alert, energetic, and ready for action. It will increase your

heartbeat, blood pressure, and blood-sugar level. It will also slow your digestion and cool you with perspiration. When the stress dies down (the speech is over), your **parasympathetic nervous**

system will calm you. It will conserve your energy as it decreases your heartbeat, lowers your blood sugar, and so on.

In everyday situations, the sympathetic and parasympathetic divisions work together to steady our internal state. I recently experienced my ANS in action. Before sending me into an MRI (magnetic resonance imaging) machine for a routine shoulder scan, the technician asked if I had claustrophobia issues (panic feelings when confined). "No, I'm fine," I assured her, with perhaps a hint of macho swagger. Moments later, as I found myself on my back, stuck deep inside a coffin-sized box and unable to move, my sympathetic nervous system had a different idea. As claustrophobia overtook me, my heart began pounding and I felt a desperate urge to escape. Just as I was about to cry out for release, I suddenly felt my calming parasympathetic nervous system kick in. My heart rate slowed, and my body relaxed, though my arousal surged again before the 20-minute confinement ended. "You did well!" the technician said, unaware of my ANS roller-coaster ride. ■

RETRIEVE + REMEMBER

- Match the type of neuron to its description.

Type
1. Motor neurons
2. Sensory neurons
3. Interneurons

Description
a. carry incoming messages from sensory receptors to the CNS.
b. communicate within the CNS and between incoming and outgoing messages.
c. carry outgoing messages from the CNS to muscles and glands.

ANSWERS: 1. c, 2. a, 3. b

- What bodily changes does your ANS (autonomic nervous system) direct before and after you give an important speech?

ANSWER: Responding to this challenge, your ANS' *sympathetic* division will arouse you. It increases your heartbeat, raises your blood pressure and blood sugar, slows your digestion, and cools you with perspiration. After you give the speech, your ANS' *parasympathetic* division will reverse these effects.

The Central Nervous System

From neurons "talking" to other neurons arises the complexity of the central ner-

vous system's brain and spinal cord.

It is the *brain* that enables our humanity—our thinking, feeling, and acting. According to one estimate based on human tissue samples, an adult male

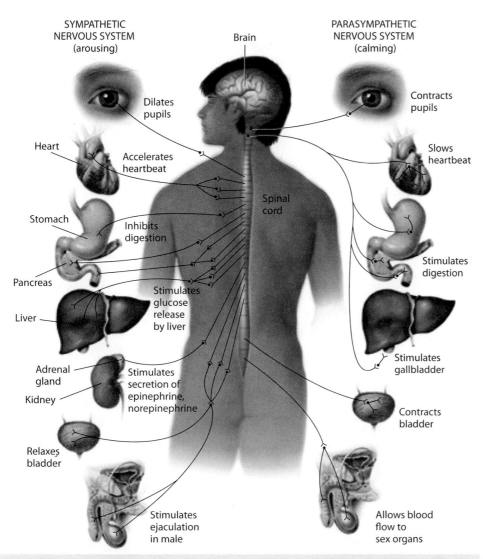

SYMPATHETIC
NERVOUS SYSTEM
(arousing)

Brain

PARASYMPATHETIC
NERVOUS SYSTEM
(calming)

Dilates
pupils

Contracts
pupils

Heart

Accelerates
heartbeat

Slows
heartbeat

Spinal
cord

Stomach

Inhibits
digestion

Stimulates
digestion

Pancreas

Stimulates
glucose
release
by liver

Liver

Stimulates
gallbladder

Adrenal
gland

Kidney

Stimulates
secretion of
epinephrine,
norepinephrine

Contracts
bladder

Relaxes
bladder

Stimulates
ejaculation
in male

Allows blood
flow to
sex organs

FIGURE 2.4 The autonomic nervous system arouses and calms Its sympathetic subdivision arouses and expends energy. Its parasympathetic subdivision calms and conserves energy, allowing routine maintenance activity. For example, sympathetic stimulation speeds up heartbeat, and parasympathetic stimulation slows it.

somatic nervous system peripheral nervous system division controlling the body's skeletal muscles. Also called the *skeletal nervous system*.

autonomic [aw-tuh-NAHM-ik] **nervous system (ANS)** peripheral nervous system division controlling the glands and the muscles of the internal organs (such as the heart). Its sympathetic subdivision arouses; its parasympathetic subdivision calms.

sympathetic nervous system autonomic nervous system subdivision that arouses the body, mobilizing its energy in stressful situations.

parasympathetic nervous system autonomic nervous system subdivision that calms the body, conserving its energy.

reflex a simple, automatic response to a sensory stimulus, such as the knee-jerk response.

© Tom Swick

"The body is made up of millions and millions of crumbs."

Stephen Colbert: "How does the brain work? Five words or less."

Steven Pinker: "Brain cells fire in patterns."

The Colbert Report, February 8, 2007

brain has about 86 billion neurons, give or take 8 billion (Azevedo et al., 2009). A grain-of-sand-sized speck of your brain contains some 100,000 neurons and one billion "talking" synapses—places where neurons meet and greet their neighbors (Ramachandran & Blakeslee, 1998). Operating this heart-of-your-smarts computing system takes energy. Your brain accounts for only about 2 percent of your body weight but uses 20 percent of your energy.

The brain's neurons cluster into work groups called *neural networks,* much as people cluster into cities rather than spreading themselves evenly across the nation (Kosslyn & Koenig, 1992). Neurons form networks with close neighbors by means of short, fast connections. Learning—to play a guitar, speak a foreign language, solve a math problem—occurs as experience strengthens those connections. Neurons that fire together wire together.

The other part of the central nervous system, the *spinal cord,* is a two-way highway connecting the brain and the peripheral nervous system. Some nerve fibers carry incoming information from your senses to your brain, while others carry outgoing motor-control information to your body parts. The neural pathways governing our **reflexes,** our automatic responses to stimuli, illustrate the spinal cord's work. A simple spinal reflex pathway is composed of a single sensory neuron and a single motor neuron. These often communicate through an interneuron. The knee-jerk response, for example, involves one such simple pathway. A headless warm body could do it.

What happens when people suffer damage to the top of their spinal cord? Their brain is truly out of touch with their body. They lose all sensation and voluntary movement in body regions that connect to the spinal cord below its injury. Given a doctor's knee-reflex test, their foot would respond with a jerk, but they would not feel the doctor's tap. Men paralyzed below the waist may be capable of an erection (a simple reflex) if their genitals are stimulated (Goldstein, 2000). Women similarly paralyzed may respond with vaginal lubrication. But, depending on where and how completely the spinal cord is severed, people may have no genital responses to erotic images and no genital feeling (Kennedy & Over, 1990; Sipski & Alexander, 1999). To produce physical pain or pleasure, the sensory information must reach the brain.

The Endocrine System

2-6 How does the endocrine system transmit information and interact with the nervous system?

◎ So far, we have focused on the body's speedy electrochemical information system. But your body has a second communication system, the **endocrine system** (FIGURE 2.5). Glands in this system secrete **hormones,** another form of chemical messenger, which travel through our bloodstream and influence our behaviors and emotions.

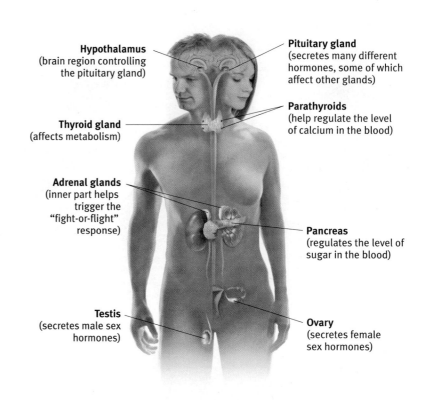

FIGURE 2.5 The endocrine system

Some hormones are chemically identical to neurotransmitters. The endocrine system and nervous system are therefore close relatives. Both produce molecules that act on receptors elsewhere. Like many relatives, they also differ. The speedy nervous system zips messages from eyes to brain to hand in a fraction of a second. Endocrine messages trudge along in the bloodstream, taking several seconds or more to travel from the gland to the target tissue. The nervous system delivers information to specific receptor sites with text-message speed. The endocrine system is more like sending a letter through the mail.

But slow and steady sometimes wins the race. The effects of endocrine messages tend to outlast those of neural messages. Have you ever felt angry, for no apparent reason? You may have experienced an "endocrine hangover" from lingering emotion-related hormones. Angry feelings can hang on, beyond our awareness of what set them off. When this happens, we need a little time to simmer down.

The endocrine system's hormones influence many aspects of our lives: growth, reproduction, metabolism, mood. They work with our nervous system to keep everything in balance as we respond to stress, hard work, and our own thoughts. Consider what happens behind the scenes when you hear burglar-like noises outside your window. Your ANS may order your **adrenal glands** to release *epinephrine* and *norepinephrine* (also called *adrenaline* and *noradrenaline*). In response, your heart rate, blood pressure, and blood sugar will rise, giving you a surge of energy known as the *fight-or-flight response*. When the "burglar" turns out to be a playful friend, the hormones—and your alert, aroused feelings—will linger a while.

The endocrine glands' control center is the **pituitary gland.** This pea-sized structure is located in the brain's core, where it is controlled by a nearby brain area, the *hypothalamus* (more on that shortly). Among the hormones released by the pituitary is a growth hormone that stimulates physical development. Another is *oxytocin*, which enables contractions during birthing, milk flow in nursing, and orgasm. Oxytocin also promotes social interactions. Its pleasant release accompanies couples bonding, feelings of group togetherness, and experiences of social trust (De Dreu et al., 2010).

Pituitary secretions also direct other endocrine glands to release their hormones. The pituitary, then, is a master gland (whose own master is the hypothalamus). For example, under the brain's influence, the pituitary triggers your sex glands to release sex hormones. These in turn influence your brain and behavior.

This feedback system (brain → pituitary → other glands → hormones → body and brain) reveals the interplay between the nervous and endocrine systems. The nervous system directs endocrine secretions, which then affect the nervous system. In charge of this whole electrochemical orchestra is that master conductor we call the brain. ■

The Brain

◎ When you think *about* your brain, you're thinking *with* your brain—sending billions of neurotransmitter molecules across countless millions of synapses. Indeed, say neuroscientists, "the mind is what the brain does" (Minsky, 1986).

Even in a permanently motionless body, the brain—and mind—may, in some cases, be active. One hospitalized 23-year-old woman showed no outward signs of conscious awareness after being in a traffic accident. Nevertheless, when researchers asked her to *imagine* playing tennis or moving around her home, brain scans revealed activity like that of healthy volunteers (Owen et al., 2006). As she imagined playing tennis, for example, an area of her brain controlling arm and leg movements became active.

Close-Up: Tools of Discovery, on the next page, describes some tools scientists use to explore the brain-mind connection. For centuries, we had no device high-powered yet gentle enough to reveal a living brain's activity. Now we are living in the golden age of brain science, moving closer and closer to understanding where and how the mind's functions are tied to the brain. To be learning about the brain now is like studying geography while the early explorers were mapping the world. Let's begin our own exploration of the brain.

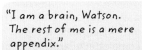

"I am a brain, Watson. The rest of me is a mere appendix."

Sherlock Holmes, in Arthur Conan Doyle's "The Adventure of the Mazarin Stone"

Older Brain Structures

Brain structures determine our abilities. In sharks and other primitive vertebrates (animals with backbones), a not-so-complex brain mainly handles basic survival functions: breathing, resting, and feeding. In lower mammals, such as rodents, a more complex brain enables emotion and greater memory. In advanced mammals, such as humans, a brain that processes more information also enables the ability to plan ahead.

This increasing complexity arises from new brain systems built on top of the old, much as new layers cover old ones in the Earth's landscape. Digging down, one discovers the fossil remnants of the past—brainstem components performing for us much as they did for our distant ancestors. Let's start with the brain's basement and work up.

The Brainstem

2-8 What are the functions of the brainstem and its related structures?

The brain's oldest and innermost region is the **brainstem**. It begins where the spinal cord swells slightly after entering the skull. This slight swelling is the

endocrine [EN-duh-krin] **system** the body's "slow" chemical communication system; a set of glands that secrete hormones into the bloodstream.

hormones chemical messengers that are manufactured by the endocrine glands, travel through the bloodstream, and affect other tissues.

adrenal [ah-DREEN-el] **glands** pair of endocrine glands that sit just above the kidneys and secrete hormones (epinephrine and norepinephrine) that help arouse the body in times of stress.

pituitary gland most influential endocrine gland. Under the influence of the hypothalamus, the pituitary regulates growth and controls other endocrine glands.

brainstem the oldest part and central core of the brain, beginning where the spinal cord swells as it enters the skull; responsible for automatic survival functions.

Tools of Discovery—Having Our Head Examined

2-7 What are some techniques for studying the brain?

In the past, brain injuries provided clues to brain-mind connections. For example, damage to one side of the brain often caused paralysis on the body's opposite side. Noting this, physicians guessed that the body's right side is wired to the brain's left side, and vice versa. Others linked vision problems with damage to the back of the brain, and speech problems with damage to the left-front brain. Gradually, a map of the brain began to emerge.

Now a new generation of mapmakers is at work charting formerly unknown territory, stimulating various brain parts and watching the results. Some use microelectrodes to snoop on the messages of individual neurons. Some attach larger electrodes to the scalp to eavesdrop with an **EEG (electroencephalograph)** on the chatter of billions of neurons. Others use scans that peer into the thinking, feeling brain and give us a Superman-like ability to see what's happening.

The **PET (positron emission tomography) scan** tracks the brain's favorite food, the sugar glucose. Knowing that active neurons are glucose hogs, researchers give the person a form of temporarily radioactive glucose. The PET scan then detects where this "food for thought" goes by locating the radioactivity. Rather like weather radar showing rain activity, PET-scan "hot spots" show which brain areas are most active as the person solves math problems, looks at images of faces, or daydreams.

MRI (magnetic resonance imaging) scans capture images of brain structures by briefly disrupting activity in brain molecules. Researchers first position the person's head in a strong magnetic field, which aligns the spinning atoms of brain molecules. Then, with a brief pulse of radio waves, they disrupt the spinning. When the atoms return to their normal spin, they give off signals that provide a detailed picture of soft tissues, including the brain. MRI scans have revealed, for example, that some people with schizophrenia, a disabling psychological disorder, have enlarged fluid-filled brain areas (FIGURE 2.6).

A special application of MRI, **fMRI (functional MRI),** also reveals the brain's *functions*. Where the brain is especially active, blood goes. By comparing MRI scans taken less than a second apart, researchers can watch parts of the brain activate as a person thinks or acts in certain ways. As the person looks at a photo, for example, the fMRI shows blood rushing to the back of the brain, which processes visual information (see Figure 2.17). The technology enables a very crude sort of mind reading, as some neuroscientists showed. They scanned 129 people's brains as they did eight different mental tasks (such as reading, gambling, and rhyming). Later, viewing another person's brain images, they were able, with 80 percent accuracy, to predict which of these mental tasks the person was doing (Poldrack et al., 2009).

What the telescope did for astronomy, these brain-snooping tools are doing for psychology. By revealing how the living, working brain divides its labor, these tools have taught us more about the brain in the past 30 years than we had learned in the prior 30,000 years. ■

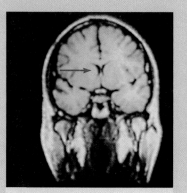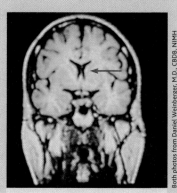

Both photos from Daniel Weinberger, M.D., CBDB, NIMH

FIGURE 2.6 MRI scan of a healthy individual (left) **and a person with schizophrenia** (right) Note the enlarged fluid-filled brain region in the image on the right.

RETRIEVE + REMEMBER

- Match the scanning technique with the correct description.

Technique

1. fMRI scan
2. PET scan
3. MRI scan

Description

a. tracks radioactive glucose to reveal brain activity.

b. tracks successive images of brain tissue to show brain function.

c. uses magnetic fields and radio waves to show brain anatomy.

ANSWERS: 1. b, 2. a, 3. c

EEG (electroencephalograph) device that uses electrodes placed on the scalp to record waves of electrical activity sweeping across the brain's surface. (The record of those brain waves is an *electroencephalogram*.)

PET (positron emission tomography) scan a view of brain activity showing where a radioactive form of glucose goes while the brain performs a given task.

MRI (magnetic resonance imaging) a technique that uses magnetic fields and radio waves to produce computer-generated images of soft tissue. MRI scans show brain anatomy.

fMRI (functional MRI) a technique for revealing bloodflow and, therefore, brain activity by comparing successive MRI scans. fMRI scans show brain function.

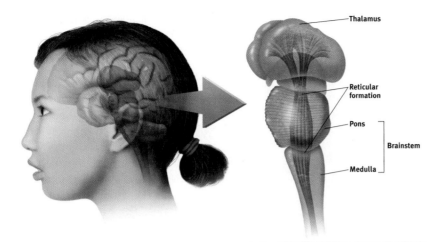

FIGURE 2.7 **The brainstem and thalamus** The brainstem, including the medulla and pons, is an extension of your spinal cord. The thalamus is attached to its top. The reticular formation passes through both structures.

medulla **(FIGURE 2.7)**. Here lie the controls for your heartbeat and breathing. As some severely brain-damaged patients illustrate, no higher brain or conscious mind is needed to orchestrate our heart's pumping and lungs' breathing. The brainstem handles those tasks.

Just above the medulla sits the *pons,* a brainstem area that helps coordinate movements. If a cat's brainstem is severed from the rest of the brain above it, the animal will still breathe. It will even run, climb, and groom (Klemm, 1990). But cut off from the brain's higher regions, it won't *purposefully* run or climb to get food.

The brainstem is a crossover point. Here, you'll find a peculiar sort of cross-wiring, with most nerves to and from each side of the brain connecting to the body's opposite side. Thus, the right brain controls the left side of the body, and vice versa **(FIGURE 2.8)**. This cross-wiring is one of the brain's many surprises. ■

The Thalamus

Sitting at the top of the brainstem is the **thalamus.** This joined pair of egg-shaped structures acts as the brain's sensory control center. The thalamus receives information from all your senses except smell, and it forwards the messages to brain regions that deal with seeing, hearing, tasting, and touching. Messages flow through this hub on their way to their final destination. In addition to incoming sensory messages, your thalamus receives replies from some higher brain regions. It forwards these replies to other brain areas (your medulla and cerebellum) for processing.

The Reticular Formation

Inside the brainstem, between your ears, lies your **reticular** ("netlike") **formation.** This neuron network extends upward from your spinal cord, through your brainstem, and into your thalamus (see Figure 2.7). This long structure acts as a filter for some of the sensory messages traveling from your spinal cord to your thalamus, relaying important information to other brain areas, and controlling arousal.

In 1949, researchers discovered that electrically stimulating the reticular formation of a sleeping cat almost instantly produced an awake, alert animal (Moruzzi & Magoun, 1949). When a cat's reticular formation was cut off from higher brain regions, without damaging the nearby sensory pathways, the effect was equally dramatic. The cat lapsed into a coma and never awakened. The conclusion? The reticular formation enables arousal.

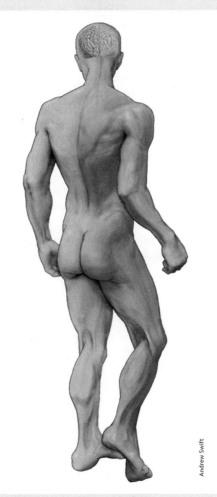

Andrew Swift

FIGURE 2.8 **The body's cross-wiring** Nerves from one side of the brain are mostly linked to the body's opposite side.

medulla [muh-DUL-uh] the base of the brainstem; controls heartbeat and breathing.

thalamus [THAL-uh-muss] area at the top of the brainstem; directs sensory messages to the cortex and transmits replies to the cerebellum and medulla.

reticular formation nerve network running through the brainstem and thalamus; plays an important role in controlling arousal.

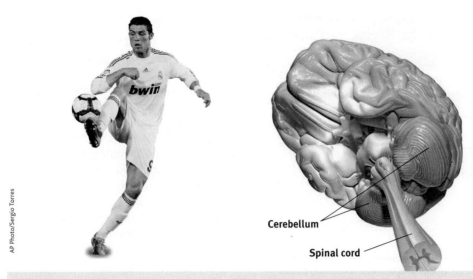

Cerebellum

Spinal cord

FIGURE 2.9 **The brain's organ of agility** Hanging at the back of the brain, the cerebellum coordinates our voluntary movements, as when soccer star Cristiano Ronaldo controls the ball.

The Cerebellum

At the rear of the brainstem is the **cerebellum,** meaning "little brain," which is what its two wrinkled halves resemble (**FIGURE 2.9**). This baseball-sized structure plays an important role in a lot that happens just outside your awareness. Quickly answer these questions. How much time has passed since you woke up this morning? Does your chair feel different from the back of your hand? How's your mood? If you answered those questions easily, thank your cerebellum.

Your cerebellum helps you judge time, discriminate sounds and textures, and control your emotions (Bower & Parsons, 2003). It also coordinates voluntary movement. When soccer player Ronaldo masterfully controls the ball, give his cerebellum some credit. If you injured your cerebellum or drugged it with alcohol, you would have trouble walking, keeping your balance, or shaking hands. The cerebellum also helps process and store memories for things we cannot consciously recall, such as how we ride a bicycle. (Stay tuned for more about this in Chapter 7.)

* * *

Note: These older brain functions all occur without any conscious effort.

Once again, we see one of our Big Ideas at work: *Our two-track brain processes most information outside of our awareness.* We are aware of the *results* of our brain's labor (say, our current visual experience) but not of *how* we construct the visual image. Likewise, whether we are asleep or awake, our brainstem manages its life-sustaining functions, freeing our newer brain regions to think, talk, dream, or savor a memory. ■

RETRIEVE + REMEMBER

- In what brain region would damage be most likely to (1) disrupt your ability to skip rope? (2) disrupt your ability to hear and taste? (3) perhaps leave you in a coma? (4) cut off the very breath and heartbeat of life?

ANSWER: 1. cerebellum, 2. thalamus, 3. reticular formation, 4. medulla

The Limbic System

2-9 What are the structures and functions of the limbic system?

. . . .

We've traveled through the brain's oldest parts, but we've not yet reached its newest and highest regions, the *cere-*

bral hemispheres (the two halves of the brain). Between the oldest and newest brain areas lies the **limbic system** (*limbus* means "border"). The limbic system contains the *amygdala,* the *hypothalamus,* and the *hippocampus* (**FIGURE 2.10**). The hippocampus processes conscious memories. Animals or humans who lose their hippocampus to surgery or injury also lose their ability to form new memories of facts and events. Chapter 7 explains how our two-track mind processes our memories. For now, let's look at the limbic system's links to emotions such as fear and anger, and to basic motives such as those for food and sex.

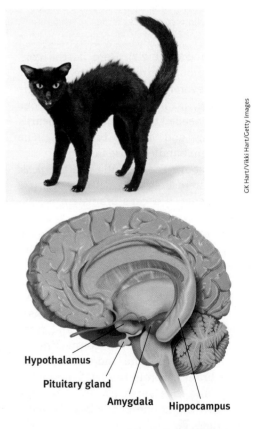

Hypothalamus

Pituitary gland

Amygdala   Hippocampus

FIGURE 2.10 **The limbic system** This neural system sits between your brain's older parts and its cerebral hemispheres. The limbic system's hypothalamus controls the nearby pituitary gland. Electrical stimulation of a cat's amygdala provokes reactions such as the one shown here, suggesting its role in emotions such as rage.

THE AMYGDALA The **amygdala**—two lima-bean-sized neural clusters—enable aggression and fear. In 1939, researchers surgically removed a rhesus monkey's amygdala, turning the normally ill-tempered animal into the most mellow of creatures (Klüver & Bucy, 1939).

What, then, might happen if we electrically stimulated the amygdala of a normally mellow domestic animal, such as a cat? Do so in one spot and the cat prepares to attack, hissing with its back arched, its pupils wide, its hair on end (see Figure 2.10). Move the electrode only slightly within the amygdala, cage the cat with a small mouse, and now it cowers in terror.

These experiments have confirmed the amygdala's role in emotions, including the processing of emotional memories and the perception of rage and fear. Consider a woman whose amygdala was destroyed by a rare genetic disease. Whether facing a snake, doing public speaking, or being threatened with a gun, she experiences no fear (Feinstein et al., 2010).

A critical thinker should be careful here. The brain is not neatly organized into structures that reflect our types of behaviors and feelings. When we feel or act in aggressive and fearful ways, there is neural activity in all levels of our brain, not just in the amygdala. If you charge a car's dead battery, you can activate the engine. Yet the battery is merely one link in the whole working system. ■

THE HYPOTHALAMUS Just below (hypo) your thalamus is your **hypothalamus,** an important link in the chain of command for bodily maintenance. Some neural clusters in the hypothalamus influence hunger. Others regulate thirst, body temperature, and sexual behavior. Together, they help you maintain a steady internal state.

As the hypothalamus monitors your body state, it tunes in to your blood chemistry and any incoming orders from other brain parts. For example, picking up signals from your brain's information-processing center, the *cerebral cortex,* that you are thinking about sex, your hypothalamus will secrete hormones. These hormones will in turn trigger the nearby gland of the endocrine system, your pituitary (see Figure 2.10), to influence your sex glands to release their hormones. These will intensify the thoughts of sex in your cerebral cortex. Once again, we see the interplay between the nervous and endocrine systems: The brain influences the endocrine system, which in turn influences the brain.)

A remarkable discovery about the hypothalamus illustrates how progress in science often occurs—when curious, smart-thinking investigators keep an open mind. Two young psychologists, James Olds and Peter Milner (1954), were trying to implant electrodes in rats' reticular formations when they made a magnificent mistake. In one rat, they placed the electrode incorrectly. Curiously, the rat kept returning to the location where it had been stimulated by this misplaced electrode, as if seeking more stimulation. When Olds and Milner discovered that they had actually placed the device in a region of the hypothalamus, they realized they had stumbled upon a brain center that provides pleasurable rewards (Olds, 1975).

In later studies, when rats were allowed to control their own stimulation in these and other areas, they did so at a feverish pace—pressing a pedal up to 7000 times an hour, until they dropped

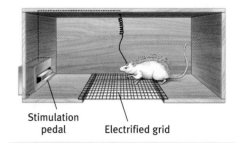

Stimulation pedal   Electrified grid

FIGURE 2.11 Pain for pleasure This rat has an electrode implanted in a reward center of its hypothalamus. It will cross an electric grid, accepting painful shocks, in order to press a lever that sends impulses to its reward center.

from exhaustion. Moreover, to get this stimulation, they would even cross an electrified floor that a starving rat would not cross to reach food (**FIGURE 2.11**).

Similar reward centers in or near the hypothalamus were later discovered in many other species, including goldfish, dolphins, and monkeys. In fact, animal research has revealed both a general reward system that triggers the release of the neurotransmitter dopamine, and specific centers associated with the pleasures of eating, drinking, and sex. Animals, it seems, come equipped with built-in systems that reward activities essential to survival.

Do you and I have limbic centers for pleasure? Indeed we do. When hearing or anticipating music that gives

cerebellum [sehr-uh-BELL-um] the "little brain" at the rear of the brainstem; functions include processing sensory input and coordinating movement output and balance.

limbic system neural system (including the *hippocampus, amygdala,* and *hypothalamus*) located below the cerebral hemispheres; associated with emotions and drives.

amygdala [uh-MIG-duh-la] two lima-bean-sized neural clusters in the limbic system; linked to emotion.

hypothalamus [hi-po-THAL-uh-muss] a neural structure lying below (hypo) the thalamus; directs several maintenance activities (eating, drinking, body temperature), helps govern the endocrine system via the pituitary gland, and is linked to emotion and reward.

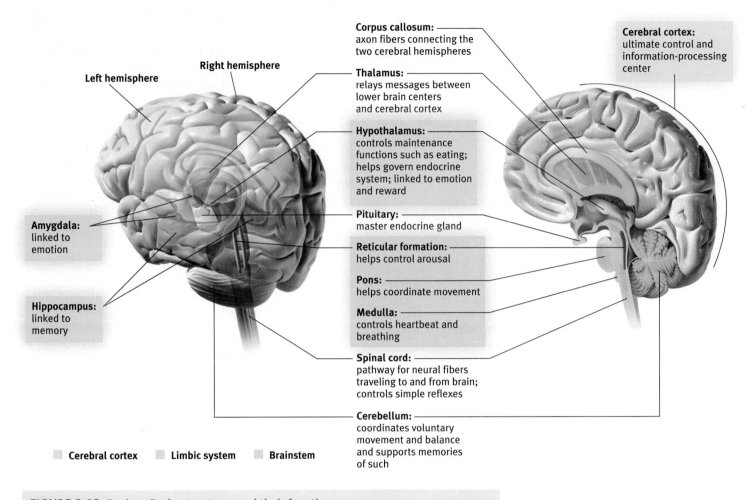

Left hemisphere

Right hemisphere

Corpus callosum: axon fibers connecting the two cerebral hemispheres

Thalamus: relays messages between lower brain centers and cerebral cortex

Hypothalamus: controls maintenance functions such as eating; helps govern endocrine system; linked to emotion and reward

Pituitary: master endocrine gland

Reticular formation: helps control arousal

Pons: helps coordinate movement

Medulla: controls heartbeat and breathing

Spinal cord: pathway for neural fibers traveling to and from brain; controls simple reflexes

Cerebellum: coordinates voluntary movement and balance and supports memories of such

Cerebral cortex: ultimate control and information-processing center

Amygdala: linked to emotion

Hippocampus: linked to memory

■ **Cerebral cortex**   ■ **Limbic system**   ■ **Brainstem**

FIGURE 2.12 Review: Brain structures and their functions

us great pleasure, our brain releases large amounts of dopamine (Salimpoor et al., 2011). To calm violent patients, one neurosurgeon implanted electrodes in such limbic system areas. Stimulated patients reported mild pleasure. Unlike Olds' rats, however, they were not driven to a frenzy (Deutsch, 1972; Hooper & Teresi, 1986).

* * *

We've finished our tour of the older brain structures. **FIGURE 2.12** will help you place the key brain areas we've discussed, as well as the cerebral cortex, our next topic. ■

RETRIEVE + REMEMBER

• What are the three key structures of the limbic system, and what functions do they serve?

ANSWER: (1) The *amygdala* is involved in aggression and fear responses. (2) The *hypothalamus* is involved in bodily maintenance, pleasurable rewards, and control of the hormonal systems. (3) The *hippocampus* processes memory.

The Cerebral Cortex

Older brain networks sustain basic life functions and enable memory, emotions, and basic drives. High above these older structures are the two large cerebral hemispheres, which contribute 85 per-

cent of the brain's weight. Covering those hemispheres, like bark on a tree, is the **cerebral cortex,** a thin surface layer of interconnected neurons. Its newer neural networks form specialized work teams that enable your thinking, sensing, and speaking. The cerebral cortex is your brain's thinking crown, your body's ultimate control and information-processing center.

Structure of the Cortex

2-10 What are the four lobes of the cerebral cortex, and where are they located?

If you opened a human skull, exposing the brain, you would see a wrinkled organ, shaped somewhat like the meat of an oversized walnut. Without these wrinkles, a flattened cerebral cortex would require triple the area—roughly that of a very large pizza. The brain's left and right hemispheres are filled mainly with axons connecting the cortex to the brain's other regions. The cerebral cortex—that thin surface layer—contains some 20 to 23 billion nerve cells and 300 trillion synaptic connections (de Courten-Myers, 2005). Being human takes a lot of nerve.

Each hemisphere's cortex is subdivided into four *lobes*, separated by deep folds (FIGURE 2.13). You can roughly trace the four lobes, starting with both hands on your forehead. The **frontal lobes** lie directly behind your forehead. As you move your hands over the top of your head, toward the rear, you're sliding over your **parietal lobes**. Continuing to move down, toward the back of your head, you'll slide over your **occipital lobes**. Now move each hand forward, to the sides of your head, and just above each ear you'll find your **temporal lobes**. Each

hemisphere has these four lobes. Each lobe carries out many functions. And many functions require the cooperation of several lobes.

Functions of the Cortex

2-11 What are the functions of the motor cortex, somatosensory cortex, and association areas?

More than a century ago, surgeons found damaged areas of the cerebral cortex during autopsies of people who had been partially paralyzed or speechless. This rather crude evidence was interesting, but it did not prove that specific parts of the cortex control complex functions like movement or speech. After all, if the entire cortex controlled speech and movement, damage to almost any area might produce the same effect. A TV with a cut power cord would go dead, but we would be fooling ourselves if we thought we had "localized" the picture in the cord.

MOTOR FUNCTIONS Early scientists had better luck showing simpler brain-

behavior links. In 1870, for example, German physicians Gustav Fritsch and Eduard Hitzig made an important discovery. By electrically stimulating parts of a dog's cortex, they could make other parts of its body move. The movement happened only when they stimulated an arch-shaped region at the back of the dog's frontal lobe, running roughly ear-to-ear across the top of the brain. Moreover, if they stimulated this region in the left hemisphere, the dog's right leg would move. And if they stimulated part of the right hemisphere, the opposite leg—on the left—reacted. Fritsch and Hitzig had discovered what is now called the **motor cortex.**

Lucky for brain surgeons and their patients, the brain has no sensory receptors. Knowing this, Otfrid Foerster and Wilder Penfield were able to map the motor cortex in hundreds of wide-awake patients by stimulating different cortical areas and observing the body's responses. They discovered that body areas requiring precise control, such as the fingers and mouth, occupied the greatest amount of cortical space (**FIGURE 2.14**, on the next page).

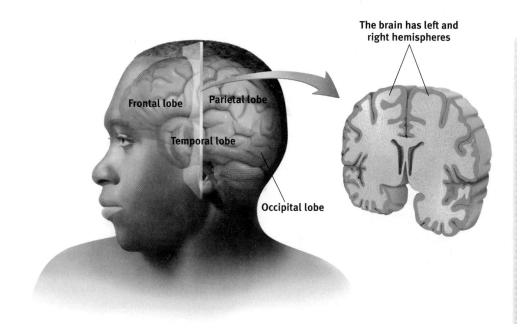

The brain has left and right hemispheres

Frontal lobe   Parietal lobe

Temporal lobe

Occipital lobe

FIGURE 2.13 The cortex and its basic subdivisions Lobes define broad divisions of each hemisphere of the cerebral cortex.

cerebral [seh-REE-bruhl] **cortex** thin layer of interconnected neurons covering the cerebral hemispheres; the body's ultimate control and information-processing center.

frontal lobes portion of the cerebral cortex lying just behind the forehead; involved in speaking and muscle movements and in making plans and judgments.

parietal [puh-RYE-uh-tuhl] **lobes** portion of the cerebral cortex lying at the top of the head and toward the rear; receives sensory input for touch and body position.

occipital [ahk-SIP-uh-tuhl] **lobes** portion of the cerebral cortex lying at the back of the head; includes areas that receive information from the visual fields.

temporal lobes portion of the cerebral cortex lying roughly above the ears; includes areas that receive information from the ears.

motor cortex cerebral cortex area at the rear of the frontal lobes; controls voluntary movements.

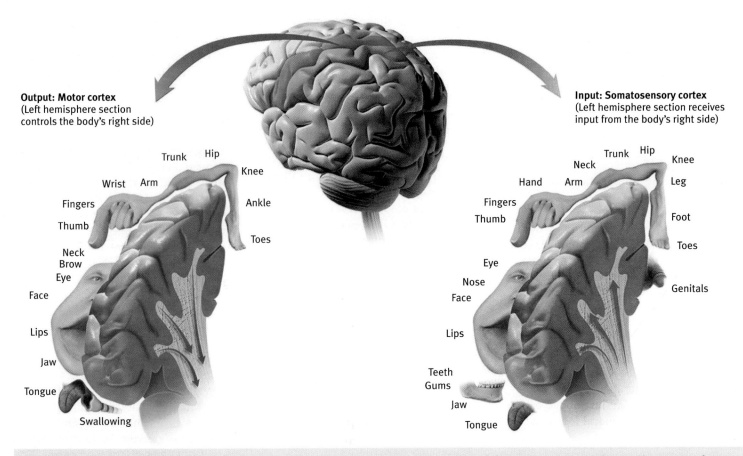

Output: Motor cortex
(Left hemisphere section controls the body's right side)

Trunk   Hip
Wrist   Arm   Knee
Fingers   Ankle
Thumb
              Toes
Neck
Brow
Eye
Face
Lips
Jaw
Tongue
  Swallowing

Input: Somatosensory cortex
(Left hemisphere section receives input from the body's right side)

        Trunk   Hip
  Neck   Knee
Hand   Arm   Leg
Fingers   Foot
Thumb
                Toes
Eye
Nose   Genitals
Face
Lips
Teeth
Gums
  Jaw
  Tongue

FIGURE 2.14 **Left hemisphere tissue devoted to each body part in the motor cortex and the somatosensory cortex** The amount of cortex devoted to a body part is not proportional to that part's size. Your brain devotes more tissue to sensitive areas and to areas requiring precise control. Thus, your fingers occupy more cortex space than does your upper arm.

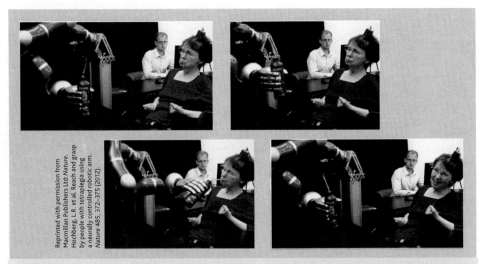

Reprinted with permission from Macmillan Publishers Ltd:*Nature.* Hochberg, L.R. et al. Reach and grasp by people with tetraplegia using a neurally controlled robotic arm. *Nature 485*, 372–375 (2012).

FIGURE 2.15 **Mind over matter** A series of strokes left Cathy paralyzed for 15 years, unable to make even simple arm movements. Now, thanks to a tiny, 96-electrode implant in her brain's motor cortex, she is learning to direct a robotic arm with her thoughts (Hochberg et al., 2012).

As is so often the case in science, new answers triggered new questions. We now know that electrically stimulating the motor cortex can cause body parts to move. What might happen, some researchers are asking, if we implanted a device to detect motor cortex activity? Could brain-controlled computer devices direct a robotic limb to move in soldiers who have lost arms or legs during combat? Could they help severely paralyzed people learn to command a cursor to send texts or e-mails or work online? Clinical trials are now under way with people who have suffered paralysis or amputation (Andersen et al., 2010; Nurmikko et al., 2010) **(FIGURE 2.15).** ■

RETRIEVE + REMEMBER

- Try moving your right hand in a circular motion, as if polishing a car. Then start your right foot doing the same motion as your hand. Now reverse the right foot's motion, but not the hand's. Finally, try moving the *left* foot opposite to the right hand.

  1. Why is reversing the right foot's motion so hard?

  2. Why is it easier to move the left foot opposite to the right hand?

ANSWER: 1. The right limbs' activities interfere with each other because both are controlled by the same (left) side of your brain. 2. Opposite sides of your brain control your left and right limbs, so the reversed motion causes less interference.

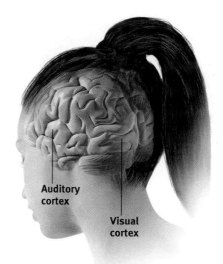

FIGURE 2.16 The visual cortex and auditory cortex The visual cortex of the occipital lobes at the rear of your brain receives input from your eyes. The auditory cortex, in your temporal lobes—above your ears—receives information from your ears.

Auditory cortex

Visual cortex

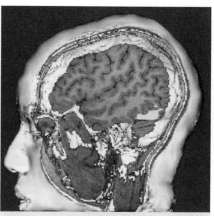

FIGURE 2.17 Watching the brain in action As this person looks at a photo, the fMRI (functional MRI) scan shows increased activity (color represents more bloodflow) in the visual cortex in the occipital lobes. When the person stops looking, the region instantly calms down.

SENSORY FUNCTIONS The motor cortex sends messages out to the body. What parts of the cortex receive incoming messages from our senses of touch and movement? Penfield supplied the answer: the **somatosensory cortex,** which runs parallel to the motor cortex and just behind it at the front of the parietal lobes (see Figure 2.14). Stimulate a point on the top of this band of tissue, and a person reports being touched on the shoulder. Stimulate some point on the side, and the person feels something on the face.

The more sensitive a body region, the larger the somatosensory cortex area devoted to it. Why do we kiss with our lips rather than rub elbows? Our supersensitive lips project to a larger brain area than do our arms (see Figure 2.14). Similarly, rats have a large brain area devoted to their whisker sensations, and owls to their hearing sensations.

Your somatosensory cortex is a very powerful tool for processing information from your skin senses and from movements of your body parts. But it isn't the only area of the cortex that receives input from your senses. If you have normal vision, you are at this moment receiving visual information in the *visual cortex* in your occipital lobes,

at the back of your brain (**FIGURE 2.16**). A friend of mine, who lost much of his right occipital lobe when a tumor was removed, became blind to the left half of his field of vision. Stimulated in your occipital lobes, you might see flashes of light or dashes of color. (In a sense, we *do* have eyes in the back of our head!) From your occipital lobes, visual information goes to other areas that specialize in tasks such as identifying words, detecting emotions, and recognizing faces (**FIGURE 2.17**).

Any sound you now hear is processed by your *auditory cortex* in your temporal lobes (just above your ears; see Figure 2.16). Most of this auditory information travels a roundabout route from one ear to the auditory receiving area above your opposite ear. If stimulated in your auditory cortex, you alone might hear a sound. People with schizophrenia sometimes have auditory **hallucinations** (false sensory experiences). MRI scans taken during these hallucinations show active auditory areas in the temporal lobes (Lennox et al., 1999). ■

RETRIEVE + REMEMBER

- Our brain's _____ cortex registers and processes body touch and movement sensations. The _____ cortex controls our voluntary movements.

ANSWERS: somatosensory; motor

ASSOCIATION AREAS So far, we have pointed out small areas of the cortex that receive messages from our senses, and other small areas that send messages to our muscles. Together, these areas occupy about one-fourth of the human brain's thin, wrinkled cover. What, then, goes on in the vast remaining regions of the cortex? In these **association areas** (peach colored in

somatosensory cortex cerebral cortex area at the front of the parietal lobes; registers and processes body touch and movement sensations.

hallucination false sensory experience, such as hearing something in the absence of an external auditory stimulus.

association areas cerebral cortex areas involved primarily in higher mental functions, such as learning, remembering, thinking, and speaking.

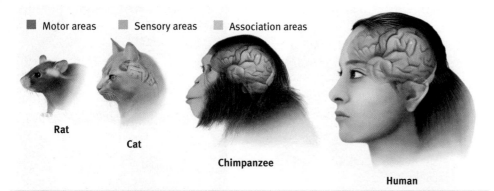

Motor areas   Sensory areas   Association areas

Rat

Cat

Chimpanzee

Human

FIGURE 2.18 Areas of the cortex in four mammals More intelligent animals have increased "uncommitted" or association areas of the cortex. These vast brain areas interpret, integrate, and act on sensory information and link it with stored memories.

FIGURE 2.18), neurons are busy with higher mental functions—many of the tasks that make us human.

Electrically probing an association area won't trigger any observable response. So, unlike the sensory and motor areas, association area functions can't be neatly mapped. Their silence has led to what Donald McBurney (1996, p. 44) called "one of the hardiest weeds in the garden of psychology"—the claim that we really use only 10 percent of our brain. (Time for some critical thinking: Wouldn't that mean that there is a 90 percent chance that a bullet to your brain would land in an unused area?) Brain-damaged animals and humans provide evidence that association areas are not unused. Rather, these brain areas interpret, integrate, and act on sensory information and link it with stored memories—a very important part of thinking.

Association areas are found in all four lobes. In the frontal lobes, they enable judgment, planning, and processing of new memories. People with damaged frontal lobes may have intact memories, high intelligence scores, and great cake-baking skills. Yet they would not be able to plan ahead to *begin* baking a cake for a loved one's birthday (Huey et al., 2006).

Frontal lobe damage can also alter personality and remove a person's inhibitions. Consider the classic case of railroad worker Phineas Gage. One after-noon in 1848, Gage, then 25 years old, was using an iron rod to pack gunpowder into a rock. A spark ignited the gunpowder, shooting the rod up through his left cheek and out the top of his skull, causing massive damage to his frontal lobes (FIGURE 2.19a). To everyone's amazement, he was immediately able to sit up and speak, and after the wound healed, he returned to work. But the friendly, soft-spoken Phineas Gage was now irritable, profane, and dishonest. This person, said his friends, was "no longer Gage." His mental abilities and memories were intact, but his person-ality was not. (Although Gage lost his railroad job, he did, over time, adapt to his injury and find work as a stagecoach driver [Macmillan & Lena, 2010].)

With his frontal lobes ruptured, Gage's moral compass had disconnected from his behavior. More recent studies of people with damaged frontal lobes have revealed similar losses. Without the frontal lobe brakes on their impulses they, too, became less inhibited. Moreover, their moral judgments seem untouched by normal emotions. Would you agree with the idea of pushing someone in front of a runaway train to save five others? Most people do not, but those with damage to a brain area behind the eyes often do (Koenigs et al., 2007).

Damage to association areas in other lobes would result in different losses. If a stroke or head injury destroyed part of your parietal lobes, you might lose mathematical and spatial reasoning. If the damaged area was on the underside of the right temporal lobe, which lets you recognize faces, you would still be able to describe facial features and to recognize someone's gender and approximate age. Yet you would be strangely unable to identify the person as, say, Lady Gaga or even your grandmother.

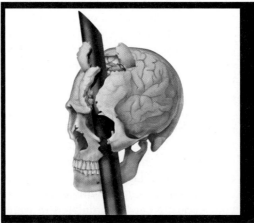

(a)   (b)

Collection of Jack and Beverly Wilgus

FIGURE 2.19 A blast from the past (a) Phineas Gage's skull was kept as a medical record. Using measurements and modern neuroimaging techniques, researchers have reconstructed the probable path of the rod through Gage's brain (Van Horn et al., 2012). (b) This recently discovered photo shows Gage after his accident. (This image has been reversed to show the features correctly. Early photos, including this one, were actually mirror images.)

Nevertheless, complex mental functions don't reside in any one place. There is no one spot in a rat's small association cortex that, when damaged, will wipe out its ability to learn or remember a maze. And as we'll see in Chapter 8, distinct neural networks in the human brain work together to enable language. Memory, language, and attention are the products of interaction among distinct brain areas (Knight, 2007). Ditto for religious experience. More than 40 brain regions become active in different religious states, such as prayer and meditation, indicating that there is no simple "God spot" (Fingelkurts & Fingelkurts, 2009). *The point to remember:* Our mental experiences arise from coordinated brain activity. ■

The Brain's Plasticity

2-12 When damaged, can the brain repair or reorganize itself?

Our brains are sculpted not only by our genes but also by our experiences. In Chapter 3, we'll focus more on how experience molds the brain. For now, let's turn to another aspect of the brain's **plasticity:** its ability to modify itself after damage.

Some brain-damage effects described earlier can be traced to two hard facts:

• Severed neurons, unlike cut skin, usually do not repair themselves. (If your spinal cord were severed, you probably would be permanently paralyzed.)

• Some brain functions seem forever linked to specific areas. One newborn who suffered damage to the facial recognition areas on both temporal lobes later remained unable to recognize faces (Farah et al., 2000).

But there is good news: Thanks to the brain's impressive plasticity, some brain tissue can *reorganize* in response to damage. Under the surface of our awareness, the brain is constantly changing, building new pathways as it adjusts to little mishaps and new experiences.

On a larger, more dramatic scale, plasticity sometimes occurs after serious damage, especially in young children (Kolb, 1989). If a slow-growing left-hemisphere tumor disrupts language, the right hemisphere may take over the task (Thiel et al., 2006). If a finger is lost, the somatosensory cortex that received its input will begin to pick up signals from the neighboring fingers, which then become more sensitive (Fox, 1984). Blindness or deafness makes unused brain areas available for other uses (Amedi et al., 2005). This plasticity helps explain why deaf people who learned

BRAIN PLASTICITY Although the brains of young children show the greatest ability to reorganize and adapt to damage, adult brains also have some capacity for self-repair. Former Arizona Congresswoman Gabrielle Giffords lost her ability to speak after suffering a left-hemisphere gunshot wound. Her medical care included music therapy, where she worked on forming words to familiar songs such as "Happy Birthday." Giffords has since partly recovered her speaking ability. Two years after the shooting, she was able to speak as a surprise witness at a 2013 U.S. Senate hearing on gun legislation.

MIKE THEILER/UPI/Newscom

sign language before any other may have better-than-average peripheral vision (Bosworth & Dobkins, 1999). Without stimulation from sounds, a temporal lobe area normally dedicated to hearing is free to process other signals, such as those from the visual system.

Although the brain often attempts self-repair by reorganizing existing tissue, it sometimes tries to mend itself by producing new neurons. This process, known as **neurogenesis,** has been found in adult mice, birds, monkeys, and humans (Jessberger et al., 2008). These baby neurons are born deep in the brain. They may then migrate elsewhere and form connections with neighboring neurons (Aimone et al., 2010; Gould, 2007).

Might new drugs spur the production of new nerve cells? Stay tuned. As you read this sentence, companies are working on such possibilities. In the meantime, we can all benefit from natural aids to neurogenesis, such as exercise, sleep, and nonstressful but stimulating environments (Iso et al., 2007; Pereira et al., 2007; Stranahan et al., 2006).

Our Divided Brain

2-13 What is a split brain, and what does it reveal about the functions of our left and right hemispheres?

Our brain's look-alike left and right hemispheres serve different functions. This *lateralization* is clear after some types of brain damage. Language processing seems to reside mostly in your left hemisphere. More than a century's research has shown that left hemisphere accidents, strokes, and tumors could leave you unable to read, write, speak, do arithmetic, and understand others. Similar right hemisphere damage seldom has such dramatic effects.

plasticity the brain's ability to change, especially during childhood, by reorganizing after damage or by building new pathways based on experience.

neurogenesis formation of new neurons.

Does this mean that the right hemisphere is just along for the ride—a silent junior partner or "minor" hemisphere? Many believed this was the case until 1960, when researchers found that the "minor" right hemisphere was not so limited after all. The unfolding of this discovery is another one of psychology's fascinating stories.

> "You wouldn't want to have a date with the right hemisphere."
> Michael Gazzaniga, 2002

Splitting the Brain: One Skull, Two Minds

In 1961, two neurosurgeons believed that the uncontrollable seizures of some patients with severe epilepsy could be caused by abnormal brain activity bouncing back and forth between the two cerebral hemispheres. If so, they wondered, could they put an end to this biological tennis game by cutting through the **corpus callosum**, the wide band of axon fibers connecting the two hemispheres and carrying messages between them (FIGURE 2.20)? The neurosurgeons knew that psychologists Roger Sperry, Ronald Myers, and Michael Gazzaniga had divided cats' and monkeys' brains in this manner, with no serious ill effects.

So the surgeons operated. The result? The seizures all but disappeared. The patients with these **split brains** were surprisingly normal, their personality and intellect hardly affected. Waking from surgery, one even joked that he had a "splitting headache" (Gazzaniga, 1967). By sharing their experiences with us, these patients have greatly expanded our understanding of interactions between the intact brain's two hemispheres.

To appreciate these studies, we need to focus for a minute on the peculiar nature of our visual wiring, illustrated in FIGURE 2.21. Note that each eye receives sensory information from the entire visual field. In each eye, information from the left half of your field of vision goes to your right hemisphere, and information from the right half of your visual field goes to your left hemisphere, which usually controls speech. In an intact brain, data received by either hemisphere are quickly transmitted to the other side, across the corpus callosum. In a person with a severed corpus callosum, this information sharing does not take place.

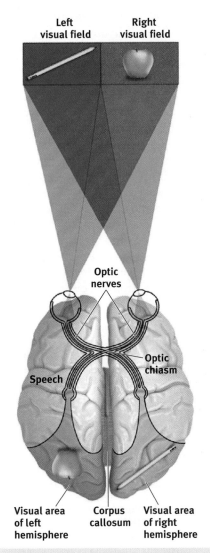

FIGURE 2.21 The information highway from eye to brain

Knowing these facts, Sperry and Gazzaniga could send information to a patient's left hemisphere by having the person stare at a dot and by then flashing a stimulus (a word or photo) to the right of the dot. To send a message to the right hemisphere, they would flash the item to the left of the dot.

They could do this with you, too, but in your intact brain the hemisphere receiving the information would instantly pass the news to the other side. Because the split-brain surgery had cut the communication lines between

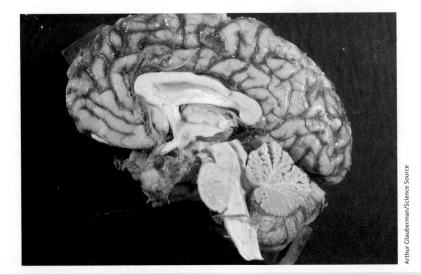

Arthur Glauberman/Science Source

FIGURE 2.20 **The corpus callosum** This large band of neural fibers connects the two brain hemispheres. To photograph the half brain shown above, a surgeon separated the hemispheres by cutting through the corpus callosum and lower brain regions.

the hemispheres, the researchers could, with these patients, quiz each hemisphere separately.

In an early experiment, Gazzaniga (1967) flashed the word *HEART* across the screen in such a way that *HE* appeared to the left of the dot, and *ART* appeared to the right (FIGURE 2.22b). Asked to *say* what they saw, the patients reported the letters sent to the left hemisphere—"*ART*." Asked to *point* with their left hand to what they saw, they pointed to the letters sent to the right hemisphere—"*HE*" (Figure 2.22c). One skull was housing two minds.

A few people who have had split-brain surgery have been bothered for a time by the unruly independence of their left hand. It seemed the left hand truly didn't know what the right hand was doing. One hand might unbutton a shirt while the other buttoned it, or put grocery store items back on the shelf after the other hand put them in the cart. It was as if each hemisphere was thinking, "I've half a mind to wear my green (blue) shirt today." Indeed, said Sperry (1964), split-brain surgery leaves people "with two separate minds" (FIGURE 2.23).

Which hemisphere resolves disagreements when the "two minds" are at odds? If a split-brain patient follows an order ("Walk") sent to the right hemisphere, the left hemisphere won't know why it did so. But rather than say "I don't know," the left hemisphere does a strange thing. It instantly invents—and apparently believes—an explanation ("I'm going into the house to get a Coke"). Thus, Gazzaniga (1989), who has called split-brain patients "the most fascinating people on Earth," concluded that the conscious left hemisphere is an "interpreter" that instantly constructs theories to explain our behavior. And so it goes for us all. The brain runs largely on autopilot: Often it feels and acts and then explains later (Kahneman, 2011). ■

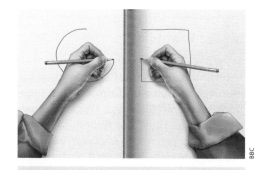

FIGURE 2.23 Try this! A split-brain patient can simultaneously draw two different shapes.

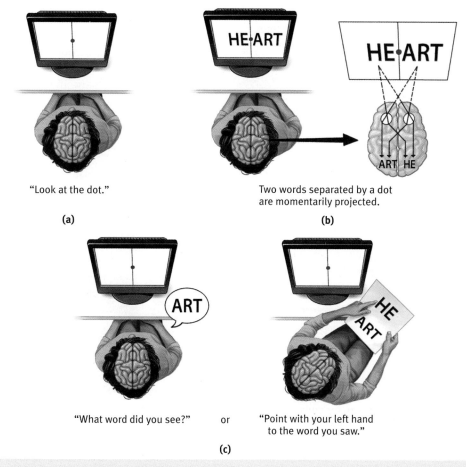

"Look at the dot."

(a)

Two words separated by a dot are momentarily projected.

(b)

"What word did you see?"   or   "Point with your left hand to the word you saw."

(c)

FIGURE 2.22 Testing the divided brain (From Gazzaniga, 1983.)

corpus callosum [KOR-pus kah-LOW-sum] large band of neural fibers connecting the two brain hemispheres and carrying messages between them.

split brain condition in which the brain's two hemispheres are isolated by cutting the fibers (mainly those of the corpus callosum) connecting them.

Right-Left Differences in Intact Brains

So, what about the 99.99+ percent of us with undivided brains? Does each of *our* hemispheres also perform distinct functions? Several different types of studies indicate they do. When a person performs a *perceptual* task, for example, brain waves, bloodflow, and glucose consumption reveal increased activity in the *right* hemisphere. When the person speaks or calculates, activity increases in the *left* hemisphere.

If you could peek into an operating room at the beginning of some types of brain surgery, you could watch a dramatic demonstration of lateralization. To locate the patient's language centers, the surgeon injects a sedative into the neck artery feeding blood to the left hemisphere, which usually controls speech. Before the injection, the patient is lying down, arms in the air, chatting with the doctor. Can you predict what probably happens when the drug puts the left hemisphere to sleep? Within seconds, the patient's right arm falls limp. If the left hemisphere is controlling language, the patient will be speechless until the drug wears off.

To the brain, language is language, whether spoken or signed. Just as hearing people usually use the left hemisphere to process spoken language, deaf people usually use the left hemisphere to process sign language (Corina et al., 1992; Hickok et al., 2001). Thus, a left-hemisphere stroke disrupts a deaf person's signing, much as it would disrupt a hearing person's speaking (Corina, 1998). The same brain area is involved in both. (For more on how the brain enables language, see Chapter 8.)

The left hemisphere is good at making quick, exact interpretations of language. But the right hemisphere excels in high-level language processing (Beeman & Chiarello, 1998; Bowden & Beeman, 1998; Mason & Just, 2004). Given an insight problem— "What word goes with *boot, summer,* and *ground?*"—the right hemisphere more

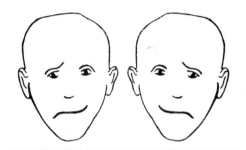

FIGURE 2.24 Which one is happier? Look at the center of one face, then the other. Does one appear happier? Most people say the right face does (Jaynes, 1976, p. 120). Some researchers believe we make this choice because our right hemisphere, which is skilled in emotion processing, receives information from the left half of each face (when looking at its center).

quickly than the left achieves the solution: *camp.* As one patient explained after a right-hemisphere stroke, "I understand words, but I'm missing the subtleties." The right side of the brain is also better than the left at copying drawings, recognizing faces, noticing differences, perceiving emotion, and expressing emotion through the more expressive left side of the face (**FIGURE 2.24**). Right-hemisphere damage can greatly disrupt these abilities.

Simply looking at the two hemispheres, so alike to the naked eye, who would suppose they contribute uniquely to the harmony of the whole? Yet a variety of observations—of people with split brains and those with intact brains, and even of other species' brains— leaves little doubt that we have unified brains with specialized parts (Hopkins & Cantalupo, 2008; MacNeilage et al., 2009).

Brain States and Consciousness

2-14 What do we mean by *consciousness,* and how does selective attention direct our perceptions?

 In the lively field of neuroscience, researchers are addressing many

exciting questions. Among the most interesting are those in the subfield of *cognitive neuroscience,* in which people from many disciplines join forces to study connections between brain activity and mental processes, including states of consciousness.

Consciousness is our awareness of ourselves and our environment. It arises not from any one brain area but from the coordinated activity of the whole brain (Gaillard et al., 2009; Koch & Greenfield, 2007; Schurger et al., 2010). A telltale sign of conscious awareness appears in brain scans as a pattern of strong signals bouncing from one brain area to another (Boly et al., 2011).

Consciousness lets you assemble information from many sources as you reflect on the past, plan for the future, and focus on the present. You'll encounter aspects of consciousness throughout this text. Conscious awareness forms one track of the dual-track mind, one of the four themes running through this text. In Chapter 5, we'll consider hypnosis and its use to relieve pain. In Chapter 13,

ALTERED STATES OF CONSCIOUSNESS In addition to normal, waking awareness, consciousness comes to us in altered states, including meditating, daydreaming, sleeping, and drug-induced hallucinating.

we'll look closely at consciousness-altering drugs and their effects. Here we explore the role of attention and the altered states of consciousness we all experience—sleep and dreams.

Selective Attention

Through **selective attention,** your awareness focuses, like a flashlight beam, on a *very* limited aspect of all that you experience. Until reading this sentence, you have been unaware that your shoes are pressing against your feet or that your nose is in your line of vision. Now, suddenly, the spotlight shifts. Your feet feel encased, your nose stubbornly intrudes on the words before you. While focusing on these words, you've also been blocking other parts of your environment from awareness, though your peripheral vision would let you see them easily. You can change that. As you stare at the X below, notice what surrounds these sentences (the edges of the page, the desktop, the floor).

X

Talk on the phone or attend to a music player or GPS while driving, and your selective attention will shift back and forth between the road and its electronic competition. But when a demanding situation requires it, you'll probably give the road your full attention. You'll probably also blink less, as we do when focused on a task (Smilek et al., 2010). So why not use a cell phone while driving? Because we pay a toll for switching atten-

"I wasn't texting. I was building this ship in a bottle."

tional gears, especially when we shift to complex tasks, like noticing and avoiding cars around us. The toll is a slight delay in coping (Rubenstein et al., 2001). In experiments that mimicked actual driving conditions, students talking on cell phones—either handheld or hands-free—have been slower to detect and respond to traffic signals, billboards, and other cars (Horrey & Wickens, 2006; Strayer & Watson, 2012).

Another study tracked long-haul truck drivers for 18 months. The video cameras mounted in their cabs showed they were at 23 times greater risk of a collision while texting (VTTI, 2009). Mindful of such findings, the United States in 2010 banned texting by truckers and bus drivers while driving (Halsey, 2010). Because our attention is selective—in one place at a time—multitasking comes at a cost. In 28 percent of all U.S. vehicle crashes, people were talking on cell phones or texting (National Safety Council, 2010).

We consciously process only a tiny sliver of the immense ocean of visual stimuli constantly before us. In one famous study, people watched a one-minute video of basketball players, three in black shirts and three in white shirts, tossing a ball (Becklen & Cervone, 1983; Neisser, 1979). Researchers told the viewers to press a key each time they saw a blackshirted player pass the ball. Most were so intent on the game that they failed to notice a young woman carrying an umbrella stroll across the screen midway through the clip. During a replay they were amazed to see her! Their attention focused elsewhere, the viewers suffered from **inattentional blindness.** Would a gorilla-suited assistant thumping his chest and moving through the swirl of players be more visible? No—

FIGURE 2.25 Hard to miss? Would you notice a clown unicycling past you on campus? In this study, most students on cell phones did *not* notice the clown; students who were off the phone generally did notice.

half the pass-counting viewers failed to see him, too (Simons & Chabris, 1999).

In another follow-up experiment, only 1 in 4 students absorbed in a cell-phone conversation while crossing a campus square noticed a clown-suited unicyclist in their midst (Hyman et al., 2010). (Most of those not on the phone did notice.) (See **FIGURE 2.25.**)

Given that most of us miss people strolling by in gorilla and clown suits while our attention is focused elsewhere, imagine the fun that magicians can have by distracting us. Misdirect our attention and we will miss the hand slipping into the pocket. "Every time you perform a magic trick, you're engaging in experimental psychology," says magician Teller, a master of mind-messing methods (2009).

Magicians also exploit our **change blindness.** By selectively riveting our attention

---

consciousness our awareness of ourselves and our environment.

selective attention focusing conscious awareness on a particular stimulus.

inattentional blindness failure to see visible objects when our attention is directed elsewhere.

change blindness failure to notice changes in the environment.

FIGURE 2.26 **Change blindness** While a man (white hair) provides directions to a construction worker, two experimenters rudely pass between them carrying a door. During this interruption, the original worker switches places with another person wearing different colored clothing. Most people, focused on their direction giving, do not notice the switch.

on their left hand's dramatic act, we fail to notice changes made with their other hand. In laboratory experiments, viewers didn't notice that, after a brief visual interruption, a big Coke bottle had disappeared, a railing had risen, or clothing color had changed (Chabris & Simons, 2010; Resnick et al., 1997). **FIGURE 2.26** shows a drawing imitating the idea behind one study in which two-thirds of the people giving directions to a construction worker failed to notice when he was replaced by another worker. Out of sight, out of mind.

The point to remember: Attention is powerfully selective. Our conscious mind is in one place at a time. But outside our conscious awareness, the other track of our two-track mind remains active—even during sleep, as we see next. ■

Sleep and Dreams

Now playing at an inner theater near you: the premiere showing of a sleeping person's vivid dream. This never-before-seen mental movie features engaging characters wrapped in a plot that is original and unlikely, yet seemingly real.

Waking from a dream, we may wonder how our brain can so creatively, colorfully, and completely construct this inner-space world. Caught for a moment between our dreaming and waking consciousness, we may even be unsure which world is real.

Sleep's mysteries have puzzled scientists for centuries. Now, in laboratories around the world, some of these mysteries are being solved as people sleep, attached to recording devices, while others observe. By recording brain waves and muscle movements, and by watching and sometimes waking sleepers, researchers are glimpsing things that a thousand years of common sense never told us.

Biological Rhythms and Sleep

2-15 What is the circadian rhythm, and what are the stages of our nightly sleep cycle?

Like the ocean, life has its rhythmic tides. Let's look more closely at two of these biological rhythms—our 24-hour biological clock and our 90-minute sleep cycle.

> "I love to sleep. Do you? Isn't it great? It really is the best of both worlds. You get to be alive and unconscious."
> Comedian Rita Rudner, 1993

CIRCADIAN RHYTHM Try pulling an all-nighter, or working an occasional night shift. You will feel groggiest in the middle of the night but may gain new energy around the time you would normally wake up. Your body is reacting in part to its own wake-up call. The human body is kept roughly in tune with the 24-hour cycle of day and night by an internal biological clock called the **circadian rhythm** (from the Latin *circa*, "about," and *diem*, "day"). As morning approaches, body temperature rises, then peaks during the day, dips for a time in early afternoon (when many people take naps), and begins to drop again in the evening. Thinking is sharpest and memory most accurate when we are at our daily peak in circadian arousal.

Age and experience can alter our circadian rhythm. After about age 20 (slightly earlier for women), we begin to shift from being evening-energized "owls" to being morning-loving "larks" (Roenneberg et al., 2004). Most college students are owls, with performance improving across the day (May & Hasher, 1998). Most older adults are larks, with performance declining as the day wears on. By mid-evening, when the night has hardly begun for many young adults, most retirement homes are quiet.

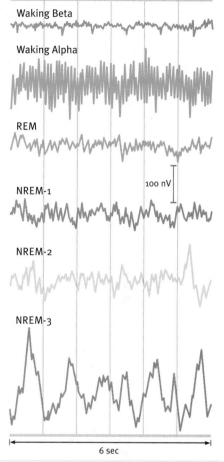

SLEEP STAGES Sooner or later, sleep overtakes us and consciousness fades as different parts of our brain's cortex stop communicating (Massimini et al., 2005). But rather than emitting a constant dial tone, the sleeping brain has its own biological rhythm.

About every 90 minutes, we cycle through distinct sleep stages. This basic fact apparently was unknown until 8-year-old Armond Aserinsky went to bed one night in 1952. His father, Eugene, needed to test an electroencephalograph he had repaired that day (Aserinsky, 1988; Seligman & Yellen, 1987). Placing electrodes near Armond's eyes to record the rolling eye movements then believed to occur during sleep, Aserinsky watched the machine go wild, tracing deep zigzags on the graph paper. Could the machine still be bro-

ken? As the night proceeded and the activity recurred, Aserinsky realized that the periods of fast, jerky eye movements were accompanied by energetic brain activity. Awakened during one such episode, Armond reported having a dream. Aserinsky had discovered what we now know as **REM sleep** (rapid *eye movement* sleep).

Similar procedures used with thousands of volunteers showed the cycles were a normal part of sleep (Kleitman, 1960). To appreciate these studies, imagine yourself as a participant. As the hour grows late, you feel sleepy and get ready for bed. A researcher comes in and tapes electrodes to your scalp (to detect your brain waves), on your chin (to detect muscle tension), and just outside the corners of your eyes (to detect eye movements) (**FIGURE 2.27**). Other devices will record your heart rate, respiration rate, and genital arousal.

When you are in bed with your eyes closed, the researcher in the next room sees on the EEG the relatively slow **alpha waves** of your awake but relaxed state (**FIGURE 2.28**). As you adapt to all this

FIGURE 2.28 Brain waves and sleep stages The beta waves of an alert, waking state and the regular alpha waves of an awake, relaxed state differ from the slower, larger delta waves of deep NREM-3 sleep. Although the rapid REM sleep waves resemble the near-waking NREM-1 sleep waves, the body is more aroused during REM sleep than during NREM sleep.

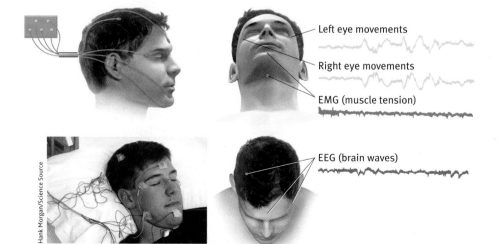

FIGURE 2.27 Measuring sleep activity As this man sleeps, attached electrodes are picking up weak electrical signals from his brain, eyes, and facial muscles. (From Dement, 1978.)

circadian [ser-KAY-dee-an] **rhythm** internal biological clock; regular bodily rhythms (for example, of temperature and wakefulness) that occur on a 24-hour cycle.

REM (rapid eye movement) sleep recurring sleep stage during which vivid dreams commonly occur. Also known as *paradoxical sleep*, because the muscles are relaxed (except for minor twitches) but other body systems are active.

alpha waves relatively slow brain waves of a relaxed, awake state.

equipment, you grow tired and, in a moment you won't remember, you slip into **sleep.** The transition is marked by the slowed breathing and the irregular brain waves of non-REM stage 1 sleep. In the new American Academy of Sleep Medicine classification of sleep stages, this stage is called *NREM-1* sleep (Silber et al., 2008).

During this brief NREM-1 sleep you may experience fantastic images resembling hallucinations. You may have a sensation of falling (at which moment your body may suddenly jerk) or of floating weightlessly. These *hypnagogic* sensations may later be incorporated into your memories. ("Hypnagogic" comes from the Greek root words meaning "leading to sleep.") People who claim to have been abducted by aliens—often shortly after getting into bed—commonly recall being floated off (or pinned down on) their beds (Clancy, 2005).

You then relax more deeply and begin about 20 minutes of *NREM-2* sleep, with its bursts of rapid, rhythmic brain-wave activity (see Figure 2.28). Although you could still be awakened without too much difficulty, you are now clearly asleep.

Then you enter the deep sleep of *NREM-3.* During this slow-wave sleep, which lasts for about 30 minutes, your brain emits large, slow **delta waves.** You would be hard to awaken. (It is at the end of the deep, slow-wave NREM-3 sleep that children may wet the bed.)

REM SLEEP About an hour after you first dive into sleep, a strange thing happens. You reverse course. From NREM-3, then back through NREM-2 (where you spend about half your night), you enter the most puzzling sleep phase—REM sleep **(FIGURE 2.29).** And the show begins. For about 10 minutes, your brain waves become rapid and saw-toothed, more like those of the nearly awake NREM-1 sleep. But unlike NREM-1, during REM sleep your heart rate rises and your breathing becomes rapid and irregular. Every half-minute or so, your eyes dart around in a brief burst of activity behind closed lids. These eye movements announce the beginning of a

dream—often emotional, usually story-like, and richly hallucinatory.

Except during very scary dreams, your genitals become aroused during REM sleep. You have an erection or increased vaginal lubrication and clitoral engorgement, regardless of whether the dream's content is sexual (Karacan et al., 1966). Men's common "morning erection" stems from the night's last REM period, often just before waking. (Many men troubled by *erectile disorder* [impotence] still have sleep-related erections, suggesting the problem is not between their legs.)

Your brain's motor cortex is active during REM sleep, but your brainstem blocks its messages. This leaves your muscles relaxed, so much so that, except for an occasional finger, toe, or

"Boy are my eyes tired! I had REM sleep all night long."

facial twitch, you are essentially paralyzed. Moreover, you cannot easily be awakened. REM sleep is thus sometimes called *paradoxical* sleep: The body

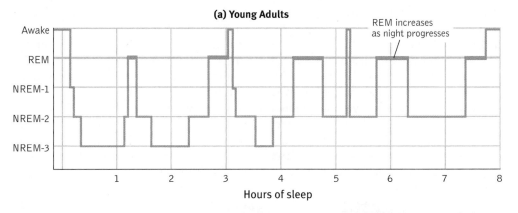

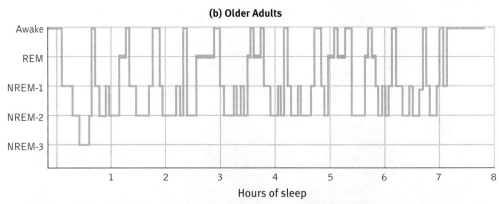

FIGURE 2.29 The stages in a typical night's sleep People pass through a multistage sleep cycle several times each night. As the night goes on, the periods of deep sleep diminish and REM sleep increases. For older adults, sleep becomes more fragile and awakenings more common (Kamel & Gammack, 2006; Neubauer, 1999).

is internally aroused and externally calm—except for those darting eyes.

The sleep cycle repeats itself about every 90 minutes for younger adults (somewhat more often for older adults). As the night wears on, deep NREM-3 sleep grows shorter and disappears. REM and NREM-2 sleep periods get longer (see Figure 2.29). By morning, we have spent 20 to 25 percent of an average night's sleep— some 100 minutes—in REM sleep. Thirty-seven percent of people have

> *Horses, which spend 92 percent of each day standing and can sleep standing, must lie down for muscle-paralyzing REM sleep (Morrison, 2003).*

> *2004 Gallup poll:*
> *"Usually, how many hours of sleep do you get at night?"*
>
> | | |
> |---|---|
> | 5 or less | 14% |
> | 6 | 26% |
> | 7 | 28% |
> | 8 | 25% |
>
> *2004 average = 6.8 hours*
> *1942 average = 7.6 hours*

reported rarely or never having dreams "that you can remember the next morning" (Moore, 2004). Yet even they, more than 80 percent of the time, will recall a dream if awakened during REM sleep. Each year, we spend about 600 hours experiencing some 1500 dreams. Over a typical lifetime, this adds up to more than 100,000 dreams—all swallowed by the night but not acted out, thanks to REM's protective paralysis. ■

Why Do We Sleep?

2-16 How do our sleep patterns differ? What five theories describe our need to sleep?

The idea that "everyone needs 8 hours of sleep" is untrue. Newborns often sleep two-thirds of their day, most adults no more than one-third. Still, there is more to our sleep differences than age. Some of us thrive with fewer than 6 hours a night. Others regularly rack up 9 hours or more (Coren, 1996). Heredity influences sleep patterns (Hor & Tafti, 2009). In studies of fraternal and identical twins, only the identical twins had strikingly similar patterns (Webb & Campbell, 1983).

But we should not overstress biology. Remember another of this book's themes: *Individual and social-cultural forces also affect behavior.* Sleep patterns are culturally influenced. In industrialized nations, people now sleep less than they did a century ago. Thanks to modern lighting, shift work, and social diversions, those who would have gone to bed at 9:00 P.M. are now up until 11:00 P.M. or later.

Bright light at night can disrupt our biological clock, tricking the brain into thinking it's morning. The process begins in the retinas in our eyes, which contain light-sensitive proteins. Normally, morning light sets off an internal alarm by activating these proteins, which then signal neural clusters in the brain (Foster, 2004). The brain interprets these signals as orders to decrease production of the sleep-inducing hormone *melatonin*. In sleep as in waking behavior, environment and biology interact.

SLEEP THEORIES So our sleep patterns differ from person to person and from culture to culture. But why do we *need* to

Uriel Sinai/Getty Images

RETRIEVE + REMEMBER

- Why would communal sleeping provide added protection for these soldiers?

  ANSWER: With each soldier cycling through the sleep stages independently, it is very likely that at any given time at least one of them will be awake or easily wakened in the event of a threat.

- What are the four sleep stages, and in what order do we normally travel through those stages?

  ANSWER: REM, NREM-1, NREM-2, NREM-3; normally we move through NREM-1, then NREM-2, then NREM-3, then back up through NREM-2 before we experience REM sleep.

- Can you match the cognitive experience with the sleep stage?

1. NREM-1	a. story-like dreams
2. NREM-3	b. fleeting images
3. REM	c. minimal awareness

  ANSWERS: 1.b, 2.c, 3.a

sleep periodic, natural loss of consciousness— as distinct from unconsciousness resulting from a coma, general anesthesia, or hibernation. (Adapted from Dement, 1999.)

delta waves the large, slow brain waves associated with deep sleep.

sleep? Psychologists offer five possible reasons why sleep evolved.

1. **Sleep protects.** When darkness shut down the day's hunting, food gathering, and travel, our distant ancestors were better off asleep in a cave, out of harm's way. Those who didn't try to navigate around rocks and cliffs at night were more likely to leave descendants. This fits a broader principle: A species' sleep patterns tend to suit its place in nature. Animals with the greatest need to graze and the least ability to hide tend to sleep less (see **FIGURE 2.30**).

2. **Sleep helps us recover.** Sleep helps restore and repair brain tissue. Bats and many other small animals burn a lot of calories, producing a lot of *free radicals,* molecules that are toxic to neurons. Sleeping a lot gives resting neurons time to repair and reorganize themselves (Gilestro et al., 2009; Siegel, 2003). Think of it this way: When consciousness leaves your house, brain construction workers come in for a makeover.

3. **Sleep helps us remember.** During sleep, we restore and rebuild our memories of the day's experiences. People trained to perform tasks recall them better after a night's sleep, or even after a short nap, than after several hours awake (Stickgold & Ellenbogen, 2008). Sleep strengthens neural memory traces and makes them more stable (Racsmány et al., 2010; Rasch & Born, 2008). After sleeping well, older people remember more. And the neural activity that takes place during slow-wave sleep seems to let humans (and rats) relive earlier experiences, and to remember them better (Peigneux et al., 2004; Ribeiro et al., 2004). Sleep, it seems, strengthens memories in a way that being awake does not.

4. **Sleep feeds creative thinking.** A full night's sleep boosts our thinking and learning. After working on a task, then sleeping on it, people solve problems more insightfully than do those who stay awake (Wagner et al., 2004). They also are better at spotting connections among novel pieces of information (Ellenbogen et al., 2007). To think smart and see connections, it often pays to sleep on it.

5. **Sleep supports growth.** During deep sleep, the pituitary gland releases a hormone we need for muscle development. A regular full night's sleep can *"dramatically improve your athletic ability"* (Maas & Robbins, 2010). Well-rested athletes have faster reaction times, more energy, and greater endurance. Teams that build 8 to 10 hours of daily sleep into their training show improved performance.

> One study of a decade's 24,121 Major League Baseball games found a circadian disadvantage. Teams that had crossed three time zones before playing a multiday series had nearly a 60 percent chance of losing their first game (Winter et al., 2009).

> *"Sleep faster, we need the pillows."*
> Yiddish proverb

Given all the benefits of sleep, it's no wonder that sleep loss hits us so hard. ■

Sleep Deprivation and Sleep Disorders

2-17 How does sleep loss affect us, and what are the major sleep disorders?

Sleep commands roughly one-third of our lives—some 25 years, on average. When our body yearns for sleep but does not get it, we feel terrible. Trying to stay awake, we will eventually lose. In the tiredness battle, sleep always wins.

THE EFFECTS OF SLEEP LOSS Today, more than ever, our sleep patterns leave us not only sleepy but drained of energy and feelings of well-being. After a series of 5-hour nights, we run up a sleep debt that can't be repaid with one long sleep. "The brain keeps an accurate count of sleep debt for at least two weeks," reported sleep researcher William Dement (1999, p. 64).

With enough sleep, we awake refreshed and in a better mood. We work more efficiently and accurately. College and university students are especially

FIGURE 2.30 Animal sleep times Would you rather be a brown bat and sleep 20 hours a day or a giraffe and sleep 2 hours (data from NIH, 2010)?

Kruglov_Orda/Shutterstock; Courtesy of Andrew D. Myers; © Anna63/Dreamstime.com; Steffen Foerster Photography/Shutterstock; The Agency Collection/Punchstock; Eric Isselée/Shutterstock; pandapaw/Shutterstock.

sleep deprived. In one national survey, 69 percent reported "feeling tired" or "having little energy" on several or more days in the last two weeks (AP, 2009). Small wonder so many fall asleep in class. When the going gets boring, the students start snoring. Even when awake, they often function below their peak.

Sleep deprivation slows reactions and increases errors on some visual attention tasks (Lim & Dinges, 2010). When sleepy frontal lobes confront an unexpected situation, slow responses can spell disaster. Driver fatigue has contributed to an estimated 20 percent of American traffic accidents (Brody, 2002). One two-year study examined the driving accident rates of more than 20,000 Virginia 16- to 18-year-olds in two major cities. In one city, the high schools started 75 to 80 minutes later than in the other. The late starters had about 25 percent fewer crashes (Vorona et al., 2011).

Twice each year, most Americans participate in a sleep-manipulation experiment—the "spring forward" to daylight savings time and "fall backward" to standard time. A search of millions of records showed that in both Canada and the United States, accidents increased

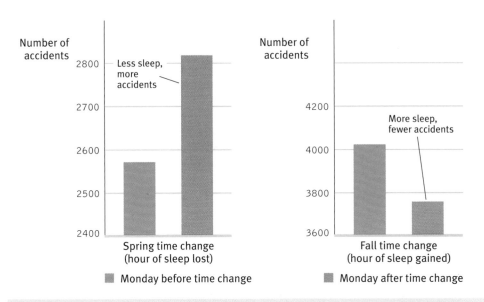

FIGURE 2.31 **Canadian traffic accidents** On the Monday after the spring time change, when people lose one hour of sleep, accidents increased, as compared with the Monday before. In the fall, traffic accidents normally increase because of greater snow, ice, and darkness, but they diminished after the time change. (Adapted from Coren, 1996.)

immediately after the time change that shortened sleep (**FIGURE 2.31**). *The bottom line:* Less sleep can mean more accidents.

When tired, the trouble people have concentrating leads to more "cyberloafing"—frittering away time online. On the Monday after daylight savings time begins, entertainment-related Google searches have been 3.1 percent higher than on the preceding Monday, and 6.4 higher than on the following Monday (Wagner, 2012). In another study, researchers had students wear a sleep-monitoring bracelet overnight. Those who were sleep deprived spent more time cyberloafing during a 42-minute video lecture.

Another effect of chronic sleep loss is immune system suppression. With sleep deprivation, we produce fewer immune cells, which battle viral infections and cancer (Beardsley, 1996; Irwin et al., 1994). One experiment exposed volunteers to a cold virus. Those who had been averaging less than 7 hours of sleep a night were three times more likely to develop the cold than were those sleeping 8 or more hours a night (Cohen et al., 2009).

Sleep loss can also predict depression. In a study of 15,500 young people (12 to 18 years old) the risk of depression among those who slept 5 or fewer hours a night was 71 percent higher than among others who slept 8 hours or more

SLEEPLESS AND SUFFERING These fatigued, sleep-deprived earthquake rescue workers in China may experience a depressed immune system, impaired concentration, and greater vulnerability to accidents.

(Gangwisch et al., 2010). Studies of nearly 70,000 adults have revealed a doubled risk of future depression among people with ongoing problems going to sleep or staying asleep (Baglioni et al., 2011). REM sleep's processing of emotional experiences helps protect against depression (Walker & van der Helm, 2009). After a good night's sleep, we often feel better the next day.

Can lack of sleep make you gain weight? Yes, by increasing *ghrelin,* a hunger-arousing hormone, and decreasing its hunger-suppressing partner, *leptin.* Sleep deprivation also increases *cortisol,* a stress hormone that triggers fat production. Sure enough, children and adults who sleep less than normal are fatter than those who sleep more (Chen et al., 2008; Knutson et al., 2007; Schoenborn & Adams, 2008). And in experiments,

> *Some students have a sleep schedule like that of the fellow who stayed up all night to see where the Sun went. (Then it dawned on him.)*

adults deprived of sleep had increased appetites and ate more (Nixon et al., 2008; Patel et al., 2006; Spiegel et al., 2004; Van Cauter et al., 2007). This may help explain the common weight gain among sleep-deprived college students.

FIGURE 2.32 summarizes these and other effects of sleep deprivation. But there is good news! Psychologists have discovered a treatment that strengthens memory, increases concentration, boosts mood, moderates hunger and obesity, fortifies the disease-fighting immune system, and lessens the risk of fatal accidents. Even better news: The treatment feels good, it can be self-administered, the supplies are limitless, and it's free! If you

> *"Sleep is like love or happiness. If you pursue it too ardently it will elude you."*
>
> Wilse Webb (1992)

are a typical college-age student, often going to bed near 2:00 A.M. and dragged out of bed 6 hours later by the dreaded alarm, the treatment is simple: Each night just add an hour to your sleep.

MAJOR SLEEP DISORDERS To manage your life with enough sleep to awaken naturally and well rested is to be more alert, productive, happy, healthy, and safe. But for many people, that goal is hard to achieve. The major sleep disorders include *insomnia; narcolepsy; sleep apnea;* and *sleepwalking, sleeptalking, and night terrors.*

No matter what their normal need for sleep, some 1 in 10 adults, and 1 in 4 older adults, complain of **insomnia.** These people have ongoing problems in falling or staying asleep, not just an occasional loss of sleep when anxious or excited.

Many who complain of insomnia overestimate their actual sleep loss and underestimate their sleep time (Harvey & Tang, 2012). Many others with true insomnia turn to popular quick fixes, such as sleeping pills and alcohol. Far from "fixing" the problem, these substances can make things worse because they reduce REM sleep and leave the person with the next-day blahs. They can also lead to *tolerance*—a state in which increasing doses are needed to produce an effect. An ideal sleep aid would mimic the natural chemicals abundant during sleep, reliably producing sound sleep without side effects. Until scientists can supply this magic pill, experts have offered some tips for getting better quality sleep (TABLE 2.2).

Falling asleep is not the problem for people with **narcolepsy** (from *narco,* "numbness," and *lepsy,* "seizure"), who have sudden attacks of overwhelming sleepiness, usually lasting less than 5 minutes. Narcolepsy attacks can occur at the worst times, perhaps just after taking a terrific swing at a softball or when laughing loudly, shouting angrily, or having

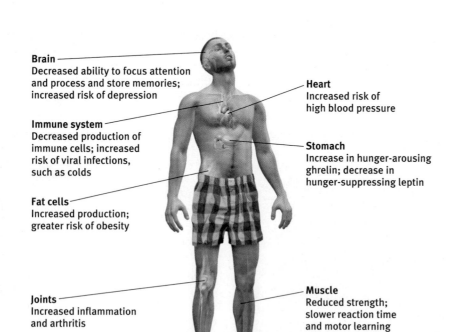

Brain
Decreased ability to focus attention and process and store memories; increased risk of depression

Heart
Increased risk of high blood pressure

Immune system
Decreased production of immune cells; increased risk of viral infections, such as colds

Stomach
Increase in hunger-arousing ghrelin; decrease in hunger-suppressing leptin

Fat cells
Increased production; greater risk of obesity

Joints
Increased inflammation and arthritis

Muscle
Reduced strength; slower reaction time and motor learning

FIGURE 2.32 How sleep deprivation affects us

TABLE 2.2   Looking for a Better Night's Sleep?

- Exercise regularly, but not in the late evening. (Late afternoon is best.)

- Avoid caffeine after early afternoon, and avoid food and drink near bedtime. The exception would be a glass of milk, which provides raw materials for the manufacture of serotonin, a neurotransmitter that promotes sleep.

- Relax before bedtime, using dimmer light.

- Sleep on a regular schedule (rise at the same time even after a restless night) and avoid naps.

- Hide the clock face so you aren't tempted to check it repeatedly.

- Reassure yourself that temporary loss of sleep causes no great harm.

- Realize that for any stressed organism, being vigilant is natural and adaptive. A personal conflict during the day often means a fitful sleep that night.

- If all else fails, settle for less sleep, either going to bed later or getting up earlier.

sex (Dement, 1978, 1999). In severe cases, the person collapses directly into a brief period of REM sleep, with loss of muscle control. People with narcolepsy—1 in 2000 of us, estimated the Stanford University Center for Narcolepsy (2002)—must therefore live with extra caution. As a traffic menace, "snoozing is second only to boozing," said the American Sleep Disorders Association, and those with narcolepsy are especially at risk (Aldrich, 1989).

Sleep apnea also puts millions of people—1 in 20 of us—at increased risk of traffic accidents (Teran-Santos et al., 1999). *Apnea* means "with no breath," and during sleep, people with this condition stop breathing over and over again. After an airless minute or so, their blood oxygen drops enough to jolt them awake, and they snort in air for a few seconds. This happens hundreds of times each night, depriving these people of slow-wave sleep and leaving them feeling fatigued and depressed the next day. Because they don't recall these episodes the next day, many apnea sufferers are unaware of their disorder (Peppard et al., 2006).

Sleep apnea is linked with obesity, particularly among overweight men, including some football players (Keller, 2007). In addition to loud snoring, other warning signs are daytime sleepiness, irritability, and (possibly) high blood pressure (Dement, 1999). If one doesn't mind looking a little goofy in the dark, the treatment—a masklike device with an air pump that keeps the sleeper's airway open (imagine a snorkeler at a slumber party)—can effectively relieve apnea symptoms.

Sleepwalking and *sleeptalking* are usually childhood disorders, and they run in families. If a fraternal twin sleepwalks, the odds are about 1 in 3 that the other twin will also sleepwalk. But if twins are genetically identical, the odds increase to 1 in 2. The same is true for sleeptalking (Hublin et al., 1997, 1998). Sleepwalking is usually harmless. After returning to bed on their own or with the help of a family member, few sleepwalkers recall their trip the next morning.

Sleepwalking happens during NREM-3 sleep. So do *night terrors*, which are not nightmares. During an attack, a child may sit up or walk around, talk nonsense, and appear terrified. The child's heart and breathing rates may double. Luckily, children remember little or nothing of the fearful event the next day (Hartmann, 1981). Children have the deepest and longest NREM-3 sleep, so it's no surprise that they most often have night terrors and sleepwalk. As deep NREM-3 sleep decreases with age, these disorders become more and more rare.

insomnia recurring problems in falling or staying asleep.

narcolepsy sleep disorder in which a person has uncontrollable sleep attacks, sometimes lapsing directly into REM sleep.

sleep apnea a sleep disorder in which a sleeping person repeatedly stops breathing until blood oxygen is so low it awakens the person just long enough to draw a breath.

ECONOMIC RECESSION AND STRESS CAN ROB SLEEP: A National Sleep Foundation (2009) survey found 27 percent of people reporting sleeplessness related to the economy, their personal finances, and employment, as seems evident in this man looking for work.

AP Photo/Paul Sakuma, File

DID BRAHMS NEED HIS OWN LULLABIES?
Cranky, overweight, and nap-prone, classical composer Johannes Brahms exhibited common symptoms of sleep apnea (Margolis, 2000).

Dreams

2-18 What do we dream about, and what are five theories of *why* we dream?

Our two-track mind is clearly at work during sleep. Consider all the events happening outside our waking conscious awareness. We may stop breathing (sleep apnea), stroll around (sleepwalking), talk to imaginary people (sleeptalking), or *dream*.

Each of us spends about six years of our life in dreams—adventures that remain locked behind our moving eyelids and usually vanish with the new day. The discovery of the link between REM sleep and dreaming gave us a key to that lock. Now, instead of relying on a dreamer's hazy recall hours or days after waking, researchers can catch dreams as they happen. They can awaken people during or within 3 minutes after a REM sleep period and hear a vivid account.

WHAT WE DREAM REM **dreams**—the sleeping mind's hallucinations—are vivid, emotional, and often bizarre (Loftus & Ketcham, 1994). Unlike daydreams, the dreams of REM sleep are so vivid we may

confuse them with reality. Awakening from a nightmare, a 4-year-old may scream in fear of the bear in the house.

Few dreams are sweet. For both women and men, 8 in 10 dreams are bad dreams (Domhoff, 2007). Common themes are failing in an attempt to do something; being attacked, pursued, or rejected; or experiencing misfortune (Hall et al., 1982). Dreams with sexual imagery occur less often than you might think. In one study, only 1 in 10 dreams among young men and 1 in 30 among young women had sexual overtones (Domhoff, 1996). More commonly, our dreams feature people and places from the day's nonsexual experiences (De Koninck, 2000).

Our two-track mind is monitoring our environment even while we sleep. Sensory stimuli—a particular odor or a phone's ringing—may be instantly woven into a dream story. In a classic experiment, researchers lightly sprayed cold water on dreamers' faces (Dement & Wolpert, 1958). Compared with sleepers who did not get the cold-water treatment, these people were more likely to dream about a waterfall, a leaky roof, or even about being sprayed by someone.

A popular sleep myth: If you dream you are falling and hit the ground (or if you dream of dying), you die. Unfortunately, those who could confirm these ideas are not around to do so. Many people, however, have had such dreams and are alive to report them.

WHY WE DREAM Dream theorists have proposed several explanations of why we dream, including these five:

1. *To satisfy our own wishes.* In 1900, Sigmund Freud offered what he thought was "the most valuable of all the discoveries it has been my good fortune to make." He proposed that dreams act as a safety valve, discharging feelings that cannot be expressed in public. He called the dream's remembered story line its **manifest content**. For Freud, this apparent content was a censored, symbolic version of the dream's underlying meaning—the **latent content,** or unconscious drives and wishes that would be threatening if expressed directly. Most dreams have no openly sexual imagery. Freud nevertheless believed that most adult dreams could be "traced back by analysis to erotic wishes." Thus, a gun appearing in a dream could be a penis in disguise.

Freud's critics say it is time to wake up from Freud's dream theory, which is a scientific nightmare. Scientific studies offer "no reason to believe

MAXINE

© 2001 Marian Henley
www.maxine.net   © 2001 Marian Henley   mkhenley@prodigy.net

any of Freud's specific claims about dreams and their purposes," said dream researcher William Domhoff (2000). Maybe a dream about a gun is really just a dream about a gun. Legend has it that even Freud, who loved to smoke cigars, agreed that "sometimes, a cigar is just a cigar." Other critics have noted that dreams may be interpreted in many different ways.

2. **To file away memories.** The *information-processing* perspective proposes that dreams may help sift, sort, and fix the day's events in our memory. Some studies support this view. When tested the day after learning a task, those who had slept undisturbed did better than those who had been deprived of both slow-wave and REM sleep (Stickgold et al., 2000, 2001).

   Students, take note. Sleep researcher Robert Stickgold (2000) believes many students suffer from a kind of sleep bulimia, binge sleeping on the weekend. The weekday sleep deprivation leaves not enough time for memory consolidation (the sleep-aided processing and storing of memories). From Stickgold's information-processing perspective he warns, "If you don't get good sleep and enough sleep after you learn new stuff, you won't integrate it effectively into your memories." In one study, high-achieving secondary students with top grades averaged 25 minutes more sleep a night and went to bed 40 minutes earlier than their lower-achieving classmates (Wolfson & Carskadon, 1998).

   Brain scans have confirmed the link between REM sleep and memory. Brain regions that were active as rats learned to navigate a maze (or as people learned to perform a visual-discrimination task) were active again later during REM sleep (Louie & Wilson, 2001; Maquet, 2001). So precise were these activity patterns that scientists could tell where in the maze the rat would be if awake.

3. **To develop and preserve neural pathways.** Dreams, or the brain activity linked to REM sleep, may give the sleeping brain a workout that helps it develop. As we'll see in Chapter 3, stimulating experiences preserve and expand the brain's neural pathways. Infants, whose neural networks are fast developing, spend much of their abundant sleep time in REM sleep.

4. **To make sense of neural static.** Other theories propose that dreams are born when random neural activity spreads upward from the brainstem (Antrobus, 1991; Hobson, 2003, 2004, 2009). Our ever-alert brain attempts to make sense of the activity, pasting the random bits of information into a meaningful image, much as children construct storybooks from snippets of magazine photos.

5. **To reflect cognitive development.** Some dream researchers see dreams as a reflection of brain maturation and cognitive development (Domhoff, 2010, 2011; Foulkes, 1999). For example, before age 9, children's dreams seem more like a slide show and less like an active story in which the child is an actor. Dreams at all ages tend to feature the kind of thinking and talking we demonstrate when awake. They seem to draw on our current knowledge and concepts we understand.

TABLE 2.3 compares these major dream theories. There is one thing today's dream researchers agree on: We need REM sleep. Deprived of it in sleep labs or in real life, people return more and more

dream sequence of images, emotions, and thoughts passing through a sleeping person's mind.

manifest content according to Freud, the remembered story line of a dream.

latent content according to Freud, the underlying meaning of a dream.

TABLE 2.3 Dream Theories		
Theory	**Explanation**	**Critical Considerations**
Wish satisfaction	Dreams provide a "psychic safety valve"—expressing otherwise unacceptable feelings; contain manifest (remembered) content and a deeper layer of latent content (a hidden meaning).	Lacks any scientific support; dreams may be interpreted in many different ways.
Information processing	Dreams help us sort out the day's events and consolidate our memories.	But why do we sometimes dream about things we have not experienced?
Neural preservation and development	Regular brain stimulation from REM sleep may help develop and preserve neural pathways.	This does not explain why we experience *meaningful* dreams.
Neural activation	REM sleep triggers neural activity that evokes random visual memories, which our sleeping brain weaves into stories.	The individual's brain is weaving the stories, which still tells us something about the dreamer.
Cognitive development	Dream content reflects dreamers' cognitive development—their knowledge and understanding.	Does not address the neuroscience of dreams.

quickly to the REM stage when finally allowed to sleep undisturbed. They literally sleep like babies—with increased REM sleep, known as **REM rebound.** Withdrawing REM-suppressing sleeping pills also increases REM sleep, often with nightmares. ■

RETRIEVE + REMEMBER

• What five theories explain why we dream?

ANSWER: (1) Freud's wish fulfillment (dreams as a psychic safety valve), (2) information processing (dreams sort the day's events and form memories), (3) physiological function (dreams pave neural pathways), (4) neural activation (REM sleep triggers random neural activity that the mind weaves into stories), (5) cognitive development (dreams reflect the dreamer's developmental stage)

* * *

We have glimpsed the truth of this chapter's overriding principle: *Everything psychological is simultaneously biological.* You and I are privileged to live in a time when the pace of discoveries about the interplay of our biology and our behavior and mental processes is truly breathtaking. Yet what is unknown still dwarfs what is known. We can describe the brain. We can learn the functions of its parts. We can study how the parts communicate. We can observe sleeping and waking brains. But how do we get mind out of meat? How does the electrochemical whir in a hunk of tissue the size of a head of lettuce give rise to a feeling of joy, a creative idea, or a crazy dream?

The mind seeking to understand the brain—that is indeed among the ultimate scientific challenges. And so it will always be. To paraphrase scientist John Barrow, a brain simple enough to be understood is too simple to produce a mind able to understand it.

REM rebound the tendency for REM sleep to increase following REM sleep deprivation.

CHAPTER REVIEW

The Biology of Mind and Consciousness

Test yourself by taking a moment to answer each of these Learning Objective Questions (repeated here from within the chapter). Then turn to Appendix D, Complete Chapter Reviews, to check your answers. Research suggests that trying to answer these questions on your own will improve your long-term memory of the concepts (McDaniel et al., 2009).

Biology and Behavior

2-1: Why are psychologists concerned with human biology?

Neural Communication

2-2: What are the parts of a neuron?

2-3: How do neurons communicate?

2-4: How do neurotransmitters affect our mood and behavior?

The Nervous System

2-5: What are the two major divisions of the nervous system, and what are their basic functions?

The Endocrine System

2-6: How does the endocrine system transmit information and interact with the nervous system?

The Brain

2-7: What are some techniques for studying the brain?

2-8: What are the functions of the brainstem and its related structures?

2-9: What are the structures and functions of the limbic system?

2-10: What are the four lobes of the cerebral cortex, and where are they located?

2-11: What are the functions of the motor cortex, somatosensory cortex, and association areas?

2-12: When damaged, can the brain repair or reorganize itself?

2-13: What is a split brain, and what does it reveal about the functions of our left and right hemispheres?

Brain States and Consciousness

2-14: What do we mean by *consciousness,* and how does selective attention direct our perceptions?

2-15: What is the circadian rhythm, and what are the stages of our nightly sleep cycle?

2-16: How do our sleep patterns differ? What five theories describe our need to sleep?

2-17: How does sleep loss affect us, and what are the major sleep disorders?

2-18: What do we dream about, and what are five theories of *why* we dream?

TERMS AND CONCEPTS TO REMEMBER

Test yourself on these terms by trying to write down the definition in your own words before flipping back to the referenced page to check your answer.

biological psychology, p. 30

neuron, p. 30

dendrites, p. 30

axon, p. 30

action potential, p. 30

glial cells (glia), p. 30

synapse [SIN-aps], p. 30

threshold, p. 31

all-or-none response, p. 31

neurotransmitters, p. 31

opiate, p. 32

endorphins [en-DOR-fins], p. 32

nervous system, p. 33

central nervous system (CNS), p. 33

peripheral nervous system (PNS), p. 33

nerves, p. 33

sensory neuron, p. 33

motor neuron, p. 33

interneuron, p. 33

somatic nervous system, p. 34

autonomic [aw-tuh-NAHM-ik] nervous system (ANS), p. 34

sympathetic nervous system, p. 34

parasympathetic nervous system, p. 34

reflex, p. 35

endocrine [EN-duh-krin] system, p. 36

hormones, p. 36

adrenal [ah-DREEN-el] glands, p. 36

pituitary gland, p. 36

brainstem, p. 37

EEG (electroencephalograph), p. 38

PET (positron emission tomography) scan, p. 38

MRI (magnetic resonance imaging), p. 38

fMRI (functional MRI), p. 38

medulla [muh-DUL-uh], p. 39

thalamus [THAL-uh-muss], p. 39

reticular formation, p. 39

cerebellum [sehr-uh-BELL-um], p. 40

limbic system, p. 40

amygdala [uh-MIG-duh-la], p. 41

hypothalamus [hi-po-THAL-uh-muss], p. 41

cerebral [seh-REE-bruhl] cortex, p. 42

frontal lobes, p. 43

parietal [puh-RYE-uh-tuhl] lobes, p. 43

occipital [ahk-SIP-uh-tuhl] lobes, p. 43

temporal lobes, p. 43

motor cortex, p. 43

somatosensory cortex, p. 45

hallucination, p. 45

association areas, p. 45

plasticity, p. 47

neurogenesis, p. 47

corpus callosum [KOR-pus kah-LOW-sum], p. 48

split brain, p. 48

consciousness, p. 50

selective attention, p. 51

inattentional blindness, p. 51

change blindness, p. 51

circadian [ser-KAY-dee-an] rhythm, p. 52

REM (rapid eye movement) sleep, p. 53

alpha waves, p. 53

sleep, p. 54

delta waves, p. 54

insomnia, p. 58

narcolepsy, p. 58

sleep apnea, p. 59

dream, p. 60

manifest content, p. 60

latent content, p. 60

REM rebound, p. 62

CHAPTER TEST

Test yourself repeatedly throughout your studies. This will not only help you figure out what you know and don't know; the testing itself will help you learn and remember the information more effectively thanks to the *testing effect*.

1. The neuron fiber that passes messages through its branches to other neurons or to muscles and glands is the _____axon_____.

2. The tiny space between the axon of one neuron and the dendrite or cell body of another is called the
   a. axon terminal.
   b. branching fiber.
   c. synaptic gap.
   d. threshold.

3. Regarding a neuron's response to stimulation, the intensity of the stimulus determines
   a. whether or not an impulse is generated.
   b. how fast an impulse is transmitted.
   c. how intense an impulse will be.
   d. whether reuptake will occur.

4. In a sending neuron, when an action potential reaches an axon terminal, the impulse triggers the release of chemical messengers called _neurotransmitters_

5. Endorphins are released in the brain in response to
   a. morphine or heroin.
   b. pain or vigorous exercise.
   c. the all-or-none response.
   d. all of the above.

6. The autonomic nervous system controls internal functions, such as heart rate and glandular activity. The word *autonomic* means
   a. calming.
   b. voluntary.
   c. self-regulating.
   d. arousing.

7. The sympathetic nervous system arouses us for action and the parasympathetic nervous system calms us down. Together, the two systems make up the _automatic_ nervous system.

8. The neurons of the spinal cord are part of the _____ nervous system.

9. The most influential endocrine gland, known as the master gland, is the
   a. pituitary.
   b. hypothalamus.
   c. thyroid.
   d. pancreas.

10. The _____ _____ secrete(s) epinephrine and norepinephrine, helping to arouse the body during times of stress.

11. The part of the brainstem that controls heartbeat and breathing is the
    a. cerebellum.
    b. medulla.
    c. cortex.
    d. thalamus.

12. The thalamus functions like a
    a. memory bank.
    b. balance center.
    c. breathing regulator.
    d. sensory control center.

13. The lower brain structure that governs arousal is the
    a. spinal cord.
    b. cerebellum.
    c. reticular formation.
    d. medulla.

14. The part of the brain that coordinates voluntary movement and balance is the _____.

15. Two parts of the limbic system are the amygdala and the
    a. cerebral hemispheres.
    b. hippocampus.
    c. thalamus.
    d. pituitary.

16. A cat's ferocious response to electrical brain stimulation would lead you to suppose the electrode had touched the _____.

17. The neural structure that most directly regulates eating, drinking, and body temperature is the
    a. endocrine system.
    b. hypothalamus.
    c. hippocampus.
    d. amygdala.

18. The initial reward center discovered by Olds and Milner was located in the _____.

19. If a neurosurgeon stimulated your right motor cortex, you would most likely
    a. see light.
    b. hear a sound.
    c. feel a touch on the right arm.
    d. move your left leg.

20. How do different neural networks communicate with one another to let you respond when a friend greets you at a party?

21. Which of the following body regions has the greatest representation in the somatosensory cortex?
    a. Upper arm
    b. Toes
    c. Lips
    d. All regions are equally represented.

22. Judging and planning are enabled by the _____ lobes.

23. What would it be like to talk on the phone if you didn't have temporal lobe association areas? What would you hear? What would you understand?

24. The "uncommitted" areas that make up about three-fourths of the cerebral cortex are called _____ _____.

25. Plasticity is especially evident in the brains of
    a. split-brain patients.
    b. young adults.
    c. young children.
    d. right-handed people.

26. An experimenter flashes the word HERON across the visual field of a man whose corpus callosum has been severed. HER is transmitted to his right hemisphere and ON to his left hemisphere. When asked to indicate what he saw, the man says he saw _____ but points to _____.

27. Studies of people with split brains and brain scans of those with undivided brains indicate that the left hemisphere excels in
    a. processing language.
    b. visual perceptions.
    c. making inferences.
    d. neurogenesis.

28. Damage to the brain's right hemisphere is most likely to reduce a person's ability to
    a. recite the alphabet rapidly.
    b. make inferences.
    c. understand verbal instructions.
    d. solve arithmetic problems.

29. Failure to see visible objects because our attention is occupied elsewhere is called _____ _____.

30. Inattentional blindness and change blindness are forms of _____ attention.

31. Our body temperature tends to rise and fall in sync with a biological clock, which is referred to as our _____ _____.

32. During the NREM-1 sleep stage, a person is most likely to experience

    a. deep sleep.

    b. hallucinations.

    c. night terrors or nightmares.

    d. rapid eye movements.

33. The brain emits large, slow delta waves during _____ sleep.

34. As the night progresses, what happens to the REM stage of sleep?

35. Which of the following is NOT one of the theories that have been proposed to explain why we need sleep?

    a. Sleep has survival value.

    b. Sleep helps us recuperate.

    c. Sleep rests the eyes.

    d. Sleep plays a role in the growth process.

36. What is the difference between narcolepsy and sleep apnea?

37. In interpreting dreams, Freud was most interested in their

    a. information-processing function.

    b. physiological function.

    c. manifest content, or story line.

    d. latent content, or hidden meaning.

38. What is the *neural activation* theory of dreaming?

39. "For what one has dwelt on by day, these things are seen in visions of the night" (Menander of Athens, *Fragments*). How might the information-processing perspective on dreaming interpret this ancient Greek quote?

40. The tendency for REM sleep to increase following REM sleep deprivation is referred to as _____ _____.

Find answers to these questions in Appendix E, in the back of the book.

IN YOUR EVERYDAY LIFE

Answering these questions will help you make these concepts more personally meaningful, and therefore more memorable.

1. Can you think of a time when endorphins may have saved you or a friend from feeling intense pain? What happened?

2. Think back to a time when you felt your autonomic nervous system kick in. What was your body preparing you for?

3. Do you remember feeling the lingering effects of hormones after a really stressful event? How did it feel? How long did it last?

4. In what ways has learning about the physical brain influenced your thoughts about human nature?

5. If most information in the brain is processed outside of our awareness, how can we ever really know ourselves?

6. Why do you think humans are not driven to a frenzy, as the rats were, by stimulation of their "reward centers" in the limbic system?

7. Why do you think our brain evolved into so many interconnected structures with varying functions?

8. How would you respond if your friend complained, "I wish I were more right-brained"?

9. Can you think of a time when you focused your attention on one thing so much that you did not notice something else? What happened?

10. Do you ever text, watch TV, or talk on the phone while studying? What impact do you think this multitasking has on your learning?

11. What have you learned about sleep that you could apply to yourself?

12. Which explanation for why we dream makes the most sense to you? How well does it explain your own dreams?

experience
more of the
testing
effect

CHAPTER OVERVIEW

③ Developing Through the Life Span

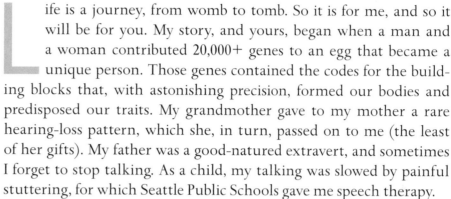

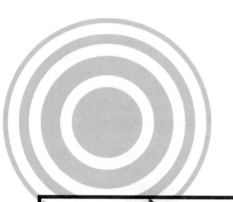

Life is a journey, from womb to tomb. So it is for me, and so it will be for you. My story, and yours, began when a man and a woman contributed 20,000+ genes to an egg that became a unique person. Those genes contained the codes for the building blocks that, with astonishing precision, formed our bodies and predisposed our traits. My grandmother gave to my mother a rare hearing-loss pattern, which she, in turn, passed on to me (the least of her gifts). My father was a good-natured extravert, and sometimes I forget to stop talking. As a child, my talking was slowed by painful stuttering, for which Seattle Public Schools gave me speech therapy.

Along with my parents' nature, I also received their nurture. Like you, I was born into a particular family and culture, with its own way of viewing the world. My values have been shaped by a family culture filled with talking and laughter, by a religious culture that speaks of love and justice, and by an academic culture that encourages critical thinking (asking, *What do you mean? How do you know?*).

We are formed by our genes, and by our contexts, so our stories will differ. But in many ways we are each like nearly everyone else on Earth. Being human, you and I have a need to belong. My mental video library, which began after age 4, is filled with scenes of social attachment. Over time, my attachments to parents loosened as peer friendships grew. After lacking confidence to date in high school, I fell in love with a college classmate and married at age 20. Natural selection disposes us to survive and pass on our genes. Sure enough, two years later a child entered our lives and I experienced a new form of love that surprised me with its intensity.

But life is marked by change. That child now lives 2000 miles away, and one of his two siblings calls South Africa her home. The tight rubber bands linking parent and child have loosened, as yours likely have as well.

Change marks most vocational lives as well. I spent my teen years working in the family insurance agency, then became a premed chemistry major and a hospital aide. After discarding my half-completed medical school applications, I found my calling as a psychology professor and author. I predict that in 10 years you, too, will be doing things not in your current plan.

Stability also marks our development. When I look in the mirror I do not see the person I once was, but I feel like the person I have always been. I am the same person who, as a late teen, played basketball and discovered love. A half-century later, I still play basketball. And I still love—with less passion but more security—the life partner with whom I have shared life's griefs and joys.

We experience a continuous self, but that self morphs through stages—typically growing up, raising children, enjoying a career, and, eventually, life's final stage, which will demand my presence. As I make my way through this cycle of life to death, I am mindful that life's journey is a continuing process of development. That process is seeded by nature and shaped by nurture, animated by love and focused by work, begun with wide-eyed curiosity and completed, for those blessed to live to a good old age, with peace and never-ending hope.

*   *   *

Across the life span, we grow from newborn to toddler to teen to mature adult. At each stage of life's journey there are physical, cognitive, and social milestones. Let's begin at the very beginning.

3-1 What are the three major issues studied by developmental psychologists?

Developmental psychology examines our physical, cognitive, and social development across the life span, with a focus on three major issues:

1. *Nature and nurture:* How does our genetic inheritance (our *nature*) interact with our experiences (our *nurture*) to influence our development?

2. *Continuity and stages:* What parts of development are gradual and continuous, like riding an escalator? What parts change abruptly in separate stages, like climbing rungs on a ladder?

3. *Stability and change:* Which of our traits persist through life? What changes as we age?

You will read about these issues throughout this chapter. At the end of our infancy and childhood discussion, we will focus on nature and nurture. At the end of our adolescence discussion, we will focus on continuity and stages. At the end of our adulthood discussion, we will focus on stability and change.

Prenatal Development and the Newborn

Conception

3-2 How does conception occur, and what are chromosomes, DNA, genes, and the genome? How do genes and the environment interact?

Nothing is more natural than a species reproducing itself, yet nothing is more wondrous. For humans, the process begins when a woman's ovary releases a mature egg, a cell roughly the size of the period at the end of this sentence. The 200 million or more sperm deposited by the man then begin their race upstream. Like space voyagers approaching a huge planet, the sperm approach a cell 85,000 times their own size. Only a small number will reach the egg. Those that do will release enzymes that eat away the egg's protective coating (**FIGURE 3.1a**). As soon as one sperm breaks through that coating (Figure 3.1b), the egg's surface will block out the others. Before half a day passes, the egg nucleus and the sperm nucleus will fuse. The two have become

one. Consider it your most fortunate of moments. Among 200 million sperm, the one needed to make you, in combination with that one particular egg, won the race, and so also for each of your ancestors through all human history. Lucky you.

Contained within the new single cell is a master code. This code will interact with your experience, creating you—a being in many ways like all other humans, but in other ways like no other human. Each of your trillions of cells carry this code in its **chromosomes**. These threadlike structures contain the **DNA** we hear so much about. **Genes** are pieces of DNA, and they can be active (*expressed*) or inactive. External influences can "turn on" genes much as a cup of hot water "turns on" a teabag and lets it "express" its flavor.

When turned on, your genes will provide the code for creating protein molecules, your body's building blocks. **FIGURE 3.2** summarizes these elements that make up your **heredity**.

Genetically speaking, every other human is close to being your identical twin. It is our shared genetic profile—our human **genome**—that makes us humans, rather than chimpanzees or tulips. "Your DNA and mine are 99.9 percent the same," noted former Human Genome Project director Francis Collins

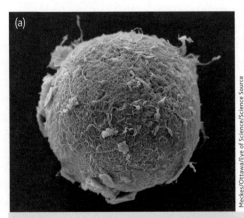
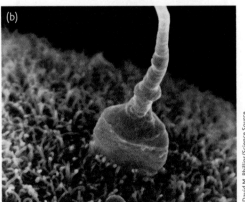

Meckes/Ottawa/Eye of Science/Science Source

David M. Phillips/Science Source

FIGURE 3.1 Life is sexually transmitted (a) Sperm cells surround an egg. (b) As one sperm penetrates the egg's jellylike outer coating, a series of events begins that will cause sperm and egg to fuse into a single cell. If all goes well, that cell will subdivide again and again to emerge 9 months later as a 100-trillion-cell human being.

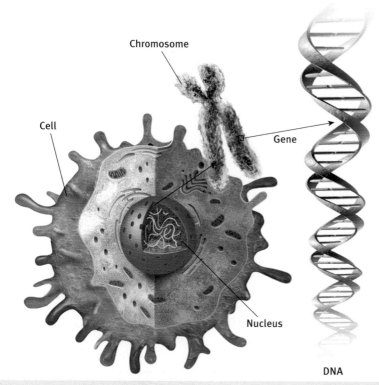

Cell

Chromosome

Gene

Nucleus

DNA

FIGURE 3.2 **The genes: Their location and composition** Contained in the nucleus of each cell in your body are chromosomes. Each chromosome contains a coiled chain of the molecule DNA. Genes are DNA segments that, when expressed (turned on), direct the production of proteins and influence our individual biological development.

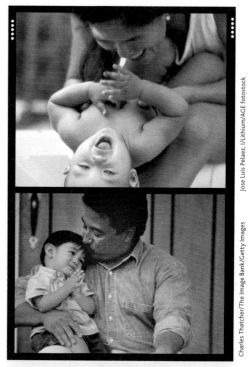

THE NURTURE OF NATURE Parents everywhere wonder: Will my baby grow up to be peaceful or aggressive? Homely or attractive? Successful or struggling at every step? What comes built in, and what is nurtured—and how? Research reveals that nature and nurture together shape our development—every step of the way.

(2007). "At the DNA level, we are clearly all part of one big worldwide family."

The slight person-to-person variations found at particular gene sites in the DNA give clues to our uniqueness. They help explain why one person has a disease that another does not, why one person is short and another tall, why one is outgoing and another shy.

> *"We share half our genes with the banana."*
> Evolutionary biologist Robert May, president of Britain's Royal Society, 2001

Most of our traits are influenced by many genes. How tall you are, for example, reflects the height of your face, the length of your leg bones, and so forth. Each of those is influenced by different genes. Complex traits such as intelligence, happiness, and aggressiveness are similarly influenced by a whole orchestra of genes (Holden, 2008).

Our human differences are also shaped by our **environment**—by every external influence, from maternal nutrition while in the womb, to social support while nearing the tomb. Your height, for example, may be influenced by your diet.

How do heredity and environment **interact?** Let's imagine two babies with two different sets of genes. Malia is a beautiful child and is also sociable and easygoing. Kalie is plain, shy, and colicky. Malia's pretty, smiling

"Thanks for almost everything, Dad."

developmental psychology branch of psychology that studies physical, cognitive, and social change throughout the life span.

chromosomes threadlike structures made of DNA molecules that contain the genes.

DNA *(deoxyribonucleic acid)* a molecule containing the genetic information that makes up the chromosomes.

genes the biochemical units of heredity that make up the chromosomes; segments of DNA.

heredity the genetic transfer of characteristics from parents to offspring.

genome the complete instructions for making an organism, consisting of all the genetic material in that organism's chromosomes.

environment every external influence, from prenatal nutrition to social support in later life.

interaction the interplay that occurs when the effect of one factor (such as environment) depends on another factor (such as heredity).

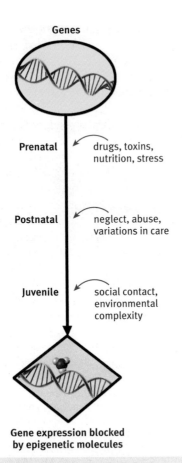

Gene expression blocked by epigenetic molecules

FIGURE 3.3 How environment influences gene expression Beginning in the womb, life experiences lay down *epigenetic marks,* which are often organic molecules. These molecules can block the expression of any gene in the DNA segment they affect. (From Frances Champagne, 2010.)

face attracts more affectionate and stimulating care. This in turn helps her develop into an even warmer and more outgoing person. Kalie's fussiness often leaves her caretakers tired and stressed. As the two children grow older, Malia, the more naturally outgoing child, often seeks activities and friends that increase her social confidence. Shy Kalie has few friends and becomes even more withdrawn. *Our genetically influenced traits affect how others respond.* And vice versa, *our environments trigger gene activity.*

The growing field of **epigenetics** explores the nature–nurture meeting place. *Epigenetics* means "in addition to" or "above and beyond" genetics. This field studies how the environment can cause genes to be either active (expressed) or inactive (not expressed). Genes can influence development, but the environment can switch genes on or off.

The molecules that trigger or block genetic expression are called *epigenetic marks.* When one of these molecules attaches to part of a DNA strand, it instructs the cell to ignore any gene present in that DNA stretch (**FIGURE 3.3**). Diet, drugs, stress, and other experiences can affect these epigenetic molecules. Thus, from conception onward, heredity and experience dance together.

Prenatal Development

3-3 How does life develop before birth, and how do teratogens put prenatal development at risk?

Fertilized eggs, fewer than half of which survive beyond two weeks, are called **zygotes.** For the survivors, one cell becomes two, then four—each just like the first—until this cell division has produced some 100 identical cells within the first week. Then the cells begin to specialize. How identical cells do this—as if one decides "I'll become a brain, you become intestines!"—is a puzzle that scientists are just beginning to solve.

About 10 days after conception, the zygote attaches to the wall of the mother's uterus. So begins about 37 weeks of the closest human relationship. The tiny clump of cells forms two parts. The inner cells become the **embryo** (**FIGURE 3.4**). The outer cells become the *placenta,* the life-link transferring nutrition and oxygen between embryo and mother. Over the next 6 weeks, the embryo's organs begin to form and function. The heart begins to beat.

For about 1 in 270 sets of parents there is a bonus. Two heartbeats will reveal that the zygote, during its early days of development, has split into two (**FIGURE 3.5**). If all goes well, some eight months

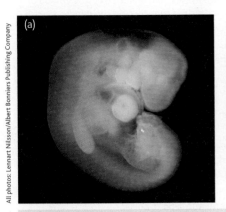
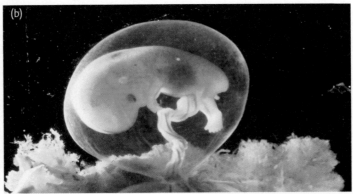
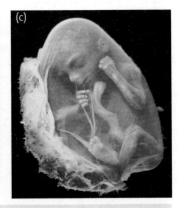

FIGURE 3.4 Prenatal development (a) The embryo grows and develops rapidly. At 40 days, the spine is visible and the arms and legs are beginning to grow. (b) By the end of the second month, when the fetal period begins, facial features, hands, and feet have formed. (c) As the fetus enters the fourth month, its 3 ounces could fit in the palm of your hand.

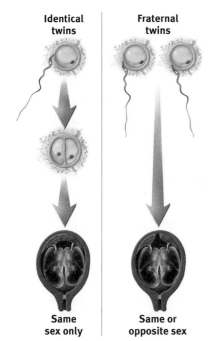

Identical twins | Fraternal twins

Same sex only | Same or opposite sex

FIGURE 3.5 Same fertilized egg, same genes; different eggs, different genes Identical twins develop from a single fertilized egg, fraternal twins from two different eggs.

later two genetically identical babies will emerge from their underwater world.

Identical (*monozygotic*) **twins** are nature's own human clones. They develop from a single fertilized egg, and they share the same genes. They also share the same uterus, and usually the same birth date and cultural history. **Fraternal** (*dizygotic*) **twins** develop from separate fertilized eggs. As wombmates, they share the same prenatal environment but not the same genes. Genetically, they are no more similar than non-twin brothers and sisters. (For more on how psychologists use twin studies to judge the influences of heredity and environment see Close-Up: Twin and Adoption Studies, on the next page.)

By 9 weeks after conception, an embryo looks unmistakably human. It is now a **fetus** (Latin for "offspring" or "young one"). During the sixth month, organs will develop enough to give the fetus a good chance of survival if born prematurely.

Remember: *Heredity and environment interact.* This is true even in the prenatal period. In addition to transferring nutrients and oxygen from mother to fetus, the placenta screens out many harmful substances. But some slip by. **Teratogens** are agents such as viruses and drugs that can damage an embryo or fetus. This is one reason pregnant women are advised not to drink alcoholic beverages. A pregnant woman never drinks alone. As alcohol enters her bloodstream—and her fetus'—it depresses activity in both their central nervous systems.

Even light drinking or occasional binge drinking can affect the fetal brain (Braun, 1996; Ikonomidou et al., 2000; Sayal et al., 2009). Persistent heavy drinking puts the fetus at risk for birth defects and for future behavior and intelligence problems. For 1 in about 800 infants, the effects are visible as **fetal alcohol syndrome (FAS),** marked by lifelong physical and mental abnormalities (May & Gossage, 2001). The fetal damage may occur because alcohol has an epigenetic effect. It leaves chemical marks on DNA that switch genes to abnormal on or off states (Liu et al., 2009). ■

> *Prenatal development*
> *zygote:* conception to 2 weeks
> *embryo:* 2 weeks through 8 weeks
> *fetus:* 9 weeks to birth

RETRIEVE + REMEMBER

• The first two weeks of prenatal development is the period of the _____. The period of the _____ lasts from 9 weeks after conception until birth. The time between those two prenatal periods is considered the period of the _____.

ANSWER: zygote; fetus; embryo

The Competent Newborn

3-5 What are some of the newborn's abilities and traits?

Having survived prenatal hazards, we arrive as newborns with automatic **reflex** responses ideally suited for our survival. (Recall Chapter 2's discussion of the neural

basis of reflexes.) New parents are often in awe of the finely tuned set of reflexes by which their baby gets food. When something touches their cheek, babies turn toward that touch, open their mouth, and actively *root* for a nipple. Finding one, they quickly close on it and begin *sucking*. Sucking has its own set of reflexes—*tonguing, swallowing,* and *breathing.* Failing to find satisfaction, the hungry baby may *cry*—a behavior parents find highly unpleasant, and very rewarding to relieve.

Even as newborns, we search out sights and sounds linked with other humans. We turn our heads in the direction of human voices. We prefer to look at objects 8 to 12 inches away. Wonder of wonders, that just happens to be the

epigenetics the study of environmental influences on gene expression that occur without a DNA change.

zygote the fertilized egg; it enters a 2-week period of rapid cell division and develops into an embryo.

embryo the developing human organism from about 2 weeks after fertilization through the second month.

identical twins (*monozygotic twins*) twins who develop from a single fertilized egg that splits in two, creating two genetically identical siblings.

fraternal twins (*dizygotic twins*) twins who develop from separate fertilized eggs. They are genetically no closer than non-twin brothers and sisters, but they share a prenatal environment.

fetus the developing human organism from 9 weeks after conception to birth.

teratogen [tuh-RAT-uh-jen] an agent, such as a chemical or virus, that can reach the embryo or fetus during prenatal development and cause harm.

fetal alcohol syndrome (FAS) physical and mental abnormalities in children caused by a pregnant woman's heavy drinking. In severe cases, signs include a small, out-of-proportion head and abnormal facial features.

reflex a simple, automatic response to a sensory stimulus.

Twin and Adoption Studies

3-4 How do twin and adoption studies help us understand the effects of nature and nurture?

In procreation, a woman and a man shuffle their gene decks and deal a life-forming hand to their child-to-be, who is then subjected to countless influences beyond their control. How might researchers tease apart the influences of nature and nurture? To do so, they would need to

- vary the home environment while controlling heredity.
- vary heredity while controlling the home environment.

Happily for our purposes, nature has done this work for us.

Identical Versus Fraternal Twins

Identical twins have identical genes. Do these shared genes mean that identical twins also *behave* more similarly than fraternal twins (Bouchard, 2004)? Studies of some 800,000 twin pairs worldwide provide a consistent answer. Identical twins are more similar than fraternal twins in their abilities, personal traits, and interests (Johnson et al., 2009; Loehlin & Nichols, 1976).

Next question: Could shared experiences rather than shared genes explain these similarities? Again, studies of twin pairs give some answers.

Separated Twins

On a chilly February morning in 1979, some time after divorcing his first wife, Linda, Jim Lewis awoke next to his second wife, Betty. Determined that this marriage would work, Jim left love notes to Betty around the house. As he lay there he thought about his son, James Alan, and his faithful dog, Toy.

Jim loved his basement woodworking shop where he built furniture, including a white bench circling a tree. Jim also liked to drive his Chevy, watch stock-car racing, and drink Miller Lite beer. Except for an occasional migraine, Jim was healthy. His blood pressure was a little high, perhaps related to his chain-smoking. He had gained weight but had shed some of the extra pounds. After a vasectomy, he was done having children.

What was extraordinary about Jim Lewis, however, was that at that moment (I am not making this up) there was another man named Jim for whom all these things were also true.[1] This other Jim—Jim Springer—just happened, 38 years earlier, to have been Jim Lewis' womb-mate. Thirty-seven days after their birth, these genetically identical twins were separated and adopted by two blue-collar families. They grew up with no contact until the day Jim Lewis received a call from his genetic clone (who, having been told he had a twin, set out to find him).

One month later, the brothers became the first of 137 separated twin pairs tested by psychologist Thomas Bouchard and his colleagues (Miller, 2012). Given tests measuring their personality, intelligence, heart rate, and brain waves, the Jim twins were virtually as alike as the same person tested twice. Their voice patterns were so similar that, hearing a playback of an earlier interview, Jim Springer guessed "That's me." Wrong—it was his brother.

TRUE BROTHERS The identical friars Julian and Adrian Reister—two "quiet, gentle souls"—both died of heart failure, at age 92, on the same day in 2011.

This and other research on separated identical twins supports the idea that genes matter.

Twin similarities do not impress Bouchard's critics, however. If any two strangers were to spend hours comparing their behaviors and life histories, wouldn't they also discover many coincidental similarities? Moreover, critics note, identical twins share an appearance and the responses it evokes, so they have probably had similar experiences. Bouchard replies that the life choices made by separated fraternal twins are not as dramatically similar as those made by separated identical twins.

Biological Versus Adoptive Relatives

The separated-twin studies control heredity while varying environment. Nature's second type of real-life experiment—adoption—controls environment while varying heredity. Adoption creates two groups: genetic relatives (biological parents and siblings) and environmental relatives (adoptive parents and siblings). For any given trait we study, we can therefore ask three questions:

- How much do adopted children resemble their biological parents, who contributed their genes?
- How much do they resemble their adoptive parents, who contribute a home environment?
- While sharing a home environment, do adopted siblings also come to share traits?

By providing children with loving, nurturing homes, adoption matters. Yet researchers asking these questions about *personality* agree on one stunning finding, based on studies of hundreds of adoptive families. *Non-twin siblings who grow up together, whether biologically related or not, do not much resemble one another in personality* (McGue & Bouchard, 1998; Plomin et al., 1998; Rowe, 1990). In traits such as outgoingness and agreeableness, adoptees are more similar to their biological parents than to their caregiving adoptive parents. This heredity effect shows up in macaque monkeys' personalities as well (Maestripieri, 2003).

In the pages to come, twin and adoption study results will shed light on how nature and nurture interact to influence intelligence, disordered behavior, and many other traits.

[1]. Actually, this description of the two Jims errs in one respect: Jim Lewis named his son James Alan. Jim Springer named his James Allan.

FIGURE 3.6 Newborns' preference for faces When shown these two images with the same three elements, newborns spent nearly twice as long looking at the face-like image on the left (Johnson & Morton, 1991). Newborns—average age just 53 minutes in one study—seem to have an inborn preference for looking toward faces (Mondloch et al., 1999).

approximate distance between a nursing infant's eyes and its mother's eyes (Maurer & Maurer, 1988). We gaze longer at a drawing of a face-like image (**FIGURE 3.6**).

We seem especially tuned in to that human who is our mother. Can newborns distinguish their own mother's smell in a sea of others? Indeed they can. Within days after birth, our brain has picked up and stored the smell of our mother's body (MacFarlane, 1978). What's more, that smell preference lasts. One experiment was able to show this, thanks to some French nursing mothers who had used a chamomile-scented balm to prevent nipple soreness (Delaunay-El Allam et al.,

2010). Twenty-one months later, their toddlers preferred playing with chamomile-scented toys! Other toddlers who had not sniffed the scent while breast feeding did not show this preference. (This makes me wonder: Will adults, who as babies associated chamomile scent with their mother's breast, become devoted chamomile tea drinkers?)

Very young infants are competent, indeed. They smell and hear well. They see what they need to see. They are already using their sensory equipment to learn. Guided by biology and experience, those sensory and perceptual abilities will continue to develop steadily over the next months.

Yet, as most parents will tell you after having their second child, babies differ. One clear difference is in **temperament,** or emotional excitability—whether intense and fidgety, or easygoing and quiet. From the first weeks of life, some babies are *difficult*: irritable, intense, and unpredictable. Others are *easy*: cheerful and relaxed, with predictable feeding and sleeping schedules (Chess & Thomas, 1987). Temperament is genetically influenced, and the effect appears in physical differences. Anxious, inhibited infants have high and variable heart rates. They become very aroused when facing new or strange situations (Kagan & Snidman, 2004).

Our biologically rooted temperament also helps form our enduring personality (McCrae et al., 2000, 2007; Rothbart, 2007).

This effect can be seen in identical twins, who have more similar personalities—including temperament—than do fraternal twins.

Infancy and Childhood

As a flower develops in accord with its genetic instructions, so do we humans. **Maturation**—the orderly sequence of biological growth—dictates much of our shared path. We stand before we walk. We use nouns before adjectives. Severe deprivation or abuse can slow our development, but the genetic growth tendencies are inborn. Maturation (nature) sets the basic course of development; experience (nurture) adjusts it. Once again, we see genes and scenes interacting.

Physical Development

3-6 How do the brain and motor skills develop during infancy and childhood?

Brain Development

In your mother's womb, your developing brain formed nerve cells at the explosive rate of nearly one-quarter million per minute. From infancy on, your brain and your mental abilities developed together. On the day you were born, you had most of the brain cells you would ever have. However, the wiring among these cells—your nervous system—was immature. After birth, these neural networks had a wild growth spurt, branching and linking in patterns that would eventually enable you to walk, talk, and remember.

From ages 3 to 6, the most rapid brain growth was in your frontal lobes, the seat of reasoning and planning. During

PREPARED TO FEED AND EAT Animals, including humans, are predisposed to respond to their offspring's cries for nourishment.

temperament a person's characteristic emotional reactivity and intensity.

maturation biological growth processes leading to orderly changes in behavior, mostly independent of experience.

those years, your ability to control your attention and behavior developed rapidly (Garon et al., 2008; Thompson-Schill et al., 2009). Your frontal lobes continued developing into adolescence and beyond. Last to develop are the association areas—those linked with thinking, memory, and language. As they develop, mental abilities surge (Chugani & Phelps, 1986; Thatcher et al., 1987).

> "It is a rare privilege to watch the birth, growth, and first feeble struggles of a living human mind."
>
> Annie Sullivan, in Helen Keller's *The Story of My Life,* 1903

The neural pathways supporting language and agility continue their rapid growth into puberty. Then, a use-it-or-lose-it *pruning process* shuts down unused links and strengthens others (Paus et al., 1999; Thompson et al., 2000).

Your genes laid down the basic design of your brain, rather like the lines of a coloring book, but experience fills in the details (Kenrick et al., 2009). So how do early experiences shape the brain? Researchers opened a window on that process in experiments that separated young rats into two groups (Rosenzweig, 1984; Renner & Rosenzweig, 1987). Rats in one group lived alone, with little to interest or distract them. The other rats shared a cage, complete with objects and activities that might exist in a natural "rat world" (**FIGURE 3.7**). In this enriched environment, rats developed a heavier and thicker brain cortex.

The environment's effect was so great that if you viewed brief video clips, you could tell from the rats' activity and curiosity whether they had lived in solitary confinement or in the enriched setting (Renner & Renner, 1993). After 60 days in the enriched environment, some rats' brain weight increased 7 to 10 percent. The number of synapses, forming the networks between the cells (see Figure 3.7), mushroomed by about 20 percent (Kolb & Whishaw, 1998).

Touching or massaging infant rats and premature human babies has similar benefits (Field, 2010). In hospital intensive care units, medical staff now massage premature infants to help them develop faster neurologically, gain weight more rapidly, and go home sooner.

Nature and nurture together sculpt our synapses. Brain maturation provides us with a wealth of neural connections. Experience—sights and smells, touches and tugs—activate and strengthen some neural pathways while others weaken from disuse. Similar to paths through a forest, less-traveled neural pathways gradually disappear and popular ones are broadened.

During early childhood—while excess connections are still available—youngsters can most easily master such skills as the accent and correct order of words of another language. We seem to have a **critical period** for some skills. Lacking any exposure to spoken, written, or signed language before adolescence, a person will never master any language (see Chapter 8). Likewise, lacking visual experience during the early years, a person whose vision is restored by cataract removal will never achieve normal perceptions (more on this in Chapter 5). Without stimulation, the brain cells normally assigned to vision will die during the pruning process or be used for other purposes. For normal brain development, early stimulation is critical. The maturing brain's rule: Use it or lose it.

The brain's development does not, however, end with childhood. Throughout life, whether we are learning to text friends or write textbooks, we perform with increasing skill as our learning changes our brain tissue (Ambrose, 2010).

Motor Development

As their nervous system and muscles mature, babies gain greater control over their movements. Motor skills emerge, and with occasional exceptions, their sequence is universal. Babies roll over before they sit unsupported. They usually crawl on all fours before they walk. The recommended infant *back-to-sleep position* (putting babies to sleep on their backs to reduce the risk of a smothering crib death) has been associated with somewhat later crawling but not with later walking (Davis et al., 1998; Lipsitt, 2003).

There are, however, individual differences in timing. Consider walking. In the United States, 90 percent of all babies walk by age 15 months. But 25 percent walk by 11 months, and 50 percent within a week after their first birthday (Frankenburg et al., 1992).

Genes guide motor development. Identical twins typically begin walking on nearly the same day (Wilson, 1979). The rapid development of the cerebellum (at the back of the brain; see Chapter 2) helps create our eagerness to walk

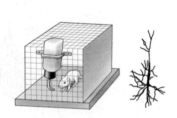 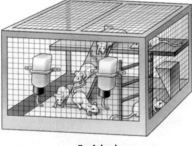

| Impoverished environment | Impoverished rat brain cell | Enriched environment | Enriched rat brain cell |

FIGURE 3.7 Experience affects brain development In this experiment, some rats lived alone in an environment without playthings. Others lived together in an environment enriched with playthings changed daily. In 14 of 16 repetitions of the experiment, rats in the enriched setting developed more cerebral cortex (relative to the rest of the brain's tissue) than was found in those raised in the impoverished environment (Renner & Rosenzweig, 1987; Rosenzweig, 1984).

PHYSICAL DEVELOPMENT Sit, crawl, walk, run—the sequence of these motor development milestones is the same the world around, though babies reach them at varying ages.

at about age 1. Maturation is likewise important for mastering other physical skills, including bowel and bladder control. Before a child's muscles and nerves mature, no amount of pleading or punishment will produce successful toilet training. ■

RETRIEVE + REMEMBER

• The biological growth process, called _____, explains why most children begin walking by about 12 to 15 months.

ANSWER: maturation

Brain Maturation and Infant Memory

Can you recall your first day of preschool or your third birthday party? Most people cannot. Psychologists call this blank space in our conscious memory *infantile amnesia*. Although we *consciously* recall little from before age 4, our brain was processing and storing information during that time. How do we know that? To see how developmental psychologists study thinking and learning in very young children, consider a surprise discovery.

In 1965, Carolyn Rovee-Collier was finishing her doctoral work in psychology. She was a new mom, whose colicky 2-month-old, Benjamin, could be calmed

by moving a mobile hung above his crib. Weary of hitting the mobile, she strung a cloth ribbon connecting the mobile to Benjamin's foot. Soon, he was kicking his foot to move the mobile.

Thinking about her unintended home experiment, Rovee-Collier realized that, contrary to popular opinion in the 1960s, babies are capable of learning. To know for sure that little Benjamin wasn't just a whiz kid, Rovee-Collier repeated the experiment with other infants (Rovee-Collier, 1989, 1999). Sure enough, they, too, soon kicked more when hitched to a mobile, both on the day of the experiment and the day after. They had learned the link between a moving leg and a moving mobile. If, however, she hitched them to a different mobile the next day, the infants showed no learning. Their actions indicated that they remembered the original mobile and recognized the difference. Moreover, when tethered to the familiar mobile a month later, they remembered the association and again began kicking.

Traces of forgotten childhood languages may also persist. One study tested English-speaking British adults who had spoken Hindi (an Indian language) or Zulu (an African language) in their childhood. Although they had no conscious memory of those languages, they could, up to age 40, relearn subtle

INFANT AT WORK Babies only 3 months old can learn that kicking moves a mobile, and they can retain that learning for a month. (From Rovee-Collier, 1989, 1997.)

Hindi or Zulu sound contrasts that other people could not learn (Bowers et al., 2009). What the conscious mind does not know and cannot express in words, the nervous system and our two-track mind somehow remembers.

Cognitive Development

3-7 How did Piaget view the developmental stages of a child's mind, and how does current thinking about cognitive development differ?

Cognition refers to all the mental activities associated with thinking, knowing, remembering, and communicating. Somewhere on your journey from egghood to childhood you became conscious. When was that, and how did your mind unfold from there? Psychologist Jean Piaget [Pee-ah-ZHAY] spent a half-century searching for answers to such

critical period a period early in life when exposure to certain stimuli or experiences is needed for proper development.

cognition all the mental activities associated with thinking, knowing, remembering, and communicating.

JEAN PIAGET (1896–1980) "If we examine the intellectual development of the individual or of the whole of humanity, we shall find that the human spirit goes through a certain number of stages, each different from the other" (1930).

questions. Thanks partly to his pioneering work, we now understand that a child's mind is not a miniature model of an adult's. Children reason *differently*, in "wildly illogical ways about problems whose solutions are self-evident to adults" (Brainerd, 1996).

Piaget's interest began in 1920, when he was developing questions for children's intelligence tests in Paris. Looking over the test results, Piaget noticed something interesting. At certain ages, children made strikingly similar mistakes. Where others saw childish mistakes, Piaget saw intelligence at work.

Piaget's studies led him to believe that a child's mind develops through a series of stages. This upward march begins with the newborn's simple reflexes, and it ends with the adult's abstract reasoning power. Moving through these stages, Piaget believed, is like climbing a ladder. A child can't easily move to a higher rung without first having a firm footing on the one below.

Tools for thinking and reasoning differ in each stage. Thus, you can tell an 8-year-old that "getting an idea is like having a light turn on in your head," and the child will understand. A 2-year-old won't get the analogy. Would a 2-year-old understand that a miniature slide is too small for sliding, or that a miniature car is much too small to get into? (See **FIGURE 3.8**.) No. But an adult mind likewise can reason in ways that an 8-year-old won't understand.

Piaget believed that the force driving us up this intellectual ladder is our struggle to make sense of our experiences. His core idea was that "children are active thinkers, constantly trying to construct more advanced understandings of the world" (Siegler & Ellis, 1996). Part of this active thinking is building **schemas**, which are concepts or mental molds into which we pour our experiences. By adulthood we have built countless schemas, ranging from what a dog is to what love is.

To explain how we use and adjust our schemas, Piaget proposed two more concepts. First, we **assimilate** new experiences—we interpret them in terms of our current understandings (schemas). Having a simple schema for dog, for example, a toddler may call all four-legged animals dogs. But as we interact with the world, we also adjust, or **accommodate,** our schemas to incorporate information provided by new experiences. Thus, the child soon learns that the original dog schema is too broad and accommodates by refining the category.

Piaget's Theory and Current Thinking

Piaget believed that children construct their understanding of the world as they interact with it. Their minds go through spurts of change, he believed, followed by greater stability as they move from one level to the next. In his view, cognitive development consisted of four major stages—*sensorimotor, preoperational, concrete operational,* and *formal operational.*

SENSORIMOTOR STAGE The **sensorimotor stage** begins at birth and lasts to nearly age 2. In this stage, babies take in the world through their senses and actions—through looking, hearing, touching, mouthing, and grasping. As their hands and limbs begin to move, they learn to make things happen.

Very young babies seem to live in the present. Out of sight is out of mind. In one test, Piaget showed an infant an appealing toy and then flopped his hat over it. Before the age of 6 months, the infant acted as if the toy no longer existed. Young infants lack **object permanence**—the awareness that objects continue to exist when out of sight (**FIGURE 3.9**). By about 8 months, infants begin to show that they do remember things they can no longer see. If you hide a toy, an 8-month-old will briefly look for it. Within another month or two, the infant will look for it even after several seconds have passed.

So does object permanence in fact blossom at 8 months, much as tulips blossom in spring? Today's researchers think not. They believe object permanence unfolds gradually, and they view development as more continuous than Piaget did.

They also think that young children are more competent than Piaget and his followers believed. For example, infants seem to have an inborn grasp of simple physical laws—they have "baby physics." Like adults staring in disbelief at a magic trick (the *"Whoa!"* look), infants look longer at an unexpected and unfamiliar scene of a car seeming to pass

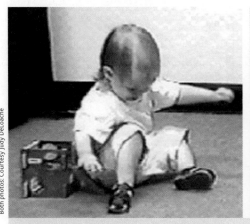

Both photos: Courtesy Judy DeLoache

FIGURE 3.8 Scale errors Children age 18 to 30 months may fail to take the size of an object into account when trying to perform impossible actions with it. At left, a 21-month-old attempts to slide down a miniature slide. At right, a 24-month-old opens the door to a miniature car and tries to step inside (DeLoache et al., 2004).

© Doug Goodman

FIGURE 3.9 Object permanence Infants younger than 6 months seldom understand that things continue to exist when they are out of sight. But for this older infant, out of sight is definitely not out of mind.

through a solid object. They also stare longer at a ball stopping in midair, or at an object that seems to magically disappear (Baillargeon, 1995, 2008; Wellman & Gelman, 1992). Even as babies, we had a lot on our minds.

PREOPERATIONAL STAGE Piaget believed that until about age 6 or 7, children are in a **preoperational stage**—too young to perform *mental operations* (such as imagining an action and mentally reversing it).

Conservation Consider a 5-year-old, who objects that there is too much milk in a tall, narrow glass. "Too much" may become an acceptable amount if you pour that milk into a short, wide glass. Focusing only on the height dimension, the child cannot perform the operation of mentally pouring the milk back into the tall glass. Before about age 6, said Piaget, young children lack the concept of **conservation**—the idea that the amount remains the same even if it changes shape (**FIGURE 3.10**).

Pretend Play A child who can perform mental operations can think in symbols and therefore begins to enjoy *pretend play*. Contemporary researchers have found symbolic thinking at an earlier age than Piaget supposed. One researcher showed children a model of a room and hid a miniature stuffed dog behind its miniature couch (DeLoache & Brown, 1987). The 2½-year-olds easily remembered where to find the miniature toy in the model, but that knowledge didn't transfer to the real world. They could not use the model to locate an actual stuffed dog behind a couch

schema a concept or framework that organizes and interprets information.

assimilation interpreting our new experiences in terms of our existing schemas.

accommodation adapting our current understandings (schemas) to incorporate new information.

sensorimotor stage in Piaget's theory, the stage (from birth to nearly 2 years of age) during which infants know the world mostly in terms of their sensory impressions and motor activities.

object permanence the awareness that things continue to exist even when not perceived.

preoperational stage in Piaget's theory, the stage (from about 2 to 6 or 7 years of age) in which a child learns to use language but cannot yet perform the mental operations of concrete logic.

conservation the principle (which Piaget believed to be a part of concrete operational reasoning) that properties such as mass, volume, and number remain the same despite changes in shapes.

Bianca Moscatelli/Worth Publishers

FIGURE 3.10 Piaget's test of conservation This preoperational child does not yet understand the principle of conservation. When the milk is poured into a tall, narrow glass, it suddenly seems like "more" than when it was in the shorter, wider glass. In another year or so, she will understand that the amount stays the same even though it looks different.

in a real room. Three-year-olds—only 6 months older—usually went right to the actual stuffed animal in the real room, showing they *could* think of the model as a symbol for the room. Piaget did not view the change from one stage to another as an abrupt shift. Even so, he probably would have been surprised to see symbolic thinking at such a young age.

Egocentrism Piaget also believed that preschool children are **egocentric:** They have difficulty imagining things from another's point of view. Asked to "show Mommy your picture," 2-year-old Gabriella holds the picture up facing her own eyes. Told to hide, 3-year-old Gray puts his hands over his eyes, assuming

"It's too late, Roger—they've seen us."

Roger has not outgrown his early childhood egocentrism.

that if he can't see you, you can't see him.

Contemporary research supports preschoolers' egocentrism. This is helpful information when a TV-watching preschooler blocks your view of the screen. The child probably assumes that you see what she sees. At this age, children simply are not yet able to take another's viewpoint. Even we adults may overestimate the extent to which others share our views. Have you ever mistakenly assumed that something would be clear to a friend because it was clear to you? Or sent a text mistakenly thinking that the receiver would "hear" your "just kidding" intent (Epley et al., 2004; Kruger et al.,

2005)? As children, we were even more prone to such egocentricism.

Theory of Mind When Little Red Riding Hood realized her "grandmother" was really a wolf, she swiftly revised her ideas about the creature's intentions and raced away. Preschoolers develop this ability to read others' mental states when they begin forming a **theory of mind.**

When children can imagine another person's viewpoint, all sorts of new skills emerge. They can tease, because they now understand what makes a playmate angry. They may be able to convince a sibling to share. Knowing what might make a parent buy a toy, they may try to persuade.

Between about 3½ and 4½, children worldwide use their new theory-of-mind skills to realize that others may hold false beliefs (Callaghan et al., 2005; Sabbagh et al., 2006). One research team asked preschoolers what was inside a Band-Aids box (Jenkins & Astington, 1996). Expecting Band-Aids, the children were surprised to see that the box contained pencils. Then came the theory-of-mind question. Asked what a child who had never seen the box would think was inside, 3-year-olds typically answered "pencils." By age 4 to 5, children knew better. They anticipated their friends' false belief that the box would hold Band-Aids.

AUTISM SPECTRUM DISORDER This therapist is using music to help a young man with ASD to improve his language skills. ASD is marked by limited communication ability and difficulty understanding others' states of mind.

Children with **autism spectrum disorder (ASD)** have an *impaired theory of mind* (Rajendran & Mitchell, 2007; Senju et al., 2009). They have difficulty reading other people's thoughts and feelings. Most children learn that another child's pouting mouth signals sadness, and that twinkling eyes mean happiness or mischief. A child with ASD fails to understand these signals (Frith & Frith, 2001).

ASD has differing levels of severity. "High-functioning" individuals generally have normal intelligence, and they often have an exceptional skill or talent in a specific area. But they lack social and communication skills, and they tend to become distracted by minor and unimportant stimuli (Remington et al., 2009). Those at the spectrum's lower end are unable to use language at all.

Biological factors, including genetic influences and abnormal brain development, contribute to ASD (State and Šestan, 2012). Childhood measles, mumps, and rubella (MMR) vaccinations do not (Demicheli et al., 2012). Based on a fraudulent 1998 study—"the most damaging medical hoax of the last 100 years" (Flaherty, 2011)—some parents were misled into thinking that the childhood MMR vaccine increased risk of ASD. The unfortunate result was a drop in vaccination rates and an increase in cases of measles and mumps. Some unvaccinated children suffered long-term harm or even death.

ASD afflicts four boys for every girl. Psychologist Simon Baron-Cohen believes this hints at another way to understand this disorder. He has argued that ASD represents an "extreme male brain" (2008, 2009). Although there is some overlap between the sexes, he believes that boys are better "systemizers." They understand things according to rules or laws, for example, as in mathematical and mechanical systems. Children exposed to high levels of the male sex hormone *testosterone* in the womb may develop more masculine and ASD-related traits (Auyeung et al., 2009).

"AUTISM" CASE NUMBER 1 In 1943, Donald Gray Triplett, an "odd" child with unusual gifts and social weaknesses, was the first person to receive the diagnosis of "autism." (After a 2013 change in the diagnosis manual, his condition is now called autism spectrum disorder.) In 2010, at age 77, Triplett was still living in his family home and Mississippi town, where he often played golf (Donvan & Zucker, 2010).

In contrast, girls are naturally predisposed to be "empathizers," Baron-Cohen contends. They are better at reading facial expressions and gestures, though less so if given testosterone (van Honk et al., 2011). Why is reading faces such a challenging task for those with ASD? The underlying cause seems to be poor communication among brain regions that normally work together to let us take another's viewpoint. This effect appears to result from ASD-related genes interacting with the environment (State & Šestan, 2012).

CONCRETE OPERATIONAL STAGE By age 6 or 7, said Piaget, children enter the **concrete operational stage.** Given concrete (physical) materials, they begin to grasp conservation. Understanding that change in form does not mean change in quantity, they can mentally pour milk back and forth between glasses of different shapes. They also enjoy jokes that allow them to use this new understanding:

> Mr. Jones went into a restaurant and ordered a whole pizza for his dinner. When the waiter asked if he wanted it cut into 6 or 8 pieces, Mr. Jones said, "Oh, you'd better make it 6, I could never eat 8 pieces!" (McGhee, 1976)

Piaget believed that during the concrete operational stage, children become able to understand simple math and conservation. When my daughter, Laura, was 6, I was astonished at her inability to reverse simple arithmetic. Asked, "What is 8 plus 4?" she required 5 seconds to compute "12," and another 5 seconds to then compute 12 minus 4. By age 8, she could answer a reversed question instantly.

FORMAL OPERATIONAL STAGE By age 12, said Piaget, our reasoning expands to include abstract thinking. We are no longer limited to purely concrete reasoning, based on actual experience. As children approach adolescence, many become capable of abstract *if . . . then* thinking: *If* this happens, *then* that will happen. Piaget called this new systematic reasoning ability **formal operational** thinking. (Stay tuned for more about adolescents' thinking abilities later in this chapter.) **TABLE 3.1** summarizes the four stages in Piaget's theory.

egocentrism in Piaget's theory, the preoperational child's difficulty taking another's point of view.

theory of mind people's ideas about their own and others' mental states—about their feelings, perceptions, and thoughts, and the behaviors these might predict.

autism spectrum disorder (ASD) a disorder that appears in childhood and is marked by significant deficiencies in communication and social interaction, and by rigidly fixated interests and repetitive behaviors.

concrete operational stage in Piaget's theory, the stage of cognitive development (from about 6 or 7 to 11 years of age) during which children gain the mental operations that enable them to think logically about concrete events.

formal operational stage in Piaget's theory, the stage of cognitive development (normally beginning about age 12) during which people begin to think logically about abstract concepts.

TABLE 3.1	Piaget's Stages of Cognitive Development	
Typical Age Range	**Stage and Description**	**New Developments**
Birth to nearly 2 years	*Sensorimotor* Experiencing the world through senses and actions (looking, hearing, touching, mouthing, and grasping)	• Object permanence • Stranger anxiety
About 2 to 6 or 7 years	*Preoperational* Representing things with words and images; using intuitive rather than logical reasoning	• Pretend play • Egocentrism
6 or 7 to 11 years	*Concrete operational* Thinking logically about concrete events; grasping concrete analogies and performing arithmetical operations	• Conservation • Mathematical transformations
About 12 through adulthood	*Formal operational* Reasoning abstractly	• Abstract logic • Potential for mature moral reasoning

PRETEND PLAY

An Alternative Viewpoint: Vygotsky and the Social Child

As Piaget was forming his theory of cognitive development, Russian psychologist Lev Vygotsky was also studying how children think and learn. He noted that by age 7, children are more able to think and solve problems with words. They do this, he said, by no longer thinking aloud. Instead they internalize their culture's language and rely on inner speech (Fernyhough, 2008). Parents who say *"No, no!"* when pulling a child's hand away from a cake are giving the child a self-control tool. When the child later needs to resist temptation, he may likewise think *"No, no!"* Talking to themselves, whether out loud or inside their heads, helps children to control their behavior and emotions and to master new skills.

Piaget emphasized how the child's mind grows through interaction with the physical environment. Vygotsky emphasized how the child's mind grows through interaction with the *social* environment. If Piaget's child was a young scientist, Vygotsky's was a young apprentice. By guiding children and giving them new words, parents and others provide a temporary *scaffold* from which children can step to higher levels of thinking (Renninger & Granott, 2005). Language is an important ingredient of social guidance, and it provides the building blocks for thinking, noted Vygotsky. (For more on children's development of language, see Chapter 8.)

Reflecting on Piaget's Theory

What remains of Piaget's ideas about the child's mind? Plenty. *Time* magazine singled him out as one of the twentieth century's 20 most influential scientists and thinkers. And a survey of British psychologists rated him as the greatest twentieth-century psychologist (Psychologist, 2003). Piaget identified significant cognitive milestones and stimulated worldwide interest in how the mind develops. His emphasis was less on the ages at which children typically reach specific milestones than on their sequence. Studies around the globe, from Algeria to North America, have confirmed that human cognition unfolds basically in the sequence Piaget described (Lourenco & Machado, 1996; Segall et al., 1990).

However, today's researchers see development as more continuous than did Piaget. By detecting the beginnings of each type of thinking at earlier ages, they have revealed conceptual abilities Piaget missed. Moreover, they view formal logic as a smaller part of cognition than he did. Piaget would not be surprised that today, as part of our own cognitive development, we are adapting his ideas to accommodate new findings.

Piaget's insights can nevertheless help teachers and parents understand young children. Remember this: Young children cannot think with adult logic and cannot take another's viewpoint. What seems simple and obvious to us—getting off a teeter-totter will cause a friend on the other end to crash—may never occur to a 3-year-old. Also remember that children are not empty containers waiting to be filled with knowledge. By building on what children already know, we can engage them in concrete demonstrations and stimulate them to think for themselves. Finally, accept children's cognitive immaturity as adaptive. It is nature's strategy for keeping children close to protective adults and providing time for learning and socialization (Bjorklund & Green, 1992). ■

James V. Wertsch/Washington University

LEV VYGOTSKY (1896–1934) Vygotsky, pictured here with his daughter, was a Russian developmental psychologist. He studied how children's minds feed on the language of social interaction.

RETRIEVE + REMEMBER

- Object permanence, pretend play, conservation, and abstract logic are developmental milestones for which of Piaget's stages, respectively?

ANSWER: Object permanence for the sensorimotor stage, pretend play for the preoperational stage, conservation for the concrete operational stage, and abstract logic for the formal operational stage.

- Match each developmental ability (1–6) to the correct cognitive developmental stage (a–d).

a. Sensorimotor

b. Preoperational

c. Concrete operational

d. Formal operational

1. Thinking about abstract concepts, such as "freedom."
2. Enjoying imaginary play (such as dress-up).
3. Understanding that physical properties stay the same even when objects change form.
4. Having the ability to reverse math operations.
5. Understanding that something is not gone for good when it disappears from sight, as when Mom "disappears" behind the shower curtain.
6. Having difficulty taking another's point of view (as when blocking someone's view of the TV).

ANSWERS: 1. d, 2. b, 3. c, 4. c, 5. a, 6. b

Social Development

From birth, babies all over the world are social creatures, developing an intense bond with their caregivers. Infants come to prefer familiar faces and voices, then to coo and gurgle when given their mother's or father's attention. Have you ever wondered why tiny infants can happily be handed off to admiring visitors, but after a certain age pull back? By about 8 months, soon after object permanence emerges and children become mobile, a curious thing happens: They develop **stranger anxiety.** When handed to a stranger they may cry and reach for a parent. "No! Don't leave me!" their distress seems to say. At about this age, children have schemas for familiar faces—mental images of how caretakers should look. When the new face does not fit one of these remembered images, they become distressed (Kagan, 1984). Once again, we see an important principle: *The brain, mind, and social-emotional behavior develop together.*

Origins of Attachment

3-8 How do the bonds of attachment form between caregivers and infants?

One-year-olds typically cling tightly to a parent when they are frightened or expect separation. Reunited after being apart, they shower the parent with smiles and hugs. No social behavior is more striking than this intense and mutual infant-parent bond. This **attachment** bond is a powerful survival impulse that keeps infants close to their caregivers.

Infants become attached to people—typically their parents—who are comfortable and familiar. For many years, psychologists reasoned that infants grew attached to those who satisfied their need for nourishment. It made sense. But an accidental finding overturned this idea.

During the 1950s, University of Wisconsin psychologists Harry Harlow and Margaret Harlow bred monkeys for their learning studies. Shortly after birth, they separated the infants from their mothers and placed each infant in a sanitary individual cage with a cheesecloth baby blanket (Harlow et al., 1971). Then came a surprise: When their soft blankets were taken to be laundered, the infant monkeys became distressed.

Imagine yourself as one of the Harlows, trying to figure out why the monkey infants were so intensely attached to their blankets. Psychologists believed that infants became attached to those who nourish them. Might comfort instead be the key? How could you test that idea? The Harlows decided to pit the drawing power of a food source against

FIGURE 3.11 The Harlows' mothers The Harlows' infant monkeys much preferred contact with a comfortable cloth mother, even while feeding from a wire nourishing mother.

the contact comfort of the blanket by creating two artificial mothers. One was a bare wire cylinder with a wooden head and an attached feeding bottle. The other was a cylinder wrapped with terry cloth.

For the monkeys, it was no contest. They overwhelmingly preferred the comfy cloth mother (**FIGURE 3.11**). Like anxious infants clinging to their live mothers, the monkey babies would cling to their cloth mothers when anxious. When exploring their environment, they used her as a *secure base*. They acted as though they were attached to her by an invisible elastic band that stretched only so far before pulling them back. Researchers soon learned that other qualities—rocking, warmth, and feeding—made the cloth mother even more appealing.

Human infants, too, become attached to parents who are soft and warm and

STRANGER ANXIETY A newly emerging ability to evaluate people as unfamiliar and possibly threatening helps protect babies 8 months and older. Babies display this same adaptive response, whether in the United States or Togo, West Africa.

stranger anxiety the fear of strangers that infants commonly display, beginning by about 8 months of age.

attachment an emotional tie with another person; shown in young children by their seeking closeness to the caregiver, and showing distress on separation.

who rock, pat, and feed. Much parent-infant emotional communication occurs via touch (Hertenstein et al., 2006), which can be either soothing (snuggles) or arousing (tickles). The human parent also provides a safe haven for a distressed child and a secure base from which to explore.

Attachment Differences

3-9 Why do secure and insecure attachments matter, and how does an infant develop basic trust?

Children's attachments differ. To study these differences, Mary Ainsworth (1979) designed the *strange situation* experiment. She observed mother-infant pairs at home during their first six months. Later she observed the 1-year-old infants in a strange situation (usually a laboratory playroom) without their mothers. Such research shows that about 60 percent of infants display *secure attachment*. In their mother's presence, they play comfortably, happily exploring their new environment. When she leaves, they become upset. When she returns, they seek contact with her.

Other infants avoid attachment or show *insecure attachment*, marked by either *anxiety* or *avoidance* of trusting relationships. They are less likely to explore their surroundings. Anxiously attached infants may cling to their mother. When she leaves, they might cry loudly and remain upset. Avoidantly attached infants seem not to notice or care about her departure and return (Ainsworth, 1973, 1989; Kagan, 1995; van IJzendoorn & Kroonenberg, 1988).

Ainsworth and others found that sensitive, responsive mothers—those who noticed what their babies were doing and responded appropriately—had infants who were securely attached (De Wolff & van IJzendoorn, 1997). Insensitive, unresponsive mothers—mothers who attended to their babies when they felt like doing so but ignored them at other times—often had infants who were insecurely attached. The Harlows' monkey studies, with unre-

FIGURE 3.12 Social deprivation and fear In the Harlows' experiments, monkeys raised with artificial mothers were terror-stricken when placed in strange situations without those mothers.

sponsive artificial mothers, produced even more striking effects. When put in strange situations without their artificial mothers, the deprived infants were terrified (**FIGURE 3.12**).

Today's climate of greater respect for animal welfare would prevent primate studies like the Harlows'. Many now remember Harry Harlow especially as the researcher who tortured helpless monkeys. But others support the Harlows' work. "Harry Harlow, whose name has [come to mean] cruel monkey experiments, actually helped put an end to cruel child-rearing practices," said primatologist Frans de Waal (2011). Harry Harlow defended their methods: "Remember, for every mistreated monkey there exist a million untreated children." He expressed the hope that this research would sensitize people to child abuse and neglect. His biographer agreed. "No one who knows [the Harlows'] work could ever argue that babies do fine without companionship, that a caring mother doesn't matter. And since we . . . didn't fully believe that before . . . , then perhaps we needed—just once—to be smacked really hard with that truth so that we could never again doubt" (Blum, 2010, pp. 292, 307).

So caring parents matter. But is attachment style the *result* of parenting? Or are other factors also at work?

TEMPERAMENT AND ATTACHMENT

How does *temperament*—a person's characteristic emotional reactivity and intensity—affect attachment style? As we saw earlier in this chapter, temperament is genetically influenced. Some babies tend to be difficult—irritable, intense, and unpredictable. Others are easy—cheerful, relaxed, and feeding and sleeping on predictable schedules (Chess & Thomas, 1987). Parenting studies that neglect such inborn differences, critics say, might as well be "comparing foxhounds reared in kennels with poodles reared in apartments" (Harris, 1998). To separate the effects of nature and nurture on attachment, we would need to vary parenting while controlling temperament. (Pause and think: If you were the researcher, how might you do this?)

One researcher's solution was to randomly assign 100 temperamentally difficult infants to two groups. Half of the 6- to 9-month-olds were in the experimental group, in which mothers received personal training in sensitive responding. The other half were in a control group, in which mothers did not receive this training (van den Boom, 1990, 1995). At 12 months of age, 68 percent of the infants in the first group were rated

FULL-TIME DAD Financial analyst Walter Cranford, shown here with his baby twins, is one of a growing number of stay-at-home dads. Cranford says the experience has made him appreciate how difficult the work can be: "Sometimes at work you can just unplug, but with this you've got to be going all the time."

securely attached, as were only 28 percent of the control group infants. Other studies support the idea that such programs can increase parental sensitivity and, to some extent, infant attachment security (Bakermans-Kranenburg et al., 2003; Van Zeijl et al., 2006).

Children's anxiety over separation from parents peaks at around 13 months, then gradually declines (Kagan, 1976). This happens whether they live with one parent or two, are cared for at home or in a day-care center, live in North America, Guatamala, or the Kalahari Desert. As the power of early attachment relaxes, we humans begin to move out into a wider range of situations. We communicate with strangers more freely. And we stay attached emotionally to loved ones despite distance.

At all ages, we are social creatures. But as we mature, our secure base and safe haven shift—from parents to peers and partners (Cassidy & Shaver, 1999). We gain strength when someone offers, by words and actions, a safe haven: "I will be here. I am interested in you. Come what may, I will actively support you" (Crowell & Waters, 1994).

ATTACHMENT STYLES AND LATER RELATIONSHIPS Developmental theorist Erik Erikson (1902–1994), working with his wife, Joan Erikson, believed that securely attached children approach life with a sense of **basic trust**—a sense that the world is predictable and reliable. This lifelong attitude of trust rather than fear, they said, flows from children's interactions with sensitive, loving caregivers.

Do our early attachments form the foundation for adult relationships, including our comfort with *intimacy?* Many researchers now believe they do (Birnbaum et al., 2006; Fraley et al., 2013). People who report that they had secure relationships with their parents tend to enjoy secure friendships (Gorrese & Ruggieri, 2012). Our adult styles of romantic love likewise exhibit either secure, trusting attachment; insecure, anxious

attachment; or the avoidance of attachment (Feeney, 2008; Shaver & Mikulincer, 2007). Feeling insecurely attached to others during childhood, for example, may take two main forms in adulthood (Fraley et al., 2011). One is anxiety, in which people constantly crave acceptance but are overly alert to signs of possible rejection. The other is avoidance, in which people experience discomfort getting close to others and use avoidant strategies to maintain distance from others.

Deprivation of Attachment

If secure attachment fosters social trust, what happens when circumstances prevent a child from forming attachments? In all of psychology, there is no sadder research literature. Some of these babies were raised in institutions without a regular caregiver's stimulation and attention. Others were locked away at home under conditions of abuse or extreme neglect. Most were withdrawn, frightened, even speechless. Those abandoned in Romanian orphanages during the 1980s looked "frighteningly like Harlow's monkeys" (Carlson, 1995). The longer they were institutionalized, the more they bore lasting emotional scars (Chisholm, 1998; Nelson et al., 2009).

The Harlows' monkeys bore similar scars if raised in total isolation, without even an artificial mother. As adults, when placed with other monkeys their age, they either cowered in fright or lashed out in aggression. When they reached sexual maturity, most were incapable of mating. Females who did have babies were often neglectful, abusive, even murderous toward them.

In humans, too, the unloved sometimes become the unloving. Some 30 percent of those who have been abused do later abuse their own children. This is four times the U.S. national rate of child abuse (Dumont et al., 2007; Widom, 1989a,b). Abuse victims have a doubled risk of later depression (Nanni et al., 2012). They are especially at risk for depression if they carry a gene variation that spurs stress-hormone production (Bradley et al., 2008). As we will see again and again, behavior and emotion arise from a particular environment interacting with particular genes.

Recall that, depending on our experience, genes may or may not

basic trust according to Erik Erikson, a sense that the world is predictable and trustworthy; said to be formed during infancy by appropriate experiences with responsive caregivers.

THE DEPRIVATION OF ATTACHMENT In this 1980s Romanian orphanage, the 250 children between ages 1 and 5 outnumbered caregivers 15 to 1. When such children were tested after Romania's dictator was assassinated, they had lower intelligence scores and double the 20 percent rate of anxiety symptoms found in children assigned to quality foster care settings (Nelson et al., 2009).

Mike Carroll mike@carrollmj.com

be "expressed" (active), and that epigenetics studies how experience puts molecular marks on genes that influence their expression. Severe child abuse, for example, can affect the expression of genes (Labonté et al., 2012). Extreme childhood trauma can also leave footprints on the brain. Normally placid golden hamsters that are repeatedly threatened and attacked while young grow up to be cowards when caged with same-sized hamsters, or bullies when caged with weaker ones (Ferris, 1996). Young children who are terrorized through physical abuse or wartime atrocities (being beaten, witnessing torture, and living in constant fear) often suffer other lasting wounds. Many have reported nightmares, depression, and an adolescence troubled by substance abuse, binge eating, or aggression (Kendall-Tackett et al., 1993, 2004; Polusny & Follette, 1995; Trickett & McBride-Chang, 1995). So too with childhood sexual abuse. Especially if severe and prolonged, it places children at increased risk for health problems, psychological disorders, substance abuse, and criminality (Freyd et al., 2005; Tyler, 2002).

Still, many children successfully survive abuse. It's true that most abusive parents—and many condemned murderers—were indeed abused. It's also true that most children growing up in harsh conditions don't become violent criminals or abusive parents. Indeed, hardship short of trauma often boosts mental toughness (Seery, 2011). When you face adversity, consider the silver lining. Your coping may strengthen your *resilience*—your ability to bounce back and go on to lead a better life.

Parenting Styles

3-10 What are three primary parenting styles, and what outcomes are associated with each?

Child-raising practices vary. Some parents are strict, some are lax. Some show little affection, some liberally hug and kiss. Do parenting-style differences affect children?

The most heavily researched aspect of parenting has been how, and to what extent, parents seek to control their children. Investigators have identified three parenting styles:

1. *Authoritarian* parents set the rules and expect obedience: "Don't interrupt." "Keep your room clean." "Don't stay out late or you'll be grounded." "Why? Because I said so."

2. *Permissive* parents give in to their children's desires. They make few demands and use little punishment.

3. *Authoritative* parents are both demanding and responsive. They exert control by setting rules, but especially with older children, they encourage open discussion and allow exceptions.

Too hard, too soft, and just right, these styles have been called. Studies reveal that children with authoritarian parents tend to have less social skill and self-esteem, and those with permissive parents tend to be more aggressive and immature. The children with the highest self-esteem, self-reliance, and social competence usually have warm, concerned, *authoritative* parents (Baumrind, 1996; Buri et al., 1988; Coopersmith, 1967). Two studies of thousands of Germans found that the parenting-competence link extended far into the future. Young adults whose parents had imposed a childhood curfew were better adjusted and had achieved more, compared with those who had permissive parents (Haase et al., 2008).

A *word of caution:* The association between certain parenting styles (being firm but open) and certain childhood outcomes (social competence) is correlational. *Correlation is not causation.* Perhaps you can imagine other possible explanations for this parenting-competence link.

Remember, too, that parenting doesn't happen in a vacuum. One of the forces that influences parenting styles is culture.

"To be frank, officer, my parents never set boundaries."

CULTURE AND CHILD RAISING *Culture,* as we noted in Chapter 1, is the set of enduring behaviors, ideas, attitudes, values, and traditions shared by a group of people and handed down from one generation to the next (Brislin, 1988). In Chapter 4, we'll explore the effects of culture on gender. In later chapters we'll consider the influence of culture on psychological disorders and social interactions. For now, let's look at the way that child-raising practices reflect cultural values.

Cultural values vary from place to place and, even in the same place, from one time to another. Do you prefer children who are independent, or children who comply with what others think? The Westernized culture of the United States today favors independence. "You are responsible for yourself," Western families and schools tell their children. "Follow your conscience. Be true to yourself. Discover your gifts. Think through your personal needs." A half-century ago and more, however, Western cultural values placed greater priority on obedience, respect, and sensitivity to others (Alwin, 1990; Remley, 1988). "Be true to your traditions," parents then taught their children. "Be loyal to your heritage and country. Show respect toward your parents and other superiors." Cultures can change.

Children across place and time have thrived under various child-raising

Phil Noble/Reuters

Francis Dean/Dean Pictures/The Image Works

CULTURES VARY Parents everywhere care about their children, but raise and protect them differently depending on the surrounding culture. In metropolitan centers, such as New York City, parents keep children close. In smaller, close-knit communities, such as Stromness, Scotland, social trust has enabled parents to park their toddlers outside shops.

systems. Upper-class British parents traditionally handed off routine caregiving to nannies, then sent their 10-year-olds away to boarding school. Many Americans now give children their own bedrooms and entrust them to day care.

Many Asian and African cultures place less value on independence and more on a strong sense of *family self*. They feel that what shames the child shames the family, and what brings honor to the family brings honor to the self. These cultures also value emotional closeness, and infants and toddlers may sleep with their mothers and spend their days close to a family member (Morelli et al., 1992; Whiting & Edwards, 1988). Sending children away would be shocking to an African Gusii family. Their babies nurse freely but spend most of the day on their mother's back, with lots of body contact but little face-to-face and language interaction. If the mother becomes pregnant again, the toddler is weaned and handed over to another family member. Westerners may wonder about the negative effects of the lack of verbal interaction, but then the African Gusii may in turn wonder about Western mothers pushing their babies around in strollers and leaving them in playpens and car seats (Small, 1997). Such diversity in child raising cautions us against presuming

that our culture's way is the only way to raise children successfully. ▪

RETRIEVE + REMEMBER

- The three parenting styles have been called "too hard, too soft, and just right." Which one is "too hard," which one "too soft," and which one "just right," and why?

ANSWER: The authoritarian style would be too hard, the permissive style too soft, and the authoritative style just right. Parents using the authoritative style tend to have children with high self-esteem, self-reliance, and social competence.

Thinking About Nature and Nurture

The unique gene combination created when our mother's egg engulfed our father's sperm helped form us as individuals. Genes predispose both our shared humanity and our individual differences.

But it also is true that our experiences form us. In the womb, in our families, and in our peer relationships, we learn ways of thinking and acting. Even differences initiated by our nature may be amplified by our nurture. We are not formed by either nature or nurture, but by the interaction between them. Biological, psychological, and social-cultural forces interact (**FIGURE 3.13**).

Mindful of how others differ from us, however, we often fail to notice the similarities stemming from our shared biology. Regardless of our culture, we humans share the same life cycle. We speak to our infants in similar ways and respond similarly to their coos and cries (Bornstein et al., 1992a,b). All over the world, the children of warm and supportive parents feel better about themselves and are less hostile than are the children of punishing and rejecting parents (Rohner, 1986; Scott et al., 1991). Although Hispanic, Asian, Black, and White Americans differ

Biological influences:
- Shared human genome
- Individual genetic variations
- Prenatal environment

Psychological influences:
- Gene-environment interaction
- Neurological effect of early experiences
- Responses evoked by our own traits
- Beliefs, feelings, and expectations

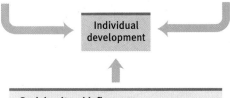

Individual development

Social-cultural influences:
- Parental influences
- Peer influences
- Cultural emphasis on group or individual
- Chance events
- Other social influences

FIGURE 3.13 The biopsychosocial approach to development

in school achievement and delinquency, the differences are "no more than skin deep" (Rowe et al., 1994). To the extent that family structure, peer influences, and parental education predict behavior in one of these ethnic groups, they do so for the others as well. Compared with the person-to-person differences within groups, the differences between groups are small. We share a human nature.

Adolescence

During **adolescence** we morph from child to adult. Adolescence starts with a physical event—bodily changes that mark the beginning of sexual maturity. It ends with a social event—independent adult status, which means that in cultures where teens are self-supporting, adolescence hardly exists.

Physical Development

3-11 What defines adolescence, and what major physical changes occur during adolescence?

Adolescence begins with **puberty,** the time when we mature sexually. Puberty

follows a surge of hormones, which may intensify moods and which trigger a series of bodily changes, outlined in Chapter 4, Gender and Sexuality.

Just as in the earlier life stages, we all go through the same *sequence* of changes in puberty. All girls, for example, develop breast buds and pubic hair before *menarche,* their first menstrual period. The *timing* of such changes is less predictable. Some girls start their growth spurt at 9, some boys as late as age 16. Maturing earlier or later than your peers has little effect on adult physical features, such as your final height. It is not when we mature that counts, but how people react to our physical development.

For boys, early maturation has mixed effects. Boys who are stronger and more athletic during their early teen years tend to be more popular, self-assured, and independent, though also more at risk for alcohol use, delinquency, and premature sexual activity (Conley & Rudolph, 2009; Copeland et al., 2010; Lynne et al., 2007). For girls, early maturation can be a challenge (Mendle et al., 2007). If a young girl's body and hormone-fed feelings are too far beyond her emotional maturity and her friends' physical development and experiences, she may search out older teens or may suffer teasing or sexual harassment (Ge & Natsuaki, 2009).

At a five-year high school reunion, former best friends may be surprised at their differences; a decade or more later, they may have trouble sustaining a conversation.

An adolescent's brain is also a work in progress. This is the time when unused neurons and their connections are pruned (Blakemore, 2008). What we don't use, we lose.

As teens mature, their frontal lobes also continue to develop. But frontal lobe maturation lags behind the development of the emotional limbic system. When puberty's hormonal surge combines with limbic system development and unfinished frontal lobes, it's no wonder teens feel stressed. Impulsiveness, risky behaviors, and emotional storms—slamming doors and turning up the music—happen (Casey et al., 2008). Not yet fully equipped for making long-term plans and curbing impulses, young teens may give in to the lure of smoking. (Adult smokers often tell them that they will later regret that move.) Teens typically know the risks of smoking, fast driving, unprotected sex. They just, reasoning from their gut, weigh the benefits of risky behaviors more heavily (Reyna & Farley, 2006; Steinberg, 2010). They seek thrills and rewards, but they can't always locate the brake pedal controlling their impulses.

HEIGHT DIFFERENCES Throughout childhood, boys and girls are similar in height. At puberty, girls surge ahead briefly, but then boys overtake them at about age 14. (Data from Tanner, 1978.)

"Young man, go to your room and stay there until your cerebral cortex matures."

So, when Junior drives recklessly and academically self-destructs, should his parents reassure themselves that "he can't help it; his frontal cortex isn't yet fully grown"? They can at least take hope: The brain with which Junior begins his teens differs from the brain with which he will end his teens. Unless he slows his brain development with heavy drinking, his frontal lobes will continue maturing until about age 25 (Beckman, 2004). Better communication between the frontal lobes and other brain regions will bring improved judgment, impulse control, and the ability to plan for the long term.

In 2004, the American Psychological Association joined seven other medical and mental health associations in filing U.S. Supreme Court briefs arguing against the death penalty for 16- and 17-year-olds. They presented evidence for the teen brain's immaturity "in areas that bear upon adolescent decision making." Teens are "less guilty by reason of adolescence," suggested psychologist Laurence Steinberg and law professor Elizabeth Scott (2003; Steinberg et al., 2009). In 2005, by a 5-to-4 margin, the Court agreed, declaring juvenile death penalties unconstitutional.

Cognitive Development

3-12 How did Piaget, Kohlberg, and later researchers describe cognitive and moral development during adolescence?

During the early teen years, reasoning is often self-focused. Adolescents may think their private experiences are unique, something parents just couldn't understand: "But, Mom, *you* don't really know how it feels to be in love" (Elkind, 1978). Capable of thinking about their own thinking and about other people's thinking, they also begin imagining what other people are thinking about *them*. (They might worry less if they understood their peers' similar self-focus.) Gradually, though, most begin to reason more abstractly.

Developing Reasoning Power

When adolescents achieve the intellectual peak Jean Piaget called *formal operations,* they apply their new abstract thinking tools to the world around them. They may debate human nature, good and evil, truth and justice. Having left behind the concrete images of early childhood, they may search for a deeper meaning of life (Elkind, 1970; Worthington, 1989). They can now reason logically. They can spot hypocrisy and detect inconsistencies in others' reasoning (Peterson et al., 1986). (Can you remember having a heated debate with your parents? Did you perhaps even vow silently never to lose sight of your own ideals?)

Developing Morality

Two crucial tasks of childhood and adolescence are determining right from wrong and developing character—the psychological muscles for controlling impulses. To be a moral person is to *think* morally and *act* accordingly. Jean Piaget and Lawrence Kohlberg proposed that moral reasoning guides moral actions. A more recent view builds on psychology's game-changing new recognition that much of our functioning occurs not on the "high road" of deliberate, conscious thinking but on the "low road" of unconscious, automatic thinking.

MORAL THINKING Piaget (1932) believed that children's moral judgments build on their cognitive development. Agreeing with Piaget, Lawrence Kohlberg (1981, 1984) sought to describe the development of *moral reasoning,* the thinking that occurs as we consider right and wrong. Kohlberg posed moral dilemmas—for example, should a person steal medicine to save a loved one's life? He then asked children,

adolescence the transition period from childhood to adulthood, extending from puberty to independence.

puberty the period of sexual maturation, during which a person becomes capable of reproducing.

DEMONSTRATING THEIR REASONING ABILITY Although they supported different candidates in the 2012 U.S. presidential election, these teens were all demonstrating their ability to think logically about abstract topics. According to Piaget, they were in the final cognitive stage, formal operations.

TABLE 3.2   Kohlberg's Levels of Moral Thinking

Level (approximate age)	Focus	Example
Preconventional morality (before age 9)	Self-interest; obey rules to avoid punishment or gain concrete rewards.	"If you save your dying wife, you'll be a hero."
Conventional morality (early adolescence)	Uphold laws and rules to gain social approval or maintain social order.	"If you steal the drug for her, everyone will think you're a criminal."
Postconventional morality (adolescence and beyond)	Actions reflect belief in basic rights and self-defined ethical principles.	"People have a right to live."

Adam Hunger/Reuters

MORAL REASONING Some Staten Island, New York, residents faced a moral dilemma in 2012 when Superstorm Sandy caused disastrous flooding. Should they risk their lives to try to rescue family, friends, and neighbors in dangerously flooded areas? Their reasoning likely reflected different levels of moral thinking, even if they behaved similarly.

adolescents, and adults whether the action was right or wrong. He believed their answers would give evidence of stages of moral thinking. His findings led him to propose three basic levels of moral thinking, *preconventional, conventional,* and *postconventional* (**TABLE 3.2**). Kohlberg claimed these levels form a moral ladder. As with all stage theories, the sequence never changes. We begin on the bottom rung and rise to varying heights. Kohlberg's critics have noted that his postconventional level is culturally limited. It appears mostly among people who prize *individualism*—giving priority to one's own goals (Eckensberger, 1994; Miller & Bersoff, 1995). This theory, add its critics, is biased against *collectivist* (group-centered) societies, such as China and India, which place more value on group goals.

MORAL INTUITION According to psychologist Jonathan Haidt (2002, 2006, 2010) much of our morality is rooted in *moral intuitions*—"quick gut feelings." In this view, the mind makes moral judgments quickly and automatically. We *feel* elevation—a tingly, warm, glowing feeling in the chest—when seeing people display exceptional generosity, compassion, or courage. Such feelings in turn trigger moral reasoning, says Haidt.

This viewpoint on morality finds support in a study of moral decisions. Imagine seeing a runaway trolley headed for five people. All will certainly be killed unless you throw a switch that diverts the trolley onto another track, where it will kill one person. Should you throw the switch? Most say *Yes.* Kill one, save five.

Now imagine the same dilemma, with one change. This time, your opportunity to save the five requires you to push a large stranger onto the tracks, where he will die as his body stops the trolley. Kill one, save five? The logic is the same, but most say *No.* Seeking to understand why, researchers used brain imaging to spy on people's neural responses as they considered such problems (Greene, 2001). Despite the identical logic, only the body-pushing type of moral choice activated their brain's emotion areas. The point: Emotions feed moral intuitions.

While the new research shows that moral intuitions can beat moral reasoning, other research reaffirms the importance of moral reasoning. The religious and moral reasoning of the Amish, for example, shapes their practices of forgiveness, communal life, and modesty (Narvaez, 2010). Joshua Greene (2010) likens our moral cognition to a camera. Usually, we rely on the automatic point-and-shoot mode. But sometimes we use reason to manually override the camera's automatic impulse.

MORAL ACTION Today's character-education programs focus both on moral reasoning and on *doing* the right thing. They teach children *empathy* for others' feelings. They also teach the self-discipline needed to restrain one's own impulses—to delay small pleasures now to earn bigger rewards later. Those who have learned to *delay gratification*

have become more socially responsible, academically successful, and productive (Funder & Block, 1989). In one of psychology's famous experiments, Walter Mischel (1988, 1989) gave 4-year-old preschoolers a choice between one marshmallow now, or two marshmallows when he returned a few minutes later. The children who had the willpower to delay gratification went on to have higher college completion rates and incomes, and less often suffered addiction problems.

In service-learning programs, where teens have tutored, cleaned up their neighborhoods, and assisted older adults, everyone has benefited. The teens' sense of competence and their desire to serve have increased, and their school absenteeism and drop-out rates have decreased (Andersen, 1998; Piliavin, 2003). Moral action feeds moral attitudes. ■

RETRIEVE + REMEMBER

- According to Kohlberg, _____ morality focuses on upholding laws and social rules, _____ morality focuses on self-interest, and _____ morality focuses on self-defined ethical principles.

ANSWER: conventional; preconventional; postconventional

Social Development

3-13 According to Erikson, what stages—and accompanying tasks and challenges—mark our psychosocial development?

Erik Erikson (1963) believed that we must resolve a specific crisis at each stage of life. Thus, each stage has its own *psychosocial* task. Young children wrestle with issues of *trust*, then *autonomy* (independence), then *initiative*. School-age children strive for *competence*—feeling able and productive. The adolescent's task is to blend past, present, and future possibilities into a clearer sense of self. Adolescents wonder, "Who am I as an individual? What do I want to do with my life? What values should I live by? What do I believe in?" Such questions, said Erikson, are part of the adolescent's *search for identity* (**TABLE 3.3**).

Forming an Identity

To refine their sense of identity, adolescents in Western cultures usually try out different "selves" in different situations. They may act out one self at home, another with friends, and still another at school or on Facebook. Sometimes these separate worlds overlap. Do you remember having your friend world and family world bump into each other, and wondering, "Which self should I be? Which is the real me?" Most of us make peace with our various selves. In time, we blend them into a stable and comfortable sense of who we are—an **identity.**

For both adolescents and adults, our group identities are often formed by how we differ from those around us. When living in Britain, I become conscious of my Americanness. When spending time with my daughter in Africa, I become conscious of my minority White race. When surrounded by women, I am mindful of my gender identity. For international students, for those of a minority ethnic group, for people with a disability, for gays and lesbians, a **social identity** often forms around their distinctiveness.

TABLE 3.3	Erikson's Stages of Psychosocial Development	
Stage (approximate age)	**Issues**	**Description of Task**
Infancy (to 1 year)	Trust vs. mistrust	If needs are dependably met, infants develop a sense of basic trust.
Toddlerhood (1 to 3 years)	Autonomy vs. shame and doubt	Toddlers learn to exercise their will and do things for themselves, or they doubt their abilities.
Preschool (3 to 6 years)	Initiative vs. guilt	Preschoolers learn to initiate tasks and carry out plans, or they feel guilty about their efforts to be independent.
Elementary school (6 years to puberty)	Competence vs. inferiority	Children learn the pleasure of applying themselves to tasks, or they feel inferior.
Adolescence (teen years into 20s)	Identity vs. role confusion	Teenagers work at refining a sense of self by testing roles and then blending them to form a single identity, or they become confused about who they are.
Young adulthood (20s to early 40s)	Intimacy vs. isolation	Young adults struggle to form close relationships and to gain the capacity for intimate love, or they feel socially isolated.
Middle adulthood (40s to 60s)	Generativity vs. stagnation	In middle age, people discover a sense of contributing to the world, usually through family and work, or they may feel a lack of purpose.
Late adulthood (late 60s and up)	Integrity vs. despair	Reflecting on his or her life, an older adult may feel a sense of satisfaction or failure.

COMPETENCE VS. INFERIORITY

INTIMACY VS. ISOLATION

But not always. Erikson noticed that some adolescents bypass this period. Some forge their identity early, simply by taking on their parents' values and expectations. Others may adopt the identity of a particular peer group—jocks, preps, geeks, goths.

Cultural values may influence teens' search for an identity. Traditional, more collectivist cultures teach adolescents who they are, rather than encouraging them to decide on their own. In individ-ualist Western cultures, young people may continue to try out possible roles well into their late teen years, when many people begin attending college or working full time. During the early to mid-teen years, self-esteem falls and, for girls, depression scores often increase. Then, during the late teens and twenties,

identity our sense of self; according to Erikson, the adolescent's task is to solidify a sense of self by testing and blending various roles.

social identity the "we" aspect of our self-concept; the part of our answer to "Who am I?" that comes from our group memberships.

"She says she's someone from your past who gave birth to you, and raised you, and sacrificed everything so you could have whatever you wanted."

self-image bounces back (Erol & Orth, 2011; Robins et al., 2002; Twenge & Nolen-Hoeksema, 2002). Agreeableness and emotional stability also increase during late adolescence and early adulthood (Klimstra et al., 2009; Lucas and Donnellan, 2011).

Erikson believed that the adolescent identity formation (which continues into adulthood) is followed in young adulthood by a developing capacity for **intimacy,** the ability to form emotionally close relationships. With a clear and comfortable sense of who you are, said Erikson, you are ready for close relationships. Such relationships are, for most of us, a source of great pleasure.

Parent and Peer Relationships

3-14 To what extent are adolescent lives shaped by parental and peer influences?

As adolescents in Western cultures seek to form their own identities, they begin to pull away from their parents (Shanahan et al., 2007). The preschooler who can't be close enough to her mother, who loves to touch and cling to her, becomes the 14-year-old who wouldn't be caught dead holding hands with Mom. The transition occurs gradually, but this period is typically a time when parental influence wanes and peer influence grows. As ancient Greek philosopher Aristotle long ago recognized, we humans are "the social

animal." At all ages, but especially during childhood and the teen years, we seek to fit in with our groups and are influenced by them (Harris, 1998, 2000). Consider:

- Children who hear English spoken with one accent at home and another in the neighborhood and at school will adopt the accent of the peers, not the parents. Accents (and slang) reflect culture, "and children get their culture from their peers," noted Judith Rich Harris (2007).

- Teens who start smoking typically have friends who model smoking, suggest its pleasures, and offer cigarettes (J. S. Rose et al., 1999; R. J. Rose et al., 2003). Part of this peer similarity may result from a *selection effect,* as kids seek out peers with similar attitudes and interests. Those who smoke (or don't) may select as friends those who also smoke (or don't).

- When researchers used a beeper to sample the daily experiences of American teens, they found them unhappiest when alone and happiest when with friends (Csikszentmihalyi & Hunter, 2003).

By adolescence, parent-child arguments occur more often, usually over ordinary things—household chores, bedtime, homework (Tesser et al., 1989). For a minority of families, these arguments lead to real splits and great stress (Steinberg & Morris, 2001). But most disagreements are at the level of harmless bickering. With sons, the issues often are behavior problems, such as acting out or hygiene. For daughters, the conflict commonly involves relationships, such as dating and friendships (Schlomer et al., 2011). Nevertheless, most adolescents—6000 of them in 10 countries, from Australia to Bangladesh to Turkey—have said they like their parents (Offer et al., 1988). They often report, "We usually get along but . . ." (Galambos, 1992; Steinberg, 1987).

> *"Men resemble the times more than they resemble their fathers."*
> Ancient Arab proverb

Positive parent-teen relations and positive peer relations often go hand in hand. High school girls who had the most affectionate relationships with their mothers tended also to enjoy the most intimate friendships with girlfriends (Gold & Yanof, 1985). And teens who felt close to their parents have tended to be healthy and happy and to do well in school (Resnick et al., 1997). But pause now to think critically. Look what happens if you state this association another way: Teens in trouble are more likely to have tense relationships with parents and other adults. Remember: *Correlations don't prove cause and effect.*

As we saw earlier, heredity does much of the heavy lifting in forming individual temperament and personality differences. Parents and peers influence teens' behaviors and attitudes. (See Thinking Critically About: How Much Credit or Blame Do Parents Deserve?)

Most teens are herd animals. They talk, dress, and act more like their peers than their parents. What their friends are, they often become, and what "everybody's doing," they often do. Part of what everybody's doing is networking—a lot. On a typical day, the average U.S. teen sends 60 text messages (Pew, 2012). Many become absorbed by social networking, sometimes with a compulsive use that produces "Facebook fatigue." Online communication prompts intimate self-disclosure, both for better (support groups) and for worse (online predators and extremist groups) (Subrahmanyam & Greenfield, 2008; Valkenburg & Peter, 2009).

For those who feel excluded by their peers, the pain is acute. "The social atmosphere in most high schools is poisonously clique-driven and exclusionary," observed social psychologist Elliot Aronson (2001). Most excluded teens "suffer in silence. . . . A small number act out in violent ways against their classmates." Those who withdraw are vulnerable to loneliness, low self-esteem,

How Much Credit or Blame Do Parents Deserve?

3-15 Does parenting matter?

Parents usually feel enormous satisfaction in their children's successes, and feel guilt or shame over their failures. They beam over the child who wins an award. They wonder where they went wrong with the child who is repeatedly called into the principal's office. Freudian psychiatry and psychology have been among the sources of such ideas, by blaming problems from asthma to schizophrenia on "bad mothering." Society has reinforced parent blaming. Believing that parents shape their offspring as a potter molds clay, people readily praise parents for their children's virtues and blame them for their children's vices.

But do parents really damage these future adults by being (take your pick from the toxic-parenting lists) overbearing—or uninvolved? Pushy—or weak? Overprotective—or distant? Are children really so easily wounded? If so, should we then blame our parents for our failings, and ourselves for our children's failings? Or does all the talk of wounding fragile children through normal parental mistakes trivialize the brutality of real abuse?

Parents do matter. The power of parenting is clearest at the extremes: the abused who become abusive, the neglected who become neglectful, the loved but firmly handled children who become self-confident and socially competent. The power of the family environment also appears in the remarkable academic and vocational successes of children of people who fled from Vietnam and Cambodia—successes attributed to close-knit, supportive, even demanding families (Caplan et al., 1992).

Yet in personality measures, shared environmental influences from the womb onward typically account for less than 10 percent of children's personality differences. In the words of Robert Plomin and Denise Daniels (1987; Plomin, 2011), "Two children in the same family are [apart from their shared genes] as different from one another as are pairs of children selected randomly from the population." To developmental psychologist Sandra Scarr (1993), this meant that "parents should be given less credit for kids who turn out great and blamed less for kids who don't." Knowing that children are not easily sculpted by parental nurture, perhaps parents can relax a bit more and love their children for who they are.

The genetic leash may limit the family environment's influence on personality, but does it mean that adoptive parenting is a fruitless venture? *No.* Parents do influence their children's attitudes, values, manners, faith, and politics (Brodzinsky & Schechter, 1990). A pair of adopted children or identical twins *will*, if raised together, have more similar religious beliefs, especially during adolescence (Kelley & De Graaf, 1997; Koenig et al., 2005; Rohan & Zanna, 1996).

Child neglect, abuse, and parental divorce are rare in adoptive homes, in part because adoptive parents are carefully screened. Despite a somewhat greater risk of psychological disorder, most adopted children thrive, especially when adopted as infants (Benson et al., 1994; Wierzbicki, 1993). Seven in eight report feeling strongly attached to one or both adoptive parents. As children of self-giving parents, they themselves grow up to be more self-giving than average (Sharma et al., 1998). Many score higher than their biological parents on intelligence tests, and most grow into happier and more stable adults. Regardless of personality differences between parents and their adoptees, children benefit from adoption. Parenting matters!

"It's you who don't understand me—I've been fifteen, but you have never been forty-eight."

ADOPTION MATTERS As country music singer Faith Hill and Apple co-founder Steve Jobs have known, children benefit from one of the biggest gifts of love: adoption.

Nine times out of ten, it's all about peer pressure.

and depression (Steinberg & Morris, 2001). Peer approval matters.

Teens see their parents as having more influence in other areas—for example, in shaping their religious faith and in thinking about college and career choices (*Emerging Trends*, 1997). A Gallup Youth Survey revealed that most share their parents' political views (Lyons, 2005).

Howard Gardner (1998) has concluded that parents and peers are complementary:

Parents are more important when it comes to education, discipline, responsibility, orderliness, charitableness, and ways of interacting with authority figures. Peers are more important for learning cooperation, for finding the road to popularity, for inventing styles of interaction among people of the same age. Youngsters may find their peers more interesting, but they will

intimacy in Erikson's theory, the ability to form close, loving relationships; a primary developmental task in early adulthood.

look to their parents when contemplating their own futures. Moreover, parents [often] choose the neighborhoods and schools that supply the peers.

The investment in raising a child buys many years not only of joy and love but of worry and irritation. Yet for most people who become parents, a child is one's biological and social legacy—one's personal investment in the human future. To paraphrase psychiatrist Carl Jung, we reach backward into our parents and forward into our children, and through their children into a future we will never see, but about which we must therefore care. ∎

> "I love u guys."
> Emily Keyes' final text message to her parents before dying in a Colorado school shooting, 2006.

- What is the *selection effect,* and how might it affect a teen's decision to join sports teams at school?

ANSWER: Adolescents tend to select similar others and to sort themselves into like-minded groups. For an athletic teen, this could lead to finding other athletic teens and joining school teams together.

Emerging Adulthood

3-16 What are the characteristics of emerging adulthood?

In the Western world, adolescence now roughly equals the teen years. At earlier times, and in other parts of the world today, this slice of life has been much smaller (Baumeister & Tice, 1986). Shortly after sexual maturity, teens would assume adult responsibilities and status. The event might be celebrated with an elaborate initiation—a public rite of passage. The new adult would then work, marry, and have children.

Where schooling became compulsory, independence was put on hold until after graduation. And as educational goals rose, so did the age of independence. Now, from Europe to Australia, adolescents are taking more time to finish college, leave the nest, and establish

careers. In 1960, three-quarters of all U.S. women and two-thirds of all U.S. men had, by age 30, finished school, left home, become financially independent, married, and had a child. Today, fewer than half of 30-year-old women and one-third of 30-year-old

"*When I was your age, I was an adult.*"

men have met these five milestones (Henig, 2010).

Delayed independence has overlapped with an earlier onset of puberty, widening the once-brief gap between child and adult (**FIGURE 3.14**). In well-off communities, the time from 18 to the mid-twenties is an increasingly not-yet-settled phase of life, which some now call **emerging adulthood** (Arnett, 2006, 2007). No longer adolescents, these emerging adults, having not yet assumed adult responsibilities and independence, feel "in between." Those in college or the job market after high school may be setting their own goals and managing their own time more than ever before. Yet they may still be living in their parents' home, unable to afford their own place and perhaps still emotionally dependent as well. Recognizing today's more gradually emerging adulthood, the U.S. government now allows children up to age 26 to remain on their parents' health insurance (Cohen, 2010). ∎

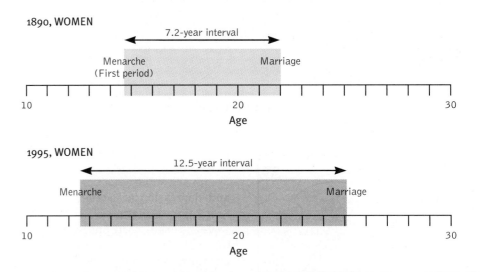

FIGURE 3.14 Transition to adulthood is being stretched from both ends In the 1890s, the average time between a woman's first menstrual period and marriage, which typically marked a transition to adulthood, was about 7 years. By 1995 in industrialized countries, that gap had widened to about 12 years (Guttmacher, 1994, 2000). Although many adults are unmarried, later marriage combines with prolonged education and earlier menarche to help stretch out the transition to adulthood.

RETRIEVE + REMEMBER

- Match the psychosocial development stage below (1–8) with the issue that Erikson believed we wrestle with at that stage (a–h).

1. Infancy
2. Toddlerhood
3. Preschool
4. Elementary school
5. Adolescence
6. Young adulthood
7. Middle adulthood
8. Late adulthood

a. Generativity vs. stagnation
b. Integrity vs. despair
c. Initiative vs. guilt
d. Intimacy vs. isolation
e. Identity vs. role confusion
f. Competence vs. inferiority
g. Trust vs. mistrust
h. Autonomy vs. shame and doubt

ANSWERS: 1. g, 2. h, 3. c, 4. f, 5. e, 6. d, 7. a, 8. b

"First, I did things for my parents' approval, then I did things for my parents' disapproval, and now I don't know why I do things."

Barbara Smaller/Funny Times

Thinking About Continuity and Stages

Let's stop now and consider the second developmental issue introduced at the beginning of this chapter—*continuity and stages*. Do adults differ from infants as a giant redwood differs from its seedling—differences mostly created by constant, gradual growth? Or do we change in some ways as a caterpillar differs from a butterfly—in distinct stages?

Generally speaking, researchers who focus on experience and learning view development as a slow, ongoing process. Those who emphasize the influence of our biology tend to see development as a process of maturation, as we pass through a series of stages or steps, guided by instructions programmed into our genes. Progress through the various stages may be quick or slow, but we all pass through the stages in the same order.

Are there clear-cut stages of psychological development, as there are physical stages such as walking before running? We have considered the stage theories of Jean Piaget on cognitive development, Lawrence Kohlberg on moral development, and Erik Erikson on psychosocial development (summarized in FIGURE 3.15). And we have seen their stage theories criticized. Young children have some abilities Piaget believed they developed only in later stages. Kohlberg's work reflected an individual-ist worldview and emphasized thinking over acting. And, as you will see in the next section, adult life does not progress through a fixed, predictable series of steps. Chance events can influence us in ways we would never have predicted.

Although research casts doubt on the idea that life proceeds through neatly defined, age-linked stages, the concept of *stage* remains useful. The human brain does experience growth spurts during childhood and puberty that correspond

emerging adulthood a period from about age 18 to the mid-twenties, when many in Western cultures are no longer adolescents but have not yet achieved full independence as adults.

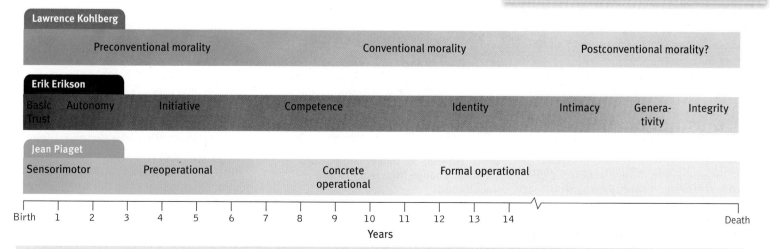

FIGURE 3.15 Comparing the stage theories (With thanks to Dr. Sandra Gibbs, Muskegon Community College, for inspiring this.)

roughly to Piaget's stages (Thatcher et al., 1987). And stage theories help us focus our attention on the forces and interests that affect us at different points in the life span. This close attention can help us understand how people of one age think and act differently when they arrive at a later age. ■

TOO MUCH COFFEE MAN   BY SHANNON WHEELER

Shannon Wheeler

Stages of the life cycle

Barbara Smaller/Funny Times

"I just don't know what to do with myself in that long stretch after college but before social security."

Adulthood

The unfolding of people's adult lives continues across the life span. Earlier in this chapter, we considered what we all share in life's early years. Making such statements about the adult years is much more difficult. If we know that James is a 1-year-old and Jamal is a 10-year-old, we can say a great deal about each child. Not so with adults who differ by a decade. A 20-year-old may be a parent who supports a child or a child who gets an allowance. A new mother may be 25 or 45. A boss may be 30 or 60.

Nevertheless, our life courses are in some ways similar. Physically, cognitively, and especially socially, we differ at age 60 from our 25-year-old selves. In the discussion that follows, we recognize these differences and use three terms: *early adulthood* (roughly twenties and thirties), *middle adulthood* (to age 65), and *late adulthood* (the years after 65). Remember, though, that within each of these stages, people vary widely in physical, psychological, and social development.

Rick Doyle/Corbis

ADULT ABILITIES VARY WIDELY Ninety-seven-year-olds: Don't try this. In 2012, George Blair maintained his place in the record books as the world's oldest barefoot water skier. (He is shown here in 2002 when he first set the record, at age 87!)

Physical Development

3-17 How do our bodies and sensory abilities change from early to late adulthood?

Early Adulthood

Our physical abilities—our muscular strength, reaction time, sensory keen-

ness, and cardiac output—all crest by our mid-twenties. Like the declining daylight at the end of summer, the pace of our physical decline is a slow creep. Athletes are often the first to notice. World-class sprinters and swimmers peak by their early twenties. Women, who mature earlier than men, also peak earlier. But few of us notice. Unless our daily lives require us to be in top physical condition, we hardly perceive the early signs of decline.

Middle Adulthood

During early and middle adulthood, physical vigor has less to do with age than with a person's health and exercise habits. Many of today's sedentary 25-year-olds find themselves huffing and puffing up two flights of stairs. When they make it to the top and glance out the window, they may see their physically fit 50-year-old neighbor jog by on a daily 4-mile run.

Physical decline is gradual, but as most athletes know, the pace of that decline gradually picks up. As a lifelong basketball player, I find myself increasingly not racing for that loose ball. The good news is that even diminished vigor is enough for normal activities.

Aging also brings a gradual decline in fertility. For a 35- to 39-year-old woman, the chances of getting pregnant after a single act of intercourse are only half those of a woman 19 to 26 (Dunson et al., 2002). Women experience **menopause,** the end of the menstrual cycle, usually within a few years of age 50. Does she see this as a sign that she is losing her femininity and growing old? Or does she view it as liberation from menstrual periods and fears of pregnancy? The answer depends on her expectations and attitudes.

There is no male menopause—no end of fertility or sharp drop in sex hormones. Men experience a more gradual decline in sperm count, testosterone level, and speed of erection and ejaculation.

"Happy fortieth. I'll take the muscle tone in your upper arms, the girlish timbre of your voice, your amazing tolerance for caffeine, and your ability to digest french fries. The rest of you can stay."

Late Adulthood

Is old age "more to be feared than death" (Juvenal, *Satires*)? Or is life "most delightful when it is on the downward slope" (Seneca, *Epistulae ad Lucilium*)? What is it like to grow old?

Although physical decline begins in early adulthood, we are not usually acutely aware of it until later life. Vision changes. We have trouble seeing fine details, and our eyes take longer to adapt to changes in light levels. As the eye's pupil shrinks and its lens grows cloudy, less light reaches the *retina*—the light-sensitive inner portion of the eye. In fact, a 65-year-old retina receives only about one-third as much light as its 20-year-old counterpart (Kline & Schieber, 1985). Thus, to see as well as a 20-year-old

when reading or driving, a 65-year-old needs three times as much light—a reason for buying cars with untinted windshields. This also explains why older people sometimes ask younger people, "Don't you need better light for reading?"

Aging also levies a tax on the brain. The small, gradual net loss of brain cells begins in early adulthood. By age 80, the brain has lost about 5 percent of its former weight. This loss is a bit slower in women, who worldwide live an average 3.5 years longer than men (Salomon et al., 2012). But in both women and men, some of the brain regions that shrink during aging are the areas important for memory (Schacter, 1996). The frontal lobes, which help restrain impulsivity, also shrink, which helps explain older people's occasional blunt comments and questions ("Have you put on weight?") (von Hippel, 2007).

Up to the teen years, we process information with greater and greater speed (Fry & Hale, 1996; Kail, 1991). But compared with teens and young adults, older people take a bit more time to react, to solve perceptual puzzles, even to remember names (Bashore et al., 1997; Verhaeghen & Salthouse, 1997). This neural processing lag is greatest on complex tasks (Cerella, 1985;

"I am still learning."
Michelangelo, 1560, at age 85

Poon, 1987). At video games, most 70-year-olds are no match for a 20-year-old.

Some good news: As noted earlier, exercise slows aging. Fit bodies support fit minds. Physical exercise enhances muscles, bones, and energy and helps to prevent obesity and heart disease. It also stimulates brain cell development and neural connections, thanks perhaps to increased oxygen and nutrient flow (Erickson et al., 2010; Pereira et al., 2007). That may help explain why sedentary older adults randomly assigned to aerobic exercise programs exhibit enhanced memory, sharpened judgment, and reduced risk of *neurocognitive disorder* (formerly called "dementia") (Colcombe et al., 2004; Liang et al., 2010; Nazimek, 2009). Exercise promotes neurogenesis (the birth of new nerve cells) in the hippocampus, a brain region important for memory.

Exercise also helps maintain the *telomeres,* which protect the ends of chromosomes (Cherkas et al., 2008; Erickson, 2009;

menopause the end of menstruation. In everyday use, it can also mean the biological transition a woman experiences from before until after the end of menstruation.

WORLD RECORD FOR LONGEVITY? Frenchwoman Jeanne Calment, the oldest human in history with authenticated age, died in 1998 at age 122. At age 100, she was still riding a bike. At age 114, she became the oldest film actor ever, by portraying herself in *Vincent and Me.*

Pereira et al., 2007). With age, telomeres wear down, much as the tip of a shoelace frays. Smoking, obesity, or stress can speed up this wear. As telomeres shorten, aging cells may die without being replaced with perfect genetic copies (Epel, 2009).

The message for seniors is clear: We are more likely to rust from disuse than to wear out from overuse.

Muscle strength, reaction time, and stamina also diminish noticeably in late adulthood. The fine-tuned senses of smell, hearing, and distance perception that we took for granted in our twenties and thirties will become distant memories. In later life, the stairs get steeper, the print gets smaller, and other people seem to mumble more.

Clever manufacturers have found a new market in this age-related difference in hearing. Some stores have reduced teen loitering by installing a device that emits a shrill, high-pitched sound that almost no one over 30 can hear (Barr, 2008; Lyall, 2005). Other teens have learned they can use that pitch to their advantage with cell-phone ringtones their instructors cannot hear (Vitello, 2006).

For those growing older, there is both bad and good news about health. The bad news: The body's disease-fighting immune system weakens, putting older adults at higher risk for

> "For some reason, possibly to save ink, the restaurants had started printing their menus in letters the height of bacteria."
> Dave Barry, *Dave Barry Turns Fifty*, 1998

life-threatening ailments, such as cancer and pneumonia. The good news: Thanks partly to a lifetime's collection of antibodies, those over 65 suffer fewer short-term ailments, such as common flu and cold viruses. One study found they were half as likely as 20-year-olds and one-fifth as likely as preschoolers to suffer upper respiratory flu each year (National Center for Health Statistics, 1990). No wonder older

> "The things that stop you having sex with age are exactly the same as those that stop you riding a bicycle (bad health, thinking it looks silly, no bicycle)."
> Alex Comfort, *The Joy of Sex*, 2002

workers have lower absenteeism rates (Rhodes, 1983).

For both men and women, sexual activity also remains satisfying after middle age. When does sexual desire diminish? In one sexuality survey, age 75 was the point when most women and nearly half the men reported little sexual desire (DeLamater, 2012; DeLamater & Sill, 2005). In another study, 75 percent of those surveyed nevertheless reported being sexually active into their eighties (Schick et al., 2010).

Cognitive Development
Aging and Memory

3-18 How does memory change with age?

As we age, we remember some things well. Looking back in later life, people asked to recall the one or two most important events over the last half-century tend to name events from their teens or twenties (Conway et al., 2005; Rubin et al., 1998). Whatever people experienced around this time of life—World War II, the civil rights movement, the Vietnam war, or the Iraq war—gets remembered (Pillemer, 1998; Schuman & Scott, 1989). Our teens and twenties are also the time when we experience many of our big "firsts"—first date, first job, first day at college, first meeting with parents-in-law.

Early adulthood is indeed a peak time for some types of learning and remembering. Consider one experiment in which 1205 people were invited to learn some names (Crook & West, 1990). They watched video clips in which 14 strangers said their names, using a common format: "Hi, I'm

> If you are within five years of 20, what experiences from your last year will you likely never forget? (When you are 70, this is the time of your life you may best remember.)

Aging researchers

Larry." Then those strangers reappeared and gave additional details. For example, they said "I'm from Philadelphia," which gave viewers more visual and voice cues for remembering the person's name. After a second and third replay of the introductions, everyone remembered more names, but younger adults were consistently better than older adults.

Perhaps it is not surprising, then, that nearly two-thirds of people over age 40 say their memory is worse than it was 10 years ago (KRC, 2001). In fact, how well older people remember depends on the task. When asked to *recognize* words they had earlier tried to memorize, people showed only a slight decline in memory. When asked to *recall* that information without clues, the decline was greater (FIGURE 3.16).

No matter how quick or slow we are, remembering seems also to depend on the type of information we are trying to retrieve. If the information is meaningless—nonsense syllables or unimportant events—then the older we are, the more errors we make. If the information is *meaningful,* older people's rich web of existing knowledge will help them to hold it. But they may take longer than younger adults to *produce* the words and things they know: Quick-thinking game show winners are usually young or middle-aged adults (Burke & Shafto, 2004).

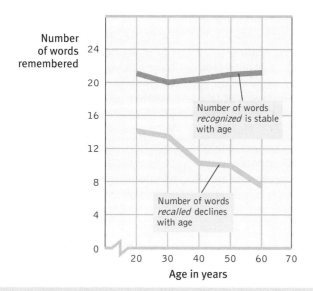

FIGURE 3.16 Recall and recognition in adulthood In this experiment, the ability to *recall* new information declined during early and middle adulthood. The ability to *recognize* new information did not. (From Schonfield & Robertson, 1966.)

Chapter 8 explores another dimension of cognitive development: intelligence. As we will see, *cross-sectional studies* (comparing people of different ages) and *longitudinal studies* (restudying the same people over time) have identified mental abilities that do and do not change as people age. Age is less a predictor of memory and intelligence than is the nearness of death. Tell me whether someone is 8 months or 8 years from death and, regardless of age, you've given me a clue to that person's mental ability. Especially in the last three or four years of life, the rate of cognitive decline typically increases (Wilson et al., 2007). Researchers call this near-death drop *terminal decline* (Backman & MacDonald, 2006).

Sustaining Mental Abilities

Recently, psychologists who study the aging mind have been debating whether "brain-fitness" computer-training programs can build "mental muscles" and hold off cognitive decline. Given what we know about the brain's plasticity, can exercising our brains—with memory, visual tracking speed, and problem-solving exercises—prevent us from los-

ing our minds? "At every point in life, the brain's natural plasticity gives us the ability to improve how our brains function," says one neuroscientist-entrepreneur (Merzenich, 2007). One study of nearly 3000 people found that 10 cognitive training sessions, with follow-up booster sessions, led to improved cognitive scores on tests related to their training (Boron et al., 2007; Willis et al., 2006).

Based on such findings, some computer-game makers are marketing daily brain-exercise programs for older people. But a veteran researcher of cognitive aging advises caution (Salthouse, 2010). The available evidence, he argues, does not indicate that the benefits of brain-mind exercise programs generalize to other tasks. A British study of 11,430 people who either completed one of two sets of brain-training activities over six weeks, or instead completed a control task, confirms the limited benefits. Although the training improved the practiced skills, it did not boost overall cognitive fitness (Owens et al., 2010). More encouraging results come from an impressive body of experiments showing that mental abilities gain a boost from aerobic exercise (Hertzog et al., 2008).

Social Development

3-19 What are adulthood's two primary commitments, and how do chance events and the social clock influence us?

Adulthood's Commitments

Two basic aspects of our lives dominate adulthood. Erik Erikson called them *intimacy* (forming close relationships) and *generativity* (being productive and supporting future generations). Sigmund Freud (1935) put it most simply: The healthy adult, he said, is one who can *love* and *work*.

LOVE We typically flirt, fall in love, and commit—one person at a time. "Pair-bonding is a trademark of the human animal," observed anthropologist Helen Fisher (1993). From an evolutionary perspective, this pairing makes sense. Parents who cooperated to nurture their children to maturity were more likely to have their gene-carrying children survive and reproduce.

Romantic attraction is often influenced by chance encounters (Bandura, 1982). Psychologist Albert Bandura (2005) recalled the true story of a book editor who came to one of Bandura's lectures on the "Psychology of Chance Encounters and Life Paths"—and ended up marrying the woman who happened to sit next to him.

Consider one study of identical twins and their spouses. Twins, especially identical twins, make similar choices of friends, clothes, vacations, jobs, and so on. So, if your identical twin became engaged to someone, wouldn't you (being in so many ways the same as your twin) expect to also feel attracted to this person? Surprisingly, only half the identical twins recalled really liking their co-twin's selection, and only 5 percent said, "I could have fallen for my twin's partner." This finding fits one explanation of romantic love: Given repeated exposure to someone after childhood, you may become attached to almost any available person who has

LOVE Intimacy, attachment, commitment—love by whatever name—is central to healthy and happy adulthood.

a roughly similar background and level of attractiveness and who returns your affections (Lykken & Tellegen, 1993).

Bonds of love are most satisfying and enduring when two adults share similar interests and values and offer mutual emotional and material support. One of the ties that binds couples is *self-disclosure*—revealing intimate aspects of oneself to others (see Chapter 12).

The chances that a marriage will last also increase when couples marry after age 20 and are well educated. Shouldn't this mean that fewer marriages would end in divorce today? Compared with their counterparts of 60 years ago, people in Western countries *are* better educated and marrying later. But in fact, they are nearly twice as likely to divorce today. (Both Canada and the United States now have about one divorce for every two marriages. In Europe, divorce is only slightly less common.) The divorce rate partly reflects women's increased ability to support themselves, but it also reflects other changes. Both men and women now expect more than an enduring bond when they marry. Most hope for a mate who is a wage earner, caregiver, intimate friend, and warm and responsive lover.

Might test-driving life together in a "trial marriage" reduce divorce risk? In one Gallup survey of American twenty-somethings, 62 percent thought it would (Whitehead & Popenoe, 2001). In reality, in Europe, Canada, and the United States, those living together before marriage have had *higher* rates of divorce and marital troubles than those who have not lived together (Jose et al., 2010). The risk appears greatest for those who live together before becoming engaged (Goodwin et al., 2010; Rhoades et al., 2009). These couples tend to be initially less committed to the ideal of enduring marriage, and they become even less marriage-supporting while living together.

Nonetheless, the institution of marriage endures. Worldwide, reports the United Nations, 9 in 10 heterosexual adults marry. And marriage is a predictor of happiness, sexual satisfaction, income, and mental health (Scott et al., 2010). Neighborhoods with high marriage rates typically have low rates of crime, delinquency, and emotional disorders among children. Since 1972, surveys of nearly 50,000 Americans have revealed that 40 percent of married adults report being "very happy," compared with 23 percent of unmarried adults. Lesbian couples, too, report greater well-being than those who are alone (Peplau & Fingerhut, 2007; Wayment & Peplau, 1995).

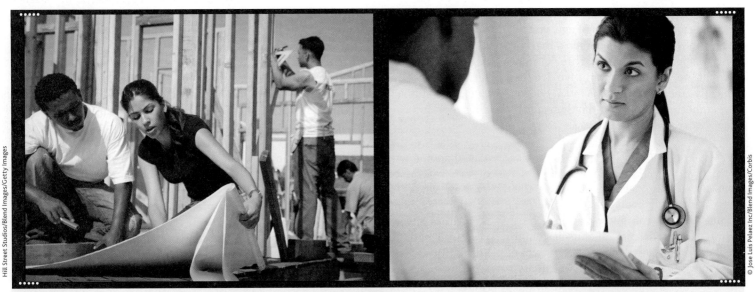

JOB SATISFACTION AND LIFE SATISFACTION Work can provide us with a sense of identity and competence and opportunities for accomplishment. Perhaps this is why challenging and interesting occupations enhance people's happiness.

Often, love bears children. For most people, this most enduring of life changes is a happy event. "I feel an overwhelming love for my children unlike anything I feel for anyone else," said 93 percent of American mothers in a national survey (Erickson & Aird, 2005). Many fathers feel the same. A few weeks after the birth of my first child I was suddenly struck by a realization: "So *this* is how my parents felt about me!"

Children eventually leave home. This departure is a significant and sometimes difficult event. For most people, however, an empty nest is a happy place (Adelmann et al., 1989; Gorchoff et al., 2008). Many parents experience a "post-launch honeymoon," especially if they maintain close relationships with their children (White & Edwards, 1990). As Daniel Gilbert (2006) concluded, "The only known symptom of 'empty nest syndrome' is increased smiling."

WORK Having work that fits your interests provides a sense of competence and accomplishment. For many adults, the answer to "Who are you?" depends a great deal on the answer to "What do you do?" Choosing a career path is difficult, especially during bad economic times. (See Appendix B: Psychology at Work for more on building work satisfaction.)

For both men and women, there exists a **social clock**—a culture's definition of "the right time" to leave home, get a job, marry, have children, and retire. It's the expectation people have in mind when saying "I married early" or "I started college late." Today the clock still ticks, but people feel freer about keeping their own time. ◼

Well-Being Across the Life Span

3-20 What factors affect our well-being in later life?

To live is to grow older. This moment marks the oldest you have ever been and the youngest you will henceforth be. That means we all can look back with satisfaction or regret, and forward with hope or dread. When asked what they would have done differently if they could relive their lives, people most often answer, "Taken my education more seriously and worked harder at it" (Kinnier & Metha, 1989; Roese & Summerville, 2005). Other regrets—"I should have told my father I loved him," "I regret that I never went to Europe"—have also focused less on mistakes made than on the things one *failed* to do (Gilovich & Medvec, 1995).

> How will you look back on your life 10 years from now? Are you making choices that someday you will recollect with satisfaction?

> "At 20 we worry about what others think of us. At 40 we don't care what others think of us. At 60 we discover they haven't been thinking about us at all."
>
> Anonymous

From the teens to midlife, people's sense of identity, confidence, and self-esteem typically grows stronger (Huang, 2010; Robins & Trzesniewski, 2005). In later life, challenges arise. Income often shrinks. Work is often taken away. The body declines. Recall fades. Energy wanes. Family members and friends die or move away. The great enemy, death, looms ever closer.

Small wonder that most believe that happiness declines in later life (Lacey et al., 2006; Lachman et al., 2008). Data collected from nearly 170,000 people in 16 nations show otherwise (Inglehart, 1990). People over 65 report as much happiness and satisfaction with life as younger people do (FIGURE 3.17).

If anything, positive feelings, supported by better emotional control, grow after midlife, and nega-

social clock the culturally preferred timing of social events such as marriage, parenthood, and retirement.

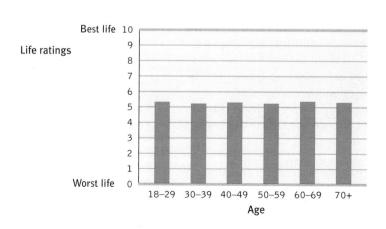

FIGURE 3.17   Age and life satisfaction The Gallup Organization asked 142,682 people worldwide to rate their lives on a ladder, from 0 ("the worst possible life") to 10 ("the best possible life"). Age gave no clue to life satisfaction (Crabtree, 2010).

tive feelings decline (Stone et al., 2010; Urry & Gross, 2010). Older adults increasingly express positive emotions (Pennebaker & Stone, 2003). Compared with younger adults, they pay more attention to positive news and are slower to perceive negative faces (Carstensen & Mikels, 2005; Scheibe & Carstensen, 2010). Older adults report less anger, stress, and worry, and have fewer problems in their social relationships (Fingerman & Charles, 2010). Like people of all ages, they are happiest when not alone (FIGURE 3.18).

Throughout the life span, the bad feelings tied to negative events fade faster than the good feelings linked with positive events (Walker et al., 2003). This contributes to most older people's comforting sense that life, on balance, has been mostly good. As the years go by, feelings mellow (Costa et al., 1987; Diener et al., 1986). Highs become less high, lows less low.

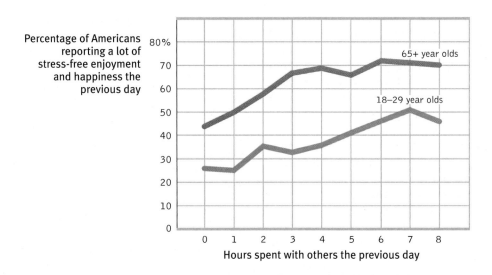

FIGURE 3.18 **Humans are social creatures** Both younger and older adults report greater happiness when spending time with others. (Note: This correlation could also reflect happier people being more social.) Gallup survey data reported by Crabtree (2011).

Death and Dying

3-21 How do people vary in their responses to a loved one's death?
. . . .

Warning: If you begin reading the next paragraph, you will die.

But of course, if you hadn't read this, you would still die in due time. Death is our unavoidable end. Most of us will also have to suffer and cope with the death of a close relative or friend. Usually, the most difficult separation is from one's spouse or partner—a loss suffered by five times more women than men. When, as usually happens, death comes at an expected late-life time—the "right time" on the social clock—the grieving usually passes. (FIGURE 3.19 shows the typical emotional path before and after a spouse's death.)

Grief is especially severe when a loved one's death comes suddenly and before its expected time. The sudden illness or accident that claims a 45-year-old life partner or a child may trigger a year or more of memory-filled mourning.

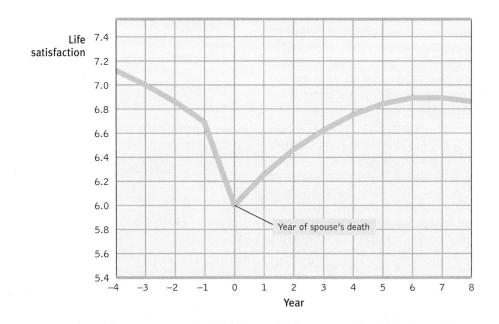

FIGURE 3.19 **Life satisfaction before, during the year of, and after a spouse's death** In periodic lifetime surveys of more than 30,000 Germans, researchers identified 513 widowed people who had not remarried after the death of a spouse. They found that life satisfaction began to dip during the year before the spouse's death, dropped significantly during the year of the death itself, and then eventually rebounded to nearly the earlier level (Lucas et al., 2003).

Eventually, this may give way to a mild depression (Lehman et al., 1987).

For some, however, the loss is unbearable. One study tracked more than 17,000 people who had suffered the death of a child under 18. In the five years following that death, 3 percent of them were hospitalized for the first time in a psychiatric unit. This rate is 67 percent higher than the rate recorded for parents who had not lost a child (Li et al., 2005).

Why do grief reactions vary so widely? Some cultures encourage public weeping and wailing. Others expect mourners to hide their emotions. In all cultures, some individuals grieve more intensely and openly. Some popular beliefs, however, are *not* confirmed by scientific studies.

- Those who immediately express the strongest grief do not purge their grief faster (Bonanno & Kaltman, 1999; Wortman & Silver, 1989).

- Grief therapy and self-help groups offer support, but there is similar healing power in the passing of time, the support of friends, and the act of giving support and help to others (Baddeley & Singer, 2009; Brown et al., 2008; Neimeyer & Carrier, 2009). After a spouse's death, those who talk often with others or who receive grief counseling adjust about as well as those who grieve more privately (Bonanno, 2009; Stroebe et al., 2005).

- Terminally ill and grief-stricken people do not go through identical stages, such as denial before anger (Friedman & James, 2008; Nolen-Hoeksema & Larson, 1999). Given similar losses, some people grieve hard and long, others grieve less (Ott et al., 2007).

We can be grateful for the waning of death-denying attitudes. Facing death with dignity and openness helps people complete the life cycle with a sense of

> "Love—why, I'll tell you what love is: It's you at 75 and her at 71, each of you listening for the other's step in the next room, each afraid that a sudden silence, a sudden cry, could mean a lifetime's talk is over."
>
> Brian Moore, *The Luck of Ginger Coffey*, 1960

life's meaningfulness and unity—the sense that their existence has been good and that life and death are parts of an ongoing cycle. Although death may be unwelcome, life itself can be affirmed even at death. This is especially so for people who review their lives not with despair but with what Erik Erikson called a sense of *integrity*—a feeling that one's life has been meaningful and worthwhile. ∎

RETRIEVE + REMEMBER

- What are some of the most significant challenges and rewards of growing old?

ANSWER: Challenges: decline of muscular strength, reaction times, stamina, sensory keenness, cardiac output, and immune system functioning. Rewards: positive feelings tend to grow, negative emotions are less intense, and anger, stress, worry, and social-relationship problems decrease.

Thinking About Stability and Change

It's time to address our third developmental issue. As we follow lives through time (in longitudinal studies), do we find more evidence for stability or change? If reunited with a long-lost grade-school friend, do we instantly realize that "it's the same old Andy"? Or do people we befriend during one period of life seem like total strangers at a later period? (At least one man I know would choose the second option. He failed to recognize a former classmate at his 40-year college reunion. That upset classmate eventually pointed out that she was his long-ago first wife!)

Developmental psychologists' research reveals that we experience both stability and change. Some of our characteristics, such as temperament, are very stable. As we noted earlier in this chapter, temperament seems to be something we're born with. When a research team studied 1000 people from age 3 to 32, they were struck by the consistency of temperament and emotionality across time (Slutske et al., 2012). Out-of-control 3-year-olds were the most likely, at age 32, to be out-of-control gamblers. In other studies, 5-year-olds who demanded a lot of teacher attention tended to become 12-year-olds who still demanded a lot of teacher attention (Houts et al., 2010). And the widest smilers in childhood and college photos were, years later, the adults most likely to enjoy enduring marriages (Hertenstein et al., 2009).

SMILES PREDICT MARITAL STABILITY In one study of 306 college graduates, 1 in 4 with yearbook expressions like the one on the left later divorced. Only 1 in 20 with smiles like the one on the right divorced (Hertenstein et al., 2009).

As adults grow older, there is continuity of self.

We cannot, however, predict all of our eventual traits based on our early years (Kagan et al., 1978, 1998). Some traits, such as social attitudes, are much less stable than temperament, especially during the impressionable late adolescent years (Krosnick & Alwin, 1989; Moss & Susman, 1980). And older children and adolescents can learn new ways of coping. It is true that delinquent children later have high rates of work problems, substance abuse, and crime, but many confused and troubled children have blossomed into mature, successful adults (Moffitt et al., 2002; Roberts et al., 2001; Thomas & Chess, 1986). Happily for them, life is a process of becoming.

In some ways, we *all* change with age. Most shy, fearful toddlers begin opening up by age 4. In the years after adolescence, most people become more conscientious, self-disciplined, agreeable, and self-confident (Lucas & Donnellan, 2011; Roberts et al., 2003, 2006; Shaw et al., 2010). Conscientiousness increases especially during the twenties, and agreeableness during the thirties (Srivastava et al., 2003). Many a 20-year-old goof-off has matured into a 40-year-old business or cultural leader. (If you are the former, you aren't done yet.) Such changes can occur without changing a person's position *relative to others* of the same age. The hard-driving young adult may mellow by later life, yet still be a relatively hard-driving senior citizen.

Life requires *both* stability and change. Stability increasingly marks our personality as we age (Ferguson, 2010; Hopwood et al., 2011; Kandler et al., 2010). ("As at 7, so at 70," says a Jewish proverb.) And stability gives us our identity. It lets us depend on others and be concerned about the healthy development of the children in our lives. Our trust in our ability to change gives us hope for a brighter future and lets us adapt and grow with experience. ■

RETRIEVE + REMEMBER

- What findings in psychology support the idea of stability in personality across the life span? What findings challenge these ideas?

ANSWER: Some traits, such as temperament, do exhibit remarkable stability across many years. But we do change in other ways, such as in our social attitudes, especially during life's early years.

CHAPTER REVIEW

Developing Through the Life Span

Test yourself by taking a moment to answer each of these Learning Objective Questions (repeated here from within the chapter). Then turn to Appendix D, Complete Chapter Reviews, to check your answers. Research suggests that trying to answer these questions on your own will improve your long-term memory of the concepts (McDaniel et al., 2009).

3-1: What are the three major issues studied by developmental psychologists?

Prenatal Development and the Newborn

3-2: How does conception occur, and what are chromosomes, DNA, genes, and the genome? How do genes and the environment interact?

3-3: How does life develop before birth, and how do teratogens put prenatal development at risk?

3-4: How do twin and adoption studies help us understand the effects of nature and nurture?

3-5: What are some of the newborn's abilities and traits?

Infancy and Childhood

3-6: How do the brain and motor skills develop during infancy and childhood?

3-7: How did Piaget view the developmental stages of a child's mind, and how does current thinking about cognitive development differ?

3-8: How do the bonds of attachment form between caregivers and infants?

3-9: Why do secure and insecure attachments matter, and how does an infant develop basic trust?

3-10: What are three primary parenting styles, and what outcomes are associated with each?

Adolescence

3-11: What defines adolescence, and what major physical changes occur during adolescence?

3-12: How did Piaget, Kohlberg, and later researchers describe cognitive and moral development during adolescence?

3-13: According to Erikson, what stages—and accompanying tasks and challenges—mark our psychosocial development?

3-14: To what extent are adolescent lives shaped by parental and peer influences?

3-15: Does parenting matter?

3-16: What are the characteristics of emerging adulthood?

Adulthood

3-17: How do our bodies and sensory abilities change from early to late adulthood?

3-18: How does memory change with age?

3-19: What are adulthood's two primary commitments, and how do chance events and the social clock influence us?

3-20: What factors affect our well-being in later life?

3-21: How do people vary in their responses to a loved one's death?

TERMS AND CONCEPTS TO REMEMBER

Test yourself on these terms by trying to write down the definition in your own words before flipping back to the referenced page to check your answer.

developmental psychology, p. 68

chromosomes, p. 68

DNA *(deoxyribonucleic acid)*, p. 68

genes, p. 68

heredity, p. 68

genome, p. 68

environment, p. 69

interaction, p. 69

epigenetics, p. 70

zygote, p. 70

embryo, p. 70

identical twins (monozygotic twins), p. 71

fraternal twins (dizygotic twins), p. 71

fetus, p. 71

teratogen [tuh-RAT-uh-jen], p. 71

fetal alcohol syndrome (FAS), p. 71

reflex, p. 71

temperament, p. 73

maturation, p. 73

critical period, p. 74

cognition, p. 75

schema, p. 76

assimilation, p. 76

accommodation, p. 76

sensorimotor stage, p. 76

object permanence, p. 76

preoperational stage, p. 77

conservation, p. 77

egocentrism, p. 78

theory of mind, p. 78

autism spectrum disorder (ASD), p. 78

concrete operational stage, p. 79

formal operational stage, p. 79

stranger anxiety, p. 81

attachment, p. 81

basic trust, p. 83

adolescence, p. 86

puberty, p. 86

identity, p. 89

social identity, p. 89

intimacy, p. 90

emerging adulthood, p. 92

menopause, p. 95

social clock, p. 99

CHAPTER TEST

Test yourself repeatedly throughout your studies. This will not only help you figure out what you know and don't know; the testing itself will help you learn and remember the information more effectively thanks to the *testing effect*.

1. The three major issues that interest developmental psychologists are nature/nurture, stability/change, and _____/_____.

2. Body organs first begin to form and function during the period of the _____; within 6 months, during the period of the _____, the organs are sufficiently functional to allow a good chance of survival.

   a. zygote; embryo

   b. zygote; fetus

   c. embryo; fetus

   d. placenta; fetus

3. Chemicals that pass through the placenta's screen and may harm an embryo or fetus are called _____.

4. Stroke a newborn's cheek and the infant will root for a nipple. This illustrates

   a. a reflex.

   b. nurture.

   c. differentiation.

   d. continuity.

5. Between ages 3 and 6, the human brain experiences the greatest growth in the _____ lobes, which we use for rational planning, and which continue developing at least into adolescence.

6. Which of the following is true of motor-skill development?

   a. It is determined solely by genetic factors.

   b. The sequence, but not the timing, is universal.

   c. The timing, but not the sequence, is universal.

   d. It is determined solely by environmental factors.

7. Why can't we consciously recall how we learned to walk when we were infants?

8. Use Piaget's first three stages of cognitive development to explain why young children are not just miniature adults in the way they think.

9. Although Piaget's stage theory continues to inform our understanding of children's thinking, many researchers believe that

   a. Piaget's "stages" begin earlier and development is more continuous than he realized.

   b. children do not progress as rapidly as Piaget predicted.

   c. few children really progress to the concrete operational stage.

   d. there is no way of testing much of Piaget's theoretical work.

10. An 8-month-old infant who reacts to a new babysitter by crying and clinging to his father's shoulder is showing _____ _____.

11. In a series of experiments, the Harlows found that monkeys raised with artificial mothers tended, when afraid, to cling to their cloth mother, rather than to a wire mother holding the feeding bottle. Why was this finding important?

12. From the very first weeks of life, infants differ in their characteristic emotional reactions, with some infants being intense and anxious, while others are easygoing and relaxed. These differences are usually explained as differences in _____.

13. Adolescence is marked by the onset of

   a. an identity crisis.

   b. puberty.

   c. separation anxiety.

   d. parent-child conflict.

14. According to Piaget, a person who can think logically about abstractions is in the _____ _____ stage.

15. In Erikson's stages, the primary task during adolescence is

   a. attaining formal operations.

   b. forging an identity.

   c. developing a sense of intimacy with another person.

   d. living independent of parents.

16. Some developmental psychologists now refer to the period that occurs in some Western cultures from age 18 to the mid-twenties and beyond (up to the time of social independence) as _____ _____.

17. Developmental researchers who emphasize learning and experience are supporting _____; those who emphasize biological maturation are supporting _____.

   a. nature; nurture

   b. continuity; stages

   c. stability; change

   d. randomness; predictability

18. By age 65, a person would be most likely to experience a cognitive decline in the ability to

   a. recall and list all the important terms and concepts in a chapter.

   b. select the correct definition in a multiple-choice question.

   c. recall their own birth date.

   d. practice a well-learned skill, such as knitting.

19. Freud defined the healthy adult as one who is able to love and work. Erikson agreed, observing that the adult struggles to attain intimacy and _____.

20. Contrary to what many people assume,

   a. older people are much happier than adolescents.

   b. men in their forties express much greater dissatisfaction with life than do women of the same age.

   c. people of all ages report similar levels of happiness.

   d. those whose children have recently left home—the empty nesters—have the lowest level of happiness of all groups.

21. Although development is lifelong, there is stability of personality over time. For example,

   a. most personality traits emerge in infancy and persist throughout life.

   b. temperament tends to remain stable throughout life.

   c. few people change significantly after adolescence.

   d. people tend to undergo greater personality changes as they age.

Find answers to these questions in Appendix E, in the back of the book.

IN YOUR EVERYDAY LIFE

Answering these questions will help you make these concepts more personally meaningful, and therefore more memorable.

1. What impresses you the most about infants' abilities, and why?

2. What do you think about the idea that, genetically speaking, we are all nearly identical twins?

3. What kinds of mistakes do you think parents of the past made? What mistakes do you think today's parents might be making?

4. What skills did you practice the most as a child? Which have you continued to use? How do you think this affected your brain development?

5. Imagine your friend says, "Personality (or intelligence) is in the genes." How would you respond?

6. What are the most positive or most negative things you remember about your own adolescence? Who do you credit or blame more—your parents or your peers?

7. Think about a difficult decision you had to make as a teenager. What did you do? Would you do things differently now?

8. What do you think makes a person an adult? Do you feel like an adult? Why or why not?

9. Imagining the future, how do you think you might change? How might you stay the same?

experience
more of the
testing
effect

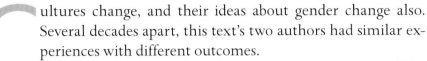

4 Gender and Sexuality

A note to our readers: I am delighted to welcome Nathan DeWall as co-author for this edition of Psychology in Everyday Life. He led our shared revision work for this chapter and three others (Chapters 10, 11, and 14).

Cultures change, and their ideas about gender change also. Several decades apart, this text's two authors had similar experiences with different outcomes.

In 1972, as the young chair of our psychology department, I [DM] was proud to make the announcement: We had concluded our search for a new colleague. We had found just who we were looking for—a bright, warm, enthusiastic woman about to receive her Ph.D. in developmental psychology. The vote was unanimous. Alas, our aging chancellor rejected our recommendation. "As a mother of a preschooler," he said, "she should be home with her child, *not* working full time." No amount of pleading or arguing (for example, that it might be possible to parent a child while employed) could change his mind. So, with a heavy heart, I drove to her city to explain, face to face, my embarrassment in being able to offer her only a temporary position.

This case ended well. She accepted the temporary position and quickly became a beloved, tenured colleague. She also went on to found our college's women's studies program. Today, she and I marvel at how swiftly our culture's thinking about gender has changed.

In 2011, I [ND] experienced something quite different. We, too, were concluding our search for a new colleague. Our department faculty had assessed several candidates, and the top two vote-getters were a man and a woman. Our faculty hiring committee would make the final choice. Before they announced their decision, a senior committee member spoke out. "Look around the table. We're all men. We need to consider that." The accomplished woman was offered the position.

Our ideas about the "proper" behavior for women and men have undergone an extreme makeover. More and more women work in formerly male-dominated professions, and more and more men work in formerly female-dominated professions (England, 2010). Yet women still earn less than men. Women continue to struggle to reach the top of the ladder. In 2011, only 2 percent of the chief executives of Fortune 500 companies were women. And expectant parents in many cultures still hope for a son. Nevertheless, our views of women and men continue to evolve.

In this chapter, we'll consider some ways nature and nurture interact to form our unique gender identities. We'll see what researchers tell us about how alike we are as males and females, and how and why we differ. And we'll gain insight from psychological science about the psychology and biology of sexual attraction and sexual intimacy. As part of the journey, we'll see how evolutionary psychologists explain our sexuality.

Let's start at the beginning. What is gender, and how does it develop?

Gender Development

◎ We humans share an irresistible urge to organize our worlds into simple categories (Chapter 8). Among the ways we classify people—as tall or short, young or old, smart or dull—one stands out. Before or after your birth, everyone wanted to know, "Boy or girl?" The simple answer described your *sex*, your biological status, defined by your chromosomes and anatomy. For most people, those biological traits help define their **gender,** their culture's expectations about what it means to be male or female. (You may recall from Chapter 1 that *culture* refers to everything that is shared by a group and transmitted across generations.)

Consider baby outfits. If you celebrate the birth of a boy with a gift of a pink outfit, his parents may frown at you. But in 1918, you probably would have received a big smile. "The generally accepted rule is pink for the boy and blue for the girl," declared the publication *Earnshaw's Infants' Department* in June 1918 (Maglaty, 2011). "The reason is that pink being a more decided and stronger color is more suitable for the boy, while blue, which is more delicate and dainty, is prettier for the girls." The way cultures define *male* and *female* varies, and it can change over time.

How Are We Alike? How Do We Differ?

4-1 What are some gender similarities and differences in aggression, social power, and social connectedness?

Whether male or female, each of us receives 23 chromosomes from our mother and 23 from our father. Of those 46 chromosomes, 45 are shared by men and women. Our similar biology helped our evolutionary ancestors face similar adaptive challenges. Both men and

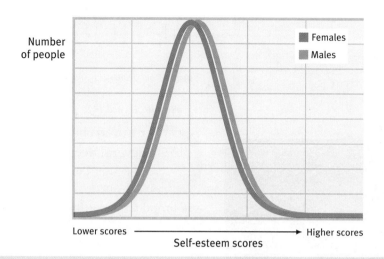

FIGURE 4.1 Different? Yes, but not by much The two bell-shaped curves in this graph show the distribution of self-esteem scores for women (red) and men (blue). These are average scores based on all available samples (Hyde, 2005). As you can see, the variation among women or among men is much greater than the difference between the average woman (highest point on red line) and the average man (highest point on blue line.)

women needed to survive, reproduce, and avoid predators, and so today we are in most ways alike. Tell me whether you are male or female and you give me no clues to your vocabulary, happiness, or ability to see, hear, learn, and remember. Women and men, on average, are similarly creative and intelligent and feel the same emotions and longings. Our similarities as male and female cannot be overstressed. Our "opposite" sex is, in reality, our very similar sex.

But in some areas, males and females do differ, and differences command attention. Some much talked-about gender differences (like the difference in self-esteem shown in **FIGURE 4.1**) are actually quite modest (Hyde, 2005). Other differences are more striking. The average woman enters puberty 2 years sooner than the average man, and her life span is 5 years longer. She carries 70 percent more fat, has 40 percent less muscle, and is 5 inches shorter. She expresses emotions more freely, can detect fainter odors, and receives offers of help more often. She also has twice the risk of developing depression and anxiety and 10 times the risk of developing an eating disorder. Yet the average man is 4 times more likely to die by

suicide or to develop alcohol use disorder. His "more likely" list includes a childhood diagnosis of autism spectrum disorder, color-blindness, or attention-deficit/hyperactivity disorder. And as an adult, he is more at risk for antisocial personality disorder. Each gender has its share of risks.

Gender differences are well studied, with 6500 related research articles appearing each year (Eagly et al., 2012). Let's take a closer look at some differences in aggression, social power, and social connectedness.

Gender and Aggression

Are men more aggressive than women? Think of the most aggressive people you heard about last year. Were most of them men? Chances are good that they were. Men generally admit to more **aggression.** They also commit more extreme physical violence (Bushman & Huesmann, 2010). In romantic relationships between men and women, minor acts of physical aggression, such as slaps, are roughly equal, but extremely violent acts are mostly committed by men (Archer, 2000; Johnson, 2008).

Here's another question: Think of stories about people harming others by passing along hurtful gossip, or by shutting someone out of a social group or situation. Were most of those people men? Perhaps not. Those behaviors are acts of **relational aggression,** and women are slightly more likely than men to commit them (Archer, 2004, 2006, 2009).

Laboratory experiments have demonstrated a gender gap in aggression. Men have been more willing to blast people with what they believed was intense and prolonged noise (Bushman et al., 2007). They have more readily zapped strangers with what they believed were intense electric shocks (Giancola, 2003). The gender gap also appears in real-life violent crime. Who commits more violent crimes worldwide? Men do (Antonaccio et al., 2011; Caddick & Porter, 2012; Frisell et al., 2012). Men also take the lead in hunting, fighting, warring, and supporting war (Wood & Eagly, 2002, 2007). More American men than American women, for example, consistently supported the Iraq war (Newport et al., 2007).

Gender and Social Power

Imagine walking into a job interview. You sit down and peer across the table at your two interviewers. The unsmiling person on the left oozes self-confidence and independence and maintains steady eye contact with you. The person on the right gives you a warm, welcoming smile but makes less eye contact and seems to expect the other interviewer to take the lead.

Which interviewer is male?

If you said the person on the left, you're not alone. Around the world, from Nigeria to New Zealand, people have perceived gender differences in power (Williams & Best, 1990). Indeed, in most societies men *do* place more importance on power and achievement and *are* socially dominant (Schwartz & Rubel-Lifschitz, 2009).

1. When groups form, whether as juries or companies, leadership tends to go to males (Colarelli et al., 2006).

2. When salaries are paid, those in traditionally male occupations receive more.

3. When people run for election, women who appear hungry for political power experience less success than their power-hungry male counterparts (Okimoto & Brescoll, 2010).

4. When political leaders are elected, they usually are men, who held 80 percent of the seats in the world's governing parliaments in 2011 (IPU, 2011).

Women's 2011 representation in national parliaments ranged from 11 percent in the Arab States to 42 percent in Scandinavia (IPU, 2011).

Men and women also lead differently. Men tend to be more *directive,* telling people what they want and how to achieve it. Women tend to be more *democratic,* more welcoming of others' input in decision making (Eagly & Carli, 2007; van Engen & Willemsen, 2004). When interacting, men are more likely to offer opinions, women to express support (Aries, 1987; Wood, 1987). In everyday behavior, men tend to act as powerful people often do: talking assertively, interrupting, initiating touches, and staring. And they smile and apologize less (Leaper & Ayres, 2007; Major et al., 1990; Schumann & Ross, 2010). Such behaviors help sustain men's greater social power.

Gender and Social Connections

Whether male or female, we humans cherish social connections. We all have a *need to belong* (more on this in Chapter 9). But males and females satisfy this need in different ways (Baumeister, 2010). Males tend to be *independent.* Females tend to be more *interdependent.* This difference in *social connectedness* surfaces in children's play. Boys typically form large groups. Their games tend to be active and competitive, with little intimate discussion (Rose & Rudolph, 2006). Girls usually play in small groups, often with one friend. They compete less and imitate social relationships more (Maccoby, 1990; Roberts, 1991).

Gender differences in the way we interact continue in our adult years. Women's social networks are larger than men's (Igarsh et al., 2005). Women take more pleasure in talking face to face,

EVERY MAN FOR HIMSELF, OR TEND AND BEFRIEND? Gender differences in the way we interact with others begin to appear at a very young age.

Getty Images/Gallo Images

© Ocean/Corbis

gender the roles and characteristics that a culture expects from those defined as *male* and *female.*

aggression any act intended to harm someone physically or emotionally.

relational aggression an act of aggression (physical or verbal) intended to harm a person's relationship or social standing.

and they more often use conversation to explore relationships. Men enjoy doing activities side by side and tend to use conversation to find solutions to problems (Tannen, 1990; Wright, 1989). Given these differences, perhaps it's not surprising that the average U.S. teen girl sends and receives twice as many text messages as the average teen boy (Lenhart, 2010).

> "In the long years liker must they grow; The man be more of woman, she of man."
>
> Alfred Lord Tennyson, *The Princess*, 1847

Worldwide, women's interests and occupations reflect this focus on people rather than things (Eagly, 2009; Lippa, 2005, 2006, 2008). One study analyzed responses from more than half a million people. The results showed that "men prefer working with things and women prefer working with people" (Su et al., 2009). One of the things men seem to prefer working with is computers. American college men are seven times more likely than women to declare an interest in computer science (Pryor et al., 2011).

At home, women have been five times more likely than men to claim primary responsibility for taking care of children (*Time*, 2009). This may help explain why women in the workplace have been less driven by money and status and more often opted for reduced work hours (Pinker, 2008).

When searching for understanding from someone who will share their worries and hurts, people usually turn to women. Both men and women have reported their friendships with women to be more intimate, enjoyable, and nurturing (Rubin, 1985; Sapadin, 1988). In one study, 69 percent said they had a close relationship with their father, while 90 percent said they felt close to their mother (Hugick, 1989).

But how do they cope with their own stress? Compared with men, women are more likely to turn to others for support. They are said to *tend and befriend* (Tamres et al., 2002; Taylor, 2002).

Gender differences in both social connectedness and power peak in late ado-lescence and early adulthood—the prime years for dating and mating. Teenage girls become less assertive and more flirtatious, and boys appear more dominant and less expressive. Gender differences in attitudes and behavior often peak after the birth of a child. Mothers especially may become more traditional (Ferriman et al., 2009; Katz-Wise, 2010). By age 50, most parent-related gender differences subside. Men become less domineering and more empathic, and women—especially those with paid employment—become more assertive and self-confident (Kasen et al., 2006; Maccoby, 1998).

Is gender an either-or characteristic, or do we vary in the extent to which we are male or female? Does biology dictate gender? How much do our cultures and other experiences shape us? Read on. ■

RETRIEVE + REMEMBER

- _____ (Men/Women) are more likely to commit relational aggression, and _____ (men/women) are more likely to commit physical aggression.

  ANSWERS: Women; men

- Worldwide, _____ (men/women) have tended to express more personal and professional interest in people and less interest in things.

  ANSWER: women

The Nature of Gender: Our Biological Sex

4-2 How is our biological sex determined, and how do sex hormones influence prenatal and adolescent development?

Men and women use similar solutions when faced with challenges: sweating to cool down, guzzling an energy drink or coffee to get going in the morning, or finding darkness and quiet to sleep. When looking for a mate, men and women also prize many of the same traits. They prefer having a mate who is "kind," "honest," and "intelligent." But according to evolutionary psychologists, in mating-related domains, males differ from females whether they're chimpanzees or elephants, rural peasants or corporate presidents (Geary, 2010). Our biology may influence our gender differences in two ways: genetically, through our differing *sex chromosomes*, and physiologically, through our differing concentrations of *sex hormones*.

Our gender is a product of the interplay among our biological makeup, our developmental experiences, and our current situations (Eagly & Wood, 2013). Biology does not *dictate* gender, but it can influence it in two ways:

- Genetically—males and females have differing *sex chromosomes*.
- Physiologically—males and females have differing concentrations of *sex hormones*.

These two sets of influences began to form you long before you were born, when your tiny body started developing in ways that determined your sex.

Prenatal Sexual Development

Six weeks after you were conceived, you and someone of the other sex looked much the same. Then, as your genes kicked in, your biological sex became more apparent. Whether you are male or female, your mother's contribution to your twenty-third chromosome pair—the two sex chromosomes—was an

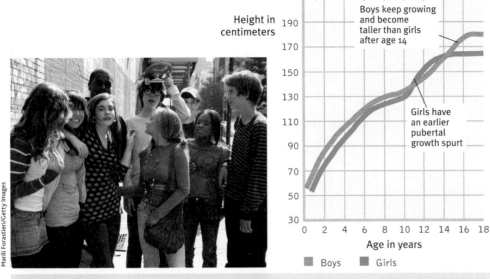

Height in centimeters

Boys keep growing and become taller than girls after age 14

Girls have an earlier pubertal growth spurt

Age in years

■ Boys   ■ Girls

FIGURE 4.2 Height differences Throughout childhood, boys and girls are similar in height. At puberty, girls surge ahead briefly, but then boys overtake them at about age 14. (Data from Tanner, 1978.) Recent studies suggest that sexual development and growth spurts are beginning somewhat earlier than was the case a half-century ago (Herman-Giddens et al., 2001).

X chromosome. It was your father's contribution that determined your sex. From him, you received the one chromosome that is not unisex—either another X chromosome, making you a girl, or a **Y chromosome,** making you a boy.

About seven weeks after conception, a single gene on the Y chromosome throws a master switch. "Turned on," this switch triggers the testes to develop and to produce **testosterone,** the principal male hormone that promotes development of male sex organs. Females also have testosterone, but less of it. Later, during the fourth and fifth prenatal months, sex hormones will bathe the fetal brain and tilt its wiring toward female or male patterns (Hines, 2004; Udry, 2000).

Adolescent Sexual Development

During adolescence, boys and girls enter **puberty** and mature sexually. Pronounced physical differences emerge as a surge of hormones triggers a two-year period of rapid physical develop-ment. A variety of changes begin at about age 11 in girls and at about age 13 in boys. A year or two before that, boys and girls often feel the first stirrings of sexual attraction (McClintock & Herdt, 1996).

Girls' slightly earlier entry into puberty can at first propel them to greater height than boys of the same age (**FIGURE 4.2**). But boys catch up when they begin puberty and by age 14 are usually taller than girls. During these growth spurts, the **primary sex characteristics**—the reproductive organs and external genitalia—develop dramatically. So do the **secondary sex characteristics.** Girls develop breasts and larger hips. Boys' facial hair begins growing and their voices deepen. Pubic and underarm hair emerges in both girls and boys (**FIGURE 4.3** on the next page).

For boys, puberty's landmark is the first ejaculation, which often occurs first during sleep (as a "wet dream"). This event, called **spermarche** (sper-MAR-key), usually happens by about age 14.

Pubertal boys may not at first like their sparse beard. (But then it grows on them.)

In girls, the landmark is the first menstrual period (**menarche**—meh-NAR-key), usually within a year of age 12½ (Anderson et al., 2003). Early menarche is more likely following stresses related to father absence, sexual abuse, insecure attachments, or a history of a mother's smoking during pregnancy (Belsky et al., 2010; Shrestha et al., 2011; Vigil et al., 2005; Zabin et al., 2005). In various countries, girls are developing breasts earlier (sometimes before age 10) and reaching puberty earlier than in the past. Suspected triggers include increased body fat, more hormone-mimicking chemicals in their diet, and greater stress due to family disruption (Biro et al., 2010).

Girls who are prepared for menarche usually experience it positively (Chang et al., 2009). Most women recall their first menstrual period with mixed emotions—pride, excitement, embarrassment, and apprehension (Greif & Ulman,

X chromosome the sex chromosome found in both men and women. Females have two X chromosomes; males have one. An X chromosome from each parent produces a female child.

Y chromosome the sex chromosome found only in males. When paired with an X chromosome from the mother, it produces a male child.

testosterone the most important male sex hormone. Both males and females have it, but the additional testosterone in males stimulates the growth of the male sex organs in the fetus and the development of the male sex characteristics during puberty.

puberty the period of sexual maturation, during which a person becomes capable of reproducing.

primary sex characteristics the body structures (ovaries, testes, and external genitalia) that make sexual reproduction possible.

secondary sex characteristics nonreproductive sexual traits, such as female breasts and hips, male voice quality, and body hair.

spermarche [sper-MAR-key] first ejaculation.

menarche [meh-NAR-key] the first menstrual period.

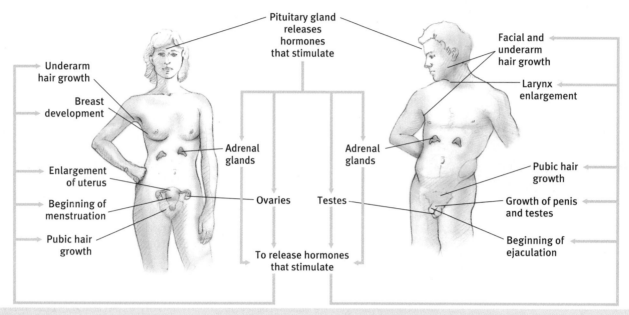

Underarm hair growth

Breast development

Enlargement of uterus

Beginning of menstruation

Pubic hair growth

Pituitary gland releases hormones that stimulate

Adrenal glands

Ovaries

To release hormones that stimulate

Facial and underarm hair growth

Larynx enlargement

Adrenal glands

Testes

Pubic hair growth

Growth of penis and testes

Beginning of ejaculation

FIGURE 4.3 Body changes at puberty At about age 11 in girls and age 13 in boys, a surge of hormones triggers a variety of physical changes.

1982; Woods et al., 1983). Men report mostly positive emotional reactions to spermarche (Fuller & Downs, 1990). ■

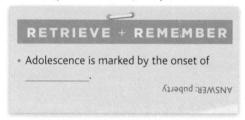

RETRIEVE + REMEMBER

- Adolescence is marked by the onset of
  _____.

ANSWER: puberty

Variations on Sexual Development

Sometimes nature blurs the biological line between males and females. When a fetus is exposed to unusual levels of sex hormones or is especially sensitive to those hormones, the individual may develop characteristics of both sexes. These **intersex** individuals may be born with combinations of male and female physical features. A genetic male, for example, may have normal male hormones and testes but no penis or a very small one.

In the past, medical professionals often recommended surgery to create a female identity for these children. One study reviewed 14 cases of boys who

had undergone early sex-reassignment surgery and had been raised as girls. Of those cases, 6 had later declared themselves male, 5 were living as females, and 3 reported an unclear gender identity (Reiner & Gearhart, 2004).

Sex-reassignment surgery can create confusion and distress among those not born with an intersex condition. In one famous case, a little boy lost his penis during a botched circumcision. His parents followed a psychiatrist's advice to raise him as a girl rather than as a damaged boy. Alas, "Brenda" Reimer was not like most other girls. "She" didn't like dolls. She tore her dresses with rough-and-tumble play. At puberty she wanted no part of kissing boys. Finally, Brenda's parents explained what had happened, whereupon "Brenda" immediately rejected the assigned female identity. He cut his hair and chose a male name, David. He eventually married a woman and became a stepfather. And, sadly, he later committed suicide (Colapinto, 2000).

The bottom line: "Sex matters," concluded the National Academy of Sciences (2001), insofar as sex-related genes and physiology "result in behavioral and cognitive differences between males and females." Yet environmental factors

matter too, as we will see next. Nature and nurture work together.

GENDER IN THE SPOTLIGHT Dramatic improvements in South African track star Caster Semenya's race times prompted the International Association of Athletics Federations to undertake sex testing in 2009. Semenya was reported to be intersex—with physical characteristics of both males and females. She was officially cleared to continue competing as a woman. Semenya declared, "God made me the way I am and I accept myself. I am who I am" (YOU, 2009).

REUTERS/Michael Dalder

The Nurture of Gender: Our Culture and Experiences

4-3 How do gender roles and gender typing influence gender development?

In many cases, biological sex and gender exist together in harmony. Biology draws the outline, and culture provides the details.

Gender Roles

Cultures shape our behaviors by defining how we ought to behave in a particular social position, or **role**. We can see this shaping power in **gender roles**—the social expectations that guide our behavior as men or as women.

Gender roles shift over time and place. A century ago, North American women could not vote in national elections, serve in the military, or divorce a husband without cause. And if a woman worked for pay outside the home, she might have been a servant or a seamstress.

Gender roles can change dramatically in a thin slice of history. At the beginning of the twentieth century, only one country in the world—New Zealand—granted women the right to vote (Briscoe, 1997). Today, worldwide, only Saudi Arabia *denies* women the right to vote. Even there, the culture shows signs of shifting toward women's voting rights

THE GENDERED TSUNAMI In Sri Lanka, Indonesia, and India, the gendered division of labor helps explain the excess of female deaths from the 2004 tsunami. In some villages, 80 percent of those killed were women, who were mostly at home while the men were more likely to be at sea fishing or doing out-of-the-home chores (Oxfam, 2005).

(Alsharif, 2011). More U.S. women than men now graduate from college, and nearly half the U.S. workforce is female (Fry & Cohn, 2010). The modern economy has produced jobs that rely not on brute strength but on social intelligence, open communication, and the ability to sit still and focus (Rosin, 2010). What changes might the next hundred years bring?

Our gender roles are not everyone's gender roles. In nomadic societies of food-gathering people, there is little division of labor by sex. Boys and girls receive much the same upbringing. In agricultural societies, where women work in the nearby fields and men roam while herding livestock, the culture has shaped children to assume more distinct gender roles (Segall et al., 1990; Van Leeuwen, 1978).

Take a minute to check your own gender expectations. Would you agree that "When jobs are scarce, men should have more rights to a job"? In the United States, Britain, and Spain, a little over 12 percent of adults agree. In Nigeria, Pakistan, and India, about 80 percent of adults agree (Pew, 2010). This question taps people's views on the idea that men and women should be treated equally. We're all human, but my, how our views differ. Australia and the Scandinavian countries offer the greatest gender equity, Middle Eastern and North African countries the least (Social Watch, 2006).

How Do We Learn to Be Male or Female?

A *gender role* describes how others expect us to act. Our **gender identity** is our personal sense of being male or female. How do we develop that personal viewpoint?

Social learning theory assumes that we acquire our gender identity in childhood, by observing and imitating others' gender-linked behaviors and by being

"Sex brought us together, but gender drove us apart."

intersex possessing biological sexual characteristics of both sexes.

role a set of expectations (norms) about a social position, defining how those in the position ought to behave.

gender role a set of expected behaviors for males or for females.

gender identity our sense of being male or female.

social learning theory the theory that we learn social behavior by observing and imitating and by being rewarded or punished.

rewarded or punished for acting in certain ways. ("Tatiana, you're such a good mommy to your dolls"; "Big boys don't cry, Armand.") Some critics think there's more to gender identity than imitating parents and being repeatedly rewarded for certain behaviors. They ask us to consider how much **gender typing**—taking on the traditional male or female role—varies from child to child (Tobin et al., 2010). No matter how much parents encourage or discourage traditional gender behavior, children may drift toward what feels right to them. Some organize themselves into "boy worlds" and "girl worlds," each guided by rules. Others seem to prefer **androgyny:** A blend of male and female roles feels right to them. Androgyny has benefits. Androgynous people are more adaptable. They show greater flexibility in behavior and career choices (Bem, 1993). They tend to be more resilient and self-accepting and experience less depression (Lam & McBride-Chang, 2007; Mosher & Danoff-Burg, 2008; Ward, 2000).

How you feel matters, but so does how you think. As you grew up, you formed *schemas,* or concepts that helped you make sense of your world. You use many of these schemas to think about your identity, about who you are. Your *gender schema* organizes your experiences of male-female characteristics (Bem, 1987, 1993; Martin et al., 2002).

Gender schemas form early in life. As a young child, you (like other children) were a "gender detective" (Martin & Ruble, 2004). Before your first birthday, you knew the difference between a male and female voice or face (Martin et al., 2002). After you turned 2, language forced you to label the world in terms of gender. English classifies people as *he* and *she*. Other languages classify objects as masculine ("*le train*") or feminine ("*la table*").

Once children grasp that two sorts of people exist—and that they are of one sort—they search for clues about gender. Hints arise not only from language, but also from clothes, toys, books, shows, and games. Having divided the human world in half, 3-year-olds will then like their own kind better and seek them out for play. "Girls," they may decide, are the ones who watch *Dora the Explorer* and have long hair. "Boys" watch battles from *Kung Fu Panda* and don't wear dresses. Armed with their newly collected "proof," they then adjust their behaviors to fit their concept of gender. These rigid stereotypes peak at about age 5 or 6. If the new neighbor is a boy, a 6-year-old girl may assume that she cannot share his interests. For young children, gender looms large.

Parents help to transmit their culture's views on gender. In one analysis of 43 studies, parents with traditional gender schemas were more likely to have gender-typed children who shared their culture's expectations about how males

> "The more I was treated as a woman, the more woman I became."
>
> Writer Jan Morris, male-to-female transsexual

and females should act (Tenenbaum & Leaper, 2002). For **transgender** people, however, comparisons with their culture's concept of gender produces feelings of confusion and discord. For transgender persons, *gender identity* (one's sense of being male or female) or *gender expression* (behavior or appearance) differs from what's typical for one's birth sex (APA, 2010). A transgender person may feel like a man in a woman's body, or a woman in a man's body. Some transgender people are also *transsexual:* They prefer to live as members of the other sex. Some transsexual people (about three times as many men as women) may seek medical treatment (including sex-reassignment surgery) to achieve their preferred gender identity (Van Kesteren et al., 1997).

THE SOCIAL LEARNING OF GENDER Children observe and imitate parental models.

TRANSGENDER CONTESTANT In 2012, Jenna Talackova became the first transgender beauty pageant contestant in this Miss Universe Canada contest in Toronto. Talackova was born a male but had sex-reassignment surgery.

Note that *gender identity* is distinct from *sexual orientation* (the direction of one's sexual attraction). Transgender people may be sexually attracted to people of the opposite birth sex (*heterosexual*), the same birth sex (*homosexual*), both sexes (*bisexual*), or to no one at all (*asexual*).

Transgender people may express their gender identity by dressing as a person of the other biological sex typically would. Most who dress this way are biological males who are attracted to women (APA, 2010). The British comedian Eddie Izzard, who regularly dresses in women's clothes during his performances, explains: "Most transvestites fancy girls." ■

Human Sexuality

◎ As you've probably noticed, we can hardly talk about gender without talking about our sexuality. For all but the tiny fraction of us considered **asexual**, dating and mating become a priority from puberty on. Both our body and our mind affect our sexual feelings and behaviors.

In a British survey of 18,876 people, 1 percent were seemingly asexual, having "never felt sexually attracted to anyone at all" (Bogaert, 2004, 2006b).

The Physiology of Sex

Unlike hunger, sex is not an actual *need*. (Without it, we may feel like dying, but we will not.) Yet sex and hunger share this: The pleasure we take in eating is nature's method of getting our body nourishment. The desires and pleasures of sex are nature's clever way of enabling our species' survival. Sex is part of life. Had this not been so for all your ancestors, you would not be reading this book. Life is sexually transmitted.

Hormones and Sexual Behavior

4-4 How do hormones influence human sexual motivation?

Among the forces driving sexual behavior are the *sex hormones*. The main male sex hormone is *testosterone*. The main female sex hormones are the **estrogens,** such as estradiol. Sex hormones influence us at many points in the life span:

• During the prenatal period, they direct our development as males or females.

• During puberty, a sex hormone surge ushers us into adolescence.

• After puberty and well into the late adult years, sex hormones help activate sexual behavior.

In most mammals, sexual interest and fertility overlap. Females become sexually receptive when their estrogen levels peak at ovulation. By injecting female animals with estrogens, researchers can increase their sexual interest. Hormone injections do not manipulate male animals' sexual behavior as easily because male hormone levels are more constant (Piekarski et al., 2009). Nevertheless, male hamsters that have had their testes (which manufacture testosterone) surgically removed will gradually lose much of their interest in receptive females. They gradually regain it if injected with testosterone.

Hormones also influence human sexual behavior, but in a looser way, and researchers are debating whether women's preferences for masculine or dominant-seeming men varies across the menstrual cycle (Gildersleeve et al., 2013; Wood et al., 2012). Among women with mates, sexual desire rises slightly at ovulation (Pillsworth et al., 2004). One study invited women with partners to keep a diary of their sexual activity. On the days around ovulation, intercourse was 24 percent more frequent (Wilcox et al., 2004).

Research by Kristina Durante, Elizabeth Pillsworth, and others also suggests that ovulation motivates women to attract male partners by wearing sexier clothing and choosing products that enhance their sexual features (Durante et al., 2011; Pillsworth & Haselton, 2006). Small wonder, then, that men tend to rate ovulating women as more attractive.

More than other mammalian females, women are responsive to their own testosterone levels (van Anders & Dunn, 2009). (Recall that women have testosterone, though less than men have.) If a woman's natural testosterone level drops, as happens with the removal of the ovaries or adrenal glands, her sexual interest may plummet (Davison & Davis, 2011; Lindau et al., 2007). But testosterone-replacement therapy can often restore sexual desire, arousal, and activity (Braunstein et al., 2005; Buster et al., 2005; Petersen & Hyde, 2011).

gender typing the acquisition of a traditional masculine or feminine role.

androgyny displaying both traditional masculine and feminine psychological characteristics.

transgender an umbrella term describing people whose gender identity or expression differs from that associated with their birth sex.

asexual having no sexual attraction to others.

estrogens sex hormones that contribute to female sex characteristics and are secreted in greater amounts by females than by males. In nonhuman female mammals, estrogen levels peak during ovulation, promoting sexual receptivity.

Testosterone-replacement therapy also increases sexual functioning in men with abnormally low testosterone levels (Khera et al., 2011). But normal ups and downs in testosterone levels (from man to man and hour to hour) have little effect on sexual drive (Byrne, 1982). In fact, male hormones sometimes vary in *response* to sexual stimulation. One Australian study tested whether the presence of an attractive woman would affect heterosexual male skateboarders' performance. The result? Their testosterone surged, as did their riskier moves and crash landings (Ronay & von Hippel, 2010). Thus, sexual arousal can be a *cause* as well as a result of increased testosterone levels.

Large hormonal surges or declines do affect men and women's desire. These shifts take place at two predictable points in the life span, and sometimes at an unpredictable third point:

1. *During puberty, the surge in sex hormones triggers development of sex characteristics and interests.* If this hormonal surge is prevented, sex characteristics and sexual desire do not develop normally (Peschel & Peschel, 1987). This happened in Europe during the 1600s and 1700s, when boy sopranos were castrated to preserve their voices for Italian opera.

2. *In later life, estrogen and testosterone levels fall.* As sex hormone levels decline, the frequency of sexual fantasies and intercourse declines as well (Leitenberg & Henning, 1995).

3. *For some, surgery or drugs may cause hormonal shifts.* After surgical castration, men's sex drive typically falls as testosterone levels decline sharply (Hucker & Bain, 1990). When male sex offenders took a drug that reduced their testosterone level to that of a boy before puberty, they also lost much of their sexual urge (Bilefsky, 2009; Money et al., 1983).

To recap, as sex hormones rise and fall, they influence our sexual characteristics and behaviors. But biology alone cannot fully explain human sexual behavior. Hormones may fuel our sex drive, but psychological stimuli turn on the engine, keep it running, and shift it into high gear. Let's now see just where that drive usually takes us. ∎

RETRIEVE + REMEMBER

- The primary male sex hormone is _____. The primary female sex hormones are the _____.

ANSWERS: testosterone; estrogens

The Sexual Response Cycle

4-5 What is the human sexual response cycle, and how do sexual dysfunctions and paraphilias differ?

In the 1960s, two researchers—gynecologist-obstetrician William Masters, and his colleague, Virginia Johnson (1966)—made headlines with their studies of sexual behavior. They recorded the physiological responses of 382 female and 312 male volunteers who came to their lab to masturbate or have intercourse. With the help of this atypical sample of people able and willing to display arousal and orgasm while scientists observed, the researchers identified a four-stage **sexual response cycle:**

1. *Excitement:* The genital areas fill with blood, causing a woman's clitoris and a man's penis to swell. A woman's vagina expands and secretes lubricant. Her breasts and nipples may enlarge.

2. *Plateau:* Excitement peaks as breathing, pulse, and blood pressure rates continue to rise. A man's penis becomes fully engorged. Some fluid—frequently containing enough live sperm to enable conception—may appear at its tip. A woman's vaginal secretion contin-

A nonsmoking 50-year-old male has about a 1-in-a-million chance of a heart attack during any hour. This increases to merely 2-in-a-million in the two hours during and following sex (with no increase for those who exercise regularly). Compared with risks associated with heavy exertion or anger (see Chapter 10), this risk seems not worth losing sleep (or sex) over (Jackson, 2009; Muller et al., 1996).

ues to increase, and her clitoris retracts. Orgasm feels imminent.

3. *Orgasm:* Muscles contract all over the body. Breathing, pulse, and blood pressure rates continue to climb. (Later studies showed that a woman's arousal and orgasm aid conception. They help propel semen from the penis, position the uterus to receive sperm, and draw the sperm further inward [Furlow & Thornhill, 1996].) Men and women don't differ much in the delight they receive from sexual release. PET scans have shown that the same brain regions are active in men and women during orgasm (Holstege et al., 2003a,b).

4. *Resolution:* The body gradually returns to its unaroused state as genital blood vessels release their accumulated blood. This happens relatively quickly if orgasm has occurred, relatively slowly otherwise. (It's like the nasal tickle that goes away rapidly if you have sneezed, slowly otherwise.) Men then enter a **refractory period,** a resting period that lasts from a few minutes to a day or more. During this time, they cannot achieve another orgasm. Women have a much shorter refractory period, enabling them to have another orgasm if restimulated during or soon after resolution.

Sexual Dysfunctions and Paraphilias

Masters and Johnson had two goals: to describe the human sexual response cycle, and to understand and treat problems that prevent people from completing that cycle. **Sexual dysfunctions** impair sexual arousal or functioning. Some involve sexual motivation, especially lack of sexual energy and arousability. For men, one common problem (and the subject of many TV commercials) is **erectile disorder,** an inability to have or maintain an erection. Another is **premature ejaculation,** reaching a sexual climax before the man or his partner wishes. For some women, pain during attempted intercourse may prevent them from completing the sexual response cycle. Others may experience **female orgasmic disorder,** distress over infrequently or never having an orgasm. In surveys of some 35,000 American women, about 4 in 10 reported a sexual problem, such as female orgasmic disorder or low desire. Only about 1 in 8 said that the problem caused them personal distress (Lutfey et al., 2009; Shifren et al., 2008). Most women who have reported sexual distress have connected it with their emotional relationship with their sexual partner (Bancroft et al., 2003).

Therapy can help men and women with sexual dysfunction. Behaviorally oriented therapy, for example, can help men learn ways to control their urge to ejaculate, or help women learn to bring themselves to orgasm. Starting with the introduction of Viagra in 1998 and now including Levitra and Cialis, erectile disorder has been routinely treated by taking a pill. Equally effective drug treatments for *female sexual interest/arousal disorder* are not yet available.

Sexual dysfunction involves problems with arousal or sexual functioning. People with **paraphilias** do experience sexual desire, but they direct it in unusual ways. The American Psychiatric Association only classifies such behavior as disordered if

- a person experiences distress from his or her unusual sexual interest *or*
- it entails harm or risk of harm to others.

The serial killer Jeffrey Dahmer had *necrophilia,* a sexual attraction to corpses. People with the paraphilic disorder *pedophilia* experience sexual arousal toward children who haven't entered puberty. Those with *exhibitionism* derive pleasure from exposing themselves sexually to others, without consent.

Sexually Transmitted Infections

4-6 How can sexually transmitted infections be prevented?

Life is sexually transmitted, but so are STIs—*sexually transmitted infections.* Rates of STIs (also called STDs, for *sexually transmitted diseases*) have ballooned in recent years, especially in people under 25 (CASA, 2004). Teenage girls, because of their less mature biological development and lower levels of protective antibodies, are especially at risk (Dehne & Riedner, 2005; Guttmacher, 1994). A Centers for Disease Control study of sexually experienced 14- to 19-year-old U.S. females found 39.5 percent had STIs (Forhan et al., 2008).

To understand the mathematics of infection, imagine this scenario. Over the course of a year, Pat has sex with 9 people. Over the same period, each of Pat's partners has sex with 9 other people, who in turn have sex with 9 others. How many "phantom" sex partners (past partners of partners) will Pat have? The actual number—511—is more than five times the estimate given by the average student (Brannon & Brock, 1993).

Condoms are very effective in blocking the spread of some STIs. When Thailand promoted 100 percent condom use by commercial sex workers, condom use soared from 14 to 94 percent over a four-year period. During that time, the number of bacterial STIs reported each year plummeted 93 percent—from 410,406 to 27,362 (WHO, 2000).

Condoms offer only limited protection against certain skin-to-skin STIs, such as herpes. But their ability to reduce other risks has saved lives (Medical Institute, 1994; NIH, 2001). When used by people with an infected partner, condoms have been 80 percent effective in preventing transmission of HIV (*human immunodeficiency virus*—the virus that causes **AIDS**) (Weller & Davis-Beaty, 2002; WHO, 2003). Women's AIDS rates are increasing fastest, partly because the virus is passed from man to woman much more often than from woman to

man. A man's semen can carry more of the virus than can a woman's vaginal and cervical secretions. The HIV-infected semen can also linger for days in a woman's vagina and cervix, increasing her exposure time (Allen & Setlow, 1991; WHO, 2004).

Most Americans with AIDS have been in midlife and younger—ages 25 to 44 (U.S. Centers for Disease Control and Prevention, 2007). Given AIDS' long incubation period, this means that many of these young people were infected as teens. In 2011, the death of 1.7 million people with AIDS worldwide left behind countless grief-stricken partners and millions of orphaned children (UNAIDS, 2013). In sub-Saharan Africa, home to two-thirds of those with HIV, medical treatment and care for the dying are sapping social resources. AIDS can be transmitted by other means, such as needle sharing during drug use, but its sexual transmission is most common.

Although many people think oral sex is "safe sex," there is a significant link

---

sexual response cycle the four stages of sexual responding described by Masters and Johnson—excitement, plateau, orgasm, and resolution.

refractory period a resting period after orgasm, during which a man cannot achieve another orgasm.

sexual dysfunction a problem that consistently impairs sexual arousal or functioning.

erectile disorder inability to develop or maintain an erection due to insufficient blood-flow to the penis.

premature ejaculation sexual climax that occurs before the man or his partner wishes.

female orgasmic disorder distress due to infrequently or never experiencing orgasm.

paraphilias sexual arousal from fantasies, behaviors, or urges involving nonhuman objects, the suffering of self or others, and /or nonconsenting persons.

AIDS (acquired immune deficiency syndrome) a life-threatening, sexually transmitted infection caused by the *human immunodeficiency virus* (HIV). AIDS depletes the immune system, leaving the person vulnerable to infections.

between oral sex and STIs, such as the *human papilloma virus (HPV)* (Ballini et al., 2012). Risks rise with the number of sexual partners (Gillison et al., 2012). Thanks to a relatively new vaccine, most HPV infections can now be prevented if people are vaccinated before they become sexually active. ■

The Psychology of Sex

4-7 How do external and imagined stimuli contribute to sexual arousal?

Biological factors powerfully influence our sexual motivation and behavior. But despite the shared biology that underlies sexual motivation, the 281 expressed reasons for having sex (at last count) ranged widely—from "to get closer to God" to "to get my boyfriend to shut up" (Buss, 2008; Meston & Buss, 2007).

Our most important sex organ may be the one resting above our shoulders: our brain. Our sophisticated brain allows us to experience sexual arousal both from what is real and from what is imagined.

External Stimuli

Men and women become aroused when they see, hear, or read erotic material (Heiman, 1975; Stockton & Murnen, 1992). Gender matters. Men generally become aroused when erotic material aligns with the direction of their own sexual interests. Thus, heterosexual men's arousal is greater when they watch men having sex

with women than when they watch men having sex with men. Homosexual men show the opposite pattern.

Women's arousal is more complicated, and the context and the intensity of the sexual experience matter more than the gender of the people they watch (Both et al., 2005; Laan et al., 1995b). Women—whether heterosexual or lesbian—become aroused when watching men having sex with women or watching women having sex with women (Chivers et al., 2004; Laan et al., 1995a).

Does viewing pornography produce any lingering effects? In some studies, people have viewed scenes in which women were forced to have sex and appeared to enjoy it. Those viewers were more accepting of the false idea that women like to be raped. Male viewers were also more willing to hurt women and to commit rape (Allen et al., 1995, 2000; Foubert et al., 2011; Malamuth & Check, 1981; Zillmann, 1989). Viewing pornography may also decrease people's satisfaction with their own sexual partner (Lambert et al., 2012). What is more, the erotic material that increases arousal today won't produce the same level of arousal a year from now. With repeated exposure to any stimulus, including an erotic stimu-

lus, our response lessens—we *habituate*. During the 1920s, when Western women's rising hemlines first reached the knee, many male hearts fluttered when viewing a woman's leg. Today, many men wouldn't notice.

Imagined Stimuli

Sexual arousal and desire can also be products of our imagination. People who are left with no genital sensation after a spinal cord injury can still feel sexual desire (Sipski et al., 1999; Willmuth, 1987). Three years after experiencing a spinal cord injury, 90 percent of men in one study were engaging in sexual intercourse (Donohue & Gebhard, 1995).

Wide-awake people become sexually aroused not only by memories of prior sexual activities but also by fantasies. About 95 percent of both men and women report having sexual fantasies. The sexual fantasies of men—whether straight or gay—tend to be more frequent, more physical, and less romantic than women's. In books and videos, men also prefer less personal and faster-paced sexual content (Leitenberg & Henning, 1995).

Does fantasizing about sex indicate a sexual problem or dissatisfaction? *No.* If anything, sexually active people have *more* sexual fantasies.

Teen Pregnancy

4-8 What factors influence teenagers' sexual behaviors and use of contraceptives?

Compared with European teens, American teens have a higher rate of STIs and also of teen pregnancy (Call et al., 2002; Sullivan/Anderson, 2009). What environmental factors contribute to teen pregnancy?

1. Minimal communication about birth control Many teenagers feel uncomfortable discussing contraception. But those who talk freely with their parents, and who are in an exclusive relationship with a

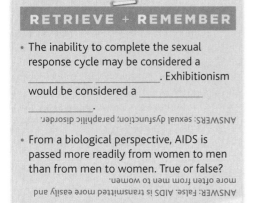

"Condoms should be used on every conceivable occasion."

Anonymous

partner with whom they communicate openly, are more likely to use contraceptives (Aspy et al., 2007; Milan & Kilmann, 1987). Jamie Lynn Spears, former television star and younger sister of pop icon Britney Spears, said she didn't use birth control (and became pregnant at age 16) because "like many young girls, I was really scared to go to the doctor . . . I was on the *Nickelodeon* show, and it felt especially embarrassing to ask someone to put me on birth control."

2. *Passion overwhelming self-control* When sexually aroused, people perform poorly on measures of impulse control (Macapagal et al., 2006). Teens who intend to delay sexual activity may also delay using contraceptives. Sexual arousal reduces intentions to use contraception, such as condoms (Ariely & Loewenstein, 2006). If passion overwhelms intentions, unexpected sexual activity may result in pregnancy (Gerrard & Luus, 1995; MacDonald & Hynie, 2008). In one survey, 72 percent of sexually active 12- to 17-year-old American girls said they regretted having had sex (Reuters, 2000).

3. *Alcohol use* Sexually active teens are typically alcohol-using teens (Mason et al., 2010; Zimmer-Gembeck & Helfand, 2008). And those who use alcohol prior to sex are less likely to use condoms (Kotchick et al., 2001). Alcohol disarms normal restraints by depressing the brain centers that control judgment, inhibition, and self-awareness.

4. *Mass media norms of unprotected promiscuity* Media help write the *social scripts* that shape our expectations about how to act in social situations. So what sexual scripts do today's media write on our minds? One script portrays the sexualization of girls (see Close-Up: The Sexualization of Girls on the next page). Another script plays out in video and online games. An analysis of the 60 top-selling video games found 489 characters, 86 percent of whom were males

(like most of the game players). The female characters were much more likely than the male characters to be *hypersexualized*—partially nude or revealingly clothed, with large breasts and tiny waists (Downs & Smith, 2010). Television has freely modeled sexual activity in which partners were unmarried, with no prior romantic relationship, and little concern for birth control or STIs (Brown et al., 2002; Kunkel, 2001; Sapolsky & Tabarlet, 1991). Adolescents learn from these scripts. Con-trolled studies show that the more sexual content adolescents view, the more likely they are to perceive their peers as sexually active, to develop sexually permissive attitudes, and to experience early intercourse (Escobar-Chaves et al., 2005; Martino et al., 2005; Ward & Friedman, 2006).

What are the characteristics of teens who delay having sex?

- *High intelligence* In two dozen studies, intelligence was associated with delaying immediate pleasure for the sake of one's future (Shamosh & Gray, 2008). Smarter teens often delay the here-and-now pleasures of sex in order to focus on future achievements.

- *Religious engagement* Many religious teachings encourage followers to restrain their sexual impulses. Actively religious teens, especially young women, often reserve sexual activity for adulthood (Štulhofer et al., 2011). The most common reason U.S. teens give for not having sex is that it conflicts with their "religion or morals" (Guttmacher Institute, 2012).

- *Father presence* Studies that followed hundreds of New Zealand and U.S. girls from age 5 to 18 found that having Dad around reduces

risk factors for teen pregnancy. A father's presence was linked to lower sexual activity before age 16 and to lower teen pregnancy rates (Ellis et al., 2003).

- *Participation in service learning programs* Teens who have volunteered as tutors or teachers' aides, or participated in community projects, have had lower pregnancy rates than other teens randomly assigned to control groups (Kirby, 2002; O'Donnell et al., 2002). Does service learning promote a sense of personal competence, control, and responsibility? Does it encourage more future-oriented thinking? Or does it simply reduce opportunities for unprotected sex? Researchers don't have those answers yet.

* * *

We have considered some biological, psychological, and social-cultural influences on human sexuality. Because of these influences, sexual motivation and behavior vary widely over time, across place, and among individuals (**FIGURE 4.4** on next page).

It's important to remember that scientific research on human sexuality does not aim to define the personal meaning of sex in our own lives. We could know every available fact about sex—that the initial spasms of male and female orgasm come at 0.8-second intervals, that systolic blood pressure rises some 60 points and respiration rate to 40 breaths per minute, that the female nipples expand 10 millimeters at the peak of sexual arousal—but fail to understand the human significance of sexual intimacy.

Sex is a socially significant act. Men and women can achieve orgasm alone. Yet most people find greater satisfaction—and experience a much greater surge in the *prolactin* hormone associated with sexual satisfaction and satiety—after intercourse and orgasm with their

Eidos/Scripps Howard Photo Service

CLOSE-UP

The Sexualization of Girls

Surely you've noticed. Just about all media—TV, the Internet, music videos and lyrics, movies, magazines, sports media, and advertising—share a tendency. They portray women and even girls as sexual objects. The frequent result, according to the 2007 American Psychological Association (APA) Task Force on the Sexualization of Girls, is harm to their self-image and unhealthy sexual development. In 2010, the Scottish Parliament agreed.

Sexualization occurs when girls

- are led to value themselves in terms of their sexual appeal.

- compare themselves to narrowly defined beauty standards.

- see themselves as sexual beings for others' use.

In experiments, the APA Task Force reported, being made self-conscious about one's body, such as by wearing a swimsuit, disrupts thinking when doing math computations or logical reasoning. Sexualization also contributes to eating disorders, to depression, and to unrealistic expectations regarding sexuality.

Mindful of today's sexualizing media, the APA has some suggestions for countering these messages. Parents, teachers, and others can teach girls "to value themselves for who they are rather than how they look." They can teach boys "to value girls as friends, sisters, and girlfriends, rather than as sexual objects." And they can help girls and boys develop *media literacy skills* that enable them to recognize and resist the message that women are sexual objects and that a thin, sexy look is all that matters.

Biological influences:
- sexual maturity
- sex hormones, especially testosterone

Psychological influences:
- exposure to stimulating conditions
- sexual fantasies

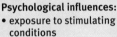

Sexual motivation

Social-cultural influences:
- family and society values
- religious and personal values
- cultural expectations
- media

FIGURE 4.4 Levels of analysis for sexual motivation Our sexual motivation is influenced by biological factors, but psychological and social-cultural factors play an even bigger role.

SHARING LOVE For most adults, a sexual relationship fulfills not only a biological motive but also a social need for intimacy.

loved one (Brody & Tillmann, 2006). One study of 2035 married people found that couples who reported being in a deeply committed relationship before having sex also reported greater relationship satisfaction and stability—and better sex (Busby et al., 2010). Sex at its human best is life uniting and love renewing.

* * *

In the rest of this chapter, we will consider two special topics: *sexual orientation* (the direction of our sexual interests), and evolutionary psychology's explanation of our sexual motivation. ■

RETRIEVE + REMEMBER

- What factors influence our sexual motivation and behavior?

  ANSWER: Influences include biological factors such as sexual maturity and sex hormones, psychological factors such as environmental stimuli and fantasies, and social-cultural factors such as the values and expectations absorbed from family and the surrounding culture.

- Which THREE of the following five factors contribute to unplanned teen pregnancies?

  a. Alcohol use

  b. Higher intelligence level

  c. Unprotected sex

  d. Mass media models

  e. Increased communication about options

  ANSWERS: a, c, d

Sexual Orientation: Why Do We Differ?

4-9 What has research taught us about sexual orientation?

As noted earlier in this chapter, we express the *direction* of our sexual interest in our **sexual orientation**—our enduring sexual attraction toward others. Sexual orientation appears to exist along a continuum, ranging from exclusive interest in our own sex to complete interest in the other sex. Those of us attracted to people of

- our own sex have a *homosexual* (gay or lesbian) orientation.
- the other sex have a *heterosexual* (straight) orientation.
- both sexes have a *bisexual* orientation.

As far as we know, in all cultures, heterosexuality has prevailed and bisexuality and homosexuality have endured. But as survey results show, cultures vary widely in their social norms for acceptable partners. In Kenya and Nigeria, 98 percent have said that homosexuality is "never justified" (Pew, 2006). In the United States, 60 percent of people say that homosexuality should be accepted, which lags behind countries such as Spain (88 percent), Germany (87 percent), France (77 percent), and Britain (76 percent) (Pew, 2013). In the United States, a smaller but increasing majority (60 percent) have recently supported accepting homosexuality.

A large number of Americans—13 percent of women and 5 percent of men—say they have had some same-sex sexual contact during their lives (Chandra et al., 2011). Still more have had an occasional same-sex fantasy. Far fewer (3.4 percent) identify themselves as lesbian, gay, bisexual, or transgender (Gates & Newport, 2012).

How many people in Europe and the United States are exclusively homosexual? About 10 percent, as the popular press has often assumed? Nearly 25 percent, as Americans, on average, estimated in a 2011 Gallup survey (Morales, 2011)? The most accurate figure seems to be about 3 percent of men and 1 or 2 percent of women (Chandra et al., 2011; Herbenick et al., 2010a; Wells et al., 2011). Active bisexuality is rarer (less than 1 percent). In one survey of 7076 Dutch adults, only 12 people said they were actively bisexual (Sandfort et al., 2001).

Heterosexuals may wonder what it feels like to be the "odd man out" in a straight culture. Imagine that you have found "the one"—a perfect partner of the other sex. How would you feel if you weren't sure who you could trust with knowing you had these feelings? How would you react if most movies, TV shows, and advertisements showed only same-sex relationships? How would you like hearing that many people wouldn't vote for a political candidate who favors other-sex marriage? And how would you feel if children's organizations and adoption agencies thought you might not be safe or trustworthy because you're attracted to people of the other sex?

Facing such reactions, homosexual people may at first try to ignore or deny their desires, hoping they will go away. They may even try to change, through psychotherapy, willpower, or prayer. But the feelings typically persist, as do those of heterosexual people—who are similarly unable to become homosexual on command (Haldeman, 1994, 2002; Myers & Scanzoni, 2005).

Most psychologists view sexual orientation as neither willfully chosen nor willfully changed. "Efforts to change sexual orientation are unlikely to be successful and involve some risk of harm," declared a 2009 American Psychological Association report. In 1973, the American Psychiatric Association dropped homosexuality from its list of "mental illnesses." In 1993, The World Health Organization did the same, as did Japan's and China's psychiatric associations in 1995 and 2001.

Some have noted that rates of depression and attempted suicide are higher among gays and lesbians. Many psychologists believe, however, that these symptoms may result from experiences with bullying and discrimination (Sandfort et al., 2001; Warner et al., 2004). "Homosexuality, in and of itself, is not associated with mental disorders or emotional or social problems," declared the American Psychological Association (2007).

DRIVEN TO SUICIDE In 2010, Rutgers University student Tyler Clementi jumped off this bridge after his intimate encounter with another man reportedly became known. Reports then surfaced of other gay teens who had reacted in a similarly tragic fashion after being taunted. Since 2010, Americans—especially those under 30—have been increasingly supportive of those with same-sex orientations.

STAN HONDA/AFP/Getty Images/Newscom

Sexual orientation usually endures, especially for men (Chivers, 2005; Diamond, 2008; Peplau & Garnets, 2000). Women's sexual orientation tends to be less strongly felt and more variable (Baumeister et al., 2000). This may help explain why more women than men report having had at least one same-sex sexual contact, even though the male homosexuality rate exceeds the female rate (Chandra et al., 2011).

sexual orientation an enduring sexual attraction toward members of either one's own sex (homosexual orientation), the other sex (heterosexual orientation), or both sexes (bisexual orientation).

Environment and Sexual Orientation

So, if we do not choose our sexual orientation and (especially for males) seem unable to change it, where do these preferences come from? See if you can predict the answers (*Yes* or *No*) to these questions:

1. Is homosexuality linked with problems in a child's relationships with parents, such as with an overpowering mother and a weak father, or a possessive mother and a hostile father?

2. Does homosexuality involve a fear or hatred of people of the other sex, leading individuals to direct their desires toward members of their own sex?

3. Is sexual orientation linked with levels of sex hormones currently in the blood?

4. As children, were most homosexuals molested, seduced, or other-

> *Note that the scientific question is not "What causes homosexuality?" (or "What causes heterosexuality?") but "What causes differing sexual orientations?" In pursuit of answers, psychological science compares the backgrounds and physiology of people whose sexual orientations differ.*

wise sexually victimized by an adult homosexual?

Hundreds of studies have indicated that the answers to these questions have been *No, No, No,* and *No* (Storms, 1983). In a search for possible environmental influences on sexual orientation, Kinsey Institute investigators interviewed nearly 1000 homosexual and 500 heterosexual people. They assessed almost every imaginable psychological cause of homosexuality—parental relationships, childhood sexual experiences, peer relationships, and dating experiences (Bell et al., 1981; Hammersmith, 1982). Their findings: Homosexual people were no more likely than heterosexual people to have been smothered by maternal love or neglected by their father. And consider this: If "distant fathers" were more likely to produce homosexual sons, then shouldn't boys growing up in father-absent homes more often be gay? (They are not.) And shouldn't the rising number of such homes have led to a noticeable increase in the gay population? (It has not.) Most children raised by gay or lesbian parents grow up to be heterosexual and well-adjusted adults (Gartrell & Bos, 2010).

What have we learned from a half-century's theory and research? If there are environmental factors that influence sexual orientation, we haven't yet found them.

Biology and Sexual Orientation

The lack of evidence for environmental influences on homosexuality has led re-

searchers to explore several lines of biological evidence:

- Same-sex attraction in other species
- Gay-straight brain differences
- Genetic influences
- Prenatal influences
- Gay-straight trait differences

Same-Sex Attraction in Other Species

In Boston's Public Gardens, caretakers solved the mystery of why a much-loved swan couple's eggs never hatched. Both swans were female. In New York City's Central Park Zoo, penguins Silo and Roy spent several years as devoted same-sex partners. Same-sex sexual behaviors have also been observed in several hundred other species, including grizzlies, gorillas, monkeys, flamingos, and owls (Bagemihl, 1999). Among rams, for example, some 7 to 10 percent (to sheep-breeding ranchers, the "duds") display same-sex attraction by shunning ewes and seeking to mount other males (Perkins & Fitzgerald, 1997). Homosexual behavior seems a natural part of the animal world.

Gay-Straight Brain Differences

Might the structure and function of heterosexual and homosexual brains differ? With this question in mind, researcher Simon LeVay (1991) studied sections of the hypothalamus taken from deceased heterosexual and homosexual people. (The hypothalamus is a brain structure linked to sexual behavior.) As a homosexual man, LeVay wanted to do "something connected with my gay identity." To avoid biasing the results, he did a *blind study:* He didn't know which donors were gay or straight. After nine months of peering through his microscope at a cell cluster that came in different sizes, he consulted the donor records. The cell cluster was reliably larger in heterosexual men than in women and homosexual men. "I was almost in a state of shock," LeVay said (1994). "I took a walk by myself on the cliffs over the ocean. I

PERSONAL VALUES AFFECT SEXUAL ORIENTATION LESS THAN THEY AFFECT OTHER FORMS OF SEXUAL BEHAVIOR Compared with people who rarely attend religious services, for example, those who attend regularly are one-third as likely to have lived together before marriage. They also report having had many fewer sex partners. But (if male) they are just as likely to be homosexual (Smith, 1998).

JULIET AND JULIET Boston's beloved swan couple, "Romeo and Juliet," were discovered actually to be, as are many other animal partners, a same-sex pair.

©John Tlumacki/The Boston Globe via Getty

sat for half an hour just thinking what this might mean."

It should not surprise us that brains differ with sexual orientation. Remember, *everything psychological is simultaneously biological*. But when did the brain difference begin? At conception? During childhood or adolescence? Did experience produce the difference? Or was it genes or prenatal hormones (or genes via prenatal hormones)?

LeVay does not view this cell cluster as an "on-off button" for sexual orientation. Rather, he believes it is part of a brain pathway that is active during sexual behavior. He agrees that sexual behavior patterns could influence the brain's anatomy. Neural pathways in our brain do grow stronger with use. In fish, birds, rats, and humans, brain structures vary with experience—including sexual experience (Breedlove, 1997). But LeVay believes it more likely that brain anatomy influences sexual orientation. His hunch seems confirmed by the discovery of a similar difference found between the 7 to 10 percent of male sheep that display same-sex

> "Gay men simply don't have the brain cells to be attracted to women."
>
> Simon LeVay, *The Sexual Brain,* 1993

attraction and the 90+ percent attracted to females (Larkin et al., 2002; Roselli et al., 2002, 2004). Moreover, such differences seem to develop soon after birth, perhaps even before birth (Rahman & Wilson, 2003).

Since LeVay's brain *structure* discovery, other researchers have replicated his study with similar results (Byne et al., 2001). Still others have reported additional differences in the way that gay and straight brains *function*. Gay men show the greatest brain arousal when they view images of other men, straight men when viewing women (Safron et al., 2007). When straight women were given a whiff of a scent derived from men's sweat (which contains traces of male hormones), an area of their hypothalamus became active (Savic et al., 2005). Gay men's brains responded similarly to the men's scent. Straight men's brains did not. For them, only a female scent triggered the arousal response. In a similar study, lesbians' responses differed from those of straight women (Kranz & Ishai, 2006; Martins et al., 2005). Clearly, the brain is a sex organ.

Genetic Influences

Findings from three sets of studies suggest a genetic influence on sexual orientation.

- *Family studies:* Human sexuality researchers report that homosexuality appears to run in families (Mustanski & Bailey, 2003) and that male homosexuality is often transmitted through the mother's side of the family (Plomin et al., 1997).

- *Twin studies:* Twin studies show that a homosexual orientation is somewhat more likely to be shared by identical twins (who have identical genes) than by fraternal twins (whose genes are not identical) (Alanko et al., 2010; Långström et al., 2008, 2010). However, sexual orientation differs in many identical twin pairs (especially female twins). This means that other factors besides genes must play a role.

- *Fruit fly studies:* Laboratory experiments on fruit flies have changed their sexual orientation and behavior by altering a single gene (Dickson, 2005). During courtship, females acted like males (pursuing other females) and males acted like females (Demir & Dickson, 2005).

It's likely that multiple genes, possibly interacting with other influences, shape human sexual orientation. In search of such genetic markers, one study financed by the U.S. National Institutes of Health is analyzing the genes of more than 1000 gay brothers.

Prenatal Influences

Twins share not only genes, but also a prenatal environment. In explaining sexual orientation, two sets of findings indicate that the prenatal environment matters.

HORMONAL ACTIVITY A critical period for human brain development occurs between the middle of the second and fifth months after conception (Ellis & Ames, 1987; Gladue, 1990; Meyer-Bahlburg, 1995).

A fetus (either male or female) exposed to typical female hormone levels during this period may be attracted to males in later life. When pregnant sheep were injected with testosterone during a similar critical period, their female offspring later showed homosexual behavior (Money, 1987).

> "Modern scientific research indicates that sexual orientation is . . . partly determined by genetics, but more specifically by hormonal activity in the womb."
> Glenn Wilson and Qazi Rahman, *Born Gay: The Psychobiology of Sex Orientation*, 2005

MATERNAL IMMUNE SYSTEM RESPONSES Men who have older brothers are somewhat more likely to be gay—about one-third more likely for each additional older brother (Blanchard, 1997, 2008; Bogaert, 2003) (**FIGURE 4.5**). If the odds of homosexuality are roughly 2 percent among first sons, they would rise to nearly 3 percent among second sons, 4 percent for third sons, and so on for each additional older brother. This curious effect is called the *older-brother* or *fraternal birth-order effect*. Its cause seems biological: The effect does not occur among adopted brothers (Bogaert, 2006). Researchers suspect the mother's immune system may have a defensive response to substances produced by male fetuses. After each pregnancy with a male fetus, antibodies in her system may grow stronger and may prevent the fetal brain from developing in a typical male pattern. Curiously, the older-brother effect is found only among right-handed men.

Gay-Straight Trait Differences

On several traits, gays and lesbians appear to fall midway between straight females and males (LeVay, 2011; Rahman & Koerting, 2008). Gay men tend to be shorter and lighter than straight men—a difference that appears even at birth. Women in same-sex marriages were mostly heavier than average at birth (Bogaert, 2010; Frisch & Zdravkovic, 2010). Data from 20 studies have also revealed handedness differences: Homosexual participants were 39 percent more likely not to be right-handed (Blanchard, 2008; Lalumière et al., 2000).

Beyond physical differences, gay-straight spatial abilities also differ. On mental rotation tasks such as the one illustrated in **FIGURE 4.6**, straight men tend to outscore straight women. The scores of gay men and lesbians fall in between (Rahman et al., 2003, 2008). But both straight women and gay men outperform straight men at remembering objects' spatial locations in tasks like those found in memory games (Hassan & Rahman, 2007).

TABLE 4.1 summarizes these and other gay-straight differences.

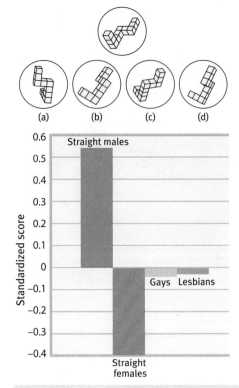

FIGURE 4.6 Spatial abilities and sexual orientation Which of the four figures can be rotated to match the target figure at the top? Straight males tend to find this an easier task than do straight females, with gays and lesbians intermediate. (From Rahman et al., 2003, with 60 people tested in each group.)

Answer: Figures a and d.

> "There is no sound scientific evidence that sexual orientation can be changed."
> UK Royal College of Psychiatrists, 2009

* * *

Taken together, the brain, genetic, and prenatal findings offer strong support for a biological explanation of sexual orientation (LeVay, 2011; Rahman & Koerting, 2008). Although "much remains to be discovered," concludes Simon LeVay (2011, p. xvii), "the same processes that are involved in the biological development of our bodies and brains as male or female are also involved in the development of sexual orientation." ◼

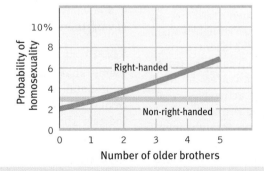

FIGURE 4.5 The fraternal birth-order effect Researcher Ray Blanchard (2008) offered these approximate curves depicting a man's likelihood of homosexuality as a function of his number of older brothers. This correlation has been found in several studies, but only among right-handed men (as about 9 in 10 men are).

TABLE 4.1 Biological Correlates of Sexual Orientation

Gay-straight trait differences

Sexual orientation is part of a package of traits. Studies—some in need of replication—indicate that homosexuals and heterosexuals differ in the following biological and behavioral traits:

- spatial abilities
- fingerprint ridge counts
- auditory system development
- handedness
- occupational preferences
- relative finger lengths

- gender nonconformity
- age of onset of puberty in males
- birth weight and size
- sleep length
- physical aggression
- walking style

On average (the evidence is strongest for males), results for gays and lesbians fall between those of straight men and straight women. Three biological influences—brain, genetic, and prenatal—may contribute to these differences.

Brain differences

- One hypothalamic cell cluster is smaller in women and gay men than in straight men.
- Gay men's hypothalamus reacts as do straight women's to the smell of sex-related hormones.

Genetic influences

- Shared sexual orientation is higher among identical twins than among fraternal twins.
- Sexual attraction in fruit flies can be genetically manipulated.
- Male homosexuality often appears to be transmitted from the mother's side of the family.

Prenatal influences

- Altered prenatal hormone exposure may lead to homosexuality in humans and other animals.
- Men with several older biological brothers are more likely to be gay, possibly due to a maternal immune-system reaction.

RETRIEVE + REMEMBER

- Which THREE of the following five factors have researchers found to have an effect on sexual orientation?
  a. An overpowering mother
  b. Size of certain cell clusters in the hypothalamus
  c. Prenatal hormone exposure
  d. A weak or distant father
  e. For men, having multiple older biological brothers

ANSWERS: b, c, e

An Evolutionary Explanation of Human Sexuality

4-10 How might evolutionary psychologists explain gender differences in sexuality and mating preferences?

Having faced many similar challenges throughout history, men and women have adapted in similar ways. Whether male or female, we eat the same foods, avoid the same predators, and perceive, learn, and remember in much the same way. It is only in areas where we have faced differing adaptive challenges—most obviously in behaviors

related to reproduction—that we differ, say **evolutionary psychologists**.

Gender Differences in Sexuality

And differ we do. Consider women's and men's sex drives. Who desires more frequent sex? Thinks more about sex? Masturbates more often? Sacrifices more to gain sex? Initiates more sex? The answers—*men, men, men, men,* and *men* (Baumeister et al., 2001). To see if you can predict such gender differences, take the quiz in **TABLE 4.2** on the next page.

Compared with lesbians, gay men (like straight men) report more interest in uncommitted sex, more responsiveness to visual sexual stimuli, and more concern with their partner's physical attractiveness (Bailey et al., 1994; Doyle, 2005; Schmitt, 2007). Gay male couples report having sex more often than do lesbian couples (Peplau & Fingerhut, 2007). And in the first year of Vermont's same-sex civil unions, and among the first 12,000 Massachusetts same-sex marriages, a striking fact emerged. Although men are roughly two-thirds of the gay population, they were only about one-third of those electing legal partnership (Crary, 2009; Rothblum, 2007).

"Not tonight, hon, I have a concussion."

evolutionary psychology the study of how our behavior and mind have changed in adaptive ways over time due to natural selection.

TABLE 4.2   Predict the Responses

Researchers asked samples of U.S. men and women whether they agreed or disagreed with the following statements. For each item below, give your best guess about the percentage of men and women who agreed with the statement.

Statement	Percentage of men who agreed	Percentage of women who agreed
1. If two people really like each other, it's all right for them to have sex even if they've known each other for a very short time.	_____	_____
2. I can imagine myself being comfortable and enjoying "casual" sex with different partners.	_____	_____
3. Affection was the reason I first had intercourse.	_____	_____
4. I think about sex every day, or several times a day.	_____	_____

Answers: (1) men, 58 percent; women, 34 percent. (2) men, 48 percent; women, 12 percent. (3) men, 25 percent; women, 48 percent. (4) men, 54 percent; women, 19 percent.

Sources: (1) Pryor et al., 2005; (2) Bailey et al., 2000; (3 and 4) Adapted from Laumann et al., 1994.

Natural Selection and Mating Preferences

The principle of **natural selection** proposes that nature selects traits and appetites that contribute to survival and reproduction. Evolutionary psychologists use this principle to explain how men and women differ more in the bedroom than in the

> "It's not that gay men are oversexed; they are simply men whose male desires bounce off other male desires rather than off female desires."
>
> Steven Pinker, *How the Mind Works,* 1997

boardroom. Our natural yearnings, they say, are our genes' way of reproducing themselves. "Humans are living fossils— collections of mechanisms produced by prior selection pressures" (Buss, 1995).

Why do women tend to be choosier than men when selecting sexual partners? Women have more at stake. To send their genes into the future, a woman must—at a minimum—nurture and protect the fetus growing inside her body for up to nine (often uncomfortable) months. And unlike men, women are limited in how many children they can have between puberty and menopause. No surprise, then, that women prefer partners who will stick around and offer their joint offspring support and

protection. Heterosexual women also prefer men who appear mature, dominant, bold, and wealthy (Asendorpf et al., 2011; Gangestad & Simpson, 2000; Singh, 1995). One study of hundreds of Welsh pedestrians asked people to rate a driver pictured at the wheel of a humble Ford Fiesta or a swanky Bentley. Men said a female driver was equally attractive in both cars. Women, however, found a male driver more attractive if he was in the luxury car (Dunn & Searle, 2010). If you put a man in a mating mind-set, how will he try to show he is a "catch"? He'll buy showy items, express aggressive intentions, and take risks (Baker & Maner, 2009; Griskevicius et al., 2009; Shan et al., 2012; Sundie et al., 2011). Thus, argue evolutionary psychologists, men pair widely; women pair wisely.

For heterosexual men, some desired traits, such as a woman's smooth skin and youthful shape, cross place and time (Buss, 1994). To evolutionary psychologists, these traits convey health and fertility. A man who mates with such women thus stands a better chance of sending his genes into the future. And sure enough, men feel most attracted to women whose waists (thanks to their genes or their surgeons) are roughly a

THE MATING GAME Evolutionary psychologists are not surprised that older men, including Bruce Willis, 58 (pictured here with his wife Emma Heming, 34), often prefer younger women whose features suggest fertility.

third narrower than their hips—a sign of future fertility (Perilloux et al., 2010). Even blind men show this preference for women with a low waist-to-hip ratio (Karremans et al., 2010).

There is a principle at work here, say evolutionary psychologists: Nature selects behaviors that increase the likelihood of sending one's genes into the future. As mobile gene machines, we are designed to prefer whatever worked for our ancestors in their environments. They were predisposed to act in ways that would produce grandchildren. Had they not been, we wouldn't be here. And as carriers of their genetic legacy, we are similarly predisposed.

Why might "gay genes" persist? Same-sex couples cannot naturally reproduce. Evolutionary psychologists suggest a possible answer: the *fertile female* theory. The theory goes like this. In generations before the birth of a homosexual man, women in that family have tended to have larger-than-normal families (Camperio-Caini et al., 2004; Iemmola & Camperio-Caini, 2009). Might the genes that dispose women to be strongly attracted to men, and therefore to have more children, also dispose some men to be attracted to men (LeVay, 2011)? If so, this could help explain why "gay genes" exist.

Critiquing the Evolutionary Perspective

4-11 What are the key criticisms of evolutionary explanations of human sexuality, and how do evolutionary psychologists respond?

Most psychologists agree that natural selection prepares us for survival and reproduction. But critics say there is a weakness in the reasoning evolutionary psychologists use to explain our mating preferences. Let's consider how an evolutionary psychologist might explain the findings in a startling study (Clark & Hatfield, 1989), and how a critic might object.

Participants were approached by a "stranger" of the other sex (someone working for the experimenter). The stranger remarked, "I have been noticing you around campus. I find you to be very attractive," and then asked one of three questions:

1. Would you go out with me tonight?
2. Would you come over to my apartment tonight?
3. Would you go to bed with me tonight?

What percentage of men and women do you think agreed to each offer?

According to the evolutionary explanation of genetic differences in sexuality, women will be choosier than men in selecting their sexual partners and will be less willing to hop in bed with a complete stranger. In fact, not a single woman—and 70 percent of men—agreed to question 3. A recent repeat of this study produced a similar result in France (Guéguen, 2011). The research seemed to support an evolutionary explanation.

Or did it? Critics note that evolutionary psychologists start with an effect—in this case, that men are more likely to accept casual sex offers—and work backward to explain what happened. What if research showed the opposite effect? If men refused an offer for casual sex, might we not reason that men who partner with one woman for life make better fathers, whose children more often survive?

Other critics ask why we should try to explain today's behavior based on decisions our ancestors made thousands of years ago. They believe social learning theory offers a better, more immediate explanation for these results. Perhaps women learn scripts by watching and imitating others in their cultures. Those scripts may teach them that sexual encounters with strangers are dangerous, and that men who ask for casual sex will not offer women much sexual pleasure (Conley, 2011). This explanation of the study's effects proposes that women react to sexual encounters in ways that their modern culture teaches them.

A third criticism focuses on the social consequences of accepting an evolutionary explanation. Are heterosexual men truly hard-wired to have sex with any woman who approaches them? If so, does this mean that men have no moral responsibility to remain faithful to their partners? Does this explanation

natural selection the principle that, among the range of inherited trait variations, those that lead to increased reproduction and survival will most likely be passed on to succeeding generations.

excuse men's sexual aggression—"boys will be boys"—because of our evolutionary history?

Evolutionary psychologists agree that much of who we are is *not* hard-wired. "Evolution forcefully rejects a genetic determinism," insisted one research team (Confer et al., 2010). Evolutionary psychologists also remind us that men and women, having faced similar adaptive problems, are far more alike than different. Natural selection has prepared us to be flexible. We humans have a great capacity for learning and social progress. We adjust and respond to varied environments. We adapt and survive, whether we live in the Arctic or the desert.

Evolutionary psychologists also agree with their critics that some traits and behaviors, such as suicide, are hard to explain in terms of natural selection (Barash, 2012; Confer et al., 2010). But they ask us to remember evolutionary psychology's testable predictions. We can, for example, scientifically test hypotheses such as: Do we tend to favor others to the extent that they share our genes or can later return our favors? (The answer is *Yes*.) And they remind us that the study of how we *came to be* need not dictate how we *ought to be*. Understanding our tendencies sometimes helps us overcome them. ∎

RETRIEVE + REMEMBER

- How do evolutionary psychologists explain gender differences in sexuality?

  ANSWER: Evolutionary psychologists theorize that women have inherited their ancestors' tendencies to be more cautious sexually, because of the challenges associated with incubating and nurturing offspring. Men have inherited an inclination to be more casual about sex, because their act of fathering requires a smaller investment.

- What are the three main criticisms of the evolutionary explanation of human sexuality?

  ANSWER: (1) It starts with an effect and works backward to propose an explanation. (2) Unethical and immoral men could use such explanations to rationalize their behavior toward women. (3) This explanation may overlook the effects of cultural expectations and socialization.

Reflections on Gender, Sexuality, and Nature–Nurture Interaction

◎ Our ancestral history helped form us as a species. Where there is variation, natural selection, and heredity, there will be evolution. Our genes form us. This is a great truth about human nature.

But our culture and experiences also shape us. If their genes and hormones predispose males to be more physically aggressive than females, culture can amplify this gender difference by supporting norms that shower benefits on macho men and on gentle women. If men are encouraged toward roles that demand physical power, and women toward more nurturing roles, each may act accordingly. By exhibiting the actions expected of those who fill such roles, men and women shape their own traits. Presidents in time become more presidential, servants more servile. Gender roles similarly shape us.

In many modern cultures, gender roles are merging. Brute strength is becoming increasingly less important for power and status (think Mark Zuckerberg and Hillary Clinton). From 1960 into the next century, women soared from 6 percent to 50 percent of U.S. medical school students (AMA, 2010). In the mid-1960s, U.S. married women devoted seven times as many hours to housework as did their husbands; by 2003 this gap had shrunk to twice as many (Bianchi et al., 2000, 2006). Such swift changes signal that biology does not fix gender roles.

If nature and nurture jointly form us, are we "nothing but" the product of nature and nurture? Are we rigidly determined?

We *are* the product of nature and nurture, but we're also an open system. Genes are all-pervasive but not all-powerful. People may reject their evolutionary role as transmitters of genes and choose not to reproduce. Culture, too, is all-pervasive. Culture bends the genders. But culture is not all-powerful. People may rebel against peer pressures and do the opposite of the expected.

We can't excuse our failings by blaming them solely on bad genes or bad influences. In reality, we are both the creatures and the creators of our worlds. So many things about us—including our gender identity and mating behaviors—are the products of our genes and environments. Yet the future-shaping stream of causation runs through our present choices. Our decisions today design our environments tomorrow. Mind matters. The human environment is not like the weather—something that just happens randomly. We are its architects. Our hopes, goals, and expectations influence our future. And that is what enables cultures to vary and to change.

San Diego Museum of Man, photograph by Rose Tyson

CULTURE MATTERS As this exhibit at San Diego's Museum of Man illustrates, children learn their culture. A baby's foot can step into any culture.

For Those Troubled by the Scientific Understanding of Human Origins

I [DM] know from my mail that some readers feel troubled by the naturalism and evolutionism of contemporary science. They worry that a science of behavior (and evolutionary science in particular) will destroy our sense of the beauty, mystery, and spiritual significance of the human creature. For those concerned, I offer some reassuring thoughts.

When Isaac Newton explained the rainbow in terms of light of differing wavelengths, British poet John Keats feared that Newton had destroyed the rainbow's mysterious beauty. Yet, nothing about the science of optics need diminish our appreciation for the drama of a rainbow arching across a rain-darkened sky.

When Galileo assembled evidence that the Earth revolved around the Sun, not vice versa, he did not offer absolute proof for his theory. Rather he offered an explanation that pulled together a variety of observations, such as the changing shadows cast by the Moon's mountains. His explanation eventually won the day because it described and explained things in a way that made sense, that hung together. Darwin's theory of evolution likewise offers an organizing principle that makes sense of many observations.

Some people of faith may find the scientific idea of human origins troubling. Many others find that it fits with their own spirituality. Pope John Paul II in 1996 welcomed a science-religion dialogue, finding it noteworthy that evolutionary theory "has been progressively accepted by researchers, following a series of discoveries in various fields of knowledge."

Meanwhile, many people of science are awestruck at the emerging understanding of the universe and the human creature. It boggles the mind—the entire universe popping out of a point some 14 billion years ago, and instantly inflating to cosmological size. Had the energy of this Big Bang been the tiniest bit less, the universe would have collapsed back on itself. Had it been the tiniest bit more, the result would have been a soup too thin to support life. Had gravity been a teeny bit stronger or weaker, or had the weight of a carbon proton been a wee bit different, our universe just wouldn't have worked.

What caused this almost-too-good-to-be-true, finely tuned universe? Why is there something rather than nothing? How did it come to be, in the words of Harvard-Smithsonian astrophysicist Owen Gingerich (1999), "so extraordinarily right, that it seemed the universe had been expressly designed to produce intelligent, sentient beings"? Is there a benevolent superintelligence behind it all? On such matters, a humble, awed, scientific silence is appropriate, suggested philosopher Ludwig Wittgenstein: "Whereof one cannot speak, thereof one must be silent."

Rather than fearing science, we can welcome its enlarging our understanding and awakening our sense of awe. In a short 4 billion years, life on Earth has come from nothing to structures as complex as a 6-billion-unit strand of DNA and the incomprehensible intricacy of the human brain. Nature seems cunningly and ingeniously devised to produce extraordinary, self-replicating, information-processing systems—us (Davies, 1992, 1999, 2004). Although we appear to have been created from dust, over eons of time, the end result is a priceless creature, one rich with potential beyond our imagining.

CHAPTER REVIEW

Gender and Sexuality

Test yourself by taking a moment to answer each of these Learning Objective Questions (repeated here from within the chapter). Then turn to Appendix D, Complete Chapter Reviews, to check your answers. Research suggests that trying to answer these questions on your own will improve your long-term memory of the concepts (McDaniel et al., 2009).

Gender Development

4-1: What are some gender similarities and differences in aggression, social power, and social connectedness?

4-2: How is our biological sex determined, and how do sex hormones influence prenatal and adolescent development?

4-3: How do gender roles and gender typing influence gender development?

Human Sexuality

4-4: How do hormones influence human sexual motivation?

4-5: What is the human sexual response cycle, and how do sexual dysfunctions and paraphilias differ?

4-6: How can sexually transmitted infections be prevented?

4-7: How do external and imagined stimuli contribute to sexual arousal?

4-8: What factors influence teenagers' sexual behaviors and use of contraceptives?

Sexual Orientation: Why Do We Differ?

4-9: What has research taught us about sexual orientation?

An Evolutionary Explanation of Human Sexuality

4-10: How might evolutionary psychologists explain gender differences in sexuality and mating preferences?

4-11: What are the key criticisms of evolutionary explanations of human sexuality, and how do evolutionary psychologists respond?

Reflections on Gender, Sexuality, and Nature–Nurture Interaction

TERMS AND CONCEPTS TO REMEMBER

Test yourself on these terms by trying to write down the definition in your own words before flipping back to the referenced page to check your answer.

gender, p. 108

aggression, p. 108

relational aggression, p. 109

X chromosome, p. 111

Y chromosome, p. 111

testosterone, p. 111

puberty, p. 111

primary sex characteristics, p. 111

secondary sex characteristics, p. 111

spermarche, p. 111

menarche [meh-NAR-key], p. 111

intersex, p. 112

role, p. 113

gender role, p. 113

gender identity, p. 113

social learning theory, p. 113

gender typing, p. 114

androgyny, p. 114

transgender, p. 114

asexual, p. 115

estrogens, p. 115

sexual response cycle, p. 116

refractory period, p. 116

sexual dysfunction, p. 116

erectile disorder, p. 117

premature ejaculation, p. 117

female orgasmic disorder, p. 117

paraphilias, p. 117

AIDS (acquired immune deficiency syndrome), p. 117

sexual orientation, p. 121

evolutionary psychology, p. 125

natural selection, p. 126

CHAPTER TEST

Test yourself repeatedly throughout your studies. This will not only help you figure out what you know and don't know; the testing itself will help you learn and remember the information more effectively thanks to the *testing effect.*

1. Females and males are very similar to each other. But one way they differ is that

   a. women are more physically aggressive than men.

   b. men are more democratic than women in their leadership roles.

   c. girls tend to play in small groups, while boys tend to play in large groups.

   d. women are more likely to commit suicide.

2. The fertilized egg will develop into a boy if it receives a(n) _____ chromosome from its father.

3. Primary sex characteristics relate to _____; secondary sex characteristics refer to _____.

   a. ejaculation; menarche

   b. breasts and facial hair; ovaries and testes

   c. emotional maturity; hormone surges

   d. reproductive organs; nonreproductive traits

4. On average, girls begin puberty at about the age of _____, boys at about the age of _____.

5. Those born with sexual anatomy that differs from "standard" male or female babies may be considered

6. *Gender role* refers to our

   a. sense of being male or female.

   b. expectations about the way males and females should behave.

   c. biological sex.

   d. unisex characteristics.

7. When children have developed a _____, they have a sense of being male or female.

8. A striking effect of hormonal changes on human sexual behavior is the

   a. end of sexual desire in men over 60.

   b. sharp rise in sexual interest at puberty.

   c. decrease in women's sexual desire at the time of ovulation.

   d. increase in testosterone levels in castrated males.

9. In describing the sexual response cycle, Masters and Johnson noted that

   a. a plateau phase follows orgasm.

   b. men experience a refractory period during which they cannot experience orgasm.

   c. the feeling that accompanies orgasm is stronger in men than in women.

   d. testosterone is released equally in women and men.

10. What is the difference between sexual dysfunctions and paraphilias?

11. The use of condoms during sex _does_ (does/doesn't) reduce the risk of getting HIV and _doesn't_ (does/doesn't) fully protect against skin-to-skin STIs.

12. An example of an external stimulus that might influence sexual behavior is
    a. blood level of testosterone.
    b. the onset of puberty.
    c. a sexually explicit film.
    d. an erotic fantasy or dream.

13. Factors contributing to unplanned teen pregnancies include
    a. low levels of testosterone during adolescence.
    b. higher intelligence level.
    c. too much communication.
    d. alcohol use.

14. Which factors have researchers thus far found to be *unrelated* to the development of our sexual orientation?

15. Evolutionary psychologists are most likely to focus on
    a. how we differ from one another.
    b. the social consequences of sexual behaviors.
    c. natural selection of the fittest adaptations.
    d. cultural expectations about the "right" ways for men and women to behave.

Find answers to these questions in Appendix E, in the back of the book.

IN YOUR EVERYDAY LIFE

Answering these questions will help you make these concepts more personally meaningful, and therefore more memorable.

1. How gender-typed are you? What has influenced your feelings of masculinity or femininity?

2. What do you think would be an effective strategy for reducing teen pregnancy?

3. Especially among younger people, there is increasing acceptance of homosexual orientation. Yet some disapproval of same-sex relationships persists in the population at large. Why do you think this is the case?

4. How has reading about the causes of sexual orientation influenced your views?

5. What do you think about the evolutionary perspective on sexual behavior? To what extent do you think genetics affects our sexual behavior?

experience
more of the
testing
effect

5 Sensation and Perception

My friend, Heather Sellers, an acclaimed writer and teacher, cannot recognize faces. Her vision is perfect, but her perception is not. In her book, *You Don't Look Like Anyone I Know* (2010), she tells of awkward moments resulting from her lifelong *prosopagnosia*—face blindness.

> In college . . . I returned from the bathroom and plunked myself down in the wrong booth, facing the wrong man. I remained unaware he was not my date even as my date (a stranger to me) accosted Wrong Booth Guy, and then stormed out. . . . I do not recognize myself in photos or videos. I can't recognize my stepsons in the soccer pick-up line; I failed to determine which husband was mine at a party, in the mall, at the market.

People sometimes see Sellers as snobby or cold. "Why did you walk past me?" a neighbor might later ask. Hoping to avoid offending others, Sellers sometimes fakes recognition. She smiles at people she passes, in case she knows them. She may pretend to know the person with whom she is talking. But there is an upside to these perception failures. When she runs into someone who previously irritated her, she typically feels no ill will. She doesn't recognize the person.

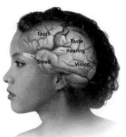

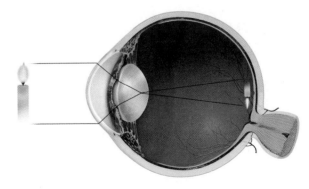

Unlike Sellers, most of us have an area on the underside of our brain's right hemisphere that helps us recognize a familiar human face as soon as we detect it—in only one-seventh of a second (Jacques & Rossion, 2006). This ability is an example of a broader principle. *Nature's sensory gifts enable each animal to obtain essential information.* Some examples:

"Time's fun when you're having flies."
Kermit the Frog

- Frogs, which feed on flying insects, have cells in their eyes that fire only in response to small, dark, moving objects. A frog could starve to death knee-deep in motionless flies. But let one zoom by and the frog's "bug detector" cells snap awake.

- Male silkworm moths' odor receptors can detect one-billionth of an ounce of sex attractant per second released by a female one mile away. That is why there continue to be silkworms.

- Human ears are most sensitive to sound *frequencies* that include human voices, especially a baby's cry.

In this chapter, we'll look more closely at what psychologists have learned about how we sense and perceive the world around us. We begin with some basic principles.

Basic Principles of Sensation and Perception

5-1 What are *sensation* and *perception*? What do we mean by *bottom-up processing* and *top-down processing*?

Sellers' curious mix of "perfect vision" and face blindness illustrates the distinction between *sensation* and *perception*. When she looks at a friend, her **sensation** is normal: Her senses detect the same information yours would, and they transmit that information to

her brain. And her **perception**—the processes by which her brain organizes and interprets the sensory input—is *almost normal*. Thus, she may recognize people from their hair, walk, voice, or peculiar build, just not from their face. Her experience is much like the struggle you or I would have trying to recognize a specific penguin.

In our everyday experiences, sensation and perception blend into one process. In this chapter, we slow down that process to study its parts. In real life, our sensory and perceptual processes work together to help us decipher the world around us.

- Our **bottom-up processing** starts at the very basic level of sensory receptors (more on those below) and works up to higher levels of processing.

- Our **top-down processing** constructs perceptions from the sensory input by drawing on our experience and expectations.

As your brain absorbs the information in **FIGURE 5.1**, bottom-up processing enables your sensory systems to detect the lines, angles, and colors that form the flower and leaves. Using top-down processing, you interpret what your senses detect.

But *how* do you do it? How do you create meaning from the blizzard of sensory stimuli bombarding your body 24 hours a day? Meanwhile, in a silent, cushioned, inner world, your brain floats in utter darkness. By itself, it sees nothing. It hears nothing. It feels nothing. *So, how does the world out there get in?* To phrase the question scientifically: How do we construct our representations of the external world? How do a campfire's flicker, crackle, and smoky scent activate neural (brain) connections? And how, from this living neurochemistry, do we create our conscious experience of the fire's motion and temperature, its aroma and beauty? In search of answers to such questions, let's look at some processes that cut across all our sensory systems. ■

FIGURE 5.1 What's going on here? Our sensory and perceptual processes work together to help us sort out the complex images, including the hidden couple in Sandro Del-Prete's drawing, *The Flowering of Love.*

© Sandro Del-Prete/www.sandrodelprete.com

RETRIEVE + REMEMBER

- What is the rough distinction between sensation and perception?

ANSWER: *Sensation* is the bottom-up process by which the physical sensory system receives and represents stimuli. *Perception* is the top-down mental process of organizing and interpreting sensory input.

From Outer Energy to Inner Brain Activity

5-2 What three steps are basic to all our sensory systems?

Every second of every day, your sensory systems perform an amazing feat: They convert one form of energy into another. Vision processes light energy. Hearing processes sound waves. All your senses

- *receive* sensory stimulation, often using specialized receptor cells.

- *transform* that stimulation into neural impulses.

• *deliver* the neural information to your brain.

The process of converting one form of energy into another form that your brain can use is called **transduction.** Later in this chapter, we'll focus on individual sensory systems. How do we see? Hear? Feel pain? Taste? Smell? Keep our balance? In each case, we'll consider these three steps—receiving, transforming, and delivering the information to the brain.

First, though, let's explore some strengths and weaknesses in our ability to detect and interpret stimuli in the vast sea of energy around us.

Thresholds

5-3 How do *absolute thresholds* and *difference thresholds* differ, and what is Weber's law?

At this moment, you and I are being struck by X-rays and radio waves, ultraviolet and infrared light, and sound waves of very high and very low frequencies. To all of these we are blind and deaf. Other animals with differing needs detect a world that lies beyond our experience (Hughes, 1999). Migrating birds stay on course aided by an internal magnetic compass. Bats and dolphins locate prey using sonar, bouncing sounds off objects. Bees navigate on cloudy days by detecting aspects of sunlight we cannot see.

The shades on our senses are open just a crack, giving us only a tiny glimpse of the energy around us. But for our needs, this is enough.

Absolute Thresholds

To some kinds of stimuli we are amazingly sensitive. Standing atop a mountain on an utterly dark, clear night, most of us could see a candle flame atop another mountain 30 miles away. We could feel the wing of a bee falling on

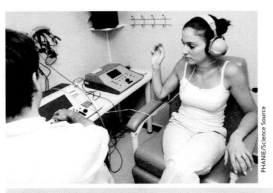

FIGURE 5.2 Absolute threshold Can I detect this sound? An *absolute threshold* is the intensity at which a person can detect a stimulus half the time. Hearing tests locate these thresholds for various frequency levels. Stimuli below your absolute threshold are subliminal.

PHANIE/Science Source

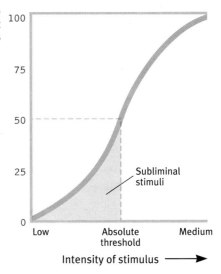

our cheek. We could smell a single drop of perfume in a three-room apartment (Galanter, 1962).

Our awareness of these faint stimuli illustrates our **absolute thresholds**—the minimum stimulation needed to detect a particular light, sound, pressure, taste, or odor 50 percent of the time. To test your absolute threshold for sounds, a hearing specialist would send tones, at varying levels, into each of your ears. The tester would then record whether or not you could hear each tone. The test results would show the point where half the time you could detect the sound and half the time you could not. That 50-50 point would define your absolute threshold for that sound.

Stimuli you cannot detect 50 percent of the time are **subliminal**—below your absolute threshold (**FIGURE 5.2**). Under certain conditions, you can be affected by stimuli so weak that you don't notice them. An unnoticed image or word can briefly **prime** your response to a later question. Let's see how this might work in a laboratory experiment. You've been asked to view slides of people and to give them either positive or negative ratings. But the trickster researchers also flash another image an instant before showing you each slide. Some of the flashed images will be emotionally positive (kittens, a romantic couple) and some will

be negative (a werewolf, a dead body). You will consciously perceive these images only as flashes of light. Will they affect your ratings?

In this real experiment, people somehow looked nicer if their photo imme-

sensation the process by which our sensory receptors and nervous system receive and represent stimulus energies from our environment.

perception the process by which our brain organizes and interprets sensory information, transforming it into meaningful objects and events.

bottom-up processing analysis that begins with the sensory receptors and works up to the brain's integration of sensory information.

top-down processing information processing guided by higher-level mental processes, as when we construct perceptions drawing on our experience and expectations.

transduction changing one form of energy into another. In sensation, the transforming of stimulus energies, such as sights, sounds, and smells, into neural impulses our brain can interpret.

absolute threshold the minimum stimulation needed to detect a particular stimulus 50 percent of the time.

subliminal below our absolute threshold for conscious awareness.

priming activating, often unconsciously, associations in our mind, thus setting us up to perceive, remember, or respond to objects or events in certain ways.

THINKING CRITICALLY ABOUT

Can Subliminal Messages Control Our Behavior?

5-4 Can we be persuaded by subliminal stimuli?

Hoping to penetrate our unconscious, marketers offer audio and video programs to help us lose weight, stop smoking, or improve our memories. Soothing ocean sounds may mask messages we cannot consciously hear, such as "I am thin," "Cigarette smoke tastes bad," or "I do well on tests. I have total recall of information." These subliminal messages, below our absolute threshold of awareness, supposedly change our lives. Such claims make two assumptions: (1) We can unconsciously sense subliminal stimuli. (2) Without our awareness, these stimuli have extraordinary persuasive powers. Can we? Do they?

As we have seen, subliminal *sensation* is a fact. Remember that an "absolute" threshold is merely the point at which we can detect a stimulus *half the time.* At or slightly below this threshold, we will still detect the stimulus some of the time.

But does this mean that claims of subliminal *persuasion* are also facts? Can subliminal recordings really help us make lasting behavioral changes, such as eating less or quitting smoking? Research results from 16 experiments on the influence of subliminal self-help recordings all reached one conclusion. The effect of subliminal stimuli is subtle and

fleeting, with no powerful, enduring influence on behavior. Not one of the recordings helped more than a placebo (Greenwald et al., 1991, 1992). And placebos work only because we *believe* they will work.

SUBLIMINAL PERSUASION? Although subliminally presented stimuli can subtly influence people, experiments discount attempts at subliminal advertising and self-improvement. (The playful message here is not actually subliminal—because you can easily perceive it.)

Babs Reingold

---

diately followed unperceived kittens rather than an unperceived werewolf (Krosnick et al., 1992). This *priming effect* happened even though the viewer's brain did not have enough time to consciously perceive the flashed images. As other experiments confirm, we may evaluate a stimulus even when we are not consciously aware of it (Ferguson & Zayas, 2009). Once again, we see the two-track mind at work: *Much of our information processing occurs automatically, out of sight, off the radar screen of our conscious mind.* Our conscious minds are upstairs executives who have delegated routine tasks to downstairs mental workers.

Can we be controlled by subliminal messages? For more on that question, see Thinking Critically About: Can Subliminal Messages Control Our Behavior?

Difference Thresholds

To function effectively, we need absolute thresholds low enough to allow us to detect important sights, sounds, textures, tastes, and smells. We also need to detect small differences among stimuli. A musician must detect tiny dif-

> The LORD is my shepherd;
>   I shall not want.
> He maketh me to lie down
>   in green pastures:
>   he leadeth me
>   beside the still waters.
> He restoreth my soul:
>   he leadeth me
>   in the paths of righteousness
>   for his name's sake.
> Yea, though I walk through the valley
>   of the shadow of death,
>   I will fear no evil:
>   for thou art with me;
>   thy rod and thy staff
>   they comfort me.
> Thou preparest a table before me
>   in the presence of mine enemies:
>   thou anointest my head with oil,
>   my cup runneth over.
> Surely goodness and mercy
>   shall follow me
>   all the days of my life:
>   and I will dwell
>   in the house of the LORD
>   for ever.

THE DIFFERENCE THRESHOLD In this world literature classic poem, the "Twenty-third Psalm," each line of the typeface increases slightly. How many lines did you read before detecting a *just noticeable difference?*

ferences when tuning an instrument. Parents must detect the sound of their own child's voice amid other children's voices. Even after I had lived two years in Scotland, sheep *baa*'s all sounded alike to my ears. But not to those of ewes, as I observed. After shearing, they would streak

directly to the *baa* of their lamb amid the chorus of other distressed lambs.

Many of life's important decisions depend on our ability to detect such small differences. The minimum difference a person can detect between any two stimuli half the time is called a **difference threshold** (or a *just noticeable difference [jnd]*). That detectable difference increases with the size of the stimulus. Thus, if you add 1 ounce to a 10-ounce weight, you will detect the difference. If you add 1 ounce to a 100-ounce weight, you probably will not.

In the nineteenth century, Ernst Weber noted something so simple and so useful that we still refer to it as **Weber's law.** This law states that for an average person to perceive a difference, two stimuli must differ by a constant minimum *percentage* (not a constant *amount*). The exact percentage varies, depending on the stimulus. Two lights, for example, must differ in intensity by 8 percent. Two objects must differ in weight by 2 percent. And two tones must differ in frequency by only 0.3 percent (Teghtsoonian, 1971). ∎

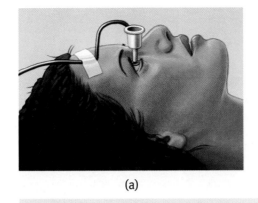

(a)

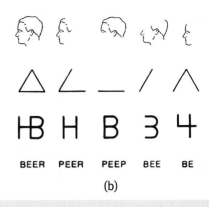

(b)

FIGURE 5.3 Sensory adaptation: Now you see it, now you don't! (a) A projector mounted on a contact lens makes the projected image move with the eye. (b) At first, the person sees the whole image, but soon it begins to break into fragments that fade and reappear. (From "Stabilized images on the retina," by R. M. Pritchard. Copyright © 1961, Scientific American, Inc. All Rights Reserved.)

Sensory Adaptation

5-5 What is the function of sensory adaptation?

Entering your neighbors' living room, you smell a musty odor. You wonder how they can stand it, but within minutes you no longer notice it. **Sensory adaptation** has come to your rescue. When we are constantly exposed to a stimulus that does not change, we become less aware of it because our nerve cells fire less frequently. (To experience sensory adaptation, move your watch up your wrist an inch. You will feel it—but only for a few moments.)

Why, then, if we stare at an object without flinching, does it *not* vanish from sight? Because, unnoticed by us, our eyes are always moving. This continual flitting from one spot to another ensures that stimulation on the eyes' receptors is always changing.

What if we actually could stop our eyes from moving? Would sights seem to vanish, as odors do? To find out, psychologists have designed clever instruments that maintain a constant image on the eye's inner surface. Imagine that we have fitted a volunteer, Mary, with one of these instruments—a miniature projector mounted on a contact lens

> "My suspicion is that the universe is not only queerer than we suppose, but queerer than we can suppose."
>
> J.B.S. Haldane, *Possible Worlds*, 1927

(FIGURE 5.3a). When Mary's eye moves, the image from the projector moves as well. So everywhere that Mary looks, the scene is sure to go.

If we project images through this instrument, what will Mary see? At first, she will see the complete image. But within a few seconds, as her sensory system begins to tire, things will get weird. Bit by bit, the image will vanish, only to reappear and then disappear—often in fragments (Figure 5.3b).

Although sensory adaptation reduces our sensitivity, it offers an important benefit. It frees us to focus on *informative* changes in our environment without being distracted by background chatter. Stinky or heavily perfumed people don't notice their odor because, like you and me, they adapt to what's constant and detect only change. Our sensory receptors are alert to novelty; bore them with repetition and they free our attention for more important things. We will see this principle again and again: *We perceive the world not exactly as it is, but as it is useful for us to perceive it.*

Our sensitivity to changing stimulation helps explain television's attention-getting power. Cuts, edits, zooms, pans, and sudden noises demand our atten-

tion. Even TV researchers marvel at its attention-grabbing power. One noted that even during interesting conversations, "I cannot for the life of me stop from periodically glancing over to the screen" (Tannenbaum, 2002).

Sensory adaptation even influences our perceptions of emotions. By creating a 50-50 morphed blend of an angry and a scared face, researchers showed that our visual system adapts to a static facial expression by becoming less responsive to that expression (Butler et al., 2008) (**FIGURE 5.4** on the next page).

Sensory adaptation and sensory thresholds are important ingredients in our perceptions of the world around us. But much of what we perceive comes not just from what's "out there" but also from the expectations that live behind our eyes and between our ears. ■

---

difference threshold the minimum difference between two stimuli required for detection 50 percent of the time. We experience the difference threshold as a *just noticeable difference* (or *jnd*).

Weber's law the principle that, to be perceived as different, two stimuli must differ by a constant minimum percentage (rather than a constant amount).

sensory adaptation reduced sensitivity in response to constant stimulation.

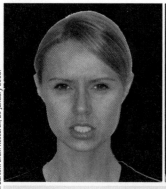

FIGURE 5.4 **Emotion adaptation** Gaze at the angry face on the left for 20 to 30 seconds, then look at the center face (looks scared, yes?). Then gaze at the scared face on the right for 20 to 30 seconds, before returning to the center face (now looks angry, yes?).

RETRIEVE + REMEMBER

- Why is it that after wearing shoes for a while, you cease to notice them (until questions like this draw your attention back to them)?

ANSWER: The shoes provide constant stimulation. *Sensory adaptation* allows us to focus on changing stimuli.

Perceptual Set

5-6 How do our expectations, assumptions, contexts, and even our motivations and emotions affect our perceptions?

As everyone knows, to see is to believe. As we also know, but less fully appreciate, to believe is to see. Through experience, we come to *expect* certain results. Those expectations may give us a **perceptual** **set,** a set of mental tendencies and assumptions that affects (top-down) what we perceive.

Perceptual set can influence what we hear, taste, feel, and see. In 1972, a British newspaper published "the most amazing pictures ever taken"—of a lake "monster" in Scotland's Loch Ness. If this information creates in you the same expectations it did in most of the paper's readers, you, too, will see the monster in a similar photo in **FIGURE 5.5**. But when a skeptical researcher approached the photos with different expectations, he saw a curved tree limb—as had others the day the photo was shot (Campbell, 1986). With this different perceptual set, you may now notice that the object is float-

> When shown the phrase
> Mary had a
>   a little lamb
>
> many people perceive
> what they expect and
> miss the repeated word.
> Did you?

ing motionless, with ripples outward in all directions around it—hardly what we would expect of a lively monster.

Perceptual set can also affect what we hear. Consider the kindly airline pilot who, on a takeoff run, looked over at his unhappy co-pilot and said, "Cheer up." Expecting to hear the usual "Gear up," the co-pilot promptly raised the wheels—before they left the ground (Reason & Mycielska, 1982).

Perceptual set similarly affects taste. One experiment invited bar patrons to sample free beer (Lee et al., 2006). When researchers added a few drops of vinegar to a brand-name beer, the tasters preferred it—unless they had been told they were drinking vinegar-laced beer. Then they expected, and usually experienced, a worse taste. In another experiment, preschool children, by a 6 to 1 margin, thought french fries tasted better when served in a McDonald's bag rather than a plain white bag (Robinson et al., 2007).

Context Effects

The effects of perceptual set show how experience helps us construct perception. But the immediate context also plays a role. Some examples:

- What is above the woman's head in **FIGURE 5.6**? In one study, most East Africans who were asked this question said that the woman was balancing a metal box or can on her head and that the family was sitting under a tree. Most Westerners, for whom head-carrying is less common and boxlike architecture is more common, said the woman was sitting under a window, indoors with her family. Cultural context helps form our perceptions.

- Does the pursuing dog in **FIGURE 5.7** look larger than the pursued one? If so, you experienced a context effect.

IT'S AMAZING HOW PEOPLE SLOW DOWN WHEN YOU POINT A HAIR DRYER AT THEM.

Keystone/Getty Images

FIGURE 5.5 **Believing is seeing** What do you perceive? Is this Nessie, the Loch Ness monster, or a log?

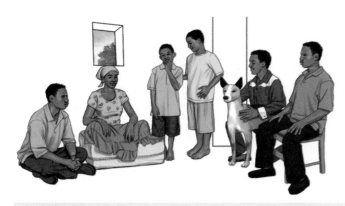

FIGURE 5.6 Culture and context effects What is above the woman's head? East African and Western viewers have responded differently to this question, reflecting their experiences in their own cultures. (Adapted from Gregory & Gombrich, 1973.)

- How tall is the shorter player in FIGURE 5.8? Here again, context creates expectations.

Context can even influence the meaning of spoken words. Hearing sad rather than happy music can tilt the mind toward hearing *mourning* rather than *morning*, *die* rather than *dye*, *pain* rather than *pane* (Halberstadt et al., 1995).

Perceptions are also influenced, top-down, by our motivations and emotions. In experiments, objects people desired, such as a water bottle when they were thirsty, seemed closer than they really were (Balcetis & Dunning, 2010). Angry people more often perceive neutral objects as guns (Baumann & DeSteno, 2010). In each case, motivation creates a bias that energizes people's perception.

Emotions can similarly shove our social perceptions in one direction or another. Spouses who feel loved and appreciated perceive less threat in stressful marital events—"He's just having a bad day" (Murray et al., 2003). Professional referees, if told a soccer team has a history of aggressive behavior, will assign more penalty cards when watching recorded play (Jones et al., 2002). Lee Ross has invited us to recall our own perceptions in different contexts: "Ever notice that when you're driving you hate pedestrians, the way they saunter through the crosswalk, almost daring you to hit them, but when you're walking you hate drivers?" (Jaffe, 2004).

* * *

The processes we've discussed so far are features shared by all our sensory systems. Let's turn now to the ways those systems are unique. We'll start with our most prized and complex sense, vision. ■

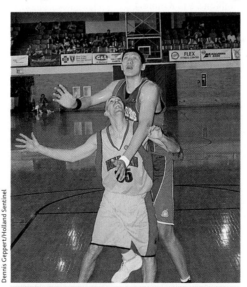

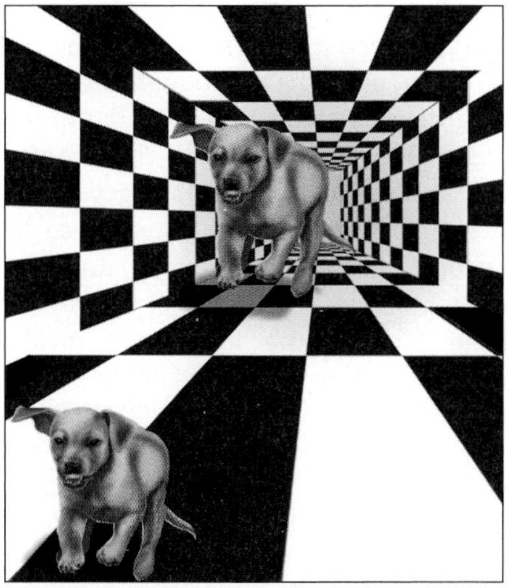

FIGURE 5.7 Context and emotional perception The context makes the pursuing dog look larger than the pursued. It isn't.

Dennis Geppert/Holland Sentinel

FIGURE 5.8 Big and "little" The "little guy" shown here is actually a 6'9" former Hope College basketball center who towers over most of us. But he seemed like a short player when matched in a semi-pro game against the world's tallest basketball player at that time—7'9" Sun Ming Ming from China.

RETRIEVE + REMEMBER

- In the context of sensation and perception, what does it mean to say that "believing is seeing"?

ANSWER: Because of *perceptual set*, our experiences, assumptions, and expectations shape our views of reality.

- Does *perceptual set* involve bottom-up or top-down processing? Why?

ANSWER: It involves top-down processing, drawing on our experiences, assumptions, and expectations.

Vision

Your eyes receive light energy and transform it into neural messages that your brain then processes into what you consciously see. How does such a taken-for-granted yet remarkable thing happen?

Light Energy: From the Environment Into the Brain

5-7 What are the characteristics of the energy we see as light?

When you look at a bright red tomato, what strikes your eyes are not bits of the color red but pulses of energy that your visual system perceives as red. What we see as visible light is but a thin slice of the wide spectrum of electro-

perceptual set a mental predisposition to perceive one thing and not another.

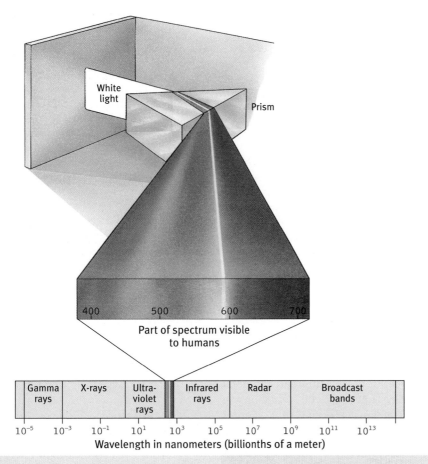

FIGURE 5.9 The wavelengths we see What we see as light is only a tiny slice of a wide spectrum of electromagnetic energy. The wavelengths visible to the human eye (shown enlarged) extend from the shorter waves of blue-violet light to the longer waves of red light.

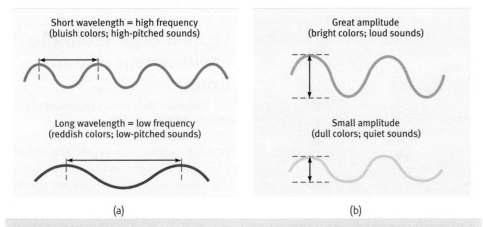

FIGURE 5.10 The physical properties of waves (a) Waves vary in *wavelength,* the distance between successive peaks. *Frequency,* the number of complete wavelengths that can pass a point in a given time, depends on the length of the wave. The shorter the wavelength, the higher the frequency. Wavelength determines the perceived color of light (and also the *pitch* of sound). (b) Waves also vary in *amplitude,* the height from peak to trough (top to bottom). Wave amplitude determines the *brightness* of colors (and also the *loudness* of sounds).

magnetic energy shown in **FIGURE 5.9.** On one end of this spectrum are the short gamma waves, no longer than the diameter of an atom. On the spectrum's other end are the mile-long waves of radio transmission. In between is the narrow band most of us can see as visible light. Other portions are visible to other animals. Bees, for instance, cannot see what we perceive as red but can see ultraviolet light.

Light travels in waves, and the shape of those waves influences what we see. Light's **wavelength**—the distance from one wave peak to the next (**FIGURE 5.10a**)—determines its **hue** (the color we experience, such as a tomato's red skin). A light wave's *amplitude,* or height, determines its **intensity**—the amount of energy it contains. Intensity influences brightness (**FIGURE 5.10b**).

Understanding the characteristics of the physical energy we see as light is one part of understanding vision. But to appreciate how we transform that energy into color and meaning, we need to know more about vision's window, the eye.

The Eye

5-8 How does the eye transform light energy into neural messages?

What color are your eyes? Asked this question, most people describe the color of their *irises.* This doughnut-shaped ring of muscle adjusts the size of your *pupil,* the small opening that controls the amount of light entering your eye. After passing through your *cornea* (the eyeball's protective covering) and pupil, light hits the *lens* in your eye. The lens then focuses the light rays into an image on your eyeball's inner surface, the **retina.**

For centuries, scientists knew that when an image of a candle passes through a small opening, it casts an upside-down mirror image on a dark wall behind. They wondered how, if the eye's structure casts this sort of image on the retina (as in **FIGURE 5.11**), can we see the world right side up?

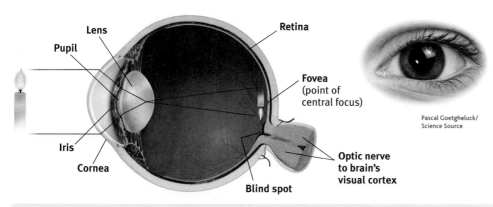

FIGURE 5.11 The eye Light rays reflected from a candle pass through the cornea, pupil, and lens. The curve and thickness of the lens change to bring nearby or distant objects into focus on the retina. Rays from the top of the candle strike the bottom of the retina. Those from the left side of the candle strike the right side of the retina. The candle's image appears on the retina upside down and reversed.

Eventually the answer became clear: The retina doesn't "see" a whole image. Rather, its millions of receptor cells behave like the prankster engineering students who make news by taking a car apart and rebuilding it in a friend's third-floor bedroom. The retina's millions of cells convert the particles of light energy into neural impulses and forward those to the brain. The brain reassembles them into what we perceive as an upright object.

The Retina

Let's follow a single light-energy particle as it makes its way to the back of your eye. Having traveled through your eye's cornea, pupil, and lens, the particle passes through your retina's outer layer of cells. As the particle reaches the retina's buried receptor cells, the **rods** and **cones,** the light energy triggers chemical changes (**FIGURE 5.12**). Those changes activate nearby *bipolar cells,* causing them to send out neural signals. These signals in turn activate neighboring *ganglion cells.* The ganglion cells' axons twine together like strands of a rope to form the **optic nerve** that will carry the information from your eye to your brain. After a momentary stopover at the thalamus, rather like changing planes in Chicago, the information flies on to its final destination, your visual cortex, at the back of your brain.

The optic nerve can send nearly 1 million messages at once through its nearly 1 million ganglion fibers. We pay a small price for this high-speed eye-to-brain highway. Where the optic nerve leaves the eye, there are no receptor cells—creating a **blind spot** (**FIGURE 5.13** on the next page). Close one eye and you won't see a black hole on your TV screen, however. Without seeking your approval, your brain fills in the hole. ■

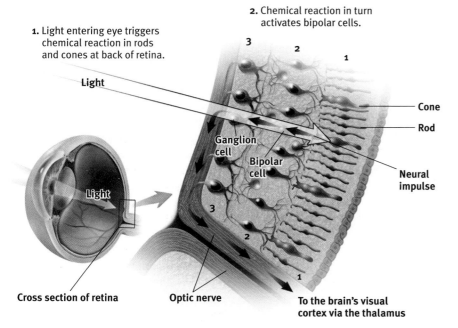

1. Light entering eye triggers chemical reaction in rods and cones at back of retina.

2. Chemical reaction in turn activates bipolar cells.

3. Bipolar cells then activate the ganglion cells, whose combined axons form the optic nerve. This nerve transmits information (via the thalamus) to the brain.

FIGURE 5.12 The retina's reaction to light

wavelength the distance from the peak of one light or sound wave to the peak of the next.

hue the dimension of color that is determined by the wavelength of light; what we know as the color names *blue, green,* and so forth.

intensity the amount of energy in a light wave or sound wave, which influences what we perceive as brightness or loudness. Intensity is determined by the wave's amplitude (height).

retina the light-sensitive inner surface of the eye; contains the receptor rods and cones plus layers of neurons that begin the processing of visual information.

rods retinal receptors that detect black, white, and gray; necessary for peripheral and twilight vision, when cones don't respond.

cones retinal receptor cells that are concentrated near the center of the retina; in daylight or well-lit conditions, cones detect fine detail and give rise to color sensations.

optic nerve the nerve that carries neural impulses from the eye to the brain.

blind spot the point at which the optic nerve leaves the eye; this part of the retina is "blind" because it has no receptor cells.

FIGURE 5.13 The blind spot

RETRIEVE + REMEMBER

- There are no receptor cells where the optic nerve leaves the eye. This creates a blind spot in your vision. To demonstrate, first close your left eye, look at the spot in Figure 5.13, and move your face away from the page to a distance at which one of the cars disappears. (Which one do you predict it will be?) Repeat with your right eye closed—and note that now the other car disappears. Can you explain why?

ANSWER: Your blind spot is on the nose side of each retina, which means that objects to your right may fall onto the right eye's blind spot. Objects to your left may fall on the left eye's blind spot. The blind spot does not normally impair your vision, because with but one eye open, your brain still fills in the blank spot.

Rods and cones differ in what they do and where they're found (TABLE 5.1). *Cones* enable you to see fine details and to perceive color. In dim light, cones don't function well, which is why the

Science Source

TABLE 5.1	Receptors in the Human Eye: Rod-Shaped Rods and Cone-Shaped Cones	
	Cones	**Rods**
Number	6 million	120 million
Location in retina	Center	Periphery
Sensitivity in dim light	Low	High
Color sensitive?	Yes	No
Detail sensitive?	Yes	No

world looks colorless at night. Cones cluster around the retina's area of central focus (the *fovea*). Many have their own hotline to the brain. Each of those cones transmits to a single bipolar cell that helps relay that cone's individual message to the visual cortex. These direct connections preserve the cones' precise information, which is why cones are better at detecting fine details.

Rods are located around the outer regions (the periphery) of your retina. Rods enable black-and-white vision, and they remain sensitive in dim light. Rods have no hotlines to the brain. Several rods pool their faint energy output and funnel it onto a single bipolar cell.

Thus, cones and rods each provide a special sensitivity:

- Cones are sensitive to detail and color.
- Rods are sensitive to faint light.

Stop for a minute and experience the rod-cone difference in sensitivity to details. Pick a word in this sentence and stare directly at it, focusing its image on the cones in the center of your eye. Notice that words a few inches off to the side appear blurred? Their image lacks details because it is striking your retina's outer regions, where most rods are found. ■

RETRIEVE + REMEMBER

Kruglov_Orda/ Shutterstock

- Some night-loving animals, such as toads, mice, rats, and bats, have impressive night vision thanks to having many more _____ (rods/cones) than _____ (rods/cones) in their retinas. These creatures probably have very poor _____ (color/black-and-white) vision.

ANSWERS: rods; cones; color

- Cats are able to open their _____ much wider than we can, which allows more light into their eyes so they can see better at night.

ANSWER: pupils

Visual Information Processing

5-9 What roles do feature detection and parallel processing play in the brain's visual information processing?

The retina's receptor cells don't just pass along electrical impulses. They begin processing sensory information by coding and analyzing it. By the time visual information travels up your optic nerve to your brain, it is on a pathway headed toward a specific location in your visual cortex, in the back of your brain. In an important stop on that journey, the optic nerve links up with neurons in the thalamus (**FIGURE 5.14**).

Feature Detection

In your brain's visual cortex, specialized nerve cells receive the information sent by individual ganglion cells in your retina. These specialized cells are called **feature detectors.** David Hubel and Torsten Wiesel (1979) received a Nobel Prize for their discovery that these cells respond to a scene's specific features— to particular edges, lines, and angles. Feature detector cells pass this information to other cortical areas, where teams of cells respond to more complex patterns, such as recognizing faces. The resulting brain activity varies depending on what's viewed. Thus, with the help of brain scans, "we can tell if a person is looking at a shoe, a chair, or a face," noted one researcher (Haxby, 2001).

One temporal lobe area by your right ear (**FIGURE 5.15**) enables you to perceive faces and, thanks to a specialized neural network, to recognize them from many viewpoints (Connor, 2010). If this region is damaged, people still may recognize other forms and objects, but, like Heather Sellers, they cannot recognize familiar faces. How do we know this? In part because in laboratory experiments, researchers have used magnetic pulses to disrupt that brain area, producing a temporary loss of face recognition.

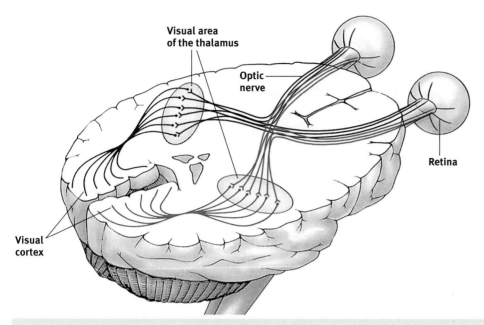

FIGURE 5.14 Pathway from the eyes to the visual cortex The retina's ganglion axons form the optic nerve. In the thalamus, the optic nerve axons connect with other neurons that run to the visual cortex.

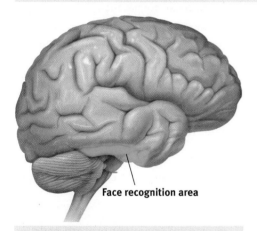

FIGURE 5.15 Face recognition processing In social animals such as humans, a large right temporal lobe area (shown here in a right-facing brain) is dedicated to the crucial task of face recognition.

Parallel Processing

One of the most amazing aspects of visual information processing is the brain's ability to divide a scene into its parts. Using **parallel processing,** your brain assigns different teams of nerve cells the separate tasks of simultaneously processing a scene's movement, form, depth, and color (**FIGURE 5.16**). You then construct your perceptions by integrating the work of these different visual teams (Livingstone & Hubel, 1988).

Destroy or disable the neural workstation for a visual subtask, and something peculiar results, as happened to "Mrs. M." (Hoffman, 1998). Since a stroke damaged areas near the rear of both sides of her brain, she has been unable to perceive movement. People in a room seem "suddenly here or there but I have not seen them moving." Pouring tea into a cup is a challenge because the fluid appears frozen—she cannot perceive it rising in the cup.

Color Vision

5-10 What theories help us understand color vision?

We talk as though objects possess color: "A tomato is red." Perhaps you have heard the old question, "If a tree falls in the forest and no one hears it, does it make a sound?" We can ask the same of color: If no one sees the tomato, is it red?

The answer is *No.* First, the tomato is everything but red, because it rejects (reflects) the long wavelengths of red. Second, the tomato's color is our mental construction. As the famous physicist Sir Isaac Newton (1704) observed more than three centuries ago, "The [light] rays are not colored." Color, like all aspects of vision, resides not in the object but in the theater of our brain. Even while dreaming, we may perceive things in color.

One of vision's most basic and intriguing mysteries is how we see the world in color. How, from the light energy striking your retina, does your brain manu-

feature detectors nerve cells in the brain that respond to specific features of a stimulus, such as edges, lines, and angles.

parallel processing the processing of many aspects of a problem or scene at the same time; the brain's natural mode of information processing for many functions, including vision.

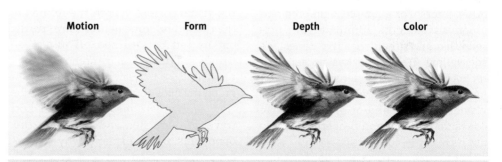

FIGURE 5.16 Parallel processing Studies of patients with brain damage suggest that the brain delegates the work of processing a scene's motion, form, depth, and color to different areas. After taking the scene apart, the brain integrates these parts into a whole perceived image.

facture your experience of color—and of so many colors? By one estimate, we can see differences among more than 1 million color variations (Neitz et al., 2001). At least most of us can. About 1 in 50 of us is "color-blind." That person is usually male, because the defect is genetically sex linked. Most people with this condition are not actually blind to all colors. They simply have trouble perceiving the difference between red and green. To understand why, we need to understand how normal color vision works.

Modern detective work on the mystery of color vision began in the nineteenth century, when Hermann von Helmholtz built on the insights of an English physicist, Thomas Young. The clue that led to their breakthrough was the knowledge that any color can be created by combining the light waves of three primary colors—red, green, and blue. Young and von Helmholtz inferred that the eye must have three types of receptors, one for each color.

Years later, researchers measured the response of various cones to different color stimuli. Their results confirmed the **Young-Helmholtz trichromatic (three-color) theory:** The eye's receptors do their color magic in teams of three. Indeed, the retina has three types of color receptors, each especially sensitive to the wavelengths of one of three colors. And those colors are, in fact, red, green, and blue. When light stimulates combinations of these cones, we see other colors. For example, when red and green wavelengths stimulate both red-sensitive and green-sensitive cones, we see yellow. The retina has no separate receptors especially sensitive to yellow. In most people with color-deficient vision, the red- and/or green-sensitive cones do not function properly. They do not have three-color vision.

Why, then, does yellow appear to be a pure color, not a mixture of red and green, the way purple is of red and blue? As Ewald Hering soon noted, trichro-

> "Only mind has sight and hearing; all things else are deaf and blind."
>
> Epicharmus, *Fragments*, 550 B.C.E.

FIGURE 5.17 Afterimage effect Stare at the center of the flag for a minute and then shift your eyes to the dot in the white space beside it. What do you see? (After tiring your neural response to black, green, and yellow, you should see their opponent colors.) Stare at a white wall and note how the size of the flag grows with the projection distance!

matic theory leaves some parts of the color vision mystery unsolved.

Hering, a physiologist, had found a clue in *afterimages*. Stare at a green square for a while and then look at a white sheet of paper, and you will see red, green's *opponent color*. Stare at a yellow square and its opponent color, blue, will appear on the white paper. (To experience this, try the flag demonstration in **FIGURE 5.17**.) Hering proposed that there must be two other color processes: One must be responsible for red-versus-green perception, and the other for blue-versus-yellow.

A century later, researchers confirmed Hering's proposal, which is now called the **opponent-process theory.** They found that color vision depends on three sets of opponent retinal processes—*red-green, yellow-blue,* and *white-black.* Recall that impulses from the retina are relayed to the thalamus on their way to the visual cortex. In both the retina and the thalamus, some neurons are "turned on" by red but "turned off" by green. Others are turned on by green but off by red (DeValois & DeValois, 1975). Like red and green marbles sent down a narrow tube, "red" and "green" messages cannot both travel at once. Red and green are thus opponents, which explains why we don't experience mixed red and green light stimuli as a reddish green. But red and blue travel in separate channels, so we *can* see a reddish-blue, or purple.

How does opponent-process theory help us understand afterimages, such as in the flag demonstration? Here's the answer (for the green changing to red):

- First, you stared at green bars, which tired the green part of the green-red pairing in your eyes.
- Then you stared at a white area. White contains all colors, including red.
- Because you had tired your green response, only the red part of the green-red pairing fired normally.

The present solution to the mystery of color vision is therefore roughly this: Color processing occurs in two stages.

1. The retina's red, green, and blue cones respond in varying degrees to different color stimuli, as the Young-Helmholtz trichromatic theory suggested.

2. The cones' responses are then processed by opponent-process cells, as Hering's theory proposed. ■

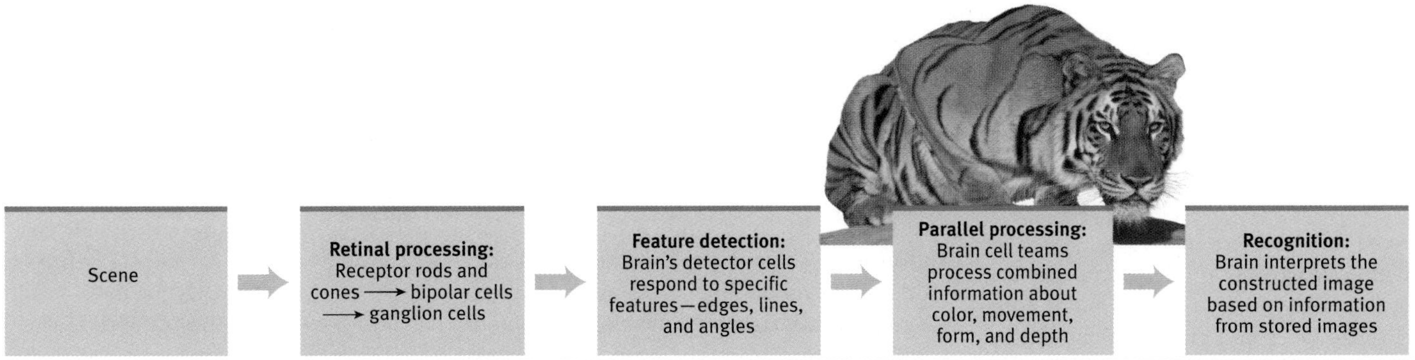

FIGURE 5.18 A simplified summary of visual information processing

Scene → **Retinal processing:** Receptor rods and cones ⟶ bipolar cells ⟶ ganglion cells → **Feature detection:** Brain's detector cells respond to specific features—edges, lines, and angles → **Parallel processing:** Brain cell teams process combined information about color, movement, form, and depth → **Recognition:** Brain interprets the constructed image based on information from stored images

Tom Walker/Photographer's Choice/Getty Images

---

* * *

Think about the wonders of visual processing. As you look at that tiger in the zoo, information enters your eyes, where it is taken apart and turned into millions of neural impulses sent to your brain. As your brain buzzes with activity, various areas focus on different aspects of the tiger's image. Finally, in some mysterious yet magnificent way, these separate teams pool their work to produce a meaningful image. You compare this with previously stored images and recognize it—a crouching tiger (FIGURE 5.18).

> "I am fearfully and wonderfully made."
> King David, Psalm 139:14

Think, too, about what is happening as you read this page. The letters are reflecting light rays into your retina, which is sending formless nerve impulses to several areas of your brain, which integrates the information and discovers meaning. And that is how we transfer information across time and space from my mind to yours. That all of this happens instantly, effortlessly, and continuously is awe-inspiring. ∎

Visual Organization

5-11 What was the main message of Gestalt psychology, and how do figure-ground and grouping principles help us perceive forms?

It's one thing to understand how we see shapes and colors. But how do we organize and interpret those sights (or sounds or tastes or smells) so that they become meaningful perceptions—a rose in bloom, a familiar face, a sunset? First, let's explore how we perceive form and depth, and how in changing conditions our perceptions remain stable.

Early in the twentieth century, a group of German psychologists noticed that people who are given a cluster of sensations tend to organize them into a **gestalt,** a German word meaning a "form" or a "whole." For example, look at FIGURE 5.19. Note that the individual elements of this figure, called a *Necker cube,* are really nothing but eight blue circles, with three white lines meeting near the center. When we view these elements all together, however, we see a cube that sometimes reverses direction. The Necker cube nicely illustrates a favorite saying of Gestalt psychologists: In perception, the whole may exceed the sum of its parts.

Over the years, the Gestalt psychologists demonstrated some principles we use to organize our sensations into perceptions. Underlying all of them is a basic truth: *Our brain does more than register*

FIGURE 5.19 A Necker cube What do you see: circles with white lines, or a cube? If you stare at the cube, you may notice that it reverses location, moving the tiny X in the center from the front edge to the back. At times the cube may seem to float in front of the page, with circles behind it. At other times, the circles may become holes in the page through which the cube appears, as though it were floating behind the page. There is far more to perception than meets the eye. (From Bradley et al., 1976.)

Young-Helmholtz trichromatic (three-color) theory the theory that the retina contains three different color receptors—one most sensitive to red, one to green, one to blue. When stimulated in combination, these cells can produce the perception of any color.

opponent-process theory the theory that opposing retinal processes (red-green, yellow-blue, white-black) enable color vision. For example, some cells are "turned on" by green and "turned off" by red; others are turned on by red and off by green.

gestalt an organized whole. Gestalt psychologists emphasized our tendency to integrate pieces of information into meaningful wholes.

information about the world. Perception is not just opening a camera's shutter and letting a picture print itself on the brain. We filter incoming information and we construct perceptions. Mind matters.

Form Perception

Imagine designing a video-computer system that, like your eye-brain system, could recognize faces at a glance. What abilities would it need?

FIGURE AND GROUND To start with, the video-computer system would need to separate faces from their backgrounds. Likewise, in our eye-brain system, our first perceptual task is to perceive any object (the *figure*) as distinct from its surroundings (the *ground*). As you hear voices at a party, the one you attend to becomes the figure; all others are part of the ground. As you read, the words are the figure; the surrounding white space is the ground. Sometimes, the same stimulus can trigger more than one perception. In **FIGURE 5.20**, for example, the **figure-ground** relationship continually reverses as we see the arrows, then the firefighters running. But always we perceive a figure standing out from a ground.

GROUPING While telling figure from ground, we (and our video-computer

system) also organize the figure into a *meaningful* form. Some basic features of a scene—such as color, movement, and light-dark contrast—we process instantly and automatically (Treisman, 1987). Our mind brings order and form to stimuli by following certain rules for **grouping.** These rules, identified by the Gestalt psychologists, and applied even by infants, illustrate how the perceived whole differs from the sum of its parts (Quinn et al., 2002; Rock & Palmer, 1990). Three examples:

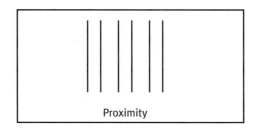

Proximity

Proximity We group nearby figures together. We see not six separate lines, but three sets of two lines.

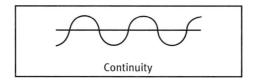

Continuity

Continuity We perceive smooth, continuous patterns rather than discontinuous ones. This pattern could be a series of alternating semicircles, but we perceive it as two continuous lines—one wavy, one straight.

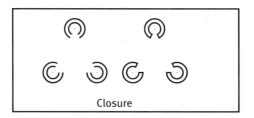

Closure

Closure We fill in gaps to create a complete, whole object. Thus, we assume that the circles on the left are complete but partially blocked by the (illusory) triangle. Add nothing more than little lines to close off the circles, and your brain stops constructing a triangle. ∎

FIGURE 5.20 Reversible figure and ground.

Depth Perception

5-12 How do we use binocular and monocular cues to see the world in three dimensions?

From the two-dimensional images falling on our retinas, our amazing brain creates three-dimensional perceptions. **Depth perception** lets us estimate an object's distance from us. At a glance, we can estimate the distance of an oncoming car or the height of a house. This ability is partly present at birth. Eleanor Gibson and Richard Walk (1960) discovered this using a model of a cliff with a drop-off area (which was covered by sturdy glass). These experiments were a product of Gibson's scientific curiosity, which kicked in while she was picnicking on the rim of the Grand Canyon. She wondered: Would a toddler peering over the rim perceive the dangerous drop-off and draw back?

Back in their laboratory, Gibson and Walk placed 6- to 14-month-old infants on the edge of a safe canyon—a **visual cliff (FIGURE 5.21)**. Their mothers then coaxed them to crawl out onto the glass. Most infants refused to do so, indicating that they could perceive depth.

Had they *learned* to perceive depth? Learning seems to be part of the answer, because crawling, no matter when it begins, seems to increase an infant's fear of heights (Campos et al., 1992). Yet, as the researchers observed, mobile newborn animals come prepared to

FIGURE 5.21 Visual cliff Eleanor Gibson and Richard Walk devised this miniature cliff with a glass-covered drop-off to find out whether crawling infants can perceive depth. Even when coaxed, most infants refuse to climb onto the sturdy glass over the cliff.

perceive depth. Even those with no visual experience—including young kittens, a day-old goat, and newly hatched chicks—will not venture across the visual cliff. Thus, it seems that biology prepares us to be wary of heights, and experience amplifies that fear.

How do we do it? *How* do we perceive depth—transforming two differing two-dimensional retinal images into a single three-dimensional perception? Our brain constructs these perceptions using information supplied by one or both eyes.

BINOCULAR CUES People who see with two eyes perceive depth thanks partly to **binocular cues.** Here's an example. With both eyes open, hold two pens or pencils in front of you and touch their tips together. Now do so with one eye closed. A more difficult task, yes?

We use binocular cues to judge the distance of nearby objects. One such cue is **retinal disparity.** Because your eyes are about 2½ inches apart, your retinas receive slightly different images of the world. By comparing these two images, your brain can judge how close an object is to you. The greater the disparity (the difference) between the two retinal

images, the closer the object. Try it. Hold your two index fingers, with the tips about half an inch apart, directly in front of your nose, and your retinas will receive quite different views. If you close one eye and then the other, you can see the difference. (You may also create a finger sausage, as in **FIGURE 5.22.**) At a greater distance—say, when you hold your fingers at arm's length—the disparity is smaller.

We could very easily build this feature into our video-computer system. Moviemakers can exaggerate retinal disparity by filming a scene with two cameras placed a few inches apart. Viewers then wear glasses that allow the left eye to see only the image from the left camera, and the right eye to see only the image from the right camera. The resulting 3-D effect, as 3-D movie fans know, mimics or exaggerates normal retinal disparity.

MONOCULAR CUES How do we judge whether a person is 10 or 100 yards away? Retinal disparity won't help us here, because there won't be much difference between the images cast on our right and left retinas. At such distances, we depend on **monocular cues** (depth cues available to each eye separately). See **FIGURE 5.23** on the next page for some examples. ∎

figure-ground the organization of the visual field into objects (the *figures*) that stand out from their surroundings (the *ground*).

grouping the perceptual tendency to organize stimuli into meaningful groups.

depth perception the ability to see objects in three dimensions, although the images that strike the retina are two-dimensional; allows us to judge distance.

visual cliff a laboratory device for testing depth perception in infants and young animals.

binocular cue a depth cue, such as retinal disparity, that depends on the use of two eyes.

retinal disparity a binocular cue for perceiving depth. By comparing images from the two eyes, the brain computes distance—the greater the disparity (difference) between the two images, the closer the object.

monocular cue a depth cue, such as interposition or linear perspective, available to either eye alone.

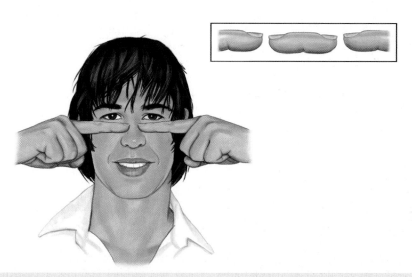

FIGURE 5.22 The floating finger sausage Hold your two index fingers about 5 inches in front of your eyes, with their tips half an inch apart. Now look beyond them and note the weird result. Move your fingers out farther, and the retinal disparity—and the finger sausage—will shrink.

Light and shadow
Shading produces a sense of depth consistent with our assumption that light comes from above. If you turn this illustration upside down, the hollow will become a hill.

Direction of passenger's motion ➡

Relative motion
As we move, objects that are actually stable may appear to move. If while riding on a bus you fix your gaze on some point—say, a house—the objects beyond the fixation point will appear to move with you. Objects in front of the point will appear to move backward. The farther an object is from the fixation point, the faster it will seem to move.

FIGURE 5.23 Monocular depth cues

Relative size
If we assume two objects are similar in size, *most* people perceive the one that casts the smaller retinal image as farther away.

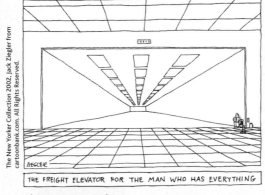

Linear perspective
Parallel lines appear to meet in the distance. The sharper the angle of convergence, the greater the perceived distance.

Interposition
Interpose means "to come between." If one object partially blocks our view of another, we perceive it as closer. The depth cues provided by interposition make this an impossible scene.

Relative height
We perceive objects higher in our field of vision as farther away. Because we assume the lower part of a figure-ground illustration is closer, we perceive it as figure (Vecera et al., 2002). Turn the illustration upside down and the black will become ground, like a night sky.

RETRIEVE + REMEMBER

- How do we normally perceive depth?

ANSWER: We are normally able to perceive depth thanks to (1) binocular cues (that are based on our retinal disparity), and (2) monocular cues (that include relative height, relative size, interposition, linear perspective, light and shadow, and relative motion).

Perceptual Constancy

5-13 How do perceptual constancies help us construct meaningful perceptions?

So far, we have noted that our video-computer system must perceive objects as we do—as having a distinct form and location. Its next task is to recognize objects without being deceived by changes in their color, shape, or size. We call this top-down process **perceptual constancy.** This feat would be an enormous challenge for a video-computer system.

COLOR CONSTANCY Our experience of color depends on an object's *context*. This would be clear if you viewed an isolated tomato through a paper tube. As the light—and thus the tomato's reflected wavelengths—changed over the course of the day, the tomato's color would also seem to change. But if you viewed that tomato without the tube, as one item in a bowl of fresh fruit and vegetables, its color would remain roughly constant as the lighting shifts. This perception of consistent color is known as **color constancy.**

> "From there to here, from here to there, funny things are everywhere."
>
> Dr. Seuss, *One Fish, Two Fish, Red Fish, Blue Fish,* 1960

Color constancy is amazing. A blue poker chip under indoor lighting will, in sunlight, reflect wavelengths that match those reflected by a sunlit gold chip (Jameson, 1985). Yet bring a goldfinch indoors and it won't look like a bluebird. The color is not in the bird's feathers. You and I see color thanks to our brain's ability to decode the meaning of the light reflected by an object *relative to the objects surrounding it.* FIGURE 5.24 dramatically illustrates the ability of a blue object to appear very different in three different contexts. Yet we have no trouble seeing these disks as blue. Paint manufacturers have learned this lesson. Knowing that your perception of a paint color will be determined by other colors in your home, many now offer trial samples you can test in that context. The take-home lesson: *Comparisons govern our perceptions.*

SHAPE AND SIZE CONSTANCIES
Thanks to *shape constancy,* we usually perceive the form of familiar objects, such as the door in FIGURE 5.25, as constant even while our retinas receive changing images of them.

Thanks to *size constancy,* we perceive objects as having a constant size even while our distance from them varies. We assume a car is large enough to carry people, even when we see its tiny image from two blocks away. This assumption also shows the close connection between perceived *distance* and perceived *size.* Perceiving an object's distance gives us cues to its size. Likewise, knowing its general size—that the object is a car—provides us with cues to its distance.

Even in size-distance judgments, however, we consider an object's context. The dogs in Figure 5.7 earlier in this chapter cast identical images on our retinas. Using linear perspective as a cue (see Figure 5.23), our brain assumes that the pursuing dog is farther away. We therefore perceive it as larger. It isn't.

The interplay between perceived size and perceived distance helps explain

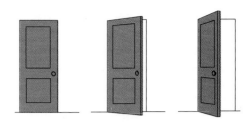

FIGURE 5.25 Shape constancy An opening door looks more and more like a trapezoid. Yet we still perceive it as a rectangle.

several well-known illusions, including the *Moon illusion.* The Moon looks up to 50 percent larger when near the horizon than when high in the sky. Can you imagine why? One reason is that cues to objects' distances make the horizon Moon—like the distant dog in Figure 5.7—appear farther away. If it's farther away, our brain assumes, it must be larger than the Moon high in the night sky (Kaufman & Kaufman, 2000). Take away the distance cues—by looking at the horizon Moon (or each dog) through a paper tube—and the object will immediately shrink.

Mistaken judgments like these reveal the workings of our normally effective perceptual processes. The perceived relationship between distance and size is usually valid. But under special circumstances it can lead us astray—as when helping to create the Moon illusion.

Form perception, depth perception, and perceptual constancy illuminate how we organize our visual experiences. Perceptual organization applies to our other senses, too. It explains why we may perceive a clock's steady tick not as a *tick-tick-tick-tick* but as grouped sounds,

(a)   (b)

FIGURE 5.24 Color depends on context (a) Believe it or not, these three blue disks are identical in color. (b) Remove the surrounding context and see what results.

R. Beau Lotto at University College, London

perceptual constancy perceiving objects as unchanging (having consistent color, brightness, shape, and size) even as illumination and retinal images change.

color constancy perceiving familiar objects as having consistent color, even if changing illumination alters the wavelengths reflected by the object.

say *TICK-tick, TICK-tick*. Perception, however, is more than organizing stimuli. Perception also requires what would be a challenge to our video-computer system: interpretation—finding meaning in what we perceive.

Visual Interpretation

The debate over whether our perceptual abilities spring from our nature or our nurture has a long history. To what extent do we learn to perceive? German philosopher Immanuel Kant (1724–1804) maintained that knowledge comes from our *inborn* ways of organizing sensory experiences. Psychology's findings support this idea. We do come equipped to process sensory information. But British philosopher John Locke (1632–1704) argued that through our experiences we also *learn* to perceive the world. Psychology also supports this idea. We do learn to link an object's distance with its size. So, just how important is experience? How much does it shape our perceptual interpretations?

Experience and Visual Perception

5-14 What does research on restored vision, sensory restriction, and perceptual adaptation reveal about the effects of experience on perception?

RESTORED VISION AND SENSORY RESTRICTION Writing to John Locke, a friend wondered what would happen if "a man *born* blind, and now adult, [was] taught by his *touch* to distinguish between a cube and a sphere." Could he, if made to see, visually distinguish the two? Locke's answer was *No*, because the man would never have learned to see the difference.

This clever question has since been put to the test with a few dozen adults who, though blind from birth, have later gained sight (Gregory, 1978; von Senden, 1932). Most were born with cataracts—clouded lenses that allowed them to see only light and shadows, rather as someone might see a foggy image through

LEARNING TO SEE At age 3, Mike May lost his vision in an explosion. Decades later, after a new cornea restored vision to his right eye, he got his first look at his wife and children. Alas, although signals were now reaching his visual cortex, it lacked the experience to interpret them. May could not recognize expressions, or faces, apart from features such as hair. Yet he can see an object in motion and has learned to navigate his world and to marvel at such things as dust floating in sunlight (Abrams, 2002).

a Ping-Pong ball sliced in half. After surgery that removed the cataracts, the patients could tell the difference between figure and ground, and they could sense colors. This suggests that we are born with these aspects of perception. But much as Locke supposed, they often could not visually recognize objects that were familiar by touch.

In experiments, researchers have outfitted infant kittens and monkeys with goggles through which they could see only diffuse, unpatterned light (Wiesel, 1982). After infancy, when the goggles were removed, the animals' reactions were much like those of humans born with cataracts. They could distinguish color, but not form. Their eyes were healthy. Their retinas still sent signals to their visual cortex. But the brain's cortical cells had not developed normal connections. Thus, the animals remained functionally blind to shape. Experience guides the brain's development as it forms pathways that affect our perceptions.

In humans and other animals, similar sensory restrictions later in life do no permanent harm. When researchers

cover an adult animal's eye for several months, its vision will be unaffected after the eye patch is removed. When surgeons remove cataracts that develop during late adulthood, most people are thrilled at the return to normal vision.

The effect of sensory restriction on infant cats, monkeys, and humans suggests there is a *critical period* (Chapter 3) for normal sensory and perceptual development. Nurture sculpts what nature has endowed. In less dramatic ways, it continues to do so throughout our lives. Our visual experience matters. For example, despite concerns about their social costs (more on this in Chapter 14), action video games sharpen spatial skills such as visual attention, eye-hand coordination and speed, and tracking multiple objects (Spence & Feng, 2010).

PERCEPTUAL ADAPTATION Given a new pair of glasses, we may feel a little strange, even dizzy. Within a day or two, we adjust. Our **perceptual adaptation** to changed visual input makes the world seem normal again. But imagine a far more dramatic new pair of glasses—one that shifts the apparent location of objects 40 degrees to the left. When you first put them on and toss a ball to a friend, it sails off to the left. Walking forward to shake hands with the person, you veer to the left.

Could you adapt to this distorted world? Baby chicks cannot. When fitted with such lenses, they have continued to peck where food grains *seemed* to be (Hess, 1956; Rossi, 1968). But we humans adapt to distorting lenses quickly. Within a few minutes, your throws would again be accurate, your stride on target. Remove the lenses and you would experience an aftereffect. At first your throws would err in the *opposite* direction, sailing off to the right. But again, within minutes you would adjust.

Indeed, given an even more radical pair of glasses—one that literally turns the world upside down—you could still adapt. Psychologist George Stratton (1896) experienced this when he invented, and for eight days wore, a device that flipped

PERCEPTUAL ADAPTATION "Oops, missed," thinks researcher Hubert Dolezal as he views the world through inverting goggles. Yet, believe it or not, kittens, monkeys, and humans can adapt to an upside-down world.

left to right *and* up to down, making him the first person to experience a right-side-up retinal image while standing upright. The ground was up, the sky was down.

At first, when Stratton wanted to walk, he found himself searching for his feet, which were now "up." Eating was nearly impossible. He became nauseated and depressed. But Stratton persisted, and by the eighth day he could comfortably reach for an object in the right direction and walk without bumping into things. When Stratton finally removed the headgear, he readapted quickly.

In later experiments, people wearing such optical gear have even been able to ride a motorcycle, ski the Alps, and fly an airplane (Dolezal, 1982; Kohler, 1962). The world around them still seemed above their heads or on the wrong side. But by actively moving about in these topsy-turvy worlds, they adapted to the context and learned to coordinate their movements.

The Nonvisual Senses

For humans, vision is the major sense. More of our brain cortex is devoted to vision than to any other sense. Yet without hearing, touch, taste, smell, and body position and movement, our experience of the world would be vastly diminished.

Hearing

Like our other senses, our hearing, or **audition,** helps us adapt and survive. For those of us who communicate invisibly—by shooting unseen air waves across space and receiving back the same—hearing provides information and enables relationships. Hearing loss is therefore an invisible disability. To not catch someone's name, to not grasp what someone is asking, and to miss the hilarious joke is to be deprived of what others know, and sometimes to feel excluded. (As a person with hearing loss, I know the feeling.)

Most of us, however, can hear a wide range of sounds, and the ones we hear best are those in a range similar to that of the human voice. With normal hearing, we are remarkably sensitive to faint sounds, such as a child's whimper. (If our ears were much more sensitive, we would hear a constant hiss from the movement of air molecules.) Our distant ancestors' survival may have depended on this keen hearing when hunting or being hunted.

We also are acutely sensitive to sound differences. Among thousands of possible voices, we easily detect a friend's on the phone, from the moment she says "Hi." A fraction of a second after such events stimulate the ear's receptors, millions of neurons have worked together to extract the essential features, compare them with past experience, and identify the sound (Freeman, 1991). For hearing as for seeing, we wonder: How do we do it?

Sound Waves: From the Environment Into the Brain

5-15 What are the characteristics of the air pressure waves that we hear as meaningful sounds?

Hit a piano key and you will unleash the energy of sound waves. Jostling molecules of air, each bumping into the next, create waves of compressed and expanded air, like the ripples on a pond circling out from a tossed stone. Our ears detect these brief air pressure changes.

Like light waves, sound waves vary in shape. The height, or *amplitude,* of sound waves determines their *loudness.* Their length, or **frequency,** determines the **pitch** we experience. Long waves have low frequency—and low pitch. Short waves have high frequency—and high pitch. Sound waves produced by a violin are much shorter and faster than those produced by a cello or a bass guitar.

We measure sounds in *decibels,* with zero decibels representing the absolute threshold for hearing. Normal conver-

THE SOUNDS OF MUSIC A violin's short, fast waves create a high pitch. The longer, slower waves of a cello or bass create a lower pitch. Differences in the waves' height, or amplitude, also create differing degrees of loudness. (To review the physical properties of light and sound waves, see Figure 5.10.)

perceptual adaptation in vision, the ability to adjust to an artificially displaced or even inverted visual field.

audition the sense or act of hearing.

frequency the number of complete wavelengths that pass a point in a given time (for example, per second).

pitch a tone's experienced highness or lowness; depends on frequency.

sation registers at about 60 decibels. A whisper falls at about 20 decibels, and a jet plane passing 500 feet overhead registers at about 110 decibels. Prolonged exposure to any sounds above 85 decibels can produce hearing loss. ■

RETRIEVE + REMEMBER

- The amplitude of a sound wave determines our perception of _____ (loudness/pitch).

  ANSWER: loudness

- The longer the sound waves are, the _____ (lower/higher) their frequency is and the _____ (higher/lower) their pitch.

  ANSWERS: lower; lower

Decoding Sound Waves

5-16 How does the ear transform sound energy into neural messages?

. . . .

How does vibrating air morph into nerve impulses that your brain can decode as sounds? The process begins when sound waves entering your outer ear trigger a mechanical chain reaction. In the first step, your outer ear channels the waves into the *auditory canal*, where they bump against your *eardrum*, causing this tight membrane to vibrate (**FIGURE 5.26a**). In your middle ear, three tiny bones (the *hammer, anvil,* and *stirrup*), pick up the vibrations and transmit them to the **cochlea,** a snail-shaped tube in your inner ear. The incoming vibrations then cause the cochlea's membrane (the

oval window) to vibrate, creating ripples in the fluid inside the cochlea (**FIGURE 5.26b**). The ripples bend the *hair cells* lining the *basilar membrane* on the cochlea's surface, like wind bending a wheat field. The hair cell movements in turn trigger impulses in nerve cells. Axons from those nerve cells combine to form the *auditory nerve,* which carries the neural messages to the thalamus and then on to your *auditory cortex* in your brain's temporal lobe. From vibrating air to fluid waves to electrical impulses to the brain: You hear!

My vote for the most magical part of the hearing process is the hair cells— "quivering bundles that let us hear" thanks to their "extreme sensitivity and extreme speed" (Goldberg, 2007). A cochlea has 16,000 of these cells, which sounds like a lot until we compare that with an eye's 130 million or so receptors. But consider a hair cell's responsiveness. Deflect the tiny bundles of *cilia* on its tip by only the width of an atom (thinking

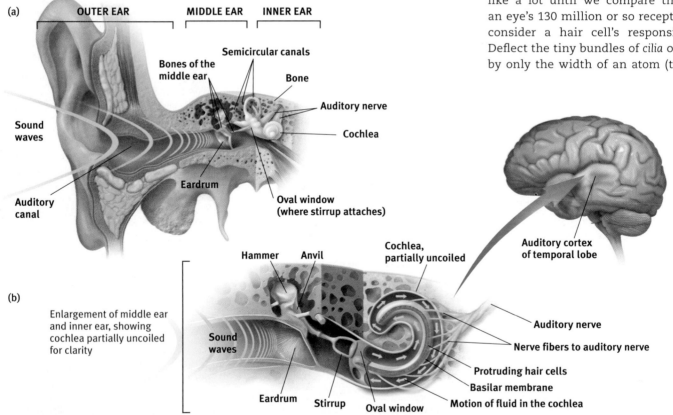

FIGURE 5.26 **Hear here: How we transform sound waves into nerve impulses that our brain interprets** (a) The outer ear funnels sound waves to the eardrum. The bones of the middle ear (hammer, anvil, and stirrup) amplify and relay the eardrum's vibrations through the oval window into the fluid-filled cochlea. (b) As shown in this detail of the middle and inner ear, the resulting pressure changes in the cochlear fluid cause the basilar membrane to ripple, bending the hair cells on its surface. Hair cell movements trigger impulses at the base of the nerve cells, whose fibers join together to form the auditory nerve. That nerve sends neural messages to the thalamus and on to the auditory cortex.

big, imagine moving the top of the Eiffel Tower half an inch), and the alert hair cell will trigger a neural response (Corey et al., 2004).

At the highest frequency you can perceive, your ears' hair cells can switch their neural current on and off a thousand times per second! As you might expect of something so sensitive, they are, however, delicate. Blast them with hunting rifle shots or blaring iPods (as teen boys more than girls do), and the hair cells' cilia will begin to wither or fuse together. No wonder men's hearing tends to be less acute than women's (Zogby, 2006).

Hearing loss that results from damage to hair cell receptors or their associated nerves is called **sensorineural hearing loss** (or nerve deafness). Occasionally, disease damages hair cell receptors, but more often the culprits are biological changes linked with heredity, aging, and prolonged exposure to ear-splitting noise or music. Sensorineural hearing loss is more common than **conduction**

THAT BAYLEN MAY HEAR The crowd roared as Super Bowl–winning quarterback Drew Brees celebrated New Orleans' 2010 victory. To protect the delicate hair cells of his son, Baylen, Brees had him wear ear muffs.

hearing loss, which is caused by damage to the mechanical system that conducts sound waves to the cochlea.

Hair cells have been compared to carpet fibers. Walk around on them and they will spring back with a quick vacuuming. But leave a heavy piece of furniture on them and they may never rebound. As a general rule, any noise we cannot talk over (loud machinery, fans screaming at a sports event, iPods blasting at maximum volume) may be harmful, especially if we are exposed to it often or for a long time (Roesser, 1998). And if our ears ring after such experiences, we have been bad to our unhappy hair cells. As pain alerts us to possible bodily harm, ringing in the ears alerts us to possible hearing damage. It is hearing's version of bleeding. People who spend many hours in a loud club, behind a power mower, or above a jackhammer should wear earplugs, or they risk needing a hearing aid later. "Condoms or, safer yet, abstinence," say sex educators. "Earplugs or walk away," say hearing educators.

Nerve deafness cannot be reversed. For now, the only way to restore hearing is a sort of bionic ear—a **cochlear implant.** These electronic devices translate sounds into electrical signals that, wired into the cochlea's nerves, transmit information about sound to the brain. By 2009, some 188,000 people worldwide had undergone surgery to have the devices implanted (NIDCD, 2011). When given to deaf kittens and human infants, cochlear implants have seemed to trigger an "awakening" of brain areas normally used in hearing (Klinke et al., 1999; Sireteanu, 1999). They can help children become skilled in oral communication (especially if they receive them as preschoolers or even before age 1) (Dettman et al., 2007; Schorr et al., 2005).

How Do We Locate Sounds?

Why don't we have one big ear—perhaps above our one nose? "All the better to hear you with," as the wolf in the

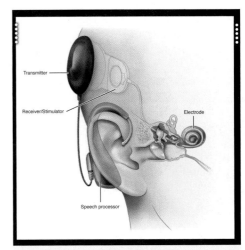

HARDWARE FOR HEARING Cochlear implants work by translating sounds into electrical signals that are transmitted to the cochlea and, via the auditory nerve, on to the brain.

fairy tale said to Red Riding Hood. The placement of our two ears allows us to hear two slightly different messages. We benefit in two ways. If a car to the right honks, the right ear receives a more *intense* sound, and it receives the sound slightly *sooner* than the left ear does. Because sound travels 750 miles per hour and our ears are only 6 inches apart, the intensity difference and the time lag are very small. Lucky for us, our supersensitive sound system can detect such tiny differences (Brown &

cochlea [KOHK-lee-uh] a coiled, bony, fluid-filled tube in the inner ear; sound waves traveling through the cochlear fluid trigger nerve impulses.

sensorineural hearing loss hearing loss caused by damage to the cochlea's receptor cells or to the auditory nerves; also called *nerve deafness*.

conduction hearing loss hearing loss caused by damage to the mechanical system that conducts sound waves to the cochlea.

cochlear implant a device for converting sounds into electrical signals and stimulating the auditory nerve through electrodes threaded into the cochlea.

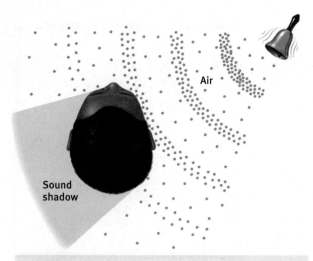

FIGURE 5.27 **Why two ears are better than one**
Sound waves strike one ear sooner and more intensely than the other. From this information, our brain can compute the sound's location. As you might therefore expect, people who lose all hearing in one ear often have difficulty locating sounds.

Deffenbacher, 1979; Middlebrooks & Green, 1991) **(FIGURE 5.27)**.

Touch

5-17 **What are the four basic touch sensations, and which of them has identifiable receptors?**

If you had to lose one sense, which would you give up? If you could have only one, which would you keep?

Although not the first sense to come to mind, touch might be a good choice for keeping. Right from the start, touch is essential to our development. Infant monkeys allowed to see, hear, and smell—but not touch—their mothers become desperately unhappy (Suomi et al., 1976). Those separated by a screen with holes that allow touching are much less miserable. As we noted in Chapter 3, premature babies gain weight faster and go home sooner if they are stimulated by hand massage. As lovers, we yearn to touch—to kiss, to stroke, to snuggle.

Humorist Dave Barry may have been right to jest that your skin "keeps people from seeing the inside of your body, which is repulsive, and it prevents your organs from falling onto the ground."

But skin does much more. Our "sense of touch" is actually a mix of distinct skin senses for *pressure, warmth, cold,* and *pain.* Other skin sensations are variations of the basic four. For example, stroking side-by-side pressure spots creates a tickle. Repeated gentle stroking of a pain spot creates an itching sensation. Touching side-by-side cold and pressure spots triggers a sense of wetness (which you can experience by touching dry, cold metal).

Surprisingly, there is no simple relationship between what we feel at a given spot and the type of specialized nerve ending found there. Only pressure has identifiable receptors.

Touch sensations involve more than the feelings on our skin, however. A self-administered tickle activates a smaller area of the brain's cortex than the same tickle would from something or someone else (Blakemore et al., 1998). (The brain is wise enough to be most sensitive to unexpected stimulation.)

Pain

5-18 **What influences our feelings of pain, and how can we treat pain?**

Be thankful for occasional pain. Pain is your body's way of telling you something has gone wrong. Drawing your attention to a burn, a break, or a sprain, pain tells you to change your behavior immediately. "Stay off that turned ankle!" The rare people born without the ability to feel pain may experience severe injury or even die before early adulthood. Without the discomfort that makes us shift positions, their joints fail from excess strain. Without the warnings of pain, infections run wild, and injuries can multiply (Neese, 1991).

Many more people live with chronic pain, which is rather like an alarm that won't shut off. Backaches, arthri-

"PAIN IS A GIFT" So said a doctor studying 13-year-old Ashlyn Blocker. Ashlyn has a rare genetic mutation that prevents her from feeling pain. At birth she didn't cry. As a child, she ran around for two days on a broken ankle. She has put her hands on a hot machine and burned the flesh off. And she has reached into boiling water to retrieve a dropped spoon. "Everyone in my class asks me about it, and I say, 'I can feel pressure, but I can't feel pain.' *Pain!* I cannot feel it!" (Heckert, 2010).

tis, headaches, and cancer-related pain prompt two questions: What is pain? And how might we control it?

UNDERSTANDING PAIN Our pain experiences vary widely. As a group, women tend to be more sensitive to pain. This was confirmed in a study of disease-related pain reported in the medical records of 11,000 patients (Ruau et al., 2012). But our individual sensitivity to pain also varies.

Your experience of pain depends in part on the genes you inherited and on your physical characteristics. Your feeling of pain is a physical event. It is in part a property of your senses, of the region where you feel it. But your pain system differs from some of your other senses. There is no simple neural cord

AP Photo/Reinhold Matay

DISTRACTED FROM THE PAIN After a tackle in the first half of a competitive game, BK Hacken soccer player Mohammed Ali Khan (in white) said he "had a bit of pain" but thought it was "just a bruise." With his attention focused on the game, he played on. In the second half he was surprised to learn from an attending doctor that the leg was broken and would need two months to heal.

running from a sensing device on your skin to a specific area in your brain. No one type of stimulus triggers pain (as light triggers vision). The human body has no special receptors (like the retina's rods and cones) for pain. Instead, different sensory receptors (*nociceptors*) in your skin detect hurtful temperatures, pressure, or chemicals. Thus, like the other touch senses, pain is in part a bottom-up property of your senses. But it is more than that. It is also a product of your attention, your expectations, and your culture (Gatchel et al., 2007; Reimann et al., 2010). Your experience of pain is also a top-down product of your brain.

With pain, as with sights and sounds, the brain sometimes gets its signals crossed. Consider people's experiences of *phantom limb sensations*. After having a limb amputated, some 7 in 10 people feel pain or movement in

limbs that no longer exist (Melzack, 1992, 1993). Some try to step off a bed onto a phantom leg or to lift a cup with a phantom hand. Even those born without a limb sometimes feel sensations in the missing part. The brain comes prepared to anticipate "that it will be getting information from a body that has limbs" (Melzack, 1998).

Phantoms may haunt our other senses, too. People with hearing loss often experience the sound of silence: *tinnitus*, a phantom sound of ringing in the ears. Those who lose vision to glaucoma, cataracts, diabetes, or macular degeneration may experience phantom sights—non-threatening hallucinations (Ramachandran & Blakeslee, 1998). And damage to nerves in the systems for tasting and smelling can give rise to phantom tastes or smells, such as ice water that seems sickeningly sweet or fresh air that reeks of rotten food (Goode, 1999). The point to remember: *We see, hear, taste, smell, and feel pain with our brain.*

CONTROLLING PAIN If pain is where body meets mind—if pain is both a physical and a psychological event—then it should be treatable both physically and psychologically.

We have some built-in pain controls. Our brain releases a natural painkiller—*endorphins*—in response to severe pain or even vigorous exercise. The release of these neurotransmitters has a soothing effect so that the pain we experience may be greatly reduced. People who carry a gene that boosts the normal supply of endorphins are less bothered by pain, and their brain is less responsive to it (Zubieta et al., 2003). Others, who carry a gene that disrupts the neural pain circuit, may be unable to experience pain (Cox et al., 2006). These discoveries point the way toward future pain medications that mimic the genetic effects.

When endorphins combine with distraction, amazing things can happen.

> "Pain is increased by attending to it."
>
> Charles Darwin, *Expression of Emotions in Man and Animals,* 1872

Sports injuries may go unnoticed until the after-game shower (thus demonstrating that the pain in sprain is mainly in the brain). During a 1989 basketball game, Ohio State University player Jay Burson broke his neck—and kept playing. Halfway through his lap of the 2012 Olympics 1600 meter relay, Manteo Mitchell broke one of his leg bones—and kept running.

Health care professionals understand the value of distractions and may divert patients' attention with a pleasant image ("*Think of a warm, comfortable environment*") or a request to perform some task ("*Count backward by 3s*"). These are effective ways to activate brain pathways that decrease pain and increase tolerance (Edwards et al., 2009). A well-trained nurse may chat with needle-shy patients and ask them to look away when the needle is inserted. For burn victims receiving painful wound care, an even more effective distraction is escaping into a computer-generated 3-D world, like the snow scene in **FIGURE 5.28** on the next page. Functional MRI (fMRI) scans reveal that playing in the virtual reality reduces the brain's pain-related activity (Hoffman, 2004).

The brain-pain connection is also clear in our *memories* of pain. The pain we experience may not be the pain we remember. In experiments, and after medical procedures, people tend to overlook how long a pain lasted. Their memory snapshots may instead record its *peak moment* and also how much pain they felt at the *end*. Researchers discovered this when they asked people to put one hand in painfully cold water for 60 seconds, and then the other hand in the same painfully cold water for 60 seconds, followed by a slightly less painful 30 seconds more (Kahneman et al., 1993). Which of these experiences would you expect to recall as most painful?

Curiously, when asked which trial they would prefer to repeat, most pre-

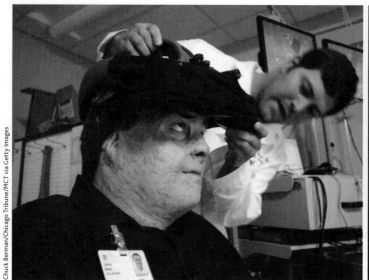

Chuck Berman/Chicago Tribune/MCT via Getty Images

Chuck Berman/Chicago Tribune/MCT via Getty Images

FIGURE 5.28 Virtual-reality pain control For burn victims undergoing painful skin repair, escaping into virtual reality (like the icy playground shown here) can be a powerful distraction. With attention focused elsewhere, pain and the brain's response to painful stimulation decrease.

ferred the longer trial, with more net pain—but less pain at the end. A physician used this principle with patients undergoing colon exams—lengthening the discomfort by a minute, but lessening its intensity at the end (Kahneman, 1999). Patients experiencing this taperdown treatment later recalled the exam as less painful than those whose pain ended abruptly. (As a painful root canal is coming to an end, if the oral surgeon asks if you'd like to go home, or to have a few more minutes of milder discomfort, there's a case to be made for prolonging your hurt.)

Because pain is in the brain, hypnosis may also bring relief.

HYPNOSIS AND PAIN RELIEF Imagine you are about to be hypnotized. The hypnotist invites you to sit back, fix your gaze on a spot high on the wall, and relax. In a quiet, low voice the hypnotist suggests, "Your eyes are growing tired . . . Your eyelids are becoming heavy . . . now heavier and heavier . . . They are beginning to close . . . You are becoming more deeply relaxed . . . Your breathing is now deep and regular . . . Your muscles are becoming more and more relaxed. Your whole body is beginning to feel like lead."

After a few minutes of this *hypnotic induction,* you may experience **hypnosis.** Hypnotists have no magical mind-control power; they merely focus people on certain images or behaviors. To some extent, we are all open to suggestion. But highly hypnotizable people—such as the 20 percent who can carry out a suggestion not to react to an open bottle of smelly ammonia—are especially suggestible and imaginative (Barnier & McConkey, 2004; Silva & Kirsch, 1992).

Has hypnosis proved useful in relieving pain? *Yes.* When unhypnotized people put their arms in an ice bath, they felt intense pain within 25 seconds (Druckman & Bjork, 1994; Jensen, 2008). When hypnotized people did the same after being given suggestions to feel no pain, they indeed reported feeling little pain. As some dentists know, light hypnosis can reduce fear, and thus hypersensitivity to pain.

Hypnosis inhibits pain-related brain activity. In surgical experiments, hypnotized patients have required less medication, recovered sooner, and left the hospital earlier than unhypnotized control patients (Askay & Patterson, 2007; Hammond, 2008; Spiegel, 2007). Nearly 10

percent of us can become so deeply hypnotized that even major surgery can be performed without anesthesia. Half of us can gain at least some relief from hypnosis. The surgical use of hypnosis has flourished in Europe, where one Belgian medical team has performed more than 5000 surgeries with a combination of hypnosis, local anesthesia, and a mild sedative (Song, 2006).

Psychologists have proposed two explanations for how hypnosis works. One theory proposes that hypnosis produces a *dissociation*—a split—between normal sensations and conscious awareness. Dissociation theory seeks to explain why, when no one is watching, hypnotized people may carry out **posthypnotic suggestions** (which are made during hypnosis but carried out after the person is no longer hypnotized) (Perugini et al., 1998). It also offers an explanation for why people hypnotized for pain relief may show brain activity in areas that receive sensory information, but not in areas that normally process pain-related information.

Those who reject the hypnosis-as-dissociation view believe that hypnosis is instead a form of normal *social influ-*

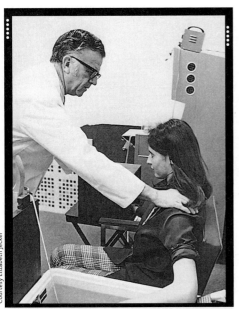

Courtesy Elizabeth Jecker

DISSOCIATION OR SOCIAL INFLUENCE? A hypnotized woman being tested by famous researcher Ernest Hilgard showed no pain when her arm was placed in an ice bath. But asked to press a key if some part of her felt the pain, she did so. To Hilgard (1986, 1992), this was evidence of *dissociation,* or divided consciousness. The *social influence* perspective, however, maintains that people responding this way are caught up in playing the role of "good subject."

ence (Lynn et al., 1990; Spanos & Coe, 1992). In this view, hypnosis is a by-product of normal social and mental processes. Like actors caught up in their roles, people begin to feel and behave in ways appropriate for "good hypnotic subjects." They may allow the hypnotist to direct their attention and fantasies away from pain. ■

RETRIEVE + REMEMBER

• Which of the following options has NOT been proven to reduce pain?

a. Distraction

b. Hypnosis

c. Phantom limb sensations

d. Endorphins

ANSWER: c

Taste

5-19 How are our senses of taste and smell similar?

Like touch, our sense of taste involves several basic sensations. Until recently, these sensations were thought to be *sweet, sour, salty,* and *bitter* (McBurney & Gent, 1979). In recent decades, many researchers have searched for specialized fibers that might act as nerve pathways for those four taste sensations. During this search, they discovered a receptor for a fifth sensation—the savory, meaty taste of *umami.* You may have experienced umami as the flavor enhancer monosodium glutamate (MSG), often used in Chinese or Thai food.

Tastes exist for more than our pleasure. Nice tastes attracted our ancestors to protein- or energy-rich foods that enabled their survival (see **TABLE 5.2**). Unpleasant tastes warned them away from new foods that might contain toxins and lead to food poisoning, which can be especially deadly for children. The taste preferences of today's 2- to 6-year-olds reflect this inherited biological wisdom. At this age, children are typically fussy eaters and often turn away from new meat dishes or bitter-tasting vegetables, such as spinach and brussels sprouts (Cooke et al., 2003). But another tool in our early ancestors' survival kit was learning. Across the globe, frustrated parents have happily discovered that when children are given repeated small tastes of disliked new foods, they typi-

TABLE 5.2	The Survival Functions of Basic Tastes
Taste	**Indicates**
Sweet	Energy source
Salty	Sodium essential to biological processes
Sour	Potentially toxic acid
Bitter	Potential poisons
Umami	Proteins to grow and repair tissue

(Adapted from Cowart, 2005.)

Lauren Burke/Digital Vision/Getty Images

cally learn to accept these foods (Wardle et al., 2003).

Taste is a chemical sense. Inside each little bump on the top and sides of your tongue are 200 or more taste buds. Each bud contains a pore. Projecting into each of these pores are antenna-like hairs from 50 to 100 taste receptor cells. These hairs detect information about molecules of food chemicals and carry it back to your taste receptor cells. Some receptors respond mostly to sweet-tasting molecules, others to salty-, sour-, umami-, or bitter-tasting ones. All send their messages to your brain.

It doesn't take much to trigger those responses. If a stream of water is pumped across your tongue, the addition of a concentrated salty or sweet taste for only one-tenth of a second will get your attention (Kelling & Halpern, 1983). When a friend asks for "just a taste" of your soft drink, you can squeeze off the straw after an eyeblink.

Taste receptors reproduce themselves every week or two, so if hot food burns your tongue, it hardly matters. However,

hypnosis a social interaction in which one person (the subject) responds to a suggestion by another person (the hypnotist) that certain perceptions, feelings, thoughts, or behaviors will spontaneously occur.

posthypnotic suggestion a suggestion, made during a hypnosis session, to be carried out after the subject is no longer hypnotized; used by some clinicians to help control undesired symptoms and behaviors.

as you grow older, it may matter more, because the number of taste buds in your mouth will decrease, as will your taste sensitivity (Cowart, 1981). (No wonder adults enjoy strong-tasting foods that children resist.) Smoking and alcohol can speed up the loss of taste buds.

Expectations can influence taste. When told a sausage roll was "vegetarian," people in one experiment judged it inferior to its identical partner labeled "meat" (Allen et al., 2008). In another experiment, hearing that a wine cost $90 rather than its real $10 price made it taste better and triggered more activity in a brain area that responds to pleasant experiences (Plassman et al., 2008). There's more to taste than meets the tongue.

Smell

Life begins with an inhale and ends with an exhale. Between birth and death, you will daily inhale and exhale nearly 20,000 breaths of life-sustaining air, bathing your nostrils in a stream of scent-laden molecules. Our experience of smell (*olfaction*) is strikingly intimate. With every breath, we inhale something of whatever or whoever it is we smell.

Smell, like taste, is a chemical sense. We smell something when molecules of a substance carried in the air reach a tiny cluster of receptor cells at the top of each nasal cavity. These 20 million olfactory receptor cells, waving like sea anemones on a reef, respond selectively—to the aroma of a cake baking, to a wisp of smoke, to a friend's fragrance. Instantly (bypassing the brain's sensory control center, the thalamus), they alert the brain.

Aided by smell, a mother fur seal returning to a beach crowded with pups will find her own. Human mothers and nursing infants also quickly learn to recognize each other's scents (McCarthy, 1986). Our sense of smell is, however, less impressive than our senses of seeing and hearing. Looking out across a garden, we see its forms and colors in wonderful detail and hear a variety of birds

THE NOSE KNOWS Humans have some 20 million olfactory receptors. A bloodhound has 220 million (Herz, 2007).

Layne Bailey/The Charlotte Observer/AP Photo

singing. Yet we smell few of the garden's scents without sticking our nose into the blossoms.

Odor molecules come in many shapes and sizes—so many, in fact, that it takes hundreds of different receptors, designed by a large family of genes, to recognize these molecules (Miller, 2004). We do not have one distinct receptor for each detectable odor. Instead, different combinations of receptors send messages to the brain's olfactory cortex. As the English alphabet's 26 letters can combine to form many words, so olfactory receptors can produce different patterns to identify the 10,000 odors we can detect (Malnic et al., 1999). These different combinations activate different neural patterns (Zou & Buck, 2006). And that is what allows us to smell the difference between fresh-brewed and hours-old coffee.

Odors can evoke memories (**FIGURE 5.29**). Though it's difficult to recall odors by name, we have a remarkable capacity to recognize long-forgotten smells and their associated personal tales (Engen, 1987; Schab, 1991). Pleasant odors can call up pleasant memories (Ehrlichman & Halpern, 1988). The smell of the sea, the

scent of a perfume, or an aroma of a favorite relative's kitchen can bring to mind a happy time. It's a link one British travel agent chain understood well. To

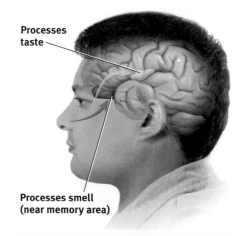

Processes taste

Processes smell (near memory area)

FIGURE 5.29 Taste, smell, and memory Information from the taste buds (yellow arrow) travels to an area between the frontal and temporal lobes of the brain. It registers in an area not far from where the brain receives information from our sense of smell, which interacts with taste. The brain's circuitry for smell (red area) also connects with areas involved in memory storage, which helps explain why a smell can trigger a memory.

evoke memories of relaxing on sunny, warm beaches, the company once piped the aroma of coconut sunscreen into its shops (Fracassini, 2000).

Our brain's circuitry helps explain an odor's power to evoke feelings, memories, and behaviors. A hotline runs between the brain area that receives information from the nose and brain centers associated with emotions and memories. Thus, when put in a foul-smelling room, people expressed harsher judgments of lying or keeping a found wallet and more negative attitudes toward gays (Inbar et al., 2011; Schnall et al., 2008). And when riding on a train car with the citrus scent of a cleaning product, people leave less rubbish behind (de Lange et al., 2012). ■

BODIES IN SPACE These high school competitive cheer team members can thank their vestibular sense for the information that enables their brains to monitor their bodies' position so expertly.

RETRIEVE + REMEMBER

- How does our system for sensing smell differ from our sensory systems for vision, touch, and taste?

ANSWER: We have two types of retinal receptors, four basic touch senses, and five taste sensations. But we have no basic smell receptors. Instead, different combinations of odor receptors send messages to the brain, enabling us to recognize some 10,000 different smells.

Body Position and Movement

5-20 How do we sense our body's position and movement?

Using only the five familiar senses we have so far considered, you could not put food in your mouth, stand up, or reach out and touch someone. Nor could you perform the "simple" act of moving your arm to grasp someone's hand. That act requires a sixth sense that informs you about the current position of your arms and hands and their changing positions as you move them. Just taking one step forward requires feedback from, and instructions to, some 200 muscles. The brain power engaged in all this exceeds even the mental activity involved in reasoning. Let's take a closer look.

You came equipped with millions of position and motion sensors. They are all over your body—in your muscles, tendons, and joints—and they are continually feeding information to your brain. Twist your wrist one degree, and these sensors provide an immediate update. This sense of your body parts' position and movement is **kinesthesia.**

You can momentarily imagine being blind or deaf. Close your eyes, plug your ears, and experience the dark stillness. But what would it be like to live without being able to sense the positions of your limbs when you wake during the night? Ian Waterman of Hampshire, England, knows. In 1972, at age 19, Waterman contracted a rare viral infection that destroyed the nerves that enabled his sense of light touch and of body position and movement. People with this condition report feeling disconnected from their body, as though it is dead, not real, not theirs (Sacks, 1985). With prolonged practice, Waterman has learned to walk and eat—by visually focusing on his limbs and directing them accordingly. But if the lights go out, he crumples to the floor (Azar, 1998).

For all of us, vision interacts with kinesthesia. Stand with your right heel in front of your left toes. Easy. Now close your eyes and you will probably wobble.

Working hand in hand with kinesthesia is our **vestibular sense.** This companion sense monitors your head's (and thus your body's) position and movement. Controlling this sense of equilibrium are two structures in your inner ear. The first, your *semicircular canals,* look like a three-dimensional pretzel (Figure 5.26a). The second, connecting those canals with the cochlea, is the pair of *vestibular sacs,* which contain fluid that moves when your head rotates or tilts. When this movement stimulates hairlike receptors, sending messages to the cerebellum at the back of your brain, you sense your body position and maintain your balance.

If you twirl around and then come to an abrupt halt, it takes a few seconds for the fluid in your semicircular canals and for your kinesthetic receptors to return to their neutral state. The aftereffect fools your dizzy brain with the sensation that you're still spinning. This illustrates a principle underlying perceptual illu-

kinesthesia [kin-ehs-THEE-see-a] the system for sensing the position and movement of individual body parts.

vestibular sense the sense of body movement and position, including the sense of balance.

sions: *Mechanisms that normally give us an accurate experience of the world can, under special conditions, fool us.* Understanding how we get fooled provides clues to how our perceptual system works. ■

* * *

TABLE 5.3 summarizes the sensory systems we have discussed.

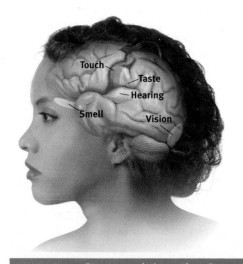

Sensory Interaction

5-21 How do our senses interact?

◎ Our senses are not totally separate information channels. In interpreting the world, our brain blends their inputs. Consider what happens to your sense of taste if you hold your nose, close your eyes, and have someone feed you various foods. A slice of apple may be indistinguishable from a chunk of raw potato. A piece of steak may taste like cardboard. Without their smells, a cup of cold coffee may be hard to distinguish from a glass of red wine. To savor a taste, we normally breathe the aroma through our nose—which is why eating is not much fun when you have a bad cold. Smell can also change our perception of taste: A drink's strawberry odor enhances our perception of its sweetness. Even touch can influence taste. Depending on its texture, a potato chip "tastes" fresh or stale (Smith, 2011). This is **sensory interaction** at work—the principle that one sense may influence another. Smell + texture + taste = flavor.

Vision and hearing may similarly interact. We can see a tiny flicker of

Action on Hearing Loss

FIGURE 5.30 Sensory interaction When a hard-of-hearing listener sees an animated face forming the words being spoken at the other end of a phone line, the words become easier to understand (Knight, 2004).

light more easily if it is accompanied by a short burst of sound (Kayser, 2007). And we can more easily hear soft sounds if they are paired with visual cues (**FIGURE 5.30**). If I (as a person with hearing loss) watch a video with on-screen captions, I have no trouble hearing the words I see. But if I then decide I don't need the captions, and turn them off, I will quickly realize I do need them. The eyes guide the ears.

What do you suppose happens if the eyes and ears disagree? What if we *see* a speaker saying one syllable while we *hear* another? Surprise: We may perceive a third syllable that blends both inputs. Seeing the mouth movements for *ga* while hearing *ba*, we may perceive *da*. This is known as the *McGurk effect,* after one of its discoverers (McGurk & MacDonald, 1976).

We have seen that our perceptions have two main ingredients: Our bottom-up sensations and our top-down cognitions (such as expectations, attitudes, thoughts, and memories). The brain circuits processing our bodily sensations may sometimes interact with brain circuits responsible for cognition.

TABLE 5.3	Summarizing the Senses	
Sensory System	**Source**	**Receptors**
Vision	Light waves striking the eye	Rods and cones in the retina
Hearing	Sound waves striking the outer ear	Cochlear hair cells in the inner ear
Touch	Pressure, warmth, cold on the skin	Skin receptors detect pressure, warmth, cold, and pain
Taste	Chemical molecules in the mouth	Basic tongue receptors for sweet, sour, salty, bitter, and umami
Smell	Chemical molecules breathed in through the nose	Millions of receptors at top of nasal cavity
Body position—kinesthesia	Any change in position of a body part, interacting with vision	Kinesthetic sensors in joints, tendons, and muscles
Body movement—vestibular sense	Movement of fluids in the inner ear caused by head/body movement	Hairlike receptors in the inner ear's semicircular canals and vestibular sacs

The result is **embodied cognition.** Some examples:

- *Physical warmth may promote social warmth.* After holding a warm drink rather than a cold one, people are more likely to rate someone more warmly, feel closer to them, and behave more generously (IJzerman & Semin, 2009; Williams & Bargh, 2008).

- *Social exclusion can literally feel cold.* After being given the cold shoulder by others in an experiment, people judge the room as colder than do those who were treated warmly (Zhong & Leonardelli, 2008).

- *Political expressions may mimic body positions.* When leaning to the left—by sitting in a left- rather than right-leaning chair, or squeezing a handgrip with their left hand, or using a mouse with their left hand—people lean more toward the left in their expressed political attitudes (Oppenheimer & Trail, 2010).

In a few rare individuals, the brain circuits for two or more senses become joined in a condition called *synesthesia*. In these cases, one sort of sensation (such as hearing sound) produces another (such as seeing color). Thus, hearing music may activate color-sensitive cortex regions, triggering a sensation of color (Brang et al., 2008; Hubbard et al., 2005). Seeing the number 3 may evoke a taste sensation (Ward, 2003).

Sensation and cognition, as we have seen, are the two streams that feed the river of perception. If perception is the product of these two sources, what can we say about *extrasensory perception*, which claims that perception can occur apart from sensory input? For more on that question, see Thinking Critically About: ESP—Perception Without Sensation?

* * *

Most of us will never know what it is like to see colorful music, to feel pressure but never pain, or to be unable to recognize the faces of friends and family. But within our ordinary sensation and perception lies much that is truly extraordinary. More than a century of research has revealed many of the secrets of sensation and perception, yet for future generations of researchers, there remain profound and genuine mysteries to solve.

sensory interaction the principle that one sense may influence another, as when the smell of food influences its taste.

embodied cognition the influence of bodily sensations, gestures, and other states on cognitive preferences and judgments.

THINKING CRITICALLY ABOUT

ESP—Perception Without Sensation?

5-22 How do ESP claims hold up when put to the test by scientists?

Without sensory input, are we capable of **extrasensory perception (ESP)?** Nearly half of Americans believe we are (AP, 2007; Moore, 2005).

Are there indeed people—*any* people—who can read minds, see through walls, or correctly predict the future? Before we evaluate claims of ESP, let's review them. The most testable and, for this chapter, most relevant ESP claims are

- *telepathy:* mind-to-mind communication.

- *clairvoyance:* perceiving remote events, such as a house on fire in another state.

- *precognition:* perceiving future events, such as an unexpected death in the next month.

Closely linked with these are claims of *psychokinesis,* or "mind over matter," such as using mind power alone to raise a table or affect the roll of a die. (The claim is illustrated by the wry request, "Will all those who believe in psychokinesis please raise my hand?")

WHEN PSYCHICS PROPOSE

Dan Piraro/Bizarro.com

Facts or Fantasies?

Most research psychologists and scientists—including 96 percent of the scientists in one U.S. National Academy of Sciences survey—are skeptical of ESP claims (McConnell, 1991). No greedy—or charitable—psychic has been able to choose the winning lottery jackpot ticket, or make billions on the stock market. In 30 years, unusual predictions have almost never come true, and psychics have virtually never anticipated any of the year's headline events (Emery, 2004, 2006). The new-century psychics failed to anticipate the big-news events such as the horror of 9/11. (Where were the psychics on 9/10 when we needed them?)

extrasensory perception (ESP) the controversial claim that perception can occur apart from sensory input, such as through *telepathy, clairvoyance,* and *precognition.*

(continued)

ESP—Perception Without Sensation? (continued)

What about the hundreds of visions offered by psychics working with the police? When asked, 65 percent of the police departments of America's 50 largest cities said they had never used psychics (Sweat & Durm, 1993). Of those that had, not one had found them helpful. Psychics' police work has been no more accurate than guesses made by others (Nickell, 1994, 2005; Reiser, 1982).

Are everyday people's "visions" any more accurate? Do our dreams predict the future, or do they only seem to do so when we recall or reconstruct them in light of what has already happened? After aviator Charles Lindbergh's baby son was kidnapped and murdered in 1932 but before the body was discovered, two psychologists invited people to report their dreams about the child (Murray & Wheeler, 1937). How many replied? 1300. How many accurately saw the child dead? 65. How many also correctly anticipated the body's location—buried among trees? Only 4. Although this number was surely no better than chance, to those 4 dreamers the accuracy of their *apparent* prior knowledge must have seemed uncanny.

Given the billions of events in the world each day and given enough days, some stunning coincidences are sure to occur. By one careful estimate, chance alone would predict that more than a thousand times a day someone on Earth will think of another person and then within the next five minutes will learn of that person's death (Charpak & Broch, 2004). With enough time and people, the improbable becomes inevitable.

TESTING PSYCHIC POWERS IN THE BRITISH POPULATION
Psychologists created a "mind machine" to see if people could influence or predict a coin toss (Wiseman & Greening, 2002). Using a touch-sensitive screen, visitors to British festivals were given four attempts to call heads or tails, playing against a computer that kept score. By the time the experiment ended, nearly 28,000 people had predicted 110,959 tosses—with 49.8 percent correct.

Testing ESP

When faced with claims of mind reading or out-of-body travel or communication with the dead, how can we separate bizarre ideas from those that sound strange but are true? At the heart of science is a simple answer: *Test them to see if they work.* If they do, so much the better for the ideas. If they don't, so much the better for our skepticism.

How might we test ESP claims in a controlled experiment? An experiment differs from a staged demonstration. In the laboratory, the experimenter controls what the "psychic" sees and hears. On stage, the "psychic" controls what the audience sees and hears.

Daryl Bem, a respected social psychologist, once joked that "a psychic is an actor playing the role of a psychic" (1984). Yet this one-time skeptic has reignited hopes for scientific evidence of ESP with nine experiments that seemed to show people anticipating future events (2011). In one, for example, people guessed when an erotic scene would appear on a screen in one of two randomly selected positions. Participants guessed right 53.1 percent of the time, beating 50 percent by a small but statistically significant margin.

Bem's research survived critical reviews by a top-tier journal. But other critics found the methods "badly flawed" (Alcock, 2011) or the statistical analyses "biased" (Wagenmakers et al., 2011). Still others predicted the results could not be repeated by "independent and skeptical researchers" (Helfand, 2011).

Anticipating such skepticism, Bem has made his computer materials available to anyone who wishes to replicate his studies. Regardless of the outcomes, science has done its work. It has been open to a find-

> *"A person who talks a lot is sometimes right."*
> Spanish proverb

ing that challenges its own worldview, and follow-up research is now assessing the validity of that finding. And that is how science sifts crazy-sounding ideas, leaving most on the historical waste heap while occasionally surprising us.

One skeptic, magician James Randi, has a long-standing offer of $1 million to be given "to anyone who proves a genuine psychic power under proper observing conditions" (Randi, 1999; Thompson, 2010). French, Australian, and Indian groups have made similar offers of up to 200,000 euros (CFI, 2003). Large as these sums are, the scientific seal of approval would be worth far more. To silence those who say there is no ESP, one need only produce a single person who can demonstrate a single, reproducible ESP event. (To silence those who say pigs can't talk would take but one talking pig.) So far, no such person has emerged.

RETRIEVE + REMEMBER

- If an ESP event occurred under controlled conditions, what would be the next best step to confirm that ESP really exists?

ANSWER: The ESP event would need to be reproduced in other scientific studies.

CHAPTER REVIEW

Sensation and Perception

Test yourself by taking a moment to answer each of these Learning Objective Questions (repeated here from within the chapter). Then turn to Appendix D, Complete Chapter Reviews, to check your answers. Research suggests that trying to answer these questions on your own will improve your long-term memory of the concepts (McDaniel et al., 2009).

Basic Principles of Sensation and Perception

5-1: What are *sensation* and *perception*? What do we mean by *bottom-up processing* and *top-down processing*?

5-2: What three steps are basic to all our sensory systems?

5-3: How do *absolute thresholds* and *difference thresholds* differ, and what is Weber's law?

5-4: Can we be persuaded by subliminal stimuli?

5-5: What is the function of sensory adaptation?

5-6: How do our expectations, assumptions, contexts, and even our motivations and emotions affect our perceptions?

Vision

5-7: What are the characteristics of the energy we see as light?

5-8: How does the eye transform light energy into neural messages?

5-9: What roles do feature detection and parallel processing play in the brain's visual information processing?

5-10: What theories help us understand color vision?

5-11: What was the main message of Gestalt psychology, and how do figure-ground and grouping principles help us perceive forms?

5-12: How do we use binocular and monocular cues to see the world in three dimensions?

5-13: How do perceptual constancies help us construct meaningful perceptions?

5-14: What does research on restored vision, sensory restriction, and perceptual adaptation reveal about the effects of experience on perception?

The Nonvisual Senses

5-15: What are the characteristics of the air pressure waves that we hear as meaningful sounds?

5-16: How does the ear transform sound energy into neural messages?

5-17: What are the four basic touch sensations, and which of them has identifiable receptors?

5-18: What influences our feelings of pain, and how can we treat pain?

5-19: How are our senses of taste and smell similar?

5-20: How do we sense our body's position and movement?

Sensory Interaction

5-21: How do our senses interact?

5-22: How do ESP claims hold up when put to the test by scientists?

TERMS AND CONCEPTS TO REMEMBER

Test yourself on these terms by trying to write down the definition in your own words before flipping back to the referenced page to check your answer.

sensation, p. 134
perception, p. 134
bottom-up processing, 134
top-down processing, 134
transduction, p. 135
absolute threshold, p. 135
subliminal, p. 135
priming, p. 135
difference threshold, p. 136
Weber's law, p. 136
sensory adaptation, p. 137
perceptual set, p. 138

wavelength, p. 140
hue, p. 140
intensity, p. 140
retina, p. 140
rods, p. 141
cones, p. 141
optic nerve, p. 141
blind spot, p. 141
feature detectors, p. 142
parallel processing, p. 143
Young-Helmholtz trichromatic (three-color) theory, p. 144

opponent-process theory, p. 144
gestalt, p. 145
figure-ground, p. 146
grouping, p. 146
depth perception, p. 146
visual cliff, p. 146
binocular cue, p. 147
retinal disparity, p. 147
monocular cue, p. 147
perceptual constancy, p. 148
color constancy, p. 149
perceptual adaptation, p. 150
audition, p. 151
frequency, p. 151

pitch, p. 151
cochlea [KOHK-lee-uh], p. 152
sensorineural hearing loss, 153
conduction hearing loss, 153
cochlear implant, p. 153
hypnosis, p. 156
posthypnotic suggestion, 156
kinesthesia [kin-ehs-THEE-see-a], p. 159
vestibular sense, p. 159
sensory interaction, p. 160
embodied cognition, p. 161
extrasensory perception (ESP), p. 161

CHAPTER TEST

Test yourself repeatedly throughout your studies. This will not only help you figure out what you know and don't know; the testing itself will help you learn and remember the information more effectively thanks to the *testing effect*.

1. Sensation is to _____ as perception is to _____.
   a. absolute threshold; difference threshold
   b. bottom-up processing; top-down processing
   c. interpretation; detection
   d. grouping; priming

2. The process by which we organize and interpret sensory information is called _____.

3. Subliminal stimuli are
   a. too weak to be processed by the brain in any way.
   b. consciously perceived more than 50 percent of the time.
   c. always strong enough to affect our behavior.
   d. below our absolute threshold for conscious awareness.

4. Another term for difference threshold is the _____ _____ _____.

5. Weber's law states that for a difference to be perceived, two stimuli must differ by
   a. a fixed or constant energy amount.
   b. a constant minimum percentage.
   c. a constantly changing amount.
   d. more than 7 percent.

6. Sensory adaptation helps us focus on
   a. visual stimuli.
   b. auditory stimuli.
   c. constant features of the environment.
   d. important changes in the environment.

7. Our perceptual set influences what we perceive. This mental tendency reflects our
   a. experiences, assumptions, and expectations.
   b. perceptual adaptation.
   c. priming ability.
   d. difference thresholds.

8. The characteristic of light that determines the color we experience, such as blue or green, is _____.

9. The amplitude of a sound wave determines our perception of loudness. The amplitude of a light wave determines our perception of _____.
   a. brightness.   c. meaning.
   b. color.   d. distance.

10. The blind spot in your retina is located where
    a. there are rods but no cones.
    b. there are cones but no rods.
    c. the optic nerve leaves the eye.
    d. the bipolar cells meet the ganglion cells.

11. Cones are the eye's receptor cells that are especially sensitive to _____ light and are responsible for our _____ vision.
    a. bright; black-and-white
    b. dim; color
    c. bright; color
    d. dim; black-and-white

12. The cells in the visual cortex that respond to certain lines, edges, and angles are called _____ _____.

13. The brain's ability to process many aspects of an object or a problem simultaneously is called _____ _____.

14. Two theories together account for color vision. The Young-Helmholtz trichromatic (three-color) theory shows that the eye contains _____, and the opponent-process theory accounts for the nervous system's having _____.
    a. opposing retinal processes; three pairs of color receptors
    b. opponent-process cells; three types of color receptors
    c. three pairs of color receptors; opposing retinal processes
    d. three types of color receptors; opponent-process cells

15. What mental processes allow you to perceive a lemon as yellow?

16. Our tendencies to fill in the gaps and to perceive a pattern as continuous are two different examples of the organizing principle called
    a. interposition.
    b. depth perception.
    c. shape constancy.
    d. grouping.

17. In listening to a concert, you attend to the solo instrument and perceive the orchestra as accompaniment. This illustrates the organizing principle of
    a. figure-ground.
    b. shape constancy.
    c. grouping.
    d. depth perception.

18. The visual cliff experiments suggest that
    a. infants have not yet developed depth perception.
    b. crawling human infants and very young animals perceive depth.
    c. we have no way of knowing whether infants can perceive depth.
    d. unlike other species, humans are able to perceive depth in infancy.

19. Depth perception underlies our ability to
    a. group similar items in a gestalt.
    b. perceive objects as having a constant shape or form.
    c. judge distances.
    d. fill in the gaps in a figure.

20. Two examples of _____ depth cues are interposition and linear perspective.

21. Perceiving a tomato as consistently red, despite lighting shifts, is an example of
    a. shape constancy.
    b. perceptual constancy.
    c. a binocular cue.
    d. continuity.

22. After surgery to restore vision, patients who had been blind from birth had difficulty
    a. recognizing objects by touch.
    b. recognizing objects by sight.
    c. distinguishing figure from ground.
    d. distinguishing between bright and dim light.

23. In experiments, people have worn glasses that turned their visual fields upside down. After a period of adjustment, they learned to function quite well. This ability is called _____ _____.

24. The snail-shaped tube in the inner ear, where sound waves are converted into neural activity, is called the _____.

25. What are the basic steps in transforming sound waves into perceived sound?

26. Of the four skin senses that make up our sense of touch, only _____ has its own identifiable receptor cells.
    a. pressure
    b. warmth
    c. cold
    d. pain

27. We have specialized nerve receptors for detecting which five tastes? How did this ability aid our ancestors?

28. _____ is your sense of body position and movement. Your _____ _____ specifically monitors your head's movement, with sensors in the inner ear.

29. Why do you feel a little dizzy immediately after a roller-coaster ride?

30. A food's aroma can greatly enhance its taste. This is an example of
    a. sensory adaptation.
    b. chemical sensation.
    c. kinesthesia.
    d. sensory interaction.

31. Which of the following ESP events is supported by solid, replicable scientific evidence?
    a. Telepathy
    b. Clairvoyance
    c. Precognition
    d. None of these answers

Find answers to these questions in Appendix E, in the back of the book.

IN YOUR EVERYDAY LIFE

Answering these questions will help you make these concepts more personally meaningful, and therefore more memorable.

1. What types of sensory adaptation have you experienced in the last 24 hours?

2. Can you recall a time when your expectations influenced how you perceived a person (or group of people)? What happened?

3. People often compare the human eye to a camera. Do you think this is an accurate comparison? Why or why not?

4. What would your life be like without perceptual constancy?

5. How would you respond if, after you were injured, a friend said, "The pain is just in your head"?

experience
more of the
testing
effect

6 Learning

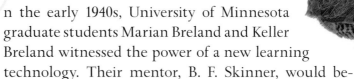

In the early 1940s, University of Minnesota graduate students Marian Breland and Keller Breland witnessed the power of a new learning technology. Their mentor, B. F. Skinner, would become famous for *shaping* rat and pigeon behaviors, by delivering well-timed rewards as the animals inched closer and closer to a desired behavior. Impressed with Skinner's results, the Brelands began shaping the behavior of cats, chickens, parakeets, turkeys, pigs, ducks, and hamsters (Bailey & Gillaspy, 2005). The rest is history. The company they formed spent the next half-century training more than 15,000 animals from 140 species for movies, traveling shows, amusement parks, corporations, and the government. The Brelands also trained trainers, including Sea World's first training director.

While writing a book about animal trainers, Amy Sutherland wondered if shaping had uses closer to home (2006a,b). If baboons could be trained to skateboard and elephants to paint, might "the same techniques . . . work on that stubborn but lovable species, the American husband"? Step by step, she "began thanking Scott if he threw one dirty shirt into the hamper. If he threw in two, I'd kiss him [and] as he basked in my appreciation, the piles became smaller." After two years of "thinking of my husband as an exotic animal species," she reports, "my marriage is far smoother, my husband much easier to love."

Like husbands and other animals, much of what we do we learn from experience. Indeed, nature's most important gift may be our *adaptability*—our capacity to learn new behaviors that help us cope with our changing world. We can learn how to build grass huts or snow shelters, submarines or space stations, and thereby adapt to almost any environment.

Learning breeds hope. What is learnable we may be able to teach—a fact that encourages animal trainers, and also parents, educators, and coaches. What has been learned we may be able to change by new learning—an assumption underlying stress management and counseling programs. No matter how unhappy, unsuccessful, or unloving we are, we can learn and change.

No topic is closer to the heart of psychology than *learning,* the process of acquiring, through experience, new and relatively enduring information or behaviors. (Learning acquires information, and memory—our next chapter topic—retains it.) In earlier chapters we considered the learning of sleep patterns, of gender roles, of visual perceptions. In later chapters we will see how learning shapes our thoughts, our emotions, our personality, and our attitudes. This chapter examines some core processes of three types of learning: *classical conditioning, operant conditioning,* and *cognitive learning.*

How Do We Learn?

6-1 What are some basic forms of learning?

◎ One way we **learn** is by *association*. Our minds naturally connect events that occur in sequence. Suppose you see and smell freshly baked bread, eat some, and find it satisfying. The next time you see and smell fresh bread, you will expect that eating it will again be satisfying. So, too, with sounds. If you associate a sound with a frightening consequence, hearing the sound alone may trigger your fear. As one 4-year-old said after watching a TV character get mugged, "If I had heard that music, I wouldn't have gone around the corner!" (Wells, 1981).

Learned associations also feed our habitual behaviors (Wood & Neal, 2007). Habits can form when we repeat behaviors in a given context—sleeping in the same comfy position in bed, walking the same path to class, eating buttery popcorn in the local theater. As behavior becomes linked with the context, our next experience of that context will evoke our habitual response.

How long does it take to form such habits? To find out, researchers asked 96 university students to choose some healthy behavior, such as running before dinner or eating fruit with lunch, and to perform it daily for 84 days. The students also recorded whether the behavior felt automatic (something they did without thinking and would find it hard not to do). When did the behaviors turn into habits? On average after about 66 days (Lally et al., 2010). (Is there something you'd like to make a routine part of your life? Just do it every day for two months, or a bit longer for exercise, and you likely will find yourself with a new habit.)

Other animals also learn by association. To protect itself, the sea slug *Aplysia* withdraws its gill when squirted with water. If the squirts continue, as happens naturally in choppy water, the withdrawal response weakens. But if the sea slug repeatedly receives an electric shock just after being squirted, its response to the squirt instead grows stronger. The animal has learned that the squirt signals an upcoming shock.

Complex animals can learn to link outcomes with their own responses. An aquarium seal will repeat behaviors, such as slapping and barking, that prompt people to toss it a herring.

By linking two events that occur close together, the sea slug and the seal are exhibiting **associative learning**. The sea slug associated the squirt with an upcoming shock. The seal associated its slapping and barking with a herring treat. Each animal has learned something important to its survival: predicting the immediate future.

This process of learning associations is *conditioning*, and it takes two main forms:

- In *classical conditioning*, we learn to associate two stimuli and thus to anticipate events. (A **stimulus** is any event or situation that evokes a response.) We learn that a flash of lightning will be followed by a crack of thunder, so when lightning flashes nearby, we start to brace ourselves (**FIGURE 6.1**).

- In *operant conditioning*, we learn to associate a response (our behavior) and its consequence. Thus, we (and other animals) learn to repeat acts followed by good results (**FIGURE 6.2**) and to avoid acts followed by bad results.

Conditioning is not the only form of learning. Through **cognitive learning** we acquire mental information that guides our behavior. *Observational learning,* one form of cognitive learning, lets us learn from others' experiences. Chimpanzees, for example, sometimes learn behaviors merely by watching others. If one animal sees another solve a puzzle and gain a food reward, the observer may perform the trick more quickly. So, too, in humans: We look and we learn.

By learning, we humans are able to adapt to our environments. We learn to expect and prepare for significant events such as food or pain (*classical conditioning*). We learn to repeat acts that bring good results and to avoid acts that bring bad results (*operant conditioning*). We learn new behaviors by observing events and by

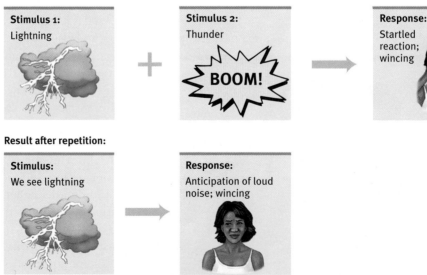

Two related events:

Stimulus 1: Lightning + Stimulus 2: Thunder BOOM! → Response: Startled reaction; wincing

Result after repetition:

Stimulus: We see lightning → Response: Anticipation of loud noise; wincing

FIGURE 6.1 Classical conditioning

(a) Response: Being polite   (b) Consequence: Getting a treat   (c) Behavior strengthened

FIGURE 6.2 Operant conditioning

watching others, and through language we learn things we have neither experienced nor observed (*cognitive learning*). ■

RETRIEVE + REMEMBER

- Why are habits, such as having something sweet with that cup of coffee, so hard to break?

ANSWER: Habits form when we repeat behaviors in a given context and, as a result, learn associations—often without our awareness. For example, we may have eaten a sweet pastry with a cup of coffee often enough to associate the flavor of the coffee with the treat, so that the cup of coffee alone just doesn't seem right anymore!

Classical Conditioning

◎ For many people, the name Ivan Pavlov (1849–1936) rings a bell. His early twentieth-century experiments—now psychology's most famous research—are classics. The process he explored we justly call **classical conditioning.**

Pavlov's Experiments

6-2 What is classical conditioning, and how does it demonstrate associative learning?

For his studies of digestion, Pavlov (who held a medical degree) earned Russia's first Nobel Prize in 1904. But his novel experiments on learning, which con-

sumed the last three decades of his life, earned Pavlov his place in history.

Pavlov's new direction came when his creative mind seized on what seemed to others an unimportant detail. Without fail, putting food in a dog's mouth caused the animal to drool—to *salivate.* Moreover, the dog began salivating not only to the taste of the food but also to the mere sight of the food or the food dish. The dog even drooled at the sight of the person delivering the food or the sound of that person's approaching footsteps. At first, Pavlov considered these "psychic secretions" an annoyance. Then he realized they pointed to a simple but important form of learning.

Pavlov and his assistants tried to imagine what the dog was thinking and feeling as it drooled in anticipation of

IVAN PAVLOV "Experimental investigation . . . should lay a solid foundation for a future true science of psychology" (1927).

Peanuts reprinted with permission of United Features Syndicate

the food. This only led them into useless debates. So, to make their studies more objective, they experimented. To rule out other possible influences, they isolated the dog in a small room, placed it in a harness, and attached a device to measure its saliva. Then, from the next room, they presented food. First, they slid in a food bowl. Later, they blew meat powder into the dog's mouth at a precise moment. Finally, they paired various **neutral stimuli (NS)**—events the dog could see or hear but didn't associ-

learning the process of acquiring, through experience, new and relatively enduring information or behaviors.

associative learning learning that certain events occur together. The events may be two stimuli (as in classical conditioning) or a response and its consequences (as in operant conditioning).

stimulus any event or situation that evokes a response.

cognitive learning the acquisition of mental information, whether by observing events, by watching others, or through language.

classical conditioning a type of learning in which we learn to link two or more stimuli and anticipate events.

neutral stimulus (NS) in classical conditioning, a stimulus that evokes no response before conditioning.

ate with food—with food in the dog's mouth. If a sight or sound regularly signaled the arrival of food, would the dog learn the link? If so, would it begin salivating in anticipation of the food?

The answers proved to be *Yes* and *Yes*. Just before placing food in the dog's mouth to produce salivation, Pavlov sounded a tone. After several pairings of tone and food, the dog got the message. Anticipating the meat powder, it began salivating to the tone alone. In later experiments, a buzzer, a light, a touch on the leg, even the sight of a circle set off the drooling.

A dog doesn't *learn* to salivate in response to food in its mouth. Food in the mouth automatically, *unconditionally*, triggers this response. Thus, Pavlov called the drooling an **unconditioned response (UR)**. And he called the food an **unconditioned stimulus (US)**.

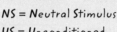

Remember:
NS = Neutral Stimulus
US = Unconditioned Stimulus
UR = Unconditioned Response
CS = Conditioned Stimulus
CR = Conditioned Response

Salivating in response to a tone, however, is learned. Because it is *conditional* upon the dog's linking the tone with the food (FIGURE 6.3), we call this response the **conditioned response (CR)**. The stimulus that used to be neutral (in this case, a previously meaningless tone that now triggers drooling) is the **conditioned stimulus (CS)**. Remembering the difference between these two kinds of stimuli and responses is easy: Conditioned = learned; *unconditioned* = *unlearned*.

If Pavlov's demonstration of associative learning was so simple, what did he do for the next three decades? What discoveries did his research factory publish in his 532 papers on salivary conditioning (Windholz, 1997)? He and his associates explored five major conditioning processes: *acquisition, extinction, spontaneous recovery, generalization,* and *discrimination.* ■

RETRIEVE + REMEMBER

- An experimenter sounds a tone just before delivering an air puff to your blinking eye. After several repetitions, you blink to the tone alone. What is the NS? The US? The UR? The CS? The CR?

ANSWERS: NS = tone before conditioning; US = air puff; UR = blink to air puff; CS = tone after conditioning; CR = blink to tone.

Acquisition

6-3 What parts do acquisition, extinction, spontaneous recovery, generalization, and discrimination play in classical conditioning?

Acquisition is the first stage in classical conditioning. This is the point when Pavlov's dogs learned the link between the NS (the tone, the light, the touch) and the US (the food). To understand this stage, Pavlov and his associates wondered: How much time should pass between presenting the neutral stimulus

BEFORE CONDITIONING

US (food in mouth) → UR (salivation)

An unconditioned stimulus (US) produces an unconditioned response (UR).

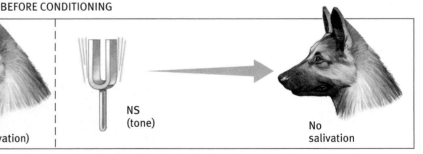

NS (tone) → No salivation

A neutral stimulus (NS) produces no salivation response.

DURING CONDITIONING

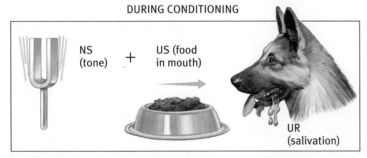

NS (tone) + US (food in mouth) → UR (salivation)

The US is repeatedly presented just after the NS. The US continues to produce a UR.

AFTER CONDITIONING

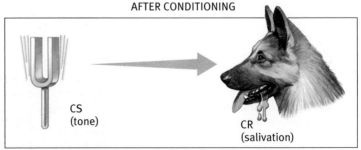

CS (tone) → CR (salivation)

The previously neutral stimulus alone now produces a conditioned response (CR), thereby becoming a conditioned stimulus (CS).

FIGURE 6.3 Pavlov's classic experiment Pavlov presented a neutral stimulus (a tone) just before an unconditioned stimulus (food in mouth). The neutral stimulus then became a conditioned stimulus, producing a conditioned response.

and the food? In most cases, not much—half a second usually works well.

What do you suppose would happen if the food (US) appeared before the tone (NS) rather than after? Would conditioning occur? Not likely. With only a few exceptions, conditioning doesn't happen when the NS follows the US. *Remember, classical conditioning is biologically adaptive because it helps humans and other animals prepare for good or bad events.* To Pavlov's dogs, the originally neutral tone became a CS after signaling an important biological event—the arrival of food (US). To deer in the forest, the snapping of a twig (CS) may signal a predator's approach (US). If the good or bad event has already occurred, the tone or the sound won't help the animal prepare.

More recent research on male Japanese quail shows how a CS can signal another important biological event (Domjan, 1992, 1994, 2005). Just before presenting a sexually approachable female quail, the researchers turned on a red light. Over time, as the red light continued to announce the female's arrival, the light caused the male quail to become excited. They developed a preference for their cage's red-light district. When a female appeared, they mated with her more quickly and released more semen and sperm (Matthews et al., 2007). All in all, the quail's capacity for classical conditioning gives it a reproductive edge.

Can objects, sights, and smells associated with sexual pleasure become conditioned stimuli for human sexual arousal, too? Indeed they can (Byrne, 1982). Onion breath does not usually produce sexual arousal (**FIGURE 6.4**). But when repeat-

Eric Isselée/Shutterstock

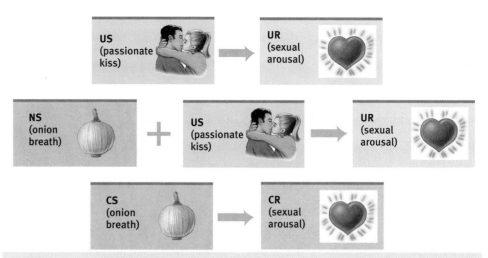

FIGURE 6.4 An unexpected CS Psychologist Michael Tirrell (1990) recalled: "My first girlfriend loved onions, so I came to associate onion breath with kissing. Before long, onion breath sent tingles up and down my spine. Oh what a feeling!"

edly paired with a passionate kiss, it can become a CS and do just that. The larger lesson: *Conditioning helps an animal survive and reproduce—by responding to cues that help it gain food, avoid dangers, locate mates, and produce offspring* (Hollis, 1997). ∎

RETRIEVE + REMEMBER

- In horror movies, sexually arousing images of women are sometimes paired with violence against women. Based on classical conditioning principles, what might be an effect of this pairing?

ANSWER: If viewing an attractive nude or semi-nude woman (a US) elicits sexual arousal (a UR), then pairing the US with a new stimulus (violence) could turn the violence into a conditioned stimulus (CS) that also becomes sexually arousing, a conditioned response (CR).

Extinction and Spontaneous Recovery

What would happen, Pavlov wondered, if after conditioning, the CS occurred repeatedly without the US? If the tone sounded again and again, but no food appeared, would the tone still trigger drooling? The answer was mixed. The dogs salivated less and less, a reaction known as **extinction**—a drop-off in responses when a CS (tone) no longer signals an upcoming US (food). But the

dogs began drooling to the tone again if Pavlov scheduled several tone-free hours. This **spontaneous recovery**—the

unconditioned response (UR) in classical conditioning, an unlearned, naturally occurring response (such as salivation) to an unconditioned stimulus (US) (such as food in the mouth).

unconditioned stimulus (US) in classical conditioning, a stimulus that unconditionally—naturally and automatically—triggers a response (UR).

conditioned response (CR) in classical conditioning, a learned response to a previously neutral (but now conditioned) stimulus (CS).

conditioned stimulus (CS) in classical conditioning, an originally irrelevant stimulus that, after association with an unconditioned stimulus (US), comes to trigger a conditioned response (CR).

acquisition in classical conditioning, the initial stage, when we link a neutral stimulus and an unconditioned stimulus so that the neutral stimulus begins triggering the conditioned response. (In operant conditioning, the strengthening of a reinforced response.)

extinction in classical conditioning, the weakening of a conditioned response when an unconditioned stimulus does not follow a conditioned stimulus. (In operant conditioning, the weakening of a response when it is no longer reinforced.)

spontaneous recovery the reappearance, after a pause, of an extinguished conditioned response.

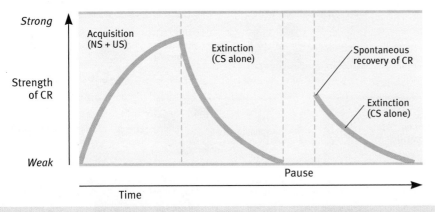

FIGURE 6.5 **Acquisition, extinction, and spontaneous recovery** The rising curve (simplified here) shows that the CR rapidly grows stronger as the NS becomes a CS as it is repeatedly paired with the US *(acquisition).* The CS weakens when it is presented alone *(extinction).* After a pause, the CR reappears *(spontaneous recovery).*

RETRIEVE + REMEMBER

"I don't care if she's a tape dispenser. I love her."

- What conditioning principle is affecting the snail's affections?

ANSWER: generalization

Pavlov's Legacy

6-4 Why is Pavlov's work important, and how is it being applied?

What remains today of Pavlov's ideas? A great deal. Most psychologists now agree that classical conditioning is a basic form of learning. Judged by today's knowledge, including our understanding of the biological and cognitive influences on conditioning, Pavlov's ideas were incomplete. But if we see further than Pavlov did, it is because we stand on his shoulders.

Why does Pavlov's work remain so important? If he had merely taught us that old dogs can learn new tricks, his experiments would long ago have been forgotten. Why should we care that dogs can be conditioned to drool at the sound of a tone? The importance lies first in this finding: *Many other responses to many other stimuli can be classically conditioned in many other creatures*—in fact, in every species tested, from earthworms to fish to dogs to monkeys to people (Schwartz, 1984). Thus, classical conditioning is one way that virtually all animals learn to adapt to their environment.

Second, *Pavlov showed us how a process such as learning can be studied objectively.* He was proud that his methods were not based on guesswork about a dog's mind. The salivary response is a behavior we can measure in cubic centimeters of saliva. Pavlov's success therefore

reappearance of a (weakened) CR after a pause—suggested to Pavlov that extinction was *suppressing* the CR rather than eliminating it (FIGURE 6.5). ■

RETRIEVE + REMEMBER

- The first step of classical conditioning, when an NS becomes a CS, is called _____. When a US no longer follows the CS, and the CR becomes weakened, this is called _____.

ANSWERS: acquisition; extinction

Generalization

Pavlov and his students noticed that a dog conditioned to the sound of one tone also responded somewhat to the sound of a new and different tone. Likewise, a dog conditioned to salivate when rubbed would also drool a bit when scratched or when touched on a different body part (Windholz, 1989). This tendency to respond similarly to stimuli that resemble the CS is called **generalization.**

Generalization can be adaptive, as when toddlers taught to fear moving cars also become afraid of moving trucks and motorcycles. And generalized fears can linger. One Argentine writer who had been tortured still flinches when he sees black shoes—his

first glimpse of his torturers as they approached his cell. This generalized fear response was found in laboratory studies comparing abused and non-abused children (Pollak et al., 1998). When an angry face appeared on a computer screen, abused children's brain-wave responses were dramatically stronger and longer lasting.

Generalization helps to explain why we like unfamiliar people more if they look like someone we've learned to like rather than dislike. (Researchers demonstrated this by subtly morphing the facial features of someone people had learned to like or dislike onto a novel face [Verosky & Todorov, 2010].)

In all these human examples, people's emotional reactions to one stimulus have generalized to similar stimuli.

Discrimination

Pavlov's dogs also learned to respond to the sound of a particular tone and *not* to other tones. This learned ability to *distinguish* between a conditioned stimulus (which predicts the US) and other irrelevant stimuli is called **discrimination**. Being able to recognize differences is adaptive. Slightly different stimuli can be followed by vastly different results. Confronted by a guard dog, your heart may race; confronted by a guide dog, it probably will not. ■

suggested a scientific model for how the young field of psychology might proceed. That model was to isolate the basic building blocks of complex behaviors and study them with objective laboratory procedures. ■

Classical Conditioning in Everyday Life

Other chapters in this text—on motivation and emotion, stress and health, psychological disorders, and therapy—show how Pavlov's principles can influence human health and well-being. Two examples:

• Drugs given as cancer treatments can trigger nausea and vomiting. Patients may then develop classically conditioned nausea (and sometimes anxiety) to the sights, sounds, and smells associated with the clinic (Hall, 1997). Merely entering the clinic's waiting room or seeing the nurses can provoke these feelings (Burish & Carey, 1986).

• Former drug users often feel a craving when they are again in the drug-using context. They associate particular people or places with previous highs. Thus, drug counselors advise addicts to steer clear of people and settings that may trigger these cravings (Siegel, 2005).

Does Pavlov's work help us understand our own emotions? John B. Watson thought so. He believed that human emotions and behaviors, though biologically influenced, are mainly a bundle of conditioned responses (1913). Working with an 11-month-old, Watson and Rosalie Rayner (1920; Harris, 1979) showed how specific fears might be conditioned. Like most infants, "Little Albert" feared loud noises but not white rats. Watson and Rayner presented a white rat and, as Little Albert reached to touch it, struck a hammer against a steel bar just behind the infant's head. After seven repeats of seeing the rat and hearing the frightening noise, Albert burst into tears at the mere sight of the rat. Five days later, he had generalized this startled fear reaction to the sight of a rabbit, a dog, and a sealskin coat, but not to dissimilar objects, such as toys.

For years, people wondered what became of Little Albert. Not until 2009 did some psychologist-sleuths identify him. It seems he was Douglas Merritte, the son of a campus hospital wet nurse who received $1 for her tot's participation. Sadly, this famous child died at age 6 from complications related to a disease he had suffered since birth (Beck et al., 2009, 2010; Fridlund et al., 2012a, b).

People also wondered what became of Watson. After losing his Johns Hopkins professorship over an affair with Rayner (whom he later married), he joined an advertising agency as the company's resident psychologist. There he used his knowledge of associative learning in many successful advertising campaigns. One of them, for Maxwell House, helped make the "coffee break" an American custom (Hunt, 1993).

The treatment of Little Albert would be unacceptable by today's ethical standards. Also, some psychologists, noting that the infant's fear wasn't learned quickly, had difficulty repeating Watson and Rayner's findings with other children. Nevertheless, Little Albert's learned fears led many psychologists to wonder whether each of us might be a walking storehouse of conditioned emotions. If so, might extinction procedures or even new conditioning help us change our unwanted responses to emotion-arousing stimuli?

Comedian-writer Mark Malkoff extinguished his fear of flying by doing just that. With support from an airline, he faced his fear. Living on an airplane for 30 days and taking 135 flights, he spent 14 hours a day in the air. After a week and a half, Malkoff's fear had faded, and he began playing games with fellow passengers (NPR, 2009). (His favorite: He'd put one end of a toilet paper roll in the toilet, unroll the rest down the aisle, and flush—sucking down the whole roll in 3 seconds.) In Chapters 13 and 14, we will see more examples of how psychologists use behavioral techniques to treat emotional disorders and promote personal growth. ■

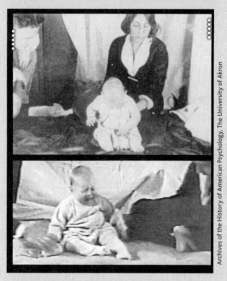

• In Watson and Rayner's experiments, "Little Albert" learned to fear a white rat after repeatedly experiencing a loud noise as the rat was presented. In this experiment, what was the US? The UR? The NS? The CS? The CR?

ANSWERS: The US was the loud noise; the UR was the fear response; the NS was the rat before it was paired with the noise; the CS was the rat after pairing; the CR was fear of the rat.

Archives of the History of American Psychology, The University of Akron

generalization in classical conditioning, the tendency, after conditioning, to respond similarly to stimuli that resemble the conditioned stimulus.

discrimination in classical conditioning, the learned ability to distinguish between a conditioned stimulus and other irrelevant stimuli.

Operant Conditioning

6-5 What is operant conditioning, and how is operant behavior reinforced and shaped?

◎ It's one thing to classically condition a dog to drool at the sound of a tone, or a child to fear moving cars. To teach an elephant to walk on its hind legs or a child to say *please*, we must turn to another type of learning—*operant conditioning*.

Classical conditioning and operant conditioning are both forms of associative learning, yet their difference is straightforward:

- In *classical conditioning*, an animal (dog, child, sea slug) forms associations between two events it does not control. Classical conditioning involves **respondent behavior**—automatic responses to a stimulus (such as salivating in response to meat powder and later in response to a tone).

- In **operant conditioning,** animals associate their own actions with consequences. Actions followed by a rewarding event increase; those followed by a punishing event decrease. Behavior that *operates* on the environment to *produce* rewarding or punishing events is called **operant behavior.**

We can therefore distinguish our classical from our operant conditioning by asking two questions. *Are we learning associations between events we do not control (classical conditioning)? Or are we learning associations between our behavior and resulting events (operant conditioning)?* ■

Skinner's Experiments

B. F. Skinner (1904–1990) was a college English major who had set his sights on becoming a writer. Then, seeking a new direction, he became a graduate student in psychology, and, eventually, modern *behaviorism's* most influential and controversial figure.

Skinner's work built on a principle that psychologist Edward L. Thorndike (1874–1949) called the **law of effect:** Rewarded behavior is likely to be repeated **(FIGURE 6.6)**. From this starting point, Skinner went on to develop experiments that would reveal principles of *behavior control.* Using these principles, he taught pigeons to walk a figure 8, play Ping-Pong®, and keep a missile on course by pecking at a screen target.

For his studies, Skinner designed an **operant chamber,** popularly known as a *Skinner box* **(FIGURE 6.7)**. The box has a bar or button that an animal presses or pecks to release a food or water reward. It also has a device that records these responses. This design creates a stage on which rats and other animals act out Skinner's concept of **reinforcement:** any event that strengthens (increases the frequency of) a preceding response. What is reinforcing depends on the animal and the conditions. For people, it may be praise, attention, or a paycheck. For hungry and thirsty rats, food and water work well. Skinner's experiments have done far more than teach us how to pull habits out of a rat. They have explored the precise conditions that foster efficient and enduring learning.

Shaping Behavior

Imagine that you wanted to condition a hungry rat to press a bar. Like Skinner, you could tease out this action with **shaping,** gradually guiding the rat's actions toward the desired behavior. First, you would watch how the animal naturally behaves, so that you could build on its existing behaviors. You might give the rat a bit of food each time it approaches the bar. Once the rat is approaching regularly, you would

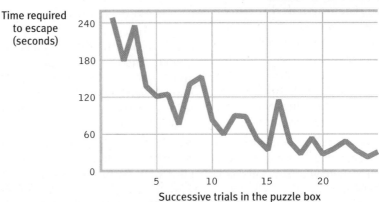

FIGURE 6.6 Cat in a puzzle box Thorndike used a fish reward to entice cats to find their way out of a puzzle box through a series of maneuvers. The cats' performance tended to improve with successive trials, illustrating Thorndike's *law of effect*. (Adapted from Thorndike, 1898.)

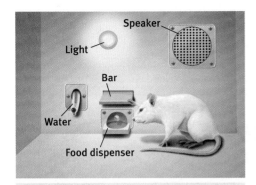

FIGURE 6.7 **A Skinner box** Inside the box, the rat presses a bar or button for a food reward. Outside, measuring devices (not shown here) keep records of the animal's responses.

TABLE 6.1	Ways to Increase Behavior	
Operant Conditioning Term	Description	Examples
Positive reinforcement	Give something that's desired	Pet a dog that comes when you call it; pay the person who paints your house
Negative reinforcement	End something that's undesired	Take painkillers to end pain; fasten seat belt to end loud beeping noise

give the treat only when it moves close to the bar, then closer still. Finally, you would require it to touch the bar to get food. With this method of *successive approximations*, you reward responses that are ever-closer to the final desired behavior. By giving rewards only for desired behaviors and ignoring all other responses, researchers and animal trainers gradually shape complex behaviors.

Shaping can also help us understand what nonverbal organisms perceive. Can a dog see red and green? Can a baby hear the difference between lower- and higher-pitched tones? If we can shape them to respond to one stimulus and not to another, then we know they can perceive the difference. Such experiments have even shown that some animals can form concepts. When experimenters reinforced pigeons for pecking after seeing a human face, but not after seeing other images, the pigeons learned to recognize human faces (Herrnstein & Loveland, 1964). After being trained to discriminate among classes of events or objects—flowers, people, cars, chairs—pigeons were usually able to identify the category in which a new pictured object belonged (Bhatt et al., 1988; Wasserman, 1993).

In everyday life, we continually reinforce and shape others' behavior, said Skinner, though we may not mean to do

so. Isaac's whining, for example, annoys his dad, but look how he responds:

Isaac: *Could you take me to the mall?*

Dad: (Ignores Isaac and stays focused on his phone.)

Isaac: *Dad, I need to go to the mall.*

Dad: (distracted) *Uh, yeah, just a minute.*

Isaac: *DAAAD! The mall!!*

Dad: *Show me some manners! Okay, where are my keys . . .*

Isaac's whining is reinforced, because he gets something desirable—his dad's attention. Dad's response is reinforced because it ends something *aversive* (unpleasant)—Isaac's whining.

Or consider a teacher who sticks gold stars on a wall chart beside the names of children scoring 100 percent on spelling tests. As everyone can then see, some children always score 100 percent. The others, who take the same test and may have worked harder than the academic all-stars, get no stars. Using operant conditioning principles, what advice could you offer the teacher to help all students do their best work?[1]

Types of Reinforcers

6-6 How do positive and negative reinforcement differ, and what are the basic types of reinforcers?

Up to now, we've mainly been discussing **positive reinforcement,** which strengthens a response by *presenting* a typically pleasurable stimulus after a response.

But, as we saw in the whining Isaac story, there are two basic kinds of reinforcement (**TABLE 6.1**). **Negative reinforcement** strengthens a response by *reducing or removing* something undesirable or unpleasant. Isaac's whining was *positively* reinforced, because Isaac got something desirable—his father's attention.

respondent behavior behavior that occurs as an automatic response to some stimulus.

operant conditioning a type of learning in which behavior is strengthened if followed by a reinforcer or diminished if followed by a punisher.

operant behavior behavior that operates on the environment, producing consequences.

law of effect Thorndike's principle that behaviors followed by favorable consequences become more likely, and that behaviors followed by unfavorable consequences become less likely.

operant chamber in operant conditioning research, a chamber (also known as a *Skinner box*) containing a bar or key that an animal can manipulate to obtain a food or water reinforcer; attached devices record the animal's rate of bar pressing or key pecking.

reinforcement in operant conditioning, any event that *strengthens* the behavior it follows.

shaping an operant conditioning procedure in which reinforcers guide actions closer and closer toward a desired behavior.

positive reinforcement increases behaviors by presenting positive stimuli, such as food. A positive reinforcer is anything that, when *presented* after a response, strengthens the response.

negative reinforcement increases behaviors by stopping or reducing negative stimuli, such as shock. A negative reinforcer is anything that, when *removed* after a response, strengthens the response. (*Note:* Negative reinforcement is *not* punishment.)

---

[1] You might advise the teacher to apply operant conditioning principles. To shape students, reinforce them all for gradual improvements, as their spelling gets closer and closer to the goal.

REINFORCERS VARY WITH CIRCUMSTANCES
What is reinforcing (a heat lamp) to one animal (a cold meerkat) may not be to another (an overheated child). What is reinforcing in one situation (an unusual cold snap at the Taronga Zoo in Sydney, Australia) may not be in another (a sweltering summer day in Texas).

RETRIEVE + REMEMBER

• How is operant conditioning at work in this cartoon?

HI AND LOIS

ANSWER: The baby negatively reinforces her parents when she stops crying once they grant her wish. Her parents positively reinforce her cries by letting her sleep with them.

His dad's response to the whining (doing what Isaac wanted) was *negatively* reinforced, because it got rid of Isaac's annoying whining. Similarly, taking aspirin may relieve your headache and hitting *snooze* will silence your annoying alarm. These welcome results provide negative reinforcement and increase the odds that you will repeat these behaviors. For drug addicts, the negative reinforcement of ending withdrawal pangs can be a compelling reason to resume using (Baker et al., 2004).

Note that *negative reinforcement is not punishment.* (Some friendly advice: Repeat the last five words in your mind.) Rather, negative reinforcement *removes* a punishing event. Think of negative reinforcement as something that provides relief—from that whining teenager, bad headache, or annoying alarm. Whether it works by getting rid of something we *don't* enjoy, or by giving us something we *do* enjoy, *reinforcement is any consequence that strengthens behavior.* ▪

PRIMARY AND CONDITIONED REINFORCERS Getting food when hungry or having a painful headache go away is innately (naturally) satisfying. These **primary reinforcers** are unlearned. **Conditioned reinforcers,** also called *secondary reinforcers,* get their power through learned associations with primary reinforcers. If a rat in a Skinner box learns that a light reliably signals a food delivery, the rat will work to turn on the light. The light has become a secondary reinforcer linked with food. Our lives are filled with conditioned reinforcers—money, good grades, a pleasant tone of voice—each of which has been linked with a more basic reward—food and shelter, safety, social support.

IMMEDIATE AND DELAYED REINFORCERS In shaping experiments, rats are conditioned with immediate rewards.

"Oh, not bad. The light comes on, I press the bar, they write me a check. How about you?"

You want the rat to press the bar, it sniffs the bar, and it immediately gets a food pellet. If a distraction delays your giving the rat its prize, the rat won't learn to link the bar sniffing with the food pellet reward.

Unlike rats, humans *do* respond to delayed reinforcers. We associate the paycheck at the end of the week, the good grade at the end of the semester, the trophy at the end of the season with our earlier actions. Indeed, learning to control our impulses in order to achieve more valued rewards is a big step toward maturity (Logue, 1998a,b). Chapter 3 described a famous finding in which children did curb their impulses and delay gratification, choosing two marshmallows later over one now. Those same children achieved greater educational and vocational success later in life (Mischel et al., 1988, 1989).

Sometimes, however, small but immediate pleasures (the enjoyment of watching late-night TV, for example) blind us to big but delayed consequences (feeling alert tomorrow). For many teens, the immediate gratification of impulsive, unprotected sex wins over the delayed gratification of safe sex or saved sex (Loewenstein & Furstenberg, 1991). And for too many of us, the immediate rewards of today's gas-guzzling vehicles, air travel, and air conditioning win over the bigger future consequences of climate change, rising seas, and extreme weather.

Reinforcement Schedules

6-7 How do continuous and partial reinforcement schedules affect behavior?

In most of our examples, the desired response has been reinforced every time it occurs. This is **continous reinforcement**. But **reinforcement schedules** vary, and they influence our learning. Continuous reinforcement is a good choice for mastering a behavior because learning occurs rapidly. But there's a catch: Extinction also occurs rapidly. When reinforcement stops—when we stop delivering food after the rat presses the bar—the behavior soon stops. If a normally dependable candy machine fails to deliver a chocolate bar twice in a row, we stop putting money into it (although a week later we may exhibit spontaneous recovery by trying again).

Real life rarely provides continuous reinforcement. Salespeople don't make a sale with every pitch. But they persist because their efforts are occasionally rewarded. And that's the good news about **partial (intermittent) reinforcement** schedules, in which responses are sometimes reinforced, sometimes not. Learning is slower than with continuous reinforcement, but *resistance to extinction* is greater. Imagine a pigeon that has learned to peck a key to obtain food. If you gradually phase out the food delivery until it occurs only rarely, in no predictable pattern, the pigeon may peck 150,000 times without a reward (Skinner, 1953). Slot machines reward gamblers in much the same way—occasionally and unpredictably. And like pigeons, slot players keep trying,

Vitaly Titov & Maria Sidelnikova/ Shutterstock

again and again. With intermittent reinforcement, hope springs eternal.

Lesson for parents: Partial reinforcement also works with children. What happens when we occasionally give in to children's tantrums for the sake of peace and quiet? We have intermittently reinforced the tantrums. This is the best way to make a behavior persist.

Skinner (1961) and his collaborators compared four schedules of partial reinforcement. Some are rigidly fixed, some unpredictably variable (**TABLE 6.2**).

Fixed-ratio schedules reinforce behavior after a set number of responses. Coffee shops may reward us with a free drink after every 10 purchased. In the laboratory, rats may be reinforced on a fixed ratio of, say, one food pellet for every 30 responses. Once conditioned, the rats will pause only briefly to munch on the pellet before returning to a high rate of responding.

Variable-ratio schedules provide reinforcers after an unpredictable number of responses. This is what slot-machine players and fly-casting anglers experience—unpredictable reinforcement. And it's what makes gambling and fly fishing so hard to extinguish even when both are getting nothing for something. Because reinforcers increase as the number of responses increases, variable-ratio schedules produce high rates of responding.

Fixed-interval schedules reinforce the first response after a fixed time period. Pigeons on a fixed-interval schedule peck more rapidly as the time for reinforcement draws near. People waiting for an important letter check more often as delivery time approaches. A hungry cook peeks into the oven frequently to see if cookies are brown. This produces a choppy stop-start pattern rather than a steady rate of response.

Variable-interval schedules reinforce the first response after unpredictable time intervals. At varying times,

TABLE 6.2 Schedules of Partial Reinforcement

	Fixed	Variable
Ratio	*Every so many:* reinforcement after every *nth* behavior, such as buy 10 coffees, then get 1 free, or get paid per shirt sewn	*After an unpredictable number:* reinforcement after a random number of behaviors, as when playing slot machines or fly fishing
Interval	*Every so often:* reinforcement for behavior after a fixed time, such as Tuesday discount prices	*Unpredictably often:* reinforcement for behavior after a random amount of time, as in checking for a Facebook response

primary reinforcer an event that is innately reinforcing, often by satisfying a biological need.

conditioned reinforcer (also known as *secondary reinforcer*) an event that gains its reinforcing power through its link with a primary reinforcer.

continuous reinforcement reinforcing a desired response every time it occurs.

reinforcement schedule a pattern that defines how often a desired response will be reinforced.

partial (intermittent) reinforcement reinforcing a response only part of the time; results in slower acquisition but much greater resistance to extinction than does continuous reinforcement.

fixed-ratio schedule in operant conditioning, a reinforcement schedule that reinforces a response only after a specified number of responses.

variable-ratio schedule in operant conditioning, a reinforcement schedule that reinforces a response after an unpredictable number of responses.

fixed-interval schedule in operant conditioning, a reinforcement schedule that reinforces a response only after a specified time has elapsed.

variable-interval schedule in operant conditioning, a reinforcement schedule that reinforces a response at unpredictable time intervals.

longed-for responses finally reward persistence in rechecking Facebook or e-mail. And at unpredictable times, a food pellet rewarded Skinner's pigeons for persistence in pecking a key. Variable-interval schedules tend to produce slow, steady responding. This makes sense, because there is no knowing when the waiting will be over.

In general, response rates are higher when reinforcement is linked to the number of responses (a ratio schedule) rather than to time (an interval schedule). But responding is more consistent when reinforcement is unpredictable (a variable schedule) than when it is predictable (a fixed schedule).

Animal behaviors differ, yet Skinner (1956) contended that the reinforcement principles of operant conditioning are universal. It matters little, he said, what response, what reinforcer, or what species you use. The effect of a given reinforcement schedule is pretty much the same: "Pigeon, rat, monkey, which is which? It doesn't matter. . . . Behavior shows astonishingly similar properties." ■

RETRIEVE + REMEMBER

- Telemarketers are reinforced by which schedule? People checking the oven to see if the cookies are done are on which schedule? Airline frequent-flyer programs that offer a free flight after every 25,000 miles of travel are using which reinforcement schedule?

ANSWERS: Telemarketers are reinforced on a variable-ratio schedule (after a varying number of calls). Cookie checkers are reinforced on a fixed-interval schedule. Frequent-flyer programs use a fixed-ratio schedule.

Punishment

6-8 How does punishment differ from negative reinforcement, and how does punishment affect behavior?

Reinforcement increases a behavior; **punishment** does the opposite. A *punisher* is any consequence that *decreases* the frequency of the behavior it follows **(TABLE 6.3)**. Swift and sure punishers can

TABLE 6.3   Ways to Decrease Behavior

Type of Punisher	Description	Examples
Positive punishment	Give something that's undesired	Spray water on a barking dog; give a parking ticket
Negative punishment	End something that's desired	Take away a teen's driving privileges; cancel a library card for failure to pay fines

powerfully restrain unwanted behaviors. The rat that is shocked after touching a forbidden object and the child who is burned by touching a hot stove will learn not to repeat those behaviors.

Criminal behavior, much of it impulsive, is also influenced more by swift and sure punishers than by the threat of severe sentences (Darley & Alter, 2011). Thus, when Arizona introduced an exceptionally harsh sentence for first-time drunk drivers, the drunk-driving rate changed very little. But when Kansas City police patrols started patrolling a high crime area to increase the sureness and swiftness of punishment, that city's crime rate dropped dramatically.

What do punishment studies tell us about parenting practices? Should we physically punish children to change their behavior? Many psychologists and supporters of nonviolent parenting say No, pointing out four major drawbacks of physical punishment (Gershoff, 2002; Marshall, 2002).

1. *Punished behavior is suppressed, not forgotten. This temporary state may (negatively) reinforce parents' punishing behavior.* The child swears, the parent swats, the parent hears no more swearing and feels the punishment successfully stopped the behavior. No wonder spanking is a hit with so many U.S. parents of 3- and 4-year-olds—more than 9 in 10 of whom admit spanking their children (Kazdin & Benjet, 2003).

2. *Punishment teaches discrimination among situations.* In operant conditioning, *discrimination* occurs when we learn that some responses, but not others, will be reinforced. Did the punishment effectively end the child's swearing?

Or did the child simply learn that it's not okay to swear around the house, but it is okay to swear elsewhere?

3. *Punishment can teach fear.* In operant conditioning, *generalization* occurs when our responses to similar stimuli are also reinforced. A punished child may associate fear not only with the undesirable behavior but also with the person who delivered the punishment or the place it occurred. Thus, children may learn to fear a punishing teacher and try to avoid school, or may become more anxious (Gershoff et al., 2010). For such reasons, most European countries and most U.S. states now ban hitting children in schools and child-care institutions (www.stophitting.com). In addition, 33 countries outlaw hitting by parents, giving children the same legal protection given to spouses.

4. *Physical punishment may increase aggression by modeling aggression as a way to cope with problems.* Studies find that spanked children are at increased risk for aggression (and depression and low self-esteem). We know, for example, that many aggressive delinquents and abusive parents come from abusive families (Straus et al., 1997). Some researchers have noted a problem with this logic. Well, yes, they've said, physically punished children may be more aggressive, for the same reason that people who have undergone psychotherapy are more likely to suffer depression—because they had preexisting problems that triggered the treatments (Larzelere, 2000, 2004). Which is the chicken and which is the egg? Correlations don't hand us an answer.

CHILDREN SEE, CHILDREN DO? Children who often experience physical punishment tend to display more aggression.

If one adjusts for preexisting antisocial behavior, then an occasional single swat or two to misbehaving 2- to 6-year-olds looks more effective (Baumrind et al., 2002; Larzelere & Kuhn, 2005). That is especially so if two other conditions are met:

1. The swat is used only as a backup when milder disciplinary tactics, such as a time-out (removing them from reinforcing surroundings), fail.

2. The swat is combined with a generous dose of reasoning and reinforcing.

But the debate continues. Other researchers note that frequent spankings predict future aggression—even when studies control for preexisting bad behavior (Taylor et al., 2010).

Parents of delinquent youths may not know how to achieve desirable behaviors without screaming at or hitting their children (Patterson et al., 1982). Training programs can help them translate dire threats ("Apologize right now or I'm taking that cell phone away!") into positive incentives ("You're welcome to have

your phone back when you apologize"). Stop and think about it. Aren't many threats of punishment just as forceful, and perhaps more effective, when rephrased positively? Thus, "If you don't get your homework done, I'm not giving you money for a movie!" would better be phrased as . . .

In classrooms, too, teachers can give feedback on papers by saying "No, but try this . . ." and "Yes, that's it!" Such responses reduce unwanted behavior while reinforcing more desirable alternatives. Remember: *Punishment tells you what not to do; reinforcement tells you what to do.*

What punishment often teaches, said Skinner, is how to avoid it. The bottom line: Most psychologists now favor an emphasis on reinforcement: Notice people doing something right and affirm them for it. ▪

RETRIEVE + REMEMBER

- Fill in the blanks below with one of the following terms: negative reinforcement (NR), positive punishment (PP), and negative punishment (NP). The first answer, positive reinforcement (PR), is provided for you.

Type of Stimulus	Give It	Take It Away
Desired (for example, a teen's use of the car):	1. PR	2.
Undesired/aversive (for example, an insult):	3.	4.

ANSWERS: 1. PR (positive reinforcement); 2. NP (negative punishment); 3. PP (positive punishment); 4. NR (negative reinforcement)

Skinner's Legacy

6-9 Why were Skinner's ideas controversial, and how are educators, managers, and parents applying operant principles?

B. F. Skinner stirred a hornet's nest with his outspoken beliefs. He repeatedly insisted that external influences (not internal thoughts and feelings) shape behavior. And he urged people to use operant principles to influence others' behavior at school, work, and home. Knowing that behavior is shaped by its results, he said, we should use rewards to evoke more desirable behavior.

Skinner's critics objected, saying that by neglecting people's personal freedom and trying to control their actions, he treated them as less than human. Skinner's reply: External consequences already control people's behavior. So why not steer those consequences toward human betterment? Wouldn't reinforcers be more humane than the punishments used in homes, schools, and prisons? And if it is humbling to think that our history has shaped us, doesn't

B. F. SKINNER "I am sometimes asked, 'Do you think of yourself as you think of the organisms you study?' The answer is yes. So far as I know, my behavior at any given moment has been nothing more than the product of my genetic endowment, my personal history, and the current setting" (1983).

punishment an event that decreases the behavior it follows.

this very idea also give us hope that we can shape our future?

Applications of Operant Conditioning

In later chapters we will see how psychologists apply operant conditioning principles to help people reduce high blood pressure or gain social skills. Reinforcement techniques are also at work in schools, workplaces, and homes (Flora, 2004).

AT SCHOOL More than 50 years ago, Skinner and others worked toward a day when "machines and textbooks" would shape learning in small steps, by immediately reinforcing correct responses. Such machines and texts, they said, would revolutionize education and free teachers to focus on each student's special needs. "Good instruction demands two things," said Skinner (1989). "Students must be told immediately whether what they do is right or wrong and, when right, they must be directed to the step to be taken next."

Skinner might be pleased to know that many of his ideals for education are now possible. Teachers used to find it difficult to pace material to each student's rate of learning, and to provide prompt feed-

COMPUTER-ASSISTED LEARNING Electronic technologies have helped realize Skinner's goal of individually paced instruction with immediate feedback.

back. Electronic adaptive quizzing (such as the system available with this text) does both. Students move through quizzes at their own pace, according to their own level of understanding. And they get immediate feedback on their efforts.

AT WORK Skinner's ideas also show up in the workplace. Knowing that reinforcers influence productivity, many organizations have invited employees to share the risks and rewards of company ownership. Others have focused on reinforcing a job well done. Rewards are most likely to increase productivity if the desired performance is well defined and is achievable. How might managers successfully motivate their employees? *Reward specific, achievable behaviors, not vaguely defined "merit."*

Operant conditioning also reminds us that reinforcement should be *immediate*. IBM legend Thomas Watson understood. When he observed an achievement, he wrote the employee a check on the spot (Peters & Waterman, 1982). But rewards don't have to be material, or lavish. An effective manager may simply walk the floor and sincerely praise people for good work, or write notes of appreciation for a completed project. As Skinner said, "How much richer would the whole world be if the reinforcers in daily life were more effectively contingent on productive work?"

AT HOME As we have seen, parents can learn from operant conditioning practices. Parent-training researchers remind us that by saying "Get ready for bed" and then caving in to protests or defiance, parents reinforce such whining and arguing. Exasperated, they may then yell or make threatening gestures. When the child, now frightened, obeys, that in turn reinforces the parents' angry behavior. Over time, a destructive parent-child relationship develops.

To disrupt this cycle, parents should remember the basic rule of shaping: *Notice people doing something right and affirm them for it.* Give children attention and other reinforcers when they are

behaving *well* (Wierson & Forehand, 1994). Target a specific behavior, reward it, and watch it increase. When children misbehave or are defiant, do not yell at or hit them. Simply explain what they did wrong and give them a time-out.

Operant conditioning principles can also help us change our own behaviors. For some tips, see Close-Up: Using Operant Conditioning to Build Your Own Strengths. ■

Contrasting Classical and Operant Conditioning

6-10 How does classical conditioning differ from operant conditioning?

Both classical and operant conditioning are forms of *associative learning* (TABLE 6.4). In both, we *acquire* behaviors that may later become *extinct* and then *spontaneously reappear*. We often *generalize* our responses but learn to *discriminate* among different stimuli.

Classical and operant conditioning also differ: Through classical conditioning, we associate different events that we don't control, and we respond automatically (*respondent behaviors*). Through operant conditioning, we link our own behaviors that act on our environment to produce rewarding or punishing events (*operant behaviors*) with their consequences.

Using Operant Conditioning to Build Your Own Strengths

Want to stop smoking? Eat less? Study or exercise more? To reinforce your own desired behaviors and extinguish the undesired ones, psychologists suggest taking five steps.

1. *State your goal in measurable terms and announce it.* You might, for example, aim to boost your study time by an hour a day and share that goal with friends.

2. *Decide how, when, and where you will work toward your goal.* Take time to plan. Those who list specific steps showing how they will reach their goals more often achieve them (Gollwitzer & Oettingen, 2012).

3. *Monitor how often you engage in your desired behavior.* You might log your current study time,

"I wrote another five hundred words. Can I have another cookie?"

© The New Yorker Collection, 2001, Mick Stevens from cartoonbank.com. All Rights Reserved.

noting under what conditions you do and don't study. (When I began writing textbooks, I logged how I spent my time each day and was amazed to discover how much time I was wasting.)

4. *Reinforce the desired behavior.* To increase your study time, give yourself a reward (a snack or some activity you enjoy) only after you finish your extra hour of study. Agree with your friends that you will join them for weekend activities only if you have met your realistic weekly studying goal.

5. *Reduce the rewards gradually.* As your new behaviors become habits, give yourself a mental pat on the back instead of a cookie.

As we shall next see, our *biology* and our *thought* processes influence both classical and operant conditioning. ■

- Salivating in response to a tone paired with food is a(n) _____ behavior; pressing a bar to obtain food is a(n) _____ behavior.

ANSWER: respondent; operant

Biology, Cognition, and Learning

◎ From drooling dogs, running rats, and pecking pigeons, we have learned much about the basic processes of learning. But conditioning principles don't tell us the whole story. Once again we see one of psychology's big ideas at work. Our learning is the product of the interaction of biological, psychological, and social-cultural influences.

Biological Limits on Conditioning

6-11 What limits does biology place on conditioning?

Evolutionary theorist Charles Darwin proposed that *natural selection* favors traits that aid survival. In the middle of the twentieth century, researchers fur-

---

TABLE 6.4	Comparison of Classical and Operant Conditioning	
	Classical Conditioning	**Operant Conditioning**
Basic idea	Learning associations between events we don't control	Learning associations between our own behavior and its consequences
Response	Involuntary, automatic	Voluntary, operates on environment
Acquisition	Associating events; NS is paired with US and becomes CS	Associating response with a consequence (reinforcer or punisher)
Extinction	CR decreases when CS is repeatedly presented alone	Responding decreases when reinforcement stops
Spontaneous recovery	The reappearance, after a rest period, of an extinguished CR	The reappearance, after a rest period, of an extinguished response
Generalization	Responding to stimuli similar to the CS	Responses to similar stimuli are also reinforced
Discrimination	Learning to distinguish between a CS and other stimuli that do not signal a US	Learning that some responses, but not others, will be reinforced

ther showed that there are **biological constraints** on learning. Each species comes predisposed (biologically prepared) to learn those things crucial to its survival.

Limits on Classical Conditioning

A discovery by John Garcia and Robert Koelling in the 1960s helped end a popular and widely held belief in psychology: that environments rule our behavior. Part of this idea was that almost any stimulus (whether a taste, sight, or sound) could serve equally well as a conditioned stimulus. Garcia and Koelling's work put that idea to the test and proved it wrong. They noticed that rats would avoid a taste—but not sights or sounds—associated with becoming sick, even hours later (1966). This response, which psychologists call *taste aversion*, makes adaptive sense. For rats, the easiest way to identify tainted food is to taste it. Taste aversion makes it tough to wipe out an invasion of "bait-shy" rats by poisoning. After being sickened by the bait, they are biologically prepared to avoid that taste ever after.

JOHN GARCIA As the laboring son of California farmworkers, Garcia attended school only in the off season during his early childhood years. After entering junior college in his late twenties, and earning his Ph.D. in his late forties, he received the American Psychological Association's Distinguished Scientific Contribution Award "for his highly original, pioneering research in conditioning and learning." He was also elected to the National Academy of Sciences.

Humans, too, seem biologically prepared to learn some things rather than others. If you become violently ill four hours after eating a tainted hamburger, you will probably develop an aversion to the taste of hamburger. But you usually won't avoid the sight of the associated restaurant, its plates, the people you were with, or the music you heard there.

Though Garcia and Koelling's taste-aversion research began with the discomfort of some laboratory animals, it later enhanced the welfare of many others. In one taste-aversion study, coyotes and wolves were tempted into eating sheep carcasses laced with a sickening poison. Ever after, they avoided sheep meat (Gustavson et al., 1974, 1976). Two wolves penned with a live sheep seemed actually to fear it. These studies not only saved the sheep from their predators, but also saved the sheep-shunning coyotes and wolves from angry ranchers and farmers. In later experiments, conditioned taste aversion has successfully prevented baboons from raiding African gardens, raccoons from attacking chickens, ravens and crows from feeding on crane eggs, and Mexican wolves from preying on sheep. In all these cases, research helped preserve both the prey and their predators (Dingfelder, 2010; Garcia & Gustavson, 1997).

Such research supports Darwin's principle that natural selection favors traits that aid survival. Our ancestors who readily learned taste aversions were unlikely to eat the same toxic food again and were more likely to survive and leave descendants. Nausea, like anxiety, pain, and other bad feelings, serves a good purpose. Like a car's low-oil warning light, each alerts the body to a threat (Neese, 1991).

This tendency to learn behaviors favored by natural selection may help explain why we humans seem naturally disposed to learn associations between the color red and sexuality. Female primates display red when nearing ovulation. In human females, enhanced bloodflow produces the red blush of flirtation and sexual excitation. Does the frequent pair-

TASTE AVERSION As an alternative to killing wolves and coyotes that prey on sheep, some ranchers have sickened the animals with lamb laced with a drug to help them develop a taste aversion.

ing of red and sex—with Valentine's hearts, red-light districts, and red lipstick—naturally enhance men's attraction to women? Experiments **(FIGURE 6.8)** indicate that it does (Elliot et al., 2013; Pazda & Elliot, 2012). ■

RETRIEVE + REMEMBER

- How did Garcia and Koelling's taste-aversion studies help disprove the belief that almost any stimulus (tastes, sights, sounds) could serve equally well as a conditioned stimulus? Explain.

ANSWER: Garcia and Koelling demonstrated that rats may learn an aversion to tastes, on which their survival depends, but not to sights or sounds.

Limits on Operant Conditioning

As with classical conditioning, nature sets limits on each species' capacity for operant conditioning. Author and humorist Mark Twain (1835–1910) said it well: "Never try to teach a pig to sing. It wastes your time and annoys the pig."

Courtesy of Kathryn Brownson, Hope College

FIGURE 6.8 Romantic red In a series of experiments that controlled for other factors (such as the brightness of the image), men found women more attractive and sexually desirable when framed in red (Elliot & Niesta, 2008).

We most easily learn and retain behaviors that reflect our biological predispositions. Thus, using food as a reinforcer, you could easily condition a hamster to dig or to rear up, because these are among the animal's natural food-searching behaviors. But you won't be so successful if you use food to try to shape face washing and other hamster behaviors that normally have no link to food or hunger (Shettleworth, 1973). Similarly, you could easily teach pigeons to flap their wings to avoid being shocked, and to peck to obtain food. That's because fleeing with their wings and eating with their beaks are natural pigeon behaviors. However, pigeons have a hard time learning to peck to avoid a shock, or to flap their wings to obtain food (Foree & LoLordo, 1973). The principle: *Our biology predisposes us to learn associations that are naturally adaptive.*

Karen Moskowitz/Getty Images

NATURAL ATHLETES Animals can most easily learn and retain behaviors that draw on their biological predispositions, such as small dogs' inborn ability to stand on their hind legs.

Cognitive Influences on Conditioning

6-12 How do cognitive processes affect classical and operant conditioning?

Cognition and Classical Conditioning

John B. Watson, of the "Little Albert" research discussed earlier in this chapter,

JOHN B. WATSON Watson (1924) admitted to "going beyond my facts" when offering his famous boast: "Give me a dozen healthy infants, well-formed, and my own specified world to bring them up in and I'll guarantee to take any one at random and train him to become any type of specialist I might select—doctor, lawyer, artist, merchant-chief, and, yes, even beggar-man and thief, regardless of his talents, penchants, tendencies, abilities, vocations, and race of his ancestors."

was one of many psychologists who built on Ivan Pavlov's work. The two researchers shared many beliefs. They rejected "mentalistic" concepts (such as consciousness) that referred to inner thoughts, feelings, and motives (Watson, 1913). They also maintained that the basic laws of learning are the same for all animals—whether dogs or humans. Thus, the science of psychology should study how organisms respond to stimuli in their environments, said Watson. "Its theoretical goal is the prediction and control of behavior." This view, that psychology should be an objective science based on observable behavior, was called **behaviorism,** and it influenced North American psychology during the first half of the twentieth century.

Later research has shown that Pavlov's and Watson's views of learning underestimated two important sets of influences. The first, as we have seen, is the way that biological predispositions limit our learning. The second is the effect of our *cognitive processes*—our thoughts, perceptions, and expectations—on learning. For example, people being treated for alcohol use disorder may be given alcohol spiked with a nauseating drug. However, their *awareness* that the drug, not the alcohol, causes the nausea tends to weaken the association between drinking alcohol and feeling sick. In classical conditioning, it is (especially with humans) not simply the CS-US pairing, but also the thought that counts.

Cognition and Operant Conditioning

B. F. Skinner granted the biological underpinnings of behavior and the existence of private thought processes. Nevertheless,

biological constraints evolved biological tendencies that predispose animals' behavior and learning. Thus, certain behaviors are more easily learned by some animals than others.

behaviorism the view that psychology (1) should be an objective science that (2) studies behavior without reference to mental processes. Most research psychologists today agree with (1) but not with (2).

TABLE 6.5 Biological and Cognitive Influences on Conditioning		
	Classical Conditioning	**Operant Conditioning**
Biological predispositions	Biological tendencies limit the types of stimuli and responses that can easily be associated. Involuntary, automatic.	Animals most easily learn behaviors similar to their natural behaviors; associations that are not naturally adaptive are not easily learned.
Cognitive processes	Thoughts, perceptions, and expectations can weaken the association between the CS and the US.	Animals may develop expectation that a response will be reinforced or punished; latent learning may occur without reinforcement.

many psychologists criticized him for discounting cognition's importance.

A mere eight days before dying of leukemia in 1990, Skinner stood before those of us attending the American Psychological Association convention. In this final address, he again rejected the growing belief that cognitive processes have a necessary place in the science of psychology and even in our understanding of conditioning. For Skinner, thoughts and emotions were behaviors that follow the same laws as other behaviors.

Nevertheless, the evidence of cognitive processes cannot be ignored. For example, rats exploring a maze, given no obvious rewards, seem to develop a **cognitive map,** a mental representation of the maze. In one study, when an experimenter placed food in the maze's goal box, these roaming rats ran the maze as quickly as (and even faster than) other rats that had always been

LATENT LEARNING Animals, like people, can learn from experience, with or without reinforcement. In a classic experiment, rats in one group repeatedly explored a maze, always with a food reward at the end. Rats in another group explored the maze with no food reward. But once given a food reward at the end, rats in the second group thereafter ran the maze as quickly as (and even faster than) the always-rewarded rats. (From Tolman & Honzik, 1930.)

rewarded with food for reaching the goal. Like people sightseeing in a new town, the exploring rats seemingly experienced **latent learning** during their earlier tours. Their latent learning became evident only when they had some reason to demonstrate it.

The cognitive perspective shows the limits of rewards. Promising people a reward for a task they already enjoy can backfire. Excessive rewards can destroy **intrinsic motivation**—the desire to do something well, for its own sake. In experiments, rewarding children with toys or candy for reading shortens the time they spend reading (Marinak & Gambrell, 2008). It is as if they think, "If I have to be bribed into doing this, it must not be worth doing for its own sake."

To sense the difference between intrinsic motivation and **extrinsic motivation** (behaving in certain ways to gain external rewards or to avoid threatened punishment), think about your experience in this course. Are you feeling pressured to finish this reading before a deadline? Worried about your grade? Eager for the credits that will count toward graduation? If *Yes*, then you are extrinsically motivated (as, to some extent, almost all students must be). Are you also finding the material interesting? Does learning it make you feel more competent? If there were no grade at stake, might you be curious enough to want to learn the material for its own sake? If *Yes*, intrinsic motivation also fuels your efforts.

Nevertheless, rewards that signal a job well done—rather than to bribe or to control someone—can be effective (Boggiano et al., 1985). "Most improved player" awards, for example, can boost feelings of competence and increase enjoyment of a

sport. Rightly administered, rewards can raise performance and spark creativity (Eisenberger & Rhoades, 2001; Henderlong & Lepper, 2002). And extrinsic rewards—such as the admissions, scholarships, and jobs that often follow hard work and good grades—are here to stay.

To sum up, **TABLE 6.5** compares the biological and cognitive influences on classical and operant conditioning. ■

RETRIEVE + REMEMBER

- Latent learning is an example of what important idea?

ANSWER: The success of operant conditioning is affected not just by environmental cues, but also by cognitive factors.

Learning by Observation

6-13 How does observational learning differ from associative learning? How may observational learning be enabled by mirror neurons?

Cognition is certainly a factor in **observational learning,** in which higher animals learn without direct experience, by watching and imitating others. A child who sees his sister burn her fingers on a hot stove learns, without getting burned himself, that hot stoves can burn us. We learn our native languages and all kinds of other specific behaviors by observing and imitating others, a process called **modeling.**

Picture this scene from an experiment by Albert Bandura, the pioneering researcher of observational learning

ALBERT BANDURA "The Bobo doll follows me wherever I go. The photographs are published in every introductory psychology text and virtually every undergraduate takes introductory psychology. I recently checked into a Washington hotel. The clerk at the desk asked, 'Aren't you the psychologist who did the Bobo doll experiment?' I answered, 'I am afraid that will be my legacy.' He replied, 'That deserves an upgrade. I will put you in a suite in the quiet part of the hotel'" (2005).

(Bandura et al., 1961). A preschool child works on a drawing. In another part of the room, an adult is building with Tinkertoys. As the child watches, the adult gets up and for nearly 10 minutes pounds, kicks, and throws around the room a large, inflated Bobo doll, yelling, "Sock him in the nose.... Hit him down.... Kick him."

The child is then taken to another room filled with appealing toys. Soon the experimenter returns and tells the child she has decided to save these good toys "for the other children." She takes the now-frustrated child to a third room containing a few toys, including a Bobo doll. Left alone, what does the child do?

Compared with other children in the study, those who viewed the model's actions were much more likely to lash out at the doll. Apparently, observing the aggressive outburst lowered their inhibitions. But *something more* was also at work, for the children often imitated the very acts they had observed and used the very words they had heard **(FIGURE 6.9)**.

That "something more," Bandura suggested, was this: By watching models, we *vicariously* (in our imagination) experience what they are experiencing. Through *vicarious reinforcement* or *vicarious punishment*, we learn to anticipate a behavior's consequences in situations like those we are observing. We are especially likely to experience their outcomes vicariously if we identify with them—if we perceive them as

- similar to ourselves.
- successful.
- admirable.

Functional MRI (fMRI) scans show that when people observe someone winning a reward, their own brain reward systems become active, much as if they themselves had won the reward (Mobbs et al., 2009).

Mirrors and Imitation in the Brain

In one of those quirky events that appear in the growth of science, researchers made an amazing discovery.

On a 1991 hot summer day in Parma, Italy, a lab monkey awaited its researchers' return from lunch. The researchers had implanted a monitoring device in the monkey's brain, in a frontal lobe region important for planning and acting out movements. The device would alert

cognitive map a mental image of the layout of one's environment.

latent learning learning that is not apparent until there is an incentive to demonstrate it.

intrinsic motivation a desire to perform a behavior well for its own sake.

extrinsic motivation a desire to perform a behavior to gain a reward or avoid punishment.

observational learning learning by observing others.

modeling the process of observing and imitating a specific behavior.

Courtesy of Albert Bandura, Stanford University

FIGURE 6.9 The famous Bobo doll experiment Notice how the children's actions directly imitate the adult's.

the researchers to activity in that region. When the monkey moved a peanut into its mouth, for example, the device would buzz. That day, the monkey stared as one of the researchers entered the lab carrying an ice cream cone in his hand. As the researcher raised the cone to lick it, the monkey's monitor buzzed—as if the motionless monkey had itself made some movement (Blakeslee, 2006; Iacoboni, 2009). The same buzzing had been heard earlier, when the monkey watched humans or other monkeys move peanuts to their mouths.

This quirky event, the researchers believed, marked an amazing discovery: a previously unknown type of neuron (Rizzolatti, 2002, 2006). In their view, these **mirror neurons** provided a neural basis for everyday imitation and observational learning. When a monkey grasps, holds, or tears something, these neurons fire. They likewise fire when the monkey observes another doing so. When one monkey sees, these neurons mirror what another monkey does. (Other researchers continue to debate the existence and importance of mirror neurons and related brain networks [Gallese et al., 2011].)

It's not just monkey business. Imitation occurs in various animal species, but it is most striking in humans. Our catchphrases, fashions, ceremonies, foods, traditions, morals, and fads all spread by one person copying another. Imitation shapes even very young humans' behavior (Bates & Byrne, 2010). Shortly after birth, a baby may imitate an adult who sticks out his tongue. By 8 to 16 months, infants imitate various novel gestures (Jones, 2007). By age 12 months, they begin looking where an adult is looking (Meltzoff et al., 2009). And by 14 months, children imitate acts modeled on TV (Meltzoff & Moore, 1997). Even as 2½-year-olds, when many of their mental abilities are near those of adult chimpanzees, young humans surpass chimps at social tasks such as imitating another's solution to a problem (Herrmann et al., 2007). Children see, children do.

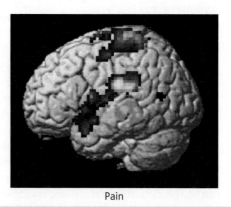
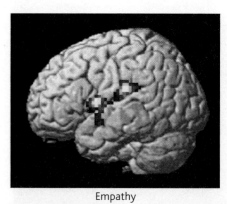

Pain   Empathy

FIGURE 6.10 **Experienced and imagined pain in the brain** Brain activity related to actual pain (left) is mirrored in the brain of an observing loved one (right). Empathy in the brain shows up in areas that process emotions, but not in the areas that register physical pain.

Because of the brain's responses, emotions are contagious. As we observe others' postures, faces, voices, and writing styles, we unconsciously mimic them. And by doing that, we grasp others' states of mind. We mentally imagine their experience and we feel what they are feeling (Bernieri et al., 1994; Ireland & Pennebaker, 2010).

Seeing a loved one's pain, our faces mirror the loved one's emotion. And so do our brains. In the fMRI scan in **FIGURE 6.10**, the pain imagined by an empathic romantic partner triggered some of the same brain activity experienced by the loved one in actual pain (Singer et al., 2004). Even fiction reading may trigger such activity, as we vicariously experience the feelings and actions described (Mar & Oatley, 2008; Speer et al., 2009).

So real are these mental instant replays that we may remember an action we have observed as an action we have actually performed (Lindner et al., 2010). The bottom line: *Brain activity underlies our intensely social nature.*

Applications of Observational Learning

6-14 What is the impact of prosocial modeling and of antisocial modeling?

So the big news from Bandura's studies and the mirror-neuron research is that we look, we mentally imitate, and we learn. Models—in our family or neighbor-

hood, or on TV—may have effects, good and bad.

PROSOCIAL EFFECTS The good news is that **prosocial** (positive, helpful) **behavior** models can have prosocial effects. People who model nonviolent, helpful behavior can prompt similar behavior in others. India's Mahatma Gandhi and America's Martin Luther King, Jr., both drew on the power of modeling, making nonviolent action a powerful force for social change in both countries. Parents are also powerful models. European Christians who risked their lives to rescue Jews from the Nazis usually had a close relationship with at least one parent who modeled a strong moral or humanitarian concern. This was also true for U.S. civil rights activists in the 1960s (London, 1970; Oliner & Oliner, 1988).

Models are most effective when their actions and words are consistent. Sometimes, however, models say one thing and do another. To encourage children to read, read to them and surround them with books and people who read. To increase the odds that your children will practice your religion, worship and attend religious activities with them. Many parents seem to operate according to the principle "Do as I *say*, not as I *do*." Experiments suggest that children learn to do both (Rice & Grusec, 1975; Rushton, 1975). Exposed to a hypocrite, they tend to imitate the hypocrisy—by doing

MODEL OF GIVING Children, such as this boy volunteering with his dad for a neighborhood revitalization project, learn positive behaviors and attitudes from the prosocial models in their lives.

what the model did and saying what the model said.

ANTISOCIAL EFFECTS The bad news is that observational learning may have *antisocial effects*. This helps us understand why abusive parents might have aggressive children, and why many men who beat their wives had wife-battering fathers (Stith et al., 2000). Critics note that being aggressive could be passed along by parents' genes. But with monkeys, we know it can be environmental. In study after study, young monkeys separated from their mothers and subjected to high levels of aggression grew up to be aggressive themselves (Chamove, 1980). The lessons we learn as children are not easily unlearned as adults, and they are sometimes visited on future generations.

TV shows and Internet videos are a powerful source of observational learning. While watching TV and videos, children may "learn" that bullying is an effective way to control others, that free and easy sex brings pleasure without later misery or disease, or that men should be tough and women gentle.

And they have ample time to learn such lessons. During their first 18 years, most children in developed countries spend more time watching TV shows than they spend in school. In the United States, the average teen watches TV shows more than 4 hours a day, the average adult 3 hours (Robinson & Martin, 2009; Strasburger et al., 2010).

TV-show viewers are learning about life from a rather peculiar storyteller, one with a taste for violence. During one closely studied year, nearly 6 in 10 U.S. network and cable programs featured violence. Of those acts, 74 percent went unpunished, and the victims usually showed no pain. Nearly half the events were portrayed as "justified," and nearly half the attackers were attractive (Donnerstein, 1998).

These conditions define the recipe for the violence-viewing effect, described in many studies (Donnerstein, 1998, 2011). To read more about this effect, see Thinking Critically About: Does Viewing Media Violence Trigger Violent Behavior? on the next page.

Screen time's greatest effect may stem from what it displaces. Children and adults who spend several hours a day in front of a screen spend that many fewer hours in other pursuits—talking, studying, playing, reading, or socializing in real time with friends. What would you have done with your extra time if you had spent even half as many hours in front of a screen, and how might you therefore be different? ■

mirror neuron neuron that fires when we perform certain actions and when we observe others performing those actions; neural basis for imitation and observational learning.

prosocial behavior positive, constructive, helpful behavior. The opposite of antisocial behavior.

RETRIEVE + REMEMBER

- Jason's parents and older friends all smoke, but they advise him not to. Juan's parents and friends don't smoke, but they say nothing to deter him from doing so. Will Jason or Juan be more likely to start smoking?

ANSWER: Jason may be more likely to smoke, because observational learning studies suggest that children tend to do as others do and say what they say.

- Match the learning examples (items 1–5) to the following concepts (a–e):

  a. Classical conditioning
  b. Operant conditioning
  c. Latent learning
  d. Observational learning
  e. Biological predispositions

  1. Knowing the way from your bed to the bathroom in the dark
  2. Speaking the language your parents speak
  3. Salivating when you smell brownies in the oven
  4. Disliking the taste of chili after being violently sick a few hours after eating chili
  5. Your dog racing to greet you on your arrival home

ANSWERS: 1. c (You've probably learned your way by latent learning.) 2. d (Observational learning may have contributed to your imitating the language modeled by your parents.) 3. a (Through classical conditioning you have associated the smell with the anticipated tasty result.) 4. e (You are biologically predisposed to develop a conditioned taste aversion to foods associated with illness.) 5. b (Through operant conditioning your dog may have come to associate your arrival with attention, petting, and a treat.)

Does Viewing Media Violence Trigger Violent Behavior?

Was the judge who in 1993 tried two British 10-year-olds for their murder of a 2-year-old right to suspect that the pair had been influenced by "violent video films"? Were the American media right to wonder if Adam Lanza, the 2012 mass killer of young children and their teachers at Connecticut's Sandy Hook Elementary School, was influenced by his playing of the violent video games found stockpiled in his home? To understand whether violence viewing leads to violent behavior, researchers have done both correlational and experimental studies (Anderson & Gentile, 2008).

Correlational studies do support this link:

- In the United States and Canada, homicide rates doubled between 1957 and 1974, just when TV was introduced and spreading. Moreover, census regions with later dates for TV service also had homicide rates that jumped later.

- Elementary schoolchildren with heavy exposure to media violence (via TV, videos, and video games) tend to get into more fights (FIGURE 6.11). As teens, they also are at greater risk for violent behavior (Boxer et al., 2009).

But as we know from Chapter 1, correlation does not *prove* causation. So these studies do not prove that viewing violence causes aggression (Ferguson, 2009; Freedman, 1988; McGuire, 1986). Maybe aggressive children prefer violent programs. Maybe abused or neglected children are both more aggressive and more often left in front of the TV or computer. Maybe violent programs reflect, rather than affect, violent trends.

To pin down cause and effect, psychologists use experiments. In this case, researchers randomly assigned some viewers to observe violence

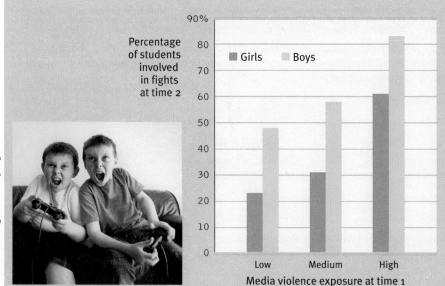

"Don't you understand? This is life, this is what is happening. We can't switch to another channel."

and others to watch entertaining nonviolence. Does viewing cruelty prepare people, when irritated, to react more cruelly? To some extent, it does. This is especially so when an attractive person commits seemingly justified, realistic violence that goes unpunished and causes no visible pain or harm (Donnerstein, 1998).

This *violence-viewing effect* seems to stem from at least two factors.

- More than 100 studies confirm that media models glorifying risk-taking behaviors (dangerous driving, extreme sports, unprotected sex) prompt *imitation* (Fischer et al., 2011; Geen & Thomas, 1986). As children watch violent models, their brains mimic the behavior. After this rehearsal, they become more likely to act out what they've observed. In one experiment, violent play increased sevenfold immediately after children viewed *Power Rangers* episodes (Boyatzis et al., 1995). As happened in the Bobo doll experiment, children often precisely imitated the model's violent acts—in this case, flying karate kicks.

- Prolonged exposure to violence *desensitizes* viewers. It fosters indifference. After spending three evenings watching sexually violent movies, men became less and less bothered by the rapes and slashings shown. Compared with others in a control group, the film watchers later expressed less sympathy for domestic violence victims. And they rated the victims' injuries as less severe (Mullin & Linz, 1995).

Drawing on such findings, the American Academy of Pediatrics (2009) has advised pediatricians that "media violence can contribute to aggressive behavior, desensitization to violence, nightmares, and fear of being harmed."

Percentage of students involved in fights at time 2

90%
80
70
60
50
40
30
20
10
0

■ Girls   ■ Boys

Low   Medium   High
Media violence exposure at time 1

FIGURE 6.11 Heavy exposure to media violence predicts future aggressive behavior Researchers studied more than 400 third- to fifth-graders. After controlling for existing differences in hostility and aggression, the researchers reported increased aggression in those heavily exposed to violent TV, videos, and video games (Gentile et al., 2004).

CHAPTER REVIEW

Learning

Test yourself by taking a moment to answer each of these Learning Objective Questions (repeated here from within the chapter). Then turn to Appendix D, Complete Chapter Reviews, to check your answers. Research suggests that trying to answer these questions on your own will improve your long-term memory of the concepts (McDaniel et al., 2009).

How Do We Learn?

6-1: What are some basic forms of learning?

Classical Conditioning

6-2: What is classical conditioning, and how does it demonstrate associative learning?

6-3: What parts do acquisition, extinction, spontaneous recovery, generalization, and discrimination play in classical conditioning?

6-4: Why is Pavlov's work important, and how is it being applied?

Operant Conditioning

6-5: What is operant conditioning, and how is operant behavior reinforced and shaped?

6-6: How do positive and negative reinforcement differ, and what are the basic types of reinforcers?

6-7: How do continuous and partial reinforcement schedules affect behavior?

6-8: How does punishment differ from negative reinforcement, and how does punishment affect behavior?

6-9: Why were Skinner's ideas controversial, and how are educators, managers, and parents applying operant principles?

6-10: How does classical conditioning differ from operant conditioning?

Biology, Cognition, and Learning

6-11: What limits does biology place on conditioning?

6-12: How do cognitive processes affect classical and operant conditioning?

Learning by Observation

6-13: How does observational learning differ from associative learning? How may observational learning be enabled by mirror neurons?

6-14: What is the impact of prosocial modeling and of antisocial modeling?

TERMS AND CONCEPTS TO REMEMBER

Test yourself on these terms by trying to write down the definition in your own words before flipping back to the referenced page to check your answer.

learning, p. 168
associative learning, p. 168
stimulus, p. 168
cognitive learning, p. 168
classical conditioning, p. 169
neutral stimulus (NS), p. 169
unconditioned response (UR), p. 170
unconditioned stimulus (US), p. 170
conditioned response (CR), p. 170

conditioned stimulus (CS), p. 170
acquisition, p. 170
extinction, p. 171
spontaneous recovery, p. 171
generalization, p. 172
discrimination, p. 172
respondent behavior, p. 174
operant conditioning, p. 174
operant behavior, p. 174
law of effect, p. 174

operant chamber, p. 174
reinforcement, p. 174
shaping, p. 174
positive reinforcement, p. 175
negative reinforcement, p. 175
primary reinforcer, p. 176
conditioned reinforcer, p. 176
continuous reinforcement, p. 177
reinforcement schedule, p. 177
partial (intermittent) reinforcement, p. 177
fixed-ratio schedule, p. 177
variable-ratio schedule, p. 177
fixed-interval schedule, p. 177

variable-interval schedule, p. 177
punishment, p. 178
biological constraints, p. 182
behaviorism, p. 183
cognitive map, p. 184
latent learning, p. 184
intrinsic motivation, p. 184
extrinsic motivation, p. 184
observational learning, p. 184
modeling, p. 184
mirror neuron, p. 186
prosocial behavior, p. 186

CHAPTER TEST

Test yourself repeatedly throughout your studies. This will not only help you figure out what you know and don't know; the testing itself will help you learn and remember the information more effectively thanks to the *testing effect*.

1. Learning is defined as "the process of acquiring, through experience, new and relatively enduring _____ or _____."

2. Two forms of associative learning are classical conditioning, in which we associate _____, and operant conditioning, in which we associate _____.

    a. two or more responses; a response and consequence

    b. two or more stimuli; two or more responses

    c. two or more stimuli; a response and consequence

    d. two or more responses; two or more stimuli

3. In Pavlov's experiments, the tone started as a neutral stimulus, and then became a(n) _____ stimulus.

4. Dogs have been taught to salivate to a circle but not to a square. This process is an example of _____.

5. After Watson and Rayner classically conditioned Little Albert to fear a white rat, the child later showed fear in response to a rabbit, a dog, and a sealskin coat. This illustrates

    a. extinction.

    b. generalization.

    c. spontaneous recovery.

    d. discrimination between two stimuli.

6. "Sex sells!" is a common saying in advertising. Using classical conditioning terms, explain how sexual images in advertisements can condition your response to a product.

7. Thorndike's law of effect was the basis for _____ work on operant conditioning and behavior control.

8. One way to change behavior is to reward natural behaviors in small steps, as they get closer and closer to a desired behavior. This process is called _____.

9. Your dog is barking so loudly that it's making your ears ring. You clap your hands, the dog stops barking, your ears stop ringing, and you think to yourself, "I'll have to do that when he barks again." The end of the barking was for you a

    a. positive reinforcer.

    b. negative reinforcer.

    c. positive punishment.

    d. negative punishment.

10. How could your psychology instructor use negative reinforcement to encourage you to pay attention during class?

11. Reinforcing a desired response only some of the times it occurs is called _____ reinforcement.

12. A restaurant is running a special deal. After you buy four meals at full price, your fifth meal will be free. This is an example of a _____ schedule of reinforcement.

    a. fixed-ratio

    b. variable-ratio

    c. fixed-interval

    d. variable-interval

13. The partial reinforcement schedule that reinforces a response after unpredictable time periods is a _____-_____ schedule.

14. An old saying notes that "a burnt child dreads the fire." In operant conditioning, the burning would be an example of a

    a. primary reinforcer.

    b. negative reinforcer.

    c. punisher.

    d. positive reinforcer.

15. Which research showed that conditioning can occur even when the unconditioned stimulus (US) does not immediately follow the neutral stimulus (NS)?

    a. The Little Albert experiment

    b. Pavlov's experiments with dogs

    c. Watson's behaviorism studies

    d. Garcia and Koelling's taste-aversion studies

16. Taste-aversion research has shown that some animals develop aversions to certain tastes but not to sights or sounds. This finding supports

    a. Pavlov's demonstration of generalization.

    b. Darwin's principle that natural selection favors traits that aid survival.

    c. Watson's belief that psychologists should study observable behavior, not mentalistic concepts.

    d. the early behaviorists' view that any organism can be conditioned to any stimulus.

17. Evidence that cognitive processes play an important role in learning comes in part from studies in which rats

    a. spontaneously recover previously learned behavior.

    b. develop cognitive maps.

    c. exhibit respondent behavior.

    d. generalize responses.

18. Rats that explored a maze without any reward were later able to run the maze as well as other rats that had received food rewards for running the maze. The rats that had learned without reinforcement demonstrated _____ _____.

19. Children learn many social behaviors by imitating parents and other models. This type of learning is called _____ _____.

20. According to Bandura, we learn by watching models because we experience _____ reinforcement or _____ punishment.

21. Parents are most effective in getting their children to imitate them if

    a. their words and actions are consistent.

    b. they have outgoing personalities.

    c. one parent works and the other stays home to care for the children.

    d. they carefully explain why a behavior is acceptable in adults but not in children.

22. Some scientists believe that the brain has _____ neurons that enable observation and imitation.

23. Most experts agree that repeated viewing of TV violence

    a. makes all viewers significantly more aggressive.

    b. has little effect on viewers.

    c. dulls viewers' sensitivity to violence.

    d. makes viewers angry and frustrated.

    Find answers to these questions in Appendix E, in the back of the book.

IN YOUR EVERYDAY LIFE

Answering these questions will help you make these concepts more personally meaningful, and therefore more memorable.

1. How have your emotions or behaviors been classically conditioned?

2. Can you recall a time when a teacher, coach, family member, or employer helped you learn something by shaping your behavior in little steps until you achieved your goal?

3. Think of a bad habit of yours or of someone you know. How could you use operant conditioning to break it?

4. Is your behavior in this class influenced more by intrinsic motivation or extrinsic motivation?

5. Who has been a significant role model for you? What did you learn from observing this person? Are you a role model for someone else?

experience more of the testing effect

Multiple-format self-tests and more may be found at www.worthpublishers.com/myers.

7 Memory

This chapter was revised after collaborating with Janie Wilson, Professor of Psychology at Georgia Southern University and Vice President for Programming of the Society for the Teaching of Psychology.

Memory is learning we retain over time. Imagine life without being able to form new conscious memories. For 55 years after having brain surgery to stop severe seizures, this was life for Henry Molaison, or H. M., as psychologists knew him until his 2008 death. H. M. was intelligent and did daily crossword puzzles. Yet, reported neuroscientist Suzanne Corkin (2005), "I've known H. M. since 1962, and he still doesn't know who I am." For about 20 seconds during a conversation he could keep something in mind. When distracted, he would lose what was just said or what had just occurred. Thus, he never could name the current president of the United States (Ogden, 2012).

My own father suffered a similar problem after a small stroke at age 92. His upbeat personality was intact. He enjoyed poring over family photo albums and telling stories about his pre-stroke life. But he could not tell me what day of the week it was, or what he'd had for dinner. Told repeatedly of his brother-in-law's death, he was surprised and saddened each time he heard the news.

At the other extreme are people with "supermemories" who would be gold medal winners in a memory Olympics. Russian journalist Shereshevskii, or S, had merely to listen while other reporters scribbled notes (Luria, 1968). You and I could parrot back a string of 7 or so numbers. If numbers were read about 3 seconds apart in an otherwise silent room, S could repeat up to 70. Moreover, he could recall them (and words, too) backward as easily as forward. His accuracy was perfect, even when recalling a list 15 years later. "Yes, yes," he might recall. "This was a series you gave me once when we were in your apartment. . . . You were sitting at the table and I in the rocking chair. . . . You were wearing a gray suit. . . ."

Amazing? Yes, but consider your own impressive memory. You remember countless faces, places, and happenings; tastes, smells, and textures; voices, sounds, and songs. In one study, students listened to snippets—a mere four-tenths of a second—from popular songs. How often did they recognize the artist and song? More than 25 percent of the time (Krumhansl, 2010). We often recognize songs as quickly as we recognize someone's voice saying "Hi" from behind us. So, too, with faces and places. In another experiment, people were exposed to 2800 images for only 3 seconds each. Later, viewing these and other images in a second round, they spotted the repeats with 82 percent accuracy (Konkle et al., 2010).

How do we accomplish such memory feats? How can we remember things we have not thought about for years, yet forget the name of someone we met a minute ago? How are our memories stored in our brain? Why, when I ask you later in this chapter, will you be likely to have trouble recalling this sentence: *"The angry rioter threw the rock at the window"*? In this chapter, we'll consider these fascinating questions and more, including some tips on how we can improve our own memories.

Studying Memory

7-1 What is memory, and how do information-processing models help us study memory?

◎ Be thankful for **memory**—your storehouse of accumulated learning. Your memory enables you to recognize family, speak your language, find your way home, and locate food and water. Your memory enables you to enjoy an experience and then mentally replay it and enjoy it again. Without memory there would be no savoring of past achievements, no guilt or anger over painful past events. You would instead live in an endless present, each moment fresh. Each person would be a stranger, every language foreign, every task—dressing, cooking, biking—a new challenge. You would even be a stranger to yourself, lacking that ongoing sense of self that extends from your distant past to your momentary present.

Earlier, in the Sensation and Perception chapter, we considered one of psychology's big questions: How does the world out there enter your brain? In this chapter we consider a related question: How does your brain pluck information out of the world around you and store it for a lifetime of use? Said simply, how does your brain construct your memories?

To help clients imagine future buildings, architects create miniature models. Similarly, psychologists create models of memory to help us think about how our brain forms and retrieves memories. One such model, known as the *information-processing model,* compares human memory to a computer's operation. It assumes that, to remember something, we must

- *get information into our brain,* a process called **encoding.**

- *retain that information,* a process called **storage.**

- later *get the information back out,* a process called **retrieval.**

Let's take a closer look.

An Information-Processing Model

7-2 What is the three-stage information-processing model, and how has later research updated this model?

Richard Atkinson and Richard Shiffrin (1968) proposed that we form memories in three stages.

1. We first record to-be-remembered information as a fleeting **sensory memory.**

2. From there, we process information into **short-term memory,** where we encode it through *rehearsal.*

3. Finally, information moves into **long-term memory** for later retrieval.

Other psychologists later updated this model to include important newer concepts, including *working memory* and *automatic processing* (**FIGURE 7.1**).

Working Memory

So much active processing takes place in the middle stage that psychologists now prefer the term **working memory**. In Atkinson and Shiffrin's original model, the second stage appeared to be a temporary shelf for holding recent thoughts and experiences. We now know that this working-memory stage is more like an active desktop—where your brain processes important information, making sense of new input and linking it with long-term memories. When you process verbal information, your *active* working memory connects new information to what you already know or imagine (Cowan, 2010; Kail & Hall, 2001). If you hear someone say eye-screem, you may encode it as "ice cream" or "I scream," depending on both the context (snack shop or horror film) and your experience.

The information you are now reading may enter your working memory through vision. You may also silently repeat the information using auditory rehearsal. Integrating these memory inputs with your existing long-term memory requires focused attention. Alan Baddeley (2002) suggested a *central executive* handles this focused processing (**FIGURE 7.2**).

Without focused attention, information often fades. In one experiment, people read and typed new information they would later need, such as "An ostrich's eye is bigger than its brain." If they knew the information would be available online, they invested less energy in remembering it, and they remembered it less well (Sparrow et al., 2011). ■

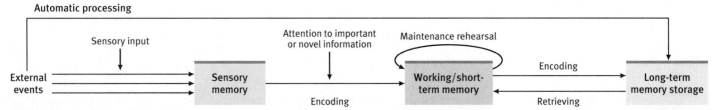

FIGURE 7.1 A modified three-stage information-processing model of memory Atkinson and Shiffrin's classic three-step model helps us to think about how memories are processed, but today's researchers recognize other ways long-term memories form. For example, some information slips into long-term memory via a "back door," without our consciously attending to it *(automatic processing).* And so much active processing occurs in the short-term memory stage that many now prefer to call that stage *working memory.*

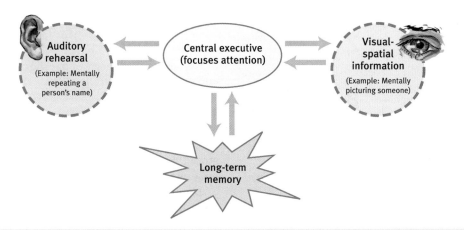

FIGURE 7.2 Working memory Alan Baddeley's (2002) model of working memory, simplified here, includes *visual* and *auditory rehearsal* of new information. Part of the brain functions like a manager, a *central executive* focusing attention and pulling information from long-term memory to help make sense of new information.

Building Memories: Encoding

Our Two-Track Memory System

7-3 How do explicit and implicit memories differ?

As we have seen throughout this text, our mind operates on two tracks. This theme appears again in the way we process memories:

- On one track, we process our **explicit memories** of the facts and experiences we can consciously know and declare. (Explicit memories are also called *declarative memories*.) We encode explicit memories through conscious, **effortful processing**. The Atkinson-Shiffrin model can help us understand how this memory track operates.

- On the second track, other information skips the Atkinson-Shiffrin stages and barges directly into storage, without our awareness. These **implicit memories** (also called *nondeclarative memories*) form without our conscious effort. Implicit memories, formed through **automatic processing,** bypass the conscious encoding track.

Automatic Processing and Implicit Memories

7-4 What information do we automatically process?

Your implicit memories include automatic skills (such as how to ride a bike) and classically conditioned *associations*. Visiting your dentist, you may find your palms sweating, thanks to a conditioned association that links the dentist's office with the painful drill. You didn't plan to feel that way when you got to the dentist's office; it happened *automatically*.

Without conscious effort, you also automatically process information about

- *space.* While studying, you often encode the place on a page where certain material appears. Later, when trying to recall how automatic processing works, you may picture that information on this page.

- *time.* While you are going about your day, your brain is working behind the scenes, jotting down the sequence of your day's events. Later, if you realize you've left your coat somewhere, you can call up that sequence and retrace your steps.

- *frequency.* Your behind-the-scenes mind also keeps track of how often things have happened, thus enabling you to realize, "This is the third time I've run into her today!"

Your two-track mind processes information efficiently. As one track automatically tucks away routine details, the other track focuses on conscious, effortful processing. This division of labor illustrates Chapter 5's description of parallel processing. Mental feats such as vision may seem to be single abilities, but they are not. Rather, your brain assigns different subtasks to separate areas for simultaneous processing.

Effortful Processing and Explicit Memories

Automatic processing happens so effortlessly that it is difficult to shut off. When you see words in your native language, you can't help but register their meaning. *Learning* to read was not automatic. You at first worked hard to pick out letters and connect them to certain sounds. But with experience and practice, your reading became automatic. Imagine now learning to read reversed sentences like this:

.citamotua emoceb nac gnissecorp luftroffE

At first, this requires effort, but with practice it becomes more automatic. We develop many skills in this way. With effort we learn to drive, to text, to speak a new language. With practice, these tasks become automatic.

Sensory Memory

7-5 How does sensory memory work?

Sensory memory (recall Figure 7.1) is the first stage in forming explicit memo-

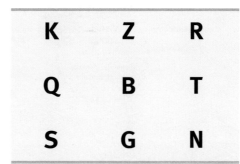

FIGURE 7.3 Total recall—briefly When George Sperling (1960) flashed a group of letters similar to this for one-twentieth of a second, people could recall only about half the letters. But when signaled to recall any one row immediately after the letters had disappeared, they could do so with near-perfect accuracy.

ries. A memory-to-be enters by way of the senses, feeding very brief images of scenes, or echoes of sounds, into our working memory. But *sensory memory,* like a lightning flash, is fleeting. How fleeting? In one experiment, people viewed three rows of three letters each for only one-twentieth of a second (**FIGURE 7.3**). Then the nine letters disappeared. How many letters could people recall? Only about half of them.

Was it because they had too little time to see them? *No*—the researcher, George Sperling (1960), demonstrated that people actually had seen, and could recall, all the letters, but only briefly. He sounded a tone immediately *after* flashing the nine letters. A high tone directed people to report the top row of letters; a medium tone, the middle row; a low tone, the bottom row. With these cues, they rarely missed a letter, showing that all nine were briefly available for recall.

This fleeting sensory memory of the flashed letters was an *iconic memory.* For a few tenths of a second, our eyes retain a picture-image memory of a scene. Then our visual field clears quickly, and new images replace old ones. We also have a fleeting sensory memory of sounds. It's called *echoic memory,* because the sound echoes in our mind for 3 or 4 seconds.

Capacity of Short-Term and Working Memory

7-6 What is the capacity of our short-term and working memory?

Recall that working memory is an active stage, where your brain makes sense of incoming information and links it with stored memories. What are the limits of what we can hold in this middle stage?

Memory researcher George Miller (1956) proposed that we can store about seven bits of information (give or take two) in this middle stage. Miller's Magical Number Seven is psychology's contribution to the list of magical sevens—the seven wonders of the world, the seven seas, the seven deadly sins, the seven primary colors, the seven musical scale notes, the seven days of the week—seven magical sevens. After Miller's 2012 death, his daughter recalled his best moment of golf: "He made the one and only hole-in-one of his life at the age of 77, on the seventh green . . . with a seven iron. He loved that" (quoted by Vitello, 2012).

Other researchers have confirmed that we can, if nothing distracts us, recall about seven digits, or about six letters or five words (Baddeley et al., 1975). How quickly do our short-term memories disappear? To find out how quickly, researchers have asked people to remember groups of three consonants, such as CHJ (Peterson & Peterson, 1959). To prevent rehearsal, they distracted them (asking them, for example, to start at 100 and count backward by threes). Without active processing, people's short-term memories of the consonants disappeared. After 3 seconds, they recalled the letters only about half the time. After 12 seconds, they seldom recalled them at all (**FIGURE 7.4**).

Working-memory capacity varies, depending on age and other factors. Compared with children and older adults, young adults have more working-memory capacity. They use their mental workspace more efficiently. Even so, whatever our age, our work is better and

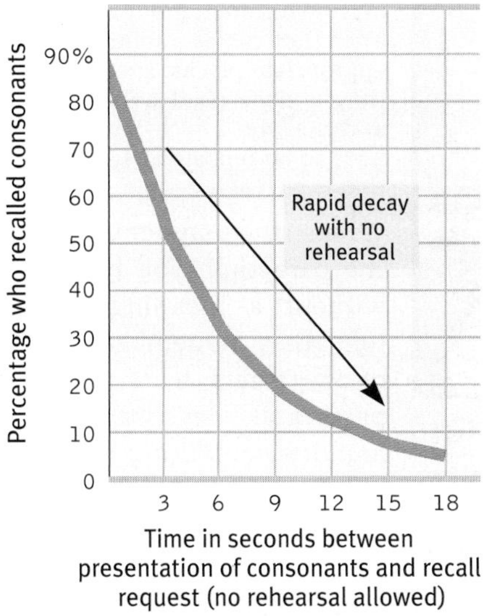

FIGURE 7.4 Short-term memory decay Unless rehearsed, verbal information may be quickly forgotten. (From Peterson & Peterson, 1959; see also Brown, 1958.)

more efficient when we focus on one task at a time, without distractions. *The bottom line:* It's probably a bad idea to try to watch TV, text your friends, and write a psychology paper all at the same time (Willingham, 2010)!

Effortful Processing Strategies

7-7 What are some effortful processing strategies that can help us remember new information?

Let's recap. To form an explicit memory (a lasting memory of a fact or an experience) it helps to *focus our attention* and *make a conscious effort* to remember. But our working memory desktop has limited space, and images, sounds, and other distractions compete for our attention.

We can boost our ability to form new explicit memories by using specific effortful processing strategies, such as *chunking* and *mnemonics*.

- ***Chunking:*** When we **chunk** information, we organize items into familiar, manageable units. Glance for a few seconds at row 1 of FIGURE 7.5, then look away and try to draw those forms. Impossible, yes? But you can easily reproduce row 2, which is just as complex. And row 4 is probably much easier to remember than row 3, although both contain the same letters. As you can see, chunking information helps us to recall it more easily.

  Chunking usually occurs so naturally that we take it for granted. Try remembering 43 individual numbers and letters. It would be impossible, unless chunked into, say, seven meaningful chunks, such as "Try remembering 43 individual numbers and letters." ☺

- ***Mnemonics:*** In ancient Greece, scholars and public speakers needed memory aids to help them encode long passages and speeches. They developed **mnemonics**, which often rely on vivid imagery. We are particularly good at remembering mental pictures. Concrete words that create these mental images are easier to remember than other words that describe abstract ideas. (When I quiz you later, which three of these words—*bicycle, void, cigarette, inherent, fire, process*—will you most likely recall?) Do you still recall the rock-throwing rioter sentence mentioned at the beginning of this chapter? If so, it is probably not only because of the meaning you encoded but also because the sentence painted a mental image.

  The *peg-word* system harnesses our visual-imagery skill. To use this strategy, you memorize a jingle: "*One is a bun; two is a shoe; three is a tree; four is a door; five is a hive; six is sticks; seven is heaven; eight is a gate; nine is swine; ten is a hen.*" Without much effort, you will soon be able to count by peg words instead of numbers: *bun, shoe, tree.* Then you create mental images to link the peg words with items you want to remember. Imagine a grocery list to remember. Carrots? Stick them into the imaginary bun. Milk? Fill the shoe with it. Paper towels? Drape them over the tree branch. Think *bun, shoe, tree* and you see their associated images: carrots, milk, paper towels. With few errors, you will be able to recall the items in any order and to name any given item (Bugelski et al., 1968). Memory whizzes understand the power of such systems. A study of star performers in the World Memory Championships showed them not to have exceptional intelligence, but rather to be superior at using mnemonic strategies (Maguire et al., 2003).

1. 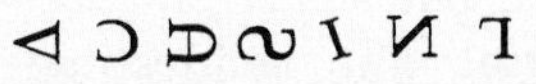

2. K L C I S N E

3. KLCISNE NVESE YNA NI CSTTIH TNDO
4. NICKELS SEVEN ANY IN STITCH DONT

5. NICKELS SEVEN ANY IN STITCH DONT SAVES AGO A SCORE TIME AND NINE WOODEN FOUR YEARS TAKE

6. DONT TAKE ANY WOODEN NICKELS FOUR SCORE AND SEVEN YEARS AGO A STITCH IN TIME SAVES NINE

FIGURE 7.5 Chunking effects Organizing information into meaningful units, such as letters, words, and phrases, helps us recall it more easily. (From Hintzman, 1978.)

* * *

Effortful processing requires closer attention and effort, and chunking and mnemonics help us form meaningful and accessible memories. But memory researchers have also discovered other important influences on how we capture information and hold it in memory. ■

chunking organizing items into familiar, manageable units; often occurs automatically.

mnemonics [nih-MON-iks] memory aids, especially techniques that use vivid imagery and organizational devices.

David Myers

MAKING THINGS MEMORABLE For suggestions on how to apply the *testing effect* to your own learning, watch this 5-minute YouTube animation: tinyurl.com/HowToRemember

Spaced Study and Self-Assessment

7-8 Why is cramming ineffective, and what is the testing effect?

We retain information (such as classmates' names) better when our encoding is spread over time. Psychologists call this the **spacing effect,** and more than 300 experiments over the past century have confirmed that *distributed practice* produces better long-term recall (Cepeda et al., 2006). *Massed practice* (cramming) can produce speedy short-term learning and feelings of confidence. But to paraphrase pioneering memory researcher Hermann Ebbinghaus (1880–1909), those who learn quickly also forget quickly. You'll retain material better if, rather than cramming, you space your study, with reviewing time later. How much later? If you need to remember something 10 days from now, practice it again tomorrow. If you need to remember something 6 months from now, practice it again a month from now (Cepeda et al., 2008). Spreading your learning over several months, rather than over a shorter term, can help you retain information for a lifetime.

One effective way to distribute practice is *repeated self-testing,* often called the **testing effect** (Roediger & Karpicke, 2006). Testing does more than assess learning;

it improves it (Karpicke, 2012; McDaniel, 2012). In this text, for example, the Retrieve + Remember questions and Chapter Tests offer self-testing opportunities. Better to practice retrieval (as any exam will demand) than merely to reread material (which may lull you into a false sense of mastery). As one memory expert explains, "What we recall becomes more recallable in the future" (Bjork, 2011).

The point to remember: Spaced study and self-assessment beat cramming and rereading. Practice may not make perfect, but smart practice—occasional rehearsal with self-testing—makes for lasting memories.

Making New Information Meaningful

Spaced practice helps, but if new information is not meaningful or related to your experience, you will have trouble processing it. Put yourself in the place of the students asked to remember this passage (Bransford & Johnson, 1972):

> The procedure is actually quite simple. First you arrange things into different groups. Of course, one pile may be sufficient depending on how much there is to do. . . . After the procedure is completed one arranges the materi-

als into different groups again. Then they can be put into their appropriate places. Eventually they will be used once more and the whole cycle will then have to be repeated. However, that is part of life.

When the students heard the paragraph you just read, without a meaningful context, they remembered little of it. Others were told the paragraph described doing laundry (something meaningful to them). They remembered much more of it—as you probably could now after rereading it.

Can you repeat the sentence about the angry rioter (from this chapter's opening section)?

Was the sentence "The angry rioter threw the rock *through* the window" or "The angry rioter threw the rock *at* the window"? If the first looks more correct, you—like the participants in the original study—may have recalled the meaning you encoded, not the words that were written (Brewer, 1977). In making such mistakes, our minds are like theater directors who, given a raw script, imagine a finished stage production (Bower & Morrow, 1990).

We can avoid some encoding errors by translating what we see and hear into personally meaningful terms. From his experiments on himself, Hermann Ebbinghaus estimated that, compared with learning nonsense material, learning meaningful material required one-tenth the effort. As another memory researcher noted, "The time you spend thinking about material you are reading and relating it to previously stored material is about the most useful thing you can do in learning any new subject matter" (Wickelgren, 1977, p. 346).

The point to remember: You can profit from taking time to find personal meaning in what you are studying. ∎

> Here is another sentence I will ask you about later: The fish attacked the swimmer.

• Which strategies are better for long-term retention: cramming and rereading material, or spreading out learning over time and repeatedly testing yourself?

ANSWER: Although cramming may lead to short-term gains in knowledge, distributed practice and repeated self-testing will result in the greatest long-term retention.

Memory Storage

7-9 What is the capacity of long-term memory? Are our long-term memories processed and stored in specific locations?

◉ In Arthur Conan Doyle's *A Study in Scarlet,* Sherlock Holmes offers a popular theory of memory capacity:

> I consider that a man's brain originally is like a little empty attic, and you have to stock it with such furniture as you choose. . . . It is a mistake to think that that little room has elastic walls and can distend to any extent. Depend upon it, there comes a time when for every addition of knowledge you forget something that you knew before.

Contrary to Holmes' "memory model," our capacity for storing long-term memories has no real limit. Many endure for a lifetime. Our brains are not like attics, which, once filled, can store more items only if we discard old ones.

Retaining Information in the Brain

I marveled at my aging mother-in-law, a retired pianist and organist. At age 88, her blind eyes could no longer read music. But let her sit at a keyboard and she would flawlessly play any of hundreds of hymns, including ones she had not thought of for 20 years. Where did her brain store those thousands of note patterns?

For a time, some surgeons and memory researchers marveled at what appeared to be vivid memories triggered by stimu-lating the brain during surgery. Did this prove that our whole past, not just well-practiced music, is "in there," just waiting to be relived? Further research disproved this idea. The vivid flashbacks were actually new creations of a stressed brain, not real memories (Loftus & Loftus, 1980). We do not store information in single, specific spots, as libraries store their books. As with perception, language, emotion, and much more, memory requires brain networks. Many parts of our brain interact as we encode, store, and retrieve information.

Explicit-Memory System: The Hippocampus and Frontal Lobes

7-10 What roles do the hippocampus and frontal lobes play in memory processing?

Separate brain regions process our explicit and implicit memories. We know this from scans of the brain in action, and from autopsies of people who suffered different types of memory loss.

New explicit memories of names, images, and events are laid down via the **hippocampus,** a limbic system neural center that is our brain's equivalent of a "save" button (**FIGURE 7.6**). When brain scans capture the brain forming an explicit memory, they reveal hippocampus activity. Your hippocampus

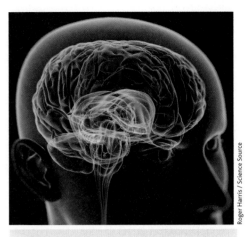

FIGURE 7.6 **The hippocampus** Explicit memories for facts and episodes are processed in the hippocampus (orange) and fed to other brain regions for storage.

Roger Harris / Science Source

acts as a loading dock where your brain registers and temporarily stores aspects of an event—its smell, feel, sound, and location. Then, like older files shifted to a storeroom, memories migrate for storage elsewhere. This storage process is called *memory consolidation.*

Your brain's right and left frontal lobes store different information. Recalling a password and holding it in working memory, for example, would activate your left frontal lobes. Calling up a visual image of last night's party would more likely activate your right frontal lobe.

A good night's sleep supports memory consolidation, both in humans and in rats. In experiments, rats have learned the location of a tasty new food. If their hippocampus is removed 3 hours after they locate the food, no long-term

off the mark.com   by Mark Parisi

THE BAD NEWS IS WE LEFT A CLAMP IN YOUR TEMPORAL LOBE... THE GOOD NEWS IS THAT YOU WON'T REMEMBER WHAT I JUST SAID...

offthemark.com/Mark Parisi dist. by UFS INC.

spacing effect the tendency for distributed study or practice to yield better long-term retention than is achieved through massed study or practice.

testing effect enhanced memory after retrieving, rather than simply rereading, information. Also sometimes referred to as the *retrieval practice effect* or *test-enhanced learning.*

hippocampus a neural center located in the limbic system; helps process explicit memories for storage.

memory will form (Tse et al., 2007). If their hippocampus is removed 48 hours later, after doing its work, they still remember that location. During sleep, the hippocampus and brain cortex display rhythmic patterns of activity, as if they were talking to each other (Ji & Wilson, 2007; Mehta, 2007). Researchers suspect that the brain is replaying the day's experiences as it transfers them to the cortex for long-term storage.

Implicit Memory System: The Cerebellum and Basal Ganglia

7-11 What roles do the cerebellum and basal ganglia play in memory processing?

You could lose your hippocampus and still—thanks to automatic processing—lay down *implicit* memories of newly conditioned associations and skills (such as golfing). Memory loss following brain damage left one patient unable to recognize her physician as, each day, he shook her hand and introduced himself. One day, after reaching for his hand, she yanked hers back, for the physician had pricked her with a tack in his palm. When he next introduced himself, she refused to shake his hand but couldn't explain why. Having been *classically conditioned,* she just wouldn't do it (LeDoux, 1996).

Your *cerebellum,* a brain region extending out from the rear of your brainstem, plays an important role in forming and storing memories created by classical conditioning. People with a damaged cerebellum cannot develop some conditioned reflexes. They can't, for example, link a tone with an oncoming puff of air, so they don't blink just before the puff, as you and I would learn to do (Daum & Schugens, 1996; Green & Woodruff-Pak, 2000). Implicit memory formation needs the cerebellum.

Your memories of physical skills—walking, cooking, dressing—are also implicit memories. Your *basal ganglia,* deep brain structures involved in motor movement, help form your memories for these skills (Mishkin, 1982; Mishkin et al., 1997). If you have learned how to

ride a bike, thank your basal ganglia.

Although not part of our conscious adult memory system, the reactions and skills we learned during infancy reach far into our future. Can you remember learning to talk and walk as a baby? If you cannot, you are not alone. As adults, our *conscious* memory of our first three years is blank, an experience called *infantile amnesia.* To form and store explicit memories, we need a command of language and a well-developed hippocampus. Before age 3, we don't have those learning tools. ∎

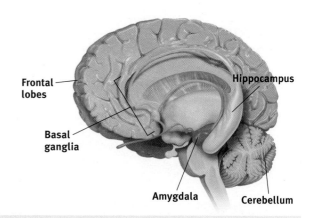

FIGURE 7.7 Review key memory structures in the brain

Frontal lobes and hippocampus: explicit memory formation
Cerebellum and basal ganglia: implicit memory formation
Amygdala: emotion-related memory formation

RETRIEVE + REMEMBER

- Which parts of the brain are important for *implicit* memory processing, and which parts play a key role in *explicit* memory processing?

  ANSWER: The cerebellum and basal ganglia are important for *implicit* memory processing. The frontal lobes and hippocampus are key to *explicit* memory formation.

- Your friend has experienced brain damage in an accident. He can remember how to tie his shoes but has a hard time remembering anything told to him during a conversation. What's going on here?

  ANSWER: Our *explicit* conscious memories differ from our *implicit* memories of skills and classically conditioned responses. The brain areas that process implicit memories apparently escaped damage during the accident.

The Amygdala, Emotions, and Memory

7-12 How do emotions affect our memory processing?

Arousal can sear certain events into the brain (Birnbaum et al., 2004; Strange & Dolan, 2004). Excitement or stress (perhaps a time you performed in front of a crowd) triggers your glands to produce stress

hormones. By making more glucose energy available to fuel brain activity, stress hormones signal the brain that something important has happened. They also provoke the *amygdala* (two limbic system, emotion-processing clusters) to boost activity in the brain's memory-forming areas (Buchanan, 2007; Kensinger, 2007) (FIGURE 7.7).

The resulting emotions often persist without our conscious awareness of what caused them, as one clever experiment demonstrated. The participants were patients with hippocampal damage, which left them unable to form new explicit memories. Researchers first showed them a sad film, and later a happy film. Although the viewers could not consciously recall the films, the sad or happy emotion lingered (Feinstein et al., 2010).

After horrific experiences—a wartime ambush, a house fire, a rape—vivid memories of the event may intrude again and again. The result is "stronger, more reliable memories" (McGaugh, 1994, 2003). The persistence of such memories is adaptive. They alert us to future dangers. By giving us a mental tunnel vision of the remembered event, they reduce our attention to minor details and focus our attention on the central event (Mather & Sutherland, 2012).

Weaker emotions mean weaker memories. In one study, people received a drug that blocked the effects of stress hormones. Later, they had trouble remembering the details of an upsetting story (Cahill, 1994).

Why are some memories so much stronger than others? Emotion-triggered hormonal changes help explain why we long remember exciting or shocking events, such as our first kiss or our whereabouts when learning of a loved one's death. Psychologists call them **flashbulb memories.** It's as if the brain commands, "Capture this!" Ask any adult American where he or she first heard the news of the 9/11 terrorist attacks—that fateful day that the *New York Times* called "one of those moments in which history splits and we define the world as 'before and after.'" Five years later, 95 percent of surveyed Americans said they remembered where they were or what they were doing (Pew, 2006). With time, some errors crept in (compared with earlier reports taken right after 9/11). Mostly, however, people's memories of 9/11 remained consistent over the next two to three years (Conway et al., 2009; Hirst et al., 2009; Kvavilashvili et al., 2009).

Dramatic experiences remain bright and clear in our memory in part because we rehearse them. We think about them and describe them to others. Memories of our best experiences, which we enjoy recalling and recounting, also endure. One study invited 1563 Boston Red Sox and New York Yankees fans to recall the baseball championship games between their two teams in 2003 (Yankees won) and 2004 (Red Sox won). Fans recalled much better the game their team won (Breslin & Safer, 2011).

> *"The biology of the mind will be as scientifically important to this [new] century as the biology of the gene [was] to the twentieth century."*
> Eric Kandel, acceptance remarks for his 2000 Nobel Prize

> Which is more important—your experiences or your memories of them?

Synaptic Changes

7-13 How do changes at the synapse level affect our memory processing?

As you read this chapter and learn about memory processes, your brain is changing. Activity in some brain pathways is increasing. Neural network connections are forming and strengthening. Changes are taking place at your *synapses*—the sites where nerve cells communicate with one another by means of chemical messengers. Experience alters the brain's neural networks (see Chapter 3).

Eric Kandel and James Schwartz (1982) were able to catch a new memory leaving tracks in neurons of the California sea slug. This simple animal's nerve cells are unusually large, and researchers have been able to observe how they change during learning. Using electric shocks, they have classically conditioned sea slugs to withdraw their gills when squirted with water, much as we might jump when lightning strikes nearby. By observing the slugs' neural connections before and after this conditioning, Kandel and Schwartz pinpointed changes. As a slug learns, it releases more of the neurotransmitter *serotonin* into certain cells. These cells then become more efficient at transmitting signals. Experience and learning can increase—even double—the number of synapses, even in slugs (Kandel, 2012). No wonder the brain area that processes spatial memory grows larger the longer London cab drivers have navigated the maze of streets (Woolett & Maguire, 2011).

As synapses become more efficient, so do neural networks. Sending neurons now release their neurotransmitters more easily. Receiving neurons may grow additional receptor sites. This increased neural efficiency, called **long-term potentiation (LTP),** enables learning and memory (Lynch, 2002; Whitlock et al., 2006). Several lines of evidence confirm that LTP is a physical basis for memory.

- Rats given a drug that enhanced synaptic efficiency (LTP) learned to run a maze with half the usual number of mistakes (Service, 1994).
- Drugs that block LTP interfere with learning (Lynch & Staubli, 1991).
- Mice that could not produce an enzyme needed for LTP could not learn their way out of a maze (Silva et al., 1992).

After LTP has occurred, an electric current passing through the brain won't erase old memories. Before LTP, the same current can wipe out very recent memories. This often happens when severely depressed people receive electroconvulsive therapy (Chapter 14). Sports

MEMORY SLUG The much-studied California sea slug, *Aplysia,* has increased our understanding of the neural basis of learning.

© Donna Ikenberry/Art Directors & TRIP/Alamy

flashbulb memory a clear memory of an emotionally significant moment or event.

long-term potentiation (LTP) an increase in a synapse's firing potential. Believed to be a neural basis for learning and memory.

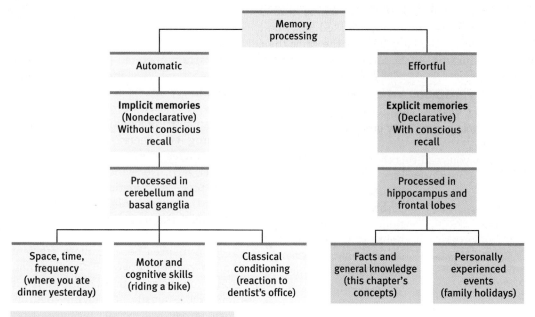

FIGURE 7.8 Our two memory systems

concussions can also wipe out recent memories. Football players and boxers knocked unconscious typically have no memory of events just before the blow to the head (Yarnell & Lynch, 1970). Their working memory had no time to process the information into long-term memory before the shutdown.

FIGURE 7.8 summarizes the brain's two-track memory processing and storage system for implicit (automatic) and explicit (effortful) memories. ■

Retrieval: Getting Information Out

◎ Remembering an event requires more than getting information into our brain and storing it there. To use that information, we must retrieve it. How do psychologists test whether learning has been retained over time? What triggers retrieval?

Measuring Retention

7-14 How do psychologists assess memory with recall, recognition, and relearning?

Memory is learning that persists over time. Three types of evidence indicate whether something has been learned and retained:

• **Recall**—drawing information out of storage and into your conscious awareness. Example: a fill-in-the-blank question.

• **Recognition**—identifying items you previously learned. Example: a multiple-choice question.

• **Relearning**—learning something more quickly when you learn it a second or later time. Example: Reviewing the first weeks of coursework to prepare for your final exam, you will relearn the material more easily than you did originally.

Long after you cannot recall most of your high school classmates, you may still be able to recognize their yearbook pictures in a photo lineup and spot their names in a list of names. One research team found that people who had graduated 25 years earlier could not *recall* many of their old classmates, but they could *recognize* 90 percent of their pictures and names (Bahrick et al., 1975).

Our recognition memory is quick and vast. "Is your friend wearing a new or old outfit?" *Old.* "Is this 5-second movie clip from a film you've ever seen?" *Yes.* "Have you ever before seen this person—this minor variation on normal human features?" *No.* Before our mouth can form an answer to any of millions of such questions, our mind knows, and knows that it knows.

Speed of *relearning* also reveals memory. Memory explorer Ebbinghaus showed this long ago by studying his own learning and memory.

Put yourself in Ebbinghaus' shoes. How could you produce new items to learn? Ebbinghaus' answer was to form a list of all possible nonsense syllables by sandwiching a vowel between two consonants. Then, for a particular experiment, he would randomly select a sample of the syllables, practice them, and test himself. To get a feel for his experiments, rapidly read aloud the following list, repeating it eight times (from Baddeley, 1982). Then, without looking, try to recall the items:

JIH, BAZ, FUB, YOX, SUJ, XIR, DAX, LEQ, VUM, PID, KEL, WAV, TUV, ZOF, GEK, HIW.

REMEMBERING THINGS PAST Even if Taylor Swift and Leonardo DiCaprio had not become famous, their high school classmates would most likely still recognize them in these photos.

As rehearsal increases, relearning time decreases.

Time (in minutes) to relearn list on day 2

Number of repetitions of list on day 1

FIGURE 7.9 **Ebbinghaus' retention curve** The more times he practiced a list of nonsense syllables on day 1, the fewer practice sessions he needed to *relearn* it on day 2. Speed of relearning is one way to measure whether something was learned and retained. (From Baddeley, 1982.)

The day after learning such a list, Ebbinghaus recalled only a few of the syllables. But were they entirely forgotten? No. The more often he practiced the list aloud on day 1, the fewer times he would have to practice it to *relearn* it on day 2 (FIGURE 7.9).

The point to remember: Tests of recognition and of time spent relearning demonstrate that *we remember more than we can recall.* ■

RETRIEVE + REMEMBER

- Multiple-choice questions test our

  a. recall.

  b. recognition.

  c. relearning.

  d. sensory memory.

  ANSWER: b

- Fill-in-the blank questions test our _____.

  ANSWER: recall

- If you want to be sure to remember what you're learning for an upcoming test, would it be better to use *recall* or *recognition* to check your memory? Why?

  ANSWER: It would be better to test your memory with *recall* (such as with short-answer or fill-in-the-blank self-test questions) rather than *recognition* (such as with multiple-choice questions). Recalling information is harder than recognizing it. So if you can recall it, that means your retention of the material is better than if you could only recognize it. Your chances of test success are therefore greater.

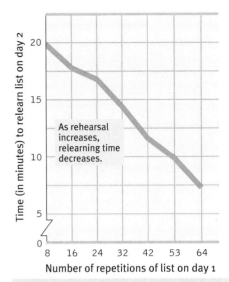

WELL, FOR CRYING OUT LOUD! AL TOWBRIDGE! WHAT IS IT, NINE YEARS, SEVEN MONTHS, AND TWELVE DAYS SINCE I LAST RAN INTO YOU? TEN-THIRTY-TWO A.M., A SATURDAY, FELCHER'S HARDWARE STORE. YOU WERE BUYING SEALER FOR YOUR BLACKTOP DRIVEWAY. TELL ME, AL, HOW DID THAT SEALER WORK? DID IT HOLD UP?

MR. TOTAL RECALL

Retrieval Cues

7-15 How do external events, internal moods, and order of appearance affect memory retrieval?

Imagine a spider suspended in the middle of her web, held up by the many strands extending outward from her in all directions to different points. You could begin at any one of these anchor points and follow the attached strand to the spider.

Retrieving a memory is similar. Memories are held in storage by a web of associations, each piece of information connected to many others. Suppose you encode into your memory the name of the person sitting next to you in class. With that name, you will also encode other bits of information, such as your surroundings, mood, seating position,

recall memory demonstrated by retrieving information learned earlier, as on a fill-in-the-blank test.

recognition memory demonstrated by identifying items previously learned, as on a multiple-choice test.

relearning memory demonstrated by time saved when learning material a second time.

and so on. These bits serve as **retrieval cues,** anchor points for pathways you can follow to access your classmate's name when you need to recall it later. The more retrieval cues you've encoded, the better your chances of finding a path to the memory suspended in this web of information.

Priming

The best retrieval cues come from associations you form at the time you encode a memory—smells, tastes, and sights that can call up your memory of the associated person or event. When trying to recall something, you may mentally place yourself in the original context. For most of us, that includes visual information. After losing his sight, British scholar John Hull (1990, p. 174) described his difficulty recalling such details:

> I knew I had been somewhere, and had done particular things with certain people, but where? I could not put the conversations . . . into a context. There was no background, no features against which to identify the place. Normally, the memories of people you have spoken to during the day are stored in frames which include the background.

Often associations are activated without your awareness. Seeing or hearing the word *rabbit* can activate associations with *hare,* even though you may not recall having seen or heard *rabbit* (FIGURE 7.10). Although this process, called **priming,** happens without your conscious awareness, it can influence your attitudes and your behavior.

Want to impress your friends with your new knowledge? Ask them two rapid-fire questions:

1. How do you pronounce the word spelled by the letters *s-h-o-p?*

2. What do you do when you come to a green light?

If they answer *stop* to the second question, you have demonstrated priming.

Context Effects

To prime your memory of something, it may help to return to the context where you experienced it. In one study, scuba

Seeing or hearing the word *rabbit*

↓

Activates concept

↓

Primes spelling the spoken word *hair/hare* as *h-a-r-e*

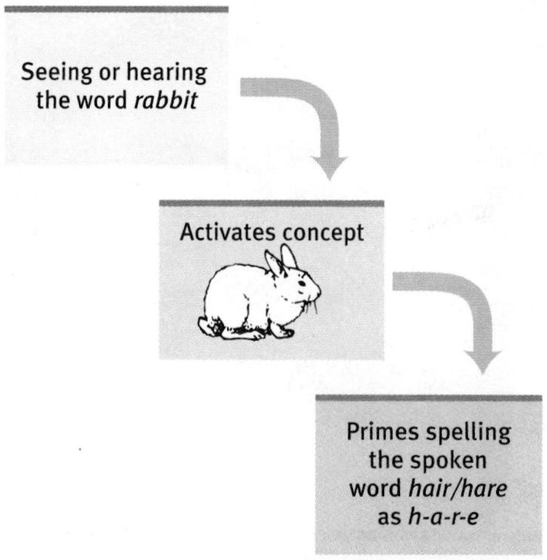

FIGURE 7.10 Priming—awakening associations After seeing or hearing *rabbit,* we are later more likely to spell the spoken word as *h-a-r-e.* Associations unconsciously activate related associations. This process is called priming. (Adapted from Bower, 1986.)

divers listened to a list of words in two different settings, either 10 feet underwater or sitting on the beach (Godden & Baddeley, 1975). Later, the divers recalled more words when they were retested in the same place (FIGURE 7.11).

You may have experienced similar context effects. Imagine this: While taking notes from this book, you realize you need to sharpen your pencil. You get up and walk to another room, but then you cannot remember why. After you return to your desk, it hits you: "I wanted to sharpen this pencil!" What happens to create this frustrating experience? In one context (desk, reading psychology), you realize your pencil needs sharpening. When you go to the other room and are in a different context, you have few cues to lead you back to that thought. But back at your desk, you are once again in the context in which you encoded the thought ("*This pencil is dull.*").

State-Dependent Memory

State-dependent memory is closely related to context-dependent memory. What we learn in one state—be it drunk or sober—may be more easily recalled when we are again in that state. What people learn when drunk they don't recall well in *any* state (alcohol disrupts storage). But they recall it slightly better when again drunk. Someone who hides money when drunk may forget the location until drunk again.

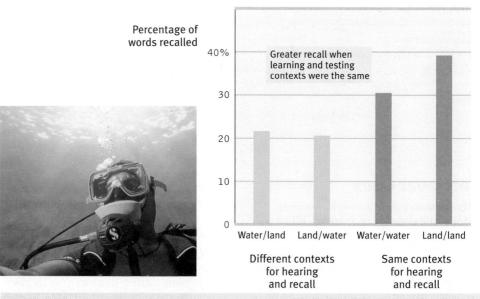

Percentage of words recalled

Greater recall when learning and testing contexts were the same

40%

30

20

10

0

Water/land   Land/water   Water/water   Land/land

Different contexts for hearing and recall   Same contexts for hearing and recall

Alexis Rosenfeld/Science Source

FIGURE 7.11 The effect of context on memory Words heard underwater were best recalled underwater; words heard on land were best recalled on land. (Adapted from Godden & Baddeley, 1975.)

Moods are also states that influence what we remember. Being happy primes sweet memories. Being angry or depressed primes sour ones. Say you have a terrible evening. Your date canceled, you lost your phone, and now a new red sweatshirt somehow made its way into your white laundry batch. Your bad mood may trigger other unhappy memories. If a friend or family member walks in at this point, your mind may fill with bad memories of that person.

This tendency to recall events that fit our mood is called **mood-congruent memory.** If put in a great mood—whether under hypnosis or just by the day's events (a World Cup soccer victory for German participants in one study)—people recall the world through rose-colored glasses (DeSteno et al., 2000; Forgas et al., 1984; Schwarz et al., 1987). They judge themselves competent and effective. They view other people as kind and giving. And they're sure happy events happen more often than unhappy ones.

Knowing this mood-memory connection, we should not be surprised that in some studies *currently* depressed people have recalled their parents as rejecting and punishing. *Formerly* depressed people have described their parents in more positive ways—much as do those who have never been depressed (Lewinsohn & Rosenbaum, 1987; Lewis, 1992). Similarly, adolescents' ratings of parental warmth in one week have offered few clues to how they would rate their parents six weeks later (Bornstein et al., 1991). When teens were down, their parents seemed inhuman. As moods brightened, those devil parents became angels.

Mood effects on retrieval help explain why our moods persist. When happy, we recall happy events and see the world as a happy place, which prolongs our good mood. When depressed, we recall sad events, which darkens our view of current events. For those predisposed to depression, this process can help maintain a vicious, dark cycle.

Serial Position Effect

Another memory-retrieval quirk, the **serial position effect,** can leave you wondering why you have large holes in your memory of a list of recent events. Imagine it's your first day in a new job, and your manager is introducing co-workers. As you meet each person, you silently repeat everyone's name, starting from the beginning. As the last person smiles and turns away, you hope you'll be able to greet your new co-workers by name the next day.

Don't count on it. Because you have spent more time rehearsing the earlier names than the later ones, those are the names you'll probably recall more easily the next day. In experiments, when people viewed a list of items (words, names, dates, even odors) and immediately tried to recall them in any order, they fell prey to the serial position effect (Reed, 2000). They briefly recalled the last items especially quickly and well, perhaps because those last items were still in working memory. But after a delay, when they shifted their attention away from the last items, their recall was best for the first items (**FIGURE 7.12**). ■

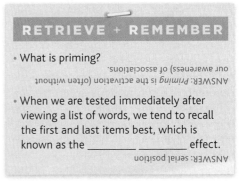

RETRIEVE + REMEMBER

• What is priming?

ANSWER: *Priming* is the activation (often without our awareness) of associations.

• When we are tested immediately after viewing a list of words, we tend to recall the first and last items best, which is known as the _____ _____ effect.

ANSWER: serial position

retrieval cue any stimulus (event, feeling, place, and so on) linked to a specific memory.

priming the activation, often unconsciously, of particular associations in memory.

mood-congruent memory the tendency to recall experiences that are consistent with your current good or bad mood.

serial position effect our tendency to recall best the last and first items in a list.

"I can't remember what we're arguing about, either. Let's keep yelling, and maybe it will come back to us."

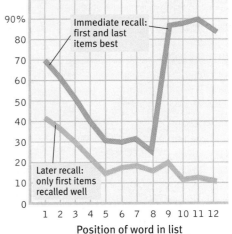

Ian West-WPA Pool/Getty Images

Percentage of words recalled

Immediate recall: first and last items best

Later recall: only first items recalled well

Position of word in list

FIGURE 7.12 The serial position effect Immediately after the royal newlyweds, William and Kate, made their way through the receiving line of special guests, they would probably have recalled the names of the last few people best. But later they may have been able to recall the first few people best.

Forgetting

7-16 Why do we forget?

If a memory-enhancing pill becomes available, it had better not be too effective. To discard the clutter of useless information—outfits worn last month, e-mail addresses now out of date, restaurant orders already cooked and served—is surely a blessing. Remember meeting the Russian memory whiz S earlier in this chapter? His junk heap of memories dominated his conscious mind. He had difficulty thinking abstractly—generalizing, organizing, evaluating. So does "A. J.," who is Jill Price in real life. She reports that her supermemory interferes with her life, with one memory cuing another (Parker et al., 2006): "It's like a running movie that never stops."

More often, however, our quirky memories fail us when we least expect it. My own memory can easily call up such episodes as that wonderful first kiss with the woman I love, or trivial facts like the air mileage from London to Detroit. Then

THE WOMAN WHO CAN'T FORGET "A. J." in real life is Jill Price. With writer Bart Davis, Price told her story in a 2008 published memoir. She remembers every day of her life since age 14 with detailed clarity, including both the joys and the unforgotten hurts.

"Oh, is that today?"

it abandons me when I discover that I have failed to encode, store, or retrieve a student's name or the spot where I left my sunglasses.

Forgetting and the Two-Track Mind

For some, memory loss is severe and permanent, as it was for Henry Molaison, whom you met earlier in this chapter. Molaison could recall his past, but he could not form new conscious memories. Neurologist Oliver Sacks (1985, pp. 26–27) described another patient, Jimmie, who was stuck in 1945, the year of his brain injury. When Jimmie gave his age as 19, Sacks set a mirror before him: "Look in the mirror and tell me what you see. Is that a 19-year-old looking out from the mirror?"

"Waiter, I'd like to order, unless I've eaten, in which case bring me the check."

Jimmie turned pale, gripped the chair, cursed, then became frantic: "What's going on? What's happened to me? Is this a nightmare? Am I crazy? Is this a joke?" When his attention was directed to some children playing baseball, his panic ended, the dreadful mirror forgotten.

Sacks showed Jimmie a photo from *National Geographic*. "What is this?" he asked.

"It's the Moon," Jimmie replied.

"No, it's not," Sacks answered. "It's a picture of the Earth taken from the Moon."

"Doc, you're kidding? Someone would've had to get a camera up there!"

"Naturally."

"Hell! You're joking—how the hell would you do that?" Jimmie's wonder was that of a bright young man from the 1940s, amazed by his travel back to the future.

Careful testing of these unique people reveals something even stranger. Although they cannot recall new facts or anything they have done recently, they can learn new skills and can be classically conditioned. Shown hard-to-find figures in pictures (in the *Where's Waldo?* series), they can quickly spot them again later. They can find their way to the bathroom, though without being able to tell you where it is. They can master mirror-image writing, jigsaw puzzles, and even complicated job skills (Schacter, 1992, 1996; Xu & Corkin, 2001). However, *they do all these things with no awareness of having learned them*. They suffer **amnesia**.

Molaison and Jimmie lost their ability to form new explicit memories, but their automatic processing ability remained intact. They could learn *how* to do something, but they had no conscious recall of learning their new skill. Such sad cases confirm that we have two distinct memory systems, controlled by different parts of the brain.

For most of us, forgetting is a less drastic process. Let's consider some of the reasons we forget.

STUDYING A FAMOUS BRAIN Jacopo Annese and other scientists at the University of California, San Diego's Brain Observatory are preserving Henry Molaison's brain for the benefit of future generations. Their careful work will result in a freely available online brain atlas.

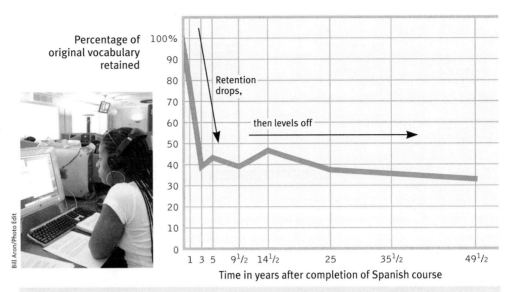

FIGURE 7.14 **The forgetting curve for Spanish learned in school** Compared with others just completing a Spanish language-learning course, people 3 years out of the course remember much less. Compared with the 3-year group, however, those who studied Spanish even longer ago did not forget much more. (Adapted from Bahrick, 1984.)

Encoding Failure

Much of what we sense we never notice, and what we fail to encode, we will never remember (**FIGURE 7.13**). Age can affect encoding ability. When young adults encode new information, areas of their brain jump into action. In older adults, these areas are slower to respond. Learning and retaining a new neighbor's name or mastering a new computer becomes more of a challenge. This encoding lag helps explain age-related memory decline (Grady et al., 1995).

But no matter how young we are, we pay conscious attention to only a limited portion of the vast number of sights and sounds bombarding us. When texting during class, students may fail to encode lecture details that their more attentive classmates are encoding. Without effort, many might-have-been memories never form.

Storage Decay

Even after encoding something well, we may later forget it. That master of nonsense-syllable learning, Hermann Ebbinghaus, also studied how long memories last. After learning his lists of nonsense syllables, such as YOX and JIH, he measured how much he remembered at various times, from 20 minutes to 30 days later. The result was his famous forgetting curve: *The course of forgetting is rapid at first, then levels off with time* (Wixted & Ebbesen, 1991).

People studying Spanish as a foreign language showed this forgetting curve for Spanish vocabulary (Bahrick, 1984). Compared with others who had just completed a high school or college Spanish course, people 3 years out of school had forgotten much of what they had learned. However, what they remembered then, they still remembered 25 and more years later. Their forgetting had leveled off (**FIGURE 7.14**).

One explanation for these forgetting curves is a gradual fading of the physical **memory trace,** which is a physical change in the brain as a memory forms. Researchers are getting closer to solving the mystery of the physical storage and decay of memories. But memories fade for many reasons, including other learning that disrupts our retrieval.

Retrieval Failure

We can compare forgotten events to books you can't find in your local library. Some aren't available because they were never acquired (not encoded). Others

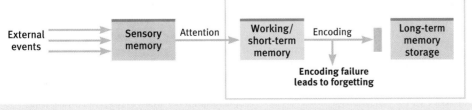

FIGURE 7.13 **Forgetting as encoding failure** We cannot remember what we have not encoded.

amnesia literally "without memory"—a loss of memory, often due to brain trauma, injury, or disease.

memory trace lasting physical changes in the brain as a memory forms.

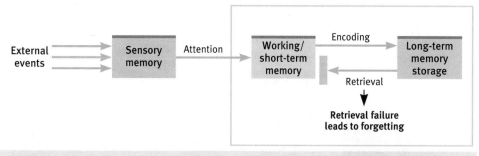

FIGURE 7.15 Retrieval failure Sometimes even stored information cannot be accessed, which leads to forgetting.

have been discarded (stored memories decay).

But there is a third possibility. The book—or memory—may be out of reach because we don't have enough information to access it. For example, what causes frustrating "tip-of-the-tongue" forgetting? (Deaf people fluent in sign language may experience a parallel "tip-of-the-fingers" feeling [Thompson et al., 2005].) These are retrieval problems **(FIGURE 7.15)**. Given retrieval cues (*"It begins with an M"*), you may easily retrieve the memory. Older adults more frequently have these frustrating tip-of-the-tongue experiences (Abrams, 2008).

Here's a question to test your memory. Do you recall the second sentence I asked you to remember—about the swimmer? If not, does the word *shark* serve as a retrieval cue? Experiments show that *shark* (the image you probably visualized) more readily retrieves the image you stored than does the sentence's actual word, *fish* (Anderson et al., 1976). (The sentence was *"The fish attacked the swimmer."*)

Retrieval problems occasionally stem from inteference or, perhaps, from motivated forgetting.

Interference

As you collect more and more information, your mental attic never fills, but it gets cluttered. Sometimes the clutter interferes, as new and old learning bump into each other and compete for your attention. **Proactive** (forward-looking) **interference** occurs when an older memory makes it more difficult

to remember new information. Your well-rehearsed Facebook password may interfere with your retrieval of your new bank log-in.

Retroactive (backward-acting) **interference** occurs when new learning disrupts your memory of older information. If someone sings new words to the tune of an old song, you may have trouble remembering the original. It is rather like a second stone being tossed in a pond, disrupting the waves rippling out from the first.

New learning in the hour before we fall asleep is protected from retroactive interference because the chances of disruption are few (Diekelmann & Born, 2010; Nesca & Koulack, 1994). Researchers first discovered this in a now-classic experiment (Jenkins & Dallenbach, 1924). Day

after day, two people each learned some nonsense syllables. When they tried to recall them after a night's sleep, they could retrieve more than half the items **(FIGURE 7.16)**. But when they learned the material and then stayed awake and involved with other activities, they forgot more, and sooner.

The hour before sleep is a good time to commit information to memory (Scullin & McDaniel, 2010), but not the *seconds* just before sleep. Information presented as the window of consciousness slams shut doesn't have a chance to be encoded (Wyatt & Bootzin, 1994). And if you're considering learning *while* sleeping, forget it. We have little memory for information played aloud in the room during sleep, although our ears do register it (Wood et al., 1992).

Old and new information do not always compete, of course. Knowing Latin may actually help us to learn French. This effect is called *positive transfer*.

Motivated Forgetting

To remember our past is often to revise it. Years ago, the huge cookie jar in our kitchen was jammed with freshly baked chocolate chip cookies. Still more were cooling across racks on the counter. Twenty-four hours later, not a crumb was left. Who had taken them? During

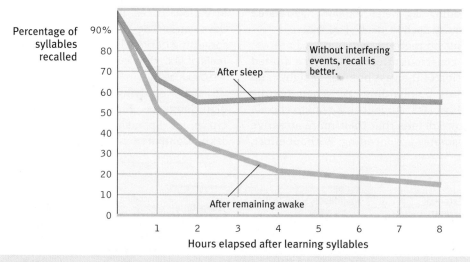

FIGURE 7.16 Retroactive interference People forgot more when they stayed awake and experienced other new material. (From Jenkins & Dallenbach, 1924.)

that time, my wife, three children, and I were the only people in the house. So while memories were still fresh, I conducted a little memory test. Andy admitted wolfing down as many as 20. Peter thought he had eaten 15. Laura guessed she had stuffed her then-6-year-old body with 15 cookies. My wife, Carol, recalled eating 6, and I remembered consuming 15 and taking 18 more to the office. We sheepishly accepted responsibility for 89 cookies. Still, we had not come close; there had been 160.

Why were our estimates so far off? FIGURE 7.17 reminds us that as we process information, we sift, change, or lose much of it. So was our cookie confusion an *encoding* problem? (Did we just not notice what we had eaten?) Was it a *storage* problem? (Might our memories of cookies, like Ebbinghaus' memory of nonsense syllables, have melted away

almost as fast as the cookies themselves?) Or was the information still intact but not *retrievable* because it would be embarrassing to remember?[1]

Sigmund Freud might have argued that our memory systems self-censored this information. He proposed that we **repress** painful or unacceptable memories to protect our self-concept and to minimize anxiety. But the repressed memory lingers, he believed, and can be retrieved by some later cue or during therapy. Repression was central to Freud's psychoanalytic theory (more on that in Chapter 11) and was a popular idea in mid-twentieth-century psychology and beyond. In one study, 9 in 10 university students agreed that "memories for painful experiences are sometimes pushed into unconsciousness" (Brown et al., 1996). Some therapists assume it. Today, however, increasing numbers of memory researchers think repression rarely, if ever, occurs. People's deliberate attempts to forget often succeed when the material is neutral, but not when it is emotional (Payne & Corrigan, 2007). Thus, we may have intrusive memories of the very traumas we would most like to forget. ■

RETRIEVE + REMEMBER

- What are three ways we forget, and how does each of these happen?

ANSWER: (1) *Encoding failure:* Unattended information never entered our memory system. (2) *Storage decay:* Information fades from our memory. (3) *Retrieval failure:* We cannot access stored information accurately, sometimes due to interference or motivated forgetting.

Memory Construction Errors

7-17 How do misinformation, imagination, and source amnesia influence our memory construction? How do we decide whether a memory is real or false?

Memory is not exact. Like scientists who infer a dinosaur's appearance from its remains, we infer our past from stored tidbits of information plus what we later imagined, expected, saw, and heard. We don't just retrieve memories; we reweave them (Gilbert, 2006). And every time we "replay" a memory, we replace the original with a slightly modified version (Hardt et al., 2010). (Memory researchers call this *reconsolidation*.) So, in a sense, said Joseph LeDoux (2009), "your memory is only as good as your last memory. The fewer times you use it, the more [unchanged] it is." This means that, to

proactive interference the disruptive effect of prior learning on the recall of new information.

retroactive interference the disruptive effect of new learning on the recall of old information.

repression in psychoanalytic theory, the basic defense mechanism that banishes from consciousness the thoughts, feelings, and memories that arouse anxiety.

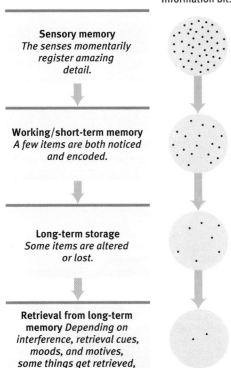

FIGURE 7.17 When do we forget? Forgetting can occur at any memory stage. As we process information, we filter, alter, or lose much of it.

Information bits

Sensory memory *The senses momentarily register amazing detail.*

Working/short-term memory *A few items are both noticed and encoded.*

Long-term storage *Some items are altered or lost.*

Retrieval from long-term memory *Depending on interference, retrieval cues, moods, and motives, some things get retrieved, some don't.*

some degree, all memory is false (Bernstein & Loftus, 2009).

Despite knowing all this, I recently rewrote my own past. It happened at an international conference, where memory researcher Elizabeth Loftus (2012) was demonstrating how memory works. Loftus showed us a handful of individual faces that we were later to identify, as if in a police lineup. Later, she showed us some pairs of faces, one face we had seen earlier and one we had not, and asked us to identify the one we had seen. But one pair she had slipped in included *two* new faces, one of which was rather *like* a face we had seen earlier. Most of us understandably but wrongly identified this face as one we had previously seen. To climax the demonstration, when she showed us the originally seen face and the previously chosen wrong face, most of us picked the wrong face! As a result of our memory reconsolidation, we—an audience of psychologists who should have known better—had replaced the original memory with a false memory.

How do we do it? How do we so easily rewrite our own history? Some memory research findings offer some clues.

Misinformation and Imagination Effects

In more than 200 experiments involving more than 20,000 people, Loftus has shown how eyewitnesses reconstruct their memories when questioned after a crime or an accident. In one study, two groups of people watched a film of a traffic accident and then answered questions about what they had seen (Loftus & Palmer, 1974). Those asked, "About how fast were the cars going when they *smashed* into each other?" gave higher speed estimates than those asked, "About how fast were the cars going when they *hit* each other?" A week later, when asked whether they recalled seeing any broken glass, people who had heard *smashed* in the leading (suggestive) version of the question were more than twice as likely to report seeing

glass fragments (**FIGURE 7.18**). In fact, the film showed no broken glass.

In many follow-up experiments around the world, others have witnessed an event. Then they have received or not received misleading information about it. And then they have taken a memory test. The repeated result is a **misinformation effect.** Exposed to misleading information, we tend to misremember (Loftus et al., 1992). Coke cans become peanut cans. Breakfast cereal becomes eggs. A clean-shaven man morphs into a man with a mustache.

Just hearing a vivid retelling of an event may implant false memories. One experiment falsely suggested to some Dutch university students that, as children, they had become ill after eating spoiled egg salad (Geraerts et al., 2008). After absorbing that suggestion, they were less likely to eat egg-salad sandwiches, both immediately and four months later.

Even repeatedly *imagining* fake actions and events can create false memories. American and British university students were asked to imagine certain childhood events, such as breaking a window with their hand or having a skin

> "Memory is insubstantial. Things keep replacing it. Your batch of snapshots will both fix and ruin your memory. . . . You can't remember anything from your trip except the wretched collection of snapshots."
>
> Annie Dillard, "To Fashion a Text," 1988

sample removed from a finger. One in four of them later recalled the imagined event as something that had really happened (Garry et al., 1996; Mazzoni & Memon, 2003).

Should we be surprised that digitally altered photos have produced the same result? In experiments, researchers have altered photos from a family album to show some family members taking a hot-air balloon ride. After viewing these photos (rather than photos showing just the balloon), children "remembered" the faked experience. And days later, they reported even richer details of their false memories (Strange et al., 2008; Wade et al., 2002).

In British and Canadian university surveys, nearly one-fourth of students have reported personal memories that they later realized were not accurate (Mazzoni et al., 2010). I empathize. For decades, my cherished earliest memory was of my parents getting off the bus and walking to our house, bringing my baby brother home from the hospital. When, in middle age, I shared that memory with my father, he assured me they did *not* bring their newborn home on

Leading question:
"About how fast were the cars going when they smashed into each other?"

Image of actual accident

Memory construction

FIGURE 7.18 Memory construction In this experiment, people viewed a film of a car accident (left). Those who later were asked a leading question recalled a more serious accident than they had witnessed. (From Loftus, 1979.)

the Seattle Transit System. The human mind, it seems, comes with built-in Photoshopping software.

Source Amnesia

Among the frailest parts of a memory is its source. Have you ever recognized someone but had no idea where you had met the person? Or dreamed about an event and later wondered whether it really happened? Or misrecalled *how* you learned about something (Henkel et al., 2000)? If so, you experienced **source amnesia**—you retained the memory of the event but not of its context. Source amnesia, along with the misinformation effect, is at the heart of many false memories. Authors and songwriters sometimes suffer from it. They think an idea came from their own creative imagination, when in fact they are unintentionally plagiarizing something they earlier read or heard.

Psychologist Donald Thompson became part of his own research on memory distortion when police brought him in for questioning about a rape. Although he was a near-perfect match to the victim's memory of the rapist, Thompson had an airtight alibi. Just before the rape occurred, he was being interviewed on live TV and could not possibly have made it to the crime scene. Then it came to light that the victim had been watching the interview—ironically about face recognition—and had experienced source amnesia. She had confused her memories of Thompson with those of the rapist (Schacter, 1996).

Source amnesia also helps explain **déjà vu** (French for "already seen"). Two-thirds of us have experienced this fleeting, eerie sense that "I've been in this exact situation before." It happens most commonly to well-educated, imaginative young adults, especially when tired or stressed (Brown, 2003, 2004; McAneny, 1996). Some wonder, "How could I recognize a situation I'm experiencing for the first time?" Others may think of reincarnation ("I must have experienced this in a previous life") or precognition ("I viewed this scene in my mind before experiencing it").

The key to déjà vu seems to be that we are familiar with a stimulus or one like it but can't recall where we ran into it before (Cleary, 2008). Normally, we expe-

> "Do you ever get that strange feeling of vujà dé? Not déjà vu; vujà dé. It's the distinct sense that, somehow, something just happened that has never happened before. Nothing seems familiar. And then suddenly the feeling is gone. Vujà dé."
>
> Comedian George Carlin (1937–2008), *Funny Times*, December 2001

rience a feeling of *familiarity* (thanks to temporal lobe processing) before we consciously remember details (thanks to hippocampus and frontal lobe processing). Sometimes, though, we may have a feeling of familiarity without conscious recall. As our amazing brain tries to make sense of this source amnesia, we get an eerie feeling that we're reliving some earlier part of our life.

Recognizing False Memories

We often are confident of our inaccurate memories. Because the misinformation effect and source amnesia happen outside our awareness, it is hard to sift

misinformation effect when a memory has been corrupted by misleading information.

source amnesia faulty memory for how, when, or where information was learned or imagined.

déjà vu that eerie sense that "I've experienced this before." Cues from the current situation may unconsciously trigger retrieval of an earlier experience.

DOONESBURY

false memories from real ones (Schooler et al., 1986). Perhaps you can recall describing a childhood experience to a friend and filling in memory gaps with reasonable guesses. We all do it. After more retellings, those guessed details—now absorbed into your memory—may feel as real as if you had actually observed them (Roediger et al., 1993). False memories, like fake jewelry, seem so real.

False memories can be very persistent. Imagine that I were to read aloud a list of words such as *candy, sugar, honey,* and *taste.* Later, I ask you to recognize those words in a larger list. If you are at all like the people in a famous experiment (Roediger & McDermott, 1995), you would err three out of four times—by falsely remembering a new but similar word, such as *sweet.* We more easily remember the *gist*—the general idea—than the words themselves.

Memory construction errors can help us understand why some people have been sent to prison for crimes they never committed. Of 200 people who were later proven not guilty by DNA testing, 79 percent had been convicted because of faulty eyewitness identification (Garrett, 2008). "Hypnotically refreshed" memories of crimes often contain similar errors. If a hypnotist asks leading questions (*"Did you hear loud noises?"*), witnesses may weave that false information into their memory of the event.

Children's Eyewitness Recall

7-18 How reliable are young children's eyewitness descriptions, and why are reports of repressed and recovered memories so hotly debated?

If memories can be sincere, yet sincerely wrong, how can jurors decide cases in which children's memories of sexual abuse are the only evidence?

Stephen Ceci (1993) thinks "it would be truly awful to ever lose sight of the enormity of child abuse." Yet Ceci and Maggie Bruck's (1993, 1995) studies have

made them aware of how easily children's memories can be molded. For example, they asked 3-year-olds to show on anatomically correct dolls where a pediatrician had touched them. Of the children who had not received genital examinations, 55 percent pointed to either genital or anal areas.

In other experiments, the researchers studied the effect of suggestive interviewing techniques (Bruck & Ceci, 1999, 2004). In one study, children chose a card from a deck of possible happenings, and an adult then read the card to them. For example, "Think real hard, and tell me if this ever happened to you. Can you remember going to the hospital with a mousetrap on your finger?" In weekly interviews, the same adult repeatedly asked children to think about several real and fictitious events. After 10 weeks of this, a new adult asked the same questions. The stunning result: 58 percent of preschoolers produced false (often vivid) stories about one or more events they had never experienced (Ceci et al., 1994). Here's one of those stories.

> My brother Colin was trying to get Blowtorch [an action figure] from me, and I wouldn't let him take it from me, so he pushed me into the wood pile where the mousetrap was. And then my finger got caught in it. And then we went to the hospital, and my mommy, daddy, and Colin drove me there, to the hospital in our van, because it was far away. And the doctor put a bandage on this finger.

Given such detailed stories, professional psychologists who specialize in interviewing children could not reliably separate the real memories from the false ones. Nor could the children themselves. The child quoted above,

reminded that his parents had told him several times that the mousetrap event never happened—that he had imagined it—protested. "But it really did happen. I remember it!"

Such findings do not mean that children can never be accurate eyewitnesses. When a neutral person has asked nonleading questions soon after the event, using words the children could understand, children often accurately recalled what happened and who did it (Goodman & Quas, 2008; Pipe et al., 2004).

Repressed or Constructed Memories of Abuse?

The source amnesia and misinformation effect findings raise concerns about therapist-guided "recovered" memories. There are two tragedies related to adult recollections of childhood abuse. One happens when people don't believe abuse survivors who tell their secret. The other happens when innocent people are falsely accused.

Some well-intentioned therapists have reasoned with patients that "people who've been abused often have your symptoms, so you probably were abused. Let's see if, aided by hypnosis or drugs, or helped to dig back and visualize your trauma, you can recover it." Patients exposed to such techniques may then form an image of a threatening person. With rehearsal, the image grows more vivid, as it did for the little boy who came to believe he had caught his finger in a mousetrap. The patient ends up stunned, angry, and ready to confront or sue the remembered abuser. The accused person, equally stunned, vigorously denies the accusation.

Critics are not questioning the professionalism of most therapists. Nor are they questioning the accusers' sincerity; even if false, their memories feel real.

Critics instead question "memory work" techniques, such as "guided imagery," hypnosis, and dream analysis. "Thousands of families were cruelly ripped apart," with

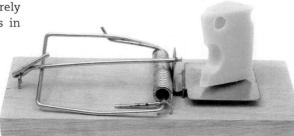

© Darren Matthews/Alamy

ELIZABETH LOFTUS "The research findings for which I am being honored now generated a level of hostility and opposition I could never have foreseen. People wrote threatening letters, warning me that my reputation and even my safety were in jeopardy if I continued along these lines. At some universities, armed guards were provided to accompany me during speeches." (Elizabeth Loftus, on receiving the Association for Psychological Science's William James Fellow Award, 2001.)

"previously loving adult daughters" suddenly accusing fathers (Gardner, 2006). Angry clinicians have countered that those who argue that recovered memories of abuse never happen are adding to abused people's trauma and playing into the hands of child molesters.

In an effort to find a sensible common ground that might resolve psychology's "memory war," professional organizations (the American Medical, American Psychological, and American Psychiatric Associations, among others) set up study panels and issued public statements. Those committed to protecting abused children and those committed to protecting wrongly accused adults have agreed on the following.

- *Sexual abuse happens.* And it happens more often than we once supposed. There is no characteristic "survivor syndrome"—no group of symptoms that lets us spot victims of sexual abuse (Kendall-Tackett et al., 1993). However, sexual abuse can leave its victims at risk for problems ranging from sexual dysfunction to depression (Freyd et al., 2007).

- *Injustice happens.* Some innocent people have been falsely convicted. And some guilty people have avoided punishment by casting doubt on their truth-telling accusers.

- *Forgetting happens.* Many of those actually abused were either very young when it happened or may not have understood the meaning of their experience. These are circumstances under which forgetting is common. Forgetting isolated past events, both negative and positive, is an ordinary part of everyday life.

- *Recovered memories are commonplace.* Cued by a remark or an experience, we all recover memories of long-forgotten events, both pleasant and unpleasant. What skeptical psychologists question is this: Does the unconscious mind *forcibly repress* painful experiences, and if so, can these experiences be retrieved by certain therapist-aided techniques (McNally & Geraerts, 2009)? Memories that surface naturally are more likely to be true (Geraerts et al., 2007).

- *Memories of things happening before age 3 are unreliable.* We cannot reliably recall happenings from our first three years. As noted earlier, this infantile amnesia happens because our brain pathways have not yet developed enough to form the kinds of memories we will form later in life. Most psychologists, including most clinical and counseling psychologists, therefore doubt "recovered" memories of abuse during infancy

> "When memories are 'recovered' after long periods of amnesia, particularly when extraordinary means were used to secure the recovery of memory, there is a high probability that the memories are false."
> Royal College of Psychiatrists Working Group on Reported Recovered Memories of Child Sexual Abuse (Brandon et al., 1998)

(Gore-Felton et al., 2000; Knapp & VandeCreek, 2000). The older a child was when suffering sexual abuse, and the more severe the abuse, the more likely it is to be remembered (Goodman et al., 2003).

- *Memories "recovered" under hypnosis are especially unreliable.* Under hypnosis, people will incorporate all kinds of suggestions into their memories, even memories of "past lives."

- *Memories, whether real or false, can be emotionally upsetting.* Both the accuser and the accused may suffer; what was born of mere suggestion can become, like an actual event, a stinging memory that drives bodily stress (McNally, 2003b, 2007).

So, does *repression* of threatening memories ever occur? Or is this concept—the cornerstone of Freud's theory and of so much popular psychology—misleading? In Chapter 11, we will return to this hotly debated issue. For now, this much appears certain: The most common response to a traumatic experience (witnessing a loved one's murder, being terrorized by a hijacker or a rapist, losing everything in a natural disaster) is not banishing the experience into the unconscious. Rather, such experiences are typically etched on the mind as vivid, persistent, haunting memories (Porter & Peace, 2007). As Robert Kraft (2002) said of

TODAY'S SPECIAL GUEST

BRUNDAGE MORNALD, OF BATTLE CREEK, MONTANA

UNDER HYPNOSIS, MR. MORNALD RECOVERED LONG-BURIED MEMORIES OF A PERFECTLY NORMAL, HAPPY CHILDHOOD.

the experience of those trapped in the Nazi death camps, "Horror sears memory, leaving . . . the consuming memories of atrocity." ∎

RETRIEVE + REMEMBER

- What—given the commonness of source amnesia—might life be like if we remembered all our daily experiences and all our dreams?

ANSWER: Real experiences would be confused with those we dreamed. When meeting someone, we might therefore be unsure whether we were reacting to something they previously did or to something we dreamed they did.

Improving Memory

7-19 How can you use memory research findings to do better in this course and in others?

Biology's findings benefit medicine. Botany's findings benefit agriculture. Can psychology's research on memory benefit your performance in class and on tests? You bet! Here, for easy ref-

© Sigrid Olsson/PhotoAlto/Corbis

THINKING AND MEMORY What's the best way to retain new information? Think actively as you read. That includes rehearsing and relating ideas and making the material personally meaningful.

erence, is a summary of research-based suggestions that could help you remember information when you need it. The SQ3R—Survey, Question, Read, Retrieve, Review—study technique introduced in Chapter 1 includes several of these strategies:

Rehearse repeatedly. To master material, use distributed (spaced) practice. To learn a concept, give yourself many separate study sessions. Take advantage of life's little intervals— riding a bus, walking across campus, waiting for class to start. New memories are weak; exercise them and they will strengthen. To memorize specific facts or figures, Thomas Landauer (2001) has advised, "rehearse the name or number you are trying to memorize, wait a few seconds, rehearse again, wait a little longer, rehearse again, then wait longer still and rehearse yet again. The waits should be as long as possible without losing the information." Rehearsal will help you retain material. It pays to study actively.

Make the material meaningful. You can build a network of retrieval cues by taking text and class notes in your own words. You can increase retrieval cues by forming as many associations as possible. Apply the concepts to your own life. Form images. Understand and organize information. Relate the material to what you already know or have experienced. As William James (1890) suggested, "Knit each new thing on to some acquisition already there." Restate concepts in your own words. Mindlessly repeating someone else's words won't supply many retrieval cues. On an exam, you may find yourself stuck when a question uses terms different from the ones you memorized.

Activate retrieval cues. Mentally re-create the situation in which your original

In the discussion of mnemonics, I gave you six words and told you I would quiz you about them later. How many of those words can you now recall? Of these, how many are concrete, vivid-image words? How many describe abstract ideas? (You can check your list against the one below.)

Bicycle, void, cigarette, inherent, fire, process

learning occurred. Imagine returning to the same location and being in the same mood. Jog your memory by allowing one thought to cue the next.

Use mnemonic devices. Associate items with peg words. Make up a story that uses vivid images of the items. Chunk information for easier retrieval.

Minimize interference. Study before sleeping. Do not schedule back-to-back study times for topics that are likely to interfere with each other, such as Spanish and French.

Sleep more. During sleep, the brain reorganizes and consolidates information for long-term memory. Sleep deprivation disrupts this process.

Test your own knowledge, both to rehearse it and to find out what you don't yet know. Don't become overconfident because you can *recognize* information. Test your *recall* using the Retrieve + Remember items found throughout each chapter, and the numbered Learning Objective questions and Chapter Test questions at the end of each chapter. Outline sections on a blank page. Define the terms and concepts listed at each chapter's end before turning back to their definitions. Take practice tests; the websites and study guides that accompany many texts, including this one, are a good source for such tests. ∎

RETRIEVE + REMEMBER

- What are the recommended memory strategies you just read about?

ANSWER: Rehearse repeatedly to boost long-term recall. Schedule spaced (not crammed) study times. Spend more time rehearsing or actively thinking about the material. Make the material personally meaningful, with well-organized and vivid associations. Refresh your memory by returning to contexts and moods to activate retrieval cues. Use mnemonic devices. Minimize interference. Plan for a complete night's sleep. Test yourself repeatedly—retrieval practice is a proven retention strategy.

CHAPTER REVIEW

Memory

Test yourself by taking a moment to answer each of these Learning Objective Questions (repeated here from within the chapter). Then turn to Appendix D, Complete Chapter Reviews, to check your answers. Research suggests that trying to answer these questions on your own will improve your long-term memory of the concepts (McDaniel et al., 2009).

Studying Memory

7-1: What is memory, and how do information-processing models help us study memory?

7-2: What is the three-stage information-processing model, and how has later research updated this model?

Building Memories: Encoding

7-3: How do explicit and implicit memories differ?

7-4: What information do we automatically process?

7-5: How does sensory memory work?

7-6: What is the capacity of our short-term and working memory?

7-7: What are some effortful processing strategies that can help us remember new information?

7-8: Why is cramming ineffective, and what is the testing effect?

Memory Storage

7-9: What is the capacity of long-term memory? Are our long-term memories processed and stored in specific locations?

7-10: What roles do the hippocampus and frontal lobes play in memory processing?

7-11: What roles do the cerebellum and basal ganglia play in memory processing?

7-12: How do emotions affect our memory processing?

7-13: How do changes at the synapse level affect our memory processing?

Retrieval: Getting Information Out

7-14: How do psychologists assess memory with recall, recognition, and relearning?

7-15: How do external events, internal moods, and order of appearance affect memory retrieval?

Forgetting

7-16: Why do we forget?

Memory Construction Errors

7-17: How do misinformation, imagination, and source amnesia influence our memory construction? How do we decide whether a memory is real or false?

7-18: How reliable are young children's eyewitness descriptions, and why are reports of repressed and recovered memories so hotly debated?

Improving Memory

7-19: How can you use memory research findings to do better in this course and in others?

TERMS AND CONCEPTS TO REMEMBER

Test yourself on these terms by trying to write down the definition in your own words before flipping back to the referenced page to check your answer.

CHAPTER TEST

Test yourself repeatedly throughout your studies. This will not only help you figure out what you know and don't know; the testing itself will help you learn and remember the information more effectively thanks to the *testing effect*.

1. The psychological terms for taking in information, retaining it, and later getting it back out are _____, _____, and _____.

2. The concept of working memory
   a. clarifies the idea of short-term memory by focusing on the active processing that occurs in this stage.
   b. splits short-term memory into two substages—sensory memory and working memory.
   c. splits short-term memory into two areas—working (retrievable) memory and inaccessible memory.
   d. clarifies the idea of short-term memory by focusing on space, time, and frequency.

3. Sensory memory may be visual (_____ memory) or auditory (_____ memory).

4. Our short-term memory for new information is limited to about _____ items.

5. Memory aids that use visual imagery (such as peg words) or other organizational devices are called _____.

6. The hippocampus seems to function as a
   a. temporary processing site for explicit memories.
   b. temporary processing site for implicit memories.
   c. permanent storage area for emotion-based memories.
   d. permanent storage area for iconic and echoic memories.

7. Amnesia following hippocampus damage typically leaves people unable to learn new facts or recall recent events. However, they may be able to learn new skills, such as riding a bicycle, which is an _____ (explicit/implicit) memory.

8. Long-term potentiation (LTP) refers to
   a. emotion-triggered hormonal changes.
   b. the role of the hippocampus in processing explicit memories.
   c. an increase in a cell's firing potential after brief, rapid stimulation.
   d. aging people's potential for learning.

9. A psychologist who asks you to write down as many objects as you can remember having seen a few minutes earlier is testing your _____.

10. Specific odors, visual images, emotions, or other associations that help us access a memory are examples of
    a. relearning.
    b. déjà vu.
    c. declarative memories.
    d. retrieval cues.

11. When you feel sad, why might it help to look at pictures that reawaken some of your best memories?

12. When tested immediately after viewing a list of words, people tend to recall the first and last items more readily than those in the middle. When retested after a delay, they are most likely to recall
    a. the first items on the list.
    b. the first and last items on the list.
    c. a few items at random.
    d. the last items on the list.

13. When forgetting is due to encoding failure, meaningless information has not been transferred from
    a. the environment into sensory memory.
    b. sensory memory into long-term memory.
    c. long-term memory into short-term memory.
    d. short-term memory into long-term memory.

14. Ebbinghaus' "forgetting curve" shows that after an initial decline, memory for novel information tends to
    a. increase slightly.
    b. decrease noticeably.
    c. decrease greatly.
    d. level out.

15. The hour before sleep is a good time to memorize information, because going to sleep after learning new material minimizes _____ interference.

16. Freud proposed that painful or unacceptable memories are blocked from consciousness through a mechanism called _____.

17. One reason false memories form is our tendency to fill in memory gaps with our reasonable guesses and assumptions, sometimes based on misleading information. This tendency is an example of
    a. proactive interference.
    b. the misinformation effect.
    c. retroactive interference.
    d. the forgetting curve.

18. Eliza's family loves to tell the story of how she "stole the show" as a 2-year-old, dancing at her aunt's wedding reception. Even though she was so young, Eliza can recall the event clearly. How is this possible?

19. We may recognize a face at a social gathering but be unable to remember how we know that person. This is an example of _____ _____.

20. When a situation triggers the feeling that "I've been here before," you are experiencing _____ _____.

21. Children can be accurate eyewitnesses if

   a. interviewers give the children hints about what really happened.

   b. a neutral person asks nonleading questions soon after the event, in words the children can understand.

   c. the children have a chance to talk with involved adults before the interview.

   d. interviewers use precise technical and medical terms.

22. Psychologists involved in the study of memories of abuse tend to DISAGREE about which of the following statements?

   a. Memories of events that happened before age 3 are not reliable.

   b. We tend to repress extremely upsetting memories.

   c. Memories can be emotionally upsetting.

   d. Sexual abuse happens.

   Find answers to these questions in Appendix E, in the back of the book.

IN YOUR EVERYDAY LIFE

Answering these questions will help you make these concepts more personally meaningful, and therefore more memorable.

1. What has your memory system encoded, stored, and retrieved today?

2. How do you make psychology terms more personally meaningful so you remember them better? Could you do this more often?

3. Can you recall a time when stress helped you remember something? Has stress ever made it more difficult to remember something?

4. In what ways do you notice your moods coloring your memories, perceptions, or expectations?

5. Most people wish for a better memory. Is that true of you? Do you ever wish you were better at forgetting certain memories?

6. If you were on a jury in a trial involving recovered memories of abuse, do you think you could be impartial? Would it matter whether the defendant was a parent accused of sexual abuse, or a therapist being sued for creating a false memory?

7. Think of a memory you frequently recall. How might you have changed it without conscious awareness?

8. Which of the study and memory strategies suggested at the end of this chapter do you plan to try?

8 Thinking, Language, and Intelligence

Throughout history, we humans have celebrated our wisdom and bemoaned our foolishness. In this book we have seen many reasons to take pride in our smartness. As our brains develop, our minds grow from the surprising abilities of the newborn to the logic of adolescence and the wisdom of older age. Our visual system converts countless sensations into nerve impulses sent to multiple brain sites. Then the results come together, forming colorful perceptions. Meanwhile, our two-track mind is processing, interpreting, and storing vast amounts of information, with and without our awareness. Not bad for the cabbage-sized three pounds of wet tissue jammed in our skull.

Yet we have also seen that in some other ways we are either simple or error-prone. Our species is kin to the other animals. The same principles that produce learning in rats and pigeons and even slugs influence our learning. Our thinking sometimes fails us. My geographical intuition tells me that Reno is east of Los Angeles, that Rome is south of New York, and that Atlanta is east of Detroit. But I am wrong, wrong, and wrong. People are good at making mistakes. We not-so-wise humans are easily fooled by perceptual illusions, fake psychic claims, and false memories.

In this chapter, we find more examples of these two images—the rational and irrational human. We will consider how we intelligently use—and sometimes ignore or misuse—the information we receive, perceive, store, and retrieve. We will look at our gifts for language and intelligence. And we will reflect on how deserving we are of the meaning of our species' name, *Homo sapiens*—wise human.

Thinking

Concepts

8-1 What is cognition, and what are the functions of concepts?

Psychologists who study **cognition** focus on the mental activities associated with thinking, knowing, remembering, and communicating information. One of these activities is forming **concepts**—mental groupings of similar objects, events, ideas, and people. The concept *chair* includes many items—a baby's high chair, a reclining chair, a dentist's chair.

Concepts simplify our thinking. Imagine life without them. We would need a different name for every person, event, object, and idea. We could not ask a child to "throw the ball" because there would be no concept of *throw* or *ball*. We could not say "They were angry." We would have to describe expressions and words. Concepts such as *ball* and *anger* give us much information with little mental effort.

We often form our concepts by developing a **prototype**—a mental image or best example of a category (Rosch, 1978). People more quickly agree that "a robin is a bird" than that "a penguin is a bird." For most of us, the robin is the birdier (more prototypical) bird; it more closely resembles our *bird* prototype. When something closely matches our proto-

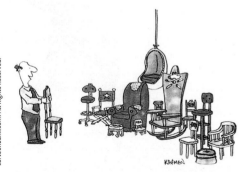

"Attention, everyone! I'd like to introduce the newest member of our family."

type of a concept, we readily recognize it as an example of the concept.

Sometimes, though, our experiences don't match up neatly with our prototypes. When this happens, our category boundaries may blur. Is a 17-year-old female a girl or a woman? Is a whale a fish or a mammal? Is a tomato a fruit? Because a tomato fails to match our *fruit* prototype, we are slower to recognize it as a fruit.

Similarly, when symptoms don't fit one of our disease prototypes, we are slow to perceive an illness (Bishop, 1991). People whose heart attack symptoms (shortness of breath, exhaustion, a dull weight in the chest) don't match their *heart attack* prototype (sharp chest pain) may not seek help. Concepts speed and guide our thinking. But they don't always make us wise.

Solving Problems

8-2 What strategies help us solve problems, and what tendencies work against us?

One tribute to our rationality is our impressive problem-solving skill. What's the best route around this traffic jam? How should we handle a friend's criticism? How can we get in the house without our keys?

Some problems we solve through *trial and error*. Thomas Edison tried thousands of light bulb filaments before stumbling upon one that worked. For other problems, we use **algorithms,** step-by-step procedures that guarantee a solution. But following the steps in an algorithm takes time and effort—sometimes a lot of time and effort. To find a word using the 10 letters in *SPLOYOCHYG*, for example, you could construct a list, with each letter in each of the 10 positions. But your list of 907,200 different combinations would be very long! In such cases, we often resort to **heuristics,** simpler thinking strategies. Thus, you might reduce the number of options in the *SPLOYOCHYG* example by grouping letters that often appear together (CH

and *GY*) and avoiding rare combinations (such as *YY*). By using heuristics and then applying trial and error, you may hit on the answer. Have you guessed it?[1]

Sometimes we puzzle over a problem, with no feeling of getting closer to the answer. Then, suddenly the pieces fall together in a flash of **insight**—an abrupt, true-seeming, and often satisfying solution (Knoblich & Oellinger, 2006; Topolinski & Reber, 2010). Ten-year-old Johnny Appleton had one of these Aha! moments and solved a problem that had stumped many adults. How could they rescue a young robin that had fallen into a narrow, 30-inch-deep hole in a cement-block wall? Johnny's solution: slowly pour in sand, giving the bird enough time to keep its feet on top of the constantly rising mound (Ruchlis, 1990).

Sudden flashes of insight are associated with bursts of brain activity (Kounios & Beeman, 2009; Sandkühler & Bhattacharya, 2008). In one study (Jung-Beeman et al., 2004), researchers asked people to think of a word that forms a compound word or phrase with each of three words in a set (such as *pine, crab,* and *sauce*). When people knew the answer, they were to press a button, which would sound a bell. (Need a hint? The word is a fruit.[2]) About half the solutions were by a sudden Aha! insight. Before the Aha! moment, the problem solvers' frontal lobes (which are involved in focusing attention) were active. Then, as the insight occurred, there was a burst of activity in their right temporal lobe, just above the ear (FIGURE 8.1).

Insight gives us a sense of satisfaction, a feeling of happiness. The joy of a joke is similarly a sudden "I get it!" reaction to double meaning or a surprise ending: "You don't need a parachute to skydive. You only need a parachute to skydive twice." Comedian Groucho Marx was a master at this: "I once shot an elephant in my pajamas. How he got into my pajamas I'll never know."

---

1   Answer to SPLOYOCHYG problem: PSYCHOLOGY
2   The word is apple: pineapple, crabapple, applesauce.

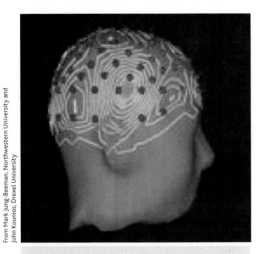

FIGURE 8.1 The Aha! moment A burst of right temporal lobe EEG activity (yellow area) accompanied insight solutions to word problems (Jung-Beeman et al., 2004). The red dots show placement of the EEG electrodes. The light gray lines show patterns of brain activity during insight.

Insightful as we are, other cognitive tendencies may lead us astray. **Confirmation bias** is our tendency to seek evidence *for* our ideas more eagerly than we seek evidence against them (Klayman & Ha, 1987; Skov & Sherman, 1986). Peter Wason (1960) demonstrated confirmation bias in a now-classic study. He gave students a set of three numbers (2-4-6) and told them the sequence was based on a rule. Their task was to guess the rule. (It was simple: Each number must be larger than the one before it.) Before giving their answers, students formed their own three-number sets, and Wason told them whether their sets worked with his rule. When they felt certain they had the rule, they were to announce it. The result? They were seldom right but never in doubt. Most students formed a wrong idea ("Maybe it's counting by twos") and then searched only for evidence confirming the wrong rule (by testing 6-8-10, 100-102-104, and so forth).

In real life, this tendency can have grave results. Once people form a belief—that gun control does (or does not) save lives—they prefer information that supports their belief. Confirmation bias also

helped launch a war. The United States invaded Iraq on the belief that dictator Saddam Hussein possessed weapons of mass destruction (WMD) that posed an immediate threat. The belief turned out to be false. A U.S. Senate Select Committee on Intelligence (2004), with members from both political parties, later investigated and found confirmation bias partly to blame. Administration analysts "had a tendency to accept information which supported [their beliefs] . . . more readily than information which contradicted" them, the report stated. Sources denying such weapons were viewed to be "either lying or not knowledgeable about Iraq's problems." Sources that reported ongoing WMD activities were seen as "having provided valuable information."

Once we get hung up on an incorrect view of a problem, it's hard to approach it from a different angle. This obstacle to problem solving is called **fixation.** Can you solve the matchstick problem in FIGURE 8.2? If not, you may be experiencing fixation. (Turn the page to see the solution in FIGURE 8.3.)

FIGURE 8.2 The matchstick problem How would you arrange six matches to form four equilateral triangles?

Making Good (and Bad) Decisions and Judgments

8-3 What is intuition, and how can the availability heuristic, overconfidence, belief perseverance, and framing influence our decisions and judgments?

Each day holds hundreds of judgments and decisions. *Is it worth the bother to take a jacket? Can I trust this person? Should I shoot*

the basketball or pass to the player who's hot? As we judge the odds and make our decisions, we seldom take the time and effort to reason systematically. We just follow our **intuition,** our fast, automatic, unreasoned feelings and thoughts. After interviewing leaders in government, business, and education, one social psychologist concluded that they often made decisions without considered thought and reflection. How did they usually reach their decisions? "If you ask, they are likely to tell you . . . they do it mostly by *the seat of their pants*" (Janis, 1986).

Quick-Thinking Heuristics

When we need to act quickly, the mental shortcuts we call *heuristics* enable snap judgments. Without conscious awareness, we use automatic, intuitive strategies that are usually both fast and

cognition all the mental activities associated with thinking, knowing, remembering, and communicating.

concept a mental grouping of similar objects, events, ideas, and people.

prototype a mental image or best example of a category. Matching new items to a prototype provides a quick and easy method for sorting items into categories (as when comparing feathered creatures to a prototypical bird, such as a robin).

algorithm a methodical, logical rule or procedure that guarantees you will solve a particular problem. Contrasts with the usually speedier—but also more error-prone—use of *heuristics*.

heuristic a simple thinking strategy that often allows you to make judgments and solve problems efficiently; usually speedier but also more error prone than *algorithms*.

insight a sudden realization of the solution to a problem; it contrasts with strategy-based solutions.

confirmation bias a tendency to search for information that supports our preconceptions and to ignore or distort evidence that contradicts them.

fixation the inability to see a problem from a new perspective; an obstacle to problem solving.

intuition an effortless, immediate, automatic feeling or thought, as contrasted with explicit, conscious reasoning.

"The problem is I can't tell the difference between a deeply wise, intuitive nudge from the Universe and one of my own bone-headed ideas!"

"In creating these problems, we didn't set out to fool people. All our problems fooled us, too." (Amos Tversky, 1985)

"Intuitive thinking [is] fine most of the time. . . . But sometimes that habit of mind gets us in trouble." (Daniel Kahneman, 2005)

effective. But not always, as research by cognitive psychologists Amos Tversky and Daniel Kahneman (1974) showed.[3] These generally helpful shortcuts sometimes lead even the smartest people into quick but dumb decisions. Consider the **availability heuristic,** which operates when we estimate how common an event is, based on how easily it comes to mind (its mental availability). Casinos know this. They entice us to gamble by making even small wins mentally avail-

able with noisy bells and flashing lights. The big losses are soundlessly invisible.

The availability heuristic can distort our judgments of other people. Anything that makes information "pop" into mind can make it seem commonplace. If someone from a particular religious of ethnic group commits a terrorist act, as happened on September 11, 2001, our readily available memory of the dramatic event may shape our impression of the whole group. Even during that horrific year, terrorist acts claimed comparatively few lives. Despite the much greater risk

of death from other causes (**FIGURE 8.4**), the 9/11 terror was more memorable. Emotion-laden images of terror fed our fears (Sunstein, 2007).

We often fear the wrong things (see Thinking Critically About: The Fear Factor on the next page). Thanks to readily available images, we may fear extremely rare events. We fear flying because we play old air disaster films in our heads. We fear swimming in ocean waters because we replay *Jaws* with ourselves as victims. How many shark attacks kill Americans each year? About

---

3 Tversky and Kahneman's joint work on decision making received a 2002 Nobel Prize; sadly, only Kahneman was alive to receive the honor.

FIGURE 8.3 Solution to the matchstick problem Were you, by chance, fixated on two-dimensional solutions? Solving problems often requires taking a new angle on the situation.

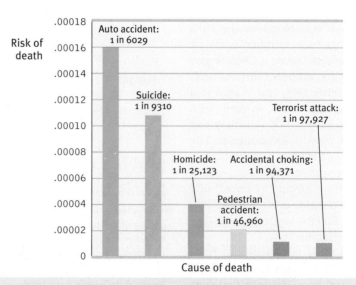

FIGURE 8.4 Risk of death from various causes in the United States, 2001 (Data assembled from various government sources by Randall Marshall et al., 2007.)

one. How many does heart disease kill? 600,000. But the vivid image (a shark bite!) often wins, and thus many of us fear sharks more than cheeseburgers and cigarettes (Daley, 2011).

Dramatic outcomes make us gasp; probabilities we hardly grasp. We over-feel and underthink. In one experiment, donations to a starving 7-year-old were greater when her image appeared alone, without statistics describing the millions of needy African children like her (Small et al., 2007). "If I look at the mass I will never act," Mother Teresa reportedly said. "If I look at the one, I will." "The more who die, the less we care," noted one psychologist (Slovic, 2010). We reason emotionally.

Overconfidence: Was There Ever Any Doubt?

Sometimes our judgments and decisions go awry because we are more confident than correct. When answering factual questions such as, "Is absinthe a liqueur or a precious stone?" only 60 percent of people in one study answered correctly. (It's a licorice-flavored liqueur.) Yet those answering felt, on average, 75 percent confident (Fischhoff et al., 1977). This ten-

PREDICT YOUR OWN BEHAVIOR When will you finish reading this chapter?

dency to overestimate our accuracy is **overconfidence.**

History is full of leaders who, when waging war, were more confident than correct. And classrooms are full of over-confident students who expect to finish assignments and write papers ahead of schedule (Buehler et al., 1994, 2002). In fact, the projects generally take about twice the number of days predicted.

We often overestimate our future free time (Zauberman & Lynch, 2005). Surely we'll have more free time next month than we do today. So we happily accept invitations, only to discover we're just as busy when the day rolls around. And believing we'll surely have more money next year, we take out loans or buy on credit. Despite our past overconfident predictions, we remain overly confident of our next one.

Overconfidence can have adaptive value. Believing that their decisions are right and they have time to spare, self-confident people tend to live happily. They make tough decisions more easily, and they seem believable (Baumeister, 1989; Taylor, 1989). Moreover, we can learn from our mistakes. When given prompt and clear feedback—as weather forecasters receive after each day's predictions—we learn to be more realistic about the accuracy of our judgments (Fischhoff, 1982). The wisdom to know when we know a thing and when we do not is born of experience.

Our Beliefs Live On— Sometimes Despite Evidence

Our overconfidence in our judgments is startling. Equally startling is our tendency to cling to our beliefs even when the evidence proves us wrong. **Belief perseverance** often fuels social conflict. Consider a classic study of people with opposing views of the death penalty (Lord et al., 1979). Both sides were asked to read the same material—two new research reports. One reported that the death penalty lowers the crime rate; the other showed that it has no effect on the crime rate. Each side was impressed by

the study supporting its own beliefs, and quick to criticize the other study. Thus, showing the two groups the *same* mixed evidence actually *increased* their disagreement about the value of capital punishment.

So how can smart thinkers avoid belief perseverance? A simple remedy is to *consider the opposite.* In a repeat of the death penalty study, researchers asked some participants to be "as *objective* and *unbiased* as possible" (Lord et al., 1984). This plea did nothing to reduce people's biases. They also asked another group to consider "whether you would have made the same high or low evaluations had exactly the same study produced results on the *other* side of the issue." In this group, people's views did change. After imagining the *opposite* findings, they judged the evidence in a much less biased way.

The more we come to appreciate why our beliefs might be true, the more tightly we cling to them. Once we have explained to ourselves why we believe a child is "gifted" (or has a "learning disorder"), or why candidate X or Y will be a better commander-in-chief, we tend to ignore evidence that challenges our belief. Prejudice persists. Once beliefs take root, it takes stronger evidence to change them than it did to create them. Beliefs often persevere.

Framing: Let Me Put It This Way . . .

Framing—the way we present an issue—can be a powerful tool of persuasion.

availability heuristic judging the likelihood of an event based on its availability in memory; if an event comes readily to mind (perhaps because it was vivid), we assume it must be common.

overconfidence the tendency to be more confident than correct—to overestimate the accuracy of our beliefs and judgments.

belief perseverance clinging to beliefs and ignoring evidence that proves they are wrong.

framing the way an issue is posed; framing can significantly affect decisions and judgments.

THINKING CRITICALLY ABOUT

The Fear Factor—Why We Fear the Wrong Things

After 9/11, many people feared flying more than driving. In a 2006 Gallup survey, only 40 percent of Americans reported being "not afraid at all" to fly. Yet from 2007 to 2009, Americans were—mile for mile—200 times more likely to die in a motor vehicle accident than on a scheduled flight (National Safety Council, 2012). In 2009 alone, 33,808 Americans were killed in motor vehicle accidents—that's 650 dead people *each week.* Meanwhile, in 2009 (as in 2007 and 2008), *zero* died from accidents on scheduled airline flights.

In a late 2001 essay, I calculated that if—because of 9/11—we flew 20 percent less and instead drove half those unflown miles, about 800 more people would die in the year after 9/11 (Myers, 2001). German psychologist Gerd Gigerenzer (2004, 2006; Gaissmaier & Gigerenzer, 2012) later checked this estimate against actual accident data. (Why didn't I think to do that?) U.S. traffic deaths did indeed increase significantly in the last three months of 2001 (FIGURE 8.5). By the end of 2002, Gigerenzer estimated, 1600 Americans had "lost their lives on the road by trying to avoid the risk of flying." Despite our greater fear of flying, flying's greatest danger is, for most people, the drive to the airport.

How can our intuition about risk be so wrong? Psychologists have identified four forces that feed fear and cause us to ignore higher risks.

1. *We fear what our ancestral history has prepared us to fear.* Human emotions were road-tested in the Stone Age. Our old brain prepares us to fear yesterday's risks: snakes, lizards, and spiders (which combined now kill a tiny fraction of the number killed by modern-day threats, such as cars and cigarettes). Yesterday's risks also prepare us to fear confinement and heights, and therefore flying.

2. *We fear what we cannot control.* Driving we control; flying we do not.

3. *We fear what is immediate.* The dangers of flying are mostly in the moments of takeoff and landing. The dangers of driving are diffused across many moments to come, each trivially dangerous.

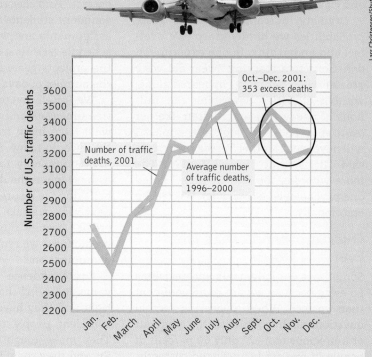

FIGURE 8.5 **Scaring us onto deadly highways** Images of 9/11 etched a sharper image in American minds than did the millions of fatality-free flights on U.S. airlines during 2002 and after. Dramatic events are readily available to memory, and they shape our perceptions of risk. In the three months after 9/11, those faulty perceptions led more Americans to travel, and some to die, by car. (Adapted from Gigerenzer, 2004.)

Consider how the framing of options can nudge people toward beneficial decisions (Thaler & Sunstein, 2008):

- *Life and death.* Imagine two surgeons explaining the risk of surgery. One tells patients that during this surgery 10 percent of people die. The other tells patients that 90 percent survive. The information is the same. The effect is not. In surveys, both patients and physicians said the risk seems greater when they hear that 10 percent will die (Marteau, 1989; McNeil et al., 1988; Rothman & Salovey, 1997).

- *Why choosing to be an organ donor depends on where you live.* In many European countries, as well as in the United States, people decide whether to be organ donors when renewing their driver's license. In some countries, the assumed answer is *Yes,* unless you opt out. Nearly 100 percent of the people in the opt-out countries agree to be donors. In the United States, Britain, and Germany, the assumed answer has been *No,* unless you opt in. In these countries, only about 25 percent have agreed to be donors (Johnson & Goldstein, 2003).

- *How to help employees decide to save for their retirement.* A 2006 U.S. pension law recognized the framing effect. Before that law, employees who wanted to contribute to a 401(k) retirement plan typically had to choose a lower take-home pay, which few people will do. Companies can now automatically enroll their employees in the plan but allow them to opt out (which would raise the employees' take-home pay). In both plans, the decision to contribute is the employee's. But under the new opt-out arrangement, enrollments among 3.4 million workers soared—from 59 percent to 86 percent (Rosenberg, 2010).

4. *Thanks to the availability heuristic, we fear what is most readily available in memory.* Powerful, vivid images, like that of United Flight 175 slicing into the World Trade Center, feed our judgments of risk. Thousands of safe car trips lull us into a comfortable, safe feeling. Similarly, we remember (and fear) disasters (hurricanes, tornadoes, school massacres) that kill people dramatically, in bunches. But we fear too little the less dramatic threats that claim lives quietly, one by one, into the distant future. Horrified citizens and commentators renewed calls for U.S. gun control in 2012, after 20 children and 6 adults were slain in a Connecticut elementary school. Yet, even more Americans are murdered with guns one by one every day, though less dramatically. Bill Gates has noted that each year a half-million children worldwide die from rotavirus. This is the equivalent of four 747s full of children dying *every day,* and we hear nothing of it (Glass, 2004).

As one risk analyst explained, "If it's in the news, don't worry about it. The very definition of *news* is 'something that hardly ever happens'" (Schneier, 2007). But the news, and our own memorable experiences, can make us fear the least likely events. Although many people fear dying in a terrorist attack on an airplane, the first decade of the twenty-first century produced one terrorist attempt for every 10.4 million flights. That's less than one-twentieth the chance of any one of us being struck by lightning (Silver, 2009).

The point to remember: Critical thinkers—smart thinkers—will check their fears against the facts and resist those who tempt us to fear the wrong things.

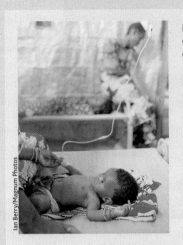

DRAMATIC DEATHS IN BUNCHES CAUSE CONCERN—AND CONTRIBUTIONS The memorable 2010 Haitian earthquake that killed some 250,000 people stirred an outpouring of justified concern. Meanwhile, according to the World Health Organization, a silent earthquake of poverty-related malaria was killing about that many people, mostly in Africa, *every four months.* Private donors gave $1839 per person affected by the visible horror of Hurricane Katrina, and $10 per person diagnosed with the subdued horror of AIDS (Epstein, 2006).

Ian Berry/Magnum Photos

© Transtock/Corbis

- Why can news be described as "something that hardly ever happens"? How does knowing this help us assess our fears?

ANSWER: If a tragic event such as a plane crash makes the news, it is noteworthy and unusual, unlike much more common bad events such as traffic accidents. Knowing this, we can worry less about unlikely events and think more about improving the safety of our everyday activities. (For example, we can wear a seat belt when in a vehicle and use the crosswalk when walking.)

The point to remember: Framing influences decisions.

The Perils and Powers of Intuition

8-4 How do smart thinkers use intuition?

We have seen how our unreasoned thinking can plague our efforts to solve problems, assess risks, and make wise decisions. Moreover, these perils of intuition persist even when people are offered extra pay for thinking smart or when asked to justify their answers. And they persist even among those with high intelligence, including expert physicians or clinicians (Shafir & LeBoeuf, 2002; Stanovich & West, 2008).

But psychological science is also revealing intuition's powers.

- *Intuition is analysis "frozen into habit"* (Simon, 2001). It is implicit knowledge—what we've learned but can't fully explain. We see this in chess masters who, when playing speed chess, intuitively know the right move (Burns, 2004). We see it in the smart and quick judgments of seasoned nurses, firefighters, art critics, car mechanics, and hockey players. And in you, too, for anything in which you have developed a deep and special knowledge, based on experience. In each case, what feels like instant intuition is an acquired ability to size up a situation in an eyeblink.

- *Intuition is usually adaptive.* Our fast and frugal heuristics let us intuitively assume that fuzzy-looking objects are far away—which they usually are, except on foggy mornings. Our learned associations surface as gut feelings, right or wrong: Seeing a stranger who looks like someone who has harmed or threatened us in the past, we may automatically react with distrust.

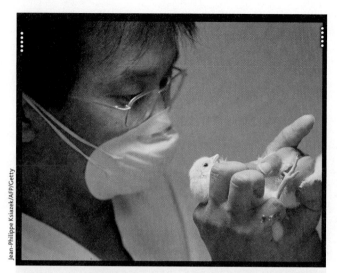

HMM . . . MALE OR FEMALE? When acquired expertise becomes an automatic habit, it feels like intuition. At a glance, experienced chicken sexers just know, yet they cannot easily tell you *how* they know.

- *Intuition is huge.* Today's cognitive science offers many examples of unconscious automatic influences on our judgments (Custers & Aarts, 2010). Imagine participating in an experiment on decision making (Strick et al., 2010). Three groups of participants receive complex information about four apartment options. Those in the first group state their choice immediately after reading the information. Those in the second group analyze the information before choosing one of the options. Your group, the third, is distracted for a time and then asked to give your decision. Which group will make the smartest decision? Most people guess that the more complex the choice, the smarter it is to make decisions rationally rather than intuitively (Inbar et al., 2010). Actually, when making complex decisions, we benefit by letting a problem "incubate" while we attend to other things (Sio & Ormerod, 2009; Strick et al., 2010, 2011). The third group, given the distraction, made the best choice. Facing a decision involving a lot of facts, we're wise to gather all the information we can, and then say, "Give me some time *not* to think about this." By taking time even to sleep on it, we let our unconscious mental machinery work, and then await the intuitive result of this automatic processing.

The bottom line: Our two-track mind makes sweet harmony as smart, critical thinking listens to the creative whispers of our vast unseen mind and then evaluates evidence, tests conclusions, and plans for the future.

Thinking Creatively

8-5 What is creativity, and what fosters it?

Creativity is the ability to produce ideas that are both novel and valuable (Hennessey & Amabile, 2010). Consider Princeton mathematician Andrew Wiles' incredible, creative moment. Pierre de Fermat (1601–1665), a mischief-loving genius, dared scholars to match his solutions to various number theory problems. Three centuries later, one of those problems continued to baffle the greatest mathematical minds, even after a $2 million prize (in today's money) had been offered for cracking the puzzle.

Wiles had searched for the answer for more than 30 years and reached the brink of a solution. One morning, out of the blue, an "incredible revelation" struck him. "It was so . . . beautiful . . . so simple and so elegant. I couldn't understand how I'd missed it. . . . It was the most important moment of my working life" (Singh, 1997, p. 25).

Creativity like Wiles' requires a certain level of *aptitude* (ability to learn). Thirteen-year-olds who score exceptionally high on aptitude tests, for example, are later more likely to take advanced degrees in science and math and to create published or patented work (Park et al., 2008; Robertson et al., 2010). But creativity is more than school smarts, and it requires a different kind of thinking. Aptitude tests (such as the SAT® Reasoning Test) typically require **convergent thinking**—an ability to provide a single correct answer. Creativity tests (*How many uses can you think of for a brick?*) require **divergent thinking**—the ability to consider many different options and to think in novel ways.

Robert Sternberg and his colleagues (1988, 2003; Sternberg & Lubart, 1991, 1992) believe creativity has five ingredients.

1. *Expertise*—a solid knowledge base—furnishes the ideas, images, and phrases we use as mental building blocks. The more blocks we have, the more novel ways we have to combine them. Wiles' well-developed base of mathematical knowledge gave him access to many combinations of ideas and methods.

2. *Imaginative thinking skills* give us the ability to see things in novel ways, to recognize patterns, and to make connections. Wiles' imaginative solution combined two partial solutions.

3. A *venturesome personality* seeks new experiences, tolerates gray areas, takes risks, and continues despite obstacles. Wiles said he worked in near-isolation from the mathematics community, partly to stay focused and avoid distraction. This kind of focus and dedication is an enduring trait.

4. *Intrinsic motivation* (as explained in Chapter 6) arises internally rather than from outside rewards or external pressures (extrinsic motivation) (Amabile & Hennessey, 1992). Creative people seem driven by the pleasure and challenge of the work itself, not by outside rewards, such as meeting deadlines, impressing people, or making money. As Wiles said, "I was so obsessed by this problem

that . . . I was thinking about it all the time—[from] when I woke up in the morning to when I went to sleep at night" (Singh & Riber, 1997).

5. *A creative environment* sparks, supports, and refines creative ideas. Colleagues are an important part of creative environments. In one study of 2026 leading scientists and inventors, the best known of them had challenging and supportive relationships with colleagues (Simonton, 1992). Many creative environments also minimize stress and foster focused awareness (Byron & Khazanchi, 2011). Jonas Salk solved a problem that led to the polio vaccine while in a monastery. Later, when he designed the Salk Institute, he provided quiet spaces where scientists could think and work without interruption (Sternberg, 2006). Serenity seeds spontaneity.

For those seeking to boost the creative process, see Close-Up: Fostering Your Own Creativity on the next page.

* * *

TABLE 8.1 summarizes the cognitive processes and strategies discussed in this section. ■

"For the love of God, is there a doctor in the house?"

IMAGINATIVE THINKING Cartoonists often display creativity as they see things in new ways or make unusual connections.

creativity the ability to produce new and valuable ideas.

convergent thinking narrows the available problem solutions to determine the single best solution.

divergent thinking expands the number of possible problem solutions (creative thinking that diverges in different directions).

TABLE 8.1 Comparing Cognitive Processes and Strategies			
Process or Strategy	**Description**	**Powers**	**Perils**
Algorithm	Methodical rule or procedure	Guarantees solution	Requires time and effort
Heuristics	Simple thinking shortcuts, such as the *availability heuristic*, which estimates likelihood based on how easily events come to mind	Lets us act quickly and efficiently	Puts us at risk for errors
Insight	Sudden Aha! reaction	Provides instant realization of solution	May not happen
Confirmation bias	Tendency to search for support for our own views and ignore contradictory evidence	Lets us quickly recognize supporting evidence	Hinders recognition of contradictory evidence
Fixation	Inability to view problems from a new angle	Focuses thinking	Hinders creative problem solving
Intuition	Fast, automatic feelings and thoughts; includes insight, heuristics, and other forms of unconscious processing	Is based on our experience; huge and adaptive	Can lead us to overfeel and underthink
Overconfidence	Overestimating the accuracy of our beliefs and judgments	Allows us to be happy and to make decisions easily	Puts us at risk for errors
Belief perseverance	Ignoring evidence that proves our beliefs are wrong	Supports our enduring beliefs	Closes our mind to new ideas
Framing	Wording a question or statement so that it evokes a desired response	Can influence others' decisions	Can produce a misleading result
Creativity	Ability to produce novel and valuable ideas	Produces new products	May distract from structured, routine work

Fostering Your Own Creativity

Creative achievement springs from creativity-fostering persons and situations. Here are some tips for growing your own creativity.

- *Develop your expertise.* Become an expert at something. Ask yourself what you care about and most enjoy and then follow your passion.

- *Allow time for ideas to hatch.* A broad base of knowledge provides building blocks that can be combined in new and creative ways. During periods of inattention ("sleeping on a problem"), automatic processing can help associations to form (Zhong et al., 2008). So think hard on a problem, but then set it aside and come back to it later.

- *Set aside time for your mind to roam freely.* Detach from attention-grabbing television, social networking, and video gaming. Jog, go for a long walk, or meditate.

- *Experience other cultures and ways of thinking.* Expose yourself to multicultural experiences. Viewing life from a different perspective sets the creative juices flowing. Students who have spent time abroad are more adept at working out creative solutions to problems (Leung et al., 2008; Maddux et al., 2009, 2010). Even if you can't afford to travel abroad, you can get out of your neighborhood and spend time in a different sort of place.

A creative environment

RETRIEVE + REMEMBER

- Match the process or strategy listed below (1–10) with its description (a–j).

1. Algorithm
2. Intuition
3. Insight
4. Heuristics
5. Fixation
6. Confirmation bias
7. Overconfidence
8. Framing
9. Belief perseverance
10. Creativity

a. Inability to view problems from a new angle; focuses thinking but hinders creative problem solving.

b. Step-by-step rule or procedure that guarantees the solution but requires time and effort.

c. Your fast, automatic, effortless feelings and thoughts based on experience; huge and adaptive but can lead you to overfeel and underthink.

d. Simple thinking shortcuts that let you act quickly and efficiently but put you at risk for errors.

e. Sudden Aha! reaction that instantly reveals the solution.

f. Tendency to search for support for your own views and to ignore evidence that opposes them.

g. Holding on to your beliefs even after they are proven wrong; closing your mind to new ideas.

h. Overestimating the accuracy of your beliefs and judgments; allows you to be happier and to make decisions easily, but puts you at risk for errors.

i. Wording a question or statement so that it produces the desired response; can mislead people and influence their decisions.

j. The ability to produce novel and valuable ideas.

ANSWERS: 1. b, 2. c, 3. e, 4. d, 5. a, 6. f, 7. h, 8. i, 9. g, 10. j.

Do Other Species Share Our Cognitive Skills?

8-6 What do we know about thinking in other species?

Other animals are smarter than many humans realize. Consider some surprising findings.

USING CONCEPTS AND NUMBERS

Even pigeons—mere birdbrains—can sort objects (pictures of cars, cats, chairs, flowers) into categories, or concepts. Shown a picture of a never-before-seen chair, pigeons will reliably peck a key that represents *chairs* (Wasserman, 1995). The great apes—a group that includes chimpanzees and gorillas—also form concepts, such as *cat* and *dog*. After monkeys have learned these concepts, certain frontal lobe neurons in their brains fire in response to new "cat-like" images, others to new "dog-like" images (Freedman et al., 2001).

Until his death in 2007, Alex, an African Grey parrot, displayed jaw-dropping numerical skills. He categorized and named objects (Pepperberg, 2006, 2009). He could comprehend numbers up to 6. He could speak the number of objects. He could add two small clusters of objects and announce the sum. He could indicate which of two numbers was greater. And he gave correct answers when shown various groups of objects. Asked, for example, "What color four?" (meaning "What's the color of the objects of which there are four?"), he could speak the answer.

DISPLAYING INSIGHT Psychologist Wolfgang Köhler (1925) showed that we are not the only creatures to display insight. He placed a piece of fruit and a long stick outside the cage of a chimpanzee named Sultan, beyond his reach. Inside the cage, he placed a short stick, which

Sultan grabbed, using it to try to reach the fruit. After several failed attempts, the chimpanzee dropped the stick and seemed to survey the situation. Then suddenly (as if thinking "Aha!"), Sultan jumped up and seized the short stick again. This time, he used it to pull in the longer stick, which he then used to reach the fruit.

USING TOOLS AND TRANSMITTING CULTURE Various animals have displayed creative tool use. Forest-dwelling chimpanzees select different tools for different purposes—a heavy stick for making holes, a light, flexible stick for fishing for termites (Sanz et al., 2004). They break off the reed or stick, strip off any leaves, and carry it to a termite mound. Then they twist it just so and carefully remove it. Termites for lunch! (This is very reinforcing for a chimpanzee.) One anthropologist, trying to mimic the animal's deft fishing moves, failed miserably.

Researchers have found at least 39 local customs related to chimpanzee tool use, grooming, and courtship (Whiten & Boesch, 2001). One group may slurp termites directly from a stick, another group may pluck them off individually. One group may break nuts with a stone hammer, another with a wooden hammer.

Chris Bird & Nathan Emery

Mathias Osvath

(a)   (b)

FIGURE 8.6 Tool-using animals (a) New Caledonian crows quickly learned to raise the water level in a tube and nab a floating worm by dropping stones into the water (Bird & Emery, 2009). Other crows have used twigs to probe for insects, and bent strips of metal to reach food. (b) One male chimpanzee in Sweden's Furuvik Zoo was observed every morning collecting stones into a neat little pile. Later in the day, he used them as ammunition to pelt visitors (Osvath, 2009).

Johan Swanepoel/Alamy

Several experiments have brought chimpanzee cultural transmission into the laboratory (Horner et al., 2006). If Chimpanzee A obtains food either by sliding or by lifting a door, Chimpanzee B will then typically do the same to get food. And so will Chimpanzee C after observing Chimpanzee B. Across a chain of six animals, from Chimpanzee A to Chimpanzee F, chimpanzees see, and chimpanzees do.

Other animals have also shown surprising cognitive talents (**FIGURE 8.6**). In tests, elephants have demonstrated self-awareness by recognizing themselves in a mirror. They have also displayed their abilities to learn, remember, discriminate smells, empathize, cooperate, teach, and spontaneously use tools (Byrne et al., 2009). As social creatures, chimpanzees have shown altruism, cooperation, and group aggression. Like humans, they will kill their neighbor to gain land, and they grieve over dead relatives (Anderson et al., 2010; Biro et al., 2010; Mitani et al., 2010).

There is no question that other species display many remarkable cognitive skills. But one big question remains: Do they, like humans, exhibit language? First, let's consider what language is, and how it develops.

Language

Imagine an alien species that could pass thoughts from one head to another merely by setting air molecules in motion between them. Actually, we are those creatures! When we speak, we send air-pressure waves banging against other people's eardrums as we transfer thoughts from our brain into theirs. As cognitive scientist Steven Pinker (1998) has noted, we sometimes sit for hours "listening to other people make noise as they exhale, because those hisses and squeaks contain *information*." And thanks to all those funny sounds created from the air pressure waves we send out, we attract people's attention and we get them to do things (Guerin, 2003). Depending on how you vibrate the air after opening your mouth, you may get a scowl or a kiss.

Language is our spoken, written, or signed words, and the ways we meaningfully combine them. When I created this paragraph, my fingers on a keyboard triggered electronic signals that morphed into the squiggles in front of you. As you read these squiggles, they trigger nerve impulses that travel to areas of your brain that decode the meaning. Thanks to our shared language, information has just moved from my mind to yours. With language, we humans can transmit civilization's

language our spoken, written, or signed words and the ways we combine them to communicate meaning.

knowledge from one generation to the next. Many animals know only what they see. Thanks to language, we know much that we've never seen and that our ancestors never knew.

Language also connects us. If you were able to keep only one cognitive ability, what would it be? Without sight or hearing, you could still have friends, family, and a job. But without language, could you have these things? "Language is so fundamental to our experience, so deeply a part of being human, that it's hard to imagine life without it" (Boroditsky, 2009).

Language Development

8-7 What are the milestones in language development, and how do we acquire language?

Make a quick guess: How many words did you learn during the years between your first birthday and your high school graduation? Although you use only 150 words for about half of what you say, you probably learned about 60,000 words (Bloom, 2000; McMurray, 2007). That averages (after age 2) nearly 3500 words each year, or nearly 10 each day! How you did it—how those 3500 words could so far outnumber the roughly 200 words your schoolteachers consciously taught you each year—is one of the great human wonders.

Could you even now state your language's rules of *syntax* (the correct way to string words together to form sentences)? Most of us cannot. Yet, before you were able to add 2 + 2, you were creating your own original sentences and applying these rules. As a preschooler, your ability to understand and speak your language was so great it would put to shame college students struggling to learn a foreign language.

We humans have an astonishing knack for language. Without blinking,

Jaimie Duplass/Shutterstock

we sample tens of thousands of words in our memory, effortlessly combine them with near-perfect syntax, and spew them out, three words a second (Vigliocco & Hartsuiker, 2002). We rarely form sentences in our minds before we speak them. Rather, our sentences organize themselves on the fly as we speak. And while doing all this, we also fine-tune our language to our social and cultural setting, following rules for speaking (*How far apart should we stand?*) and listening (*Is it OK to interrupt?*). Given how many ways there are to mess up, it's amazing that we master this social dance. When and how does it happen?

When Do We Learn Language?

RECEPTIVE LANGUAGE Children's language development moves from simplicity to complexity. Infants start without language (*in fantis* means "not speaking"). Yet by 4 months of age, babies can recognize differences in speech sounds (Stager & Werker, 1997). They can also read lips. They prefer to look at a face that matches a sound, so we know they can recognize that *ah* comes from wide open lips and *ee* from a mouth with corners pulled back (Kuhl & Meltzoff, 1982). This marks the beginning of the development of babies' *receptive language,* their ability to understand what is said to and about them. At 7 months and beyond, babies grow in their power to break spoken sounds into individual words—which you and I find difficult when listening to an unfamiliar language.

PRODUCTIVE LANGUAGE Babies' *productive language,* their ability to produce words, matures after their receptive language. Before nurture molds their speech, nature allows a wide range of possible sounds in the **babbling stage,** around 4 months of age. In this stage, they seem to sample all the sounds they can make, such as *ah-goo*. Babbling is not an imitation of adult speech. We know

"Got idea. Talk better. Combine words. Make sentences."

ScienceCartoonsPlus.com

this because babbling includes sounds from languages not spoken in the household. From this early babbling, a listener could not identify an infant as being, say, French, Korean, or Ethiopian. Do deaf infants babble in sign language? They do, and those who observe their deaf parents signing begin to babble more with their hands (Petitto & Marentette, 1991).

By the time infants are about 10 months old, their babbling has changed so that a trained ear can identify the household language (de Boysson-Bardies et al., 1989). Without exposure to other languages, babies lose their ability to hear and produce sounds and tones found outside their native language (Meltzoff et al., 2009; Pallier et al., 2001). Thus, by adulthood those who speak only English cannot discriminate certain sounds in Japanese speech. Nor can Japanese adults with no training in English hear the difference between the English *r* and *l*. For a Japanese-speaking adult, *la-la-ra-ra* may sound like the same syllable repeated.

Around their first birthday, most children enter the **one-word stage.** They already know that sounds carry meanings. They now begin to use sounds—usually only one barely recognizable syllable, such as *ma* or *da*—to communicate meaning. But family members quickly learn to understand, and gradually the infant's language sounds more like the family's language. Across the world, baby's first words are often nouns that label objects or people (Tardif et al., 2008). At this one-word stage, a single word ("*Doggy!*") may equal a sentence ("*Look at the dog out there!*").

At about 18 months, children's word learning explodes, jumping from about a word each week to a word each day. By their second birthday, most have entered the **two-word stage** (TABLE 8.2). They start uttering two-word sentences in **telegraphic speech.** Like yesterday's telegrams that charged by the word (TERMS ACCEPTED. SEND MONEY), a 2-year-old's speech contains mostly nouns and verbs (*Want juice*). Also like telegrams, their speech follows rules of syntax, arranging words in a sensible order. English-speaking children typically place adjectives before nouns—*white house* rather than *house white*. Spanish reverses this order, as in *casa blanca*.

Moving out of the two-word stage, children quickly begin speaking in longer phrases (Fromkin & Rodman, 1983). What might happen if a child gets a late start on learning a particular language? This is not uncommon for children who have surgery to enable hearing, or who are adopted by a family in another country. For these late bloomers, language development follows the same sequence, though the pace is often faster (Ertmer et al., 2007; Snedeker et al., 2007). (But stay tuned: There is a limit on how long language learning can be delayed.)

By early elementary school, children understand complex sentences. They can enjoy a joke with a double meaning: "You never starve in the desert because of all the sand-which-is there." ■

How Do We Learn Grammar?

The world's 7000 or so languages are structurally very diverse (Evans & Levinson, 2009). Linguist Noam Chomsky has argued that all languages nevertheless share some basic elements, which he calls a *universal grammar*. Thus, all human languages have the same grammatical building blocks, such as nouns, verbs, and adjectives. Moreover, said Chomsky, we humans are born with a built-in readiness—a predisposition—to learn grammar rules. This helps explain why preschoolers pick up language so readily and use grammar so well. It happens so naturally—as naturally as birds learn to fly—that training hardly helps.

No matter what our language is, we start speaking mostly in nouns (*kitty, da-da*) rather than verbs and adjectives (Bornstein et al., 2004). We are not, however, born with a built-in *specific* language. Babies born in Mexico learn to speak Spanish, not Chinese. And whatever language we experience as children, whether spoken or signed, we readily learn its specific **grammar** and vocabulary (Bavelier et al., 2003). Once again, we see biology and experience working together.

CRITICAL PERIODS In *The Fragile Species* (1992), Lewis Thomas observed, "Childhood is the time for language, no doubt

CREATING A LANGUAGE Young deaf children in Nicaragua were brought together as if on a desert island (actually a school). They drew upon sign gestures from their own home to create their own Nicaraguan Sign Language, complete with words and intricate grammar. Our biological predisposition for language does not create language in a vacuum. But activated by a social context, nature and nurture work creatively together (Osborne, 1999; Sandler et al., 2005; Senghas & Coppola, 2001).

Susan Meiselas/Magnum Photos

TABLE 8.2	Summary of Language Development
Month (approximate)	Stage
4	Babbles many speech sounds ("ah-goo")
10	Babbling; resembles household language ("ma-ma")
12	One-word stage ("Kitty!")
24	Two-word speech ("Get ball.")
24+	Rapid development into complete sentences

babbling stage beginning at about 4 months, the stage of speech development in which the infant spontaneously utters various sounds at first unrelated to the household language.

one-word stage the stage in speech development, from about age 1 to 2, during which a child speaks mostly in single words.

two-word stage beginning about age 2, the stage in speech development during which a child speaks mostly two-word statements.

telegraphic speech early speech stage in which a child speaks like a telegram—"go car"—using mostly nouns and verbs.

grammar in a specific language, a system of rules that enables us to communicate with and understand others.

about it. Young children, the younger the better, are good at it; it is child's play. It is a onetime gift to the species." Childhood seems to represent a *critical* (or "sensitive") *period* for mastering certain aspects of language (Hernandez & Li, 2007; Lenneberg, 1967). Deaf children who gain hearing with cochlear implants by age 2 develop better oral speech than do those who receive implants after age 4 (Greers, 2004). For deaf or hearing children, later-than-usual exposure to language—at age 2 or 3—unleashes their brain's idle language capacity, producing a rush of language. But there is no similar rush of learning if children are not exposed to either a spoken or a signed language until age 7. Such deprived children lose their ability to master *any* language.

After the language window closes, even learning a second language becomes more difficult. Have you learned a second language as an adult? If so, you almost certainly speak it with the accent of your first, and perhaps with imperfect grammar.

The older we are when moving to a new country, the harder it is to learn the new culture and language (Cheung et al., 2011; Hakuta et al., 2003). This difficulty appeared in one study of Korean and Chinese immigrants (Johnson & Newport, 1991). Their task was to read 276 English sentences, such as "*Yesterday the hunter shoots a deer,*" and to decide whether each sentence was grammatically correct or incorrect. Everyone in the study had lived in the United States for approximately 10 years. Some had arrived as very young children, others as adults. As **FIGURE 8.7** reveals, those who had learned their second language early learned it best.

The impact of early experience is also evident in sign language learning in children who have been deaf from birth. More than 90 percent of such children are born to hearing parents who do not use sign language. These children typically do not experience signed language during their early years. Those who learn to sign as teens or adults are in some ways like the immigrants who learned a new language after childhood. They can master the basic words and learn to order them. But they are never as fluent as native signers in using and understanding subtle differences in grammar (Newport, 1990). ∎

FIGURE 8.7 New language learning gets harder with age Young children have a readiness to learn language. Ten years after coming to the United States, Asian immigrants took a grammar test. Those who arrived before age 8 understood American English grammar as well as native speakers did. Those who arrived later did not. (From Johnson & Newport, 1991.)

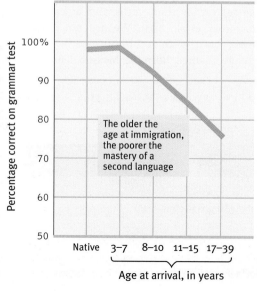

The older the age at immigration, the poorer the mastery of a second language

Percentage correct on grammar test — 100%, 90, 80, 70, 60, 50

Age at arrival, in years — Native, 3–7, 8–10, 11–15, 17–39

RETRIEVE + REMEMBER

- What was Noam Chomsky's explanation of language development?

ANSWER: Chomsky maintained that all languages share a universal grammar, and humans are biologically predisposed to learn the grammar rules of language.

- Why is it so difficult to learn a new language in adulthood?

ANSWER: Our brain's *critical period* for language learning is in childhood, when we can absorb language structure almost effortlessly. As we move past that stage in our brain's development, our ability to learn a new language drops dramatically.

The Brain and Language

8-8 What brain areas are involved in language processing and speech?

We think of speaking and reading, or writing and reading, or singing and speaking as merely different examples of the same general ability—language. But consider this curious finding: Damage to any one of several areas of the brain's cortex can impair language. Even more curious, some people with brain damage can speak fluently but cannot read (despite good vision). Others can understand what they read but cannot speak. Still others can write but not read, read but not write, read numbers but not letters, or sing but not speak. To sort out this puzzle required a lot of smart thinking by many different scientists, all seeking to answer the same question: How does the brain process language?

In 1865, French physician Paul Broca discovered that after damage to a specific area of the left frontal lobe (later called **Broca's area**) a person would struggle to *speak* words, yet could often sing familiar songs with ease. A decade later, German investigator Carl Wernicke discovered that after damage to a specific area of the left temporal lobe (**Wernicke's area**), people could speak only meaningless words and were unable to understand others' words.

Over the next century and a half, other researchers continued the search for the answer to the language-processing puzzle. Today's neuroscience has confirmed brain activity in Broca's and Wernicke's areas during language processing (**FIGURE 8.8**). But we now know that your brain processes language in other areas as well. You experience language as a single, unified stream. But functional MRI (fMRI) scans show that different neural networks in your brain are activated by nouns and verbs (or objects and actions); by different vowels; and by reading stories of visual versus motor experiences (Shapiro et al., 2006; Speer et al., 2009). And if you are lucky enough to be fluent in two languages, your hardworking brain has assigned those two functions to two different sets of neural networks. One processes your native language, and the other handles your second language (Perani & Abutalebi, 2005).

The big point to remember: In processing language, as in other forms of information processing, *the brain operates by dividing its mental functions—speaking, perceiving, thinking, remembering—into smaller tasks.* Your conscious experience of reading this page *seems* to be one task, but many different neural networks in your brain are pooling their work to compute each word's form, sound, and meaning (Posner & Carr, 1992). ∎

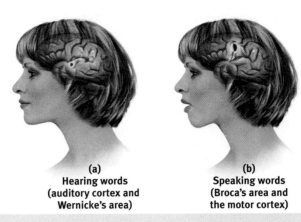

(a)
Hearing words
(auditory cortex and
Wernicke's area)

(b)
Speaking words
(Broca's area and
the motor cortex)

FIGURE 8.8 Brain activity when hearing and speaking words

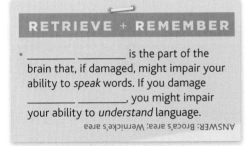

RETRIEVE + REMEMBER

- _____ _____ is the part of the brain that, if damaged, might impair your ability to *speak* words. If you damage _____ _____, you might impair your ability to *understand* language.

ANSWER: Broca's area; Wernicke's area

Thinking Without Language

8-9 How can thinking in images be useful?

To turn on the cold water in your bathroom, in which direction do you turn the handle? To answer this question, you probably thought not in words but in images—perhaps a mental picture of your hand turning the faucet.

Indeed, we often think in images. Mental practice relies on thinking in images. One year after placing second in a worldwide piano competition, pianist Liu Chi Kung was imprisoned during China's cultural revolution. Soon after his release, after seven years without touching a piano, Liu was back on tour. The critics judged his playing to be better than ever, and his fans wondered how he had continued to develop without practice. "I did practice," said Liu, "every day. I rehearsed every piece I had ever played, note by note, in my mind" (Garfield, 1986).

How does mental practice work its magic? Once you have learned a skill, even *watching* that event will trigger brain activity in the same areas that are active when you actually use the skill. As ballet dancers watch ballet videos, fMRI scans show the brain dancing along (Calvo-Merino et al., 2004). Just *imagining* a physical experience, such as pain, can have similar results. Imagining pain activates neural networks that are normally active during *actual* pain (Grèzes & Decety, 2001).

One experiment on the benefits of mental practice observed the University of Tennessee women's basketball team (Savoy & Beitel, 1996). Over 35 games, researchers tracked the team's skill at shooting free throws following standard physical practice or mental practice. After physical practice, the team scored about 52 percent of their shots. After mental practice, that score rose

to 65 percent. During mental practice, players had repeatedly imagined making free throws under various conditions, including being "trash-talked" by their opposition. In a dramatic conclusion, Tennessee won that season's national championship game in overtime, thanks in part to their free throw shooting.

Can mental rehearsal also help you reach your academic goals? Definitely! One study demonstrated this with two groups of introductory psychology students facing a midterm exam one week later (Taylor et al., 1998). (A third control group did not engage in any mental rehearsal.) The first group spent five minutes each day imagining themselves scanning the posted grade list, seeing their A, beaming with joy, and feeling proud. This daily *outcome simulation* had little effect, adding only 2 points to their average exam score. The second group spent five minutes each day imagining themselves effectively studying—reading the chapters, going over notes, eliminating distractions, declining an offer to go out. This daily *process simulation* paid off. In real life, the group began studying

Broca's area controls language expression— an area of the frontal lobe, usually in the left hemisphere, that directs the muscle movements involved in speech.

Wernicke's area controls language reception— a brain area involved in language comprehension and expression; usually in the left temporal lobe.

sooner, spent more time at it, and beat the others' average score by 8 points.

The point to remember: It's better to spend your fantasy time planning *how* to get somewhere than to focus on the imagined destination. ▪

Do Other Species Have Language?

8-10 What do we know about other species' capacity for language?

If in our use of language we humans are, as an ancient psalm says, "little lower than God," where do other animals fit in the scheme of things? Are they "little lower than humans"?

Animals display great powers of understanding and communicating. Vervet monkeys sound different alarm cries for different predators: a barking call for a leopard, a cough for an eagle, and a chuttering for a snake. Hearing the leopard alarm, other vervets climb the nearest tree. Hearing the eagle alarm, they rush into the bushes. Hearing the snake chutter, they stand up and scan the ground (Byrne, 1991). To indicate complex alarms, such as the type of threat (eagle, leopard, falling tree, neighboring group) monkeys may combine 6 different calls into a 25-call sequence (Balter, 2010). But are such communications language? This question has launched many studies with chimpanzees.

In the late 1960s, psychologists Allen Gardner and Beatrix Gardner (1969) aroused enormous scientific and public interest when they taught sign language to a young chimpanzee named Washoe. After four years, Washoe could use 132 signs. By her life's end in 2007, she was

using 250 signs (Metzler, 2011). One *New York Times* reporter, having learned sign language from his deaf parents, visited Washoe and exclaimed, "Suddenly I realized I was conversing with a member of another species in my native tongue."

During the 1970s, as more and more reports came in, it seemed apes might indeed be "little lower than human." Some were stringing signs together to form sentences. Washoe, for example, signed "You me go out, please." Some word combinations seemed very creative—saying *water bird* for "swan" or *apple which-is orange* for "orange" (Patterson, 1978; Rumbaugh, 1977).

By the late 1970s, some psychologists were growing skeptical. Were the chimps language champs or were the researchers chumps? Consider the skeptics' points:

• Ape vocabularies and sentences are simple, rather like those of a 2-year-old child. And unlike speaking or signing children, who easily soak up dozens of new words a week (and 60,000 by adulthood), apes gain their limited vocabularies only with great difficulty (Wynne, 2004, 2008). Saying that apes can learn language because they can sign words is like saying humans can fly because they can jump.

• Chimpanzees can make signs or push buttons in sequence to get a reward. But pigeons, too, can peck a sequence of keys to get grain (Straub et al., 1979). The apes' signing might be nothing more than aping their trainers' signs and learning that certain arm movements produce rewards (Terrace, 1979).

• Studies of perceptual set (see Chapter 5) show that when information is unclear, we tend to

COMPREHENDING CANINE Border collie Rico has a 200 (human) word vocabulary. If asked to retrieve a toy with a name he has never heard, Rico will pick out a new toy from a group of familiar items (Kaminski et al., 2004). Hearing that name for the second time four weeks later, Rico more often than not retrieves the same toy. Another border collie, Chaser, has set an animal record by learning 1022 object names (Pilley & Reid, 2011). Like a 3-year-old child, she can also categorize them by function and shape. She can "fetch a ball" or "fetch a doll."

SUSANNE BAUS/AFP/GETTY IMAGES/Newscom

see what we want or expect to see. Interpreting chimpanzee signs as language may be little more than the trainers' wishful thinking (Terrace, 1979). When Washoe signed *water*

BUT IS THIS LANGUAGE? Chimpanzees' ability to express themselves in American Sign Language raises questions about the very nature of language. Here, the trainer is asking, "What is this?" The sign in response is "Baby." Does the response constitute language?

Paul Fusco/Magnum Photos

bird, she may have been separately naming *water* and *bird.*

- "Give orange me give eat orange me eat orange . . ." is a far cry from the exquisite syntax of a 3-year-old (Anderson, 2004; Pinker, 1995). To the child, "You tickle" and "Tickle you" communicate different ideas. A chimpanzee, lacking human syntax, might use the same sequence of signs for both phrases.

Controversy can stimulate progress. In this case, it triggered more evidence of chimpanzees' abilities to think and communicate. One surprising finding was that Washoe trained her adopted son Loulis to sign. After her second infant died, Washoe became withdrawn when told, "Baby dead, baby gone, baby finished." Two weeks later, researcher caretaker Roger Fouts (1992, 1997) signed better news: "I have baby for you." Washoe reacted with instant excitement. Hair on end, she swaggered and panted while signing over and again, "Baby, my baby." It took several hours for the foster mom and infant to warm to each other. But then Washoe broke the ice by signing, "Come baby" and cuddling Loulis. In the months that followed, Loulis picked up 68 signs. He did this without human assistance, simply by observing Washoe and three other language-trained chimps signing together.

Even more stunning was a report that Kanzi, a bonobo, with a reported 384-word vocabulary, could understand syntax in spoken English (Savage-Rumbaugh et al., 1993, 2009). Kanzi has responded appropriately when asked, "Can you show me the light?" and "Can you bring me the [flash]light?" and "Can you turn the light on?" Given stuffed animals and asked—for the first time—to "make the dog bite the snake," he put the snake to the dog's mouth.

So, how should we interpret these studies? Are humans the only language-using species? If by *language* we mean verbal or signed expression of complex grammar, most psychologists would now agree that humans alone possess language. If we mean, more simply, an ability to communicate through a meaningful sequence of symbols, then apes are indeed capable of language.

One thing is certain. Studies of animal language and thinking have moved psychologists toward a greater appreciation of other species' remarkable abilities (Friend, 2004; Rumbaugh & Washburn, 2003). In the past, many psychologists doubted that other species could plan, form concepts, count, use tools, show compassion, or use language (Thorpe, 1974). Today, thanks to animal researchers, we know better. Other animals exhibit insight, show family loyalty, communicate with one another, care for one another, and transmit cultural patterns across generations. Working out what this means for the moral rights of other animals is an unfinished task.

* * *

Thinking about other species' abilities brings us back to a question raised earlier in this chapter: How smart are we? Do we deserve the label *Homo sapiens?* Let's pause to issue an interim report card. On decision making and judgment, our smart but error-prone species might rate a B–. On problem solving and creativity, where humans are inventive yet subject to confirmation bias and fixation, we would probably receive better marks, perhaps a B+. On cognitive skills, our quick though sometimes faulty heuristics earn us an A. And when it comes to language and the processing that occurs outside of con-sciousness, the awestruck experts would surely award the human species an A+. ■

RETRIEVE + REMEMBER

- If your dog barks at a stranger at the front door, does this qualify as language? What if the dog yips in a telltale way to let you know she needs to go out?

ANSWER: These are definitely communications. But if *language* consists of words and the grammatical rules we use to combine them to communicate meaning, few scientists would label a dog's barking and yipping as language.

Intelligence

◎ So far, we have considered how we humans think and communicate. But we do so with differing abilities. School boards, courts, and scientists debate the use of tests that assess people's mental abilities. One of the most heated questions has been whether each of us has some general mental aptitude, or ability to learn, that can be measured and assigned a number.

In this section, we consider some findings from a century of searching for answers to these questions and more:

- What is intelligence? Is it one general ability, or many different abilities?
- How can we best assess intelligence?
- How do nature (heredity) and nurture (environment) together weave the fabric of intelligence?

What Is Intelligence?

8-11 How do psychologists define *intelligence,* and what are the arguments for general intelligence *(g)?*

Intelligence is not a quality like height or weight, which has the same meaning in all generations, worldwide. People assign the term *intelligence* to the qualities that enable success in their own time and place (Sternberg & Kaufman, 1998). In the Amazon rain forest, intelligence may be

ScienceCartoonsPlus.com

"Although humans make sounds with their mouths and occasionally look at each other, there is no solid evidence that they actually communicate with each other."

understanding the medicinal qualities of local plants. In a North American high school, it may be mastering difficult concepts in tough courses. In both places, **intelligence** is the ability to learn from experience, solve problems, and use knowledge to adapt to new situations.

You probably know some people with talents in science or history, and others gifted in athletics, art, music, or dance. You may also know a terrific artist who is stumped by the simplest math problem, or a brilliant math student with little talent for writing term papers. Are all these people intelligent? Could you rate their intelligence on a single scale? Or would you need several different scales? Simply put: Is intelligence a single overall ability or several specific abilities?

Spearman's General Intelligence (g)

Charles Spearman (1863–1945) believed we have one **general intelligence** (often shortened to *g*) that is at the heart of our smarts, from sailing the sea to sailing through school. People often have special, outstanding abilities, he noted, but those who score high in one area (such as verbal ability) typically score above average in other areas (such as spatial or reasoning ability). Spearman's belief stemmed in part from his work with *factor analysis,* a statistical tool that searches for clusters of related items.

In Spearman's view, mental abilities are much like physical abilities. The ability to run fast is distinct from the eye-hand coordination required to throw a ball on target. Yet there remains some tendency for good things to come packaged together. Running speed and throwing accuracy, for example, often correlate, thanks to general athletic ability. Similarly, intelligence involves distinct abilities, which correlate enough to define a small general intelligence factor.

Other psychologists have questioned the extent of the *g factor,* or common skill set. Howard Gardner and Robert Sternberg believe there are several different kinds of intelligence.

Theories of Multiple Intelligences

8-12 What are two theories of multiple intelligences, and what criticisms have they faced?

. . . .

GARDNER'S EIGHT INTELLIGENCES

Howard Gardner (1983, 2006, 2011; Davis et al., 2011) views intelligence as multiple abilities that come in different packages. He asks us to consider people with brain damage, who may lose one ability while others remain intact. He sees other evidence of multiple intelligences in people with **savant syndrome.** Despite their island of brilliance (their special talent), these people often score low on intelligence tests and may have limited or no language ability (Treffert & Wallace, 2002). Some can render incredible art work or musical performances. Others can compute numbers as quickly and accurately as an electronic calculator, or identify almost instantly the day of the week that matches any given date in history (Miller, 1999).

Four in five people with savant syndrome are males. Many also have *autism spectrum disorder (ASD)* (see Chapter 3). The late memory whiz Kim Peek (who did not have ASD) was the inspiration for the movie *Rain Man.* In 8 to 10 seconds, Peek could read and remember a page. During his lifetime, he memorized 9000 books, including Shakespeare's plays and the Bible. He learned maps from the front of phone books, and he could provide GPS-like travel directions within any major U.S. city. Yet he could not button his clothes, and he had little capacity for abstract concepts. Asked by his father at a restaurant to "lower your voice," he slid lower in his chair to lower his voice box. Asked for Lincoln's Gettysburg Address, he responded, "227 North West Front Street. But he only stayed there one night—he gave the speech the next day" (Treffert & Christensen, 2005).

Gardner has identified a total of eight *relatively independent intelligences,* including the verbal and mathematical aptitudes assessed by standard tests (FIGURE 8.9). Thus, the computer programmer, the poet, the street-smart adolescent who becomes a crafty executive, and the basketball team's play-making point guard exhibit different kinds of intelligence (Gardner, 1998). To Gardner, a general intelligence score is like the overall rating of a city—which tells you something but doesn't give you much specific information about the city's schools, streets, or nightlife.

> "You have to be careful, if you're good at something, to make sure you don't think you're good at other things that you aren't necessarily so good at. . . . Because I've been very successful at [software development] people come in and expect that I have wisdom about topics that I don't."
>
> Bill Gates, 1998

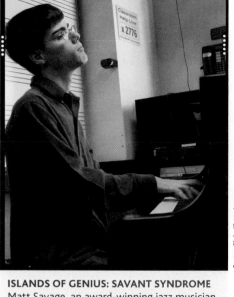

ISLANDS OF GENIUS: SAVANT SYNDROME Matt Savage, an award-winning jazz musician, is a Berklee College of Music graduate who has released many albums. His success has been hard-won given his early childhood diagnosis of what is now called autism spectrum disorder, which came with struggles to communicate and an initial inability to tolerate sounds of any kind.

Boston Globe/Getty Images

FIGURE 8.9 Gardner's eight intelligences

STERNBERG'S THREE INTELLIGENCES
Robert Sternberg (1985, 1999, 2003) agrees with Gardner that there is more to real-world success than traditional intelligence and that we have multiple intelligences. But his *triarchic theory* proposes three, not eight, intelligences:

- *Analytical intelligence* (school smarts: traditional academic problem solving)

- *Creative intelligence* (trailblazing smarts: the ability to generate novel ideas)

- *Practical intelligence* (street smarts: skill at handling everyday tasks)

Gardner and Sternberg differ in some areas, but they agree on two important points: Multiple abilities can contribute to life success, and diverse gifts add both variety to life and challenges for education. Under their influence, many teachers have been trained to appreciate such variety and to apply multiple intelligence theories in their classrooms.

"You're wise, but you lack tree smarts."

CRITICISMS OF MULTIPLE INTELLIGENCE THEORIES Wouldn't it be wonderful if the world were so just that a weakness in one area would be balanced by genius in some other area? Alas, say critics, the world is not just (Ferguson, 2009; Scarr, 1989). Recent research, using

---

intelligence mental quality consisting of the ability to learn from experience, solve problems, and use knowledge to adapt to new situations.

general intelligence (*g*) a general intelligence factor that, according to Spearman and others, underlies specific mental abilities and is therefore measured by every task on an intelligence test.

savant syndrome a condition in which a person otherwise limited in mental ability has an exceptional specific skill, such as in computation or drawing.

factor analysis, has confirmed that there is a general intelligence factor (Johnson et al., 2008). *g* matters. It predicts performance on various complex tasks and in various jobs (Arneson et al., 2011; Gottfredson, 2002a,b, 2003a,b). Youths' intelligence test scores predict their income decades later (Zagorsky, 2007).

But we do well to remember that the recipe for success is not simple. As in so many realms of life, success has two ingredients: *can do* (ability) and *will do* (motivation) (Lubinski, 2009). More than 300 studies of college and university students confirm the point. Study habits, study skills, and a "hungry (curious) mind" are important for academic success (Credé & Kuncel, 2008; von Stumm et al., 2011). High intelligence may get you into a profession (via the schools and training programs that open doors). *Grit*—your motivation and drive—will make you successful once you're there.

Highly successful people tend to be conscientious, well connected, and doggedly energetic. These qualities often translate into dedicated hard work. Researchers report a *10-year rule*: Expert performers—in chess, dancing, sports, computer programming, music, and medicine—have all spent about a decade in intense, daily practice (Ericsson, 2002, 2007; Simon & Chase, 1973). Becoming a chess master requires a certain cognitive ability. But it also requires practice—about 11,000 hours on average, and *at least* 3000 hours (Campitelli &

Gobet, 2011). (For more on how self-disciplined grit feeds success, see Appendix B.) ■

RETRIEVE + REMEMBER

- How does the existence of savant syndrome support Gardner's theory of multiple intelligences?

  ANSWER: People with savant syndrome have limited mental ability overall but possess one or more exceptional skills. According to Howard Gardner, this suggests that our abilities come in separate packages rather than being fully expressed by one general intelligence that covers all our talents.

- How do Gardner's and Sternberg's theories of multiple intelligences differ?

  ANSWER: Gardner sees intelligence as eight relatively independent abilities. Sternberg agrees with Gardner that there is more to real-world success than traditional understandings of intelligence. However, he thinks that there are just three kinds of intelligence, not eight.

Emotional Intelligence

8-13 What four abilities make up emotional intelligence?

Some psychologists have further explored our nonacademic *social intelligence*—the know-how involved in understanding social situations and managing ourselves successfully (Cantor & Kihlstrom, 1987). Psychologist Edward Thorndike first proposed the concept in 1920, noting that "the best mechanic in a factory may fail as a foreman for lack of social intelligence" (Goleman, 2006, p. 83).

Research has focused on a critical part of social intelligence, **emotional intelligence,** with its four abilities (Mayer et al., 2002, 2008).

- *Perceiving* emotions (recognizing them in faces, music, and stories)
- *Understanding* emotions (predicting them and how they may change and blend)
- *Managing* emotions (knowing how to express them in varied situations)
- *Using* emotions to enable adaptive or creative thinking

Emotionally intelligent people are both socially aware and self-aware. Those who score high on managing emotions enjoy higher-quality interactions with friends (Lopes et al., 2004). They avoid being hijacked by overwhelming depression, anxiety, or anger. They can read others' emotions and know what to say to soothe a grieving friend, encourage a workmate, and manage a conflict.

These emotionally intelligent people also perform modestly better on the job (O'Boyle et al., 2011). On and off the job, they can delay gratification in favor of long-range rewards. Simply said, they are emotionally smart. Thus, they tend to succeed in career, marriage, and parenting situations where academically smarter (but emotionally less intelligent) people often fail (Ciarrochi et al., 2006).

* * *

For a summary of Spearman's, Gardner's, and Sternberg's theories, see **TABLE 8.3**.

TABLE 8.3 Comparing Theories of Intelligence

Theory	Summary	Strengths	Other Considerations
Spearman's general intelligence (g)	A basic intelligence predicts our abilities in many different academic areas.	Different abilities, such as verbal and spatial, do have some tendency to correlate.	Human abilities are too varied to be presented as a single general intelligence factor.
Gardner's multiple intelligences	Our abilities are best viewed as eight independent intelligences, which include a broad range of skills beyond traditional school smarts.	Intelligence is more than just verbal and mathematical skills. Other equally important abilities help us adapt.	Should all abilities be considered *intelligences*? Shouldn't some be called less vital *talents*?
Sternberg's triarchic theory	Three areas of intelligence—analytical, creative, and practical—predict real-world success.	These three areas cover the different talents we call intelligence.	These three areas may be less independent than Sternberg thought and may actually share an underlying *g* factor.

Assessing Intelligence

An **intelligence test** assesses a person's mental aptitudes and compares them with those of others, using numerical scores. So, how do psychologists design these tests, and why should we believe in the results?

What Do Intelligence Tests Test?

8-14 When and why were intelligence tests created, and how do today's tests differ from early intelligence tests?

Barely more than a century ago, psychologists began designing tests to assess people's abilities. Some measured **aptitude** (ability to learn). Others assessed **achievement** (what people have already learned).

ALFRED BINET: PREDICTING SCHOOL ACHIEVEMENT Modern intelligence testing traces its birth to early twentieth-century France, where a new law required all children to attend school. French officials knew that some children, including many newcomers to Paris, would need special classes. But how could the schools make fair judgments about children's learning potential? Teachers might assess children who had little prior education as slow learners. Or they might sort children into classes on the basis of their social backgrounds. France's minister of public education took action to minimize such bias in 1904. He gave Alfred Binet and others, including Théodore Simon, the task of studying this problem.

Binet and Simon began by assuming that all children follow the same course of intellectual development but that some develop more rapidly. A "dull" child should therefore score much like a typical younger child, and a "bright" child like a typical older child. Binet and Simon now had a clear goal. They would measure each child's **mental age,** the level of performance typically associated with a certain chronological age. The average 8-year-old, for example, has

ALFRED BINET (1857–1911) Adaptations of Binet's pioneering intelligence test were sometimes used to discriminate against immigrant and minority groups. But his intent was to match children with appropriate schooling, not to label them and limit their opportunities.

a mental age of 8. An 8-year-old with a below-average mental age (perhaps performing at the level of a typical 6-year-old) would struggle with schoolwork considered normal for 8-year-olds.

Binet and Simon tested a variety of reasoning and problem-solving questions on Binet's two daughters, and then on "bright" and "backward" Parisian schoolchildren. The items they developed predicted how well French children would handle their schoolwork.

LEWIS TERMAN: THE INNATE IQ Soon after Binet's death in 1911, others adapted his tests for wider use. One of them was Lewis Terman (1877–1956), a Stanford University professor. Terman found that the Paris-developed questions and age norms worked poorly with California schoolchildren. He adapted some items, added others, and established new standards for various ages. He also extended the upper end of the test's range from teenagers to "superior adults." He gave his revision the name it still has today—the **Stanford-Binet.** For Terman, intelligence tests revealed the intelligence with which a person was born.

German psychologist William Stern's contribution to intelligence testing was the famous term **intelligence quotient,** or **IQ.** The IQ was simply a person's mental age divided by *chronological age* (age in years) and multiplied by 100 to get rid of the decimal point.

Thus, an average child, whose mental age (8) and chronological age (8) are the same, has an IQ of 100. But an 8-year-old who answers questions at the level of a typical 10-year-old has an IQ of 125:

$$IQ = \frac{\text{mental age of } 10}{\text{chronological age of } 8} \times 100 = 125$$

The original IQ formula worked fairly well for children but not for adults. (Should a 40-year-old who does as well on the test as an average 20-year-old be assigned an IQ of only 50?) Most current intelligence tests, including the Stanford-Binet, no longer compute an IQ (though the term *IQ* still lingers in everyday vocabulary as short for "intelligence test score"). Instead, they represent the test-taker's performance *relative to the average performance of others the same age.*

emotional intelligence the ability to perceive, understand, manage, and use emotions.

intelligence test a method for assessing an individual's mental aptitudes and comparing them with those of others, using numerical scores.

aptitude test a test designed to predict a person's future performance; *aptitude* is the capacity to learn.

achievement test a test designed to assess what a person has learned.

mental age a measure of intelligence test performance devised by Binet; the chronological age that most typically corresponds to a given level of performance. Thus, a child who does as well as an average 8-year-old is said to have a mental age of 8.

Stanford-Binet the widely used American revision (by Terman at Stanford University) of Binet's original intelligence test.

intelligence quotient (IQ) defined originally as the ratio of mental age *(ma)* to chronological age *(ca)* multiplied by 100 (thus, IQ = *ma* ÷ *ca* × 100). On contemporary intelligence tests, the average performance for a given age is assigned a score of 100.

MATCHING PATTERNS A block design puzzle like this one can test children's visual abstract processing ability. Wechsler's individually administered intelligence test comes in forms suited for adults and children.

This average performance is arbitrarily assigned a score of 100. Most people—68 percent of those taking an intelligence test—fall between 85 and 115. (We'll return to these figures later in this chapter, in the discussion of the *normal curve*.)

DAVID WECHSLER: SEPARATE SCORES FOR SEPARATE SKILLS Psychologist David Wechsler created what is now the most widely used intelligence test, the **Wechsler Adult Intelligence Scale (WAIS)**. There is a version for school-age children (the *Wechsler Intelligence Scale for Children* [WISC]), and another for preschool children. The WAIS (2008 edition) consists of 15 subtests, broken into verbal and performance areas, including these:

- *Similarities*—Considering the commonality of two objects or concepts, such as "In what way are wool and cotton alike?"

- *Vocabulary*—Naming pictured objects, or defining words ("What is a guitar?")

- *Block design*—Visual abstract processing, such as "Using the four blocks, make one just like this."

- *Letter-number sequencing*—On hearing a series of numbers and letters, repeat the numbers in ascending order, and then the letters in alphabetical order: "R-2-C-1-M-3."

The WAIS yields both an overall intelligence score and separate scores for verbal comprehension, perceptual organization, working memory, and processing speed. Striking differences among these scores can provide clues to strengths or weaknesses. For example, a person who scores low on verbal comprehension but has high scores on other subtests may have a reading or language disability. Other comparisons can help health care workers design a therapy plan for a stroke patient. In such ways, tests help realize Binet's aim: to identify opportunities for improvement and strengths that teachers and others can build upon. ◼

RETRIEVE + REMEMBER

- What did Binet hope to achieve by establishing a child's *mental age?*

ANSWER: Binet hoped that the child's *mental age* (the age that typically corresponds to the child's level of performance) would help identify appropriate school placements with children of similar abilities.

- An employer with a pool of applicants for a single available position is interested in testing each applicant's potential. To help her decide whom she should hire, she should use an _____ (achievement/aptitude) test. That same employer wishing to test the effectiveness of a new, on-the-job training program would be wise to use an _____ (achievement/aptitude) test.

ANSWER: aptitude; achievement

- What is the IQ of a 4-year-old with a mental age of 5?

ANSWER: 125 (5 ÷ 4 × 100 = 125)

Three Tests of a "Good" Test

8-15 What is a normal curve, and what does it mean to say that a test has been standardized and is reliable and valid?

To be widely accepted, a psychological test must be *standardized, reliable,* and

valid. The Stanford-Binet and Wechsler tests meet these requirements.

WAS THE TEST STANDARDIZED? The number of questions you answer correctly on an intelligence test would tell you almost nothing about how well you performed. For a score to be meaningful, you need some basis for comparison. That's why test-makers give new tests to a representative sample of people. The scores from this pretested group become the basis for future comparisons. If you later take the test following the same procedures, your score will be meaningful when compared with others. This process is called **standardization**.

One way to compare scores is to graph them. No matter what trait we measure—height, weight, or mental aptitude—people's scores tend to form a bell-shaped pattern called the **normal curve**. The highest point of a symmetrical bell curve is the average score. Moving out from the average, toward either extreme, we find fewer and fewer people.

On an intelligence test, the average score has a value of 100 (FIGURE 8.10). For the Stanford-Binet and the Wechsler tests, your score would indicate whether your performance fell above or below that average. A score of 130, for example, would indicate that only 2 percent of all test-takers had scores higher than yours. About 95 percent of all people score within 30 points above or 30 points below 100.

IS THE TEST RELIABLE? Knowing how your score compares with those in the standardization group still won't tell you much unless the test has **reliability**. A reliable test gives consistent scores, no matter who takes the test or when they take it. To check a test's reliability, researchers test many people many times. They may retest people using the same test, or they may split the test in half and see whether odd-question scores and even-question scores agree. If the two sets of scores gen-

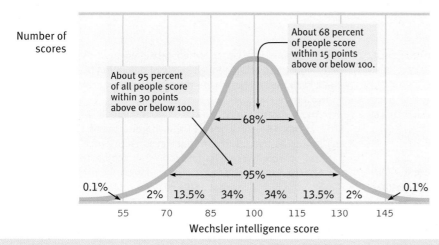

FIGURE 8.10 The normal curve Scores on aptitude tests tend to form a normal, or bell-shaped, curve around an average score. For the Wechsler scale, for example, the average score is 100.

erally agree, the test is reliable. The tests we have considered so far—the Stanford-Binet, the WAIS, and the WISC—all are very reliable. When retested, people's scores generally match their first score closely—even over a lifetime (Deary et al., 2004, 2009).

IS THE TEST VALID? A **valid** test measures or predicts what it promises. A test can be reliable but not valid. Imagine buying a tape measure with faulty markings. If you use it to measure people's heights, your results will be very reliable. No matter how many times you measure, people's heights will be the same. But your faulty results will not be valid.

Valid tests have *content validity* when they measure what they are supposed to measure. The road test for a driver's license has content validity because it samples the tasks a driver routinely faces. A course exam has content validity if it tests what you learned in the course. But we also expect intelligence tests to have *predictive validity*. Intelligence tests should predict future performance, and to some extent, they do. (See Close-Up: Extremes of Intelligence on the next page.) Past grades—which reflect both aptitude and motivation—are better predictors of future achievements. ■

RETRIEVE + REMEMBER

- What are the three requirements that a psychological test must meet in order to be widely accepted? Explain.

ANSWER: A psychological test must be *standardized* (pretested on a similar group of people), *reliable* (yielding consistent results), and *valid* (measuring or predicting what it is supposed to measure or predict).

The Nature and Nurture of Intelligence

8-17 How is intelligence influenced by nature and nurture? What does it mean when we say that a trait is heritable?

Intelligence runs in families. But why? Are our intellectual abilities mostly inherited? Or are they molded by our environment? Few issues in psychology arouse so much passion. Let's look at some of the evidence.

What Do Twin and Adoption Studies Tell Us?

Does sharing the same genes also mean sharing the same mental abilities? As you can see from **FIGURE 8.11** (turn the page), which summarizes many studies, the answer is *Yes*.

Identical twins who grow up together have intelligence test scores nearly as similar as those of the same person taking the same test twice (Haworth et al., 2009; Lykken, 1999). Identical twins are also very similar in specific talents, such as music, math, and sports (Vinkhuyzen et al., 2009). (Fraternal twins, who share only about half their genes, are much less similar.) Even when identical twins are adopted by two different families, their intelligence test scores are nearly the same.

There is, however, no known "genius" gene. Many, many genes contribute to intelligence, and each of them accounts for much less than 1 percent of our differences (Butcher et al., 2008; Davies et al., 2011). Intelligence is thus like height (Johnson, 2010). Working together, 54 specific gene variations account for only 5 percent of our individual height differences.

So genes matter, but environment matters too. Fraternal twins are genetically no more alike than any other siblings. But they usually share an environment and, because they are the same age, are often treated more alike. They also tend to score more alike than other siblings. Moreover, adoption of mistreated or neglected children enhances intelligence scores (van IJzendoorn & Juffer, 2005, 2006). So does adoption from poverty into middle-class homes (Nisbett et al., 2012).

Wechsler Adult Intelligence Scale (WAIS) the most widely used intelligence test; contains verbal and performance (nonverbal) subtests.

standardization defining uniform testing procedures and meaningful scores by comparison with the performance of a pretested group.

normal curve the bell-shaped curve that describes the distribution of many physical and psychological attributes. Most scores fall near the average, and fewer and fewer scores lie near the extremes.

reliability the extent to which a test yields consistent results, as assessed by the consistency of scores on two halves of the test, on alternative forms of the test, or on retesting.

validity the extent to which a test measures or predicts what it is supposed to.

Extremes of Intelligence

8-16 What are the traits of those at the low and high intelligence extremes?

One way to glimpse the validity and significance of any test is to compare people who score at the two extremes of the normal curve. The two groups should differ noticeably, and they do.

The Low Extreme

At one extreme of the intelligence test normal curve are those with unusually low scores. To be given a diagnosis of **intellectual disability**, a person must have both

- an intelligence score of 70 or below.
- difficulty adapting to life demands.

Intellectual disability is a developmental condition that exists before age 18, sometimes with a known physical cause. **Down syndrome,** for example, is a disorder of varying intellectual and physical severity caused by an extra copy of chromosome 21.

The High Extreme

In one famous project begun in 1921, psychologist Lewis Terman studied more than 1500 California schoolchildren with IQ scores over 135. These high-scoring children (later called the "Termites") were healthy, well-adjusted, and unusually successful academically (Koenen et al., 2009;

Lubinski, 2009a; Stanley, 1997). When restudied over the next seven decades, most had attained high levels of education (Austin et al., 2002; Holahan & Sears, 1995). Many were doctors, lawyers, professors, scientists, and writers.

A more recent study focuses on young people who aced the math SAT® at age 13—by scoring in the top quarter of 1 percent of their age group. At age 33, these math aces were twice as likely to have patents as were those who had scored in the bottom quarter *of the top 1 percent* (Wai et al., 2005). Compared with the math stars, 13-year-olds scoring high on verbal aptitude were more likely to have become humanities professors or written a novel (Park et al., 2007). About 1 percent of Americans earn doctorates. But among those scoring in the top 1 in 10,000 on the SAT® at age 12 or 13, more than half have done so (Lubinski, 2009b).

These whiz kids remind me of Jean Piaget, the twentieth century's most famous developmental psychologist. By age 15, he was already publishing scientific articles on mollusks (Hunt, 1993). Children with extraordinary academic gifts are sometimes more isolated, introverted, and in their own worlds (Winner, 2000). But most thrive.

---

intellectual disability a condition of limited mental ability, indicated by an intelligence test score of 70 or below and difficulty adapting to the demands of life. (Formerly referred to as *mental retardation*.)

Down syndrome a condition of mild to severe intellectual disability and associated physical disorders caused by an extra copy of chromosome 21.

Claudia Daut/Reuters

MAINSTREAMING IN CHILE Most Chilean children with Down syndrome attend separate schools for students with special needs. However, this boy attends the Altamira School, where children with differing abilities share the classroom.

Joe Klamar/AFP/Getty Images

THE EXTREMES OF INTELLIGENCE Moshe Kai Cavalin completed his third college degree by the time he was 14, when the math major graduated from UCLA. According to his mother, he first picked up a college textbook and started reading it at age 2.

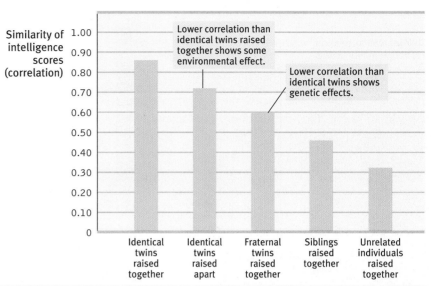

Similarity of intelligence scores (correlation)

Lower correlation than identical twins raised together shows some environmental effect.

Lower correlation than identical twins shows genetic effects.

| Identical twins raised together | Identical twins raised apart | Fraternal twins raised together | Siblings raised together | Unrelated individuals raised together |

FIGURE 8.11 Intelligence: Nature and nurture The most genetically similar people have the most similar intelligence scores. Remember: 1.0 indicates a perfect correlation; zero indicates no correlation at all. (Data from McGue et al., 1993.)

Should we therefore expect that several biologically unrelated children who are adopted into the same family will share similar aptitudes? Seeking to untangle the effects of genes and environment, researchers have compared the intelligence test scores of adopted children with those of their

- *biological* parents (the providers of their genes).
- *adoptive* parents (the providers of their home environment).
- *adoptive* siblings (who share that home environment).

During childhood, adoptive siblings' test scores correlate modestly. What do you think happens as the years go by and adopted children settle in with their adoptive families? Would you expect the shared-home-environment effect to grow stronger, and the shared-gene effect to shrink?

If you said *Yes*, I have a surprise for you. Mental similarities between adopted children and their adoptive families lessen with age. By adulthood they drop to roughly zero (McGue et al., 1993). Genetic influences—not environmental ones—become more apparent as we accumulate life experience. Identical twins' similarities, for example, continue or increase into their eighties (Deary et al., 2009). Similarly, in verbal ability, adopted children become more like their biological parents as the years go by (**FIGURE 8.12** on the next page). Who would have guessed?

To read more about genetic influences on intelligence, see Close-Up: What Is Heritability? on the next page.

How Does Environment Influence Intelligence?

We have seen that biology and experience intertwine. Nowhere is this more apparent than in the most hopeless human environments. Severe deprivation

DEVASTATING NEGLECT Some Romanian orphans, such as this child in the Lagunul Pentro Copii orphanage in 1990, had minimal interaction with caregivers. They suffered delayed development.

"I told my parents that if grades were so important they should have paid for a smarter egg donor."

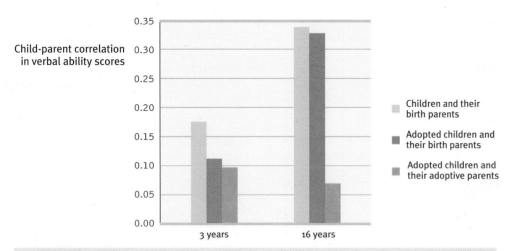

FIGURE 8.12 **In verbal ability, adopted children resemble their birth parents** As the years went by in their adoptive families, children's verbal ability scores became more like their biological parents' scores. (Adapted from Plomin & DeFries, 1998.)

leaves footprints on the brain, as J. McVicker Hunt (1982) observed in one Iranian orphanage. The typical child Hunt observed there could not sit up unassisted at age 2 or walk at age 4. The little care the infants received was not in response to their crying, cooing, or other behaviors, so the children developed little sense of personal control over their environment. They were instead becoming passive "glum lumps." Extreme deprivation was crushing native intelligence—a finding confirmed by other studies of children raised in poorly run orphanages in Romania and elsewhere (Nelson et al., 2009; van IJzendoorn et al., 2008).

Mindful of the effect of early experiences and early intervention, Hunt began a training program for caregivers, teaching them to play language-fostering games with 11 infants. They learned to imitate the babies' babbling. They

CLOSE-UP

What Is Heritability?

Heritability of intelligence is the portion of the variation among people's test scores that we can assign to genetic factors. This genetically influenced portion is often estimated to be 50 percent or more (Johnson et al., 2009). Does this mean your genes are responsible for 50 percent of your intelligence and your environment is responsible for the rest? *No.* It means we credit heredity with 50 percent of the *variation in intelligence among people being studied.* This point is so often misunderstood that I repeat: Heritability never applies to an *individual,* only to *why people in a group differ from one another.*

Heredity's influence on the range of test scores varies from study to study. Where environments vary widely, as they do among children of less-educated parents, environmental differences are better predictors of intelligence scores (Rowe et al., 1999). To see why, consider humorist Mark Twain's fantasy of raising boys in barrels until age 12, feeding them through a hole. Let's take his joke a step further and say we'll give all those boys an intelligence test at age 12. Since their environments were all equal, any differences in their test scores could only be due to their heredity. In this "study," heritability would be 100 percent. But what if a mad scientist cloned 100 boys and raised them in drastically different environments (some in barrels and others in mansions)? In this case, their heredity would be equal, so any test-score differences could only be due to their environment. The environmental effect would be 100 percent, and heritability would be zero.

In the real world, your genes and your environment work together. Suppose that (thanks to your genes) you are just slightly taller and quicker than others (Flynn, 2003, 2007). If you try out for a basketball team, you will more likely be picked. Once on the team, you will probably play more often than others (getting more practice and experience) and you will receive more coaching. The same would be true for your separated identical twin—who might, *not just for genetic reasons,* also become a basketball star. *Our genes shape the experiences that shape us.* (Recall from Chapter 3 that *epigenetics* is the field that studies this nature–nurture meeting place.) If you have a natural aptitude for academics, you will more likely stay in school, read books, and ask questions—all of which will increase your brain power. In these gene-environment interactions, small genetic advantages can trigger social experiences that multiply our original skills. ◼

RETRIEVE + REMEMBER

- A check on your understanding of heritability: If environments become more equal, the heritability of intelligence would

    a. increase.   **b.** decrease.   **c.** be unchanged.

ANSWER: a. (Heritability—variation explained by genetic influences—will increase as environmental variation decreases.)

heritability the portion of variation among individuals that we can attribute to genes. The heritability of a trait may vary, depending on the population and the environment.

engaged them in vocal follow-the-leader. And, finally, they taught the infants sounds from the Persian language. The results were dramatic. By 22 months of age, the infants could name more than 50 objects and body parts. They so charmed visitors that most were adopted—an impressive new success rate for the orphanage.

So, malnutrition, sensory deprivation, and social isolation can slow normal brain development. Is the reverse also true? Will an "enriched" environment give normal children a superior intellect? Most experts are doubtful (Bruer, 1999). In experiments, infants' word learning has been unaffected by exposure to educational DVDs (DeLoache et al., 2010; Reichert et al., 2010). All babies should have normal exposure to sights, sounds, and speech. Beyond that, developmental psychologist Sandra Scarr's (1984) verdict is still widely shared: "Parents who are very concerned about providing special educational lessons for their babies are wasting their time." There is no environmental recipe for fast-forwarding a normal infant into a genius.

Intelligence Across the Life Span: Stability or Change?

8-18 How stable are intelligence scores across people's lives, and how do psychologists study this question?

Intelligence endures. By age 4, children's intelligence test scores begin to predict their adolescent and adult scores. By late adolescence, intelligence and other aptitude scores display remarkable stability. How do we know this?

● **Cross-sectional studies** compare people of different ages with one another.

● **Longitudinal studies** restudy and retest the same people over a long period of time.

Scottish researcher Ian Deary and his colleagues (2004, 2009) set a record for a long-term study, and their story is one of

psychology's great tales. On June 1, 1932, Scotland did what no other nation has done before or since. To identify working-class children who would benefit from further education, the government gave every child born in Scotland in 1921 an intelligence test—87,498 eleven-year-olds in all.

On June 1, 1997, sixty-five years later to the day, Patricia Whalley, the wife of Deary's co-worker, Lawrence Whalley, discovered the test results on dusty store-room shelves at the Scottish Council for Research in Education, not far from Deary's Edinburgh University office. "This will change our lives," Deary replied when Whalley told him the news. And so it has, with dozens of studies of the stability and the predictive capacity of these early test results.

For example, 542 survivors from the 1932 test group were retested at age 80 (Deary et al., 2004). After nearly 70 years of varied life experiences, the test-takers' two sets of scores showed a striking correlation of +.66. When 207 survivors were again retested at age 87, the correlation with their age 11 scores was +.51 (**FIGURE 8.13**). A later study that followed Scots born in 1936 from ages 11

to 70 confirmed the remarkable stability of intelligence, independent of life circumstance (Johnson et al., 2010).

Another interesting finding was that high-scoring 11-year-olds outlived others in the study. As 77-year-olds, they were more likely to be living independently and less likely to have Alzheimer's disease (Starr et al., 2000; Whalley et al., 2000). World War II had prematurely ended the lives of many of the male test-takers, but female scores showed a striking difference. Seventy percent who had scored in the top quarter as 11-year-olds were still alive at age 76. Only 45 percent of those scoring in the lowest quarter were still alive. Follow-up studies with other large samples from different groups have confirmed this finding: *More intelligent children and adults live healthier and longer lives* (Calvin et al., 2011; Deary et al., 2010; Snowdon et al., 1996).

Pause a moment: Have you any ideas why more intelligent people might live

cross-sectional study a study in which people of different ages are compared with one another.

longitudinal study research in which the same people are restudied and retested over a long period.

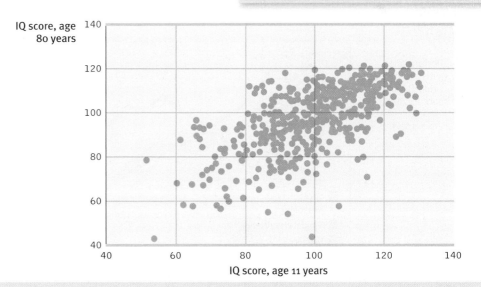

IQ score, age 80 years

IQ score, age 11 years

FIGURE 8.13 Intelligence endures When Ian Deary and his colleagues (2004) retested 80-year-old Scots, using an intelligence test they had taken as 11-year-olds, their scores across seven decades correlated +.66. (When 207 survivors were again retested at age 87, the correlation with their age 11 scores was +.51 [Gow et al., 2011].)

longer? Deary (2008) offered four possible explanations:

- Intelligence gives people better access to more education, better jobs, and a healthier environment.
- Intelligence encourages healthy living: less smoking, better diet, more exercise.
- Prenatal events or early childhood illnesses could influence both intelligence and health.
- A "well-wired body," as evidenced by fast reaction speeds, may foster both intelligence and longer life.

So, intelligence is strikingly stable. And high intelligence is a predictor of health and long life. Yet, with age, our knowledge and our mental agility change, as we see next.

Crystallized and Fluid Intelligence

8-19 What are crystallized and fluid intelligence, and how does aging affect them?

What happens to our intellectual powers as we age? The answer to that question

depends on the task and the type of ability it represents (Cattell, 1963; Horn, 1982; Salthouse, 2004, 2009).

- **Crystallized intelligence**—our accumulated knowledge, as reflected in vocabulary and word-power tests—*increases* as we age, into middle age.
- **Fluid intelligence**—our ability to reason speedily and abstractly, as when solving unfamiliar logic problems—decreases as we age (Park et al., 2002). It declines gradually until about age 75, and then, especially after age 85, decreases more rapidly.

With age we lose and we win. We lose recall memory and processing speed, but we gain vocabulary knowledge (**FIGURE 8.14**). Our decisions also become less distorted by negative emotions such as anxiety, depression, or anger (Blanchard-Fields, 2007; Carstensen & Mikels, 2005).

These life-span differences in mental abilities help explain why older adults are less likely to embrace new technologies (Charness & Boot, 2009). In 2010, only 31 percent of Americans ages 65 and older had broadband Internet at home, com-

pared with 80 percent of adults under 30 (Pew, 2010).

The age-related differences also help explain some curious findings about creativity. Mathematicians and scientists, who draw on their fluid intelligence, produce much of their most creative work during their late twenties or early thirties. Prose authors, historians, and philosophers, who depend more on crystallized intelligence, tend to hit their peak in their forties, fifties, and beyond (Simonton, 1988, 1990).

Group Differences in Intelligence Test Scores

If there were no group differences in aptitude scores, psychologists could politely debate hereditary and environmental influences in their ivory towers. But there are group differences. What are they? And what do they mean?

Gender Similarities and Differences

8-20 How and why do the genders differ in mental ability scores?

In science, as in everyday life, differences, not similarities, excite interest. Compared with the many ways men and women are physically alike, our differences are fairly minor. In the 1932 testing of all Scottish 11-year-olds, for example, girls' average intelligence score was 100.6 and boys' was 100.5 (Deary et al., 2003, 2009). So far as *g* is concerned, boys and girls, men and women, are the same species.

Yet, most people find differences more newsworthy. Girls outpace boys in spelling, verbal fluency, and locating objects. They are better emotion detectors and are more sensitive to touch, taste, and color (Halpern et al., 2007). In math computation and overall math performance, girls and boys hardly differ (Else-Quest et al., 2010; Hyde & Mertz, 2009; Lindberg et al., 2010). But in tests of spatial ability and complex math problems, boys outperform girls.

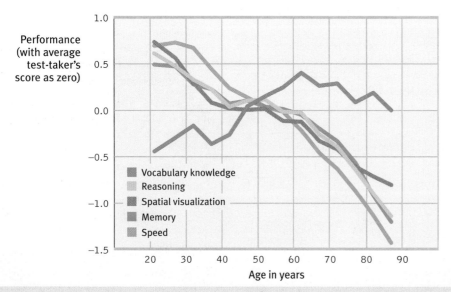

FIGURE 8.14 With age we lose and we win Studies reveal that word power grows with age, while fluid intelligence declines (Salthouse, 2010b).

Males' mental ability scores also vary more than females'. Worldwide, boys outnumber girls at both the low extreme and the high extreme (Johnson et al., 2008; Machin & Pekkarinen, 2008; Strand et al., 2006). Boys, for example, are more often found in special education classes. And among American 12- to 14-year-olds with extremely high SAT® math scores (700 or above), boys outnumber girls 4 to 1 (Wai et al., 2010).

The most reliable male edge appears in spatial ability tests like the one shown in **FIGURE 8.15**. To solve the problem, you must quickly rotate three-dimensional objects in your mind (Collins & Kimura, 1997; Halpern, 2000). Today, such skills help when fitting suitcases into a car trunk, playing chess, or doing certain types of geometry problems. Evolutionary psychologists believe these same skills would have had survival value for our ances-

tral fathers, helping them to track prey and make their way home (Geary, 1995, 1996; Halpern et al., 2007). The survival of our ancestral mothers may have benefited more from a keen memory for the location of edible plants. That legacy lives today in women's superior memory for objects and their location.

But remember that our experiences form pathways in the brain. Playing action video games boosts spatial abilities (Feng et al., 2007). And who spends more time playing video or computer games? Among entering American collegians, six times as many men (23 percent) as women (4 percent) report playing these games six or more hours a week (Pryor et al., 2010). Experience matters.

Social expectations and opportunities also matter. Gender-equal cultures, such as Sweden and Iceland, exhibit little of the gender math gap found in gender-

unequal cultures, such as Turkey and Korea (Guiso et al., 2008). In Russia, Asia, and even the Middle East—where science and engineering are not considered masculine subjects—15-year-old girls slightly outperformed boys on an international science exam (Fairfield, 2012).

Racial and Ethnic Similarities and Differences

8-21 How and why do racial and ethnic groups differ in mental ability scores?

Fueling the group-differences debate are two other disturbing but agreed-upon facts:

- Racial and ethnic groups differ in their average intelligence test scores.

- High-scoring people (and groups) are more likely to achieve high levels of education and income.

There are many group differences in average intelligence test scores. In New Zealand, people of European descent outscore people of native Maori decent. In Israel, Jews outscore Arabs. In Japan, most Japanese outscore most Burakumin, a stigmatized minor-

Which two circles contain an object identical to the one in the circle on the left?

Standard

Choices

FIGURE 8.15 The mental rotation test This is a test of spatial abilities. (From Vandenberg & Kuse, 1978.) See answer below.

ANSWERS: The first and fourth responses.

crystallized intelligence our accumulated knowledge and verbal skills; tends to increase with age.

fluid intelligence our ability to reason speedily and abstractly; tends to decrease during late adulthood.

ity group. And in the United States, White Americans have outscored Black Americans. This difference has been somewhat smaller in recent years, especially among children (Dickens & Flynn, 2006; Nisbett, 2009).

One more agreed-upon fact is that *group* differences provide little basis for judging individuals. Worldwide, women outlive men by four years, but knowing that you are male or female won't tell us much about how long you will live.

We have seen that heredity contributes to *individual* differences in intelligence. But group differences in a heritable trait may be entirely environmental, as in our earlier boys-in-barrels versus boys-in-mansions example. Consider one of nature's experiments: Allow some children to grow up hearing their culture's dominant language, while others, born deaf, do not. Then give both groups an intelligence test rooted in the dominant language. The result? No surprise. Those with expertise in the dominant language will score higher than those who were born deaf (Braden, 1994; Steele, 1990; Zeidner, 1990). Within each group, the differences between individuals are mainly a reflection of genetic differences. Between the two groups, the difference is mainly environmental (FIGURE 8.16).

Might racial and ethnic gaps be similarly environmental? Consider:

Genetics research reveals that under the skin, the races are remarkably alike. The average genetic difference between two Icelandic villagers or between two Kenyans greatly exceeds the group difference between Icelanders and Kenyans (Cavalli-Sforza et al., 1994; Rosenberg et al., 2002). Moreover, looks can deceive. Lightskinned Europeans and dark-skinned Africans are genetically closer than are dark-skinned Africans and dark-skinned Aboriginal Australians.

Race is not a neatly defined biological category. Many social scientists think *race* is no longer a meaningful term. They view race primarily as a social category without well-defined physical boundaries. Each racial group, they point out, blends seamlessly into its geographical neighbors (Helms et al., 2005; Smedley & Smedley, 2005). Moreover, with increasingly mixed ancestries, fewer and fewer people fit neatly into any one category, and more and more identify themselves as multiracial (Pauker et al., 2009).

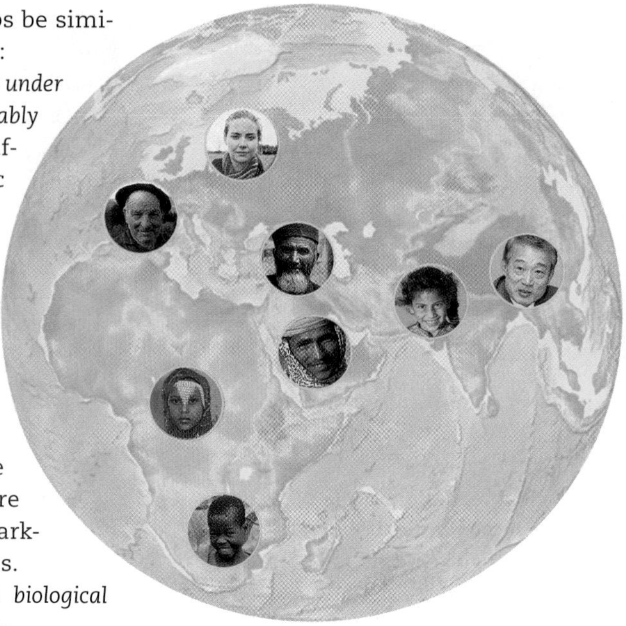

NATURE'S OWN MORPHING Nature draws no sharp boundaries between races, which blend gradually one into the next around the Earth. But the human urge to classify causes people to socially define themselves in racial categories, which become catchall labels for physical features, social identity, and nationality.

© John-Francis Bourke/zefa/Corbis; © Owen Franken/Corbis; © Richard T. Nowitz/Corbis; © Haruyoshi Yamaguchi/Corbis; © David Turnley/Corbis; © Dave Bartruff/Corbis; © Rob Howard/Corbis; © Barbara Bannister/Gallo Images/Corbis.

Within the same population, there are generation-to-generation differences in test scores. Test scores of today's better-fed, better-educated, and more test-prepared population exceed the scores

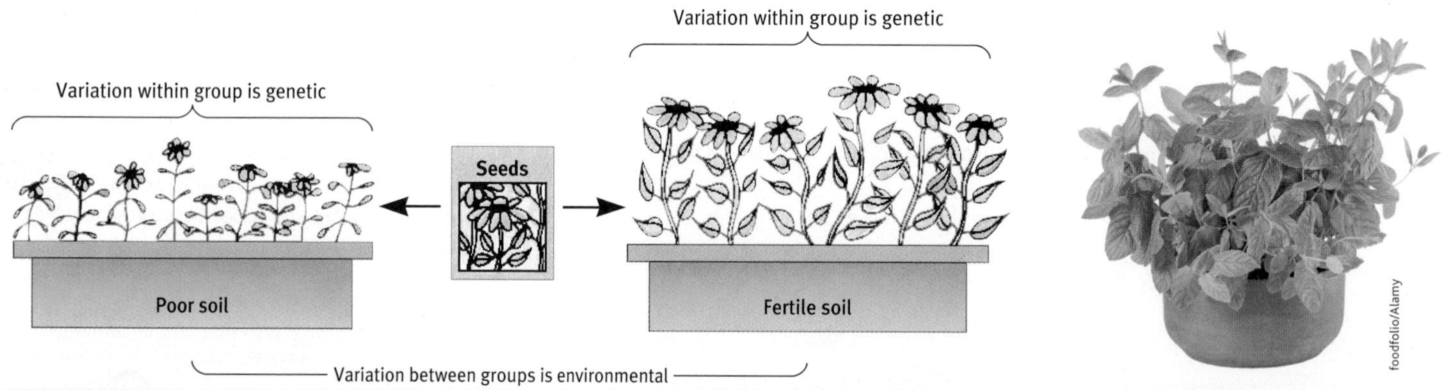

FIGURE 8.16 Group differences and environmental impact Even if the variation between members within a group reflects genetic differences, the average difference between groups may be wholly due to the environment. Imagine that seeds from the same mixture are sown in different soils. Although height differences *within* each window box of flowers will be genetic, the height difference *between* the two groups will be environmental. (From Lewontin, 1976.)

of the 1930s population (Flynn, 2007). The two generations differ by a greater margin than the intelligence test score of the average White today exceeds that of the average Black. The average intelligence test performance of today's sub-Saharan Africans is the same as British adults in 1948, with the possibility of more gains to come, given improved nutrition, economic development, and education (Wicherts et al., 2010). No one credits the generation-to-generation differences to genetics.

Given the same information, Blacks and Whites show similar information-processing skills. Research findings indicate that cultural differences in access to information may account for racial differences in intelligence test performance (Fagan & Holland, 2007).

Schools and culture matter. A country's rich-poor wealth gap correlates with its rich-poor intelligence test score gap (Nisbett, 2009). Moreover, educational policies—such as kindergarten attendance, school discipline, and instructional time per year—predict national differences in intelligence and knowledge tests (Rindermann & Ceci, 2009). An example: Asian students have outperformed North American students on math achievement and aptitude tests. This difference may reflect culture more than inborn abilities (Fagan & Holland, 2007). Compared with Americans, Asian students attend school 30 percent more days per year, and they spend much more time studying math in and out of school (Geary et al., 1996; Larson & Verma, 1999; Stevenson, 1992).

In different eras, different ethnic groups have experienced golden ages—periods of remarkable achievement. Twenty-five hundred years ago, it was the Greeks and the Egyptians, then the Romans. In the eighth and ninth centuries, genius seemed to reside in the Arab world. Five hundred years ago, the Aztecs and North Europeans took the lead. Today, we marvel at Asians' technological genius and Jews' cultural success. Cultures rise and fall over centuries. Genes do not. That fact makes it difficult to believe in the natural genetic superiority of any racial or ethnic group. ■

Are Test Questions Biased?

8-22 Are intelligence tests biased and discriminatory?

Knowing there are group differences in intelligence test scores leads us to wonder whether those differences are built into the tests. Are intelligence tests biased? The answer depends on how we define *bias*.

One way a test can be biased is if scores are influenced by a person's cultural experience. This in fact happened to Eastern European immigrants in the early 1900s. Lacking the experience to answer questions about their new culture, many were classified as feeble-minded.

The *scientific* meaning of *bias* hinges on a test's validity. A valid intelligence test should predict future behavior for all groups of test-takers, not just for some. For example, if the SAT® accurately predicted the college achievement of women but not that of men, then the test would be biased. Almost all psychologists agree that in this scientific sense, the major U.S. aptitude tests are *not* biased (Hunt & Carlson, 2007; Neisser et al., 1996; Wigdor & Garner, 1982). Their predictive validity is roughly the same for women and men, for various races, and for rich and poor. If an intelligence test score of 95 predicts slightly below-

"Math class is tough!"
"Teen talk" talking Barbie doll (introduced February 1992, recalled October 1992)

average grades, that rough prediction usually applies equally to both genders and all ethnic and economic groups. ■

STEREOTYPE THREAT Our expectations and attitudes can influence our perceptions and behaviors. They can also influence our performance on intelligence tests. If you worry that your group or "type" often doesn't do well on a certain kind of test, your self-doubts and self-monitoring may hijack your working memory and hurt your performance (Schmader, 2010). This self-confirming concern that you will be evaluated based on a negative viewpoint is called **stereotype threat,** and it may impair your attention and learning (Inzlicht & Kang, 2010; Rydell et al., 2010).

In one study, equally capable men and women took a difficult math test. The women did not do as well as the men—except when they had been led to expect that women usually do as well as men on the test (Spencer et al., 1997). Without this helpful hint, women apparently expected they would not do well. This feeling then led them to live *down* to their own expectations. Stereotype threat appeared again when Black students were reminded of their race just before taking verbal aptitude tests

stereotype threat a self-confirming concern that we will be judged based on a negative stereotype.

and performed worse (Steele et al., 2002). Negative stereotypes may undermine people's academic potential (Nguyen & Ryan, 2008; Walton & Spencer, 2009).

Stereotype threat helps explain why Blacks have scored higher when tested by Blacks than when tested by Whites (Danso & Esses, 2001; Inzlicht & Ben-Zeev, 2000). It gives us insight into why women have scored higher on math tests with no male test-takers present, and why women's internet chess play drops sharply when they think they are playing a male opponent (Maass et al., 2008). It also explains "the Obama effect"—the finding that African-American adults performed better if they took a verbal aptitude test immediately after watching then-candidate Barack Obama's stereotype-defying nomination-acceptance speech, or just after his 2008 presidential victory (Marx et al., 2009).

Could remedial "minority support" programs function as a stereotype that can erode performance? Some researchers believe they can, by telling students they probably won't succeed. College programs that challenge minority students to believe in their potential, or to focus on the idea that intelligence is not fixed, have had good results. Students' grades were markedly higher, and their dropout rates lower (Wilson, 2006).

Believing that intelligence is changeable, rather than biologically fixed, can foster a *growth mind-set* (Dweck, 2012). Collegians with a growth mind-set tend to flourish happily (Howell, 2009). Fostering a growth mind-set means teaching young teens that the brain is like a muscle that grows stronger with use as neuron connections grow. Recall the 10-year rule discussed earlier. Superior achievements in fields from sports to science to music arise from disciplined effort and sustained practice (Ericsson et al., 2007). To reach your potential, the formula is simple: Believe in your ability to learn and apply yourself with sustained effort.

> What time is it now? Earlier in this chapter, did you underestimate or overestimate how quickly you would finish the chapter?

* * *

Perhaps, then, our goals for tests of mental abilities should be threefold.

- We should realize the benefits Alfred Binet foresaw—to enable schools to recognize who might profit most from early intervention.

- We must remain alert to Binet's fear that intelligence test scores may be misinterpreted as literal measures of a person's worth and potential.

- We must remember that the competence that general intelligence tests sample is important; without such tests, those who decide on jobs and admissions would rely more on other considerations, such as personal opinion. But these tests reflect only one aspect of personal competence. Our practical intelligence and emotional intelligence matter, too, as do other forms of creativity, talent, and character.

The point to remember: There are many ways of being successful: Our differences are variations of human adaptability. Life's great achievements result not only from abilities but also from motivation. Competence + Diligence = Accomplishment.

CHAPTER REVIEW

Thinking, Language, and Intelligence

Test yourself by taking a moment to answer each of these Learning Objective Questions (repeated here from within the chapter). Then turn to Appendix D, Complete Chapter Reviews, to check your answers. Research suggests that trying to answer these questions on your own will improve your long-term memory of the concepts (McDaniel et al., 2009).

Thinking

8-1: What is cognition, and what are the functions of concepts?

8-2: What strategies help us solve problems, and what tendencies work against us?

8-3: What is intuition, and how can the availability heuristic, overconfidence, belief perseverance, and framing influence our decisions and judgments?

8-4: How do smart thinkers use intuition?

8-5: What is creativity, and what fosters it?

8-6: What do we know about thinking in other species?

Language

8-7: What are the milestones in language development, and how do we acquire language?

8-8: What brain areas are involved in language processing and speech?

8-9: How can thinking in images be useful?

8-10: What do we know about other species' capacity for language?

Intelligence

8-11: How do psychologists define *intelligence,* and what are the arguments for general intelligence *(g)?*

8-12: What are two theories of multiple intelligences, and what criticisms have they faced?

8-13: What four abilities make up emotional intelligence?

8-14: When and why were intelligence tests created, and how do today's tests differ from early intelligence tests?

8-15: What is a normal curve, and what does it mean to say that a test has been standardized and is reliable and valid?

8-16: What are the traits of those at the low and high intelligence extremes?

8-17: How is intelligence influenced by nature and nurture? What does it mean when we say that a trait is heritable?

8-18: How stable are intelligence scores across people's lives, and how do psychologists study this question?

8-19: What are crystallized and fluid intelligence, and how does aging affect them?

8-20: How and why do the genders differ in mental ability scores?

8-21: How and why do racial and ethnic groups differ in mental ability scores?

8-22: Are intelligence tests biased and discriminatory?

TERMS AND CONCEPTS TO REMEMBER

Test yourself on these terms by trying to write down the definition in your own words before flipping back to the referenced page to check your answer.

cognition, p. 220

concept, p. 220

prototype, p. 220

algorithm, p. 220

heuristic, p. 220

insight, p. 220

confirmation bias, p. 221

fixation, p. 221

intuition, p. 221

availability heuristic, p. 222

overconfidence, p. 223

belief perseverance, p. 223

framing, p. 223

creativity, p. 226

convergent thinking, p. 226

divergent thinking, p. 226

language, p. 229

babbling stage, p. 230

one-word stage, p. 230

two-word stage, p. 231

telegraphic speech, p. 231

grammar, p. 231

Broca's area, p. 232

Wernicke's area, p. 232

intelligence, p. 236

general intelligence *(g)*, p. 236

savant syndrome, p. 236

emotional intelligence, p. 238

intelligence test, p. 239

aptitude test, p. 239

achievement test, p. 239

mental age, p. 239

Stanford-Binet, p. 239

intelligence quotient (IQ), p. 239

Wechsler Adult Intelligence Scale (WAIS), p. 240

standardization, p. 240

normal curve, p. 240

reliability, p. 240

validity, p. 241

intellectual disability, p. 242

Down syndrome, p. 242

heritability, p. 244

cross-sectional studies, p. 245

longitudinal studies, p. 245

crystallized intelligence, p. 246

fluid intelligence, p. 246

stereotype threat, p. 249

CHAPTER TEST

Test yourself repeatedly throughout your studies. This will not only help you figure out what you know and don't know; the testing itself will help you learn and remember the information more effectively thanks to the testing effect.

1. A mental grouping of similar things is called a
   _____.

2. The most systematic procedure for solving a problem is a(n) _____.

3. Oscar describes his political beliefs as "strongly liberal," but he has decided to explore opposing viewpoints. How might he be affected by *confirmation bias* and *belief perseverance* in this effort?

4. A major obstacle to problem solving is fixation, which is a(n)
   a. tendency to base our judgments on vivid memories.
   b. tendency to wait for insight to occur.
   c. inability to view a problem from a new perspective.
   d. rule of thumb for judging the likelihood of an event in terms of our mental image of it.

5. After the 9/11 attacks by foreign-born terrorists, some observers initially assumed that the 2003 U. S. East Coast blackout was probably also the work of foreign-born terrorists. This assumption illustrates the _____ heuristic.

6. When consumers respond more positively to ground beef described as "75 percent lean" than to the same product labeled "25 percent fat," they have been influenced by _____.

7. Which of the following is NOT a characteristic of a creative person?

   a. Expertise

   b. Extrinsic motivation

   c. A venturesome personality

   d. Imaginative thinking skills

8. Children reach the one-word stage of speech development at about

   a. 4 months.

   b. 6 months.

   c. 1 year.

   d. 2 years.

9. When young children speak in short phrases using mostly verbs and nouns, this is referred to as _____ _____.

10. According to Chomsky, all languages share a(n) _____ _____.

11. Most researchers agree that apes can

   a. communicate through symbols.

   b. reproduce most human speech sounds.

   c. master language in adulthood.

   d. surpass a human 3-year-old in language skills.

12. Charles Spearman suggested we have one _____ _____ underlying success across a variety of intellectual abilities.

13. The existence of savant syndrome seems to support

   a. Sternberg's distinction among three types of intelligence.

   b. criticism of multiple intelligence theories.

   c. Gardner's theory of multiple intelligences.

   d. Thorndike's view of social intelligence.

14. Sternberg's three types of intelligence are _____, _____, and _____.

15. Emotionally intelligent people tend to

   a. seek immediate gratification.

   b. understand their own emotions but not those of others.

   c. understand others' emotions but not their own.

   d. succeed in their careers.

16. The IQ of a 6-year-old with a measured mental age of 9 would be

   a. 67.   c. 86.

   b. 133.   d. 150.

17. The Wechsler Adult Intelligence Scale (WAIS) is best able to tell us

   a. what part of an individual's intelligence is determined by genetic inheritance.

   b. whether the test-taker will succeed in a job.

   c. how the test-taker compares with other adults in vocabulary and arithmetic reasoning.

   d. whether the test-taker has specific skills for music and the performing arts.

18. The Stanford-Binet, the Wechsler Adult Intelligence Scale, and the Wechsler Intelligence Scale for Children yield consistent results, for example on retesting. In other words, these tests have high _____.

19. The strongest support for heredity's influence on intelligence is the finding that

   a. identical twins, but not other siblings, have nearly identical intelligence test scores.

   b. the correlation between intelligence test scores of fraternal twins is higher than that for other siblings.

   c. mental similarities between adopted siblings increase with age.

   d. children in impoverished families have similar intelligence scores.

20. To say that the heritability of intelligence is about 50 percent means that 50 percent of

   a. an individual's intelligence is due to genetic factors.

   b. the similarities between two groups of people are attributable to genes.

   c. the variation in intelligence within a group of people is attributable to genetic factors.

   d. intelligence is due to the mother's genes and the rest is due to the father's genes.

21. The environmental influence that has the clearest, most profound effect on intellectual development is

   a. exposing normal infants to educational DVDs before age 1.

   b. growing up in an economically disadvantaged home or neighborhood.

   c. being raised in conditions of extreme deprivation.

   d. being an identical twin.

22. In prosperous country X everyone eats all they want. In country Y the rich are well fed, but the semistarved poor are often thin. In which country will the heritability of body weight be greater?

23. _____ _____ can lead to poor performance on tests by undermining test-takers' belief that they can do well on the test.

Find answers to these questions in Appendix E, in the back of the book.

IN YOUR EVERYDAY LIFE

Answering these questions will help you make these concepts more personally meaningful, and therefore more memorable.

1. What are the things you fear? Are some of those fears out of proportion to statistical risk? Are there other areas of your life where you need to take more precautions?

2. Can you recall a time when contradictory information challenged one of your views? Was it hard for you to consider the opposite view? Did you change your mind?

3. Do you think that young children should be required to learn a second language? Why or why not?

4. How could you use mental practice to improve your performance in some area of your life?

5. Can you think of a time when you felt an animal was communicating with you? How might you put that to a test?

6. The concept of multiple intelligences suggests that different people have different gifts. What are yours?

7. How have environmental influences shaped your ability to reach your academic potential?

9 Motivation and Emotion

Having bagged nearly all of Colorado's tallest peaks, experienced climber Aron Ralston went canyon hiking alone one spring day in 2003. The Saturday morning outing seemed so risk-free he did not bother to tell anyone where he was going. In Utah's narrow Bluejohn Canyon, just 150 yards above his final drop, he was climbing over an 800-pound rock when disaster struck. The rock shifted and pinned his right wrist and arm. He was, as the title of his book says, caught *Between a Rock and a Hard Place*.

Realizing that no one would be rescuing him, Ralston tried with all his might to dislodge the rock. Then, with a dull pocket knife, he tried chipping away at the rock. When that failed, he rigged up ropes to lift the rock. Alas, nothing worked. Hour after hour, then cold night after cold night, he was stuck.

By Tuesday, he had run out of food and water. On Wednesday, as thirst and hunger gnawed, he began saving and sipping his own urine. Using his video recorder, he said his good-byes to family and friends, for whom he now felt intense love. "So again love to everyone. Bring love and peace and happiness and beautiful lives into the world in my honor. Thank you. Love you."

On Thursday, surprised to find himself still alive, Ralston had a seemingly divine insight into his reproductive future. In his vision, he saw a preschool boy being scooped up by a one-armed man. Inspired by his vision, he summoned his remaining strength and his enormous will to live. Over the next hour, he willfully broke his bones and then proceeded to use his dull knife to cut off his arm. After slowing his bloodflow with a tourniquet, he chopped through the last piece of skin and, after 127 hours, broke free. Holding his bleeding half-arm close, he climbed down the 65-foot cliff and hiked 5 miles before finding someone. Ralston (2004) described the moment when he broke free. "[I was] just reeling with this euphoria . . . having been dead and standing in my grave, leaving my last will and testament, etching 'Rest in peace' on the wall, all of that, gone and then replaced with having my life again. It was undoubtedly the sweetest moment that I will ever experience."

Aron Ralston's thirst and hunger, his sense of belonging to others, and his brute will to live and become a father highlight the force of *motivation*: a need or desire that *energizes* behavior and *directs* it toward a goal. The intense love and joy he felt demonstrate the close ties between our *emotions* and our motivated behaviors, two areas we explore in this chapter.

Motivational Concepts

9-1 What is motivation, and what are three key perspectives that help us understand motivated behaviors?

◎ Our **motivations** arise from the interplay between nature (the bodily "push") and nurture (the "pulls" from our personal experiences, thoughts, and culture). Let's consider three perspectives that psychologists have used to understand motivated behaviors.

Drive-Reduction Theory

Drive-reduction theory makes three assumptions:

- We have **physiological needs,** such as the need for food or water.

- If a need is not met, it creates a *drive,* an aroused, motivated state, such as hunger or thirst.

- That drive pushes us to reduce the need by, say, eating or drinking.

The goal of this three-step process (**FIGURE 9.1**), from need to drive-reducing behavior, is **homeostasis,** our body's natural tendency to maintain a steady internal state. (*Homeostasis* means "staying the same.") The body's heat-regulation system, which works like a room's thermostat, is an example of homeostasis. Both systems monitor temperature and feed information to a control device. If the room's temperature cools, the control device switches on the furnace. Likewise, if our body's temperature cools, our blood vessels narrow to conserve warmth,

"What do you think . . . should we get started on that motivation research or not?"

and we search for warmer clothes or a warmer environment.

We also are pulled by **incentives**—environmental stimuli that attract or repel us, depending on our individual learning histories. If you are hungry, the aroma of good food will motivate you. Whether that aroma comes from fresh-baked bread or toasted ants will depend on your culture and experience.

When there is both a need and an incentive, we feel strongly driven. Let's assume you are motivated more by fresh-baked bread than by fresh-toasted ants. You've skipped lunch and you can smell bread baking in your friend's kitchen. You will feel a strong drive to satisfy your hunger, and the baking bread will be a powerful incentive that will motivate your actions.

For each motive, we can therefore ask, "How are we pushed by our inborn bodily needs and pulled by incentives in the environment?"

Arousal Theory

We are much more than homeostatic systems, however. When we are aroused, we are physically energized, or tense. Some motivated behaviors actually *increase* arousal (**FIGURE 9.2**). Well-fed animals with no clear, need-based drive will

leave a safe shelter to explore and gain information. Curiosity drives monkeys to monkey around trying to figure out how to unlock a latch that opens nothing, or how to open a window that allows them to see outside their room (Butler, 1954). Curiosity drives 9-month-old infants who check out every corner of the house. It drives the scientists whose work this text discusses. And it drives adventurers such as Aron Ralston and George Mallory. Asked why he wanted to climb Mount Everest, the *New York Times* reported that Mallory answered, "Because it is there." Those who, like Mallory and Ralston, enjoy high arousal are most likely to enjoy intense music, novel foods, and risky behaviors (Zuckerman, 1979). They are "sensation seekers."

We humans hunger for information (Biederman & Vessel, 2006). When we find that all our biological needs have been

FIGURE 9.2 Curiosity worldwide These Israeli college students exploring at an archeological site (top) and this Berber shepherd boy in Morocco meeting a digital camera for the first time (bottom) are all driven by their curiosity, and they are maintaining an optimum level of arousal.

Need (food, water)	→	Drive (hunger, thirst)	→	Drive-reducing behaviors (eating, drinking)

FIGURE 9.1 Drive-reduction theory Drive-reduction motivation arises from *homeostasis*—our body's natural tendency to maintain a steady internal state. Thus, if we are water deprived, our thirst drives us to drink and to restore the body's normal state.

Murray Close/Lionsgate/Photofest

FIGURE 9.3 Maslow's hierarchy of needs Reduced to near-starvation by their rulers, inhabitants of Suzanne Collins' fictional nation, Panem, hunger for food and survival.

Self-transcendence needs
Need to find meaning and identity beyond the self

Self-actualization needs
Need to live up to our fullest and unique potential

Esteem needs
Need for self-esteem, achievement, competence, and independence; need for recognition and respect from others

Belongingness and love needs
Need to love and be loved, to belong and be accepted; need to avoid loneliness and separation

Safety needs
Need to feel that the world is organized and predictable; need to feel safe, secure, and stable

Physiological needs
Need to satisfy hunger and thirst

met, we feel bored and seek stimulation to increase our arousal. But not *too* much stimulation, for that brings stress and sends us looking for ways to decrease arousal. Arousal theory describes this search for the right arousal level, a search that energizes and directs our behavior. ■

A Hierarchy of Needs

Some needs are more important than others. At this moment, with your needs for air and water satisfied, other motives are directing your behavior. But if you were deprived of water, your thirst would take over your thoughts. Just ask Aron Ralston. Or ask the semistarved people of the fictional Panem, whose districts, represented by a boy and girl selected by lottery, must compete in mortal *Hunger Games*. Food matters. Yet in Panem, as in our world, we do not live by bread alone. People also have needs for safety, connection, and self-worth.

Abraham Maslow (1970) viewed human motives as a pyramid—a **hierarchy of needs** (FIGURE 9.3). At the pyramid's base are physiological needs, such as those for food. If those are unmet, life is a hunger game. Only after these needs are met, said Maslow (1971), do we try to meet our need for safety, and then to satisfy our needs to give and receive love and to enjoy self-esteem. At the peak of the pyramid are the highest human needs. At the *self-actualization* level, people seek to realize their own potential. At the very top is *self-transcendence*, which Maslow proposed near the end of his life. At this level, some people strive for meaning, purpose, and identity that is *transpersonal*—beyond (*trans*) the self (Koltko-Rivera, 2006).

There are exceptions to Maslow's hierarchy. For example, people have starved themselves to make a political statement. Nevertheless, some needs are indeed more basic than others. In poorer nations, money—and the food and shelter it buys—more strongly commands attention and predicts feelings of well-being. In wealthy nations, where most are able to meet their basic needs,

motivation a need or desire that energizes and directs behavior.

drive-reduction theory the idea that a physiological need creates an aroused state (a drive) that motivates us to satisfy the need.

physiological need a basic bodily requirement.

homeostasis a tendency to maintain a balanced or constant internal state; the regulation of any aspect of body chemistry, such as blood glucose, around a particular level.

incentive a positive or negative environmental stimulus that motivates behavior.

hierarchy of needs Maslow's pyramid of human needs; at the base are physiological needs. These basic needs must be satisfied before higher-level safety needs, and then psychological needs, become active.

home-life satisfaction is a better predictor of well-being (Oishi et al., 1999).

Let's take a closer look now at two specific motives: the basic-level motive, *hunger,* and the higher-level *need to belong.* As you read about these motives, watch for ways that incentives (the psychological "pull") interact with bodily needs (the biological "push"). ■

RETRIEVE + REMEMBER

- How do drive-reduction theory and arousal theory contribute to our understanding of motivated behavior?

ANSWER: From drive-reduction theory, we know that our physiological needs (such as hunger) create an aroused state that drives us to reduce the need (for example, by eating). Arousal theory suggests we need to maintain an optimal level of arousal, which helps explain our motivation toward behaviors that meet no physiological need.

- After hours of driving alone in an unfamiliar city, you finally see a diner. Although it looks deserted and a little creepy, you stop because you are *really* hungry. How would Maslow's hierarchy of needs explain your behavior?

ANSWER: According to Maslow, our drives to meet the physiological needs of hunger and thirst take priority over safety needs, prompting us to take risks at times in order to eat.

Hunger

◎ The power of physiological needs to hijack our minds was vividly demonstrated when Ancel Keys and his research team (1950) did a now-classic study. First, they fed 36 male volunteers just enough to maintain their initial weight. Then, for six months, they cut this food level in half. The effects soon became visible. Without thinking about it, the men began conserving energy. They appeared sluggish and dull. After dropping rapidly, their body weights stabilized at about 25 percent below their starting point.

As Maslow might have guessed, the men became obsessed with food. They talked about it. They daydreamed about it. They collected recipes, read cookbooks, and feasted their eyes on tasty but forbidden food. Focused on their unmet basic need, they lost interest in sex and social activities. One man reported, "If we see a show, the most interesting [parts are] scenes where people are eating. I couldn't laugh at the funniest picture in the world, and love scenes are completely dull." As journalist Dorothy Dix (1861–1951) observed, "Nobody wants to kiss when they are hungry."

Motives can capture our consciousness. When we're hungry, thirsty, fatigued, or sexually aroused, little else seems to matter. When we're not, food, water, sleep, or sex just don't seem like such big things in life, now or ever. (You may recall from Chapter 7 a parallel effect of our current good or bad mood on our memories.) Shop for food on an empty stomach and you are more likely to see those jelly-filled doughnuts as just what you've always loved and will be wanting tomorrow. *Motives matter mightily.*

The Physiology of Hunger

9-2 What physiological factors cause us to feel hungry?

Deprived of a normal food supply, Keys' volunteers were clearly hungry. What triggers hunger? Does it arise from the pangs of an empty stomach? So it seemed to A. L. Washburn. Working with Walter Cannon (Cannon & Washburn, 1912), Washburn agreed to swallow a balloon that was attached to a recording device **(FIGURE 9.4)**. When inflated to fill his stomach, the balloon tracked his stomach contractions. Washburn supplied information about his *feelings* of hunger by pressing a key each time he felt a hunger pang. The discovery: When Washburn felt hungry, he was indeed having stomach contractions.

Can hunger exist without stomach pangs? To answer that question, researchers removed some rats' stomachs and created a direct path to their small intestines (Tsang, 1938). Did the rats continue to eat? Indeed they did. Some hunger persists similarly in humans whose stomachs have been removed as a treatment for ulcers or cancer. So the pangs of an empty stomach cannot be the *only* source of hunger. What else might trigger hunger?

Body Chemistry and the Brain

Somehow, somewhere, your body is keeping tabs on the energy it takes in and the energy it uses. This balancing act enables you to maintain a stable body weight. A major source of energy in your body is the **glucose** circulating in your bloodstream. If your blood glucose level drops, you won't consciously feel this change. But your brain, which automatically monitors your blood chemistry and your body's internal state, will trigger your feeling of hunger.

How does the brain sound the alarm? The work is done by several neural areas, some housed deep in the brain within the *hypothalamus* **(FIGURE 9.5)**. This neural traffic intersection includes areas that influ-

"Never hunt when you're hungry."

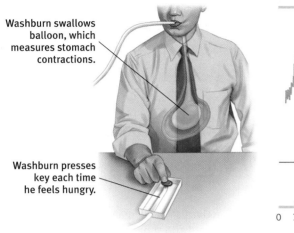

Washburn swallows balloon, which measures stomach contractions.

Washburn presses key each time he feels hungry.

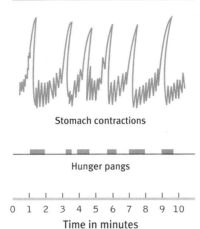

Stomach contractions

Hunger pangs

0 1 2 3 4 5 6 7 8 9 10
Time in minutes

FIGURE 9.4 **Monitoring stomach contractions**

ence eating. In one neural area (called the *arcuate nucleus*), a center pumps out appetite-stimulating hormones, and another center pumps out appetite-suppressing hormones. When researchers stimulate an appetite-enhancing center in this or another neural area, well-fed animals will begin to eat. If they destroy the area, even starving animals lose interest in food. The opposite occurs when the appetite-suppressing area is stimulated: The animal will stop eating. Destroy this area and animals become extremely fat (Duggan & Booth, 1986; Hoebel & Teitelbaum, 1966) **(FIGURE 9.6).**

Blood vessels connect the hypothalamus to the rest of the body, so it can respond to our current blood chemistry and other incoming information. One of its tasks is monitoring levels of appetite hormones, such as *ghrelin,* a hunger-arousing hormone secreted by an empty stomach. When people have surgery for severe obesity, surgeons seal off part of the stomach. The remaining stomach then produces much less ghrelin, and the person's appetite lessens (Lemonick, 2002). Other appetite hormones include *insulin, leptin, orexin,* and PYY. **FIGURE 9.7** on the next page describes how they influence your feelings of hunger.

The interaction of appetite hormones and brain activity suggests that the body has a "weight thermostat." When semistarved rats fall below their normal weight, this system signals their bodies to restore the lost weight: Their hunger increases and their energy output decreases. If body weight rises—as happens when rats are force-fed—hunger decreases and energy output increases. In this way, rats (and humans) tend to hover around a stable weight, or **set point**, influenced in part by heredity (Keesey & Corbett, 1983).

We humans (and other species, too) vary in our **basal metabolic rate,** a measure of how much energy we use to maintain basic body functions when our body is at rest. But we share a common response to decreased food intake: our basal metabolic rate drops. So it did for the participants in Keys' experiment. After 24 weeks of semistarvation, they stabilized at three-quarters of their normal weight, although they were taking in only *half* their previous calories. How did their bodies achieve this dieter's nightmare? They reduced the amount of energy they were using—partly by being

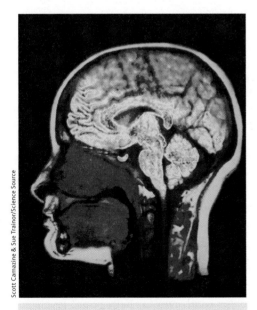

Scott Camazine & Sue Trainor/Science Source

FIGURE 9.5 **The hypothalamus** The hypothalamus (colored green) performs various body maintenance functions. One of these functions is control of hunger.

Olivier Voisin/Science Source

FIGURE 9.6 **Evidence for the brain's control of eating** The fat mouse on the left has nonfunctioning receptors in the appetite-suppressing part of the hypothalamus.

glucose the form of sugar that circulates in the blood and provides the major source of energy for body tissues. When its level is low, we feel hunger.

set point the point at which your "weight thermostat" is supposedly set. When your body falls below this weight, increased hunger and a lowered metabolic rate may combine to restore lost weight.

basal metabolic rate the body's resting rate of energy output.

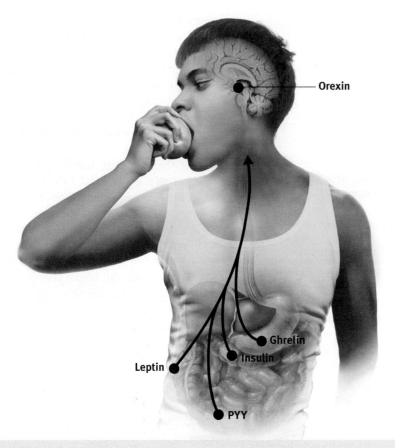

FIGURE 9.7 The appetite hormones

Ghrelin: Hormone secreted by empty stomach; sends "I'm hungry" signals to the brain.

Insulin: Hormone secreted by pancreas; controls blood glucose.

Leptin: Protein hormone secreted by fat cells; when abundant, causes brain to increase metabolism and decrease hunger.

Orexin: Hunger-triggering hormone secreted by hypothalamus.

PYY: Digestive tract hormone; sends "I'm *not* hungry" signals to the brain.

less active, but partly by dropping their basal metabolic rate by 29 percent.

Some researchers have suggested that the idea of a biologically *fixed* set point is too rigid to explain why slow, steady changes in body weight can alter a person's set point (Assanand et al., 1998), or why, when we have unlimited access to various tasty foods, we tend to overeat and gain weight (Raynor & Epstein, 2001). Thus, some researchers prefer the looser term *settling point* to indicate the level at which a person's weight settles in response to caloric intake and energy use. As we will see next, environment matters as well as biology. ■

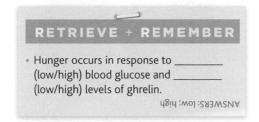

"Never get a tattoo when you're drunk and hungry."

activity. Yet there is more to hunger than meets the stomach. This was strikingly apparent when trickster researchers tested two patients who had no memory for events occurring more than a minute ago (Rozin et al., 1998). If offered a second lunch 20 minutes after eating a normal lunch, both patients readily ate it . . . and usually a third meal offered 20 minutes after they finished the second. This suggests that one part of our decision to eat is our memory of the time of our last meal. As time passes, we think about eating again, and that thought triggers feelings of hunger.

Psychological influences on eating behavior affect all of us at some point. But consider this: Over the next 40 years you will eat about 20 tons of food. If during those years you give in to the environmental stimuli bombarding you, and you increase your daily intake by just .01 ounce more than required for your energy needs, you will gain 24 pounds (Martin et al., 1991).

Taste Preferences: Biology and Culture

Both body chemistry and environment play a role in our feelings of hunger and in what we hunger for—our taste preferences. When feeling tense or depressed, do you crave starchy, carbohydrate-laden foods? High-carb foods, such as pasta, chips, and sweets, help boost levels of the neurotransmitter serotonin, which has calming effects. When stressed, even rats find it extra rewarding to scarf Oreos (Artiga et al., 2007; Boggiano et al., 2005).

RETRIEVE + REMEMBER

- Hunger occurs in response to _____ (low/high) blood glucose and _____ (low/high) levels of ghrelin.

ANSWERS: low; high

The Psychology of Hunger

9-3 How do psychological, biological, cultural, and situational factors affect our taste preferences and eating habits?

We have seen that our eagerness to eat is pushed by our body chemistry and brain

Our preferences for sweet and salty tastes are genetic and universal. Other taste preferences are learned. People given highly salted foods, for example, develop a liking for excess salt (Beauchamp, 1987). People who become violently ill after eating a particular food often develop a dislike of it. (The frequency of children's illnesses provides many chances for them to learn to avoid certain foods.)

Our culture teaches us that some foods are acceptable but others are not. Bedouins enjoy eating the eye of a camel, which most North Americans would find repulsive. North Americans and Europeans also shun horse, dog, and rat meat, all of which are prized elsewhere.

We also may learn to prefer some tastes because they are adaptive. In hot climates (where food spoils more quickly), recipes often include spices that slow the growth of bacteria (FIGURE 9.8). India averages nearly 10 spices per meat recipe, Finland 2 spices. Pregnancy-related food dislikes—and the nausea associated with them—are another example of adaptive taste preferences. These dislikes peak about the tenth week, when the developing embryo is most vulnerable to toxins.

Rats tend to avoid unfamiliar foods (Sclafani, 1995). So do we, especially those that are animal-based. This surely was

Spices per recipe

The hotter the climate, the more spices used.

Mean annual temperature (degrees Celsius)

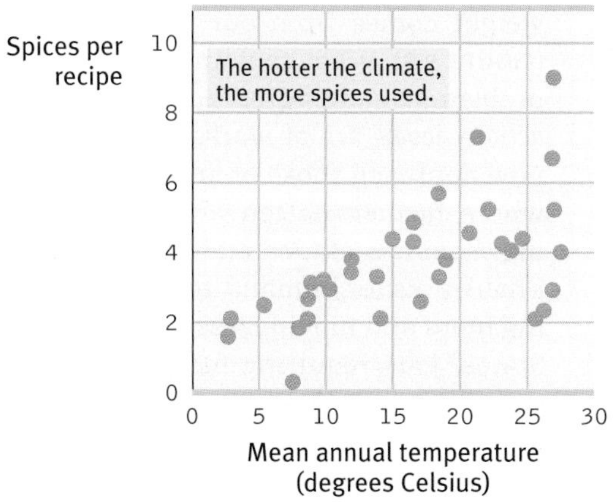

FIGURE 9.8 Hot cultures like hot spices (Sherman & Flaxman, 2001).

adaptive for our ancestors by protecting them from potentially toxic substances.

Tempting Situations

Would it surprise you to know that situations also control your eating? Psychologists call this effect the *ecology of eating*.

- *Friends and food* Do you eat more when eating with others? Most of us do (Herman et al., 2003; Hetherington et al., 2006). The presence of others tends to amplify our natural behavior tendencies. (This is *social facilitation* and you'll hear more about it in Chapter 12.)

- *Serving size is significant* French waistlines are smaller than American waistlines. From soda drinks to yogurt sizes, the French offer foods in smaller portion sizes. Does it matter? (One could as well order two small sandwiches as one large one.) To find out, researchers offered people varieties of free snacks (Geier et al., 2006). For example, in the lobby of an apartment house, they laid out either full or half pretzels, big or little Tootsie Rolls, or a big bowl of M&M's with either a small or large serving scoop. Their consistent result: Offered a supersized portion, people put away more calories. Other studies confirm that we eat more when given supersized servings, bigger food packages, and larger serving containers (Herman & Polivy, 2008; Wansink, 2007). Offered pasta, people eat more when given a big plate (Van Ittersum & Wansink, 2012). Offered ice cream, people take and eat more when given a big bowl and big scoop. They pour and drink more from short, wide glasses than from tall, narrow glasses. And they take more of easier-to-reach foods on buffet lines (Marteau et al., 2012). Portion size matters.

- *Selections stimulate* Food variety promotes eating. Offered a

dessert buffet, we eat more than we do when choosing a portion from one favorite dessert. For our early ancestors, eating more when foods were abundant and varied was adaptive. Consuming a wide range of vitamins and minerals and storing fat offered protection later, during winter cold or famine. When bad times hit, they could eat less, hoarding their small food supply until winter or famine ended (Polivy et al., 2008; Remick et al., 2009). ■

RETRIEVE + REMEMBER

- After an eight-hour hike without food, your long-awaited favorite dish is placed in front of you, and your mouth waters in anticipation. Why?

ANSWER: You have learned to respond to the sight and aroma that signal the food about to enter your mouth. Both physiological cues (low blood sugar) and psychological cues (anticipation of the tasty meal) heighten your experienced hunger.

Obesity and Weight Control

9-4 What factors predispose some people to become and remain obese?

Obesity has physical health risks, but it can also be socially toxic, by affecting both how you feel about yourself and how others treat you. Obese 6- to 9-year olds are 60 percent more likely to suffer bullying (Lumeng et al., 2010). Adult obesity is linked with lower psychological well-being, increased depression, and discrimination in employment (de Wit et al., 2010; Luppino et al., 2010; Mendes, 2010; Roehling et al., 1999, 2009, 2010). Yet few overweight people win the battle of the bulge. Why? And why do some people gain weight while others eat the same amount and seldom add a pound?

The Survival Value—and Health Risks—of Fat

The answers lie partly in our history. Fat is stored energy. It is a fuel reserve that can carry us through times when food is scarce, which were common in our prehistoric ancestors' world. (Think of that spare tire around the middle as an energy storehouse—biology's counterpart to a hiker's waist-borne snack pack.) In Europe in earlier centuries, and in parts of the world today, obesity signaled wealth and social status (Furnham & Baguma, 1994).

Our hungry distant ancestors were well served by a simple rule: *When you find energy-rich fat or sugar, eat it!* That rule is no longer adaptive in a world where food and sweets are abundantly available. Pretty much everywhere this book is being read, people have a growing problem. Worldwide, obesity has doubled since 1980, with 1.46 billion adults now overweight. Some 502 million are *obese,* which is defined as a *body mass index (BMI)* of 30 or more (Swinburn et al., 2011). (See cdc.gov/healthyweight/assessing/bmi to calculate your BMI.) In the United States, 36 percent of adults are now obese (Flegal et al., 2012).

PhotoObjects.net/Jupiterimages/Getty

Significant obesity can shorten your life, reduce your quality of life, and increase your health care costs (de Gonzales et al., 2010; Jarrett et al., 2010; Sun, 2009). It increases the risk of diabetes, high blood pressure, heart disease, gallstones, arthritis, and certain types of cancer. Women's obesity has been linked to a higher risk of late-life cognitive decline, including Alzheimer's disease and brain tissue loss (Bruce-Keller et al., 2009; Whitmer et al., 2008). In one experiment, memory performance improved 12 weeks after severely obese people had weight-loss surgery and lost significant weight. Those *not* having the surgery showed some further cognitive decline (Gunstad et al., 2011).

So why don't obese people just drop that excess baggage? Because their bodies fight back.

A SLUGGISH METABOLISM Once we become fat, we require less food to maintain our weight than we did to gain it. Compared with muscle tissue, fat has a lower metabolic rate—it takes less food energy to maintain. When an overweight person's body drops below its previous set (or settling) point, the person's hunger increases and metabolism decreases. Thus, the body adapts to starvation by burning off fewer calories.

Lean people and overweight people differ in their rates of resting metabolism. Lean people seem naturally disposed to move about, and in doing so, they burn more calories. Overweight people tend to sit still longer and conserve their energy (Levine et al., 2005). This helps explain why two people of the same height and age can maintain the same weight, even if one of them eats much more than the other does. (Who said life is fair?)

A GENETIC HANDICAP It's true: Our genes influence the size of our jeans. Consider:

- Adopted children share meals with their adoptive siblings and parents. Yet their body weights more closely resemble those of their biological family (Grilo & Pogue-Geile, 1991).

- Identical twins have closely similar weights, even when raised apart (Plomin et al., 1997; Stunkard et al., 1990). Fraternal twins' weights are much less similar. Such findings suggest that genes explain two-thirds of the person-to-person differences in body mass (Maes et al., 1997).

SLEEP, FRIENDS, FOOD, ACTIVITY— THEY ALL MATTER! Genes tell an important part of the obesity story. But environmental factors are mighty important, too.

Studies in Europe, Japan, and the United States show that children and adults who suffer from *sleep loss* are more at risk for obesity (Keith et al., 2006; Nedeltcheva et al., 2010; Taheri, 2004a,b). Deprived of sleep, our bodies produce less leptin (which reports body fat to the brain) and more ghrelin (the appetite-stimulating stomach hormone).

Social influence is another factor. One 32-year study of 12,067 people found them most likely to become obese when a friend became obese (Christakis & Fowler, 2007). The odds of becoming obese almost tripled when the obese friend was a close one. Moreover, the correlation among friends' weights was not simply a matter of seeking out similar people as friends.

Friends matter, but the strongest evidence that environment influences weight comes from our *fattening world* (**FIGURE 9.9**). What explains this growing problem? Changing *food consumption* and *activity levels* are at work. Our lifestyles now approach those of animal feedlots, where farmers fatten animals by giving them lots of food and little exercise. That works for humans, too. We are eating more and moving less. In the United States, jobs requiring moderate physical activity declined from about 50 percent in 1960 to 20 percent in 2011 (Church et al., 2011).

Stadiums, theaters, and subway cars—but not airplanes—are widening seats to accommodate the new "bottom"

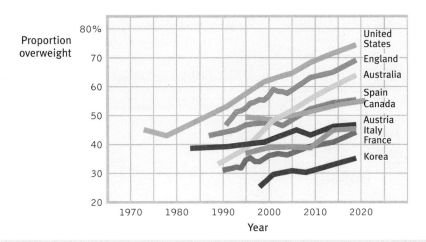

FIGURE 9.9 Past and projected overweight rates, by the Organisation for Economic Co-operation and Development

line (Hampson, 2000; Kim & Tong, 2010). Washington State Ferries abandoned a 50-year-old standard: "Eighteen-inch butts are a thing of the past" (Shepherd, 1999). New York City, facing a large problem with Big Apple bottoms, has mostly replaced 17.5-inch bucket-style subway seats with bucketless seats (Hampson, 2000). In the end, today's people need more room.

* * *

The obesity research findings reinforce a familiar lesson from Chapter 8's study of intelligence. There can be high levels of *heritability* (genetic influence on individual differences) without heredity being the only explanation of group differences. Genes mostly determine why you are heavier or leaner than your friends. Environment mostly determines why you and your friends are heavier than your parents and grandparents were at your age.

Our eating behavior once again demonstrates one of this book's big ideas: Biological, psychological, and social-cultural factors interact. We have seen

> *"We put fast food on every corner, we put junk food in our schools, we got rid of [physical education classes], we put candy and soda at the checkout stand of every retail outlet you can think of. The results are in. It worked."*
>
> Harold Goldstein, Executive Director of the California Center for Public Health Advocacy, 2009, when imagining a vast U.S. national experiment to encourage weight gain

many biological and psychological forces working against those who want to shed excess pounds. Indeed, short of drastic surgery to tie off part of the stomach and small intestine, most who have succeeded on weightloss programs have eventually regained most of the weight (Mann et al., 2007).

Setting Realistic Goals

Nearly two-thirds of American women and half of American men have said that they want to lose weight. About half of those people have said they are "seriously trying" (Moore, 2006).

So what advice can psychology offer? Permanent weight loss is not easy. For some helpful hints, see Close-Up: Waist Management on the next page. ■

RETRIEVE + REMEMBER

Why can two people of the same height, age, and activity level maintain the same weight, even if one of them eats much less than the other does?

ANSWER: Individuals have very different set points and genetically influenced metabolism levels, causing them to burn calories differently.

The Need to Belong

9-5 What evidence points to our human need to belong?

◎ Imagine yourself like the fictional Robinson Crusoe, dropped on an island . . . alone . . . for the rest of your life. Food, shelter, and comfort are yours—but there are no fellow humans, no social media, no story but your own. Do you savor the stressless serenity?

Surely not. We are what Greek philosopher Aristotle called the *social animal.* Cut off from friends or family—alone in prison or in a new school or in a foreign land—most people feel keenly their lost connections with important others. This deep *need to belong* seems a basic human motivation (Baumeister & Leary, 1995). Josh Silverman (2008), president of Internet communication company Skype, understood the need to belong: "There's no question in my mind about what stands at the heart of the communication revolution—the human desire to connect." And connect we do.

The Benefits of Belonging

Social bonds boosted our ancestors' chances of survival. These bonds helped keep children close to their caregivers, protecting them from many threats. As adults, those who formed attachments were more likely to reproduce and co-nurture their offspring to maturity. To be "wretched" literally means, in its Middle English origin (*wrecche*), to be without kin nearby.

Survival also was supported by cooperation. In solo combat, our ancestors were not the toughest predators. But as hunters, they learned that eight hands were better than two. As food gatherers, they gained protection from their enemies by traveling in groups. Those who felt a need to belong survived and

Waist Management

Perhaps you are shaking your head: "Slim chance I have of becoming and staying thin." People struggling with obesity should seek medical evaluation and guidance. For others who wish to take off a few pounds, researchers have offered these tips.

Begin only if you feel motivated and self-disciplined. For most people, permanent weight loss means making a career of staying thin. It requires a lifelong change in eating habits, combined with increased exercise.

Exercise and get enough sleep. Inactive people are often overweight (FIGURE 9.10). Especially when supported by 7 to 8 nightly hours of sleep, exercise empties fat cells, builds muscle, speeds up metabolism, and helps lower your settling point (Bennett, 1995; Kolata, 1987; Thompson et al., 1982).

Minimize exposure to tempting food cues. Food shop only on a full stomach. Keep tempting foods out of the house or out of sight.

Limit variety and eat healthy foods. Given more variety, people consume more; so, eat simple meals with whole grains, fruits, and vegetables. Healthy fats, such as those found in olive oil and fish, help regulate appetite and artery-clogging cholesterol (Taubes, 2001, 2002). Better crispy greens than Krispy Kremes.

Reduce portion sizes. Serve food with smaller bowls, plates, and utensils.

Don't starve all day and eat one big meal at night. This pattern, common among overweight people, slows metabolism. By late morning, most of us are more alert and less fatigued if we have eaten a balanced breakfast (Spring et al., 1992).

Beware of the binge. Especially for men, eating slowly can lead to eating less (Martin et al., 2007). Even when people consciously control their eating, drinking alcohol or feeling anxious or depressed can unleash the urge to overeat (Herman & Polivy, 1980).

Before eating with others, decide how much you want to eat. Eating with friends can distract us from monitoring our own eating (Ward & Mann, 2000).

Remember, most people occasionally lapse. A lapse need not become a full collapse.

Connect to a support group. Share your goals and progress by joining others, either face to face or online (Freedman, 2011).

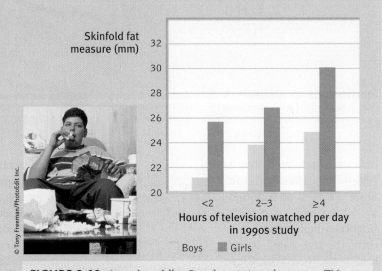

FIGURE 9.10 American idle: Couch potatoes beware—TV watching correlates with obesity As lifestyles have become less active and TV watching has increased, so has the percentage of overweight people in Britain, Canada, and the United States (Pagani et al., 2010). When California children were placed in a TV-reduction educational program, they watched less—and lost weight (Robinson, 1999). Don't watch TV? Then watch out for other screen time that keeps your motor idling.

reproduced most successfully, and their genes now rule.

People in every society on Earth belong to groups (and, as Chapter 12 explains, prefer and favor "us" over "them"). With the need to belong satisfied by close, supportive relationships, we feel included, accepted, and loved, and our self-esteem rides high. Indeed, *self-esteem* is a measure of how valued and accepted we feel (Leary et al., 1998). When our need for relatedness is satisfied in balance with two other basic psychological needs—*autonomy* (a sense of personal control) and *competence*—the result is a deep sense of well-being (Deci & Ryan, 2002; Patrick et al., 2007; Sheldon & Niemiec, 2006). To feel free, capable, and connected is to enjoy a good life.

Is it surprising, then, that so much of our social behavior aims to increase our feelings of belonging? To win friendship and avoid rejection, we generally conform to group standards. We monitor our behavior, hoping to make a good impression. We spend billions on clothes, cosmetics, diet, and fitness—all motivated by our search for love and acceptance.

By drawing a sharp circle around "us," the need to belong

Photodisc/Getty

THE NEED TO CONNECT Six days a week, women from the Philippines work as "domestic helpers" in 154,000 Hong Kong households. On Sundays, they throng to the central business district to picnic, dance, sing, talk, and laugh. "Humanity could stage no greater display of happiness," reported one observer (*Economist*, 2001).

feeds both deep attachments and menacing threats. Out of our need to define a "we" come loving families, faithful friendships, and team spirit, but also teen gangs, ethnic rivalries, and fanatic nationalism.

For good or for bad, we work hard to form and maintain our relationships. Familiarity breeds liking, not contempt. Thrown together at work, on a hiking trip, in groups at school, we behave like magnets, moving closer, forming bonds. Parting, we feel distress. We promise to call, to write, to come back for reunions.

Even when bad relationships break, people suffer. In one 16-nation survey, and in repeated U.S. surveys, separated and divorced people have been half as likely as married people to say they were "very happy" (Inglehart, 1990; NORC, 2007). Divorce also predicts earlier mortality. In an analysis of 755,000 divorces in 11 different countries, divorce was associated with dying earlier (Sbarra et al., 2011). After such separations, loneliness and anger—and sometimes even a strange desire to be near the former partner—linger. For those in abusive relationships, the fear of being alone sometimes seems

worse than the certainty of emotional or physical pain. Children who move through a series of foster homes also know the fear of being alone. After repeated breaks in budding attachments, children may have difficulty forming deep attachments. The evidence is clearest at the extremes—children who grow up in institutions without a sense of belonging to anyone, or who are locked away at home and severely neglected. They become pathetic creatures, withdrawn, frightened, speechless.

No matter how secure our early years were, we all experience anxiety, loneliness, jealousy, or guilt when something threatens or dissolves our social ties. Many of life's best moments occur when close relationships begin: making a new friend, falling in love, having a baby. And many of life's worst moments happen when close relationships end (Jaremka et al., 2011). At such times, we may feel life is empty, pointless. For those moving alone to new places, the stress and loneliness can be depressing. After years of placing individual refugee and immigrant families in isolated communities, U.S. agencies today encourage *chain migration* (Pipher, 2002). The second refugee Sudanese family settling in a town generally has an easier adjustment than the first.

The Pain of Being Shut Out

Sometimes our need to belong is denied. Can you recall a time when you felt excluded or ignored or shunned? Perhaps you were unfriended on a social networking site, ignored in a chat room, or

had a text message or e-mail go unanswered. Or perhaps others gave you the silent treatment, avoided you, looked away, mocked you, or shut you out in some other way.

This is *ostracism*—social exclusion (Williams, 2007, 2009). Worldwide, humans use many forms of ostracism—exile, imprisonment, solitary confinement—to punish, and therefore control, social behavior. For children, even a brief time-out in isolation can be punishing. Among prisoners, half of all suicides occur among those experiencing the extreme exclusion of solitary confinement (Goode, 2012).

Being shunned threatens our need to belong (Williams & Zadro, 2001). Lea, a lifelong victim of the silent treatment by her mother and grandmother, described the effect. "It's the meanest thing you can do to someone, especially if you know they can't fight back. I never should have been born." Like Lea, people often respond to ostracism with depressed moods, efforts to restore their acceptance, and then withdrawal. After two years of silent treatment by his employer, Richard reported, "I came home every night

SOCIAL ACCEPTANCE AND REJECTION Successful participants on the reality TV show *Survivor* form alliances and gain acceptance among their peers. The rest receive the ultimate social punishment as they are "voted off the island."

and cried. I lost 25 pounds, had no self-esteem, and felt that I wasn't worthy."

Rejected and powerless, people may seek new friends. Or they may turn nasty, as did college students made to feel rejected in one series of experiments (Baumeister et al., 2002; Twenge et al., 2001, 2002, 2007). Some students were told that a personality test they had taken showed that they were "the type likely to end up alone later in life." Others heard that people they had met didn't want them in a group that was forming. Still others heard good news. These lucky people would have "rewarding relationships throughout life," or "everyone chose you as someone they'd like to work with." How did students react after being told they weren't wanted or would end up alone? They were much more likely to engage in self-defeating behaviors and to underperform on aptitude tests. When later interacting with those who had excluded them, they also were more likely to act in mean or aggressive ways (blasting people with noise, for example). "If intelligent, well-adjusted, successful . . . students can turn aggressive in response to a small laboratory experience of social exclusion," noted the research team, "it is disturbing to imagine the aggressive tendencies that might arise from . . . chronic exclusion from desired groups in actual social life." (At the end of the experiments, the study was fully explained and the participants left feeling reassured.)

Ostracism is a real pain. Brain scans show increased activity in areas that also activate in response to physical pain (Kross et al., 2011; Eisenberger, 2012a,b). That helps explain another surprising finding. Acetaminophen, found in such products as Tylenol and Anacin, and taken to relieve physical pain, also lessens social pain (DeWall et al., 2010). Psychologically, we seem to experience social pain with the same emotional unpleasantness that marks physical pain. And across cultures, we use the same words (for example, *hurt*,

crushed) for social pain and physical pain (MacDonald & Leary, 2005).

The opposite of ostracism—feelings of love—activate brain areas associated with rewards and satisfaction. Loved ones activate a brain region that dampens feelings of physical pain (Eisenberger et al., 2011). In one experiment, university students felt markedly less pain when looking at their beloved's picture, rather than at someone else's photo (Younger et al., 2010).

The bottom line: Social isolation and rejection foster depressed moods or emotional numbness, and they can trigger aggression (Baumeister et al., 2009; Gerber & Wheeler, 2009). They can put us at risk for mental decline and ill health (Cacioppo & Hawkley, 2009). But love is a natural painkiller. When feelings of acceptance and connection build, so do self-esteem, positive feelings, and the desire to help rather than hurt others (Buckley & Leary, 2001). ■

RETRIEVE + REMEMBER

- How have students reacted in studies where they were made to feel rejected and unwanted? What helps explain these results?

ANSWER: These students' basic need to belong seems to have been disrupted. They engaged in more self-defeating behaviors, underperformed on aptitude tests, and displayed less empathy and more aggression.

Connecting and Social Networking

9-6 How does social networking influence us?

As social creatures, we live for connection. Researcher George Vaillant (2009) was asked what he had learned from studying 238 Harvard University men from the 1930s to the end of their lives. He replied, "The only thing that really matters in life are your relationships to other people." A South African Zulu saying captures the idea: *Umuntu ngumuntu ngabantu*—"a person is a person through other persons."

It keeps me from looking at my phone . . .

Mobile Networks and Social Media

Look around and see humans connecting: talking, texting, posting, chatting, social gaming, e-mailing. The changes in how we connect have been fast and vast.

- At the end of 2013, the world had 7.1 billion people and 6.8 billion mobile cell-phone subscriptions (ITU, 2013). But phone talking now accounts for less than half of U.S. mobile network traffic (Wortham, 2010). In Canada and elsewhere, e-mailing is being displaced by texting, Facebook, and other messaging technology (IPSOS, 2010a). Speedy texting is not really writing, said one observer (McWhorter, 2012), but rather a new form of conversation—"fingered speech."

- Three in four U.S. teens text. Half (mostly females) send 60 or more texts daily (Lenhart, 2012). For many, it's as though friends, for better or worse, are always present.

- How many of us are using social networking sites, such as Facebook or Twitter? Among 2010's entering American collegians, 94 percent were (Pryor et al., 2011). With a "critical mass" of your friends on a social network, its lure becomes hard to resist. Such is our need to belong. Check in or miss out.

The Net Result: Social Effects of Social Networking

By connecting like-minded people, the Internet serves as a social amplifier. In

times of social crisis or personal stress, it provides information and supportive connections. It also functions as an online dating matchmaker (more on those topics in Chapter 12). As electronic communication has become part of the "new normal," researchers have explored how these changes have affected our relationships.

HAVE SOCIAL NETWORKING SITES MADE US MORE, OR LESS, SOCIALLY ISOLATED?

In the Internet's early years, online communication in chat rooms and during social games was mostly between strangers. In that period, the adolescents and adults who spent more time online spent less time with friends; as a result, their offline relationships suffered (Kraut et al., 1998; Mesch, 2001; Nie, 2001). Even in more recent times, lonely people have tended to spend greater-than-average time online (Bonetti et al., 2010; Stepanikova et al., 2010). Social networkers have been less likely to know their real-world neighbors and "64 percent less likely than non-

Internet users to rely on neighbors for help in caring for themselves or a family member" (Pew, 2009).

But the Internet has also diversified our social networks. (I am now connected to other hearing-technology advocates across the world.) And despite the decrease in neighborliness, social networking is mostly strengthening our connections with people we already know (DiSalvo, 2010; Valkenburg & Peter, 2010). If your social networking helps you connect with friends, stay in touch with extended family, or find support when facing challenges, then you are not alone (Rainie et al., 2011). So social networks connect us. But they can also, as you've surely noticed, become a gigantic time- and attention-sucking distraction. If you are like most other students, two days without social networking access would be followed by a glut of online time, much as a two-

day food fast would be followed by a period of feasting (Sheldon et al., 2011).

DOES ELECTRONIC COMMUNICATION STIMULATE HEALTHY SELF-DISCLOSURE?

Self-disclosure is sharing ourselves—our joys, worries, and weaknesses—with others. As we will see in Chapter 10, confiding in others can be a healthy way of coping with day-to-day challenges. When communicating electronically rather than face to face, we often are less focused on others' reactions. We are less self-conscious and thus less inhibited. Sometimes this is taken to an extreme, as when teens send photos of themselves they later regret, or cyberbullies hound a victim, or hate groups post messages promoting bigotry or crimes. More often, however, the increased self-disclosure serves to deepen friendships (Valkenburg & Peter, 2010).

Although electronic networking pays dividends, nature has designed us for face-to-face communication, which appears to be a better predictor of life satisfaction (Killingsworth & Gilbert, 2010; Lee et al., 2011). Texting and e-mailing are rewarding, but eye-to-eye conversation with family and friends is even more so.

DO SOCIAL NETWORKING PROFILES AND POSTS REFLECT PEOPLE'S ACTUAL PERSONALITIES?

We've all heard stories of Internet predators hiding behind false personalities, values, and motives. Generally, however, social networks reveal a person's real personality. In one study, participants completed a personality test twice. In one test, they described their "actual personality"; in the other, they described their "ideal self." Other volunteers then used the

Thomas Northcut/Getty images

participants' Facebook profiles to create an independent set of personality ratings. The Facebook-profile ratings were much closer to the participants' actual personalities than to their ideal personalities (Back et al., 2010). In another study, people who seemed most likable on their Facebook page also seemed most likable in face-to-face meetings (Weisbuch et al., 2009). Your online profiles may indeed reflect the real you!

DOES SOCIAL NETWORKING PROMOTE NARCISSISM? *Narcissism* is self-esteem gone wild. Narcissistic people are self-important, self-focused, and self-promoting. Some personality tests assess narcissism with items such as "I like to be the center of attention." People with high narcissism test scores are especially active on social networking sites. They collect more superficial "friends." They offer more staged, glamorous photos. And, not surprisingly, they *seem* more narcissistic to strangers viewing their pages (Buffardi & Campbell, 2008).

For narcissists, social networking sites are more than a gathering place; they are a feeding trough. In one study, college students were randomly assigned either to edit and explain their online profiles for 15 minutes, or to use that time to study and explain a Google Maps routing (Freeman & Twenge, 2010). After completing their tasks, all were tested. Who then scored higher on a narcissism measure? Those who had spent the time focused on themselves.

Maintaining Balance and Focus

In both Taiwan and the United States, excessive online socializing and gaming have been associated with lower grades (Chen & Fu, 2008; Kaiser Family Foundation, 2010). In one U.S. survey, 47 percent of the heaviest users of the Internet and other media were receiving mostly C grades or lower, as were 23 percent of the lightest users (Kaiser Family Foundation, 2010). Except when sleeping, the heaviest users may be almost constantly connected.

In today's world, each of us is challenged to maintain a healthy balance between our real-world time with family and friends and our online sharing. Experts offer some practical suggestions for balancing online connecting and real-world responsibilities.

- *Monitor your time.* Keep a log of how you use your time. Then ask yourself, "Does my time use reflect my priorities? Am I spending more or less time online than I intended? Is my time online interfering with school or work performance? Have family or friends commented on this?"

- *Monitor your feelings.* Ask yourself, "Am I emotionally distracted by my online interests? When I disconnect and move to another activity, how do I feel?"

- *"Hide" your more distracting online friends.* And in your own postings, practice the golden rule. Before you post, ask yourself, "Is this something I'd care about reading if someone else posted it?"

- *Try turning off your mobile devices or leaving them elsewhere.* Selective attention—the flashlight of your mind—can be in only one place at a time. When we try to do two things at once, we don't do either one of them very well (Willingham, 2010). If you want to study or work productively, resist the temptation to check for messages, posts, or e-mails. Disable sound alerts and pop-ups, which can hijack your attention just when you've managed to get focused. (I am proofing and editing this chapter in a coffee shop, where I escape the distractions of my computer and office phone.)

- *Try a social networking fast* (give it up for an hour, a day, or a week) *or a time-controlled social media diet* (check in only after homework is done, or only during a lunch break). Take notes on what you're losing and gaining on your new "diet."

- *Refocus by taking a nature walk.* People learn better after a peaceful walk in the woods, which—unlike a walk on a busy street—refreshes our capacity for focused attention (Berman et al., 2008).

As psychologist Steven Pinker (2010) said, "The solution is not to bemoan technology but to develop strategies of self-control, as we do with every other temptation in life." ∎

RETRIEVE + REMEMBER

- Social networking tends to _____ (strengthen/weaken) your relationships with people you already know, _____ (increase/decrease) your self-disclosure, and _____ (reveal/hide) your true personality.

ANSWERS: strengthen; increase; reveal

Emotion: Arousal, Behavior, and Cognition

9-7 What are the three parts of an emotion, and what theories help us to understand our emotions?

Motivated behavior is often connected to powerful emotions. My own need to belong was unforgettably challenged one day when I went to a huge store to drop off film and brought along Peter, my toddler first-born child. As I set Peter down on his feet and prepared to complete the paperwork, a passerby warned, "You'd better be careful or you'll lose that boy!" Not more than a few breaths later, after dropping the film in the slot, I turned and found no Peter beside me.

With mild anxiety, I peered around one end of the counter. No Peter in sight. With slightly more anxiety, I peered

Courtesy of David G. Myers

around the other end. No Peter there, either. Now, with my heart pounding, I circled the neighboring counters. Still no Peter anywhere. As anxiety turned to panic, I began racing up and down the store aisles. He was nowhere to be found. Seeing my alarm, the store manager used the public-address system to ask customers to assist in looking for a missing child. Soon after, I passed the customer who had warned me. "I told you that you were going to lose him!" he now scorned. With visions of kidnapping (strangers routinely admired that beautiful child), I braced for the possibility that my neglect had caused me to lose what I loved above all else, and—dread of all dreads—that I might have to return home and face my wife without our only child. Never before or since have I felt such panic.

But then, as I passed the customer service counter yet again, there he was, having been found and returned by some obliging customer! In an instant, the arousal of terror spilled into ecstasy. Clutching my son, with tears suddenly flowing, I found myself unable to speak my thanks and stumbled out of the store awash in grateful joy.

Where do such emotions come from? Why do we have them? What are they made of? Emotions don't exist just to give us interesting experiences. They are our body's adaptive response, supporting our survival. When we face chal-

lenges, emotions focus our attention and energize our action (Cyders & Smith, 2008). Our heart races. Our pace quickens. All our senses go on high alert. Receiving unexpected good news, we may find our eyes tearing up. We raise our hands in triumph. We feel joy and a newfound confidence.

As my panicked search for Peter illustrates, **emotions** are a mix of

- *bodily arousal* (heart pounding).
- *expressive behaviors* (quickened pace).
- *conscious experience* including thoughts *("Is this a kidnapping?")* and feelings (fear, panic, joy).

Psychologists' task is fitting these three pieces together. To do that, we need answers to two big questions:

1. A chicken-and-egg debate: Does your bodily arousal come *before* or *after* your emotional feelings? (Did I first notice my racing heart and faster step, and then feel terror about losing Peter? Or did my sense of fear come first, stirring my heart and legs to respond?)

2. How do *thinking* (cognition) and *feeling* interact? Does cognition always come before emotion? (Did I think about a kidnapping threat before I reacted emotionally?)

Historic theories of emotion, as well as current research, have tried to answer these questions.

Historic Emotion Theories

James-Lange Theory: Arousal Comes Before Emotion

Common sense tells most of us that we cry because we are sad, lash out because we are angry, tremble because we are afraid. First comes conscious awareness, then the feeling. But to pioneering psychologist William James, this commonsense view of emotion had things backward. Rather, "We feel sorry because we cry, angry because we strike, afraid because we tremble" (1890, p. 1066). James'

Reuters/Matt Sullivan

JOY EXPRESSED IS JOY FELT According to the James-Lange theory, we don't just smile because we share our teammates' joy. We also share the joy because we are smiling with them.

idea was also proposed by Danish physiologist Carl Lange, and so is called the **James-Lange theory.** James and Lange might have guessed that I noticed my racing heart and then, shaking with fright, felt the whoosh of emotion—that my feeling of fear *followed* my body's response.

Cannon-Bard Theory: Arousal and Emotion Happen at the Same Time

Physiologist Walter Cannon (1871–1945) disagreed with James and Lange. Does a racing heart signal fear, anger, or love? The body's responses—heart rate, perspiration, and body temperature—are too similar to *cause* the different emotions, said Cannon. He and another physiologist, Philip Bard, concluded that our bodily arousal and emotional experience occur together. So, according to

emotion a response of the whole organism, involving (1) bodily arousal, (2) expressive behaviors, and (3) conscious experience.

James-Lange theory the theory that our experience of emotion is our awareness of our physiological responses to emotion-arousing stimuli.

the **Cannon-Bard theory,** my heart began pounding *as* I experienced fear. The emotion-triggering stimulus traveled to my sympathetic nervous system, causing my body's arousal. *At the same time,* it traveled to my brain's cortex, causing my awareness of my emotion. My pounding heart did not cause my feeling of fear, nor did my feeling of fear cause my pounding heart. Bodily responses and experienced emotions are separate.

The Cannon-Bard theory has been challenged by studies of people with severed spinal cords, including a survey of 25 injured World War II soldiers (Hohmann, 1966). Those with *lower-spine injuries,* who had lost sensation only in their legs, reported little change in their emotions' intensity. Those with *high spinal cord injuries,* who could feel nothing below the neck, did report changes. Some reactions were much less intense than before the injuries. Anger, one man confessed, "just doesn't have the heat to it that it used to. It's a mental kind of anger." Other emotions, those expressed mostly in body areas above the neck, were felt *more* intensely. These men reported increases in weeping, lumps in the throat, and getting choked up when saying good-bye, worshipping, or watching a touching movie. Such evidence has led some researchers to view feelings as "mostly shadows" of our bodily responses and behaviors (Damasio, 2003).

But most researchers now agree that our emotions also involve cognition (Averill, 1993; Barrett, 2006). Whether we fear the man behind us on the dark street depends entirely on whether we interpret his actions as threatening or friendly.

Schachter-Singer Two-Factor Theory: Arousal + Label = Emotion

Stanley Schachter and Jerome Singer (1962) proposed a third theory: Our physical reactions and our thoughts (perceptions, memories, and interpretations) together create emotion. In their **two-factor theory,** emotions therefore have two ingredients: *physical arousal* and *cognitive appraisal.* In their view, an emotional experience requires a conscious interpretation of arousal.

Sometimes our arousal spills over from one event to the next, influencing our response. Imagine arriving home after a fast run and finding a message that you got a longed-for job. With arousal lingering from the run, will you feel more excited than you would be if you hear this news after awakening from a nap?

To explore this *spillover effect,* Schachter and Singer injected college men with *epinephrine,* a hormone that triggers feelings of arousal. Picture yourself as a participant. After receiving the injection, you go to a waiting room. You find yourself with another person (actually an accomplice of the experimenters) who is acting either joyful or irritated. As you observe this person, you begin to feel your heart race, your body flush, and your breathing become more rapid. If you had been told to expect these effects from the injection, what would you feel? The actual volunteers felt little emotion—because they assumed their arousal was caused by the drug. But if you had been told the injection would produce no effects, what would you feel? Perhaps you would react as another group of participants did. They "caught" the apparent emotion of the other person in the waiting room. They became happy if the accomplice was acting joyful, and testy if the accomplice was acting irritated.

We can experience a stirred-up state as one emotion or another, depending on how we interpret and label it. Dozens of experiments have demonstrated this effect (Reisenzein, 1983; Sinclair et al., 1994; Zillmann, 1986). As one happiness researcher noted, "Feelings that one

THE SPILLOVER EFFECT Arousal from a soccer match can fuel anger, which can descend into rioting or other violent confrontations.

© Reuters/Corbis

interprets as fear in the presence of a sheer drop may be interpreted as lust in the presence of a sheer blouse" (Gilbert, 2006).

The point to remember: Arousal fuels emotion; cognition channels it.

Zajonc, LeDoux, and Lazarus: Emotion and the Two-Track Brain

Is the heart always subject to the mind? Must we *always* interpret our arousal before we can experience an emotion? No, said Robert Zajonc [ZI-yence] (1980, 1984a). He argued that we actually have many emotional reactions apart from, or even before, our interpretation of a situation. Can you recall liking something or someone immediately, without knowing why? These reactions often reflect the automatic processing that takes place in our two-track mind.

Our emotional responses are the final step in a process that can follow two different pathways in our brain, both via the thalamus. Some emotions, especially our more complex feelings, like hatred and love, travel a "high road" to the brain's cortex (**FIGURE 9.11a**). There, we analyze and label information before

TABLE 9.1   Summary of Emotion Theories

Theory	Explanation of Emotions	Example
James-Lange	Our awareness of our specific bodily response to emotion-arousing stimuli	We observe our heart racing after a threat and then feel afraid.
Cannon-Bard	Bodily response + simultaneous subjective experience	Our heart races at the same time that we feel afraid.
Schachter-Singer	Two factors: general arousal + a cognitive label	We may label our arousal as fear or excitement, depending on context.
Zajonc; LeDoux	Instant, before cognitive appraisal	We automatically feel startled by a sound in the forest before we label it a threat.
Lazarus	Appraisal ("Is it danger or not?")—sometimes without our awareness—defines emotion	The sound is "just the wind."

we order a response via the amygdala (an emotion-control center).

But sometimes our emotions (especially simple likes, dislikes, and fears) take what Joseph LeDoux (2002) has called the "low road." This neural shortcut bypasses the cortex (Figure 9.11b). Following the low road, a fear-provoking stimulus travels from the eye or the ear directly to the amygdala. This shortcut enables our greased-lightning emotional response ("Life in danger!") before our brain interprets the exact source of danger. Like speedy reflexes that also operate apart from the brain's thinking cortex, the amygdala's reactions are so fast that we may not be aware of what's happened (Dimberg et al., 2000).

The amygdala's structure makes it easier for our feelings to hijack our thinking than for our thinking to rule our feelings (LeDoux & Armony, 1999). It sends more neural projections up to the cortex than it receives back. In the forest, we can jump when we hear rustling in nearby bushes and leave it to our cortex (via the high road) to decide later whether the sound was made by a snake or by the wind. Such experiences support Zajonc's belief that *some* of our emotional reactions involve no deliberate thinking.

Emotion researcher Richard Lazarus (1991, 1998) agreed that our brain processes vast amounts of information without our conscious awareness, and that some emotional responses do not require *conscious* thinking. Much of our emotional life operates via the automatic, speedy low road. But, he asked, how would we *know* what we are reacting to if we did not in some way appraise the situation? The appraisal may be effortless and we may not be conscious of it, but it is still a mental function. To know whether a stimulus is good or bad, the brain must have some idea of what it is (Storbeck et al., 2006). Thus, said Lazarus, emotions arise when we *appraise* an event as harmless or dangerous, whether we truly *know* it is or not. We appraise the sound of the rustling bushes as the presence of a threat. Later, we learn that it was "just the wind."

Let's sum up (see also **TABLE 9.1**). As Zajonc and LeDoux have demonstrated, some emotional responses—especially simple likes, dislikes, and fears—involve no conscious thinking. We may fear a big spider, even if we "know" it is harmless. Such responses are difficult to alter by changing our thinking. We may automatically like one person more than another. This instant appeal can even influence our political decisions if we vote (as many people do) for the candidate we *like*

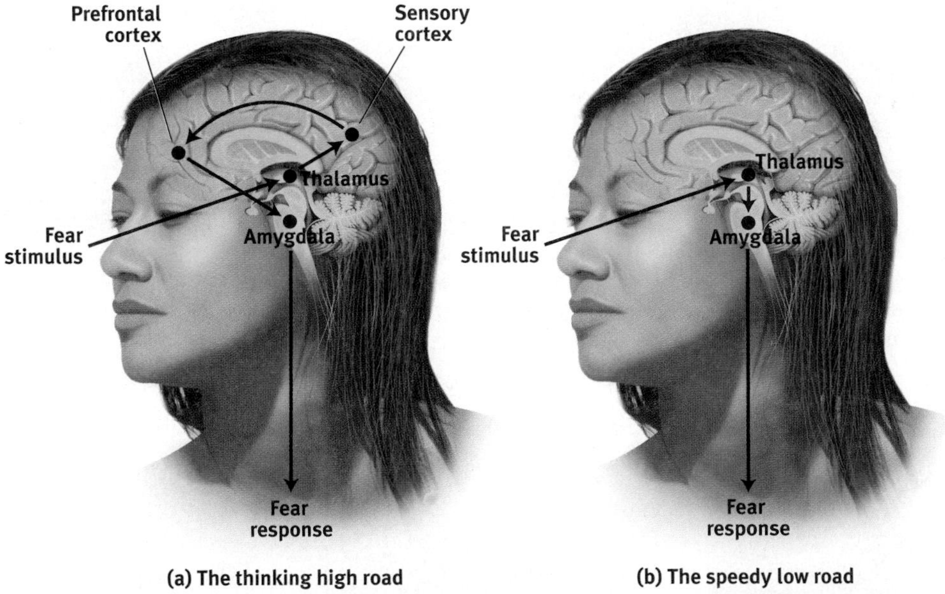

FIGURE 9.11   The brain's pathways for emotions The two-track brain processes sensory input on two different pathways. (a) Some input travels to the cortex (via the thalamus) for analysis and is then sent to the amygdala. (b) Other input travels directly to the amygdala (via the thalamus) for an instant emotional reaction.

(a) The thinking high road

(b) The speedy low road

Cannon-Bard theory the theory that an emotion-arousing stimulus simultaneously triggers (1) physiological responses and (2) the subjective experience of emotion.

two-factor theory Schachter and Singer's theory that to experience emotion we must (1) be physically aroused and (2) cognitively label the arousal.

over the candidate expressing positions closer to our own (Westen, 2007).

But other emotions—including moods such as depression, and complex feelings such as hatred and love—are, as Lazarus, Schachter, and Singer predicted, greatly affected by our interpretations, memories, and expectations. For these emotions, we have more conscious control. As you will see in Chapter 12, learning to *think* more positively about ourselves and the world around us can help us *feel* better. ▪

RETRIEVE + REMEMBER

- According to the Cannon-Bard theory, (a) our *physiological response* to a stimulus (for example, a pounding heart), and (b) the *emotion* we experience (for example, fear) occur _____ (simultaneously/ sequentially). According to the James-Lange theory, (a) and (b) occur _____ (simultaneously/sequentially).

ANSWERS: simultaneously; sequentially (first the physiological response, and then the experienced emotion)

- According to Schachter and Singer, two factors lead to our experience of an emotion: (1) physiological arousal and (2) _____ appraisal.

ANSWER: cognitive

- Emotion researchers have disagreed about whether emotional responses occur in the absence of cognitive processing. How would you characterize the approach of each of the following researchers: Zajonc, LeDoux, Lazarus, Schachter, and Singer?

ANSWER: Zajonc and LeDoux suggested that we experience some emotions without any conscious, cognitive appraisal. Lazarus, Schachter, and Singer emphasized the importance of appraisal and cognitive labeling in our experience of emotion.

Embodied Emotion

◎ Whether you are falling in love or grieving a loved one's death, you need little convincing that emotions involve the body. Feeling without a body

is like breathing without lungs. Some physical responses are easy to notice; others happen without your awareness. Indeed, many take place at the level of your brain's neurons.

The Basic Emotions

9-8 What are some basic emotions?

Carroll Izard (1977) isolated 10 basic emotions: joy, interest-excitement, surprise, sadness, anger, disgust, contempt, fear, shame, and guilt. Most are present in infancy (**FIGURE 9.12**). Although others believe that pride and love are basic emotions (Shaver et al., 1996; Tracey & Robins, 2004), Izard has argued that they are combinations of the basic 10. Other researchers have asked a different question: Do our different emotions have distinct arousal footprints? Before answering that question, let's review what happens in your

autonomic nervous system when your body becomes aroused.

Emotions and the Autonomic Nervous System

9-9 What is the link between emotional arousal and the autonomic nervous system?

As we saw in Chapter 2, in a crisis, the *sympathetic division* of your *autonomic nervous system* (ANS) mobilizes your body for action (**FIGURE 9.13**). It triggers your adrenal glands to release stress hor-

(a) Joy (mouth forming smile, cheeks lifted, twinkle in eye)

Petr Jilek/Shutterstock

FIGURE 9.12 Infants' naturally occurring emotions
To identify the emotions present from birth, Carroll Izard analyzed the facial expressions of infants.

(b) Anger (brows drawn together and downward, eyes fixed, mouth squarish)

Patrick Donehue/Science Source

(c) Interest (brows raised or knitted, mouth softly rounded, lips may be pursed)

© Emma Kim/cultura/Corbis

(d) Disgust (nose wrinkled, upper lip raised, tongue pushed outward)

lina aidukaite/Flickr RF/Getty Images

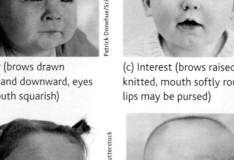
(e) Surprise (brows raised, eyes widened, mouth rounded in oval shape)

Samuel Borges Photography/Shutterstock

(f) Sadness (brows' inner corners raised, mouth corners drawn down)

iStock/Thinkstock

(g) Fear (brows level, drawn in and up, eyelids lifted, mouth corners retracted)

Vladimir Godnik/Getty

Autonomic Nervous System Controls Physiological Arousal

Sympathetic division (arousing)		Parasympathetic division (calming)
Pupils open wider	EYES	Pupils become smaller
Decreases	SALIVATION	Increases
Perspires	SKIN	Dries
Increases	RESPIRATION	Decreases
Speeds up	HEART	Slows
Slows	DIGESTION	Speeds up
Increased stress hormones	ADRENAL GLANDS	Decreased stress hormones
Reduced	IMMUNE SYSTEM FUNCTIONING	Enhanced

FIGURE 9.13 Emotional arousal In a crisis, the ANS' sympathetic division arouses us. When the crisis passes, the parasympathetic division calms us.

mones. To provide energy, your liver pours extra sugar into your bloodstream. To help burn the sugar, your breathing rate increases to supply needed oxygen. Your heart rate and blood pressure increase. Your digestion slows, allowing blood to move away from your internal organs and toward your muscles. With blood sugar driven into the large muscles, running becomes easier. Your pupils open wider, letting in more light. To cool your stirred-up body, you perspire. If you were wounded, your blood would clot more quickly.

After your next crisis, think of this: Without any conscious effort, your body's response to danger is wonderfully coordinated and adaptive—preparing you for *fight or flight*. When the crisis passes, the *parasympathetic division* of your ANS gradually calms your body, as stress hormones slowly leave your bloodstream.

The Physiology of Emotions

9-10 How do our body states relate to specific emotions? How effective are polygraphs in using body states to detect lies?

Imagine another scene. You are conducting an experiment, measuring the body's responses to different emotions. In each of four rooms, you have someone watching a movie. In the first, the person is viewing a horror show. In the second, the viewer watches an anger-provoking film. In the third, someone is watching a sexually arousing film. In the fourth, the person is viewing an utterly boring movie. From the control center, you are tracking each person's physical responses, measuring perspiration, breathing, and heart rate. Do you think you could tell who is frightened? Who is angry? Who is sexually aroused? Who is bored?

With training, you could probably pick out the bored viewer. But spotting the bodily differences among fear, anger, and sexual arousal would be much more difficult (Barrett, 2006). Different emotions do not have sharply different biological signatures.

Despite similar bodily responses, sexual arousal, fear, and anger *feel* different to you and me, and they often *look* different to others. We may appear "para-

"No one ever told me that grief felt so much like fear. I am not afraid, but the sensation is like being afraid. The same fluttering in the stomach, the same restlessness, the yawning. I keep on swallowing."
C. S. Lewis, *A Grief Observed*, 1961

lyzed with fear" or "ready to explode."

With the help of sophisticated laboratory tools, researchers have pinpointed some subtle indicators of different emotions (Lench et al., 2011). The finger temperatures and hormone secretions that accompany fear and rage do sometimes differ (Ax, 1953; Levenson, 1992). Fear and joy stimulate different facial muscles. During fear, your brow muscles tense. During joy, muscles in your cheeks and under your eyes pull into a smile (Witvliet & Vrana, 1995).

Brain scans and EEGs reveal that some emotions also differ in their brain circuits (Panksepp, 2007). When you experience negative emotions such as disgust, your right frontal cortex is more active than your left frontal cortex. People who are prone to depression, or who have generally negative personalities, also show more activity in their right frontal lobe (Harmon-Jones et al., 2002). One not-unhappy wife reported that her husband, who had lost part of his right frontal lobe in brain surgery, became less

EMOTIONAL AROUSAL Intense, happy excitement and panicky fear are accompanied by similar states of bodily arousal. That allows us to flip rapidly between the two emotions.

irritable and more affectionate (Goleman, 1995). My father, after a right-hemisphere stroke at age 92, lived the last two years of his life with happy gratitude and nary a complaint or negative emotion.

When you experience positive moods—when you are enthusiastic, energized, and happy—your left frontal lobe will be more active. Increased left frontal lobe activity is found in people with positive personalities—jolly infants and alert, energetic, and persistently goal-directed adults (Davidson, 2012; Urry et al., 2004). When you're happy and you know it, your brain will surely show it.

To sum up, we can't easily see differences in emotions from tracking heart rate, breathing, and perspiration. But facial expressions and brain activity can vary from one emotion to another. So do we, like Pinocchio, give off telltale signs when we lie? For more on that question, see Thinking Critically About: Lie Detection. ■

THINKING CRITICALLY ABOUT

Lie Detection

Can a *lie detector*—a **polygraph**—reveal lies? Polygraphs don't really detect lies. Instead, they measure emotion-linked changes in breathing, heart rate, and perspiration. Imagine yourself attached to one of these machines, trying to relax. An examiner asks you questions and monitors your responses. She asks, "In the last 20 years, have you ever taken something that didn't belong to you?" This item is a *control question*, aimed at making everyone a little nervous. If you lie and say "*No!*" (as many people do), your nervousness will register as arousal, which the polygraph will detect. This response will give the examiner a baseline, a useful comparison for your responses to *critical questions*. (*"Did you ever steal anything from your previous employer?"*) If your responses to critical questions are weaker than to control questions, the examiner will infer you are telling the truth. The idea is that only a thief becomes nervous when denying a theft.

Critics point out two problems. First, our bodily arousal is much the same from one emotion to another. Our bodies react to anxiety, irritation, and guilt in very similar ways. Second, many innocent people *do* get tense and nervous when accused of a crime or bad act. Many rape victims, for example, have "failed" these tests because they had strong emotional reactions while telling the truth about the rapist (Lykken, 1991). About one-third of the time, polygraph test results are just wrong (FIGURE 9.14).

A 2002 U.S. National Academy of Sciences report noted that "no spy has ever been caught [by] using the polygraph." It is not for lack of trying. The CIA is one of several U.S. agencies that together have spent millions of dollars testing tens of thousands of employees. Did the test catch Aldrich Ames, a Russian spy within the CIA who enjoyed a very lavish lifestyle? Ames took many "polygraph tests and passed them all," noted physicist Robert Park (1999). "Nobody thought to investigate the source of his sudden wealth—after all, he was passing the lie detector tests."

A more effective approach to lie detection uses a *guilty knowledge test*, with questions focused on specific crime-scene details known only

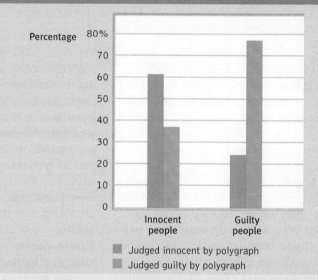

FIGURE 9.14 How often do lie detectors lie? In one study, polygraph experts interpreted the test results of 100 people who had been suspects in theft crimes (Kleinmuntz & Szucko, 1984). Half the suspects were guilty and had confessed. The other half had been proven innocent. If the polygraph experts had been the judges, more than one-third of the innocent would have been declared guilty, and one-fourth of the guilty would have been declared innocent.

to the police and the guilty person (Ben-Shakhar & Elaad, 2003). If a camera and computer had been stolen, for example, only a guilty person should react strongly to the brand names of the stolen items. Given enough such specific probes, an innocent person will seldom be wrongly accused.

polygraph a machine, commonly used in attempts to detect lies, that measures some bodily responses (such as changes in perspiration, heart rate, and breathing) accompanying emotion.

Expressed and Experienced Emotion

There is a simple method of detecting people's emotions: Read their body language, listen to their voice tones, and study their faces. People's expressive behavior reveals their emotion. Does this nonverbal language vary with culture, or is it the same everywhere? And do our expressions influence what we feel?

Detecting Emotion in Others

9-11 How do we communicate nonverbally? How do women and men differ in these abilities?

All of us communicate without words. Westerners "read" a firm handshake as evidence of an outgoing, expressive personality (Chaplin et al., 2000). A glance or a stare can communicate intimacy, submission, or dominance (Kleinke, 1986). When two people are passionately in love, they typically spend time—quite a bit of time—gazing into each other's eyes (Rubin, 1970). Would such gazes stir these feelings between strangers? To find out, researchers asked male-female pairs of strangers to gaze intently for 2 minutes either at each other's hands or into each other's eyes. After separating, the eye gazers reported feeling a tingle of attraction and affection (Kellerman et al., 1989).

Most of us read nonverbal cues fairly well. Shown 10 seconds of video from the end of a speed-dating interaction, people can often detect whether one person is attracted to the other (Place et al., 2009). We are especially good at detecting nonverbal threats. A single angry face will "pop out" of a crowd faster than a single happy one (Fox et al., 2000; Hansen & Hansen, 1988; Öhman et al., 2001). Even when hearing another language, most people can easily detect anger (Scherer et al., 2001).

OBVIOUS EMOTIONS Graphic novel authors use facial expressions and other design elements to express emotion, reducing the need to explain how the characters are feeling.

Despite our brain's emotion-detecting skill, we find it difficult to detect deceiving expressions (Porter & ten Brinke, 2008). When researchers summarized 206 studies of sorting truth from lies, people were just 54 percent accurate—barely better than a coin toss (Bond & DePaulo, 2006). Are experts more skilled at spotting lies? No. With the possible exception of police professionals in high-stakes situations, even they don't beat chance by much (Bond & DePaulo, 2008; O'Sullivan et al., 2009). The behavioral differences between liars and truth tellers are too slight for most of us to detect (Hartwig & Bond, 2011).

Some of us are, however, more skilled than others at reading emotions. In one study, hundreds of people were asked to name the emotion displayed in brief film clips. The clips showed portions of a person's emotionally expressive face or body, sometimes accompanied by a garbled voice (Rosenthal et al., 1979). For example,

one 2-second scene revealed only the face of an upset woman. After watching the scene, viewers would state whether the woman was criticizing someone for being late or was talking about her divorce. Given such "thin slices," women have generally been the better emotion detectors (Hall, 1984, 1987). Women have also surpassed men in other assessments of emotional cues, such as deciding whether a male-female couple is a genuine romantic couple or a posed phony couple (Barnes & Sternberg, 1989).

Women's skill at decoding emotions may help explain why women tend to respond with greater emotion (Vigil, 2009). In studies of 23,000 people from 26 cultures, women more than men have reported themselves open to feelings (Costa et al., 2001). That helps explain the extremely strong perception (nearly all 18- to 29-year-old Americans in one survey) that emotionality is "more true of women" (Newport, 2001).

One exception: Quickly—imagine an angry face. What gender is the person? If you're like 3 in 4 Arizona State University students in the original study, you imagined a male (Becker et al., 2007). The researchers also found that when a gender-neutral face was made to look angry, most people perceived it as male. If the face was smiling, they were more likely to perceive it as female (FIGURE 9.15). Anger strikes most people as a more masculine emotion.

FIGURE 9.15 Male or female? Researchers manipulated a gender-neutral face. People were more likely to see it as a male when it wore an angry expression, and as a female when it wore a smile (Becker et al., 2007).

Are there gender differences in empathy? If you have *empathy*, you identify with others and imagine what it must be like to walk in their shoes. You rejoice with those who rejoice and weep with those who weep. In surveys, women are far more likely than men to describe themselves as empathic. Actually, measures of body responses, such as one's heart rate while seeing another's distress, reveal a much smaller gender gap (Eisenberg & Lennon, 1983; Rueckert et al., 2010).

Nevertheless, females are somewhat more likely to *express* empathy—to cry and to report distress when observing someone in distress. As **FIGURE 9.16** shows, this gender difference was clear in videotapes of men and women watching film clips that were sad (children with a dying parent), happy (slapstick comedy), or frightening (a man nearly falling off the ledge of a tall building) (Kring & Gordon, 1998; Vigil, 2009). Women also more deeply experience emotional events, such as viewing mutilation pictures. (Brain scans show more activity in areas sensitive to emotion.) Women also tend to remem-

ber the scenes better three weeks later (Canli et al., 2002). ■

Culture and Emotional Expression

9-12 How are nonverbal expressions of emotion understood within and across cultures?

The meaning of *gestures* varies from culture to culture. U.S. President Richard Nixon learned this while traveling in Brazil. He made the North American "A-OK" sign before a welcoming crowd, not knowing it was a crude insult in that country. In 1968, North Korea publicized photos of supposedly happy officers from a captured U.S. Navy spy ship. In the photo, three men had raised their middle fingers, telling their captors—

who didn't recognize the cultural gesture—it was a "Hawaiian good luck sign" (Fleming & Scott, 1991).

Do *facial expressions* also have different meanings in different cultures? To find out, researchers showed photographs of some facial expressions to people in different parts of the world and asked them to guess the emotion (Ekman et al., 1975, 1987, 1994; Izard, 1977, 1994). You can try this matching task yourself by pairing the six emotions with the six faces of **FIGURE 9.17**.

Regardless of your cultural background, you probably did pretty well. A smile's a smile the world around. Ditto for anger, and to a lesser extent the other basic expressions (Elfenbein & Ambady, 1999). (There is no culture where people frown when they are happy.) We do slightly better when judging emotional displays from our own culture (Elfenbein & Ambady, 2002, 2003a,b). Nevertheless, the

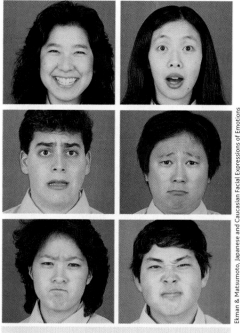

FIGURE 9.17 Culture-specific or culturally universal expressions? As people of differing cultures, do our faces speak the same language or different languages? Which face expresses disgust? Anger? Fear? Happiness? Sadness? Surprise? (From Matsumoto & Ekman, 1989.)

Answers, from left to right, top to bottom: happiness, surprise, fear, sadness, anger, disgust.

Ekman & Matsumoto, Japanese and Caucasian Facial Expressions of Emotions

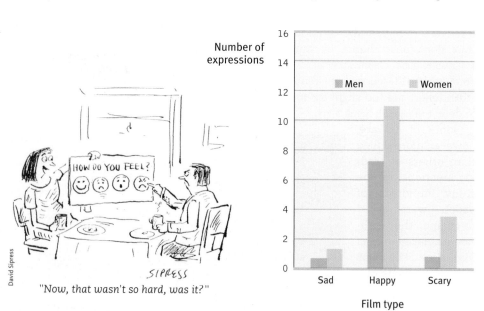

David Sipress

"Now, that wasn't so hard, was it?"

FIGURE 9.16 Gender and expressiveness Male and female film viewers did not differ dramatically in self-reported emotions or physiological responses. But the women's faces *showed* much more emotion. (From Kring & Gordon, 1998.)

UNIVERSAL EMOTIONS No matter where on Earth you live, you have no trouble knowing which photo depicts Michael Owen and his fans feeling distraught (after missing a goal) and triumphant (after scoring it).

outward signs of emotion are generally the same across cultures.

Musical expressions of emotions also cross cultures. Happy and sad music feels happy and sad around the world. Whether you live in an African village or a European city, fast-paced music seems happy, and slow-paced music seems sadder (Fritz et al., 2009).

Do these shared emotional categories reflect shared *cultural* experiences, such as movies and TV programs that are seen around the world? Apparently not. Paul Ekman and his team asked isolated people in New Guinea to respond to such statements as, "Pretend your child has died." When North American collegians viewed the taped responses, they easily read the New Guineans' facial reactions.

So we can say that facial muscles speak a fairly universal language. This discovery would not have surprised Charles Darwin (1809–1882). In *The Expression of the Emotions in Man and Animals* (1872), Darwin argued that in prehistoric times, before our ancestors

"For news of the heart, ask the face."

Guinean proverb

communicated in words, they communicated threats, greetings, and submission with facial expressions. Such expressions helped them survive and became part of our shared heritage (Hess & Thibault, 2009). A sneer, for example, retains elements of an animal's baring its teeth in a snarl. Emotional expressions may enhance our survival in other ways, too. Surprise raises our eyebrows and widens our eyes, helping us take in more information. Disgust wrinkles our nose, closing out foul odors.

Smiles are social as well as emotional events. Bowlers seldom smile when they score a strike. They smile when they turn to face their companions (Jones et al., 1991; Kraut & Johnston, 1979). Olympic gold medalists typically don't smile when they are awaiting their ceremony. But they wear broad grins when interacting with officials and facing the crowd and cameras (Fernández-Dols & Ruiz-Belda, 1995). Even natively blind athletes, who have never observed smiles, display the same social smiles in such situations (Matsumoto & Willingham, 2006, 2009).

Although we humans share a universal facial language, it has been adaptive for us to interpret faces in particular contexts (**FIGURE 9.18**, next page). People judge an angry face set in a frightening situation as afraid, and a fearful face set in a painful situation as pained (Carroll & Russell, 1996). Movie directors harness this tendency by creating contexts and soundtracks that amplify our perceptions of particular emotions. ■

The Effects of Facial Expressions

9-13 How do facial expressions influence our feelings?

As famed psychologist William James (1890) struggled with feelings of depression and grief, he came to believe that we can control our emotions by going

FIGURE 9.18 We read faces in context Tears on a face (above left) make its expression seem sadder (Provine et al., 2009, 2011).

Whether we perceive the man's face on the far right as disgusted or angry depends on which body his face appears on (Aviezer et al., 2008).

R. R. Provine. Emotional tears and NGF: A biographical appreciation and research beginning. Archives Italiennes de Biologie, 149, 271–276.

"Angry, Disgusted, or Afraid? Studies on the Malleability of Emotion Perception," Hillel Aviezer, Ran R. Hassin, Jennifer Ryan, Cheryl Grady, Josh Susskind, Adam Anderson, Morris Moscovitch, Shlomo Bentin

"through the outward movements" of any emotion we want to experience. "To feel cheerful," he advised, "sit up cheerfully, look around cheerfully, and act as if cheerfulness were already there."

Was James right? Can our outward expressions and movements trigger our inner feelings and emotions? You can test his idea: Fake a big grin. Now scowl. Can you feel the "smile therapy" difference? Participants in dozens of experiments have felt a difference. For example, researchers tricked students into making a frowning expression by asking them to "contract these muscles" and "pull your brows together" (Laird et al., 1974, 1984, 1989). (The students thought they were helping the researchers attach facial electrodes.) The result? The students reported feeling a little angry. So, too, for other basic emotions. For example, people reported feeling more fear than anger, disgust, or sadness when made to construct a fearful expression (Duclos et al., 1989). (They were told, "Raise your eyebrows. And open your eyes wide. Move your whole head back, so that your chin is tucked in a little bit, and let your mouth relax and hang open a little.") This **facial feedback effect** has been repeated many times, in many places, for many basic emotions (**FIGURE 9.19**). Just activating one of the smiling muscles by holding a pen in the teeth (rather than with the lips, which activates a frowning muscle) is enough to make cartoons seem more amusing (Strack et al., 1988).

So, your face is more than a billboard that displays your feelings; it also feeds your feelings. No wonder depressed patients reportedly feel better after between-the-eyebrows Botox injections that freeze their frown muscles (Wollmer et al., 2012). Botox paralysis of the frowning muscles also slows people's reading of sadness- or anger-related sentences, and it slows activity in emotion-related brain circuits (Havas et al., 2010; Hennenlotter et al., 2008). In such ways, Botox smooths life's emotional wrinkles.

Other studies have noted a similar *behavior feedback effect* (Flack, 2006; Snodgrass et al., 1986). Try it. Walk for a few minutes with short, shuffling steps, keeping your eyes downcast. Now walk around taking long strides, with your arms swinging and your eyes looking straight ahead. Can you feel your mood shift? Going through the motions awakens the emotions.

You can use your understanding of feedback effects to become more empathic—to feel what others feel. See what happens if you let your own face mimic another person's expression. Acting as another acts helps us feel what another feels (Vaughn & Lanzetta, 1981). Indeed, natural mimicry of others' emotions helps explain why emotions are contagious (Dimberg et al., 2000; Neumann & Strack, 2000).

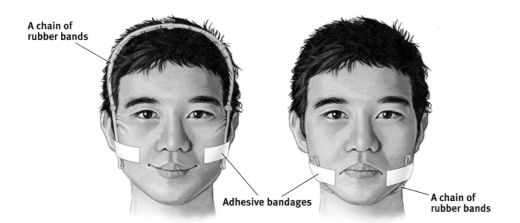

A chain of rubber bands

Adhesive bandages

A chain of rubber bands

FIGURE 9.19 How to make people smile without telling them to smile Do as Kazuo Mori and Hideko Mori (2009) did with students in Japan: Attach rubber bands to the sides of the face with adhesive bandages, and then run them either over the head or under the chin.

RETRIEVE + REMEMBER

- (1) Based on the *facial feedback effect,* how might students in this experiment report feeling when the rubber bands raise their cheeks as though in a smile? (2) How might they report feeling when the rubber bands pull their cheeks downward?

ANSWERS: (1) Most report feeling more happy than sad when their cheeks are raised upward. (2) Most report feeling more sad than happy when their cheeks are pulled downward.

* * *

We have seen how our motivated behaviors, triggered by the forces of nature and nurture, often go hand in hand with emotional responses. Our psychological emotions likewise come equipped with physical reactions. Nervous about an upcoming date, we feel stomach butterflies. Anxious over public speaking, we head for the bathroom. Smoldering over a family conflict, we get a splitting headache. Negative emotions and the prolonged high arousal that may accompany them can tax the body and harm our health. You'll hear more about this in Chapter 10. In that chapter, we'll also take a closer look at the emotion of happiness. ■

facial feedback effect the tendency of facial muscle states to trigger corresponding feelings such as fear, anger, or happiness.

CHAPTER REVIEW

Motivation and Emotion

Test yourself by taking a moment to answer each of these Learning Objective Questions (repeated here from within the chapter). Then turn to Appendix D, Complete Chapter Reviews, to check your answers. Research suggests that trying to answer these questions on your own will improve your long-term memory of the concepts (McDaniel et al., 2009).

Motivational Concepts

9-1: What is motivation, and what are three key perspectives that help us understand motivated behaviors?

Hunger

9-2: What physiological factors cause us to feel hungry?

9-3: How do psychological, biological, cultural, and situational factors affect our taste preferences and eating habits?

9-4: What factors predispose some people to become and remain obese?

The Need to Belong

9-5: What evidence points to our human need to belong?

9-6: How does social networking influence us?

Emotion: Arousal, Behavior, and Cognition

9-7: What are the three parts of an emotion, and what theories help us to understand our emotions?

Embodied Emotion

9-8: What are some basic emotions?

9-9: What is the link between emotional arousal and the autonomic nervous system?

9-10: How do our body states relate to specific emotions? How effective are polygraphs in using body states to detect lies?

Expressed and Experienced Emotion

9-11: How do we communicate nonverbally? How do women and men differ in these abilities?

9-12: How are nonverbal expressions of emotion understood within and across cultures?

9-13: How do facial expressions influence our feelings?

TERMS AND CONCEPTS TO REMEMBER

Test yourself on these terms by trying to write down the definition in your own words before flipping back to the referenced page to check your answer.

motivation, p. 256
drive-reduction theory, p. 256

physiological need, p. 256
homeostasis, p. 256

incentive, p. 257
hierarchy of needs, p. 257
glucose, p. 258
set point, p. 259
basal metabolic rate, p. 259
emotion, p. 269

James-Lange theory, p. 269
Cannon-Bard theory, p. 270
two-factor theory, p. 270
polygraph, p. 274
facial feedback effect, p. 278

CHAPTER TEST

Test yourself repeatedly throughout your studies. This will not only help you figure out what you know and don't know; the testing itself will help you learn and remember the information more effectively thanks to the *testing effect*.

1. An example of a physiological need is _____. An example of a psychological drive is _____.

   a. hunger; a "push" to find food

   b. a "push" to find food; hunger

   c. curiosity; a "push" to reduce arousal

   d. a "push" to reduce arousal; curiosity

2. Jan walks into a friend's kitchen, smells bread baking, and begins to feel very hungry. The smell of baking bread is a(n) _____ (incentive/drive).

3. _____ theory attempts to explain behaviors that do NOT reduce physiological needs.

4. With a challenging task, such as taking a difficult exam, performance is likely to peak when arousal is

   a. very high.

   b. moderate.

   c. very low.

   d. absent.

5. According to Maslow's hierarchy of needs, our most basic needs are physiological, including the need for food and water; just above these are _____ needs.

   a. safety

   b. self-esteem

   c. belongingness

   d. self-transcendence

6. Journalist Dorothy Dix (1861–1951) once remarked, "Nobody wants to kiss when they are hungry." Which motivation theory best supports her statement?

7. According to the concept of set point, our body maintains itself at a particular weight level. This "weight thermostat" is an example of _____.

8. Which of the following is a genetically predisposed response to food?

   a. An aversion to eating cats and dogs

   b. An interest in novel foods

   c. A preference for sweet and salty foods

   d. An aversion to carbohydrates

9. The blood sugar _____ provides the body with energy. When it is _____ (low/high), we feel hungry.

10. The rate at which your body expends energy while at rest is referred to as the _____ _____ rate.

11. Obese people find it very difficult to lose weight permanently. This is due to several factors, including the fact that

    a. it takes less energy to maintain weight than it did to gain it.

    b. the set point of obese people is lower than average.

    c. with dieting, metabolism increases.

    d. there is a genetic influence on body weight.

12. Sanjay recently adopted the typical college diet high in fat and sugar. He knows he may gain weight, but he figures it's no big deal because he can lose the extra pounds in the future. How would you evaluate Sanjay's plan?

13. Which of the following is NOT part of the evidence presented to support the view that humans are strongly motivated by a need to belong?

    a. Students who rated themselves as "very happy" also tended to have satisfying close relationships.

    b. Social exclusion—such as exile or solitary confinement—is considered a severe form of punishment.

    c. As adults, adopted children tend to resemble their biological parents and to yearn for an affiliation with them.

    d. Children who are extremely neglected become withdrawn, frightened, and speechless.

14. What are some ways to manage our social networking time successfully?

15. The _____-_____ theory of emotion maintains that a physiological response happens BEFORE we know what we are feeling.

16. Assume that after spending an hour on a treadmill, you receive a letter saying that your scholarship request has been approved. The two-factor theory of emotion would predict that your physical arousal will

    a. weaken your happiness.

    b. intensify your happiness.

    c. transform your happiness into relief.

    d. have no particular effect on your happiness.

17. Zajonc and LeDoux maintain that some emotional reactions occur before we have had the chance to label or interpret them. Lazarus disagreed. These psychologists differ about whether emotional responses occur in the absence of

    a. physical arousal.

    b. the hormone epinephrine.

    c. cognitive processing.

    d. learning.

18. What does a polygraph measure and why are its results questionable?

19. When people are induced to assume fearful expressions, they often report feeling a little fear. This result is known as the _____ _____ effect.

Find answers to these questions in Appendix E, in the back of the book.

IN YOUR EVERYDAY LIFE

Answering these questions will help you make these concepts more personally meaningful, and therefore more memorable.

1. How often do you satisfy what Maslow called "self-actualization" needs? What about "self-transcendence" needs?

2. Does boredom ever motivate you to do things just to figure out something new? When was the last time that happened, and what did you find?

3. Do you usually eat only when your body sends hunger signals? How much does the sight or smell of delicious food tempt you even when you're full?

4. Have you or a loved one ever tried unsuccessfully to lose weight? What happened? What weight-loss strategies might have been more successful?

5. Do you think that texting, e-mailing, or posting online increases your sense of belonging or leaves you feeling more isolated?

6. Can you remember a time when you began to feel upset or uneasy and only later labeled those feelings? What was that like?

7. Can you think of a recent time when you noticed your body's reactions to a stressful experience? How did you interpret the situation? What emotion did you feel?

8. Imagine one situation in which you would like to change the way you feel. How could you do so by altering your facial expressions or the way you carry yourself?

experience more of the testing effect

Multiple-format self-tests and more may be found at www.worthpublishers.com/myers.

10 Stress, Health, and Human Flourishing

A note to our readers: I am delighted to welcome Nathan DeWall as co-author for this edition of Psychology in Everyday Life. *He led our shared revision work for this chapter and Chapters 4, 11, and 14.*

For many students, the transition to college (or back to college) has not been easy. College is a happy time, but it presents challenges. Debt piles up. Deadlines loom. New relationships form, and sometimes fail. Family demands continue. Big exams or class presentations make you tense. Stuck in traffic, late to class or work, your mood may turn sour. It's enough to give you a headache or disrupt your sleep. No wonder 85 percent of college students have reported occasional or frequent stress during the past three months (AP, 2009).

Stress often strikes without warning. Imagine being 21-year-old Ben Carpenter on the world's wildest and fastest wheelchair ride. As he crossed an intersection on a sunny summer afternoon in 2007, the light changed. A large truck, whose driver didn't see him, started moving into the intersection. As they bumped, Ben's wheelchair turned to face forward, and its handles got stuck in the truck's grille. Off they went, the driver unable to hear Ben's cries for help.

As they sped down the highway about an hour from my [DM] home, passing motorists caught the bizarre sight of a truck pushing a wheelchair at 50 miles per hour and started calling 911. (The first caller: "You are not going to believe this. There is a semi truck pushing a guy in a wheelchair on Red Arrow highway!") Lucky for Ben, one passerby was an undercover police officer. Pulling a quick U-turn, he followed the truck to its destination a couple of miles from where the wild ride had started, and informed the disbelieving driver that he had a passenger hooked in his grille. "It was very scary," said Ben, who has muscular dystrophy.

In this chapter we explore stress—what it is, how it affects us, and how we can reduce it. Then we'll take a close look at happiness—an important measure of whether we are flourishing. Let's begin with some basic terms.

Stress: Some Basic Concepts

10-1 How does our appraisal of an event affect our stress reaction, and what are the three main types of stressors?

Stress is a slippery concept. In everyday life, we may use the word to describe threats or challenges ("Ben was under under a lot of stress") or to describe our responses to those events ("Ben experienced acute stress"). Psychologists use more precise terms. The challenge or event (Ben's dangerous truck ride) is a *stressor*. Ben's physical and emotional responses are a *stress reaction*. And the process by which he interpreted the threat is *stress*.

Thus, **stress** is the process of appraising an event as threatening or challenging, and responding to it (Lazarus, 1998). If you have prepared for an important math test, you may welcome it as a challenge. You will be aroused and focused, and you will probably do well (**FIGURE 10.1**). Championship athletes, successful entertainers, and great teachers and leaders all thrive and excel when aroused by a challenge (Blascovich & Mendes, 2010).

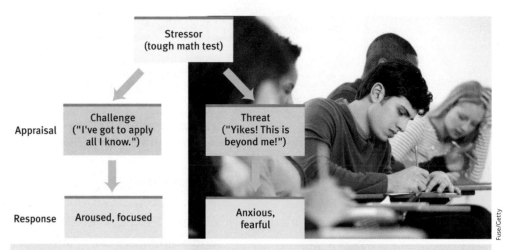

FIGURE 10.1 Stress appraisal The events of our lives flow through a psychological filter. How we appraise an event influences how much stress we experience and how effectively we respond.

Stressors that we appraise as threats, not challenges, can instead lead to strong *negative* reactions. If prevented from preparing for your math test, you will appraise the disruption as a threat, and your response will be distress.

Extreme or prolonged stress can harm us. Demanding jobs that mentally exhaust workers also damage their physical health (Huang et al., 2010). Pregnant women with overactive stress systems tend to have shorter pregnancies, which pose health risks for their infants (Entringer et al., 2011).

So there is an interplay between our head and our health. Before we explore that interplay, let's take a closer look at types of stressors and stress reactions.

Stressors—Things That Push Our Buttons

Stressors fall into three main types: catastrophes, significant life changes, and daily hassles. All can be toxic—they can increase our risk of disease and death.

Catastrophes

Catastrophes are unpredictable large-scale events, such as earthquakes, floods, wildfires, and storms. Even though we often give aid and comfort to one another after such events, the damage to emotional and physical health is significant.

In surveys taken in the three weeks after the 9/11 terrorist attacks, for example, 58 percent of Americans said they were experiencing greater than average arousal and anxiety (Silver et al., 2002). In the four months after Hurricane Katrina, New Orleans reportedly experienced a tripled suicide rate (Saulny, 2006).

Significant Life Changes

During catastrophes, misery often has company. But during significant life changes, we may experience stress alone. Even a happy life change, such as marrying the love of your life, can be a stressor. So can other personal events—leaving home, becoming divorced, having a loved one die. These life changes often happen during young adulthood. The stress of those years was clear in a recent survey that asked, "Are you trying to take on too many things at once?" Who reported the highest stress levels? Women and younger adults (APA, 2009). About half of people in their twenties, but only one-fifth of those over 65, reported experiencing stress during "a lot of the day yesterday" (Newport & Pelham, 2009).

How does stress related to life changes affect our health? Long-term studies indicate that people recently widowed, fired, or divorced are more disease-prone (Dohrenwend et al., 1982; Strully, 2009). In one study of 96,000 wid-

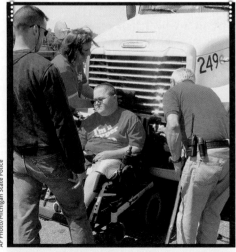

EXTREME STRESS Ben Carpenter experienced the wildest of rides after his wheelchair got stuck in a truck's grille.

owed people, their risk of death doubled in the week following their partner's death (Kaprio et al., 1987). Experiencing a cluster of crises (perhaps losing a job and an important relationship while falling behind in schoolwork) puts one even more at risk.

Daily Hassles

Events don't have to remake our lives to cause stress. Stress also comes from *daily hassles*—spotty cell-phone connections, irritating housemates, long lines at the store, too many things to do, e-mail and text spam, and loud cell-phone talkers (Lazarus, 1990; Pascoe & Richman, 2009; Ruffin, 1993). Some people simply shrug off such hassles. Others find them hard to ignore. This is especially the case for the many Americans who wake up each day facing budgets that won't stretch to the next payday, housing problems, solo parenting, poor health, perceived discrimination, and unreachable goals. Such stressors can take a toll on physical and mental well-being.

> "It's not the large things that send a man to the madhouse . . . no, it's the continuing series of small tragedies . . . not the death of his love but the shoelace that snaps with no time left."
>
> American author Charles Bukowski (1920–1994)

TOXIC STRESS On the day of its 1994 earthquake, Los Angeles experienced a fivefold increase in sudden-death heart attacks. Most occurred in the first two hours after the quake and near its center and were unrelated to physical exertion (Muller & Verrier, 1996). The 2010 Haiti earthquake surely also triggered stress-related ills.

AFP/Getty Images

Stress Reactions—From Alarm to Exhaustion

10-2 How does the body respond to stress?

Our response to stress is part of a unified mind-body system. Walter Cannon (1929) first realized this in the 1920s. He found that extreme cold, lack of oxygen, and emotion-arousing events all trigger an outpouring of stress hormones from the adrenal glands. When your brain sounds an alarm, your *sympathetic nervous system* (Chapter 2) responds. It increases your heart rate and respiration, diverts blood from your digestive organs to your skeletal muscles, dulls your feeling of pain, and releases sugar and fat from your body's stores. All this prepares your body for the wonderfully adaptive **fight-or-flight response** (see Figure 9.13 in Chapter 9).

Hans Selye (1936, 1976) extended Cannon's findings. His studies of animals' reactions to various stressors, such as electric shock and surgery, helped make stress a major concept in both psychology and medicine. Selye discovered that the body's adaptive response to stress was so general that it was like a single burglar alarm that sounds, no matter what intrudes. He named this response the **general adaptation syndrome (GAS),** and he saw it as a three-stage process (**FIGURE 10.2** on the next page). Here's how those stages, or phases, might look if you suffered a physical or emotional trauma:

- In Phase 1, you have an *alarm reaction,* as your sympathetic nervous system suddenly activates. Your heart rate soars. Blood races to your skeletal muscles. You feel the faintness of shock.

- During Phase 2, *resistance,* your temperature, blood pressure, and respiration remain high. With your resources mobilized, you are ready to fight back. Your adrenal glands pump stress hormones into your bloodstream. You are fully engaged, summoning all your resources to meet the challenge.

- In Phase 3, constant stress causes *exhaustion.* As time passes, with no relief from stress, your reserves begin to run out. Your body copes well with temporary stress, but prolonged stress can damage it. You become more vulnerable to illness or even, in extreme cases, collapse and death. Rats show similar patterns. The most fearful and easily stressed rats die about 15 percent sooner than their more confident counterparts (Cavigelli & McClintock, 2003).

There are other options for dealing with stress. One is a common response to a loved one's death: Withdraw. Pull back. Conserve energy. Faced with an extreme disaster, such as a car sinking in a body of water, some people become paralyzed by fear. They stay strapped in their seatbelt instead of paddling to safety. Another option for dealing with stress is to seek and give support. Perhaps you have participated in this

> **stress** the process by which we perceive and respond to certain events, called *stressors,* that we appraise as threatening or challenging.
>
> **fight-or-flight response** an emergency response, including activity of the sympathetic nervous system, that mobilizes energy and activity for attacking or escaping a threat.
>
> **general adaptation syndrome (GAS)** Selye's concept of the body's adaptive response to stress in three stages—alarm, resistance, exhaustion.

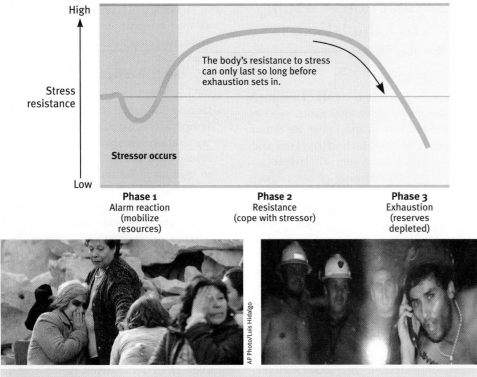

The body's resistance to stress can only last so long before exhaustion sets in.

High

Stress resistance

Stressor occurs

Low

Phase 1
Alarm reaction
(mobilize
resources)

Phase 2
Resistance
(cope with stressor)

Phase 3
Exhaustion
(reserves
depleted)

AP Photo/Luis Hidalgo

AP Photo/Chile's Presidency

FIGURE 10.2 Selye's general adaptation syndrome When a gold and copper mine in Chile collapsed in 2010, family and friends rushed to the scene, fearing the worst. Many of those holding vigil outside the mine were nearly exhausted with the stress of waiting and worrying. Then—good news! After waiting and worrying for 18 days, they heard that all 33 men inside the mine were alive and well.

Krista Kennell/AFP/Getty Images

TENDING TO TRAUMA Arizona's 2013 wildfires claimed the lives of 19 elite firefighters. Juliann Ashcroft's (left) husband, Andrew, was among those lost. Women suffering such tragedies often show a tend-and-befriend coping response by joining together and nurturing each other.

tend-and-befriend response by contributing help after some natural disaster.

The tend-and-befriend response is found especially among women (Taylor et al., 2000, 2006). Facing stress, men more often than women tend to socially withdraw, turn to alcohol, or become aggressive. Women more often respond to stress by nurturing and banding together, which may be due to *oxytocin*. This stress-moderating hormone is associated with pair-bonding in animals and is released by cuddling, massage, and breast feeding in humans (Taylor, 2006). Women in distressed relationships have higher levels of oxytocin, which may help them seek out and receive support from others (Taylor et al., 2010).

It often pays to spend our physical and mental resources in fighting or fleeing an external threat. But we do so at a cost. When our stress is momentary, the

cost is small. When stress persists, we may pay a much higher price, with lowered resistance to infections and other threats to mental and physical health. ■

Stress Effects and Health

10-3 How does stress influence our immune system?

How do you try to stay healthy? Avoid sneezers? Get extra rest? Wash your hands? You should add stress management to that list. Why? Because, as we have seen throughout this text, everything psychological is also biological. Stress is no exception. Stress contributes to high blood pressure and headaches. Stress also leaves us less able to fight off disease. To manage stress, we need to understand these connections.

The field of **psychoneuroimmunology** studies our mind-body interactions (Kiecolt-Glaser, 2009). That mouthful of a word makes sense when said slowly. Your emotions (*psycho*) affect your brain (*neuro*), which controls the stress hormones that influence your disease-fighting *immune* system. And this field is the study of (*ology*) those interactions. Let's start by focusing on the immune system.

Your immune system resembles a complex security system. When it functions properly, it keeps you healthy by capturing and destroying bacteria, viruses, and other invaders. Four types of cells carry out these search-and-destroy missions (FIGURE 10.3). Two are types of white blood cells, called **lymphocytes.** B lymphocytes release antibodies that fight bacterial infections. T lymphocytes attack cancer cells, viruses, and foreign substances—even "good" ones, such as transplanted organs. The third cell type is the *macrophage* ("big eater"), which identifies, traps, and destroys harmful invaders and worn-out cells. And, finally, the *natural killer cells* (NK cells) attack diseased cells (such as those infected by viruses or cancer).

Your age, nutrition, genetics, body temperature, and stress all influence your immune system's activity. When your immune system doesn't function properly, it can err in two directions:

1. Responding too strongly, it may attack the body's own tissues, causing some forms of arthritis or an allergic reaction. Women have stronger immune systems, making them less likely than men to get infections. But this very strength also puts women at higher risk for self-attacking diseases, such as lupus and multiple sclerosis (Nussinovitch & Schoenfeld, 2012; Schwartzman-Morris & Putterman, 2012).

2. Underreacting, the immune system may allow a bacterial infection to flare, a dormant herpes virus to erupt, or cancer cells to multiply. Surgeons may deliberately suppress the pa-tient's immune system to protect transplanted organs (viewed as foreign invaders).

A flood of stress hormones can also suppress the immune system. In laboratories, immune suppression appears when animals are stressed by physical restraints, unavoidable electric shocks, noise, crowding, cold water, social defeat, or separation from their mothers (Maier et al., 1994). In one such study, monkeys were housed with new roommates—three or four new monkeys— each month for six months (Cohen et al., 1992). If you know the stress of adjusting to even one new roommate, you can imagine how trying it would be to repeat this experience monthly. By the experiment's end, the socially stressed monkeys' immune systems were weaker than those of other monkeys left in stable groups.

Human immune systems react similarly. Two examples:

- *Surgical wounds heal more slowly in stressed people.* In one experiment, two groups of dental students received punch wounds (small holes punched in the skin). Punch-wound healing was 40 percent slower in the group wounded three days before a major exam than in the group wounded during summer vacation (Kiecolt-Glaser et al., 1998).

- *Stressed people develop colds more readily.* Researchers dropped a cold virus in the noses of people with high and low life-stress scores (FIGURE 10.4 on the next page). Among those living stress-filled lives, 47 percent developed colds. Among those living relatively free of stress, only 27 percent did (Cohen et al., 1999, 2003, 2006a,b).

- *Low stress may increase the effectiveness of vaccinations.* Nurses gave older adults a flu vaccine and then measured how well their bodies fought off bacteria and viruses. The vaccine was most effective among older adults who had a healthy body

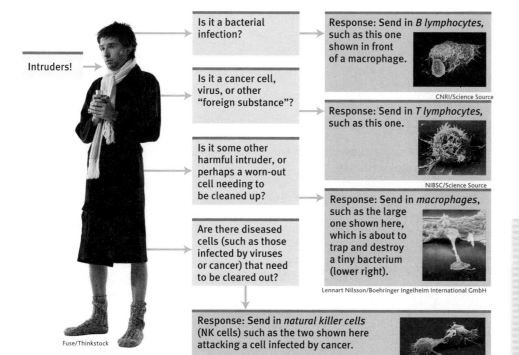

Intruders!

Is it a bacterial infection? → Response: Send in *B lymphocytes*, such as this one shown in front of a macrophage.

CNRI/Science Source

Is it a cancer cell, virus, or other "foreign substance"? → Response: Send in *T lymphocytes*, such as this one.

NIBSC/Science Source

Is it some other harmful intruder, or perhaps a worn-out cell needing to be cleaned up? → Response: Send in *macrophages*, such as the large one shown here, which is about to trap and destroy a tiny bacterium (lower right).

Lennart Nilsson/Boehringer Ingelheim International GmbH

Are there diseased cells (such as those infected by viruses or cancer) that need to be cleaned out? → Response: Send in *natural killer cells* (NK cells) such as the two shown here attacking a cell infected by cancer.

Eye of Science/Science Source

Fuse/Thinkstock

FIGURE 10.3 **A simplified view of immune responses**

tend-and-befriend response under stress, people (especially women) often provide support to others *(tend)* and bond with and seek support from others *(befriend)*.

psychoneuroimmunology the study of how psychological, neural, and endocrine processes combine to affect our immune system and health.

lymphocytes the two types of white blood cells that are part of the body's immune system: *B lymphocytes* release antibodies that fight bacterial infections; *T lymphocytes* attack cancer cells, viruses, and foreign substances.

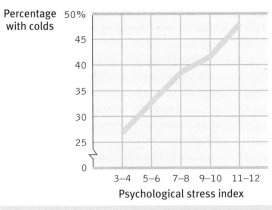

FIGURE 10.4 Stress and colds People with the highest life-stress scores were also most likely to develop colds when exposed to an experimentally delivered virus (Cohen et al., 1999).

weight and experienced low stress (Segerstrom et al., 2012).

The stress effect on immunity makes sense. It takes energy to track down invaders, produce swelling, and maintain fevers (Maier et al., 1994). Stress hormones drain this energy away from the disease-fighting white blood cells. When you are ill, your body demands less activity and more sleep, in part to cut back on the energy your muscles usually use. Stress does the opposite. During an aroused fight-or-flight reaction, your stress responses draw energy away from your disease-fighting immune system and send it to your muscles and brain (see Figure 9.13 in Chapter 9). This competing energy need leaves you more open to illness.

The bottom line: Stress does not make us sick. But it does reduce our immune system's ability to function, and that leaves us less able to fight infection.

Let's look now at how stress might affect AIDS, cancer, and heart disease. ■

RETRIEVE + REMEMBER

- _____ focuses on mind-body interactions, including the effects of psychological, neural, and endocrine functioning on the immune system and overall health.

ANSWER: Psychoneuroimmunology

- What general effect does stress have on our overall health?

ANSWER: Stress tends to reduce our immune system's ability to function properly, so that those who regularly experience higher stress also have a higher risk of physical illness.

Stress and AIDS

We know that stress suppresses immune system functioning. What does this mean for people suffering from AIDS (acquired immune deficiency syndrome)? People with AIDS already have a damaged immune system. The name of the virus that triggers AIDS tells us that. "HIV" stands for *human immunodeficiency virus.*

Stress can't give people AIDS. But could stress and negative emotions speed the transition from HIV infection to AIDS in someone already infected? Might stress predict a faster decline in those with AIDS? An analysis of 33,252 participants from around the world suggests the answer to both questions

is *Yes* (Chida & Vedhara, 2009). The greater the stress that HIV-infected people experience, the faster their disease progresses.

Could reducing stress help control AIDS? The answer again appears to be *Yes*. Although drug treatments are more effective, educational programs, grief support groups, talk therapy, relaxation training, and exercise programs that reduce distress have all had good results for HIV-positive people (Baum & Posluszny, 1999; McCain et al., 2008; Schneiderman, 1999).

Stress and Cancer

Stress does not create cancer cells. But in a healthy, functioning immune system, lymphocytes, macrophages, and NK cells search out and destroy cancer cells and cancer-damaged cells. If stress weakens the immune system, might this weaken a person's ability to fight off cancer? To find out, researchers implanted tumor cells in rodents. Next, they exposed some of the rodents to uncontrollable stress (for example, inescapable restraint). Compared with their unstressed counterparts, the stressed rodents had weaker immune function, lower body weight, and grew larger tumors (Frick et al., 2009).

Does this stress-cancer link apply to humans? The results are mixed. Some studies have found that people are at increased risk for cancer within a year after experiencing depression, helplessness, or grief. In one large study, the risk of colon cancer was 5.5 times greater among people with a history of workplace stress than among those who did not report such problems. The difference was not due to group differences in age, smoking, drinking, or physical characteristics (Courtney et al., 1993). Other studies, however, have found no link between stress and a risk of cancer in humans (Edelman & Kidman, 1997; Fox, 1998; Petticrew et al., 1999, 2002). Concentration camp survivors and former prisoners of war, for example, do not have elevated cancer rates. So this research story is still being written.

There is a danger in hyping reports on attitudes and cancer. Can you imagine how a woman dying of breast cancer might react to a report on the effects of stress on the speed of decline in cancer patients? She could wrongly blame herself for her illness. ("If only I had been more expressive, relaxed, and hopeful.") Her loved ones could become haunted by the notion that they caused her illness. ("If only I had been less stressful to my mom.")

> "I didn't give myself cancer."
>
> Mayor Barbara Boggs Sigmund (1939–1990), Princeton, New Jersey

It's important enough to repeat: *Stress does not create cancer cells.* At worst, stress may affect their growth by weakening the body's natural defenses against multiplying cancer cells (Antoni & Lutgendorf, 2007). Although a relaxed, hopeful state may enhance these defenses, we should be aware of the thin line that divides science from wishful thinking. The powerful biological processes at work in advanced cancer or AIDS are not likely to be completely derailed by avoiding stress or maintaining a relaxed but determined spirit (Anderson, 2002; Kessler et al., 1991).

Stress and Heart Disease

10-4 How does stress increase coronary heart disease risk?

Depart from reality for a moment. In this new world, you wake up each day, eat your breakfast, and check the news. Political coverage buzzes, local events snap up airtime, and your favorite sports team occasionally wins. But there is a fourth story: Four 747 jumbo jet airlines crashed yesterday and all 1642 passengers died. You finish your breakfast, grab your books, and head to class. It's just an average day.

Replace airline crashes with **coronary heart disease,** the United States' leading cause of death, and you have re-entered reality. About 600,000 Americans die annually from heart disease (CDC, 2013). Heart disease occurs when the blood vessels that nourish the heart muscle gradually close. High blood pressure

and a family history of the disease increase the risk. So do smoking, obesity, a high-fat diet, physical inactivity, and a high cholesterol level.

Stress and personality also play a big role in heart disease. The more psychological trauma people experience, the more their bodies generate *inflammation,* which is associated with heart and other health problems (O'Donovan et al., 2012). Plucking a hair and measuring its level of *cortisol* (a stress hormone) can help predict whether a person will have a future heart attack (Pereg et al., 2011).

In some classic studies, Meyer Friedman, Ray Rosenman, and their colleagues measured the blood cholesterol level and clotting speed of 40 U.S. male tax accountants during unstressful and stressful times of year (Friedman & Rosenman, 1974; Friedman & Ulmer, 1984). From January through March, the accountants showed normal results. But as the accountants began scrambling to finish their clients' tax returns before the April 15 filing deadline, their cholesterol and clotting measures rose to dangerous levels. In May and June, with the deadline passed, their health measures returned to normal. Stress predicted heart attack risk for the accountants, with rates going up during their most stressful times.

A more recent study showed similar effects, with Americans' blood pressure increasing two months after the 9/11 World Trade Center attacks compared with the two months preceding the attacks (Gerin et al., 2005). Blood pressure also rises as students approach everyday academic stressors (Conley & Lehman, 2012). So, are some of us at high risk of stress-related coronary disease? To answer this question, the researchers who studied the tax accountants launched a classic nine-year study of more than 3000 healthy men, aged 35 to 59.

At the start of the study, the researchers interviewed each man for 15 minutes, noting his work and eating habits, manner of talking, and other behavioral patterns. Some men reacted strongly. These men, whom they labeled **Type A,** were competitive, hard-driving, impatient, time-conscious, super-motivated, verbally aggressive, and easily angered. The roughly equal number who were more easygoing they called **Type B.** Which group do you suppose turned out to be the most coronary-prone?

Nine years later, 257 men in the study had suffered heart attacks, and 69 percent of them were Type A. Moreover, not one of the "pure" Type Bs—the most

TYPE A PERSONALITY / TYPE B PERSONALITY

Because it's there! / Because it's there!

BANNERMAN © 7/94

Bannerman © 7/94

PhotoSpin, Inc./Alamy

coronary heart disease the clogging of the vessels that nourish the heart muscle; the leading cause of death in the United States and many other countries.

Type A Friedman and Rosenman's term for competitive, hard-driving, impatient, verbally aggressive, and anger-prone people.

Type B Friedman and Rosenman's term for easygoing, relaxed people.

mellow and laid-back of their group—had suffered a heart attack.

As often happens in science, this exciting discovery provoked enormous public interest. But after that initial honeymoon period, researchers wanted to know more. Was the finding reliable? If so, what exactly is so toxic about the Type A profile: Time-consciousness? Competitiveness? Anger? Further research revealed the answer. Type A's toxic core is negative emotions—especially anger (Smith, 2006; Williams, 1993). Type A individuals are more often "combat ready." When these people are threatened or challenged by a stressor, they react aggressively. As their often active sympathetic nervous system redistributes bloodflow to the muscles, it pulls blood away from internal organs. One of these internal organs, the liver, which normally removes cholesterol and fat from the blood, can't do its job. Excess cholesterol and fat continue to circulate in the blood and are deposited around the heart. Further stress—sometimes conflicts brought on by their own traits—may trigger altered heart rhythms. In people with weakened hearts, this altered pattern can cause sudden death (Kamarck & Jennings, 1991). Our heart and mind interact.

> *"The fire you kindle for your enemy often burns you more than him."*
> Chinese proverb

Hundreds of other studies of young and middle-aged men and women have confirmed that people who react with anger over little things are the most coronary-prone (Chida & Hamer, 2008; Chida & Steptoe, 2009). One study followed 13,000 middle-aged people for five years. Among those with normal blood pressure, people who had scored high on anger were three times more likely to have had heart attacks, even after researchers controlled for smoking and weight (Williams et al., 2000). Another study followed 1055 male medical students over an average of 36 years. Those who had reported being hot-tempered were five times more likely to have had a heart attack by age 55 (Chang et al., 2002). As others have noted, rage "seems to lash back and strike us in the heart muscle" (Spielberger & London, 1982).

In recent years, another personality type has interested stress and heart disease researchers. For these *Type D* individuals, the negative emotion they experience during social interactions is mainly *distress* (Denollet, 2005; Denollet et al., 1996). Type A individuals direct their negative emotion toward dominating others. Type D people suppress their negative emotion to avoid social disapproval. In one analysis of 12 studies, Type D personality significantly increased risk for mortality and nonfatal heart attack (Grande et al., 2012).

Depression, too, can be lethal, as the evidence from 57 studies has shown (Wulsin et al., 1999). In one study, people with high scores for depression were four times more likely than their low-scoring counterparts to develop further heart problems (Frasure-Smith & Lesperance, 2005). In a British study that followed 61,349 people over three to six years, depression predicted risk of death as well as did smoking (Mykletun et al., 2009). It is still unclear why depression poses such a serious risk for heart disease, but this much seems clear: Depression is disheartening.

* * *

So, in many ways stress can affect our health (**FIGURE 10.5**). Our stress-related susceptibility to disease is a price we pay for the benefits of stress. Stress enriches our lives. It arouses and motivates us. An unstressed life would not be challenging or productive.

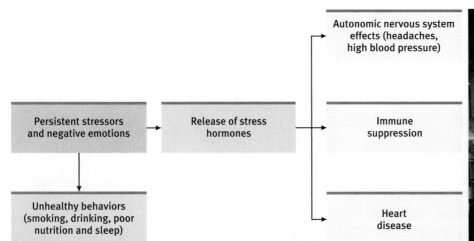

FIGURE 10.5 Stress can have a variety of health-related consequences This is especially so when stress is experienced by angry, depressed, or anxious people. Job and income loss caused by the recent economic recession has created stress for many people, such as this jobless Japanese man living in a Tokyo "capsule hotel."

Coping With Stress

10-5 What are two basic ways that people cope with stress?

◎ Stressors are unavoidable. That's the reality we live with. One way we can develop our strengths and protect our health is to learn better ways to **cope** with our stress.

We need to find new ways to feel, think, and act when we are dealing with stressors. We address some stressors directly, with **problem-focused coping.** For example, if our impatience leads to a family fight, we may go directly to that family member to work things out. We tend to use problem-focused strategies when we feel a sense of control over a situation and think we can change the circumstances, or at least change ourselves to deal with the circumstances more capably.

We turn to **emotion-focused coping** when we cannot—or *believe* we cannot—change a situation. If, despite our best efforts, we cannot get along with a family member, we may search for relief from stress by confiding in friends and reaching out for support and comfort.

Emotion-focused strategies can move us toward better long-term health, as when we attempt to gain emotional distance from a damaging relationship or keep busy with hobbies to avoid thinking about an old addiction. Emotion-focused strategies can also be maladaptive, however, as when students worried about not keeping up with the reading in class go out to party or play video games to get it off their mind. Sometimes a problem-focused strategy (catching up with the reading) will reduce stress more effectively and promote long-term health and satisfaction.

Our success in coping depends on several factors. Let's look at four of them: personal control, an optimistic outlook, social support, and finding meaning in life's ups and downs. ■

RETRIEVE + REMEMBER

- To cope with stress, we tend to use _____-focused (emotion/problem) strategies when we feel in control of our world. When we believe we cannot change a situation, we may try to relieve stress with _____-focused (emotion/problem) strategies.

ANSWERS: problem; emotion

Personal Control, Health, and Well-Being

10-6 How does our sense of control influence stress and health?

Personal control refers to how much we perceive having control over our environment. Psychologists study the effect of personal control (or any personality factor) in two ways:

1. They *correlate* people's feelings of control with their behaviors and achievements.

2. They *experiment*, by raising or lowering people's sense of control and noting the effects.

At times, we all feel helpless, hopeless, and depressed after experiencing a series of bad events beyond our control. For some animals and people, a series of uncontrollable events creates a state of **learned helplessness**, with feelings of passive resignation (**FIGURE 10.6**). In one series of experiments, dogs were strapped in a harness and given repeated shocks, with no opportunity to avoid them (Seligman & Maier, 1967). When later placed in another situation where they could escape the punishment by simply leaping a hurdle, the dogs cow-ered as if without hope. Other dogs that had been able to escape the first shocks reacted differently. They had learned they were in control, and in the new situation they easily escaped the shocks (Seligman & Maier, 1967). In other experiments, people have shown similar patterns of learned helplessness (Abramson et al., 1978, 1989; Seligman, 1975).

Learned helplessness is a dramatic form of loss of control, but we've all felt a loss of control at times. Our health can suffer as our level of stress hormones (such as *cortisol*) rise, our blood pressure increases, and our immune responses weaken (Rodin, 1986; Sapolsky, 2005). One study found these effects among nurses, who reported their workload and their level of personal control on the job. The greater their workload, the higher their cortisol level and blood pressure—but *only* among nurses who reported little control over their environment (Fox et al., 1993). Stress effects have also been observed among captive animals. Those in captivity are more prone to disease than their wild counterparts, which have more control over their lives (Roberts, 1988). Similar effects are found when humans are crowded together in

coping reducing stress using emotional, cognitive, or behavioral methods.

problem-focused coping attempting to reduce stress directly—by changing the stressor or the way we interact with that stressor.

emotion-focused coping attempting to reduce stress by avoiding or ignoring a stressor and attending to emotional needs related to our stress reaction.

personal control our sense of controlling our environment rather than feeling helpless.

learned helplessness the hopelessness and passive resignation an animal or person learns when unable to avoid repeated aversive events.

| Uncontrollable bad events | → | Perceived lack of control | → | Generalized helpless behavior |

FIGURE 10.6 Learned helplessness When animals and people experience no control over repeated bad events, they often learn helplessness.

high-density neighborhoods, prisons, and even college dorms (Fleming et al., 1987; Fuller et al., 1993; Ostfeld et al., 1987). Feelings of control drop, and stress hormone levels and blood pressure rise.

Proposals to improve health and morale by increasing control have included (Humphrey et al., 2007; Ruback et al., 1986; Warburton et al., 2006):

- Allowing prisoners to move chairs and control room lights and the TV.

- Having workers participate in decision making. Simply allowing people to personalize their workspace has been linked with higher (55 percent) engagement with their work (Krueger & Killham, 2006).

- Offering nursing home patients choices about their environment. In one famous study, 93 percent of nursing home patients who were encouraged to exert more control became more alert, active, and happy (Rodin, 1986).

"Perceived control is basic to human functioning," concluded researcher Ellen Langer (1983, p. 291). "For the young and old alike," she suggested, environments should enhance people's sense of control over their world. No wonder mobile

HAPPY TO HAVE CONTROL After working on the building—alongside Habitat for Humanity volunteers—for several months, this family is finally experiencing the joy of having their own new home.

devices and DVRs, which enhance our control of the content and timing of our entertainment, are so popular.

Google incorporates these principles effectively. Each week, Google employees can spend 20 percent of their working time on projects they find personally interesting. This Innovation Time Off program increases employees' personal control over their work environment, and it has paid off. Gmail was developed this way.

The power of having personal control also shows up at national levels. People thrive when they live in conditions of personal freedom and empowerment. For example, citizens of stable democracies report higher levels of happiness (Inglehart et al., 2008).

So, some freedom and control are better than none. But does ever-increasing choice breed ever-happier lives? Some researchers have suggested that today's Western cultures offer an "excess of freedom"—too many choices. The result can be decreased life satisfaction, increased depression, or even behavior paralysis (Schwartz, 2000, 2004). In one study, people offered a choice of one of 30 brands of jam or chocolate were less satisfied with their decision than were others who had chosen from only 6 options (Iyengar & Lepper, 2000). This *tyranny of choice* brings information overload and a greater likelihood that we will feel regret over some of the things we left behind. (Do you, too, ever waste time agonizing over too many choices?)

Who Controls Your Life?

Do you believe that your life is out of control? That the world is run by a few powerful people? That getting a good

job depends mainly on being in the right place at the right time? Or do you more strongly believe that you control your own fate? That each of us can influence our government's decisions? That being a success is a matter of hard work?

Hundreds of studies have compared people who differ in their perceptions of control:

- Those who have an **external locus of control** believe that chance or outside forces control their fate.

- Those who have an **internal locus of control** believe they control their own destiny.

EXTREME SELF-CONTROL Our ability to exert self-control increases with practice, and some of us have practiced more than others! Magician David Blaine (left) endured standing on a pillar in New York City for 72 hours in a 20-pound protective suit while being bombarded with electrical jolts from Tesla coils. A number of performing artists make their living as very convincing human statues, as does this actress (right) performing on the Royal Mile in Edinburgh, Scotland.

Does it matter which view we hold? In study after study comparing people with these two viewpoints, the "internals" have achieved more in school and work, acted more independently, enjoyed better health, and felt less depressed

(Lefcourt, 1982; Ng et al., 2006). In one long-term study of more than 7500 people, those who had expressed a more internal locus of control at age 10 exhibited less obesity, lower blood pressure, and less distress at age 30 (Gale et al., 2008).

Another way to say that we believe we are in control of our own life is to say we have *free will,* or that we can control our own willpower. Studies show that people who believe in their freedom learn better, perform better at work, and behave more helpfully (Job et al., 2010; Stillman et al., 2010).

So we differ in our perceptions of whether we have control over our world. Why? Compared with their parents' generation, more young Americans now endorse an external locus of control (Twenge et al., 2004). This shift may help explain an associated increase in rates of depression and other psychological disorders (Twenge et al., 2010).

Coping With Stress by Boosting Self-Control

Google trusted its belief in the power of personal control, and the company and its employees reaped the benefits. Could we reap similar benefits by actively managing our own behavior? One place to start might be increasing our *self-control*—the ability to control impulses and delay immediate gratification. Strengthening our self-control may not pay off with a Gmail invention, but self-control has been linked to health and well-being (Moffitt et al., 2011; Tangney et al., 2004). People with more self-control earn higher grades, accumulate more wealth, enjoy better mental health, and have stronger relationships. In one study that followed eighth-graders over a school year, better self-control was more than twice as important as intelligence score in predicting academic success (Duckworth & Seligman, 2005).

Self-control is constantly changing—from day to day, hour to hour, and even minute to minute. We can compare self-control to a muscle: It weakens after use, recovers after rest, and grows stronger with exercise (Baumeister & Exline, 2000; Hagger et al., 2010; Vohs & Baumeister, 2011).

When you use your self-control, you have less of it available to use when you need it later (Gailliot et al., 2007). In one experiment, hungry people who had resisted eating tempting chocolate chip cookies abandoned a frustrating task sooner than people who had not resisted the cookies (Baumeister et al., 1998). When people feel provoked, those who have used up their self-control energy have acted more aggressively toward strangers and intimate partners (DeWall et al., 2007). In one experiment, frustrated participants with low self-control energy stuck more pins into a voodoo doll that represented their romantic partner. Participants whose self-control energy was left intact used fewer pins (Finkel et al., 2012).

Exercising self-control uses up the blood sugar and brain energy needed for mental focus (Inzlicht & Gutsell, 2007). Some people can spend their self-control energy on losing weight. Others may do so to stop smoking. But given our limited reservoir of self-control, few can do both simultaneously. (It often pays to work on one thing at a time.)

What, then, might be the effect of deliberately boosting people's blood sugar when their self-control energy has been used up? In one study, energy-boosting sugar (in a naturally rather than an artificially sweetened lemon-ade) had a sweet effect. It strengthened people's conscious thought processes and reduced their financial impulsiveness and aggression (Denson et al., 2010; Masicampo & Baumeister, 2008; Wang & Dvorak, 2010). Even dogs experiencing self-control energy loss seemed to bounce back after this sweet treatment (Miller et al., 2010).

Decreased mental energy after exercising self-control is a short-term effect. The long-term effect of exercising self-control is *increased* self-control, much as a hard physical workout leaves you temporarily tired out, but stronger in the long term. Strengthened self-control improves people's performance on laboratory tasks as well as their self-management of eating, drinking, smoking, and household chores (Oaten & Cheng, 2006a,b).

The point to remember: Develop self-discipline in one area of your life, and your strengthened self-control may spill over into other areas as well, making for a less stressed life.

Is the Glass Half Full or Half Empty?

10-7 How do optimists and pessimists differ, and why does our outlook on life matter?

Another part of coping with stress is our outlook—how we perceive the world. **Optimists** agree with statements such as, "In uncertain times, I usually expect the best" (Scheier & Carver, 1992). Optimists expect to have control, to cope well with stressful events, and to enjoy good health. **Pessimists** don't share these expectations. They expect things to go

"We just haven't been flapping them hard enough."

external locus of control the perception that chance or outside forces beyond our personal control determine our fate.

internal locus of control the perception that we control our own fate.

optimism the anticipation of positive outcomes. Optimists are people who expect the best and expect their efforts to lead to good things.

pessimism the anticipation of negative outcomes. Pessimists are people who expect the worst and doubt that their goals will be achieved.

badly (Aspinwall & Tedeschi, 2010; Carver et al., 2010; Rasmussen et al., 2009). And when bad things happen, pessimists knew it all along. They lacked the necessary skills ("I can't do this"). The situation prevented them from doing well ("There is nothing I can do about it"). They expected the worst and their expectations were fulfilled.

Optimism, like a feeling of personal control, pays off. Optimists respond to stress with smaller increases in blood pressure, and they recover more quickly from heart bypass surgery. And during the stressful first few weeks of classes, U.S. law school students who were optimistic ("It's unlikely that I will fail") enjoyed better moods and stronger immune systems (Segerstrom et al., 1998). When American dating couples wrestle with conflicts, optimists and their partners see each other as engaging constructively. They tend to feel more supported and satisfied with the resolution and with their relationship (Srivastava et al., 2006). Optimism also predicts well-being and success elsewhere, including China and Japan (Qin & Piao, 2011).

Is an optimistic outlook related to living a longer life? Possibly. One research team followed 941 Dutch people, aged 65 to 85, for nearly a decade (Giltay et al., 2004, 2007). They split the sample into four groups according to their optimism scores. Only 30 percent of those with the highest optimism died during the study, as did 57 percent of those with the lowest optimism.

The optimism–long-life correlation also appeared in a famous study of 180 American Catholic nuns. At about 22 years of age, each of these women had written a brief autobiography. In the decades that followed, they lived similar lifestyles. Those who had expressed happiness, love, and other pos-

itive feelings in their autobiographies lived an average of seven years longer than did the more negative nuns (Danner et al., 2001). By age 80, only 24 percent of the most positive-spirited had died, compared with 54 percent of those expressing few positive emotions.

Optimism runs in families, so some people truly are born with a sunny, hopeful outlook. With identical twins, if one is optimistic, the other often will be as well (Mosing et al., 2009). One genetic marker of optimism is a gene that enhances the social-bonding hormone oxytocin (Saphire-Bernstein et al., 2011).

Positive thinking pays dividends, but so does a dash of realism (Schneider, 2001). Realistic anxiety over possible *future* failures—worrying about being able to pay a bill on time, or fearing you will do badly on an exam—can cause you to try extra hard to avoid failure (Goodhart, 1986; Norem, 2001; Showers, 1992). Students concerned about failing an upcoming exam may study more, and therefore outperform equally able but more confident peers. This may help explain the impressive academic achievements of some Asian-American students. Compared with European-Americans, these students express somewhat greater pessimism (Chang, 2001). Success requires enough optimism to provide hope and enough pessimism to keep you on your toes.

Excessive optimism can blind us to real risks (Weinstein, 1980, 1982, 1996). Most college students display an *unrealistic optimism*. They view themselves as less likely than their average classmate to develop drinking problems, drop out of school, or have a heart attack. Most older adolescents see themselves as much less likely than their peers to contract the AIDS virus (Abrams, 1991; Gold, 2006) or to develop skin cancer. Many

LAUGHTER AMONG FRIENDS IS GOOD MEDICINE Laughter arouses us, massages muscles, and then leaves us feeling relaxed (Robinson, 1983). Humor (though not hostile sarcasm) may defuse stress, ease pain, and strengthen immune activity (Ayan, 2009; Berk et al., 2001; Kimata, 2001). People who laugh a lot also tend to have lower rates of heart disease (Clark et al., 2001).

> "God grant us the serenity to accept the things we cannot change, courage to change the things we can, and wisdom to know the difference."
>
> Alcoholics Anonymous Serenity Prayer (attributed to Reinhold Niebuhr)

credit-card users choose cards with low fees and high interest, causing them to pay more because they are unrealistically optimistic that they will always pay off the monthly balance (Yang et al., 2006). Blinded by optimism, people young and old echo the statement famed basketball player Magic Johnson made (1993) after contracting HIV: "I didn't think it could happen to me."

Social Support

10-8 How do social support and finding meaning in life influence health?

Which of these factors has the strongest association with poor health: smoking 15 cigarettes daily, being obese, being

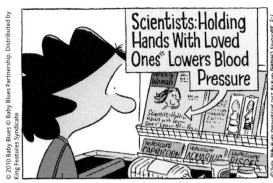

poor health. In one analysis of 32 studies involving more than 6.5 million people, divorced people were 23 percent more likely to die early (Sbarra et al., 2011).

Social support helps us fight illness in at least two ways. First, it calms our cardiovascular system, which lowers blood pressure and stress hormone levels (Uchino et al., 1996, 1999). To see if social support might calm people's response to threats, one research team subjected happily married women, while lying in an fMRI machine, to the threat of electric shock to an ankle (Coan et al., 2006). During the experiment, some women held their husband's hand. Others held a stranger's hand or no hand at all. While awaiting the occasional shocks, the women's brains reacted differently. Those who held their husband's hand had less activity in threat-responsive areas. This soothing benefit was greatest for women reporting the highest-quality marriages. A follow-up experiment suggested that simply viewing a supportive

inactive, or lacking strong social connections? This is a trick question, because each factor has a roughly similar impact (Cacioppo & Patrick, 2008). That's right! *Social support*—feeling liked and encouraged by intimate friends and family—promotes both happiness and health. It helps you cope with stress. Not having this support can affect your health as much as smoking nearly a pack per day.

Seven massive investigations that followed thousands of people over several years reached similar conclusions. People supported by close relationships are less likely to die early (Uchino, 2009). These relationships may be with friends, family, fellow workers, members of our faith community, or some other support group. Even pets can help us cope with stress. (See Close-Up: Pets Are Friends, Too.)

Happy marriages bathe us in social support. People in low-conflict marriages live longer, healthier lives than the unmarried (Kaplan & Kronick, 2006; Wilson & Oswald, 2002). This correlation holds regardless of age, sex, race, and income (National Center for Health Statistics, 2004). One seven-decade-long study found that at age 50, healthy aging is better predicted by a good marriage than by a low cholesterol level (Vaillant, 2002). On the flip side, divorce is a predictor of

CLOSE-UP

Pets Are Friends, Too

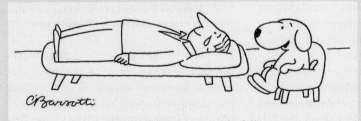

"Well, I think you're wonderful"

Have you ever wished for a friend who would love you just as you are? One who would never judge you? Who would be there for you, no matter your mood? For many tens of millions of people that friend exists, and it is a loyal dog or a friendly cat.

Many people describe their pet as a beloved family member who helps them feel calm, happy, and valued. Can pets also help people handle stress? If so, might pets have healing power? Karen Allen has reported that the answers are *Yes* and *Yes*. For example, women's blood pressure rises as they struggle with challenging math problems in the presence of a best friend or even a spouse, but it rises much less in the presence of their dog (Allen, 2003). Pets increase the odds of survival after a heart attack. They relieve depression among AIDS patients. And they lower the level of fatty acids in the blood that increase the risk of heart disease.

So, would pets be good medicine for people who do not have pets? To find out, Allen experimented. The participants were a group of stockbrokers. They all lived alone, described their work as stressful, and had high blood pressure. She randomly selected half to adopt an animal shelter cat or dog. Did these new companions help their owners handle stress better? Indeed they did. When later facing stress, all participants experienced higher blood pressure. But among the new pet owners, the increase was only half as high as the increases in the no-pet group. The effect was greatest for pet owners with few social contacts or friends. Allen's conclusion: For lowering blood pressure, pets are no substitute for effective drugs and exercise. But for those who enjoy animals, and especially for those who live alone, they are a healthy pleasure.

romantic partner's picture was enough to reduce painful discomfort (Master et al., 2009). One study of women with ovarian cancer suggests that social support may slow the progression of cancer. Researchers found that women with the highest levels of social support had the lowest levels of a stress hormone linked to cancer progression.

Social support helps us cope with stress in a second way. It helps us fight illness by fostering stronger *immune functioning*. We have seen that stress puts us at risk for disease because it steals disease-fighting energy from our immune system. Social support seems to reboot our immune system. In one series of studies, research volunteers with strong support systems showed greater resistance to cold viruses (Cohen et al., 1997, 2004). After inhaling nose drops loaded with a cold virus, two groups of healthy volunteers were isolated and observed for five days. (The volunteers each received $800 to endure this experience.) The researchers then took a cold hard look at the results. After controlling for age, race, sex, smoking, and other health habits, they found that people with close social ties in their everyday lives were least likely to catch a cold. If they did catch one, they produced less mucus. The effect of social ties is nothing to sneeze at!

When we are trying to cope with stressors, social ties can tug us toward or away from our goal. Are you trying to exercise more, drink less, quit smoking, or eat better? If so, think about whether your social network can help or hinder you. That social net covers not only the people you know but friends of your friends, and friends of their friends. That's three degrees of separation between you and the most remote people. Within that network, others can influence your thoughts, feelings, and actions without your awareness (Christakis & Fowler, 2009). Obesity, for example, spreads within networks, and it is not merely a reflection of our tendency to seek out similar others. Three degrees of separation seems to be the limit for this type of social influence.

Finding Meaning

Catastrophes and significant life changes can leave us confused and distressed as we try to make sense of what happened. At such times, an important part of coping with stress is finding meaning in life—some redeeming purpose in our suffering (Taylor, 1983). Unemployment is very threatening, but it may free up time to spend with children. The loss of a loved one may force us to expand our social network. A heart attack may trigger a shift toward healthy, active living. Some have argued that the search for meaning is fundamental. We constantly seek to maintain meaning when our expectations are not met (Heine el al., 2006). As psychiatrist Viktor Frankl (1962), who had been imprisoned in a Nazi concentration camp, observed, "Life is never made unbearable by circumstances, but only by lack of meaning and purpose."

Close relationships offer an opportunity for "open heart therapy"—a chance to *confide* painful feelings and sort things out (Frattaroli, 2006). Talking about things that push our buttons may arouse us in the short term. But in the long term, it calms us by reducing activity in our limbic system (Lieberman et al., 2007; Mendolia & Kleck, 1993). Talking or writing about our experiences helps us make sense of our stress and find meaning in it (Esterling et al., 1999). In one study, 33 Holocaust survivors spent two hours recalling their experiences, many in intimate detail never before disclosed (Pennebaker et al., 1989). In the weeks following, most watched a tape of their recollections and showed it to family and friends. Those who were most self-disclosing had the most improved health 14 months later. Confiding is good for the body and the soul. Another study surveyed surviving spouses of people who had committed suicide or died in car accidents. Those who bore their grief alone had more health problems than those who could express it openly (Pennebaker & O'Heeron, 1984). ■

Managing Stress Effects

◎ Having a sense of control, nurturing an optimistic outlook, building our social support, and finding meaning can help us *experience* less stress and thus improve our health. What do we do when we cannot avoid stress? At such times, we need to *manage* our stress. Aerobic exercise, relaxation, meditation, and active spiritual engagement may help us gather inner strength and lessen stress effects.

Aerobic Exercise

10-9 How well does aerobic exercise help manage stress and improve well-being?

It's hard to find a medicine that works for most people most of the time. But **aerobic exercise**—sustained activity that increases heart and lung fitness—is one of these rare near-perfect "medicines." By one estimate, moderate exercise adds not only to your quantity of life—two additional years, on average—but also to your quality of life, with more energy and better mood (Seligman, 1994; Wang et al., 2011).

Throughout this book, we have revisited one of psychology's basic themes: Heredity and environment interact. Physical activity can weaken the influence of genetic risk factors for obesity.

THE MOOD BOOST When energy or spirits are sagging, few things reboot the day better than exercising (as I [DM] can confirm from my noontime basketball, and as I [ND] can confirm from my running).

In one analysis of 45 studies, that risk fell by 27 percent (Kilpeläinen et al., 2012). Exercise also helps fight heart disease. It strengthens your heart, increases blood-flow, keeps blood vessels open, lowers overall blood pressure, and reduces the hormone and blood pressure reaction to stress (Ford, 2002; Manson, 2002). Compared with inactive adults, people who exercise suffer half as many heart attacks (Powell et al., 1987; Visich & Fletcher, 2009). Exercise makes the muscles hungry for the fats that, if not used by the muscles, contribute to clogged arteries (Barinaga, 1997).

Many studies suggest that aerobic exercise reduces stress, depression, and anxiety. For example, half of Americans have reported exercising at least 30 minutes three times a week (Mendes, 2009). People at this level of activity manage stressful situations better, show more self-confidence and energy, and feel less depressed and anxious than their inactive peers (McMurray, 2004; Puetz et al., 2006; Smits et al., 2011). Going from active exerciser to couch potato can increase risk for depression—by 51 percent in two years for the women in one study (Wang et al., 2011). But we could state these observations another way: Stressed and depressed people exercise less. It's that old correlation problem again—cause and effect are not clear.

To sort out cause and effect, researchers experiment. They randomly assign people either to an aerobic exercise group or to a control group. Next, they measure whether aerobic exercise (compared with a control activity) produces a change in stress, depression, anxiety, or some other health-related outcome. In one such experiment (McCann & Holmes, 1984), researchers randomly assigned mildly depressed female college students to one of three groups:

- Group 1 completed an aerobic exercise program.

- Group 2 completed a relaxation program.

- Group 3 functioned as a pure control group and did not complete any special activity.

As **FIGURE 10.7** shows, 10 weeks later the women in the aerobic exercise program reported the greatest decrease in depression. Many of them had, quite literally, run away from their troubles.

Another experiment randomly assigned depressed people to an exercise group, an antidepressant group, or a placebo pill group. Again, exercise diminished depression levels. And it did so as effectively as antidepressants, with longer-lasting effects (Hoffman et al., 2011). Aerobic exercise counteracts depression in two ways. First, it increases arousal. Second, it does naturally what some prescription drugs do chemically: It increases the brain's serotonin activity.

More than 150 other studies have confirmed that exercise reduces depression and anxiety. Aerobic exercise has therefore taken a place, along with antidepressant drugs and psychotherapy, on the list of effective treatments for depression and anxiety (Arent et al., 2000; Berger & Motl, 2000; Dunn et al., 2005).

Relaxation and Meditation

10-10 In what ways might relaxation and meditation influence stress and health?

Sit with your back straight, getting as comfortable as you can. Breathe a deep, single breath of air through your nose. Now exhale that air through your mouth as

aerobic exercise sustained activity that increases heart and lung fitness; may also reduce depression and anxiety.

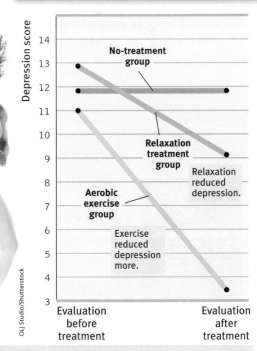

FIGURE 10.7 Aerobic exercise reduced depression (From McCann & Holmes, 1984.)

slowly as you can. As you exhale, repeat a focus word, phrase, or prayer—something from your own belief system. Do this five times. Do you feel more relaxed?

Why Relaxation Is Good

Like aerobic exercise, relaxation can improve our well-being. Did you notice in Figure 10.7 that women in the relaxation treatment group also experienced reduced depression? More than 60 studies have found that relaxation procedures can also provide relief from headaches, high blood pressure, anxiety, and insomnia (Nestoriuc et al., 2008; Stetter & Kupper, 2002).

Researchers have even used relaxation to help Type A heart attack survivors reduce their risk of future attacks (Friedman & Ulmer, 1984). They randomly assigned hundreds of these middle-aged men to one of two groups. The first group received standard advice from cardiologists about medications, diet, and exercise habits. The second group received similar advice, but they also were taught ways of modifying their lifestyle. They learned to slow down and relax by walking, talking, and eating more slowly. They learned to smile at others and laugh at themselves. They learned to admit

AP Photo/David Goldman

FURRY FRIENDS FOR FINALS WEEK Some schools bring cuddly critters on campus for finals week as a way to help students relax and bring disruptive stress levels down. This student at Emory University is relaxing with dogs and puppies. Other schools offer petting zoos or encourage instructors to bring in their own pets that week.

their mistakes, to take time to enjoy life, and to renew their religious faith. The training paid off spectacularly (**FIGURE 10.8**). During the next three years, the lifestyle modification group had half as many repeat heart attacks as did the first group. A British study supported this

finding. Lifestyle modification cut the risk of heart attack in half over 13 years for heart-attack-prone people (Eysenck & Grossarth-Maticek, 1991).

Time may heal all wounds, but relaxation can help speed that process. In one study, surgery patients were randomly assigned to two groups. Both groups received standard treatment, but the second group also experienced a 45-minute relaxation exercise and received relaxation recordings to use before and after surgery. A week after surgery, patients in the second group reported lower stress and showed better wound healing (Broadbent el al., 2012).

Learning to Reflect and Accept

Meditation is a modern practice with a long history in a variety of world religions. Meditation was originally used to reduce suffering and improve awareness, insight, and compassion. Today, it has found a new home in stress management programs, such as **mindfulness meditation.** If you were taught this practice, you would relax and silently attend to your inner state, without judging it (Kabat-Zinn, 2001). You would sit down, close your eyes, and mentally scan your body from head to toe. Zooming your focus on certain body parts and responses, you would remain aware and accepting. You would also pay attention to your breathing, attending to each breath as if it were a material object.

Djomas/Shutterstock

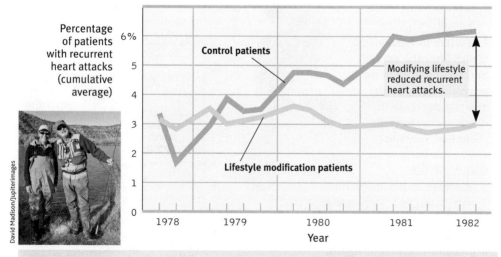

David Madison/Jupiterimages

FIGURE 10.8 Recurrent heart attacks and lifestyle modification The San Francisco Recurrent Coronary Prevention Project offered counseling from a cardiologist to survivors of heart attacks. Those who were also guided in modifying their Type A lifestyle suffered fewer repeat heart attacks. (From Friedman & Ulmer, 1984.)

Practicing mindfulness may improve many health measures. One study analyzed 39 experiences, involving 1140 people. Some received mindfulness-based therapy for several weeks. Others did not. Levels of anxiety and depression were lower among those who received the therapy (Hofmann et al., 2010). In another study, mindfulness training improved immune system functioning and coping in a group of women newly diagnosed with early-stage breast cancer (Witek-Janusek et al., 2008). Mindfulness practices have also been linked with improvements in other areas, including reducing sleep problems, cigarette use, binge eating, and alcohol and other substance abuse (Bowen et al., 2006; Brewer et al., 2011; Cincotta et al., 2011; de Dios et al., 2012; Kristeller et al., 2006).

So, what's going on in the brain as we practice mindfulness? Correlational and experimental studies offer three explanations for how mindfulness helps us make positive changes:

- *It strengthens connections among regions in our brain.* The affected regions are those associated with focusing our attention, processing what we see and hear, and being reflective and aware (Ives-Deliperi et al., 2011; Kilpatrick et al., 2011).

- *It activates brain regions associated with more reflective awareness* (Davidson et al., 2003; Way et al., 2010). When labeling emotions, "mindful people" show less activation in the amygdala, a brain region associated with fear, and more activation in the prefrontal cortex, which aids emotion regulation (Creswell et al., 2007).

- *It calms brain activation in emotional situations.* This lower activation was clear in one study in which participants watched two movies— one sad, one neutral. Those in the control group, who were not trained in mindfulness, showed strong differences in brain activation when watching the two movies. Those who had received mindfulness

training showed little change in brain response to the two movies (Farb et al., 2010). Emotionally unpleasant images also trigger weaker electrical brain responses in mindful people than in their less mindful counterparts (Brown et al., 2013). A mindful brain is strong, reflective, and soothing.

Exercise and meditation are not the only routes to healthy relaxation. Massage helps relax both premature infants (Chapter 3) and those suffering pain (Chapter 5). An analysis of 17 experiments revealed another benefit: Massage therapy relaxes muscles and helps reduce depression (Hou et al., 2010).

Faith Communities and Health

10-11 Does religious involvement relate to health?

A wealth of studies has revealed another curious correlation, called the *faith factor.* Religiously active people tend to live longer than those who are not religiously active. In one 16-year study, researchers tracked 3900 Israelis living in one of two groups of communities (Kark et al., 1996). The first group contained 11 religiously orthodox collective settlements. The second group contained 11 matched, nonreligious collective settlements. The researchers found that "belonging to a religious collective was associated with

a strong protective effect" not explained by age or economic differences. In every age group, religious community members were about half as likely to have died as were those in the nonreligious community.

How should we interpret such findings? Remember that correlation does not mean causation. What other factors might explain these protective effects? Here's one possibility: Women are more religiously active than men, and women outlive men. Does religious involvement reflect this gender-longevity link? No. Although the spirituality-longevity correlation is stronger among women, it also appears among men (McCullough et al., 2000, 2005). In study after study— some lasting 28 years, and some studying more than 20,000 people—the faith factor holds (Chida et al., 2009; Hummer et al., 1999; Schnall et al., 2010). And it holds after researchers control for age, sex, race, ethnicity, education, and region. In one study, this effect translated into a life expectancy at age 20 of 83 years for attenders at religious services (more than weekly) and only 75 years for nonattenders (FIGURE 10.9 on the next page).

Does this mean that nonattenders who start attending services and change nothing else will live longer? Again, the answer is *No.* But we can say that religious involvement *predicts* health and longevity, just as nonsmoking and exercise do. Religiously active people have

© MaRoDee Photography/Alamy
Fuse/Jupiterimages
Sura Nualpradid/Shutterstock
casejustin/Shutterstock
© Georgios Kollidas/Alamy
Georgios Kollidas/Shutterstock
ppart/Shutterstock

mindfulness meditation attending to current experiences in a nonjudgmental and accepting manner.

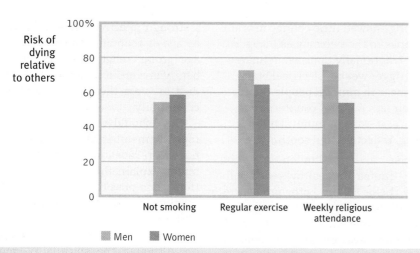

FIGURE 10.9 Predictors of longer life: Regular religious attendance, frequent exercise, and not smoking One 28-year study followed more then 5200 adults (Oman et al., 2002; Strawbridge et al., 1997, 1999). After adjusting for age and education, the researchers found that religious attendance, regular exercise, and not smoking all predicted a lowered risk of death in any given year. Women attending weekly religious services, for example, were only 54 percent as likely to die in a typical study year as were nonattenders.

demonstrated healthier immune functioning, fewer hospital admissions, and, for AIDS patients, fewer stress hormones and longer survival (Ironson et al., 2002; Koenig & Larson, 1998; Lutgendorf et al., 2004).

Can you imagine why religiously active people might be healthier and live longer than others? Here are three factors that help explain the correlation:

- *Healthy lifestyles* Religiously active people have healthier lifestyles. For example, they smoke and drink less (Islam & Johnson, 2003; Koenig & Vaillant, 2009; Koopmans et al., 1999). In one Gallup survey of 550,000 Americans, 15 percent of the very religious were smokers, compared with 28 percent of nonreligious people (Newport et al., 2010). But healthy lifestyles are not the complete answer. In studies that have controlled for unhealthy behaviors, such as inactivity and smoking, about 75 percent of the life-span difference remained (Musick et al., 1999).

- *Social support* Those who belong to a faith community have access to a support network. When misfortune strikes, religiously active people can turn to each other for support.

Moreover, religions encourage marriage, another predictor of health and longevity. In the Israeli religious settlements, for example, divorce has been almost nonexistent. But even after controlling for social support, gender, unhealthy behaviors, and preexisting health problems, much of the original religious engagement correlation remains (Chida et al., 2009; George et al., 2000; Powell et al., 2003).

- *Positive emotions* Researchers speculate that a third set of influences help protect religiously

active people from stress and enhance their well-being (FIGURE 10.10). Religiously active people have a stable worldview, a sense of hope for the long-term future, and feelings of ultimate acceptance. They may also benefit from the relaxed meditation of prayer or Sabbath observance. Taken together, these positive emotions and expectations may have a protective effect on well-being.

* * *

Let's summarize what we've learned so far: Sustained emotional reactions to stressful events can be damaging. However, some qualities and influences can help us cope with life's challenges by making us emotionally and physically stronger. These include a sense of control, an optimistic outlook, relaxation, healthy habits, social support, a sense of meaning, and spirituality (FIGURE 10.11).

In the remainder of this chapter, we'll take a closer look at our pursuit of happiness and how it relates to our human flourishing. ■

RETRIEVE + REMEMBER

- What are some of the tactics that help people manage the stress they cannot avoid?

ANSWERS: Aerobic exercise, relaxation procedures, mindfulness meditation, and religious engagement

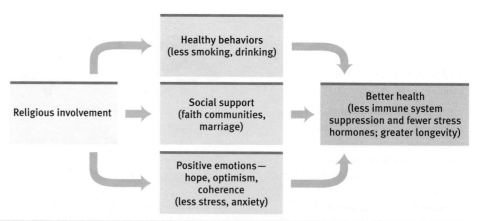

FIGURE 10.10 Possible explanations for the correlation between religious involvement and health/longevity

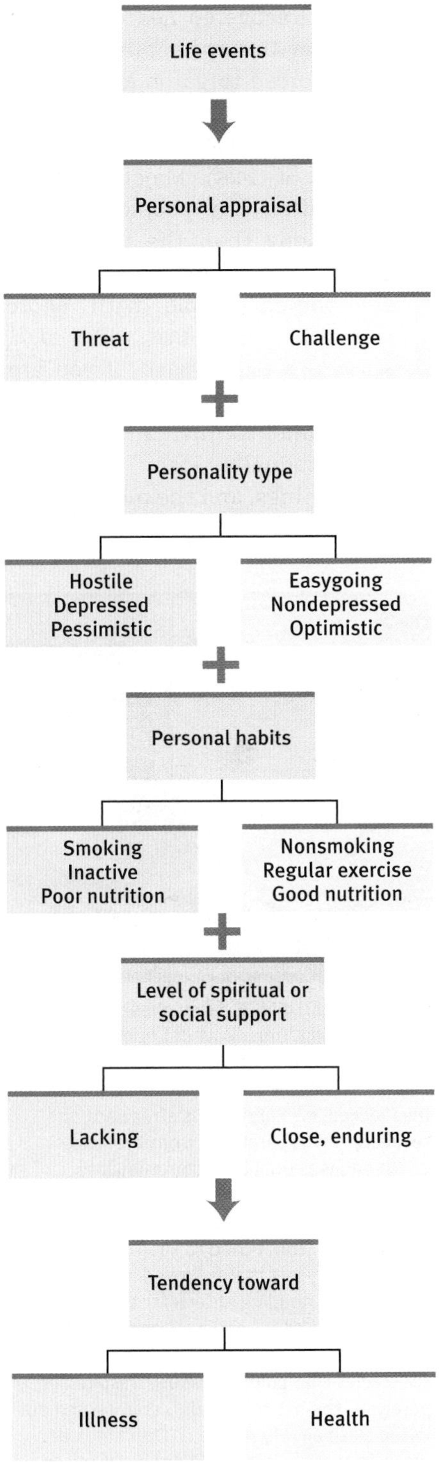

Life events

↓

Personal appraisal

Threat | Challenge

+

Personality type

Hostile
Depressed
Pessimistic | Easygoing
Nondepressed
Optimistic

+

Personal habits

Smoking
Inactive
Poor nutrition | Nonsmoking
Regular exercise
Good nutrition

+

Level of spiritual or
social support

Lacking | Close, enduring

↓

Tendency toward

Illness | Health

FIGURE 10.11 How to flourish

Happiness

10-12 What are the causes and consequences of happiness?

In *The How of Happiness*, psychologist Sonja Lyubomirsky (2008) tells the true story of Randy. By any measure, Randy lived a hard life. His dad and best friend died by suicide. Growing up, his mother's boyfriend treated him poorly. Randy's own first marriage was troubled. His wife was unfaithful, and they divorced. Despite these setbacks, Randy is a happy person whose endless optimism can light up a room. He remarried and enjoys his role as stepfather to three boys. He also finds his work life to be rewarding. Randy says he survived his life stressors by seeing the "silver lining in the cloud."

Bouncing back from serious losses, as Randy did, people may feel a stronger sense of self-esteem and a deeper sense of purpose. Tough challenges, especially early in life, can foster personal growth and emotional **resilience** (Landauer & Whiting, 1979).

Are you a person who makes everyone around you smile and laugh? Have you, like Randy, bounced back from serious challenges and become stronger because of it? Our state of happiness or unhappiness colors our thoughts and our actions. Happy people perceive the world as a safer place. They are more decisive and cooperate more easily. They live healthier and more energized and satisfied lives (Briñol et al., 2007; Liberman et al., 2009; Mauss et al., 2011). We all get gloomy sometimes. When that happens, life as a whole may seem depressing and meaningless. Let your mood brighten, and your thinking broadens and becomes more playful and creative (Baas et al., 2008; Forgas, 2008b; Fredrickson, 2006). Your relationships, your self-image, and your hopes for the future seem more promising.

This helps explain why college students' happiness helps predict their life

course. In one study, which surveyed thousands of U.S. college students in 1976 and restudied them at age 37, happy students had gone on to earn significantly more money than their less-happy-than-average peers (Diener et al., 2002). In another, the happiest 20-year-olds were not only more likely to marry, but also less likely to divorce (Stutzer & Frey, 2006).

Moreover—and this is one of psychology's most consistent findings—when we feel happy we become more helpful. Psychologists call it the **feel-good, do-good phenomenon** (Salovey, 1990). Happiness doesn't just feel good, it does good. In study after study, a mood-boosting experience (finding money, succeeding on a challenging task, recalling a happy event) has made people more likely to give money, pick up someone's dropped papers, volunteer time, and do other good deeds.

The reverse is also true: Doing good promotes feeling good. One survey of more than 200,000 people in 136 countries found that, pretty much everywhere, people report feeling happier after spending money on others rather than themselves (Aknin et al., 2013). Some happiness coaches and instructors harness this force by asking their clients to perform a daily "random act of kindness" and to record how it made them feel.

William James was writing about the importance of happiness ("the secret motive for all [we] do") as early as 1902. With the rise of *positive psychology* in the twenty-first century (Chapter 1), the study of happiness has become a main area of research. It is a key part of one of our big ideas in this text: Psychology explores human strengths as well as challenges. Part of happiness research is

resilience the personal strength that helps most people cope with stress and recover from adversity and even trauma.

feel-good, do-good phenomenon our tendency to be helpful when already in a good mood.

the study of **subjective well-being**— our feelings of happiness (sometimes defined as a high ratio of positive to negative feelings) or sense of satisfaction with life. This information, combined with objective measures of well-being, such as a person's physical and economic condition, is helping us understand our quality-of-life judgments.

The Short Life of Emotional Ups and Downs

Are some days of the week happier than others? In what is surely psychology's biggest-ever data sample, one social psychologist (Kramer, 2010—at my [DM] request and in cooperation with Facebook) did a naturalistic observation of emotion words in "billions" of status updates. After eliminating exceptional days, such as holidays, he tracked the frequency of positive and negative emotion words by day of the week. The days with the most positive moods? Friday and Saturday (**FIGURE 10.12**). A similar analysis of emotion-related words in 59 million Twitter messages found Friday to Sunday the

TAKE HEART! TOMORROW WILL BE A NEW DAY Car trouble can happen at the worst possible times. But this young man's bad mood will almost certainly clear by tomorrow, when he may even experience a better-than-normal good mood.

week's happiest days (Golder & Macy, 2011). For you, too?

Over the long run, our emotional ups and downs tend to balance out. This is true even over the course of the day. Positive emotion rises over the early to middle part of most days and then drops off (Kahneman et al., 2004; Watson, 2000). So, too, with day-to-day moods. A stressful event—an argument, a sick child, a car problem—triggers a bad mood. No surprise there. But by the next day, the gloom nearly always lifts (Affleck et al., 1994; Bolger et al., 1989; Stone & Neale, 1984). If anything, people tend to bounce back from a bad day to a better-than-usual good mood the following day. Even when negative events drag us down for longer periods, our bad mood usually ends. We may feel that our heart has broken during a romantic breakup, but eventually the wound heals.

Grief over the loss of a loved one or anxiety after a

severe trauma can linger. But usually, even tragedy is not permanently depressing. People who have become blind or paralyzed have usually recovered near-normal levels of day-to-day happiness. So have those forced to go on kidney dialysis or to have permanent colostomies (Gerhart et al., 1994; Riis et al., 2005; Smith et al., 2009). Major disabilities have often left people somewhat less happy than the average person, yet considerably happier than able-bodied people with depression (Kübler et al., 2005; Lucas, 2007a,b; Schwartz & Estrin, 2004). "If you are a paraplegic," explained psychologist Daniel Kahneman (2005), "you will gradually start thinking of other things, and the more time you

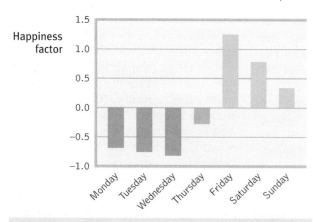

HUMAN RESILIENCE Seven weeks after her 1994 wedding, Anna Putt of South Midlands, England, shown here with her husband, Des, suffered a brainstem stroke that left her "locked in." For months afterward, she recalled, "I was paralyzed from the neck down and was unable to communicate. These were VERY frightening times. But with encouragement from family, friends, faith, and medical staff, I tried to keep positive." In the three years that followed, she learned to "talk" (by nodding at letters), to steer an electric wheelchair with her head, and to use a computer (by nodding while wearing spectacles that guide a cursor). Despite her paralysis, she has reported, "I enjoy going out in the fresh air. My motto is 'Don't look back, move forward.' God would not want me to stop trying and I have no intention of doing so. Life is what you make of it!"

FIGURE 10.12 Using web science to track happy days Adam Kramer (personal correspondence, 2010) tracked positive and negative emotion words in many "billions" (the exact number is proprietary information) of status updates of U.S. users of Facebook between September 7, 2007, and November 17, 2010.

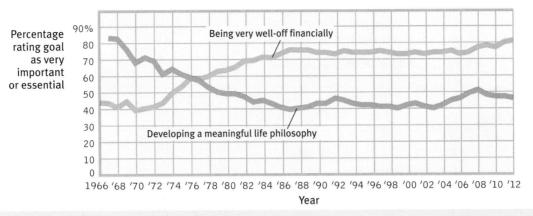

FIGURE 10.13 The changing materialism of entering college students Yearly surveys of more than 200,000 entering U.S. college students have, since 1970, revealed an increasing desire for wealth. (From *The American Freshman* surveys, UCLA, 1966 to 2012.)

spend thinking of other things, the less miserable you are going to be." Contrary to what many people believe, even most patients "locked in" a motionless body do not indicate they want to die (Nizzi et al., 2012; Smith & Delargy, 2005; 2011). The surprising reality: *We overestimate the duration of our emotions and underestimate our resilience—our ability to bounce back.*

Wealth and Well-Being

Would you be happier if you made more money? In a 2006 Gallup poll, 73 percent

"Researchers say I'm not happier for being richer, but do you know how much researchers make?"

of Americans thought they would be. How important is "Being very well off financially"? *Very important,* say many entering U.S. collegians (FIGURE 10.13).

Having enough money to buy your way out of hunger and to enable a sense of control over your life does buy some happiness (Fischer & Boer, 2011). Money's power to buy happiness also depends on your current income. A $1000 annual wage increase would do a lot more for the average person in a very poor country than for the average person in a very rich one. But once one has enough money for comfort and security, piling up more and more matters less and less.

Consider: During the last four decades, the average U.S. citizen's buying power almost tripled. Did this greater wealth—enabling twice as many cars per person, not to mention iPads, smart phones, and HDTVs—also buy more happiness? As FIGURE 10.14 on the next page shows, the average American, though certainly richer, is not a bit happier. In 1957, some 35 percent said they were "very happy," as did slightly fewer— 29 percent—in 2010. Ditto China, where living standards have risen but happiness has not (Davey & Rato, 2012; Easterlin et al., 2012). These findings lob a bombshell at modern materialism: *Economic growth in wealthy countries has provided no apparent boost to morale or social well-being.*

Why Can't Money Buy More Happiness?

Why is it that, for those who are not poor, more and more money does not buy more and more happiness? More generally, why do our emotions seem to be attached to elastic bands that pull us back from highs or lows? Psychology has proposed two answers. Each suggests that happiness is relative.

My Happiness Is Relative to My Own Experience

We tend to judge new events by comparing them with our past experiences. Psychologists call this the **adaptation-level phenomenon.** Our past experiences act as *neutral* levels—sounds that seem neither loud nor soft, temperatures that seem neither hot nor cold, events that seem neither pleasant nor unpleasant. We then notice and react to variations up or down from these levels.

subjective well-being self-perceived happiness or satisfaction with life. Used along with measures of objective well-being (for example, physical and economic indicators) to judge our quality of life.

adaptation-level phenomenon our tendency to form judgments (of sounds, of lights, of income) relative to a neutral level defined by our past experiences.

"Money won't make you happy, Waldron. So instead of a raise, I'm giving a Prozac."

So, could we ever create a permanent social paradise? Probably not (Campbell, 1975; Di Tella et al., 2010). People who have experienced a recent windfall—from the lottery, an inheritance, or a surging economy—typically feel joy and satisfaction (Diener & Oishi, 2000; Gardner & Oswald, 2007). You would, too, if you woke up tomorrow with all your wishes granted. Wouldn't you love to live in a world with no bills, no ills, perfect grades, and someone who loves you unreservedly? But after a time, you would gradually adapt, and you would adjust your neutral level to include these new experiences. Before long, you would again sometimes feel joy and satisfaction (when events exceed your expectations), sometimes feel let down (when they fall below), and sometimes feel neutral.

The point to remember: Feelings of satisfaction and dissatisfaction, success and failure are judgments we make about ourselves, based on our prior experience.

My Happiness Is Relative to Your Success

We are always comparing ourselves with others. And whether we feel good or bad depends on our perception of just how successful those others are (Lyubomirsky, 2001). We are slow-witted or clumsy only when others are smarter or more graceful. This sense that we are worse off than

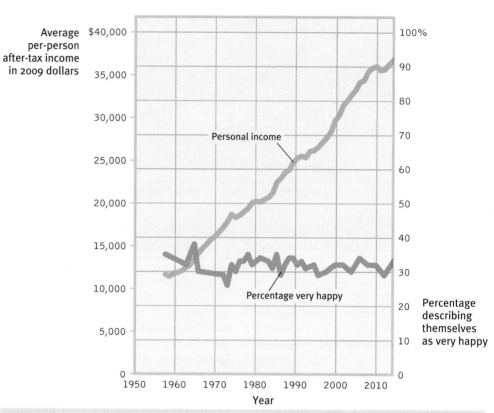

FIGURE 10.14 Does money buy happiness? Money surely helps us to avoid certain types of pain. Yet, though buying power has almost tripled since the 1950s, the average American's reported happiness has remained almost unchanged. (Happiness data from National Opinion Research Center surveys; income data from Historical Statistics of the United States and Economic Indicators.)

others with whom we compare ourselves is called **relative deprivation.**

When expectations soar above achievements, the result is disappointment. Thus, the middle- and upper-income people in a given country, who can compare themselves with the relatively poor, tend to be more satisfied with life than are their less-fortunate fellow citizens. Nevertheless, once people reach a moderate income level, further increases buy smaller increases in happiness. Why? Because as people climb the ladder of success, they mostly compare themselves with local peers who are at or above their current level (Gruder, 1977; Suls & Tesch, 1978; Zell & Alicke, 2010).

HI & LOIS

TABLE 10.1 Happiness Is . . .

Researchers Have Found That Happy People Tend to	However, Happiness Seems Not Much Related to Other Factors, Such as
Have high self-esteem (in individualist countries).	Age.
Be optimistic, outgoing, and agreeable.	Gender (women are more often depressed, but also more often joyful).
Have close friendships or a satisfying marriage.	Education level.
Have work and leisure that engage their skills.	Parenthood (having children or not).
Have a meaningful religious faith.	Physical attractiveness.
Sleep well and exercise.	

Source: Summarized from DeNeve & Cooper (1998), Diener et al. (2003), Headey et al. (2010), Lucas et al. (2004), Myers (1993, 2000), Myers & Diener (1995, 1996), and Steel et al. (2008).

Just as comparing ourselves with those who are better off creates envy, so counting our blessings as we compare ourselves with those worse off boosts our contentment. In one study, University of Wisconsin–Milwaukee women considered others' suffering (Dermer et al., 1979). They viewed vivid images of how grim life was in Milwaukee in 1900. They imagined and then wrote about various personal tragedies, such as being burned and disfigured. Later, the women expressed greater satisfaction with their own lives. Similarly, when mildly depressed people have read about some-one who was even more depressed, they felt somewhat better (Gibbons, 1986). "I cried because I had no shoes," states a Persian saying, "until I met a man who had no feet."

Predictors of Happiness

Happy people share many characteristics (**TABLE 10.1**). But what makes one person so filled with joy, day after day, and others so gloomy? Here, as in so many other areas, the answer is found in the interplay between nature and nurture.

Genes matter. Studies of hundreds of identical and fraternal twins indicate that heredity accounts for about 50 percent of the difference among people's happiness ratings (Gigantesco et al., 2011; Lykken & Tellegen, 1996). Identical twins raised apart are often similarly happy.

But our personal history and our culture matter, too. On the personal level, as we saw earlier, our emotions tend to balance around a level defined by our experiences. On the cultural level, groups vary in the traits they value. Self-esteem matters more to Westerners, who value individualism. Social acceptance and harmony matter more to those in other cultures, such as in Japan, that stress family and community (Diener et al., 2003; Uchida & Kitayama, 2009).

Depending on our genes, our outlook, and our recent experiences, our happiness seems to vary around our "happiness set point." Some of us seem to be ever upbeat; others, more negative. Even so, our satisfaction with life is not fixed (Fujita & Diener, 2005; Mroczek & Spiro, 2005). As researchers studying human strengths will tell you, happiness rises and falls, and we can control some of the factors that make us more or less happy (Sin & Lyubomirsky, 2009). For more on this idea, see Close-Up: Want to Be Happier?

If we can enhance our happiness on an *individual* level, could we use happiness research to refocus our *national* priorities more on advancing psychological well-being? Many psychologists believe we could. More than 50 of them have joined together to propose ways in which nations might measure national well-being and assess the impacts of various public policies (Diener et al., 2006, 2009). Happy societies are not only prosperous but are also places where people trust one another, feel free, and enjoy close relationships (Oishi & Schimmack, 2010; Sachs, 2012). Thus, when debating such issues as economic inequality, tax rates, divorce laws, and health care, people's psychological well-being should be a prime consideration. The Canadian, French, German, and British governments have each added well-being measures to their national agendas (Cohen, 2011; Gertner, 2010; Stiglitz, 2009). Such measures may help guide nations toward policies that decrease stress and foster human flourishing. ■

"I could cry when I think of the years I wasted accumulating money, only to learn that my cheerful disposition is genetic."

relative deprivation the perception that we are worse off relative to those with whom we compare ourselves.

Want to Be Happier?

Your happiness, like your cholesterol level, is genetically influenced. Yet as cholesterol is also influenced by diet and exercise, so happiness is to some extent under your personal control (Nes, 2010; Sin & Lyubomirsky, 2009). Here are some research-based suggestions for building your personal strengths to increase your satisfaction with life.

Realize that enduring happiness doesn't come from financial success. We adapt to change by adjusting our expectations. Neither wealth, nor any other circumstance we long for, will guarantee happiness.

Take control of your time. Happy people feel in control of their lives. To master your use of time, set goals and divide them into daily aims. This may be frustrating at first because we all tend to overestimate how much we will accomplish in any given day. The good news is that we generally *underestimate* how much we can accomplish in a year, given just a little progress every day.

Act happy. As you saw earlier in Chapter 9, people who have been manipulated into a smiling expression felt better. So put on a happy face. Talk *as if* you feel positive self-esteem, are optimistic, and are outgoing. We can often act our way into a happier state of mind.

Seek work and leisure that engage your skills. Happy people often are in a zone called *flow*—absorbed in tasks that challenge but don't overwhelm them. Passive forms of leisure (watching TV) often provide less flow experience than exercising, socializing, or expressing your musical interests. And frequent small positive experiences make for more lasting happiness than big but rare positive events. Money also buys more happiness when spent on experiences you can look forward to, enjoy, and remember than when spent on material stuff (Carter & Gilovich, 2010).

Photodisc/Jupiterimages

Join the "movement" movement. Aerobic exercise can relieve mild depression and anxiety as it promotes health and energy. Sound minds reside in sound bodies. Off your duffs, couch potatoes!

Give your body the sleep it wants. Happy people live active lives yet save time for renewing sleep. Many people—high school and college students, especially—suffer from sleep debt. The result is fatigue, diminished alertness, and gloomy moods.

Give priority to close relationships. Confiding is good for soul and body. Those who care deeply about you can help you weather difficult times. Compared with unhappy people, happy people engage in less small talk and more meaningful conversations (Mehl et al., 2010). You can nurture your closest relationships by not taking your loved ones for granted. This means being as kind to them as you are to others, affirming them, playing together, and sharing together.

Focus beyond self. Reach out to those in need. Happiness increases helpfulness (those who feel good do good). But doing good also makes us feel good.

Count your blessings and record your gratitude. Keeping a gratitude journal heightens well-being (Emmons, 2007; Seligman et al., 2005). Each day, savor the good moments and positive events and record why they occurred. Express your gratitude to others.

Nurture your spiritual self. For many people, faith provides a support community, a reason to focus beyond self, and a sense of purpose and hope. That helps explain why people active in faith communities report greater-than-average happiness and often cope well with crises.

Digested from David G. Myers, The Pursuit of Happiness (Harper).

CHAPTER REVIEW

Stress, Health, and Human Flourishing

Test yourself by taking a moment to answer each of these Learning Objective Questions (repeated here from within the chapter). Then turn to Appendix D, Complete Chapter Reviews, to check your answers. Research suggests that trying to answer these questions on your own will improve your long-term memory of the concepts (McDaniel et al., 2009).

Stress: Some Basic Concepts

10-1: How does our appraisal of an event affect our stress reaction, and what are the three main types of stressors?

10-2: How does the body respond to stress?

Stress Effects and Health

10-3: How does stress influence our immune system?

10-4: How does stress increase coronary heart disease risk?

Coping With Stress

10-5: What are two basic ways that people cope with stress?

10-6: How does our sense of control influence stress and health?

10-7: How do optimists and pessimists differ, and why does our outlook on life matter?

10-8: How do social support and finding meaning in life influence health?

Managing Stress Effects

10-9: How well does aerobic exercise help manage stress and improve well-being?

10-10: In what ways might relaxation and meditation influence stress and health?

10-11: Does religious involvement relate to health?

Happiness

10-12: What are the causes and consequences of happiness?

TERMS AND CONCEPTS TO REMEMBER

Test yourself on these terms by trying to write down the definition in your own words before flipping back to the referenced page to check your answer.

stress, p. 284
fight-or-flight response, p. 285
general adaptation syndrome (GAS), p. 285
tend-and-befriend reponse, p. 286

psychoneuroimmunology, p. 286
lymphocytes, p. 287
coronary heart disease, p. 289
Type A, p. 289
Type B, p. 289

coping, p. 291
problem-focused coping, p. 291
emotion-focused coping, p. 291
personal control, p. 291
learned helplessness, p. 291
external locus of control, p. 292
internal locus of control, p. 292
optimism, p. 293
pessimism, p. 293

aerobic exercise, p. 296
mindfulness meditation, p. 298
resilience, p. 301
feel-good, do-good phenomenon, p. 301
subjective well-being, p. 302
adaptation-level phenomenon, p. 303
relative deprivation, p. 304

CHAPTER TEST

Test yourself repeatedly throughout your studies. This will not only help you figure out what you know and don't know; the testing itself will help you learn and remember the information more effectively thanks to the *testing effect*.

1. Selye's general adaptation syndrome (GAS) consists of an alarm reaction followed by _____, then _____.

2. When faced with stress, women are more likely than men to experience the _____-and-_____ response.

3. The number of short-term illnesses and stress-related psychological disorders was higher than usual in the months following an earthquake. Such findings suggest that

   a. daily hassles have adverse health consequences.

   b. experiencing a very stressful event increases a person's vulnerability to illness.

   c. the amount of stress a person feels is directly related to the number of stressors experienced.

   d. small, bad events don't cause stress, but large ones can be toxic.

4. Which of the following is NOT one of the three main types of stressors?

   a. Catastrophes

   b. Significant life changes

   c. Daily hassles

   d. Threatening events that we hear about

5. Stress hormones released in response to a signal from the brain suppress _____, the immune cells that ordinarily attack bacteria, viruses, cancer cells, and other foreign substances.

6. Research has shown that people are at increased risk for cancer a year or so after experiencing depression, helplessness, or bereavement. In describing this link, researchers are quick to point out that

   a. accumulated stress causes cancer.

   b. anger is the negative emotion most closely linked to cancer.

   c. stress does not create cancer cells, but it weakens the body's natural defenses against them.

   d. feeling optimistic about chances of survival ensures that a cancer patient will get well.

7. A Chinese proverb warns, "The fire you kindle for your enemy often burns you more than him." How is this true of Type A individuals?

8. The components of the Type A personality that have been linked most closely to coronary heart disease are anger and other _____ feelings.

9. When faced with a situation over which you feel you have no control, it is most effective to use _____ (emotion/problem)-focused coping.

10. Research has showed that a dog will respond with learned helplessness if it has received repeated shocks and has had

    a. the opportunity to escape.

    b. no control over the shocks.

    c. pain or discomfort.

    d. no food or water prior to the shocks.

11. When elderly patients take an active part in managing their own care and surroundings, their morale and health tend to improve. Such findings indicate that people do better when they experience an _____ (internal/external) locus of control.

12. People who have close relationships are less likely to die prematurely than those who do not, supporting the idea that

    a. social ties can be a source of stress.

    b. gender influences longevity.

    c. Type A behavior is responsible for many premature deaths.

    d. social support has a beneficial effect on health.

13. Because it triggers the release of mood-boosting neurotransmitters such as serotonin, _____ exercise raises energy levels and helps alleviate depression and anxiety.

14. Research on the faith factor has found that

    a. pessimists tend to be healthier than optimists.

    b. our expectations influence our feelings of stress.

    c. religiously active people tend to outlive those who are not religiously active.

    d. religious engagement promotes isolation, repression, and ill health.

15. One of the most consistent findings of psychological research is that happy people are also

    a. more likely to express anger.

    b. generally luckier than others.

    c. concentrated in the wealthier nations.

    d. more likely to help others.

16. After moving to a new apartment, you find the street noise irritatingly loud, but after a while, it no longer bothers you. This reaction illustrates the

    a. relative deprivation principle.

    b. adaptation-level phenomenon.

    c. feel-good, do-good phenomenon.

    d. catharsis principle.

17. A philosopher observed that we cannot escape envy, because there will always be someone more successful, more accomplished, or richer with whom to compare ourselves. In psychology, this observation is embodied in the _____ _____ principle.

Find answers to these questions in Appendix E, in the back of the book.

IN YOUR EVERYDAY LIFE

Answering these questions will help you make these concepts more personally meaningful, and therefore more memorable.

1. In what ways have you experienced the stress adaptation phases of alarm, resistance, and exhaustion in your life as a student?

2. Do you think you are Type A, Type B, or somewhere in between? In what ways has this been helpful to you, and in what ways has this been a challenge?

3. Can you remember a time when you felt better after discussing a problem with a loved one, or even after playing with your pet? How did it help you to cope?

4. What strategies have you used to cope with stress in your own life? How well are they working? What other strategies could you try?

5. How much control do you feel you have over your life? What changes could you make to increase your sense of control?

experience
more of the
testing
effect

11 Personality

Lady Gaga dazzles millions with her unique musical arrangements, tantalizing outfits, and provocative performance theatrics. In shows around the world, Lady Gaga's most predictable feature is her unpredictability. She has worn a meat dress to an award show, performed in a plastic bubble dress, and caused President Barack Obama to describe his interaction with her as "a little intimidating" in light of the 16-inch heels she wore.

Lady Gaga's fans and critics can depend on her openness to new experiences and the energy she gets from the spotlight. But they can also rely on her careful, painstaking dedication to her music and performances. She describes herself in high school as "very dedicated, very studious, and very disciplined." Now, in adulthood, she shows similar self-discipline: "I'm very detailed—every minute of the show has got to be perfect."

Lady Gaga exhibits distinctive and enduring ways of thinking, feeling, and behaving. Earlier chapters focused on the similar ways we develop, perceive, learn, remember, think, and feel. This chapter emphasizes what makes us unique—our **personality.**

Much of this book deals with personality. Earlier chapters considered biological influences on personality, personality development across the life span, and how personality relates to learning, motivation, emotion, and health. Later chapters will study social influences on personality and disorders of personality. This chapter focuses on personality itself—what it is and how researchers study it.

We begin with two historically important grand theories of personality that have become part of our cultural legacy. Sigmund Freud's *psychoanalytic theory* proposed that childhood sexuality and unconscious motivations influence personality. The *humanistic approach* focused on our inner abilities for growth and self-fulfillment.

The chapter then explores today's more scientific study of personality. We'll look at the traits that define our uniqueness. We'll see how biology, psychology, and environment together influence personality. Finally, we'll note how our concept of self— that sense of "Who I am"—helps organize our thoughts, feelings, and behaviors.

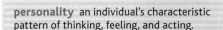

personality an individual's characteristic pattern of thinking, feeling, and acting.

Psychodynamic Theories

◎ **Psychodynamic theories** of personality view human behavior as a lively (dynamic) interaction between the conscious and unconscious mind, and they consider our related motives and conflicts. These theories came from Sigmund Freud's **psychoanalysis**, a historically important theory of personality that included methods for treating psychological disorders. Freud's work was the first to focus clinical attention on our unconscious mind.

Freud's Psychoanalytic Perspective: Exploring the Unconscious

11-1 How did Sigmund Freud's treatment of psychological disorders lead to his view of the unconscious mind?

Freud was not psychology's most important figure, but he is definitely the most famous. Ask 100 people on the street to name a deceased psychologist, suggested Keith Stanovich (1996, p. 1), and "Freud would be the winner hands down." His influence lingers in books, movies, and psychological therapies. Who was Freud, what did he teach, and why do we still study his work?

Like all of us, Sigmund Freud was a product of his times. His Victorian era was a time of great discovery and scientific advancement, but it is also known today as a time of sexual repression and male dominance. Men's and women's roles were clearly defined, with male superiority assumed and only male sexuality generally acknowledged (discreetly).

After graduating from the University of Vienna medical school, Freud specialized in nervous disorders. Before long, he began hearing complaints that made no medical sense. One patient had lost all

SIGMUND FREUD (1856–1939) "I was the only worker in a new field."

feeling in one hand. Yet there is no nerve pathway that, if damaged, would numb the entire hand and nothing else. Freud wondered: What could cause such disorders? His search for the answer led in a direction that would challenge our self-understanding.

Could these strange disorders have mental rather than physical causes? Freud decided they could. Many meetings with patients led to Freud's "discovery" of the **unconscious.** In Freud's view, this deep well keeps unacceptable thoughts, wishes, feelings, and memories hidden away so thoroughly that we are no longer aware of them. But despite our best efforts, bits and pieces of these ideas seep out. Thus, according to Freud, patients might have an odd loss of feeling in their hand because they have an unconscious fear of touching their genitals. Or their unexplained blindness might be caused by unconsciously not wanting to see something that makes them anxious.

Basic to Freud's theory was his belief that the mind is mostly hidden. Below the surface lies a large unconscious region where unacceptable passions and thoughts lurk. Freud believed we

"I know how hard it is for you to put food on your family."
Former U.S. President George W. Bush, 2000

repress these unconscious feelings and ideas, blocking them from awareness, because admitting them would be too unsettling. Nevertheless, he said, these repressed feelings and ideas powerfully influence us.

For Freud, nothing was ever accidental. He saw the unconscious seeping not only into people's troubling symptoms but also, in disguised forms, into their work, their beliefs, and their daily habits. He also glimpsed the unconscious in slips of the tongue and pen, as when a financially stressed patient, not wanting any large pills, said, "Please do not give me any bills, because I cannot swallow them." Jokes, too, were expressions of repressed sexual and aggressive tendencies traveling in disguise. Dreams, he said, were the "royal road to the unconscious." He thought the dreams we remember are really censored versions of our unconscious wishes.

Hoping to unlock the door to the unconscious, Freud first tried hypnosis, but with poor results. He then turned to **free association,** telling patients to relax and say whatever came to mind, no matter how unimportant or silly. Freud believed that free association would trace a path from the troubled present into a patient's distant past. The chain of thought would lead back to the patient's unconscious, the hiding place of painful past memories, often from childhood. His goal was to find these forbidden thoughts and release them.

"Good morning, beheaded—uh, I mean beloved."

Personality Structure

11-2 What was Freud's view of personality?

In Freud's view, human personality arises from a conflict between impulse and restraint. People who evolved from "lower animals" are born with aggressive, pleasure-seeking urges, Freud famously said. "Man is wolf to man." He believed that as we are socialized, we internalize social restraints against these urges. Personality is the result of our efforts to resolve basic conflict—to express these impulses in ways that bring satisfaction without guilt or punishment.

To understand the mind's conflicts, Freud proposed three interacting systems: the *id, ego,* and *superego.* Psychologists have found it useful to view the mind's structure as an iceberg (FIGURE 11.1).

The **id** stores unconscious energy. It tries to satisfy our basic drives to survive, reproduce, and be aggressive. The id operates on the *pleasure principle:* It seeks immediate gratification. To see

"Fifty is plenty."   "Hundred and fifty."

The ego struggles to reconcile the demands of superego and id, said Freud.

the id's power, think of newborn infants crying out the moment they feel a need, wanting satisfaction now. Or think of people who abuse drugs, partying now rather than sacrificing today's pleasure for future success and happiness (Keough et al., 1999).

The mind's second part, the **ego,** operates on the *reality principle.* The ego is the conscious mind. It tries to satisfy the id's impulses in realistic ways that will bring long-term benefits rather than pain or destruction.

As the ego develops, the young child learns to cope with the real world. Around age 4 or 5, Freud theorized, a child's ego begins to recognize the demands of the **superego,** the voice of our moral compass, or *conscience.* The superego forces the ego to consider not only the real but the ideal. It focuses on how one *ought* to behave in a perfect world. It judges actions and produces positive feelings of pride or negative feelings of guilt.

As you may have guessed, the superego's demands often oppose the id's. It is the ego's job to reconcile the two. As the

psychodynamic theories view of personality with a focus on the unconscious and the importance of childhood experiences.

psychoanalysis Freud's theory of personality that attributes thoughts and actions to unconscious motives and conflicts; the techniques used in treating psychological disorders by seeking to expose and interpret unconscious tensions.

unconscious according to Freud, a reservoir of mostly unacceptable thoughts, wishes, feelings, and memories. According to contemporary psychologists, information processing of which we are unaware.

free association in psychoanalysis, a method of exploring the unconscious in which the person relaxes and says whatever comes to mind, no matter how unimportant or embarrassing.

id a reservoir of unconscious psychic energy that, according to Freud, strives to satisfy basic sexual and aggressive drives. The id operates on the *pleasure principle,* demanding immediate gratification.

ego the largely conscious, "executive" part of personality that, according to Freud, balances the demands of the id, superego, and reality. The ego operates on the *reality principle,* satisfying the id's desires in ways that will realistically bring pleasure rather than pain.

superego the part of personality that, according to Freud, represents internalized ideals and provides standards for judgment (the conscience) and for future goals.

Ego
(mostly conscious; makes peace between the id and the superego)

Conscious mind

Superego
(internalized ideals)

Id
(unconscious energy)

Unconscious mind

FIGURE 11.1 Freud's idea of the mind's structure Icebergs hide most of their bulk beneath the surface of the water. Psychologists often use this image to show Freud's idea that the mind is mostly hidden beneath the surface of our awareness. Unlike the parts of a frozen iceberg, however, the id, ego, and superego interact.

TABLE 11.1 Freud's Psychosexual Stages	
Stage	**Focus**
Oral (0–18 months)	Pleasure centers on the mouth—sucking, biting, chewing
Anal (18–36 months)	Pleasure focuses on bowel and bladder elimination; coping with demands for control
Phallic (3–6 years)	Pleasure zone is the genitals; coping with incestuous sexual feelings
Latency (6 to puberty)	Dormant sexual feelings
Genital (puberty on)	Maturation of sexual interests

"Oh, for goodness' sake! Smoke!"

personality's "executive," the ego juggles the impulsive demands of the id, the restraining demands of the superego, and the real-life demands of the external world.

Personality Development

11-3 **What developmental stages did Freud propose?**

Freud believed that personality formed during life's first few years. He was convinced that children pass through a series of **psychosexual stages,** from oral to genital **(TABLE 11.1).** In each stage, the id's pleasure-seeking energies focus on an *erogenous zone,* a distinct pleasure-sensitive area of the body.

Freud believed that during the third stage, the *phallic stage,* boys seek genital

"I heard that as soon as we become aware of our sexual impulses, whatever they are, we'll have to hide them."

stimulation, and they develop unconscious sexual desires for their mother. They feel jealousy and hatred for their father, who is a rival for their mother's attention. These feelings lead to guilt and a lurking fear that their father will punish them, perhaps by castration. Freud called this cluster of feelings the **Oedipus complex,** after the Greek legend of Oedipus, who unknowingly killed his father and married his mother. Some psychoanalysts in Freud's era believed that girls experienced a parallel *Electra complex.*

Children learn to cope with these feelings by repressing them, said Freud. They identify with the "rival" parent and try to become like him or her. It's as though something inside the child decides, "If you can't beat 'em, join 'em." This **identification** process strengthens children's superegos as they take on many of their parents' values. Freud believed that identification with the same-sex parent provides what psychologists now call our *gender identity*—our sense of being male or female.

Other conflicts could arise at other childhood stages. But whatever the stage, unresolved conflicts can cause trouble in adulthood. The result, Freud believed, would be **fixation,** locking the person's pleasure-seeking energies at the unresolved stage. A child who is either orally overindulged or orally deprived (perhaps by abrupt, early weaning) might become stalled at the

oral stage, for example. As an adult, this orally fixated person might continue to seek oral gratification by smoking or excessive eating. In such ways, Freud suggested, the twig of personality is bent at an early age.

Defense Mechanisms

11-4 **How did Freud think people defended themselves against anxiety?**

Anxiety, said Freud, is the price we pay for civilization. As members of social groups, we must control our sexual and aggressive impulses, not act them out. Sometimes the ego fears losing control of this inner war between the id and superego, which results in a dark cloud of generalized anxiety. We feel unsettled, but we don't know why.

Freud proposed that the ego distorts reality in an effort to protect itself from anxiety. **Defense mechanisms** help achieve this goal by disguising threatening impulses and preventing them from reaching consciousness. Note that, for Freud, *all defense mechanisms function indirectly and unconsciously.* Just as the body unconsciously defends itself against disease, so also does the ego unconsciously defend itself against anxiety. For example, **repression** banishes anxiety-arousing wishes and feelings from consciousness. According to Freud,

TABLE 11.2 Six Defense Mechanisms

Freud believed that *repression*, the basic mechanism that banishes anxiety-arousing impulses, enables other defense mechanisms, including these six.

Defense Mechanism	Unconscious Process Employed to Avoid Anxiety-Arousing Thoughts or Feelings	Example
Regression	Retreating to a more infantile psychosexual stage, where some psychic energy remains fixated.	A little boy reverts to the oral comfort of thumb sucking on the way to his first day of school.
Reaction formation	Switching unacceptable impulses into their opposites.	Repressing angry feelings, a person displays exaggerated friendliness.
Projection	Disguising one's own threatening impulses by attributing them to others.	An El Salvadoran saying captures the idea: "The thief thinks everyone else is a thief."
Rationalization	Offering self-justifying explanations in place of the real, more threatening unconscious reasons for one's actions.	A habitual drinker says she drinks with her friends "just to be sociable."
Displacement	Shifting sexual or aggressive impulses toward a more acceptable or less threatening object or person.	A little girl kicks the family dog after her mother puts her in time-out.
Denial	Refusing to believe or even perceive painful realities.	A partner denies evidence of his loved one's affair.

REGRESSION Faced with a stressor, children and young orangutans may regress, retreating to the comfort of earlier behaviors.

repression underlies all of the other defense mechanisms. However, because repression is often incomplete, repressed urges may appear as symbols in dreams or as slips of the tongue in casual conversation. TABLE 11.2 describes six other well-known defense mechanisms. ■

The Neo-Freudian and Later Psychodynamic Theorists

11-5 Which of Freud's ideas did his followers accept or reject?

Freud's writings caused a lot of debate. Living in a historical period when people never talked about sex, and certainly not unconscious desires for sex with one's parent, Freud was constantly criticized. In a letter to a trusted friend, Freud wrote, "In the Middle Ages, they would have burned me. Now they are content with burning my books." Despite the controversy, Freud attracted followers. Several young, ambitious physicians formed an inner circle around the strong-minded Freud. These *neo-Freudians*, such as Alfred Adler, Karen Horney [HORN-eye], and Carl Jung [Yoong], accepted Freud's basic ideas:

- Personality has three parts: id, ego, and superego.
- The unconscious is key.
- Personality is shaped in childhood.
- We use defense mechanisms to ward off anxiety.

But the neo-Freudians differed from Freud in two important ways. First, they placed more emphasis on the role of the *conscious* mind. Second, they doubted that sex and aggression were all-consuming motivations. Instead, they tended to emphasize loftier motives and social interactions.

psychosexual stages the childhood stages of development (oral, anal, phallic, latency, genital) during which, according to Freud, the id's pleasure-seeking energies focus on distinct erogenous zones.

Oedipus [ED-uh-puss] **complex** according to Freud, a boy's sexual desires toward his mother and feelings of jealousy and hatred for the rival father.

identification the process by which, according to Freud, children incorporate their parents' values into their developing superegos.

fixation according to Freud, a lingering focus of pleasure-seeking energies at an earlier psychosexual stage, in which conflicts were unresolved.

defense mechanisms in psychoanalytic theory, the ego's protective methods of reducing anxiety by unconsciously distorting reality.

repression in psychoanalytic theory, the basic defense mechanism that banishes from consciousness the thoughts, feelings, and memories that arouse anxiety.

ALFRED ADLER (1870–1937) Adler believed that childhood feelings of insecurity can drive behavior, triggering strivings for power and superiority. Adler coined the term *inferiority complex*.

KAREN HORNEY (1885–1952) Horney proposed that children's feelings of dependency give rise to feelings of helplessness and anxiety. These feelings trigger adult desires for love and security. Horney believed Freud's views of personality showed a masculine bias.

CARL JUNG (1875–1961) Jung shared Freud's view of the power of the unconscious. He also proposed a human *collective unconscious,* derived from our species' experiences in the distant past. Today's psychology rejects the idea that experiences can be inherited.

Some of Freud's ideas have been incorporated into the diversity of modern perspectives that make up psychodynamic theory. Theorists and clinicians who study personality from a psychodynamic perspective assume, with Freud and with much support from today's psychological science, that much of our mental life is unconscious. They believe we often struggle with inner conflicts among our wishes, fears, and values, and respond defensively. And they agree that childhood shapes our personality and ways of becoming attached to others. But in other ways, they differ from Freud. "Most contemporary [psychodynamic] theorists and therapists are not wedded to the idea that sex is the basis of personality," noted psychologist Drew Westen (1996). They "do not talk about ids and egos, and do not go around classifying their patients as oral, anal, or phallic characters."

Assessing Unconscious Processes

11-6 What are projective tests, how are they used, and how are they criticized?

Personality tests reflect the basic ideas of particular personality theories. So, what might be the tool of choice for someone working in the Freudian tradition?

To find a way into the unconscious mind, you would need a sort of "psychological X-ray." The test would have to see through the top layer of social politeness, revealing hidden conflicts and impulses. **Projective tests** aim to provide this view by asking test-takers to describe an unclear image or tell a story about it. The image itself has no real meaning, but what the test-takers say about it offers a glimpse into their unconscious. (Recall that in Freudian theory, *projection* is a defense mechanism that disguises threatening impulses by "seeing" them in other people.)

The most famous projective test, the **Rorschach inkblot test,** was introduced in 1921. Swiss psychiatrist Hermann Rorschach [ROAR-shock] based it on a game he and his friends played as children. They would drip ink on paper, fold it, and then say what they saw in the resulting blot (Sdorow, 2005). The assumption is that what you see in a series of 10 inkblots reflects your inner feelings and conflicts. Do you see predatory animals or

> *"We don't see things as they are; we see things as we are."*
> The Talmud

weapons in **FIGURE 11.2**? Perhaps you have aggressive tendencies.

Is this a reasonable assumption? Let's see how well the Rorschach test measures up to the two primary criteria of a good test (Chapter 8):

- *Reliability* (consistency of results): Raters trained in different Rorschach

FIGURE 11.2 The Rorschach test In this projective test, people tell what they see in a series of symmetrical inkblots. Some who use this test are confident that the interpretation of unclear images will reveal unconscious parts of the test-taker's personality.

"The forward thrust of the antlers shows a determined personality, yet the small sun indicates a lack of self-confidence. . . ."

scoring systems show little agreement (Sechrest et al., 1998).

- *Validity* (predicting what it's supposed to): The Rorschach test is not very successful at predicting behavior or at discriminating between groups (for example, identifying who is suicidal and who is not). Inkblot results diagnose many normal adults as disordered (Wood et al., 2003, 2006).

Thus, the Rorschach test has neither much reliability nor great validity. In fact, the Rorschach test appears to have "the dubious distinction of being simultaneously the most cherished and most reviled of all psychological assessment instruments" (Hunsley & Bailey, 1999, p. 266, as quoted in Lilienfeld et al., 2000). A research-based, computer-aided coding and interpretation tool aims to improve agreement among raters and enhance the test's validity (Erdberg, 1990; Exner, 2003). But Freud himself might have been uncomfortable with a tool that tried to diagnose patients based on tests. He probably would have been more interested in the therapist-patient interactions that take place during the test.

Evaluating Freud's Psychoanalytic Perspective and Modern Views of the Unconscious

11-7 How do today's psychologists view Freud's psychoanalysis?

"Many aspects of Freudian theory are indeed out of date, and they should be: Freud died in 1939, and he has been slow to undertake further revisions," observed one researcher (Westen, 1998). In Freud's time, there were no neurotransmitter or DNA studies. More than eight decades of scientific breakthroughs in human development, thinking, and emotion were yet to come. Criticizing Freud's theory by comparing it with current concepts is therefore, some say, like comparing Henry Ford's Model T with today's hybrid cars. (How tempting it always is to judge people in the past from our perspective in the present.)

But Freud's admirers and critics agree that recent research contradicts many of his specific ideas. Developmental psychologists now see our development as lifelong, not fixed in childhood. They doubt that infant brain networks are mature enough to process emotional trauma in the ways Freud assumed. Some think Freud overestimated parental influence and underestimated peer influence (and abuse). They also doubt that conscience and gender identity form as the child resolves the Oedipus complex at age 5 or 6. Our gender identity develops much earlier, and we become masculine or feminine even without a same-sex parent present. And they note that Freud's ideas about childhood sexuality have a shaky basis, in part because Freud didn't believe his female patients' stories of childhood sexual abuse. He apparently thought such stories reflected childhood sexual wishes and conflicts (Esterson, 2001; Powell & Boer, 1994).

Freud believed that dreams were the royal road to the unconscious, but they aren't. Modern dream researchers disagree with Freud's idea that dreams disguise unfulfilled wishes lurking in our unconscious (Chapter 2). And slips of the tongue can be explained as competition between similar word choices in our memory network. Someone who says, "I don't want to do that—it's a lot of brothel" may simply be blending *bother* and *trouble* (Foss & Hakes, 1978).

Psychology's strength comes from its use of the same scientific method that biologists, chemists, and physicists use to test their theories. Psychologists must ask the same question about Freud's theory that they ask about other theories. Remember that a good theory organizes observations and predicts behaviors or events (Chapter 1). How does Freudian theory stand up to the scientific tests?

Freud's theory rests on few objective observations, and it has produced few hypotheses to verify or reject. (For Freud, his own interpretations of patients' free associations, dreams, and slips of the tongue were evidence enough.) Moreover, say the critics, Freud's theory offers after-the-fact explanations of behaviors and traits, but it fails to predict them. There is also no way to disprove this theory. If you feel angry when your mom dies, you illustrate his theory because "your unresolved childhood dependency needs are threatened." If you do not feel angry, you again illustrate his theory because "you are repressing your anger." That, say critics "is like betting on a horse after the race has been run" (Hall & Lindzey, 1978, p. 68).

Freud's supporters object. To criticize Freudian theory for not making testable

projective test a personality test, such as the Rorschach, that provides an unclear image designed to trigger projection of the test-taker's unconscious thoughts or feelings.

Rorschach inkblot test the most widely used projective test; a set of 10 inkblots, designed by Hermann Rorschach; seeks to identify people's inner feelings by analyzing their interpretations of the blots.

predictions is, they say, like criticizing baseball for not being an aerobic exercise, something it was never intended to be. Freud never claimed that psychoanalysis was predictive science. He merely claimed that, looking back, psychoanalysts could find meaning in their clients' mental state (Rieff, 1979).

Freud's supporters also note that some of his ideas *are* enduring. It was Freud who drew our attention to the unconscious and the irrational, when such ideas were not popular. Today many researchers study our irrationality (Ariely, 2010). Psychologist Daniel Kahneman won the 2002 Nobel Prize in Economics with his studies of our faulty decision making. Freud also drew our attention to the importance of human sexuality. He made us aware of the tension between our biological impulses and our social well-being. He challenged our self-righteousness, pointed out our self-protective defenses, and reminded us of our potential for evil.

Modern Research Challenges the Idea of Repression

Psychoanalytic theory hinges on the assumption that our mind *represses* offending wishes. Repression supposedly banishes emotions into the unconscious until they resurface, like long-lost books in a dusty attic. Today's memory researchers find that we do sometimes spare our egos by ignoring threatening information (Green et al., 2008). Yet they also find that repression, if it ever occurs, is a rare mental response to terrible trauma. "Repression folklore is . . . partly refuted, partly untested, and partly untestable," said Elizabeth Loftus (1995). Even those who have witnessed a parent's murder or survived Nazi death camps retain their unrepressed memories of the horror (Helmreich, 1992, 1994; Malmquist, 1986; Pennebaker, 1990). This led one prominent personality researcher to conclude, "Dozens of formal studies have yielded not a single convincing case of repression in the entire literature on trauma" (Kihlstrom, 2006).

Some researchers believe that extreme, prolonged stress, such as the stress some severely abused children experience, might disrupt memory by damaging the hippocampus (Schacter, 1996). But the far more common reality is that high stress and associated stress hormones *enhance* memory. Indeed, rape, torture, and other traumatic events haunt survivors, who experience unwanted flashbacks. They are seared onto the soul. "You see the babies," said Holocaust survivor Sally H. (1979). "You see the screaming mothers. You see hanging people. You sit and you see that face there. It's something you don't forget."

The Modern Unconscious Mind

11-8 How has modern research developed our understanding of the unconscious?

Freud was right that we do indeed have limited access to all that goes on in our minds (Erdelyi, 1985, 1988, 2006; Kihlstrom, 1990). Our two-track mind has a vast out-of-sight realm. Some researchers even argue that "most of a person's everyday life is determined by unconscious thought processes" (Bargh & Chartrand, 1999). But the unconscious mind studied by cognitive researchers today is not the place Freud thought it was for storing our censored anxiety-producing thoughts and seething passions. Rather, it is a part of our two-track mind, where cooler information processing occurs without our awareness, such as

- the right-hemisphere brain activity that enables the split-brain patient's left hand to carry out an instruction the patient cannot verbalize. (Chapter 2).

- the parallel processing of different aspects of vision and thinking, and the schemas that automatically control our perceptions and interpretations (Chapter 5).

- the implicit memories that operate without our conscious recall, even among those with amnesia (Chapter 7).

- the emotions we experience instantly, before conscious analysis (Chapter 9).

- the self-concept and stereotypes that automatically and unconsciously influence how we process information about ourselves and others (Chapter 12).

More than we realize, we fly on autopilot. Our mind wanders, activating the brain's "default network" (Mason et al., 2007). Unconscious processing occurs constantly. Like an enormous ocean, the unconscious mind is huge.

There is also research support for two of Freud's defense mechanisms. For example, one study demonstrated *reaction formation* (trading unacceptable impulses for their opposite). Men who reported strong anti-gay attitudes experienced greater physiological arousal when watching videos of homosexual men having sex (as measured with an instrument that measures bloodflow to the penis) even though they said the films did not make them sexually aroused (Adams et al., 1996). Likewise, preliminary evidence suggests that people who unconsciously identify as homosexual—but who consciously identify as straight—report more negative attitudes toward gays and less support for pro-gay policies (Weinstein et al., 2012). Freud's *projection* (attributing our own threatening impulses to others) has been confirmed. People do tend to see their traits, attitudes, and goals in others (Baumeister et al., 1998; Maner et al., 2005). Today's researchers call this the *false consensus effect*—the tendency to overestimate the extent to which others share our beliefs and behaviors. People who binge-drink or break speed limits tend to think many others do the same. However, defense mechanisms don't work exactly as Freud supposed. They seem motivated less by the seething impulses he imagined than by our need to protect our self-image. ■

- What are three values that Freud's work in psychoanalytic theory has contributed? What are three ways in which Freud's work has been criticized?

ANSWER: Freud first drew attention to (1) the importance of childhood experiences, (2) the existence of the unconscious mind, and (3) our self-protective defense mechanisms. Freud's work has been criticized as (1) not scientifically testable—drawing on after-the-fact explanations, (2) focusing too much on sexual conflicts in childhood, and (3) based upon the idea of repression, which has not been supported by modern research.

- Which elements of traditional psychoanalysis do modern-day psychodynamic theorists and therapists retain, and which elements have they mostly left behind?

ANSWER: Today's psychodynamic theories still tend to focus on childhood experiences and attachments, unresolved conflicts, and unconscious influences. However, they are not likely to focus on fixation at any psychosexual stage, or the idea that sexual issues influence our personality.

Humanistic Theories

11-9 How did humanistic psychologists view personality, and what was their goal in studying personality?

◎ By the 1960s, some personality psychologists decided that their field needed fresh ideas and a new direction. They thought Freud's views were too negative. They were equally uncomfortable with the strict behaviorism of John Watson and B. F. Skinner (Chapter 6), judging it to be too mechanical. This movement helped produce *humanistic psychologists* such as Abraham Maslow (1908–1970) and Carl Rogers (1902–1987). In contrast to Freud's emphasis on disorders born out of dark conflicts, the humanistic psychologists focused on the ways "healthy" people strive for self-determination and self-realization. In contrast to behaviorism's objective laboratory experiments, they asked people to report their own experiences and feelings.

Abraham Maslow's Self-Actualizing Person

Abraham Maslow proposed that human motivations form a pyramid-shaped **hierarchy of needs** (Chapter 9). At the base are bodily needs. If those are met, we become concerned with the next-higher level of needs, personal safety. If we feel secure, we then seek to love, to be loved, and to love ourselves. With our love needs satisfied, we seek self-esteem (feelings of self-worth). Having achieved self-esteem, we strive for the top-level needs for **self-actualization** and **self-transcendence**. These motives, at the pyramid's peak, involve reaching our full potential.

Maslow (1970) formed his ideas by studying healthy, creative people rather than troubled clinical cases. His description of self-actualization grew out of his study of people, such as Abraham Lincoln, who had lived rich and productive lives. They were self-aware and self-accepting. They were open and spontaneous. They were loving and caring. They didn't worry too much about other people's opinions. Yet they were not self-centered. Curious about the world, they embraced uncertainties and stretched themselves to seek out new experiences (Kashdan, 2009). Once they focused their energies on a particular task, they often regarded that task as their life mission, or "calling" (Hall & Chandler, 2005). Most enjoyed a few deep relationships rather than many shallow ones. Many had been moved by spiritual or personal *peak experiences* that were beyond normal consciousness.

Maslow considered these to be mature adult qualities. These healthy people had outgrown their mixed feelings toward their parents. They had found their calling. They had "acquired enough courage to be unpopular, to be unashamed about being openly virtuous." Maslow's work with college students led him to believe that those likely to become self-actualizing adults were likable, caring young people who were "privately affectionate to those of their elders who deserve it," and "secretly uneasy about the cruelty,

ABRAHAM MASLOW (1908–1970) "Any theory of motivation that is worthy of attention must deal with the highest capacities of the healthy and strong person as well as with the defensive maneuvers of crippled spirits" (*Motivation and Personality*, 1970).

hierarchy of needs Maslow's pyramid of human needs; at the base are physiological needs that must be satisfied before higher-level safety needs, and then psychological needs, become active.

self-actualization according to Maslow, the psychological need that arises after basic physical and psychological needs are met and self-esteem is achieved; the motivation to fulfill our potential.

self-transcendence according to Maslow, the striving for identity, meaning, and purpose beyond the self.

meanness, and mob spirit so often found in young people."

Carl Rogers' Person-Centered Perspective

Carl Rogers agreed that people have self-actualizing tendencies. Rogers' *person-centered perspective* held that people are basically good. Like plants, we are primed to reach our potential if we are given a growth-promoting environment. People nurture our growth, and we nurture theirs, he said, in three ways (Rogers, 1980).

- Be *genuine*. If we are genuine to another person, we are open with our own feelings. We drop our false fronts and are transparent and self-disclosing.

- Be *accepting*. If we are accepting, we offer the other person what Rogers called **unconditional positive regard.** This is an attitude of total acceptance. We value the person even knowing the person's failings. We all find it a huge relief to drop our pretenses, confess our worst feelings, and discover that we are still accepted. In a good marriage, a close family, or an intimate friendship, we are free to be ourselves without fearing what others will think.

"Just remember, son, it doesn't matter whether you win or lose—unless you want Daddy's love."

A father *not* offering unconditional positive regard.

- Be *empathic*. If we are empathic, we share another's feelings and reflect that person's meanings back to them. "Rarely do we listen with real understanding, true empathy," said Rogers. "Yet listening, of this very special kind, is one of the most potent forces for change that I know." Consider a conversation where you knew someone was waiting for their turn to speak instead of listening to you. Now consider the last time someone heard you with empathy. How did those two experiences differ?

Genuineness, acceptance, and empathy are the water, sun, and nutrients that enable people to grow like vigorous oak trees, according to Rogers. For "as persons are accepted and prized, they tend to develop a more caring attitude toward themselves" (Rogers, 1980, p. 116). As persons are empathically heard, "it becomes possible for them to listen more accurately to the flow of inner experiencing."

Rogers called for genuineness, acceptance, and empathy in the relationship between therapist and client. But he also believed that these three qualities nurture growth between any two human beings—between leader and group, teacher and student, manager and staff member, parent and child, friend and friend.

Writer Calvin Trillin (2006) recalls an example of parental genuineness and acceptance at a camp for children with severe disorders, where his wife, Alice, worked. L., a "magical child," had genetic diseases that meant she had to be tube-fed and could walk only with difficulty. Alice recalled,

> . . . One day, when we were playing duck-duck-goose, I was sitting behind her and she asked me to hold her mail for her while she took her turn to be chased around the circle. It took her a while to make the circuit, and I had time to see that on top of the pile [of mail] was a note from her mom. Then I did something truly awful. . . . I simply had to know what this child's parents could have done to make her so spec-

THE PICTURE OF EMPATHY Being open and sharing confidences is easier when the listener shows real understanding. Within such relationships people can relax and fully express their true selves.

tacular, to make her the most optimistic, most enthusiastic, most hopeful human being I had ever encountered. I snuck a quick look at the note, and my eyes fell on this sentence: "If God had given us all of the children in the world to choose from, L., we would only have chosen you." Before L. got back to her place in the circle, I showed the note to Bud, who was sitting next to me. "Quick. Read this," I whispered. "It's the secret of life."

From "Alice, Off the Page" by Calvin Trillin. Originally appeared in *The New Yorker*. Copyright ©2006 by Calvin Trillin. Reprinted by permission of Lescher & Lescher, Ltd. All rights reserved.

Maslow and Rogers would have smiled knowingly. For them, a central feature of personality is one's **self-concept**—all the thoughts and feelings we have in response to the question, "Who am I?" If our self-concept is positive, we tend to act and perceive the world positively. If it is negative—if in our own eyes we fall far short of our *ideal self*—we feel dissatisfied and unhappy. A worthwhile goal for all of us—therapists, parents, teachers, and friends—is therefore to help others know, accept, and be true to themselves, said Rogers.

Assessing the Self

11-10 How did humanistic psychologists assess a person's sense of self?

Humanistic psychologists sometimes assessed personality by asking people to fill out questionnaires that would evaluate their self-concept. One questionnaire, inspired by Carl Rogers, asked people to describe themselves both as they would *ideally* like to be and as they *actually* are. When the ideal and the actual self are nearly alike, said Rogers, the self-concept is positive. Assessing his clients' personal growth during therapy, he looked for closer and closer ratings of actual and ideal selves.

Some humanistic psychologists believed that any standardized assessment of personality, even a questionnaire, is depersonalizing. Rather than forcing the person to respond to narrow categories, these humanistic psychologists presumed that interviews and intimate conversation would provide a better understanding of each person's unique experiences.

Evaluating Humanistic Theories

11-11 How have humanistic theories influenced psychology? What criticisms have they faced?

Just as Freudian concepts have seeped into modern culture, humanistic psychology has had a far-reaching impact. Maslow's and Rogers' ideas have influenced counseling, education, child raising, and management. And they laid the groundwork for today's scientific positive psychology (Chapter 10).

These theorists have also influenced—sometimes in ways they did not intend—much of today's popular psychology. Is a positive self-concept the key to happiness and success? Do acceptance and empathy nurture positive feelings about ourselves? Are people basically good and capable of improving? Many would answer Yes,

Yes, and Yes. By 1992, nine in ten people responding to a *Newsweek* Gallup poll rated self-esteem as very important for "motivating a person to work hard and succeed." In 2006, U.S. high school students reported notably higher self-esteem and greater expectations of future career success than did students living in 1975 (Twenge & Campbell, 2008). When you hear talk about the importance of "loving yourself," you can give some credit to the humanistic theories.

Many psychologists have criticized the humanistic perspective. First, said the critics, its concepts are vague and based on the theorists' personal opinions, rather than on scientific methods. Consider Maslow's description of self-actualizing people as open, spontaneous, loving, self-accepting, and productive. Is this a scientific description? Or is it merely a description of Maslow's own values and ideals, as viewed in his own personal heroes (Smith, 1978)? Imagine another theorist with a different set of heroes, such as Napoleon and former Vice President Dick Cheney. This theorist might have described self-actualizing people as "desiring power," "willing to go to war," and "self-assured."

Other critics objected to the attitudes that humanistic psychology encourages. Rogers, for example, said, "The only question which matters is, 'Am I living in a way which is deeply satisfying to me, and which truly expresses me?'" (quoted by Wallach & Wallach, 1985). Imagine working on a group project with people who refuse to complete any task that is not deeply satisfying or does not truly express their identity. Such attitudes could lead to self-indulgence, selfishness, and a lack of moral restraint (Campbell & Specht, 1985; Wallach & Wallach, 1983).

Humanistic psychologists have countered that a secure, nondefensive self-acceptance is the important first step toward loving others. Indeed, people who recall feeling liked and accepted by a romantic partner—for who they are, not just for their achievements—report being happier in their relationships and acting more kindly toward their partner (Gordon & Chen, 2010).

A final criticism has been that humanistic psychology fails to appreciate our human capacity for evil. Faced with global climate change, overpopulation, terrorism, and the spread of nuclear weapons, we may be paralyzed by either of two ways of thinking. One is a naive optimism that denies the threat ("People are basically good; everything will work out"). The other is a dark despair ("It's hopeless; why try?"). Action requires enough realism to fuel concern and enough optimism to provide hope. Humanistic psychology, said the critics, encourages the needed hope but not the equally necessary realism about evil. ■

"We do pretty well when you stop to think that people are basically good."

unconditional positive regard according to Rogers, an attitude of total acceptance toward another person.

self-concept all our thoughts and feelings about ourselves, in answer to the question, "Who am I?"

STEPHEN COLBERT: THE EXTRAVERT Trait labels such as extraversion can describe our temperament and typical behaviors.

Trait Theories

11-12 How do psychologists use traits to describe personality?

Freudian and humanistic theories shared a common goal: Explain how our personality develops. They focused on the forces that act upon us. **Trait** researchers, led by the work of Gordon Allport (1897–1967), have been less concerned with *explaining* traits than with *describing* them. They define per-

sonality as a *stable and enduring pattern of behavior,* such as Lady Gaga's consistent sociability, openness to new experiences, and self-discipline. These three traits help describe her personality.

Exploring Traits

Imagine that you've been hired by an Internet dating service. Your job is to construct a questionnaire that will help people describe themselves to those seeking dates and mates. With millions of people using such services each year, the need to understand and incorporate psychological science grows more important (Finkel et al, 2012a,b). What personality traits might give an accurate sense of the person filling out the questionnaire? You might begin by thinking of how we describe a pizza. We place it along several trait dimensions. It's small, medium, or large; it has one or more toppings; it has a thin or thick crust. By likewise placing people on trait dimensions, we can begin to describe them.

Basic Factors

An even better way to identify our personality is to identify **factors**—clusters of

behavior tendencies that occur together. People who describe themselves as outgoing, for example, may also say that they like excitement and practical jokes and dislike quiet reading. This cluster of behaviors reflects a basic factor, or trait—in this case, *extraversion.* (For more about extraversion's opposite, see Thinking Critically About: The Stigma of Introversion.)

So how many traits will be just the right number for your Internet dating questionnaire? If psychologists Hans Eysenck and Sybil Eysenck [EYE-zink] had been hired to do your job, they would have said two. They believed that we can reduce many normal human variations to two basic factors: Extraversion–introversion and emotional stability–instability (**FIGURE 11.3**). People in 35 countries,

UNSTABLE

INTROVERTED	EXTRAVERTED
Moody	Touchy
Anxious	Restless
Rigid	Aggressive
Sober	Excitable
Pessimistic	Changeable
Reserved	Impulsive
Unsociable	Optimistic
Quiet	Active
Passive	Sociable
Careful	Outgoing
Thoughtful	Talkative
Peaceful	Responsive
Controlled	Easygoing
Reliable	Lively
Even-tempered	Carefree
Calm	Leadership

STABLE

FIGURE 11.3 Two personality factors Mapmakers can tell us a lot by using two axes (north–south and east–west). Two primary personality factors (extraversion–introversion and stability–instability) are similarly useful as axes for describing personality variation. Varying combinations define other, more specific traits. (From Eysenck & Eysenck, 1963.) Those who are naturally introverted, such as primatologist Jane Goodall, may be particularly gifted in field studies. Successful politicians, including former U.S. President Bill Clinton, are often natural extraverts.

THINKING CRITICALLY ABOUT

The Stigma of Introversion

AMC/The Kobal Collection/Art Resource

Psychologists describe personality, but they don't advise which traits people should or should not have. Society does this. Western cultures prize extraversion more than all personality traits. Being introverted means that you don't have the "right stuff" (Cain, 2012).

Our superheroes have extraverted personalities. Extraverted Superman is bold and energetic. His introverted alter ego, Clark Kent, is mild-mannered and writes for a living. The message is clear: To show people you're a superhero, show them you're an extravert.

TV shows also portray heartthrobs and examples of success as extraverts. Donald Draper, the highly successful, attractive advertising executive in the hit show *Mad Men* is a classic extravert. He is dominant and charismatic. Women clamor for his attention. Again, the message is plain: Extraversion equals success, and introversion doesn't.

Why does our culture celebrate extraversion and belittle introversion? Many people may not understand what introversion really is. People tend to equate introversion with shyness, but the two concepts are quite different. Introverted people seek low levels of stimulation from their environment because they're very sensitive. One classic study suggested that introverted people even have greater taste sensitivity. When given lemon juice, introverted people salivated more than extraverted people (Corcoran, 1964). Shy people, in contrast, remain quiet because they fear others will evaluate them negatively.

People may also believe that introversion acts as a barrier to success. On the contrary, introverts experience tremendous achievement. They show greater receptiveness when their employees voice their ideas, challenge existing norms, and take charge. Under these circumstances, introverted leaders outperform extraverted ones (Grant et al., 2011). Perhaps the best example of the misperception that introversion hinders career success lies in the American presidency. The American president who is most consistently ranked number one of all time was introverted. His name was Abraham Lincoln.

So, introversion should not be a sign of disgrace. Those who need a quiet break from a loud party are not broken, unacceptable, or incapable of great things. They simply know how to pick an environment where they can thrive. It's important for extraverts to understand that not everyone needs the high levels of stimulation that they do. It's not a crime to unwind.

© Bettmann/CORBIS

from China to Uganda to Russia, have taken the Eysenck Personality Questionnaire. The extraversion and emotionality factors emerged as basic personality dimensions (Eysenck, 1990, 1992).

Biology and Personality

As you may recall from the twin and adoption studies discussed in Chapter 3, our genes have much to say about the temperament and behavioral style that help define our personality. Children's shyness, for example, seems related to differences in their autonomic nervous systems. Infants with reactive autonomic nervous systems respond to stress with greater anxiety and inhibition (Kagan, 2010).

Erik Lam/Shutterstock

Brain activity appears to vary with personality as well. Brain-activity scans suggest that extraverts seek stimulation because their normal brain arousal is relatively low. Also, a frontal lobe area involved in restraining behavior is less active in extraverts than in introverts (Johnson et al., 1999).

Personality differences among dogs are as obvious to researchers as they are to dog owners. Such differences (in energy, affection, reactivity, and curious intelligence) are as evident, and as consistently judged, as personality differences among humans (Gosling et al., 2003; Jones & Gosling, 2005). Monkeys, chimpanzees, orangutans, and even birds also have stable personalities (Weiss et al., 2006). Among the Great Tit (a European relative of the American chickadee), bold birds more quickly inspect new objects and explore trees (Groothuis & Carere, 2005; Verbeek et al., 1994). By selective breeding, researchers can produce bold or shy birds. Both have their place in natural history. In lean years, bold birds are more likely to find food; in abundant years, shy birds feed with less risk. ■

RETRIEVE + REMEMBER

• Which two primary dimensions did Hans and Sybil Eysenck propose for describing personality variation?

ANSWER: introversion–extraversion and emotional stability–instability

trait a characteristic pattern of behavior or a tendency to feel and act in a certain way, as assessed by self-reports on a personality test.

factor a cluster of behavior tendencies that occur together.

Assessing Traits

11-13 What are personality inventories?

It helps to know that a potential date is an introvert or an extravert, or even that the person is emotionally stable or unstable. But wouldn't you like more information about the test-taker's personality before matching people as romantic partners? The **Minnesota Multiphasic Personality Inventory (MMPI)** might help. **Personality inventories,** including the famous MMPI, are long sets of questions covering a wide range of feelings and behaviors. Although the MMPI was originally developed to identify emotional disorders, it also assesses people's personality traits. Unlike projective tests such as the Rorschach, personality inventories are scored objectively—so objectively that a computer can administer and score them. Objectivity does not, however, guarantee validity. People taking the MMPI for employment purposes can give the answers they know will create a good impression. But in so doing they may also score high on a *lie scale* that assesses faking (as when people respond *False* to a universally true statement, such as "I get angry sometimes"). The objectivity of the MMPI has contributed to its popularity and to its translation into more than 100 languages.

The Big Five Factors

11-14 Which traits seem to provide the most useful information about personality variation?

Today's trait researchers rely on five factors (called the Big Five) to understand personality—conscientiousness, agreeableness, neuroticism, openness, and extraversion **(TABLE 11.3)** (Costa & McCrae, 2011; John & Srivastava, 1999). Work by Paul Costa, Robert McCrae, and others shows that where we fall on these five dimensions reveals much of what there is to say about our personality.

As the dominant model in personality psychology, Big Five research has explored various questions:

- *How stable are these traits?* One research team analyzed 1.25 million participants ages 10 to 65. They learned that personality continues to develop and change through late childhood and adolescence. By adulthood, our traits have become fairly stable, though conscientiousness, agreeableness, openness, and extraversion continue to increase over the life span, and neuroticism (emotional instability) decreases (Soto et al., 2011). Some other dimensions of the Big Five (in addition to neuroticism) decrease as people become older (Lucas & Donnellan, 2011).

- *Have these traits changed over time?* Cultures change over time, which can influence shifts in personality. Within the United States and the Netherlands, extraversion and conscientiousness have increased over time (Mroczek & Spiro, 2003; Smits et al., 2011; Twenge, 2001).

- *Do we inherit these traits?* Roughly 50 percent of our individual differences on the Big Five can be credited to our genes (Jang et al., 2006; Krueger & Johnson, 2008; Loehlin et al., 1998).

- *Do these traits reflect differing brain structure or function?* The size of different brain regions does correlate with several Big Five traits (DeYoung et al., 2010). For example, those who score high on conscientiousness tend to have a larger frontal lobe area that aids in planning and controlling behavior. Brain connections also influence the Big Five traits (Adelstein et al., 2011). For example, people high in openness have brains that are wired to experience intense imagination, curiosity, and fantasy.

- *How well do these traits apply to various cultures?* The Big Five dimensions describe personality in various cultures reasonably well (Schmitt et al., 2007; Yamagata et al., 2006). "Features of personality traits are common to all human groups," concluded Robert McCrae and 79 co-researchers (2005) from their 50-culture study.

- *Do the Big Five traits predict our actual behavior?* Yes. For example, our traits appear in our language patterns. In blog posts, extraversion predicts use of personal pronouns (we, our, us). Agreeableness predicts positive-emotion words. Neuroticism predicts negative-emotion words (Yarkoni, 2010).

If you work the Big Five traits into your dating questionnaire, your mission should be accomplished—assuming people act the same way at all times and in all situations. Next, we ask, do they? ■

TABLE 11.3	The "Big Five" Personality Factors	
(*Memory tip:* Picturing a **CANOE** will help you recall these.)		
Disorganized, careless, impulsive	Conscientiousness	Organized, careful, disciplined
Ruthless, suspicious, uncooperative	Agreeableness	Soft-hearted, trusting, helpful
Calm, secure, self-satisfied	Neuroticism (emotional stability vs. instability)	Anxious, insecure, self-pitying
Practical, prefers routine, conforming	Openness	Imaginative, prefers variety, independent
Retiring, sober, reserved	Extraversion	Sociable, fun-loving, affectionate

Source: Adapted from McCrae & Costa (1986, 2008).

Steve Wisbauer/Getty Images

RETRIEVE + REMEMBER

- What are the Big Five personality factors, and why are they scientifically useful?

ANSWER: The Big Five personality factors are conscientiousness, agreeableness, neuroticism (emotional stability vs. instability), openness, and extraversion (CANOE). These factors may be objectively measured, and research suggests that these factors are relatively stable across the life span and apply to all cultures in which they have been studied.

Evaluating Trait Theories

11-15 Does research support the consistency of personality traits over time and across situations?

To be useful indicators of personality, traits would have to persist over time and across situations. Friendly people, for example, would have to act friendly at different times and places. In some ways, our personality seems stable. Cheerful, friendly children tend to become cheerful, friendly adults. But it's also true that a fun-loving jokester can suddenly be serious and respectful at a job interview. The personality traits we express change from one situation to another.

The Person-Situation Controversy

Many researchers have studied personality stability over the life span. A group of 152 long-term studies compared early trait scores with scores for the same traits seven years later. These comparisons were done for several different age groups, and for each group, the scores were positively correlated. But the correlations were strongest for comparisons done in adulthood. For young children, the correlation between early and later scores was +0.3. For collegians, the correlation was +0.54. For 70-year-olds, the correlation was +0.73. (Remember that 0 indicates no relationship, and +1.0 would mean that one score perfectly predicts the other.)

As we grow older, our personality traits stabilize. Interests may change—the devoted collector of tropical fish may become the devoted gardener. Careers may change—the determined salesperson may become a determined social worker. Relationships may change—the hostile spouse may start over with a new partner. But most people recognize their traits as their own.

The consistency of specific *behaviors* from one situation to the next is another matter. People are not always predictable. What relationship would you expect to find between a student's being conscientious on one occasion (say, showing up for class on time) and being conscientious on another occasion (say, turning in assignments on time)? If you've noticed how outgoing you are in some situations and how reserved you are in others, perhaps you said, "very little." That's what researchers have found—only a small correlation (Mischel, 1968, 1984, 2004). This inconsistency makes personality traits weak predictors of behaviors. Personality traits predict a person's behavior *across many different situations*. They do not neatly predict a person's behavior *in any one specific situation* (Mischel, 1968, 1984; Mischel & Shoda, 1995).

If we remember such results, we will be more careful about labeling other people (Mischel, 1968, 2004). We will recognize how difficult it is to predict whether someone is likely to violate parole, commit suicide, or be an effective employee. Years in advance, science can tell us the distance of the Earth from the Sun for any given date. A day in advance, meteorologists can often predict the weather. Yet psychologists have not yet solved the riddle of how you will feel and act tomorrow, or even a few hours from now.

Does this mean that psychological science has nothing meaningful to say about personality traits? No! Remember that traits do a good job at predicting people's *average* behavior (outgoingness, happiness, carelessness) over *many* situations (Epstein, 1983a,b).

Even when we try to restrain them, our traits may assert themselves. During my [DM] noontime pickup basketball games with friends, I keep vowing to cut back on my jabbering and joking. But without fail, the irrepressible chatterbox reoccupies my body moments later. I [ND] have a similar experience each time I try to stay quiet when riding in taxis, but somehow always end up chatting!

Our personality traits lurk in some unexpected places.

- *Music preferences:* Your playlist says a lot about who

It's not just personality that stablizes with age.

Minnesota Multiphasic Personality Inventory (MMPI) the most widely researched and clinically used of all personality tests. Originally developed to identify emotional disorders (still considered its most appropriate use), this test is now used for many other screening purposes.

personality inventory a questionnaire (often with true-false or agree-disagree items) on which people respond to items designed to gauge a wide range of feelings and behaviors; used to assess selected personality traits.

OUR SPACES EXPRESS OUR PERSONALITY
Even at "zero acquaintance," people can catch a glimpse of others' personality from looking at their website, bedroom, or office. So, what's your read on this person's office?

you are. Classical, jazz, blues, and folk music lovers tend to be open to experience and verbally intelligent. Extraverts tend to prefer upbeat and energetic music. Country, pop, and religious music lovers tend to be cheerful, outgoing, and conscientious (Langmeyer et al., 2012; Rentfrow & Gosling, 2003).

- *Bedrooms and offices:* Our personal spaces—our scattered papers or neat surfaces—display our personality. After just a few minutes' inspection of someone's living and working spaces, you could give a fairly accurate summary of their conscientiousness, openness to new experience, and even emotional stability (Gosling, 2008).

- *Electronic communications:* Have you ever felt you could detect others' personality from their writing voice? You are right!! What a cool, exciting finding!!! (If you catch my drift.) You can predict levels of extraversion, neuroticism, and agreeableness by analyzing the content of a person's

last 20 texts (Holtgraves, 2011). For example, those who score high in extraversion draw attention to themselves by using more first-person singular pronouns (for example, "I" and "me"). Those high in neuroticism use more negative emotion words. And those high in agreeableness use fewer swear words. You can also gauge a person's extraversion and neuroticism by reading their e-mails (Gill et al., 2006; Oberlander & Gill, 2006).

- *Social networking sites:* Online profiles and personal websites are a canvas for self-expression. They offer clues to a person's extraversion, agreeableness, conscientiousness, and openness (Back et al., 2010). Even mere photos, with their associated clothes, expressions, and postures, can give clues to personality (Naumann et al., 2009).

In unfamiliar, formal situations—perhaps as a guest in the home of a person from another culture—our traits remain hidden as we carefully attend to social cues. In familiar, informal situations—just hanging out with friends—we feel more relaxed, and our traits emerge (Buss, 1989). In these informal situations, our expressive styles—our animation, manner of speaking, and gestures—are impressively consistent. Viewing "thin slices" of someone's behavior—such as seeing a photo for a mere fraction of a second or seeing three 2-second video clips of a teacher in action—can tell us a lot about the person's basic personality traits (Ambady, 2010; Rule et al., 2009).

To sum up, we can say that the immediate situation powerfully influences our behavior, *especially when the situation makes clear demands* (Cooper & Withey, 2009). We can better predict drivers' behavior at traffic lights from knowing the color of the lights than from knowing the drivers' personalities. Averaging our behavior across many occasions does, however, reveal distinct personality

traits. Traits exist, and they leave tracks in our lives. We differ. And our differences matter. ■

Social-Cognitive Theories

11-16 How do social-cognitive theorists view personality development, and how do they explore behavior?

Reciprocal Influences

So, our personal traits interact with our environment to influence our behavior. Albert Bandura (1986, 2006, 2008) called this process **reciprocal determinism.** "Behavior, internal personal factors, and environmental influences," he said, "all operate as interlocking determinants of each other" (FIGURE 11.4).

The **social-cognitive** theories of personality (including Bandura's and others) are especially focused on in the many ways our individual traits and thoughts interact with our social world as we move from one situation to another. We bring a lot to any social situation we enter. We bring our past learning, often picked up through conditioning or by observing others. We bring our **self-efficacy**—our expectations about whether we will succeed in (and attempt) new challenges (Bandura, 1977). We also bring our ways of thinking about specific situations. But situations themselves place different demands on us. Most of us know the general social rules for acceptable behavior at a grandparent's funeral, for example. We also

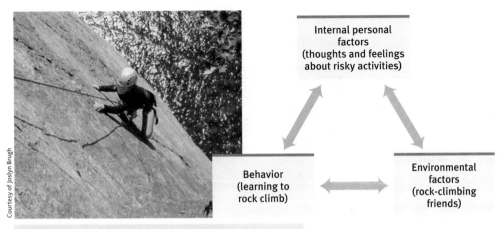

FIGURE 11.4 **Reciprocal determinism**

know that a different set of rules outlines what's acceptable at a friend's New Year's Eve party. In the end, our behavior in any situation is in part the result of our own characteristics and in part the result of the situation.

For psychologists who study personality from a social-cognitive perspective, this interaction is a fascinating area of research. Roughly speaking, the short-term, outside influences on behavior are the focus of social psychology (Chapter 12), and the lasting, inner influences are the focus of personality psychology. In actuality, behavior always depends on the interaction of persons with situations.

We can see this interaction in the habits people develop in relationships. For example, Romena's history of romantic relationships (past behavior) influences her attitudes toward relationships in general (internal factor), which impacts how she now responds to Jordan (environmental factor). Social-cognitive theorists explore the *interaction* among the three sets of influence:

1. *Different people choose different environments.* What school do you attend? What do you read? What shows do you watch? What music do you listen to? With whom do you enjoy spending time? All these choices are part of an environment you are choosing, based partly on your personality (Ickes et al., 1997). We choose our environment, and then it shapes us.

2. *Our personalities shape how we interpret and react to events.* Anxious people tend to attend and react strongly to relationship threats (Campbell & Marshall, 2011). If we perceive the world as threatening, we will watch for threats and be prepared to defend ourselves.

3. *Our personalities help create situations to which we react.* How we view and treat people influences how they then treat us. If we expect that others will not like us, our desperate attempts to seek their approval might cause them to reject us. Depressed people often engage in this excessive reassurance seeking, which confirms their negative self-views (Coyne, 1976a, b).

In addition to the interaction of internal personal factors, the environment, and our behaviors, we also experience *heredity-environment interaction* (Chapter 3). Our genetically influenced traits evoke certain responses from others, which may nudge us in one direction or another. In one classic study, those with the interacting factors of (1) having a specific gene associated with aggression, and (2) being raised in a difficult environment were most likely to demonstrate adult antisocial behavior (Caspi et al., 2002).

In such ways, we are both the products and the architects of our environments. Boiling water turns an egg hard and a noodle soft. Academic challenges turn one person into a success and another toward collapse (Harms et al., 2006). At every moment, our behavior is influenced by our biology, our social and cultural experiences, and our thought processes and traits (**FIGURE 11.5**).

reciprocal determinism the interacting influences of behavior, internal personal factors, and environment.

social-cognitive perspective views behavior as influenced by the interaction between persons (and their thinking) and their social context.

self-efficacy our sense of competence and effectiveness.

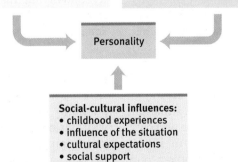

FIGURE 11.5 **The biopsychosocial approach to the study of personality**

Assessing Behavior in Situations

To predict behavior, social-cognitive psychologists often observe behavior in realistic situations.

Military and educational organizations and many Fortune 500 companies are using such strategies (Bray & Byham, 1991, 1997; Eurich et al., 2009). AT&T has observed prospective managers doing simulated managerial work. Many colleges assess students' potential via internships and student teaching and assess potential faculty members' teaching abilities by observing them teach. Armies assess their soldiers by observing them during military exercises. Most American cities with populations of 50,000 or more have used such strategies in evaluating police officers and firefighters (Lowry, 1997).

These assessment exercises have some limitations. They may not reveal less visible but important characteristics, such as inner achievement drive (Bowler & Woehr, 2006). These procedures do exploit a valid principle: The best way to predict future behavior is neither a personality test nor an interviewer's intuition; rather, *it is the person's past behavior patterns in similar situations* (Mischel, 1981; Ouellette & Wood, 1998; Schmidt & Hunter, 1998).

Evaluating Social-Cognitive Theories

11-17 What criticisms have social-cognitive theorists faced?

Social-cognitive theories of personality emphasize how situations affect, and are affected by, individuals. More than other personality theories (TABLE 11.4), they build from psychological research on learning and cognition.

Critics charge that social-cognitive theories focus so much on the situation that they fail to appreciate the person's inner traits. They note that in many instances our unconscious motives, our emotions, and our traits shine through. Personality traits have been shown to predict behavior at work, love, and play. Consider Percy Ray Pridgen and Charles Gill. Each faced the same situation: They had jointly won a $90 million lottery jackpot (Harriston, 1993). When Pridgen learned of the winning numbers, he began trembling uncontrollably, huddled with a friend behind a bathroom door while confirming the win, then sobbed. When Gill heard the news, he told his wife and then went to sleep. ■

ASSESSING BEHAVIOR IN SITUATIONS Reality TV shows, such as Donald Trump's *The Apprentice,* may take "show me" job interviews to the extreme, but they do illustrate a valid point. Seeing how a potential employee behaves in a job-relevant situation helps predict job performance.

> **RETRIEVE + REMEMBER**
>
> • According to the social-cognitive perspective, what is the best way to predict a person's future behavior?
>
> ANSWER: Examine the person's past behavior patterns in similar situations.

Exploring the Self

11-18 Why has psychology generated so much research on the self? How important is self-esteem to psychology and to our well-being?

We can think of our *self-image* as our internal view of our personality. Underlying this idea is the notion that the **self** is the center of personality—the organizer of our thoughts, feelings, and actions.

Consider the concept of *possible selves* (Cross & Markus, 1991; Markus & Nurius, 1986). Your possible selves include your visions of the self you dream of becoming—the rich self, the successful self, the loved and admired self. Your possible selves also include the self you fear becoming—the unemployed self, the academically failed self, the lonely and unpopular self. Possible selves motivate us to lay out specific goals that direct our energy effectively and efficiently. High school students enrolled in a gifted program for math and science were more likely to become scientists if they had a clear vision of themselves as successful scientists (Buday et al., 2012).

Carried too far, our self-focus can lead us to fret that others are noticing and evaluating us. Researchers demonstrated this **spotlight effect** by having some students wear Barry Manilow T-shirts and enter a room filled with other students (Gilovich, 1996). Feeling self-conscious, the T-shirt wearers guessed that nearly half of the other students would notice the shirt as they walked in. How many did notice? Only half as many as they feared—fewer than one in four. We stand out less than we imagine, even with dorky clothes or bad hair, and even after a blunder like setting off a library alarm (Gilovich & Savitsky, 1999; Savitsky et al., 2001).

To turn down the brightness of the spotlight, we

Timothy Large/Shutterstock
Barry Manilow: Trinity Mirror/Mirrorpix/Alamy

TABLE 11.4 Comparing the Major Personality Theories

Personality Theory	Key Proponents	Assumptions	View of Personality	Personality Assessment Methods
Psychoanalytic	Freud	Emotional disorders spring from unconscious dynamics, such as unresolved sexual and other childhood conflicts, and fixation at various developmental stages. Defense mechanisms fend off anxiety.	Personality consists of pleasure-seeking impulses (the id), a reality-oriented executive (the ego), and an internalized set of ideals (the superego).	Free association, projective tests, dream analysis
Psychodynamic	Jung, Adler, Horney	The unconscious and conscious minds interact. Childhood experiences and defense mechanisms are important.	The dynamic interplay of conscious and unconscious motives and conflicts shapes our personality.	Projective tests, therapy sessions
Humanistic	Rogers, Maslow	Rather than examining the struggles of sick people, it's better to focus on the ways healthy people strive for self-realization.	If our basic human needs are met, we will strive toward self-actualization. In a climate of unconditional positive regard, we can develop self-awareness and a more realistic and positive self-concept.	Questionnaires, therapy sessions
Trait	Allport, Eysenck, McCrae, Costa	We have certain stable and enduring characteristics, influenced by genetic predispositions.	Scientific study of traits has isolated important dimensions of personality, such as the Big Five traits (conscientiousness, agreeableness, neuroticism, openness, and extraversion).	Personality inventories
Social-Cognitive	Bandura	Our traits and the social context interact to produce our behaviors.	Conditioning and observational learning interact with cognition to create behavior patterns.	Our behavior in one situation is best predicted by considering our past behavior in similar situations.

Image Source/Getty Images

TRYING OUT A POSSIBLE SELF As an apprentice, this young man has a chance to see how it feels to be a woodworker, while learning valuable life skills in the process.

can use two strategies. The first is simply knowing about the spotlight effect. Public speakers who understand that their natural nervousness is not obvious to the audience perform better (Savitsky & Gilovich, 2003). The second is to take the perspective of

> *Do people put themselves before others? "Who in the world am I? Ah, that's the great puzzle!"*
>
> Lewis Carroll, *Alice in Wonderland* (as quoted in Schlegel et al., 2011)

an audience member. When we imagine how much an audience member empathizes with our situation, we tend to expect we will not be judged as harshly (Epley et al., 2002).

The Benefits of Self-Esteem

If we like our self-image, we probably have high **self-esteem.** This feeling of high self-worth will translate into more restful nights and less pressure to conform. We'll be more persistent at difficult tasks. We'll be less shy, anxious, and lonely, and, in the future, we'll be just plain happier (Greenberg, 2008; Orth et al., 2008, 2009; Swann et al., 2007). Self-esteem tends to increase during adolescence and then stay fairly consistent over time (Erol & Orth, 2011).

Self-esteem is a household word. College students even report wanting high self-esteem more than food or sex (Bushman et al., 2011). But most research challenges the idea that high self-esteem is really "the armor that protects kids" from life's problems (Baumeister, 2006; Dawes, 1994; Leary, 1999; Seligman, 1994, 2002). Problems and failures lower self-esteem. So, maybe self-esteem simply reflects reality. Maybe it's a side effect of meeting challenges and getting through difficulties. Maybe kids with high self-esteem do better in school because doing better in school raises their self-esteem. Maybe self-esteem is a gauge that reports the state of our relationships with others. If so, isn't pushing the gauge artificially higher (with empty compliments) much like forcing a car's low-fuel gauge to display "full"?

If feeling good *follows* doing well, then giving praise in the absence of good per-

self your image and understanding of who you are; in modern psychology, the idea that this is the center of personality, organizing your thoughts, feelings, and actions.

spotlight effect overestimating others' noticing and evaluating our appearance, performance, and blunders (as if we presume a spotlight shines on us).

self-esteem our feelings of high or low self-worth.

formance may actually harm people. After receiving weekly self-esteem-boosting messages, struggling students earned *lower* than expected grades (Forsyth et al., 2007). Other research showed that giving people random rewards hurt their productivity. Martin Seligman said, "We found that . . . when good things occurred that weren't earned, like nickels coming out of slot machines, it did not increase people's well-being. It produced helplessness. People gave up and became passive."

There is, however, an important *effect* of low self-esteem. People who feel negatively about themselves also tend to behave negatively toward others (Amabile, 1983; Baumgardner et al., 1989; Pelham, 1993). Deflating a person's self-esteem produces similar effects. Researchers have temporarily lowered people's self-esteem—for example, by telling them they did poorly on a test or by insulting them. These participants were then more likely to insult others or to express racial prejudice (vanDellen et al., 2011; Van Dijk et al., 2011; Ybarra, 1999). But inflated self-esteem can also cause problems. When studying insult-triggered aggression, researchers found that "conceited, self-important individuals turn nasty toward those who puncture their bubbles of self-love" (Baumeister, 2001; Bushman et al., 2009). *Narcissistic* people forgive others less, take a game-playing approach to their romantic relationships, and make poor leaders (Campbell et al., 2002; Exline et al., 2004; Nevicka et al., 2011).

Self-Serving Bias

11-19 What evidence reveals self-serving bias, and how do defensive and secure self-esteem differ?

Imagine dashing to class, hoping not to miss the first few minutes. You arrive five minutes late, huffing and puffing. As you sink into your seat, what thoughts go through your mind? Do you go through a negative door, with thoughts such as, "I hate myself" and "I'm worthless"? Or do you go through a positive door, saying to yourself, "At least I made it to class" and "I really tried to get here on time"?

Personality psychologists have found that most people choose the second door, which leads to positive self-thoughts. We have a good reputation with ourselves. We show a **self-serving bias**—a readiness to perceive ourselves favorably (Myers, 2010; Von Hippel & Trivers, 2011). Consider these two findings:

People accept more responsibility for good deeds than for bad, and for successes than for failures. When athletes succeed, they credit their own talent. When they fail, they blame poor weather, bad luck, lousy officials, or the other team's amazing performance. Most students who received poor grades on a test blame the test (or the professor), not themselves. On insurance forms, drivers have explained accidents in such words as "An invisible car came out of nowhere, struck my car, and vanished." "As I reached an intersection, a hedge sprang up, obscuring my vision, and I did not see the other car." "A pedestrian hit me and went under my car." The question "What have I done to deserve this?" is one we usually ask of our troubles, not our successes.

> "If you are like most people, then like most people, you don't know you're like most people. Science has given us a lot of facts about the average person, and one of the most reliable of these facts is the average person doesn't see herself as average."
>
> Daniel Gilbert, *Stumbling on Happiness*, 2006

Most people see themselves as better than average. Compared with most other people, how nice are you? How easy to get along with? How appealing are you as a friend or romantic partner? Where would you rank yourself from 0 to 100th percentile? Most people put themselves well above the 50th percentile. This better-than-average effect applies for nearly any common, socially desirable behavior. Most business executives say they are more ethical than the average executive. At least 90 percent of business managers and college professors rate their performance as superior to that of their average peer. This tendency is less striking in Asia, where people value modesty (Heine & Hamamura, 2007). Yet self-serving biases have been observed worldwide: among Dutch, Australian, and Chinese students; Japanese drivers; Indian Hindus; and French people of most walks of life. In every one of 53 countries surveyed, people expressed self-esteem above the midpoint of the most widely used scale (Schmitt & Allik, 2005).

TOO MUCH COFFEE MAN BY SHANNON WHEELER

AND GOD CREATED SELF-WORTH

Shannon Wheeler

Most people even see themselves as more immune than others to self-serving bias (Pronin, 2007). That's right, people believe they are above average at not believing they are above average. (Isn't psychology fun?) We also are quicker to believe flattering descriptions of ourselves than unflattering ones, and we are impressed with psychological tests that make us look good.

Self-serving bias often underlies conflicts, such as blaming a spouse for marriage problems or an assistant for work problems. All of us tend to see our own group as superior (whether it's our school, our ethnic group, or our country). Ethnic pride fueled Nazi horrors and Rwandan genocide. No wonder religion and literature so often warn against the perils of self-love and pride.

If the self-serving bias is so common, why do so many people put themselves down? For four reasons:

1. Some negative thoughts—"How could I have been so stupid!"—*protect us from repeating mistakes*.

2. Self put-downs are sometimes meant to *prompt positive feedback*. Saying "No one likes me" may at least get you "But not everyone has met you!"

3. Put-downs can help *prepare us for possible failure*. The coach who talks about the superior strength of the upcoming opponent makes a loss understandable, a victory noteworthy.

4. We often put down *our old selves*, not our current selves (Wilson & Ross, 2001). Chumps yesterday, but champs today: "At 18, I was a jerk; today I'm more sensitive."

Despite our self-serving bias, all of us some of the time, and some of us much of the time, do feel inferior. As we saw in Chapter 10, this often happens when we compare ourselves with those who are a step or two higher on the ladder of status, looks, income, or ability. For example, Olympians who win silver medals, barely missing gold, show greater sadness on the award podium compared with the bronze medal winners (Medvec et al., 1995).

The more deeply and frequently we have such feelings, the more unhappy, even depressed, we are. Positive self-esteem predicts happiness and *persistence after failure* (Baumeister et al., 2003). So maybe it helps that, for most people, thinking has a naturally positive bias.

Researchers have shown the value of separating self-esteem into two categories—*defensive* and *secure* (Kernis, 2003; Lambird & Mann, 2006; Ryan & Deci, 2004).

- *Defensive self-esteem is fragile*. Its goal is to sustain itself, which makes failures and criticism feel threatening. Defensive self-esteem feeds anger and disordered responses to threats (Crocker & Park, 2004). It correlates with aggressive and antisocial behavior (Donnellan et al., 2005).

- *Secure self-esteem is sturdy*. It relies less on other people's evaluations. If we feel accepted for who we are, and not for our looks, wealth, or fame, we are free of pressures to succeed. We can focus beyond ourselves, losing ourselves in relationships and purposes larger than self. Secure self-esteem thus leads to greater quality of life. Such findings are in line with Maslow's and Rogers' ideas about the benefits of a healthy self-image. ■

Culture and the Self

11-20 How do individualist and collectivist cultures influence people?

The meaning of *self* varies from culture to culture. How much of your identity is defined by your social connections? Your answer may depend on your culture, and whether it gives greater priority to the *independent self* or to the *interdependent self*.

If you are an **individualist,** you have an independent sense of "me," and an awareness of your unique personal convictions and values. Individualists give higher priority to personal goals. They define their identity mostly in terms of personal traits. They strive for personal control and individual achievement.

Although within cultures we vary, different cultures tend to emphasize either individualism or **collectivism.** The

A COLLECTIVIST CULTURE Although the United States is largely individualist, many cultural subgroups remain collectivist. This is true for many Alaska Natives, who demonstrate respect for tribal elders, and whose identity springs largely from their group affiliations.

self-serving bias our readiness to perceive ourselves favorably.

individualism giving priority to our own goals over group goals and defining our identity in terms of personal traits rather than group membership.

collectivism giving priority to the goals of our group (often our extended family or work group) and defining our identity accordingly.

CONSIDERATE COLLECTIVISTS Japan's collectivist values, including duty to others and social harmony, were on display after the devastating 2011 earthquake and tsunami. Virtually no looting was reported, and residents remained calm and orderly, as shown here while waiting for drinking water.

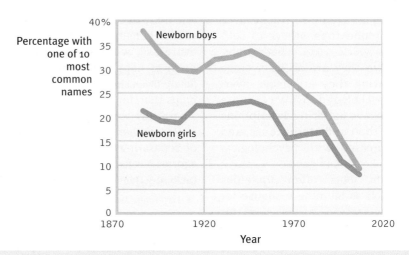

FIGURE 11.6 A child like no other Americans' individualist tendencies are reflected in their choice of names for their babies. In recent years, the percentage of American babies receiving one of that year's 10 most common names has plunged. (Adapted from Twenge et al., 2010.)

United States is mostly an individualist culture. Founded by settlers who wanted to differentiate themselves from others, Americans still cherish the "pioneer" spirit (Kitayama et al., 2010). Some 85 percent of Americans say it is possible "to pretty much be who you want to be" (Sampson, 2000). Being more self-contained, individualists also move in and out of social groups more easily. They change relationships, towns, and jobs with ease.

Over the past several decades, U.S. individualism has only increased. American high school and college students in 2012 reported greater interest in obtaining benefits for themselves and lower concern for others than ever before (Twenge et al., 2012). The need for uniqueness has even crept into the names people choose for their children (FIGURE 11.6). Even within the United States, parents from more recently settled states (for example, Utah and Arizona) give their children more distinctive names compared with parents who live in more established states (for example, New York and Massachusetts) (Varnum & Kitayama, 2011).

People in competitive, individualist cultures have more personal freedom (TABLE 11.5). They take more pride in personal achievements, are less geographically bound to their families, and enjoy more privacy. But these benefits come at the cost of more loneliness, divorce, homicide, and stress-related disease (Popenoe, 1993; Triandis et al., 1988). People in individualist cultures also demand more romance and personal fulfillment in marriage, which puts relationships under more pressure (Dion & Dion, 1993). In one survey, "keeping romance alive" was rated as important to a good marriage by 78 percent of U.S. women but only 29 percent of Japanese women (*American Enterprise*, 1992).

If you are a collectivist, your identity may be closely tied to family, groups, and loyal friends. These connections define who you are. *Group identifications* provide a sense of belonging and a set of values in collectivist cultures. In Korea, for example, people place less value on expressing a consistent, unique self-concept, and more on tradition and shared practices (Choi & Choi, 2002).

TABLE 11.5 Value Contrasts Between Individualism and Collectivism

Concept	Individualism	Collectivism
Self	Independent (identity from individual traits).	Interdependent (identity from belonging to groups).
Life task	Discover and express your own uniqueness.	Maintain connections, fit in, perform your role.
What matters	Me—personal achievement and fulfillment; rights and liberties; self-esteem.	Us—group goals and solidarity; social responsibilities and relationships; family duty.
Coping method	Change reality.	Adjust to reality.
Morality	Defined by the individual (self-based).	Defined by social networks (duty-based).
Relationships	Many, often temporary or casual; confrontation is acceptable.	Few, close, and enduring; harmony is valued.
Attributing behavior	Behavior reflects the individual's personality and attitudes.	Behavior reflects social norms and roles.

Sources: Adapted from Thomas Schoeneman (1994) and Harry Triandis (1994).

Collectivists are like athletes who take more pleasure in their team's victory than in their own performance. They find satisfaction in advancing their groups' interests, even at the expense of personal needs. Preserving group spirit and avoiding social embarrassment are important goals. Collectivists therefore avoid direct confrontation, blunt honesty, and uncomfortable topics. They value humility, not self-importance (Bond et al., 2012). Instead of dominating conversations, collectivists hold back and display shyness when meeting strangers (Cheek & Melchior, 1990). Elders receive great respect. In some collectivist cultures, it is even against the law to disrespect elders. For example, the Law of the People's Republic of China on Protection of the Rights and Interests of the Elderly states that parents aged 60 or above can sue their sons and daughters if they fail to follow through on their legal obligation of "providing for the elderly, taking care of them and comforting them, and cater[ing] to their special needs" (Chapter 11, Article 11).

> Individualist proverb: "The squeaky wheel gets the grease."
>
> Collectivist proverb: "The quacking duck gets shot."

Collectivist cultures place little expectation or value on having a consistent, coherent self-concept because one's identity depends on others in the social context (Heine & Buchtel, 2009). Even if East Asians report inconsistency in their self-concept across different relationship partners, they still feel authentic (English & Chen, 2011). In contrast, European-Americans do not feel authentic if their self-concept changes across relationship partners.

* * *

From Freud's psychoanalysis and Maslow's and Rogers' humanistic perspective, to the trait and social-cognitive theories, to today's study of the self, our understanding of personality has come a long way! This is a good base from which to explore Chapter 12's questions: How and why do some people suffer from disordered thinking and emotions? ■

RETRIEVE + REMEMBER

- How do individualist and collectivist cultures differ?

ANSWER: Individualists give priority to personal goals over group goals and tend to define their identity in terms of their own personal attributes. Collectivists give priority to group goals over individual goals and tend to define their identity in terms of group identifications.

CHAPTER REVIEW

Personality

Test yourself by taking a moment to answer each of these Learning Objective Questions (repeated here from within the chapter). Then turn to Appendix D, Complete Chapter Reviews, to check your answers. Research suggests that trying to answer these questions on your own will improve your long-term memory of the concepts (McDaniel et al., 2009).

Psychodynamic Theories

11-1: How did Sigmund Freud's treatment of psychological disorders lead to his view of the unconscious mind?

11-2: What was Freud's view of personality?

11-3: What developmental stages did Freud propose?

11-4: How did Freud think people defended themselves against anxiety?

11-5: Which of Freud's ideas did his followers accept or reject?

11-6: What are projective tests, how are they used, and how are they criticized?

11-7: How do today's psychologists view Freud's psychoanalysis?

11-8: How has modern research developed our understanding of the unconscious?

Humanistic Theories

11-9: How did humanistic psychologists view personality, and what was their goal in studying personality?

11-10: How did humanistic psychologists assess a person's sense of self?

11-11: How have humanistic theories influenced psychology? What criticisms have they faced?

Trait Theories

11-12: How do psychologists use traits to describe personality?

11-13: What are personality inventories?

11-14: Which traits seem to provide the most useful information about personality variation?

11-15: Does research support the consistency of personality traits over time and across situations?

Social-Cognitive Theories

11-16: How do social-cognitive theorists view personality development, and how do they explore behavior?

11-17: What criticisms have social-cognitive theorists faced?

Exploring the Self

11-18: Why has psychology generated so much research on the self? How important is self-esteem to psychology and to our well-being?

11-19: What evidence reveals self-serving bias, and how do defensive and secure self-esteem differ?

11-20: How do individualist and collectivist cultures influence people?

TERMS AND CONCEPTS TO REMEMBER

Test yourself on these terms by trying to write down the definition in your own words before flipping back to the referenced page to check your answer.

personality, p. 311

psychodynamic theories, p. 312

psychoanalysis, p. 312

unconscious, p. 312

free association, p. 312

id, p. 313

ego, p. 313

superego, p. 313

psychosexual stages, p. 314

Oedipus [ED-uh-puss] complex, p. 314

identification, p. 314

fixation, p. 314

defense mechanisms, p. 314

repression, p. 314

projective test, p. 316

Rorschach inkblot test, p. 316

hierarchy of needs, p. 319

self-actualization, p. 319

self-transcendence, p. 319

unconditional positive regard, p. 320

self-concept, p. 320

trait, p. 322

factor, p. 322

Minnesota Multiphasic Personality Inventory (MMPI), p. 324

personality inventory, p. 324

reciprocal determinism, p. 326

social-cognitive perspective, p. 326

self-efficacy, p. 326

self, p. 328

spotlight effect, p. 328

self-esteem, p. 329

self-serving bias, p. 330

individualism, p. 331

collectivism, p. 331

CHAPTER TEST

Test yourself repeatedly throughout your studies. This will not only help you figure out what you know and don't know; the testing itself will help you learn and remember the information more effectively thanks to the testing effect.

1. Freud believed that we may block painful or unacceptable thoughts, wishes, feelings, or memories from consciousness through an unconscious process called

   _____.

2. According to Freud's view of personality structure, the "executive" system, the _____, seeks to gratify the impulses of the _____ in more acceptable ways.

   a. id; ego

   b. ego; superego

   c. ego; id

   d. id; superego

3. Freud proposed that the development of the "voice of conscience" is related to the _____, which internalizes ideals and provides standards for judgments.

4. According to the psychoanalytic view of development, we all pass through a series of psychosexual stages, including the oral, anal, and phallic stages. Conflicts unresolved at any of these stages may lead to

   a. dormant sexual feelings.

   b. fixation at that stage.

   c. unconscious blocking of impulses.

   d. a distorted gender identity.

5. Freud believed that defense mechanisms are unconscious attempts to distort or disguise reality, all in an effort to reduce our _____.

6. _____ tests ask test-takers to respond to an ambiguous stimulus, for example, by describing it or telling a story about it.

7. In general, neo-Freudians such as Adler and Horney accepted many of Freud's views but placed more emphasis than he did on

   a. development throughout the life span.

   b. the collective unconscious.

   c. the role of the id.

   d. social interactions.

8. Modern-day psychodynamic theorists and therapists agree with Freud about

   a. the existence of unconscious mental processes.

   b. the Oedipus complex.

   c. the predictive value of Freudian theory.

   d. the superego's role as the executive part of personality.

9. Which of the following is NOT part of the contemporary view of the unconscious?

   a. Repressed memories of anxiety-provoking events

   b. Schemas that influence our perceptions and interpretations

   c. Parallel processing that occurs without our conscious knowledge

   d. Instantly activated emotions and implicit memories of learned skills

10. Maslow's hierarchy of needs proposes that we must satisfy basic physiological and safety needs before we seek ultimate psychological needs, such as self-actualization. Maslow based his ideas on

    a. Freudian theory.

    b. his experiences with patients.

    c. a series of laboratory experiments.

    d. his study of healthy, creative people.

11. How might Freud and Rogers differ in their explanations of how the environment influences the development of a criminal?

12. The total acceptance Rogers advocated as part of a growth-promoting environment is called _____ _____ _____.

13. The _____ theory of personality focuses on describing characteristic behavior patterns, such as agreeableness or extraversion.

14. One famous personality inventory is the
    a. Extraversion–Introversion Scale.
    b. Person–Situation Inventory.
    c. MMPI.
    d. Rorschach.

15. Which of the following is NOT one of the Big Five personality factors?
    a. Conscientiousness
    b. Anxiety
    c. Extraversion
    d. Agreeableness

16. Our scores on personality tests best predict
    a. our behavior on a specific occasion.
    b. our average behavior across many situations.
    c. behavior involving a single trait, such as conscientiousness.
    d. behavior that depends on the situation or context.

17. The social-cognitive perspective proposes our personality is shaped by a process called reciprocal determinism, as personal factors, environmental factors, and behaviors interact. An example of an environmental factor is
    a. the presence of books in a home.
    b. a preference for outdoor play.
    c. the ability to read at a fourth-grade level.
    d. the fear of violent action on television.

18. Critics say that _____ - _____ personality theory is very sensitive to an individual's interactions with particular situations, but that it gives too little attention to the person's enduring traits.

19. Researchers have found that low self-esteem tends to be linked with life problems. How should this link be interpreted?
    a. Life problems cause low self-esteem.
    b. The answer isn't clear because the link is correlational and does not indicate cause and effect.
    c. Low self-esteem leads to life problems.
    d. Because of the self-serving bias, we must assume that external factors cause low self-esteem.

20. A fortune cookie advises, "Love yourself and happiness will follow." Is this good advice?

21. Individualist cultures tend to value _____; collectivist cultures tend to value _____.
    a. interdependence; independence
    b. independence; interdependence
    c. group solidarity; uniqueness
    d. duty to family; personal fulfillment

Find answers to these questions in Appendix E, in the back of the book.

IN YOUR EVERYDAY LIFE

Answering these questions will help you make these concepts more personally meaningful, and therefore more memorable.

1. How would you describe your personality? What are your typical patterns of thinking, feeling, and acting?

2. What did you think or know about Freud before you read this chapter? Have your thoughts changed now that you have learned more about him?

3. Has someone in your life accepted you unconditionally? Has this person helped you know yourself better or improve your self-image?

4. Where would you place yourself on the Big Five personality dimensions—conscientiousness, agreeableness, neuroticism, openness, and extraversion? Would your family and friends agree with you?

5. Look around your personal spaces, such as your bedroom, car, or your social media profiles. How do you think these spaces reflect your personality?

6. How have your experiences shaped your personality? How has your personality helped shape your environment?

7. What possible selves do you dream of—or fear—becoming? To what extent do these imagined selves motivate you now?

8. Do you consider yourself to be more of a collectivist or an individualist? How do you think this has influenced your behavior, emotions, or thoughts?

experience
more of the
testing
effect

12 Social Psychology

On a winter day in 1569, Dirk Willems faced a moment of decision. He had just escaped from prison, where he was facing torture and death for belonging to a persecuted religious minority. Willems fled across an ice-covered pond in Asperen, Holland, with his stronger and heavier jailer close behind. Then, suddenly, his jailer fell through the ice. Unable to climb out, he pleaded for help to escape the icy waters.

With his freedom in front of him, Willems acted with ultimate selflessness: He turned back and rescued his pursuer. The jailer, following his orders, took Willems back to prison where, a few weeks later, he was burned alive. For his martyrdom, present-day Asperen has named a street in honor of its folk hero (Toews, 2004).

What drives people to feel and act so heartlessly toward those, like Willems, who differ from them? What motivates the selflessness of the responses of so many who have died trying to save others?

What leads us to like or even love another? Do birds of a feather flock together—or do opposites attract? Does absence make the heart grow fonder—or does out of sight more often mean out of mind? Do good looks attract us—or does a good personality matter more?

As such questions demonstrate, we are social animals. We may assume the worst or the best in others. We may approach them with closed fists or open arms. But as the novelist Herman Melville remarked, "We cannot live for ourselves alone. Our lives are connected by a thousand invisible threads." In this chapter, we explore some of these connections and see how social psychologists study them.

What Is Social Psychology's Focus?

12-1 What are three main focuses of social psychology?

◎ **Social psychologists** use *scientific methods* to study how we *think about, influence,* and *relate to* one another. When the unexpected occurs, we want to understand why people act as they do. Personality psychologists (Chapter 11) study the personal traits and processes that explain why we as *individuals* may act differently *in a given situation*. (Would you have acted as Willems did, helping the jailer out of the icy water?) Social psychologists study the social forces that explain why people act differently in *different situations*. (Might Willems' jailer have released him if the circumstances had been different?)

Social Thinking

◎ When we try to explain people's actions, our search for answers often leaves us with two choices. We

AN ETCHING OF DIRK WILLEMS BY DUTCH ARTIST JAN LUYKEN (from *The Martyrs Mirror,* 1685)

Mennonite Library and Archives/Bethel College

can attribute behavior to a person's stable, enduring traits. Or we can attribute behavior to the situation (Heider, 1958). Our explanations, or *attributions,* affect our feelings and actions.

The Fundamental Attribution Error

12-2 How does the fundamental attribution error describe how we tend to explain others' behavior compared with our own?

In class, we notice that Juliette seldom talks. Over coffee, Jack talks nonstop. That must be the sort of people they are, we decide. Juliette must be shy and Jack outgoing. Are they? Perhaps. People do have enduring personality traits. But often our explanations are wrong. We fall prey to the **fundamental attribution error:** We give too much weight to the influence of personality and too little to the influence of situations. In class, Jack may be as quiet as Juliette. Catch Juliette at a party and you may hardly recognize your quiet classmate.

Researchers demonstrated this tendency in an experiment with college students (Napolitan & Goethals, 1979). They had students talk, one at a time, with a young woman who acted either cold and critical or warm and friendly. Before the talks, the researchers told half the students that the woman's behavior would be normal and natural. They told the other half the truth—that they had instructed her to *act* friendly (or unfriendly).

Did hearing the truth affect students' impressions of the woman? Not at all! If the woman acted friendly, both groups decided she really was a warm person. If she acted unfriendly, both decided she really was a cold person. In other words, they attributed her behavior to her personal traits, *even when they were told that her behavior was part of the experimental situation.*

The fundamental attribution error appears more often in some cultures than in others. Individualist Westerners

more often attribute behavior to people's personal traits. People in East Asian cultures are more sensitive to the power of situations (Masuda & Kitayama, 2004). This difference appeared in experiments in which people were asked to view scenes, such as a big fish swimming. Americans focused more on the individual fish; Japanese people focused on the whole scene (Chua et al., 2005; Nisbett, 2003).

To see how easily we make the fundamental attribution error, answer this question: Is your psychology instructor shy or outgoing?

If you're tempted to answer "outgoing," remember that you know your instructor from one situation—the classroom, which demands outgoing behavior. Your instructor (who observes his or her own behavior not only in the classroom, but also with family, friends, and colleagues) might say, "Me, outgoing? It all depends on the situation. In class or with good friends, yes, I'm outgoing. But at professional meetings I'm really rather shy." Outside the classroom, professors seem less professorial, students less studious.

When we explain *our own* behavior, we are sensitive to how behavior changes with the situation (Idson & Mischel, 2001). We also are sensitive to the power of the situation when we explain the behavior of people we have seen in many different contexts. So, when are we most likely to commit the fundamental attribution error? The odds are highest when a stranger acts badly. Having never seen this person in other situations, we assume he must be a bad person. But outside the stadium, that red-faced man screaming at the referee may be a great neighbor and a good father.

As we act, our eyes look outward; we see others' faces, not our own. If we could take an observer's point of view, would we become more aware of our own personal style? To test this idea, researchers have filmed two people interacting with a camera behind each person. Then they showed each person a replay of their interaction—filmed from the other person's perspective. It worked. Seeing their behavior from the other person's perspective, participants better appreciated the power of the situation (Lassiter & Irvine, 1986; Storms, 1973).

Reflecting on our past selves of 5 or 10 years ago also switches our perspective. Our present self adopts the observer's perspective and attributes our past behavior mostly to our traits (Pronin & Ross, 2006). In another 5 or 10 years, your current self may seem like another person.

The way we explain others' actions, attributing them to the person or the situation, can have important real-life effects (Fincham & Bradbury, 1993; Fletcher et al., 1990). A person must decide whether another's warm greeting reflects friendliness or a romantic interest. A jury must decide whether a shooting was an attack or an act of self-defense. A voter must judge whether a candidate's promises are sincere or soon to be forgotten. A partner must decide whether a loved one's acid-tongued remark reflects a bad day or a serious rejection.

Finally, consider the social effects of attribution. How should we explain poverty or unemployment? In Britain, India, Australia, and the United States, political conservatives have tended to place the blame on the personal traits of the poor and unemployed (Furnham, 1982; Pandey et al., 1982; Wagstaff, 1982; Zucker & Weiner, 1993). "People generally get what they deserve. Those who don't work are often freeloaders. Anybody who tries hard can still get ahead." In experiments, after reflecting on the power of choice—either by recalling their own choices or taking note of another's choices—people are less bothered by inequality. They are more likely to think people get what they deserve (Savani & Rattan, 2012). Those not asked to consider the power of choice are more likely to blame past and present situations. So are political liberals.

The point to remember: Our attributions—to someone's personal traits or to the situation—have real consequences.

"Otis, shout at that man to pull himself together."

Attitudes and Actions

12-3 What is an attitude, and how do attitudes and actions affect each other?

Attitudes are feelings, often based on our beliefs, that can influence how we respond to particular objects, people, and events. If we *believe* someone is mean, we may *feel* dislike for the person and *act* unfriendly. That helps explain a noteworthy finding. If people in a country intensely dislike the leaders of another country, their country is more likely to produce terrorist acts against that country (Krueger & Malecková, 2009). Hateful attitudes breed violent behavior.

Attitudes Affect Actions

Attitudes affect our behavior, but other factors, including the situation, also influence behavior. For example, in roll-call votes, situational pressures can control behavior. Forced to state publicly their support or opposition, politicians may vote as their supporters demand, despite privately disagreeing with those demands (Nagourney, 2002).

When are attitudes most likely to affect behavior? Under these conditions (Glasman & Albarracin, 2006):

- External influences are minimal.
- The attitude is stable.
- The attitude is specific to the behavior.
- The attitude is easily recalled.

One experiment used vivid, easily recalled information to persuade people that sustained tanning put them at risk for future skin cancer. One month later, 72 percent of the participants, and only 16 percent of those in a waitlist control group, had lighter skin (McClendon & Prentice-Dunn, 2001). Changed attitudes can change behavior.

Actions Affect Attitudes

People also come to believe in what they have stood up for. Many streams of evidence confirm that *attitudes follow behavior* (**FIGURE 12.1**).

FOOT-IN-THE-DOOR PHENOMENON How would you react if someone got

FIGURE 12.1 Attitudes follow behavior Cooperative actions, such as those performed by people on sports teams, feed mutual liking. Such attitudes, in turn, promote positive behavior.

social psychology the scientific study of how we think about, influence, and relate to one another.

fundamental attribution error the tendency, when analyzing others' behavior, to overestimate the influence of personal traits and underestimate the effects of the situation.

attitude feelings, often based on our beliefs, that predispose us to respond in a particular way to objects, people, and events.

you to act against your beliefs? Would you change your beliefs? Many people do. During the Korean war, many U.S. prisoners were held in Chinese communist camps. Without using brutality, the Chinese captors gained prisoners' cooperation in various activities. Some merely did simple tasks to gain privileges. Others made radio appeals and false confessions. Still others informed on other prisoners and revealed military information. When the war ended, 21 prisoners chose to stay with the communists. More returned home "brainwashed"—convinced that communism was good for Asia.

How did the Chinese captors achieve these amazing results? A key ingredient was their effective use of the **foot-in-the-door phenomenon.** They knew that people who agree to a small request will find it easier to agree later to a larger one. The Chinese began with harmless requests, such as copying a trivial statement. Gradually, they made bigger demands (Schein, 1956). The next statement to be copied might contain a list of the flaws of capitalism. Then, to gain privileges, the prisoners took part in group discussions, wrote self-criticisms, or made public confessions. After taking this series of small steps, some of the Americans changed their beliefs to be more in line with their public acts. The point is simple. To get people to agree to something big, start small and build (Cialdini, 1993). A trivial act makes the next act easier. Give in to a temptation and you will find the next temptation harder to resist.

In dozens of experiments, researchers have coaxed people into acting against their attitudes or violating their moral standards, with the same result. Doing becomes believing. After giving in to a request to harm an innocent victim—by making nasty comments or delivering electric shocks—people begin to look down on their victim. After speaking or writing in support of a position they have doubts about, they begin to believe their own words.

Fortunately, the principle that attitudes follow behavior works as well for good deeds as for bad. After U.S. schools were desegregated and the 1964 Civil Rights Act was passed, White Americans expressed lower levels of racial prejudice. And as Americans in different regions came to *act* more alike—thanks to more uniform national standards against discrimination—they began to *think* more alike. Experiments confirm the observation: Moral action strengthens moral convictions.

ROLE-PLAYING AFFECTS ATTITUDES

How many new **roles** have you adopted recently? Becoming a college student is a new role. Perhaps you've started a new job, or a new relationship, or even become engaged or married. If so, you may have realized that people expected you to behave a little differently. At first, your behaviors may have felt phony, because you were acting a role. Soldiers may at first feel they are playing war games. Newlyweds may feel they are "playing house." Before long, however, what began as play-acting in the theater of life becomes you. (This fact is reflected in the Alcoholics Anonymous advice: "Fake it until you make it.")

Role-playing morphed into real life in one famous study in which male college students volunteered to spend time in a mock prison (Zimbardo, 1972). Psychologist Philip Zimbardo randomly assigned some volunteers to be guards. He gave them uniforms, clubs, and whistles and instructed them to enforce certain rules. Others became prisoners, locked in barren cells and forced to wear humiliating outfits. For a day or two, the volunteers self-consciously played their roles. Then it became clear that the "play" had become real—too real. Most guards developed bad attitudes. Some set up cruel routines. One by one, the prisoners broke down, rebelled, or became passively resigned. After only six days, Zimbardo called off the study.

Role-playing can also train people to become torturers in the real world (Staub, 1989). Yet people differ. In Zimbardo's prison simulation, and in other atrocity-producing situations, some people gave in to the situation and others did not

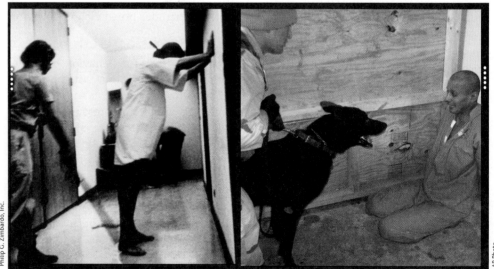

THE POWER OF THE SITUATION In his 1972 Stanford Prison study, Philip Zimbardo created a toxic situation (left). Those assigned to the guard role soon began to abuse those playing the role of prisoners. In real life in 2004, some U.S. military guards abused Iraqi prisoners at the U.S.-run Abu Ghraib prison (right). To Zimbardo (2004, 2007), a bad barrel, not a few bad apples, led to the abuse: "When ordinary people are put in a novel, evil place, such as most prisons, Situations Win, People Lose."

(Carnahan & McFarland, 2007; Haslam & Reicher, 2007; Mastroianni & Reed, 2006; Zimbardo, 2007). Persons and situations interact.

COGNITIVE DISSONANCE: RELIEF FROM TENSION We have seen that actions can affect attitudes, sometimes turning prisoners into collaborators, doubters into believers, and guards into abusers. But why? One explanation is that when we become aware of a mismatch between our attitudes and actions, we experience mental discomfort, or *cognitive dissonance*. Indeed, the brain regions that become active when people experience cognitive conflict and negative arousal also become active when people experience cognitive dissonance (Kitayama et al., 2013). To relieve this tension, according to Leon Festinger's **cognitive dissonance theory,** we often bring our attitudes into line with our actions.

Dozens of experiments have tested this attitudes-follow-behavior principle. Many have made people feel responsible for behavior that clashed with their attitudes. As a participant in one of these experiments, you might agree for a mere $2 to help a researcher by writing an essay that supports something you don't believe in (perhaps a tuition increase). Feeling responsible for your written statements (which don't reflect your attitudes), you would probably feel dissonance, especially if you thought an administrator would be reading your essay. How could you reduce the uncomfortable tension? One way would be to start believing your phony words. It's as if we tell ourselves, "If I chose to do it (or say it), I must believe in it." Thus, we may change our attitudes to help justify the act.

The attitudes-follow-behavior principle can also help us become better people. We cannot control all our feelings, but we can influence them by altering our behavior. (Recall from Chapter 9 the emotional effects of facial expressions and of body postures.) If we are down in the dumps, we can do as cognitive therapists advise: We can talk in more positive, self-accepting ways with

fewer self-put-downs. If we are unloving, we can become more loving: We can do thoughtful things, express affection, give support.

The point to remember: Cruel acts shape the self. But so do acts of good will. Act as though you like someone, and you soon may. Changing our behavior can change how we think about others and how we feel about ourselves. ■

RETRIEVE + REMEMBER

- Driving to school one snowy day, Marco narrowly misses a car that slides through a red light. "Slow down! What a terrible driver," he thinks to himself. Moments later, Marco himself slips through an intersection and yelps, "Wow! These roads are awful. The city plows need to get out here." What social psychology principle has Marco just demonstrated? Explain.

  ANSWER: By attributing the other person's behavior to personal traits ("what a terrible driver") and his own to the situation ("these roads are awful"), Marco has exhibited the *fundamental attribution error.*

- How do our attitudes and our actions affect each other?

  ANSWER: Our attitudes often influence our actions, as we behave in ways consistent with our beliefs. However, our attitudes also follow our actions; we come to believe in what we have done.

- When people act in a way that is not in keeping with their attitudes, and then change their attitudes to match those actions, _____ _____ theory attempts to explain why.

  ANSWER: cognitive dissonance

Social Influence

◎ Social psychology's great lesson is the enormous power of social influence. We adjust our views to match the desires of those around us. We follow orders. We behave as others in our group behave. On campus, jeans are the dress code. On New York's Wall Street, dress suits are the norm. Let's examine the pull of these social strings. How strong are they? How do they operate? When do we break them?

Conformity and Obedience

12-4 What do experiments on conformity and obedience reveal about the power of social influence?

Fish swim in schools. Birds fly in flocks. And humans, too, tend to go with their group—to think what it thinks and do what it does. Behavior is catching. If one of us laughs, coughs, yawns, or stares at the sky, others in our group will soon do the same. Like the chameleon lizards that take on the color of their surroundings, we humans take on the emotional tones of those around us (Totterdell et al., 1998). We are natural mimics, unconsciously imitating others' expressions, postures, and voice tones.

Researchers demonstrated this *chameleon effect* in a clever experiment (Chartrand & Bargh, 1999). They had students work in a room beside another person, who was actually the experimenter's assistant. Sometimes the assistants rubbed their own face. Sometimes they shook their foot. Sure enough, the students tended to rub their face when with the face-rubbing person and shake their foot when with the foot-shaking person.

Automatic mimicry helps us to *empathize*, to feel what others feel. This helps explain why we feel happier around happy people than around depressed ones. The more we mimic, the greater our empathy, and the more people tend to like us.

---

foot-in-the-door phenomenon the tendency for people who have first agreed to a small request to comply later with a larger request.

role a set of expectations about a social position, defining how those in the position ought to behave.

cognitive dissonance theory the theory that we act to reduce the discomfort (dissonance) we feel when two of our thoughts (cognitions) clash. For example, when we become aware that our attitudes and our actions don't match, we may change our attitudes so that we feel more comfortable.

Group Pressure and Conformity

To study **conformity**—adjusting our behavior or thinking toward some group standard—Solomon Asch (1955) designed a simple test. As a participant in what you believe is a study of visual perception, you arrive in time to take a seat at a table with five other people. The experimenter asks the group to state, one by one, which of three comparison lines is identical to a standard line. You see clearly that the answer is Line 2, and you await your turn to say so. Your boredom begins to show when the next set of lines proves equally easy.

Now comes the third trial, and the correct answer seems just as clear-cut (FIGURE 12.2). But the first person gives what strikes you as a wrong answer: "Line 3." When the second person and then the third and fourth give the same wrong answer, you sit up straight and squint. When the fifth person agrees with the first four, you feel your heart begin to pound. The experimenter then looks to you for your answer. Torn between the agreement voiced by the five others and the evidence of your own eyes, you feel tense and suddenly unsure of yourself. You wait a bit before answering, wondering whether you should suffer the pain of being the odd-ball. What answer do you give?

CONFORMING TO NONCONFORMITY Are these students asserting their individuality, or identifying themselves with others of the same microculture?

In Asch's experiments, college students experienced this conflict. Answering questions alone, they were wrong less than 1 percent of the time. But the odds were quite different when several others—people actually working for Asch—answered incorrectly. Although most people told the truth even when others did not, Asch was disturbed by his result. More than one-third of the time, these "intelligent and well-meaning" college students were then "willing to call white black" by going along with the group.

Experiments reveal that we are more likely to conform when we

- are made to feel incompetent or insecure.
- are in a group with at least three people.
- are in a group in which everyone else agrees. (If just one other person disagrees, we will almost surely disagree.)
- admire the group's status and attractiveness.

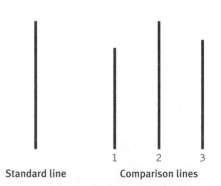

Standard line   Comparison lines

FIGURE 12.2 Asch's conformity experiments Which of the three comparison lines on the right is equal to the standard line? The photo on the left (from one of the experiments) was taken after five people, who were actually working for Asch, had answered, "Line 3." The student in the center shows the severe discomfort that comes from disagreeing with the responses of other group members.

BODY PIERCINGS: YESTERDAY'S NONCONFORMITY, TODAY'S CONFORMITY? As body piercings become perceived as fashion conformity, their popularity may wane.

- have not already committed ourselves to any response.
- know that others in the group will observe our behavior.
- are from a culture that strongly encourages respect for social standards.

Why do we so often think what others think and do what they do? Why in college residence halls do students' attitudes become more similar to those living near them (Cullum & Harton, 2007)? Why in classrooms are hand-raised answers to controversial questions more alike than answers given by anonymous electronic clicker responses (Stowell et al., 2010)? Why do we clap when others clap, eat as others eat, believe what others believe, even see what others see? Sometimes it's to avoid rejection or to gain social approval. So we respond to social

norms—a group's rules for "proper" behavior. But groups also provide information that can benefit open-minded people. "Those who never retract their opinions love themselves more than they love truth," observed Joseph Joubert, an eighteenth-century French essayist.

Is conformity good or bad? The answer depends on our values. When people conform to influences that support what we approve, we applaud them for being "open-minded" and "sensitive" enough to be "responsive." When they conform to influences that support what we disapprove, we scorn their "blind, thoughtless" willingness to give in to others' wishes.

Our values, as we saw in Chapter 11, are influenced by our culture. Western Europeans and people in most English-speaking countries tend to prize *individualism*. People in many Asian, African, and Latin American countries place a higher value on honoring group standards (*collectivism*). It's perhaps not surprising, then, that in social influence experiments across 17 countries, conformity rates are lower in individualist cultures than in collectivist cultures (Bond & Smith, 1996). In the United States, for example, university students tend to see themselves as less conforming than others (Pronin et al., 2007). We are, in our own eyes, individuals amid a flock of sheep. ▪

> "Have you ever noticed how one example—good or bad—can prompt others to follow? How one illegally parked car can give permission for others to do likewise? How one racial joke can fuel another?"
>
> Marian Wright Edelman,
> *The Measure of Our Success*, 1994

RETRIEVE + REMEMBER

- Which of the following strengthens conformity to a group?
  a. Finding the group attractive
  b. Feeling secure
  c. Coming from an individualist culture
  d. Having already decided on a response

ANSWER: a

Obedience

Social psychologist Stanley Milgram (1963, 1974), a student of Solomon Asch and a high school classmate of Phillip Zimbardo, knew that people often give in to social pressure. But how would they respond to outright commands? To find out, he undertook experiments that have become social psychology's most famous and most hotly debated.

Imagine yourself as one of the nearly 1000 people who took part in Milgram's 20 experiments. You have responded to an ad for participants in a Yale University psychology study of the effect of punishment on learning. Professor Milgram's assistant asks you and another person to draw slips from a hat to see who will be the "teacher" and who will be the "learner." You draw the "teacher" slip and are asked to sit down in front of a machine, which has a series of labeled switches. The "learner" is led to a nearby room and strapped into a chair. From the chair, wires run through the wall to "your" machine. You are given your task: Teach and then test the learner on a list of word pairs. If the

STANLEY MILGRAM (1933–1984) This social psychologist's obedience experiments "belong to the self-understanding of literate people in our age" (Sabini, 1986).

---

conformity adjusting our behavior or thinking to coincide with a group standard.

norm an understood rule for accepted and expected behavior in a given group.

learner gives a wrong answer, you are to flip a switch to deliver a brief electric shock. For the first wrong answer, you will flip the switch labeled "15 Volts—Slight Shock." With each succeeding error, you will move to the next higher voltage. The researcher demonstrates by flipping the first switch. Lights flash, relay switches click on, and an electric buzzing fills the air.

The experiment begins, and you deliver the shocks after the first and second wrong answers. If you continue, you hear the learner grunt when you flick the third, fourth, and fifth switches. After you flip the eighth switch ("120 Volts—Moderate Shock"), the learner cries out that the shocks are painful. After the tenth switch ("150 Volts—Strong Shock"), he begins shouting. "Get me out of here! I won't be in the experiment anymore! I refuse to go on!" You draw back, but the experimenter prods you. "Please continue—the experiment requires that you continue." You resist, but the experimenter insists, "It is absolutely essential that you continue," or "You have no other choice, you *must* go on."

If you obey, you hear the learner shriek in agony as you continue to raise the shock level after each new error. After the 330-volt level, the learner refuses to answer and falls silent. Still, the experimenter pushes you toward the final, 450-volt switch. Ask the question, he says, and if no correct answer is given, administer the next shock level.

Would you follow an experimenter's commands to shock someone? At what level would you refuse to obey? Milgram asked that question in a survey before he started his experiments. Most people were sure they would stop playing such a sadistic-seeming role soon after the learner first indicated pain, certainly before he shrieked in agony. Forty psychiatrists agreed with that prediction when Milgram asked them. Were the predictions accurate? Not even close. When Milgram actually conducted the experiment with men aged 20 to 50, he was amazed. More than 60 percent followed orders—right up to the last switch. Even when Milgram ran a new study, with 40 new teachers, and the learner complained of a "slight heart condition,"

the results were the same. A full 65 percent of the new teachers obeyed every one of the experimenter's commands, right up to 450 volts (FIGURE 12.3).

How can we explain these findings? Could they be a product of the 1960s culture? Would people today be less likely to obey an order to hurt someone? *No.* When researchers replicated Milgram's basic experiment, 70 percent of the participants obeyed up to the 150-volt point (Burger, 2009). This is only a slight reduction from Milgram's 80 percent at that level. And in a French reality TV show replication, 80 percent of people, egged on by a cheering audience, obeyed and tortured a screaming victim (de Moraes, 2010).

Could Milgram's findings reflect some aspect of gender behavior found only in males? Again, the answer is *No.* In 10 later studies, women obeyed at rates similar to men (Blass, 1999).

Did the teachers figure out the hoax—that no real shock was being delivered and the learner was in fact an assistant only pretending to feel pain? Did they realize the experiment was really testing their willingness to obey commands

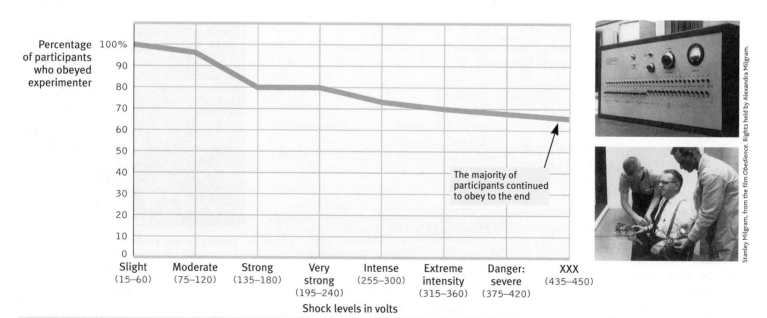

FIGURE 12.3 Milgram's follow-up obedience experiment In a repeat of the earlier experiment, 65 percent of the adult male "teachers" fully obeyed the experimenter's commands to continue. They did so despite the "learner's" earlier mention of a heart condition and despite hearing cries of protest after they delivered what they thought were 150 volts, and agonized protests after 330 volts. (Data from Milgram, 1974.)

to inflict punishment? No, the teachers were typically genuinely distressed. They perspired, trembled, laughed nervously, and bit their lips.

In later experiments, Milgram discovered some things that did influence people's behavior. When he varied some details of the situation, the percentage of participants who fully obeyed ranged from 0 to 93 percent. Obedience was highest when

- the person giving the orders was close at hand and was perceived to be a legitimate authority figure.

- the authority figure was supported by a respected, well-known institution (Yale University).

- the victim was depersonalized or at a distance, even in another room. Similarly, many soldiers in combat either do not fire their rifles at an enemy they can see or do not aim them properly. Such refusals to kill are rare among those who kill from a distance. (Veterans who operated remotely piloted drones have suffered less posttraumatic stress than is found among on-the-ground Afghanistan and Iraq war veterans [Miller, 2012; Padgett, 1989].)

- there were no role models for defiance. (Teachers did not see any other participant disobey the experimenter.)

The power of legitimate, close-at-hand authorities is dramatically apparent in stories of those who followed orders to carry out the Holocaust atrocities. Obedience alone does not explain the Holocaust. Anti-Semitic ideology produced eager killers as well (Mastroianni, 2002). But obedience was a factor. In the summer of 1942, nearly 500 middle-aged German reserve police officers were dispatched to German-occupied Jozefow, Poland. On July 13, the group's visibly upset commander informed his recruits, mostly family men, of their orders. They were to round up the village's Jews, who were said to

STANDING UP FOR DEMOCRACY Some individuals—roughly one in three in Milgram's experiments—resist social pressure to act against their beliefs. This unarmed man single-handedly challenged an advancing line of tanks in Tiananmen Square in 1989. This was one day after the Chinese government had suppressed a student uprising there.

be aiding the enemy. Able-bodied men would be sent to work camps, and all the rest were to be shot on the spot.

The commander gave the recruits a chance to refuse to participate in the executions. Only about a dozen immediately refused. Within 17 hours, the remaining 485 officers killed 1500 helpless women, children, and elderly, shooting them in the back of the head as they lay face down. Hearing the victims' pleas and seeing the gruesome results, some 20 percent of the officers did eventually disobey. They did so either by missing their victims or by wandering away and hiding until the slaughter was over (Browning, 1992). In real life, as in Milgram's experiments, those who resisted did so early, and they were the minority.

Another story was being played out in the French village of Le Chambon. There, French Jews were being sheltered by villagers who openly defied orders to cooperate with the "New Order." The villagers'

> "I was only following orders."
>
> Adolf Eichmann,
> Director of Nazi deportation
> of Jews to concentration camps

ancestors had themselves been persecuted. Their pastors had been teaching them to "resist whenever our adversaries will demand of us obedience contrary to the orders of the Gospel" (Rochat, 1993). Ordered by police to give a list of sheltered Jews, the head pastor modeled defiance. "I don't know of Jews, I only know of human beings." These resistors had no idea how long and terrible the war would be, or how much punishment and poverty they would suffer. But early on, they made a commitment to resist. After that, they drew support from their beliefs, their role models, their interactions with one another, and their own early actions. They remained defiant to the war's end.

Lessons From the Conformity and Obedience Studies

12-5 What do the social influence studies teach us about ourselves? How much power do we have as individuals?

How do the laboratory experiments on social influence relate to everyday life? Psychology's experiments aim not to re-create the exact behaviors of everyday life but to explore what influences them. Solomon Asch and Stanley Milgram devised experiments that forced a choice: Do I remain true to my own standards or do I respond to others? That's a dilemma we all face.

In Milgram's experiments and their modern replications (Burger, 2009), participants were also torn. Should they respond to the pleas of the victim or the orders of the experimenter? Their moral sense warned them not to harm another. But that same sense also prompted them to obey the experimenter and to be a good research participant. With kindness and obedience on a collision course, obedience usually won.

These experiments demonstrated that strong social influences can make people conform to falsehoods or give in to cruelty. Milgram saw this as the most basic lesson of his work. "Ordinary people, simply doing their jobs, and without any particular hostility on their part, can become agents in a terrible destructive process" (1974, p. 6).

Using the foot-in-the-door effect, Milgram began with a little tickle of electricity and advanced step by step. In the minds of those throwing the switches, the small action became justified, making the next act tolerable.

In any society, great evils sometimes grow out of people's acceptance of lesser evils. The Nazi leaders suspected that most German civil servants would resist shooting or gassing Jews directly. But they found them surprisingly willing to handle the paperwork of the Holocaust (Silver & Geller, 1978). Milgram found a similar reaction in his experiments. When he asked 40 men to give the learning test while someone else delivered the shocks, 93 percent agreed. Cruelty does not require devilish villains. All it takes is ordinary people corrupted by an evil situation. Ordinary students may follow orders to haze new members joining their group. Ordinary employees may follow orders to produce and market harmful products. Ordinary soldiers may follow orders to torture prisoners (Lankford, 2009).

In Jozefow and Le Chambon, as in Milgram's experiments, those who resisted usually did so early. After the first acts of obedience or resistance, attitudes began to follow and justify behavior.

What have social psychologists learned about the power of the individual? *Social control* (the power of the situation) and *personal control* (the power of the individual) interact. Much as water dissolves salt but not sand, so rotten situations turn some people into bad apples while others resist (Johnson, 2007).

People do resist. When feeling pressured, some react by doing the opposite of what is expected (Brehm & Brehm, 1981). Rosa Parks' refusal to sit at the back of the bus ignited the U.S. civil rights movement.

The power of one or two individuals to sway majorities is *minority influence* (Moscovici, 1985). In studies, one finding repeatedly stands out. When you are the minority, you are far more likely to sway the majority if you hold firmly to your position and don't waffle. This tactic won't make you popular, but it may make you influential, especially if your self-confidence stimulates others to consider why you react as you do. Even when a minority's influence is not yet visible, people may privately develop sympathy for the minority position and rethink their views (Wood et al., 1994). The powers of social influence are enormous, but so are the powers of the committed individual. ■

RETRIEVE + REMEMBER

- In psychology's most famous obedience experiments, most participants obeyed an authority figure's demands to inflict presumed life-threatening shocks on an innocent person. Social psychologist _____ _____ conducted these experiments.

ANSWER: Stanley Milgram

- In the obedience experiments, people were most likely to follow orders in four situations. What were those situations?

ANSWER: The Milgram studies showed that people were most likely to follow orders when (a) the person giving the orders was nearby and was a legitimate authority figure, (b) the authority figure was supported by a respected institution, (c) the victim was not nearby, and (d) there were no models for defiance.

Group Influence

12-6 How does the presence of others influence our actions, via social facilitation, social loafing, or deindividuation?

Imagine yourself standing in a room, holding a fishing pole. Your task is to wind the reel as fast as you can. On some occasions you wind in the presence of another participant who is also winding as fast as possible. Will the other's presence affect your own performance?

In one of social psychology's first experiments, Norman Triplett (1898)

GANDHI As the life of Hindu nationalist and spiritual leader Mahatma Gandhi (right) powerfully testified, a consistent and persistent minority voice can sometimes sway the majority. His nonviolent appeals and fasts helped India win its independence from Britain in 1947.

found that adolescents would wind a fishing reel faster in the presence of someone doing the same thing. He and later social psychologists studied how the presence of others affects our behavior. Group influences operate in such simple groups—one person in the presence of another—and in more complex groups.

Social Facilitation

Triplett's finding—that our responses on an individual task are stronger in

SOCIAL FACILITATION Skilled athletes often find they are "on" before an audience. What they do well, they do even better when people are watching.

the presence of others—is called **social facilitation.** Later studies revealed that the presence of others sometimes helps and sometimes hurts performance (Guerin, 1986; Zajonc, 1965). Why? Because when others observe us, we become aroused, and this arousal amplifies our other reactions. It strengthens our most likely response—the correct one on an easy task, an incorrect one on a difficult task. Thus, when others observe us, we perform well-learned tasks more quickly and accurately. But on new and difficult tasks, we perform less quickly and accurately.

This effect helps explain the home-team advantage. Studies of more than 80,000 college and professional athletic events in Canada, the United States, and England show that the home team advantage is real (TABLE 12.1). An enthusiastic audience seems to energize the home sports team. In about 6 in 10 games (somewhat fewer for baseball and football, somewhat more for basketball and soccer), home teams win.

The point to remember: What you do well, you are likely to do even better in front of an audience, especially a friendly audience. What you normally find difficult may seem all but impossible when you are being watched.

Social facilitation also helps explain a funny effect of crowding. Comedians and actors know that a "good house" is a full one. What they may not know is that crowding triggers arousal, which, as you have seen, strengthens other reactions. Comedy routines that are mildly amusing to people in an uncrowded room seem funnier in a densely packed room (Aiello et al., 1983; Freedman & Perlick, 1979). And when you seat participants close to one another, they like a friendly person even more, an unfriendly person even less (Schiffenbauer & Schiavo, 1976; Storms & Thomas, 1977). You can use this finding to increase the chances of lively interaction at your next gathering. Choose a room or set up seating that will just barely hold all your guests.

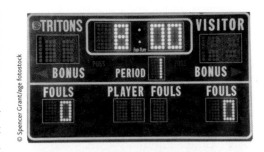
© Spencer Grant/age fotostock

TABLE 12.1	Home Advantage in Major Team Sports	
Sport	Games Studied	Home Team Winning Percentage
Baseball	23,034	53.5%
Football	2,592	57.3
Ice hockey	4,322	61.1
Basketball	13,596	64.4
Soccer	37,202	69.0

Source: From Courneya & Carron (1992).

Social Loafing

Does the presence of others have the same arousal effect when we perform a task as a group? In a team tug-of-war, do we exert more than, less than, or the same amount of effort as in a one-on-one tug-of-war? If you said, "less than," you're right. In one experiment, students who believed three others were also pulling behind them exerted only 82 percent as much effort as when they knew they were pulling alone (Ingham et al.,

WORKING HARD, OR HARDLY WORKING? In group projects, such as this Earth Day beach cleanup,, social loafing often occurs, as individuals free ride on the efforts of others.
Lawrence Migdale/Photo Researchers, Inc.

1974). And consider what happened when blindfolded people seated in a group clapped or shouted as loud as they could while hearing (through headphones) other people clapping or shouting (Latané, 1981). In one round of noise-making, the participants believed the researchers could identify their individual sounds. In another round, they believed their clapping and shouting was blended with other people's. When they thought they were part of a group effort, the participants produced about one-third less noise than when clapping "alone."

This lessened effort is called **social loafing** (Jackson & Williams, 1988; Latané, 1981). Experiments in the United States, India, Thailand, Japan, China, and Taiwan have recorded social loafing on various tasks. It was especially common among men in individualist cultures (Karau & Williams, 1993). What causes social loafing? Three things:

- People acting as part of a group feel less accountable, so they worry less about what others think of them.
- Group members may not believe their individual contributions make a difference (Harkins & Szymanski, 1989; Kerr & Bruun, 1983).
- Loafing is its own reward. When group members share equally in the benefits regardless of how much they contribute, some may slack off. (If you've worked on group assignments, you're probably already aware of this.) People who are not highly motivated, who don't identify strongly with the group, may *free ride* on others' efforts.

Deindividuation

We've seen that the presence of others can arouse people or it can make them

social facilitation improved performance on simple or well-learned tasks in the presence of others.

social loafing the tendency for people in a group to exert less effort when pooling their efforts toward attaining a common goal than when individually accountable.

feel less responsible. But sometimes the presence of others does both, triggering behavior that can range from a food fight to vandalism or rioting. This process of losing self-awareness and self-restraint is called **deindividuation**. It often occurs when group participation makes people feel aroused and anonymous. In one experiment, some female students dressed in Ku Klux Klan–style hoods that concealed their identity. Others in a control group did not wear the hoods. Those wearing hoods delivered twice as much electric shock to a victim (Zimbardo, 1970). (As in all such experiments, the "victim" did not actually receive the shocks.)

Deindividuation thrives, for better or for worse, in many different settings. The anonymity of Internet discussion boards and blog comment sections can unleash mocking or cruel words. Tribal warriors wearing face paints or masks have been more likely than those with exposed faces to kill, torture, or mutilate captured enemies (Watson, 1973). Internet trolls and bullies, who would never say "You're a fraud" to someone's face, will hide behind their online anonymity. When we shed self-awareness and self-restraint—whether in a mob, at a rock concert, at a ballgame, or at worship—we become

more responsive to the group experience—bad or good.

Group Polarization

12-7 How can group interaction enable group polarization and groupthink?
· ·

Over time, differences between groups of college students tend to grow. If the first-year students at College X tend to be more artistic, and those at College Y tend to be more business-savvy, those differences will probably be even greater by the time they graduate.

In each case, the beliefs and attitudes students bring to a group grow stronger as they discuss their views with others who share them. This process, called **group polarization**, can have positive results, as when low-prejudice students become even more accepting while discussing racial issues. It can also have negative results (**FIGURE 12.4**), as when high-prejudice students discuss racial issues and become more prejudiced (Myers & Bishop, 1970).

Researchers captured group polarization in a 2005 "Deliberation Day" exper-

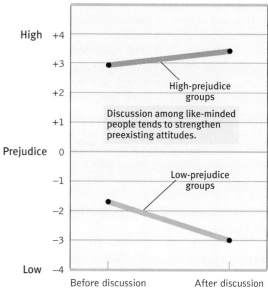

FIGURE 12.4 Group polarization If a group is like-minded, discussion strengthens existing opinions. Talking about racial issues increased prejudice in a high-prejudice group of high school students and decreased it in a low-prejudice group (Myers & Bishop, 1970).

iment (Schkade et al., 2006). They chose a random sample of people from the voter rolls of liberal Boulder, Colorado. They then divided the sample into five-person groups to discuss global climate change, affirmative action, and same-sex civil unions. In Colorado Springs, the researchers followed the same procedure with its more conservative voters. After the discussions, those in Boulder had moved further left, and those in Colorado Springs further right.

The polarizing effect of interaction among like-minded people applies also to suicide terrorists. The terrorist mentality does not erupt suddenly on a whim (McCauley, 2002; McCauley & Segal, 1987; Merari, 2002). It usually begins slowly, among people who get together because of a grievance. As group members interact in isolation (sometimes with other "brothers" and "sisters" in camps), their views grow more and more extreme. Increasingly, they divide the world into "us" against "them" (Moghaddam, 2005; Qirko, 2004).

DEINDIVIDUATION During England's 2011 riots and looting, rioters were disinhibited by social arousal and by the anonymity provided by darkness and their hoods and masks. Later, some of those arrested expressed bewilderment over their own behavior.

The Internet as Social Amplifier

I cut my eyeteeth in social psychology with experiments on *group polarization*—the tendency for face-to-face discussion to amplify group members' existing opinions. Never then did I imagine the potential dangers, or the creative possibilities, of polarization in *virtual* groups.

Electronic communication and social networking have created virtual town halls where people can isolate themselves from those with different opinions. As the Internet connects the like-minded and pools their ideas, climate-change skeptics, UFO abductees, and conspiracy theorists find support for their shared ideas and suspicions. White supremacists may become more racist. Cyberbullies may become more abusive. And militia members may become violent. In the echo chambers of virtual worlds, as in the real world, separation + conversation = polarization.

But the Internet-as-social-amplifier can also work for good. Social networking sites connect friends and family members sharing common interests or coping with challenges. Peacemakers, cancer survivors, and bereaved parents can find strength and support from kindred spirits. By amplifying shared concerns and ideas, Internet-enhanced communication can also foster social ventures. (I know this personally from social networking with others with hearing loss to transform American assistive listening technology.)

The point to remember: By linking and magnifying the inclinations of like-minded people, the Internet can be very, very bad, but also very, very good.

© Hero Images/Corbis

The Internet provides an easily accessible medium for group polarization. For more on this, see Thinking Critically About: The Internet as Social Amplifier.

Groupthink

So group interaction can influence our personal decisions. Can it also influence important national decisions? It can and it does. In one famous decision, it led to what is now known as the "Bay of Pigs fiasco." President John F. Kennedy and his advisers decided in 1961 to invade Cuba with 1400 CIA-trained Cuban exiles. When the invaders were easily captured and quickly linked to the U.S. government, the president wondered in hindsight, "How could I have been so stupid?"

Reading a historian's account of the ill-fated blunder, social psychologist Irving Janis (1982) found some clues in the invasion's decision-making procedures. The morale of the popular and recently elected president and his advisers was

soaring. Their confidence was almost unlimited. To preserve the good feeling, group members with differing views kept quiet, especially after President Kennedy voiced his enthusiasm for the scheme. Since no one spoke strongly against the idea, everyone assumed the support was unanimous. **Groupthink** was at work: The desire for harmony had replaced realistic judgment.

Groupthink later contributed to the escalation of the Vietnam war, the Chernobyl nuclear reactor accident in Russia, and the U.S. space shuttle *Challenger* explosion (Esser & Lindoerfer, 1989; Reason, 1987). Most recently, it surfaced in U.S. discussions of the Iraq war, which was launched on the false idea that Iraq had weapons of mass destruction (WMD). The bipartisan U.S. Senate Intelligence Committee (2004) reported that "personnel involved in the Iraq WMD issue demonstrated several aspects of groupthink: examining

few alternatives, selective gathering of information, pressure to conform within the group or withhold criticism, and collective rationalization." This mode of thinking led analysts to interpret some evidence as proof of a WMD program and to "ignore or minimize evidence that Iraq did not have [WMD] programs."

In the Iraq war discussions, groupthink was fed by overconfidence, conformity, self-justification, and group polarization. How can we prevent groupthink? Knowing that two heads are often

deindividuation the loss of self-awareness and self-restraint occurring in group situations that foster arousal and anonymity.

group polarization strengthening of a group's preexisting attitudes through discussions within the group.

groupthink the mode of thinking that occurs when the desire for harmony in a decision-making group overrides a realistic appraisal of alternatives.

better than one, leaders can welcome open debate, invite experts' critiques of developing plans, and assign people to identify possible problems.

The point to remember: None of us is as smart as all of us, especially when we welcome open debate. ∎

Social Relations

◎ We have sampled how we *think* *about* and *influence* one another. Now we come to social psychology's third focus—how we *relate* to one another. What causes us to harm or to help or to fall in love? How can we transform the closed fists of aggression into the open arms of compassion? We will ponder the bad and the good: from prejudice and aggression to attraction, altruism, and peacemaking.

Prejudice

12-8 What are the three parts of prejudice, and how has prejudice changed over time?

Prejudice means "prejudgment." It is an unfair negative attitude toward some group. The target of the prejudice is often a different cultural, ethnic, or gender group.

Prejudice is a three-part mixture of

• *beliefs* (called **stereotypes**).

• *emotions* (for example, hostility, envy, or fear).

• *predispositions* to action (to discriminate).

Some stereotypes may be at least partly accurate. If you presume that young men tend to drive faster than elderly women, you may be right. But to *believe* that obese people are gluttonous, and to *feel* dislike for an obese person, and to *pass* over all the obese people on a dating site is to be *prejudiced*. Prejudice is a negative *attitude*. **Discrimination** is a negative *behavior*.

Our ideas influence what we notice and how we interpret events. In one 1970s study, most White participants who saw a White man shoving a Black man said they were "horsing around." When they saw a Black man shoving a White man, they interpreted the same act as "violent" (Duncan, 1976). The ideas we bring to a situation can color our perceptions.

> "Unhappily the world has yet to learn how to live with diversity."
> Pope John Paul II, Address to the United Nations, 1995

How Prejudiced Are People?

To assess prejudice, we can observe what people say and what they do. What Americans say about gender and race has changed dramatically in the last 70 years. In 1937, one-third of Americans told Gallup pollsters they would vote for a qualified woman whom their party nominated for president. That number soared to 89 percent by 2007 (Gallup Brain, 2008; Jones & Moore, 2003). Nearly everyone now agrees that men and women should receive the same pay for doing the same job, and that children of all races should attend the same schools.

Support for all forms of racial contact, including interracial dating (FIGURE 12.5), has also dramatically increased. Among 18- to 29-year-old Americans, 9 in 10 now say they would be fine with a family member marrying someone of a different race (Pew, 2010).

Yet as *open* prejudice wanes, *subtle* prejudice lingers. As shown in FIGURE 12.5, Americans' approval of interracial marriage has soared over the past half-century (Gallup surveys reported by Carroll, 2007). Yet many people admit that in socially intimate settings (dating, dancing, marrying) they would feel uncomfortable with someone of another race. Many Americans also say they would feel upset with someone making racist slurs. Actually, when hearing racist comments, many respond indifferently (Kawakami et al., 2009). Recent experiments illustrate that prejudice can be not only subtle but also automatic and unconscious (see Close-Up: Automatic Prejudice on the next page).

Sometimes it is not so subtle. When experimenters have sent thousands of resumes in response to employment ads, "Eric" has been more likely than "Hassan" to get a reply. "Emily" has received more replies than "Lakisha." And those whose past activities included "Treasurer, Progressive and Socialist Alliance" received more replies than those who had been "Treasurer, Gay and Lesbian Alliance" (Agerström et al., 2012; Bertrand & Mullainathan, 2003; Drydakis, 2009).

In most places in the world, gays and lesbians cannot comfortably acknowledge who they are and whom they love (Katz-Wise & Hyde, 2012; United Nations, 2011). Gender prejudice and discrimination persist, too. Despite gender equality in intelligence scores, people have tended

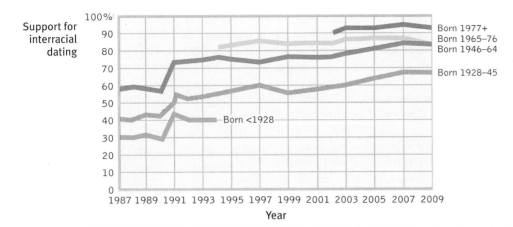

FIGURE 12.5 Prejudice over time Americans' approval of interracial dating has soared over the past quarter-century. (Pew, 2010)

to perceive their fathers as more intelligent than their mothers (Furnham & Wu, 2008). In Saudi Arabia, women are still not allowed to drive. In Western countries, we still pay more to those (usually men) who care for our streets than to those (usually women) who care for our children. Worldwide, women have been more likely to live in poverty (Lipps, 1999). And among adults who cannot read, two-thirds are women (CIA, 2010).

Unwanted female infants are no longer left on a hillside to die of exposure, as was the practice in ancient Greece. Yet the normal male-to-female newborn ratio (105 to 100) hardly explains the world's estimated 163 million (say that number slowly) "missing women" (Hvistendahl, 2011). In many places, sons are valued more than daughters. If men could choose their children's gender, "we'd get a few decades of incredible

football," comedian Aaron Karo (2012) wryly suggested, but the human race would die out.

Social Roots of Prejudice

12-9 What factors contribute to the social roots of prejudice, and how does scapegoating illustrate the emotional roots of prejudice?

Why does prejudice arise? Social inequalities and social divisions are partly responsible.

SOCIAL INEQUALITIES Some people have money, power, and prestige. Others do not. In this situation, the "haves" usually develop attitudes that justify things

---

prejudice an unjustifiable and usually negative attitude toward a group and its members. Prejudice generally involves stereotyped beliefs, negative feelings, and a predisposition to discriminatory action.

stereotype a generalized (sometimes accurate but often overgeneralized) belief about a group of people.

discrimination unjustifiable negative behavior toward a group and its members.

CLOSE-UP

Automatic Prejudice

Again and again throughout this book, we have seen that the human mind processes thoughts, memories, and attitudes on two different tracks. Sometimes that processing is *explicit*—on the radar screen of our awareness. More often, it is *implicit*—below the radar, out of sight. Modern studies indicate that prejudice is often implicit, an automatic attitude that is more of an unthinking knee-jerk response than a decision. Consider these findings.

Implicit racial associations Even people who deny harboring racial prejudice may carry negative associations (Fisher & Borgida, 2012; Greenwald et al., 1998). For example, 9 in 10 White respondents took longer to identify pleasant words (such as *peace* and *paradise*) as "good" when the words were paired with Black-sounding names (such as *Latisha* and *Darnell*) rather than White-sounding names (such as *Katie* and *Ian*). Such tests are useful for studying automatic prejudice. But critics caution against using them to assess or label individuals as prejudiced (Blanton et al., 2006, 2007, 2009).

Race-influenced perceptions Our expectations influence our perceptions. Consider the shooting of an unarmed man in the doorway of his Bronx apartment building several years ago. The officers thought he had pulled a gun from his pocket. In fact, he had pulled

out his wallet. Curious about this tragic killing of an innocent man, several research teams reenacted the situation (Correll et al., 2002, 2007; Greenwald et al., 2003; Sadler et al., 2012). They asked viewers to press buttons quickly to "shoot" or not shoot men who suddenly appeared on screen. Some of the on-screen men held a gun. Others held a harmless object, such as a flashlight or bottle. People (both Blacks and Whites, in one study) more often shot Black men holding the harmless object.

Reflexive bodily responses Even people who consciously express little prejudice may give off telltale signals as their body responds selectively to another person's race. Neuroscientists can detect these signals when people look at images of White and Black faces. The viewers' implicit prejudice shows up in different responses in their facial muscles and in their amygdala, an emotion-processing center (Cunningham et al., 2004; Eberhardt, 2005; Vanman et al., 2004).

Are you sometimes aware that you have feelings you would rather not have about other people? If so, remember this: It is what we do with our feelings that matters. By monitoring our feelings and actions, and by replacing old habits with new ones based on new friendships, we can free ourselves of prejudice.

as they are. The **just-world phenomenon** assumes that good is rewarded and evil is punished. From this it is but a short leap to assume that those who succeed must be good and those who suffer must be bad. Such reasoning enables the rich to see both their own wealth and the misfortune of the poor as justly deserved.

Are women naturally unassertive but sensitive? Such stereotypes just happen to "justify" holding women responsible for the caretaking tasks they have traditionally performed (Hoffman & Hurst, 1990). In an extreme case, slave "owners" developed attitudes that they then used to "justify" slavery. They stereotyped the people they enslaved as being innately lazy, ignorant, and irresponsible. Stereotypes rationalize inequalities.

Victims of discrimination may react with either self-blame or anger (Allport, 1954). Either reaction can feed prejudice through the classic blame-the-victim dynamic. Do the circumstances of poverty breed a higher crime rate? If so, that higher crime rate can be used to justify discrimination against those who live in poverty.

US AND THEM: INGROUP AND OUTGROUP We have inherited our Stone Age ancestors' need to belong—to live and love in groups. We cheer for our groups, kill for them, die for them. Indeed, we define who we are partly in terms of our groups. Through our *social identities* we associate ourselves with certain groups and contrast ourselves with others (Hogg, 1996; Turner, 1987). When Marc identifies himself as a man, an American, a political Independent, a Hudson Community

College student, a Catholic, and a part-time letter carrier, he knows who he is, and so do we.

Evolution prepared us, when meeting strangers, to make instant judgments: friend or foe? Those from our group, those who look like us, and also those who *sound* like us—with accents like our own—we instantly tend to like, from childhood onward (Gluszek & Dovidio, 2010; Kinzler et al., 2009). Mentally drawing a circle defines "us," the **ingroup.** But the social definition of who we are also states who we are not. People outside that circle are "them," the **outgroup.** An **ingroup bias**—a favoring of our own group— soon follows. Even forming us-them groups by tossing a coin creates this bias. In experiments, people have favored their own new group when dividing any rewards (Tajfel, 1982; Wilder, 1981).

Ingroup bias explains why active supporters of political parties may see what they expect to see (Cooper, 2010; Douthat, 2010). In the United States in the late 1980s, most Democrats believed inflation had risen under Republican president Ronald Reagan. (They were wrong: It had dropped.) In 2010, most Republicans believed that taxes had increased under Democrat president Barack Obama. (They were wrong: For most, they had decreased.)

> "All good people agree,
> And all good people say
> All nice people, like Us,
> are We
> And everyone else is They."
>
> Rudyard Kipling,
> "We and They," 1926

Emotional Roots of Prejudice

Prejudice springs not only from the divisions of society but also from the passions of the heart. **Scapegoat theory** proposes that when things go wrong, finding someone to blame can provide an outlet for anger. Following the 9/11 terrorist attacks, negative stereotypes blossomed. Some outraged people lashed out at innocent Arab-Americans. Others called for eliminating Saddam Hussein, the Iraqi leader whom Americans had been grudgingly tolerating. "Fear and anger create aggression, and aggression against citizens of different ethnicity or race creates racism and, in turn, new forms of terrorism," noted Philip Zimbardo (2001).

Evidence for the scapegoat theory of prejudice comes from two sources:

- Prejudice levels tend to be high among economically frustrated people.

- In experiments, a temporary frustration increases prejudice.

THE INGROUP Scotland's famed "Tartan Army" soccer fans, shown here during a match against archrival England, share a social identity that defines "us" (the Scottish ingroup) and "them" (the English outgroup).

| 100% Chinese | 80% Chinese 20% Caucasian | 60% Chinese 40% Caucasian | 40% Chinese 60% Caucasian | 20% Chinese 80% Caucasian | 100% Caucasian |

Dr. Jamin Halberstadt

FIGURE 12.6 **Categorizing mixed-race people** When New Zealanders quickly classified 104 photos by race, those of European descent more often than those of Chinese descent classified the ambiguous middle two as Chinese (Halberstadt et al., 2011).

Students made to feel temporarily insecure have often restored their self-esteem by speaking badly of a rival school or another person (Cialdini & Richardson, 1980; Crocker et al., 1987). Those made to feel loved and supported have become more open to and accepting of others who differ (Mikulincer & Shaver, 2001).

Negative emotions nourish prejudice. When facing death, fearing threats, or experiencing frustration, we cling more tightly to our ingroup and our friends. The terror of death heightens patriotism. It also produces anger and aggression toward "them"—those who threaten our world (Pyszczynski et al., 2002, 2008).

Cognitive Roots of Prejudice

12-10 What are the cognitive roots of prejudice?

Prejudice springs from a culture's divisions, the heart's passions, and also from the mind's natural workings. Stereotyped beliefs are a by-product of how we cognitively simplify the world.

FORMING CATEGORIES One way we simplify our world is to sort things into categories. A chemist sorts molecules into categories of "organic" and "inorganic." Therapists categorize psychological disorders. All of us categorize people by race, with mixed-race people often assigned to their minority identity. Despite his mixed-race background and being raised by a White mother and White grandparents, President Barack Obama

has been perceived by White Americans as Black. Researchers believe this happens because, after learning the features of a familiar racial group, the observer's selective attention is drawn to the distinctive features of the less-familiar minority. In one study, New Zealanders viewed images of blended Chinese-Caucasian faces (Halberstadt et al., 2011). Some participants were of European descent; others were of Chinese descent. Those of European descent more readily classified ambiguous faces as Chinese (see **FIGURE 12.6**).

When we categorize people into groups, we often overestimate their similarities. "They"—the members of that other social or ethnic group—seem to look alike (Rhodes & Anastasi, 2012; Young et al., 2012). In personality and attitudes, too, they seem more alike than they really are, while "we" differ from

one another (Bothwell et al., 1989). This greater recognition for own-race faces is called the **other-race effect** (also called the *cross-race effect* or *own-race bias*). It emerges during infancy, between 3 and 9 months of age (Kelly et al., 2007).

REMEMBERING VIVID CASES Cognitive psychologists tell us that we often judge the likelihood of events by recalling vivid cases that readily come to mind. In a classic experiment, researchers showed two groups of student volunteers lists containing information about 50 men (Rothbart et al., 1978). The first group's list included 10 men arrested for *nonviolent* crimes, such as forgery. The second group's list included 10 men arrested for *violent* crimes, such as assault. Later, both groups were asked how many men on their list had committed *any* sort of crime. The second

YOU'RE BOB? SORRY, YOU RESEARCHERS ALL LOOK ALIKE TO ME.

© Dave Coverly

just-world phenomenon the tendency to believe that the world is just and people therefore get what they deserve and deserve what they get.

ingroup "us"—people with whom we share a common identity.

outgroup "them"—those perceived as different or apart from our group.

ingroup bias the tendency to favor our own group.

scapegoat theory the theory that prejudice offers an outlet for anger by providing someone to blame.

other-race effect the tendency to recall faces of one's own race more accurately than faces of other races.

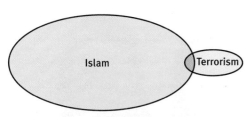

FIGURE 12.7 Vivid cases feed stereotypes The 9/11 Muslim terrorists created, in many minds, an exaggerated stereotype of Muslims as terrorism prone. Actually, reported a U.S. National Research Council panel on terrorism, when offering this inexact illustration, most terrorists are not Muslim. "The vast majority of Islamic people have no connection with and do not sympathize with terrorism" (Smelser & Mitchell, 2002).

group overestimated the number. Vivid (violent) cases are readily available to our memory and feed our stereotypes (**FIGURE 12.7**).

BELIEVING THE WORLD IS JUST As noted earlier, people often justify their prejudices by blaming the victims. If the world is just, "people must get what they deserve." As one German civilian is said to have remarked when visiting the Bergen-Belsen concentration camp shortly after World War II, "What terrible criminals these prisoners must have been to receive such treatment."

People have a basic tendency to justify their culture's social systems (Jost et al., 2009; Kay et al., 2009). We're inclined to see the way things are as the way they ought to be. This natural conservatism makes it difficult to legislate major social changes, such as civil rights laws or Social Security or health care reform. But once such policies are in place, our "system justification" tends to preserve them. ▮

RETRIEVE + REMEMBER

• When a prejudiced attitude causes us to blame an innocent person for our problems, we have used that person as a _____.

ANSWER: scapegoat

Aggression

12-11 What biological factors predispose us to be aggressive?

The most destructive force in our social relations is aggression. In psychology, **aggression** is any verbal or physical behavior intended to hurt or destroy, whether it is passing along a vicious rumor or engaging in a physical attack.

Aggressive behavior emerges when biology interacts with experience. For a gun to fire, the trigger must be pulled. With some people, as with hair-trigger guns, it doesn't take much to trip an explosion. Let's look first at some biological factors that influence our thresholds for aggressive behavior. Then we'll turn to the psychological and social-cultural factors that pull the trigger.

The Biology of Aggression

Is aggression an unlearned instinct? The wide variation from culture to culture, era to era, and person to person argues against that idea. But biology does *influence* aggression at three levels—genetic, biochemical, and neural.

GENETIC INFLUENCES Genes influence aggression. We know this because animals have been bred for aggressiveness—sometimes for sport, sometimes for research. The effect of genes also appears in human twin studies (Miles & Carey, 1997; Rowe et al., 1999). If one identical twin admits to "having a violent temper," the other twin will often independently admit the same. Fraternal twins are much less likely to respond similarly. Researchers continue to search for genetic markers, or predictors, in those who commit the most violence. One is already well known and is carried by half the human race: the Y chromosome.

BIOCHEMICAL INFLUENCES Our genes engineer our individual nervous systems, which operate electrochemically. The hormone testosterone, for example, circulates in the bloodstream and influences the neural systems that control aggression. A raging bull becomes a gen-

tle Ferdinand when castration reduces its testosterone level. The same is true of mice. When injected with testosterone, gentle, castrated mice once again become aggressive.

In humans, high testosterone is associated with irritability, assertiveness, impulsiveness, and low tolerance for frustration. These qualities make people somewhat more prone to aggressive responses when provoked or when competing for status (Dabbs et al., 2001b; McAndrew, 2009; Montoya et al., 2012). Among both teenage boys and adult men, high testosterone levels have been linked with delinquency, hard drug use, and *aggressive-bullying* responses to frustration (Berman et al., 1993; Dabbs & Morris, 1990; Olweus et al., 1988). Drugs that sharply reduce testosterone levels subdue men's aggressive tendencies. As men age, their testosterone levels—and their aggressiveness—diminish. Hormonally charged, aggressive 17-year-olds mature into hormonally quieter and gentler 70-year-olds.

Another drug that sometimes circulates in the bloodstream—alcohol—also unleashes aggressive responses to frustration. Aggression-prone people are more likely to drink, and when intoxicated they are more likely to become violent (White et al., 1993). National crime

A LEAN, MEAN FIGHTING MACHINE— THE TESTOSTERONE-LADEN FEMALE HYENA Unusual prenatal development pumps testosterone into female hyena fetuses. The result is revved-up young females that seem born to fight.

Karl Ammann/Getty Images

data indicate that 73 percent of Russian homicides and 57 percent of U.S. homicides were influenced by alcohol (Landberg & Norström, 2011). Alcohol's effects are both biological and psychological. Just *thinking* you've been drinking alcohol can increase aggression (Bègue et al., 2009). But so, too, does unknowingly drinking an alcohol-laced beverage.

NEURAL INFLUENCES

There is no one spot in the brain that controls aggression. Aggression is a complex behavior, and it occurs in particular contexts. But animal and human brains have neural systems that, given provocation, will either inhibit or facilitate aggression (Denson, 2011; Moyer, 1983; Wilkowski et al., 2011). Consider:

- Researchers implanted a radio-controlled electrode in the brain of the domineering leader of a caged

In the last 40 years in the United States, well over 1 million people—more than all deaths in all wars in American history—have been killed by firearms in nonwar settings. Compared with people of the same sex, race, age, and neighborhood, those who keep a gun in the home (ironically, often for protection) are almost three times more likely to be murdered in the home. Nearly always, the shooter is a family member or close acquaintance. For every self-defense use of a gun in the home, there have been 4 unintentional shootings, 7 criminal assaults or homicides, and 11 attempted or completed suicides.
(Kellermann et al., 1993, 1997, 1998; see also Branas et al., 2009)

monkey colony. The electrode was in an area that, when stimulated, inhibits aggression. When researchers placed the control button for the electrode in the colony's cage, one small monkey learned to push it every time the boss became threatening.

- A neurosurgeon implanted an electrode in the brain of a mild-mannered woman to diagnose a disorder. The electrode was in her amygdala, within her limbic system. Because the brain has no sensory receptors, she did not feel the stimulation. But at the flick of a switch, she snarled, "Take my blood pressure. Take it now," then stood up and began to strike the doctor.

- Studies of violent criminals have revealed diminished activity in the frontal lobes, which help control impulses. If the frontal lobes are damaged, inactive, disconnected, or not yet fully mature, aggression may be more likely (Amen et al., 1996; Davidson et al., 2000; Raine, 1999, 2005).

Psychological and Social-Cultural Influences on Aggression

12-12 What psychological and social-cultural factors may trigger aggressive behavior?

Biological factors create the hair trigger for aggression. But what psychological and social-cultural factors pull that trigger?

"It's a guy thing."

AVERSIVE EVENTS Suffering sometimes builds character. In laboratory experiments, however, those made miserable have often made others miserable (Berkowitz, 1983, 1989). This reaction is called the **frustration-aggression principle.** Frustration creates anger, which can spark aggression. One Major League Baseball analysis of 27,667 hit-by-pitch incidents between 1960 and 2004 revealed this link (Timmerman, 2007). Pitchers were most likely to hit batters when

- they had been frustrated by the previous batter hitting a home run.

- the current batter hit a home run the last time at bat.

- a teammate had been hit by a pitch in the previous half-inning.

Other aversive stimuli—hot temperatures, physical pain, personal insults, foul odors, cigarette smoke, crowding, and a host of others—can also trigger anger. When people get overheated, they think, feel, and act more aggressively. Simply thinking about words related to hot temperatures is enough to increase hostile thoughts (DeWall & Bushman, 2009). In baseball games, the number of hit batters rises with the temperature (Reifman

aggression any act intended to harm someone physically or emotionally.

frustration-aggression principle the principle that frustration—the blocking of an attempt to achieve some goal—creates anger, which can generate aggression.

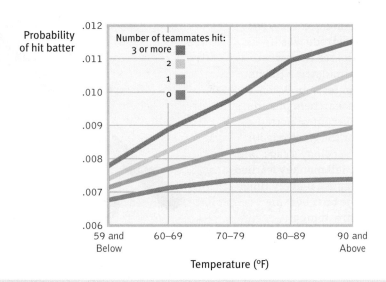

Probability of hit batter

Number of teammates hit:
3 or more
2
1
0

Temperature (°F)

59 and Below   60–69   70–79   80–89   90 and Above

FIGURE 12.8 **Temperature and retaliation** Richard Larrick and his colleagues (2011) looked for occurrences of batters hit by pitchers during 4,566,468 pitcher-batter matchups across 57,293 Major League Baseball games since 1952. The probability of a hit batter increased if one or more of the pitcher's teammates had been hit, and also with temperature.

AGGRESSION-REPLACEMENT PROGRAM Part of the rehabilitation of these juvenile offenders at the Missouri Division of Youth Services' Rosa Parks Center involves learning anger management and peaceful ways to resolve disputes. Here they "circle up" to resolve a problem peacefully.

et al., 1991; see **FIGURE 12.8**). And in the wider world, violent crime and spousal abuse rates have been higher during hotter years, seasons, months, and days (Anderson et al., 1997). One projection, based on the available data, estimates that global warming of 4 degrees Fahrenheit (about 2 degrees Celsius) could induce tens of thousands of additional assaults and murders (Anderson et al., 2000, 2011). And that's before the added violence inducement from climate-change-related drought, poverty, food insecurity, and migration.

REINFORCEMENT, MODELING, AND SELF-CONTROL Aggression may naturally follow aversive events, but learning can alter natural reactions. As Chapter 6 points out, we learn when our behavior is reinforced, and we learn by watching others. Children whose aggression successfully intimidates other children may become bullies. Animals that have successfully fought to get food or mates become increasingly ferocious. To foster a kinder, gentler world, we had best model and reward sensitivity and cooperation from an early age, perhaps by training parents to discipline without modeling violence.

Parents of delinquent youth frequently cave in to (and thus reward) their children's tears and temper tantrums. Then, frustrated, they discipline with beatings (Patterson et al., 1982, 1992). Parent-training programs often advise parents to avoid modeling violence by screaming and hitting. Instead, parents should reinforce desirable behaviors and frame statements positively. ("When you finish loading the dishwasher, you can go play," rather than "If you don't load the dishwasher, there'll be no playing.")

Self-control curbs aggressive and criminal behavior. Alas, physical and mental challenges, such as exhaustion and food and sleep deprivation, often deplete our self-control (Vohs et al., 2011). Picture yourself after a long, challenging day at school or work, or after missing a meal or when sleep deprived. Might you, without realizing what's happening, begin to snap at your friends or partner?

Poor self-control is "one of the strongest known correlates of crime" (Pratt & Cullen, 2000, p. 952). To foster self-

"Why do we kill people who kill people to show that killing people is wrong?"

National Coalition to Abolish the Death Penalty, 1992

control, one *aggression-replacement program* worked with juvenile offenders and gang members and their parents. It taught both generations new ways to control anger, and more thoughtful approaches to moral reasoning (Goldstein et al., 1998). The result? The youths' re-arrest rates dropped.

Different cultures model, reinforce, and evoke different tendencies toward violence. For example, U.S. men are less approving of male-to-female violence between romantic partners than are men from India, Japan, and Kuwait (Nayak et al., 2003). Crime rates have also been higher and average happiness has been lower in times and places marked by a great income gap between rich and poor (Messias et al., 2011; Oishi et al., 2011; Wilkinson & Pickett, 2009). In the United States, high rates of violence and youth imprisonment have been found in cultures and families with minimal or no father care (Harper & McLanahan, 2004; Triandis, 1994).

MEDIA MODELS FOR VIOLENCE Parents are not the only aggression models. In the United States and elsewhere, TV shows, films, and video games offer supersized portions of violence. Repeatedly viewing on-screen violence tends to make us less sensitive to cruelty (Montag et al., 2012). It also primes us to respond aggressively when provoked. And it teaches us **social scripts**—culturally provided mental files for how to act. When we find ourselves in new situations, uncertain how to behave, we rely on social scripts. After watching so many action films, adolescent boys may acquire a script that plays in their head when they face real-life conflicts. Challenged, they may "act like a man" by intimidating or eliminating the threat. More than 100 studies together confirm that people sometimes imitate what they've viewed. Watching risk-glorifying behaviors (dangerous driving, extreme sports, unprotected sex) increases viewers' real-life risk-taking (Fischer et al., 2011).

Music lyrics also write social scripts. In experiments, German university men who listened to woman-hating song lyrics administered the most hot chili sauce to a woman. They also recalled more negative feelings and beliefs about women. Man-hating song lyrics had a similar effect on the aggressive behavior of women listeners (Fischer & Greitemeyer, 2006).

Sexual scripts depicted in X-rated films are often toxic. People heavily exposed to televised crime perceive the world as more dangerous. People heavily exposed to pornography see the world as more sexual. Repeatedly watching X-rated films, even nonviolent films, has many effects (Kingston et al., 2009). One's own partner seems less attractive (Chapter 4). Extramarital sex seems less troubling (Zillmann, 1989). Women's friendliness seems more sexual. Sexual aggression seems less serious (Harris, 1994).

In one experiment, undergraduates viewed six brief, sexually explicit films each week for six weeks (Zillmann & Bryant, 1984). A control group viewed films with no sexual content during the same six-week period. Three weeks later, both groups read a newspaper report about a man convicted of raping a hitchhiker and were asked to suggest an appropriate prison term. Sentences recommended by those viewing the sexually explicit films were only half as long as the sentences recommended by the control group.

Research on the effects of violent versus nonviolent erotic films indicates that it's not the sexual content of films that most directly affects men's aggression against women. It's the sexual *violence*, whether in R-rated slasher films or X-rated films. A statement by 21 social scientists noted, "Pornography that portrays sexual aggression as pleasurable for the victim increases the acceptance of the use of coercion in sexual relations" (Surgeon General, 1986). Contrary to much popular opinion, viewing such scenes does not provide an outlet for bottled-up impulses. Rather, "in laboratory studies measuring short-term effects, exposure to violent pornography increases punitive behavior toward women."

To a lesser extent, nonviolent pornography can also influence aggression. One set of studies exploring pornography's effects on aggression against relationship partners found that pornography consumption predicted both self-reported aggression and laboratory noise blasts to their partner (Lambert et al., 2011). Abstaining from customary pornography consumption decreased aggression. Abstaining from their favorite food did not.

DO VIOLENT VIDEO GAMES TEACH SOCIAL SCRIPTS FOR VIOLENCE?

Experiments in North America, Western Europe, Singapore, and Japan indicate that playing positive games produces positive effects (Gentile et al., 2009; Greitemeyer & Osswald, 2010). For example, playing *Lemmings*, where a goal is to help others, increases real-life helping. So, might a parallel effect occur after playing games that enact violence? Violent video games became an issue for public debate after teenagers in more than a dozen places seemed to mimic the carnage in the shooter games they had so often played (Anderson, 2004a).

In 2002, two Grand Rapids, Michigan, teens and a man in his early twenties spent part of a night drinking beer and playing *Grand Theft Auto III*. Using simulated cars, they ran down pedestrians, then beat them with fists, leaving a bloody body behind (Kolker, 2002). These same teens and man then went out for a real drive. Spotting a 38-year-old man on a bicycle, they ran him down with their car, got out, stomped and punched him, and returned home to play the game some more. (The victim, a father of three, died six days later.)

Such violent mimicry causes some to wonder: What will be the effect of actively role-playing aggression? Will young people become less sensitive to violence and more open to violent acts? Nearly 400 studies of 130,000 people offer an answer, report some researchers (Anderson et al., 2010). Video games can prime aggres-

COINCIDENCE OR CAUSE? In 2011, Norwegian Anders Behring Breivik bombed government buildings in Oslo, and then went to a youth camp, where he shot and killed 69 people, mostly teens. As a player of first-person shooter games, Breivik stirred debate when he commented that "I see *MW2 [Modern Warfare 2]* more as a part of my training-simulation than anything else." Did his violent game playing contribute to his violence, or was it a mere coincidental association? To explore such questions, psychologists experiment.

social script culturally modeled guide for how to act in various situations.

sive thoughts, decrease empathy, and increase aggression. University men who spend the most hours playing violent video games have also tended to be the most physically aggressive (Anderson & Dill, 2000). (For example, they more often acknowledged having hit or attacked someone else.) And people randomly assigned to play a game involving bloody murders with groaning victims (rather than to play nonviolent *Myst*) became more hostile. On a follow-up task, they also were more likely to blast intense noise at a fellow student.

Studies of young adolescents reveal that those who play a lot of violent video games see the world as more hostile (Gentile, 2009). Compared with nongaming kids, they get into more arguments and fights and get worse grades.

Ah, but is this merely because naturally hostile kids are drawn to such games? Apparently not. Comparisons of gamers and nongamers who scored low in hostility revealed a difference in the number of fights they reported. Almost 4 in 10 violent-game players had been in fights. Only 4 in 100 of the nongaming kids reported fights (Anderson, 2004a). Some researchers believe that, due partly to the more active participation and rewarded violence of game play, violent video games have even greater effects on aggressive behavior and cognition than do violent TV shows and movies (Anderson & Warburton, 2012).

Other researchers are unimpressed by such findings (Ferguson & Kilburn, 2010; Ferguson et al., 2011). They note that from 1996 to 2006, youth violence was declining while video game sales were increasing, and that other factors—depression, family violence, peer influence—better predict aggression. Moreover, some point out that avid game players are quick and sharp: They develop speedy reaction times and enhanced visual skills (Dye et al., 2009; Green et al., 2010). The focused fun of game playing can satisfy basic needs for a sense of competence, control, and social connection (Przbylski et al., 2010). In 2011, a U.S. Supreme Court

decision overturned a California state law that banned violent video game sales to children (modeled after the bans on sales of sexually explicit materials to children). The First Amendment's free speech guarantee protects even offensive games, said the court's majority, which was unpersuaded by the evidence of harm. So, the debate continues.

* * *

To sum up, research reveals biological, psychological, and social-cultural influences on aggressive behavior. Complex behaviors, including violence, have many causes, making any single explanation an oversimplification. Asking what causes violence is therefore like asking what causes cancer. Those who study the effects of asbestos exposure on cancer rates may remind us that asbestos is indeed a cancer cause, but it is only one among many. Like so much else, aggression is a biopsychosocial phenomenon.

A happy concluding note: Historical trends suggest that the world is increasingly nonviolent (Pinker, 2011). That people vary over time and place reminds us that environments differ. Yesterday's plundering Vikings have become today's peace-promoting Scandinavians. Like all behavior, aggression arises from the interaction of persons and situations. ■

> ### RETRIEVE + REMEMBER
>
> • What psychological, biological, and social-cultural influences interact to produce aggressive behaviors?
>
> ANSWER: Our biology (our genes, biochemistry, and neural systems—including testosterone and alcohol levels) influences our tendencies to be aggressive. Psychological factors (such as frustration, previous rewards for aggressive acts, and observation of others' aggression) can trigger any aggressive tendencies we may have. Social influences, such as exposure to violent media and cultural factors, can also affect our aggressive responses.

Attraction

Pause a moment and think about your relationships with two people—a close friend, and someone who has stirred in you feelings of romantic love. These spe-

cial sorts of attachments help us cope with all other relationships. What is the psychological chemistry that binds us together? Social psychology suggests some answers.

The Psychology of Attraction

12-13 Why do we befriend or fall in love with some people but not others?

We endlessly wonder how we can win others' affection and what makes our own affections flourish or fade. Does familiarity breed contempt or affection? Do birds of a feather flock together, or do opposites attract? Is beauty only skin deep, or does attractiveness matter greatly? To explore these questions, let's consider three ingredients of our liking for one another: proximity, physical attractiveness, and similarity.

PROXIMITY Before friendships become close, they must begin. Proximity—geographic nearness—is friendship's most powerful predictor. Being near another person gives us opportunities for aggression, but much more often it breeds liking. Study after study reveals that people are most inclined to like, and even to marry, those who are nearby. We are drawn to those who live in the same neighborhood, sit nearby in class, work in the same office, share the

FAMILIARITY BREEDS ACCEPTANCE When this rare white penguin was born in the Sydney, Australia, zoo, his tuxedoed peers shunned him. Zookeepers thought they would need to dye him black to gain acceptance. But after three weeks of contact, the other penguins came to accept him.

Rex USA/Brendan Beirne/Rex

same parking lot, eat in the same dining hall. Look around. Mating starts with meeting. (For a look at modern ways to connect people not in physical proximity, see Close-Up: Online Matchmaking and Speed Dating.)

Proximity breeds liking partly because of the **mere exposure effect.** Repeated exposure to novel stimuli increases our liking for them. This applies to nonsense syllables, musical selections, geometric figures, Chinese characters, human faces, and the letters of our own name (Moreland & Zajonc, 1982; Nuttin, 1987; Zajonc, 2001). People are even somewhat more likely to marry some-one whose first or last name resembles their own (Jones et al., 2004).

So, within certain limits, familiarity breeds fondness (Bornstein, 1989, 1999). Researchers demonstrated this by having four equally attractive women silently attend a 200-student class for zero, 5, 10, or 15 class sessions (Moreland & Beach, 1992). At the end of the course, students were shown slides of each woman and asked to rate her attractiveness. The most attractive? The ones they'd seen most often. These ratings would come as no surprise to the young Taiwanese man who wrote more than 700 letters to his girlfriend, urging her to marry him. She did marry—the mail carrier (Steinberg, 1993).

PHYSICAL ATTRACTIVENESS So proximity offers contact. What most affects our first impressions? The person's sincerity? Intelligence? Personality? The answer is physical appearance. This finding is unnerving for most of us who were taught that "beauty is only skin deep" and that "appearances can be deceiving."

> **mere exposure effect** the phenomenon that repeated exposure to novel stimuli increases liking of them.

CLOSE-UP

Online Matchmaking and Speed Dating

If you have not found a romantic partner in your immediate proximity, why not cast a wider net? Each year, an estimated 30 million people search for love on one of the 1500 online dating services (Ellin, 2009). Online matchmaking seems to work mostly by expanding the pool of potential mates (Finkel et al., 2012a,b).

How effective are Internet matchmaking services? Published research is sparse. But here's a surprising finding: Compared with relationships formed in person, Internet-formed friendships and romantic relationships are, on average, more likely to last beyond two years (Bargh et al., 2002, 2004; McKenna & Bargh, 1998, 2000; McKenna et al., 2002). In one study, people disclosed more, with less posturing, to those whom they met online. When chatting online with someone for 20 minutes, they felt more liking for that person than they did for someone they had met and talked with face to face. This was true even when (unknown to them) it was the same person! Internet friendships often feel as real and important to people as in-person relationships. Small wonder that one survey found a leading online matchmaker enabling more than 500 U.S. marriages a day (Harris Interactive, 2010). By one estimate, online dating now is responsible for about a fifth of U.S. marriages (Crosier et al., 2012).

Dating sites collect trait information, but that accounts for only a thin slice of what makes for successful long-term relationships. What matters more, say researchers, is what emerges only after two people get to know each other, such as how they communicate and resolve disagreements (Finkel et al., 2012a,b). Skeptics are calling for controlled studies. To establish that some matchmaking secret sauce does actually work, they say, experiments need to match people by either using the data sites' matchmaking formulas or not. And, of course, the participants should not know the basis of their match.

AND DO YOU, FUNNYGRL@BIZONE.NET, TAKE HARLEY99@COMCO.COM...

THEY MET ONLINE.

© Dave Coverly

Speed dating pushes the search for romance into high gear. In a process pioneered by a matchmaking Jewish rabbi, people meet a succession of would-be partners, either in person or via webcam (Bower, 2009). After a 3- to 8-minute conversation, people move on to the next person. (In an in-person meeting, one partner—usually the woman—remains seated and the other circulates.) Those who want to meet again can arrange for future contacts. For many participants, 4 minutes is enough time to form a feeling about a conversational partner and to register whether the partner likes them (Eastwick & Finkel, 2008a,b).

Researchers have quickly realized that speed dating offers a unique opportunity for studying influences on our first impressions of potential romantic partners. Among recent findings are these:

- *Men are more transparent.* Observers (male or female) watching videos of speed dating can read a man's level of romantic interest more accurately than a woman's (Place et al., 2009).

- *Given more options, people make more superficial choices.* They focus on more easily assessed characteristics, such as height and weight (Lenton & Francesconi, 2010, 2012). This was true even when researchers controlled for time spent with each partner.

- *Men wish for future contact with more of their speed dates; women tend to be more choosy.* This gender difference disappears if the conventional roles are reversed, so that men stay seated while women circulate (Finkel & Eastwick, 2009).

Ben Pruchnie/Getty Images

WHICH IS THE REAL MAGGIE SMITH? They both are, but the mere exposure effect may have influenced your choice. The left and right sides of the human face differ a bit, so the face we see in the mirror is not the same as the one others see. The person actor Maggie Smith sees in the mirror each morning is shown at right, and that's the photo she would probably prefer. We might feel more comfortable with the reverse image (left), the one we see (Mita et al., 1977).

In one early study, researchers randomly matched new students for a Welcome Week dance (Walster et al., 1966). Before the dance, the researchers gave each student a battery of personality and aptitude tests, and they rated each student's level of physical attractiveness. On the night of the blind date, the couples danced and talked for more than two hours and then took a brief break to rate their dates. What determined whether they liked each other? Only one thing seemed to matter: appearance. Both the men and the women liked good-looking dates best. Women are more likely than men to say that another's looks don't affect them (Lippa, 2007). But studies show that a man's looks do affect women's behavior (Feingold, 1990; Sprecher, 1989; Woll, 1986). Speed-dating experiments confirm that attractiveness influences first impressions for both sexes (Belot & Francesconi, 2006; Finkel & Eastwick, 2008).

Physical attractiveness also predicts how often people date and how popular they feel. We don't assume that attractive people are more compassionate,

but we do perceive them as healthier, happier, more sensitive, more successful, and more socially skilled (Eagly et al., 1991; Feingold, 1992; Hatfield & Sprecher, 1986). Attractive, well-dressed people have been more likely to make a favorable impression on potential employers, and they have tended to be more successful in their jobs (Cash & Janda, 1984; Langlois et al., 2000; Solomon, 1987). There is a premium for beauty in the workplace, and a penalty for plainness or obesity (Engemann & Owyang, 2005).

Judging from their gazing times, even babies seem to prefer attractive over unattractive faces (Langlois et al., 1987). So do some blind people. University of Birmingham professor John Hull (1990, p. 23) discovered this after going blind himself. A colleague's remarks about a woman's beauty would strangely affect his feelings. He found this "deplorable. What can it matter to me what sighted men think of women . . . yet I do care what sighted men think, and I do not seem able to throw off this prejudice."

For those of us who find the importance of looks unfair and short-sighted, two other findings may be reassuring. First, people's attractiveness has been found to be surprisingly unrelated to their self-esteem and happiness (Diener et al., 1995; Major et al., 1984). Unless we have just compared ourselves with superattractive people, few of us (thanks, perhaps, to the mere exposure effect) view ourselves as unattractive (Thornton & Moore, 1993). Second, strikingly attractive people are sometimes suspicious that praise

for their work may simply be a reaction to their looks. Less attractive people have been more likely to accept praise as sincere (Berscheid, 1981).

Beauty is in the eye of the culture. Hoping to look attractive, people across the globe have pierced and tattooed various body parts, lengthened their necks, bound their feet, and dyed or painted their skin and hair. Cultural ideals also change over time. In the United States, the soft, voluptuous Marilyn Monroe ideal of the 1950s has been replaced by today's lean yet busty ideal.

If we're not born attractive, we may try to buy beauty. Americans now spend more on beauty supplies than on education and social services combined. Still not satisfied, millions undergo plastic surgery, teeth capping and whitening, Botox skin smoothing, and laser hair removal (ASPS, 2010).

Do any aspects of attractiveness cross place and time? *Yes.* As we noted in Chapter 4, men in many cultures, from Australia to Zambia, judge women as more attractive if they have a youthful, fertile appearance, suggested by a low waist-to-hip ratio (Karremans et al., 2010; Perilloux et al., 2010; Platek & Singh, 2010). Women feel attracted to healthy-looking men, but especially—and the more so when ovulating—to those who seem mature, dominant, masculine, and wealthy (Gallup & Frederick, 2010; Gangestad et al., 2010). But faces matter, too.

When people separately rate opposite-sex faces and bodies, the face tends to be the better predictor of overall physical attractiveness (Currie & Little, 2009; Peters et al., 2007).

Our feelings also influence our attractiveness judgments. Imagine two people: One is honest, humorous, and polite. The other is rude, unfair, and abusive. Which one is more attractive? Most people perceive the person with the appealing traits as more attrac-

Percentage of Men and Women Who "Constantly Think About Their Looks"		
	Men	Women
Canada	18%	20%
United States	17	27
Mexico	40	45
Venezuela	47	65

From Roper Starch survey, reported by McCool (1999).

tive (Lewandowski et al., 2007). Or imagine being paired with an opposite-sex stranger who listened well to your self-disclosures (rather than seeming not tuned into your thoughts and feelings). If you are heterosexual, might you feel a twinge of sexual attraction toward that person? Student volunteers did, in several experiments (Birnbaum & Reis, 2012). Our feelings influence our perceptions.

In a Rodgers and Hammerstein musical, Prince Charming asks Cinderella, "Do I love you because you're beautiful, or are you beautiful because I love you?" Chances are it's both. As we see our loved ones again and again, we notice their physical imperfections less, and their attractiveness grows more obvious (Beaman & Klentz, 1983; Gross & Crofton, 1977). Shakespeare said it in *A Midsummer Night's Dream:* "Love looks not with the eyes, but with the mind." Come to love someone and watch beauty grow.

SIMILARITY So you've met someone, and your appearance has made a decent first impression. What now influences whether you will become friends? As you get to know each other, will the chemistry be better if you are opposites or if you are alike?

It makes a good story—extremely different types liking or loving each other: Frog and Toad in Arnold Lobel's books, Edward and Bella in the *Twilight* series. The stories delight us by expressing what we seldom experience, for in real life, opposites retract (Rosenbaum, 1986). Birds that flock together usually are of a feather. Compared with randomly paired people, friends and couples are far more likely to share attitudes, beliefs, and interests (and, for that matter, age, religion, race, education, intelligence, smoking behavior, and economic status). Journalist Walter Lippmann was right to suppose that love lasts "when the lovers love many things together, and not merely each other."

Proximity, attractiveness, and similarity are not the only forces that influence attraction. We also like those who like us. This is especially so when

WHAT DO WE MEAN BY "ATTRACTIVE"? The answer varies by culture and over time. Yet some adult physical features, such as a youthful form and face, seem attractive everywhere.

our self-image is low. When we believe someone likes us, we feel good and respond warmly. Our warm response in turn leads them to like us even more (Curtis & Miller, 1986). To be liked is powerfully rewarding.

Indeed, all the findings we have considered so far can be explained by a simple *reward theory of attraction.* We will like those whose behavior is rewarding to us, and we will continue relationships that offer more rewards than costs. When people live or work in close proximity with us, it costs less time and effort to develop the friendship and enjoy its benefits. When people are attractive, they are aesthetically pleasing, and associating with them can be socially rewarding. When people share our views, they reward us by confirming our own. ■

Romantic Love

12-14 How does romantic love typically change as time passes?

Sometimes people move from first impressions, to friendship, to the more intense, complex, and mysterious state of romantic love. If love endures, temporary *passionate love* will mellow into a lingering *companionate love* (Hatfield, 1988).

PASSIONATE LOVE A key ingredient of **passionate love** is arousal. The two-factor theory of emotion (Chapter 9) can help us understand this intense, positive state of feeling fully absorbed in another (Hatfield, 1988). That theory makes two assumptions:

- Emotions have two ingredients— physical arousal and cognitive appraisal.
- Arousal from any source can enhance an emotion, depending on how we interpret and label the arousal.

In one famous experiment, researchers studied people crossing two bridges above British Columbia's rocky Capilano River (Dutton & Aron, 1974, 1989). One, a swaying footbridge, was 230 feet above

passionate love an aroused state of intense positive absorption in another, usually present at the beginning of a love relationship.

Snapshots at jasonlove.com

Bill looked at Susan, Susan at Bill. Suddenly death didn't seem like an option. This was love at first sight.

the rocks. The other was low and solid. The researchers had an attractive young woman stop men coming off each bridge and ask their help in filling out a short questionnaire. She then offered her phone number in case they wanted to hear more about her project. Which men accepted the number and later called the woman? Far more of those who had just crossed the high bridge—which left their hearts pounding. To experience a stirred-up state and to associate some of that feeling with a desirable person is to experience the pull of passion. Adrenaline makes the heart grow fonder. Sexual desire + a growing attachment = the passion of romantic love (Berscheid, 2010).

COMPANIONATE LOVE Passionate romantic love seldom endures. The intense absorption in the other, the thrill of the romance, the giddy "floating on a cloud" feeling typically fade. Are the French correct in saying that "love makes the time pass and time makes love pass"? The evidence indi-

"When two people are under the influence of the most violent, most insane, most delusive, and most transient of passions, they are required to swear that they will remain in that excited, abnormal, and exhausting condition continuously until death do them part."

George Bernard Shaw, "Getting Married," 1908

cates that, as love matures, it becomes a steadier **companionate love**—a deep, affectionate attachment (Hatfield, 1988). Like a passing storm, the flood of passion-feeding hormones (testosterone, dopamine, adrenaline) gives way. But another hormone, oxytocin, remains, supporting feelings of trust, calmness, and bonding with the mate. In the most satisfying of marriages, attraction and sexual desire endure, minus the obsession of early- stage romance (Acevedo & Aron, 2009).

There may be adaptive wisdom to this shift from passion to attachment (Reis & Aron, 2008). Passionate love often produces children, whose survival is aided by the parents' waning obsession with one another. Failure to appreciate passionate love's limited half-life can doom a relationship (Berscheid et al., 1984). Indeed, recognizing the short duration of passionate love, some societies judge such feelings to be a poor reason for marrying. Better, these cultures say, to choose (or have someone choose for you) a partner who shares your background and interests. Non-Western cultures, where people rate love less important for marriage, do have lower divorce rates (Levine et al., 1995). Do you think you could be happy in a marriage someone else arranged for you, by matching you with someone who shared your interests and traits? Many people in many cultures around the world live seemingly happy lives in such marriages.

One key to a satisfying and enduring relationship is **equity,** as both partners receive in proportion to what they give (Gray-Little & Burks, 1983; Van Yperen & Buunk, 1990). In one national survey, "sharing

LOVE IS AN ANCIENT THING In 2007, skeletons of a 5000- to 6000-year-old "Romeo and Juliet" young couple were unearthed, locked in an embrace, near Rome.

household chores" ranked third, after "faithfulness" and a "happy sexual relationship," on a list of nine things Americans associated with successful marriages. "I like hugs. I like kisses. But what I really love is help with the dishes," summarized the Pew Research Center (2007).

Equity's importance extends beyond marriage. Mutually sharing self and possessions, making decisions together, giving and getting emotional support, promoting and caring about each other's welfare—all these acts are at the core of every type of loving relationship (Sternberg & Grajek, 1984). It's true for lovers, for parent and child, and for close friends.

Another vital ingredient of loving relationships is **self-disclosure,** revealing intimate details about ourselves—our likes and dislikes, our dreams and worries, our proud and shameful moments. As one person reveals a little, the other returns the gift. The first then reveals more, and on and on, as friends or lovers move to deeper and deeper intimacy (Baumeister & Bratslavsky, 1999).

One study marched pairs of students through 45 minutes of increasingly self-disclosing conversation—from "When did you last sing to yourself" to "When did you last cry in front of another person? By yourself?" Others spent the time with small-talk questions, such as "What was your high school like?" (Aron et al., 1997). By the experiment's end, those experiencing the escalating intimacy felt remarkably close to their conversation partner, much closer than did the small-talkers.

In the mathematics of love, self-disclosing intimacy + mutually supportive equality = enduring companionate love. ■

Altruism

12-15 What is altruism? When are we most—and least—likely to help?

Altruism is an unselfish concern for the welfare of others, such as Dirk Willems displayed when he rescued his jailer. Another heroic example of altruism took place in an underground New York City subway station. Construction worker Wesley Autrey and his 6- and 4-year-old daughters were waiting for their train when they saw a nearby man collapse in a convulsion. The man then got up, stumbled to the platform's edge, and fell onto the tracks. With train headlights approaching, Autrey later recalled, "I had to make a split decision" (Buckley, 2007).

SUBWAY HERO WESLEY AUTREY "I don't feel like I did something spectacular; I just saw someone who needed help."

His decision, as his girls looked on in horror, was to leap onto the track, push the man off the rails and into a foot-deep space between them, and lie on top of him. As the train screeched to a halt, five cars traveled just above his head, leaving grease on his knitted cap. When Autrey cried out, "I've got two daughters up there. Let them know their father is okay," the onlookers erupted into applause.

Such selfless goodness made New Yorkers proud to call that city home. Another New York story, four decades earlier, had a different ending. In 1964,

a stalker repeatedly stabbed Kitty Genovese, then raped her as she lay dying outside her Queens, New York, apartment at 3:30 A.M. "Oh, my God, he stabbed me!" Genovese screamed into the early morning stillness. "Please help me!" Windows opened and lights went on as neighbors heard her screams. Her attacker fled. Then he returned to stab and rape her again. Not until he had fled for good did anyone so much as call the police, at 3:50 A.M.

Bystander Intervention

In an emergency, some people intervene, as Wesley Autrey did, but others, like the Genovese bystanders, fail to offer help. Why do some people become heroes in emergencies while others just stand and watch? Social psychologists John Darley and Bibb Latané (1968b) believed three conditions were necessary for bystanders to help (**FIGURE 12.9**). They

• *notice* the incident.
• *interpret* the event as an emergency.
• *assume responsibility* for helping.

companionate love the deep affectionate attachment we feel for those with whom our lives are intertwined.

equity a condition in which people receive from a relationship in proportion to what they give to it.

self-disclosure revealing intimate aspects of ourselves to others.

altruism unselfish concern for the welfare of others.

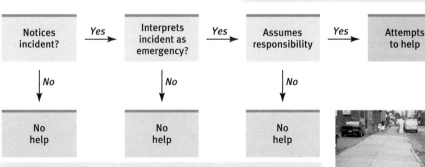

FIGURE 12.9 The decision-making process for bystander intervention Before helping, one must first notice an emergency, then correctly interpret it, and then feel responsible. For Wesley Autrey, the quick answer to each question was *Yes*. (From Darley & Latané, 1968b.)

At each step, the presence of others can turn people away from the path that leads to helping. Darley and Latané (1968a) reached these conclusions after interpreting the results of a series of experiments. For example, they staged a fake emergency in their laboratory as students participated in a discussion over an intercom. Each student was in a separate cubicle, and only the person whose microphone was switched on could be heard. When his turn came, one student (who was actually working for the experimenters) made sounds as though he were having an epileptic seizure, and he called for help.

How did the other students react? As FIGURE 12.10 shows, those who believed only they could hear the victim—and therefore thought they alone were responsible for helping him—usually went to his aid. Students who thought others also could hear the victim's cries were more likely to react as Kitty Genovese's neighbors had. When more people shared responsibility for helping—when no one person was clearly responsible—each listener was less likely to help.

Hundreds of additional experiments have confirmed this **bystander effect**. For example, researchers and their assistants took 1497 elevator rides in three cities and "accidentally" dropped coins or pencils in front of 4813 fellow passengers (Latané & Dabbs, 1975). When alone with the person in need, 40 percent helped; in the presence of five other bystanders, only 20 percent helped.

Observations of behavior in thousands of situations—relaying an emergency phone call, aiding a stranded motorist, donating blood, picking up dropped books, contributing money, giving time, and more—show that the best odds of our helping someone occur when

- the person appears to need and deserve help.
- the person is in some way similar to us.
- the person is a woman.
- we have just observed someone else being helpful.
- we are not in a hurry.
- we are in a small town or rural area.
- we are feeling guilty.
- we are focused on others and not preoccupied.
- we are in a good mood.

This last result, that happy people are helpful people, is one of the most consistent findings in all of psychology. As poet Robert Browning (1868) observed, "Oh, make us happy and you make us good!" It doesn't matter how we

are cheered. Whether by being made to feel successful and intelligent, by thinking happy thoughts, by finding money, or even by receiving a posthypnotic suggestion, we become more generous and more eager to help (Carlson et al., 1988).

So happiness breeds helpfulness. But it's also true that helpfulness breeds happiness. Making charitable donations activates brain areas associated with reward (Harbaugh et al., 2007). That helps explain a curious finding: People who give money away are happier than those who spend it almost entirely on themselves. In one experiment, researchers gave people an envelope with cash and instructions either to spend it on themselves or to spend it on others (Dunn et al., 2008). Which group was happiest at the day's end? It was, indeed, those assigned to the spend-it-on-others condition. ∎

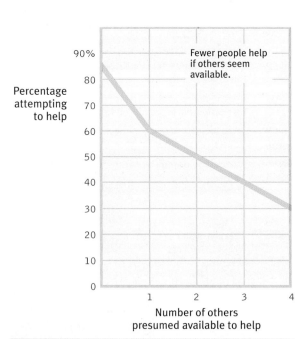

FIGURE 12.10 Responses to a staged physical emergency When people thought they alone heard the calls for help from a person they believed to be having an epileptic seizure, they usually helped. But when they thought four others were also hearing the calls, fewer than a third responded. (From Darley & Latané, 1968a.)

RETRIEVE + REMEMBER

- Why didn't anybody help Kitty Genovese? What social relations principle did this incident illustrate?

ANSWER: In the presence of others, an individual is less likely to notice a situation, correctly interpret it as an emergency, and then take responsibility for offering help. The Kitty Genovese case demonstrated this *bystander effect*, as each witness assumed many others were also aware of the event.

The Norms for Helping

12-16 How do social norms explain helping behavior?

Why do we help? Sometimes we go to the aid of another because we have been socialized to do so, through norms that prescribe how we *ought* to behave. Through socialization, we learn the **reciprocity norm,** the expectation that we should return help, not harm, to those who have helped us. In our relations with others of similar status, the reciprocity norm compels us to give (in favors, gifts, or social invitations) about as much as we receive.

The reciprocity norm kicked in after Dave Tally, a Tempe, Arizona, homeless man, found $3300 in a backpack that had been lost by an Arizona State University student headed to buy a used car (Lacey, 2010). Tally could have used the cash for much-needed bike repairs, food, and shelter. Instead, he turned the backpack in to the social service agency where he volunteered. To reciprocate Tally's help, the student thanked him with a monetary reward. Hearing about Tally's self-giving deeds, dozens of others also sent him money and job offers.

We also learn a **social-responsibility norm:** We should help those who depend on us. So we help young children and others who cannot give back as much as they receive. People who attend weekly religious services are often urged to practice the social-responsibility norm, and sometimes they do. Between 2006 and 2008, Gallup polls sampled more than 300,000 people across 140 countries, comparing those "highly religious" (who said religion was important to them and who had attended a religious service in the prior week) with those less religious. The highly religious, despite being poorer, were about 50 percent more likely to report having "donated money to a charity in the last month" and to have volunteered time to an organization (Pelham & Crabtree, 2008).

Although positive social norms encourage generosity and enable group living, conflicts often divide us.

Conflict and Peacemaking

12-17 What social processes fuel conflict? How can we transform feelings of prejudice and conflict into behaviors that promote peace?

We live in surprising times. With astonishing speed, recent democratic movements have swept away totalitarian rule in Eastern European and Arab countries. Yet *every day,* the world continues to spend more than $3 billion for arms and armies—money that could have been used for housing, nutrition, education, and health care. Knowing that wars begin in human minds, psychologists have wondered: What in the human mind causes destructive conflict? How might the perceived threats of our differences be replaced by a spirit of cooperation?

To a social psychologist, a **conflict** is the perception that actions, goals, or ideas are incompatible. The elements of conflict are much the same, whether we are speaking of nations at war, cultural groups feuding within a society, or partners sparring in a relationship. In each situation, people become tangled in a destructive process that can produce results no one wants.

Enemy Perceptions

Psychologists have noticed a curious tendency: People in conflict form evil images of one another. These distorted images are so similar that we call them **mirror-image perceptions.** As we see "them"—untrustworthy, with evil intentions—so "they" see us.

Mirror-image perceptions can feed a vicious cycle of hostility. If Juan believes Maria is annoyed with him, he may snub her. In return, she may act annoyed, justifying his perceptions. As with individuals, so with countries. Perceptions can become self-fulfilling prophecies.

We tend to see our own actions as responses to provocation, not as the causes of what happens next. Perceiving ourselves as returning tit for tat, we often hit back harder, as University College London volunteers did in one experiment (Shergill et al., 2003). After feeling pressure on their own finger, they were to use a mechanical device to press on another volunteer's finger. Although told to reciprocate with the same amount of pressure, they typically responded with about 40 percent more force than they had just experienced. Despite seeking only to respond in kind, their touches soon escalated to hard presses, much as when each child after a fight claims that "I just poked him, but he hit me harder."

The point is not that truth must lie midway between conflicting views (one may be more accurate). The point is that enemy perceptions often form mirror images. Moreover, as enemies change, so do perceptions. In American minds and media, the "bloodthirsty, cruel, treacherous" Japanese of World War II became "intelligent, hardworking, self-disciplined, resourceful allies" (Gallup, 1972).

Promoting Peace

How can we change perceptions and make peace? Can contact and cooperation transform the anger and fear fed by prejudice and conflicts into peaceful attitudes? Research indicates that, in some cases, they can.

---

bystander effect the tendency for any given bystander to be less likely to give aid if other bystanders are present.

reciprocity norm an expectation that people will help, not hurt, those who have helped them.

social-responsibility norm an expectation that people will help those dependent upon them.

conflict a perceived incompatibility of actions, goals, or ideas.

mirror-image perceptions mutual views often held by conflicting people, as when each side sees itself as ethical and peaceful and views the other side as evil and aggressive.

CONTACT Does it help to put two conflicting parties into close contact? It depends. When contact is free of competition and between parties with equal status, such as fellow store clerks, it typically helps. Initially prejudiced co-workers of different races have, in such circumstances, usually come to accept one another. Across a quarter-million people studied in 38 nations, friendly contact with ethnic minorities, older people, and people with disabilities has usually led to less prejudice (Pettigrew & Tropp, 2011). Some examples:

- With interracial contact, South African Whites' and Blacks' "attitudes [have moved] into closer alignment" (Dixon et al., 2007; Finchilescu & Tredoux, 2010).

- Heterosexuals' attitudes toward gay people are influenced not only by what they know but also by whom they know (Smith et al., 2009). In surveys, the reason people most often give for becoming more supportive of same-sex marriage is "having friends, family, or acquaintances who are gay or lesbian" (Pew, 2013).

- Even indirect contact with an outgroup member (via story reading or through a friend who has an outgroup friend) has reduced prejudice (Cameron & Rutland, 2006; Pettigrew et al., 2007).

However, contact is not always enough. In most desegregated schools, ethnic groups resegregate themselves in the lunchrooms and on the school grounds (Alexander & Tredoux, 2010; Clack et al., 2005; Schofield, 1986). People in each group often think they would welcome more contact with the other group, but they assume the other group does not share their interest (Richeson & Shelton, 2007). When these mirror-image untruths are corrected, friendships can form and prejudices melt.

COOPERATION To see if enemies could overcome their differences, researcher Muzafer Sherif (1966) manufactured a conflict. He separated 22 boys into two separate camp areas. Then he had the two groups compete for prizes in a series of activities. Before long, each group became intensely proud of itself and hostile to the other group's "sneaky," "smart-alecky stinkers." Food wars broke out. Cabins were ransacked. Fistfights had to be broken up by camp counselors. Brought together, the two groups avoided each other, except to taunt and threaten. Little did they know that within a few days, they would be friends.

Sherif accomplished this reconciliation by giving them **superordinate goals**—shared goals that could be achieved only through cooperation. When he arranged for the camp water supply to "fail," all 22 boys had to work together to restore water. To rent a movie in those pre-Netflix days, they all had to pool their resources. To move a stalled truck, all the boys had to combine their strength, pulling and pushing together. Sherif used shared predicaments and goals to turn enemies into friends. What reduced conflict was not mere contact, but *cooperative* contact.

A shared predicament likewise had a powerfully unifying effect in the weeks after the 9/11 terrorist attack. Patriotism soared as Americans felt "we" were under attack. Gallup-surveyed approval of "our President" shot up from 51 percent the week before the attack to a highest-ever 90 percent level just 10 days after (Newport, 2002). In chat groups and everyday speech, even the word *we* (relative to *I*) surged in the immediate aftermath (Pennebaker, 2002).

At such times, cooperation can lead people to define a new, inclusive group that dissolves their former subgroups (Dovidio & Gaertner, 1999). If this were a social psychology experiment, you might seat members of two groups not on opposite sides, but alternately around a table. Give them a new, shared name. Have them work together. Then watch "us" and "them" become "we." After 9/11, one 18-year-old New Jersey man described this shift in his own social identity. "I just thought of myself as Black. But now I feel like I'm an American, more than ever" (Sengupta, 2001).

If superordinate goals and shared threats help bring rival groups together, might this principle bring people together in multicultural schools? Could interracial friendships replace competitive classroom situations with cooperative ones? Could cooperative learning maintain or even enhance student achievement? Experiments with teens from 11 countries confirm that, in each case, the answer is *Yes* (Roseth et al., 2008). In the classroom as in the sports arena, members of interracial groups

> *"You cannot shake hands with a clenched fist."*
> Indira Gandhi, 1971

KOFI ANNAN "Most of us have overlapping identities which unite us with very different groups. We *can* love what we are, without hating what—and who—we are *not*. We can thrive in our own tradition, even as we learn from others" (Nobel lecture, 2001).

AP Photo/Shawn Baldwin

"To begin with, I would like to express my sincere thanks and deep appreciation for the opportunity to meet with you. While there are still profound differences between us, I think the very fact of my presence here today is a major breakthrough."

who work together on projects typically come to feel friendly toward one another. Knowing this, thousands of teachers have made interracial cooperative learn-ing part of their classroom experience.

The power of cooperative activity to make friends of former enemies has led psychologists to urge increased international exchange and cooperation. Let us engage in mutually beneficial trade, working together to protect our common destiny on this fragile planet and becoming more aware that our hopes and fears are shared. By taking such steps, we can change misperceptions that drive us apart and instead join together in a common cause based on common interests. As working toward shared goals reminds us, we are more alike than different. ■

superordinate goals shared goals that override differences among people and require their cooperation.

CHAPTER REVIEW

Social Psychology

Test yourself by taking a moment to answer each of these Learning Objective Questions (repeated here from within the chapter). Then turn to Appendix D, Complete Chapter Reviews, to check your answers. Research suggests that trying to answer these questions on your own will improve your long-term memory of the concepts (McDaniel et al., 2009).

What Is Social Psychology's Focus?

12-1: What are three main focuses of social psychology?

Social Thinking

12-2: How does the fundamental attribution error describe how we tend to explain others' behavior compared with our own?

12-3: What is an attitude, and how do attitudes and actions affect each other?

Social Influence

12-4: What do experiments on conformity and obedience reveal about the power of social influence?

12-5: What do the social influence studies teach us about ourselves? How much power do we have as individuals?

12-6: How does the presence of others influence our actions, via social facilitation, social loafing, or deindividuation?

12-7: How can group interaction enable group polarization and groupthink?

Social Relations

12-8: What are the three parts of prejudice, and how has prejudice changed over time?

12-9: What factors contribute to the social roots of prejudice, and how does scapegoating illustrate the emotional roots of prejudice?

12-10: What are the cognitive roots of prejudice?

12-11: What biological factors predispose us to be aggressive?

12-12: What psychological and social-cultural factors may trigger aggressive behavior?

12-13: Why do we befriend or fall in love with some people but not others?

12-14: How does romantic love typically change as time passes?

12-15: What is altruism? When are we most—and least—likely to help?

12-16: How do social norms explain helping behavior?

12-17: What social processes fuel conflict? How can we transform feelings of prejudice and conflict into behaviors that promote peace?

TERMS AND CONCEPTS TO REMEMBER

Test yourself on these terms by trying to write down the definition in your own words before flipping back to the referenced page to check your answer.

social psychology, p. 338

fundamental attribution error, p. 338

attitude, p. 339

foot-in-the-door phenomenon, p. 340

role, p. 340

cognitive dissonance theory, p. 341

conformity, p. 342

norm, p. 343

social facilitation, p. 347

social loafing, p. 347

deindividuation, p. 348

group polarization, p. 348

groupthink, p. 349

prejudice, p. 350

stereotype, p. 350

discrimination, p. 350

just-world phenomenon, p. 352

ingroup, p. 352

outgroup, p. 352

ingroup bias, p. 352

scapegoat theory, p. 352

other-race effect, p. 353

aggression, p. 354

frustration-aggression principle, p. 355

social script, p. 357

mere exposure effect, p. 359

passionate love, p. 361

companionate love, p. 362

equity, p. 362

self-disclosure, p. 362

altruism, p. 363

bystander effect, p. 364

reciprocity norm, p. 365

social-responsibility norm, p. 365

conflict, p. 365

mirror-image perceptions, p. 365

superordinate goals, p. 366

CHAPTER TEST

Test yourself repeatedly throughout your studies. This will not only help you figure out what you know and don't know; the testing itself will help you learn and remember the information more effectively thanks to the testing effect.

1. If we encounter a person who appears to be high on drugs, and we make the fundamental attribution error, we will probably attribute the person's behavior to

   a. moral weakness or an addictive personality.

   b. peer pressure.

   c. the easy availability of drugs on city streets.

   d. society's acceptance of drug use.

2. We tend to agree to a larger request more readily if we have already agreed to a small request. This tendency is called the _____ -_____ - _____ - _____ phenomenon.

3. Jamal's therapist has suggested that Jamal should "act as if" he is confident, even though he feels insecure and shy. Which social psychological theory would best support this suggestion, and what might the therapist be hoping to achieve?

4. Researchers have found that a person is most likely to conform to a group if

   a. the group members have diverse opinions.

   b. the person feels competent and secure.

   c. the person admires the group's status.

   d. no one else will observe the person's behavior.

5. In Milgram's experiments, the rate of obedience was highest when

   a. the "learner" was at a distance from the "teacher."

   b. the "learner" was close at hand.

   c. other "teachers" refused to go along with the experimenter.

   d. the "teacher" disliked the "learner."

6. Dr. Huang, a popular music professor, delivers fascinating lectures on music history but gets nervous and makes mistakes when describing exam statistics in front of the class. Why does his performance vary by task?

7. In a group situation that fosters arousal and anonymity, a person sometimes loses self-consciousness and self-control. This phenomenon is called _____.

8. Sharing our opinions with like-minded others tends to strengthen our views, a phenomenon referred to as _____ _____.

9. Prejudice toward a group involves negative feelings, a tendency to discriminate, and overly generalized beliefs referred to as _____.

10. If several well-publicized murders are committed by members of a particular group, we may tend to react with fear and suspicion toward all members of that group. In other words, we

   a. blame the victim.

   b. overgeneralize from vivid, memorable cases.

   c. view the world as just.

   d. rationalize inequality.

11. The other-race effect occurs when we assume that other groups are _____ (more/less) homogeneous than our own group.

12. Evidence of a biochemical influence on aggression is the finding that

    a. aggressive behavior varies widely from culture to culture.

    b. animals can be bred for aggressiveness.

    c. stimulation of an area of the brain's limbic system produces aggressive behavior.

    d. a higher-than-average level of the hormone testosterone is associated with violent behavior in males.

13. Studies show that parents of delinquent young people tend to use beatings to enforce discipline. This suggests that aggression can be

    a. learned through direct rewards.

    b. triggered by exposure to violent media.

    c. learned through observation of aggressive models.

    d. caused by hormone changes at puberty.

14. A statement by 21 social scientists studying the effects of pornography noted that violent pornography

    a. has little effect on most viewers.

    b. is the primary cause of reported and unreported rapes.

    c. leads viewers to be more accepting of coercion in sexual relations.

    d. has no effect, other than short-term arousal and entertainment.

15. The aspect of X-rated films that most directly influences men's aggression toward women seems to be the

    a. length of the film.   c. depictions of sexual violence.

    b. eroticism portrayed.   d. attractiveness of the actors.

16. The more familiar a stimulus becomes, the more we tend to like it. This exemplifies the _____ _____ effect.

17. A happy couple celebrating their 50th wedding anniversary is likely to experience deep _____ love, even though their _____ love has probably decreased over the years.

18. After vigorous exercise, you meet an attractive person, and you are suddenly seized by romantic feelings for that person. This response supports the two-factor theory of emotion, which assumes that emotions, such as passionate love, consist of physical arousal plus

    a. a reward.

    b. proximity.

    c. companionate love.

    d. our interpretation of that arousal.

19. Due to the bystander effect, a particular bystander is less likely to give aid if

    a. the victim is similar to the bystander in appearance.

    b. no one else is present.

    c. other people are present.

    d. the incident occurs in a deserted or rural area.

20. Our enemies often have many of the same negative impressions of us as we have of them. This exemplifies the concept of _____ - _____ perceptions.

21. One way of resolving conflicts and fostering cooperation is by giving rival groups shared goals that help them override their differences. These are called _____ goals.

Find answers to these questions in Appendix E, in the back of the book.

IN YOUR EVERYDAY LIFE

Answering these questions will help you make these concepts more personally meaningful, and therefore more memorable.

1. Do you have an attitude or tendency you would like to change? How could you use the attitudes-follow-behavior idea to change it?

2. What example of social influence have you experienced this week? How did you respond to the power of the situation?

3. What could you do to discourage social loafing in a group project assigned for a class?

4. What negative attitudes might professors and students have toward each other? What strategies might change those attitudes?

5. In what ways have you been affected by social scripts for aggression? How have TV shows or video games contributed such scripts?

6. To what extent have your closest relationships been affected by proximity, physical attractiveness, and similarity?

7. What could you do to motivate your friends to contribute their time or money to a cause that is important to you?

8. Think of a conflict between friends or family members. What strategies would you suggest to help them reconcile their relationships?

experience
more of the
testing
effect

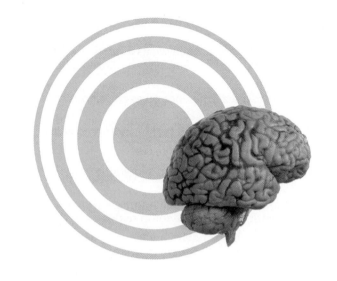

13 Psychological Disorders

TABLE 13.1 Percentage of Americans Reporting Certain Psychological Disorders in the Past Year

Disorder	Percentage
Generalized anxiety	3.1
Social anxiety disorder	6.8
Phobia of specific object or situation	8.7
Mood disorder	9.5
Obsessive-compulsive disorder (OCD)	1.0
Schizophrenia	1.1
Posttraumatic stress disorder (PTSD)	3.5
Attention-deficit/hyperactivity disorder (ADHD)	4.1

Source: National Institute of Mental Health, 2008.

I felt the need to clean my room at home in Indianapolis every Sunday and would spend four to five hours at it. I would take every book out of the bookcase, dust and put it back. At the time I loved doing it. Then I didn't want to do it anymore, but I couldn't stop. The clothes in my closet hung exactly two fingers apart. . . . I made a ritual of touching the wall in my bedroom before I went out because something bad would happen if I didn't do it the right way. I had a constant anxiety about it as a kid, and it made me think for the first time that I might be nuts.

Marc, diagnosed with obsessive-compulsive disorder (from Summers, 1996)

Whenever I get depressed it's because I've lost a sense of self. I can't find reasons to like myself. I think I'm ugly. I think no one likes me. . . . I become grumpy and short-tempered. Nobody wants to be around me. I'm left alone. Being alone confirms that I am ugly and not worth being with. I think I'm responsible for everything that goes wrong.

Greta, diagnosed with depression (from Thorne, 1993, p. 21)

Voices, like the roar of a crowd, came. I felt like Jesus; I was being crucified. It was dark. I just continued to huddle under the blanket, feeling weak, laid bare and defenseless in a cruel world I could no longer understand.

Stuart, diagnosed with schizophrenia (from Emmons et al., 1997)

Now and then, all of us feel, think, or act in ways that resemble a psychological disturbance. We get anxious, depressed, withdrawn, or suspicious, just less intensely and more briefly. So it's no wonder that we sometimes see ourselves in the psychological disorders we study. "To study the abnormal is the best way of understanding the normal," said William James (1842–1910).

Either personally or through friends or family, many of us will know the confusion and pain of unexplained physical symptoms, irrational fears, or a feeling that life is not worth living. Worldwide, some 450 million people suffer from mental or behavioral disorders (WHO, 2010). The National Institute of Mental Health (2012) estimates that 26 percent of adult Americans "suffer from a diagnosable mental disorder in a given year" (**TABLE 13.1**). Rates and symptoms vary by culture, but no known society is free of two terrible disorders—major depression and schizophrenia (Baumeister & Härter, 2007; Draguns, 1990a,b, 1997). This chapter examines these disorders and others. Chapter 14 considers their *treatment.* First, though, let's address some basic questions.

What Is a Psychological Disorder?

"They're trying to figure out whether it's a chemical thing or I'm just a crybaby."

Most of us would agree that a family member who is depressed and refuses to get out of bed for three months has a psychological disorder. But what should we say about a grieving father who can't resume his usual social activities three months after his child has died? Where do we draw the line between clinical depression and understandable grief? Between bizarre irrationality and zany creativity? Between abnormality and normality?

In their search for answers, theorists and clinicians consider several perspectives:

- How should we *define* psychological disorders?

- How should we *understand* disorders? How do underlying biological factors contribute to disorder? How do troubling environments influence our well-being? And how do these effects of nature and nurture interact?

- How should we *classify* psychological disorders? How can we use labels to guide treatment without stigmatizing people or excusing their behavior?

Defining Psychological Disorders

13-1 How should we draw the line between normal behavior and psychological disorder?

A **psychological disorder** is a syndrome marked by a "clinically significant disturbance in an individual's cognitions, emotion regulation, or behavior" (American Psychiatric Association, 2013).

Disturbed, or *dysfunctional,* thoughts, emotions, or behaviors interfere with normal day-to-day life—they are *maladaptive.* An intense fear of spiders may

be abnormal, but if it doesn't interfere with your life, it is not a disorder. Believing that your home must be thoroughly cleaned every weekend is not a disorder. But when cleaning rituals interfere with work and leisure, as Marc's did in this chapter's opening, they may be signs of a disorder. And occasional sad moods that persist and become disabling may likewise signal a psychological disorder.

People are often distressed by their dysfunctional thoughts, emotions, or behaviors. Marc, Greta, and Stuart all experienced distress about their behaviors or emotions.

The diagnosis of specific disorders has varied from culture to culture and even over time in the same culture. By 1973, mental health workers no longer considered same-sex attraction as inherently dysfunctional or distressing. The American Psychiatric Association therefore dropped homosexuality from its list of disorders. On the other hand, high-energy children, who might have been viewed as normal youngsters running a bit wild in the 1970s, may today receive a diagnosis of *attention-deficit/hyperactivity disorder (ADHD).* (See Thinking Critically About: ADHD—Normal High Energy or Disordered Behavior?) Times change, and research and clinical practices change, too.

Understanding Psychological Disorders

13-3 How is our understanding of psychological disorders affected by whether we use a medical model or a biopsychosocial approach?

The way we view a problem influences how we try to solve it. In earlier times, people often thought that strange behaviors were evidence that strange forces were at work. Had you lived during the Middle Ages, you might have said, "The devil made him do it." To drive out demons, "mad" people were sometimes caged or given "therapies" such as beatings, genital mutilations, removal of teeth or lengths of intestine, or transfusions of animal blood (Farina, 1982).

Reformers such as Philippe Pinel (1745–1826) in France opposed such brutal treatments. Madness is not demon possession, he insisted, but a sickness of the mind caused by severe stress and inhumane conditions. Curing the sickness requires "moral treatment," including boosting patients' morale by unchaining them and talking with them. He and others worked to replace brutality with gentleness, isolation with activity, and filth with clean air and sunshine.

"MORAL TREATMENT" Under Philippe Pinel's influence, hospitals sometimes sponsored patient dances, often called "lunatic balls," depicted in this painting by George Bellows *(Dance in a Madhouse).*

THINKING CRITICALLY ABOUT

ADHD—Normal High Energy or Disordered Behavior?

13-2 Why is there controversy over attention-deficit/hyperactivity disorder?

Eight-year-old Todd has always been full of energy. At home, he chatters away and darts from one activity to the next. He rarely settles down to read a book or focus on a game. At play, he is reckless. He overreacts when playmates bump into him or take one of his toys. At school, he fidgets, and his teacher complains that he doesn't listen, follow instructions, or stay in his seat and do his lessons.

If taken for a psychological evaluation, Todd may be diagnosed with **attention-deficit/hyperactivity disorder (ADHD).** Some 11 percent of American 4- to 17-year-olds receive this diagnosis after displaying its key symptoms (extreme inattention, hyperactivity, and impulsivity) (Schwarz & Cohen, 2013). Studies also find that 2.5 percent of adults—though the number grows smaller with age—have ADHD symptoms (Simon et al., 2009). (Psychiatry's new diagnostic manual has loosened the criteria for adult ADHD, leading critics to fear increased diagnosis and overuse of prescription drugs [Frances, 2012].)

To skeptics, being distractible, fidgety, and impulsive sounds like a "disorder" caused by a single genetic variation: a Y chromosome (the male sex chromosome). And sure enough, ADHD is diagnosed more than twice as often in boys as in girls. Does energetic child + boring school = ADHD overdiagnosis?

Skeptics think so. Depending on where they live, children who are "a persistent pain in the neck in school" are often diagnosed with ADHD and given powerful prescription drugs (Gray, 2010). But the problem may reside less in the child than in today's abnormal environment that forces children to do what evolution has not prepared them to do—to sit for long hours in chairs. In more natural outdoor environments, these healthy schoolchildren might seem perfectly normal.

Rates of medication for presumed ADHD vary by age, sex, and location. Prescription drugs are more often given to teens than to younger children. Boys are nearly three times more likely to receive them than are girls. And location matters. Among 4- to 17-year-olds, prescription rates have varied from 1 percent in Nevada to 9 percent in North Carolina (CDC, 2013). Some students seek out the stimulant drugs—calling them the "good-grade pills." They hope to increase their focus and achievement, but the risk is eventual addiction and mood disorder (Schwarz, 2012).

Not everyone agrees that ADHD is being overdiagnosed. Some argue that today's more frequent diagnoses reflect increased awareness of the disorder, especially in those areas where rates are highest. They also note that diagnoses can be inconsistent—ADHD is not as clearly defined as, for example, a broken arm is. Nevertheless, declared the World Federation for Mental Health (2005), "there is strong agreement among the international scientific community that ADHD is a real neurobiological disorder whose existence should no longer be debated." A consensus statement by 75 researchers noted that in neuroimaging studies, ADHD has associations with abnormal brain activity patterns (Barkley et al., 2002).

What, then, is known about ADHD's causes? It is not caused by too much sugar or poor schools. ADHD often coexists with a learning disorder or with defiant and temper-prone behavior. ADHD is *heritable,* and research teams are sleuthing the culprit gene variations and abnormal neural pathways (Nikolas & Burt, 2010; Poelmans et al., 2011; Volkow et al., 2009; Williams et al., 2010). It is treatable with medications such as Ritalin and Adderall, which are considered stimulants but help calm hyperactivity and increase one's ability to sit and focus on a task—and to progress normally in school (Barbaresi et al., 2007). Psychological therapies, such as those focused on shaping behaviors in the classroom and at home, have also helped address the distress of ADHD (Fabiano et al., 2008).

The bottom line: Extreme inattention, hyperactivity, and impulsivity can derail social, academic, and vocational achievements, and these symptoms can be treated with medication and other therapies. But the debate continues over whether normal high energy is too often diagnosed as a psychiatric disorder, and whether there is a cost to the long-term use of stimulant drugs in treating ADHD.

> **attention-deficit/hyperactivity disorder (ADHD)** a psychological disorder marked by extreme inattention and/or hyperactivity and impulsivity.

The Medical Model

By the 1800s, a medical breakthrough prompted further reform. Researchers discovered that syphilis, a sexually transmitted infection, invades the brain and distorts the mind. This discovery triggered an excited search for physical causes of other mental disorders, and for treatments that would cure them. Hospitals replaced madhouses, and the **medical model** of mental disorders was born. This model is reflected in words we still use today. We speak of the mental *health* movement. A mental *illness* needs to be *diagnosed* on the basis of its *symptoms.* It needs to be *cured* through *therapy,*

> **psychological disorder** a syndrome marked by a clinically significant disturbance in a person's thoughts, feelings, or behaviors.
>
> **medical model** the concept that diseases, in this case psychological disorders, have physical causes that can be *diagnosed, treated,* and, in most cases, *cured,* often through *treatment* in a *hospital.*

"I'm always like this, and my family was wondering if you could prescribe a mild depressant."

ScienceCartoonsPlus.com

which may include *treatment* in a psychiatric *hospital*. Recent discoveries that abnormal brain structures and biochemistry contribute to some disorders have energized the medical perspective.

The Biopsychosocial Approach

To call psychological disorders "sicknesses" tilts research heavily toward the influence of biology and away from the influence of our personal histories and social and cultural surroundings. But as we have seen throughout this text, our behaviors, our thoughts, and our feelings are formed by the interaction of our biology, our psychology, and our social-cultural environment. As individuals, we differ in the amount of stress we experience and in the ways we cope with stress. Cultures also differ in the ways people experience and cope with stress.

The environment's influence on disorders can be seen in culture-related symptoms (Beardsley, 1994; Castillo, 1997). Anxiety, for example, may be exhibited in differ-

ent ways in different cultures. In Latin American cultures, people may suffer from *susto,* a condition marked by severe anxiety, restlessness, and a fear of black magic. In Japanese culture, people may experience *taijin-kyofusho*—social anxiety about their appearance, combined with a readiness to blush and a fear of eye contact. The eating disorder *bulimia nervosa* occurs mostly in food-abundant Western cultures. Increasingly, however, North American disorders, along with McDonalds and MTV, have spread the globe (Watters, 2010).

Other disorders, such as depression and schizophrenia, have appeared more consistently worldwide. From Asia to Africa and across the Americas, people with schizophrenia often act irrationally and speak in disorganized ways. Such disorders reflect genes and physiology, as well as psychological dynamics and cultural circumstances. The biopsychosocial approach reminds us that mind and body are inseparable. We are mind embodied. ■

also attempts to predict the disorder's future course and to suggest treatment. And it prompts research into causes. To study a disorder we must first name and describe it.

The most common tool for describing disorders and estimating how often they occur is the American Psychiatric Association's 2013 *Diagnostic and Statistical Manual of Mental Disorders,* now in its fifth edition (**DSM-5**). (Many examples in this chapter were drawn from the case studies in a previous DSM edition.) Physicians and mental health workers use the detailed "diagnostic criteria and codes" in the DSM-5 to guide medical diagnoses and define who is eligible for treatments, including medication (and corresponding insurance coverage). For example, a person may be diagnosed with and treated for "insomnia disorder" if he or she meets *all* of the following criteria:

- Is dissatisfied with sleep quantity or quality (difficulty initiating, maintaining, or returning to sleep)
- Sleep disturbance causes distress or impairment in everyday functioning
- Occurs at least three nights per week
- Present for at least three months
- Occurs despite adequate opportunity for sleep
- Is not explained by another sleep disorder (such as narcolepsy)
- Is not caused by substance use or abuse
- Is not caused by other mental disorders or medical conditions

In this new edition, some diagnostic labels have changed. As noted in Chapter 3, the conditions formerly called "autism" and "Asperger's syndrome" have now been combined under the label *autism spectrum disorder.* "Mental retardation" has become *intellectual disability.* New categories include *hoarding disorder,* and *binge-eating disorder.*

Some new or altered diagnoses are controversial. *Disruptive mood dysregulation disorder* is a new DSM-5 diagno-

RETRIEVE + REMEMBER

- Are psychological disorders culture-specific? Explain with examples.

ANSWER: Some psychological disorders are culture-specific. For example, bulimia nervosa occurs mostly in food-rich Western cultures, and *taijin-kyofusho* appears largely in Japan. Other disorders, such as schizophrenia, appear across cultures.

- What is the biopsychosocial perspective, and why is it important in our understanding of psychological disorders?

ANSWER: Biological, psychological, and social-cultural influences combine to produce psychological disorders. This broad perspective stresses that our well-being is affected by the interaction of many forces: our genes, brain functioning, inner thoughts and feelings, and the influences of our social and cultural environment.

Classifying Disorders— and Labeling People

13-4 How and why do clinicians classify psychological disorders, and why do some psychologists criticize the use of diagnostic labels?

In biology, classification creates order and helps us communicate. To say that an animal is a "mammal" tells us a great deal—that it is warm-blooded, has hair or fur, and produces milk to feed its young.

In psychiatry and psychology, classification also tells us a great deal. To classify a disorder as "schizophrenia" implies that the person speaks in a disorganized way, has bizarre beliefs, shows either little emotion or inappropriate emotion, or is socially withdrawn. "Schizophrenia" is a quick way of describing a complex set of behaviors.

But diagnostic classification does more than give us a thumbnail sketch of a person's disordered behavior. In psychiatry and psychology, classification

sis for children "who exhibit persistent irritability and frequent episodes of behavior outbursts three or more times a week for more than a year." Will this diagnosis assist parents who struggle with unstable children, or will it "turn temper tantrums into a mental disorder" and lead to overmedication, as the chair of the previous DSM edition has warned (Frances, 2012)? Another change that has triggered some debate is that prolonged bereavement can now be diagnosed as depression. Patients with this diagnosis are now eligible for insurance coverage for antidepressant drugs. Companies that market those drugs will benefit. Some protest that depression after a loved one's death should not be considered abnormal; others argue that depression is depression, regardless of its trigger.

Real-world tests (*field trials*) have assessed clinician agreement when using the new DSM-5 categories (Freedman et al., 2013). Some diagnoses, such as *adult posttraumatic stress disorder* and *childhood autism spectrum disorder*, fared well—with agreement near 70 percent. (If one psychiatrist or psychologist diagnosed someone with autism spectrum disorder, there was a 70 percent chance that another mental health worker would independently give the same diagnosis.) Others, such as *antisocial personality disorder* and *generalized anxiety disorder,* fared poorly.

Critics have long faulted the DSM manual for casting too wide a net and bringing "almost any kind of behavior within the compass of psychiatry" (Eysenck et al., 1983). They worry that the DSM-5 will extend the pathologizing of everyday life—for example, by turning bereavement grief into depression and boyish rambunctiousness into ADHD (Frances, 2013). Others respond that depression and hyperactivity, though needing careful definition, are genuine disorders—even, for example, those triggered by a major life stress such as a death when the grief does not go away (Kendler, 2011; Kupfer, 2012).

Other critics have registered a more basic complaint—that these labels are just society's value judgments (Farina, 1982). Labels can change reality by putting us on the alert for evidence that confirms our view. When teachers are told certain students are "gifted," they may act in ways that bring out the creative behavior they expect (Snyder, 1984). If we hear that a new co-worker is a difficult person, we may treat the person suspiciously. He or she may in turn respond to us as a difficult person would. Labels can be self-fulfilling.

The biasing power of labels was clear in a now-classic study. David Rosenhan (1973) and seven others went to hospital admissions offices, complaining (falsely) of "hearing voices" saying *empty, hollow,* and *thud.* Apart from this complaint and giving false names and occupations, they answered questions truthfully. All eight of these normal people were misdiagnosed with disorders.

Should we be surprised? As one psychiatrist noted, if someone swallows blood, goes to an emergency room, and spits it up, should we blame the doctor for diagnosing a bleeding ulcer? Surely not. But what followed the diagnosis in the Rosenhan study was startling. Until being released an average of 19 days later, these eight "patients" showed no other symptoms. Yet after analyzing their (quite normal) life histories, clinicians were able to "discover" the causes of their disorders, such as having mixed emotions about a parent. Even routine note-taking behavior was misinterpreted as a symptom.

When people in another experiment watched videotaped interviews, those told that they were watching job applicants perceived the people as normal (Langer et al., 1974, 1980). Others, who were told they were watching psychiatric or cancer patients, perceived them as "different from most people." Labels matter. One therapist who thought he was watching an interview of a psychiatric patient described the person as "frightened of his own aggressive impulses," a

"passive, dependent type," and so forth. As Rosenhan discovered, a label can have "a life and an influence of its own."

The power of labels is just as real outside the laboratory. Getting a job or finding a place to rent can be a challenge for people recently released from a mental hospital. Label someone as "mentally ill" and people may fear them as potentially violent (see Close-Up: Are People With Psychological Disorders Dangerous? on the next page). That reaction seems to be fading as people better understand that many psychological disorders are diseases of the brain, not failures of character (Solomon, 1996). Public figures have helped foster this new understanding by speaking openly about their own struggles with disorders such as depression.

Despite their risks, diagnostic labels have benefits. They help mental health professionals communicate about their cases, pinpoint underlying causes, and share information about effective treatments. They are useful in research that explores the causes and treatments of disorders. And clients are often glad that the nature of their suffering has a name, and that they are not alone in experiencing this collection of symptoms. ∎

RETRIEVE + REMEMBER

- What is the value, and what are the dangers, of labeling individuals with disorders?

ANSWER: Therapists and others use disorder labels to communicate with one another in a common language. Clients may benefit from knowing they are not the only ones with these symptoms. Insurance companies require a diagnosis (a label) before they will pay for therapy. The danger of labeling people is that they will begin to act as they have been labeled, and also that labels can trigger assumptions that will change our behavior toward the people we label.

DSM-5 the American Psychiatric Association's *Diagnostic and Statistical Manual of Mental Disorders,* Fifth Edition; a widely used system for classifying psychological disorders.

CLOSE-UP

Are People With Psychological Disorders Dangerous?

Movies and television sometimes portray people with psychological disorders as homicidal. Mass killings in 2012 by apparently disturbed people in a Colorado theater and a Connecticut elementary school reinforced public perceptions that people with psychological disorders are dangerous (Jorm et al., 2012). Thus, "People who have mental issues should not have guns," said New York's governor (Kaplan & Hakim, 2013).

Do disorders actually increase risk of violence, and can clinicians predict who is likely to do harm? In real life, the vast majority of violent crimes are committed by those with no diagnosed disorder (Fazel & Grann, 2006). Moreover, mental disorders seldom lead to violence, and clinical prediction of violence is unreliable.

The few people with disorders who do commit violent acts tend to be either those who experience threatening delusions and hallucinated voices that command them to act, or those who abuse substances (Douglas et al., 2009; Elbogen & Johnson, 2009; Fazel et al., 2009, 2010). People with disorders also are more likely to be *victims* than perpetrators of violence (Marley & Bulia, 2001). Indeed, reported the U.S. Surgeon General's Office (1999, p. 7), "There is very little risk of violence or harm to a stranger from casual contact with an individual who has a mental disorder." People with mental illness commit proportionately little gun violence. Thus, focusing gun restrictions only on mentally ill people is unlikely to significantly reduce gun violence (Friedman, 2012).

Better predictors of violence are use of alcohol or drugs, previous violence, and gun availability. The mass-killing shooters had one

HOW TO PREVENT MASS SHOOTINGS? Following the Newtown, Connecticut, slaughter of 20 young children and 6 adults, people wondered: Could those at risk for violence be identified in advance by mental health workers and reported to police? Would laws that require such reporting discourage disturbed gun owners from seeking mental health treatment?

more thing in common: They were young males. "We could avoid two-thirds of all crime simply by putting all able-bodied young men in a cryogenic sleep from the age of 12 through 28," said one psychologist (Lykken, 1995).

Anxiety Disorders, OCD, and PTSD

13-5 What are the main anxiety disorders, and how do anxiety disorders differ from the ordinary worries and fears we all experience?

Anxiety is part of life. Have you ever felt anxious when speaking in front of a class, peering down from a high ledge, or waiting to play in a big game? We all feel anxious at times. We may occasionally feel enough anxiety to avoid making eye contact or talking with someone—"shyness," we call it. Fortunately for most of us, our uneasiness is not intense and persistent.

Some of us, however, are especially prone to notice and remember threats (Mitte, 2008). This tendency may place us at risk for one of the **anxiety disorders,** marked by distressing, persistent anxiety or by maladaptive behaviors that reduce anxiety. For example, a man with a fear of social settings may avoid going out. This behavior is maladaptive because it reduces his anxiety but does not help him cope with his world.

In this section we focus on three anxiety disorders:

- *Generalized anxiety disorder,* in which a person is constantly tense and uneasy for no apparent reason.

- *Panic disorder,* in which a person experiences sudden episodes of intense dread and often lives in fear of when the next attack might strike.

- *Phobias,* in which a person feels irrationally and intensely afraid of a specific object or situation.

Two other disorders involve anxiety, though the DSM-5 now classifies them separately:

- *Obsessive-compulsive disorder,* in which a person is troubled by repetitive thoughts or actions.

- *Posttraumatic stress disorder,* in which a person has lingering memories, nightmares, and other symptoms for weeks after a severely threatening, uncontrollable event.

Generalized Anxiety Disorder

Tom is a 27-year-old electrician. For the past two years, he has been bothered by dizziness, sweating palms, irregular heartbeat, and ringing in his ears. He feels on edge and sometimes finds himself shaking. Tom has been fairly successful at hiding his symptoms from his family and co-workers, but sometimes he has to leave work. He allows himself few other social contacts. Neither his family doctor nor a neurologist has been able to find any physical problem.

Tom's restless, unfocused, out-of-control, and agitated feelings suggest **generalized anxiety disorder.** The symptoms of this disorder are commonplace; their persistence is not. People with this condition worry continually, and they are often jittery, on edge, and sleep deprived. Concentration is difficult, as attention switches from worry to worry. Their tension may leak out through furrowed brows, twitching eyelids, trembling, sweating, or fidgeting.

The person may not be able to identify and therefore relieve or avoid the tension's cause. To use Sigmund Freud's term, the anxiety is *free-floating* (not linked with a specific stressor or threat). Generalized anxiety disorder and depression often go hand in hand, but even without depression this disorder tends to be disabling (Hunt et al., 2004; Moffitt et al., 2007b). Moreover, it may lead to physical problems, such as high blood pressure.

Two-thirds of those with generalized anxiety disorder are women. The

LIVING WITH AN ANXIETY DISORDER NBA basketball player Royce White speaks openly about his generalized anxiety disorder and associated fear of flying (Wrenn, 2012).

anxiety gender difference appeared in a Gallup poll taken eight months after 9/11. More U.S. women (34 percent) than men (19 percent) said they were still less willing than before 9/11 to go into skyscrapers or fly on planes. And in early 2003, more women (57 percent) than men (36 percent) said they were "somewhat worried" about becoming a terrorist victim (Jones, 2003).

Some people with generalized anxiety disorder were treated badly and felt inhibited when they were children (Moffitt et al., 2007a). As time passes, emotions tend to mellow. By age 50, generalized anxiety disorder becomes rare (Rubio & López-Ibor, 2007).

Panic Disorder

In **panic disorder,** anxiety suddenly escalates into a terrifying *panic attack*—a minutes-long feeling of intense fear that something horrible is about to happen. Irregular heartbeat, chest pains, shortness of breath, choking, trembling, or dizziness may accompany the fear. One woman recalled suddenly feeling "hot and as though I couldn't breathe. My heart was racing and I started to sweat and tremble and I was sure I was going to faint. Then my fingers started to feel numb and tingly and things seemed unreal. It was so bad I wondered if I was dying and asked my husband to take me to the emergency room. By the time we got there (about 10 minutes) the worst of the attack was over and I just felt washed out" (Greist et al., 1986). This anxiety tornado strikes suddenly, does its damage, and disappears, but it is not forgotten. After experiencing even a few panic attacks, people may come to fear the fear itself.

Those having (or observing) a panic attack often misread the symptoms as an impending heart attack or other serious physical ailment. Smokers have at least a doubled risk of a panic attack (Zvolensky & Bernstein, 2005). Because nicotine is a stimulant, lighting up doesn't lighten up.

PLAYING THROUGH PANIC Golfer Charlie Beljan suffered panic and a racing pulse during a 2012 PGA golf tournament. After finishing, he left in an ambulance and spent the night in a hospital before returning the next day and winning $846,000.

Phobias

We all live with some fears. People with **phobias** are consumed by a persistent, irrational fear and avoidance of some object or situation. Marilyn, an otherwise healthy and happy 28-year-old, so fears thunderstorms that she feels anxious as soon as a weather forecast mentions possible storms later in the week. If her husband is away and a storm is forecast, she may stay with a close relative. During a storm, she hides from windows and buries her head to avoid seeing the lightning. *Specific phobias* such as Marilyn's typically focus on particular animals,

anxiety disorders psychological disorders characterized by distressing, persistent anxiety or maladaptive behaviors that reduce anxiety.

generalized anxiety disorder an anxiety disorder in which a person is continually tense, fearful, and in a state of autonomic nervous system arousal.

panic disorder an anxiety disorder marked by unpredictable minutes-long episodes of intense dread in which a person may experience terror and accompanying chest pain, choking, or other frightening sensations, followed by worry about a possible next attack.

phobia an anxiety disorder marked by a persistent, irrational fear and avoidance of a specific object or situation.

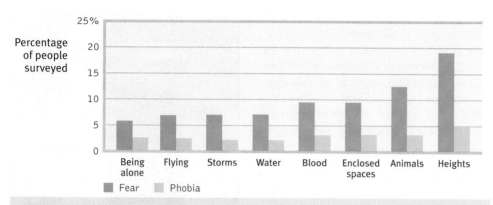

FIGURE 13.1 Some common and uncommon specific fears Researchers surveyed Dutch people to identify the most common events or objects they feared. A strong fear becomes a phobia if it provokes a compelling but irrational desire to avoid the dreaded object or situation. (From Depla et al., 2008.)

insects, heights, blood, or enclosed spaces (**FIGURE 13.1**).

Not all phobias are so specific. The constant fear of having another panic attack can lead people with panic disorder to avoid situations where panic might strike. Their avoidance itself may lead to a diagnosis of *agoraphobia*, the fear of again experiencing the dreaded tornado of anxiety. The fear of being unable to escape or get help during an attack may cause people with agoraphobia to avoid being outside the home, in a crowd, or on a bus. Those with *social anxiety disorder* (formerly called social phobia) may also avoid going out, but for different reasons. Their intense fear of being judged by others may cause them to avoid social situations such as speaking up, eating out, or going to parties, or they may sweat or tremble when doing so. ∎

Obsessive-Compulsive Disorder (OCD)

13-6 What is OCD?

As with generalized anxiety and phobias, we can see aspects of our own behavior in **obsessive-compulsive disorder (OCD)**. *Obsessive thoughts* (recall Marc's focus on cleaning his room) are unwanted and so repetitive it may seem they will never go away. *Compulsive behaviors* are responses to those thoughts (cleaning and cleaning and cleaning).

All of us are at times obsessed with senseless or offensive thoughts that will not go away. Have you ever caught yourself behaving compulsively, per-

SNAPSHOTS

Obsessing about obsessive-compulsive disorder.

haps rigidly checking, ordering, and cleaning before guests arrive, or lining up books and pencils "just so" before you begin studying? On a small scale, obsessive thoughts and compulsive behaviors are part of everyday life. They cross the fine line between normality and disorder when they *interfere* with everyday life and cause us distress. Checking to see if you locked the door is normal; checking 10 times is not. Washing your hands is normal; washing so often that your skin becomes raw is not. Normal rehearsals and fussy behaviors become a disorder when the obsessive thoughts are so haunting, the compulsive rituals so senselessly time-consuming, that effective functioning becomes impossible.

Posttraumatic Stress Disorder (PTSD)

13-7 What is PTSD?

As an Iraq war soldier, Jesse "saw the murder of children and women. It was just horrible for anyone to experience." After calling in a helicopter strike on one house where he had seen ammunition crates carried in, he heard the screams of children from within. "I didn't know there were kids there," he recalled. Back home in Texas, he suffered "real bad flashbacks" (Welch, 2005).

Jesse is not alone. In one study of 103,788 veterans returning from Iraq and Afghanistan, 25 percent were diagnosed with a psychological disorder (Seal et al., 2007). The most frequent diagnosis was **posttraumatic stress disorder (PTSD)**. Typical symptoms include recurring haunting memories and nightmares, a numb feeling of social withdrawal, jumpy anxiety, and trouble sleeping (Hoge et al., 2004, 2006, 2007; Kessler, 2000). Many battle-scarred veterans have been diagnosed with PTSD. Survivors of accidents, disasters, and violent and sexual assaults (including an estimated two-thirds of prostitutes) have also experi-

BRINGING THE WAR HOME During his three deployments to Iraq, this Marine staff sergeant suffered traumatic brain injury. After his return home, he was diagnosed with posttraumatic stress disorder. He regularly travels two hours each way with his wife to Bethesda Naval Hospital for psychiatric and medical appointments.

enced these symptoms (Brewin et al., 1999; Farley et al., 1998; Taylor et al., 1998).

The greater one's emotional distress during a trauma, the higher the risk for posttraumatic symptoms (Ozer et al., 2003). Among American military personnel in Afghanistan, 7.6 percent of combatants and 1.4 percent of noncombatants developed PTSD (McNally, 2012). Among New Yorkers who witnessed or responded to the 9/11 terrorist attacks, most did not experience PTSD (Neria et al., 2011). After experiencing a traumatic life event, about 5 to 10 percent of people develop PTSD (Bonanno et al., 2011). PTSD diagnoses among survivors who had been inside the World Trade Center during the attack were, however, double the rates found among those who were outside (Bonanno et al., 2006).

About half of us will experience at least one traumatic event in our lifetime. Why do some people develop PTSD

A $125 million, five-year U.S. Army program is currently assessing the well-being of 800,000 soldiers and training them in emotional resilience (Stix, 2011).

after a traumatic event, but others don't? Some people may have more sensitive emotion-processing limbic systems that flood their bodies with stress hormones (Kosslyn, 2005; Ozer & Weiss, 2004). The odds of getting this disorder after a traumatic event are higher for women (about 1 in 10) than for men (1 in 20) (Olff et al., 2007; Ozer & Weiss, 2004).

Some psychologists have suggested that PTSD has been overdiagnosed, due partly to a broader definition of *trauma* (Dobbs, 2009; McNally, 2003). Also, too often, say some critics, PTSD gets stretched to include normal bad memories and dreams after a bad experience. In such cases, some well-intentioned procedures used to treat PTSD may make people feel worse (Wakefield & Spitzer, 2002). For example, survivors may be "debriefed" right after a trauma and asked to revisit the experience and vent their emotions. This tactic has been generally ineffective and sometimes harmful (Devilly et al., 2006; McNally et al., 2003; Rose et al., 2003). Nevertheless, people diagnosed with PTSD can benefit from other therapies, some of which are discussed in Chapter 14.

Most people, male and female, display an impressive *survivor resiliency*, or ability to recover after severe stress (Bonanno, 2004, 2005, 2006). For more on human resilience, and on the *posttraumatic growth* that some experience, see Chapter 14. ■

Understanding Anxiety Disorders, OCD, and PTSD

13-8 How do learning and biology contribute to the feelings and thoughts found in anxiety disorders, OCD, and PTSD?

Anxiety is both a feeling and a thought—a doubt-laden appraisal of one's safety or social skill. How do these anxious feelings and thoughts arise? Sigmund Freud's psychoanalytic theory (Chapter 11) proposed that, beginning in childhood, people *repress* certain impulses, ideas, and feelings. This submerged mental energy sometimes, he thought, leaks out in odd symptoms, such as anxious hand washing. Few of today's psychologists interpret anxiety this way. Most believe that three modern perspectives—conditioning, cognition, and biology—are more helpful.

Conditioning

We are more likely to develop anxiety or PTSD when bad events happen unpredictably and uncontrollably (Field, 2006; Mineka & Zinbarg, 2006). In experiments, researchers have shown how classical conditioning can link our fear responses to formerly neutral objects and events. You may recall from Chapter 6 that the infant called "Little Albert" learned to fear furry objects that were paired with loud noises. And by giving rats unpredictable electric shocks, researchers have created anxious animals (Schwartz, 1984). The rats, like assault victims who report feeling anxious when returning to the scene of the crime, became uneasy

obsessive-compulsive disorder (OCD) a disorder characterized by unwanted repetitive thoughts (obsessions) and/or actions (compulsions).

posttraumatic stress disorder (PTSD) a disorder characterized by haunting memories, nightmares, social withdrawal, jumpy anxiety, numbness of feeling, and/or insomnia lingering for four weeks or more after a traumatic experience.

in their lab environment. The lab had become a cue for fear.

Such research helps explain how panic-prone people come to associate anxiety with certain cues and why anxious or traumatized people are so attentive to possible threats. In one survey, 58 percent of those with social anxiety disorder said their disorder began after a traumatic event (Ost & Hugdahl, 1981).

Two other conditioning processes, *stimulus generalization* and *reinforcement,* can magnify a single painful and frightening event into a full-blown phobia. Stimulus generalization occurs when a person experiences a fearful event and later develops a fear of similar events. My car was once struck by another whose driver missed a stop sign. For months afterward, I felt a twinge of unease when any car approached from a side street. My fear eventually disappeared, but for others, fear may linger and grow. Marilyn's phobia of thunderstorms (a phobia shared by recording artist Madonna) may have similarly generalized after a terrifying or painful experience during a thunderstorm.

Once phobias develop and generalize, they can be maintained by reinforcement, a part of operant conditioning. Anything that helps us avoid or escape from a feared situation reduces our anxiety. This feeling of relief can reinforce phobic behaviors. Fearing a panic attack, a person may decide not to leave the house. Reinforced by feeling calmer, the person is likely to repeat that maladaptive behavior in the future (Antony et al., 1992). Compulsive behaviors operate similarly. If washing your hands relieves your feelings of anxiety, you may wash your hands again when those feelings return.

Cognition

We learn some fears by observing others. For example, why do nearly all monkeys raised in the wild fear snakes, yet lab-raised monkeys do not? Surely, most wild monkeys do not actually suffer snake bites. Do they learn their fear through observation? To find out, one researcher experimented (Mineka, 1985, 2002). Her study focused on six monkeys raised in the wild (all strongly fearful of snakes) and their lab-raised offspring (none of which feared snakes). The young monkeys repeatedly observed their parents or peers refusing to reach for food in the presence of a snake. Can you predict what happened? The young monkeys also developed a strong fear of snakes. When they were retested three months later, their learned fear persisted. We humans learn many of our own fears by observing others (Olsson et al., 2007).

Our interpretations and expectations also shape our reactions. Whether we panic in response to a creaky sound in an old house depends on whether we interpret the sound as the wind or as a possible knife-wielding intruder. These misinterpretations can develop into irrational beliefs. A pounding heart is seen as a sign of a heart attack. A lone spider near the bed becomes a likely infestation. An everyday disagreement with a partner or boss spells possible doom for the relationship. These thoughts can trigger the overly watchful state known as *hypervigilance.* Feelings of anxiety are common when people cannot switch off such intrusive thoughts and perceive a loss of control and a sense of helplessness (Franklin & Foa, 2011).

Biology

There is, however, more to anxiety disorders, OCD, and PTSD than learning. Why will some of us develop lasting phobias or PTSD after suffering traumas? Why are some of us more vulnerable to learned fears? Why do we all learn some

Hemera Technologies/Jupiterimages/Getty

Tim Boyles/Getty Images

FEARLESS? The biological perspective helps us understand why most of us have more fear of heights than does Nik Wallenda, shown here crossing the Grand Canyon in 2013 without a security harness or safety net.

fears more easily than others? The biological perspective offers insight.

GENES Genes matter. Among monkeys, fearfulness runs in families. A monkey reacts more strongly to stress if its close biological relatives have sensitive, high-strung temperaments (Suomi, 1986).

So, too, with people. Some of us have genes that make us like orchids—fragile, yet capable of beauty under favorable circumstances. Others of us are like dandelions—hardy, and able to thrive in varied circumstances (Ellis & Boyce, 2008). Thus, some of us are genetically predisposed to anxiety, OCD, and PTSD. If one identical twin has an anxiety disorder, the other is likewise at risk (Hettema et al., 2001; Kendler et al., 2002a,b; Taylor, 2011). Even when raised separately, identical twins may develop similar phobias (Carey, 1990; Eckert et al., 1981). One pair of separated identical twins independently became so afraid of water that, even at age 35, they would wade into the ocean backwards and only up to their knees. Researchers have found genes associated with OCD (Dodman et al., 2010; Hu et al., 2006) and with typical anxiety disorder symptoms (Hovatta et al., 2005).

THE BRAIN Traumatic experiences alter our brain, paving new pathways. These fear pathways create easy inroads for more fear experiences (Armony et al., 1998). Generalized anxiety, panic attacks, phobias, and PTSD reflect a brain danger detection system gone hyperactive—producing anxiety when no danger exists.

Generalized anxiety disorder, panic attacks, PTSD, and OCD express themselves biologically as overarousal of brain areas involved in impulse control and habitual behaviors. When the disordered brain detects that something is wrong, it seems to generate a mental hiccup of repeating thoughts or actions (Gehring et al., 2000). Our brain's frontal lobes—where we make plans and form judgments—are among the affected areas. Brain scans of people with OCD show elevated activity in specific frontal lobe brain areas during behaviors such as compulsive hand washing, checking, ordering, or hoarding (Insel, 2010; Mataix-Cols et al., 2004, 2005).

NATURAL SELECTION No matter how fearful or fearless we are, we humans seem biologically prepared to fear the threats our ancestors faced—spiders and snakes, enclosed spaces and heights, storms and darkness. (In the distant past, those who did not fear these threats were less likely to survive and leave descendants.) Thus, even in Britain, which has only one poisonous snake species, people often fear snakes. And we have these fears at very young ages. Preschool children detect snakes in a scene faster than they spot flowers, caterpillars, or frogs (LoBue & DeLoache, 2008). Our Stone Age fears are easy to condition and hard to extinguish (Davey, 1995; Öhman, 1986).

Some of our modern fears may also stem from our evolutionary past. For example, a fear of flying may have grown from a fear of confinement and heights, which can be traced to our biological past. Our phobias focus on dangers our ancestors faced.

Compare these easily conditioned fears to what we humans *don't* easily learn to fear. World War II air raids, for example, produced remarkably few lasting phobias. As the air strikes continued,

Martin Harvey/Jupiterimages

the British, Japanese, and German populations did not become more and more panicked. Rather, they grew more indifferent to planes outside their immediate neighborhood (Mineka & Zinbarg, 1996). Evolution has not prepared us to fear bombs dropping from the sky.

Just as our phobias focus on dangers faced by our ancestors, our compulsive acts typically exaggerate behaviors that contributed to our species' survival. Grooming gone wild becomes hair pulling. Washing up becomes ritual hand washing. Checking territorial boundaries becomes repeatedly rechecking an already locked door (Rapoport, 1989).

The biological perspective explains a great deal, but it cannot explain the sharp increase in the anxiety levels of U.S. children and college students over the last half-century. That increase appears related to unrealistic expectations, a greater focus on the self than on the community, and a loss of social support (Twenge, 2000). Thus, natural selection shapes our anxious tendencies, but culture and experience also influence our reactions. ■

RETRIEVE + REMEMBER

• Researchers believe that anxiety disorders, OCD, and PTSD are influenced by conditioning and cognition. What other factors contribute to these disorders?

ANSWER: Biological factors also play a role. They may include inherited temperament and other gene variations; learned fears that have altered brain pathways; and outdated, inherited responses that had survival value for our distant ancestors.

Substance Use and Addictive Disorders

13-9 What are substance use disorders, and what role do tolerance, withdrawal, and addiction play in these disorders?

Most of us manage to use some nonprescription drugs—caffeine, alcohol, and painkillers, for example—in moderation and without disrupting our lives. But some of us develop a self-harming **substance use disorder** (TABLE 13.2 on the next page). People with these disorders may have trouble completing schoolwork, maintaining healthy relationships, or holding a job. They may be unable to care for their children. They may drive dangerously or lose control of machinery while "under the influence." Conflicts over getting, using, or not using the substance may be frequent enough to interfere with their daily life. The substances they are using are **psychoactive drugs,** chemicals that change perceptions and mood.

A drug's overall effect depends not only on its *biological* effects but also on the *psychology* of the user's expectations, which vary with *cultures* (Scott-Sheldon et al., 2012; Ward, 1994). If one culture assumes that a particular drug produces good feelings or aggression or sexual arousal, and another does not, each culture may find its expectations fulfilled. In the pages that follow, we'll take a closer look at these interacting forces in the use and potential abuse of particular psychoactive drugs. But first, let's see how our bodies react to the ongoing use of psychoactive drugs.

substance use disorder continued substance craving and use despite significant life disruption and/or physical risk.

psychoactive drug a chemical substance that alters perceptions and mood.

TABLE 13.2   When Is Drug Use a Disorder?

A person may be diagnosed with *substance use disorder* when drug use continues despite significant life disruption. Resulting brain pathway changes may persist after quitting use of the substance (leading to strong cravings when with people and situations that trigger memories of drug use). Severity ranges from *mild* (two to three symptoms) to *moderate* (four to five symptoms) to *severe* (six or more symptoms) (American Psychiatric Association, 2013).

Impaired Control

1. Uses more substance, or for longer, than intended
2. Tries unsuccessfully to regulate substance use
3. Spends much time gaining, using, or recovering from substance use
4. Craves the substance

Social Impairment

5. Use disrupts obligations at work, school, or home
6. Continues use despite social problems
7. Causes reduced social, recreational, and work activities

Risky Use

8. Continues use despite hazards
9. Continues use despite worsening physical or psychological problems

Drug Action

10. Experiences tolerance (needing more substance for the desired effect)
11. Experiences withdrawal when attempting to end use

Tolerance and Addiction

Why might a person who rarely drinks alcohol get buzzed on one can of beer, while a long-term drinker shows few effects until the second six-pack? The answer is **tolerance.** With continued use of alcohol and some other drugs (marijuana is an exception), the user's brain chemistry adapts to offset the drug's effect. To experience the same result, the user needs to take larger and larger doses of the substance (**FIGURE 13.2**).

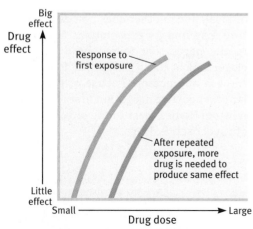

FIGURE 13.2 Drug tolerance

Ever-increasing doses of most psychoactive drugs can pose a serious threat to health. In some cases, they lead to **addiction:** The person craves and uses the substance despite harmful consequences. Sometimes even *behaviors* become compulsive and dysfunctional, much like abusive drug taking. Thus, the DSM-5 now includes behavior addictions, such as gambling disorder and hoarding disorder, and proposes Internet gaming disorder "for further study" (American Psychiatric Association, 2013).

Those with addictions often try to fight them. But abruptly stopping the drug or behavior can lead to the undesirable side effects of **withdrawal.** Heavy coffee drinkers who skip their usual caffeine know the feeling when a headache or grogginess strikes.

The three major categories of psychoactive drugs are *depressants, stimulants,* and *hallucinogens.* All do their work at the brain's synapses. They stimulate, inhibit, or mimic the activity of the brain's own chemical messengers, the neurotransmitters. ∎

Depressants

13-10 How do depressants, such as alcohol, influence neural activity and behavior?

Depressants are drugs such as alcohol, barbiturates (tranquilizers), and opiates that calm (depress) neural activity and slow body functions.

ALCOHOL True or false? In large amounts, alcohol is a depressant; in small amounts, it is a stimulant. *False.* Low doses of alcohol may, indeed, enliven a drinker, but they do so by acting as a *disinhibitor*—they slow brain activity that controls judgment and inhibitions.

Unleashing urges. Alcohol is an equal-opportunity drug. It increases helpful tendencies, as when tipsy restaurant patrons leave big tips (Lynn, 1988). And it increases harmful tendencies (Hirsh et al., 2011). Thus, sexually aggressive college men, knowing that "beauty is in the eyes of the beer holder," may lower their dates' inhibitions by getting them to drink (Abbey, 1991; Mosher & Anderson, 1986). Each year, drinking has contributed to some 1400 deaths, 70,000 sexual assaults, and 500,000 injuries of U.S. college students (Hingson et al., 2002).

In one survey of 18,000 students at 140 colleges and universities, almost

"That is not one of the seven habits of highly effective people."

9 in 10 students reported harm or abuse by intoxicated peers. That abuse included sleep and study interruption, insults, sexual advances, and property damage (Wechsler et al., 1994). In a follow-up survey, 44 percent of students admitted binge drinking within the previous two weeks (Wechsler et al., 2002). *The point to remember:* The urges you would feel if sober are the ones you will more likely act upon after drinking.

Slowed neural processing. Low doses of alcohol relax the drinker by slowing sympathetic nervous system activity. Larger doses cause reactions to slow, speech to slur, and skilled performance to deteriorate. Paired with lack of sleep, alcohol is a potent sedative. Add these physical effects to lowered inhibitions, and the result can be deadly. Worldwide, several hundred thousand lives are lost each year in alcohol-related accidents and violent crime. When sober, most drinkers believe that driving under the influence of alcohol is wrong, and they insist they would not do so. That belief disappears as blood-alcohol level rises and moral judgments become fuzzy. Most will drive home from a bar, even if given a breathalyzer test and told they are intoxicated (Denton & Krebs, 1990; MacDonald et al., 1995).

Memory disruption. Some people drink to forget their troubles. And forget they do—alcohol disrupts the processing of recent experiences into long-term memories.

Thus, heavy drinkers may not recall people they met the night before or what they said or did while drunk. These blackouts result in part because alcohol suppresses REM sleep, the part of the sleep cycle that helps fix the day's experiences into permanent memories. Heavy drinking can also have long-term effects on the brain. In rats, at a development period corresponding to human adolescence, binge drinking contributes to the death of nerve cells and reduces the birth rates of new nerve cells. It also impairs the growth of synaptic connections (Crews et al., 2006, 2007).

In those with **alcohol use disorder,** prolonged and excessive drinking can shrink the brain. Women **(FIGURE 13.3)** are especially vulnerable because they have less of a stomach enzyme that digests alcohol (Wuethrich, 2001). Girls and young women can become addicted to alcohol more quickly than boys and young men do. They also suffer lung, brain, and liver damage at lower consumption levels (CASA, 2003).

A strong correlation between early drinking and later addiction appeared in a national survey of 43,000 adults. Of those who began drinking alcohol before age 14, about half (47 percent) later became addicted (Hingson et al., 2006). Of those who began drinking at age 21 or after, only 9 percent showed this addiction. These correlations remained after researchers controlled for smoking, family alcohol history, and antisocial behaviors.

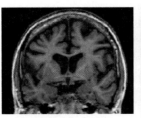
Scan of woman with alcohol use disorder

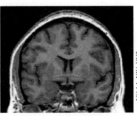
Scan of woman without alcohol use disorder

FIGURE 13.3 Alcohol use disorder shrinks the brain MRI scans show brain shrinkage in women with alcohol use disorder (left) compared with women in a control group (right).

TABLE 13.3 Warning Signs of Alcohol Use Disorder
• Drinking binges
• Craving alcohol
• Use results in unfulfilled work, school, or home tasks
• Continued use when risky
• Failing to honor a resolve to drink less
• Avoiding family or friends when drinking

Few college and university students believe they have an alcohol problem. In fact, many meet the criteria for alcohol use disorder **(TABLE 13.3)**. College and university students drink more alcohol than their nonstudent peers. They spend more on alcohol than on books and other beverages combined. Fraternity and sorority members drink three times as much as other students (Atwell, 1986; Malloy, 1994; Slutske, 2005). As students mature with age, they drink less (Marlatt, 1991).

Effects of expectations. As with other psychoactive drugs, alcohol users' expectations influence their behavior. When people *believe* that alcohol affects social behavior in certain ways, and *believe,* rightly or wrongly, that they have been drinking alcohol, they will behave accordingly (Scott-Sheldon et al., 2012). In one experiment (supposedly a study on "alcohol and sexual stimulation"), researchers gave college male volun-

tolerance with repeated use, the desired effect requires larger doses.

addiction compulsive craving of drugs or certain behaviors (such as gambling) despite known harmful consequences.

withdrawal the discomfort and distress that follow discontinuing an addictive drug or behavior.

depressants drugs (such as alcohol, barbiturates, and opiates) that reduce (depress) neural activity and slow body functions.

alcohol use disorder (popularly known as *alcoholism*). Alcohol use marked by tolerance, withdrawal, and a drive to continue problematic use.

DRINKING DISASTER DEMO Firefighters re-enacted the trauma of an alcohol-related car accident, providing a memorable demonstration for these high school students. Alcohol consumption leads to feelings of invincibility, which become especially dangerous behind the wheel of a car.

teers either an alcoholic or a nonalcoholic drink (Abrams & Wilson, 1983). (Each drink had a strong taste that masked the presence or absence of alcohol.) In each group, half the participants thought they were drinking alcohol and half thought they were not. After watching an erotic movie clip, the men who *thought* they had consumed alcohol were more likely to report having strong sexual fantasies and feeling guilt-free. Being able to explain their sexual responses as reactions to alcohol released their inhibitions—whether or not they had actually consumed any alcohol. If, as commonly believed, liquor is the quicker pick-her-upper, the effect lies partly in that powerful sex organ, the mind.

BARBITURATES Like alcohol, the **barbiturate** drugs, or *tranquilizers,* depress nervous system activity. Barbiturates such as Nembutal, Seconal, and Amytal are sometimes prescribed to induce sleep or reduce anxiety. In larger doses, they can impair memory and judgment. If combined with alcohol, the total depressive effect on body functions can lead to death. This sometimes happens when people take a sleeping pill after an evening of heavy drinking.

OPIATES The **opiates**—opium and its offshoots, such as heroin, also depress

nervous system activity. (Opiates include the narcotics, such as codeine and morphine, which physicians prescribe for pain relief.) As blissful pleasure replaces pain and anxiety, the user's pupils constrict, breathing slows, and *lethargy* (a feeling of extreme relaxation and a lack of energy) sets in. For this short-term pleasure, the person may pay a long-term price: a gnawing craving for another fix, a need for progressively larger doses (as tolerance develops), and the extreme discomfort of withdrawal. (*Methadone,* a synthetic opiate drug prescribed as a substitute for heroin or for relief of chronic pain, can also produce tolerance.) When repeatedly flooded with an artificial opiate, the brain eventually stops producing *endorphins,* its own feel-good opiates. If the artificial opiate is then withdrawn, the brain lacks the normal level of these natural painkillers. Those who cannot or choose not to endure this state may pay an ultimate price—death by overdose. ■

RETRIEVE + REMEMBER

• Alcohol, barbiturates, and opiates are all in a class of drugs called _____.

ANSWER: depressants

Stimulants

13-11 How do the major stimulants affect neural activity and behavior?

A **stimulant** excites neural activity and speeds up body functions. Pupils dilate. Heart and breathing rates increase. Blood-sugar levels rise, causing a drop in appetite. Energy and self-confidence also rise.

Stimulants include caffeine, nicotine, the **amphetamines,** cocaine, methamphetamine, and Ecstasy (NIDA, 2002, 2005). People use stimulants to feel alert, lose weight, or boost mood or athletic performance.

> *"There is an overwhelming medical and scientific consensus that cigarette smoking causes lung cancer, heart disease, emphysema, and other serious diseases in smokers. Smokers are far more likely to develop serious diseases, like lung cancer, than nonsmokers."*
> Philip Morris Companies Inc., 1999

NIC-A-TEEN Virtually nobody starts smoking past the vulnerable teen years. Eager to hook customers whose addiction will give them business for years to come, cigarette companies target teens. Portrayals of smoking by popular actors, such as Robert Pattinson in *Remember Me,* entice teens to imitate.

Unfortunately, stimulants can be addictive, as you may know if you are one of the many who use caffeine daily in your coffee, tea, soda, or energy drinks. Cut off from your usual dose, you may crash into fatigue, headaches, irritability, and depression (Silverman et al., 1992).

NICOTINE One of the most addictive stimulants is **nicotine,** found in cigarettes and other tobacco products. Are tobacco products at least as addictive as heroin and cocaine? *Yes* (see **TABLE 13.4**). Attempts to quit even within the first weeks of smoking often fail (DiFranza, 2008). And, as with other addictions, smokers develop *tolerance.* If you are a smoker who has tried unsuccess-

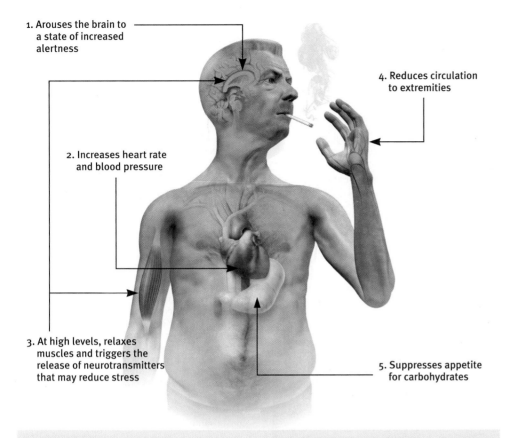

1. Arouses the brain to a state of increased alertness

2. Increases heart rate and blood pressure

3. At high levels, relaxes muscles and triggers the release of neurotransmitters that may reduce stress

4. Reduces circulation to extremities

5. Suppresses appetite for carbohydrates

FIGURE 13.4 Where there's smoke . . . : The physiological effects of nicotine Nicotine reaches the brain within 7 seconds, twice as fast as intravenous heroin. Within minutes, the amount in the blood soars.

fully to kick your habit, you probably aren't surprised. Addicted customers are loyal customers. Nearly 1 billion of them will be rewarded for their loyalty with a tobacco-related death (WHO, 2012).

A burning cigarette is a portable nicotine dispenser. Within 7 seconds (twice as fast as intravenous heroin), a rush of nicotine signals the central nervous

TABLE 13.4 The Odds of Getting Hooked After Trying Various Drugs	
Marijuana	9%
Alcohol	15
Cocaine	17
Heroin	23
Tobacco	32

Source: National Academy of Science, Institute of Medicine (Brody, 2003).

system to release a flood of neurotransmitters (**FIGURE 13.4**). Epinephrine and norepinephrine diminish appetite and boost alertness and mental efficiency. Dopamine and opioids calm anxiety and reduce sensitivity to pain (Nowak, 1994; Scott et al., 2004).

These mood-altering effects are very reinforcing, and they are especially potent when combined with the punishment of nicotine-withdrawal symptoms, which include craving, insomnia, anxiety, and irritability. The combined package keeps people smoking, even among the 8 in 10 smokers who wish they could stop (Jones, 2007). Each year, fewer than 1 in 7 smokers who want to quit will be able to resist. Even those who know they are committing slow-motion suicide may be unable to stop (Saad, 2002).

Nevertheless, repeated attempts seem to pay off. Half of all Americans who have ever smoked have quit, and more than 90 percent did so on their own. Success is equally likely whether smokers quit abruptly or gradually (Fiore et al., 2008; Lichtenstein et al., 2010; Lindson et al., 2010). The acute craving and withdrawal symptoms do go away gradually over six months (Ward et al., 1997). After a year's abstinence, only 10 percent return to smoking (Hughes et al., 2008). ■

RETRIEVE + REMEMBER

- Why do tobacco companies try so hard to get customers hooked as teens?

ANSWER: Nicotine is powerfully addictive, expensive, and deadly. Those who start paying the neural pathways when young may find it very hard to stop using nicotine. As a result, tobacco companies may have lifelong customers.

COCAINE Cocaine users travel a fast track from flying high to crashing to earth. The recipe for Coca-Cola originally included an extract of the coca plant, creating a tonic laced with a small amount of cocaine for tired elderly people. Between 1896 and 1905, Coke was indeed "the real thing." But no longer. Cocaine is now snorted, injected, or smoked. It enters the bloodstream quickly, producing a rush of *euphoria*—feelings of great happiness and well-being. Those feelings continue until the brain's supply of the neurotransmitters

barbiturates drugs that depress the activity of the central nervous system, reducing anxiety but impairing memory and judgment.

opiates opium and its derivatives, such as morphine and heroin; they depress neural activity, temporarily lessening pain and anxiety.

stimulants drugs (such as caffeine, nicotine, and the more powerful amphetamines, cocaine, Ecstasy, and methamphetamines) that excite neural activity and speed up body functions.

amphetamines drugs that stimulate neural activity, causing speeded-up body functions and associated energy and mood changes.

nicotine a stimulating and highly addictive psychoactive drug in tobacco.

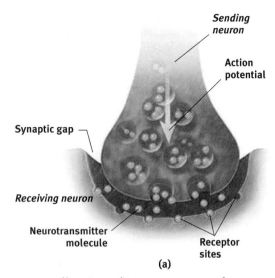

(a)

Neurotransmitters carry a message from a sending neuron across a synapse to receptor sites on a receiving neuron.

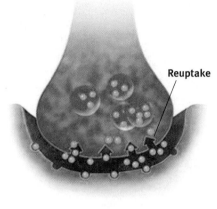

(b)

The sending neuron normally reabsorbs excess neurotransmitter molecules, a process called *reuptake*.

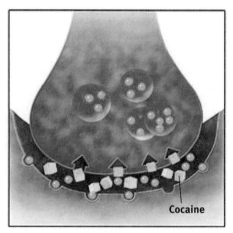

(c)

By binding to the sites that normally reabsorb neurotransmitter molecules, cocaine blocks reuptake of dopamine, norepinephrine, and serotonin (Ray & Ksir, 1990). The extra neurotransmitter molecules therefore remain in the synapse, intensifying their normal mood-altering effects and producing a euphoric rush. When the cocaine level drops, the absence of these neurotransmitters produces a crash.

FIGURE 13.5 Cocaine euphoria and crash

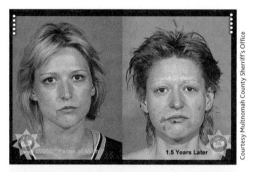

DRAMATIC DRUG-INDUCED DECLINE This woman's methamphetamine addiction led to obvious physical changes just 18 months after she started.

dopamine, serotonin, and norepinephrine drops off (**FIGURE 13.5**). Then, within a mere 15 to 30 minutes, a crash of agitated depression follows. Many regular cocaine users chasing this high become addicted. In the lab, cocaine-addicted monkeys have pressed levers more than 12,000 times to gain one cocaine injection (Siegel, 1990). Cocaine-addicted adults likewise may take extreme action, including crime, to gain more doses.

Cocaine's psychological effects depend in part on the dosage and form consumed, but the situation and the user's expectations and personality also play a role. Given a placebo, cocaine users who *thought* they were taking cocaine often had a cocaine-like experience (Van Dyke & Byck, 1982).

METHAMPHETAMINE The highly addictive **methamphetamine** triggers the release of the neurotransmitter dopamine, which stimulates brain cells that enhance energy and mood. Eight or so hours of heightened energy and mood then follow. Aftereffects may include irritability, insomnia, high blood pres-

sure, seizures, periods of disorientation, and occasional violent behavior. Over time, methamphetamine use appears to permanently reduce the brain's normal output of dopamine.

ECSTASY Ecstasy is the street name for **MDMA** (methylenedioxymethamphetamine). This powerful drug is both a stimulant and a mild hallucinogen. (*Hallucinogens,* as we will see in the next section, distort perceptions and lead to false sensory images.) Ecstasy is an amphetamine derivative that triggers the brain's release of dopamine. But its major effect is releasing stored serotonin and blocking its reuptake, thus

prolonging serotonin's feel-good flood (Braun, 2001). Users feel the effect about a half-hour after taking an Ecstasy pill. For three or four hours, they experience high energy and emotional elevation. They feel intimately connected to the people around them. ("I love everyone.")

During the late 1990s, Ecstasy's popularity soared as a "club drug" taken at nightclubs and all-night raves (Landry, 2002). There are, however, reasons not to be ecstatic about Ecstasy. One is its ability to cause dehydration. With prolonged dancing, Ecstasy's side effects can lead to severe overheating, increased blood pressure, and death. Long-term, repeated use can also damage serotonin-producing neurons. Serotonin does more than just make us feel good. It helps regulate our body rhythms (including sleep), our disease-fighting immune system, and our memory and other cognitive functions (Laws & Kokkalis, 2007; Pacifici et al., 2001; Schilt et al., 2007). Ecstasy interferes with all of these functions. The decreased serotonin output can be permanent and can lead to a permanently depressed mood (Croft et al., 2001; McCann et

Courtesy Multnomah County Sheriff's Office

al., 2001; Roiser et al., 2005). Ecstasy delights for the night but darkens the tomorrow.

Hallucinogens

13-12 What are the physiological and psychological effects of LSD and marijuana?

Among the least addictive drugs are the **hallucinogens.** These substances distort perceptions and call up sensory images (such as sounds or sights) without any input from the senses. This helps explain why these drugs are also called *psychedelics,* meaning "mind-manifesting." Some are synthetic. The best known synthetic hallucinogens are MDMA (Ecstasy), discussed earlier, and LSD. Others, such as the mild hallucinogen marijuana, are natural substances.

LSD In 1943, Albert Hofmann reported perceiving "an uninterrupted stream of fantastic pictures, extraordinary shapes with an intense, kaleidoscopic play of colors" (Siegel, 1984). Hofmann, a chemist, created and accidentally ingested **LSD** (lysergic acid diethylamide). LSD, like Ecstasy, interferes with the serotonin neurotransmitter system. An LSD "trip" can take users to unexpected places. Emotions may vary from euphoria to detachment to panic, depending in part on the person's current mood and expectations.

Even so, the perceptual distortions and hallucinations have some things in common. Whether provoked to hallucinate by drugs, loss of oxygen, or extreme sensory deprivation, the brain hallucinates in basically the same way (Siegel, 1982). The experience typically begins with simple geometric forms, such as a criss-cross, a cobweb, or a spiral. The next phase consists of more meaningful images. Some may be seen in front of a tunnel, others may be replays of past emotional experiences. As the hallucination peaks, users frequently feel separated from their bodies. Dreamlike scenes feel so real that people may become panic-stricken or harm themselves.

From Hallucinations by Ronald K. Siegel, *Scientific American 237*, 132–139 (1977)

FIGURE 13.6 Hallucination or near-death vision? People under the influence of hallucinogenic drugs often see "a bright light in the center of the field of vision.... The location of this point of light create[s] a tunnel-like perspective" (Siegel, 1977). This is very similar to others' reported near-death experiences.

These sensations are strikingly similar to the **near-death experience.** This altered state of consciousness is reported by about one-third of those who survive a brush with death, as when revived from cardiac arrest (Moody, 1976; Ring, 1980; Schnaper, 1980). Many describe visions of tunnels (**FIGURE 13.6**), bright lights or beings of light, a replay of old memories, and out-of-body sensations (Siegel, 1980). Oxygen deprivation and other insults to the brain can produce hallucinations. Following temporal lobe seizures, for example, patients have reported similarly profound mystical experiences. So have solitary sailors and polar explorers while enduring monotony, isolation, and cold (Suedfeld & Mocellin, 1987). Under stress, the brain can manufacture seeming near-death experiences.

MARIJUANA For 5000 years, hemp has been cultivated for its fiber. The leaves and flowers of this plant, which are sold as *marijuana,* contain **THC** (delta-9-tetrahydrocannabinol). Marijuana is a difficult drug to classify. Whether smoked (getting to the brain in a mere 7

seconds) or eaten (producing slower, less intense effects), THC produces a mix of effects. Marijuana is a mild hallucinogen, increasing sensitivity to colors, sounds, tastes, and smells. But like alcohol, marijuana also relaxes, disinhibits, and may produce a euphoric high. Both drugs impair the motor coordination, perceptual skills, and reaction time necessary for safely operating an automobile or other machine. "THC causes animals to misjudge events," reported Ronald Siegel (1990, p. 163). "Pigeons wait too long to respond to buzzers or lights that tell them food is available for brief periods; and rats turn the wrong way in mazes."

Marijuana and alcohol differ in other ways. The body eliminates alcohol within hours. THC and its by-products linger in the body for a month or more, which means that regular users may experience a less abrupt withdrawal. They may also achieve a high with smaller amounts of the drug than would be needed by an occasional user. This is contrary to the usual path of tolerance, in which repeat users need to take larger doses to feel the same effect.

A user's experience can vary with the situation. If the user feels anxious

methamphetamine a powerfully addictive drug that stimulates the central nervous system with speeded-up body functions and associated energy and mood changes; over time, appears to reduce baseline dopamine levels.

Ecstasy (MDMA) a synthetic stimulant and mild hallucinogen. Produces euphoria and social intimacy, but with short-term health risks and longer-term harm to serotonin-producing neurons and to mood and cognition.

hallucinogens psychedelic ("mind-manifesting") drugs, such as LSD, that distort perceptions and evoke sensory images in the absence of sensory input.

LSD a powerful hallucinogenic drug; also known as *acid (lysergic acid diethylamide).*

near-death experience an altered state of consciousness reported after a close brush with death (such as through cardiac arrest); often similar to drug-induced hallucinations.

THC the major active ingredient in marijuana; triggers a variety of effects, including mild hallucinations.

or depressed, marijuana may intensify these feelings. The more often the person uses it, the greater the risk of anxiety, depression, or, possibly, schizophrenia. These correlations held even after researchers controlled for other drug use and personal traits (Hall, 2006; Murray et al., 2007; Patton et al., 2002). Marijuana also disrupts memory formation and interferes with immediate recall of information learned only a few minutes before. Such effects on thinking outlast the period of smoking (Pope & Yurgelun-Todd, 1996; Smith, 1995).

To free up resources to fight crime, some states have passed laws legalizing the possession of small quantities of marijuana. In some cases, legal *medical marijuana* use has been granted to relieve the pain, nausea, and severe weight loss associated with diseases such as cancer and AIDS (Watson et al., 2000). In such cases, the Institute of Medicine recommends medical inhalers to deliver the THC without toxic marijuana smoke.

* * *

TABLE 13.5 summarizes the psychoactive drugs discussed in this section. They share some features. All trigger negative aftereffects that counter the drug's immediate positive effects. As negative aftereffects grow stronger with repetition, larger and larger doses are typically needed to produce the desired positive effect. (This

process is *tolerance*.) These increasingly larger doses produce even worse aftereffects in the drug's absence. (This process is *withdrawal*.) The worsening aftereffects in turn create a need to switch off the withdrawal symptoms by taking yet more of the drug. (This process is *addiction*.) ■

RETRIEVE + REMEMBER

How strange would appear to be this thing that men call pleasure! And how curiously it is related to what is thought to be its opposite, pain! . . . Wherever the one is found, the other follows up behind."

Plato, *Phaedo*, fourth century B.C.E.

• How does this pleasure-pain description apply to the repeated use of psychoactive drugs?

ANSWER: Psychoactive drugs create pleasure by altering brain chemistry. With repeated use of the drug, the brain develops tolerance and needs more of the drug to achieve the desired effect. (Marijuana is an exception.) Discontinuing use of the substance then produces painful or psychologically unpleasant withdrawal symptoms.

Understanding Substance Use Disorder

13-13 What biological, psychological, and social-cultural factors help explain why some people abuse mind-altering drugs?

Substance use by North American youth increased during the 1970s. Then, with

increased drug education and a shift toward more realism in media portrayals of the effects of drugs, substance use declined sharply. After the early 1990s, the cultural antidrug voice softened, and drugs for a time have again been glamorized in some music and films (**FIGURE 13.7**).

For many adolescents, occasional drug use represents thrill seeking. Why do some adolescents but not others become regular drug abusers? In search of answers, researchers have tried to sort out biological, psychological, and social-cultural influences.

Biological Influences

Are some of us biologically vulnerable to particular drugs? Evidence indicates we are (Crabbe, 2002):

- Having an identical twin with alcohol use disorder puts one at increased risk for alcohol problems. In marijuana use also, identical twins more closely resemble each other (Kendler et al., 2002). This increased risk is not found among fraternal twins.

- Boys who at age 6 are excitable, impulsive, and fearless (genetically influenced traits) are more likely as teens to smoke, drink, and abuse other drugs (Masse & Tremblay, 1997).

- Some genes are more common among people and animals

Drug	Type	Pleasurable Effects	Negative Aftereffects
Alcohol	Depressant	Initial high followed by relaxation and disinhibition	Impaired reactions, depression, memory loss, organ damage
Heroin	Depressant	Rush of euphoria, relief from pain	Depressed physiology, agonizing withdrawal
Caffeine	Stimulant	Increased alertness and wakefulness	In high doses, anxiety, restlessness, and insomnia; uncomfortable withdrawal
Nicotine	Stimulant	Arousal and relaxation, sense of well-being	Heart disease, cancer
Cocaine	Stimulant	Rush of euphoria, confidence, energy	Cardiovascular stress, suspiciousness, depressive crash
Methamphetamine	Stimulant	Euphoria, alertness, energy	Irritability, insomnia, high blood pressure, seizures
Ecstasy (MDMA)	Stimulant; mild hallucinogen	Euphoria, disinhibition	Dehydration, overheating, depressed mood, impaired cognitive and immune functioning
LSD	Hallucinogen	Visual "trip"	Risk of panic
Marijuana (THC)	Mild hallucinogen	Enhanced sensation, relief of pain, distortion of time, relaxation	Impaired learning and memory, increased risk of psychological disorders, lung damage from smoke

TABLE 13.5 A Guide to Selected Psychoactive Drugs

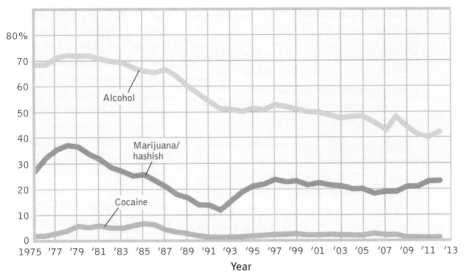

High school seniors reporting drug use

80%
70
60
Alcohol
50
40
Marijuana/ hashish
30
20
Cocaine
10
0
1975 '77 '79 '81 '83 '85 '87 '89 '91 '93 '95 '97 '99 '01 '03 '05 '07 '09 '11 '13
Year

FIGURE 13.7 Trends in drug use The percentage of U.S. high school seniors who said they had used alcohol, marijuana, or cocaine during the past 30 days peaked in the late 1970s. (From Johnston et al., 2013.)

predisposed to alcohol use disorder, and researchers are seeking genes that contribute to tobacco addiction (NIH, 2006; Nurnberger & Bierut, 2007). These genes may, for example, produce deficiencies in the brain's natural dopamine reward system.

Psychological and Social-Cultural Influences

Throughout this text, you have seen a recurring theme. Biological, psychological, and social-cultural influences interact to influence behavior. So, too, with substance use disorder. Feeling that one's life is meaningless and direction-less is a psychological influence that puts youth and young adults at risk (Newcomb & Harlow, 1986). This feeling is common among school dropouts who try to make their way in life without job skills, without privilege, and with little hope.

Sometimes, the psychological influence is obvious. Many heavy users of alcohol, marijuana, and cocaine have experienced significant stress or failure and are depressed. Girls with a history of depression, eating disorders, or sexual or physical abuse are at risk for substance addiction. So are youth undergoing school

or neighborhood transitions (CASA, 2003; Logan et al., 2002). By temporarily dulling the pain of self-awareness, psychoactive drugs may offer a way to avoid coping with depression, anger, anxiety, or insomnia. (As Chapter 6 explains, behavior is often controlled more by its immediate consequences than by its later ones.)

Especially for teenagers, substance use can also have social roots. The media offer easy access to models who

SNAPSHOTS

Once upon a time, peer pressure caused Bob to start smoking.

Twenty years later, it forces him to quit.

(c) Love A141

drink and smoke. For example, in the real world, alcohol accounts for one-sixth or less of beverage use. In TV land, people have drunk alcohol more often than other drinks—coffee, tea, soft drinks, or water—combined (Gerbner, 1990). Teens are also exposed to smoking in movies. Those with high exposure are three times as likely as other teens to try smoking and to become smokers. And that correlation is not a result of personality, parenting style, or family economics, which researchers controlled for (Heatherton & Sargent, 2009). Rates of substance use also vary across cultural and ethnic groups. Among the Amish, Mennonites, Mormons, and Orthodox Jews, alcohol and other substance addiction rates are extremely low (Trimble, 1994). Among African-American teens, rates of drinking, smoking, and cocaine use are sharply lower than among other U.S. teens (Johnston et al., 2007).

For substance use, location matters. Those whose genetic predispositions nudge them toward substance use will find more opportunities and less supervision in cities (Legrand et al., 2005). Relatively drug-free small towns and rural areas restrain substance use.

Regardless of location, peers influence drug-related attitudes and opportunities. Peers throw the parties and provide (or don't provide) the drugs. If an adolescent's friends abuse drugs, the odds are that he or she will, too. If the friends do not, the opportunity may not even arise.

Peer influence is more than what friends do and say. Adolescents' expectations—what they *believe* their friends are doing and favoring—matter too. One study surveyed sixth-graders in 22 U.S. states. How many believed their friends had smoked marijuana? About 14 percent. How many of those friends said they had smoked it? Only 4 percent (Wren, 1999). College students are not immune to such misperceptions.

Drinking dominates social occasions partly because students overestimate their fellow students' enthusiasm for alcohol (Moreira et al., 2009; Prentice & Miller, 1993; Self, 1994). As always with correlations, the traffic between friends' drug use and our own may be two-way. Our friends influence us, but we also select as friends those who share our likes and dislikes.

Teens rarely abuse drugs if they understand the physical and psychological costs, do well in school, feel good about themselves, and are in a peer group that disapproves of early drinking and abusing drugs (Bachman et al., 2007; Hingson, 2006). These findings suggest three tactics for preventing and treating substance use and addiction among young people:

- Educate people about the long-term costs of a drug's temporary pleasures.
- Boost people's self-esteem and purpose in life.
- Modify peer associations or "inoculate" youth against peer pressures by training them in refusal skills. ■

RETRIEVE + REMEMBER

- Studies have found that people who begin drinking in their early teens are much more likely to develop alcohol use disorder than are those who begin at age 21 or after. What possible explanations might there be for this correlation?

ANSWER: Possible explanations include (a) a biological predisposition to both early use and later abuse; (b) brain changes and taste preferences triggered by early use; and (c) enduring habits, attitudes, activities, or peer relationships that could foster alcohol use disorder.

Mood Disorders

13-14 What are the main mood disorders?

 Many of us have had close encounters with the emotional extremes of **mood disorders,** which appear in two principal forms:

- *Major depressive disorder* is a persistent state of hopeless depression.
- *Bipolar disorder* is an alternation between depression and overexcited hyperactivity.

In the past year, have you at some time "felt so depressed that it was difficult to function"? If so, you were not alone. In one national survey, 31 percent of American collegians answered *Yes* (ACHA, 2009). The college years are an exciting time, but they can also be stressful. Perhaps you wanted to go to college right out of high school but couldn't afford it, and now you are struggling to find time for school amid family and work responsibilities. Perhaps social stresses, such as a relationship gone sour or your feeling excluded, have made you feel isolated or plunged you into despair. Dwelling on these thoughts may have you down about your life or your future. You may lack the energy to get things done or even to force yourself out of bed. You may be unable to concentrate, eat, or sleep normally. Occasionally, you may even wonder if you would be better off dead.

To feel bad in reaction to very sad events is to be in touch with reality. In such times, depression is like a car's oil light—a signal that warns us to stop and take appropriate measures. Depression makes sense from an evolutionary perspective. As one social psychologist warned, "If someone offered you a pill that would make you permanently happy, you would be well advised to run fast and run far. Emotion is a compass that tells us what to do, and a compass that is perpetually stuck on NORTH is worthless" (Gilbert, 2006). Biologically speaking, life's purpose is survival and reproduction, not happiness. Just as coughing, vomiting, and various forms of pain protect our body from danger-ous toxins, so depression protects us from dangerous thoughts and feelings. It slows us down and gives us time to think hard and consider our options (Wrosch & Miller, 2009). It defuses aggression, cuts back on risk taking, and focuses our mind (Allen & Badcock, 2003; Andrews & Thomson, 2009).

After reassessing our life, we may redirect our energy in more promising ways. Even mild sadness can make people more discerning, and help them make complex decisions (Forgas, 2009). It can also help them process and recall faces more accurately (Hills et al., 2011). There is sense to suffering.

Sometimes, however, depression becomes seriously maladaptive. How do we recognize the difference between a normal blue mood and abnormal depression?

Major Depressive Disorder

Joy, contentment, sadness, and despair are different points on a continuum, points at which any of us may be found at any given moment. The difference between a blue mood after bad news and **major depressive disorder** is like the difference between gasping for breath after a hard run and having chronic asthma. Major depressive disorder occurs when signs of depression last two or more weeks and are not caused by drugs or a medical condition. These signs include lethargy (extreme lack of energy), feelings of worthlessness, or loss of interest in family, friends, and activities (**TABLE 13.6**). To sense what major depression feels like, imagine combining the anguish of grief with the exhaustion you feel after pulling an all-nighter.

Although phobias are more common, depression is the number one reason people seek mental health services.

Brad Wenner/Getty Images

TABLE 13.6 Diagnosing Major Depressive Disorder

The DSM-5 classifies major depressive disorder as the presence of at least five of the following symptoms (including depressed mood or loss of interest/pleasure) over a two-week period of time. The symptoms must cause near-daily distress or impairment and not be attributable to substance use or another medical or mental illness.

- Depressed mood most of the day
- Loss of interest or pleasure in activities most of the day
- Significant weight loss or gain when not dieting, or significant decrease or increase in appetite
- Insomnia or sleeping too much
- Physical agitation or lethargy
- Fatigue or loss of energy
- Feeling worthless or excessive/inappropriate guilt
- Problems in thinking, concentrating, or making decisions
- Recurrent thoughts of death and suicide

Worldwide, it is the leading cause of disability—afflicting at least 350 million people (WHO, 2012). With or without therapy, most of these people will temporarily or permanently return to their previous nondepressed state.

Adults diagnosed with *persistent depressive disorder* (also called *dysthymia*) experience a mildly depressed mood more often than not for at least two years (American Psychiatric Association, 2013). They also display at least two of depression's symptoms.

Bipolar Disorder

In **bipolar disorder,** people bounce from one emotional extreme to the other (week to week, and not day to day or moment to moment). When a depressive episode ends, an intensely happy, overly talkative, wildly energetic, and extremely optimistic state called **mania** follows. But before long, the elated mood either returns to normal or plunges again into depression.

If depression is living in slow motion, mania is fast forward. During mania, people feel little need for sleep, are easily irritated, and show fewer sexual inhibitions. Feeling extreme optimism and self-esteem, they find advice annoying. Yet they need protection from their poor judgment, which may lead to reckless spending or unsafe sex.

For some people suffering depressive disorders or bipolar disorder, symptoms may have a *seasonal pattern*. Depression may regularly return each fall or winter, and mania (or a reprieve from depression) may dependably arrive with spring. For many others, winter darkness simply means more blue moods. When asked "Have you cried today?" Americans have agreed more often in the winter (TABLE 13.7).

TABLE 13.7 Percentage Answering Yes When Asked "Have You Cried Today?"

	Men	Women
In August	4%	7%
In December	8%	21%

Source: *Time*/CNN survey, 1994.

In milder forms, mania's energy and flood of ideas can fuel creativity. Classical composer George Frideric Handel (1685–1759), who many believe suffered a mild form of bipolar disorder, composed his nearly four-hour-long *Messiah* during three weeks of intense, creative energy (Keynes, 1980). Bipolar disorder strikes more often among people who rely on emotional expression and vivid imagery, such as poets and artists, and less often among those who rely on precision and logic, such as architects, designers, and journal-

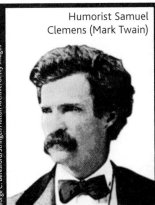

Writer Virginia Woolf

Humorist Samuel Clemens (Mark Twain)

Producer Tim Burton

CREATIVITY AND BIPOLAR DISORDERS
There are many creative artists, composers, writers, and performers with bipolar disorder.

mood disorders psychological disorders characterized by emotional extremes. See *major depressive disorder* and *bipolar disorder.*

major depressive disorder a mood disorder in which a person experiences, in the absence of drugs or a medical condition, two or more weeks with five or more symptoms, at least one of which must be either (1) depressed mood or (2) loss of interest or pleasure.

bipolar disorder a mood disorder in which the person alternates between the hopelessness and lethargy of depression and the overexcited state of mania. (Formerly called *manic-depressive disorder.*)

mania a hyperactive, wildly optimistic state.

ists (Jamison, 1993, 1995; Kaufman & Baer, 2002; Ludwig, 1995).

Bipolar disorder is as maladaptive as major depressive disorder, but it is much less common. It afflicts as many men as women. The diagnosis has risen among adolescents, whose mood swings, sometimes prolonged, range from rage to giddiness. The trend was clear in U.S. National Center for Health Statistics annual physician surveys. Between 1994 and 2003, bipolar diagnoses in under-20 people showed an astonishing 40-fold increase—from an estimated 20,000 to 800,000 (Carey, 2007; Flora & Bobby, 2008; Moreno et al., 2007). The new popularity of the diagnosis has been a boon to companies whose drugs are prescribed to lessen the mood swings. The DSM-5 will likely reduce the number of child and adolescent bipolar diagnoses, by classifying as *disruptive mood dysregulation disorder* some of those with emotional volatility (Miller, 2010).

This surge in diagnoses has prompted debate over whether normal mood swings are sometimes being labeled abnormal and then medicated.

BIPOLAR DISORDER Artist Abigail Southworth illustrates her experience of bipolar disorder.

Life as a Two-Headed Beast: Bipolar, Abigail Southworth

Suicide and Self-Injury

13-15 Why do people attempt suicide, and why do some people injure themselves?

Each year nearly 1 million despairing people worldwide will elect a permanent solution to what might have been a temporary problem (WHO, 2012). The risk of suicide is at least five times greater for those who have been depressed than for the general population (Bostwick & Pankratz, 2000). People seldom, however, elect suicide while in the depths of depression, when energy and initiative are lacking. The risk increases when they begin to rebound and become capable of following through.

Suicide is not necessarily an act of hostility or revenge. Elderly people sometimes choose death as an alternative to current or future suffering. People of all ages may view suicide as a way of switching off unendurable pain and

relieving a perceived burden on family members. "People desire death when two fundamental needs are frustrated to the point of extinction," noted one psychologist: "The need to belong with or connect to others, and the need to feel effective with or to influence others" (Joiner, 2006, p. 47). Suicidal urges typically increase when people feel disconnected from others and a burden to them (Joiner, 2010), or when they feel defeated and trapped by a situation they feel they cannot escape (Taylor et al., 2011). Thus, suicide rates increase a bit during economic recessions (Luo et al., 2011).

Looking back, families and friends may recall signs that they believe should have forewarned them—verbal hints, giving possessions away, self-inflicted injuries, or withdrawal and preoccupation with death. But few who talk or think of suicide (a number that includes one-third of all adolescents and college students) actually attempt it. Only about 1 in 25 Americans who make the attempt will complete the act (AAS, 2009). Nevertheless, about 30,000 will kill themselves—about two-thirds using guns. (Drug overdoses account for about 80 percent of suicide attempts, but only 14 percent of suicide fatalities.) States with high gun ownership are states with high suicide rates, even after controlling

for poverty and urbanization (Miller et al., 2002; Tavernise, 2013).

Suicide is not the only way to send a message or deal with distress. Some people, especially some adolescents and young adults, may engage in *nonsuicidal self-injury (NSSI)*. Such behavior includes cutting or burning the skin, hitting oneself, pulling out hair, inserting objects under the nails or skin, and self-administered tattooing (Fikke et al., 2011).

Why do people hurt themselves? Those who do so tend to be less able to tolerate emotional distress. They are often extremely self-critical, with poor communication and problem-solving skills (Nock, 2010). They may engage in NSSI to

- gain relief from intense negative thoughts through the distraction of pain.
- ask for help and gain attention.
- relieve guilt by self-punishment.
- get others to change their negative behavior (bullying, criticism).
- fit in with a peer group.

Does NSSI lead to suicide? Usually not. Those who engage in NSSI are typically "suicide gesturers," not suicide attempters (Nock & Kessler, 2006). Suicide gesturers engage in NSSI as a desperate but non-life-threatening form of communication

The emotional lives of men and women?

Paula Niedenthal

or when they are feeling overwhelmed. But NSSI is a risk factor for *future* suicide attempts (Wilkinson & Goodyer, 2011). If people do not find help, their nonsuicidal behavior may escalate to suicidal thoughts and, finally, to suicide attempts.

The point to remember: If a friend talks suicide to you or engages in NSSI, it's important to listen and to direct the person to professional help. Your friend may at least be sending a signal of feeling desperate or beyond hope.

Understanding Mood Disorders

13-16 How do mood disorders develop? What roles do biology, thinking, and social behavior play?

From thousands of studies of the causes, treatment, and prevention of mood disorders, researchers have pulled out some common threads. Here are some findings that any theory of depression must explain (Lewinsohn et al., 1985, 1998, 2003).

BEHAVIORS AND THOUGHTS CHANGE WITH DEPRESSION. People trapped in a depressed mood are inactive and feel unmotivated. They are sensitive to negative happenings (Peckham et al., 2010). They recall negative information. And they expect negative outcomes (my team will lose, my grades will fall, my love will fail). When the mood lifts, these behaviors and thoughts disappear. Nearly half the time, people with depression also have symptoms of another disorder, such as anxiety or substance use disorder.

DEPRESSION IS WIDESPREAD. Depression is found worldwide. (So, also, is schizophrenia.) This suggests that depression's causes, too, must be common.

WOMEN'S RISK OF MAJOR DEPRESSION IS NEARLY DOUBLE MEN'S. In 2009, when Gallup pollsters asked more than a quarter-million Americans if they had ever been diagnosed with depression, 13 percent of men and 22 percent of women said *Yes* (Pelham, 2009). When Gallup asked Americans if they experienced sadness "during a lot of the day yesterday," 17 percent of men and 28 percent of women answered *Yes* (Mendes & McGeeney, 2012). This gender gap has been found worldwide (**FIGURE 13.8**). The trend begins in adolescence; preadolescent girls are not more depression-prone than boys are (Hyde et al., 2008).

The depression gender gap fits a bigger pattern. Women are generally more vulnerable to disorders involving internal states, such as depression, anxiety, and inhibited sexual desire. Men's disorders tend to be more external—alcohol use disorder, antisocial conduct, lack of impulse control. When women get sad, they often get sadder than men do. When men get mad, they often get madder than women do.

MOST MAJOR DEPRESSIVE EPISODES END ON THEIR OWN. Although therapy often speeds recovery, most people suffering major depression eventually return to normal even without professional help. The black cloud of depression comes and, a few weeks or months later, it often goes. About half the time, it recurs within two years (Burcusa & Iacono, 2007). Recovery is more likely to endure (Fergusson & Woodward, 2002; Kendler et al., 2001; Richards, 2011) when

- the first episode strikes later in life.
- there were few previous episodes.

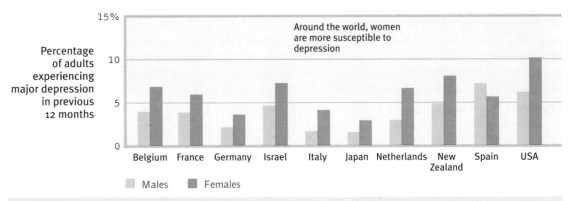

FIGURE 13.8 Gender and major depression Interviews with 89,037 adults in 18 countries (10 of which are shown here) confirm what many smaller studies have found. Women's risk of major depression is nearly double that of men's (Bromet et al., 2011).

Jennifer Graylock

LIFE AFTER DEPRESSION J. K. Rowling, author of the Harry Potter books, has reported suffering acute depression—a "dark time," with suicidal thoughts—between ages 25 and 28. It was a "terrible place," she said, but it formed a foundation that allowed her "to come back stronger" (McLaughlin, 2010).

- the person experiences minimal stress.
- there is ample social support.

STRESSFUL EVENTS SOMETIMES PRECEDE DEPRESSION. A family member's death, a job loss, a marital crisis, or a physical assault increase one's risk of depression. One long-term study tracked rates of depression in 2000 people (Kendler, 1998). Among those who had experienced no stressful life event in the preceding month, the risk of depression was less than 1 percent. Among those who had experienced three such events in that month, the risk was 24 percent. Surveys before and after Hurricane Sandy in 2012 revealed a 25 percent increase in clinical depression rates in the most affected areas (Witters & Ander, 2013).

WITH EACH NEW GENERATION, DEPRESSION IS STRIKING EARLIER IN LIFE (NOW OFTEN IN THE LATE TEENS) AND AFFECTING MORE PEOPLE. This has been true in Canada, England, France, Germany, Italy, Lebanon, New Zealand, Puerto Rico, Taiwan, and the United States (Collishaw et al., 2007; Cross-National Collaborative Group, 1992; Kessler et al., 2010; Twenge et al., 2008). In North America, today's young adults are three times more likely than their grandparents to report having recently—or ever—suffered depression. This is true even though their grandparents have been at risk for many more years.

The increased risk among young adults appears partly real, but it may also reflect increased reporting due to cultural differences. Today's young people are more willing to talk openly about their depression. Psychological processes may help explain the generational differences in reporting of depression. We tend to forget many negative experiences over time, so older generations may overlook depressed feelings they had in earlier years.

Biological Influences

Depression is a whole-body disorder that may disrupt sleep, appetite, energy, and concentration. It involves genetic predispositions and biochemical imbalances as well as negative thoughts and a gloomy mood.

GENES AND DEPRESSION We have long known that mood disorders run in families. The risk of major depression and bipolar disorder increases if you have a parent or sibling with the disorder (Sullivan et al., 2000). If one identical twin is diagnosed with major depressive disorder, the chances are about 1 in 2 that at some time the other twin will be, too. If one identical twin has bipolar disorder, the chances are 7 in 10 that the other twin will at some point be diagnosed similarly. Among fraternal twins, the corresponding odds are just under 2 in 10 (Tsuang & Faraone, 1990).

The greater similarity among identical twins holds even among twins raised apart (DiLalla et al., 1996). Summarizing the major twin studies (see **FIGURE 13.9**), one research team estimated the heritability of major depression (the extent to which individual differences are attributable to genes) at 37 percent (Bienvenu et al., 2011).

To tease out the genes that put people at risk for depression, some researchers have turned to *linkage analysis*. After finding families in which the disorder appears across several generations, geneticists examine DNA from affected and unaffected family members, looking for differences. Linkage analysis points us to a chromosome neighborhood, note behavior genetics researchers; "a house-to-house search is then needed to find the culprit gene" (Plomin & McGuffin, 2003). Such studies are reinforcing the view that depression is a complex condition. Many genes work together, producing a mosaic of small effects that interact with other factors to put some people at greater risk. If the culprit gene vari-

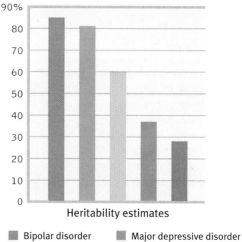

FIGURE 13.9 The heritability of various psychological disorders Researchers used data from studies of identical and fraternal twins to estimate the heritability of bipolar disorder, schizophrenia, anorexia nervosa, major depressive disorder, and generalized anxiety disorder (Bienvenu et al., 2011).

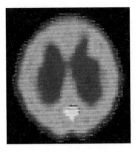
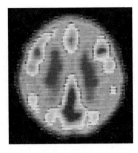
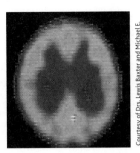

Depressed state
(May 17)

Manic state
(May 18)

Depressed state
(May 27)

Courtesy of Drs. Lewis Baxter and Michael E. Phelps, UCLA School of Medicine

FIGURE 13.10 The ups and downs of bipolar disorder PET scans show that brain energy consumption rises and falls with the patient's emotional switches. Red areas are where the brain is using energy most rapidly.

ations can be identified—with chromosome 3 genes implicated in separate British and American studies (Breen et al., 2011; Pergadia et al., 2011)—they may open the door to more effective drug therapy.

THE DEPRESSED BRAIN Scanning devices open a window on the brain's activity during depressed and manic states. During depression, brain activity slows. During mania, it increases (**FIGURE 13.10**). The left frontal lobe, which is active during positive emotions, is less active during depressed times (Davidson et al., 2002).

At least two neurotransmitter systems are at work during these periods of activity and inactivity. *Norepinephrine* increases arousal and boosts mood. It is scarce during depression and overabundant during mania. *Serotonin* is also scarce or inactive during depression (Carver et al., 2008; Plomin & McGuffin, 2003).

In Chapter 14, we will see how drugs that relieve depression tend to make more norepinephrine or serotonin available to the depressed brain. Repetitive physical exercise, such as jogging, which increases serotonin, can have a similar effect (Ilardi, 2009; Jacobs, 1994).

Psychological and Social Influences

Biological influences contribute to depression, but in the nature–nurture dance, thinking and acting also play a part. Recall that life's experiences may cause *epigenetic* changes. Our experiences can place molecular tags on our chromosomes, thereby turning genes on or off. Animal studies suggest a role for long-lasting epigenetic influences on depression (Nestler, 2011).

Thinking certainly matters, too. The *social-cognitive perspective* explores how people's assumptions and expectations influence what they perceive. Depressed people see life through dark glasses. They have intensely negative views of themselves, their situation, and their future. Listen to Norman, a college professor, recalling his depression (Endler, 1982, pp. 45–49).

> I [despaired] of ever being human again. I honestly felt subhuman, lower than the lowest vermin. Furthermore, I . . . could not understand why anyone would want to associate with me, let alone love me. . . . I was positive that I was a fraud and a phony and that I didn't deserve my Ph.D. . . . I didn't deserve the research grants I had been awarded; I couldn't understand how I had written books and journal articles. . . . I must have conned a lot of people.

Expecting the worst, depressed people magnify bad experiences and minimize good ones.

NEGATIVE THOUGHTS AND NEGATIVE MOODS INTERACT Self-defeating beliefs may arise from *learned helplessness*. As we saw in Chapter 10, both dogs and humans act depressed, passive, and withdrawn after experiencing uncontrollable painful events. Learned help-

lessness is more common in women, who may respond more strongly to stress (Hankin & Abramson, 2001; Mazure et al., 2002; Nolen-Hoeksema, 2001, 2003). Do you agree or disagree with the statement, "I feel frequently overwhelmed by all I have to do"? In a survey of women and men entering American colleges, 38 percent of the women agreed. Only 17 percent of the men agreed (Pryor et al., 2006). (Did your answer fit that pattern?)

Why are women nearly twice as vulnerable to depression (Kessler, 2001)? This higher risk may relate to women's tendency to *overthink,* to brood or ruminate (Nolen-Hoeksema, 2003). Rumination can be adaptive when it helps us focus intently on a problem (Altamirano et al., 2010; Andrews & Thomson, 2009a,b). But when it becomes relentless, self-focused rumination is not adaptive. It diverts us from thinking about other life tasks and leaves us mired in negative emotions (Kuppens et al., 2010).

Even so, why do life's unavoidable failures lead only some people—women and men—and not others to become depressed? The answer lies partly in their *explanatory style*—who or what they blame for their failures (or credit for their successes). Think how you might feel if you failed a test. If you can blame someone else ("What an unfair test!"), you are more likely to feel angry. If you blame yourself, you probably will feel stupid and depressed.

Depressed people tend to blame themselves. As **FIGURE 13.11** on the next page illustrates, they explain bad events in terms that are *stable* ("I'll never get over this"), *global* ("I can't do anything right"), and *internal* ("It's all my fault"). Their explanations are pessimistic, overgeneralized, self-focused, and self-blaming. The result may be a depressing sense of hopelessness (Abramson et al., 1989; Panzarella et al., 2006). As Martin Seligman has noted, "A recipe for severe depression is preexisting pessimism encountering failure" (1991, p. 78).

Critics point out a chicken-and-egg problem nesting in the social-cognitive

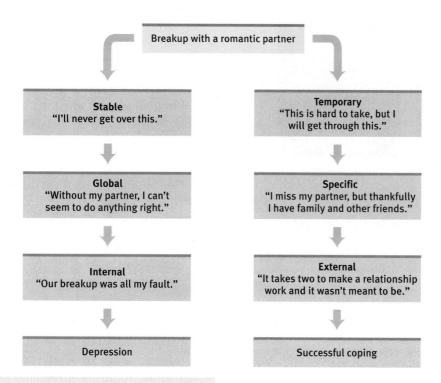

FIGURE 13.11 Outlook and depression

explanation of depression. Which comes first? The pessimistic explanatory style, or the depressed mood? Certainly, the negative explanations *coincide* with a depressed mood, and they are *indicators* of depression (Barnett & Gotlib, 1988). But do they *cause* depression, any more than a speedometer's reading 70 mph *causes* a car's speed? Before or after being depressed, people's thoughts are less negative. Perhaps a depressed mood *triggers* negative thoughts. If you temporarily put people in a bad or sad mood, their memories, judgments, and expectations do become more pessimistic.

DEPRESSION'S VICIOUS CYCLE Depression, social withdrawal, and rejection feed one another. Depression, as we have seen, is often brought on by events that disrupt our sense of who we are and why we are worthy. The stressful experience may be losing a job, getting divorced or rejected, and suffering physical trauma. Such disruptions in turn lead to brooding, which is rich

soil for growing negative feelings. And that negativity—being withdrawn, self-focused, and complaining—can cause others to reject us (Furr & Funder, 1998; Gotlib & Hammen, 1992). Indeed, people with depression are at high risk for di-

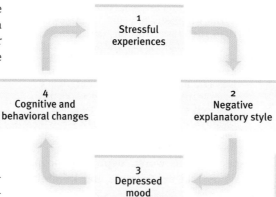

FIGURE 13.12 The vicious cycle of depressed thinking Cognitive therapists attempt to break this cycle, as we will see in Chapter 14, by changing the way depressed people process events. Psychiatrists prescribe medication to try to alter the biological roots of persistently depressed moods.

vorce, job loss, and other stressful life events. Weary of the person's fatigue, hopeless attitude, and lethargy, a spouse may threaten to leave, or a boss may begin to question the person's competence. New losses and stress then plunge the already depressed person into even deeper misery. Misery may love another's company, but company does not love another's misery.

We can now assemble pieces of the depression puzzle (**FIGURE 13.12**): (1) Stressful events interpreted through (2) a brooding, negative explanatory style create (3) a hopeless, depressed state that (4) hampers the way the person thinks and acts. These thoughts and actions in turn fuel (1) negative experiences such as rejection. Depression is a snake that bites its own tail.

It is a cycle we can all recognize. When we *feel* down, we *think* negatively and remember bad experiences. On the brighter side, each of the four points offers an exit. We could reverse our self-blame and negative outlook. We could turn our attention outward. We could engage in more pleasant activities and more competent behavior.

Britain's Prime Minister Winston Churchill called depression a "black dog" that periodically hounded him. President Abraham Lincoln was so withdrawn and brooding as a young man that his friends feared he might take his own life (Kline, 1974). As their lives remind us, people can and do struggle through depression. Most regain their capacity to love, to work, to hope, and even to succeed at the highest levels. ■

Schizophrenia

During their most severe periods, people with **schizophrenia** live in a private inner world, preoccupied with the strange ideas and images that haunt them. The word itself means "split" (*schizo*) "mind" (*phrenia*). But in this disorder, the mind is not split into multiple personalities. Rather, the mind has suffered a split from reality that shows itself in disturbed perceptions, disorganized thinking and speech, and diminished, inappropriate emotions and actions.

As you can imagine, these traits profoundly disrupt social relationships and make it difficult to hold a job. Given a supportive environment, some eventually recover to enjoy a normal life or to experience only occasional bouts of schizophrenia. Others remain socially withdrawn and isolated for much of their life.

Symptoms of Schizophrenia

13-17 What patterns of thinking, perceiving, and feeling characterize schizophrenia?

Schizophrenia patients with *positive* symptoms may have hallucinations or talk in disorganized and deluded ways. They may laugh or cry or lash out in rage at inappropriate times. Their symptoms are "positive" in the sense that inappropriate behaviors are *present*.

Those with *negative* symptoms may have toneless voices, expressionless faces, or mute and rigid bodies. Their symptoms are "negative" in the sense that actions or feelings are *absent* when you might expect them to be present.

Disorganized Speech

Imagine trying to communicate with Maxine, a young woman whose thoughts spill out in no logical order. Her biog-

ART BY SOMEONE DIAGNOSED WITH SCHIZOPHRENIA Commenting on the kind of artwork shown here (from Craig Geiser's 2010 art exhibit in Michigan), poet and art critic John Ashbery wrote: "The lure of the work is strong, but so is the terror of the unanswerable riddles it proposes."

rapher, Susan Sheehan (1982, p. 25), observed her saying aloud to no one in particular, "This morning, when I was at Hillside [Hospital], I was making a movie. I was surrounded by movie stars. . . . I'm Mary Poppins. Is this room painted blue to get me upset? My grandmother died four weeks after my eighteenth birthday."

As this strange speech illustrates, the thinking of a person with schizophrenia is fragmented and often distorted by false beliefs called **delusions.** Maxine believed she was Mary Poppins. People with paranoid tendencies often believe they are being threatened or pursued.

Disorganized thinking may appear as *word salad,* jumbled ideas that make no sense even within sentences. One young man begged for "a little more allegro in the treatment," and suggested that "liberationary movement with a view to the widening of the horizon" will "ergo extort some wit in lectures."

Disturbed Perceptions

Delusions are false *beliefs.* Hallucinations are false *perceptions.* People with schizophrenia sometimes see, feel, taste, or smell things that exist only in their minds. Most often, however, the hallucinations are sounds, often voices making insulting remarks or giving orders. The voices may tell the person that she is bad or that she must burn herself with a cigarette lighter. Imagine your own reaction if a dream broke into your waking consciousness, making it hard to separate your experience from your imagination. Stuart Emmons described his experience:

> When someone asks me to explain schizophrenia I tell them, you know how sometimes in your dreams you are in them yourself and some of them feel like real nightmares? My schizophrenia was like I was walking through a dream. But everything around me was real. At times, today's world seems so boring and I wonder if I would like to step back into the schizophrenic dream, but then I remember all the scary and horrifying experiences (Emmons et al., 1997).

When the unreal seems real, the resulting perceptions are at best bizarre, at worst terrifying.

Diminished and Inappropriate Emotions and Actions

The expressed emotions of schizophrenia are often utterly inappropriate, split off from reality (Kring & Caponigro, 2010). Maxine laughed after recalling her grandmother's death. On other occasions, she cried when others laughed, or became angry for no apparent reason. Others with schizophrenia lapse into an emotionless *flat affect,* a zombielike state of no apparent feeling. Many people with schizophrenia have difficulty reading other people's

---

schizophrenia a psychological disorder characterized by delusions, hallucinations, disorganized speech, and/or diminished, inappropriate emotional expression.

delusions false beliefs, often of persecution or grandeur, that may accompany schizophrenia and other disorders.

facial emotions and states of mind (Green & Horan, 2010; Kohler et al., 2010).

Inappropriate motor behavior takes many forms. Some patients perform senseless, compulsive acts, such as continually rocking or rubbing an arm. Others may remain motionless for hours and then become agitated.

Onset and Development of Schizophrenia

13-18 How do chronic and acute schizophrenia differ?

Nearly 1 in 100 people develop schizophrenia, with an estimated 24 million worldwide suffering from this disorder (Abel et al., 2010; WHO, 2011). It typically strikes as young people are maturing into adulthood. It knows no national boundaries, and it affects both men and women. Men tend to be struck earlier, more severely, and slightly more often (Picchioni & Murray, 2007).

For some, schizophrenia appears suddenly, seemingly as a reaction to stress. For others, as was the case with Maxine, schizophrenia develops gradually, emerging from a long history of social inadequacy. This may help explain why people predisposed to schizophrenia often are found in the lower socioeconomic levels, or even homeless.

One rule holds true around the world (WHO, 1979): When schizophrenia is a slow-developing process (called *chronic*, or *process, schizophrenia*), recovery is doubtful. Social withdrawal, a negative symptom, is common among those with chronic schizophrenia. Men more often exhibit negative symptoms and chronic schizophrenia (Räsänen et al., 2000). Recovery is much more likely when a well-adjusted person develops schizophrenia rapidly following some sort of stress (called *acute*, or *reactive, schizophrenia*).

©mikeledray/Shutterstock

Understanding Schizophrenia

13-19 What do we know about the brain chemistry, functions, and structures associated with schizophrenia, and what have we learned about prenatal risk factors?

Schizophrenia is a dreaded psychological disorder. It is also one of the most heavily researched. Most of the new research studies link it with abnormal brain tissue and activity, and with genetic predispositions. Schizophrenia is a disease of the brain exhibited in symptoms of the mind.

Brain Abnormalities

What sorts of brain abnormalities might explain schizophrenia? Biochemical imbalances? Abnormal brain activity? Problems with brain structures or functions? Researchers are taking a close look at all of these.

BRAIN CHEMISTRY Scientists have long known that strange behavior can have strange chemical causes. Have you ever heard the phrase "mad as a hatter"? The saying dates back to the behavior of British hatmakers whose brains were slowly poisoned as they used their tongue and lips to moisten the brims of mercury-laden felt hats (Smith, 1983). Could the hallucinations and other symptoms of schizophrenia have a similar biochemical key?

One possible answer emerged when researchers examined schizophrenia patients' brains after death. They found an excess number of *dopamine* receptors (Seeman et al., 1993; Wong et al., 1986).

What could this mean? Perhaps a high level of dopamine could intensify brain signals, creating positive symptoms such as hallucinations and paranoia. Sure enough, other evidence confirmed this idea. Drugs that block dopamine receptors often lessen the positive symptoms

of schizophrenia. Drugs that increase dopamine levels, such as amphetamines and cocaine, sometimes intensify them (Seeman, 2007; Swerdlow & Koob, 1987). But there's more to schizophrenia than abnormal brain chemistry.

ABNORMAL BRAIN ACTIVITY AND ANATOMY Brain scans show that abnormal brain activity and brain structures accompany schizophrenia. Some patients have abnormally low activity in the brain's frontal lobes, which are critical for reasoning, planning, and problem solving (Morey et al., 2005; Pettegrew et al., 1993; Resnick, 1992).

One study took PET scans of brain activity while people were hallucinating (Silbersweig et al., 1995). When patients heard a voice or saw something, their brain became vigorously active in several core regions. One was the thalamus, the structure that filters incoming sensory signals and transmits them to the brain's cortex. Another PET scan study of people with *paranoia* (who may have delusions of persecution) found increased activity in the amygdala, a fear-processing center (Epstein et al., 1998).

In schizophrenia, areas of the brain become enlarged and fill with fluid; cerebral tissue also shrinks (Goldman et al., 2009; Wright et al., 2000). "People with schizophrenia are losing brain tissue at a more rapid rate than healthy people," noted one researcher (Andreasen, 2008). The greater the shrinkage, the more severe the thought disorder (Collinson et al., 2003; Nelson et al., 1998; Shenton, 1992). Some studies have even found brain abnormalities in people who would *later* develop this disorder (Boos et al., 2007; Job et al., 2006).

The bottom line of various studies is clear. Schizophrenia involves not one isolated brain abnormality but problems with several brain regions and their interconnections (Andreasen, 1997, 2001).

Prenatal Environment and Risk

What causes the brain abnormalities that are found in people with schizophrenia? Some researchers blame low birth weight or lack of oxygen during delivery (Buka et al., 1999; Zornberg et al., 2000). Famine may also increase risks. People conceived during the peak of World War II's Dutch famine developed schizophrenia at twice the normal rate. Those conceived during the famine of 1959 to 1961 in eastern China also displayed this doubled rate (St. Clair et al., 2005; Susser et al., 1996).

Let's consider another possible culprit. Might a midpregnancy viral infection impair fetal brain development (Patterson, 2007)? To test this fetal-virus idea, scientists have asked these questions:

- *Are people at increased risk of schizophrenia if, during the middle of their fetal development, their country experienced a flu epidemic?* The repeated answer is Yes (Mednick et al., 1994; Murray et al., 1992; Wright et al., 1995).

- *Are people who are born in densely populated areas, where viral diseases spread more readily, at greater risk for schizophrenia?* The answer, confirmed in a study of 1.75 million Danes, is Yes (Jablensky, 1999; Mortensen, 1999).

- *Are people born during the winter and spring months—after the fall-winter flu season—also at increased risk?* The answer is again Yes, and the risk increases from 5 to 8 percent (Torrey et al., 1997, 2002).

- *In the Southern Hemisphere, where the seasons are the reverse of the Northern Hemisphere, are the months of above-average schizophrenia births similarly reversed?* Again, the answer is Yes. In Australia, people born between August and October are at greater risk. But there is an exception. For people born in the Northern Hemisphere, who later moved to Australia, the risk is greater if they were born between January and March (McGrath et al., 1995, 1999).

- *Are mothers who report being sick with influenza during pregnancy more likely to bear children who develop schizophrenia?* In one study of nearly 8000 women, the answer was Yes. The schizophrenia risk increased from the customary 1 percent to about 2 percent. But that increase applied only to mothers who were infected during their second trimester (Brown et al., 2000).

- *Does blood drawn from pregnant women whose offspring develop schizophrenia suggest a viral infection?* In a huge California study, which collected blood samples from some 20,000 pregnant women during the 1950s and 1960s, the answer was again Yes. Some children born of those pregnancies were later diagnosed with schizophrenia. Antibodies in the blood samples indicated whether the women had been exposed to influenza. When the exposure took place during the first half of the pregnancy, the child's risk of developing schizophrenia tripled. Exposure to flu during the second half of the pregnancy produced no such increase (Brown et al., 2004).

Taken together, these converging lines of evidence suggest a key to the schizophrenia puzzle: Prenatal viral infections can contribute to the development of schizophrenia. This finding strengthens the U.S. government recommendation that "women who expect to be more than three months pregnant during the flu season" should have a flu shot (CDC, 2013).

Genetics and Risk

13-20 Does research indicate a genetic contribution to schizophrenia?

Prenatal viruses increase the odds that a child will develop schizophrenia. But many women get the flu during their second trimester of pregnancy, and only 2 percent of their children develop schizophrenia. Why does prenatal exposure to the flu virus put some children at risk but not others? Could the answer be that some people are more vulnerable because they have inherited a predisposition to this disorder? The evidence indicates the answer is Yes. For most people, the odds of being diagnosed with schizophrenia are nearly 1 in 100. For those who have a sibling or parent with schizophrenia, the odds increase to 1 in 10. And if the affected sibling is an identical twin, the odds are close to 5 in 10 (FIGURE 13.13). Those odds are unchanged even if the twins are raised apart (Plomin et al., 1997). (Only a dozen or so of these cases are on record.)

But wait! Identical twins also share a prenatal environment. So it is possible that shared germs as well as shared genes produce identical twin similarities. And there is some evidence to support this idea.

About two-thirds of identical twins also share a placenta and the blood

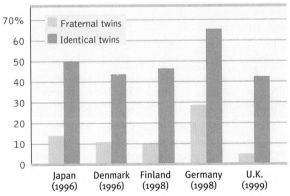
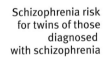

FIGURE 13.13 Risk of developing schizophrenia The lifetime risk of developing schizophrenia varies for family members of a person with this disorder. The closer the genetic relationship, the higher the risk. Across countries, barely more than 1 in 10 fraternal twins, but some 5 in 10 identical twins, share a schizophrenia diagnosis. (Adapted from Gottesman, 2001.)

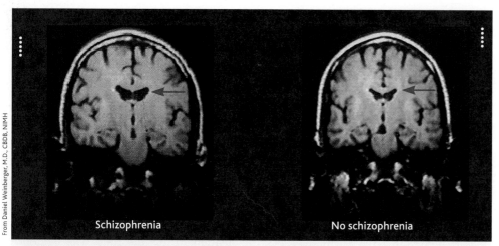

From Daniel Weinberger, M.D., CBDB, NIMH

Schizophrenia   No schizophrenia

SCHIZOPHRENIA IN IDENTICAL TWINS When twins differ, only the one afflicted with schizophrenia typically has enlarged, fluid-filled cranial cavities (left) (Suddath et al., 1990). The difference between the twins implies some nongenetic factor, such as a virus, is also at work.

it supplies. The other sets of identical twins have two separate placentas. Sharing a placenta raises the odds of later sharing a schizophrenia diagnosis. If identical twins had separate placentas, the chances are 1 in 10. If they shared a placenta, the co-twin's chances of having the disorder are 6 in 10 (Davis et al., 1995a,b; Phelps et al., 1997). A likely explanation: Identical twins who share a placenta are more likely to share the same prenatal viruses.

How, then, can we untangle the genetic influences from the environmental influences on this disorder? Adoption studies offer some clues. Children adopted by someone who develops schizophrenia seldom "catch" the disorder. Rather, adopted children have a higher risk of developing schizophrenia if one of their *biological* parents has this disorder. So, adoption studies confirm that the genetic link is real (Gottesman, 1991).

The search is on for specific genes that, in some combination, might lead to schizophrenia-inducing brain abnormalities (Levinson et al., 2011; Mitchell & Porteous, 2011; Ripke et al., 2011; Vacic et al., 2011). (It is not our genes but our brains that directly control our behavior.) Some of these genes influence the activity of dopamine and other brain

neurotransmitters. Others affect the production of *myelin*, a fatty substance that coats the axons of nerve cells and lets impulses travel at high speed through neural networks.

Although genes matter, the genetic formula is not as straightforward as the inheritance of eye color. Genome studies of thousands of individuals with and without schizophrenia indicate that schizophrenia is influenced by many genes, each with very small effects (International Schizophrenia Consortium, 2009; Pogue-Geile & Yokley, 2010). Recall again that epigenetic (literally "in addition to genetic") factors influence gene expression. Like hot water activating a tea bag, environmental factors such as viral infections, nutritional deprivation, and maternal stress can "turn on" the genes that put some of us at higher risk for this disorder. Identical twins' differing histories in the womb and beyond explain why only one may show differing gene expressions (Walker et al., 2010). As we have seen in so many different contexts, nature and nurture interact. Neither hand claps alone.

* * *

Most of us can relate more easily to the ups and downs of mood disorders than to the strange thoughts, perceptions, and

behaviors of schizophrenia. Sometimes our thoughts do jump around, but we do not talk nonsensically. Occasionally, we feel unjustly suspicious of someone, but we do not believe the world is plotting against us. Often, our perceptions err, but rarely do we see or hear things that are not there. We have felt regret after laughing at someone's misfortune, but we rarely giggle in response to bad news. At times we just want to be alone, but we do not live in social isolation. However, millions of people around the world do talk strangely, suffer delusions, hear nonexistent voices, see things that are not there, laugh or cry at inappropriate times, or withdraw into private imaginary worlds. The quest to solve the cruel puzzle of schizophrenia therefore continues, more vigorously than ever. ■

RETRIEVE + REMEMBER

- A person with schizophrenia who has _____ (positive/negative) symptoms may have an expressionless face and toneless voice.

ANSWER: negative

- What factors contribute to the onset and development of schizophrenia?

ANSWER: Biological factors include abnormalities in brain structure and function, prenatal exposure to a maternal virus, and genetic factors. However, schizophrenia is more likely to develop given a high-risk environment.

Other Disorders

Eating Disorders

13-21 What are the three major eating disorders?

Our bodies are naturally disposed to maintain a steady weight, storing energy reserves in case food becomes unavailable. But psychological influences can overwhelm biological wisdom. Nowhere is this more painfully clear than in eating disorders.

"SKELETONS ON PARADE" A newspaper article used this headline in criticizing the display of superthin models. Do such models make self-starvation fashionable?

- In **anorexia nervosa,** people—usually female adolescents—starve themselves. Anorexia often begins as an attempt to lose weight, but the dieting doesn't end. Even when far below normal weight, the self-starved person feels fat, fears being fat, and focuses obsessively on losing weight, sometimes exercising excessively. At some point in their lifetime, 0.6 percent of Americans meet the criteria for anorexia nervosa (Hudson et al., 2007). Many people with the disorder come from competitive, high-achieving families. They tend to have low self-esteem, to set impossible standards, and to fret about falling short of expectations (Polivy & Herman, 2002; Sherry & Hall, 2009).

- In **bulimia nervosa,** food binges alternate with vomiting, laxative use, fasting, and excessive exercise. Unlike anorexia, bulimia is marked by weight shifts within or above normal ranges, making this disorder

easier to hide. Binge-purge eaters are preoccupied with food (especially sweet and high-fat foods) and obsessed with their weight and appearance. They experience bouts of guilt, depression, and anxiety, especially during and following binges (Hinz & Williamson, 1987; Johnson et al., 2002). About 1 percent of Americans, mostly women in their late teens or early twenties, have had bulimia.

- In **binge-eating disorder,** significant binge eating is followed by remorse. But people with the disorder do not purge, fast, or exercise excessively after their food binges, and so may be overweight. At some point during their lifetime, 2.8 percent of Americans have had binge-eating disorder (Hudson et al., 2007).

So, how can we explain eating disorders? Heredity matters. Identical twins share these disorders somewhat more often than fraternal twins do (Culbert et al., 2009; Klump et al., 2009).

But environment also matters. Body ideals vary across culture and time. In India, women students rate their ideal body size as close to their actual shape. In impoverished areas of the world, including much of Africa—where plump means prosperous and thinness can signal poverty or illness—bigger is better (Knickmeyer, 2001; Swami et al., 2010).

Bigger does not seem better in Western cultures, where the rise in eating disorders over the last 50 years has coincided with a dramatic increase in women having a poor body image (Feingold & Mazzella, 1998). Part of the pressure on women stems from images of unnaturally thin models and celebrities (Tovee et al., 1997). Viewing such images, women—especially those who can't resist comparing their bodies with others'—often feel ashamed, depressed, and dissatisfied with their own bodies (Myers & Crowther, 2009; Posavac et al., 1998; Stice & Shaw, 1994).

In one study, researchers tested media influences by giving some ado-

lescent girls (but not others) a 15-month subscription to a teen fashion magazine (Stice et al., 2001). Vulnerable magazine readers (girls who felt dissatisfied, idealized thinness, and lacked social support) showed increased body dissatisfaction and eating disorder tendencies.

But there's much more to body dissatisfaction and anorexia than media effects, note Christopher Ferguson and his colleagues (2011). Peer influences, such as teasing, also matter. So do wealth, increased marriage age, and, especially, competition for available mates. ■

Dissociative Disorders

13-22 What are dissociative disorders, and why are they controversial?

Among the most bewildering disorders are the rare **dissociative disorders.** The person's conscious awareness is said to become separated—*dissociated*—from painful memories, thoughts, and feelings. In

anorexia nervosa an eating disorder in which a person (usually an adolescent female) maintains a starvation diet despite being significantly underweight; sometimes accompanied by excessive exercise

bulimia nervosa an eating disorder in which a person alternates binge eating (usually of high-calorie foods) with purging (by vomiting or laxative use), fasting, or excessive exercise.

binge-eating disorder significant binge eating, followed by distress, disgust, or guilt, but without the purging, fasting, or excessive exercise that marks bulimia nervosa.

dissociative disorder a disorder in which conscious awareness becomes separated (dissociated) from previous memories, thoughts, and feelings.

MULTIPLE PERSONALITIES Chris Sizemore's story, told in the book and movie, *The Three Faces of Eve,* gave early visibility to what is now called *dissociative identity disorder.*

this state, people may suddenly lose their memory or change their identity, often in response to an overwhelmingly stressful situation.

Dissociation itself is not so rare. Now and then, any one of us may have a fleeting sense of being unreal, of being separated from our body, of watching ourselves as if in a movie. But a massive dissociation of self from ordinary consciousness occurs in **dissociative identity disorder (DID)**. At different times, two or more distinct identities seem to control the person's behavior, each with its own voice and mannerisms. Thus, the person may be prim and proper one moment, loud and flirtatious the next. Typically, the original personality denies any awareness of the other(s).

Skeptics question the genuineness of DID. First, they find it suspicious that DID has such a short history. Between 1930 and 1960, the number of DID diagnoses in North America was 2 per decade. By the 1980s, when the DSM contained the first formal code for this disorder, the number of reported cases had exploded to more than 20,000 (McHugh, 1995a). The average number of displayed person-

alities also mushroomed—from 3 to 12 per patient (Goff & Simms, 1993).

Second, note the skeptics, DID is much less common outside North America, although in other cultures some people are said to be "possessed" by an alien spirit (Aldridge-Morris, 1989; Kluft, 1991). In Britain, DID—which some consider "a wacky American fad" (Cohen, 1995)—is rare. In India and Japan, it is essentially nonexistent. Such findings, say skeptics, point to a cultural explanation. They propose that this disorder is created by therapists in a particular social context (Merskey, 1992). Rather than being provoked by trauma, dissociative symptoms tend to be exhibited by suggestible, fantasy-prone people (Giesbrecht et al., 2008, 2010).

Third, instead of being a real disorder, some ask, could DID be an extension of the way we vary the "selves" we present, as when we display a goofy, loud self while hanging out with friends, and a subdued, respectful self around grandparents? If so, say the critics, clinicians who discover multiple personalities may merely have triggered role playing by fantasy-prone people. After all, patients do not enter therapy saying, "Allow me

"Would it be possible to speak with the personality that pays the bills?"

to introduce myselves." Rather, note these skeptics, some therapists go fishing for multiple personalities: "Have you ever felt like another part of you does things you can't control? Does this part of you have a name? Can I talk to the angry part of you?" Once patients permit a therapist to talk, by name, "to the part of you that says those angry things," they begin acting out the fantasy. Like actors who lose themselves in their roles, vulnerable patients may "become" the parts they are acting out. The result may be the experience of another self.

Other researchers and clinicians believe DID is a real disorder. They find support for this view in the distinct brain and body states associated with differing personalities (Putnam, 1991). DID patients have exhibited activity in brain areas linked with traumatic memories (Elzinga et al., 2007).

If DID is a real disorder, how can we best understand it? Both the psychodynamic and the learning perspectives interpret DID symptoms as ways of dealing with anxiety. Psychoanalysts see them as defenses against the anxiety caused by unacceptable impulses. In this view, an immoral second personality allows the discharge of forbidden impulses. Learning theorists see dissociative disorders as behaviors reinforced by anxiety reduction.

Other psychologists include dissociative disorders under the umbrella of posttraumatic stress disorder. In this view, DID would be a natural, protective response to traumatic experiences during childhood (Dalenberg et al., 2012). Many DID patients recall suffering physical, sexual, or emotional abuse as children (Gleaves, 1996; Lilienfeld et al., 1999). In one study of 12 murderers diagnosed with DID, 11 had suffered severe abuse, even torture, in childhood (Lewis et al., 1997). One had been set afire by his parents. Another had been used in child pornography and was scarred from being made to sit on a stove burner. Some critics wonder, however, whether vivid imagination or therapist suggestion contributes to such recollections (Kihlstrom, 2005). Disrupted sleep may also contribute, with intrusions of dreamlike experiences into waking consciousness (Lynn et al., 2012).

So the debate continues. On one side are those who believe multiple personalities are the desperate efforts of people trying to detach from a horrific existence. On the other are the skeptics who think DID is a condition constructed out of the therapist-patient interaction and acted out by fantasy-prone, emotionally vulnerable people. ■

Personality Disorders

13-23 What characteristics are typical of personality disorders in general, and what biological and psychological factors are associated with antisocial personality disorder?

There is little debate about the reality of **personality disorders.** These disruptive, inflexible, and enduring behavior patterns interfere with a person's social functioning. Some people with these disorders withdraw and avoid social contact. Some interact but do so without responding emotionally. Others show insecurity and instability as they manipulate others or pull them close, then push them away.

The most troubling and heavily researched personality disorder is **antisocial personality disorder.** A person with this disorder is typically a male who shows no conscience in his actions, even toward friends and family. When

an antisocial personality combines a keen intelligence with no conscience, the result may be a charming and clever con artist—or even a fearless, focused, ruthless soldier, CEO, or politician (Dutton, 2012).

Lack of conscience usually becomes plain before age 15, as the person begins to lie, steal, fight, or display unrestrained sexual behavior (Cale & Lilienfeld, 2002). Not all such children become antisocial adults. Those who do (about half of them) will generally be unable to keep a job, irresponsible as a spouse and parent, and violent or otherwise criminal (Farrington, 1991). People with antisocial personality disorder behave impulsively and then feel and fear little (Fowles & Dindo, 2009). Antisocial does not mean criminal (Skeem & Cooke, 2010). But do all criminals have antisocial personality disorder? Definitely not. Most criminals show concern for their friends and family members.

Antisocial personality disorder is woven of both biological and psychological strands. No single gene codes for a complex behavior such as crime. There is, however, a genetic tendency toward a fearless and uninhibited life. Twin and adoption studies reveal that biological relatives of people with antisocial and unemotional tendencies are at increased risk for antisocial behavior (Frisell et al., 2012; Tuvblad et al., 2011).

The genetic vulnerability of those with antisocial personality disorder appears as low arousal. Awaiting events that most people would find unnerving, such as electric shocks or loud noises, they show little bodily arousal (Hare, 1975; van Goozen et al., 2007). Long-term studies have shown that their levels of stress

ANTISOCIAL PERSONALITY? Dennis Rader, known as the "BTK killer" in Kansas, was convicted in 2005 of killing 10 people over a 30-year span. Rader exhibited the extreme lack of conscience that marks antisocial personality disorder.

EPA/JEFF TUTTLE/Landov

hormones were lower than average when they were youngsters, before committing any crime (FIGURE 13.14 on the next page). Even at age 3, children who were slow to develop conditioned fears were later more likely to commit a crime (Gao et al., 2010).

dissociative identity disorder (DID) a controversial, rare dissociative disorder in which a person exhibits two or more distinct and alternating personalities. Formerly called *multiple personality disorder.*

personality disorder an inflexible and enduring behavior pattern that impairs social functioning.

antisocial personality disorder a personality disorder in which the person (usually a man) exhibits a lack of conscience for wrongdoing, even toward friends and family members; may be aggressive and ruthless or a clever con artist.

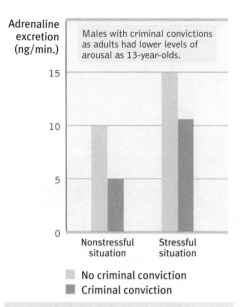

FIGURE 13.14 Cold-blooded arousability and risk of crime Levels of the stress hormone adrenaline were measured in two groups of 13-year-old Swedish boys. In both stressful and nonstressful situations, those who would later be convicted of a crime (as 18- to 26-year-olds) showed relatively low arousal as 13-year-olds. (From Magnusson, 1990.)

With antisocial behavior, as with so much else, nature and nurture interact to leave their marks on the brain. To explore the neural basis of antisocial personality disorder, scientists are identifying brain activity differences in antisocial criminals. Shown emotionally evocative photographs, such as a man holding a knife to a woman's throat, they display lower than normal heart rate and perspiration responses, and less activity in brain areas that typically respond to emotional stimuli (Harenski et al., 2010; Kiehl & Buckholtz, 2010). They also display a hyper-reactive dopamine reward system that predisposes their impulsive drive to do something rewarding, despite the consequences (Buckholtz et al., 2010). One study compared PET scans of 41 murderers' brains with those from people of similar age and sex. The murderers' frontal lobes, an area that helps control impulses, displayed reduced activity (Raine, 1999, 2005). This reduction was especially apparent in those who murdered impulsively. In a follow-up study, researchers found that violent repeat offenders had 11 percent less frontal lobe tissue than normal (Raine et al., 2000). This helps explain another finding: People with antisocial personality disorder fall far below normal in aspects of thinking such as planning, organization, and inhibition, which are all frontal lobe functions (Morgan & Lilienfeld, 2000). Such data remind us: Everything psychological is also biological.

* * *

The findings described in this chapter make clear the need for research and treatment to help the growing number of people, especially teenagers and young adults, who suffer the bewilderment and pain of a psychological disorder. Although mindful of their pain, we can also be encouraged by the many successful people who pursued brilliant careers while enduring psychological difficulties. Eighteen of them were U.S. presidents, according to one psychiatric analysis of their biographies (Davidson et al., 2006). The bewilderment, fear, and sorrow caused by psychological disorders are real. But, as Chapter 14 shows, hope, too, is real.

CHAPTER REVIEW

Psychological Disorders

Test yourself by taking a moment to answer each of these Learning Objective Questions (repeated here from within the chapter). Then turn to Appendix D, Complete Chapter Reviews, to check your answers. Research suggests that trying to answer these questions on your own will improve your long-term memory of the concepts (McDaniel et al., 2009).

What Is a Psychological Disorder?

13-1: How should we draw the line between normal behavior and psychological disorder?

13-2: Why is there controversy over attention-deficit/hyperactivity disorder?

13-3: How is our understanding of psychological disorders affected by whether we use a medical model or a biopsychosocial approach?

13-4: How and why do clinicians classify psychological disorders, and why do some psychologists criticize the use of diagnostic labels?

Anxiety Disorders, OCD, and PTSD

13-5: What are the main anxiety disorders, and how do anxiety disorders differ from the ordinary worries and fears we all experience?

13-6: What is OCD?

13-7: What is PTSD?

13-8: How do learning and biology contribute to the feelings and thoughts found in anxiety disorders, OCD, and PTSD?

Substance Use and Addictive Disorders

13-9: What are substance use disorders, and what role do tolerance, withdrawal, and addiction play in these disorders?

13-10: How do depressants, such as alcohol, influence neural activity and behavior?

13-11: How do the major stimulants affect neural activity and behavior?

13-12: What are the physiological and psychological effects of LSD and marijuana?

13-13: What biological, psychological, and social-cultural factors help explain why some people abuse mind-altering drugs?

Mood Disorders

13-14: What are the main mood disorders?

13-15: Why do people attempt suicide, and why do some people injure themselves?

13-16: How do mood disorders develop? What roles do biology, thinking, and social behavior play?

Schizophrenia

13-17: What patterns of thinking, perceiving, and feeling characterize schizophrenia?

13-18: How do chronic and acute schizophrenia differ?

13-19: What do we know about the brain chemistry, functions, and structures associated with schizophrenia, and what have we learned about prenatal risk factors?

13-20: Does research indicate a genetic contribution to schizophrenia?

Other Disorders

13-21: What are the three major eating disorders?

13-22: What are dissociative disorders, and why are they controversial?

13-23: What characteristics are typical of personality disorders in general, and what biological and psychological factors are associated with antisocial personality disorder?

TERMS AND CONCEPTS TO REMEMBER

Test yourself on these terms by trying to write down the definition in your own words before flipping back to the referenced page to check your answer.

psychological disorder, p. 372

attention-deficit/hyperactivity disorder (ADHD), p. 373

medical model, p. 373

DSM-5, p. 374

anxiety disorders, p. 376

generalized anxiety disorder, p. 377

panic disorder, p. 377

phobia, p. 377

obsessive-compulsive disorder (OCD), p. 378

posttraumatic stress disorder (PTSD), p. 378

substance use disorder, p. 381

psychoactive drug, p. 381

tolerance, p. 382

addiction, p. 382

withdrawal, p. 382

depressants, p. 382

alcohol use disorder, p. 383

barbiturates, p. 384

opiates, p. 384

stimulants, p. 384

amphetamines, p. 384

nicotine, p. 384

methamphetamine, p. 386

Ecstasy (MDMA), p. 386

hallucinogens, p. 387

LSD, p. 387

near-death experience, p. 387

THC, p. 387

mood disorders, p. 390

major depressive disorder, p. 390

bipolar disorder, p. 391

mania, p. 391

schizophrenia, p. 397

delusions, p. 397

anorexia nervosa, p. 401

bulimia nervosa, p. 401

binge-eating disorder, p. 401

dissociative disorder, p. 401

dissociative identity disorder (DID), p. 402

personality disorder, p. 403

antisocial personality disorder, p. 403

CHAPTER TEST

Test yourself repeatedly throughout your studies. This will not only help you figure out what you know and don't know; the testing itself will help you learn and remember the information more effectively thanks to the testing effect.

1. Anna is embarrassed that it takes her several minutes to parallel-park her car. She usually gets out of the car once or twice to inspect her distance both from the curb and from the nearby cars. Should she worry about having a psychological disorder?

2. Although some psychological disorders are culture-bound, others cross cultures. For example, in every known culture some people have

   a. bulimia nervosa.

   b. ADHD.

   c. schizophrenia.

   d. *susto.*

3. A therapist says that psychological disorders are sicknesses and people with these disorders should be treated as patients in a hospital. This therapist believes in the _____ model.

4. Many psychologists reject the "disorders-as-illness" view and instead contend that other factors may also be involved—for example, the person's bad habits and poor social skills. This view represents the _____ approach.

   a. medical

   b. evil spirits

   c. biopsychosocial

   d. diagnostic labels

5. Most psychologists and psychiatrists use _____ to classify psychological disorders.

   a. DSM descriptions and codes

   b. in-depth patient histories

   c. input from patients' family and friends

   d. the theories of Pinel, Rosenhan, and others

6. A feeling of intense dread that can be accompanied by chest pains, choking sensations, or other frightening sensations is called

   a. a specific phobia.

   b. a compulsion.

   c. a panic attack.

   d. an obsessive fear.

7. Anxiety that takes the form of a persistent irrational fear and avoidance of a specific object or situation is called a _____.

8. Marina became consumed with the need to clean the entire house and refused to participate in any other activities. Her family consulted a therapist, who diagnosed her as having _____ - _____ disorder.

9. The learning perspective proposes that phobias are

   a. the result of individual genetic makeup.

   b. a way of repressing unacceptable impulses.

   c. conditioned fears.

   d. a symptom of having been abused as a child.

10. Two disorders have been found to cross cultures. One is schizophrenia, and the other is _____.

11. After continued use of a psychoactive drug, the drug user needs to take larger doses to get the desired effect. This is referred to as _____.

12. The depressants include alcohol, barbiturates,

   a. and opiates.

   b. cocaine, and morphine.

   c. caffeine, nicotine, and marijuana.

   d. and amphetamines.

13. Why might alcohol make a person more helpful or more aggressive?

14. Long-term use of Ecstasy can

   a. depress sympathetic nervous system activity.

   b. deplete the brain's supply of epinephrine.

   c. deplete the brain's supply of dopamine.

   d. damage serotonin-producing neurons.

15. Near-death experiences are strikingly similar to the hallucinations evoked by _____.

16. Use of marijuana

   a. impairs motor coordination, perception, reaction time, and memory.

   b. inhibits people's emotions.

   c. leads to dehydration and overheating.

   d. stimulates brain cell development.

17. An important psychological contributor to drug use is

   a. inflated self-esteem.

   b. the feeling that life is meaningless and directionless.

   c. genetic predisposition.

   d. overprotective parents.

18. Although bipolar disorder is as maladaptive as depression, it is much less common and it affects

   a. more women than men.

   b. more men than women.

   c. women and men equally.

   d. primarily scientists and doctors.

19. The rate of depression is _____ (increasing/decreasing) among young people.

20. Depression can often be alleviated by drugs that increase supplies of the neurotransmitters _____ and _____.

21. Psychologists who emphasize the importance of negative perceptions, beliefs, and thoughts in depression are working within the _____ - _____ perspective.

22. A person with positive symptoms of schizophrenia is most likely to experience

   a. tremors.

   b. delusions.

   c. withdrawal.

   d. flat emotion.

23. People with schizophrenia may hear voices urging self-destruction, an example of a(n) _____.

24. Victor exclaimed, "The weather has been so schizophrenic lately: It's hot one day and freezing the next!" Is this an accurate comparison? Why or why not?

25. Chances for recovery from schizophrenia are best when
    a. onset is sudden, in response to stress.
    b. deterioration occurs gradually, during childhood.
    c. no environmental causes can be identified.
    d. there is a detectable brain abnormality.

26. Which of the following statements is true of bulimia nervosa?
    a. People with bulimia continue to want to lose weight even when they are underweight.
    b. Bulimia is marked by weight fluctuations within or above normal ranges.
    c. Bulimia patients often come from middle-class families that are competitive, high-achieving, and protective.
    d. If one twin is diagnosed with bulimia, the chances of the other twin's sharing the disorder are greater if they are fraternal rather than identical twins.

27. Dissociative identity disorder is controversial because
    a. dissociation is actually quite rare.
    b. it was reported frequently in the 1920s but rarely today.
    c. it is almost never reported outside North America.
    d. its symptoms are nearly identical to those of obsessive-compulsive disorder.

28. A personality disorder, such as antisocial personality, is characterized by
    a. depression.
    b. hallucinations.
    c. enduring and inflexible behavior patterns that impair social functioning.
    d. an elevated level of autonomic nervous system arousal.

29. PET scans of murderers' brains have revealed
    a. higher-than-normal activation in the frontal lobes.
    b. lower-than-normal activation in the frontal lobes.
    c. more frontal lobe tissue than normal.
    d. no differences in brain structures or activity.

Find answers to these questions in Appendix E, in the back of the book.

IN YOUR EVERYDAY LIFE

Answering these questions will help you make these concepts more personally meaningful, and therefore more memorable.

1. Can you recall a fear that you have learned? What role, if any, was played by fear conditioning or by observational learning?

2. Psychoactive drugs such as alcohol, heroin, and methamphetamine all bring pleasure followed by discomfort or depression when the substance wears off. Knowing this, what strategies do you think might keep young teens from abusing substances?

3. How has student life affected your moods? What advice would you have for new students?

4. Can you think of a time when being in a sad mood has actually helped you in some ways? Did you re-evaluate your situation or make new plans for the future?

5. Now that you know more about schizophrenia, do you think the media accurately portray the behavior of people with this disorder? Why or why not?

6. As his fans already know, comedian and TV personality Howie Mandel suffers from obsessive-compulsive disorder and a severe germ phobia. How do you think being labeled has helped or hurt Mandel?

7. Dissociative identity disorder is rare, but feeling like a "different person" at times is common. Can you recall ever feeling like a "different person" because of the situation you were in? What was that like?

experience
more of the
testing
effect

CHAPTER
OVERVIEW

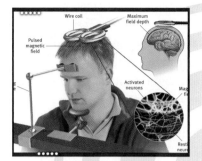

Treating Psychological Disorders

The Psychological Therapies

Psychoanalysis and Psychodynamic Therapy

Humanistic Therapies

Behavior Therapies

Cognitive Therapies

Group and Family Therapies

Evaluating Psychotherapies

Is Psychotherapy Effective?

Which Psychotherapies Work Best?

How Do Psychotherapies Help People?

How Do Culture and Values Influence
Psychotherapy?

CLOSE-UP: A Consumer's Guide to
Psychotherapists

The Biomedical Therapies

Drug Therapies

Brain Stimulation

Psychosurgery

Therapeutic Lifestyle Change

Preventing Psychological
Disorders

14 Therapy

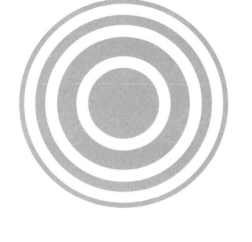

Note to our readers: I am delighted to welcome Nathan DeWall as co-author for this edition of Psychology in Everyday Life. *He led our shared revision work for this chapter and Chapters 4, 10, and 11.*

Kay Redfield Jamison is both an award-winning clinical psychologist and a world expert on the emotional extremes of bipolar disorder. She knows her subject firsthand: "For as long as I can remember, I was frighteningly, although wonderfully, beholden to moods . . . as a child, as a young girl . . . as an adolescent. . . . Caught up in the cycles of manic-depressive illness [now known as bipolar disorder] by the time I began my professional life, I became, both by necessity and intellectual [choice], a student of moods" (1995, pp. 4–5).

Jamison's life was blessed with times of intense sensitivity and passionate energy. But like her father's, it was also an emotional roller coaster. Reckless spending, racing conversation, and sleeplessness alternated with swings into "the blackest caves of the mind."

Then, "in the midst of utter confusion," she made a sane and helpful decision. Risking embarrassment, she made an appointment with a therapist, a psychiatrist she would visit weekly for years to come.

> He kept me alive a thousand times over. He saw me through madness, despair, wonderful and terrible love affairs, disillusionments and triumphs, recurrences of illness, an almost fatal suicide attempt, the death of a man I greatly loved, and the enormous pleasures and [frustrations] of my professional life. . . . He was very tough, as well as very kind. . . . Even though he understood more than anyone how much I felt I was losing . . . by taking medication, he never [lost] sight of the overall perspective of how costly, damaging, and life threatening my illness was. . . . Although I went to him to be treated for an illness, he taught me . . . the total beholdenness of brain to mind and mind to brain (pp. 87–89).

"Psychotherapy heals," Jamison noted. "It makes some sense of the confusion, reins in the terrifying thoughts and feelings, returns some control and hope and possibility from it all."

This chapter explores therapeutic options for those wanting help.

Treating Psychological Disorders

14-1 What are the differences between psychotherapy and the biomedical therapies?

The history of treatments for psychological disorders includes a mix of harsh and gentle methods. Would-be healers have cut holes in people's heads and restrained, bled, or "beat the devil" out of them. They have given them drugs and electric shocks. But they also have given people warm baths and massages, and placed them in sunny, serene settings. And they have talked with them about their experiences, feelings, thoughts, and behaviors.

The switch from harsh to gentler methods arrived because nineteenth-century reformers such as Philippe Pinel and Dorothea Dix pushed for more humane treatments and for constructing mental hospitals. Most of those hospitals now have other uses. Since the 1950s, effective drug therapies have been available, and community-based treatment programs are now common.

Today's therapies can be classified into two main categories.

- In **psychotherapy**, a trained therapist uses psychological techniques to assist someone seeking to overcome difficulties or achieve personal growth. The therapist may seek to uncover hidden meaning from a client's early relationships, to encourage the client to adopt a new way of thinking, or to replace old behaviors with new ones.

- **Biomedical therapy** offers medications and other biological treatments. For example, a person with severe depression, as we will see, may receive antidepressants, electroconvulsive shock therapy (ECT), or deep-brain stimulation.

The care provider's training and expertise, as well as the disorder itself, influence the choice of treatment. Psychotherapy and medication are often combined. Kay Redfield Jamison received psychotherapy in her meetings with her psychiatrist, and she took medications to control her wild mood swings.

Let's look first at the psychotherapy options for those treated with "talk therapies."

The Psychological Therapies

Among the dozens of psychotherapies, we will focus on the most influential. Each is built on one or more of psychology's major theories: psychodynamic, humanistic, behavioral, and cognitive. Most of these techniques can be used one-on-one or in groups. Psychotherapists often use multiple methods. Indeed, many psychotherapists describe their approach as **eclectic**, using a blend of therapies.

Psychoanalysis and Psychodynamic Therapy

14-2 What are the goals and techniques of psychoanalysis, and how have they been adapted in psychodynamic therapy?

The first major psychological therapy was Sigmund Freud's **psychoanalysis.** Although few clinicians today practice therapy as Freud did, his work deserves discussion. It helped form the foundation for treating psychological disorders, partly by influencing modern therapists working from the psychodynamic perspective.

The Goals of Psychoanalysis

Freud believed that in therapy, people could achieve healthier, less anxious living by releasing the energy they had previously devoted to id-ego-superego conflicts (Chapter 11). Freud assumed that we do not fully know ourselves. There are

DOROTHEA DIX (1802–1887) "I . . . call your attention to the state of the Insane Persons confined within this Commonwealth, in cages."

THE HISTORY OF TREATMENT Visitors to eighteenth-century mental hospitals paid to gawk at patients, as though they were viewing zoo animals. William Hogarth's (1697–1764) painting captured one of these visits to London's St. Mary of Bethlehem hospital (commonly called Bedlam).

threatening things that we seem to want not to know—things we refuse to admit.

Freud's therapy aimed to bring patients' repressed feelings into conscious awareness. By helping them reclaim their unconscious thoughts and feelings, the therapist ("analyst") would also help them gain *insight* into the origins of their disorders. This insight could in turn inspire them to take responsibility for their own growth.

The Techniques of Psychoanalysis

Psychoanalytic theory emphasizes the power of childhood experiences to mold us. Thus, its main method is historical reconstruction. It aims to excavate the past in the hope of loosening its bonds on the present. Like many of his generation, Freud began with hypnosis as a method but discarded it as unreliable. He then turned to *free association*.

Imagine yourself as a patient (or perhaps with a trusted friend) doing free association. First, you relax. You may lie on a couch or sit in a comfy chair. As the psychoanalyst sits out of your line of vision, you say aloud whatever comes to your mind. At one moment, you're relating a childhood memory. At another, you're describing a dream or recent experience.

It sounds easy, but soon you notice how often you edit your thoughts as you speak. You pause for a second before describing how embarrassed you felt giving a class presentation. You leave out details that seemed trivial or shameful. Your mind goes blank as you try to remember an important person or place. You may even joke or change the subject to something less threatening.

To an analyst, these mental blips are blocks that indicate **resistance.** They hint that anxiety lurks and you are defending against sensitive material. The analyst will note your resistance and then provide insight into its meaning. If offered at the right moment, this **interpretation**—of, say, your not wanting to talk about your mother or call, text, or message her—may reveal underlying wishes, feelings, and conflicts you are avoiding. The analyst may also offer an explanation of how this resistance fits with other pieces of your psychological puzzle, including those based on an analysis of your dreams.

Multiply that one session by dozens and your relationship patterns will surface in your interactions. You may find you have strong positive or negative feelings for your analyst. The analyst may suggest you are **transferring** feelings, such as dependency or mingled love and anger, that you experienced in earlier relationships with family members or other important people. By exposing such feelings, you may gain insight into your current relationships.

Relatively few U.S. therapists now offer traditional psychoanalysis. Much of its underlying theory is not supported by scientific research (Chapter 11). Analysts' interpretations cannot be proven or disproven. And psychoanalysis takes considerable time and money, often years of several expensive sessions each week. Some of these problems have been addressed in the modern *psychodynamic perspective* that has evolved from psychoanalysis. ■

> ### RETRIEVE + REMEMBER
>
> • In psychoanalysis, patients may experience strong feelings for their analyst, which is called _____. Patients are said to demonstrate anxiety when they put up mental blocks around sensitive memories—showing _____. The analyst will attempt to provide insight into the underlying anxiety by offering a(n) _____ of the mental blocks.
>
> ANSWERS: transference; resistance; interpretation

psychotherapy treatment involving psychological techniques; consists of interactions between a trained therapist and someone seeking to overcome psychological difficulties or achieve personal growth.

biomedical therapy prescribed medications or procedures that act directly on the person's physiology.

eclectic approach an approach to psychotherapy that, depending on the client's problems, uses techniques from various forms of therapy.

psychoanalysis Sigmund Freud's therapeutic technique. Freud believed that the patient's free associations, resistances, dreams, and transferences—and the analyst's interpretations of them—released previously repressed feelings, allowing the patient to gain self-insight.

resistance in psychoanalysis, the blocking from consciousness of anxiety-laden material.

interpretation in psychoanalysis, the analyst's noting supposed dream meanings, resistances, and other significant behaviors and events in order to promote insight.

transference in psychoanalysis, the patient's transfer to the analyst of emotions linked with other relationships (such as love or hatred for a parent).

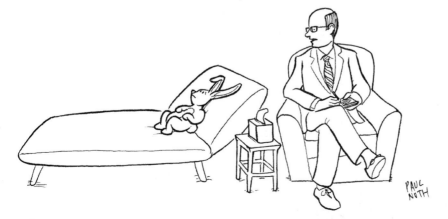

"I'm more interested in hearing about the eggs you're hiding from yourself."

Psychodynamic Therapy

Those using **psychodynamic therapy** techniques also aim to dig up their clients' pasts, but they don't talk much about id, ego, and superego. Instead, by focusing on themes across important relationships (including childhood experiences and the therapist relationship), they try to help people understand their current symptoms. "We can have loving feelings and hateful feelings toward the same person," and "we can desire something and also fear it," noted psychodynamic therapist Jonathan Shedler (2009). Client-therapist meetings take place once or twice a week (rather than several times weekly) for only a few weeks or months (rather than several years). Rather than lying on a couch, out of the therapist's line of vision, clients meet with their therapist face to face.

In these meetings, clients explore and gain perspective on defended-against thoughts and feelings, as one therapist illustrated with the case of a young man (Shapiro, 1999, p. 8). He had told women that he loved them, knowing well that he didn't. They expected it, so he said it. But later with his wife, who wished he would say that he loved her, he found he *could not* do that—"I don't know why, but I can't."

Therapist: *Do you mean, then, that if you could, you would like to?*

Patient: *Well, I don't know. . . . Maybe I can't say it because I'm not sure it's true. Maybe I don't love her.*

Further interactions revealed that the client could not express real love because it would feel "mushy" and "soft" and therefore unmanly. He was "in conflict with himself, and . . . cut off from the nature of that conflict," the therapist noted. With such patients, who are estranged from themselves, therapists using psychodynamic techniques "are in a position to introduce them to themselves. We can restore their awareness of their own wishes and feelings, and their awareness, as well, of their reac-

Tetra Images/Getty Images

FACE-TO-FACE THERAPY In this type of therapy session, the couch has disappeared. But the influence of psychoanalytic theory may not have, especially if the therapist seeks information from the patient's childhood and helps the patient reclaim unconscious feelings.

tions against those wishes and feelings" (Shapiro, 1999, p. 8).

Exploring past relationship troubles may help clients understand the origin of their current difficulties. Shedler (2010a) recalled "Jeffrey's" complaints of difficulty getting along with his colleagues and wife, who saw him as overly critical. When Jeffrey "began responding to me as if I were an unpredictable, angry adversary," Shedler seized the opportunity to help Jeffrey recognize the relationship pattern. He helped Jeffrey explore the pattern's roots in the attacks and humiliation he had experienced from his father. Jeffrey was then able to work through and let go of this defensive style of responding to people.

Humanistic Therapies

14-3 What are the basic themes of humanistic therapy, and what are the goals and techniques of Rogers' client-centered approach?

· ·

The *humanistic* perspective (Chapter 11) has emphasized people's potential for self-fulfillment. Not surprisingly, humanistic therapies attempt to reduce the inner conflicts that interfere with natural development and growth. To achieve this goal, humanistic therapies try to give people new insights. Indeed, because they share this goal, humanistic and psychodynamic therapies are often referred to as **insight therapies.** But humanistic therapies differ from psychodynamic therapies in many other ways:

- *They aim to boost people's self-fulfillment by helping them grow in self-awareness and self-acceptance.*

- *They focus on promoting growth, not curing illness.* Thus, those in therapy are called "clients" or just "persons" rather than "patients" (a change many other therapists have adopted).

- *The path to growth is taking immediate responsibility for one's feelings and actions, rather than uncovering hidden causes.*

- *Conscious thoughts are more important than the unconscious.*

- *The present and future are more important than the past.* Therapy thus focuses on exploring feelings as they occur, rather than gaining insights into the childhood origins of the feelings.

All these themes are present in a widely used humanistic technique developed by Carl Rogers (1902–1987). **Client-centered therapy,** now often called *person-centered therapy*, focuses on the person's conscious self-perceptions. It is *nondirective*—the therapist listens, without judging or interpreting, and refrains from directing the client toward certain insights.

Rogers (1961, 1980) believed that most people already possess the resources for growth. He encouraged therapists to foster growth by exhibiting *genuineness, acceptance,* and *empathy*. By being *genuine,* therapists will express their true feelings. By being *accepting,* therapists may help clients feel freer and more open to change. By showing *empathy,* by sensing and reflecting their clients' feelings, therapists can help clients experience a deeper self-understanding and self-acceptance (Hill & Nakayama, 2000). As Rogers (1980, p. 10) explained,

> Hearing has consequences. When I truly hear a person and the meanings that are important to him at that moment, hearing not simply his words, but him, and when I let him know that I have heard his own private personal meanings, many things happen. There is first of all a grateful look. He feels released. He wants to tell me more about his world. He surges forth in a new sense of freedom. He becomes more open to the process of change.
>
> I have often noticed that the more deeply I hear the meanings of the person, the more there is that happens. Almost always, when a person realizes he has been deeply heard, his eyes moisten. I think in some real sense he is weeping for joy. It is as though he were saying, "Thank God, somebody heard me. Someone knows what it's like to be me."

To Rogers, "hearing" was **active listening.** The therapist echoes, restates, and clarifies what the client expresses (verbally or nonverbally). The therapist also acknowledges those expressed feelings. Active listening is now an accepted part of counseling practices in many schools, colleges, and clinics. Counselors listen attentively. They interrupt only to restate and confirm feelings, to accept what was said, or to check their under-

ACTIVE LISTENING Carl Rogers (second from right) empathized with a client during this group therapy session.

standing of something. In the following brief excerpt, note how Rogers tried to provide a psychological mirror that would help the client see himself more clearly.

Rogers: *Feeling that now, hm? That you're just no good to yourself, no good to anybody. Never will be any good to anybody. Just that you're completely worthless, huh?—Those really are lousy feelings. Just feel that you're no good at all, hm?*

Client: *Yeah.* (Muttering in low, discouraged voice) *That's what this guy I went to town with just the other day told me.*

Rogers: *This guy that you went to town with really told you that you were no good? Is that what you're saying? Did I get that right?*

Client: *M-hm.*

Rogers: *I guess the meaning of that if I get it right is that here's somebody that meant something to you and what does he think of you? Why, he's told you that he thinks you're no good at all. And that just really knocks the props out from under you.* (Client weeps quietly.) *It just brings the tears.* (Silence of 20 seconds)

Client: (Rather defiantly) *I don't care though.*

Rogers: *You tell yourself you don't care at all, but somehow I guess some part of you cares because some part of you weeps over it.* (Meador & Rogers, 1984, p. 167)

Critics ask: Can a therapist be a perfect mirror, without selecting and interpreting what is reflected? Rogers agreed that no one can be *totally* nondirective. Nevertheless, he said, the therapist's most important contribution is to accept and understand the client. Given a nonjudgmental, grace-filled environment that provides **unconditional positive regard,** people may accept even their worst traits and feel valued and whole.

psychodynamic therapy theraputic approach derived from the psychoanalytic tradition; views individuals as responding to unconscious forces and childhood experiences, and seeks to enhance self-insight.

insight therapies therapies that aim to improve psychological functioning by increasing a person's awareness of underlying motives and defenses.

client-centered therapy a humanistic therapy, developed by Carl Rogers, in which the therapist uses techniques such as active listening within a genuine, accepting, empathic environment to promote clients' growth. (Also called *person-centered therapy*.)

active listening empathic listening in which the listener echoes, restates, and clarifies. A feature of Rogers' client-centered therapy.

unconditional positive regard a caring, accepting, nonjudgmental attitude, which Carl Rogers believed would help clients develop self-awareness and self-acceptance.

Time & Life Pictures/Getty Images

How can we develop our own communication strengths by listening more actively in our friendships? Three Rogerian hints may help:

1. *Summarize.* Check your understanding by repeating your friend's statements in your own words.

2. *Invite clarification.* "What might be an example of that?" may encourage your friend to say more.

3. *Reflect feelings.* "It sounds frustrating" might mirror what you're sensing from your friend's body language and emotional intensity.

Behavior Therapies

14-4 How do behavior therapy's assumptions and techniques differ from those of psychodynamic and humanistic therapies? What techniques are used in exposure therapies and aversive conditioning?

Insight therapies assume that self-awareness and psychological well-being go hand in hand. Psychodynamic therapies expect people's problems to lessen as they gain insight into their unresolved and unconscious tensions. Humanistic therapies expect people's problems to lessen as they get in touch with their feelings. **Behavior therapies,** however, take a different approach. Rather than searching beneath the surface for inner causes, they assume that problem behaviors *are* the problems. (You can become aware of why you are highly anxious during exams and still be anxious.) By harnessing the power of learning principles, behavior therapies offer clients useful tools for getting rid of unwanted behaviors. They view phobias, for example, as learned behaviors. So why not use conditioning techniques to replace them with new behaviors?

Classical Conditioning Techniques

One cluster of behavior therapies draws on principles developed in Ivan Pavlov's conditioning experiments (Chapter 6).

As Pavlov and others showed, we learn various behaviors and emotions through *classical conditioning.* If we're attacked by a dog, we may thereafter have a conditioned fear response when other dogs approach. (Our fear generalizes, and all dogs become conditioned stimuli.)

Could other unwanted responses also be explained by conditioning? If so, might reconditioning be a solution? Learning theorist O. H. Mowrer thought so. He developed a successful conditioning therapy for chronic bed-wetters, using a liquid-sensitive pad connected to an alarm. If the sleeping child wets the bed pad, moisture triggers the alarm, waking the child. After a number of trials, the child associates bladder relaxation with waking. In three out of four cases, the treatment has stopped the bed-wetting, and the success has boosted the child's self-image (Christophersen & Edwards, 1992; Houts et al., 1994).

Let's broaden the discussion. What triggers your worst fear responses? Public speaking? Flying? Tight spaces? Whatever the trigger, do you think you could unlearn your fear responses? With new conditioning, many people have. An example: The fear of riding in an elevator is often a learned response to the stimulus of being confined in a tight space. Therapists have successfully **counterconditioned** people with a fear of confined spaces. They pair the trigger stimulus (the enclosed space of the elevator) with a new response (relaxation) that cannot coexist with fear.

To replace unwanted responses with new responses, therapists may use *exposure therapies* and *aversive conditioning.*

EXPOSURE THERAPIES Picture the animal you fear the most. Maybe it's a snake, a spider, or even a cat or a dog. For 3-year-old Peter, it was a rabbit. To rid Peter of his fear of rabbits and other furry objects, psychologist Mary Cover Jones had a plan: Associate the fear-evoking rabbit with the pleasurable, relaxed response associated with eating.

As Peter began his midafternoon snack, she introduced a caged rabbit on the other side of the huge room. Peter, eagerly munching on his crackers and slurping his milk, hardly noticed the furry animal. Day by day, Jones moved the rabbit closer and closer. Within two months, Peter was holding the rabbit in his lap, even stroking it while he ate. His fear of rabbits and other furry objects had disappeared. It had been *countered,* or replaced, by a relaxed state that could not coexist with fear (Fisher, 1984; Jones, 1924).

Unfortunately for many who might have been helped by Jones' procedures, her story of Peter and the rabbit did not enter psychology's lore until psychiatrist Joseph Wolpe (1958; Wolpe & Plaud, 1997) refined Jones' counterconditioning technique into the **exposure therapies** used today. These therapies, in a variety of ways, try to change people's reactions by repeatedly exposing them to stimuli that trigger unwanted reactions. We all experience this process in everyday life. Why would someone who has moved to a new apartment be annoyed by loud traffic sounds nearby but only

VIRTUAL REALITY EXPOSURE THERAPY Within the confines of a room, virtual reality technology exposes people to vivid simulations of feared stimuli, such as walking across a rickety bridge high off the ground.

for a while? With repeated exposure, the person adapts. So, too, with people who have fear reactions to specific events. Exposed repeatedly to the situation that once terrified them, they can learn to react less anxiously (Rosa-Alcázar et al., 2008; Wolitzky-Taylor et al., 2008).

One form of exposure therapy widely used to treat phobias is **systematic desensitization.** You cannot be anxious and relaxed at the same time. Therefore, if you can repeatedly relax when facing anxiety-provoking stimuli, you can gradually eliminate your anxiety. The trick is to proceed gradually. Say you fear public speaking. A therapist might first ask you to make a list of situations that trigger your public speaking anxiety. Your list would range from situations that cause you to feel mildly anxious (perhaps speaking up in a small group of friends) to those that provoke feelings of panic (having to address a large audience).

The therapist would then train you in *progressive relaxation.* You would learn to relax one muscle group after another. When you have achieved a state of comfortable, complete relaxation, the therapist will ask you to imagine, with your eyes closed, a mildly anxiety-arousing situation—perhaps a mental image of having coffee with a group of friends

and trying to decide whether to speak up. You are told to signal, by raising your finger, if you feel any anxiety while imagining this scene. Seeing the signal, the therapist will instruct you to switch off the mental image and go back to deep relaxation. This imagined scene is repeatedly paired with relaxation until you feel no trace of anxiety.

The therapist will then move to the next item on your list, again using relaxation techniques to desensitize you to each imagined situation. After several sessions, you will move to actual situations and practice what you had only *imagined* before. You will begin with relatively easy tasks and gradually move to more anxiety-filled ones. Conquering your anxiety in an actual situation, not just in your imagination, will raise your self-confidence (Foa & Kozak, 1986; Williams, 1987). Eventually, you may even become a confident public speaker.

If an anxiety-arousing situation is too expensive, difficult, or embarrassing to re-create, the therapist may recommend **virtual reality exposure therapy.** You would don a head-mounted display unit that projects a three-dimensional virtual world in front of your eyes. The lifelike scenes (which shift as your head turns) would be tailored to your partic-

ular fear. Experimentally treated fears include flying, public speaking, particular animals, and heights (Parsons & Rizzo, 2008; Westerhoff, 2007). Those who fear flying can peer out a virtual window of a simulated plane. They feel the engine's vibrations and hear it roar as the plane taxis down the runway and takes off. In controlled studies, people treated with virtual reality exposure therapy have experienced significant relief from real-life fear (Hoffman, 2004; Krijn et al., 2004; Meyerbröker & Emmelkamp, 2010).

AVERSIVE CONDITIONING Exposure therapies help you learn what you *should* do. They substitute a relaxed, positive response for a negative response to a *harmless* stimulus.

Aversive conditioning helps you to learn what you *should not* do. It substitutes a negative (aversive) response for a positive response to a *harmful* stimulus.

The procedure is simple: Form a new association between the unwanted behavior and *unpleasant* feelings. Is nail

behavior therapy therapeutic approach that applies learning principles to the elimination of unwanted behaviors.

counterconditioning behavior therapy procedures that use classical conditioning to evoke new responses to stimuli that are triggering unwanted behaviors; includes *exposure therapies* and *aversive conditioning.*

exposure therapies behavioral techniques, such as *systematic desensitization* and *virtual reality exposure therapy,* that treat anxieties by exposing people (in imagination or actual situations) to the things they fear and avoid.

systematic desensitization a type of exposure therapy that associates a pleasant, relaxed state with gradually increasing, anxiety-triggering stimuli. Commonly used to treat phobias.

virtual reality exposure therapy a counterconditioning technique that treats anxiety by creative electronic simulations in which people can safely face their greatest fears, such as airplane flying, spiders, or public speaking.

aversive conditioning a type of counterconditioning that associates an unpleasant state (such as nausea) with an unwanted behavior (such as drinking alcohol).

biting the problem? The therapist might suggest painting the fingernails with a yucky-tasting nail polish (Baskind, 1997). Is alcohol abuse the problem? The therapist may offer the client appealing drinks laced with a drug that produces severe nausea. If that therapy links alcohol with violent nausea, the person's reaction to alcohol may change from positive to negative (FIGURE 14.1).

Does aversive conditioning work? In the short run it may. In one classic study, 685 patients with alcohol use disorder completed an aversion therapy program at a hospital (Wiens & Menustik, 1983). Over the next year, they returned for several booster treatments that paired alcohol with sickness. At the end of that year, 63 percent were not drinking alcohol. But after three years, only 33 percent were alcohol free.

Aversive conditioning has a built-in problem: Our thoughts can override conditioning processes (Chapter 6). People know that the alcohol-nausea link exists only in certain situations. This knowledge limits the treatment's effectiveness. Thus, therapists often combine aversive conditioning with other treatments.

Operant Conditioning

14-5 What is the basic idea of operant conditioning therapies?

If you swim, you know fear. Through trial, error, and instruction, you learned how to put your head underwater without suffocating, how to pull your body through the water, and how to dive safely. Operant conditioning shaped your swimming. You were reinforced for safe, effective behaviors. And you were naturally punished, as when you swallowed water, for improper swimming behaviors.

Remember a basic operant conditioning concept: Consequences drive our behaviors (Chapter 6). Knowing this, therapists can practice *behavior modification*. They reinforce behaviors they consider desirable. And they do not reinforce, or they sometimes punish, undesirable behavior. Using operant conditioning to solve specific behavior problems has raised hopes for some seemingly hopeless cases. Children with an intellectual disability have been taught to care for themselves. Socially withdrawn children with autism spectrum disorder have learned to interact.

People with schizophrenia have learned how to behave more rationally. In each case, therapists used positive reinforcers to *shape* behavior. In a step-by-step manner, they rewarded behaviors that came closer and closer to the desired behaviors.

In extreme cases, treatment can be intensive. One study worked with 19 withdrawn, uncommunicative 3-year-olds with autism spectrum disorder. For two years, 40 hours each week, the children's parents attempted to shape their behavior (Lovaas, 1987). They positively reinforced desired behaviors and ignored or punished aggressive and self-abusive behaviors. The combination worked wonders for some children. By first grade, 9 of the 19 were functioning successfully in school and exhibiting normal intelligence. In a control group (not receiving this treatment), only one child showed similar improvement. (Later studies suggested that positive reinforcement without punishment was most effective.)

Not everyone finds the same things rewarding. Hence, the rewards used to modify behavior vary. Some people may respond well to attention or praise. Others require concrete rewards, such as food. Even then, certain foods won't work as reinforcements for everyone. One of us [ND] finds chocolate neither rewarding nor tasty. Pizza is both, so a nice slice would better shape his behaviors.

To modify behavior, therapists sometimes create a **token economy**. When people display appropriate behavior, such as getting out of bed, washing, dressing, eating, talking meaningfully, cleaning their rooms, or playing cooperatively, they receive a token or plastic coin. Later, they can exchange a number of these tokens for rewards, such as candy, TV time, day trips, or other privileges. Token economies have worked well in various settings (homes, classrooms, hospitals, institutions for delinquent youth), and among people with various disabilities (Matson & Boisjoli, 2009). ∎

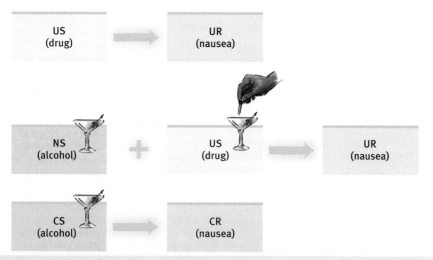

FIGURE 14.1 Aversion therapy for alcohol abuse Therapists gave people with a history of alcohol abuse a mixed drink containing alcohol and a drug that produces severe nausea. After repeated treatments, some people developed at least a temporary conditioned aversion to alcohol. (Classical conditioning terms: US is *unconditioned stimulus,* UR is *unconditioned response,* NS is *neutral stimulus,* CS is *conditioned stimulus,* and CR is *conditioned response.*)

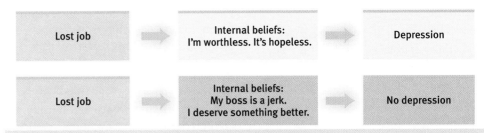

FIGURE 14.2 A cognitive perspective on psychological disorders The person's emotional reactions are produced not directly by the event but by the person's thoughts in response to the event.

Cognitive Therapies

14-6 What are the goals and techniques of the cognitive therapies and of cognitive-behavioral therapy?

People with specific fears and problem behaviors may respond to behavior therapy. But how would you modify the wide assortment of behaviors that accompany major depression? Or those associated with unfocused anxiety, which doesn't lend itself to a neat list of anxiety-triggering situations? The same *cognitive revolution* that influenced other areas of psychology during the last half-century influenced therapy as well.

Like psychodynamic approaches, the **cognitive therapies** assume that our thinking colors our feelings (**FIGURE 14.2**). Between the event and our response lies the mind. Self-blaming and overgeneralized explanations of bad events are often an important part of the vicious cycle of depression (Chapter 13). If depressed, we may interpret a suggestion as criticism, disagreement as dislike, praise as flattery, friendliness as pity. Dwelling on such thoughts sustains our bad mood and may alienate others. In one classic study, depressed and nondepressed people had a phone conversation with a stranger. Later, that stranger was given the choice of accepting or rejecting them. Depressed people were more often rejected (Coyne, 1976).

Cognitive therapies aim to help people break out of depression's vicious cycle by adopting new ways of thinking.

Beck's Therapy for Depression

Many people see the world through rose-colored glasses. They accept more responsibility for their successes than failures. They perceive themselves as above average on most desirable behaviors. And they show unrealistic optimism about their future (recall *self-serving bias* from Chapter 11). Depressed people occupy a different world, one in which they perceive their own and others' actions as dark, negative, and pessimistic. Aaron Beck developed cognitive therapy to show de-pressed clients the irrational nature of their thinking, and to reverse their negative views of themselves, their situations, and their futures.

In Beck's approach, gentle questioning seeks to reveal irrational thinking and then to persuade people to remove the dark glasses through which they view life (Beck et al., 1979, pp. 145–146):

Client: *I agree with the descriptions of me but I guess I don't agree that the way I think makes me depressed.*

Beck: *How do you understand it?*

Client: *I get depressed when things go wrong. Like when I fail a test.*

Beck: *How can failing a test make you depressed?*

Client: *Well, if I fail I'll never get into law school.*

Beck: *So failing the test means a lot to you. But if failing a test could drive people into clinical depression, wouldn't you expect everyone who failed the test to have a depression? . . . Did everyone who failed get depressed enough to require treatment?*

Client: *No, but it depends on how important the test was to the person.*

Beck: *Right, and who decides the importance?*

COGNITIVE THERAPY FOR EATING DISORDERS AIDED BY JOURNALING Cognitive therapy guides people toward new ways of explaining their good and bad experiences. By recording each day's positive events and how she has enabled them, this young woman may become more mindful of her self-control and more optimistic in her outlook.

token economy an operant conditioning procedure in which people earn a token for exhibiting a desired behavior and can later exchange the tokens for privileges or treats.

cognitive therapy therapeutic approach that teaches people new, more adaptive ways of thinking; based on the assumption that thoughts intervene between events and our emotional reactions.

Client: *I do.*

Beck: *And so, what we have to examine is your way of viewing the test (or the way that you think about the test) and how it affects your chances of getting into law school. Do you agree?*

Client: *Right.*

Beck: *Do you agree that the way you interpret the results of the test will affect you? You might feel depressed, you might have trouble sleeping, not feel like eating, and you might even wonder if you should drop out of the course.*

Client: *I have been thinking that I wasn't going to make it. Yes, I agree.*

Beck: *Now what did failing mean?*

Client: (tearful) *That I couldn't get into law school.*

Beck: *And what does that mean to you?*

Client: *That I'm just not smart enough.*

Beck: *Anything else?*

Client: *That I can never be happy.*

Beck: *And how do these thoughts make you feel?*

Client: *Very unhappy.*

Beck: *So it is the meaning of failing a test that makes you very unhappy. In fact, believing that you can never be happy is a powerful factor in producing unhappiness. So, you get yourself into a trap—by definition, failure to get into law school equals "I can never be happy."*

We often think in words. Therefore, getting people to change what they say to themselves is an effective way to change their thinking. Have you ever studied hard for an exam but felt extremely anxious before taking it? Many well-prepared students make matters worse with self-defeating thoughts: "This exam is going to be impossible. Everyone else seems so relaxed and confident. I wish I were better prepared.

> "Life does not consist mainly, or even largely, of facts and happenings; it consists mainly of the storm of thoughts that are forever blowing through one's mind."
>
> Mark Twain (1835–1910)

I'm so nervous I'll forget everything." Psychologists call this overgeneralized, self-blaming thinking *catastrophizing*.

To change such negative self-talk, therapists teach people to alter their thinking in stressful situations (Meichenbaum, 1977, 1985). Sometimes it may be enough simply to say more positive things to yourself. "Relax. The exam may be hard, but it will be hard for everyone else, too. I studied harder than most people. Besides, I don't need a perfect score to get a good grade in this class." Training people to "talk back" to negative thoughts can be effective. With such training, depression-prone children and adolescents have shown a modestly reduced rate of future depression (Brunwasser et al., 2009; Stice et al., 2009). To a great extent, it is the thought that counts. (For a sampling of commonly used cognitive therapy techniques, see **TABLE 14.1**.)

Cognitive-Behavioral Therapy

"The trouble with most therapy," said therapist Albert Ellis (1913–2007), "is that it helps you to feel better. But you don't get better. You have to back it up with action, action, action." **Cognitive-behavioral therapy** takes a double-barreled approach to depression and other disorders. This widely practiced integrated approach aims not only to alter the way people *think* but also to alter the way they *act*. Like other cognitive therapies, it seeks to make people aware of their irrational negative thinking and to replace it with new ways of thinking. Like other behavior therapies, it trains people to practice a more positive approach in everyday settings.

In therapy, people learn to make more realistic appraisals and, as homework, to practice behaviors that counter their problem (Kazantzis et al., 2010a,b; Moses & Barlow, 2006). A person with depression might keep a log of daily situations associated with negative and positive emotions and attempt to engage more in activities that lead to feeling good. Those who fear social situations might practice approaching people.

In one study, people learned to prevent their compulsive behaviors by relabeling their intrusive thoughts (Schwartz et al., 1996). Feeling the urge to wash their hands again, they would tell themselves, "I'm having a compulsive

TABLE 14.1	Selected Cognitive Therapy Techniques	
Aim of Technique	**Technique**	**Therapists' Directions**
Reveal beliefs	Question your interpretations	Explore your beliefs, revealing faulty assumptions such as "I must be liked by everyone."
	Rank thoughts and emotions	Gain perspective by ranking your thoughts and emotions from mildly to extremely upsetting.
Test beliefs	Examine consequences	Explore difficult situations, assessing possible consequences and challenging faulty reasoning.
	Decatastrophize thinking	Work through the actual worst-case consequences of the situation you face (it is often not as bad as imagined). Then determine how to cope with the real situation you face.
Change beliefs	Take appropriate responsibility	Challenge total self-blame and negative thinking, noting aspects for which you may be truly responsible, as well as aspects that aren't your responsibility.
	Resist extremes	Develop new ways of thinking and feeling to replace habits that are not adaptive. For example, change from thinking "I am a total failure" to "I got a failing grade on that paper, and I can make these changes to succeed next time."

urge." They would explain to themselves that the hand-washing urge was a result of their brain's abnormal activity, which they had previously viewed in PET scans. Then, instead of giving in, they would spend 15 minutes in an enjoyable alternative behavior, such as practicing an instrument, taking a walk, or gardening. This helped "unstick" the brain by shifting attention and engaging other brain areas. For two or three months, the weekly therapy sessions continued, with relabeling and refocusing practice at home. By the study's end, most participants' symptoms had diminished, and their PET scans revealed normalized brain activity. Other studies confirm cognitive-behavioral therapy's effectiveness for those with anxiety or depression (Covin et al., 2008).

Might clients benefit from participating in cognitive-behavioral therapy over the Internet? *Yes*, clients can learn cognitive-behavioral skills and can benefit from the therapy over the Internet (Andersson et al., 2012; Kessler et al., 2009; Marks & Cavanaugh, 2009; Stross, 2011). But does therapy over the Internet produce the same benefits as in-person therapy? It's too early to know. One thing is clear: From Freud's couch to today's Internet, the landscape of therapy is changing. ■

Group and Family Therapies

14-7 What are the aims and benefits of group and family therapy?

So far, we have focused on therapies in which one therapist treats one client. Most therapies (though not traditional psychoanalysis) can also occur in small groups. **Group therapy** does not provide the same degree of therapist involvement with each client. However, it saves therapists' time and clients' money, and often is no less effective (Fuhriman & Burlingame, 1994; Jónsson et al., 2011). Therapists frequently suggest group therapy when clients' problems stem from their interactions with others, as when families have conflicts or an individual's behavior distresses others. Up to 90 minutes a week, the therapist guides the interactions of 6 to 10 people as they confront issues and react to one another.

The social context of group sessions offers some unique benefits. It can be a relief to find that others, despite their calm appearance, share your problems and your troubling feelings. It can also be helpful to receive feedback as you try out new ways of behaving. Hearing that you look confident, even though you feel anxious and self-conscious, can be very reassuring.

One special type of group interaction, **family therapy,** assumes that no person is an island. We live and grow in relation to others, especially our family, yet we also work to find an identity outside of our family. These two opposing tendencies can create stress for the individual and the family. This helps explain why

cognitive-behavioral therapy a popular integrative therapy that combines cognitive therapy (changing self-defeating thinking) with behavior therapy (changing behavior).

group therapy therapy conducted with groups rather than individuals, providing benefits from group interaction.

family therapy therapy that treats the family as a system. Views an individual's unwanted behaviors as influenced by, or directed at, other family members.

John Moore/Getty Images News/Getty Images

FAMILY THERAPY This type of therapy often acts as a preventive mental health strategy and may include marriage therapy, as shown here at a retreat for military families. The therapist helps family members understand how their ways of relating to one another create problems. The treatment's emphasis is not on changing the individuals, but on changing their relationships and interactions.

therapists tend to view families as systems, in which each person's actions trigger reactions from others. To change these negative interactions, the therapist often attempts to guide family members toward positive relationships and improved communication. ■

Evaluating Psychotherapies

Many Americans have great confidence in psychotherapy's effectiveness. "Seek counseling" or "Ask your mate to find a therapist," advice columnists often advise. Before 1950, psychiatrists were the primary providers of mental health care. Today, many others have joined their ranks. Clinical and counseling psychologists offer psychotherapy, and so do clinical social workers; pastoral, marital, abuse, and school counselors; and psychiatric nurses.

Is the faith that millions of people place in these therapists justified? As we have seen, history offers examples of ineffective (and occasionally harmful) treatments for psychological disorders. Will psychotherapy join that list? The question, though simply put, is not simply answered.

Is Psychotherapy Effective?

14-8 Does psychotherapy work? Who decides?

Imagine that a loved one, knowing that you're studying psychology, has asked for your help. She's been feeling depressed, and she's thinking about making an appointment with a therapist. She wonders: Does psychotherapy really work? You've promised to gather some answers. Where will you start? Who decides whether psychotherapy is effective? Clients? Therapists? Friends and family members?

Clients' Perceptions

If clients' glowing comments were the only measuring stick, your job would be easy. Most clients believe that psychotherapy is effective. Consider 2900 *Consumer Reports* readers who rated their experiences with mental health professionals (1995; Kotkin et al., 1996; Seligman, 1995). How many were at least "fairly well satisfied"? Almost 90 percent (as was Kay Redfield Jamison, as we saw at this chapter's beginning). Among those who recalled feeling *fair* or *very poor* when beginning therapy, 9 in 10 now were feeling *very good, good,* or at least *so-so*. We have their word for it—and who should know better?

But clients' self-reports don't persuade everyone. Critics point out some reasons for skepticism.

- *Clients may need to justify their investment of effort and money.* If you invested dozens of hours and lots of money in something, wouldn't you be motivated to find something positive about it? Psychologists call this *effort justification.*

- *Clients generally speak kindly of their therapists.* Even if their problems remain, clients "work hard to find something positive to say. The therapist had been very understanding, the client had gained a new perspective, he learned to communicate better, his mind was eased, anything at all so as not to have to say treatment was a failure" (Zilbergeld, 1983, p. 117).

- *People often enter therapy in crisis.* Life ebbs and flows. When the crisis passes, people may assume their improvement was a therapy result.

Clinicians' Perceptions

If clinicians' perceptions were proof of therapy's effectiveness, we would have even more reason to celebrate. Case studies of successful treatment abound. Furthermore, therapists are like the rest of us. They treasure compliments from people they've tried to help—in this case, clients saying good-bye or later expressing their gratitude. The problem is that clients justify entering psychotherapy by emphasizing their unhappiness. They justify leaving by emphasizing their well-being. And they stay in touch only if satisfied. This means that therapists are most aware of the failures of *other* therapists—those whose clients, having experienced only temporary relief, are now seeking a new therapist for their recurring problems. Thus, the same person, suffering from the same old anxiety, depression, or marital difficulty, may be a "success" story in several therapists' files.

Outcome Research

How, then, can we objectively assess psychotherapy's effectiveness? How can we predict therapy *outcomes?* What types of people and problems are best helped, and by what type of psychotherapy?

In search of answers, psychologists have turned to controlled research studies. This is a well-traveled path. In the 1800s, skeptical medical doctors began to realize that many patients got better on their own and that most of the fashionable treatments (bleeding, purging) were doing no good. Sorting fact from superstition required following patients and recording outcomes with and without a particular treatment. Typhoid fever patients, for example, often improved

TRAUMA These women were mourning the tragic loss of lives and homes in the 2010 earthquake in China. Those who suffer through such trauma may benefit from counseling, though many people recover on their own, or with the help of supportive relationships with family and friends. "Life itself still remains a very effective therapist," noted psychodynamic therapist Karen Horney (*Our Inner Conflicts*, 1945).

after being bled, convincing most doctors that the treatment worked. Then came the shock. A control group was given mere bed rest, and after five weeks of fever, 70 percent improved. The study showed that bleeding was worthless (Thomas, 1992).

In the twentieth century, psychology faced a similar challenge. British psychologist Hans Eysenck (1952) launched a spirited debate when he summarized 24 studies of psychotherapy outcomes. He found that two-thirds of those receiving psychotherapy for disorders not involving hallucinations or delusions improved markedly. To this day, no one disputes that optimistic estimate.

Why, then, are we still debating psychotherapy's effectiveness? Because—as other researchers would later affirm—Eysenck found that *untreated* people, such as those on waiting lists for the same treatment, had similar rates of improvement. With or without psychotherapy, roughly two-thirds improved noticeably. Time was a great healer.

An uproar greeted Eysenck's findings. Some critics pointed out errors in his analyses. Others noted that he based his ideas on only 24 studies. Now, more than a half-century later, there are hundreds of such studies. And they confirm that psychotherapy works (Kopta et al., 1999; Leichsenring & Rabung, 2008; Shadish et al., 2000). The best of these studies are *randomized clinical trials*, in which people on a waiting list are randomly assigned to therapy or to no therapy. Later, the researchers evaluate everyone and compare the outcomes.

Therapists welcomed the result when the first statistical digest combined the results of 475 of these investigations (Smith et al., 1980). The outcome for the average therapy client was better than that for 80 percent of the untreated people (**FIGURE 14.3**).

Dozens of such summaries have echoed the results of the earlier outcome studies: *Those not undergoing therapy often improve, but those undergoing therapy are more likely to improve.*

It's good to know that psychotherapy, in general at least, is somewhat effective. But distressed people—and those paying for their therapy—really want a different question answered. How effective are *particular* treatments for *specific* problems? So what can we tell these people?

Which Psychotherapies Work Best?

14-9 Are some psychotherapies more effective than others for specific disorders?

The early statistical summaries and surveys did not find that any one type of psychotherapy was generally better than others (Smith et al., 1977, 1980). Newer studies have similarly found little connection between clients' outcomes and their clinicians' experience, training, supervision, and licensing (Bickman, 1999; Luborsky et al., 2002; Wampold, 2007). A *Consumer Reports* survey confirmed this result. Were they treated by a psychiatrist, psychologist, or social worker? Were they seen in a group or individual context? Did the therapist have extensive or relatively limited training and experience? It didn't matter. Clients seemed equally satisfied (Seligman, 1995).

So was the dodo bird in *Alice in Wonderland* right: "Everyone has won and all must have prizes"? Not quite. Some forms of psychotherapy get prizes for

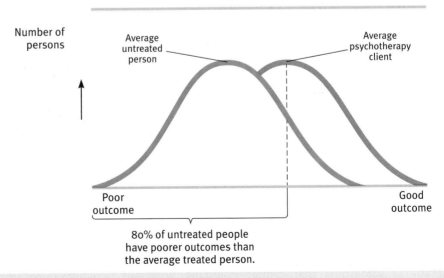

FIGURE 14.3 Treatment versus no treatment In 475 studies, the outcome for the average therapy client was better than that for 80 percent of the untreated people. (Adapted from Smith et al., 1980.)

particular problems. Behavior therapies, for example, work well for specific behavior problems, such as bed-wetting, phobias, compulsions, marital problems, and sexual dysfunctions (Bowers & Clum, 1988; Hunsley & Di Giulio, 2002; Shadish & Baldwin, 2005). Psychodynamic therapy has helped treat depression and anxiety (Driessen et al., 2010; Leichsenring & Rabung, 2008; Shedler, 2010b). Cognitive therapies are effective in helping people cope with anxiety, depression, and posttraumatic stress disorder (Aderka et al., 2012; Bisson & Andrew, 2007).

But no prizes—and little or no scientific support—would go to certain other psychotherapies (Arkowitz & Lilienfeld, 2006). We would all be wise to avoid the following unsupported approaches:

- *Energy therapies,* which seek to manipulate people's invisible energy fields.

- *Recovered-memory therapies,* which aim to unearth "repressed memories" of early childhood abuse (Chapter 7).

- *Rebirthing therapies,* which engage people in reenacting their supposed birth trauma.

This list of discredited therapies raises another question. Who should decide which psychotherapies get prizes and which do not? This question lies at the heart of a controversy—some call it psychology's civil war. What role should science play in clinical practice, and how much should science guide health care providers and insurers in setting payment policies for psychotherapy?

On one side are research psychologists who use scientific methods to extend the list of well-defined therapies with proven results in aiding people with various disorders. They worry that many clinicians "give more weight to their personal experience than to science" (Baker et al., 2008).

On the other side are the nonscientist therapists who view their practices as more art than science. They view psychotherapy as something that cannot be described in a manual or tested in an experiment. People are too complex

and psychotherapy is too intuitive for a cookie-cutter approach, many therapists say.

Between these two camps stand the science-oriented clinicians calling for **evidence-based practice** (FIGURE 14.4). Evidence-based therapists make informed decisions based on research evidence, clinical expertise, and their knowledge of the patient. If we make mental health professionals accountable for effectiveness, everyone gains, say these clinicians. The public will be protected from false therapies. And therapists will be protected from accusations of sounding like snake-oil vendors— "Trust me, I know it works, I've seen it work. It will work for you, too." ■

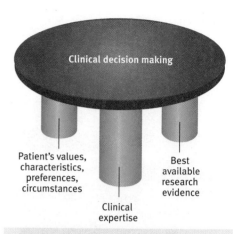

FIGURE 14.4 Evidence-based clinical decision making Ideal clinical decision making is a three-legged stool, upheld by research evidence, clinical expertise, and knowledge of the patient.

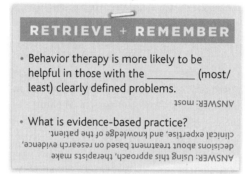

RETRIEVE + REMEMBER

- Behavior therapy is more likely to be helpful in those with the _____ (most/least) clearly defined problems.

ANSWER: most

- What is evidence-based practice?

ANSWER: Using this approach, therapists make decisions about treatment based on research evidence, clinical expertise, and knowledge of the patient.

How Do Psychotherapies Help People?

14-10 What three elements are shared by all forms of psychotherapy?

Why do therapists' training and experience appear not to influence clients' outcomes? The answer seems to be that all psychotherapies offer three basic benefits: *hope for demoralized people; a new perspective on oneself and the world;* and *an empathic, trusting, caring relationship.*

Hope for Demoralized People

Many people seek therapy because they feel anxious, depressed, and self-disapproving. They've lost their way, and they don't feel able to turn things around. What any psychotherapy offers is the expectation that things can and will get better. This belief, regardless of

therapy technique, can improve morale, create feelings of inner strength, and reduce symptoms (Prioleau et al., 1983). By harnessing the person's own healing powers, all sorts of treatments—including some folk-healing rites with no scientific support for their effectiveness—may produce cures (Frank, 1982).

A New Perspective

Every psychotherapy also offers people an explanation of their symptoms. Therapy is a new experience that can help people change their behavior and their view of themselves. Psychodynamic therapy, for example, may free people from false beliefs that are rooted in early relationships. Armed with a believable fresh perspective, people may approach life with new energy to make needed changes.

An Empathic, Trusting, Caring Relationship

No matter what technique they use, effective therapists are empathic. They seek to understand people's experiences. They communicate care and concern. And they earn trust through respectful listening, reassurance, and advice. These qualities were clear in taped therapy sessions from 36 recognized master therapists (Goldfried et al., 1998). Some took a cognitive-behavioral approach. Others emphasized psychodynamic teachings. Regardless, at key moments during the most significant parts of their sessions, they were strikingly similar. They helped clients evaluate themselves, link one aspect of their life with another, and gain insight into their interactions with others. During such interactions, an emotional bond—called the *therapeutic alliance*—forms between therapist and client. This bond is a key aspect of effective psychotherapy (Klein et al., 2003; Wampold, 2001). In one U.S. National Institute of Mental Health depression-treatment study, the most effective therapists were those who formed the closest therapeutic bonds with their clients by showing empathy and care (Blatt et al., 1996).

These three basic benefits—hope, a fresh perspective, and an empathic, caring relationship—help us understand why paraprofessionals (briefly trained caregivers) can assist so many troubled people so effectively (Christensen & Jacobson, 1994). They are an important part of what self-help and support groups offer their members. And they also are part of what traditional healers have offered (Jackson, 1992). Healers everywhere—special people to whom others disclose their suffering, whether psychiatrists, witch doctors, or shamans—have listened in order to understand. And they have empathized, reassured, advised, consoled, interpreted, and explained (Torrey, 1986). These three elements of effective psychotherapy may also explain another finding. People who feel supported by close relationships—who enjoy the fellowship and friendship of caring people—are less likely to need or seek therapy (Frank, 1982; O'Connor & Brown, 1984).

* * *

To recap, people who seek psychotherapy usually improve. So do many of those who do not undergo psychotherapy, and that is a tribute to our human resourcefulness and our capacity to care for one another. Nevertheless, though the therapist's orientation and experience appear not to matter much, people who receive some psychotherapy usually improve more than those who do not. People with clear-cut, specific problems tend to improve the most. ■

RETRIEVE + REMEMBER

- Those who undergo psychotherapy are _____ (more/less) likely to show improvement than those who do not undergo psychotherapy.

ANSWER: more

How Do Culture and Values Influence Psychotherapy?

14-11 How do culture and values influence the client-therapist relationship?

All psychotherapies offer hope. Nearly all therapists try to enhance their clients' sensitivity, openness, personal responsibility, and sense of purpose (Jensen & Bergin, 1988). But in matters of cultural and moral diversity, therapists differ from one another and may differ from their clients (Delaney et al., 2007; Kelly, 1990).

These differences can create a mismatch when a therapist from one culture interacts with a client from

A CARING RELATIONSHIP Effective counselors, such as this chaplain working aboard a ship, form a bond of trust with the people they are serving.

STEVE SZYDLOWSKI/KRT/Newsroom

another. In North America, Europe, and Australia, for example, many therapists reflect the majority culture's *individualism*, which often gives priority to personal desires and identity. Clients with a *collectivist* perspective, as with many from Asian cultures, may assume people will be more mindful of others' expectations. Such clients may have trouble relating to therapies that require them to think only of their individual well-being (Markus & Kitayama, 1991). Cultural differences help explain the reluctance of some minority populations to use mental health services and their tendency to leave therapy prematurely (Chen et al., 2009; Sue, 2006). In one experiment, Asian-American clients matched with counselors who shared their cultural values (rather than mismatched with those who did not) perceived more counselor empathy and felt more alliance with the counselor (Kim et al., 2005).

Another area of potential conflict related to values is religion. Highly religious people may prefer and benefit from therapists who share their values and beliefs (Masters, 2010; Smith et al., 2007; Wade et al., 2006). They may have trouble establishing an emotional bond with a therapist who views the world differently.

Albert Ellis, who advocated an aggressive "rational-emotive" therapy, and Allen Bergin, co-editor of the *Handbook of Psychotherapy and Behavior Change*, illustrated how sharply psychotherapists can differ. They also show how such differences can affect a therapist's view of a healthy person.

Ellis (1980) assumed that "no one and nothing is supreme." "Self-gratification" should be encouraged. "Unequivocal love, commitment, service, and . . . fidelity to any interpersonal commitment, especially marriage, leads to harmful consequences."

evidence-based practice clinical decision making that integrates the best available research with clinical expertise and patient characteristics and preferences.

A Consumer's Guide to Psychotherapists

14-12 What should a person look for when selecting a therapist?

Life for everyone is marked by a mix of calm and stress, blessings and losses, good moods and bad. So when should we seek a mental health professional's help? The American Psychological Association offers these common trouble signals:

- Feelings of hopelessness
- Deep and lasting depression
- Self-destructive behavior, such as alcohol and drug abuse
- Disruptive fears
- Sudden mood shifts
- Thoughts of suicide
- Compulsive rituals, such as hand washing
- Sexual difficulties
- Hearing voices or seeing things that others don't experience

In looking for a psychotherapist, you may want to have a preliminary meeting with two or three. College health centers are generally good starting points, and they offer some free services. In your meetings, you can describe your problem and learn each therapist's treatment approach. You can ask questions about the therapist's values, credentials (TABLE 14.2), state license, and fees. And you can assess your own feelings about each of them. The emotional bond between therapist and client is perhaps the most important factor in effective therapy.

TABLE 14.2	Therapists and Their Training
Type	**Description (includes research training)**
Clinical psychologists	Most are psychologists with a Ph.D. (includes research training) or Psy.D. (focuses on therapy), supplemented by a supervised internship and, often, postdoctoral training. About half work in agencies and institutions, half in private practice.
Psychiatrists	Psychiatrists are medical doctors who specialize in the treatment of psychological disorders. As M.D.s or D.O.s, they can prescribe medications. Many have their own private practice.
Clinical or psychiatric social workers	A two-year master of social work graduate program plus postgraduate supervision prepares some social workers to offer psychotherapy, mostly to people with everyday personal and family problems. About half have earned the National Association of Social Workers' designation of clinical social worker.
Counselors	Marriage and family counselors specialize in family relations problems. Clergy provide counseling to countless people. Abuse counselors work with substance abusers and with spouse and child abusers and their victims. Mental health and other counselors may be required to have a two-year master's degree.

Bergin (1980) viewed things differently: "Because God is supreme, humility and the acceptance of divine authority are virtues." "Self-control and committed love and self-sacrifice are to be encouraged." "Infidelity to any interpersonal commitment, especially marriage, leads to harmful consequences."

Bergin's and Ellis' values differed radically. But they agreed on at least one point: *Psychotherapists' personal beliefs and values influence their practice.* Clients tend to adopt their therapists' values (Worthington et al., 1996). For that reason, some psychologists believe therapists should express those values more openly. (For therapy options see Close-Up: A Consumer's Guide to Psychotherapists.)

The American Psychological Association recognizes the importance of a strong therapeutic alliance and it welcomes diverse therapists who can relate well to diverse clients. It accredits programs that provide training in cultural sensitivity (for example, to differing values, communication styles, and language) and that recruit underrepresented cultural groups.

The Biomedical Therapies

Psychotherapy is one way to treat psychological disorders. The other, often used with the most serious disorders, is *biomedical therapy*, which changes the brain's chemistry with drugs or affects the brain's circuitry with electrical stimulation, magnetic impulses, or psychosurgery. Primary care providers prescribe most drugs for anxiety and depression, followed by psychiatrists and, in some states, psychologists.

Drug Therapies

14-13 What are the drug therapies? How do double-blind studies help researchers evaluate a drug's effectiveness?

By far the most widely used biomedical treatments today are the drug therapies. Since the 1950s, drug researchers have written a new chapter in the treatment of people with severe disorders. Thanks to drug therapies and support from community mental health programs, the resident population of U.S. state and county mental hospitals has dropped to

"Our psychopharmacologist is a genius."

DRUG OR PLACEBO EFFECT? For many people, depression lifts while they are taking an antidepressant drug. But people given a placebo may experience the same effect. Double-blind clinical trials suggest that, especially for those with severe depression, antidepressant drugs do have at least a modest clinical effect.

a small fraction of what it was a half-century ago. In one decade alone (1996 to 2005), the number of Americans prescribed antidepressant drugs doubled, from 13 million to 27 million (Olfson & Marcus, 2009).

Almost any new treatment, including drug therapy, is greeted by an initial wave of enthusiasm as many people apparently improve. But that enthusiasm often diminishes on closer examination. To judge the effectiveness of a new treatment, we also need to know more:

- Do untreated people also improve? If so, how many, and how quickly?
- Was recovery due to the drug or to the *placebo effect?* When patients and/or mental health workers expect positive results, they may see what they expect, not what really happens.

To control for these influences when testing a new drug, researchers give half the patients the drug, and the other half a similar-appearing placebo. Because neither the staff nor the patients know who gets which, this is called a *double-blind technique.* The good news: In double-blind studies, several types of drugs

have proven useful in treating psychological disorders.

* * *

The four most common drug treatments for psychological disorders are *antipsychotic drugs, antianxiety drugs, antidepressant drugs,* and *mood-stabilizing medications.* Let's consider each of these in more detail.

Antipsychotic Drugs

Accidents sometimes launch revolutions. In this instance, an accidental discovery launched a treatment revolution for people with *psychoses.* The discovery was that some drugs used for other medical purposes calmed the hallucinations or delusions that are part of the split from reality for these patients. **Antipsychotic drugs,** such as chlorpromazine (sold as Thorazine), reduce patients' overreactions to irrelevant stimuli. Thus, they provide the most help to schizophrenia patients experiencing symptoms such as auditory hallucinations and paranoia (Lehman et al., 1998; Lenzenweger et al., 1989). (Antipsychotic drugs are not equally effective in changing symptoms such as apathy and withdrawal.)

How do antipsychotic drugs work? They mimic certain neurotransmitters.

"If this doesn't help you don't worry, it's a placebo."

Some block the activity of dopamine by occupying its receptor sites. This finding reinforces the idea that an overactive dopamine system contributes to schizophrenia. Further support for this idea comes from a side effect of another drug. L-dopa is a drug sometimes given to people with Parkinson's disease to boost their production of dopamine, which is too low in Parkinson's. L-dopa raises dopamine levels, but can you guess its occasional side effect? If you guessed hallucinations, you're right.

Do antipsychotic drugs also have side effects? *Yes,* and some are powerful. They may produce sluggishness, tremors, and twitches similar to those of Parkinson's disease (Kaplan & Saddock, 1989). Long-term use of antipsychotics can also produce *tardive dyskinesia,* with involuntary movements of the facial muscles (such as grimacing), tongue, and limbs. Although not more effective in controlling schizophrenia symptoms, many of the newer-generation antipsychotics (such as risperidone and olanzapine) have fewer of these effects. These drugs may, however, increase the risk of obesity and diabetes (Buchanan et al., 2010; Tiihonen et al., 2009).

Despite their drawbacks, antipsychotics, combined with life-skills programs and family support, have given new hope to many people with schizophrenia (Guo, 2010). Hundreds of thousands of patients have left the wards of mental hospitals and returned to work and to near-normal lives (Leucht et al., 2003). Elyn Saks, a University of Southern California law professor, knows what it means to live with schizophrenia. Thanks to her treatment, which combines an antipsychotic drug and psychotherapy, "Now I'm mostly well. I'm mostly thinking clearly. I do have episodes, but it's not like I'm struggling all of the time to stay on the right side of the line" (Saks, 2007).

antipsychotic drugs drugs used to treat schizophrenia and other forms of severe thought disorders.

Antianxiety Drugs

Like alcohol, **antianxiety drugs,** such as Xanax or Ativan, depress central nervous system activity (and so should not be used in combination with alcohol). These drugs are often used in combination with psychological therapy to treat anxiety disorders, obsessive-compulsive disorder, and posttraumatic stress disorder. They calm anxiety as the person learns to cope with frightening situations and fear-triggering stimuli.

Some critics fear that antianxiety drugs may reduce symptoms without resolving underlying problems, especially when used as an ongoing treatment. "Popping a Xanax" at the first sign of tension can provide immediate relief, which may reinforce a person's tendency to take drugs when anxious. Regular heavy use can also lead, when the person stops taking the drugs, to physical problems, such as increased anxiety and insomnia.

Antidepressant Drugs

The **antidepressant drugs** were named for their ability to lift people up from a state of depression. These drugs are now also used to treat anxiety disorders, obsessive-compulsive disorder, and post-

traumatic stress disorder. They work by increasing the availability of norepinephrine or serotonin. These neurotransmitters elevate arousal and mood and are scarce when a person experiences feelings of depression or anxiety.

Fluoxetine, which tens of millions of users worldwide have known as Prozac, lifts spirits by prolonging the time serotonin molecules remain in the brain's synapses. It does this by partially blocking the normal reuptake process (**FIGURE 14.5**). Prozac and its cousins Zoloft and Paxil are called *selective serotonin reuptake inhibitors (SSRIs)* because they slow (inhibit) the synaptic vacuuming up (reuptake) of serotonin.

Given their widening use, some professionals prefer the *SSRI drugs,* rather than antidepressants (Kramer, 2011). SSRIs begin to influence neurotransmission within hours. But their full psychological effect may take four weeks, possibly because these drugs promote the birth of new brain cells (Becker & Wojtowicz, 2007; Jacobs, 2004).

Drugs are not the only way to lift our mood. Aerobic exercise can calm people who feel anxious, energize those who feel depressed, and offer other positive

side effects. (More about that later in this chapter.) Cognitive therapy, which helps people reverse their habits of thinking negatively, can boost the drug-aided relief from depression and reduce post-treatment relapses (Hollon et al., 2002; Keller et al., 2000; Vittengl et al., 2007). The best approach seems to be attacking depression (and anxiety) from both above and below (Cuijpers et al., 2010; Walkup et al., 2008). Cognitive-behavioral therapy works from the top down to change thought processes. Antidepressant drugs work from the bottom up to affect the emotion-forming limbic system.

People with depression often improve after a month on antidepressant drugs. But after allowing for natural recovery (the return to normal called *spontaneous recovery*) and the placebo effect, how big is the drug effect? Not big, report some researchers (Kirsch et al., 1998, 2002, 2010). In double-blind clinical trials, placebos produced improvement comparable to about 75 percent of the active drug's effect. In a follow-up review that included unpublished clinical trials, the antidepressant effect was again modest (Kirsch et al., 2008). The placebo effect was less for those with severe depression,

Message is sent across synaptic gap.

Message is received; excess serotonin molecules are reabsorbed by sending neuron.

Prozac partially blocks normal reuptake of the neurotransmitter serotonin; excess serotonin in synapse enhances its mood-lifting effect.

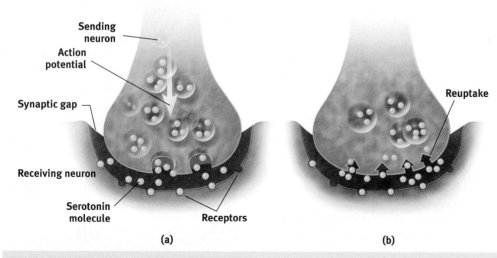
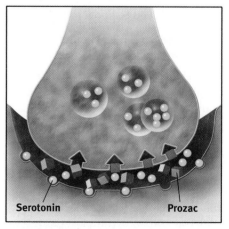

(a)   (b)   (c)

FIGURE 14.5 **Biology of antidepressants** Shown here is the action of Prozac, which partially blocks the reuptake of serotonin.

which made the added benefit of the drug somewhat greater for them (Fournier et al., 2010; Kirsch et al., 2008; Olfson & Marcus, 2009). "Given these results, there seems little reason to prescribe antidepressant medication to any but the most severely depressed patients, unless alternative treatments have failed," concluded one researcher (BBC, 2008).

Mood-Stabilizing Medications

In addition to antipsychotic, antianxiety, and antidepressant drugs, psychiatrists have *mood-stabilizing* drugs in their arsenal. One of them, Depakote, was originally used to treat epilepsy. It was also found effective in controlling the manic episodes associated with bipolar disorder. Another, the simple salt *lithium*, effectively levels the emotional highs and lows of this disorder. Australian physician John Cade discovered this in the 1940s when he administered lithium to a patient with severe mania and the patient became perfectly well in less than a week (Snyder, 1986). Although we do not understand why, lithium works. About 7 in 10 people with bipolar disorder benefit from a long-term daily dose of this cheap salt (Solomon et al., 1995). Their risk of suicide is but one-sixth that of patients with bipolar disorder not taking lithium (Tondo et al., 1997). Kay Redfield Jamison (1995, pp. 88–89) described the effect:

> Lithium prevents my seductive but disastrous highs, diminishes my depressions, clears out the wool and webbing from my disordered thinking, slows me down, gentles me out, keeps me from ruining my career and relationships,

keeps me out of a hospital, alive, and makes psychotherapy possible. ■

RETRIEVE + REMEMBER

- How do researchers evaluate the effectiveness of particular drug therapies?

  ANSWER: Researchers assign people to treatment and no-treatment conditions to see if those who receive the drug therapy improve more than those who don't. Double-blind controlled studies are most effective. If neither the therapist nor the patient knows which participants have received the drug treatment, then any difference between the treated and untreated groups will reflect the drug treatment's actual effect.

- The drugs given most often to treat depression are called _____. The drugs that are now often given to treat anxiety disorders are called _____. Schizophrenia is often treated with _____ drugs.

  ANSWERS: antidepressants; antidepressants (The antidepressants have been shown to be effective at treating both depression and anxiety.); antipsychotic

Brain Stimulation

14-14 How are brain stimulation and psychosurgery used in treating specific disorders?

Electroconvulsive Therapy

Another biomedical treatment, **electroconvulsive therapy (ECT)**, manipulates the brain by shocking it. When ECT was first introduced in 1938, the wide-awake patient was strapped to a table and jolted with roughly 100 volts of electricity to the brain. The procedure, which produced racking convulsions and brief unconsciousness, gained a barbaric image. Although that image lingers, ECT has changed. Today, the patient receives a general anesthetic and a muscle relaxant to prevent convulsions. A psychiatrist then delivers to the patient's brain 30 to 60 seconds of electric current, in briefer pulses, sometimes only to the brain's right side (FIGURE 14.6 on the next page). Within 30 minutes, the patient awakens and remembers nothing of the treatment or of the preceding hours.

Would you agree to ECT for yourself or a loved one? The decision might be difficult, but the treatment works. Shocking as it may seem, study after study con-

firms that ECT can effectively treat severe depression in patients who have not responded to drug therapy (Bailine et al., 2010; Fink, 2009; UK ECT Review Group, 2003). After three such sessions each week for two to four weeks, 80 percent or more of those receiving ECT improve markedly. They show some memory loss for the treatment period but no apparent brain damage (Bergsholm et al., 1989; Coffey, 1993). Modern ECT causes less memory disruption than earlier versions did (HMHL, 2007).

A *Journal of the American Medical Association* editorial concluded that "the results of ECT in treating severe depression are among the most positive treatment effects in all of medicine" (Glass, 2001). ECT reduces suicidal thoughts and is credited with saving many from suicide (Kellner et al., 2005).

How does ECT relieve severe depression? After more than 75 years, no one knows for sure. One patient compared ECT to the smallpox vaccine, which was saving lives before we knew how it worked. Perhaps the brief electric current calms neural centers where overactivity produces depression. ECT, like antidepressant drugs and exercise, also appears to boost the production of new brain cells (Bolwig & Madsen, 2007). ECT and antidepressants also share similarity in how they influence serotonin (Yatham et al., 2010).

Skeptics have offered another possible explanation: ECT may trigger a placebo effect. Most ECT studies have failed to include a control group of patients who were randomly assigned to receive the same general anesthesia and to undergo simulated ECT, but without the

"First of all I think you should know that last quarter's sales figures are interfering with my mood-stabilizing drugs."

antianxiety drugs drugs used to control anxiety and agitation.

antidepressant drugs drugs used to treat depression, anxiety disorders, obsessive-compulsive disorder, and posttraumatic stress disorder. (Several widely used antidepressant drugs are *selective serotonin reuptake inhibitors—SSRIs*.)

electroconvulsive therapy (ECT) a biomedical therapy for severely depressed patients in which a brief electric current is sent through the brain of an anesthetized patient.

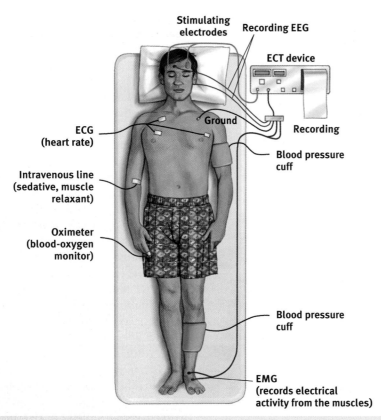

FIGURE 14.6 Electroconvulsive therapy Although controversial, ECT is often an effective treatment for severe depression that does not respond to drug therapy. "Electroconvulsive" is no longer accurate because patients are now given a drug that prevents convulsions.

shock. When given this placebo treatment, patients' expectation of positive results is therapeutic without the shock (Read & Bentall, 2010). Nevertheless, a U.S. Food and Drug Administration (2011) research review concluded that ECT is more effective than a placebo, especially in the short run.

No matter how impressive the results, the idea of electrically shocking a person's brain still strikes many as barbaric, especially given our ignorance about why ECT works. Moreover, the mood boost may not last long. About 4 in 10 ECT-treated patients have relapsed into depression within six months, with or without follow-up drug therapy (Kellner et al., 2006; Tew et al., 2007).

Nevertheless, in the minds of many psychiatrists and patients, ECT is a lesser evil than severe depression's misery, anguish, and risk of suicide. As one

psychologist reported after ECT relieved his deep depression, "A miracle had happened in two weeks" (Endler, 1982).

Alternative Neurostimulation Therapies

To jump-start the depressed brain, scientists have developed some gentler alternatives (Moreines et al., 2011). *Vagus nerve stimulation* stimulates a nerve in the neck, via an electrical device implanted in the chest. The device periodically sends signals to the brain's mood-related limbic system, increasing available serotonin by boosting the firing rates of some neurons (Fitzgerald & Daskalakis, 2008; Marangell et al., 2007).

Another experimental procedure, *deep-brain stimulation,* manipulates the depressed brain by means of a pacemaker that activates implanted electrodes in brain areas that feed negative emotions and thoughts (Lozano et al., 2008; Mayberg et al., 2005). The stimulation inhibits activity in those brain areas. With deep-brain stimulation, some patients whose depression did not respond to drugs or ECT have found their depression lifting. Others have become more responsive to drugs or psychotherapy.

Deep-brain stimulation may show promise in other treatment areas. By inhibiting activity in areas associated with pleasure and reward, it may curb an addict's urges to use drugs and alcohol (Luigjes et al., 2012). But investigators caution that the science is new and more research is needed (Hamani et al., 2009; Rabins et al., 2009).

Depressed moods also seem to improve when repeated pulses of magnetic energy are applied to a person's brain. In a painless procedure called **repetitive transcranial magnetic stimulation (rTMS),** a coiled wire held close to the skull sends a magnetic field to the brain (**FIGURE 14.7**). Unlike deep-brain stimulation, the magnetic energy penetrates only to the brain's surface.

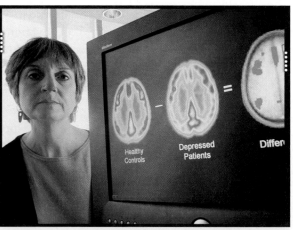

© Eric S. Lesser

A DEPRESSION SWITCH? By comparing the brains of patients with and without depression, researcher Helen Mayberg identified a brain area that appears active in people who are depressed or sad, and whose activity may be calmed by deep-brain stimulation.

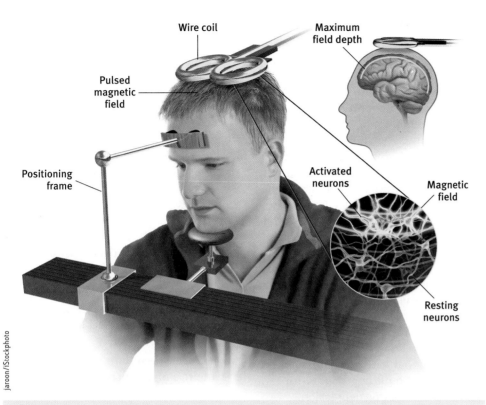

FIGURE 14.7 **Magnets for the mind** In rTMS, a painless magnetic field is sent through the skull to the surface of the brain. Pulses can stimulate or dampen activity in various areas. (From George, 2003.)

And unlike ECT, the rTMS procedure produces no memory loss or other serious side effects. (Headaches can result.) Wide-awake patients receive this treatment daily for two to four weeks.

Initial studies have found "modest" positive benefits of rTMS (Daskalakis et al., 2008; George et al., 2010; López-Ibor et al., 2008). In one study, a woman with bipolar disorder benefited more from rTMS than from ECT (Zeeuws et al., 2011). How it works is not yet clear. One possible explanation is that the stimulation energizes the brain's left frontal lobe, which is relatively inactive during depression (Helmuth, 2001). Repeated stimulation may cause nerve cells to form new functioning circuits through the process of long-term potentiation. (For more on long-term potentiation, see Chapter 7.) ■

RETRIEVE + REMEMBER

- Severe depression that has not responded to other therapy may be treated with _____ _____, which can cause memory loss. More moderate neural stimulation techniques designed to help alleviate depression include _____ _____ stimulation, _____-_____ stimulation, and _____ _____ magnetic stimulation.

ANSWERS: electroconvulsive therapy (ECT); vagus nerve; deep-brain; repetitive transcranial

Psychosurgery

Psychosurgery is surgery that removes or destroys brain tissue in an attempt to change thoughts and behaviors. Because its effects are irreversible, it is the least-used biomedical therapy.

In the 1930s, Portuguese physician Egas Moniz developed what would become the best-known psychosurgical operation: the **lobotomy**. He (and, later, other neurosurgeons) used it to calm uncontrollably emotional and violent patients. His crude but easy and inexpensive procedure took only about 10 minutes:

- *Step 1.* Shock the patient into a coma.

FAILED LOBOTOMY This 1940 photo shows Rosemary Kennedy (center) at age 22 with brother (and future U.S. president) John and sister Jean. A year later her father, on medical advice, approved a lobotomy that was promised to control her reportedly violent mood swings. The procedure left her confined to a hospital with an infantile mentality until her death in 2005 at age 86.

repetitive transcranial magnetic stimulation (rTMS) the application of repeated pulses of magnetic energy to the brain; used to stimulate or suppress brain activity.

psychosurgery surgery that removes or destroys brain tissue in an effort to change behavior.

lobotomy a psychosurgical procedure once used to calm uncontrollably emotional or violent patients. The procedure cut the nerves connecting the frontal lobes to the emotion-controlling centers of the inner brain.

- *Step* 2. Hammer an instrument shaped like an icepick through each eye socket. Drive it into the brain.

- *Step* 3. Wiggle the instrument to cut nerves connecting the frontal lobes with the emotion-controlling centers of the inner brain.

Tens of thousands of severely disturbed people received lobotomies between 1936 and 1954. By that time, some 35,000 people had been lobotomized in the United States alone.

For his work, Moniz received a Nobel Prize (Valenstein, 1986). But today, lobotomies are history. Their intention was simply to disconnect emotion from thought, and indeed, they did usually decrease misery or tension. But their effect was often more drastic, leaving people permanently listless, immature, and uncreative. During the 1950s, when calming drugs became available, psychosurgery was largely abandoned. Today, more precise micropsychosurgery is sometimes used in extreme cases. For example, if a patient has uncontrollable seizures, surgeons can destroy the specific nerve clusters that cause or transmit the convulsions. MRI-guided precision surgery is also occasionally done to cut the circuits involved in severe obsessive-compulsive disorder (Carey, 2009, 2011; Sachdev & Sachdev, 1997). Because these procedures cannot be reversed, neurosurgeons perform them only as a last resort.

Therapeutic Lifestyle Change

14-15 How, by adopting a healthier lifestyle, might people find some relief from depression?

The effectiveness of the biomedical therapies reminds us of a fundamental lesson. *We find it convenient to talk of separate psychological and biological influences, but everything psychological is also biological.* Every thought and feeling depends on the functioning brain. Every creative idea, every moment of joy or anger, every period of depression emerges from the electrochemical activity of the living brain. The influence is two-way. When psychotherapy relieves behaviors associated with obsessive-compulsive disorder or schizophrenia, PET scans reveal a calmer brain (Habel et al., 2010; Schwartz et al., 1996).

For years, we have considered the health of our body and mind separately. That neat separation no longer seems valid. Stress affects body chemistry and health. And chemical imbalances, whatever their cause, can produce psychological disorders.

That lesson is now being applied in training seminars promoting *therapeutic lifestyle change* (Ilardi, 2009). Two basic ideas behind these sessions are that human brains and bodies were designed for physical activity and social engagement, and that our ancestors hunted, gathered, and built in groups, with little evidence of disabling depression.

Those whose way of life includes regular physical activity, strong community ties, sunlight exposure, and plenty of sleep rarely experience major depression. Depression is nearly absent in America's Amish farming communities. Whether we are children or adults, outdoor activity in a natural environment—perhaps a walk in the woods—can reduce stress and promote health (NEEF, 2011; Phillips, 2011).

Research shows that regular aerobic exercise rivals the healing power of antidepressant drugs (Babyak et al., 2000; Salmon, 2001). And a complete night's sleep boosts mood and energy (Gregory et al., 2009; Walker & van der Helm, 2009). In the lifestyle change sessions, small groups of people with depression undergo a 12-week training program with the following goals:

- *Aerobic exercise,* 30 minutes a day, at least three times weekly (increases fitness and vitality, stimulates endorphins)

- *Adequate sleep,* with a goal of 7 to 8 hours a night (increases energy and alertness, boosts immunity)

- *Light exposure,* at least 30 minutes each morning with a light box (amplifies arousal, influences hormones)

- *Social connection,* with less alone time and at least two meaningful social engagements weekly (helps satisfy the human need to belong)

ENDURING SMILE Mexico's Tarahumara people have a cultural system where distance running is commonplace. Some believe that the Tarahumara's distance running skills contribute to their lower rate of depression (McDougall, 2009).

© Marcos Ferro/Aurora Photos/Alamy

Rubberball/Nicole Hill/Jupiterimages

- *Antirumination,* by identifying and redirecting negative thoughts (enhances positive thinking)
- *Nutritional supplements,* including a daily fish oil supplement with omega-3 fatty acids (aids in healthy brain functioning)

In one study of 74 people, 77 percent of those who completed the program experienced relief from depressive symptoms. In contrast, only 19 percent of those assigned to a treatment-as-usual control group showed similar results. Though in need of replication, these results are striking. Future research will try to identify which parts of the treatment produce the therapeutic effect. But there seems little reason to doubt the truth of the Latin saying, *Mens sana in corpore sano:* "A healthy mind in a healthy body" **(FIGURE 14.8).**

* * *

TABLE 14.3 summarizes the therapies discussed in this chapter. ■

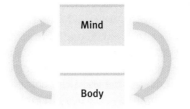

FIGURE 14.8 Mind-body interaction The biomedical therapies assume that mind and body are a unit: Affect one and you will affect the other.

RETRIEVE + REMEMBER

- What are some examples of lifestyle changes we can make to enhance our mental health?

ANSWER: Exercise regularly, get enough sleep, get more exposure to light, nurture important relationships, redirect negative thinking, and eat a diet rich in omega-3 fatty acids.

Preventing Psychological Disorders

14-16 What may help prevent psychological disorders?

We have seen that lifestyle change can help *reverse* some of the symptoms of psychological disorders. Might such change also *prevent* some disorders by building individuals' **resilience**—an ability to cope with stress and recover from adversity? When trauma blindsides us, most adults exhibit resilience. This was true of New Yorkers in the aftermath of the September 11 terror attacks, especially

resilience the personal strength that helps most people cope with stress and recover from adversity and even trauma.

Therapy	Presumed Problem	Therapy Aim	Therapy Technique
Psychodynamic	Unconscious conflicts from childhood experiences	Reduce anxiety through self-insight.	Interpret patients' memories and feelings.
Client-centered	Blocking of self-understanding and self-acceptance	Enable growth via unconditional positive regard, genuineness, and empathy.	Listen actively and reflect clients' feelings.
Behavior	Dysfunctional behaviors	Learn new adaptive behaviors; extinguish problem ones.	Use classical conditioning (via exposure or aversion therapy) or operant conditioning (as in token economies).
Cognitive	Negative, self-harmful thoughts and behaviors	Promote healthier positive thinking and self-talk.	Train people to dispute negative thoughts and attributions.
Cognitive-behavioral	Self-harmful thoughts and behaviors	Promote healthier thinking and adaptive behaviors.	Train people to counter self-harmful thoughts and to act out their new ways of thinking.
Group and family	Stressful relationships	Heal relationships.	Develop an understanding of family and other social systems, explore roles, and improve communication.
Drug therapies	Neurotransmitter malfunction	Control symptoms of psychological disorders.	Alter brain chemistry through drugs.
Brain stimulation	Severe, "treatment-resistant" depression	Alleviate depression that is unresponsive to drug therapy.	Stimulate brain through electroconvulsive shock, vagus nerve stimulation, deep-brain stimulation, or magnetic impulses.
Psychosurgery	Brain malfunction	Relieve severe disorders.	Remove or destroy brain tissue.
Therapeutic lifestyle change	Stress and unhealthy lifestyle	Restore healthy biological state.	Alter lifestyle through adequate exercise, sleep, and other changes.

those who enjoyed supportive close relationships and who had not recently experienced other stressful events (Bonanno et al., 2007). More than 9 in 10 New Yorkers, although stunned and grief-stricken by 9/11, did *not* have a dysfunctional stress reaction. Among those who did have such reactions, the stress symptoms had mostly gone away by the following January (Person et al., 2006).

Similar resilience has been observed among other groups. One study that followed 233 people for up to 2 years following a spinal cord injury reported that most experienced few psychological problems (Bonanno et al., 2012, p. 243). Even combat-stressed veterans and political rebels who have survived dozens of torture episodes usually do not later exhibit posttraumatic stress disorder (Mineka & Zinbarg, 1996).

This resilience also appeared among Holocaust survivors, most of whom went on to live productive lives. "It is not always true that 'What doesn't kill you makes you stronger,' but it is often true," psychologist Peter Suedfeld (1998, 2000) reported. "What doesn't kill you may reveal to you just how strong you really are." Suedfeld speaks from experience. As a boy, he survived the Holocaust, though his mother did not. Fellow survivor Ervin Staub has described "altruism born of suffering" (Staub & Vollhardt, 2008). Although nothing justifies terror and victimization, those who have suffered, he reports, often develop a greater-than-usual sensitivity to suffering. They have greater empathy for others who suffer, an increased sense of responsibility, and an enlarged capacity for caring. Staub is a living example of his own work. He was spared from being sent to the Auschwitz death camps, thanks to a heroic intervention. Since that time, his lifelong mission has been to understand why some people perpetrate evil, some stand by, and some help out.

Struggling with challenging crises can lead to *posttraumatic growth*. Many cancer survivors have reported a greater appreciation for life, more meaningful relationships, increased personal strength, changed priorities, and a richer spiritual life (Tedeschi & Calhoun, 2004). Americans who tried to make sense of the 9/11 terrorist attacks experienced less distress (Park et al., 2012). Out of even our worst experiences some good can come.

How might we foster such growth and human flourishing? One option might be to adopt a preventive view of human disorders.

A story about the rescue of drowning persons from a rushing river illustrates prevention. Having successfully given first aid to the first victim, the rescuer spots another struggling person and pulls her out, too. After a half-dozen repetitions, the rescuer suddenly turns and starts running away while the river sweeps yet another person into view. "Aren't you going to rescue that fellow?" asks a bystander. "Heck no," the rescuer replies. "I'm going upstream to find out what's pushing all these people in."

Preventive mental health is upstream work. It aims to prevent psychological casualties by identifying and wiping out the conditions that cause them. Poverty, meaningless work, constant criticism, unemployment, racism, and sexism can undermine people's sense of competence, personal control, and self-esteem (Albee, 1986, 2006). Such stresses increase the risk of depression, alcohol abuse, and suicide.

To prevent psychological casualties, said George Albee, caring people should therefore support programs that control or eliminate these stressful situations. We eliminated smallpox not by treating the afflicted but by vaccinating the healthy. We conquered yellow fever by controlling mosquitoes. Better to drain the swamps than just swat the mosquitos.

Preventing psychological problems means empowering those who have learned an attitude of helplessness and changing environments that breed loneliness. It means renewing fragile family ties and boosting parents' and teachers' skills at nurturing children's achievements and resulting self-concept. Indeed, "everything aimed at improving the human condition, at making life more fulfilling and meaningful, may be considered part of primary prevention of mental or emotional disturbance" (Kessler & Albee, 1975, p. 557). Prevention can sometimes provide a double payoff. People with a strong sense of life's meaning are more engaging socially (Stillman et al., 2011). If we can strengthen people's sense of meaning in life, we may also lessen their loneliness as they grow into more engaging companions.

Among the upstream prevention workers are *community psychologists*. Mindful of how people interact with their environments, they focus on creating environments that support psychological health. Through their research and social action, community psychologists aim to empower people and to enhance their competence, health, and well-being. ∎

* * *

That brings us to the end of this book. Your introduction to psychological science is complete. Navigating through the waters of psychological science has taught us—and you, too?—about our moods and memories, about the inner nooks and crannies of our unconscious, about how our biology and culture in turn shape us. Our hope, as your guides on this tour, is that you have shared some of our fascination, grown in your understanding and compassion, and sharpened your critical thinking. We hope you enjoyed the ride. We did.

With every good wish in your future endeavors,

David G. Myers
www.davidmyers.org

Nathan DeWall
www.NathanDeWall.com

CHAPTER REVIEW

Therapy

Test yourself by taking a moment to answer each of these Learning Objective Questions (repeated here from within the chapter). Then turn to Appendix D, Complete Chapter Reviews, to check your answers. Research suggests that trying to answer these questions on your own will improve your long-term memory of the concepts (McDaniel et al., 2009).

Treating Psychological Disorders

14-1: What are the differences between psychotherapy and the biomedical therapies?

The Psychological Therapies

14-2: What are the goals and techniques of psychoanalysis, and how have they been adapted in psychodynamic therapy?

14-3: What are the basic themes of humanistic therapy, and what are the goals and techniques of Rogers' client-centered approach?

14-4: How do behavior therapy's assumptions and techniques differ from those of psychodynamic and humanistic therapies? What techniques are used in exposure therapies and aversive conditioning?

14-5: What is the basic idea of operant conditioning therapies?

14-6: What are the goals and techniques of the cognitive therapies and of cognitive-behavioral therapy?

14-7: What are the aims and benefits of group and family therapy?

Evaluating Psychotherapies

14-8: Does psychotherapy work? Who decides?

14-9: Are some psychotherapies more effective than others for specific disorders?

14-10: What three elements are shared by all forms of psychotherapy?

14-11: How do culture and values influence the client-therapist relationship?

14-12: What should a person look for when selecting a therapist?

The Biomedical Therapies

14-13: What are the drug therapies? How do double-blind studies help researchers evaluate a drug's effectiveness?

14-14: How are brain stimulation and psychosurgery used in treating specific disorders?

14-15: How, by adopting a healthier lifestyle, might people find some relief from depression?

Preventing Psychological Disorders

14-16: What may help prevent psychological disorders?

TERMS AND CONCEPTS TO REMEMBER

Test yourself on these terms by trying to write down the definition in your own words before flipping back to the referenced page to check your answer.

psychotherapy, p. 410
biomedical therapy, p. 410
eclectic approach, p. 410
psychoanalysis, p. 410
resistance, p. 411
interpretation, p. 411
transference, p. 411
psychodynamic therapy, p. 412

insight therapies, p. 412
client-centered therapy, p. 413
active listening, p. 413
unconditional positive regard, p. 413
behavior therapy, p. 414
counterconditioning, p. 414
exposure therapies, p. 414

systematic desensitization, p. 415
virtual reality exposure therapy, p. 415
aversive conditioning, p. 415
token economy, p. 416
cognitive therapy, p. 417
cognitive-behavioral therapy, p. 418
group therapy, p. 419
family therapy, p. 419

evidence-based practice, p. 422
antipsychotic drugs, p. 425
antianxiety drugs, p. 426
antidepressant drugs, p. 426
electroconvulsive therapy (ECT), p. 427
repetitive transcranial magnetic stimulation (rTMS), p. 428
psychosurgery, p. 429
lobotomy, p. 429
resilience, p. 431

CHAPTER TEST

Test yourself repeatedly throughout your studies. This will not only help you figure out what you know and don't know; the testing itself will help you learn and remember the information more effectively thanks to the *testing effect*.

1. A therapist who helps patients search for the unconscious roots of their problem and offers interpretations of their behaviors, feelings, and dreams, is drawing from
   a. psychoanalysis.
   b. humanistic therapies.
   c. client-centered therapy.
   d. behavior therapy.

2. _____ therapies are designed to help individuals discover the thoughts and feelings that guide their motivation and behavior.

3. Compared with psychoanalysis, humanistic therapies are more likely to emphasize
   a. hidden or repressed feelings.
   b. childhood experiences.
   c. psychological disorders.
   d. self-fulfillment and growth.

4. A therapist who restates and clarifies the client's statements is practicing _____ _____.

5. The goal of behavior therapy is to
   a. identify and treat the underlying causes of the problem.
   b. improve learning and insight.
   c. eliminate the unwanted behavior.
   d. improve communication and social sensitivity.

6. Behavior therapies often use _____ techniques such as systematic desensitization and aversive conditioning to encourage clients to produce new responses to old stimuli.

7. The technique of _____ _____ teaches people to relax in the presence of progressively more anxiety-provoking stimuli.

8. After a near-fatal car accident, Rico developed such an intense fear of driving on the freeway that he takes lengthy alternative routes to work each day. Which psychological therapy might best help Rico overcome his phobia, and why?

9. At a treatment center, people who display a desired behavior receive coins that they can later exchange for other rewards. This is an example of a(n) _____ _____.

10. Cognitive therapy has been especially effective in treating
    a. nail biting.
    b. phobias.
    c. alcohol use disorder.
    d. depression.

11. _____ - _____ therapy helps people to change their self-defeating ways of thinking and to act out those changes in their daily behavior.

12. In family therapy, the therapist assumes that
    a. only one family member needs to change.
    b. each person's actions trigger reactions from other family members.
    c. dysfunctional families must improve their interactions or give up their children.
    d. all of the above are true.

13. The most enthusiastic or optimistic view of the effectiveness of psychotherapy comes from
    a. outcome research.
    b. randomized clinical trials.
    c. reports of clinicians and clients.
    d. a government study of treatment for depression.

14. Studies show that _____ therapy is the most effective treatment for most psychological disorders.
    a. behavior
    b. humanistic
    c. psychodynamic
    d. no one type of

15. What are the three components of evidence-based practice?

16. How does the placebo effect bias patients' attitudes about the effectiveness of drug therapies?

17. Some antipsychotic drugs, used to calm people with schizophrenia, can have unpleasant side effects, most notably
    a. hyperactivity.
    b. convulsions and momentary memory loss.
    c. sluggishness, tremors, and twitches.
    d. paranoia.

18. Drugs such as Xanax and Ativan, which depress central nervous system activity, can become addictive when used as ongoing treatment. These drugs are referred to as _____ drugs.

19. A simple salt that often brings relief to patients suffering the highs and lows of bipolar disorder is _____.

20. When drug therapies have not been effective, electroconvulsive therapy (ECT) may be used as treatment, largely for people with

    a. severe obsessive-compulsive disorder.

    b. severe depression.

    c. schizophrenia.

    d. anxiety disorders.

21. An approach that seeks to identify and alleviate conditions that put people at high risk for developing psychological disorders is called

    a. deep-brain stimulation.

    b. the mood-stabilizing perspective.

    c. spontaneous recovery.

    d. preventive mental health.

    Find answers to these questions in Appendix E, in the back of the book.

IN YOUR EVERYDAY LIFE

Answering these questions will help you make these concepts more personally meaningful, and therefore more memorable.

1. What do you think about psychodynamic and humanistic "talk therapy"? Have you ever found yourself using similar ideas when talking with upset friends or family members?

2. Critics say that behavior modification techniques, such as those used in token economies, are not humane. Do you agree or disagree? Why?

3. Have you ever had trouble reaching a goal at school or work because of your own irrational thoughts? How could you challenge these thoughts?

4. How might you use the general helping principles discussed in this chapter during a conversation with a friend who is having family problems?

5. What were your impressions of biomedical therapies before reading this chapter? Are any of your views different now? Why or why not?

6. Which lifestyle changes could you make to improve your resilience and enhance your mental health?

experience
more of the
testing
effect

Multiple-format self-tests and more may be found at www.worthpublishers.com/myers.

Statistical Reasoning in Everyday Life

In descriptive, correlational, and experimental research, statistics are tools that help us see and interpret what the unaided eye might miss. Sometimes the unaided eye misses badly, as it did when researchers asked 5522 Americans to estimate (as a percentage) the portion of the country's wealth possessed by the richest 20 percent of the population (Norton & Ariely, 2011). The average person's guess—58 percent—"dramatically underestimated" the actual figure. (The wealthiest 20 percent possess 84 percent of the wealth.)

Accurate statistical understanding benefits everyone. To be an educated person today is to be able to apply simple statistical principles to everyday reasoning. We needn't memorize complicated formulas to think more clearly and critically about data.

Off-the-top-of-the-head estimates often mis-

> Asked about the *ideal* wealth distribution in America, Democrats and Republicans were surprisingly similar. In the Democrats' ideal world, the richest 20 percent would possess 30 percent of the wealth. Republicans preferred a similar 35 percent (Norton & Ariely, 2011).

read reality and then mislead the public. Someone throws out a big, round number. Others echo it, and before long the big, round number becomes public misinformation. A few examples:

- *Ten percent of people are lesbians or gay men.* Or is it 2 to 3 percent, as suggested by various national surveys (Chapter 4)?
- *We ordinarily use but 10 percent of our brain.* Or is it closer to 100 percent (Chapter 2)?
- *The human brain has 100 billion nerve cells.* Or is it more like 40 billion, as suggested by one extrapolation from sample counts (Chapter 2)?

The point to remember: Doubt big, round, undocumented numbers.

Statistical illiteracy also feeds needless health scares (Gigerenzer et al., 2008, 2009, 2010). In the 1990s, the British press reported a study showing that women taking a particular contraceptive pill had a 100 percent increased risk of blood clots that could produce strokes. This caused thousands of women to stop taking the pill, leading to a wave of unwanted pregnancies and an estimated 13,000 additional abortions (which also are associated with increased blood clot risk). And what did the study find? A 100 percent increased risk, indeed—but only from 1 in 7000 to 2 in 7000. Such false alarms underscore the need to teach statistical reason-

ing and to present statistical information more transparently.

Describing Data

A-1 How can we describe data with measures of central tendency and variation?

Once researchers have gathered their data, they must organize them in some meaningful way. One way to do this is to convert the data into a simple *bar graph,* as in **FIGURE A.1** on the next page, which displays a distribution of different brands of trucks still on the road after a decade. When reading statistical graphs such as this, take care. It's easy to design a graph to make a difference look big (Figure A.1a) or small (Figure A.1b). The secret lies in how you label the vertical scale (the *y-axis*).

"Figures can be misleading—so I've written a song which I think expresses the real story of the firm's performance this quarter."

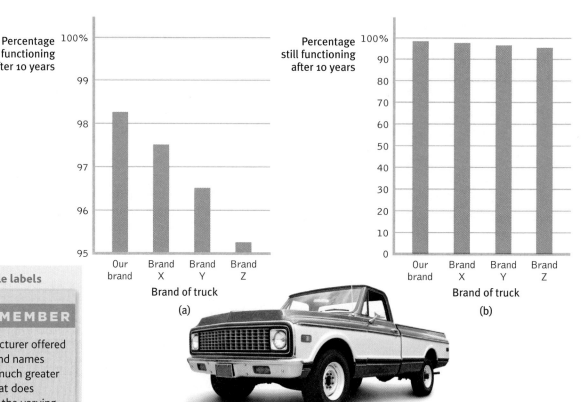

Percentage still functioning after 10 years

Brand of truck

(a)

Percentage still functioning after 10 years

Brand of truck

(b)

Brian Sullivan / Getty Images

FIGURE A.1 Read the scale labels

• An American truck manufacturer offered graph (a)—with actual brand names included—to suggest the much greater durability of its trucks. What does graph (b) make clear about the varying durability, and how is this accomplished?

ANSWER: Note how the y-axis of each graph is labeled. The range for the y-axis label in graph a is only from 95 to 100. The range for graph b is from 0 to 100. All the trucks rank as 95% and up, so almost all are still functioning after 10 years, which graph b makes clear.

The point to remember: Think smart. When viewing figures in magazines, on TV, or online, read the scale labels and note their range.

Measures of Central Tendency

The next step is to summarize the data using some *measure of central tendency,* a single score that represents a whole set of scores. The simplest measure is the **mode,** the most frequently occurring score or scores. The most familiar is the **mean,** or arithmetic average—the total sum of all the scores divided by the number of scores. The midpoint—the

The average person has one ovary and one testicle.

50th percentile—is the **median.** On a divided highway, the median is the middle. So, too, with data: If you arrange all the scores in order from the highest to the lowest, half will be above the median and half will be below it.

Measures of central tendency neatly summarize data. But consider what happens to the mean when a distribution is lopsided, or *skewed,* by a few way-out scores. With income data, for example, the mode, median, and mean often tell very different stories (**FIGURE A.2**). This happens because the mean is biased by a few extreme scores. When Microsoft co-founder Bill Gates sits down in an intimate café, its average (mean) customer instantly becomes a billionaire. But the median customers' wealth remains unchanged. Understanding this, you can see how a British newspaper could accurately run the headline "Income for 62% Is Below Average"

(Waterhouse, 1993). Because the bottom *half* of British income earners received only a *quarter* of the national income cake, most British people, like most people everywhere, made less than the mean. Mean and median tell different true stories.

The point to remember: Always note which measure of central tendency is reported. If it is a mean, consider whether a few atypical scores could be distorting it.

Measures of Variation

Knowing the value of an appropriate measure of central tendency can tell us a great deal. But the single number omits other information. It helps to know something about the amount of *variation* in the data—how similar or diverse the scores are. Averages derived from scores with low variability are more reliable than averages based on scores with high variability. Consider a basketball player who scored between 13 and 17 points in each of the season's first 10 games. Knowing this, we

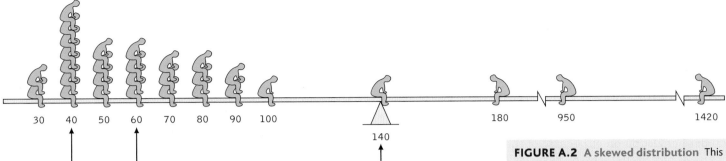

Mode (at 40) **Median** (at 60) **Mean** (at 140)

One family

140

Income per family in thousands of dollars

FIGURE A.2 **A skewed distribution** This graphic representation of the distribution of a village's incomes illustrates the three measures of central tendency—mode, median, and mean. Note how just a few high incomes make the mean—the point that balances the incomes above and below—deceptively high.

would be more confident that she would score near 15 points in her next game than if her scores had varied from 5 to 25 points.

The **range** of scores—the gap between the lowest and highest—provides only a crude estimate of variation. A couple of extreme scores in an otherwise uniform group, such as the $950,000 and $1,420,000 incomes in Figure A.2, will create a deceptively large range.

The more useful standard for measuring how much scores deviate from one another is the **standard deviation.** It better gauges whether scores are packed together or dispersed, because it uses information from each score. The computation (see **TABLE A.1**) assembles in-formation about how much individual scores differ from the mean. Note that the test scores in Class A and Class B have the same mean (80), but very different standard deviations, which tell us more about how the students in each class are really faring. If your college or university attracts students of a certain ability level, their intelligence scores will have a relatively small standard deviation compared with the more diverse community population outside your school.

You can grasp the meaning of the standard deviation if you consider how scores tend to be distributed in nature. Large numbers of data—heights, weights, intelligence scores, grades (though not

mode the most frequently occurring score(s) in a distribution.

mean the arithmetic average of a distribution, obtained by adding the scores and then dividing by the number of scores.

median the middle score in a distribution; half the scores are above it and half are below it.

range the difference between the highest and lowest scores in a distribution.

standard deviation a computed measure of how much scores vary around the mean score.

TABLE A.1   Standard Deviation Is Much More Informative Than Mean Alone

Test Scores in Class A			Test Scores in Class B		
Score	Deviation From the Mean	Squared Deviation	Score	Deviation From the Mean	Squared Deviation
72	−8	64	60	−20	400
74	−6	36	60	−20	400
77	−3	9	70	−10	100
79	−1	1	70	−10	100
82	+2	4	90	+10	100
84	+4	16	90	+10	100
85	+5	25	100	+20	400
87	+7	49	100	+20	400

Total = 640

Mean = 640 ÷ 8 = 80

Sum of (deviations)² = 204

Standard deviation =

$$\sqrt{\frac{\text{Sum of (deviations)}^2}{\text{Number of scores}}} = \sqrt{\frac{204}{8}} = 5.0$$

Total = 640

Mean = 640 ÷ 8 = 80

Sum of (deviations)² = 2000

Standard deviation =

$$\sqrt{\frac{\text{Sum of (deviations)}^2}{\text{Number of scores}}} = \sqrt{\frac{2000}{8}} = 15.8$$

incomes)—often form a symmetrical, *bell-shaped* distribution. Most cases fall near the mean, and fewer cases fall near either extreme. This bell-shaped distribution is so typical that we call the curve it forms the **normal curve.**

As **FIGURE A.3** shows, a useful property of the normal curve is that roughly 68 percent of the cases fall within one standard deviation on either side of the mean. About 95 percent of cases fall within two standard deviations. Thus, as Chapter 8 notes, about 68 percent of people taking an intelligence test will score within ±15 points of 100. About 95 percent will score within ±30 points. ∎

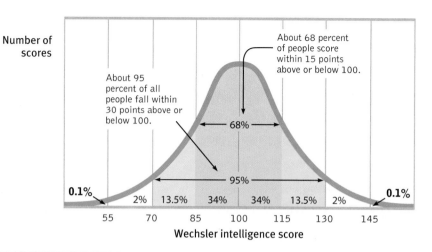

FIGURE A.3   The normal curve   Scores on aptitude tests tend to form a normal, or bell-shaped, curve. For example, the Wechsler Adult Intelligence Scale calls the average score 100.

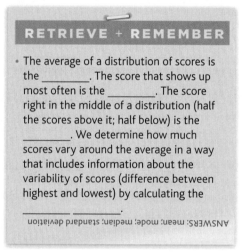

RETRIEVE + REMEMBER

- The average of a distribution of scores is the _____. The score that shows up most often is the _____. The score right in the middle of a distribution (half the scores above it; half below) is the _____. We determine how much scores vary around the average in a way that includes information about the variability of scores (difference between highest and lowest) by calculating the _____ _____.

ANSWERS: mean; mode; median; standard deviation

Correlation: A Measure of Relationships

A-2 What does it mean when we say two things are correlated?

Throughout this book we often ask how strongly two things are related: For example, how closely related are the personality scores of identical twins? How well do intelligence test scores predict vocational achievement? How closely is stress related to disease?

As we saw in Chapter 1, describing behavior is a first step toward predicting it. When naturalistic observation and surveys reveal that one trait or behavior accompanies another, we say the two *correlate.* A **correlation coefficient** is a statistical measure of relationship. In such cases, **scatterplots** can be very revealing.

Each dot in a scatterplot represents the values of two variables. The three scatterplots in **FIGURE A.4** illustrate the range of possible correlations—from a perfect positive to a perfect negative. (Perfect correlations rarely occur in the "real world.") A correlation is positive if two sets of scores, such as height and weight, tend to rise or fall together.

Saying that a correlation is "negative" says nothing about its strength or weakness. A correlation is negative if two sets of scores relate inversely, one set going up as the other goes down.

Statistics can help us see what the naked eye sometimes misses. To demonstrate this for yourself, try an imaginary project. Wondering if tall men are more or less easygoing, you collect two sets of scores: men's heights and men's temperaments. You measure the heights of 20 men, and you have someone else independently assess their temperaments (from zero for extremely calm to 100 for highly reactive).

With all the relevant data right in front of you (**TABLE A.2**), can you tell whether the correlation between height and reactive temperament is positive, negative, or close to zero?

Comparing the columns in Table A.2, most people detect very little relationship between height and temperament. In fact, the correlation in this imaginary example is positive, +0.63, as we can see if we display the data as a scatterplot. In **FIGURE A.5** moving from left to right, the upward, ovalshaped slope of the cluster of points shows that our two imaginary sets of scores (height and temperament) tend to rise together.

If we fail to see a relationship when data are presented as systematically as in Table A.2, how much less likely are we to notice them in everyday life? To see what is right in front of us, we sometimes need statistical illumination. We can easily see evidence of gender discrimination when given statistically summarized information about job level, seniority, performance, gender, and salary. But we often see no discrimination when the same information dribbles in, case by case (Twiss et al., 1989).

The point to remember: Correlation coefficients tell us nothing about cause and effect, but they can help us see the world more clearly by revealing the extent to which two things relate.

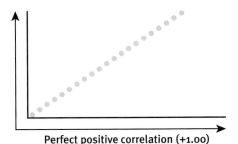
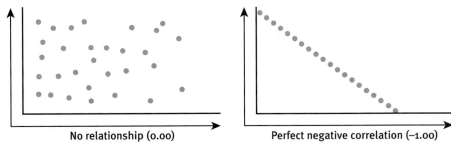

Perfect positive correlation (+1.00)   No relationship (0.00)   Perfect negative correlation (–1.00)

FIGURE A.4   Scatterplots, showing patterns of correlation   Correlations can range from +1.00 (scores on one measure increase in direct proportion to scores on another) to –1.00 (scores on one measure decrease precisely as scores rise on the other).

TABLE A.2   Height and Temperamental Reactivity of 20 Men

Person	Height in Inches	Temperament
1	80	75
2	63	66
3	61	60
4	79	90
5	74	60
6	69	42
7	62	42
8	75	60
9	77	81
10	60	39
11	64	48
12	76	69
13	71	72
14	66	57
15	73	63
16	70	75
17	63	30
18	71	57
19	68	84
20	70	39

istent relationships. When we believe there is a relationship between two things, we are likely to notice and recall instances that confirm our belief. If we believe that dreams are forecasts of actual events, we may notice and recall confirming instances more than disconfirming instances. The result is an *illusory correlation*.

Illusory correlations feed an illusion of control—that chance events are subject to our personal control. Gamblers, remembering their lucky rolls, may come to believe they can influence the

normal curve *(normal distribution)* a symmetrical, bell-shaped curve that describes the distribution of many types of data; most scores fall near the mean (about 68 percent fall within one standard deviation of it) and fewer and fewer near the extremes.

correlation coefficient a statistical index of the relationship between two things (from –1 to +1).

scatterplot a graphed cluster of dots, each of which represents the values of two variables. The slope of the points suggests the direction of the relationship between the two variables. The amount of scatter suggests the strength of the correlation (little scatter indicates high correlation).

FIGURE A.5   Scatterplot for height and reactive temperament   This display of data from 20 imagined people (each represented by a data point) reveals an upward slope, indicating a positive correlation. The considerable scatter of the data indicates the correlation is much lower than +1.0.

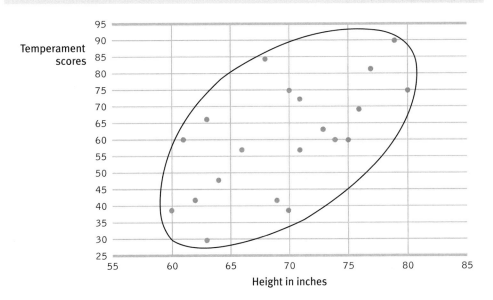

Regression Toward the Mean

A-3 What is regression toward the mean?

Correlations not only make visible the relationships we might otherwise miss, they also restrain our "seeing" nonex-

roll of the dice by again throwing gently for low numbers and hard for high numbers. The illusion that uncontrollable events correlate with our actions is also fed by a statistical phenomenon called **regression toward the mean.** Average results are more typical than extreme results. Thus, after an unusual event, things tend to return toward their average level; extraordinary happenings tend to be followed by more ordinary ones.

The point may seem obvious, yet we regularly miss it: We sometimes attribute what may be a normal regression (the expected return to normal) to something we have done. Consider two examples:

● Students who score much lower or higher on an exam than they usually do are likely, when retested, to return to their average.

● Unusual ESP subjects who defy chance when first tested nearly always lose their "psychic powers" when retested (a phenomenon parapsychologists have called the *decline effect*).

Failure to recognize regression is the source of many superstitions and of some ineffective practices as well. When day-to-day behavior has a large element of chance fluctuation, we may notice that others' behavior improves (regresses toward average) after we criticize them for very bad performance, and that it worsens (regresses toward average) after we warmly praise them for an exceptionally fine performance. Ironically, then, regression toward the average can mislead us into feeling rewarded for having criticized others and into feeling punished for having praised them (Tversky & Kahneman, 1974).

The point to remember: When a fluctuating behavior returns to normal, there is no need to invent fancy explanations

> "Once you become sensitized to it, you see regression everywhere."
> Psychologist Daniel Kahneman (1985)

for why it does so. Regression toward the mean is probably at work. ■

RETRIEVE + REMEMBER

● You hear the school basketball coach telling her friend that she rescued her team's winning streak by yelling at them after they played unusually badly in the first half of the game. What is another explanation of why the team's performance improved?

ANSWER: The team's poor performance was not their typical behavior. Their return to their normal—their winning streak—may just have been a case of regression toward the mean.

Significant Differences

A-4 How do we know whether an observed difference can be generalized to other populations?

◎ Data are "noisy." The average score in one group could conceivably differ from the average score in another group not because of any real difference but merely because of chance fluctuations in the people sampled. How confidently, then, can we infer that an observed difference is not just a fluke—a chance result from the research sample? For guidance, we can ask whether the observed difference between the two groups is reliable and significant.

When Is an Observed Difference Reliable?

In deciding when it is safe to generalize from a sample, we should keep three principles in mind:

1. **Representative samples are better than biased (unrepresentative) samples.** The best basis for generalizing is from a representative sample of cases, not from the exceptional and memorable cases one finds at the extremes. Research never randomly samples the whole human population. Thus, it pays to keep in mind what population a study has sampled. (To see how an unrepresentative sample can lead you astray, see Close-Up: Cross-Sectional and Longitudinal Studies.)

2. **Less-variable observations are more reliable than those that are more variable.** As we noted earlier, in the example of the basketball player whose game-to-game points were consistent, an average is more reliable when it comes from scores with low variability.

3. **More cases are better than fewer cases.** An eager prospective student visits two university campuses, each for a day. At the first, the student randomly attends two classes and discovers both instructors to be witty and engaging. At the next campus, the two sampled instructors seem dull and uninspiring. Returning home, the student (discounting the small sample size of only two teachers at each institution) tells friends about the "great teachers" at the first school, and the "bores" at the second. Again, we know it but we ignore it: *Averages based on many cases are more reliable* (less variable) *than averages based on only a few cases.*

The point to remember: Smart thinkers are not overly impressed by a few anecdotes. Generalizations based on a few unrepresentative cases are unreliable.

When Is an Observed Difference "Significant"?

Perhaps you've compared men's and women's scores on a laboratory test of aggression, and you've found a gender

Reprinted by permission of United Features Syndicate, Inc.

CLOSE-UP

Cross-Sectional and Longitudinal Studies

A-5 What are cross-sectional studies and longitudinal studies, and why is it important to know which method was used?

When interpreting research results, smart thinkers consider how researchers arrived at their conclusions. One way studies vary is in the time period for gathering data.

In **cross-sectional studies**, researchers compare different groups at the same time. When researchers compare intelligence test scores among people in differing age groups, older adults, on average, give fewer correct answers than do younger adults. This could suggest that mental ability declines with age, and indeed, that was the conclusion drawn from many early cross-sectional studies of intelligence.

In **longitudinal studies**, researchers study and restudy the same group at different times in their life span. Around 1920, colleges began giving intelligence tests to entering students, and several psychologists saw their chance to study intelligence longitudinally. What they expected to find was a decrease in intelligence after about age 30 (Schaie & Geiwitz, 1982). What they actually found was a surprise: Until late in life, intelligence remained stable. On some tests, it even increased.

Why did these new results differ from the earlier cross-sectional findings? In retrospect, researchers realized that cross-sectional studies that compared 70-year-olds and 30-year-olds were comparing people not only of two different ages but also of two different eras. They were comparing

- generally less-educated people (born, say, in the early 1900s) with better-educated people (born after 1950).
- people raised in large families with people raised in smaller families.
- people from less-affluent families with people from more-affluent families.

Others have since pointed out that longitudinal studies have their own pitfalls. Participants who survive to the end of longitudinal studies may be the healthiest (and brightest) people. When researchers adjust for the loss of participants, as did one study following more than 2000 people over age 75 in Cambridge, England, they find a steeper intelligence decline, especially as people age after 85 (Brayne et al., 1999).

The point to remember: When interpreting research results, pay attention to the methodology used, such as whether it was a longitudinal or cross-sectional study.

> **cross-sectional study** research in which people of different ages are compared with one another.
>
> **longitudinal study** research in which the same people are restudied and retested over a long period of time.

difference. But individuals differ. How likely is it that the difference you observed was just a fluke? Statistical testing can estimate the probability of the result occurring by chance.

Here is the underlying logic: When averages from two samples are each reliable measures of their respective populations (as when each is based on many observations that have small variability), then their *difference* is likely to be reliable as well. (Example: The less the variability in women's and in men's aggression scores, the more confidence we would have that any observed gender difference is reliable.) And when the difference between the sample averages is *large,* we have even more confidence that the difference between them reflects a real difference in their populations.

In short, when sample averages are reliable, and when the difference between them is relatively large, we say the difference has **statistical significance**. This means that the observed difference is probably not due to chance variation between the samples.

In judging statistical significance, psychologists are conservative. They are like juries who must presume innocence until guilt is proven. For most psychologists, proof beyond a reasonable doubt means not making much of a finding unless the odds of its occurring by chance, if no real effect exists, are less than 5 percent.

PEANUTS

> **regression toward the mean** the tendency for extreme or unusual scores or events to fall back (regress) toward the average.
>
> **statistical significance** a statistical statement of how likely it is that an obtained result occurred by chance.

When reading about research, you should remember that, given large enough samples, a difference between them may be "statistically significant" yet have little practical significance. For example, comparisons of intelligence test scores among hundreds of thousands of first-born and later-born individuals indicate a highly significant tendency for first-born individuals to have higher average scores than their later-born siblings (Kristensen & Bjerkedal, 2007; Zajonc & Markus, 1975). But because the scores differ by only one to three points, the difference has little practical importance.

The point to remember: Statistical significance indicates the *likelihood* that a result will happen by chance. But this does not say anything about the *importance* of the result. ∎

APPENDIX REVIEW

Statistical Reasoning in Everyday Life

Test yourself by taking a moment to answer each of these Learning Objective Questions (repeated here from within the appendix). Then turn to Appendix D, Complete Chapter Reviews, to check your answers. Research suggests that trying to answer these questions on your own will improve your long-term memory of the concepts (McDaniel et al., 2009).

Describing Data

A-1: How can we describe data with measures of central tendency and variation?

A-2: What does it mean when we say two things are correlated?

A-3: What is regression toward the mean?

Significant Differences

A-4: How do we know whether an observed difference can be generalized to other populations?

A-5: What are cross-sectional studies and longitudinal studies, and why is it important to know which method was used?

TERMS AND CONCEPTS TO REMEMBER

Test yourself on these terms by trying to write down the definition in your own words before flipping back to the referenced page to check your answer.

mode, p. A-2

mean, p. A-2

median, p. A-2

range, p. A-3

standard deviation, p. A-3

normal curve, p. A-4

correlation coefficient, p. A-4

scatterplot, p. A-4

regression toward the mean, p. A-6

cross-sectional study, p. A-7

longitudinal study, p. A-7

statistical significance, p. A-7

APPENDIX A TEST

Test yourself repeatedly throughout your studies. This will not only help you figure out what you know and don't know; the testing itself will help you learn and remember the information more effectively thanks to the *testing effect*.

1. Which of the three measures of central tendency is most easily distorted by a few very large or very small scores?

   a. The mode

   b. The mean

   c. The median

   d. They are all equally vulnerable to distortion from atypical scores.

2. The standard deviation is the most useful measure of variation in a set of data because it tells us

   a. the difference between the highest and lowest scores in the set.

   b. the extent to which the sample being used deviates from the bigger population it represents.

   c. how much individual scores differ from the mode.

   d. how much individual scores differ from the mean.

3. Another name for a bell-shaped distribution, in which most scores fall near the middle and fewer scores fall at each extreme, is a _____ _____.

4. In a _____ correlation, the scores rise and fall together; in a(n) _____ correlation, one score falls as the other rises.

   a. positive; negative   c. negative; inverse

   b. positive; illusory   d. strong; weak

5. If a study revealed that tall people were less intelligent than short people, this would suggest that the correlation between height and intelligence is _____ (positive/negative).

6. A _____ provides a visual representation of the direction and the strength of a relationship between two variables.

7. What is regression toward the mean, and how can it influence our interpretation of events?

8. In _____-_____ studies, a characteristic is assessed across different age groups at the same time.

9. When sample averages are _____ and the difference between them is _____, we can say the difference has statistical significance.

   a. reliable; large   c. due to chance; large

   b. reliable; small   d. due to chance; small

Find answers to these questions in Appendix E, in the back of the book.

experience
more of the
testing
effect

Psychology at Work

For most of us, to live is to work. Work is life's biggest single waking activity, helping to satisfy several levels of our needs. Work supports us, giving us food, water, and shelter. Work connects us, meeting our social needs. Work defines us, satisfying our self-esteem needs. Work helps us understand someone we've met for the first time. Wondering, "Who are you?" we may instead ask, "So, what do you do?"

The answer, however, may give us only a fleeting snapshot of that person at a particular time and place. On the day we retire from the workforce, few of us will look back and say we have followed a predictable career path. We will have changed jobs, some of us often. The trigger for those changes may have been a desire for better pay, happier on-the-job relationships, or more fulfilling work.

Work and Life Satisfaction

B-1 What is *flow?*

Across various occupations, attitudes toward work tend to fall into one of three categories (Wrzesniewski et al., 1997, 2001). Some people view their work as a *job,* an unfulfilling but necessary way to make money. Others view their work as a *career.* Their present position may not be ideal, but it is at least a rung on a ladder leading to increasingly better options. The third group views their work as a *calling.* For them, work is a fulfilling and socially useful activity. Of all these groups, those who see their work as a calling report the highest satisfaction with their work and their lives.

This finding would not surprise Mihaly Csikszentmihalyi (1990, 1999). He has observed that people's quality of life increases when they are purposefully engaged. Between the anxiety of being overwhelmed and stressed, and the apathy of being underwhelmed and bored, lies **flow.** In this intense, focused state, our skills are totally engaged, and we lose our awareness of self and time. Can you recall being in a zoned-out flow state while playing a video game or text messaging? If so, then perhaps you can sympathize with the two Northwest

Sometimes, notes Gene Weingarten (2002), a humor writer knows "when to just get out of the way." Here are some sample job titles from the U.S. Department of Labor *Dictionary of Occupational Titles:* animal impersonator, human projectile, banana ripening-room supervisor, impregnator, impregnator helper, dope sprayer, finger waver, rug scratcher, egg smeller, bottom buffer, cookie breaker, brain picker, hand pouncer, bosom presser, mother repairer.

LIFE DISRUPTED Playing and socializing online are ever-present sources of distraction. It takes energy to resist checking our phones, and time to refocus mental concentration after each disrupting buzz. Such regular interruptions make it difficult to be productive and to achieve flow offline, and argue for scheduled separations from our handheld devices.

Airlines pilots who in 2009 were so focused on their laptops that they missed Earth-to-pilot messages from their control tower. The pilots flew 150 miles past their Minneapolis destination—and lost their jobs.

Csikszentmihalyi (Chick-SENT-me-hi) came up with the flow concept while studying artists who spent hour after hour wrapped up in a project. After painting or sculpting for hours as if nothing else mattered, they finished and appeared to forget about the project. The artists seemed driven less by the external rewards for producing their art—money, praise,

flow a completely involved, focused state, with lowered awareness of self and time; results from full engagement of our skills.

promotion—than by the internal rewards for creating the work. They do what they love, and love what they do.

Fascinated, Csikszentmihalyi broadened his observations. He studied dancers, chess players, surgeons, writers, parents, mountain climbers, sailors, and farmers. His research included Australians, North Americans, Koreans, Japanese, and Italians. Participants ranged from the teen years to the golden years. A clear principle emerged: It's exhilarating to flow with an activity that fully engages our skills. Flow experiences boost our sense of self-esteem, competence, and well-being. Idleness may sound like bliss, but purposeful work enriches our lives. Busy people are happier (Hsee et al., 2010; Robinson & Martin, 2008). One research team interrupted people on about a quarter-million occasions (using a smart-phone app), and found people's minds wandering 47 percent of the time. They were, on average, happier when not mind-wandering (Killingsworth & Gilbert, 2010). (For some tips on enriching your own work life, see Close-Up: Finding Your Own Flow.) ▪

CLOSE-UP

Finding Your Own Flow

Want to identify your own path to flow? You can start by pinpointing your strengths and the types of work that may prove satisfying and successful. Marcus Buckingham and Donald Clifton (2001) have suggested asking yourself four questions.

1. What activities give me pleasure? (Bringing order out of chaos? Playing host? Helping others? Challenging sloppy thinking?)
2. What activities leave me wondering, "When can I do this again?" (Rather than "When will this be over?")
3. What sorts of challenges do I relish? (And which do I dread?)
4. What sorts of tasks do I learn easily? (And which do I struggle with?)

You may find your skills engaged and time flying when teaching or selling or writing or cleaning or consoling or creating or repairing. If an activity feels good, if it comes easily, if you look forward to it, then look deeper. You'll see your strengths at work (Buckingham, 2007). (To help find your own strengths, take the "Brief Strengths Test" at www.authentichappiness.sas.upenn.edu. Free registration is required.)

Top performers are "rarely well rounded" (Buckingham & Clifton, 2001, p. 26). Satisfied and successful people devote far less time to correcting their weaknesses than to sharpening their existing skills. Given how stable our traits and temperaments are, this is probably wise. There may be limits to the benefits of assertiveness training if you are shy, or of public speaking courses if you tend to be nervous and soft-spoken. Drawing classes may not help much if you express your artistic side in stick figures. But identifying your talents can help you recognize the activities you learn quickly and find absorbing. Knowing your strengths, you can develop them further.

As Robert Louis Stevenson said in *Familiar Studies of Men and Books* (1882), "To be what we are, and to become what we are capable of becoming, is the only end of life."

RETRIEVE + REMEMBER

• What is the value of finding flow in our work?

ANSWER: We become more likely to view our work as fulfilling and socially useful.

Industrial-Organizational Psychology

B-2 What are the three main subfields of industrial-organizational psychology?

◎ In developed nations, work has been changing, from farming to manufacturing to *knowledge work*. More and more work is *outsourced* to temporary employ-

ees. Consultants in remote locations now communicate electronically with the main office and with one another. (This book and its teaching package are developed and produced by a team of people in a dozen cities, from Alaska to Florida.)

The editorial team that supports the creation of this book and its teaching resources reflects a modern trend toward working remotely. Editor Nancy Fleming is in Massachusetts, publisher Kevin Feyen is in New York, editor Betty Probert and manuscript developer Don Probert are in Florida, editor Christine Brune is in Alaska, editor Trish Morgan is in Alberta, development director Tracey Kuehn is in New York, and project manager Kathryn Brownson is in Michigan.

As work changes, will our attitudes toward our work also change? Will our satisfaction with work increase or decrease? What will happen to the *psychological contract*—that two-way feeling of duty between workers and employers? These are among the questions that fascinate those interested in **industrial-organizational (I/O) psychology,** a profession that applies psychology's principles to the workplace.

I/O psychology has three main subfields (see Close-Up: I/O Psychologists on the Job). **Human factors psychology** explores how machines and environments can best be designed to fit human abilities.

industrial-organizational (I/O) psychology the application of psychological concepts and methods to human behavior in workplaces.

human factors psychology an I/O psychology subfield that explores how people and machines interact and how machines and physical environments can be made safe and easy to use.

I/O Psychologists on the Job

As scientists, consultants, and management professionals, I/O psychologists are found working in varied areas.

HUMAN FACTORS (ENGINEERING) PSYCHOLOGY

- Designing optimum work environments
- Optimizing person-machine interactions
- Developing systems technologies

PERSONNEL PSYCHOLOGY

Selecting and placing employees

- Developing and testing assessment tools for selecting, placing, and promoting workers
- Analyzing job content
- Optimizing worker placement

Training and developing employees

- Identifying needs
- Designing training programs
- Evaluating training programs

Appraising performance

- Developing guidelines
- Measuring individual performance
- Measuring organizational performance

ORGANIZATIONAL PSYCHOLOGY

Developing organizations

- Analyzing organizational structures
- Increasing worker satisfaction and productivity
- Making organizational change easier

Enhancing quality of work life

- Expanding individual productivity
- Identifying elements of satisfaction
- Redesigning jobs

Source: Adapted from the Society of Industrial and Organizational Psychology (www.siop.org).

Personnel psychology applies psychology's methods and principles to selecting, placing, training, and evaluating workers. **Organizational psychology** is the primary focus of this appendix. This subfield considers an organization's goals, work environments, and management styles, and their influence on worker motivation, satisfaction, and productivity.

Motivating Achievement

B-3 Why is it important to motivate achievement?

Organizational psychologists help motivate employees and keep them engaged. But what motivates any of us to pursue high standards or difficult goals?

Grit

Think of someone you know who seems driven to be the best—to excel at any task where performance can be judged. Now think of someone who is less driven. For psychologist Henry Murray (1938), the difference between these two people is a reflection of their **achievement motivation.** If you score high in achievement motivation, you have a desire for significant accomplishment, for mastering skills or ideas, for control, and for meeting a high standard.

Achievement motivation matters. Just how much it matters can be seen in a study that followed the lives of 1528 California children. All had scored in the top 1 percent on an intelligence test. Forty years later, researchers compared those who were most and least successful professionally. The most successful were the most highly motivated—they were ambitious, energetic, and persistent. As children, these individuals had enjoyed more active hobbies. As adults, they participated in more groups and

"Genius is 1% inspiration and 99% perspiration."
Thomas Edison (1847–1931)

preferred *playing* sports over watching sports (Goleman, 1980). Gifted children are able learners. Accomplished adults are determined doers. Most of us are energetic doers when starting and finishing a project. It's easiest—have you noticed?—to get "stuck in the middle," which is when high achievers keep going (Bonezzi et al., 2011).

Motivation differences also appear in other studies, including those of high school and college students. Self-discipline, not intelligence score, has been the best predictor of school performance, attendance, and graduation honors. Intense, sustained effort predicts success for teachers, too, especially when combined with a positive enthusiasm. Students of these motivated educators make good academic progress (Duckworth et al., 2009).

"Discipline outdoes talent," conclude researchers Angela Duckworth and Martin Seligman (2005, 2006). It also refines talent. By their early twenties, top violinists have fiddled away 10,000 hours of their life practicing. This is double the practice time of other violin students aiming to be teachers (Ericsson et al., 2001, 2006, 2007).

Similarly, a study of outstanding scholars, athletes, and artists found that all were highly motivated and self-disciplined. They dedicated hours every day to the pursuit of their goals (Bloom, 1985). These achievers became superstars through daily discipline, not just natural talent. Great achievement, it seems, mixes a teaspoon of inspiration with a gallon of perspiration.

personnel psychology an I/O psychology subfield that focuses on employee selection, placement, training, and appraisal.

organizational psychology an I/O psychology subfield that examines organizational influences on worker satisfaction and productivity and facilitates organizational change.

achievement motivation a desire for significant accomplishment; for mastery of skills or ideas; for control; and for attaining a high standard.

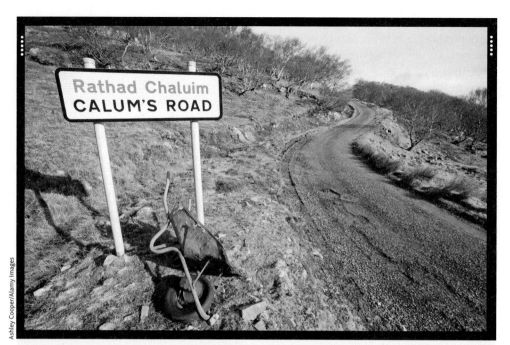

Ashley Cooper/Alamy Images

CALUM'S ROAD: WHAT GRIT CAN ACCOMPLISH Having spent his life on the Scottish island of Raasay farming a small patch of land, tending its lighthouse, and fishing, Malcolm ("Calum") MacLeod (1911–1988) felt anguished. His local government had refused to build a road that would enable electricity and vehicles to reach his north end of the island. With the once-flourishing population there having dwindled to two—MacLeod and his wife—he responded with heroic determination. One spring morning in 1964, MacLeod, then in his fifties, gathered an ax, a chopper, a shovel, and a wheelbarrow. By hand, he began to transform the existing footpath into a 1.75 mile road (Miers, 2009).

"With a road," a former neighbor explained, "he hoped new generations of people would return to the north end of Raasay," restoring its culture (Hutchinson, 2006). Day after day he worked through rough hillsides, along hazardous cliff-faces, and over peat bogs. Finally, 10 years later, he completed his supreme achievement. The road, which the government has since surfaced, remains a visible example of what vision plus determined grit can accomplish. It bids us each to ponder: What "roads"—what achievements—might we, with sustained effort, build in the years before us?

Darren Breen/The Grand Rapids Press/Landov

AN ENGAGED EMPLOYEE Mohamed Mamow, left, is joined by his employer in saying the Pledge of Allegiance as he becomes a U.S. citizen. Mamow and his wife met in a Somali refugee camp and now are parents of five children, whom he supports by working as a machine operator. Mindful of his responsibility—"I don't like to lose my job. I have a responsibility for my children and my family"—he arrives for work a half hour early and tends to every detail on his shift. "He is an extremely hard-working employee," noted his employer, and "a reminder to all of us that we are really blessed" (Roelofs, 2010).

Duckworth has a name for this passionate dedication to an ambitious, long-term goal: **grit.** Intelligence scores and many other physical and psychological traits can be displayed as a *bell-shaped curve*. Most scores cluster around an average, and fewer scores fall at the two far ends of the bell shape. Achievement scores don't follow this pattern. That is why organizational psychologists seek ways to engage and motivate ordinary people to be superstars in their own jobs. And that is why training students in *hardiness*—resilience under stress—leads to better grades (Maddi et al., 2009).

Satisfaction and Engagement

I/O psychologists know that everyone wins when workers are satisfied with their jobs. For employees, satisfaction with work feeds satisfaction with life. Moreover, lower job stress feeds improved health (Chapter 10).

How do employers benefit from worker satisfaction? Positive moods can translate into greater creativity, persistence, and helpfulness (Brief & Weiss, 2002; Kaplan et al., 2009). The correlation between individual job satisfaction and performance is modest but

real (Judge et al., 2001; Ng et al., 2009; Parker et al., 2003). One analysis tracked 4500 employees at 42 British manufacturing companies. The most productive workers tended to be those in satisfying work environments (Patterson et al., 2004). In the United States, the *Fortune* "100 Best Companies to Work For" have also produced much higher-than-average returns for their investors (Dickler, 2007).

The biggest-ever study of worker satisfaction and job performance was an analysis of Gallup data from more than 198,000 employees (Harter et al., 2002). These people were employed in

grit in psychology, grit is passion and perseverance in the pursuit of long-term goals.

TABLE B.1 Three Types of Employees

Engaged: working with passion and feeling a profound connection to their company or organization.

Not engaged: putting in the time but investing little passion or energy into their work.

Actively disengaged: unhappy workers undermining what their colleagues accomplish.

Source: Adapted from Gallup via Crabtree, 2005

nearly 8000 business units of 36 large companies, including some 1100 bank branches, 1200 stores, and 4200 teams or departments. The study focused on links between various measures of organizational success and employee engagement—the extent of workers' involvement, enthusiasm, and identification with their organizations (**TABLE B.1**). The researchers found that engaged workers (compared with not-engaged workers who are just putting in time) know what's expected of them, have what they need to do their work, feel fulfilled in their work, have regular opportunities to do what they do best, perceive that they are part of something significant, and have opportunities to learn and develop. They also found that business units with engaged employees have more loyal customers, less turnover, higher productivity, and greater profits.

But what causal arrows explain this correlation between business success and employee morale and engagement? Does success boost morale, or does high morale boost success? In a follow-up longitudinal study of 142,000 workers, researchers found that, over time, employee attitudes predicted future business success (more than the other way around) (Harter et al., 2010). Many other studies confirm that happy workers tend to be good workers (Ford et al., 2011; Seibert et al., 2011; Shockley et al., 2012). One analysis compared companies with top-quartile versus below-average employee engagement levels. Over a three-year period, earnings grew 2.6 times faster for the companies with highly engaged workers (Ott, 2007).

Leadership

B-4 How can leaders be most effective?

◎ The best leaders want their organization to be successful. They also want the people who work for them and with them to be satisfied, engaged, and productive. To achieve these ends, effective leaders harness people's strengths, set goals, and choose an appropriate leadership style.

Harnessing Strengths

Engaged employees don't just happen. Effective leaders engage their employees' interests and loyalty. They figure out people's natural talents, adjust roles to suit their talents, and develop those talents into great strengths (**FIGURE B.1**). Consider, for example, instructors at a given school. Should they all be expected to teach the same load? To advise the same number of students? To serve on the same number of committees? To take on the same number of additional responsibilities in the depart-

---

ment? Or should their job descriptions be tailored to their specific strengths? Would most schools and their students be better served if instructors' tasks were matched to their strengths?

Trying to create talents that are not there can be a waste of time. Leaders who excel spend more time developing and drawing out talents that already exist. Effective managers share certain traits (Tucker, 2002). They

- start by helping people identify and measure their talents.
- match tasks to talents and then give people freedom to do what they do best.
- care how people feel about their work.
- reinforce positive behaviors through recognition and reward.

Good managers also try not to promote people into roles ill-suited to their strengths. Imagine that you're a manager with a limited budget for training. Will you focus on your employees' weaknesses and send them to training seminars to fix those problems? Or will you focus on educating your employees about their strengths and building upon them? Good managers choose the second option. In Gallup surveys, 77 percent of engaged workers strongly agreed that "my supervisor focuses on my strengths or positive characteristics." Only 23 percent of not-engaged workers agreed with that statement (Krueger & Killham, 2005).

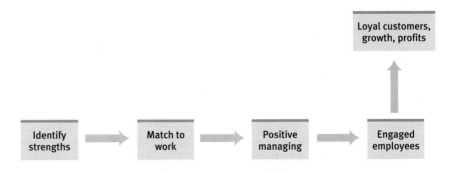

FIGURE B.1 The Gallup Organization path to organizational success (Adapted from Fleming, 2001.)

POSITIVE COACHING Larry Brown has been an adviser to the youth sports organization Positive Coaching Alliance. He was observed during practices offering his players four to five positive comments for every negative comment (Insana, 2005). In 2004, he coached his underdog Detroit Pistons to the National Basketball Association championship.

Does all this sound familiar? Bringing out the best in people within an organization builds upon a basic principle of operant conditioning (Chapter 6). To teach a behavior, catch a person doing something right and reinforce it. It sounds simple, but too many managers act like the parents who focus on the one low score on a child's almost-perfect report card. As a report by the Gallup Organization (2004) observed, "65 percent of Americans received no praise or recognition in their workplace last year."

Setting Specific, Challenging Goals

In study after study, people merely asked to do their best do not do so. Good managers know that a better way to motivate higher achievement is to set specific, challenging goals. For example, you might state your own goal in this course as "Finish studying Appendix B by Fri-

day." Specific goals focus our attention and stimulate us to work hard, persist, and try creative strategies. Such goals are especially effective when workers or team members participate in setting them. Achieving goals that are challenging yet within our reach boosts our self-evaluation (White et al., 1995).

Stated goals are most effective when combined with progress reports (Johnson et al., 2006; Latham & Locke, 2007). Action plans that break large goals into smaller steps (subgoals) and specify when, where, and how to achieve those steps will increase the chances of completing a project on time (Burgess et al., 2004; Fishbach et al., 2006; Koestner et al., 2002).

Through a task's ups and downs, people best sustain their mood and motivation when they focus on immediate goals (such as daily study) rather than distant goals (such as a course grade). Better to have one's nose to the grindstone than one's eye on the ultimate prize (Houser-Marko & Sheldon, 2008). Thus, before beginning each new edition of this book, my editor, my associates, and I manage by objectives—we agree on target dates for the completion and editing of each chapter draft. If we focus on achieving each of these short-term goals, the prize—an on-time book—takes care of itself. So, to motivate high productivity, effective leaders work with people to define explicit goals, subgoals, and implementation plans, and then they provide feedback on progress.

Choosing an Appropriate Leadership Style

What qualities produce a great leader? Psychologists and others once believed that all great leaders share certain traits. That *great person theory of leadership* now seems overstated (Vroom & Jago, 2007). The same coach may seem great or not great, depending on the team and its competition. But a leader's personality does matter (Zaccaro, 2007). Effective leaders are not overly assertive; that trait can damage social relationships within the group. They are not unassertive, because that

trait can limit their ability to lead (Ames & Flynn, 2007). Effective leaders of laboratory groups, work teams, and large corporations tend to be self-confident. They have *charisma,* which seems to have three main ingredients (House & Singh, 1987; Shamir et al., 1993).

- They have a *vision* of some goal.
- They are able to *communicate* that vision clearly and simply.
- They have enough optimism and faith to *inspire* their group to follow them.

Consider a study rating company morale at 50 Dutch firms (de Hoogh et al., 2004). Firms with the highest ratings had chief executives who inspired their colleagues "to transcend their own self-interests for the sake of the collective." This ability to motivate others to commit themselves to a group's mission is *transformational leadership.* Transformational leaders are often natural extraverts. They set their standards high, and they inspire others to share their vision. They pay attention to other people (Bono & Judge, 2004). The frequent result is a workforce that is more engaged, trusting, and effective (Turner et al., 2002). (For an impressive example of transformational leadership skills, see Close-Up: Doing Well While Doing Good.)

Women more than men tend to be transformational leaders. This may help explain why companies with women in top management positions have tended to enjoy superior financial results (Eagly, 2007). That tendency held even after researchers controlled for variables such as company size.

Leadership styles vary, depending both on the qualities of the leader and the demands of the situation. In some situations (think of a commander leading troops into battle), a *directive* style may be needed (Fiedler, 1981). In other situations, the strategies that work on the battlefield may smother creativity. If developing a comedy show, for example, a leader might get better results using a *democratic* style that welcomes team member creativity.

CLOSE-UP

Doing Well While Doing Good— "The Great Experiment"

At the end of the 1700s, the cotton mill at New Lanark, Scotland, had more than 1000 workers. Many were children drawn from Glasgow's poorhouses. They worked 13-hour days and lived in grim conditions. Education and sanitation were neglected. Theft and drunkenness were common. Most families occupied just one room.

On a visit to Glasgow, Welsh-born Robert Owen—an idealistic young cotton-mill manager—chanced to meet and fall in love with the mill owner's daughter. After their marriage, Owen, with several partners, purchased the mill. On the first day of the 1800s he took control as its manager. Before long, he began what he said was "the most important experiment for the happiness of the human race that had yet been instituted at any time in any part of the world" (Owen, 1814). The abuse of child and adult labor was, he observed, producing unhappy and inefficient workers. Owen believed that better working and living conditions could pay economic dividends.

Owen showed transformational leadership skills when he bravely began many new practices. He started a nursery for preschool children, and education for older children (with encouragement rather than corporal punishment). Workers had Sundays off. They received health care, paid sick days, and unemployment pay for days when the mill could not operate. He set up a company store, selling goods at reduced prices. When his partners resisted his changes, he bought their shares.

Owen also designed a goals and worker-assessment program, with detailed records of daily productivity and costs. By each employee's workstation, one of four colored boards indicated that person's performance for the previous day. Owen could walk through the mill and at a glance see how individuals were performing. There was, he said, "no beating, no abusive language. . . . I merely looked at the person and then at the color. . . . I could at once see by the expression [which color] was shown."

The financial success of Owen's mill supported a reform movement for better working and living conditions. By 1816, with decades of profits still ahead, Owen believed he had demonstrated "that society may be formed so as to exist without crime, without poverty, with health greatly improved, with little if any misery, and with intelligence and happiness increased a hundredfold." Although that vision has not been fulfilled, Owen's great experiment did lay the groundwork for employment practices that are accepted in much of the world today.

THE GREAT EXPERIMENT New Lanark Mills showed that industries could do well while doing good. In its time, Owen's mill was visited by many European royals and reformers who came to observe its vibrant work force and prosperous business. New Lanark today is preserved as a World Heritage Site (www.newlanark.org).

Leaders differ in the personal qualities they bring to the job. Some excel at **task leadership**—by setting standards, organizing work, and focusing attention on goals. To keep the group centered on its mission, task leaders typically use a directive style. This style can work well if the leader is smart enough to give good orders (Fiedler, 1987).

Other managers excel at **social leadership.** They explain decisions, help group members solve their conflicts, and build teams that work well together (Evans & Dion, 1991). Social leaders often have a democratic style. They share authority and welcome the opinions of team members. Social leadership is good for morale. We usually feel more satisfied and motivated and perform better when we can participate in decision making (Cawley et al., 1998; Pereira & Osburn, 2007). Moreover, when members are sensitive to one another and participate equally, groups solve problems with greater "collective intelligence" (Woolley et al., 2010).

Effective managers often exhibit a high degree of *both* task and social leadership. This finding applies in many locations, including coal mines, banks, and government offices in India, Taiwan, and Iran (Smith & Tayeb, 1989). As achievement-minded people, effective managers certainly care about how well people do their work. Yet they are sensitive to their workers' needs. That sensitivity is often repaid by worker loyalty. In one national survey of American workers, those in family-friendly organizations offering flexible hours reported feeling greater loyalty to their employers (Roehling et al., 2001).

Employee participation in decision making is common in Sweden, Japan,

---

task leadership goal-oriented leadership that sets standards, organizes work, and focuses attention on goals.

social leadership group-oriented leadership that builds teamwork, resolves conflict, and offers support.

the United States, and elsewhere (Cawley et al., 1998; Sundstrom et al., 1990). Giving workers a chance to voice their opinion before a decision is made engages them in the process. They then tend to respond more positively to the final decision (van den Bos & Spruijt, 2002). They also feel more empowered and are more creative (Hennessey & Amabile, 2010; Huang et al., 2010).

The ultimate in employee participation is the employee-owned company. One such company in my town, the Fleetwood Group, is a 165-employee manufacturer of educational furniture and wireless electronic clickers. When its founder gave 45 percent of the company to his employees, who later bought out other family stockholders, Fleetwood became one of America's first companies with an employee stock ownership plan (ESOP). Today, every employee owns part of the company, and as a group they own 100 percent. The more years employees work, the more they own, yet no one owns more than 5 percent. Like every corporate president, Doug Ruch works for his stockholders, who also just happen to be his employees.

As a company that endorses faith-inspired "servant-leadership" and "re-spect and care for each team member-owner," Fleetwood is free to place people above profits. Thus, when orders lagged during the recent recession, the employee-owners decided that job security meant more to them than profits. So the company paid otherwise idle workers to do community service—answering phones at nonprofit agencies, building Habitat for Humanity houses, and the like.

Fleetwood employees "act like they own the place"; Ruch contends that employee ownership attracts and retains talented people, "drives dedication," and gives Fleetwood "a sustainable competi-tive advantage." With stock growth averaging 17 percent a year, Fleetwood was named the 2006 National ESOP of the year. ■

RETRIEVE + REMEMBER

• What characteristics are important for transformational leaders?

ANSWER: Transformational leaders are able to inspire others to share a vision and commit themselves to a group's mission. They tend to be naturally extraverted and set high standards.

APPENDIX REVIEW

Psychology at Work

Test yourself by taking a moment to answer each of these Learning Objective Questions (repeated here from within the appendix). Then turn to Appendix D, Complete Chapter Reviews, to check your answers. Research suggests that trying to answer these questions on your own will improve your long-term memory of the concepts (McDaniel et al., 2009).

Work and Life Satisfaction

B-1: What is *flow?*

Industrial-Organizational Psychology

B-2: What are the three main subfields of industrial-organizational psychology?

Motivating Achievement

B-3: Why is it important to motivate achievement?

Leadership

B-4: How can leaders be most effective?

TERMS AND CONCEPTS TO REMEMBER

Test yourself on these terms by trying to write down the definition in your own words before flipping back to the referenced page to check your answer.

flow, p. B-1

industrial-organizational (I/O) psychology, p. B-2

human factors psychology, p. B-2

personnel psychology, p. B-2

organizational psychology, p. B-2

achievement motivation, p. B-3

grit, p. B-4

task leadership, p. B-7

social leadership, p. B-7

APPENDIX B TEST

Test yourself repeatedly throughout your studies. This will not only help you figure out what you know and don't know; the testing itself will help you learn and remember the information more effectively thanks to the testing effect.

1. What are the three main divisions within industrial-organizational psychology?

2. People who view their work as a calling often experience _____, a focused state of consciousness, with diminished awareness of themselves and of time.

   a. stress

   b. apathy

   c. flow

   d. facilitation

3. _____ psychologists study the recruitment, selection, placement, training, appraisal, and development of employees; _____ _____ psychologists focus on how people and machines interact, and on optimizing devices and work environments.

4. What type of goals will best help you stay focused and motivated to do your finest work in this class?

5. Research indicates that women are more likely than men to have a _____ leadership style.

6. Effective managers often exhibit

   a. only task leadership.

   b. only social leadership.

   c. both task and social leadership, depending on the situation and the person.

   d. task leadership for building teams and social leadership for setting standards.

   Find answers to these questions in Appendix E, in the back of the book.

experience more of the testing effect —

Subfields of Psychology

Jennifer Zwolinski, University of San Diego

What can you do with a degree in psychology? Lots!

As a psychology major, you will graduate with a scientific mind-set and an awareness of basic principles of human behavior (biological mechanisms, development, cognition, psychological disorders, social interaction). This background will prepare you for success in many areas, including business, the helping professions, health services, marketing, law, sales, and teaching. You may even go on to graduate school for specialized training to become a psychology professional. This appendix describes psychology's specialized subfields.[1] I also provide updated information about CAREERS IN PSYCHOLOGY at: www.worthpublishers.com/MyersPEL3e, where you can learn more about the many interesting options available to those with bachelor's, master's, and doctoral degrees in psychology.

If you are like most psychology students, you may be unaware of the wide variety of specialties and work settings available in psychology (Terre & Stoddart, 2000). To date, the American Psychological Association (APA) has formed 56 divisions (TABLE C.1 on the next page). The following paragraphs (arranged alphabetically) describe some careers in the main specialty areas of psychology, most of which require a graduate degree in psychology.

Clinical psychologists promote psychological health in individuals, groups, and organizations. Some clinical psychologists specialize in specific psychological disorders. Others treat a range of disorders, from adjustment difficulties to severe psychopathology. Clinical psychologists might engage in research, teaching, assessment, and consultation. Some hold workshops and lectures on psychological issues for other professionals or for the public. Clinical psychologists work in a variety of settings, including private practice, industry, mental health service organizations, schools, universities, legal systems, medical systems, counseling centers, government agencies, and military services.

To become a clinical psychologist, you will need to earn a doctorate from a clinical psychology program. The APA sets the standards for clinical psychology graduate programs, offering accreditation (official recognition) to those who meet their standards. In all U.S. states, clinical psychologists working in independent practice must obtain a license to offer services such as therapy and testing.

Cognitive psychologists study thought processes and focus on such topics as perception, language, attention, problem solving, memory, judgment and decision making, forgetting, and intelligence. Research interests include designing computer-based models of thought processes and identifying biological correlates of cognition. As a cognitive psychologist, you might work as a professor, industrial consultant, or human factors specialist in an educational or business setting.

Community psychologists move beyond focusing on specific individuals or families and deal with broad problems of mental health in community settings. These psychologists believe that human behavior is powerfully influenced by the interaction between people and their physical, social, political, and economic environments. They seek to promote psychological health by enhancing environmental

COGNITIVE CONSULTING Cognitive psychologists may advise businesses on how to operate more effectively by understanding the human factors involved.

COMMUNITY CARE This community psychologist (left) helped residents work through the emotional challenges that followed the devastating 2010 earthquake in Haiti.

---

[1] Although this text covers the world of psychology for students in many countries, this appendix draws primarily from available U.S. data. Its descriptions of psychology's subfields are, however, also applicable in many other countries.

TABLE C.1   APA Divisions by Number and Name

1. Society for General Psychology	29. Psychotherapy
2. Society for the Teaching of Psychology	30. Society of Psychological Hypnosis
3. Experimental Psychology	31. State, Provincial, and Territorial Psychological Association Affairs
4. *There is currently no Division 4.*	32. Society for Humanistic Psychology
5. Evaluation, Measurement, and Statistics	33. Intellectual and Developmental Disabilities
6. Behavioral Neuroscience and Comparative Psychology	34. Society for Environmental, Population, and Conservation Psychology
7. Developmental Psychology	35. Society for the Psychology of Women
8. Society for Personality and Social Psychology	36. Society for the Psychology of Religion and Spirituality
9. Society for the Psychological Study of Social Issues (SPSSI)	37. Society for Child and Family Policy and Practice
10. Society for the Psychology of Aesthetics, Creativity, and the Arts	38. Health Psychology
11. *There is currently no Division 11.*	39. Psychoanalysis
12. Society of Clinical Psychology	40. Society for Clinical Neuropsychology
13. Society of Consulting Psychology	41. American Psychology-Law Society
14. Society for Industrial and Organizational Psychology	42. Psychologists in Independent Practice
15. Educational Psychology	43. Society for Family Psychology
16. School Psychology	44. Society for the Psychological Study of Lesbian, Gay, Bisexual, and Transgender Issues
17. Society of Counseling Psychology	45. Society for the Psychological Study of Ethnic Minority Issues
18. Psychologists in Public Service	46. Society for Media Psychology and Technology
19. Society for Military Psychology	47. Exercise and Sport Psychology
20. Adult Development and Aging	48. Society for the Study of Peace, Conflict, and Violence: Peace Psychology Division
21. Applied Experimental and Engineering Psychology	49. Society of Group Psychology and Group Psychotherapy
22. Rehabilitation Psychology	50. Society of Addiction Psychology
23. Society for Consumer Psychology	51. Society for the Psychological Study of Men and Masculinity
24. Society for Theoretical and Philosophical Psychology	52. International Psychology
25. Behavior Analysis	53. Society of Clinical Child and Adolescent Psychology
26. Society for the History of Psychology	54. Society of Pediatric Psychology
27. Society for Community Research and Action: Division of Community Psychology	55. American Society for the Advancement of Pharmacotherapy
28. Psychopharmacology and Substance Abuse	56. Trauma Psychology

Source: American Psychological Association

settings, focusing on preventive measures and crisis intervention, with special attention to the problems of underserved groups and ethnic minorities. Given the shared emphasis on prevention, some community psychologists collaborate with professionals in other areas, such as public health. As a community psychologist, your work settings could include federal, state, and local departments of mental health, corrections, and welfare. You might conduct research or help evaluate research in health service settings, serve as an independent consultant for a private or government agency, or teach and consult as a college or university faculty member.

Counseling psychologists help people adjust to life transitions or make lifestyle changes. Although similar to clinical psychologists, counseling psychologists typically help people with adjustment problems rather than severe psychopathology. Like clinical psychologists, counseling psychologists conduct therapy and provide assessments to individuals and groups. As a counseling psychologist, you would emphasize your clients' strengths, helping them to use their own skills, interests, and abilities to cope during transitions. You might find yourself working in an academic setting as a faculty member or administrator or in a university counseling center, community mental health center, business, or private practice. As with clinical psychology, if you plan to work in independent practice you will need to obtain a state license to provide counseling services to the public.

Developmental psychologists conduct research in age-related behavioral changes and apply their scientific knowledge to educational, child-care, policy, and related settings. As a developmental psychologist, you would investigate change across a broad range of topics, including the biological, psychological, cognitive, and social aspects of development. Developmental psychology informs a number of applied fields, including educational psychology, school psychology, child psychopathology, and gerontology. The field also informs public policy in areas such as education and child-care reform, maternal and child health, and attachment and adoption. You would probably specialize in a specific stage of the life span, such as infancy, childhood, adolescence, or middle or late adulthood. Your work setting could be an educational institution, day-care center, youth group program, or senior center.

Educational psychologists are interested in the psychological processes involved in learning. They study the relationship between learning and the physical and social environments, and they develop strategies for enhancing the learning process. As an educational psychologist, working in a university psychology department or school of education, you might conduct basic research on topics related to learning or develop innovative methods of teaching to en-

hance the learning process. You might design effective tests, including measures of aptitude and achievement. You might be employed by a school or government agency or charged with designing and implementing effective employee-training programs in a business setting.

Experimental psychologists are a diverse group of scientists who investigate a variety of basic behavioral processes in humans and other animals. Prominent areas of experimental research include comparative methods of science, motivation, learning, thought, attention, memory, perception, and language. Most experimental psychologists identify with a particular subfield, such as cognitive psychology, depending on their interests and training. It is important to note that experimental research methods are not limited to the field of experimental psychology; many other subfields rely on experimental methodology to conduct studies. As an experimental psychologist, you would most likely work in an academic setting, teaching courses and supervising students' research in addition to conducting your own research.

Or you might be employed by a research institution, zoo, business, or government agency.

Forensic psychologists apply psychological principles to legal issues. They conduct research on the interface of law and psychology, help to create public policies related to mental health, help law-enforcement agencies in criminal investigations, or consult on jury selection and deliberation processes. They also provide assessment to assist the legal community. Although most forensic psychologists are clinical psychologists, they might have expertise in other areas of psychology, such as social or cognitive psychology. Some also hold law degrees. As a forensic psychologist, you might work in a university psychology department, law school, research organization, community mental health agency, law-enforcement agency, court, or correctional setting.

Health psychologists are researchers and practitioners concerned with psychology's contribution to promoting health and preventing disease. As

© ZUMA Press, Inc./Alamy

CRIMINAL INVESTIGATION Forensic psychologists may be called on to assist police officers investigating a crime scene, as here after a shooting in Florida. Most forensic work, however, occurs in the lab and for the judicial system.

applied psychologists or clinicians, they may help individuals lead healthier lives by designing, conducting, and evaluating programs to stop smoking, lose weight, improve sleep, manage pain, prevent the spread of sexually transmitted infections, or treat psychosocial problems associated with chronic and terminal illnesses. As researchers and clinicians, they identify conditions and practices associated with health and illness to help create effective interventions. In public service, health psychologists study and work to improve government policies and health care systems. As a health psychologist, you could be employed in a hospital, medical school, rehabilitation center, public health agency, college or university, or, if you are also a clinical psychologist, in private practice.

Industrial-organizational (I/O) psychologists study the relationship between people and their working environments. They may develop new ways to increase productivity, improve personnel selection, or promote job satisfaction in an organizational setting. Their interests include organizational structure and change, consumer behavior, and personnel selection and training. As an I/O psychologist, you might conduct workplace training or provide organizational analysis and development. You may find yourself working in business, industry, the government, or a college or university. Or you may be self-employed as a consultant or work for a management consulting firm.

Neuropsychologists investigate the relationship between neurological processes (structure and function of the brain and nervous system) and behavior. As a neuropsychologist you might assess, diagnose, or treat central nervous system disorders, such as Alzheimer's disease or stroke. You might also evaluate individuals for evidence of head injuries; specific learning disorder; and neurodevelopmental disorders, such as autism spectrum disorder and attention-deficit/hyperactivity disorder (ADHD). If you are a *clinical neuropsychologist,* you might work in a hospital's neurology, neurosurgery, or psychiatric unit. Neuropsychologists also work in academic settings, where they conduct research and teach.

Psychometric and quantitative psychologists study the methods and techniques used to acquire psychological knowledge. A psychometrician may update existing neurocognitive or personality tests or devise new tests for use in clinical and school settings or in business and industry. These psychologists also administer, score, and interpret such tests. Quantitative psychologists collaborate with researchers to design, analyze, and interpret the results of research programs. As a psychometric or quantitative psychologist, you would need to be well trained in research methods, statistics, and computer technology. You would most likely be employed by a university or college, testing company, private research firm, or government agency.

Rehabilitation psychologists are researchers and practitioners who work with people who have lost optimal functioning after an accident, illness, or other event. As a rehabilitation psychologist, you would probably work in a medical rehabilitation institution or hospital. You might also work in a medical school, university, state or federal vocational rehabilitation agency, or in private practice serving people with physical disabilities.

School psychologists are involved in the assessment of and intervention for children in educational settings. They diagnose and treat cognitive, social, and emotional problems that may negatively influence children's learning or overall functioning at school. As a school psychologist, you would collaborate with teachers, parents, and administrators, making recommendations to improve student learning. You

CLASS COUNSELOR School psychologists, who have their master's degree in psychology, may find themselves working with students individually or in groups, as well as in a consultative role for their school's administrators.

would work in an academic setting, a federal or state government agency, a child guidance center, or a behavioral research laboratory.

Social psychologists are interested in our interactions with others. Social psychologists study how our beliefs, feelings, and behaviors are affected by and influence other people. They study topics such as attitudes, aggression, prejudice, interpersonal attraction, group behavior, and leadership. As a social psychologist, you would probably be a college or university faculty member. You might also work in organizational consultation, market research, or other applied psychology fields. Some social psychologists work for hospitals, federal agencies, or businesses performing applied research.

Sport psychologists study the psychological factors that influence, and are influenced by, participation in sports and other physical activities. Their professional activities include coach

Phil Walter/Getty Images

CRICKET CURES Sport psychologists often work directly with athletes to help them improve their performance. Here a team psychologist consults with Brendon McCullum, a record-breaking athlete who plays international cricket for New Zealand.

education and athlete preparation, as well as research and teaching. Sport psychologists who also have a clinical or counseling degree can apply those skills to working with individuals with psychological problems, such as anxiety or substance use disorder, that might interfere with optimal performance. As a sport psychologist, if you were not working in an academic or research setting, you would most likely work as part of a team or an organization or in a private capacity.

* * *

So, the next time someone asks you what you will do with your psychology degree, tell them you have a lot of options. You might use your acquired skills and understanding to get a job and succeed in any number of fields, or you might pursue graduate school and then career opportunities in associated professions. In any case, what you have learned about behavior and mental processes will surely enrich your life (Hammer, 2003).

Complete Chapter Reviews

CHAPTER 1
Psychology's Roots, Big Ideas, and Critical Thinking Tools

Psychology's Roots

1-1: How has psychology's focus changed over time?

• Wilhelm Wundt established the first psychological laboratory in Germany in 1879, and studied the basic elements of mental experience.

• Early researchers defined psychology as "the science of mental life."

• This definition was revised under the influence of the *behaviorists* in the 1920s to the "scientific study of observable behavior."

• In the 1960s, the *humanistic psychologists* and the *cognitive psychologists* revived interest in the study of mental processes.

• *Psychology* is now defined as "the science of behavior and mental processes."

1-2: What are psychology's current perspectives, and what are some of its subfields?

• Psychology's current perspectives include neuroscience, evolutionary, behavior genetics, psychodynamic, behavioral, cognitive, and social-cultural.

• Psychology's subfields include biological, developmental, cognitive, personality, social, counseling, health, clinical, and industrial-organizational.

• Psychologists may conduct basic research to increase the field's knowledge base or applied research to solve practical problems.

Four Big Ideas in Psychology

1-3: What four big ideas run throughout this book?

• *Critical thinking* is smart thinking. It challenges our beliefs and triggers new ways of thinking.

• Behavior is a *biopsychosocial* event. The biological, psychological, and social-cultural levels of analysis each offer valuable insight into behavior and mental processes.

• We operate with a two-track mind (*dual processing*). Our brains process a surprising amount without our awareness, which affects our perception, thinking, memory, and attitudes.

• Psychology explores human strengths (*positive psychology*) as well as challenges (clinical psychology).

Why Do Psychology?

1-4: How does our everyday thinking sometimes lead us to the wrong conclusion?

• *Hindsight bias* (the I-knew-it-all-along phenomenon) is believing, after learning the outcome, that we would have foreseen it.

• Overconfidence is the human tendency to be more confident than correct.

• We perceive order in random events due to our natural eagerness to make sense of our world.

• These tendencies lead us to overestimate our intuition and common sense, and then come to the wrong conclusion.

1-5: What are the three key elements of the scientific attitude, and how do they support scientific inquiry?

• Curiosity triggers new ideas.

• Skepticism encourages attention to the facts.

• Humility helps us discard predictions that can't be verified by research.

The scientific attitude carries into life as critical thinking, which puts ideas to the test by examining assumptions, uncovering hidden values, weighing evidence, and assessing conclusions.

How Do Psychologists Ask and Answer Questions?

1-6: How do psychological theories guide scientific research?

• Psychological *theories* are explanations using principles that organize observations and predict behaviors or events.

• Theories generate *hypotheses*—predictions that can be tested using descriptive, correlational, or experimental methods.

• Research results may validate the theory, or lead to its rejection or revision.

• The precise language used in *operational definitions* allows *replication* by others. If others achieve similar results, confidence in the conclusion will be greater.

1-7: How do psychologists use case studies, naturalistic observations, and surveys to observe and describe behavior, and why is random sampling important?

- *Case studies* study one person or group in depth, in the hope of revealing things true to us all.
- *Naturalistic observation* studies examine behavior in naturally occurring situations without trying to change or control the situation.
- *Surveys* study many people in less depth, using *random sampling* to fairly represent the *population* being studied.

1-8: What are positive and negative correlations, and how can they lead to prediction but not cause-effect explanation?

- In a positive correlation, both items increase or decrease together.
- In a negative correlation, one item increases as the other decreases.
- *Correlations* tell us how well one event predicts another (using a measure called a correlation coefficient), but not whether one event caused the other, or whether some third factor influenced both events.

1-9: How do experiments clarify or reveal cause-effect relationships?

- *Experiments* create a controlled, simplified version of reality to discover cause-effect relationships.
- Psychologists manipulate one factor (the *independent variable*) while controlling others.
- The researchers can then measure changes in other factors (*dependent variables*).
- Experiments minimize confounding variables, such preexisting differences between groups (through *random assignment*).
- Experiments allow researchers to compare *experimental group* results with *control group* results.

- Experiments may use a *double-blind procedure* to control for the *placebo effect*.

Frequently Asked Questions About Psychology

1-10: How do simplified laboratory conditions help us understand general principles of behavior?

- Studying specific examples in controlled environments can reveal important general principles. The general principles that result, not the specific findings, help explain everyday behaviors.

1-11: Why do psychologists study animals, and what ethical guidelines safeguard human and animal research participants?

- Research on animals advances our understanding of other species and sometimes benefits them directly.
- Animal experimentation advances our understanding of ourselves and may help solve human problems.
- Professional ethical standards and other legal guidelines, enforced by ethics committees, protect participants.
- The APA ethics code outlines standards for safeguarding human participants' well-being, including obtaining their *informed consent* and *debriefing* them later.

1-12: How do personal values influence psychologists' research and application? Does psychology aim to manipulate people?

- Psychologists' values influence their choice of research topics, their theories and observations, their labels for behavior, and their professional advice.
- Psychology's principles could be used for good or evil, but have been used mainly to enlighten and to achieve positive ends.

Improve Your Retention— and Your Grades

1-13: How can psychological principles help you learn and remember?

- The *testing effect* shows that learning and memory are enhanced by actively retrieving, rather than simply rereading, previously studied material.
- The SQ3R study method—survey, question, read, retrieve, and review—applies principles derived from memory research and can help you learn and remember material.
- Four additional study tips are (1) distribute your study time; (2) learn to think critically; (3) process class information actively; and (4) overlearn.

CHAPTER 2
The Biology of Mind and Consciousness

Biology and Behavior

2-1: Why are psychologists concerned with human biology?

- Everything psychological is simultaneously biological.
- The links between biology and behavior are a key part of the biopsychosocial approach.
- *Biological psychologists* study these links.

Neural Communication

2-2: What are the parts of a neuron?

- *Neurons* (nerve cells) are basic building blocks of the nervous system.
- A neuron has *dendrites* (extensions of the cell body) that receive messages and an *axon* that sends messages to other neurons or cells.
- Some axons are encased in a myelin sheath, which enables faster communication.

- *Glial cells* provide myelin, and they support, nourish, and protect neurons; they may also play a role in learning and thinking.

2-3: How do neurons communicate?

- Neurons transmit information in a chemistry-to-electricity process.
- They send signals (*action potentials*) down their axons.
- They receive incoming excitatory or inhibitory signals through their dendrites and cell body.
- Neurons fire in an *all-or-none response* when combined incoming signals are strong enough to pass a minimum *threshold*.
- The response triggers a release of chemical messengers (*neurotransmitters*) across the tiny gap (*synapse*) separating a sending neuron from a receiving cell.

2-4: How do neurotransmitters affect our mood and behavior?

- Specific neurotransmitters, such as serotonin and dopamine, travel designated pathways in the brain.
- Neurotransmitters affect particular behaviors and emotions, such as hunger, movement, and arousal.
- *Endorphins* are natural opiates released in response to pain and intense exercise.
- Drugs and other chemicals affect brain chemistry at synapses.

The Nervous System

2-5: What are the two major divisions of the nervous system, and what are their basic functions?

- The *nervous system's* two major divisions are the *central nervous system (CNS)*—the brain and spinal cord—and the *peripheral nervous system (PNS)*—the sensory and motor neurons connecting the CNS to the rest of the body.
- *Interneurons* communicate within the brain and spinal cord and between *motor neurons* and *sensory neurons*.
- In the PNS, the *somatic nervous system* controls voluntary movements of the skeletal system. The *autonomic nervous system* controls the involuntary muscles and the glands.
- The subdivisions of the PNS are the *sympathetic nervous system* (which arouses) and the *parasympathetic nervous system* (which calms).

The Endocrine System

2-6: How does the endocrine system transmit information and interact with the nervous system?

- The *endocrine system* is the body's slower information system. Its glands secrete *hormones* into the bloodstream, which influence brain and behavior.
- In times of stress or danger, the autonomic nervous system (ANS) activates the *adrenal glands'* fight-or-flight response.
- The *pituitary* (the endocrine system's master gland) triggers other glands, including sex glands, to release hormones, which then affect the brain and behavior.
- This complex feedback system reveals the interplay between the nervous and endocrine systems.

The Brain

2-7: What are some techniques for studying the brain?

- To study the brain, researchers consider the effects of brain damage.
- They also use *MRI* scans to reveal brain structures.
- Researchers use *EEG* recordings and *PET* and *fMRI* (functional MRI) scans to reveal brain activity.

2-8: What are the functions of the brainstem and its related structures?

- The *brainstem,* the oldest part of the brain, controls automatic survival functions.
- The *medulla* controls heartbeat and breathing. Just above the medulla, the pons helps coordinate movements.
- The *thalamus,* sitting at the top of the brainstem, acts as the brain's sensory control center.
- The *reticular formation* controls arousal and attention.
- The *cerebellum,* attached to the rear of the brainstem, processes sensory input and coordinates muscle movement.

2-9: What are the structures and functions of the limbic system?

- The *limbic system* is linked to emotions, drives, and memory, and its neural centers include the hippocampus, amygdala, and hypothalamus:
  - The hippocampus processes conscious memories.
  - The *amygdala* is involved in aggressive and fearful responses.
  - The *hypothalamus* monitors various bodily maintenance activities, contains reward centers, and triggers the pituitary to influence other glands of the endocrine system.

2-10: What are the four lobes of the cerebral cortex, and where are they located?

- The *cerebral cortex* has two hemispheres, and each hemisphere has four lobes:
  - The *frontal lobes* (just behind the forehead) enable speaking, muscle movement, planning, and judging.
  - The *parietal lobes* (top-rear of the head) receive sensory input for touch and body position.

o The *occipital lobes* (back of the head) receive input from the visual fields.

o The *temporal lobes* (above the ears) receive input from the ears.

2-11: What are the functions of the motor cortex, somatosensory cortex, and association areas?

- The *motor cortex* (at the rear the frontal lobes) controls voluntary muscle movement.

- The *somatosensory cortex* (in front of the parietal lobes) registers and processes body touch and movement sensations.

- The cerebral cortex is mostly *association areas*, which integrate information related to higher-level functions, such as learning, remembering, thinking, and speaking. Higher-level functions require the coordination of many brain areas.

2-12: When damaged, can the brain repair or reorganize itself?

- The brain's *plasticity* allows it to modify itself after some types of damage, especially early in life.

- *Neurogenesis* is the formation of new neurons.

2-13: What is a split brain, and what does it reveal about the functions of our left and right hemispheres?

- The *corpus callosum* (a large band of nerve fibers) normally connects the two brain hemispheres. If surgically severed (often to treat severe epilepsy), a *split brain* results.

- Split-brain research shows that in most people, the hemispheres are specialized, though they work together in a normal brain.

- The left hemisphere usually specializes in verbal processing.

- The right hemisphere usually specializes in visual perception and the recognition of emotion.

Brain States and Consciousness

2-14: What do we mean by *consciousness*, and how does selective attention direct our perceptions?

- *Consciousness* is our awareness of ourselves and our environment.

- *Selective attention* is our focusing of conscious awareness on a particular stimulus. We can focus attention on only a small part of the world around us.

- *Inattentional blindness* is the failure to see visible objects when our attention is directed elsewhere.

- *Change blindness* is the failure to notice changes in our environment.

2-15: What is the circadian rhythm, and what are the stages of our nightly sleep cycle?

- The *circadian rhythm* is our internal biological clock; it regulates our daily cycles of alertness and sleepiness.

- Nightly sleep cycles every 90 minutes through recurring stages:

o NREM-1 sleep is the brief, near-waking sleep with irregular brain waves we enter (after leaving the *alpha waves* of being awake and relaxed); *hallucinations* (sensations such as falling or floating) may occur.

o NREM-2 sleep, in which we spend most of our time, includes characteristic bursts of rhythmic brain waves; lengthens as the night goes on.

o NREM-3 sleep is deep sleep in which large, slow *delta waves* are emitted; this stage shortens as the night goes on.

o REM *(rapid eye movement) sleep* is described as a paradoxical sleep stage because of internal arousal but external calm (near paralysis). It includes most dreaming and lengthens as the night goes on.

2-16: How do our sleep patterns differ? What five theories describe our need to sleep?

- Life-span, genetic, and social-cultural factors affect *sleep* patterns.

- Psychologists suggest five possible reasons why sleep evolved:

o Sleep may have played a protective role in human evolution by keeping people safe during potentially dangerous periods.

o Sleep also helps restore and repair damaged neurons.

o Sleep helps strengthen neural connections that build enduring memories.

o Sleep promotes creative problem solving the next day.

o During deep sleep, the pituitary gland secretes a growth hormone necessary for muscle development.

2-17: How does sleep loss affect us, and what are the major sleep disorders?

- Sleep loss causes fatigue and irritability, and impairs concentration, productivity, and memory consolidation. It can also lead to depression, obesity, joint pain, a suppressed immune system, and slowed performance (with greater vulnerability to accidents).

- The major sleep disorders are *insomnia* (recurring wakefulness); *narcolepsy* (sudden, uncontrollable sleepiness or lapsing into REM sleep); *sleep apnea* (the stopping of breathing while asleep); and sleepwalking, sleeptalking, and night terrors.

2-18: What do we dream about, and what are five theories of *why* we dream?

- We usually *dream* of ordinary events and everyday experiences, but dreams are vivid, emotional, and often bizarre. Most dreams are bad dreams—of personal failures, dangers, or misfortunes.

- There are five major views of the function of dreams:
  - o Freud's wish fulfillment: Dreams provide a psychic "safety valve," with *manifest content* (story line) acting as a censored version of *latent content* (underlying meaning that gratifies our unconscious wishes).
  - o Information processing: Dreams help us sort out the day's events and consolidate them in memory.
  - o Physiological function: Regular brain stimulation may help us develop and preserve neural pathways in the brain.
  - o Neural activation: The brain attempts to make sense of neural static by weaving it into a story line.
  - o Cognitive development: Dreams reflect dreamers' cognitive development—their knowledge and understanding.
- Most sleep theorists agree that REM sleep and its associated dreams serve an important function, as shown by the REM *rebound* that occurs following REM deprivation in humans and other species.

CHAPTER 3
Developing Through the Life Span

3-1: What are the three major issues studied by developmental psychologists?

- *Developmental psychologists* study physical, cognitive, and social change throughout the life span with a focus on three major issues:
  - o Nature and nurture—how our genetic inheritance (our nature) interacts with our experiences (our nurture) to influence our development.
  - o Continuity and stages—what parts of development are gradual and continuous and what parts change abruptly in separate stages.
  - o Stability and change—which traits persist through life and which change as we age.

Prenatal Development and the Newborn

3-2: How does conception occur, and what are chromosomes, DNA, genes, and the genome? How do genes and the environment interact?

- At conception, one sperm cell fuses with one egg cell.
- *Genes* are the basic units of *heredity* that make up *chromosomes*, the threadlike coils of *DNA*.
- A *genome* is the shared genetic profile that distinguishes each species.
- Heredity and environment *interact* to influence development.
- The field of *epigenetics* studies how genes guide development as they are expressed in particular *environments*.

3-3: How does life develop before birth, and how do teratogens put prenatal development at risk?

- From conception to 2 weeks, the *zygote* is in a period of rapid cell development.
- By 6 weeks, the *embryo's* body organs begin to form and function.
- By 9 weeks, the *fetus* is recognizably human.
- *Identical twins* (monozygotic twins) develop from a single fertilized egg that splits into two; *fraternal twins* (dizygotic twins) develop from separate fertilized eggs.
- *Teratogens* are potentially harmful agents that can pass through the placental screen and interfere with normal development, as happens with *fetal alcohol syndrome*.

3-4: How do twin and adoption studies help us understand the effects of nature and nurture?

- Studies of separated identical twins allow researchers to maintain the same genes while testing the effects of different home environments. Studies of adoptive families let researchers maintain the same home environment while studying the effects of genetic differences.

3-5: What are some of the newborn's abilities and traits?

- Newborns' sensory systems and *reflexes* aid their survival and social interactions with adults.
- Newborns smell and hear well, see what they need to see, and begin using their sensory equipment to learn.
- Inborn *temperament*—emotional excitability—heavily influences our developing personality.

Infancy and Childhood

3-6: How do the brain and motor skills develop during infancy and childhood?

- Most brain cells form before birth. With *maturation* and experience, their interconnections multiply rapidly and become more complex after birth. A pruning process strengthens heavily used links and weakens unused ones, and we seem to have a *critical period* for some skills, such as language.
- Complex motor skills—sitting, standing, walking—develop in a predictable sequence. Timing may vary with individual maturation and with culture.
- We have few conscious memories of events occurring before age 4, a blank space in our conscious memory psychologists call infantile amnesia.

3-7: How did Piaget view the developmental stages of a child's mind, and how does current thinking about cognitive development differ?

- In his theory of *cognitive* development, Jean Piaget proposed that children actively construct and modify an understanding of the world through the processes of *assimilation* and *accommodation*. They form *schemas* that help them organize their experiences.

- Piaget believed children construct an understanding of the world by interacting with it while moving through four cognitive stages:
  - *Sensorimotor stage*—first two years; *object permanence* develops.
  - *Preoperational stage*—about age 2 to 6 or 7; preschoolers are *egocentric* but begin to develop a *theory of mind* (except for those with *autism spectrum disorder (ASD)*, whose theory of mind is impaired).
  - *Concrete operational stage*—6 or 7 to 11 years; mastery of *conservation* and simple math.
  - *Formal operational stage*—about age 12 and up; reasoning expands to abstract thinking.

- Current research supports the sequence Piaget proposed, but finds young children more capable and their development more continuous.

- Lev Vygotsky's studies of child development focused on the ways a child's mind grows by interacting with the social environment. Parents and other caregivers provide temporary scaffolds from which children can step to higher levels of thinking.

3-8: How do the bonds of attachment form between caregivers and infants?

- Infants develop *stranger anxiety* soon after object permanence.

- Infants form *attachments* with caregivers who not only satisfy nutritional needs but, more importantly, who are comfortable, familiar, and responsive.

3-9: Why do secure and insecure attachments matter, and how does an infant develop basic trust?

- Attachment styles differ (secure or insecure) due to the child's individual temperament and the responsiveness of the child's caregivers.

- Securely attached children develop *basic trust* and tend to have healthier adult relationships.

- Neglect or abuse can disrupt the attachment process and put children at risk for physical, psychological, and social problems.

3-10: What are three primary parenting styles, and what outcomes are associated with each?

- Parenting styles—authoritarian, permissive, and authoritative—reflect varying degrees of control.

- Children with the highest self-esteem, self-reliance, and social competence tend to have authoritative parents.

- Child-raising practices reflect both individual and cultural values.

Adolescence

3-11: What defines adolescence, and what major physical changes occur during adolescence?

- *Adolescence* begins with *puberty*, a time of sexual maturation.

- The brain's frontal lobes mature during adolescence and the early twenties, enabling improved judgment, impulse control, and long-term planning.

3-12: How did Piaget, Kohlberg, and later researchers describe cognitive and moral development during adolescence?

- In Jean Piaget's view, formal operations (abstract reasoning) develop in adolescence, and this development is the basis for moral judg-ment. Research indicates that these abilities begin to emerge earlier than Piaget believed.

- Lawrence Kohlberg proposed a stage theory of moral thinking: preconventional morality (self-interest), conventional morality (gaining others' approval or doing one's duty), and postconventional morality (basic rights and self-defined ethical principles).

- Kohlberg's critics note that the postconventional level is culturally limited, representing morality only from the perspective of an individualist, middle-class society.

- Other researchers believe that morality lies in moral intuition and moral action as well as thinking.

3-13: According to Erikson, what stages—and accompanying tasks and challenges—mark our psychosocial development?

- Erik Erikson proposed eight stages of psychosocial development across the life span.

- Each life stage has its own psychosocial task, with the chief task of adolescence being solidifying one's sense of self, one's *identity*. This often means trying out a number of different roles. *Social identity* is the part of the self-concept that comes from a person's group memberships.

- Erikson believed we need to achieve the following challenges: trust, autonomy, initiative, competency, identity (in adolescence), *intimacy* (in young adulthood), generativity, and integrity.

3-14: To what extent are adolescent lives shaped by parental and peer influences?

- During adolescence, parental influence diminishes and peer influence increases, in part because of the selection effect—the tendency to choose similar others as friends.

- Nature and nurture—genes and experiences—interact to guide our development.

3-15: Does parenting matter?

- Parents influence our manners, attitudes, values, faith, and politics.
- Language and other behaviors are shaped by peer groups, as children adjust to fit in.

3-16: What are the characteristics of emerging adulthood?

- *Emerging adulthood* is the period from age 18 to the mid-twenties, when many young people in Western cultures are no longer adolescents but have not yet achieved full independence as adults.

Adulthood

3-17: How do our bodies and sensory abilities change from early to late adulthood?

- Muscular strength, reaction time, sensory abilities, and cardiac output begin to decline in the late twenties and continue to decline through middle adulthood (to age 65) and late adulthood (after 65).
- Around age 50, *menopause* ends women's period of fertility. Men do not undergo a similar sharp drop in hormone levels or fertility.
- In late adulthood, the immune system also weakens, but good health habits help to enable better health in later life.

3-18: How does memory change with age?

- Recall begins to decline, especially for meaningless information. Recognition memory remains strong.

3-19: What are adulthood's two primary commitments, and how do chance events and the social clock influence us?

- Adulthood's two major commitments are love (Erikson's intimacy—form-

ing close relationships) and work (productive activity, or what Erikson called generativity).

- Chance encounters affect many of our important decisions, such as our choice of romantic partners.
- The *social clock* is a culture's expected timing for social events, such as marriage, parenthood, and retirement.

3-20: What factors affect our well-being in later life?

- Most older people retain a sense of well-being, partly due to the tendency to focus more on positive emotions and memories.
- People over 65 report as much happiness and satisfaction with life as younger people do. Many experience what Erikson called a sense of integrity—a feeling that one's life has been meaningful.

3-21: How do people vary in their responses to a loved one's death?

- Normal grief reactions vary widely. People do not grieve in predictable stages.
- Immediate strong expression of grief does not purge the grief more quickly, and bereavement therapy is not significantly more effective than grieving without such aid.
- Death of a loved one is much harder to accept when it comes before its expected time.

CHAPTER 4
Gender and Sexuality

Gender Development

4-1: What are some gender similarities and differences in aggression, social power, and social connectedness?

- *Gender* refers to the socially constructed roles and characteristics by which a culture defines male and female.

- Males and females are more alike than different, thanks to our similar genetic makeup—we see, hear, learn, and remember similarly.
- Male-female differences include body fat, muscle, height, age of onset of puberty, life expectancy, and onset of certain disorders.
- Men admit to more *aggression* than women do, and they are more likely to be physically aggressive. Women's aggression is more likely to be *relational*.
- In most societies, men have more social power, and their leadership style tends to be directive, whereas women's is more democratic.
- Women often focus more on social connectedness than do men, and they "tend and befriend."

4-2: How is our biological sex determined, and how do sex hormones influence prenatal and adolescent development?

- Both sex chromosomes and sex hormones influence development.
- The twenty-third pair of chromosomes determines sex, with the mother contributing an X chromosome and the father contributing either an X *chromosome* (for a girl baby) or a Y *chromosome* (for a boy baby). A Y chromosome triggers additional *testosterone* release and the formation of male sex organs.
- During *puberty*, both *primary* and *secondary sex characteristics* develop. Sex-related genes and physiology influence behavioral and cognitive gender differences between males and females.
- *Intersex* individuals are born possessing biological sexual characteristics of both sexes.

4-3: How do gender roles and gender typing influence gender development?

- *Gender roles* describe how others expect us to act and vary depending on cultural expectations, which change over time and place.

- *Social learning theory* proposes that we learn our *gender identity*—our sense of being male or female—as we learn other things: through reinforcement, punishment, and observation. But critics argue that cognition also plays a role because modeling and rewards cannot explain *gender typing*.

- Some people display *androgyny,* with both traditional masculine and feminine psychological characteristics.

- *Transgender* people's gender identity or expression differs from that associated with their birth sex. Their sexual orientation may be heterosexual, homosexual, bisexual, or asexual.

Human Sexuality

4-4: How do hormones influence human sexual motivation?

- The female *estrogen* and male *testosterone* hormones influence human sexual behavior less directly than they influence sexual behavior in other species.

- These hormones direct sexual development in the prenatal period; trigger development of sexual characteristics in adolescence; and help activate sexual behavior from puberty to late adulthood.

- Women's sexuality is more responsive to testosterone level than to estrogen level.

- Short-term shifts in testosterone level are normal in men, partly in response to stimulation.

4-5: What is the human sexual response cycle, and how do sexual dysfunctions and paraphilias differ?

- William Masters and Virginia Johnson described four stages in the human *sexual response cycle:* excitement, plateau, orgasm (which seems

to involve similar feelings and brain activity in males and females), and resolution. Males then enter a *refractory period* in which renewed arousal and orgasm are impossible.

- *Sexual dysfunctions* are problems that consistently impair sexual arousal or functioning. They can often be successfully treated by behaviorally oriented therapy or drug therapy.

- *Paraphilias* are conditions, which may or may not be classified as disorders, involving nonhuman objects, the suffering of self or others, and/or nonconsenting persons.

4-6: How can sexually transmitted infections be prevented?

- Safe-sex practices help prevent sexually transmitted infections (STIs). Using condoms helps protect against most sexually transmitted infections (especially *AIDS*), but not those that are transmitted skin-to-skin.

- A vaccination administered before sexual contact can prevent most human papilloma virus (HPV) infections.

4-7: How do external and imagined stimuli contribute to sexual arousal?

- Erotic material and other external stimuli can trigger sexual arousal in both men and women.

- Viewing sexually coercive material can lead to increased acceptance of violence toward women.

- Viewing sexually explicit materials can cause people to perceive their partners as comparatively less appealing and to devalue their relationships.

- Imagined stimuli (fantasies) help trigger sexual arousal.

4-8: What factors influence teenagers' sexual behaviors and use of contraceptives?

- Rates of teen intercourse vary from culture to culture and era to era.

- Factors contributing to teen pregnancy include minimal communication about birth control with parents, partners, and peers; passion overwhelming self-control; alcohol use; and mass media norms of unprotected and impulsive sexuality.

- High intelligence, religious engagement, father presence, and participation in service learning programs have been predictors of teen sexual restraint.

Sexual Orientation: Why Do We Differ?

4-9: What has research taught us about sexual orientation?

- *Sexual orientation* is an enduring sexual attraction toward members of one's own sex (homosexual orientation), the other sex (heterosexual orientation), or both sexes (bisexual orientation).

- About 3 percent of men and 1 or 2 percent of women are homosexual, and sexual orientation seems to be enduring.

- Sexual orientation is not an indicator of mental health. There is no evidence that environmental factors influence sexual orientation.

- Evidence for biological influences on homosexuality comes from same-sex attraction in many animal species; gay-straight differences in body and brain characteristics; higher rates of homosexuality in certain families and in identical twins; exposure to certain hormones during critical periods of prenatal development; and the fraternal birth-order effect.

An Evolutionary Explanation of Human Sexuality

4-10: How might evolutionary psychologists explain gender differences in sexuality and mating preferences?

- *Evolutionary psychologists* attempt to understand how *natural selection* (how nature selects traits and appetites that contribute to survival and reproduction) has shaped behaviors found in all people.

- They reason that men's more recreational attitude toward sex results from their ability to spread their genes widely by mating with many females.

- In contrast, women's more relational approach to sex results from their need to incubate and nurse one infant at a time. Women increase their own and their children's chances of survival by searching for mates with the potential for long-term investment in their joint offspring.

4-11: What are the key criticisms of evolutionary explanations of human sexuality, and how do evolutionary psychologists respond?

- Critics argue that evolutionary psychologists (1) start with an effect and work backward to an explanation, (2) relieve people from taking responsibility for their sexual behavior, and (3) do not recognize social and cultural influences.

- Evolutionary psychologists respond that understanding our predispositions can help us overcome them. They recognize the importance of social and cultural influences, but they also cite the value of testable predictions based on evolutionary principles.

Reflections on Gender, Sexuality, and Nature–Nurture Interaction

Nature and nurture interact in the development of our gender-related traits and our mating behaviors.

CHAPTER 5
Sensation and Perception

Basic Principles of Sensation and Perception

5-1: What are *sensation* and *perception*? What do we mean by *bottom-up processing* and *top-down processing*?

- *Sensation* is the process by which our sensory receptors and nervous system receive information and transmit it to the brain.

- *Perception* is the process by which our brain organizes and interprets that information.

- *Bottom-up processing* is analysis that begins with the sensory receptors and works up to the brain.

- *Top-down processing* is information processing guided by higher-level mental processing, such as when we construct perceptions by filtering information through our experience and expectations.

5-2: What three steps are basic to all our sensory systems?

- Our senses (1) receive sensory stimulation (often using specialized receptor cells); (2) transform that stimulation into neural impulses; and (3) deliver the neural information to the brain.

- *Transduction* is the process of converting one form of energy into another.

5-3: How do *absolute thresholds* and *difference thresholds* differ, and what is Weber's law?

- Our *absolute threshold* is the minimum stimulation needed for us to be consciously aware of any stimulus 50 percent of the time. (Stimuli below that threshold are subliminal.)

- A *difference threshold* (also called the just noticeable difference, or jnd) is the minimum change needed to detect a difference between two stimuli 50 percent of the time.

- *Weber's law* states that two stimuli must differ by a constant minimum percentage (rather than a constant minimum amount).

5-4: Can we be persuaded by subliminal stimuli?

- We do sense some stimuli *subliminally*—less than 50 percent of the time—but those sensations don't have lasting behavioral effects.

5-5: What is the function of sensory adaptation?

- We grow less sensitive to constant sensory input.

- This diminished sensitivity to constant or routine odors, sounds, and touches (*sensory adaptation*) focuses our attention on informative changes in our environment.

5-6: How do our expectations, assumptions, contexts, and even our motivations and emotions affect our perceptions?

- Perception is influenced by our *perceptual set*—our mental predisposition to perceive one thing and not another.

- Our physical, emotional, and cultural context, as well as our motivation, can create expectations about what we will perceive, thus affecting those perceptions.

Vision

5-7: What are the characteristics of the energy we see as light?

- The visible light we experience is just a thin slice of the broad spectrum of electromagnetic energy.

- The *hue* (blue, green, and so forth) we perceive in a light depends on its *wavelength,* and its brightness depends on its *intensity*.

5-8: How does the eye transform light energy into neural messages?

- Light entering the eye is focused on our *retina*—the inner surface of the eye.
- The retina's light-sensitive *rods* and color-sensitive *cones* convert the light energy into neural impulses.
- After processing by bipolar and ganglion cells in the eyes' retina, neural impulses travel through the *optic nerve* to the thalamus and on to the visual cortex.

5-9: What roles do feature detection and parallel processing play in the brain's visual information processing?

- In the visual cortex, *feature detectors* respond to specific features of the visual stimulus, such as edges, lines, and angles.
- Through *parallel processing,* the brain handles many aspects of vision (color, movement, form, and depth) simultaneously. Other neural teams integrate the results, comparing them with stored information and enabling perceptions.

5-10: What theories help us understand color vision?

- According to the *Young-Helmholtz trichromatic (three-color) theory,* the retina contains three types of color receptors. Contemporary research has found three types of cones, each most sensitive to the wavelengths of one of the three primary colors of light (red, green, or blue).
- According to the *opponent-process theory,* there are three additional color processes (red-versus-green, blue-versus-yellow, black-versus-white). Contemporary research has confirmed that, on the way to the brain, neurons in the retina and the thalamus code the color-related information from the cones into pairs of opponent colors.

- These two theories, and the research supporting them, show that color processing occurs in two stages.

5-11: What was the main message of Gestalt psychology, and how do figure-ground and grouping principles help us perceive forms?

- Gestalt psychologists showed that the brain organizes bits of sensory information into *gestalts,* or meaningful forms. In pointing out that the whole may exceed the sum of its parts, they noted that we filter sensory information and construct our perceptions.
- To recognize an object, we must first perceive it as distinct (see it as a *figure*) from its surroundings (the *ground*).
- We bring order and form to sensory input by organizing it into meaningful groups, following such rules as proximity, continuity, and closure.

5-12: How do we use binocular and monocular cues to see the world in three dimensions?

- Humans and many other species perceive depth at, or very soon after, birth.
- We transform two-dimensional retinal images into three-dimensional *depth perceptions* that allow us to see objects in three dimensions and to judge distance.
- *Binocular cues,* such as *retinal disparity,* are depth cues that rely on information from both eyes.
- *Monocular cues* (such as relative size, interposition, relative height, relative motion, linear perspective, and light and shadow) let us judge depth using information transmitted by only one eye.

5-13: How do perceptual constancies help us construct meaningful perceptions?

- *Perceptual constancy* is our ability to recognize an object regardless of the changing image it casts upon our retinas due to its changing angle, distance, or illumination.
- *Color constancy* is our ability to perceive consistent color in an object, even though the lighting and wavelengths shift.
- Shape constancy is our ability to perceive familiar objects (such as an opening door) as unchanging in shape. Size constancy is our ability to perceive objects as unchanging in size despite their changing retinal images. Knowing an object's size gives us clues to its distance; knowing its distance gives clues about its size, but we sometimes misread monocular distance cues and reach the wrong conclusions, as in the Moon illusion.

5-14: What does research on restored vision, sensory restriction, and perceptual adaptation reveal about the effects of experience on perception?

- Experience guides our perceptual interpretations. Some perceptual abilities (such as color and figure-ground perception) are inborn. But people blind from birth who gain sight after surgery lack the experience to visually recognize shapes, forms, and complete faces.
- Sensory restriction research indicates that there is a critical period for some aspects of sensory and perceptual development. Without early stimulation, the brain's neural organization does not develop normally.
- Given eyeglasses that shift the world slightly to the left or right, turn it upside down, or reverse it, people can, through *perceptual adaptation,* learn to move about with ease.

The Nonvisual Senses

5-15: What are the characteristics of the air pressure waves that we hear as meaningful sounds?

- Sound waves vary in amplitude (perceived as loudness) and in *frequency* (perceived as *pitch*—a tone's highness or lowness).

- Sound energy is measured in decibels.

5-16: How does the ear transform sound energy into neural messages?

- Sound waves vary in amplitude, which we perceive as differing loudness, and in *frequency,* which we experience as differing *pitch*.

- Through a mechanical chain of events, sound waves travel from the outer ear through the auditory canal, causing tiny vibrations in the eardrum.

- The bones of the middle ear transmit the vibrations to the fluid-filled *cochlea* in the inner ear, causing waves of movement in hair cells lining the basilar membrane.

- This movement triggers nerve cells to send signals along the auditory nerve to the thalamus and then to the brain's auditory cortex.

- Small differences in the loudness and timing of the sounds received by each ear allow us to locate sounds.

- *Sensorineural hearing loss* (or nerve deafness) results from damage to the cochlea's hair cells or their associated nerves.

- *Conduction hearing loss* results from damage to the mechanical system that transmits sound waves to the cochlea.

- *Cochlear implants* can restore hearing for some people.

5-17: What are the four basic touch sensations, and which of them has identifiable receptors?

- Our sense of touch is actually several senses—pressure, warmth, cold, and pain—that combine to produce other sensations, such as "hot." Only pressure has identifiable receptors.

5-18: What influences our feelings of pain, and how can we treat pain?

- Pain reflects bottom-up sensations (such as input from nociceptors, the sensory receptors that detect hurtful temperatures, pressure, or chemicals) and top-down processes (such as experience, attention, and culture).

- Pain treatments often combine physical and psychological elements, including distractions. *Hypnosis,* which increases our response to suggestions, can help relieve pain. *Posthypnotic suggestion* is used by some clinicians to help control undesired symptoms and behavior.

5-19: How are our senses of taste and smell similar?

- Both taste and smell are chemical senses.

- Taste involves five basic sensations—sweet, sour, salty, bitter, and umami.

- Taste receptors in the taste buds carry messages to an area between the frontal and temporal lobes of the brain.

- There are no basic sensations for smell.

- Some 20 million olfactory receptor cells for smell, located at the top of each nasal cavity, send messages to the brain. These cells work together, combining their messages into patterns that vary, depending on the different odors they detect.

5-20: How do we sense our body's position and movement?

- Through *kinesthesia,* we sense the position and movement of individual body parts.

- We monitor our head's (and therefore our body's) position and movement, and maintain our balance, with our *vestibular sense.*

Sensory Interaction

5-21: How do our senses interact?

- *Sensory interaction* is the influence of one sense on another. This occurs, for example, when the smell of a favorite food enhances its taste.

- *Embodied cognition* is the influence of bodily sensations, gestures, and other states on cognitive preferences and judgments.

5-22: How do ESP claims hold up when put to the test by scientists?

- The three most testable forms of *extrasensory perception (ESP)* are telepathy (mind-to-mind communication), clairvoyance (perceiving remote events), and precognition (perceiving future events).

- Researchers have not been able to replicate (reproduce) ESP effects under controlled conditions.

CHAPTER 6
Learning

How Do We Learn?

6-1: What are some basic forms of learning?

- *Learning* is the process of acquiring new and relatively enduring information or behaviors through experience.

- In *associative learning,* we learn that certain events occur together.

- Through *cognitive learning,* we acquire mental information, such as by observation or language, that guides our behavior.

Classical Conditioning

6-2: What is classical conditioning, and how does it demonstrate associative learning?

- *Classical conditioning* is a type of learning in which we learn to link two or more stimuli and anticipate events. The process involves stimuli and responses:
  - o A *UR (unconditioned response)* is an event that occurs naturally (such as salivation), in response to some stimulus.
  - o A *US (unconditioned stimulus)* is something that naturally and automatically (without learning) triggers the unlearned response (as food in the mouth triggers salivation).
  - o A *CS (conditioned stimulus)* is originally an *NS (neutral stimulus,* such as a tone) that, through learning, becomes associated with some unlearned response (salivating).
  - o A *CR (conditioned response)* is the learned response (salivating) to the originally neutral but now conditioned stimulus.

6-3: What parts do acquisition, extinction, spontaneous recovery, generalization, and discrimination play in classical conditioning?

- In classical conditioning, the first stage is *acquisition,* or the association of the NS with the US so that the NS begins triggering the CR. Acquisition occurs most readily when the NS is presented just before (ideally, about a half-second before) a US, preparing the organism for the upcoming event. This finding supports the view that classical conditioning is biologically adaptive.
- *Extinction* is diminished responding, which occurs if the CS appears repeatedly by itself (without the US).

- *Spontaneous recovery* is the appearance of a formerly extinguished response, following a rest period.
- Responses may be triggered by stimuli similar to the CS (*generalization*) but not by dissimilar stimuli (*discrimination*).

6-4: Why is Pavlov's work important, and how is it being applied?

- Ivan Pavlov taught us how to study a psychological process objectively, and that classical conditioning is a basic form of learning that applies to all species.
- Classical conditioning is applied to further human health and well-being in many areas, including behavioral therapy for some types of psychological disorders.

Operant Conditioning

6-5: What is operant conditioning, and how is operant behavior reinforced and shaped?

- *Operant conditioning* is a type of learning in which behavior is strengthened if followed by a reinforcer or diminished if followed by a punisher.
- Expanding on Edward Thordike's *law of effect,* B. F. Skinner and others *shaped* the behavior of rats and pigeons placed in *operant chambers* by rewarding the closer and closer approximations of a desired behavior.
- In operant conditioning, *reinforcement* is any event that strengthens a preceding response.

6-6: How do positive and negative reinforcement differ, and what are the basic types of reinforcers?

- *Positive reinforcers* add a desirable stimulus to increase the frequency of a behavior.

- *Negative reinforcers* remove or reduce a negative stimulus to increase the frequency of a behavior.
- *Primary reinforcers* (such as receiving food when hungry) are naturally satisfying—no learning is required.
- *Conditioned* (or secondary) *reinforcers* (such as cash) are satisfying because we have learned to associate them with primary reinforcers.
- Reinforcers may be immediate or delayed.

6-7: How do continuous and partial reinforcement schedules affect behavior?

- A *reinforcement schedule* is a pattern that defines how often a desired response will be reinforced:
  - o In *continuous reinforcement* (reinforcing desired responses every time they occur), learning is rapid, but so is extinction if reinforcement stops.
  - o In *partial (intermittent) reinforcement* (reinforcing responses only sometimes), learning is slower, but the behavior is much more resistant to extinction.
  - o *Fixed-ratio schedules* reinforce behaviors after a set number of responses.
  - o *Variable-ratio schedules* reinforce behaviors after an unpredictable number of responses.
  - o *Fixed-interval schedules* reinforce behaviors after set time periods.
  - o *Variable-interval schedules* reinforce behaviors after unpredictable time periods.

6-8: How does punishment differ from negative reinforcement, and how does punishment affect behavior?

- *Punishment* administers an undesirable consequence (such as spanking) or withdrawing something desirable (such as taking away a favorite toy).

- Negative reinforcement aims to increase frequency of a behavior (such as putting on your seat belt) by taking away something undesirable (the annoying beeping).

- The aim of punishment is to decrease the frequency of a behavior (such as a child's disobedience).

- Punishment can have unintended drawbacks: it can (1) suppress rather than change unwanted behaviors; (2) encourage discrimination (so that the undesirable behavior appears when the punisher is absent); (3) create fear; and (4) increase aggression.

6-9: Why were Skinner's ideas controversial, and how are educators, managers, and parents applying operant principles?

- Critics say that Skinner's approach dehumanized people by neglecting their personal freedom and seeking to control their actions. Skinner replied that external forces shape us anyway, so we should direct those forces with reinforcement, which is more humane than punishment.

- Teachers can control students' behaviors with shaping techniques, and use interactive media to provide immediate feedback.

- Managers can boost productivity and morale by rewarding well-defined and achievable behaviors.

- Parents can reward desirable behaviors but not undesirable ones.

- We can shape our own behaviors by stating our goals, planning how to work toward these goals, monitoring the frequency of our desired behaviors, reinforcing these behaviors, and gradually reducing rewards as our desired behaviors become habitual.

6-10: How does classical conditioning differ from operant conditioning?

- Both types of conditioning are forms of associative learning and involve acquisition, extinction, spontaneous recovery, generalization, and discrimination.

- In classical conditioning, we associate events we do not control and respond automatically (*respondent behaviors*).

- In operant conditioning, we link our behaviors (*operant behaviors*) with their consequences.

Biology, Cognition, and Learning

6-11: What limits does biology place on conditioning?

- We come prepared to learn tendencies, such as taste aversions, that aid our survival. Learning is adaptive.

- Despite operant training, animals may revert to biologically predisposed patterns. Learning some associations is easier than learning others due to these *biological constraints*.

6-12: How do cognitive processes affect classical and operant conditioning?

- More than the *behaviorists* supposed, expectations influence conditioning. In classical conditioning, animals may learn when to expect a US and may be aware of the link between stimuli and responses.

- In operant conditioning, *cognitive mapping* and *latent learning* research illustrate learning that occurs without immediate consequences. This demonstrates the importance of cognitive processes in learning.

- Other research shows that excessive rewards (driving *extrinsic motivation*) can destroy *intrinsic motivation* for an activity.

Learning by Observation

6-13: How does observational learning differ from associative learning? How may observational learning be enabled by mirror neurons?

- *Observational learning*, as shown in Bandura's Bobo doll experiment, involves learning by watching and imitating, rather than learning associations between different events. We learn to anticipate a behavior's consequences because we experience vicarious reinforcement or vicarious punishment.

- Our brain's frontal lobes have a demonstrated ability to mirror the activity of another's brain. (Some psychologists believe *mirror neurons* enable this process.) The same areas fire when we perform certain actions (such as responding to pain or moving our mouth to form words) as when we observe someone else performing those actions.

6-14: What is the impact of prosocial modeling and of antisocial modeling?

- Children tend to imitate what a model does and says, whether the behavior *modeled* is *prosocial* (positive, helpful) or antisocial.

- If a model's actions and words are inconsistent, children may imitate the hypocrisy they observe.

CHAPTER 7
MEMORY

Studying Memory

7-1: What is memory, and how do information-processing models help us study memory?

- *Memory* is the persistence of learning over time, through the storage and retrieval of information.

- Psychologists use memory models to think about how our brain forms and retrieves memories. Information-processing models involve three processes: *encoding*, *storage*, and *retrieval*.

7-2: What is the three-stage information-processing model, and how has later research updated this model?

- The three processing stages in the Atkinson and Shiffrin classic three-stage model of memory are *sensory memory*, *short-term memory*, and *long-term memory*.
- More recent research has updated this model to include two additional concepts: (1) *working memory*, to stress the active processing occurring in the second memory stage, and (2) *automatic processing*, to address the processing of information outside of conscious awareness.

Building Memories: Encoding

7-3: How do explicit and implicit memories differ?

- Through parallel processing, we process many things at once, on dual tracks.
- *Explicit* (declarative) *memories* are our conscious memories of general knowledge, facts, and experiences. They form through *effortful processing*.
- *Implicit* (nondeclarative) *memories* are our unconscious memories of skills and classically conditioned responses. They happen without our awareness, through *automatic processing*.

7-4: What information do we automatically process?

- In addition to skills and classically conditioned associations, we automatically process incidental information about space, time, and frequency.

7-5: How does sensory memory work?

- Sensory memory feeds some information into working memory for active processing there.
- An iconic memory is a very brief (a few tenths of a second) picture-image memory of a scene; an echoic memory is a three- or four-second sensory memory of a sound.

7-6: What is the capacity of our short-term and working memory?

- Short-term memory capacity is about seven items, give or take two, but this information disappears from memory quickly without rehearsal.
- Working-memory capacity varies, depending on age and other factors.

7-7: What are some effortful processing strategies that can help us remember new information?

- Effective effortful processing strategies include *chunking* and *mnemonics*.
- Such strategies help us remember new information because we then focus our attention and make a conscious effort to remember.

7-8: Why is cramming ineffective, and what is the testing effect?

- Massed practice, or cramming, results in poorer long-term recall than encoding that is spread over time. Psychologists call this result of distributed practice the *spacing effect*.
- The *testing effect* is the finding that consciously retrieving, rather than simply rereading, information enhances memory.

Memory Storage

7-9: What is the capacity of long-term memory? Are our long-term memories processed and stored in specific locations?

- We have an unlimited capacity for storing information permanently in long-term memory.
- Memories are not stored intact in the brain in single specific spots. Many parts of the brain interact as we encode, store, and retrieve memories.

7-10: What roles do the hippocampus and frontal lobes play in memory processing?

- The frontal lobes and *hippocampus* are parts of the brain network dedicated to explicit memory formation.
- Many brain regions send information to the frontal lobes for processing. The hippocampus registers and temporarily holds elements of explicit memories before moving them for storage elsewhere.

7-11: What roles do the cerebellum and basal ganglia play in memory processing?

- The cerebellum and basal ganglia are parts of the brain network dedicated to implicit memory formation. The cerebellum is important for storing classically conditioned memories.
- The basal ganglia are involved in motor movement and help form procedural memories for skills.

7-12: How do emotions affect our memory processing?

- Emotional arousal causes an outpouring of stress hormones, which lead to activity in the brain's memory-forming areas. Significantly stressful events can trigger very clear *flashbulb memories*.

7-13: How do changes at the synapse level affect our memory processing?

- *Long-term potentiation (LTP)* appears to be the neural process for learning and memory. It involves an increase in a synapse's firing potential as neurons become more efficient and more connections between neurons develop.

Retrieval: Getting Information Out

7-14: How do psychologists assess memory with recall, recognition, and relearning?

- Psychologists assess memory by studying evidence of it in the recall, recognition, and relearning of information:
  - o *Recall* is memory demonstrated by retrieving information we learned earlier (as on a fill-in-the-blank test).
  - o *Recognition* is memory demonstrated by identifying items previously learned (as on a multiple-choice test).
  - o *Relearning* is memory demonstrated by more quickly mastering material that has been previously learned.

7-15: How do external events, internal moods, and order of appearance affect memory retrieval?

- *Retrieval cues*, such as context and mood, are information bits linked with the original encoded memory. These cues activate associations that help us retrieve memories; this process may occur without our awareness, as it does in *priming*.
- Returning to the same physical context or emotional state *(mood congruency)* in which we formed a memory can help us retrieve it.
- The *serial position effect* accounts for our tendency to recall best the last items (which may still be in working memory) and the first items (which we've spent more time rehearsing) in a list.

Forgetting

7-16: Why do we forget?

- Normal forgetting can happen because we have never encoded information (encoding failure); because the physical trace has decayed (storage decay); or because we cannot retrieve what we have encoded and stored (retrieval failure).
- Retrieval problems may result from *proactive* (forward-acting) *interference*, when prior learning interferes with recall of new information, or from *retroactive* (backward-acting) *interference*, when new learning disrupts recall of old information.
- Freud believed that motivated forgetting occurs, but researchers have found little evidence of *repression*.

Memory Construction Errors

7-17: How do misinformation, imagination, and source amnesia influence our memory construction? How do we decide whether a memory is real or false?

- We construct our memories, using both stored and new information as well as our imaginations.
- *Misinformation* (exposure to misleading information) and imagination effects corrupt our stored memories of what actually happened.
- *Source amnesia* leads to faulty memories of how, when, or where we learned something, and may help explain *déjà vu*.
- False memories feel like real memories and can be persistent but are usually limited to the gist (the general idea) of the event.

7-18: How reliable are young children's eyewitness descriptions, and why are reports of repressed and recovered memories so hotly debated?

- Children's eyewitness descriptions are subject to the same memory influences that distort adult reports. Children are susceptible to source amnesia and the misinformation effect, but if questioned in neutral words they understand, they can accurately recall events and people involved in them.
- Incest and abuse happen more than was once supposed. But unless the victim was a child too young to remember, such traumas are usually remembered vividly, not repressed.

Improving Memory

7-19: How can you use memory research findings to do better in this course and in others?

- Memory research findings suggest the following strategies for improving memory: Study repeatedly, make material meaningful, activate retrieval cues, use mnemonic devices, minimize interference, sleep more, and test yourself to be sure you can retrieve, as well as recognize, material.

CHAPTER 8
Thinking, Language, and Intelligence

Thinking

8-1: What is cognition, and what are the functions of concepts?

- *Cognition* refers to all the mental activities associated with thinking, knowing, remembering, and communicating.
- We use *concepts*, mental groupings of similar objects, events, ideas, or people, to simplify and order the world around us.
- We form most concepts around *prototypes*, or best examples of a category.

8-2: What strategies help us solve problems, and what tendencies work against us?

- An *algorithm* is a methodical, logical rule or procedure (such as a step-by-step description for evacuating a building during a fire) that guarantees a solution to a problem.

- A *heuristic* is a simpler strategy (such as running for an exit if you smell smoke) that is usually speedier than an algorithm but is also more error prone.

- *Insight* is not a strategy-based solution, but rather a sudden flash of inspiration (Aha!) that solves a problem.

- Tendencies that work against us in problem solving include *confirmation bias*, which leads us to verify rather than challenge our hypotheses, and *fixation*, which may prevent us from taking the fresh perspective that would lead to a solution.

8-3: What is intuition, and how can the availability heuristic, overconfidence, belief perseverance, and framing influence our decisions and judgments?

- *Intuition* involves fast, automatic, unreasoned feelings and thoughts, as contrasted with explicit, conscious reasoning.

- Heuristics enable snap judgments. Using the *availability heuristic,* we judge the likelihood of things based on how readily they come to mind, which often leads us to fear the wrong things.

- *Overconfidence* can lead us to overestimate the accuracy of our beliefs.

- When a belief we have formed and explained has been discredited, *belief perseverance* may cause us to cling to that belief. A remedy for belief perseverance is to consider how we might have explained an opposite result.

- *Framing* is the way a question or statement is worded. Subtle wording differences can dramatically alter our responses.

8-4: How do smart thinkers use intuition?

- As people gain expertise, they become skilled at making quick,

shrewd judgments. Smart thinkers welcome their intuitions (which are usually adaptive), but when making complex decisions they gather as much information as possible and then take time to let their two-track mind process all available information.

8-5: What is creativity, and what fosters it?

- *Creativity,* the ability to produce new and valuable ideas, requires a certain level of aptitude (ability to learn), but it is more than school smarts. Aptitude tests require *convergent thinking,* but creativity requires *divergent thinking.*

- Robert Sternberg has proposed that creativity has five components: expertise; imaginative thinking skills; a venturesome personality; intrinsic motivation; and a creative environment that sparks, supports, and refines creative ideas.

8-6: What do we know about thinking in other species?

- Evidence from studies of various species shows that other animals use concepts, numbers, and tools, and that they transmit learning from one generation to the next (cultural transmission). And, like humans, other species also show insight, self-awareness, altruism, cooperation, and grief.

Language

8-7: What are the milestones in language development, and how do we acquire language?

- *Language* is our spoken, written, or signed words and the ways we combine them to communicate meaning. Receptive language (the ability to understand what is said to or about you) develops before productive language (the ability to produce words).

- Language development's timing varies, but all children follow the same sequence:

  o By about 4 months of age, infants *babble,* making a wide range of sounds found in languages all over the world.

  o By about 10 months, babbling contains only the sounds of the household language.

  o By about 12 months, children begin to speak in *one-word* sentences.

  o *Two-word (telegraphic)* phrases happen around 24 months, followed by full sentences soon after.

- Noam Chomsky has proposed that all human languages share a universal grammar—the basic building blocks of language—and that humans are born with a predisposition (a built-in readiness) to learn language. The particular language we learn is the result of our experience.

- Childhood is a critical period for learning language.

8-8: What brain areas are involved in language processing and speech?

- Two important language- and speech-processing areas are Broca's area, a region of the frontal lobe that controls language expression, and Wernicke's area, a region in the left temporal lobe that controls language reception.

- Language processing is spread across other brain areas as well, where different neural networks handle specific linguistic subtasks.

8-9: How can thinking in images be useful?

- Thinking in images can provide useful mental practice if we focus on the steps needed to reach our goal (rather than fantasizing about having achieved the goal).

8-10: What do we know about other species' capacity for language?

- A number of chimpanzees and bonobos have (1) learned to communicate with humans by signing or by pushing buttons wired to a computer, (2) developed vocabularies of nearly 400 words, (3) communicated by stringing these words together, (4) taught their skills to younger animals, and (5) demonstrated some understanding of syntax. But only humans possess language—verbal or signed expressions of complex grammar.

Intelligence

8-11: How do psychologists define *intelligence,* and what are the arguments for general intelligence *(g)?*

- *Intelligence* is a mental quality consisting of the ability to learn from experience, solve problems, and use knowledge to adapt to new situations.
- Charles Spearman proposed that we have one *general intelligence (g)* underlying all other specific mental abilities. He helped develop factor analysis, a statistical procedure that searches for clusters of related items.

8-12: What are two theories of multiple intelligences, and what criticisms have they faced?

- *Savant syndrome* and abilities lost after brain injuries seem to support Howard Gardner's view that we have multiple intelligences. He proposed eight independent intelligences: linguistic, logical-mathematical, musical, spatial, bodily-kinesthetic, intrapersonal, interpersonal, and naturalist.
- Robert Sternberg's triarchic theory proposes three intelligence areas that predict real-world skills: analytical (academic problem-solving), creative, and practical.

- Critics note research that has confirmed a general intelligence factor. But highly successful people also tend to be conscientious, well connected, and doggedly energetic.

8-13: What four abilities make up emotional intelligence?

- *Emotional intelligence,* which is an aspect of social intelligence, is the ability to perceive, understand, manage, and use emotions. Emotionally intelligent people achieve greater personal and professional success.

8-14: When and why were intelligence tests created, and how do today's tests differ from early intelligence tests?

- *Intelligence tests* assess a person's mental aptitudes and compare them with those of others, using numerical scores.
- *Aptitude tests* measure the ability to learn; *achievement* tests measure what we have already learned.
- Alfred Binet started the modern intelligence-testing movement in France in 1904 when he developed questions to help predict children's future progress in the Paris school system.
- During the early twentieth century, Lewis Terman of Stanford University revised Binet's work for use in the United States (which resulted in the *Stanford-Binet* intelligence test).
- William Stern contributed the concept of the *IQ (intelligence quotient).*
- The most widely used intelligence tests today are the *Wechsler Adult Intelligence Scale (WAIS)* and Wechsler's tests for children. These tests differ from their predecessors in the way they offer an overall intelligence score as well as scores for various verbal and performance areas.

8-15: What is a normal curve, and what does it mean to say that a test has been standardized and is reliable and valid?

- The distribution of test scores often forms a *normal* (bell-shaped) curve around the central average score, with fewer and fewer scores at the extremes.
- *Standardization* establishes a basis for meaningful score comparisons by giving a test to a representative sample of future test-takers.
- *Reliability* is the extent to which a test yields consistent results (on two halves of the test, or when people are retested).
- *Validity* is the extent to which a test measures or predicts what it is supposed to. A test should have both content validity and predictive validity. (Aptitude tests have predictive ability if they can predict future achievements.)

8-16: What are the traits of those at the low and high intelligence extremes?

- At the low extreme are those with unusually low scores. An intelligence test score of or below 70 is one diagnostic criterion for the diagnosis of *intellectual disability;* another is difficulty adapting to life demands. One condition included in this category is *Down syndrome,* a developmental disorder caused by an extra copy of chromosome 21.
- People at the high-intelligence extreme tend to be healthy and well-adjusted, as well as unusually successful academically.

8-17: How is intelligence influenced by nature and nurture? What does it mean when we say that a trait is heritable?

- Studies of twins, family members, and adoptees indicate a significant hereditary contribution to intelligence scores. But these studies also provide evidence of environmental influences. Heredity and environment interact: Our genes shape the environments that influence us.

- Studies of children raised in extremely impoverished environments with minimal social interaction indicate that life experiences can significantly influence intelligence test performance. No evidence supports the idea that normal, healthy children can be molded into geniuses by growing up in an exceptionally enriched environment.

- *Heritability* is the portion of variation among individuals that can be attributed to genes.

8-18: How stable are intelligence scores across people's lives, and how do psychologists study this question?

- *Cross-sectional studies* (comparing people of different ages) and *longitudinal studies* (retesting the same group over a period of years) have shown that intelligence endures. The stability of intelligence test scores increases with age.

8-19: What are crystallized and fluid intelligence, and how does aging affect them?

- *Fluid intelligence,* our ability to reason speedily and abstractly, declines in older adults.

- *Crystallized intelligence,* our accumulated knowledge and verbal skills, tends to increase.

8-20: How and why do the genders differ in mental ability scores?

- Males and females tend to have the same average intelligence test scores, but they differ in some specific abilities.

- Girls are better spellers, more verbally fluent, better at locating objects, better at detecting emotions, and more sensitive to touch, taste, and color.

- Boys outperform girls at spatial ability and related mathematics, though in math computation and overall math performance, boys and girls hardly differ. Boys also outnumber girls at the low and high extremes of mental abilities.

- Evolutionary and cultural explanations have been proposed for these gender differences.

8-21: How and why do racial and ethnic groups differ in mental ability scores?

- Racial and ethnic groups differ in their average intelligence test scores. The evidence suggests that environmental differences are largely, perhaps entirely, responsible for these group differences.

8-22: Are intelligence tests biased and discriminatory?

- Aptitude tests aim to predict how well a test-taker will perform in a given situation. So they are necessarily "biased" in the sense that they are sensitive to performance differences caused by cultural experience.

- But a test should not predict less accurately for one group than for another. In this sense, most experts consider the major aptitude tests unbiased.

- *Stereotype threat,* a self-confirming concern that we will be judged based on a negative stereotype, affects performance on all kinds of tests.

CHAPTER 9
Motivation and Emotion

Motivational Concepts

9-1: What is motivation, and what are three key perspectives that help us understand motivated behaviors?

- *Motivation* is a need or desire that energizes and directs behavior.

- *Drive-reduction theory:* We feel motivated when pushed by a *physiological* need to reduce a drive (such as thirst), or when pulled by an *incentive* in our environment (an ice-cold drink). Drive-reduction's goal is *homeostasis,* maintaining a steady internal state.

- Arousal theory: We also feel motivated to behave in ways that maintain arousal (for example, curiosity-driven behaviors).

- Maslow's *hierarchy of needs:* Our levels of motivation form a pyramid of human needs, from basic needs such as hunger and thirst up to higher-level needs such as self-actualization and self-transcendence.

Hunger

9-2: What physiological factors cause us to feel hungry?

- Hunger's pangs correspond to the stomach's contractions, but hunger also has other causes. Neural areas in the brain, some within the hypothalamus, monitor blood chemistry (including level of *glucose*) and incoming information about the body's state.

- Appetite hormones include insulin (controls blood glucose); ghrelin (secreted by an empty stomach); orexin (secreted by the hypothalamus); leptin (secreted by fat cells); and PYY (secreted by the digestive tract).

- *Basal metabolic rate* is the body's resting rate of energy output. The body may have a *set point* (a biologically fixed tendency to maintain an optimum weight) or a looser settling point (which is also influenced by the environment).

9-3: How do psychological, biological, cultural, and situational factors affect our taste preferences and eating habits?

- Hunger also reflects our memory of when we last ate and our expectation of when we should eat again.

- Humans as a species prefer certain tastes (such as sweet and salty), but our individual preferences are also influenced by conditioning, culture, and situation.

- Some taste preferences, such as the avoidance of new foods, or of foods that have made us ill, have survival value.

9-4: What factors predispose some people to become and remain obese?

- Genes and environment interact to produce obesity.

- Twin and adoption studies indicate that body weight is genetically influenced.

- Environmental influences include too little sleep and exercise, an abundance of high-calorie food, and social influence.

- Those wishing to lose weight are advised to make a lifelong change in habits: Get enough sleep; boost energy expenditure through exercise; limit variety and minimize exposure to tempting food cues; eat healthy foods and reduce portion sizes; space meals throughout the day; beware of the binge; monitor eating during social events; forgive the occasional lapse; and connect to a support group.

The Need to Belong

9-5: What evidence points to our human need to belong?

- Social bonds are adaptive and help us to be healthier and happier. Feeling loved activates brain regions associated with rewards and satisfaction.

- When shunned by others, people suffer from stress and depression and may engage in self-defeating or anti-social behavior. Social isolation can put us at risk for mental decline and ill health.

9-6: How does social networking influence us?

- We connect with others through social networking, strengthening our relationships with those we already know. When networking, people tend toward increased self-disclosure.

- Working out strategies for self-control and disciplined usage can help people maintain a healthy balance between social connections and school and work performance.

Emotion: Arousal, Behavior, and Cognition

9-7: What are the three parts of an emotion, and what theories help us to understand our emotions?

- *Emotions* are psychological responses of the whole organism involving bodily arousal, expressive behaviors, and conscious experience.

- *James-Lange theory:* Emotional feelings follow our body's response to the emotion-arousing stimuli. (We observe our heart pounding and feel fear.)

- *Cannon-Bard theory:* Our body responds to emotion at the same time that we experience that emotion. (Neither causes the other.)

- Schachter-Singer *two-factor theory:* Emotions have two ingredients, physical arousal and a cognitive label, and the cognitive labels we put on our states of arousal are an essential ingredient of emotion.

- Richard Lazarus agreed that many important emotions arise from our interpretations or inferences. Robert Zajonc and Joseph LeDoux, however, believe that some simple emotional responses occur instantly, not only outside our conscious awareness, but before any cognitive processing occurs. This interplay between emotion and cognition illustrates our two-track mind.

Embodied Emotion

9-8: What are some basic emotions?

- Carroll Izard's basic emotions are joy, interest-excitement, surprise, sadness, anger, disgust, contempt, fear, shame, and guilt.

9-9: What is the link between emotional arousal and the autonomic nervous system?

- The arousal component of emotion is regulated by the autonomic nervous system's sympathetic (arousing) and parasympathetic (calming) divisions.

- In a crisis, the fight-or-flight response automatically mobilizes your body for action.

9-10: How do our body states relate to specific emotions? How effective are polygraphs in using body states to detect lies?

- The large-scale body changes that accompany sexual arousal, fear, and anger are very similar (increased perspiration, breathing, and heart rate), though they feel different. Emotions may be similarly arousing, but some subtle physiological responses (such as facial muscle movements) distinguish them.

- Emotions use different circuits in the brain. For example, greater activity in the left frontal lobe signals positive rather than negative moods.

- *Polygraphs* (lie detectors) attempt to measure physical evidence of emotions, but they are not accurate enough to justify widespread use in business and law enforcement.

- The use of guilty knowledge questions and new forms of technology may produce better indications of lying.

Expressed and Experienced Emotion

9-11: How do we communicate nonverbally? How do women and men differ in these abilities?

- We are good at detecting emotions from body movements, facial expressions, and voice tones. Even seconds-long video clips of behavior can reveal feelings.

- Women tend to read emotional cues more easily and to be more empathic. Their faces also express more emotion.

9-12: How are nonverbal expressions of emotion understood within and across cultures?

- The meaning of gestures varies by culture.

- Facial expressions, such as those of happiness and fear, are roughly similar all over the world. Research on the *facial feedback effect* shows that our facial expressions can trigger emotional feelings and signal our body to respond accordingly. We also mimic others' expressions, which helps us empathize.

9-13: How do facial expressions influence our feelings?

- Research on the *facial feedback effect* shows that our facial expressions can trigger emotional feelings and signal our body to respond accordingly. We also mimic others' expressions, which helps us empathize.

CHAPTER 10
Stress, Health, and Human Flourishing

Stress: Some Basic Concepts

10-1: How does our appraisal of an event affect our stress reaction, and what are the three main types of stressors?

- *Stress* is the process by which we appraise and respond to stressors—events that challenge or threaten us.

- If we appraise an event as challenging, we will be aroused and focused in preparation for success. If we appraise an event as a threat, we will experience a stress reaction, and our health may suffer.

- The three main types of stressors are catastrophes, significant life changes, and daily hassles.

10-2: How does the body respond to stress?

- Walter Cannon viewed our body's response to stress as a *fight-or-flight* system.

- Hans Selye proposed a general three-phase (alarm-resistance-exhaustion) *general adaptation syndrome (GAS)*.

- People may react to stress by withdrawing, turning to alcohol, or becoming aggressive (more common in men) or by showing a *tend-and-befriend response* (more common in women), such as when helping others after natural disasters.

Stress Effects and Health

10-3: How does stress influence our immune system?

- Stress takes energy away from the immune system, inhibiting the activities of its B and T *lymphocytes*, macrophages, and natural killer (NK) cells. This leaves us more vulnerable to illness and disease.

- *Psychoneuroimmunology* is the study of these mind-body interactions.

- Although stress does not cause diseases such as AIDS and cancer, it may make us more vulnerable to them and influence their progression.

10-4: How does stress increase coronary heart disease risk?

- Stress is directly connected to *coronary heart disease*, the United States' number one cause of death

- Heart disease has been linked with the competitive, hard-driving, impatient, and (especially) anger-prone *Type A* personality. Type A people secrete more stress hormones. Chronic stress contributes to persistent inflammation, which is associated with heart and other health problems.

- *Type B* personalities are more relaxed and easygoing and less likely to experience heart disease.

- The fight-or-flight stress reaction may divert blood from the liver to the muscles, leaving excess cholesterol circulating in the bloodstream. Stress can also trigger altered heart rhythms.

Coping With Stress

10-5: What are two basic ways that people cope with stress?

- We use direct, *problem-focused coping* strategies when we feel a sense of control over a situation, and these are usually most effective.

- When lacking that sense of control, we may need to use *emotion-focused coping* strategies to protect our long-term well-being. These strategies can be harmful if misused.

10-6: How does our sense of control influence stress and health?

- Feelings of loss of *personal control* can trigger physical symptoms, such as increased stress hormones and rising blood pressure. A series of uncontrollable events can lead to *learned helplessness*.

- Those with an *internal locus of control* achieve more in school and work, act more independently, enjoy better health, and feel less depressed than do those with an *external locus of control*.

- Those who develop and maintain self-control achieve more academic and social success and are healthier.

10-7: How do optimists and pessimists differ, and why does our outlook on life matter?

- *Optimists* (those expecting positive outcomes) tend to be in better health than *pessimists* (those expecting negative outcomes). Studies of people with an optimistic outlook show that their immune system is stronger, their blood pressure does not increase as sharply in response to stress, their recovery from heart bypass surgery is faster, and their life expectancy is longer. Yet realistic anxiety over possible future failures can help motivate us to do better.

10-8: How do social support and finding meaning in life influence health?

- Social support promotes health by calming us, by reducing blood pressure and stress hormones, and by fostering stronger immune function. We can significantly reduce our stress and increase our health by building and maintaining relationships with family and friends, and by finding meaning even in difficult times.

Managing Stress Effects

10-9: How well does aerobic exercise help manage stress and improve well-being?

- *Aerobic exercise* is sustained activity that increases heart and lung fitness, which leads to greater well-being.
- Exercise increases arousal and triggers serotonin activity. It may also reduce depression and anxiety.

10-10: In what ways might relaxation and meditation influence stress and health?

- Relaxation and meditation have been shown to reduce stress by relaxing muscles, lowering blood pressure, improving immune functioning, and lessening anxiety and depression.

- *Mindfulness meditation* is attending to current experiences in a nonjudgmental and accepting manner.
- Massage therapy also relaxes muscles and reduces depression.
- Counseling Type A heart attack survivors to slow down and relax has helped lower rates of recurring attacks.

10-11: Does religious involvement relate to health?

- Religious involvement predicts better health and longevity. This may be explained by the healthier lifestyles of religiously active people, the social support that comes along with practicing a faith in community, and the positive emotions often found among people who regularly attend religious services.

Happiness

10-12: What are the causes and consequences of happiness?

- A good mood brightens people's perceptions of the world. Happy people tend to be healthy, energized, and satisfied with life. They also are more willing to help others (the *feel-good, do-good phenomenon*).
- Even significant good or bad events don't usually change our *subjective well-being* for long.
- Happiness is relative to our own experiences (the *adaptation-level phenomenon*) and to others' success (the *relative deprivation* principle).
- Tips for increasing happiness levels: focus beyond finances, take charge of your schedule, act happy, seek meaningful work and leisure, exercise, sleep enough, foster friendships, focus beyond the self, and nurture gratitude and spirituality.

CHAPTER 11
Personality

Personality—an individual's characteristic pattern of thinking, feeling, and acting.

Psychodynamic Theories

Psychodynamic theories view personality from the perspective that behavior is a dynamic interaction between the conscious and unconscious mind. The theories trace their origin to Sigmund Freud's theory of *psychoanalysis*.

11-1: How did Sigmund Freud's treatment of psychological disorders lead to his view of the unconscious mind?

- In treating patients whose disorders had no clear physical explanation, Freud concluded that these problems reflected unacceptable thoughts and feelings, hidden away in the *unconscious* mind.
- To explore this hidden part of a patient's mind, Freud used *free association* and dream analysis.

11-2: What was Freud's view of personality?

- Freud believed that personality is a result of conflict among the mind's three systems: the *id* (pleasure-seeking impulses), *ego* (reality-oriented executive), and *superego* (internalized set of ideals, or conscience).

11-3: What developmental stages did Freud propose?

- He believed children pass through five *psychosexual* stages (oral, anal, phallic, latency, and genital). Unresolved conflicts at any stage can leave a person's pleasure-seeking impulses *fixated* (stalled) at that stage.

11-4: How did Freud think people defended themselves against anxiety?

- For Freud, anxiety was the product of tensions between the demands of id and superego.
- The ego copes by using unconscious *defense mechanisms*, such as *repression*, which he viewed as the basic

mechanism underlying and enabling all the others.

11-5: Which of Freud's ideas did his followers accept or reject?

- Freud's early followers, the neo-Freudians, accepted many of his ideas. They differed in placing more emphasis on the conscious mind and in stressing social motives more than sex or aggression.

- Contemporary psychodynamic theorists and therapists reject Freud's emphasis on sexual motivation. They stress, with support from modern research findings, the view that much of our mental life is unconscious, and they believe that our childhood experiences influence our adult personality and attachment patterns.

11-6: What are projective tests, how are they used, and how are they criticized?

- *Projective tests* attempt to assess personality by showing people an unclear image designed to trigger projection of the test-taker's unconscious thoughts and feelings.

- One such test, the *Rorschach inkblot test*, has low reliability and validity.

11-7: How do today's psychologists view Freud's psychoanalysis?

- Freud rightly drew our attention to the vast unconscious, to the struggle to cope with anxiety and sexuality, to the conflict between biological impulses and social restraints and for some forms of defense mechanisms (false consensus effect/projection; reaction formation).

- But his concept of repression, and his view of the unconscious as a collection of repressed and unacceptable thoughts, wishes, feelings, and memories, cannot survive scientific scrutiny.

- Freud offered after-the-fact explanations, which are hard to test scientifically.

- Research does not support many of Freud's specific ideas, such as development being fixed in childhood. (We now know it is lifelong.)

11-8: How has modern research developed our understanding of the unconscious?

- Current research confirms that we do not have full access to all that goes on in our mind, but the current view of the unconscious is that it is a separate and parallel track of information processing that occurs outside our awareness.

- This processing includes schemas that control our perceptions; implicit memories of learned skills; instantly activated emotions; and the self-concept and stereotypes that automatically influence how we process information about ourselves and others.

Humanistic Theories

11-9: How did humanistic psychologists view personality, and what was their goal in studying personality?

- Humanistic theories sought to turn psychology's attention toward human growth potential.

- Abraham Maslow thought that human motivations form a *hierarchy of needs*. If basic needs are fulfilled, people will strive toward *self-actualization* and *self-transcendence*.

- Carl Rogers believed that people are basically good, and that showing *unconditional positive regard* and being genuine, accepting, and empathic can help others develop a more realistic and positive *self-concept*.

11-10: How did humanistic psychologists assess a person's sense of self?

- Some rejected any standardized assessments and relied on interviews and conversations.

- Rogers sometimes used questionnaires in which people described their ideal and actual selves, which he later used to judge progress during therapy.

11-11: How have humanistic theories influenced psychology? What criticisms have they faced?

- Humanistic psychology helped renew interest in the concept of self.

- Critics have said that humanistic psychology's concepts were vague and subjective, its values self-centered, and its assumptions naively optimistic.

Trait Theories

11-12: How do psychologists use traits to describe personality?

- *Trait* theorists see personality as a stable and enduring pattern of behavior. They describe our differences rather than trying to explain them.

- They identify *factors*—clusters of behavior tendencies that occur together.

11-13: What are personality inventories?

- *Personality inventories* (such as the MMPI) are questionnaires on which people respond to items designed to gauge a wide range of feelings and behaviors.

- Unlike projective tests, these tests are objectively scored. But people can fake their answers to create a good impression, and the ease of computerized testing may lead to misuse of the tests.

11-14: Which traits seem to provide the most useful information about personality variation?

- The Big Five personality factors—conscientiousness, agreeableness, neuroticism, openness, and extraversion (CANOE)—currently offer the clearest picture of personality.
- These factors are stable and appear to be found in all cultures.

11-15: Does research support the consistency of personality traits over time and across situations?

- A person's average traits persist over time and are predictable over many different situations. But traits cannot predict behavior in any one particular situation.

Social-Cognitive Theories

11-16: How do social-cognitive theorists view personality development, and how do they explore behavior?

- Albert Bandura first proposed the *social-cognitive perspective,* which views personality as the product of the interaction between a person's traits (including thinking) and the situation—the social world around us.
- Social-cognitive researchers apply principles of learning, cognition, and social behavior to personality.
- *Reciprocal determinism* describes the interaction and mutual influence of behavior, internal personal factors, and environmental factors.
- A person's average traits are predictable over many different situations, but not in any one particular situation.

11-17: What criticisms have social-cognitive theorists faced?

- Critics note that social-cognitive theorists focus so much on the situation that they fail to appreciate a person's inner traits, underemphasizing the importance of unconscious motives, emotions, and personality characteristics.

Exploring the Self

11-18: Why has psychology generated so much research on the self? How important is self-esteem to psychology and to our well-being?

- The *self* is the center of personality, organizing our thoughts, feelings, and actions.
- Considering possible selves helps motivate us toward positive development, but focusing too intensely on ourselves can lead to the *spotlight effect*.
- High *self-esteem* (our feeling of self-worth) is beneficial, but unrealistically high self-esteem is dangerous (linked to aggressive behavior) and fragile.
- Psychologists are now more pessimistic about the value of unrealistically promoting children's feelings of self-worth, rather than rewarding their achievements, which leads to feelings of competence.

11-19: What evidence reveals self-serving bias, and how do defensive and secure self-esteem differ?

- *Self-serving bias* is our tendency to perceive ourselves favorably, as when viewing ourselves as better than average or when accepting credit for our successes but not blame for our failures.
- Defensive self-esteem is fragile, focuses on sustaining itself, and views failure or criticism as a threat.
- Secure self-esteem is sturdy, enabling us to feel accepted for who we are.

11-20: How do individualist and collectivist cultures influence people?

- Although individuals within countries vary, different cultures tend to emphasize either individualism or collectivism.
- People who are *individualist* are self-reliant and usually tend to define themselves in terms of personal goals and attributes.
- People who are *collectivist* are socially connected and give priority to group goals, social identity, and commitments.

CHAPTER 12
Social Psychology

What Is Social Psychology's Focus?

12-1: What are three main focuses of social psychology?

- *Social psychology* focuses on how we think about, influence, and relate to one another. Social psychologists study the social influences that explain why the same person will act differently in different situations.

Social Thinking

12-2: How does the fundamental attribution error describe how we tend to explain others' behavior compared with our own?

- We may commit the *fundamental attribution error* (especially if we come from an individualistic Western culture) when explaining others' behavior, by underestimating the influence of the situation and overestimating the effects of personality.
- When we explain our own behavior, however, we more often recognize the influence of the situation.

12-3: What is an attitude, and how do attitudes and actions affect each other?

- *Attitudes* are feelings, often based on our beliefs, that predispose us to respond in certain ways.
- Attitudes that are stable, specific, and easily recalled can affect our actions when other influences are minimal.
- Actions also modify our attitudes. This can be seen in the *foot-in-the-door*

phenomenon (complying with a large request after having agreed to a small request) and *role* playing (acting a social part by following guidelines for expected behavior).

- When our attitudes don't fit with our actions, *cognitive dissonance theory* suggests that we will reduce tension by changing our attitudes to match our actions.

Social Influence

12-4: What do experiments on conformity and obedience reveal about the power of social influence?

- Solomon Asch and others have found that we are most likely to *conform* to a group standard when (a) we feel incompetent or insecure, (b) our group has at least three people, (c) everyone else agrees, (d) we admire the group's status, (e) we have not already committed to another response, (f) we know we are being observed, and (g) our culture encourages respect for social standards.
- In Stanley Milgram's famous experiments, people usually obeyed the experimenter's orders even when they thought they were harming another person. Obedience was highest when (a) the experimenter was nearby and (b) was a legitimate authority figure supported by an important institution, (c) the victim was not nearby, and (d) there were no role models for defiance.

12-5: What do the social influence studies teach us about ourselves? How much power do we have as individuals?

- Strong social influences can make people to conform to falsehoods or give in to cruelty.
- Even a small minority sometimes sways a group, especially when the minority expresses its views consistently.

- Social control (the power of the situation) and personal control (the power of the individual) interact.

12-6: How does the presence of others influence our actions, via social facilitation, social loafing, or deindividuation?

- In *social facilitation*, the presence of others arouses us, improving performance on easy tasks but hindering it on difficult ones.
- *Social loafing* is the tendency when participating in a group project to feel less responsible, when we may free ride on others' efforts.
- When the presence of others both arouses us and makes us feel less responsible, we may experience *deindividuation*—loss of self-awareness and self-restraint.

12-7: How can group interaction enable group polarization and groupthink?

- In *group polarization*, group discussions with like-minded others cause us to feel more strongly about our shared beliefs and attitudes. Internet communication magnifies this effect, for better and for worse.
- *Groupthink* is driven by a desire for harmony within a group, causing its members to overlook important alternatives.

Social Relations

12-8: What are the three parts of prejudice, and how has prejudice changed over time?

- *Prejudice* is an unjustifiable, usually negative, attitude toward a group and its members. Prejudice's three components are (a) beliefs (often *stereotypes*), (b) emotions (negative feelings), and (c) predispositions to action (*discrimination*).
- Open prejudice has decreased, but subtle prejudice and automatic

prejudice—occurring without our awareness—continue.

12-9: What factors contribute to the social roots of prejudice, and how does scapegoating illustrate the emotional roots of prejudice?

- Social inequalities and social divisions feed prejudice. Favored social groups often justify their higher status with the *just-world phenomenon*.
- We tend to favor our own group (*ingroup bias*) as we divide ourselves into us (the *ingroup*) and them (the *outgroup*).
- We may use prejudice to protect our emotional well-being, such as when focusing anger by blaming events on a *scapegoat*.

12-10: What are the cognitive roots of prejudice?

- The cognitive roots of prejudice grow from our natural ways of processing information: forming categories, remembering vivid cases, and believing that the world is just and our culture's way of doing things is the right way.

12-11: What biological factors predispose us to be aggressive?

- *Aggression* is a complex behavior resulting from the interaction of biology and experience.
- Biology influences our threshold for aggressive behaviors at three levels: genetic (inherited traits), biochemical (such as alcohol or excess testosterone in the bloodstream), and neural (activity in key brain areas).

12-12: What psychological and social-cultural factors may trigger aggressive behavior?

- Frustration (*frustration-aggression principle*), aversive events, getting rewarded for aggression, seeing an aggressive role model, and poor self-control can all contribute to aggression.

- Viewing sexual violence contributes to greater aggression toward women.
- Media portrayals of violence provide *social scripts* that children learn to follow.

12-13: Why do we befriend or fall in love with some people but not others?

- Proximity (geographical nearness) increases liking; in part because of the *mere exposure effect*—exposure to novel stimuli increases liking of those stimuli.
- Physical attractiveness increases social opportunities and improves the way we are perceived.
- Similarity of attitudes and interests greatly increases liking, especially as relationships develop. We also like those who like us.

12-14: How does romantic love typically change as time passes?

- Intimate love relationships start with *passionate love*—an intensely aroused state.
- Over time, the strong affection of *companionate love* may develop, especially if enhanced by an *equitable* relationship and by intimate *self-disclosure*.

12-15: What is *altruism?* When are we most—and least—likely to help?

- *Altruism* is unselfish regard for the well-being of others.
- We are most likely to help when we (a) notice an incident, (b) interpret it as an emergency, and (c) assume responsibility for helping. Other factors, including our mood and our similarity to the victim, also affect our willingness to help.

- We are least likely to help if other bystanders are present (the *bystander effect*).

12-16: How do social norms explain helping behavior?

- Helping results from socialization, in which we are taught guidelines for expected behaviors in social situations, such as the *reciprocity norm* and the *social-responsibility norm*.

12-17: What social processes fuel conflict? How can we transform feelings of prejudice and conflict into behaviors that promote peace?

- *Conflicts,* perceived incompatibilities of actions goals or ideas between individuals and cultures, are often fed by distorted *mirror-image perceptions*—each party views itself as ethical and peaceful and the other as untrustworthy and evil-intentioned.
- Peace can result when individuals or groups cooperate to achieve *superordinate* (shared) goals.

CHAPTER 13
Psychological Disorders

What Is a Psychological Disorder?

13-1: How should we draw the line between normal behavior and psychological disorder?

- According to psychologists and psychiatrists, *psychological disorders* are marked by a clinically significant disturbance in an individual's cognition, emotion regulation, or behavior.

13-2: Why is there controversy over attention-deficit/hyperactivity disorder?

- A child who displays extreme inattention, hyperactivity, and impul-

sivity may be diagnosed with *attention-deficit/hyperactivity disorder (ADHD)* and treated with medication and other therapy.

- The controversy centers on whether the growing number of ADHD cases reflects overdiagnosis or increased awareness of the disorder, and on the long-term effects of stimulant-drug treatment.

13-3: How is our understanding of psychological disorders affected by whether we use a medical model or a biopsychosocial approach?

- The *medical model* assumes that psychological disorders are mental illnesses with physical causes that can be diagnosed, treated, and, in most cases, cured through therapy, sometimes in a hospital.
- The biopsychosocial approach assumes that disordered behavior comes from the interaction of biological characteristics (genes and physiology), psychological dynamics, and social-cultural circumstances.

13-4: How and why do clinicians classify psychological disorders, and why do some psychologists criticize the use of diagnostic labels?

- The American Psychiatric Association's *DSM-5 (Diagnostic and Statistical Manual of Mental Disorders, Fifth Edition)* lists and describes psychological disorders.
- Diagnostic labels provide a common language and shared concepts for communication and research.
- Some critics believe the DSM editions have become too detailed and extensive.
- Labels can create preconceptions that cause us to view a person differently, and then look for evidence to confirm that view.

Anxiety Disorders, OCD, and PTSD

13-5: What are the main anxiety disorders, and how do anxiety disorders differ from the ordinary worries and fears we all experience?

- It's common to feel uneasy; when those feelings are intense and persistent they may be classified as disordered.

- *Anxiety disorders* are psychological disorders characterized by distressing, persistent anxiety or maladaptive behaviors that reduce anxiety.

- People with *generalized anxiety disorder* feel persistently and uncontrollably tense and apprehensive for no apparent reason.

- In the more extreme *panic disorder,* anxiety escalates into episodes of intense dread.

- Those with a *phobia* show an irrational fear and avoidance of a specific object or situation.

- Two other disorders, obsessive-compulsive disorder and posttraumatic stress disorder, involve anxiety (though they are classified separately from the anxiety disorders).

13-6: What is OCD?

- Persistent and repetitive thoughts (obsessions) and actions (compulsions) mark *obsessive-compulsive disorder (OCD).*

13-7: What is PTSD?

- Symptoms of *posttraumatic stress disorder (PTSD)* include four or more weeks of haunting memories, nightmares, social withdrawal, jumpy anxiety, and sleep problems following a traumatic event.

13-8: How do learning and biology contribute to the feelings and thoughts found in anxiety disorders, OCD, and PTSD?

- The learning perspective views anxiety disorders as a product of fear conditioning, stimulus generalization, fearful-behavior reinforcement, and observational learning of others' fears and cognitions (interpretations, irrational beliefs, and hypervigilance).

- The biological perspective considers genetic predispositions and the role that fears of life-threatening animals, objects, or situations played in natural selection and evolution.

Substance Use and Addictive Disorders

13-9: What are substance use disorders, and what role do tolerance, withdrawal, and addiction play in these disorders?

- Those with a *substance use disorder* may exhibit impaired control, social disruption, risky behavior, and the physical effects of tolerance and withdrawal.

- *Psychoactive drugs* alter perceptions and moods. They may produce *tolerance*—requiring larger doses to achieve the desired effect—and *withdrawal*—significant discomfort accompanying attempts to quit.

- *Addiction* is the compulsive craving of drugs or certain behaviors (such as gambling) despite known harmful consequences.

13-10: How do depressants, such as alcohol, influence neural activity and behavior?

- *Depressants* (alcohol, *barbiturates, opiates*) dampen neural activity and slow body functions.

- Alcohol disinhibits, increasing the likelihood that we will act on our impulses, whether helpful or harmful.

- Alcohol slows neural processing, disrupts memory, and shrinks the brain in those with *alcohol use disorder* (marked by tolerance, withdrawal if use is suspended, and a drive to continue using).

- User expectations strongly influence alcohol's behavioral effects.

13-11: How do the major stimulants affect neural activity and behavior?

- *Stimulants* (caffeine, *nicotine, amphetamines,* cocaine, *methamphetamine, Ecstasy*) excite neural activity, speed up body functions, and lead to heightened energy and mood. All are highly addictive.

- Nicotine's effects make smoking a difficult habit to kick, yet the percentage of Americans who smoke has been dramatically decreasing.

- Cocaine gives users a fast high, followed shortly by a crash. Its risks include cardiovascular stress and suspiciousness.

- Methamphetamine may permanently reduce dopamine levels.

- Ecstasy (MDMA), which is also a mild hallucinogen, may damage serotonin-producing neurons and impair physical and cognitive functions.

13-12: What are the physiological and psychological effects of LSD and marijuana?

- *Hallucinogens* (*LSD,* marijuana) distort perceptions and evoke hallucinations (sensory images in the absence of sensory input), some of which resemble the altered consciousness of *near-death experiences.*

- Marijuana's main ingredient, *THC,* may trigger feelings of disinhibition, euphoria, relaxation, relief from pain, and intense sensitivity to colors, sounds, tastes, and smells. It may also increase feelings of depression or anxiety, impair motor coordination and reaction time, disrupt memory formation, and damage lung tissue (because of the inhaled smoke).

13-13: What biological, psychological, and social-cultural factors help explain why some people abuse mind-altering drugs?

- Some people are biologically more vulnerable to drugs, such as alcohol.

- Psychological factors (such as stress, depression, and hopelessness) and social-cultural influences (peer pressure, cultural values) combine to lead many people to experiment with—and sometimes become addicted to—drugs. Cultural and ethnic groups have differing rates of drug use.

Mood Disorders

13-14: What are the main mood disorders?

- *Mood disorders* are characterized by emotional extremes.

- A person with *major depressive disorder* experiences two or more weeks of seriously depressed moods and feelings of worthlessness, with little interest in most activities, that is not caused by drugs or a medical condition.

- A person with the less common condition of *bipolar disorder* experiences mood swings between depression and mania (hyperactive and wildly optimistic, impulsive feelings and behavior).

13-15: Why do people attempt suicide, and why do some people injure themselves?

- People with depression are more at risk for suicide than others are, but health status and economic and social frustration are also contributing factors.

- Forewarnings of suicide may include verbal hints, giving away possessions, self-inflicted injuries, or withdrawal and preoccupation with death. People who talk about suicide should be taken seriously.

- Nonsuicidal self-injury (NSSI) does not usually lead to suicide but may escalate to suicidal thoughts and acts if untreated. People with NSSI do not tolerate stress well and tend to be self-critical, with poor communication and problem-solving skills.

13-16: How do mood disorders develop? What roles do biology, thinking, and social behavior play?

- The biological perspective on depression focuses on genetic predispositions and on abnormalities in brain function, including those found in neurotransmitter systems.

- The social-cognitive perspective views depression as an ongoing cycle of stressful experiences (interpreted through negative beliefs, attributions, and memories) leading to negative moods and actions and fueling new stressful experiences.

Schizophrenia

13-17: What patterns of thinking, perceiving, and feeling characterize schizophrenia?

- *Schizophrenia* typically strikes during late adolescence and seems to occur in all cultures.

- Symptoms are disorganized and delusional thinking, disturbed perceptions, and diminished, inappropriate emotional expression.

- *Delusions* are false beliefs; hallucinations are sensory experiences without sensory stimulation.

- Schizophrenia symptoms may be positive (the presence of inappropriate behaviors) or negative (the absence of appropriate behaviors).

- In chronic (or process) schizophrenia, the disorder develops gradually and recovery is doubtful. In acute (or reactive) schizophrenia, the onset is sudden, in reaction to stress, and the prospects for recovery are brighter.

13-18: How do chronic and acute schizophrenia differ?

- In chronic (or process) schizophrenia, the disorder develops gradually and recovery is doubtful. In acute (or reactive) schizophrenia, the onset is sudden, in reaction to stress, and the prospects for recovery are brighter.

13-19: What do we know about the brain chemistry, functions, and structures associated with schizophrenia, and what have we learned about prenatal risk factors?

- People with schizophrenia have more receptors for dopamine, which may intensify the positive symptoms such as hallucinations and paranoia.

- Brain scans reveal abnormal activity in the frontal lobes, thalamus, and amygdala.

- Brain abnormalities associated with schizophrenia include enlarged, fluid-filled cerebral cavities and loss of cerebral cortex.

- Schizophrenia involves not one isolated brain abnormality but problems with several brain regions and their interconnections.

- Low weight or oxygen deprivation at birth, famine conditions during the mother's pregnancy, or a mid-pregnancy virus are possible contributing factors.

13-20: Does research indicate a genetic contribution to schizophrenia?

- Twin and adoption studies indicate that the predisposition to schizophrenia is inherited.

- Multiple genes probably interact to produce schizophrenia.

- No environmental causes invariably produce schizophrenia, but environmental events (such as prenatal viruses or maternal stress) may "turn on" genes for this disorder in those who are predisposed to it.

Other Disorders

13-21: What are the three major eating disorders?

- In those with eating disorders, psychological factors can overwhelm the body's tendency to maintain a normal weight.

- Despite being significantly underweight, people with *anorexia nervosa* (usually adolescent females) continue to diet and exercise excessively because they view themselves as fat.

- Those with *bulimia nervosa* (usually females in their teens and twenties) secretly binge and then compensate with purging, fasting, or excessive exercise.

- Those with *binge-eating disorder* binge but do not follow with purging, fasting, and exercise.

- Cultural pressures, low self-esteem, and negative emotions interact with stressful life experiences and genetics to produce eating disorders.

13-22: What are dissociative disorders, and why are they controversial?

- *Dissociative disorders* are conditions in which conscious awareness seems to become separated (to dissociate) from previous memories, thoughts, and feelings.

- Skeptics note that *dissociative identity disorder* (formerly known as multiple personality disorder) increased dramatically in the late twentieth century, that it is rarely found outside North America, and that it may reflect role playing by people who are vulnerable to therapists' suggestions. Others view this disorder as a protective response to traumatic experience.

13-23: What characteristics are typical of personality disorders in general, and what biological and psychological factors are associated with antisocial personality disorder?

- *Personality disorders* are disruptive, inflexible, and enduring behavior patterns that impair social functioning.

- *Antisocial personality disorder* is characterized by a lack of conscience and, sometimes, by aggressive and fearless behavior. Genetic predispositions may interact with the environment to produce the altered brain activity associated with this disorder.

CHAPTER 14
Therapy

Treating Psychological Disorders

14-1: What are the differences between psychotherapy and the biomedical therapies?

- *Psychotherapy* is treatment involving psychological techniques. It consists of interactions between a trained therapist and a person seeking to overcome difficulties or achieve personal growth. The major psychotherapies derive from psychology's psychodynamic, humanistic, behavioral, and cognitive perspectives.

- *Biomedical therapy* treats psychological disorders with medications and other biological treatments.

- Therapists who take an *eclectic approach* combine different techniques tailored to the client's problems.

The Psychological Therapies

14-2: What are the goals and techniques of psychoanalysis, and how have they been adapted in psychodynamic therapy?

- Freud's *psychoanalysis* aimed to give people self-insight and relief from their disorders by bringing anxiety-laden feelings and thoughts into conscious awareness.

- Techniques included free association, dream analysis, and *interpretation* of instances of *resistance* and *transference*.

- Like psychoanalysis, *psychodynamic therapy* focuses on childhood experiences, therapist interactions, unconscious feelings, and unresolved conflicts. Yet it is briefer, less expensive, and focuses primarily on current symptom relief. Exploring past relationship troubles may help clients understand the origin of their current difficulties.

14-3: What are the basic themes of humanistic therapy, and what are the goals and techniques of Rogers' client-centered approach?

- Both psychoanalytic and humanistic therapists are *insight therapies*—they attempt to improve functioning by increasing clients' awareness of motives and defenses.

- Humanistic therapy's goals have included helping clients grow in self-awareness and self-acceptance; promoting personal growth rather than curing illness; helping clients take responsibility for their own growth; focusing on conscious thoughts rather than unconscious motivations; and seeing the present and future as more important than the past.

- Carl Rogers' *client-centered therapy* proposed that therapists' most important contribution is to function as a psychological mirror through active listening and to provide a growth-fostering environment of *unconditional positive regard* characterized by genuineness, acceptance, and empathy.

14-4: How do behavior therapy's assumptions and techniques differ from those of psychodynamic and humanistic therapies? What techniques are used in exposure therapies and aversive conditioning?

- *Behavior therapies* are not insight therapies. The goal of behavior therapists is to apply learning principles to modify problem behaviors.

- Classical conditioning techniques, including *exposure therapies* (such as *systematic desensitization* or *virtual reality exposure therapy*) and *aversive conditioning*, attempt to change behaviors through *counterconditioning*—evoking new responses to old stimuli that trigger unwanted behaviors.

14-5: What is the basic idea of operant conditioning therapies?

- Therapy based on operant conditioning principles uses behavior modification techniques to change unwanted behaviors through positively reinforcing desired behaviors and ignoring or punishing undesirable behaviors.

- Therapists may use a *token economy*, in which desired behavior earns privileges.

14-6: What are the goals and techniques of the cognitive therapies and of cognitive-behavioral therapy?

- *Cognitive therapies*, such as Aaron Beck's therapy for depression, assume that our thinking influences our feelings, and that the therapist's role is to change clients' self-defeating thinking by training them to think in healthier ways.

- The widely researched and practiced *cognitive-behavioral therapy* combines cognitive therapy and behavior therapy by helping clients regularly act out their new ways of thinking and talking in their everyday life.

14-7: What are the aims and benefits of group and family therapy?

- *Group therapy* can help more people for less money than individual therapy. Clients may benefit from learning that others have similar problems and from getting feedback on new ways of behaving.

- *Family therapy* treats a family as an interactive system and attempts to help family members discover the roles they play and how to learn to communicate more openly and directly.

Evaluating Psychotherapies

14-8: Does psychotherapy work? Who decides?

- Clients' and therapists' positive testimonials cannot prove that psychotherapy is actually effective. Clients justify their investment, tend to speak kindly of their therapists, and often enter therapy in crisis. Sometimes they are healed by time alone.

- Therapists tend to track only their "success" stories.

- Outcome research has found that people who remain untreated often improve, but those who receive psychotherapy are more likely to improve.

14-9: Are some psychotherapies more effective than others for specific disorders?

- No one psychotherapy is superior to all others. Therapy is most effective for those with clear-cut, specific problems.

- Behavior therapies work best with specific behavior problems, such as bed-wetting, phobias, compulsions, marital problems, and sexual dysfunctions.

- Psychodynamic therapy has been effective for depression and anxiety, and cognitive therapies have been effective in helping people cope with anxiety, depression, and posttraumatic stress disorder.

- *Evidence-based practice* integrates the best available research with clinicians' expertise and patients' characteristics, preferences, and circumstances.

14-10: What three elements are shared by all forms of psychotherapy?

- All effective psychotherapies offer (1) new hope; (2) a fresh perspective; and (3) an empathic, trusting, caring relationship.

- An emotional bond of trust and understanding between therapist and client (the therapeutic alliance) is an important element in effective therapy.

14-11: How do culture and values influence the client-therapist relationship?

- Therapists differ from one another and from their clients. These differences may create problems if therapists and clients differ in their cultural or religious perspectives.

14-12: What should a person look for when selecting a therapist?

- A person seeking therapy may want to ask about the therapist's treatment approach, values, credentials, and fees. An important consideration is whether the therapy seeker feels comfortable and able to establish a bond with the therapist.

The Biomedical Therapies

14-13: What are the drug therapies? How do double-blind studies help researchers evaluate a drug's effectiveness?

- Drug therapy is the most widely used biomedical therapy.

- *Antipsychotic drugs*, used in treating schizophrenia and other forms of severe thought disorders, block dopamine activity. Side effects may include tardive dyskinesia (with involuntary movements of facial muscles, tongue, and limbs) or increased risk of obesity and diabetes.

- *Antianxiety drugs*, which depress central nervous system activity, are used to treat anxiety disorders, obsessive-compulsive disorder, and posttraumatic stress disorder, often in combination with psychotherapy. These drugs can reinforce a person's tendency to take drugs and can also cause physical problems.

- *Antidepressant drugs*, which increase the availability of various neuro-transmitters, are used for depression, anxiety disorders, obsessive-compulsive disorder, and posttraumatic stress disorder, with modest effectiveness. Given their widening use, some pro-fessionals prefer the term SSRI drugs (selective serotonin reuptake inhibi-tors) for drugs such as Prozac.

- Mood-stabilizing drugs, such as lithium and Depakote, are often prescribed for those with bipolar disorder.

- Studies may use a double-blind pro-cedure to avoid the placebo effect and researchers' and patients' poten-tial bias.

14-14: How are brain stimulation and psychosurgery used in treating specific disorders?

- In *electroconvulsive therapy (ECT)*, a brief electric current is sent through the brain of an anesthetized patient. ECT is an effective treatment for severely depressed people who have not responded to other therapy.

- Newer alternative treatments for depression include vagus nerve stim-ulation, deep-brain stimulation, and *repetitive transcranial magnetic stimula-tion (rTMS)*.

- *Psychosurgery* removes or destroys brain tissue in hopes of modifying behavior. These irreversible psychosurgical pro-cedures are used only as a last resort. *Lobotomies* are no longer performed.

14-15: How, by adopting a healthier lifestyle, might people find some relief from depression?

- Depressed people who undergo a pro-gram of aerobic exercise, adequate sleep, light exposure, social engage-ment, negative-thought reduction, and better nutrition often gain some

relief. In our integrated biopsycho-social system, stress affects our body chemistry and health; chemi-cal imbalances can produce depres-sion; and social support and other lifestyle changes can lead to relief of symptoms.

Preventing Psychological Disorders

14-16: What may help prevent psychological disorders?

- Preventive mental health programs are based on the idea that many psychological disorders could be pre-vented by changing stressful social contexts and teaching people to cope better with stress. This may help them become more *resilient*, enabling recovery from adversity.

- Community psychologists work to prevent psychological disorders by turning destructive environments into more nurturing places that foster competence, health, and well-being.

APPENDIX A
Statistical Reasoning in Everyday Life

Describing Data

A-1: How can we describe data with measures of central tendency and variation?

- A measure of central tendency is a single score that represents a whole set of scores.

- Three such measures are the *mode* (the most frequently occurring score), the *mean* (the arithmetic aver-age), and the *median* (the middle score in a group of data). Measures of variation tell us how diverse data are.

- Two measures of variation are the *range* (which describes the gap between the highest and lowest scores) and the *standard deviation*

(which states how much scores vary around the mean, or average, score).

- Scores often form a *normal* (or bell-shaped) *curve*.

A-2: What does it mean when we say that two things are correlated?

- When we say two things are corre-lated, we are saying that they accom-pany each other in their movements. The strength of their relationship is expressed as a *correlation coefficient*, which ranges from +1.00 (a perfect positive correlation) through 0 (no correlation) to –1.00 (a perfect nega-tive correlation).

- Their relationship may be displayed in a *scatterplot*, in which each dot rep-resents a value for the two variables.

- Correlations predict but cannot explain.

A-3: What is regression toward the mean?

- *Regression toward the mean* is the ten-dency for extreme or unusual scores to fall back toward their average.

Significant Differences

A-4: How do we know whether an observed difference can be generalized to other populations?

- To feel confident about general-izing an observed difference to other populations, we would want to know that the sample studied was representative of the larger population being studied; that the observations, on average, had low variability; that the sample con-sisted of more than a few cases; and that the observed difference was *statistically significant*.

A-5: What are cross-sectional studies and longitudinal studies, and why is it important to know which method is used?

- In a *cross-sectional study,* people of different ages are compared. In a *longitudinal study,* a group of people is studied periodically over a long period of time.
- To draw meaningful conclusions about a study's results, we need to know whether the study used a representative sample to draw its conclusions. Studies of intelligence and aging, for example, have drawn different conclusions depending on whether a cross-sectional or longitudinal study was used.

APPENDIX B
Psychology at Work

Work and Life Satisfaction

B-1: What is *flow?*

- *Flow* is a completely involved, focused state of consciousness with diminished awareness of self and time. It results from fully engaging one's skills.
- Work may be just a job, a somewhat fulfilling career, or a calling, which produces the highest levels of satisfaction.

Industrial-Organizational Psychology

B-2: What are the three main subfields of industrial-organizational psychology?

- *Industrial-organizational (I/O) psychology's* three subfields are human factors, personnel, and organizational psychology:
  - *Human factors psychologists* explore how people and machines interact for optimal safety and effectiveness.
  - *Personnel psychologists* use psychology's principles to select, place, train, and evaluate workers.
  - *Organizational psychologists* consider an organization's goals, environments, and management styles in an effort to improve worker motivation, satisfaction, and productivity.

Motivating Achievement

B-3: Why is it important to motivate achievement?

- *Achievement motivation* is a desire for significant accomplishment; for mastery of skills or ideas; for control; and for attaining a high standard. High achievement motivation leads to greater success, especially when combined with determined, persistent grit.
- The most satisfied and engaged employees tend to be the most productive and successful.
- Managers motivate most effectively when they make clear what is expected, provide needed materials, allow employees to do what they do best, affirm employees, and ensure opportunities to learn and develop.

Leadership

B-4: How can leaders be most effective?

- Leaders can harness strengths, by matching tasks to talents and reinforcing positive behaviors.
- They can set specific, challenging goals that stretch employees, but not beyond what they can do.
- They can choose an appropriate leadership style for the situation, such as *task leadership* when a more directive style is needed, or *social leadership* when a more democratic style fits best.
- The most effective leaders often combine task and social leadership styles.

Answers to *Chapter Test* Questions

CHAPTER 1
Psychology's Roots, Big Ideas, and Critical Thinking Tools

1. Wilhelm Wundt

2. a

3. d

4. psychiatrist

5. c

6. Critical thinking teaches us to look for evidence instead of relying on our intuition, which is often wrong. In evaluating a claim in the media, look for any signs of scientific evidence, preferably from several studies. Ask the following questions: Are claims based on scientific findings? Have several studies replicated the findings and confirmed them? Are any experts cited? If so, research their background. Are they affiliated with a credible university, college, or institution? Have they conducted or written about scientific research?

7. b

8. The environment (nurture) has an influence on us, but that influence is limited by our biology (nature). Nature and nurture interact. People predisposed to be very tall (nature), for example, are unlikely to become Olympic gymnasts, no matter how hard they work (nurture).

9. Dual processing

10. emotions; character traits; institutions

11. Hindsight bias

12. d

13. hypotheses

14. c

15. random (representative)

16. negative

17. a

18. *(a) Alcohol use is associated with violence. (One interpretation: Drinking causes, or triggers, aggressive behavior.)* Perhaps anger triggers drinking, or perhaps the same genes or child-rearing practices are making both drinking and aggression more likely. (Here researchers have learned that drinking does indeed trigger aggressive behavior.) *(b) Educated people live longer, on average, than less-educated people. (One interpretation: Education lengthens life and improves health.)* Perhaps richer people can afford more education and better health care. (Research supports this conclusion.) *(c) Teens engaged in team sports are less likely to use drugs, smoke, have sex, carry weapons, and eat junk food than are teens who do not engage in team sports. (One interpretation: Team sports encourage healthy living.)* Perhaps some third factor explains this correlation—teens who use drugs, smoke, have sex, carry weapons, and eat junk food may be "loners" who do not enjoy playing on any team. *(d) Adolescents who frequently see smoking in movies are more likely to smoke. (One interpretation: Movie stars' behavior influences teens.)* Perhaps adolescents who smoke and attend movies frequently have less parental supervision and more access to spending money than other adolescents.

19. experiments

20. placebo

21. c

22. independent variable

23. b

24. d

CHAPTER 2
The Biology of Mind and Consciousness

1. axon

2. c

3. a

4. neurotransmitters

5. b

6. c

7. autonomic

8. central

9. a

10. adrenal glands

11. b

12. d

13. c

14. cerebellum

15. b

16. amygdala

17. b

18. hypothalamus

19. d

20. The visual cortex is a neural network of sensory neurons connected via interneurons to other neural networks, including auditory networks. This allows you to integrate visual and auditory information to respond when a friend you recognize greets you at a party.

21. c

22. frontal

23. You would hear sounds, but without the temporal lobe association areas you would be unable to make sense of what you were hearing.

24. association areas

25. c

26. ON; HER

27. a
28. b
29. inattentional blindness
30. selective
31. circadian rhythm
32. b
33. NREM-3
34. It increases in duration.
35. c
36. With narcolepsy, the person periodically falls directly into sleep, sometimes REM sleep, with no warning; with sleep apnea, the person repeatedly awakens during the night.
37. d
38. The neural activation theory suggests that dreams are the brain's attempt to make sense of random neural activity.
39. The information-processing explanation of dreaming proposes that brain activity during REM sleep enables us to sift through *what one has dwelt on by day* (that is, the daily events and activities one has been thinking about).
40. REM rebound

CHAPTER 3
Developing Through the Life Span

1. continuity/stages
2. c
3. teratogens
4. a
5. frontal
6. b
7. We have little conscious memory of events occurring before age 4, in part because major brain areas have not yet matured.
8. Infants in Piaget's *sensorimotor stage* tend to be focused only on their own perceptions of the world and may, for example, be unaware that objects continue to exist when unseen. A child in the *preoperational stage* is still egocentric and incapable of appreciating simple logic, such as the reversibility of operations. A preteen in the *concrete operational stage* is beginning to think logically about concrete events but not about abstract concepts.
9. a
10. stranger anxiety
11. Before these studies, many psychologists believed that infants became attached to those who nourished them.
12. temperament
13. b
14. formal operations
15. b
16. emerging adulthood
17. b
18. a
19. generativity
20. c
21. b

CHAPTER 4
Gender and Sexuality

1. c
2. Y
3. d
4. 11; 13
5. intersex
6. b
7. gender identity
8. b
9. b
10. Sexual dysfunctions are problems that men and women may have related to sexual arousal and sexual function. Paraphilias are conditions, which may be classified as psychological disorders, where sexual arousal is associated with socially unacceptable target partners and/or suffering of self or others.
11. does; doesn't
12. c
13. d
14. Researchers have found no evidence that any environmental factor (parental relationships, childhood experiences, peer relationships, or dating experiences) influences the development of our sexual orientation.
15. c

CHAPTER 5
Sensation and Perception

1. b
2. perception
3. d
4. just noticeable difference
5. b
6. d
7. a
8. wavelength
9. a
10. c
11. c
12. feature detectors
13. parallel processing
14. d
15. Your brain constructs this perception of color in two stages. In the first stage, the lemon reflects light energy into your eyes, where it is transformed into neural messages. Three sets of cones, each sensitive to a different light frequency (red, blue, and green) process color. In this case, the light energy stimulates both red-sensitive and green-sensitive cones. In the second stage, opponent-process cells sensitive to paired opposites of color (red/green, yellow/blue, and black/white) evaluate the incoming neural messages as they pass through your optic nerve to the thalamus and visual cortex. When the yellow-sensitive opponent-process cells are stimulated, you identify the lemon as yellow.

16. d

17. a

18. b

19. c

20. monocular

21. b

22. b

23. perceptual adaptation

24. cochlea

25. The outer ear collects sound waves, which are translated into mechanical waves by the middle ear and turned into fluid waves in the inner ear. The auditory nerve then translates the energy into electrical waves and sends them to the brain, which perceives and interprets the sound.

26. a

27. We have specialized receptors for detecting sweet, salty, sour, bitter, and umami tastes. Being able to detect pleasurable tastes enabled our ancestors to seek out energy- and protein-rich foods. Detecting aversive tastes deterred them from eating toxic substances, increasing their chances of survival.

28. Kinesthesia; vestibular sense

29. Your vestibular sense regulates balance and body positioning through kinesthetic receptors triggered by fluid in your inner ear. Wobbly legs and a spinning world are signs that these receptors are still responding to the ride's turbulence. As your vestibular sense adjusts to solid ground, your balance will be restored.

30. d

31. d

CHAPTER 6
Learning

1. information; behaviors

2. c

3. conditioned

4. discrimination

5. b

6. A sexual image is a US that triggers a UR of interest or arousal. Before the advertisement pairs a product with a sexual image, the product is an NS. Over time the product can become a CS that triggers the CR of interest or arousal.

7. Skinner's

8. shaping

9. b

10. Your instructor could reinforce your attentive behavior by taking away something you dislike. For example, your instructor could offer to shorten the length of an assigned paper or replace lecture time with an in-class activity. In both cases, the instructor would remove something aversive in order to negatively reinforce your focused attention.

11. partial

12. a

13. variable-interval

14. c

15. d

16. b

17. b

18. latent learning

19. observational learning

20. vicarious; vicarious

21. a

22. mirror

23. c

CHAPTER 7
Memory

1. encoding; storage; retrieval

2. a

3. iconic; echoic

4. seven

5. mnemonics

6. a

7. implicit

8. c

9. recall

10. d

11. Memories are stored within a web of many associations, one of which is mood. When you recall happy moments from your past, you deliberately activate these positive links. You may then experience mood-congruent memory and recall other happy moments, which could improve your mood and brighten your interpretation of current events.

12. a

13. d

14. d

15. retroactive

16. repression

17. b

18. Eliza's immature hippocampus and lack of verbal skills would have prevented her from encoding an explicit memory of the wedding reception at the age of two. It's more likely that Eliza learned information (from hearing the story repeatedly) that she eventually constructed into a memory that feels very real.

19. source amnesia

20. déjà vu

21. b

22. b

CHAPTER 8
Thinking, Language, and Intelligence

1. concept

2. algorithm

3. Oscar will need to carefully guard against *confirmation bias* (searching for support for his own views and ignoring contradictory evidence) as he seeks out opposing viewpoints. Even if Oscar encounters new information that disproves his beliefs, *belief perseverance* may lead him to cling to these

views anyway. It will take more compelling evidence to change his beliefs than it took to create them.

4. c

5. availability

6. framing

7. b

8. c

9. telegraphic speech

10. universal grammar

11. a

12. general intelligence (*g*)

13. c

14. academic; practical; creative

15. d

16. d

17. c

18. reliability

19. a

20. c

21. c

22. The heritability (difference due to genes) of body weight will be greater in country X, where environmental differences in available nutrition are minimal.

23. Stereotype threat

CHAPTER 9
Motivation and Emotion

1. a

2. incentive

3. Arousal

4. b

5. a

6. Maslow's hierarchy of needs best supports this statement because it addresses the primacy of some motives over others. Once our basic physiological needs are met, safety concerns are addressed next, followed by belongingness and love needs (such as the desire to kiss).

7. homeostasis

8. c

9. glucose; low

10. basal metabolic

11. d

12. Sanjay's plan is problematic. After he gains weight, the extra fat will require less energy to maintain than it did to gain in the first place. Sanjay may have a hard time getting rid of it later, when his metabolism slows down in an effort to retain his body weight.

13. c

14. Monitor the time spent online, as well as your feelings about that time. Hide distracting online friends. Turn off or put away distracting devices. Consider a social media fast, and get outside and away from technology regularly.

15. James-Lange

16. b

17. c

18. A polygraph measures physiological changes, such as heart rate and perspiration, that are associated with emotions. Its use as a lie detector is controversial because the measure cannot distinguish between emotions with similar physiology (such as anxiety and guilt).

19. facial feedback

CHAPTER 10
Stress, Health, and Human Flourishing

1. resistance; exhaustion

2. tend; befriend

3. b

4. d

5. lymphocytes

6. c

7. Type A individuals frequently experience negative emotions (such as anger and depression), during which the sympathetic nervous system diverts blood away from the liver. This leaves fat and cholesterol circulating in the bloodstream for deposit near the heart and other organs, increasing the risk of heart disease and other health problems. Thus, Type A individuals actually harm themselves by directing anger at others.

8. negative

9. emotion

10. b

11. internal

12. d

13. aerobic

14. c

15. d

16. b

17. relative deprivation

CHAPTER 11
Personality

1. repression

2. c

3. superego

4. b

5. anxiety

6. Projective

7. d

8. a

9. a

10. d

11. Freud might argue that the criminal may have lacked the proper guidance as a child for developing a strong superego, allowing the id free rein. Rogers might assert that the criminal was raised in an environment lacking genuineness, acceptance (unconditional positive regard), and empathy, which inhibited psychological growth and led to a negative self-concept.

12. unconditional positive regard

13. trait

14. c

15. b

16. b

17. a

18. social-cognitive

19. b

20. Yes, if that self-love is of the *secure* type. Secure self-esteem promotes a focus beyond the self and a higher quality of life. Excessive self-love may promote artificially high or defensive self-esteem, which may lead to unhappiness if negative external feedback triggers anger or aggression.

21. b.

CHAPTER 12
Social Psychology

1. a

2. foot-in-the-door

3. Cognitive dissonance theory best supports this suggestion. If Jamal acts confident, his behavior will contradict his negative self-thoughts, creating cognitive dissonance. To relieve the tension, Jamal may realign his attitudes with his actions by viewing himself as more outgoing and confident.

4. c

5. a

6. The presence of a large audience generates arousal and strengthens Dr. Huang's most likely response: enhanced performance on a task he has mastered (teaching music history) and impaired performance on a task he finds difficult (statistics).

7. deindividuation

8. group polarization

9. stereotypes

10. b

11. more

12. d

13. c

14. c

15. c

16. mere exposure

17. companionate; passionate

18. d

19. c

20. mirror-image

21. superordinate

CHAPTER 13
Psychological Disorders

1. No. Anna's behavior is unusual, causes her distress, and may make her a few minutes late on occasion, but it does not appear to significantly disrupt her ability to function. Like most of us, Anna demonstrates some unusual behaviors that are not disabling or dysfunctional, so they wouldn't be considered a clinically significant disturbance. Thus, her unusual behavior does not suggest a psychological disorder.

2. c

3. medical

4. c

5. a

6. c

7. phobia

8. obsessive-compulsive

9. c

10. depression

11. tolerance

12. a

13. Alcohol is a disinhibitor—it makes us more likely to do what we would have done when sober, whether that is being helpful or being aggressive.

14. d

15. LSD

16. a

17. b

18. c

19. increasing

20. norepinephrine; serotonin

21. social-cognitive

22. b

23. hallucination

24. No. Schizophrenia involves the altered perceptions, emotions, and behaviors of a mind split from reality. It does not involve rapid changes in mood or identity, as suggested by this comparison.

25. a

26. b

27. c

28. c

29. b

CHAPTER 14
Therapy

1. a

2. Insight

3. d

4. active listening

5. c

6. counterconditioning

7. systematic desensitization

8. Behavior therapies are often the best choice for treating phobias. Viewing Rico's fear of the freeway as a learned response, a behavior therapist might help Rico learn to replace his anxious response to freeway driving with a relaxation response.

9. token economy

10. d

11. Cognitive-behavioral

12. b

13. c

14. d

15. research evidence, clinical expertise, and knowledge of the patient

16. The placebo effect is the healing power of belief in a treatment. When patients expect a treatment

to be effective, they may believe it was.

17. c

18. antianxiety

19. lithium

20. b

21. d

APPENDIX A
Statistical Reasoning in Everyday Life

1. b

2. d

3. normal curve

4. a

5. negative

6. scatterplot

7. Regression toward the mean is a statistical phenomenon describing the tendency of extreme scores or outcomes to return to normal after an unusual event. Without knowing this, we may inaccurately decide the return to normal was a result of our own behavior.

8. cross-sectional

9. a

APPENDIX B
Psychology at Work

1. human factors; personnel; organizational

2. c

3. Personnel; human factors

4. Focusing on specific, short-term goals, such as maintaining a regular study schedule, will be more helpful than focusing on more distant general goals, such as earning a good grade in this class.

5. transformational

6. c

Glossary

A

absolute threshold the minimum stimulation needed to detect a particular stimulus 50 percent of the time. (p. 135)

accommodation adapting our current understandings (schemas) to incorporate new information. (p. 76)

achievement motivation a desire for significant accomplishment; for mastery of skills or ideas; for control; and for attaining a high standard. (p. B-3)

achievement test a test designed to assess what a person has learned. (p. 239)

acquisition in classical conditioning, the initial stage, when we link a neutral stimulus and an unconditioned stimulus so that the neutral stimulus begins triggering the conditioned response. (In operant conditioning, the strengthening of a reinforced response.) (p. 170)

action potential a nerve impulse. (p. 30)

active listening empathic listening in which the listener echoes, restates, and clarifies. A feature of Rogers' client-centered therapy. (p. 413)

adaptation-level phenomenon our tendency to form judgments (of sounds, of lights, of income) relative to a neutral level defined by our past experiences. (p. 304)

addiction compulsive craving of drugs or certain behaviors (such as gambling) despite known harmful consequences. (p. 381)

adolescence the transition period from childhood to adulthood, extending from puberty to independence. (p. 86)

adrenal [ah-DREEN-el] **glands** pair of endocrine glands that sit just above the kidneys and secrete hormones (epinephrine and norepinephrine) that help arouse the body in times of stress. (p. 36)

aerobic exercise sustained activity that increases heart and lung fitness; may also reduce depression and anxiety. (p. 296)

aggression any act intended to harm someone physically or emotionally. (pp. 108, 354)

AIDS (acquired immune deficiency syndrome) a life-threatening, sexually transmitted infection caused by the *human immunodeficiency virus* (HIV). AIDS depletes the immune system, leaving the person vulnerable to infections. (p. 117)

alcohol use disorder (popularly known as *alcoholism*). Alcohol use marked by tolerance, withdrawal, and a drive to continue problematic use. (p. 382)

algorithm a methodical, logical rule or procedure that guarantees you will solve a particular problem. Contrasts with the usually speedier—but also more error-prone—use of *heuristics*. (p. 220)

all-or-none response a neuron's reaction of either firing (with a full-strength response) or not firing. (p. 31)

alpha waves relatively slow brain waves of a relaxed, awake state. (p. 53)

altruism unselfish concern for the welfare of others. (p. 363)

amnesia literally "without memory"—a loss of memory, often due to brain trauma, injury, or disease. (p. 206)

amphetamines drugs that stimulate neural activity, causing speeded-up body functions and associated energy and mood changes. (p. 383)

amygdala [uh-MIG-duh-la] two lima-bean-sized neural clusters in the limbic system; linked to emotion. (p. 41)

androgyny displaying both traditional masculine and feminine psychological characteristics. (p. 114)

anorexia nervosa an eating disorder in which a person (usually an adolescent female) maintains a starvation diet despite being significantly underweight; sometimes accompanied by excessive exercise. (p. 400)

antianxiety drugs drugs used to control anxiety and agitation. (p. 426)

antidepressant drugs drugs used to treat depression, anxiety disorders, obsessive-compulsive disorder, and posttraumatic stress disorder. (Several widely used antidepressant drugs are *selective serotonin reuptake inhibitors—SSRIs*.) (p. 426)

antipsychotic drugs drugs used to treat schizophrenia and other forms of severe thought disorders. (p. 425)

antisocial personality disorder a personality disorder in which the person (usually a man) exhibits a lack of conscience for wrongdoing, even toward friends and family members; may be aggressive and ruthless or a clever con artist. (p. 402)

anxiety disorders psychological disorders characterized by distressing, persistent anxiety or maladaptive behaviors that reduce anxiety. (p. 375)

aptitude test a test designed to predict a person's future performance; *aptitude* is the capacity to learn. (p. 239)

asexual having no sexual attraction to others. (p. 115)

assimilation interpreting our new experiences in terms of our existing schemas. (p. 76)

association areas cerebral cortex areas involved primarily in higher mental functions, such as learning, remembering, thinking, and speaking. (p. 45)

associative learning learning that certain events occur together. The events may be two stimuli (as in classical conditioning) or a response and its consequences (as in operant conditioning). (p. 168)

attachment an emotional tie with another person; shown in young children by their seeking closeness to the caregiver, and showing distress on separation. (p. 81)

attention-deficit/hyperactivity disorder (ADHD) a psychological disorder marked by extreme inattention and/or hyperactivity and impulsivity. (p. 372)

attitude feelings, often based on our beliefs, that predispose us to respond in a particular way to objects, people, and events. (p. 339)

audition the sense or act of hearing. (p. 151)

autism spectrum disorder a disorder that appears in childhood and is marked by significant deficiencies in communication and social interaction, and by rigidly fixated interests and repetitive behaviors. (p. 78)

automatic processing unconscious encoding of everyday information, such as space, time, and frequency, and of well-learned information, such as word meanings. (p. 195)

autonomic [aw-tuh-NAHM-ik] **nervous system**   peripheral nervous system division controlling the glands and the muscles of the internal organs (such as the heart). Its sympathetic subdivision arouses; its para-sympathetic subdivision calms. (p. 34)

availability heuristic   judging the likelihood of an event based on its availability in memory; if an event comes readily to mind (perhaps be-cause it was vivid), we assume it must be common. (p. 222)

aversive conditioning   a type of counterconditioning that associates an unpleasant state (such as nausea) with an unwanted behavior (such as drinking alcohol). (p. 415)

axon   neuron extension that sends messages to other neurons or cells. (p. 30)

B

babbling stage   beginning at about 4 months, the stage of speech de-velopment in which the infant spontaneously utters various sounds at first unrelated to the household language. (p. 230)

barbiturates   drugs that depress the activity of the central nervous system, reducing anxiety but impairing memory and judgment. (p. 383)

basal metabolic rate   the body's resting rate of energy output. (p. 259)

basic trust   according to Erik Erikson, a sense that the world is predict-able and trustworthy; said to be formed during infancy by appropriate experiences with responsive caregivers. (p. 83)

behavior therapy   therapeutic approach that applies learning princi-ples to the elimination of unwanted behaviors. (p. 414)

behaviorism   the view that psychology (1) should be an objective science that (2) studies behavior without reference to mental processes. Most psychologists today agree with (1) but not with (2). (pp. 3, 183)

belief perseverance   clinging to beliefs and ignoring evidence that proves they are wrong. (p. 223)

binge-eating disorder   significant binge eating, followed by distress, disgust, or guilt, but without the purging, fasting, or excessive exercise that marks bulimia nervosa. (p. 400)

binocular cue   a depth cue, such as retinal disparity, that depends on the use of two eyes. (p. 147)

biological constraints   evolved biological tendencies that predispose animals' behavior and learning. Thus, certain behaviors are more easily learned by some animals than others. (p. 182)

biological psychology   a branch of psychology concerned with the links between biology and behavior. (p. 30)

biomedical therapy   prescribed medications or procedures that act di-rectly on the person's physiology. (p. 410)

biopsychosocial approach   an approach that integrates different but complementary views from biological, psychological, and social-cultural viewpoints. (p. 6)

bipolar disorder   a mood disorder in which the person alternates be-tween the hopelessness and lethargy of depression and the overexcited state of mania. (Formerly called *manic-depressive disorder.*) (p. 390)

blind spot   the point at which the optic nerve leaves the eye; this part of the retina is "blind" because it has no receptor cells. (p. 141)

bottom-up processing   analysis that begins with the sensory receptors and works up to the brain's integration of sensory information. (p. 134)

brainstem   the oldest part and central core of the brain, beginning where the spinal cord swells as it enters the skull; responsible for auto-matic survival functions. (p. 37)

Broca's area   controls language expression—an area of the frontal lobe, usually in the left hemisphere, that directs the muscle movements in-volved in speech. (p. 232)

bulimia nervosa   an eating disorder in which a person alternates binge eating (usually of high-calorie foods) with purging (by vomiting or laxa-tive use), fasting, or excessive exercise. (p. 400)

bystander effect   the tendency for any given bystander to be less likely to give aid if other bystanders are present. (p. 364)

C

Cannon-Bard theory   the theory that an emotion-arousing stimulus simultaneously triggers (1) physiological responses and (2) the subjective experience of emotion. (p. 270)

case study   a descriptive technique in which one indivdual or group is studied in depth in the hope of revealing universal principles. (p. 14)

central nervous system (CNS)   the brain and spinal cord. (p. 33)

cerebellum [sehr-uh-BELL-um]   the "little brain" at the rear of the brainstem; functions include processing sensory input and coordinating movement output and balance. (p. 40)

cerebral [seh-REE-bruhl] **cortex**   thin layer of interconnected neurons covering the cerebral hemispheres; the body's ultimate control and information-processing center. (p. 42)

change blindness   failure to notice changes in the environment. (p. 52)

chromosomes   threadlike structures made of DNA molecules that con-tain the genes. (p. 68)

chunking   organizing items into familiar, manageable units; often oc-curs automatically. (p. 197)

circadian [ser-KAY-dee-an] **rhythm**   internal biological clock; regular bodily rhythms (for example, of temperature and wakefulness) that occur on a 24-hour cycle. (p. 52)

classical conditioning   a type of learning in which we learn to link two or more stimuli and anticipate events. (p. 169)

client-centered therapy   a humanistic therapy, developed by Carl Rogers, in which the therapist uses techniques such as active listening within a genuine, accepting, empathic environment to promote clients' growth. (Also called *person-centered therapy.*) (p. 413)

cochlea [KOHK-lee-uh]   a coiled, bony, fluid-filled tube in the inner ear; sound waves traveling through the cochlear fluid trigger nerve impulses. (p. 152)

cochlear implant   a device for converting sounds into electrical signals and stimulating the auditory nerve through electrodes threaded into the cochlea. (p. 153)

cognition   all the mental activities associated with thinking, knowing, remembering, and communicating. (pp. 75, 220)

cognitive-behavioral therapy   a popular integrative therapy that com-bines cognitive therapy (changing self-defeating thinking) with behavior therapy (changing behavior). (p. 418)

cognitive dissonance theory   the theory that we act to reduce the discomfort (dissonance) we feel when two of our thoughts (cognitions) clash. For example, when we become aware that our attitudes and our actions don't match, we may change our attitudes so that we feel more comfortable. (p. 341)

cognitive learning   the acquisition of mental information, whether by observing events, by watching others, or through language. (p. 168)

cognitive map   a mental image of the layout of one's environment. (p. 184)

cognitive neuroscience   the interdisciplinary study of the brain activity linked with mental activity (including perception, thinking, memory, and language). (p. 3)

cognitive therapy   therapeutic approach that teaches people new, more adaptive ways of thinking; based on the assumption that thoughts intervene between events and our emotional reactions. (p. 417)

collectivism   giving priority to the goals of our group (often our extended family or work group) and defining our identity accordingly. (p. 332)

color constancy   perceiving familiar objects as having consistent color, even if changing illumination alters the wavelengths reflected by the object. (p. 149)

companionate love   the deep affectionate attachment we feel for those with whom our lives are intertwined. (p. 362)

concept   a mental grouping of similar objects, events, ideas, and people. (p. 220)

concrete operational stage   in Piaget's theory, the stage of cognitive development (from about 6 or 7 to 11 years of age) during which children gain the mental operations that enable them to think logically about concrete events. (p. 79)

conditioned reinforcer   (also known as *secondary reinforcer*) an event that gains its reinforcing power through its link with a primary reinforcer. (p. 176)

conditioned response (CR)   in classical conditioning, a learned response to a previously neutral (but now conditioned) stimulus (CS). (p. 170)

conditioned stimulus (CS)   in classical conditioning, an originally irrelevant stimulus that, after association with an unconditioned stimulus (US), comes to trigger a conditioned response (CR). (p. 170)

conduction hearing loss   hearing loss caused by damage to the mechanical system that conducts sound waves to the cochlea. (p. 153)

cones   retinal receptor cells that are concentrated near the center of the retina; in daylight or well-lit conditions, cones detect fine detail and give rise to color sensations. (p. 141)

confirmation bias   a tendency to search for information that supports our preconceptions and to ignore or distort evidence that contradicts them. (p. 221)

conflict   a perceived incompatibility of actions, goals, or ideas. (p. 365)

conformity   adjusting our behavior or thinking to coincide with a group standard. (p. 342)

confounding variable   in an experiment, a factor other than the independent variable that might produce an effect. (p. 19)

consciousness   our awareness of ourselves and our environment. (p. 50)

conservation   the principle (which Piaget believed to be a part of concrete operational reasoning) that properties such as mass, volume, and number remain the same despite changes in shapes. (p. 77)

continuous reinforcement   reinforcing a desired response every time it occurs. (p. 177)

control group   in an experiment, the group *not* exposed to the treatment; the control group serves as a comparison with the experimental group for judging the effect of the treatment. (p. 18)

convergent thinking   narrows the available problem solutions to determine the single best solution. (p. 226)

coping   reducing stress using emotional, cognitive, or behavioral methods. (p. 291)

coronary heart disease   the clogging of the vessels that nourish the heart muscle; the leading cause of death in the United States and many other countries. (p. 289)

corpus callosum [KOR-pus kah-LOW-sum]   large band of neural fibers connecting the two brain hemispheres and carrying messages between them. (p. 48)

correlation   a measure of the extent to which two events vary together, and thus of how well either one predicts the other. The *correlation coefficient* is the mathematical expression of the relationship, ranging from −1.00 to +1.00, with 0 indicating no relationship. (p. 16)

correlation coefficient   a statistical index of the relationship between two things (from −1.00 to +1.00). (p. A-4)

counterconditioning   behavior therapy procedures that use classical conditioning to evoke new responses to stimuli that are triggering unwanted behaviors; includes *exposure therapies* and *aversive conditioning*. (p. 414)

creativity   the ability to produce new and valuable ideas. (p. 226)

critical period   a period early in life when exposure to certain stimuli or experiences is needed for proper development. (p. 74)

critical thinking   thinking that does not blindly accept arguments and conclusions. Rather, it examines assumptions, uncovers hidden values, weighs evidence, and assesses conclusions. (p. 6)

cross-sectional study   a study in which people of different ages are compared with one another. (p. 245)

crystallized intelligence   our accumulated knowledge and verbal skills; tends to increase with age. (p. 246)

culture   the enduring behaviors, ideas, attitudes, values, and traditions shared by a group of people and handed down from one generation to the next. (p. 7)

D

debriefing   after an experiment ends, explaining to participants the study's purpose and any deceptions researchers used. (p. 22)

defense mechanisms   in psychoanalytic theory, the ego's protective methods of reducing anxiety by unconsciously distorting reality. (p. 314)

deindividuation   the loss of self-awareness and self-restraint occurring in group situations that foster arousal and anonymity. (p. 348)

déjà vu   that eerie sense that "I've experienced this before." Cues from the current situation may unconsciously trigger retrieval of an earlier experience. (p. 211)

delta waves   the large, slow brain waves associated with deep sleep. (p. 54)

delusions   false beliefs, often of persecution or grandeur, that may accompany schizophrenia and other disorders. (p. 396)

dendrites   neuron extensions that receive messages and conduct them toward the cell body. (p. 30)

dependent variable   in an experimant, the factor that is measured; the variable that may change when the independent variable is manipulated. (p. 19)

depressants   drugs (such as alcohol, barbiturates, and opiates) that reduce (depress) neural activity and slow body functions. (p. 381)

depth perception   the ability to see objects in three dimensions, although the images that strike the retina are two-dimensional; allows us to judge distance. (p. 146)

developmental psychology   branch of psychology that studies physical, cognitive, and social change throughout the life span. (p. 68)

difference threshold the minimum difference between two stimuli required for detection 50 percent of the time. We experience the difference threshold as a *just noticeable difference* (or *jnd*). (p. 136)

discrimination (1) in classical conditioning, the learned ability to distinguish between a conditioned stimulus and other irrelevant stimuli. (p. 172) (2) in social psychology, unjustifiable negative behavior toward a group and its members. (p. 350)

dissociative disorder a disorder in which conscious awareness becomes separated (dissociated) from previous memories, thoughts, and feelings. (p. 400)

dissociative identity disorder (DID) a controversial, rare dissociative disorder in which a person exhibits two or more distinct and alternating personalities. Formerly called *multiple personality disorder.* (p. 401)

divergent thinking expands the number of possible problem solutions (creative thinking that diverges in different directions). (p. 226)

DNA *(deoxyribonucleic acid)* a molecule containing the genetic information that makes up the chromosomes. (p. 68)

double-blind procedure a procedure in which participants and research staff are ignorant (blind) about who has received the treatment or a placebo. (p. 18)

Down syndrome a condition of mild to severe intellectual disability and associated physical disorders caused by an extra copy of chromosome 21. (p. 242)

dream sequence of images, emotions, and thoughts passing through a sleeping person's mind. (p. 60)

drive-reduction theory the idea that a physiological need creates an aroused state (a drive) that motivates us to satisfy the need. (p. 256)

DSM-5 the American Psychiatric Association's *Diagnostic and Statistical Manual of Mental Disorders,* Fifth Edition; a widely used system for classifying psychological disorders. (p. 373)

dual processing the principle that, at the same time, our mind processes information on separate conscious and unconscious tracks. (p. 8)

E

eclectic approach an approach to psychotherapy that, depending on the client's problems, uses techniques from various forms of therapy. (p. 410)

Ecstasy (MDMA) a synthetic stimulant and mild hallucinogen. Produces euphoria and social intimacy, but with short-term health risks and longer-term harm to serotonin-producing neurons and to mood and cognition. (p. 385)

EEG (electroencephalograph) device that uses electrodes placed on the scalp to record waves of electrical activity sweeping across the brain's surface. (The record of those brain waves is an *electroencephalogram*.) (p. 38)

effortful processing encoding that requires attention and conscious effort. (p. 195)

ego the largely conscious, "executive" part of personality that, according to Freud, balances the demands of the id, superego, and reality. The ego operates on the *reality principle*, satisfying the id's desires in ways that will realistically bring pleasure rather than pain. (p. 313)

egocentrism in Piaget's theory, the preoperational child's difficulty taking another's point of view. (p. 78)

electroconvulsive therapy (ECT) a biomedical therapy for severely depressed patients in which a brief electric current is sent through the brain of an anesthetized patient. (p. 427)

embodied cognition the influence of bodily sensations, gestures, and other states on cognitive preferences and judgments. (p. 161)

embryo the developing human organism from about 2 weeks after fertilization through the second month. (p. 70)

emerging adulthood a period from about age 18 to the mid-twenties, when many in Western cultures are no longer adolescents but have not yet achieved full independence as adults. (p. 92)

emotion a response of the whole organism, involving (1) bodily arousal, (2) expressive behaviors, and (3) conscious experience. (p. 269)

emotional intelligence the ability to perceive, understand, manage, and use emotions. (p. 238)

emotion-focused coping attempting to reduce stress by avoiding or ignoring a stressor and attending to emotional needs related to our stress reaction. (p. 291)

encoding the process of getting information into the memory system. (p. 194)

endocrine [EN-duh-krin] **system** the body's "slow" chemical communication system; a set of glands that secrete hormones into the bloodstream. (p. 36)

endorphins [en-DOR-fins] "morphine within"—natural, opiate-like neurotransmitters linked to pain control and to pleasure. (p. 32)

environment every external influence, from prenatal nutrition to social support in later life. (p. 69)

epigenetics the study of environmental influences on gene expression that occur without a DNA change. (p. 70)

equity a condition in which people receive from a relationship in proportion to what they give to it. (p. 362)

erectile disorder inability to develop or maintain an erection due to insufficient blood flow to the penis. (p. 117)

estrogens sex hormones that contribute to female sex characteristics and are secreted in greater amounts by females than by males. In nonhuman female mammals, estrogen levels peak during ovulation, promoting sexual receptivity. (p. 115)

evidence-based practice clinical decision making that integrates the best available research with clinical expertise and patient characteristics and preferences. (p. 422)

evolutionary psychology the study of how our behavior and mind have changed in adaptive ways over time due to natural selection. (p. 125)

experiment a method in which researchers vary one or more factors (independent variables) to observe the effect on some behavior or mental process (the dependent variable). (p. 17)

experimental group in an experiment, the group exposed to the treatment, that is, to one version of the independent variable. (p. 18)

explicit memory memory of facts and personal events you can consciously retrieve. (Also called *declarative memory*.) (p. 195)

exposure therapies behavioral techniques, such as *systematic desensitization* and *virtual reality exposure therapy,* that treat anxieties by exposing people (in imagination or actual situations) to the things they fear and avoid. (p. 414)

external locus of control the perception that chance or outside forces beyond our personal control determine our fate. (p. 292)

extinction in classical conditioning, the weakening of a conditioned response when an unconditioned stimulus does not follow a conditioned stimulus. (In operant conditioning, the weakening of a response when it is no longer reinforced.) (p. 171)

extrasensory perception (ESP) the controversial claim that perception can occur apart from sensory input, such as through *telepathy, clairvoyance, and precognition.* (p. 161)

extrinsic motivation a desire to perform a behavior to gain a reward or avoid punishment. (p. 184)

F

facial feedback effect the tendency of facial muscle states to trigger corresponding feelings such as fear, anger, or happiness. (p. 278)

factor a cluster of behavior tendencies that occur together. (p. 322)

family therapy therapy that treats the family as a system. Views an individual's unwanted behaviors as influenced by, or directed at, other family members. (p. 419)

feature detectors nerve cells in the brain that respond to specific features of a stimulus, such as edges, lines, and angles. (p. 142)

feel-good, do-good phenomenon our tendency to be helpful when already in a good mood. (p. 301)

female orgasmic disorder feeling distressed due to infrequently or never experiencing orgasm. (p. 117)

fetal alcohol syndrome (FAS) physical and mental abnormalities in children caused by a pregnant woman's heavy drinking. In severe cases, signs include a small, out-of-proportion head and abnormal facial features. (p. 71)

fetus the developing human organism from 9 weeks after conception to birth. (p. 71)

fight-or-flight response an emergency response, including activity of the sympathetic nervous system, that mobilizes energy and activity for attacking or escaping a threat. (p. 285)

figure-ground the organization of the visual field into objects (the *figures*) that stand out from their surroundings (the *ground*). (p. 146)

fixation (1) in personality theory, according to Freud, a lingering focus of pleasure-seeking energies at an earlier psychosexual stage, in which conflicts were unresolved. (p. 314) (2) in thinking, the inability to see a problem from a new perspective; an obstacle to problem solving. (p. 221)

fixed-interval schedule in operant conditioning, a reinforcement schedule that reinforces a response only after a specified time has elapsed. (p. 177)

fixed-ratio schedule in operant conditioning, a reinforcement schedule that reinforces a response only after a specified number of responses. (p. 177)

flashbulb memory a clear memory of an emotionally significant moment or event. (p. 201)

flow a completely involved, focused state, with lowered awareness of self and time; results from full engagement of our skills. (p. B-1)

fluid intelligence our ability to reason speedily and abstractly; tends to decrease during late adulthood. (p. 246)

fMRI (functional MRI) a technique for revealing bloodflow and, therefore, brain activity by comparing successive MRI scans. fMRI scans show brain function. (p. 38)

foot-in-the-door phenomenon the tendency for people who have first agreed to a small request to comply later with a larger request. (p. 340)

formal operational stage in Piaget's theory, the stage of cognitive development (normally beginning about age 12) during which people begin to think logically about abstract concepts. (p. 79)

framing the way an issue is posed; framing can significantly affect decisions and judgments. (p. 223)

fraternal twins (*dizygotic twins*) twins who develop from separate fertilized eggs. They are genetically no closer than non-twin brothers and sisters, but they share a prenatal environment. (p. 71)

free association in psychoanalysis, a method of exploring the unconscious in which the person relaxes and says whatever comes to mind, no matter how unimportant or embarrassing. (p. 312)

frequency the number of complete wavelengths that pass a point in a given time (for example, per second). (p. 151)

frontal lobes portion of the cerebral cortex lying just behind the forehead; involved in speaking and muscle movements and in making plans and judgments. (p. 41)

frustration-aggression principle the principle that frustration—the blocking of an attempt to achieve some goal—creates anger, which can generate aggression. (p. 355)

fundamental attribution error the tendency, when analyzing others' behavior, to overestimate the influence of personal traits and underestimate the effects of the situation. (p. 338)

G

gender the roles and characteristics that a culture expects from those defined as *male* and *female.* (p. 108)

gender identity our sense of being male or female. (p. 113)

gender role a set of expected behaviors for males or for females. (p. 113)

gender typing the acquisition of a traditional masculine or feminine role. (p. 114)

general adaptation syndrome (GAS) Selye's concept of the body's adaptive response to stress in three stages—alarm, resistance, exhaustion. (p. 285)

general intelligence (*g*) a general intelligence factor that, according to Spearman and others, underlies specific mental abilities and is therefore measured by every task on an intelligence test. (p. 236)

generalization in classical conditioning, the tendency, after conditioning, to respond similarly to stimuli that resemble the conditioned stimulus. (p. 172)

generalized anxiety disorder an anxiety disorder in which a person is continually tense, fearful, and in a state of autonomic nervous system arousal. (p. 376)

genes the biochemical units of heredity that make up the chromosomes; segments of DNA. (p. 68)

genome the complete instructions for making an organism, consisting of all the genetic material in that organism's chromosomes. (p. 68)

gestalt an organized whole. Gestalt psychologists emphasized our tendency to integrate pieces of information into meaningful wholes. (p. 145)

glial cells (glia) cells in the nervous system that support, nourish, and protect neurons; they may also play a role in learning, thinking, and memory. (p. 30)

glucose the form of sugar that circulates in the blood and provides the major source of energy for body tissues. When its level is low, we feel hunger. (p. 258)

grammar in a specific language, a system of rules that enables us to communicate with and understand others. (p. 231)

group polarization strengthening of a group's preexisting attitudes through discussions within the group. (p. 348)

group therapy therapy conducted with groups rather than individuals, providing benefits from group interaction. (p. 419)

grouping the perceptual tendency to organize stimuli into meaningful groups. (p. 146)

groupthink the mode of thinking that occurs when the desire for harmony in a decision-making group overrides a realistic appraisal of alternatives. (p. 349)

H

hallucination false sensory experience, such as hearing something in the absence of an external auditory stimulus. (p. 45)

hallucinogens psychedelic ("mind-manifesting") drugs, such as LSD, that distort perceptions and evoke sensory images in the absence of sensory input. (p. 385)

heredity the genetic transfer of characteristics from parents to offspring. (p. 68)

heritability the portion of variation among individuals that we can attribute to genes. The heritability of a trait may vary, depending on the population and the environment. (p. 244)

heuristic a simple thinking strategy that often allows you to make judgments and solve problems efficiently; usually speedier but also more error prone than *algorithms*. (p. 200)

hierarchy of needs Maslow's pyramid of human needs; at the base are physiological needs. These basic needs must be satisfied before higher-level safety needs, and then psychological needs, become active. (pp. 257, 319)

hindsight bias the tendency to believe, after learning an outcome, that we could have predicted it. (Also known as the *I-knew-it-all-along phenomenon.*) (p. 9)

hippocampus a neural center located in the limbic system; helps process explicit memories for storage. (p. 199)

homeostasis a tendency to maintain a balanced or constant internal state; the regulation of any aspect of body chemistry, such as blood glucose, around a particular level. (p. 256)

hormones chemical messengers that are manufactured by the endocrine glands, travel through the bloodstream, and affect other tissues. (p. 36)

hue the dimension of color that is determined by the wavelength of light; what we know as the color names *blue, green,* and so forth. (p. 140)

human factors psychology an I/O psychology subfield that explores how people and machines interact and how machines and physical environments can be made safe and easy to use. (p. B-2)

humanistic psychology emphasized the growth potential of healthy people. (p. 3)

hypnosis a social interaction in which one person (the subject) responds to a suggestion by another person (the hypnotist) that certain perceptions, feelings, thoughts, or behaviors will spontaneously occur. (p. 156)

hypothalamus [hi-po-THAL-uh-muss] a neural structure lying below (*hypo*) the thalamus; directs several maintenance activities (eating, drinking, body temperature), helps govern the endocrine system via the pituitary gland, and is linked to emotion and reward. (p. 41)

hypothesis a testable prediction, often implied by a theory. (p. 12)

I

id a reservoir of unconscious psychic energy that, according to Freud, strives to satisfy basic sexual and aggressive drives. The id operates on the *pleasure principle,* demanding immediate gratification. (p. 313)

identical twins (*monozygotic twins*) twins who develop from a single fertilized egg that splits in two, creating two genetically identical siblings. (p. 71)

identification the process by which, according to Freud, children incorporate their parents' values into their developing superegos. (p. 314)

identity our sense of self; according to Erikson, the adolescent's task is to solidify a sense of self by testing and blending various roles. (p. 89)

implicit memory retaining learned skills, or classically conditioned associations, without conscious awareness. (Also called *nondeclarative memory.*) (p. 195)

inattentional blindness failure to see visible objects when our attention is directed elsewhere. (p. 51)

incentive a positive or negative environmental stimulus that motivates behavior. (p. 256)

independent variable in an experiment, the factor that is manipulated; the variable whose effect is being studied. (p. 19)

individualism giving priority to our own goals over group goals and defining our identity in terms of personal traits rather than group membership. (p. 331)

industrial-organizational (I/O) psychology the application of psychological concepts and methods to human behavior in workplaces. (p. B-2)

informed consent giving people enough information about a study to enable them to decide whether they wish to participate. (p. 22)

ingroup "us"—people with whom we share a common identity. (p. 352)

ingroup bias the tendency to favor our own group. (p. 352)

insight a sudden realization of the solution to a problem; it contrasts with strategy-based solutions. (p. 220)

insight therapies therapies that aim to improve psychological functioning by increasing a person's awareness of underlying motives and defenses. (p. 412)

insomnia recurring problems in falling or staying asleep. (p. 58)

intellectual disability a condition of limited mental ability, indicated by an intelligence score of 70 or below and difficulty adapting to the demands of life. (Formerly referred to as *mental retardation.*) (p. 242)

intelligence mental quality consisting of the ability to learn from experience, solve problems, and use knowledge to adapt to new situations. (p. 236)

intelligence quotient (IQ) defined originally as the ratio of mental age (*ma*) to chronological age (*ca*) multiplied by 100 (thus, IQ = $ma \times ca \times 100$). On contemporary intelligence tests, the average performance for a given age is assigned a score of 100. (p. 239)

intelligence test a method for assessing an individual's mental aptitudes and comparing them with those of others, using numerical scores. (p. 239)

intensity the amount of energy in a light wave or sound wave, which influences what we perceive as brightness or loudness. Intensity is determined by the wave's amplitude (height). (p. 140)

interaction the interplay that occurs when the effect of one factor (such as environment) depends on another factor (such as heredity). (p. 69)

internal locus of control the perception that we control our own fate. (p. 292)

interneuron   neurons within the brain and spinal cord; communicate internally and process information between sensory inputs and motor outputs. (p. 33)

interpretation   in psychoanalysis, the analyst's noting supposed dream meanings, resistances, and other significant behaviors and events in order to promote insight. (p. 411)

intersex   possessing biological sexual characteristics of both sexes. (p. 112)

intimacy   in Erikson's theory, the ability to form close, loving relationships; a primary developmental task in early adulthood. (p. 90)

intrinsic motivation   a desire to perform a behavior well for its own sake. (p. 184)

intuition   an effortless, immediate, automatic feeling or thought, as contrasted with explicit, conscious reasoning. (p. 221)

J

James-Lange theory   the theory that our experience of emotion is our awareness of our physiological responses to emotion-arousing stimuli. (p. 269)

just-world phenomenon   the tendency to believe that the world is just and people therefore get what they deserve and deserve what they get. (p. 352)

K

kinesthesia [kin-ehs-THEE-see-a]   the system for sensing the position and movement of individual body parts. (p. 159)

L

language   our spoken, written, or signed words and the ways we combine them to communicate meaning. (p. 229)

latent content   according to Freud, the underlying meaning of a dream. (p. 60)

latent learning   learning that is not apparent until there is an incentive to demonstrate it. (p. 184)

law of effect   Thorndike's principle that behaviors followed by favorable consequences become more likely, and that behaviors followed by unfavorable consequences become less likely. (p. 174)

learned helplessness   the hopelessness and passive resignation an animal or person learns when unable to avoid repeated aversive events. (p. 291)

learning   the process of acquiring, through experience, new and relatively enduring information or behaviors. (p. 168)

limbic system   neural system (including the *hippocampus, amygdala,* and *hypothalamus*) located below the cerebral hemispheres; associated with emotions and drives. (p. 40)

lobotomy   a psychosurgical procedure once used to calm uncontrollably emotional or violent patients. The procedure cut the nerves connecting the frontal lobes to the emotion-controlling centers of the inner brain. (p. 429)

longitudinal study   research in which the same people are restudied and retested over a long period of time. (pp. 245, A-7)

long-term memory   the relatively permanent and limitless storehouse of the memory system. Includes knowledge, skills, and experiences. (p. 194)

long-term potentiation (LTP)   an increase in a synapse's firing potential. Believed to be a neural basis for learning and memory. (p. 201)

LSD   a powerful hallucinogenic drug; also known as *acid (lysergic acid diethylamide)*. (p. 386)

lymphocytes   the two types of white blood cells that are part of the body's immune system: *B lymphocytes* release antibodies that fight bacterial infections; *T lymphocytes* attack cancer cells, viruses, and foreign substances. (p. 287)

M

major depressive disorder   a mood disorder in which a person experiences, in the absence of drugs or a medical condition, two or more weeks with five or more symptoms, at least one of which must be either (1) depressed mood or (2) loss of interest or pleasure. (p. 389)

mania   a hyperactive, wildly optimistic state. (p. 390)

manifest content   according to Freud, the remembered story line of a dream. (p. 60)

maturation   biological growth processes leading to orderly changes in behavior, mostly independent of experience. (p. 73)

mean   the arithmetic average of a distribution, obtained by adding the scores and then dividing by the number of scores. (p. A-2)

median   the middle score in a distribution; half the scores are above it and half are below it. (p. A-2)

medical model   the concept that diseases, in this case psychological disorders, have physical causes that can be *diagnosed, treated,* and, in most cases, *cured,* often through *treatment* in a *hospital.* (p. 372)

medulla [muh-DUL-uh]   the base of the brainstem; controls heartbeat and breathing. (p. 39)

memory   the persistence of learning over time through the encoding, storage, and retrieval of information. (p. 194)

memory trace   lasting physical changes in the brain as a memory forms. (p. 207)

menarche [meh-NAR-key]   the first menstrual period. (p. 111)

menopause   the end of menstruation. In everyday use, it can also mean the biological transition a woman experiences from before until after the end of menstruation. (p. 95)

mental age   a measure of intelligence test performance devised by Binet; the chronological age that most typically corresponds to a given level of performance. Thus, a child who does as well as an average 8-year-old is said to have a mental age of 8. (p. 239)

mere exposure effect   the phenomenon that repeated exposure to novel stimuli increases liking of them. (p. 359)

methamphetamine   a powerfully addictive drug that stimulates the central nervous system with speeded-up body functions and associated energy and mood changes; over time, appears to reduce baseline dopamine levels. (p. 385)

mindfulness meditation   attending to current experiences in a nonjudgmental and accepting manner. (p. 298)

Minnesota Multiphasic Personality Inventory (MMPI)   the most widely researched and clinically used of all personality tests. Originally developed to identify emotional disorders (still considered its most appropriate use), this test is now used for many other screening purposes. (p. 324)

mirror neuron   neuron that fires when we perform certain actions and when we observe others performing those actions; neural basis for imitation and observational learning. (p. 186)

mirror-image perceptions　mutual views often held by conflicting people, as when each side sees itself as ethical and peaceful and views the other side as evil and aggressive. (p. 365)

misinformation effect　when a memory has been corrupted by misleading information. (p. 210)

mnemonics [nih-MON-iks]　memory aids, especially techniques that use vivid imagery and organizational devices. (p. 197)

mode　the most frequently occurring score(s) in a distribution. (p. A-2)

modeling　the process of observing and imitating a specific behavior. (p. 184)

monocular cue　a depth cue, such as interposition or linear perspective, available to either eye alone. (p. 147)

mood disorders　psychological disorders characterized by emotional extremes. See *major depressive disorder* and *bipolar disorder*. (p. 389)

mood-congruent memory　the tendency to recall experiences that are consistent with your current good or bad mood. (p. 205)

motivation　a need or desire that energizes and directs behavior. (p. 256)

motor cortex　cerebral cortex area at the rear of the frontal lobes; controls voluntary movements. (p. 41)

motor neuron　neuron that carries outgoing information from the central nervous system to the muscles and glands. (p. 33)

MRI (magnetic resonance imaging)　a technique that uses magnetic fields and radio waves to produce computer-generated images of soft tissue. MRI scans show brain anatomy. (p. 38)

N

narcolepsy　sleep disorder in which a person has uncontrollable sleep attacks, sometimes lapsing directly into REM sleep. (p. 59)

natural selection　the principal that among the range of inherited trait variations, those that lead to increased reproduction and survival will most likely be passed on to succeeding generations. (p. 126)

naturalistic observation　a descriptive technique of observing and recording behavior in naturally occurring situations without trying to change or control the situation. (p. 14)

nature–nurture issue　the age-old controversy over the relative influence of genes and experience in the development of psychological traits and behaviors. Today's psychological science sees traits and behaviors arising from the interaction of nature and nurture. (p. 7)

near-death experience　an altered state of consciousness reported after a close brush with death (such as through cardiac arrest); often similar to drug-induced hallucinations. (p. 386)

negative reinforcement　increases behaviors by stopping or reducing negative stimuli, such as shock. A negative reinforcer is anything that, when *removed* after a response, strengthens the response. (*Note:* Negative reinforcement is *not* punishment.) (p. 175)

nerves　bundled axons that form neural cables connecting the central nervous system with muscles, glands, and sense organs. (p. 33)

nervous system　the body's speedy, electrochemical communication network, consisting of all the nerve cells of the central and peripheral nervous systems. (p. 33)

neurogenesis　formation of new neurons. (p. 47)

neuron　a nerve cell; the basic building block of the nervous system. (p. 30)

neurotransmitters　neuron-produced chemicals that cross synapses to carry messages to other neurons or cells. (p. 31)

neutral stimulus (NS)　in classical conditioning, a stimulus that evokes no response before conditioning. (p. 169)

nicotine　a stimulating and highly addictive psychoactive drug in tobacco. (p. 383)

norm　an understood rule for accepted and expected behavior in a given group. (p. 343)

normal curve　(*normal distribution*) a symmetrical, bell-shaped curve that describes the distribution of many types of data; most scores fall near the mean (about 68 percent fall within one standard deviation of it) and fewer and fewer near the extremes. (p. 240)

O

object permanence　the awareness that things continue to exist even when not perceived. (p. 76)

observational learning　learning by observing others. (p. 184)

obsessive-compulsive disorder (OCD)　a disorder characterized by unwanted repetitive thoughts (obsessions) and/or actions (compulsions). (p. 377)

occipital [ahk-SIP-uh-tuhl] **lobes**　portion of the cerebral cortex lying at the back of the head; includes areas that receive information from the visual fields. (p. 41)

Oedipus [ED-uh-puss] **complex**　according to Freud, a boy's sexual desires toward his mother and feelings of jealousy and hatred for the rival father. (p. 314)

one-word stage　the stage in speech development, from about age 1 to 2, during which a child speaks mostly in single words. (p. 230)

operant behavior　behavior that operates on the environment, producing consequences. (p. 174)

operant chamber　in operant conditioning research, a chamber (also known as a *Skinner box*) containing a bar or key that an animal can manipulate to obtain a food or water reinforcer; attached devices record the animal's rate of bar pressing or key pecking. (p. 174)

operant conditioning　a type of learning in which behavior is strengthened if followed by a reinforcer or diminished if followed by a punisher. (p. 174)

operational definition　a carefully worded statement of the exact procedures (operations) used in a research study. For example, *human intelligence* may be operationally defined as what an intelligence test measures. (p. 13)

opiates　chemicals such as opium, morphine, and heroin, that depress neural activity, temporarily lessening pain and anxiety. (pp. 32, 381)

opponent-process theory　the theory that opposing retinal processes (red-green, yellow-blue, white-black) enable color vision. For example, some cells are "turned on" by green and "turned off" by red; others are turned on by red and off by green. (p. 144)

optic nerve　the nerve that carries neural impulses from the eye to the brain. (p. 141)

optimism　the anticipation of positive outcomes. Optimists are people who expect the best and expect their efforts to lead to good things. (p. 293)

organizational psychology　an I/O psychology subfield that examines organizational influences on worker satisfaction and productivity and facilitates organizational change. (p. B-2)

other-race effect　the tendency to recall faces of one's own race more accurately than faces of other races. (p. 353)

outgroup "them"—those perceived as different or apart from our group. (p. 352)

overconfidence the tendency to be more confident than correct—to overestimate the accuracy of our beliefs and judgments. (p. 223)

P

panic disorder an anxiety disorder marked by unpredictable minutes-long episodes of intense dread in which a person may experience terror and accompanying chest pain, choking, or other frightening sensations, followed by worry about a possible next attack. (p. 376)

parallel processing the processing of many aspects of a problem or scene at the same time; the brain's natural mode of information processing for many functions, including vision. (p. 143)

paraphilias experiencing sexual arousal from fantasies, behaviors, or urges involving nonhuman objects, the suffering of self or others, and/or nonconsenting persons. (p. 117)

parasympathetic nervous system autonomic nervous system subdivision that calms the body, conserving its energy. (p. 34)

parietal [puh-RYE-uh-tuhl] **lobes** portion of the cerebral cortex lying at the top of the head and toward the rear; receives sensory input for touch and body position. (p. 41)

partial (intermittent) reinforcement reinforcing a response only part of the time; results in slower acquisition but much greater resistance to extinction than does continuous reinforcement. (p. 177)

passionate love an aroused state of intense positive absorption in another, usually present at the beginning of a love relationship. (p. 261)

perception the process by which our brain organizes and interprets sensory information, transforming it into meaningful objects and events. (p. 134)

perceptual adaptation in vision, the ability to adjust to an artificially displaced or even inverted visual field. (p. 150)

perceptual constancy perceiving objects as unchanging (having consistent color, brightness, shape, and size) even as illumination and retinal images change. (p. 148)

perceptual set a mental predisposition to perceive one thing and not another. (p. 138)

peripheral nervous system (PNS) the sensory and motor neurons connecting the central nervous system (CNS) to the rest of the body. (p. 133)

personal control our sense of controlling our environment rather than feeling helpless. (p. 291)

personality an individual's characteristic pattern of thinking, feeling, and acting. (p. 311)

personality disorder an inflexible and enduring behavior pattern that impairs social functioning. (p. 402)

personality inventory a questionnaire (often with true-false or agree-disagree items) on which people respond to items designed to gauge a wide range of feelings and behaviors; used to assess selected personality traits. (p. 324)

personnel psychology an I/O psychology subfield that focuses on employee selection, placement, training, and appraisal. (p. B-2)

pessimism the anticipation of negative outcomes. Pessimists are people who expect the worst and doubt that their goals will be achieved. (p. 293)

PET (positron emission tomography) scan a view of brain activity showing where a radioactive form of glucose goes while the brain performs a given task. (p. 38)

phobia an anxiety disorder marked by a persistent, irrational fear and avoidance of a specific object or situation. (p. 376)

physiological need a basic bodily requirement. (p. 256)

pitch a tone's experienced highness or lowness; depends on frequency. (p. 151)

pituitary gland most influential endocrine gland. Under the influence of the hypothalamus, the pituitary regulates growth and controls other endocrine glands. (p. 37)

placebo [pluh-SEE-bo; Latin for "I shall please"] an inactive substance or condition that is sometimes given to those in a control group in place of the treatment given to the experimental group. (p. 18)

placebo effect results caused by expectations alone. (p. 18)

plasticity the brain's ability to change, especially during childhood, by reorganizing after damage or by building new pathways based on experience. (p. 47)

polygraph a machine, commonly used in attempts to detect lies, that measures some bodily responses (such as changes in perspiration, heart rate, and breathing) accompanying emotion. (p. 274)

population all those in a group being studied, from which samples may be drawn. (Note: Except for national studies, this does not refer to a country's whole population.) (p. 15)

positive psychology the scientific study of human functioning, with the goals of discovering and promoting strengths and virtues that help individuals and communities to thrive. (p. 8)

positive reinforcement increases behaviors by presenting positive stimuli, such as food. A positive reinforcer is anything that, when *presented* after a response, strengthens the response. (p. 175)

posthypnotic suggestion a suggestion, made during a hypnosis session, to be carried out after the subject is no longer hypnotized; used by some clinicians to help control undesired symptoms and behaviors. (p. 156)

posttraumatic stress disorder (PTSD) a disorder characterized by haunting memories, nightmares, social withdrawal, jumpy anxiety, numbness of feeling, and/or insomnia lingering for four weeks or more after a traumatic experience. (p. 377)

prejudice an unjustifiable and usually negative attitude toward a group and its members. Prejudice generally involves stereotyped beliefs, negative feelings, and a predisposition to discriminatory action. (p. 350)

premature ejaculation sexual climax that occurs before the man or his partner wishes. (p. 117)

preoperational stage in Piaget's theory, the stage (from about 2 to 6 or 7 years of age) in which a child learns to use language but cannot yet perform the mental operations of concrete logic. (p. 77)

primary reinforcer an event that is innately reinforcing, often by satisfying a biological need. (p. 176)

primary sex characteristics the body structures (ovaries, testes, and external genitalia) that make sexual reproduction possible. (p. 111)

priming activating, often unconsciously, associations in our mind, thus setting us up to perceive, remember, or respond to objects or events in certain ways. (pp. 135, 204)

proactive interference the disruptive effect of prior learning on the recall of new information. (p. 208)

problem-focused coping attempting to reduce stress directly—by changing the stressor or the way we interact with that stressor. (p. 291)

projective test a personality test, such as the Rorschach, that provides an unclear image designed to trigger projection of the test-taker's unconscious thoughts or feelings. (p. 316)

prosocial behavior positive, constructive, helpful behavior. The opposite of antisocial behavior. (p. 186)

prototype a mental image or best example of a category. Matching new items to a prototype provides a quick and easy method for sorting items into categories (as when comparing feathered creatures to a prototypical bird, such as a robin). (p. 220)

psychoactive drug a chemical substance that alters perceptions and mood. (p. 380)

psychoanalysis (1) Sigmund Freud's theory of personality that attributes thoughts and actions to unconscious motives and conflicts. (p. 312) (2) Freud's therapeutic technique used in treating psychological disorders. Freud believed that the patient's free associations, resistances, dreams, and transferences—and the analyst's interpretations of them—released previously repressed feelings, allowing the patient to gain self-insight. (p. 410)

psychodynamic theories view of personality with a focus on the unconscious and the importance of childhood experiences. (p. 312)

psychodynamic therapy therapeutic approach derived from the psychoanalytic tradition; views individuals as responding to unconscious forces and childhood experiences, and seeks to enhance self-insight. (p. 412)

psychological disorder a syndrome marked by a clinically significant disturbance in a person's thoughts, feelings, or behaviors. (p. 371)

psychology the science of behavior and mental processes. (p. 3)

psychoneuroimmunology the study of how psychological, neural, and endocrine processes combine to affect our immune system and health. (p. 287)

psychosexual stages the childhood stages of development (oral, anal, phallic, latency, genital) during which, according to Freud, the id's pleasure-seeking energies focus on distinct erogenous zones. (p. 314)

psychosurgery surgery that removes or destroys brain tissue in an effort to change behavior. (p. 429)

psychotherapy treatment involving psychological techniques; consists of interactions between a trained therapist and someone seeking to overcome psychological difficulties or achieve personal growth. (p. 410)

puberty the period of sexual maturation, during which a person becomes capable of reproducing. (pp. 86, 111)

punishment an event that decreases the behavior it follows. (p. 178)

R

random assignment assigning participants to experimental and control groups by chance, thus minimizing any differences between the groups. (p. 18)

random sample a sample that fairly represents a population because each member has an equal chance of inclusion. (p. 15)

range the difference between the highest and lowest scores in a distribution. (p. A-3)

recall memory demonstrated by retrieving information learned earlier, as on a fill-in-the-blank test. (p. 202)

reciprocal determinism the interacting influences of behavior, internal personal factors, and environment. (p. 326)

reciprocity norm an expectation that people will help, not hurt, those who have helped them. (p. 365)

recognition memory demonstrated by identifying items previously learned, as on a multiple-choice test. (p. 202)

reflex a simple, automatic response to a sensory stimulus, such as the knee-jerk response. (pp. 36, 71)

refractory period a resting period after orgasm, during which a man cannot achieve another orgasm. (p. 116)

regression toward the mean the tendency for extreme or unusual scores or events to fall back (regress) toward the average. (p. A-6)

reinforcement in operant conditioning, any event that *strengthens* the behavior it follows. (p. 174)

reinforcement schedule a pattern that defines how often a desired response will be reinforced. (p. 177)

relational aggression an act of aggression (physical or verbal) intended to harm a person's relationship or social standing. (p. 109)

relative deprivation the perception that we are worse off relative to those with whom we compare ourselves. (p. 304)

relearning memory demonstrated by time saved when learning material a second time. (p. 202)

reliability the extent to which a test yields consistent results, as assessed by the consistency of scores on two halves of the test, on alternative forms of the test, or on retesting. (p. 240)

REM (rapid eye movement) sleep recurring sleep stage during which vivid dreams commonly occur. Also known as *paradoxical sleep,* because the muscles are relaxed (except for minor twitches) but other body systems are active. (p. 53)

REM rebound the tendency for REM sleep to increase following REM sleep deprivation. (p. 62)

repetitive transcranial magnetic stimulation (rTMS) the application of repeated pulses of magnetic energy to the brain; used to stimulate or suppress brain activity. (p. 428)

replication repeating the essence of a research study, usually with different participants in different situations, to see whether the basic finding extends to other participants and circumstances. (p. 13)

repression in psychoanalytic theory, the basic defense mechanism that banishes from consciousness the thoughts, feelings, and memories that arouse anxiety. (pp. 208, 314)

resilience the personal strength that helps most people cope with stress and recover from adversity and even trauma. (pp. 301, 431)

resistance in psychoanalysis, the blocking from consciousness of anxiety-laden material. (p. 411)

respondent behavior behavior that occurs as an automatic response to some stimulus. (p. 174)

reticular formation nerve network running through the brainstem and thalamus; plays an important role in controlling arousal. (p. 39)

retina the light-sensitive inner surface of the eye; contains the receptor rods and cones plus layers of neurons that begin the processing of visual information. (p. 140)

retinal disparity a binocular cue for perceiving depth. By comparing images from the two eyes, the brain computes distance—the greater the disparity (difference) between the two images, the closer the object. (p. 147)

retrieval the process of getting information out of memory storage. (p. 194)

retrieval cue   any stimulus (event, feeling, place, and so on) linked to a specific memory. (p. 204)

retroactive interference   the disruptive effect of new learning on the recall of old information. (p. 208)

rods   retinal receptors that detect black, white, and gray; necessary for peripheral and twilight vision, when cones don't respond. (p. 141)

role   a set of expectations (norms) about a social position, defining how those in the position ought to behave. (pp. 113, 340)

Rorschach inkblot test   the most widely used projective test; a set of 10 inkblots, designed by Hermann Rorschach; seeks to identify people's inner feelings by analyzing their interpretations of the blots. (p. 316)

S

savant syndrome   a condition in which a person otherwise limited in mental ability has an exceptional specific skill, such as in computation or drawing. (p. 236)

scapegoat theory   the theory that prejudice offers an outlet for anger by providing someone to blame. (p. 352)

scatterplot   a graphed cluster of dots, each of which represents the values of two factors. The slope of the dots suggests the direction of the relationship between the two factors. How much the dots are scattered suggests the strength of the correlation (with little scatter indicating high correlation). (pp. 16, A-4)

schema   a concept or framework that organizes and interprets information. (p. 76)

schizophrenia   a psychological disorder characterized by delusions, hallucinations, disorganized speech, and/or diminished, inappropriate emotional expression. (p. 396)

secondary sex characteristics   nonreproductive sexual traits, such as female breasts and hips, male voice quality, and body hair. (p. 111)

selective attention   focusing conscious awareness on a particular stimulus. (p. 51)

self   your image and understanding of who you are; in modern psychology, the idea that this is the center of personality, organizing your thoughts, feelings, and actions. (p. 328)

self-actualization   according to Maslow, the psychological need that arises after basic physical and psychological needs are met and self-esteem is achieved; the motivation to fulfill our potential. (p. 319)

self-concept   all our thoughts and feelings about ourselves, in answer to the question, "Who am I?" (p. 320)

self-disclosure   revealing intimate aspects of ourselves to others. (p. 362)

self-efficacy   our sense of competence and effectiveness. (p. 326)

self-esteem   our feelings of high or low self-worth. (p. 329)

self-serving bias   our readiness to perceive ourselves favorably. (p. 330)

self-transcendence   according to Maslow, the striving for identity, meaning, and purpose beyond the self. (p. 319)

sensation   the process by which our sensory receptors and nervous system receive and represent stimulus energies from our environment. (p. 134)

sensorimotor stage   in Piaget's theory, the stage (from birth to nearly 2 years of age) during which infants know the world mostly in terms of their sensory impressions and motor activities. (p. 76)

sensorineural hearing loss   hearing loss caused by damage to the cochlea's receptor cells or to the auditory nerves; also called *nerve deafness*. (p. 153)

sensory adaptation   reduced sensitivity in response to constant stimulation. (p. 137)

sensory interaction   the principle that one sense may influence another, as when the smell of food influences its taste. (p. 160)

sensory memory   the immediate, very brief recording of sensory information in the memory system. (p. 194)

sensory neuron   neuron that carries incoming information from the sensory receptors to the central nervous system. (p. 33)

serial position effect   our tendency to recall best the last and first items in a list. (p. 205)

set point   the point at which your "weight thermostat" is supposedly set. When your body falls below this weight, increased hunger and a lowered metabolic rate may combine to restore lost weight. (p. 259)

sexual dysfunction   a problem that consistently impairs sexual arousal or functioning. (p. 116)

sexual orientation   an enduring sexual attraction toward members of either one's own sex (homosexual orientation), the other sex (heterosexual orientation), or both sexes (bisexual orientation). (p. 120)

sexual response cycle   the four stages of sexual responding described by Masters and Johnson—excitement, plateau, orgasm, and resolution. (p. 116)

shaping   an operant conditioning procedure in which reinforcers guide actions closer and closer toward a desired behavior. (p. 174)

short-term memory   activated memory that holds a few items briefly (such as the seven digits of a phone number while dialing) before the information is stored or forgotten. (p. 194)

sleep   periodic, natural loss of consciousness—as distinct from unconsciousness resulting from a coma, general anesthesia, or hibernation. (Adapted from Dement, 1999.) (p. 54)

sleep apnea   a sleep disorder in which a sleeping person repeatedly stops breathing until blood oxygen is so low it awakens the person just long enough to draw a breath. (p. 59)

social clock   the culturally preferred timing of social events such as marriage, parenthood, and retirement. (p. 99)

social facilitation   improved performance on simple or well-learned tasks in the presence of others. (p. 347)

social identity   the "we" aspect of our self-concept; the part of our answer to "Who am I?" that comes from our group memberships. (p. 89)

social leadership   group-oriented leadership that builds teamwork, resolves conflict, and offers support. (p. B-7)

social learning theory   the theory that we learn social behavior by observing and imitating and by being rewarded or punished. (p. 113)

social loafing   the tendency for people in a group to exert less effort when pooling their efforts toward attaining a common goal than when individually accountable. (p. 347)

social psychology   the scientific study of how we think about, influence, and relate to one another. (p. 338)

social script   culturally modeled guide for how to act in various situations. (p. 357)

social-cognitive perspective   views behavior as influenced by the interaction between persons (and their thinking) and their social context. (p. 326)

social-responsibility norm   an expectation that people will help those dependent upon them. (p. 365)

somatic nervous system   peripheral nervous system division controlling the body's skeletal muscles. Also called the *skeletal nervous system*. (p. 34)

somatosensory cortex   cerebral cortex area at the front of the parietal lobes; registers and processes body touch and movement sensations. (p. 45)

source amnesia   faulty memory for how, when, or where information was learned or imagined. (p. 211)

spacing effect   the tendency for distributed study or practice to yield better long-term retention than is achieved through massed study or practice. (p. 198)

spermarche [sper-MAR-key]   first ejaculation. (p. 111)

split brain   condition in which the brain's two hemispheres are isolated by cutting the fibers (mainly those of the corpus callosum) connecting them. (p. 48)

spontaneous recovery   the reappearance, after a pause, of an extinguished conditioned response. (p. 171)

spotlight effect   overestimating others' noticing and evaluating our appearance, performance, and blunders (as if we presume a spotlight shines on us). (p. 328)

SQ3R   a study method incorporating five steps: Survey, Question, Read, Retrieve, Review. (p. 23)

standard deviation   a computed measure of how much scores vary around the mean score. (p. A-3)

standardization   defining uniform testing procedures and meaningful scores by comparison with the performance of a pretested group. (p. 240)

Stanford-Binet   the widely used American revision (by Terman at Stanford University) of Binet's original intelligence test. (p. 239)

statistical significance   a statistical statement of how likely it is that an obtained result occurred by chance. (p. A-7)

stereotype   a generalized (sometimes accurate but often overgeneralized) belief about a group of people. (p. 350)

stereotype threat   a self-confirming concern that we will be judged based on a negative stereotype. (p. 249)

stimulants   drugs (such as caffeine, nicotine, and the more powerful amphetamines, cocaine, Ecstasy, and methamphetamines) that excite neural activity and speed up body functions. (p. 383)

stimulus   any event or situation that evokes a response. (p. 168)

storage   the process of retaining encoded information over time. (p. 194)

stranger anxiety   the fear of strangers that infants commonly display, beginning by about 8 months of age. (p. 81)

stress   the process by which we perceive and respond to certain events, called *stressors*, that we appraise as threatening or challenging. (p. 284)

subjective well-being   self-perceived happiness or satisfaction with life. Used along with measures of objective well-being (for example, physical and economic indicators) to judge our quality of life. (p. 302)

subliminal   below our absolute threshold for conscious awareness. (p. 135)

substance use disorder   continued substance craving and use despite significant life disruption and/or physical risk. (p. 380)

superego   the part of personality that, according to Freud, represents internalized ideals and provides standards for judgment (the conscience) and for future goals. (p. 313)

superordinate goals   shared goals that override differences among people and require their cooperation. (p. 366)

survey   a descriptive technique for obtaining the self-reported attitudes or behaviors of a group, usually by questioning a representative, random sample of that group. (p. 15)

sympathetic nervous system   autonomic nervous system subdivision that arouses the body, mobilizing its energy in stressful situations. (p. 34)

synapse [SIN-aps]   junction between the axon tip of a sending neuron and the dendrite or cell body of a receiving neuron. (p. 30)

systematic desensitization   a type of exposure therapy that associates a pleasant, relaxed state with gradually increasing, anxiety-triggering stimuli. Commonly used to treat phobias. (p. 415)

T

task leadership   goal-oriented leadership that sets standards, organizes work, and focuses attention on goals. (p. B-7)

telegraphic speech   early speech stage in which a child speaks like a telegram—"go car"—using mostly nouns and verbs. (p. 231)

temperament   a person's characteristic emotional reactivity and intensity. (p. 83)

temporal lobes   portion of the cerebral cortex lying roughly above the ears; includes areas that receive information from the ears. (p. 41)

tend-and-befriend response   under stress, people (especially women) often provide support to others (*tend*) and bond with and seek support from others (*befriend*). (p. 286)

teratogen [tuh-RAT-uh-jen]   an agent, such as a chemical or virus, that can reach the embryo or fetus during prenatal development and cause harm. (p. 71)

testing effect   enhanced memory after retrieving, rather than simply rereading, information. Also sometimes called the *retrieval practice effect* or *test-enhanced learning*. (pp. 23, 198)

testosterone   the most important male sex hormone. Both males and females have it, but the additional testosterone in males stimulates the growth of the male sex organs in the fetus and the development of the male sex characteristics during puberty. (p. 111)

thalamus [THAL-uh-muss]   area at the top of the brainstem; directs sensory messages to the cortex and transmits replies to the cerebellum and medulla. (p. 39)

THC   the major active ingredient in marijuana; triggers a variety of effects, including mild hallucinations. (p. 386)

theory   an explanation using principles that organize observations and predict behaviors or events. (p. 12)

theory of mind   people's ideas about their own and others' mental states—about their feelings, perceptions, and thoughts, and the behaviors these might predict. (p. 78)

threshold   level of stimulation required to trigger a neural impulse. (p. 31)

token economy   an operant conditioning procedure in which people earn a token for exhibiting a desired behavior and can later exchange the tokens for privileges or treats. (p. 416)

tolerance   with repeated use, the desired effect requires larger doses. (p. 381)

top-down processing   information processing guided by higher-level mental processes, as when we construct perceptions drawing on our experience and expectations. (p. 134)

trait   a characteristic pattern of behavior or a tendency to feel and act in a certain way, as assessed by self-reports on a personality test. (p. 322)

transduction   changing one form of energy into another. In sensation, the transforming of stimulus energies, such as sights, sounds, and smells, into neural impulses our brain can interpret. (p. 135)

transference   in psychoanalysis, the patient's transfer to the analyst of emotions linked with other relationships (such as love or hatred for a parent). (p. 411)

transgender   an umbrella term describing people whose gender identity or expression differs from that associated with their birth sex. (p. 114)

two-factor theory   Schachter and Singer's theory that to experience emotion we must (1) be physically aroused and (2) cognitively label the arousal. (p. 270)

two-word stage   beginning about age 2, the stage in speech development during which a child speaks mostly two-word statements. (p. 231)

Type A   Friedman and Rosenman's term for competitive, hard-driving, impatient, verbally aggressive, and anger-prone people. (p. 289)

Type B   Friedman and Rosenman's term for easygoing, relaxed people. (p. 289)

U

unconditional positive regard   a caring, accepting, nonjudgmental attitude, which Carl Rogers believed would help clients develop self-awareness and self-acceptance. (pp. 320, 413)

unconditioned response (UR)   in classical conditioning, an unlearned, naturally occurring response (such as salivation) to an unconditioned stimulus (US) (such as food in the mouth). (p. 170)

unconditioned stimulus (US)   in classical conditioning, a stimulus that unconditionally—naturally and automatically—triggers a response (UR). (p. 170)

unconscious   according to Freud, a reservoir of mostly unacceptable thoughts, wishes, feelings, and memories. According to contemporary psychologists, information processing of which we are unaware. (p. 312)

V

validity   the extent to which a test measures or predicts what it is supposed to. (p. 241)

variable-interval schedule   in operant conditioning, a reinforcement schedule that reinforces a response at unpredictable time intervals. (p. 177)

variable-ratio schedule   in operant conditioning, a reinforcement schedule that reinforces a response after an unpredictable number of responses. (p. 177)

vestibular sense   the sense of body movement and position, including the sense of balance. (p. 159)

virtual reality exposure therapy   a counterconditioning technique that treats anxiety by creative electronic simulations in which people can safely face their greatest fears, such as airplane flying, spiders, or public speaking. (p. 415)

visual cliff   a laboratory device for testing depth perception in infants and young animals. (p. 146)

W

wavelength   the distance from the peak of one light or sound wave to the peak of the next. (p. 140)

Weber's law   the principle that, to be perceived as different, two stimuli must differ by a constant minimum percentage (rather than a constant amount). (p. 137)

Wechsler Adult Intelligence Scale (WAIS)   the WAIS is the most widely used intelligence test; contains verbal and performance (nonverbal) subtests. (p. 240)

Wernicke's area   controls language reception—a brain area involved in language comprehension and expression; usually in the left temporal lobe. (p. 232)

withdrawal   the discomfort and distress that follow discontinuing an addictive drug or behavior. (p. 381)

working memory   a newer understanding of short-term memory that stresses conscious, active processing of incoming auditory and visual-spatial information, and of information retrieved from long-term memory. (p. 194)

X

X chromosome   the sex chromosome found in both men and women. Females have two X chromosomes; males have one. An X chromosome from each parent produces a female child. (p. 111)

Y

Y chromosome   the sex chromosome found only in males. When paired with an X chromosome from the mother, it produces a male child. (p. 111)

Young-Helmholtz trichromatic (three-color) theory   the theory that the retina contains three different color receptors—one most sensitive to red, one to green, one to blue. When stimulated in combination, these cells can produce the perception of any color. (p. 144)

Z

zygote   the fertilized egg; it enters a 2-week period of rapid cell division and develops into an embryo. (p. 70)

Glosario

A

absolute threshold/umbral absoluto Estimulación mínima necesaria para detectar una estimulación dada el 50 por ciento del tiempo. (p. 135)

accommodation/acomodo Adaptación de nuestros entendimientos (esquemas) actuales de manera que incorporen información nueva. (p. 76)

achievement motivation/motivación de logro Deseo de lograr algo importante, para el dominio maestral de destrezas o ideas; para el control; deseo de alcanzar una norma alta. (p. B-3)

achievement test/prueba de rendimiento Prueba diseñada para evaluar lo que una persona ha aprendido. (p. 239)

acquisition/adquisición Según el condicionamiento clásico, etapa inicial en la que relacionamos un estímulo neutral con uno incondicionado, de tal modo que el estímulo neutral comience a desencadenar la respuesta condicionada. (Según el condicionamiento operante, intensificación de una respuesta reforzada). (p. 170)

action potential/potencial de acción Impulso nervioso. (p. 30)

active listening/escucha activa Escucha empática en la que el oyente hace eco, reitera y aclara. Característica de la terapia de Rogers centrada en el cliente. (p. 413)

adaptation-level phenomenon/fenómeno del nivel de adaptación Nuestra tendencia de formar juicios (de sonidos, de luces, de ingresos) con relación a un nivel neutro definido por nuestras vivencias anteriores. (p. 304)

addiction/adicción Ansia y uso compulsivo de drogas o de ciertas conductas (como participar en juegos de azar), pese a que se conozcan sus consecuencias perjudiciales. (p. 381)

adolescence/adolescencia Período de transición de la niñez a la madurez, extendiéndose de la pubertad a la independencia. (p. 86)

adrenal glands/glándulas suprarrenales Par de glándulas endocrinas ubicadas sobre los riñones que segregan hormonas (epinefrina y norepinefrina) que contribuyen a la estimulación del cuerpo en presencia de situaciones de tensión. (p. 36)

aerobic exercise/ejercicios aeróbicos Actividad sostenida que mejora la salud cardíaca y pulmonar; posiblemente reduce también la depresión y la ansiedad. (p. 296)

aggression/agresión Toda conducta que tiene por fin hacerle daño a alguien, sea física o emocionalmente. (pp. 108, 354)

AIDS (acquired immune deficiency syndrome)/sida (síndrome de inmunodeficiencia adquirida) Infección que se transmite sexualmente y que atenta contra la vida misma, causada por *el virus de inmunodeficiencia humana (VIH)*. El sida debilita el sistema inmunitario y así aumenta la vulnerabilidad de la persona a infecciones. (p. 117)

alcohol use disorder/trastorno de uso del alcohol (conocido comúnmente como *alcoholismo*) Consumo de alcohol caracterizado por tolerancia, síntomas de abstinencia cuando se interrumpe el consumo, y deseo de seguir consumiéndolo de manera problemática. (p. 382)

algorithm/algoritmo Regla o procedimiento metódico y lógico que garantiza la resolución de un problema dado. Contrasta con el empleo de la *heurística,* un método generalmente más rápido pero también más propenso a registrar errores. (p. 220)

all-or-none response/respuesta de todo o nada Reacción que produce una neurona al activarse (con una respuesta de máxima intensidad) o al no activarse. (p. 31)

alpha waves/ritmo alfa Ritmo con ondas cerebrales relativamente lentas que corresponden a un estado relajado y de vigilia. (p. 53)

altruism/altruismo Consideración desinteresada por el bienestar de los demás. (p. 363)

amnesia/amnesia Literalmente significa "sin memoria". Pérdida de la memoria, a menudo a raíz de un trauma, una lesión o una enfermedad. (p. 206)

amphetamines/anfetaminas Medicamentos que estimulan la actividad neuronal, acelerando las funciones corporales y cambiando el humor y los niveles de energía. (p. 383)

amygdala/amígdala Dos conjuntos de fibras nerviosas del tamaño de una haba que se hallan en el sistema límbico e intervienen en las emociones. (p. 41)

androgyny/androginia Que presenta características psicológicas tradicionales tanto masculinas como femeninas. (p. 114)

anorexia nervosa/anorexia nerviosa Trastorno alimentario en el cual una persona (generalmente una mujer adolescente) se somete a una dieta de hambre a pesar de padecer de delgadez extrema; a veces acompañada de ejercicios excesivos. (p. 400)

antianxiety drugs/medicamentos ansiolíticos Medicamentos recetados para aliviar los síntomas de la ansiedad y la agitación. (p. 426)

antidepressant drugs/medicamentos antidepresivos Medicamentos que se usan para tratar la depresión, los trastornos de ansiedad, obsesivo-compulsivo o de estrés postraumático. (Varios de los medicamentos más usados son *inhibidores selectivos de la recaptación de serotonina: ISRS*). (p. 426)

antipsychotic drugs/medicamentos antipsicóticos Medicamentos recetados para tratar la esquizofrenia y otros tipos de trastornos graves del pensamiento. (p. 425)

antisocial personality disorder/trastorno de personalidad antisocial Trastorno de la personalidad que se manifiesta cuando la persona (generalmente un hombre) no exhibe sentimiento de culpa por actuar con maldad, incluso hacia los amigos y miembros de la familia; puede ser agresivo y cruel o puede ser un timador listo. (p. 402)

anxiety disorders/trastornos de ansiedad Trastornos psicológicos que se caracterizan por la preocupación y tensión crónicas o por comportamientos desadaptados que reducen la ansiedad. (p. 375)

aptitude test/prueba de aptitud Prueba diseñada para predecir el desempeño de una persona en el futuro; *aptitud* es la capacidad de aprender. (p. 239)

asexual/asexual Ausencia de atracción sexual hacia otros. (p. 115)

assimilation/asimilación Interpretación de nuestras experiencias nuevas en términos de nuestros esquemas existentes. (p. 76)

association areas/áreas de asociación Áreas de la corteza cerebral principalmente relacionadas con las funciones mentales superiores como aprender, recordar, pensar y hablar. (p. 45)

associative learning/aprendizaje asociativo Aprender que ciertos eventos ocurren simultáneamente. Los eventos pueden ser dos estímulos (como en el condicionamiento clásico) o una respuesta y sus consecuencias (como en el condicionamiento operante). (p. 168)

attachment/apego   Vínculo emocional con otra persona; se observa en niños pequeños que buscan cercanía física con la persona que los cuida. Se observan señales de angustia cuando se hay una separación. (p. 81)

attention-deficit/hyperactivity disorder/trastorno por déficit de atención con hiperactividad(TDAH)   trastorno psicológico caracterizado por una falta de atención extrema y/o hiperactividad e impulsividad. (p. 372)

attitude/actitud   Sentimientos, a menudo basados en nuestras creencias, que nos predisponen para responder de una manera particular a los objetos, las personas y los eventos. (p. 339)

audition/audición   Sentido o acto de oír. (p. 151)

autism/autismo   Trastorno que se manifiesta en la niñez y que está marcado por deficiencias en las comunicaciones y en la interacción social, y por conductas repetitivas e intereses rigurosamente fijados. (p. 78)

automatic processing/procesamiento automático   Codificación inconsciente de información cotidiana, por ejemplo, de espacio, de tiempo y de frecuencia, y de información bien asimilada, tal como el significado de las palabras. (p. 195)

autonomic nervous system/sistema nervioso autónomo   División del sistema nervioso periférico que controla las glándulas y los músculos de los órganos internos (tales como el corazón). Su subdivisión simpática estimula y su subdivisión parasimpática relaja. (p. 34)

availability heuristic/heurística de disponibilidad   Acto de estimar la probabilidad de un evento, basándose en su disponibilidad en la memoria. Si un evento viene prontamente a la mente (quizás debido a su intensidad), presumimos que es un evento común. (p. 222)

aversive conditioning/condicionamiento aversivo   Tipo de contra-condicionamiento que asocia un estado desagradable (por ejemplo, náuseas) con una conducta no deseada (tal como beber alcohol). (p. 415)

axons/axones   Prolongaciones de las neuronas que transmiten mensajes a otras neuronas o células. (p. 30)

B

babbling stage/fase balbuciente   Fase del desarrollo del lenguaje que se da aproximadamente a los 4 meses de edad, y en la que el bebé espontáneamente emite diversos sonidos que al principio no se relacionan con el lenguaje que se usa en casa. (p. 230)

barbiturates/barbitúricos   Medicamentos que deprimen la actividad del sistema nervioso central, reduciendo la ansiedad pero afectando la memoria y el discernimiento. (p. 383)

basal metabolic rate/tasa de metabolismo basal   Cantidad de energía producida por el organismo en reposo absoluto. (p. 259)

basic trust/confianza básica   Según Erik Erikson, una percepción de que el mundo es predecible y fiable; se dice que se forma durante la primera infancia a través de experiencias apropiadas con cuidadores que responden con sensibilidad. (p. 83)

behavior therapy/terapia del comportamiento   Enfoque terapéutico que aplica los principios de aprendizaje para lograr la eliminación de comportamientos no deseados. (p. 414)

behaviorism/conductismo   Posición de que la psicología (1) debe ser una ciencia objetiva que (2) estudia el comportamiento sin referencia a los procesos mentales. Hoy, la mayoría de los psicólogos que realizan concuerdan con (1) pero no con (2). (pp. 3, 183)

belief perseverance/perseverancia en las creencias   Empeño en insistir en las creencias al tiempo que se hace caso omiso de las pruebas que las desacreditan. (p. 223)

binge-eating disorder/trastorno alimentario compulsivo   Ingestión excesiva de alimentos, seguida de angustia, disgusto o culpa, pero sin las purgas, el ayuno o los ejercicios físicos excesivos que caracterizan a la bulimia nerviosa. (p. 400)

binocular cue/clave binocular   Señal de profundidad, por ejemplo, la disparidad retiniana, para la que se requiere el uso de ambos ojos. (p. 147)

biological constraints/límites biológicos   Tendencias biológicas evolucionadas que predisponen la conducta y el aprendizaje por parte de los animales. Por lo tanto, ciertas conductas son más fáciles de aprender por ciertos animales que por otros. (p. 182)

biological psychology/psicología biológica   Especialidad de la psicología que estudia la relación entre la biología y el comportamiento. (p. 30)

biomedical therapy/terapia biomédica   Procedimientos o medicamentos recetados que actúan directamente sobre la fisiología de la persona. (p. 410)

biopsychosocial approach/enfoque biopsicosocial   Enfoque que integra diversos conceptos complementarios en los que se combinan perspectivas biológicas, psicológicas y socioculturales. (p. 6)

bipolar disorder/trastorno bipolar   Trastorno del estado de ánimo en el que la persona alterna entre la desesperanza y el letargo de la depresión y el estado eufórico de la manía. (Anteriormente llamado *trastorno maníaco-depresivo*). (p. 390)

blind spot/punto ciego   Punto en el cual el nervio óptico sale del ojo; esta parte de la retina es "ciega" porque carece de células receptoras. (p. 141)

bottom-up proessing/procesamiento de abajo hacia arriba   Análisis que comienza con los receptores sensoriales y marcha hacia el cerebro y su integración de la información sensorial. (p. 134)

brainstem/tronco encefálico   Parte más antigua y foco central del cerebro, empezando donde la médula espinal se inflama al entrar en el cráneo; el tronco encefálico es responsable por las funciones automáticas de supervivencia. (p. 37)

Broca's area/área de Broca   Parte del lóbulo frontal del cerebro, generalmente en el hemisferio izquierdo, que dirige los movimientos musculares relacionados con el habla y que controla la expresión del lenguaje. (p. 232)

bulimia nervosa/bulimia nerviosa   Trastorno alimentario que se caracteriza por episodios de ingestión excesiva de alimentos (generalmente de alto contenido calórico) seguidos de purgas (vómito o uso de laxantes), ayuno o ejercicios físicos excesivos. (p. 400)

bystander effect/efecto espectador   Tendencia que tienen las personas a no brindar ayuda si hay otras personas presentes. (p. 364)

C

Cannon-Bard theory/teoría de Cannon-Bard   Teoría de que un estímulo que despierta emociones simultáneamente puede provocar (1) respuestas fisiológicas y (2) la experiencia subjetiva de la emoción. (p. 270)

case study/caso de estudio   Técnica de observación en la cual se estudia a individuo o grupo a profundidad con la esperanza de revelar principios universales. (p. 14)

central nervous system (CNS)/sistema nervioso central (SNC)   El cerebro y la médula espinal. (p. 33)

cerebellum/cerebelo   Es el "cerebro pequeño" y está unido a la parte posterior del tronco encefálico. Sus funciones incluyen el procesamiento de la información sensorial y la coordinación de los movimientos y el equilibrio. (p. 40)

cerebral cortex/corteza cerebral Capa delgada de neuronas conectadas entre sí, que forman los hemisferios cerebrales; es el principal centro de control y procesamiento de información del organismo. (p. 42)

change blindness/ceguera al cambio No darse cuenta de cambios en el entorno. (p. 52)

chromosomes/cromosomas Estructuras semejantes a hilos conformadas de moléculas de ADN que contienen los genes. (p. 68)

chunking/Agrupamiento Organizar artículos en unidades conocidas y manejables; a menudo ocurre automáticamente. (p. 197)

circadian rhythm/ritmo circadiano Reloj biológico; ritmos periódicos del organismo (por ejemplo, el de temperatura y estado de vigilia) que ocurren en ciclos de 24 horas. (p. 52)

classical conditioning/condicionamiento clásico Tipo de aprendizaje en el cual aprendemos a relacionar dos o más estímulos y a anticipar sucesos. (p. 169)

client-centered therapy/terapia centrada en el cliente Tipo de terapia humanista creada por Carl Rogers, en la cual el terapeuta se vale de técnicas tales como escuchar activamente dentro de un entorno genuino, con aceptación y empatía, para facilitar el crecimiento personal del cliente. (También se denomina *terapia centrada en la persona*). (p. 413)

cochlea/cóclea Estructura tubular en forma de espiral, ósea y rellena de líquido que se halla en el oído interno; las ondas sonoras que pasan por el líquido coclear desencadenan impulsos nerviosos. (p. 152)

cochlear implant/implante coclear Dispositivo que convierte sonidos en señales eléctricas que estimulan el nervio auditivo mediante electrodos enhebrados en la cóclea. (p. 153)

cognition/cognición Todas las actividades mentales asociadas con pensar, saber, recordar y comunicar. (pp. 75, 220)

cognitive-behavioral therapy/terapia cognitivo-conductual Terapia integrada muy difundida que combina la terapia cognitiva (que cambia los pensamientos contraproducentes) con la terapia conductual (que cambia la conducta). (p. 418)

cognitive dissonance theory/teoría de disonancia cognitiva Teoría según la cual llevamos a cabo una acción con el propósito de reducir la incomodidad (disonancia) que sentimos cuando tenemos dos pensamientos (cogniciones) contradictorios. Por ejemplo, cuando tenemos consciencia de que nuestras actitudes y nuestras acciones entran en conflicto, cambiamos nuestra actitud para sentirnos más cómodos. (p. 341)

cognitive learning/aprendizaje cognitivo Adquisición de información mental, ya sea a partir de la observación de acontecimientos, la observación de otras personas o a través del lenguaje. (p. 168)

cognitive map/mapa cognitivo Imagen mental del trazado de nuestro entorno. (p. 184)

cognitive neuroscience/neurociencia cognitiva Estudio interdisciplinario de las conexiones entre la actividad mental (que incluye la percepción, el pensamiento, la memoria y el lenguaje). (p. 3)

cognitive therapy/terapia cognitiva Enfoque terapéutico en que se les enseña a los pacientes nuevas formas de pensar de un modo más adaptativo. Se basa en el supuesto de que los pensamientos intervienen entre los eventos y nuestras reacciones emocionales. (p. 417)

collectivism/colectivismo Modo de dar prioridad a las metas del grupo (a menudo de la familia extendida o el grupo de trabajo) y de definir la identidad personal según lo que dicta el grupo. (p. 332)

color constancy/constancia de color Percibir que objetos conocidos tienen un color constante, incluso si cambios en la iluminación modifican las longitudes de onda que el objeto refleja. (p. 149)

companionate love/amor compañero Apego afectuoso profundo que sentimos por aquéllos con quienes nuestras vidas se entrelazan. (p. 362)

concept/concepto Agrupamiento mental de objetos, eventos, ideas y personas que tienen un parecido. (p. 220)

concrete operational stage/etapa del pensamiento lógico-concreto En la teoría de Piaget, la fase del desarrollo cognitivo (desde aproximadamente los 6 o 7 años hasta los 11 años de edad) durante la cual los niños adquieren las operaciones mentales que les permiten pensar lógicamente sobre eventos concretos. (p. 79)

conditioned reinforcer/reforzador condicionado (También denominado *reforzador secundario*) evento que adquiere su poder de reforzamiento mediante su vínculo con el reforzador primario. (p. 176)

conditioned response (CR)/respuesta condicionada (RC) En el condicionamiento clásico, la respuesta aprendida a un estímulo previamente neutral (pero ahora condicionado). (p. 170)

conditioned stimulus (CS)/estímulo condicionado (EC) En el condicionamiento clásico, un estímulo originalmente intrascendente que, después de verse asociado con un estímulo incondicionado (EI) produce una respuesta condicionada. (p. 170)

conduction hearing loss/pérdida de la audición por conducción Sordera atribuible a daños en el sistema mecánico que conduce ondas sonoras a la cóclea. (p. 153)

cones/conos Células receptoras que se concentran cerca del centro de la retina; con la luz del día o en lugares bien iluminados, los conos detectan detalles finos y producen las sensaciones del color. (p. 141)

confirmation bias/sesgo confirmatorio Tendencia a buscar información que confirme nuestras ideas preconcebidas y de hacer caso omiso o de distorsionar las pruebas que las contradigan. (p. 221)

conflict/conflicto Incompatibilidad percibida de acciones, metas o ideas. (p. 365)

conformity/conformidad Tendencia a ajustar el comportamiento o la forma de pensar hasta hacerlos coincidir con las normas que tiene un grupo. (p. 342)

confounding variable/variable de confusión En un experimento, factor que no sea la variable independiente que podría producir un efecto. (p. 19)

consciousness/conciencia Percepción de nosotros mismos y de nuestro entorno. (p. 50)

conservation/conservación Principio (que para Piaget forma parte del razonamiento operacional concreto) de que ciertas propiedades (p. ej., masa, volumen y número) no varían pese a modificaciones en la forma de los objetos. (p. 77)

continuous reinforcement/ reforzamiento continuo Reforzar la respuesta deseada cada vez que ocurre. (p. 177)

control group/grupo control En un experimento, el grupo de participantes que *no* se expone al tratamiento; el grupo de control sirve de comparación para evaluar el efecto del tratamiento en el grupo sometido al tratamiento. (p. 18)

convergent thinking/razonamiento convergente Reduce las opciones disponibles para resolver el problema a fin de determinar cuál es la mejor solución. (p. 226)

coping/mecanismos de manejo Aminoramiento de las tensiones con métodos emocionales, cognitivos o conductuales. (p. 291)

coronary heart disease/enfermedad coronaria Obstrucción de los vasos que nutren el músculo cardíaco; causa principal de muerte en Estados Unidos y muchos otros países. (p. 289)

corto plazo. Además, a largo plazo, perjudica las neuronas que producen la serotonina, y afecta el ánimo y el proceso de cognición. (p. 385)

EEG (electroencephalogram)/(EEG) electroencefalograma Aparato que emplea electrodos colocados sobre el cuero cabelludo, que produce un registro de las ondas de actividad eléctrica que circulan por la superficie del cerebro. (El trazado de dichas ondas cerebrales es un *electroencefalograma*). (p. 38)

effortful processing/procesamiento con esfuerzo Codificación que precisa atención y esfuerzo conscientes. (p. 195)

ego/ego Parte consciente y ejecutiva de la personalidad que, según Freud, media entre las exigencias del id, el superego y la realidad. El ego opera según el *principio de realidad,* satisfaciendo los deseos del id en formas que de manera realista le brindarán placer en lugar de dolor. (p. 313)

egocentrism/egocentrismo Según la teoría de Piaget, la dificultad de los niños en la etapa preoperacional de aceptar el punto de vista ajeno. (p. 78)

electroconvulsive therapy (ECT)/terapia electroconvulsiva (TEC) Terapia biomédica para pacientes gravemente deprimidos en la que se envía una corriente eléctrica de corta duración a través del cerebro de un paciente anestesiado. (p. 427)

embodied cognition/cognición incorporada La influencia de sensaciones del organismo, y otros estados de preferencias y juicios cognitivos. (p. 161)

embryo/embrión Etapa de desarrollo del organismo humano a partir de las dos semanas después de fertilización hasta el segundo mes. (p. 70)

emerging adulthood/madurez emergente Etapa que se extiende desde los 18 hasta alrededor de los 25 años, durante la cual muchas personas en los países occidentales ya no son adolescentes pero aún no han alcanzado la independencia plena de un adulto. (p. 92)

emotion/emoción Reacción que involucra a todo el organismo e incluye (1) excitación fisiológica, (2) comportamientos expresivos y (3) experiencia consciente. (p. 269)

emotional intelligence/inteligencia emocional Habilidad de percibir, entender, administrar y hacer uso de las emociones. (p. 238)

emotion-focused coping/superación con enfoque en las emociones Medidas para sobrellevar las tensiones enfocándose en aliviar o hacer caso omiso de una situación estresante y atender las necesidades emocionales relacionadas con nuestra reacción al estrés. (p. 291)

encoding/codificación El proceso de ingresar información al sistema de memoria. (p. 194)

endocrine system/sistema endocrino Sistema "lento" de comunicación química del cuerpo; conjunto de glándulas que secretan hormonas al torrente sanguíneo. (p. 36)

endorphins/endorfinas "Morfina adentro"; neurotransmisores naturales similares a los opiáceos que están asociados con el control del dolor y con el placer. (p. 32)

environment/entorno Toda influencia externa, desde la alimentación prenatal hasta el apoyo social que se recibe más adelante en la vida. (p. 69)

epigenetics/epigenética estudio de la influencia ambiental sobre la expresión de los genes que ocurre sin un cambio de ADN. (p. 70)

equity/equidad Condición en la cual la persona recibe de manera proporcional lo que aporte a una relación. (p. 362)

erectile disorder/trastorno eréctil Incapacidad de desarrollar o mantener una erección debido a un flujo insuficiente de sangre al pene. (p. 117)

estrogens/estrógenos Hormonas sexuales secretadas en mayor cantidad en la mujer que en el hombre. En las hembras de los animales mamíferos, los niveles de estrógeno alcanzan su nivel máximo durante la ovulación, facilitando la receptividad sexual. (p. 115)

evidence-based practice/práctica basada en la evidencia toma de decisiones clínicas que integra lo mejor de las investigaciones disponibles con la pericia clínica y las características y preferencias del paciente. (p. 422)

evolutionary psychology/psicología evolutiva Estudio de la evolución del comportamiento y la mente, que emplea los principios de la selección natural para una adaptación efectiva. (p. 125)

experiment/experimento Método de investigación en el cual el investigador manipula uno o más factores (variables independientes) para observar su efecto en un comportamiento o proceso mental (variable dependiente). (p. 17)

experimental group/grupo experimental Sujetos de un experimento que están expuestos al tratamiento, o sea, a una versión de la variable independiente. (p. 18)

explicit memory/memoria explícita Memoria de hechos y vivencias personales que tenemos la capacidad de recuperar conscientemente. (p. 195)

exposure therapies/terapias de exposición Técnicas conductuales, como la *desensibilización sistemática* y la *terapia de exposición a una realidad virtual* para tratar la ansiedad exponiendo a la persona (en situaciones imaginarias o reales) a las cosas que teme y evita. (p. 414)

external locus of control/centro de control externo Impresión de que nuestro destino está determinado por el azar o por fuerzas que están más allá de nuestro control. (p. 292)

extinction/extinción Según el condicionamiento clásico, disminución de una respuesta condicionada cuando un estímulo incondicionado no sigue a un estímulo condicionado. (En el condicionamiento operante, disminución de una respuesta cuando deja de ser reforzada). (p. 171)

extrasensory perception (ESP)/percepción extrasensorial (PES) La afirmación polémica de que la percepción puede ocurrir aislada de la recepción sensorial, como a través de la *telepatía, clarividencia y premoniciones.* (p. 161)

extrinsic motivation/motivación extrínseca Deseo de realizar un comportamiento para obtener una recompensa o evitar el castigo. (p. 184)

F

facial feedback effect/efecto de reacción facial Tendencia de los músculos faciales a provocar sentimientos correspondientes como el miedo, el enojo o la felicidad. (p. 278)

factor/factor Conjunto de tendencias del comportamiento que ocurren al mismo tiempo. (p. 322)

family therapy/terapia de familia Tipo de terapia que trata a la familia como sistema y considera que los comportamientos no deseados de una persona son influenciados por otros miembros de la familia o están dirigidos hacia ellos. (p. 419)

feature detectors/detectores específicos Células nerviosas del cerebro que responden a características específicas de un estímulo, por ejemplo, a los bordes, las líneas y los ángulos. (p. 142)

feel-good, do-good phenomenon/fenómeno de sentirse bien y hacer el bien Tendencia a ayudar a los demás cuando estamos de buen humor. (p. 301)

female orgasmic disorder/trastorno orgásmico Sentirse angustiada debido a nunca haber vivido un orgasmo o a tenerlos infrecuentemente. (p. 117)

fetal alcohol syndrome (FAS)/síndrome de alcoholismo fetal (SAF) Anomalías físicas y cognitivas en los niños causadas por la intensa ingestión de alcohol de la madre durante el embarazo. En casos agudos, los síntomas incluyen la cabeza demasiado pequeña y desproporciones faciales observables. (p. 71)

fetus/feto   Organismo humano en vías de desarrollo a partir de las 9 semanas de concepción hasta el nacimiento. (p. 71)

fight-or-flight/respuesta de luchar o huir   Reacción en una emergencia que incluye actividad del sistema nervioso simpático y genera energía y actividad dirigidas a atacar o escapar ante una amenaza. (p. 285)

figure-ground/figura-trasfondo   Organización del campo visual en objetos (las *figuras*) que se distinguen de sus entornos (los *trasfondos*). (p. 146)

fixation/obsesión   (1) Según Freud, un foco persistente de energías en busca del placer en una etapa psicosexual anterior en la que los conflictos todavía no estaban resueltos. (p. 314) (2) Incapacidad de ver un problema desde una perspectiva nueva; un impedimento para resolver problemas. (p. 221)

fixed-interval schedule/cronograma de intervalo fijo   Según el condicionamiento operante, cronograma de reforzamiento que refuerza la respuesta solo después de haber transcurrido un tiempo específico. (p. 177)

fixed-ratio schedule/cronograma de proporción fija   Según el condicionamiento operante, cronograma de reforzamiento que refuerza la respuesta solo después de darse un número específico de respuestas. (p. 177)

flashbulb memory/memoria de flash   Memoria clara de un momento o evento emocionalmente significativo. (p. 201)

flow/fluidez   Estado de participación y concentración totales, con disminución de la conciencia de uno mismo y del tiempo, que ocurre cuando aprovechamos nuestras destrezas al máximo. (p. B-1)

fluid intelligence/inteligencia fluida   Capacidad que tenemos de razonar de manera rápida y abstracta; tiende a disminuir en la vejez. (p. 246)

fMRI (functional magnetic resonance imaging)/(RMF) resonancia magnética funcional   Técnica para observar la circulación de la sangre, y por lo tanto, la actividad cerebral. Consiste en comparar imágenes de resonancia magnética sucesivas. Las imágenes de resonancia magnética funcional muestran el funcionamiento del cerebro. (p. 38)

foot-in-the-door phenomenon/fenómeno de pie en la puerta   Tendencia de la gente que ha accedido a algo pequeño en primer lugar, a después satisfacer una exigencia de mayor envergadura. (p. 340)

formal operational stage/período operacional formal   En la teoría de Piaget, el período en el desarrollo cognitivo (normalmente empieza a los 12 años) durante el que la persona empieza a pensar lógicamente sobre conceptos abstractos. (p. 79)

framing/encuadre   Forma en que se presenta un asunto; el encuadre puede influenciar considerablemente las decisiones y las opiniones. (p. 223)

fraternal twins (*dizygotic twins*)**/gemelos** (*gemelos dizigóticos*)   Se desarrollan de dos óvulos fecundados. Genéticamente no están más cercanos que los hermanos y hermanas; pero comparten un entorno prenatal. (p. 71)

free association/asociación libre   En psicoanálisis, método de explorar el inconsciente en el que la persona se relaja y dice lo primero que le viene a la mente, no importa cuán poco importante o incómodo. (p. 312)

frequency/frecuencia   Número de ondas completas que pasan un punto en un tiempo dado (por ejemplo, por segundo). (p. 151)

frontal lobes/lóbulos frontales   Porción de la corteza cerebral que se halla inmediatamente detrás de la frente; se relaciona con el habla y los movimientos musculares y con la planificación y la formación de opiniones. (p. 41)

frustration-aggression principle/principio de frustración-agresión   Principio de que la frustración —el bloqueo de un intento para lograr alguna meta— crea ira, la cual puede generar agresión. (p. 355)

fundamental attribution error/error de atribución fundamental   Tendencia de los observadores, cuando analizan el comportamiento ajeno, a sobrestimar el impacto de las características personales y subestimar el impacto de la situación. (p. 338)

G

gender/género   En psicología, las características biológicas y sociales por las cuales la sociedad define *varón y mujer*. (p. 108)

gender identity/identidad de género   Nuestra sensación personal de ser varón o mujer. (p. 113)

gender role/papel del género   Conjunto de expectativas de cómo las mujeres y los hombres deben comportarse. (p. 113)

gender typing/tipificación por género   La adquisición de un papel masculino o femenino tradicional. (p. 114)

general adaptation syndrome (GAS)/síndrome de adaptación general   Término usado por Selye para referirse a la respuesta adaptiva del cuerpo al estrés que se da en tres etapas: alarma, resistencia, y agotamiento. (p. 285)

general intelligence (g)/factor g de inteligencia general   Factor de inteligencia general que según Spearman y otros subyace habilidades mentales específicas y es, por tanto, cuantificado por cada función en una prueba de inteligencia. (p. 236)

generalization/generalización   Según el condicionamiento clásico, tendencia posterior al condicionamiento, de responder de manera similar a los estímulos que se parecen al estímulo condicionado. (p. 172)

generalized anxiety disorder/trastorno de ansiedad generalizado   Trastorno de ansiedad en el cual la persona está constantemente tensa, asustada y con el sistema nervioso autónomo activado. (p. 376)

genes/genes   Unidades bioquímicas de la herencia que forman los cromosomas. Segmentos de ADN. (p. 68)

genome/genoma   Instrucciones completas para crear un organismo; consiste en todo el material genético en los cromosomas de ese organismo. (p. 68)

gestalt/Gestalt   Un todo organizado. Los psicólogos de la Gestalt enfatizan nuestra tendencia a integrar segmentos de información en todos significativos. (p. 145)

glial cells (glía)/células glíales   Células del sistema nervioso que apoya, alimentan y protegen a las neuronas; también pueden desempeñar un papel en el aprendizaje, el razonamiento y la memoria. (p. 30)

glucose/glucosa   Forma de azúcar que circula en la sangre y es la mayor fuente de energía para los tejidos del cuerpo. Cuando su nivel está bajo, sentimos hambre. (p. 258)

grammar/gramática   En un lenguaje específico, sistema de reglas que nos permite comunicarnos y entendernos con otros. (p. 231)

group polarization/efecto de polarización de grupo   Solidificación y fortalecimiento de las posiciones imperantes en un grupo mediante diálogos en el grupo. (p. 348)

group therapy/terapia de grupo   Tratamiento que se realiza con grupos en lugar de con personas individuales, que genera beneficios de la interacción del grupo. (p. 419)

grouping/agrupamiento   Tendencia de percepción que clasifica los estímulos en grupos que tienen sentido. (p. 146)

groupthink/pensamiento colectivo   Modo de pensar que ocurre cuando el deseo de armonía en un grupo que toma de decisiones colectivas anula la evaluación objetiva de las alternativas. (p. 349)

H

hallucinations/alucinaciones   Vivencia sensorial falsa, por ejemplo, cuando una persona oye algo sin haber ningún estímulo auditivo externo. (p. 45)

hallucinogens/alucinógenos   Fármacos psicodélicos ("que se manifiestan en la mente"), como el LSD, que distorsionan las percepciones y evocan imágenes sensoriales sin que intervenga ningún estímulo sensorial. (p. 385)

heredity/herencia   Transferencia genética de características, de los padres a los hijos. (p. 68)

heritability/heredabilidad   La porción de variación entre individuos que le podemos atribuir a los genes. La heredabilidad de un rasgo varía de acuerdo con la población y el medio ambiente. (p. 244).

heuristics/heurística   Estrategias de pensamiento sencilla que a menudo nos permite formar juicios y resolver problemas de manera eficiente. Por lo general es más expedita que utilizar *algoritmos*; pero también pueden conducir a más errores. (p. 200)

hierarchy of needs/jerarquía de necesidades   Pirámide de Maslow de las necesidades humanas. En la base de la pirámide están las necesidades fisiológicas, que deben satisfacerse antes que las necesidades de seguridad personal que son de más alto nivel. Las necesidades psicológicas se activan por último, después de satisfacer las anteriores. (pp. 257, 319)

hindsight bias/distorsión retrospectiva   Tendencia a creer después de saber un resultado, que uno lo habría previsto. (También conocido como el *fenómeno de ya yo lo sabía*). (p. 9)

hippocampus/hipocampo   Centro neuronal ubicado en el sistema límbico; ayuda a procesar recuerdos explícitos para almacenarlos de manera accesible. (p. 199)

homeostasis/homeostasis   Tendencia a mantener un estado interno constante o equilibrado; la regulación de todos los aspectos de la química del organismo, tal como los niveles de glucosa, alrededor de un nivel dado. (p. 256)

hormones/hormonas   Mensajeros químicos producidos por las glándulas endocrinas, que circulan por la sangre y tienen efecto en los tejidos del cuerpo. (p. 36)

hue/tono   Dimensión del color determinada por la longitud de la onda de luz; lo que conocemos como los nombres de los colores: *azul, verde,* etc. (p. 140)

human factors psychology/psicología de factores humanos   Subdivisión de la psicología I/O que explora la interacción entre las personas y las máquinas, y las maneras de hacer que las máquinas y los entornos físicos sean más seguros y fáciles de utilizar. (p. B-2)

humanistic psychology/psicología humanista   Perspectiva que enfatiza el potencial de crecimiento de las personas saludables y la capacidad de crecimiento personal de la persona. (p. 3)

hypnosis/hipnosis   Interacción social en la cual una persona (el sujeto) responde a la sugestión de otra persona (el hipnotizador) de que ciertas percepciones, sentimientos, pensamientos o comportamientos se producirán espontáneamente. (p. 156)

hypothalamus/hipotálamo   Estructura neuronal localizada bajo (hipo) del tálamo; regula actividades como comer, beber, y la temperatura del cuerpo; dirige varias actividades de mantenimiento (comer, beber, temperatura corporal); ayuda a dirigir el sistema endocrino a través de la glándula pituitaria, y está conectado a las emociones y las recompensas. (p. 41)

hypothesis/hipótesis   Predicción comprobable, a menudo implicada por una teoría. (p. 12)

I

id/id   Depósito de energía psíquica inconsciente que, según Freud, aspira a satisfacer los impulsos sexuales y agresivos esenciales. El id funciona según el *principio de placer,* exigiendo satisfacción inmediata. (p. 313)

identical twins (*monozygotic twins*)/gemelos (*gemelos monozigóticos*)   Se desarrollan de un sólo óvulo fertilizado que se subdivide en dos para así crear dos organismos genéticamente idénticos. (p. 71)

identification/identificación   Proceso en el que, según Freud, los niños incorporan los valores de sus padres en sus súper-egos en vías de desarrollo. (p. 314)

identity/identidad   Sentido de autoreconocimiento; según Erikson, la tarea del adolescente consiste en solidificar el sentido de sí mismo probando e integrando una variedad de papeles. (p. 89)

implicit memory/memoria implícita   Retención de destrezas aprendidas o asociaciones condicionadas clásicas, sin tener consciencia del aprendizaje. También se le dice *memoria no declarativa*). (p. 195)

inattentional blindness/ceguera por falta de atención   No ver los objetos visibles cuando nuestra atención se dirige a otra parte. (p. 51)

incentive/incentivo   Estímulo positivo o negativo del entorno que motiva el comportamiento. (p. 256)

independent variable/variable independiente   Factor experimental que se manipula; la variable cuyo efecto es el objeto de estudio. (p. 19)

individualism/individualismo   Darle atención prioritaria a las metas personales antes que a las metas del grupo, y definir la identidad mediante las cualidades personales y no con la pertenencia al grupo. (p. 331)

industrial-organizational (I/O) psychology/psicología industrial y organizacional   Aplicación de conceptos y métodos psicológicos al comportamiento humano en el entorno laboral. (p. B-2)

informed consent/autorización informada   Darles a las personas información suficiente sobre un estudio para permitirles decidir si desean o no participar. (p. 22)

ingroup/endogrupo   "Nosotros". Personas con quienes uno comparte una identidad común. (p. 352)

ingroup bias/estereotipo de grupo propio   Tendencia a favorecer al grupo al que se pertenece. (p. 352)

insight/agudeza   Entendimiento repentino de cómo se resuelve un problema; contrasta con las soluciones basadas en estrategias. (p. 220)

insight therapies/tratamientos con agudeza   Terapias que aspiran a mejorar el funcionamiento psicológico mediante el aumento en la conciencia de la persona de los motivos y las defensas subyacentes. (p. 412)

insomnia/insomnio   Dificultades recurrentes para dormirse y conciliar el sueño. (p. 58)

intellectual disability/discapacidad intelectual   Estado de capacidad mental limitada, que se expresa a través de una puntuación de inteligencia de 70 o menos y de la dificultad para adaptarse a las exigencias de la vida. (Anteriormente conocida como *retardo mental*.) (p. 242)

intelligence/inteligencia   Calidad mental que consiste en la habilidad de aprender de las experiencias, de resolver problemas y de utilizar el conocimiento para adaptarse a situaciones nuevas. (p. 236)

intelligence quotient (IQ)/coeficiente intelectual (CI)   Cifra definida originalmente como la edad mental (*em*) dividida entre la edad cronológica (*ec*) y el resultado multiplicado por 100 (por lo tanto, CI = *em*/*ec* × 100). En las pruebas actuales de inteligencia, al desempeño promedio para una edad dada se le asigna un puntaje de 100. (p. 239)

intelligence test/prueba de inteligencia   Método para evaluar las aptitudes mentales de la persona y compararlas con las de otras personas utilizando puntajes numéricos. (p. 239)

intensity/intensidad   Cantidad de energía en una onda de luz o en una onda sonora que percibimos como brillo o volumen. La intensidad la determina la amplitud de la onda. (p. 140)

interaction//interacción   Interacción que se produce cuando el efecto de un factor (por ejemplo, el entorno) depende de otro factor (por ejemplo, la herencia). (p. 69)

internal locus of control/foco de control interno   Impresión de que controlamos nuestro propio destino. (p. 292)

interneuron/interneurona   Neuronas dentro del cerebro y la espinal dorsal. Se comunican internamente y procesan la información entre los estímulos sensoriales y las respuestas motoras. (p. 33)

interpretation/interpretación   En psicoanálisis, las observaciones del analista con relación al significado de los sueños, las resistencias, y otras conductas y eventos significativos, a fin de promover la sagacidad. (p. 411)

intersex/intersexo   Que cuenta con características sexuales biológicas de ambos sexos. (p. 112)

intimacy/intimidad   Según la teoría de Erikson, capacidad de formar relaciones cercanas y afectivas; función primordial del desarrollo en la adolescencia y al comienzo de la vida adulta. (p. 90)

intrinsic motivation/motivación intrínseca   Deseo de comportarse de una manera precisamente por el comportamiento en sí. (p. 184)

intuition/intuición   sentimiento o pensamiento automático e inmediato, que no precisa esfuerzo alguno, que se contrasta con el razonamiento explícito y consciente. (p. 221)

J

James-Lange theory/teoría de James-Lange   Teoría que expone que nuestra experiencia emocional es la conciencia que tenemos de nuestras respuestas fisiológicas a los estímulos que despiertan emociones. (p. 269)

just-world phenomenon/hipótesis del "mundo justo"   Tendencia a creer que el mundo es justo y que por tanto, las personas obtienen lo que se merecen y se merecen lo que obtienen. (p. 352)

K

kinesthesia/cinestesia   Sistema que siente la posición y el movimiento de las partes individuales de cuerpo. (p. 159)

L

language/lenguaje   Palabras habladas, escritas o en señas y las maneras que se combinan para comunicar significado. (p. 229)

latent content/contenido latente   Según Freud, significado subyacente de un sueño. (p. 60)

latent learning/aprendizaje latente   Aprendizaje que no es aparente sino hasta que hay un incentivo para demostrarlo. (p. 184)

law of effect/ley de efecto   Principio propuesto por Thorndike en el que se propone que las conductas seguidas por consecuencias favorables se tornan más comunes, mientras que las conductas seguidas por consecuencias desfavorables se ven con menos frecuencia. (p. 174)

learned helplessness/indefensión aprendida   Desesperación y resignación pasiva que un animal o persona desarrollan cuando son incapaces de evitar repetidos eventos de aversión. (p. 291)

learning/aprendizaje   Proceso de adquirir, mediante la experiencia información o conductas nuevas y relativamente permanentes. (p. 168)

limbic system/sistema límbico   Sistema de neuronas (incluye el *hipocampo, la amígdala* y el *hipotálamo*), ubicado debajo de los hemisferios cerebrales; se lo asocia con las emociones y los impulsos. (p. 40)

lobotomy/lobotomía   Procedimiento psicoquirúrgico que otrora se usó para calmar a pacientes emocionalmente incontrolables o violentos. En el procedimiento se cortaban los nervios entre los lóbulos frontales y los centros en el interior del cerebro que controlan las emociones. (p. 429)

longitudingal study/estudio longitudinal   Investigación en la que las mismas personas se estudian una y otra vez durante un lapso de tiempo prolongado. (pp. 245, A-7)

long-term memory/memoria a largo plazo   El almacenaje relativamente permanente e ilimitado del sistema de la memoria. Incluye los conocimientos, las habilidades y las experiencias. (p. 194)

long-term potentiation (LTP)/potenciación a largo plazo   Aumento en la eficacia de una sinapsis para transmitir impulsos. Se considera la base neuronal del aprendizaje y la memoria. (p. 201)

LSD/ácido lisérgico   Poderoso fármaco alucinógeno; también se conoce como *ácido* (*ácido lisérgico y dietilamina*). (p. 386)

lymphocytes/linfocitos   Los dos tipos de glóbulos blancos que forman parte del sistema inmunitario del organismo: los *linfocitos B* liberan anticuerpos que combaten las infecciones bacterianas; los *linfocitos T* atacan células cancerosas, virus y substancias extrañas en el organismo. (p. 287)

M

major depressive disorder/trastorno depresivo mayor   Trastorno del estado de ánimo en el cual una persona —sin padecer una afección médica y sin usar drogas— pasa dos o más semanas con cinco o más síntomas, de los cuales al menos uno tiene que ser ya sea (1) un estado de ánimo deprimido o (2) la pérdida de interés o placer. (p. 389)

mania/manía   Trastorno del estado de ánimo marcado por un estado de hiperactividad, desenfreno y optimismo. (p. 390)

manifest content/contenido manifiesto   Según Freud, trama del sueño que se recuerda al despertarse. (p. 60)

maturation/maduración   Procesos de crecimiento biológico que casi siempre conducen a cambios ordenados en el comportamiento y son independientes de la experiencia. (p. 73)

mean/promedio   Promedio aritmético de una distribución que se obtiene sumando los puntajes y luego dividiendo por el número de puntajes. (p. A-2)

median/media   Puntaje central en una distribución; la mitad de los puntajes se encuentran por encima y la mitad se encuentran por dejado de la media. (p. A-2)

medical model/modelo médico   Concepto que afirma que las enfermedades, en este caso los trastornos psicológicos, tienen causas físicas que se pueden *diagnosticar, tratar* y, en la mayoría de los casos, *curar,* generalmente por medio de *tratamientos* que se llevan a cabo en un *hospital.* (p. 372)

medulla/médula   Base del tronco encefálico; controla la frecuencia cardíaca y la respiración. (p. 39)

memory/memoria   Aprender de manera persistente a través del tiempo usando la codificación, el almacenaje y la recuperación de la información. (p. 194)

memory trace/rastro de memoria   Cambios físicos duraderos que ocurren en el cerebro al formarse un recuerdo. (p. 207)

menarche/menarquia   Primer período menstrual. (p. 111)

menopause/menopausia   Cesación de la menstruación. En el uso cotidiano, el término se refiere a la transición biológica que experimenta la mujer desde antes hasta después de acabar de menstruar. (p. 95)

mental age/edad mental   Medida de desempeño en la prueba de inteligencia diseñada por Binet. La edad cronológica que característicamente corresponde a un nivel dado de desempeño. Por ende, se dice que un niño que se desempeña como una persona normal de 8 años, tiene una edad mental de 8 años. (p. 239)

mere exposure effect/efecto de la mera exposición   Fenómeno que sostiene que la exposición repetida a estímulos novedosos aumenta la atracción a tales estímulos. (p. 359)

methamphetamine/metanfetamina   Fármaco poderosamente adictivo que estimula el sistema nervioso central con funciones corporales aceleradas y los cambios correspondientes de la energía y el estado de ánimo. Con el tiempo, parece reducir los niveles de referencia de dopamina. (p. 385)

mindfulness meditation/meditación a conciencia plena   Prestarles atención a las vivencias vigentes de una manera que las acepta y no es moralizante. (p. 298)

Minnesota Multiphasic Personality Inventory (MMPI)/Inventario de Personalidad Polifacética de Minnesota   La más ampliamente investigada y utilizada de todas las pruebas de personalidad. Se creó originalmente para identificar trastornos emocionales (y todavía se le utiliza con tal fin). Esta prueba se utiliza hoy en día para muchas actividades de preselección. (p. 324)

mirror neuron/neurona espejo   Neurona que se activa cuando llevamos a cabo ciertas acciones y cuando observamos a otros realizando tales acciones. La base neuronal para el aprendizaje por imitación y por observación. (p. 186)

mirror-image perceptions/percepciones idénticas   Opiniones mutuas que generalmente sostienen las personas que discrepan o experimentan conflictos entre sí, como cuando cada parte se ve a sí misma como ética y pacífica, y a la otra parte la ve como malvada y agresiva. (p. 365)

misinformation effect/efecto de información errónea   Recuerdo que se deforma al recibir información engañosa. (p. 210)

mnemonics/nemotécnica   Ayudas para la memoria, sobre todo técnicas que utilizan imágenes brillantes y dispositivos organizacionales. (p. 197)

mode/modo   Puntaje o puntajes que ocurren con mayor frecuencia en una distribución. (p. A-2)

modeling/modelar   Proceso de observar e imitar un comportamiento en particular. (p. 184)

monocular cue/indicación monocular   Señal de profundidad como la interposición y la perspectiva lineal, que puede ser extraída de las imágenes de cada uno de los ojos. (p. 147)

mood disorders/trastornos del estado de ánimo   Trastornos psicológicos caracterizados por extremos de emociones. Ver *trastorno depresivo mayor, manía y trastorno bipolar.* (p. 389)

mood-congruent memory/memoria congruente con el estado de ánimo   Tendencia a recordar experiencias que concuerdan con el buen o mal estado de ánimo que estamos viviendo. (p. 205)

motivation/motivación   Necesidad o deseo que da energía y dirige el comportamiento. (p. 256)

motor cortex/corteza motora   Parte de la corteza cerebral en la parte posterior de los lóbulos frontales. Controla los movimientos voluntarios. (p. 41)

motor neuron/neurona motriz   Neurona que lleva la información del sistema nervioso central hacia los músculos y glándulas. (p. 33)

MRI (magnetic resonance imaging)/resonancia magnética   Técnica que emplea campos magnéticos y ondas de radio para producir imágenes computarizadas de tejidos blandos. Las imágenes de resonancia magnética nos permiten visualizar la anatomía del cerebro. (p. 38)

N

narcolepsy/narcolepsia   Trastorno caracterizado por ataques incontrolables de sueño, en el que a veces el individuo entra directamente en el sueño MOR. (p. 59)

natural selection/selección natural   Principio según el cual, de entre la variedad de rasgos heredados, aquellos que contribuyen al aumento de la reproducción y la supervivencia tienen mayor probabilidad de pasar a las generaciones futuras. (p. 126)

naturalistic observation/observación naturalista   Técnica de observar y registrar la conducta en situaciones reales sin tratar de manipular ni controlar la situación. (p. 14)

nature–nurture issue/debate de naturaleza–crianza   Controversia de antaño acerca del aporte relativo que ejercen los genes y las vivencias en el desarrollo de los rasgos y comportamientos psicológicos. En la ciencia psicológica actual se opina que los rasgos y comportamientos tienen origen en la interrelación entre la naturaleza y la crianza. (p. 7)

near-death experience/experiencia al borde de la muerte   Estado de alteración de la consciencia experimentado por personas que llegan al borde de la muerte, o que parecen morir pero luego retornan a la vida (por ejemplo, cuando se sufre un paro cardíaco). A menudo es similar a las alucinaciones inducidas por los estupefacientes. (p. 386)

negative reinforcement/reforzamiento negativo   Aumento en la expresión de comportamientos mediante la interrupción o reducción de los estímulos negativos tales como un corrientazo. Un reforzamiento negativo es cualquier cosa que, cuando *se elimina* después de una reacción, refuerza la reacción. (*Nota:* el reforzamiento negativo *no significa* castigo). (p. 175)

nerves/nervios   Haces de axones neuronales que forman "cables" de nervios y conectan el sistema nervioso central con los músculos, las glándulas y los órganos sensoriales. (p. 33)

nervous system/sistema nervioso   Veloz red electroquímica de comunicación del cuerpo que consta de todas las células nerviosas de los sistemas nerviosos central y periférico. (p. 33)

neurogenesis/neurogénesis   Formación de neuronas nuevas. (p. 47)

neuron/neurona   Célula nerviosa; el componente básico del sistema nervioso. (p. 30)

neurotransmitters/neurotransmisores   Agentes químicos producidos por las neuronas que atraviesan las sinapsis y transmiten mensajes a otras neuronas o a las células del organismo. (p. 31)

neutral stimulus (NS)/estímulos neutrales (EN)   Según el condicionamiento clásico, un estímulo que no produce respuesta antes del condicionamiento. (p. 169)

nicotine/nicotina   Fármaco estimulante, altamente adictivo y psicoactivo que se halla en el tabaco. (p. 383)

norm/norma   Una regla conocida para conductas aceptables y previstas en un grupo dado. (p. 343)

normal curve/curva normal (*distribución normal*) Curva simétrica y en forma de campana que describe la distribución de muchos tipos de datos; la mayoría de los puntajes yacen cerca de la media (alrededor del 68 porciento yace dentro de una desviación estándar de ella) y otros, cada vez menos, yacen cerca de los extremos. (p. 240)

O

object permanence/permanencia de los objetos Reconocimiento de que las cosas siguen existiendo aunque no las veamos. (p. 76)

observational learning/aprendizaje observacional Aprender observando a los demás. (p. 184)

obsessive-compulsive disorder (OCD)/trastorno obsesivo-compulsivo (TOC) Trastorno que se caracteriza por pensamientos (obsesiones) y/o acciones (compulsiones) repetitivos y no deseados. (p. 377)

occipital lobes/lóbulos occipitales Porción de la corteza cerebral ubicada en la parte posterior de la cabeza; incluye las áreas que reciben información de los campos visuales. (p. 41)

Oedipus complex/complejo de Edipo Según Freud, los deseos sexuales de un niño hacia su madre y sentimientos de celos y odio para con el padre rival. (p. 314)

one-word stage/etapa holofrástica Etapa en el desarrollo del habla, entre el primero y segundo años, en la que el niño se expresa principalmente con palabras aisladas. (p. 230)

operant behavior/comportamiento operante Comportamiento que opera en el entorno, produciendo consecuencias. (p. 174)

operant chamber/cámara operante Caja que contiene una barra o tecla que un animal puede manipular para obtener un reforzamiento de comida o agua. Está dotada de un aparato de grabación que registra la frecuencia con la que el animal dentro de la caja presiona la barra o pincha la tecla. Se emplea en investigaciones de condicionamiento operante. (También se conoce como *caja de Skinner*). (p. 174)

operant conditioning/condicionamiento operante Aprendizaje en el que el comportamiento se consolida si está seguido por un reforzamiento o se atenúa si está seguido por un castigo. (p. 174)

operational definition/definición operacional Declaración redactada con gran cuidado en la que se detallan los procedimientos (operaciones) exactos que se usan en un estudio de investigación. Por ejemplo, la *inteligencia humana* puede ser operacionalmente definida como lo que se mide en una prueba de inteligencia. (p. 13)

opiates/opiáceos Agentes químicos, tales como la morfina y la heroína, que deprimen la actividad neuronal y alivian temporalmente el dolor y la ansiedad. (pp. 32, 381)

opponent-process theory/teoría de proceso de oponentes Teoría que manifiesta que los procesos opuestos de la retina (rojo-verde, amarillo-azul, blanco-negro) posibilitan la visualización de los colores. Por ejemplo, el verde "enciende" algunas células y "apaga" otras; y el rojo "enciende" otras más y el verde las "apaga". (p. 144)

optic nerve/nervio óptico Nervio que transporta los impulsos neuronales del ojo al cerebro. (p. 141)

optimism/optimismo Anticipación de resultados positivos. Son optimistas las personas que esperan lo mejor y creen que sus esfuerzos llevan a obtener buenos resultados. (p. 293)

organizational psychology/psicología organizacional Subdivisión de la psicología I/O que examina las influencias organizacionales en la satisfacción y productividad de los trabajadores, y facilita cambios organizacionales. (p. B-2)

other-race effect/efecto de otras razas Tendencia a recordar caras de la raza de uno mismo con mayor precisión que las caras de otras razas. (p. 353)

outgroup/grupo ajeno "Ellos", o sea, las personas a las que percibimos como distintas o separadas, que no forman parte de nuestro grupo. (p. 352)

overconfidence/exceso de confianza Tendencia a ser más confiado que acertado, o sea, a sobreestimar las creencias y las opiniones propias. (p. 223)

P

panic disorder/trastorno de pánico Trastorno de ansiedad marcado por el inicio repentino y recurrente de episodios de aprehensión intensa o terror que pueden durar varios minutos. Pueden incluir dolor de pecho, sofocamiento, y otras sensaciones atemorizantes, seguidas por la inquietud de un posible atraque posterior. (p. 376)

parallel processing/procesamiento en paralelo Procesamiento simultáneo de muchos aspectos de un problema o escena; modo natural del cerebro de procesar la información de varias funciones, incluida la vista. (p. 143)

paraphilias/parafilias Sentir excitación sexual a partir de fantasías, conductas o ansias que implican objetos no humanos, sufrimiento personal o del prójimo y/o personas que no han dado su consentimiento. (p. 117)

parasympathetic nervous system/sistema nervioso autonómico parasimpático Subdivisión del sistema nervioso autonómico que calma el cuerpo conservando su energía. (p. 34)

parietal lobes/lóbulos parietales Área de la corteza cerebral en la parte superior y hacia la parte posterior de la cabeza; recibe aportes sensoriales del tacto y la posición del cuerpo. (p. 41)

partial (intermittent) reinforcement/reforzamiento parcial (intermitente) Reforzamiento de una respuesta tan sólo una parte del tiempo; tiene como resultado la adquisición más lenta de una respuesta pero mucho más resistente a la extinción que el reforzamiento continuo. (p. 177)

passionate love/amor apasionado Estado excitado de intensa y positiva absorción en otro ser. Por lo general se observa al comienzo de una relación amorosa. (p. 261)

perception/percepción Proceso mediante el cual el cerebro organiza e interpreta la información sensorial transformándola en objetos y sucesos que tienen sentido. (p. 134)

perceptual adaptation/adaptación perceptiva Hablando de la vista, habilidad de acomodarnos a un campo visual artificialmente desplazado o hasta invertido. (p. 150)

perceptual constancy/constancia perceptiva Tendencia a percibir objetos como si fueran constantes e inalterables (como si mantuvieran el color, el brillo, la forma y el tamaño), a pesar de los cambios que se produzcan en la iluminación y en las imágenes que llegan a la retina. (p. 148)

perceptual set/predisposición perceptiva Predisposición mental para percibir una cosa y no otra. (p. 138)

peripheral nervous system (PNS)/sistema nervioso periférico (SNP) Neuronas sensoriales y motrices que conectan el sistema nervioso central con el resto del organismo. (p. 133)

personal control/control personal Nuestro sentido de controlar el entorno en lugar de sentirnos impotentes. (p. 291)

personality/personalidad Forma característica de pensar, sentir y actuar de una persona. (p. 311)

personality disorders/trastornos de la personalidad   Patrón de comportamientos inflexibles y duraderos que se interponen ante el desempeño social. (p. 402)

personality inventory/inventario de personalidad   cuestionario (a menudo de preguntas de cierto/falso y de desacuerdo/acuerdo) en el que las personas responden a consultas diseñadas para medir una amplia gama de sentimientos y conductas. Se usa para evaluar ciertas características escogidas de la personalidad. (p. 324)

personnel psychology/psicología de personal   Subdivisión de la psicología I/O, que se encarga de la selección, colocación, capacitación y evaluación de los empleados. (p. B-2)

pessimism/pesimismo   Anticipación de resultados negativos. Son pesimistas las personas que esperan lo peor y dudan de que puedan alcanzar sus metas. (p. 293)

PET (positron emission tomography) scan/(TEP) tomografía por emisión de positrones   Muestra visual de la actividad cerebral que detecta hacia dónde se dirige un tipo de glucosa radiactiva en el momento en que el cerebro realiza una función dada. (p. 38)

phobia/fobia   Trastorno de ansiedad marcado por un temor persistente e irracional y la evasión de un objeto o situación específicos. (p. 376)

physiological need/necesidad fisiológica   Exigencia básica del cuerpo. (p. 256)

pitch/tono   Propiedad de los sonidos que los caracteriza como agudos o graves, en función de su frecuencia. (p. 151)

pituitary gland/glándula pituitaria   La glándula más influyente del sistema endocrino. Bajo la influencia del hipotálamo, la glándula pituitaria regula el crecimiento y controla demás glándulas endocrinas. (p. 37)

placebo/placebo   Substancia o condición inactiva que a veces se suministra a los miembros de un grupo de control en lugar del tratamiento que se le da al grupo experimental. En latín significa "complaceré". (p. 18)

placebo effect/efecto placebo   Resultados producidos por las expectativas únicamente. (p. 18)

plasticity/plasticidad   Capacidad del cerebro de modificarse, sobre todo durante la niñez, reordenándose después de un daño cerebral o formando nuevas trayectorias basadas en la experiencia. (p. 47)

polygraph/polígrafo   Máquina, utilizada comunmente con la intención de detectar mentiras, que mide ciertas reacciones corporales (como los cambios en la transpiración, el ritmo cardíaco y la respiración) que acompañan a las emociones. (p. 274)

population/población   Todos aquellos que constituyen el grupo que se está estudiando, a partir del cual se pueden tomar muestras. (*Nota:* Salvo en estudios de alcance nacional, no se refiere a la totalidad de la población de un país). (p. 15)

positive psychology/psicología positiva   Estudio científico del funcionamiento humano, que tiene las metas de descubrir y promover las fortalezas y las virtudes que ayudan a los individuos y a las comunidades a prosperar. (p. 8)

positive reinforcement/reforzamiento positivo   Aumento en la expresión de comportamientos mediante la presentación de estímulos positivos, por ejemplo, un alimento. Un reforzamiento positivo es cualquier cosa que, *presentada* después de una respuesta, refuerza la respuesta. (p. 175)

posthypnotic suggestion/sugerencia poshipnótica   Sugerencia que se hace durante una sesión de hipnotismo, que el sujeto debe realizar cuando ya no está hipnotizado; la utilizando algunos practicantes para ayudar a controlar síntomas y conductas no deseadas. (p. 156)

posttraumatic stress disorder (PTSD)/trastorno de estrés posttraumático (TTPT)   Trastorno de ansiedad caracterizado por recuerdos obsesionantes, pesadillas, aislamiento social, ansiedad asustadiza, y/o insomnio que perdura por cuatro semanas o más después de una experiencia traumática. (p. 377)

prejudice/prejuicio   Actitud injustificable y normalmente negativa hacia un grupo y sus integrantes. El prejuicio generalmente implica creencias estereotipadas, sentimientos negativos y una predisposición a acción discriminatoria. (p. 350)

premature ejaculation/eyaculación precoz   Clímax sexual que ocurre antes de que el varón o su pareja lo deseen. (p. 117)

preoperational stage/etapa preoperacional   En la teoría de Piaget, la etapa (desde alrededor de los 2 hasta los 6 o 7 años de edad) durante la que el niño aprende a utilizar el lenguaje; pero todavía no comprende las operaciones mentales de la lógica concreta. (p. 77)

primary reinforcer/reforzador primario   Suceso que es inherentemente reforzador y a menudo satisface una necesidad biológica. (p. 176)

primary sex characteristics/características primarias del sexo   Las estructuras del organismo (ovarios, testículos y aparatos genitales externos) que posibilitan la reproducción sexual. (p. 111)

priming/preparación   Activación de asociaciones en nuestra mente, a menudo de manera inconsciente, que nos dispone a percibir o recordar objetos o sucesos de una manera determinada. (pp. 135, 204)

proactive interference/interferencia proactiva   Efecto interruptor del aprendizaje anterior sobre la manera de recordar información nueva. (p. 208)

problem-focused coping/superación con enfoque en los problemas   Intento de sobrellevar el estrés de manera directa cambiando ya sea lo que produce la tensión o la forma en que nos relacionamos con dicho tensionador. (p. 291)

projective test/prueba de proyección   Tipo de prueba de la personalidad, como la prueba de Rorschach, en la cual se le da a una persona una imagen ambigua diseñada para provocar una proyección de pensamientos o sentimientos inconscientes. (p. 316)

prosocial behavior/comportamiento prosocial   Comportamiento positivo, constructivo, útil. Lo contrario del comportamiento antisocial. (p. 186)

prototype/prototipo   Imagen mental o mejor ejemplo de una categoría. Al cotejar artículos nuevos con un prototipo se trabaja con un método rápido y sencillo para clasificar artículos en categorías (tal como cuando se comparan animales de plumas con un ave prototípico, tal como un petirrojo). (p. 220)

psychoactive drug/fármaco psicoactivo   Sustancia química que altera las percepciones y el estado de ánimo. (p. 380)

psychoanalysis/psicoanálisis psychoanalysis   (1) Teoría de Freud sobre la personalidad que atribuye los pensamientos y las acciones a motivos y conflictos enconscientes. (p. 312) (2) El método terapéutico de Freud usado para tratar desórdenes psicológicos. Freud creía que las asociaciones libres, las resistencias, los sueños y las transferencias del paciente (así como la interpretación de ellas por parte del analista) liberaban sentimientos antes reprimidos, permitiendo que el paciente adquiriera agudeza introspectiva. (p. 410)

psychodynamic theories/teorías psicodinámicas   Visión de la personalidad con una concentración en el subconsciente y en la importancia de las vivencias en la niñez. (p. 312)

psychodinamic therapy/terapia psicodinámica   Enfoque terapéutico que se deriva de la tradición psicoanalítica; se observa a los individuos como si respondieran a fuerzas inconscientes y experiencias de la niñez, y se busca agudizar la introspección. (p.142)

psychological disorder/trastorno psicológico   Síndrome caracterizado por la alteración clínicamente significativa de los pensamientos, los sentimientos y los comportamientos de una persona. (p. 371)

psychology/psicología   Estudio científico de cómo los procesos psicológicos, neuronales y endocrinos se combinan para afectar nuestro sistema inmunitario y la salud en general. (p. 3)

psychoneuroimmunology (PNI)/psiconeuroinmunología (PNI)   Estudio de cómo los procesos psicológicos, neuronales y endocrinos se combinan en nuestro organismo para influenciar el sistema inmunitario y la salud en general. (p. 287)

psychosexual stages/etapas psicosexuales   Etapas del desarrollo infantil (oral, anal, fálica, latente, genital), durante las cuales, según Freud, las energías del id que buscan el placer se enfocan en zonas erógenas específicas. (p. 314)

psychosurgery/psicocirugía   Cirugía que extrae o destruye tejido cerebral para cambiar el comportamiento. (p. 429)

psychotherapy/psicoterapia   Tratamiento que incluye técnicas psicológicas; consiste en interacciones entre un terapeuta calificado y una persona que desea superar dificultades psicológicas o lograr un crecimiento personal. (p. 410)

puberty/pubertad   Período de maduración sexual durante el cual la persona adquiere la capacidad de reproducirse. (pp. 86, 111)

punishment/castigo   Evento que disminuye el comportamiento que le precede. (p. 178)

R

random assignment/asignación aleatoria   Asignación de participantes a los grupos experimental y de control. Se realiza al azar para minimizar las diferencias que pudiese haber entre los asignados. (p. 18)

random sample/muestra aleatoria   Muestra que representa justamente la población, gracias a que cada elemento de la población tiene igual oportunidad de ser seleccionado. (p. 15)

range/alcance   La diferencia entre los puntajes más alto y más bajo en una distribución. (p. A-3)

recall/recordación   Memoria que se demuestra recuperando información aprendida anteriormente, tal como en las pruebas que consisten en completar espacios en blanco. (p. 202)

reciprocal determinism/determinismo recíproco   Influencias de la interacción entre la conducta, los factores personales internos y el entorno. (p. 326)

reciprocity norm/norma de reciprocidad   Expectativa de que las personas ayudarán, y no harán daño, a aquellos que les han ayudado a ellos. (p. 365)

recognition/reconocimiento   Memoria que se demuestra identificando cosas que se aprendieron anteriormente, tal como en las pruebas de opciones múltiples. (p. 202)

reflex/reflejo   Respuesta sencilla y automática a un estímulo sensorial, tal como la reacción de la rodilla al golpearla. (pp. 36, 71)

refractory period/período refractario   Fase de descanso después del orgasmo, en la que el hombre no es capaz de tener otro orgasmo. (p. 116)

regression toward the mean/regresión hacia la media   tendencia hacia los puntajes o eventos extremos o poco comunes para asi retornar (regresar) hacia el promedio. (p. A-6)

reinforcement/reforzamiento   Según el condicionamiento operante, todo suceso que *fortalezca* el comportamiento al que sigue. (p. 174)

reinforcement schedule/plan de reforzamiento   Patrón que define la frecuencia con que se reforzará una respuesta deseada. (p. 177)

relational aggression/regresión relacional   Acto de agresión (sea física o verbal) que tiene por intención hacerle daño a las relaciones de la persona o a su estatus social. (p. 109)

relative deprivation/privación relativa   Impresión de que estamos en peor situación que aquellos con quienes nos comparamos. (p. 304)

relearning/reaprendizaje   Memoria que se demuestra por el tiempo que se ahorra cuando se aprende algo por segunda vez. (p. 202)

reliability/fiabilidad   Grado hasta el que una prueba produce resultados coherentes, comprobados por la uniformidad de los puntajes en las dos mitades de la prueba, en formas distintas de la prueba, o al retomar la prueba. (p. 240)

REM (rapid eye movement) sleep/sueño MOR (movimiento ocular rápido)   Etapa recurrente del sueño durante la cual generalmente ocurren sueños gráficos. También se conoce como *sueño paradójico* porque los músculos están relajados (salvo unos espasmos mínimos) pero los demás sistemas del cuerpo están activos. (p. 53)

REM rebound/rebote de MOR   Tendencia al aumento del sueño MOR como consecuencia de la privación del sueño MOR. (p. 62)

repetitive transcranial magnetic stimulation (rTMS)/estimulación magnética transcraneal repetitiva (EMTR)   Aplicación repetitiva de pulsos de energía magnética al cerebro. Se utiliza para estimular o suprimir actividad cerebral. (p. 428)

replication/replicación   Repetir la esencia de un estudio de investigación, por lo general con participantes diferentes y en diferentes situaciones diferentes para ver si las conclusiones básicas se extienden a otros participantes y circunstancias. (p. 13)

repression/represión   En la teoría del psicoanálisis, el mecanismo básico de defensa por medio del cual el sujeto elimina de su consciente aquellos pensamientos, emociones o recuerdos que le producen ansiedad. (pp. 208, 314)

resilience/resiliencia   Fuerza personal que ayuda a la mayoría de las personas a asumir con flexibilidad situaciones de estrés y recuperarse de la adversidad e incluso de un trauma. (pp. 301, 431)

resistance/resistencia   En el psicoanálisis, bloquear del consciente aquello que está cargado de ansiedad. (p. 411)

respondent behavior/comportamiento de respuesta   Comportamiento que ocurre como respuesta automática a un estímulo. (p. 174)

reticular formation/formación reticular   Red de nervios en el tronco encefálico que desempeña un papel importante en el control de la excitación. (p. 39)

retina/retina   Superficie en la parte interior del ojo que es sensible a la luz y que contiene los receptores de luz llamados bastoncillos y conos, además de capas de neuronas que inician el procesamiento de la información visual. (p. 140)

retinal disparity/disparidad retiniana   Clave binocular para la percepción de la profundidad. Mediante la comparación de las imágenes que provienen de ambos ojos, el cerebro calcula la distancia. Cuanto mayor sea la disparidad (diferencia) entre dos imágenes, más cerca estará el objeto. (p. 147)

retrieval/recuperación   Proceso de extraer la información que está almacenada en la memoria. (p. 194)

retrieval cue/clave de recuperación   Todo estímulo (suceso, sentimiento, lugar, etc.) relacionado con un recuerdo específico. (p. 204)

retroactive interference/interferencia retroactiva   El efecto irruptor de algo nuevo que se ha aprendido en la capacidad de recordar información vieja. (p. 208)

rods/bastoncillos Receptores de la retina que detectan el negro, el blanco y el gris; necesarios para la visión periférica y en la penumbra cuando los conos no responden. (p. 141)

role/rol Conjunto de expectativas (normas) acerca de una posición social, que definen la forma en que deben comportarse las personas que ocupan esa posición. (pp. 113, 340)

Rorschach inkblot test/prueba de Rorschach Prueba proyectiva de amplio uso. Conjunto de 10 manchas de tinta, diseñado por Hermann Rorschach; busca identificar los sentimientos internos de las personas mediante el análisis de sus interpretaciones de las manchas. (p. 316)

S

savant syndrome/síndrome de savant Condición según la cual una persona de habilidad mental limitada, cuenta con una destreza excepcional en un campo como la computación o el dibujo. (p. 236)

scapegoat theory/teoría del chivo expiatorio Teoría que expone que el prejuicio ofrece un escape para la cólera porque nos brinda a alguien a quien culpar. (p. 352)

scatterplot/gráfico de aspersión Conjunto de datos graficados, cada uno de los cuales representa los valores de dos factores. El declive de los puntos sugiere el sentido de la relación entre los dos factores. El nivel de aspersión de los puntos sugiere la fuerza de la correlación (la poca aspersión indica una correlación alta). (pp. 16, A-4)

schema/esquema Concepto o marco referencial que organiza e interpreta la información. (p. 76)

schizophrenia/esquizofrenia Trastornos psicológico caracterizado por delirios, alucinaciones, habla desorganizada y/o expresión emocional disminuida o inapropiada. (p. 396)

secondary sex characteristics/características secundarias del sexo Rasgos sexuales no relacionados con la reproducción, tales como los senos y las caderas de las mujeres, la calidad de la voz del varón, y el pelo corporal. (p. 111)

selective attention/atención selectiva Capacidad de enfocar la consciencia en un estímulo en particular. (p. 51)

self/yo Imagen que tenemos de nosotros mismos y entendimiento de quiénes somos. Según la psicología moderna, el concepto de que este es el centro de la personalidad, que organiza los pensamientos, los sentimientos y las acciones. (p. 328)

self-actualization/autorrealización Según Maslow, necesidad psicológica que surge después de satisfacer las necesidades físicas y psicológicas y de lograr la autoestima; motivación para realizar nuestro potencial pleno. (p. 319)

self-concept/concepto de uno mismo Todo lo que pensamos y sentimos acerca de nosotros mismos cuando respondemos a la pregunta: "¿Quién soy?". (p. 320)

self-disclosure/revelación personal Revelación a los demás de cosas íntimas de nuestro ser. (p. 362)

self-efficacy/autoeficacia Nuestros sentimientos de competencia y eficacia. (p. 326)

self-esteem/autoestima Sentimientos altos o bajos con que nos valoramos a nosotros mismos. (p. 329)

self-serving bias/parcialidad interesada Disposición para percibirnos a nosotros mismos de manera favorable. (p. 330)

self-transcendence/autotrascendencia Según Maslow, esfuerzo por alcanzar una identidad, un sentido y un propósito que vaya más allá de uno mismo. (p. 319)

sensation/sensación Proceso mediante el cual los receptores sensoriales y el sistema nervioso reciben las energías de los estímulos provenientes de nuestro entorno. (p. 134)

sensorimotor stage/etapa sensoriomotriz En la teoría de Piaget, la etapa (de los 0 a los 2 años de edad) durante la cual los bebés conocen el mundo principalmente en términos de sus impresiones sensoriales y actividades motoras. (p. 76)

sensorineural hearing loss/pérdida de la audición sensorineuronal Sordera causada por daños a la células receptoras de la cóclea o a los nervios de la audición. También se le dice *sordera nerviosa*. (p. 153)

sensory adaptation/adaptación sensorial Disminución en la sensibilidad como respuesta a la estimulación constante. (p. 137)

sensory interaction/interacción sensorial Principio que un sentido puede influir en otro, como cuando el olor de la comida influye en su sabor. (p. 160)

sensory memory/memoria sensorial Registro breve e inmediato de la información sensorial en el sistema de la memoria. (p. 194)

sensory neuron/neurona sensorial Neurona que recibe la información que le llega desde los receptores sensoriales al sistema nervioso central. (p. 33)

serial position effect/efecto de posición serial Tendencia a recordar con mayor facilidad los elementos del comienzo y el final de una lista. (p. 205)

set point/punto fijo Punto de supuesto equilibrio en el "termostato del peso" de una persona. Cuando el cuerpo llega a un peso debajo de este punto, se produce un aumento en el hambre y una disminución en el índice metabólico, los cuales pueden actuar para restablecer el peso perdido. (p. 259)

sexual dysfunction/disfunción sexual Problema que complica de manera constante la excitación y el funcionamiento sexuales. (p. 116)

sexual orientation/orientación sexual Atracción sexual duradera hacia miembros de nuestro mismo sexo (orientación homosexual), del sexo opuesto (orientación heterosexual), o de ambos sexos (orientación bisexual). (p. 120)

sexual response cycle/ciclo de respuesta sexual Las cuatro etapas de respuesta sexual descritas por Masters y Johnson-excitación, meseta, orgasmo y resolución. (p. 116)

shaping/modelamiento Procedimiento del condicionamiento operante en el cual los reforzadores conducen una acción con aproximaciones sucesivas hasta lograr el comportamiento deseado. (p. 174)

short-term memory/memoria a corto plazo Memoria activada que retiene algunos elementos por un corto tiempo, tales como los siete dígitos de un número telefónico mientras se marca, antes de que la información se almacene o se olvide. (p. 194)

sleep/sueño Pérdida del conocimiento que es periódica y natural. Es distinta de la inconsciencia que puede resultar del estado de coma, de la anestesia general o de la hibernación. (Adaptado de Dement, 1999). (p. 54)

sleep apnea/apnea del sueño Trastorno del sueño en el que se interrumpe repetidamente la respiración hasta tal punto de que el oxígeno en sangre llega a ser tan poco que la persona tiene que despertarse para respirar. (p. 59)

social clock/reloj social Manera que la sociedad prefiere para marcar el tiempo adecuado de los eventos sociales, tales como el matrimonio, la paternidad y la jubilación. (p. 99)

social facilitation/facilitación social Mejoramiento del desempeño en funciones sencillas o bien aprendidas en la presencia de otros. (p. 347)

social identity/identidad social   Aspecto "nosotros" del concepto de nosotros mismos; parte de nuestra respuesta a "¿Quién soy?" que proviene de nuestra pertenencia a grupos. (p. 89)

social leadership/liderazgo social   Liderazgo orientado hacia el grupo que fortalece el trabajo en equipo, que media en conflictos y que ofrece apoyo. (p. B-7)

social learning theory/teoría de aprendizaje social   Teoría que señala que aprendemos la conducta social observando e imitando, y al ser recompensados o castigados. (p. 113)

social loafing/haraganería social   Tendencia de las personas en un grupo de realizar menos esfuerzo cuando juntan sus esfuerzos para lograr una meta común que cuando son responsables individualmente. (p. 347)

social psychology/psicología social   Estudio científico de cómo pensamos, influimos y nos relacionamos con los demás. (p. 338)

social script/guión social   Guía modelada culturalmente acerca de cómo actuar en diversas situaciones. (p. 357)

social-cognitive perspective/perspectiva sociocognoscitiva   Ver la conducta como influida por la interacción entre las personas (y sus pensamientos) y su contexto social. (p. 326)

social-responsibility norm/norma de responsabilidad social   Expectativa de que las personas ayudarán a aquellos que dependen de ellas. (p. 365)

somatic nervous system/sistema nervioso somático   División del sistema nervioso periférico que controla los músculos del esqueleto. También llamado *sistema nervioso del esqueleto*. (p. 34)

somatosensory cortex/corteza somatosensorial   Área de la corteza cerebral en la parte delantera de los lóbulos parietales. Registra y procesa el tacto y las sensaciones de movimiento. (p. 45)

source amnesia/amnesia de la fuente   Recuerdo errado de cómo, cuándo o dónde se aprendió o se imaginó la información. (p. 211)

spacing effect/efecto del aprendizaje espaciado   Tendencia a que el estudio o la práctica distribuidos logren mejor retención a largo plazo que la que se logra a través del estudio o la práctica en volumen masivo. (p. 198)

spermache/espermarca   Primera eyaculación. (p. 111)

split brain/cerebro dividido   Condición en la que los dos hemisferios cerebrales se privan de la comunicación mediante el corte de las fibras que los conectan (principalmente las del cuerpo calloso). (p. 48)

spontaneous recovery/recuperación espontánea   Reaparición, después de una pausa, de una respuesta condicionada extinguida. (p. 171)

spotlight effect/efecto reflector   Sobreestimación de lo que los demás advierten y evalúan de nuestro aspecto, desempeño y desatinos (como si nos estuviera apuntando un reflector). (p. 328)

SQ3R/inspeccionar, preguntar, leer, recitar, repasar   Método de estudio en el que se siguen los pasos de inspeccionar, preguntar, leer, recitar y repasar. (p. 23)

standard deviation/desviación estándar   Medición computada de cuánto varía cierta puntuación con respecto al puntaje medio. (p. A-3)

standardization/estandarización   Definir procedimientos de medición uniformes y puntajes significativos mediante la comparación del desempeño de un grupo examinado con anterioridad. (p. 240)

Stanford-Binet/Stanford-Binet   Revisión norteamericana (por Terman en la Universidad de Stanford) de la prueba original de inteligencia de Binet. Esta prueba se usa extensamente. (p. 239)

statistical significance/significado estadístico   Declaración estadística de la probabilidad de que un resultado obtenido haya sido producto del azar. (p. A-7)

stereotype/estereotipo   Creencia (a veces acertada; pero frecuentemente demasiado generalizada) sobre las características de un grupo. (p. 350)

stereotype threat/amenaza de estereotipos   Preocupación autoconfirmada de que nos evaluarán con base en un estereotipo negativo. (p. 249)

stimulants/estimulantes   Fármacos (tales como la cafeína, la nicotina y las anfetaminas más poderosas, la cocaína y el éxtasis) que excitan la actividad neuronal y aceleran las funciones corporales. (p. 383)

stimulus/estímulo   Todo suceso o situación que provoca una respuesta. (p. 168)

storage/almacenamiento   Retención a través del tiempo de información codificada. (p. 194)

stranger anxiety/miedo a los extraños   Miedo a los extraños que los bebé manifiestan normalmente a partir de alrededor de los 8 meses de edad. (p. 81)

stress/estrés   Proceso mediante el cual percibimos y respondemos a ciertos eventos llamados *estresores*, los cuales evaluamos como amenazantes o desafiantes. (p. 284)

subjective well-being/bienestar subjetivo   Felicidad o satisfacción con la vida de uno mismo. Se emplea junto con medidas de bienestar objetivas (por ejemplo, con indicadores físicos y económicos) para evaluar nuestra calidad de vida. (p. 302)

subliminal/subliminal   Aquello que ocurre por debajo de nuestro umbral absoluto de la consciencia. (p. 135)

substance use disorders/trastornos causados por el uso de estupefacientes   Continuación de las ansias y el uso de estupefacientes pese a que ha interrumpido la vida de manera significativa y/o a que representa un riesgo físico. (p. 380)

superego/supergo   En el psicoanálisis freudiano, componente de la personalidad que representa ideales internalizados y proporciona parámetros de juicio (la consciencia) y para fijarse metas futuras. (p. 313)

superordinate goals/metas comunes   Metas compartidas que hacen caso omiso de las diferencias entre las personas y que requieren su cooperación. (p. 366)

survey/encuesta   Técnica descriptiva para obtener actitudes o conductas del grupo autoreportadas por las personas; generalmente mediante preguntas que se le plantean a una muestra aleatoria y representativa. (p. 15)

sympathetic nervous system/sistema nervioso simpático   Subdivisión del sistema nervioso autonómico que en situaciones estresantes despierta al cuerpo y moviliza su energía. (p. 34)

synapse/sinapsis   Intersección entre el extremo del axón de una neurona que envía un mensaje y la dendrita o cuerpo celular de la neurona receptora (p. 30).

systematic desensitization/desensibilización sistemática   Tipo de terapia de exposición en la cual se asocia un estado tranquilo y agradable con estímulos que van aumentando paulatinamente y que provocan ansiedad. De uso común para tratar fobias. (p. 415)

T

task leadership/liderazgo específico   Liderazgo orientado a metas específicas que establece las normas, organiza el trabajo y centra la atención en metas. (p. B-7)

telegraphic speech/habla telegráfica Etapa inicial del habla de un niño, que tiene forma de telegrama y está formada mayormente por sustantivos y verbos; por ejemplo, "ir carro". (p. 231)

temperament/temperamento Reactividad e intensidad emocionales características de una persona. (p. 83)

temporal lobes/lóbulos temporales Porción de la corteza cerebral que yace más o menos encima de las orejas; incluye las áreas que reciben información de los oídos. (p. 41)

tend and befriend response/respuesta de cuidarse y amigarse En situaciones de estrés, las personas (sobre todo las mujeres) a menudo se dan apoyo (*cuidar*), a la vez que forman vínculos y buscan apoyo de otros (*amigarse*). (p. 286)

teratogen/teratógeno Agente, podría ser químico o viral, que pueden afectar al embrión o al feto durante el desarrollo prenatal, produciéndole daño. (p. 71)

testing effect/efecto de prueba Recuerdo aumentado luego de recuperar la información, en lugar de simplemente volver a leerla. También conocido en inglés como *retrieval practice effect* o *test-enhanced learning*. (pp. 23, 198)

testosterone/testosterona La hormona sexual masculina más importante. La tienen tanto los varones como las mujeres pero la cantidad adicional en los varones estimula el crecimiento de los órganos sexuales masculinos en el feto y el desarrollo de las características sexuales masculinas secundarias durante la pubertad. (p. 111)

thalamus/tálamo Área ubicada encima del tronco encefálico; dirige mensajes sensoriales a la corteza cerebral y transmite respuestas al cerebelo y la médula. (p. 39)

THC/THC Principal sustancia activa que se encuentra en la marihuana, produce distintos efectos, inclusive alucinaciones leves. (p. 386)

theory/teoría Explicación que emplea principios que organizan observaciones y predicen comportamientos o sucesos. (p. 12)

theory of mind/teoría de la mente Conceptos que tienen las personas acerca de sus propios procesos mentales y de los de los demás; es decir, de sus sentimientos, percepciones y pensamientos y de los comportamientos que éstos podrían predecir. (p. 78)

threshold/umbral Nivel de estimulación requerido para activar un impulso neuronal. (p. 31)

token economy/economía de fichas Procedimiento del condicionamiento operante en el que las personas ganan una ficha cuando exhiben un comportamiento deseado y luego pueden intercambiar las fichas ganadas por privilegios o para darse algún gusto. (p. 416)

tolerance/tolerancia Cuando se sigue repitiendo el uso, el efecto deseado precisa de dosis siempre mayores. (p. 381)

top-down processing/procesamiento de arriba hacia abajo Procesamiento de la información orientado por procesos mentales de alto nivel, como cuando construimos percepciones basándonos en nuestras vivencias y expectativas. (p. 134)

trait/rasgo Patrón de comportamiento característico o disposición a sentirse y actuar de cierta forma, según se evalúa en los autoinformes de una prueba de la personalidad. (p. 322)

transduction/transducción Transformación de un tipo de energía en otro. En las sensaciones, transformación de las energías de los estímulos, tales como las imágenes, los sonidos y los olores, en impulsos neuronales que el cerebro tiene la capacidad de interpretar. (p. 135)

transference/transferencia En el psicoanálisis, la transferencia de emociones ligadas a otras relaciones, del paciente al analista (tales como el amor o el odio hacia uno de los padres de familia). (p. 411)

transgender/transexual Término genérico que describe a personas cuya identidad o expresión de género difiere de la que se asocia con su sexo al nacer. (p. 114)

two-factor theory/teoría de los dos factores Teoría de Schachter y Singer que propone que para experimentar emociones debemos (1) recibir estimulación física y (2) identificar el estímulo a nivel cognitivo. (p. 270)

two-word stage/etapa de dos palabras A partir de los 2 años de edad, etapa del desarrollo del lenguaje durante la cual el niño emite mayormente frases de dos palabras. (p. 231)

Type A/Tipo A Término de Friedman y Rosenman para referirse a las personas competitivas, compulsivas, impacientes, verbalmente agresivas y con tendencia a enojarse. (p. 289)

Type B/Tipo B Término de Friedman y Rosenman para referirse a las personas tolerantes, relajadas y tranquilas. (p. 289)

U

unconditional positive regard/consideración positiva incondicional Actitud de cuidado, aceptación y parcialidad. Según Carl Rogers, así los clientes desarrollarían consciencia y aceptación de sí mismos. (págs. 320, 143)

unconditioned response (UR)/respuesta incondicionada (RI) En el condicionamiento clásico, la respuesta no aprendida e innata que es producida por un estímulo incondicionado (como la salivación cuando la comida está en la boca). (p. 170)

unconditioned stimulus (US)/estímulo incondicionado (EI) En el condicionamiento clásico, estímulo que provoca una respuesta incondicionalmente (RI) y de manera natural y automática. (p. 170)

unconscious/inconciente Según Freud, un depósito de pensamientos, deseos, sentimientos y recuerdos, en su mayoría inaceptables. Según los psicólogos contemporáneos, el procesamiento de información del cual no tenemos consciencia. (p. 312)

V

validity/validez Grado en que una prueba mide o predice lo que se supone debe medir o predecir. (p. 241)

variable-interval schedule/calendario de intervalo variable Según el condicionamiento operante, calendario de reforzamientos que refuerza una respuesta en intervalos de tiempo impredecibles. (p. 177)

variable-ratio schedule/plan de proporción variable En el condicionamiento operante, plan de reforzamientos que refuerza una respuesta después de un número impredecible de respuestas. (p. 177)

vestibular sense/sentido vestibular Sentido de movimiento y posición del cuerpo, inclusive el sentido de equilibrio. (p. 159)

virtual reality exposure therapy/terapia de exposición a una realidad virtual Técnica del contracondicionamiento que trata la ansiedad mediante estimulaciones electrónicas creativas en la que las personas puede hacerles frente a más grandes temores, tales como volar en avión, ver una araña o hablar en público. (p. 415)

visual cliff/precipicio visual Dispositivo del laboratorio con el que se examina la percepción de profundidad en los bebés y en animales de corta edad. (p. 146)

W

wavelength/longitud de onda Distancia entre la cresta de una onda de luz o de sonido y la cresta de la siguiente onda afín. (p. 140)

Weber's law/ley de Weber   Principio que sostiene que para que dos estímulos se perciban como distintos, estos deben diferir por un porcentaje mínimo constante (en vez de por una cantidad constante). (p. 137)

Wechsler Adult Intelligence Scale (WAIS)/escala de la Inteligencia de Wechsler para adultos (EIWA)   Prueba de inteligencia más ampliamente utilizada. Incluye subpruebas verbales y de desempeño (no verbales). (p. 240)

Wernicke's area/área de Wernicke   Parte del cerebro generalmente ubicada en el lóbulo temporal izquierdo, que participa en la comprensión y la expresión del lenguaje, y que controla la recepción del mismo. (p. 232)

withdrawal/síndrome de abstinencia   La incomodidad y angustia que sigue cuando se deja de utilizar un estupefaciente adictivo o se suspende una conducta. (p. 381)

working memory/memoria operativa   Entendimiento más reciente de la memoria a corto plazo que el que se enfatiza el procesamiento consciente y activo de información auditiva y visual-espacial, y de información recuperada de la memoria a largo plazo. (p. 194)

X

X chromosome/cromosoma X   Cromosoma del sexo que se encuentra en el varón y la mujer. Las mujeres tienen dos cromosomas X; los hombres tienen un cromosoma X y un cromosoma Y. Con un cromosoma X del padre y otro de la madre, se produce una mujer. (p. 111)

Y

Y chromosome/cromosoma Y   Cromosoma del sexo que sólo se halla en los hombres. Cuando se aparea con un cromosoma X de la madre, produce un varón. (p. 144)

Young-Helmholtz trichromatic (three-color) theory/teoría tricromática de Young-Helmholtz   teoría de que la retina contiene tres receptores de color distintos: uno más sensible al rojo, otro al verde y otro al azul. Al estimularse en combinación, estas células son capaces de producir la percepción de cualquier color. (p. 144)

Z

Zygote/cigoto   Huevo fertilizado. Atraviesa por un período de dos semanas de división celular rápida y se convierte en un embrión. (p. 70)

References

AAS. (2009, April 25). *USA suicide: 2006 final data*. Prepared for the American Association of Suicidology by J. L. McIntosh (www.suicidology.org). (p. 392)

Abbey, A. (1991). Acquaintance rape and alcohol consumption on college campuses: How are they linked? *Journal of American College Health, 39*, 165–169. (p. 382)

Abel, K. M., Drake, R., & Goldstein, J. M. (2010). Sex differences in schizophrenia. *International Review of Psychiatry, 22*, 417–428. (p. 398)

Abrams, D. B. (1991). AIDS: What young people believe and what they do. Paper presented at the British Association for the Advancement of Science conference. (p. 294)

Abrams, D. B., & Wilson, G. T. (1983). Alcohol, sexual arousal, and self-control. *Journal of Personality and Social Psychology, 45*, 188–198. (p. 384)

Abrams, L. (2008). Tip-of-the-tongue states yield language insights. *American Scientist, 96*, 234–239. (p. 208)

Abramson, L. Y., Metalsky, G. I., & Alloy, L. B. (1989). Hopelessness depression: A theory-based subtype. *Psychological Review, 96*, 358–372. (pp. 291, 395)

Abramson, L. Y., Seligman, M. E. P., and Teasdale, J. D. (1978). Learned helplessness in humans: Critique and reformulation. *Journal of Abnormal Psychology, 87*, 49–74. (p. 291)

Acevedo, B. P., & Aron, A. (2009). Does a long-term relationship kill romantic love? *Review of General Psychology, 13*, 59–65. (p. 362)

ACHA. (2009). *American College Health Association-National College Health Assessment II: Reference group executive summary Fall 2008*. Baltimore: American College Health Association. (p. 390)

Ackerman, D. (2004). *An alchemy of mind: The marvel and mystery of the brain*. New York: Scribner. (p. 30)

Adams, H. E., Wright, L. W., Jr., & Lohr, B. A. (1996). Is homophobia associated with homosexual arousal? *Journal of Abnormal Psychology, 105*, 440–446. (p. 318)

Adelmann, P. K., Antonucci, T. C., Crohan, S. F., & Coleman, L. M. (1989). Empty nest, cohort, and employment in the well-being of midlife women. *Sex Roles, 20*, 173–189. (p. 99)

Adelstein, J. S., Shehzad, Z., Mennes, M., DeYoung, C. G., Zuo, X-N., Kelly, C., Margulies, D. S., Bloomfield, A., Gray, J. R., Castellanos, F. X., & Milham, M. P. (2011). Personality is reflected in the brain's intrinsic functional architecture. *PLoS ONE, 6*, e27633. (p. 324)

Aderka, I. M., Nickerson, A., Bøe, H. J., & Hofmann, S. G. (2012). Sudden gains during psychological treatments of anxiety and depression: A meta-analysis. *Journal of Consulting and Clinical Psychology, 80*, 93–101. (p. 422)

Affleck, G., Tennen, H., Urrows, S., & Higgins, P. (1994). Person and contextual features of daily stress reactivity: Individual differences in relations of undesirable daily events with mood disturbance and chronic pain intensity. *Journal of Personality and Social Psychology, 66*, 329–340. (p. 302)

Agerström, J., Björklund, F., Carlsson, R., & Rooth, D-O. (2012). Warm and competent Hassan = cold and incompetent Eric: A harsh equation of real-life hiring discrimination. *Basic and Applied Social Psychology, 34*, 359–366. (p. 350)

Aiello, J. R., Thompson, D. D., & Brodzinsky, D. M. (1983). How funny is crowding anyway? Effects of room size, group size, and the introduction of humor. *Basic and Applied Social Psychology, 4*, 193–207. (p. 347)

Ainsworth, M. D. S. (1973). The development of infant-mother attachment. In B. Caldwell & H. Ricciuti (Eds.), *Review of child development research* (Vol. 3). Chicago: University of Chicago Press. (p. 82)

Ainsworth, M. D. S. (1979). Infant-mother attachment. *American Psychologist, 34*, 932–937. (p. 82)

Ainsworth, M. D. S. (1989). Attachments beyond infancy. *American Psychologist, 44*, 709–716. (p. 82)

Aknin, L. B., Barrington-Leigh, C. P., Dunn, E. W., Helliwell, J. F., Burns, J., Biswas-Diener, R., & Norton, M. I. (2013). Prosocial spending and well-being: Cross-cultural evidence for a psychological universal. *Journal of Personality And Social Psychology, 104*, 635–652. (p. 301)

Alanko, K., Santtila, P., Harlaar, N., Witting, K., Varjonen, M., Jern, P., Johansson, A., von der Pahlen, B., & Sandnabba, N. K. (2010). Common genetic effects of gender atypical behavior in childhood and sexual orientation in adulthood: A study of Finnish twins. *Archives of Sexual Behavior, 39*, 81–92. (p. 123)

Albee, G. W. (1986). Toward a just society: Lessons from observations on the primary prevention of psychopathology. *American Psychologist, 41*, 891–898. (p. 432)

Albee, G. W. (2006). Historical overview of primary prevention of psychopathology: Address to the 3rd world conference on the promotion of mental health and prevention of mental and behavioral disorders September 15–17, 2004, Auckland, New Zealand. *The Journal of Primary Prevention, 27*, 449–456. (p. 432)

Alcock, J. (2011, March/April). Back from the future: Parapsychology and the Bem affair. *Skeptical Inquirer*, pp. 31–39. (p. 162)

Aldrich, M. S. (1989). Automobile accidents in patients with sleep disorders. *Sleep, 12*, 487–494. (p. 59)

Aldridge-Morris, R. (1989). *Multiple personality: An exercise in deception*. Hillsdale, NJ: Erlbaum. (p. 402)

Alexander, L., & Tredoux, C. (2010). The spaces between us: A spatial analysis of informal segregation. *Journal of Social Issues, 66*, 367–386. (p. 366)

Allen, J. R., & Setlow, V. P. (1991). Heterosexual transmission of HIV: A view of the future. *Journal of the American Medical Association, 266*, 1695–1696. (p. 117)

Allen, K. (2003). Are pets a healthy pleasure? The influence of pets on blood pressure. *Current Directions in Psychological Science, 12*, 236–239. (p. 295)

Allen, M., D'Alessio. D., & Emmers-Sommer, T. M. (2000). Reactions of criminal sexual offenders to pornography: A meta-analytic summary. In M. Roloff (Ed.), *Communication yearbook 22* (pp. 139–169). Thousand Oaks, CA: Sage. (p. 118)

Allen, M., Emmers, T. M., Gebhardt, L., & Giery, M. (1995). Pornography and rape myth acceptance. *Journal of Communication, 45*, 5–26. (p. 118)

Allen, M. W., Gupta, R., & Monnier, A. (2008). The interactive effect of cultural symbols and human values on taste evaluation. *Journal of Consumer Research, 35*, 294–308. (p. 158)

Allen, N. B., & Badcock, P. B. T. (2003). The social risk hypothesis of depressed mood: Evolutionary, psychosocial, and neurobiological perspectives. *Psychological Bulletin, 129*, 887–913. (p. 390)

Allport, G. W. (1954). *The nature of prejudice.* New York: Addison-Wesley. (pp. 14, 352)

Alsharif, A. (2011, September 25). Saudi king gives women right to vote. *Reuters.* (p. 113)

Altamirano, L. J., Miyake, A., & Whitmer, A. J. (2010). When mental inflexibility facilitates executive control: Beneficial side effects of ruminative tendencies on goal maintenance. *Psychological Science, 21*, 1377–1382. (p. 395)

Alwin, D. F. (1990). Historical changes in parental orientations to children. In N. Mandell (Ed.), *Sociological studies of child development* (Vol. 3). Greenwich, CT: JAI Press. (p. 84)

AMA. (2010, accessed 13 January). Women medical school applicants (Table 2 of Statistics History). ama-assn.org. (p. 128)

Amabile, T. M. (1983). *The social psychology of creativity.* New York: Springer-Verlag. (p. 330)

Amabile, T. M., & Hennessey, B. A. (1992). The motivation for creativity in children. In A. K. Boggiano & T. S. Pittman (Eds.), *Achievement and motivation: A social-developmental perspective.* New York: Cambridge University Press. (p. 226)

Ambady, N. (2010). The perils of pondering: Intuition and thin slice judgments. *Psychological Inquiry, 21*, 271–278. (p. 326)

Ambrose, C. T. (2010). The widening gyrus. *American Scientist, 98*, 270–274. (p. 74)

Amedi, A., Merabet, L. B., Bermpohl, F., & Pascual-Leone, A. (2005). The occipital cortex in the blind: Lessons about plasticity and vision. *Current Directions in Psychological Science, 14*, 306–311. (p. 47)

Amen, D. G., Stubblefield, M., Carmichael, B., & Thisted, R. (1996). Brain SPECT findings and aggressiveness. *Annals of Clinical Psychiatry, 8*, 129–137. (p. 355)

American Academy of Pediatrics. (2009). Policy statement—media violence. *Pediatrics, 124*, 1495–1503. (p. 188)

American Enterprise. (1992, January/February). Women, men, marriages & ministers, 106. (p. 332)

American Psychiatric Association (2013). *Diagnostic and statistical manual of mental disorders* (Fifth ed.). Arlington, VA: American Psychiatric Publishing. (pp. 372, 382, 391)

American Psychological Association. (2007). Answers to your questions about sexual orientation and homosexuality (www.apa.org. Accessed December 6, 2007). (p. 121)

Ames, D. R., & Flynn, F. J. (2007). What breaks a leader: The curvilinear relation between assertiveness and leadership. *Journal of Personality and Social Psychology, 92*, 307–324. (p. B-6)

Andersen, R. A., Burdick, J. W., Musallam, S., Pesaran, B., & Cham, J. G. (2004). Cognitive neural prosthetics. *Trends in Cognitive Sciences, 8*, 486–493. (p. 44)

Andersen, S. M. (1998). *Service learning: A National Strategy for Youth Development.* A position paper issued by the Task Force on Education Policy. Washington, DC: Institute for Communitarian Policy Studies, George Washington University. (p. 88)

Anderson, B. L. (2002). Biobehavioral outcomes following psychological interventions for cancer patients. *Journal of Consulting and Clinical Psychology, 70*, 590–610. (p. 289)

Anderson, C. A. (2004a). An update on the effects of playing violent video games. *Journal of Adolescence, 27*, 113–122. (pp. 357, 358)

Anderson, C. A., Anderson, K. B., Dorr, N., DeNeve, K. M., & Flanagan, M. (2000). Temperature and aggression. In M. P. Zanna (Ed.), *Advances in Experimental Social Psychology.* San Diego: Academic Press. (p. 356)

Anderson, C. A., Bushman, B. J., & Groom, R. W. (1997). Hot years and serious and deadly assault: Empirical tests of the heat hypothesis. *Journal of Personality and Social Psychology, 73*, 1213–1223. (p. 356)

Anderson, C. A., & Delisi, M. (2011). Implications of global climate change for violence in developed and developing countries. In J. Forgas, A. Kruglanski., & K. Williams (eds.), *The psychology of social conflict and aggression.* New York: Psychology Press. (p. 356)

Anderson, C. A., & Dill, K. E. (2000). Video games and aggressive thoughts, feelings, and behavior in the laboratory and in life. *Journal of Personality and Social Psychology, 78*, 772–790. (p. 358)

Anderson, C. A., & Gentile, D. A. (2008). Media violence, aggression, and public policy. In E. Borgida & S. Fiske (Eds.), *Beyond common sense: Psychological science in the courtroom.* Malden, MA: Blackwell. (p. 188)

Anderson, C. A., Lindsay, J. J., & Bushman, B. J. (1999). Research in the psychological laboratory: Truth or triviality? *Current Directions in Psychological Science, 8*, 3–9. (p. 21)

Anderson, C. A., Shibuya, A., Ihori, N., Swing, E. L., Bushman, B. J., Sakamoto, A., Rothstein, H. R., & Saleem, M. (2010). Violent video game effects on aggression, empathy, and prosocial behavior in Eastern and Western countries: A meta-analytic review. *Psychological Bulletin, 136*, 151–173. (p. 357)

Anderson, C. A., & Warburton, W. A. (2012). The impact of violent video games: An overview. In W. Warburton & D. Braunstein (Eds.), *Growing up fast and furious.* Annandale, NSW, Australia: The Federation Press. (p. 358)

Anderson, J. R., Gillies, A., & Lock, L. (2010). Pan thanatology. *Current Biology, 20*, R349–R351. (p. 229)

Anderson, R. C., Pichert, J. W., Goetz, E. T., Schallert, D. L., Stevens, K. V., & Trollip, S. R. (1976). Instantiation of general terms. *Journal of Verbal Learning and Verbal Behavior, 15*, 667–679. (p. 208)

Anderson, S. E., Dallal, G. E., & Must, A. (2003). Relative weight and race influence average age at menarche: Results from two nationally representative surveys of U.S. girls studied 25 years apart. *Pediatrics, 111*, 844–850. (p. 111)

Anderson, S. R. (2004). *Doctor Dolittle's delusion: Animals and the uniqueness of human language.* New Haven: Yale University Press. (p. 235)

Andersson, E., Enander, J., Andrén, P., Hedman, E., Ljótsson, B., Hursti, T., Bergström, J., Kaldo, V., Lindefors, N., Andersson, G., & Rück, C. (2012). Internet-based cognitive behaviour therapy for obsessive-compulsive disorder: A randomized controlled trial. *Psychological Medicine, 42*, 2193–2203. (p. 419)

Andreasen, N. C. (1997). Linking mind and brain in the study of mental illnesses: A project for a scientific psychopathology. *Science, 275*, 1586–1593. (p. 398)

Andreasen, N. C. (2001). *Brave new brain: Conquering mental illness in the era of the genome.* New York: Oxford University Press. (p. 398)

Andreasen, N. C. (2008, September 16). A conversation with Nancy C. Andreasen, by Claudia Dreifus. *New York Times* (www.nytimes.com). (p. 398)

Andrews, P. W., & Thomson, J. A., Jr. (2009a). The bright side of being blue: Depression as an adaptation for analyzing complex problems. *Psychological Review, 116*, 620–654. (pp. 390, 395)

Andrews, P. W., & Thomson, J. A., Jr. (2009b, January/February). Depression's evolutionary roots. *Scientific American Mind*, pp. 57–61. (p. 395)

Annan, K. A. (2001). We can love what we are, without hating who—and what—we are not. Nobel Peace Prize lecture. (p. 366)

Antonaccio, O., Botchkovar, E. V., & Tittle, C. R. (2011). Attracted to crime: Exploration of criminal motivation among respondents in three European cities. *Criminal Justice and Behavior, 38*, 1200–1221. (p. 109)

Antoni, M. H., & Lutgendorf, S. (2007). Psychosocial factors and disease progression in cancer. *Current Directions in Psychological Science, 16*, 42–46. (p. 289)

Antony, M. M., Brown, T. A., & Barlow, D. H. (1992). Current perspectives on panic and panic disorder. *Current Directions in Psychological Science, 1*, 79–82. (p. 380)

Antrobus, J. (1991). Dreaming: Cognitive processes during cortical activation and high afferent thresholds. *Psychological Review, 98*, 96–121. (p. 61)

AP. (2007). AP-Ipsos poll of 1,013 U.S. adults taken October 16–18, 2007, and distributed via Associated Press. (p. 161)

AP. (2009, May 9). AP-mtvU poll: Financial worries, stress and depression on college campus. www.hosted.ap.org. (pp. 57, 283)

APA. (2002). *Ethical principles of psychologists and code of conduct*. Washington, DC: American Psychological Association. (p. 22)

APA. (2009). *Stress in America 2009*. American Psychological Association (apa.org). (p. 284)

APA. (2010, accessed April 28). *Answers to your questions about transgender individuals and gender identity*. American Psychological Association (apa.org). (pp. 114, 115)

Archer, J. (2000). Sex differences in aggression between heterosexual partners: A meta-analytic review. *Psychological Bulletin, 126*, 651–680. (p. 108)

Archer, J. (2004). Sex differences in aggression in real-world settings: A meta-analytic review. Review of *General Psychology, 8*, 291–322. (p. 109)

Archer, J. (2007). A cross-cultural perspective on physical aggression between partners. *Issues in Forensic Psychology*, No. 6, 125–131. (p. 109)

Archer, J. (2009). Does sexual selection explain human sex differences in aggression? *Behavioral and Brain Sciences, 32*, 249–311. (p. 109)

Arent, S. M., Landers, D. M., & Etnier, J. L. (2000). The effects of exercise on mood in older adults: A meta-analytic review. *Journal of Aging and Physical Activity, 8*, 407–430. (p. 297)

Ariely, D. (2010). *Predictably irrational, revised and expanded edition: The hidden forces that shape our decisions*. New York: Harper Perennial. (p. 318)

Ariely, D., & Loewenstein, G. (2006). The heat of the moment: The effect of sexual arousal on sexual decision making. *Journal of Behavioral Decision Making, 19*, 87–98. (p. 119)

Aries, E. (1987). Gender and communication. In P. Shaver & C. Henrick (Eds.), *Review of Personality and Social Psychology, 7*, 149–176. (p. 109)

Arkowitz, H., & Lilienfeld, S. O. (2006, April/May). Psychotherapy on trial. *Scientific American: Mind*, pp. 42–49. (p. 422)

Armony, J. L., Quirk, G. J., & LeDoux, J. E. (1998). Differential effects of amygdala lesions on early and late plastic components of auditory cortex spike trains during fear conditioning. *Journal of Neuroscience, 18*, 2592–2601. (pp. 380, 381)

Arneson, J. J., Sackett, P. R., & Beatty, A. S. (2011). Ability-performance relationships in education and employment settings: Critical tests of the more-is-better and the good-enough hypotheses. *Psychological Science, 22*, 1336–1342. (p. 238)

Arnett, J. J. (2006). Emerging adulthood: Understanding the new way of coming of age. In J. J. Arnett & J. L. Tanner (Eds.), *Emerging adults in America:*

Coming of age in the 21st century. Washington, DC: American Psychological Association. (p. 92)

Arnett, J. J. (2007). Socialization in emerging adulthood: From the family to the wider world, from socialization to self-socialization. In J. E. Grusec & P. D. Hastings (Eds.), *Handbook of socialization: Theory and research*. New York: Guilford Press. (p. 92)

Aron, A., Melinat, E., Aron, E. N., Vallone, R. D., & Bator, R. J. (1997). The experimental generation of interpersonal closeness: A procedure and some preliminary findings. *Personality and Social Psychology Bulletin, 23*, 363–377. (p. 363)

Aronson, E. (2001, April 13). Newsworthy violence. E-mail to SPSP discussion list, drawing from *Nobody Left to Hate*. New York: Freeman, 2000. (p. 90)

Artiga, A. I., Viana, J. B., Maldonado, C. R., Chandler-Laney, P. C., Oswald, K. D., & Boggiano, M. M. (2007). Body composition and endocrine status of long-term stress-induced binge-eating rats. *Physiology and Behavior, 91*, 424–431. (p. 260)

Asch, S. E. (1955). Opinions and social pressure. *Scientific American, 193*, 31–35. (p. 342)

Asendorpf, J. B., Penke, L., & Back, M. D. (2011). From dating to mating and relating: Predictors of initial and long-term outcomes of speed-dating in a community sample. *European Journal of Personality, 25*, 16–30. (p. 126)

Aserinsky, E. (1988, January 17). Personal communication. (p. 53)

Askay, S. W., & Patterson, D. R. (2007). Hypnotic analgesia. *Expert Review of Neurotherapeutics, 7*, 1675–1683. (p. 156)

Aspinwall, L. G., & Tedeschi, R. G. (2010). The value of positive psychology for health psychology: Progress and pitfalls in examining the relation of positive phenomena to health. *Annals of Behavioral Medicine, 39*, 4–15. (p. 294)

ASPS. (2010). *2010 report of the 2009 statistics: National Clearinghouse of Plastic Surgery Statistics*. American Society of Plastic Surgeons (www.plasticsurgery.org). (p. 360)

Aspy, C. B., Vesely, S. K., Oman, R. F., Rodine, S., Marshall, L., & McLeroy, K. (2007). Parental communication and youth sexual behaviour. *Journal of Adolescence, 30*, 449–466. (p. 119)

Assanand, S., Pinel, J. P. J., & Lehman, D. R. (1998). Personal theories of hunger and eating. *Journal of Applied Social Psychology, 28*, 998–1015. (p. 260)

Atkinson, R. C., & Shiffrin, R. M. (1968). Human memory: A control system and its control processes. In K. Spence (Ed.), *The psychology of learning and motivation* (Vol. 2). New York: Academic Press. (p. 194)

Atwell, R. H. (1986, July 28). Drugs on campus: A perspective. *Higher Education & National Affairs*, p. 5. (p. 383)

Austin, E. J., Deary, I. J., Whiteman, M. C., Fowkes, F. G. R., Pedersen, N. L., Rabbitt, P., Bent, N., & McInnes, L. (2002). Relationships between ability and personality: Does intelligence contribute positively to personal and social adjustment? *Personality and Individual Differences, 32*, 1391–1411. (p. 242)

Auyeung, B., Baron-Cohen, S., Ashwin, E., Knickmeyer, R., Taylor, K., Hackett, G., & Hines, M. (2009). Fetal testosterone predicts sexually differentiated childhood behavior in girls and in boys. *Psychological Science, 20*, 144–148. (p. 78)

Averill, J. R. (1993). William James's other theory of emotion. In M. E. Donnelly (Ed.), *Reinterpreting the legacy of William James*. Washington, DC: American Psychological Association. (p. 270)

Aviezer, H., Hassin, R. R., Ryan, J., Grady, C., Susskind, J., Anderson, A., Moscovitch, M., & Bentin, S. (2008). Angry, disgusted, or afraid? Studies on the malleability of emotion perception. *Psychological Science, 19*, 724–732. (p. 278)

Ax, A. F. (1953). The physiological differentiation of fear and anger in humans. *Psychosomatic Medicine, 15*, 433–442. (p. 273)

Ayan, S. (2009, April/May). Laughing matters. *Scientific American Mind*, pp. 24–31. (p. 294)

Azar, B. (1998, June). Why can't this man feel whether or not he's standing up? *APA Monitor* (www.apa.org/monitor/jun98/touch.html). (p. 159)

Azevedo, F. A., Carvalho, L. R., Grinberg, L. T., Farfel, J. M., Ferretti, R. E., Leite, R. E., Jacob Filho, W., Lent, R., & Herculano-Houzel, S. (2009). Equal numbers of neuronal and nonneuronal cells make the human brain an isometrically scaled-up primate brain. *Journal of Comparative Neurology, 513*, 532–541. (p. 35)

Baas, M., De Dreu, C. K. W., & Nijstad, B. A. (2008). A meta-analysis of 25 years of mood-creativity research: hedonic tone, activation, or regulatory focus? *Psychological Bulletin, 134*, 779–806. (p. 301)

Babyak, M., Blumenthal, J. A., Herman, S., Khatri, P., Doraiswamy, M., Moore, K., Craighead, W. W., Baldewics, T. T., & Krishnan, K. R. (2000). Exercise treatment for major depression: Maintenance of therapeutic benefit at ten months. *Psychosomatic Medicine, 62*, 633–638. (p. 430)

Bachman, J., O'Malley, P. M., Schulenberg, J. E., Johnston, L. D., Freedman-Doan, P., & Messersmith, E. E. (2007). *The education-drug use connection: How successes and failures in school relate to adolescent smoking, drinking, drug use, and delinquency.* Mahwah, NJ: Erlbaum. (p. 390)

Back, M. D., Stopfer, J. M., Vazire, S., Gaddis, S., Schmukle, S. C., Egloff, B., & Gosling, S. D. (2010). Facebook profiles reflect actual personality not self-idealization. *Psychological Science, 21*, 372–274. (pp. 268, 326)

Backman, L., & MacDonald, S. W. S. (2006). Death and cognition: Synthesis and outlook. *European Psychologist, 11*, 224–235. (p. 97)

Baddeley, A. D. (1982). *Your memory: A user's guide.* New York: Macmillan. (pp. 202, 203)

Baddeley, A. D. (2002, June). Is working memory still working? *European Psychologist, 7*, 85–97. (p. 194, 195)

Baddeley, A. D., Thomson, N., & Buchanan, M. (1975). Word length and the structure of short-term memory. *Journal of Verbal Learning and Verbal Behavior, 14*, 575–589. (p. 196)

Baddeley, J. L., & Singer, J. A. (2009). A social interactional model of bereavement narrative disclosure. *Review of General Psychology, 13*, 202–218. (p. 101)

Bagemihl, B. (1999). *Biological exuberance: Animal homosexuality and natural diversity.* New York: St. Martins. (p. 122)

Baglioni, C., Battagliese, G., Feige, B., Spiegelhalder, K., Nissen, C., Voderholzer, U., Lombardo, C., & Riemann, D. (2011). Insomnia as a predictor of depression: A meta-analytic evaluation of longitudinal epidemiological studies. *Journal of Affective Disorders, 135*, 10–19. (p. 58)

Bahrick, H. P. (1984). Semantic memory content in permastore: 50 years of memory for Spanish learned in school. *Journal of Experimental Psychology: General, 111*, 1–29. (p. 207)

Bahrick, H. P., Bahrick, P. O., & Wittlinger, R. P. (1975). Fifty years of memory for names and faces: A cross-sectional approach. *Journal of Experimental Psychology: General, 104*, 54–75. (p. 202)

Bailey, J. M., Dunne, M. P., & Martin, N. G. (2000). Genetic and environmental influences on sexual orientation and its correlates in an Australian twin sample. *Journal of Personality and Social Psychology, 78*, 524–536. (p. 126)

Bailey, J. M., Gaulin, S., Agyei, Y., & Gladue, B. A. (1994). Effects of gender and sexual orientation on evolutionary relevant aspects of human mating psychology. *Journal of Personality and Social Psychology, 66*, 1081–1093. (p. 125)

Bailey, R. E., & Gillaspy, J. A., Jr. (2005). Operant psychology goes to the fair: Marian and Keller Breland in the popular press, 1947–1966. *The Behavior Analyst, 28*, 143–159. (p. 167)

Bailine, S., & 10 others. (2010). Elctroconvulsive therapy is equally effective in unipolar and bipolar depression. *Acta Psychiatrica Scandinavica, 121*, 431–436. (p. 427)

Baillargeon, R. (1995). A model of physical reasoning in infancy. In C. Rovee-Collier & L. P. Lipsitt (Eds.), *Advances in infancy research* (Vol. 9). Stamford, CT: Ablex. (p. 77)

Baillargeon, R. (2008). Innate ideas revisited: For a principle of persistence in infants' physical reasoning. *Perspectives in Psychological Science, 3*, 2–13. (p. 77)

Baker, M. & Maner, J. (2009). Male risk-taking as a context-sensitive signaling device. *Journal of Experimental Social Psychology, 45*, 1136–1139. (p. 126)

Baker, T. B., McFall, R. M., & Shoham, V. (2008). Current status and future prospects of clinical psychology: Toward a scientifically principled approach to mental and behavioral health care. *Psychological Science in the Public Interest, 9*, 67–103. (p. 422)

Baker, T. B., Piper, M. E., McCarthy, D. E., Majeskie, M. R., & Fiore, M. C. (2004). Addiction motivation reformulated: An affective processing model of negative reinforcement. *Psychological Review, 111*, 33–51. (p. 176)

Bakermans-Kranenburg, M. J., van IJzendoorn, M. H., & Juffer, F. (2003). Less is more: Meta-analyses of sensitivity and attachment interventions in early childhood. *Psychological Bulletin, 129*, 195–215. (p. 83)

Balcetis, E., & Dunning, D. (2010). Wishful seeing: More desired objects are seen as closer. *Psychological Science, 21*, 147–152. (p. 139)

Ballini, A., Cantore, S., Fatone, L., Montenegro, V., et al. (2012). Transmission of nonviral sexually transmitted infections and oral sex. *Journal of Sexual Medicine, 9*, 372–384. (p. 118)

Balter, M. (2010). Animal communication helps reveal roots of language. *Science, 328*, 969–970. (p. 234)

Bancroft, J., Loftus, J., & Long, J. S. (2003). Distress about sex: A national survey of women in heterosexual relationships. *Archives of Sexual Behavior, 32*, 193–208. (p. 117)

Bandura, A. (1977). Self-efficacy: Toward a unifying theory of behavior. *Psychological Review, 84*, 191–215. (p. 326)

Bandura, A. (1982). The psychology of chance encounters and life paths. *American Psychologist, 37*, 747–755. (p. 97)

Bandura, A. (1986). *Social foundations of thought and action: A social-cognitive theory.* Englewood Cliffs, NJ: Prentice-Hall. (p. 326)

Bandura, A. (2005). The evolution of social cognitive theory. In K. G. Smith & M. A. Hitt (Eds.), *Great minds in management: The process of theory development.* Oxford: Oxford University Press. (pp. 97, 185)

Bandura, A. (2006). Toward a psychology of human agency. *Perspectives on Psychological Science, 1*, 164–180. (p. 326)

Bandura, A. (2008). An agentic perspective on positive psychology. In S. J. Lopez (Ed.), *The science of human flourishing.* Westport, CT: Praeger. (p. 326)

Bandura, A., Ross, D., & Ross, S. A. (1961). Transmission of aggression through imitation of aggressive models. *Journal of Abnormal and Social Psychology, 63*, 575–582. (p. 185)

Barash, D. P. (2012). *Homo mysterius: Evolutionary puzzles of human nature.* New York: Oxford University Press. (p. 128)

Barbaresi. W. J., Katusic, S. KI., Colligan, R. C., Weaver, A. L., & Jacobsen, S. J. (2007). Modifiers of long-term school outcomes for children with attention-deficit/hyperactivity disorder: Does treatment with stimulant medication make a difference? Results from a population-based study. *Journal of Developmental and Behavioral Pediatrics, 28,* 274–287. (p. 373)

Bargh, J. A., & Chartrand, T. L. (1999). The unbearable automaticity of being. *American Psychologist, 54,* 462–479. (p. 318)

Bargh, J. A., & McKenna, K. Y. A. (2004). The Internet and social life. *Annual Review of Psychology, 55,* 573–590. (p. 359)

Bargh, J. A., McKenna, K. Y. A., & Fitzsimons, G. M. (2002). Can you see the real me? Activation and expression of the "true self" on the Internet. *Journal of Social Issues, 58,* 33–48. (p. 359)

Barinaga, M. B. (1997). How exercise works its magic. *Science, 276,* 1325. (p. 297)

Barkley, R. A., & 74 others. (2002). International consensus statement (January 2002). *Clinical Child and Family Psychology Review, 5,* 2. (p. 373)

Barnes, M. L., & Sternberg, R. J. (1989). Social intelligence and decoding of nonverbal cues. *Intelligence, 13,* 263–287. (p. 275)

Barnett, P. A., & Gotlib, I. H. (1988). Psychosocial functioning and depression: Distinguishing among antecedents, concomitants, and consequences. *Psychological Bulletin, 104,* 97–126. (p. 396)

Barnier, A. J., & McConkey, K. M. (2004). Defining and identifying the highly hypnotizable person. In M. Heap, R. J. Brown, & D. A. Oakley (Eds.), *High hypnotisability: Theoretical, experimental and clinical issues.* London: Brunner-Routledge. (p. 156)

Baron-Cohen, S. (2008). Autism, hypersystemizing, and truth. *Quarterly Journal of Experimental Psychology, 61,* 64–75. (p. 78)

Baron-Cohen, S. (2009). Autism: The empathizing-systemizing (E-S) theory. *The Year in Cognitive Neuroscience, 1156,* 68–80. (p. 78)

Barr, R. (2008, February 12). Stores use sonic devices to chase kids. *Associated Press* (news.yahoo.com). (p. 96)

Barrett, L. F. (2006). Are emotions natural kinds? *Perspectives on Psychological Science, 1,* 28–58. (pp. 270, 273)

Bashore, T. R., Ridderinkhof, K. R., & van der Molen, M. W. (1997). The decline of cognitive processing speed in old age. *Current Directions in Psychological Science, 6,* 163–169. (p. 95)

Baskind, D. E. (1997, December 14). Personal communication, from Delta College. (p. 416)

Bates, L. A., & Byrne, R. W. (2010, September/October). Imitation: What animal imitation tells us about animal cognition. *Wiley Interdisciplinary Reviews: Cognitive Science, 1,* 685–695. (p. 186)

Baum, A., & Posluszny, D. M. (1999). Health psychology: Mapping biobehavioral contributions to health and illness. *Annual Review of Psychology, 50,* 137–163. (p. 288)

Baumann, J., & DeSteno, D. (2010). Emotion guided threat detection: Expecting guns where there are none. *Journal of Personality and Social Psychology, 99,* 595–610. (p. 139)

Baumeister, H., & Härter, M. (2007). Prevalence of mental disorders based on general population surveys. *Social Psychiatry and Psychiatric Epidemiology, 42,* 537–546. (p. 371)

Baumeister, R. F. (1989). The optimal margin of illusion. *Journal of Social and Clinical Psychology, 8,* 176–189. (p. 223)

Baumeister, R. F. (2000). Gender differences in erotic plasticity: The female sex drive as socially flexible and responsive. *Psychological Bulletin, 126,* 347–374. (p. 121)

Baumeister, R. F. (2001, April). Violent pride: Do people turn violent because of self-hate, or self-love? *Scientific American,* 96–101. (p. 330)

Baumeister, R. F. (2006, August/September). Violent pride. *Scientific American Mind,* pp. 54–59. (p. 329)

Baumeister, R. F. (2010). *Is there anything good about men? How cultures flourish by exploiting men.* New York: Oxford. (p. 109)

Baumeister, R. F., & Bratslavsky, E. (1999). Passion, intimacy, and time: Passionate love as a function of change in intimacy. *Personality and Social Psychology Review, 3,* 49–67. (p. 363)

Baumeister, R. F., Bratslavsky, E., Muraven, M., & Tice, D. M. (1998). Ego depletion: Is the active self a limited resource? *Journal of Personality and Social Psychology, 74,* 1252–1265. (p. 319)

Baumeister, R. F., Campbell, J. D., Krueger, J. I., & Vohs, K. D. (2003). Does high self-esteem cause better performance, interpersonal success, happiness, or healthier lifestyles? *Psychological Science in the Public Interest, 4,* 1–44. (p. 331)

Baumeister, R. F., Catanese, K. R., & Vohs, K. D. (2001). Is there a gender difference in strength of sex drive? Theoretical views, conceptual distinctions, and a review of relevant evidence. *Personality and Social Psychology Review, 5,* 242–273. (p. 125)

Baumeister, R. F., Dale, K., & Sommer, K. L. (1998). Freudian defense mechanisms and empirical findings in modern personality and social psychology: Reaction formation, projection, displacement, undoing, isolation, sublimation, and denial. *Journal of Personality, 66,* 1081–1125. (p. 293)

Baumeister, R. F., DeWall, C. N., & Vohs, K. D. (2009). Social rejection, control, numbness, and emotion: How not to be fooled by Gerber and Wheeler (2009). *Perspectives on Psychological Science, 4,* 489–493. (p. 266)

Baumeister, R. F., & Exline, J. J. (2000). Self-control, morality, and human strength. *Journal of Social and Clinical Psychology, 19,* 29–42. (p. 293)

Baumeister, R. F., & Leary, M. R. (1995). The need to belong: Desire for interpersonal attachments as a fundamental human motivation. *Psychological Bulletin, 117,* 497–529. (p. 263)

Baumeister, R. F., & Tice, D. M. (1986). How adolescence became the struggle for self: A historical transformation of psychological development. In J. Suls & A. G. Greenwald (Eds.), *Psychological perspectives on the self* (Vol. 3). Hillsdale, NJ: Erlbaum. (p. 92)

Baumeister, R. F., Twenge, J. M., & Nuss, C. K. (2002). Effects of social exclusion on cognitive processes: Anticipated aloneness reduces intelligent thought. *Journal of Personality and Social Psychology, 83,* 817–827. (p. 266)

Baumgardner, A. H., Kaufman, C. M., & Levy, P. E. (1989). Regulating affect interpersonally: When low esteem leads to greater enhancement. *Journal of Personality and Social Psychology, 56,* 907–921. (p. 330)

Baumrind, D. (1996). The discipline controversy revisited. *Family Relations, 45,* 405–414. (p. 84)

Baumrind, D., Larzelere, R. E., & Cowan, P. A. (2002). Ordinary physical punishment: Is it harmful? Comment on Gershoff (2002). *Psychological Bulletin, 128,* 602–611. (p. 179)

Bavelier, D., Newport, E. L., & Supalla, T. (2003). Children need natural languages, signed or spoken. *Cerebrum, 5*(1), 19–32. (p. 231)

BBC. (2008, February 26). Anti-depressants 'of little use.' *BBC News* (www.news.bbc.co.uk). (p. 427)

Beaman, A. L., & Klentz, B. (1983). The supposed physical attractiveness bias against supporters of the women's movement: A meta-analysis. *Personality and Social Psychology Bulletin, 9,* 544–550. (p. 361)

Beardsley, L. M. (1994). Medical diagnosis and treatment across cultures. In W. J. Lonner & R. Malpass (Eds.), *Psychology and culture.* Boston: Allyn & Bacon. (p. 374)

Beardsley, T. (1996, July). Waking up. *Scientific American,* pp. 14, 18. (p. 57)

Beauchamp, G. K. (1987). The human preference for excess salt. *American Scientist, 75,* 27–33. (p. 261)

Beck, A. T., Rush, A. J., Shaw, B. F., & Emery, G. (1979). *Cognitive therapy of depression*. New York: Guilford Press. (p. 417)

Beck, H. P., Levinson, S., & Irons, G. (2009). Finding Little Albert: A journey to John B. Watson's infant laboratory. *American Psychologist, 64,* 605–614. (p. 173)

Beck, H. P., Levinson, S., & Irons, G. (2010). The evidence supports Douglas Merritte as Little Albert. *American Psychologist, 65,* 301–303. (p. 173)

Becker, D. V., Kenrick, D. T., Neuberg, S. L., Blackwell, K. C., & Smith, D. M. (2007). The confounded nature of angry men and happy women. *Journal of Personality and Social Psychology, 92,* 179–190. (p. 275)

Becker, S., & Wojtowicz, J. M. (2007). A model of hippocampal neurogenesis in memory and mood disorders. *Trends in Cognitive Sciences, 11,* 70–76. (p. 426)

Becklen, R., & Cervone, D. (1983). Selective looking and the noticing of unexpected events. *Memory and Cognition, 11,* 601–608. (p. 51)

Beckman, M. (2004). Crime, culpability, and the adolescent brain. *Science, 305,* 596–599. (p. 87)

Beeman, M. J., & Chiarello, C. (1998). Complementary right- and left-hemisphere language comprehension. *Current Directions in Psychological Science, 7,* 2–8. (p. 50)

Bègue, L., Subra, B., Arvers, P., Muller, D., Bricout, V., & Zorman, M. (2009). A message in a bottle: Extrapharmacological effects of alcohol on aggression. *Journal of Experimental Social Psychology, 45,* 137–142. (p. 355)

Bell, A. P., Weinberg, M. S., & Hammersmith, S. K. (1981). *Sexual preference: Its development in men and women*. Bloomington: Indiana University Press. (p. 122)

Belot, M., & Francesconi, M. (2006, November). *Can anyone be 'the one'? Evidence on mate selection from speed dating*. London: Centre for Economic Policy Research (www.cepr.org). (p. 360)

Belsky, J., Houts, R. M., & Fearon, R. M. P. (2010). Infant attachment security and the timing of puberty: Testing an evolutionary hypothesis. *Psychological Science, 21,* 1195–1201. (p. 111)

Bem, D. J. (1984). Quoted in *The Skeptical Inquirer, 8,* 194. (p. 162)

Bem, D. J. (2011). Feeling the future: Experimental evidence for anomalous retroactive influences on cognition and affect. *Journal of Personality and Social Psychology, 100,* 407–425. (p. 162)

Bem, S. L. (1987). Masculinity and femininity exist only in the mind of the perceiver. In J. M. Reinisch, L. A. Rosenblum, & S. A. Sanders (Eds.), *Masculinity/femininity: Basic perspectives*. New York: Oxford University Press. (p. 114)

Bem, S. L. (1993). *The lenses of gender*. New Haven, CT: Yale University Press. (p. 114)

Ben-Shakhar, G., & Elaad, E. (2003). The validity of psychophysiological detection of information with the guilt knowledge test: A meta-analytic review. *Journal of Applied Psychology, 88,* 131–151. (p. 274)

Bennett, W. I. (1995). Beyond overeating. *New England Journal of Medicine, 332,* 673–674. (p. 264)

Benson, P. L., Sharma, A. R., & Roehlkepartain, E. C. (1994). *Growing up adopted: A portrait of adolescents and their families*. Minneapolis: Search Institute. (p. 91)

Berger, B. G., & Motl, R. W. (2000). Exercise and mood: A selective review and synthesis of research employing the profile of mood states. *Journal of Applied Sports Psychology, 12,* 69–92. (p. 297)

Bergin, A. E. (1980). Psychotherapy and religious values. *Journal of Consulting and Clinical Psychology, 48,* 95–105. (p. 424)

Bergsholm, P., Larsen, J. L., Rosendahl, K., & Holsten, F. (1989). Electroconvulsive therapy and cerebral computed tomography. *Acta Psychiatrica Scandinavia, 80,* 566–572. (p. 427)

Berk, L. S., Felten, D. L., Tan, S. A., Bittman, B. B., & Westengard, J. (2001). Modulation of neuroimmune parameters during the eustress of humor-associated mirthful laughter. *Alternative Therapies, 7,* 62–76. (p. 294)

Berkowitz, L. (1983). Aversively stimulated aggression: Some parallels and differences in research with animals and humans. *American Psychologist, 38,* 1135–1144. (p. 355)

Berkowitz, L. (1989). Frustration-aggression hypothesis: Examination and reformulation. *Psychological Bulletin, 106,* 59–73. (p. 355)

Berman, M., Gladue, B., & Taylor, S. (1993). The effects of hormones, Type A behavior pattern, and provocation on aggression in men. *Motivation and Emotion, 17,* 125–138. (p. 354)

Berman, M. G., Jonides, J., & Kaplan, S. (2008). The cognitive benefits of interacting with nature. *Psychological Science, 19,* 1207–1212. (p. 268)

Bernieri, F., Davis, J., Rosenthal, R., & Knee, C. (1994). Interactional synchrony and rapport: Measuring synchrony in displays devoid of sound and facial affect. *Personality and Social Psychology Bulletin, 20,* 303–311. (p. 186)

Bernstein, D. M., & Loftus, E. F. (2009). The consequences of false memories for food preferences and choices. *Perspectives on Psychological Science, 4,* 135–139. (p. 210)

Berscheid, E. (1981). An overview of the psychological effects of physical attractiveness and some comments upon the psychological effects of knowledge of the effects of physical attractiveness. In G. W. Lucker, K. Ribbens, & J. A. McNamara (Eds.), *Psychological aspects of facial form* (Craniofacial growth series). Ann Arbor: Center for Human Growth and Development, University of Michigan. (p. 360)

Berscheid, E. (2010). Love in the fourth dimension. *Annual Review of Psychology, 61,* 1–25. (p. 362)

Berscheid, E., Gangestad, S. W., & Kulakowski, D. (1984). Emotion in close relationships: Implications for relationship counseling. In S. D. Brown & R. W. Lent (Eds.), *Handbook of counseling psychology*. New York: Wiley. (p. 362)

Bertrand, M., & Mullainathan, S. (2003). Are Emily and Greg more employable than Lakisha and Jamal? A field experiment on labor market discrimination. Massachusetts Institute of Technology, Department of Economics, Working Paper 03–22. (p. 350)

Bhatt, R. S., Wasserman, E. A., Reynolds, W. F., Jr., & Knauss, K. S. (1988). Conceptual behavior in pigeons: Categorization of both familiar and novel examples from four classes of natural and artificial stimuli. *Journal of Experimental Psychology: Animal Behavior Processes, 14,* 219–234. (p. 175)

Bianchi, S. M., Milkie, M. A., Sayer, L. C., & Robinson, J. P. (2000). Is anyone doing the housework? Trends in the gender division of household labor. *Social Forces, 79,* 191–228. (p. 128)

Bianchi, S. M., Robinson, J. P., & Milkie, M. A. (2006). *Changing rhythms of American family life*. New York: Russell Sage. (p. 128)

Bickman, L. (1999). Practice makes perfect and other myths about mental health services. *American Psychologist, 54,* 965–978. (p. 421)

Biederman, I., & Vessel, E. A. (2006). Perceptual pleasure and the brain. *American Scientist, 94,* 247–253. (p. 256)

Bienvenu, O. J., Davydow, D. S., & Kendler, K. S. (2011). Psychiatric 'diseases' *versus* behavioral disorders and degree of genetic influence. *Psychological Medicine, 41,* 33–40. (p. 394)

Bilefsky, D. (2009, March 11). Europeans debate castration of sex offenders. *New York Times* (www.nytimes.com). (p. 116)

Bird, C. D., & Emery, N. J. (2009). Rooks use stones to raise the water level to reach a floating worm. *Current Biology, 19,* 1410–1414. (p. 229)

Birnbaum, G. E., Reis, H. T., Mikulincer, M., Gillath, O., & Orpaz, A. (2006). When sex is more than just sex: Attachment orientations, sexual experience, and relationship quality. *Journal of Personality and Social Psychology, 91,* 929–943. (pp. 83, 361)

Birnbaum, S. G., Yuan, P. X., Wang, M., Vijayraghavan, S., Bloom, A. K., Davis, D. J., Gobeski, K. T., Sweatt, J. D., Manhi, H. K., & Arnsten, A. F. T. (2004). Protein kinase C overactivity impairs prefrontal cortical regulation of working memory. *Science, 306,* 882–884. (p. 200)

Biro, D., Humle, T., Koops, K., Sousa, C., Hayashi, M., & Matsuzawa, T. (2010). Chimpanzee mothers at Bossou, Guinea carry the mummified remains of their dead infants. *Current Biology, 20,* R351–R352. (p. 229)

Biro, F. M., & 9 others. (2010). Pubertal assessment method and baseline characteristics in a mixed longitudinal study of girls. *Pediatrics, 126,* e583–e590. (p. 111)

Bishop, G. D. (1991). Understanding the understanding of illness: Lay disease representations. In J. A. Skelton & R. T. Croyle (Eds.), *Mental representation in health and illness.* New York: Springer-Verlag. (p. 220)

Bisson, J., & Andrew, M. (2007). Psychological treatment of post-traumatic stress disorder (PTSD). *Cochrane Database of Systematic Reviews 2007,* Issue 3. Art. No. CD003388. (p. 422)

Bjork, E. L., & Bjork, R. (2011). Making things hard on yourself, but in a good way: Creating desirable difficulties to enhance learning. In M. A. Gernsbacher, M. A. Pew, L. M. Hough, & J. R. Pomerantz (eds.), *Psychology and the real world.* New York: Worth Publishers. (p. 24)

Bjork, R. (2011, January 20). Quoted by P. Belluck, To really learn, quit studying and take a test. *New York Times* (www.nytimes.com). (p. 198)

Bjorklund, D. F., & Green, B. L. (1992). The adaptive nature of cognitive immaturity. *American Psychologist, 47,* 46–54. (p. 80)

Blakemore, S-J. (2008). Development of the social brain during adolescence. *Quarterly Journal of Experimental Psychology, 61,* 40–49. (p. 86)

Blakemore, S-J., Wolpert, D. M., & Frith, C. D. (1998). Central cancellation of self-produced tickle sensation. *Nature Neuroscience, 1,* 635–640. (p. 154)

Blakeslee, S. (2006, January 10). Cells that read minds. *New York Times* (www.nytimes.com). (p. 186)

Blanchard-Fields, F. (2007). Everyday problem solving and emotion: An adult developmental perspective. *Current Directions in Psychological Science, 16,* 26–31. (p. 246)

Blanchard, R. (1997). Birth order and sibling sex ratio in homosexual versus heterosexual males and females. *Annual Review of Sex Research, 8,* 27–67. (p. 124)

Blanchard, R. (2008). Review and theory of handedness, birth order, and homosexuality in men. *Laterality, 13,* 51–70. (p. 124)

Blanton, H., Jaccard, J., Christie, C., & Gonzales, P. M. (2007). Plausible assumptions, questionable assumptions and post hoc rationalizations: Will the real IAT please stand up? *Journal of Experimental Social Psychology, 43,* 399–409. (p. 351)

Blanton, H., Jaccard, J., Gonzales, P. M., & Christie, C. (2006). Decoding the implicit association test: Implications for criterion prediction. *Journal of Experimental Social Psychology, 42,* 192–212. (p. 351)

Blanton, H., Jaccard, J., Klick, J., Mellers, B., Mitchell, G., & Tetlock, P. E. (2009). Strong claims and weak evidence: Reassessing the predictive validity of the IAT. *Journal of Applied Psychology, 94,* 567–582. (p. 351)

Blascovich, J. & Mendes, W. B. (2010). Social psychophysiology and embodiment. In S. T. Fiske, D. T. Gilbert, & G. Lindzey (Eds.), *The handbook of social psychology* (5th ed., pp. 194–227). New York: John Wiley & Sons Inc. (p. 284)

Blass, T. (1999). The Milgram paradigm after 35 years: Some things we now know about obedience to authority. *Journal of Applied Social Psychology, 29,* 955–978. (p. 344)

Blatt, S. J., Sanislow, C. A., III, Zuroff, D. C., & Pilkonis, P. (1996). Characteristics of effective therapists: Further analyses of data from the National Institute of Mental Health Treatment of Depression Collaborative Research Program. *Journal of Consulting and Clinical Psychology, 64,* 1276–1284. (p. 423)

Bloom, B. C. (Ed.). (1985). *Developing talent in young people.* New York: Ballantine. (p. B-3)

Bloom, P. (2000). *How children learn the meanings of words.* Cambridge, MA: MIT Press. (p. 230)

Bogaert, A. F. (2003). Number of older brothers and sexual orientation: New texts and the attraction/behavior distinction in two national probability samples. *Journal of Personality and Social Psychology, 84,* 644–652. (p. 124)

Bogaert, A. F. (2004). Asexuality: Prevalence and associated factors in a national probability sample. *Journal of Sex Research, 41,* 279–287. (p. 115)

Bogaert, A. F. (2006). Biological versus nonbiological older brothers and men's sexual orientation. *Proceedings of the National Academy of Sciences, 103,* 10771–10774. (pp. 115, 124)

Bogaert, A. F. (2010). Physical development and sexual orientation in men and women: An analysis of NATSAL-2000. *Archives of Sexual Behavior, 39,* 110–116. (p. 124)

Boggiano, A. K., Harackiewicz, J. M., Bessette, M. M., & Main, D. S. (1985). Increasing children's interest through performance-contingent reward. *Social Cognition, 3,* 400–411. (p. 184)

Boggiano, M. M., Chandler, P. C., Viana, J. B., Oswald, K. D., Maldonado, C. R., & Wauford, P. K. (2005). Combined dieting and stress evoke exaggerated responses to opioids in binge-eating rats. *Behavioral Neuroscience, 119,* 1207–1214. (p. 260)

Bolger, D. (2010). The dynamics of gender in early agricultural societies of the Near East. *Signs, 35,* 503–531. (p. 82)

Bolger, N., DeLongis, A., Kessler, R. C., & Schilling, E. A. (1989). Effects of daily stress on negative mood. *Journal of Personality and Social Psychology, 57,* 808–818. (p. 302)

Bolwig, T. G., & Madsen, T. M. (2007). Electroconvulsive therapy in melancholia: The role of hippocampal neurogenesis. *Acta Psychiatrica Scandinavica, 115,* 130–135. (p. 427)

Boly, M., Garrido, M. I., Gosseries, O., Bruno, M-A., Boveroux, P., Schnakers, C., Massimini, M., Litvak, V., Laureys, S., & Friston, K. (2011). Preserved feed-forward but impaired top-down processes in the vegetative state. *Science, 332,* 858–862. (p. 50)

Bonanno, G. A. (2004). Loss, trauma, and human resilience: Have we underestimated the human capacity to thrive after extremely aversive events? *American Psychologist, 59,* 20–28. (p. 379)

Bonanno, G. A. (2005). Adult resilience to potential trauma. *Current Directions in Psychological Science, 14,* 135–137. (p. 379)

Bonanno, G. A. (2009). *The other side of sadness: What the new science of bereavement tells us about life after loss.* New York: Basic Books. (p. 101)

Bonanno, G. A., Galea, S., Bucciarelli, A., & Vlahov, D. (2006). Psychological resilience after disaster. *Psychological Science, 17,* 181–186. (p. 379)

Bonanno, G. A., Galea, S., Bucciarelli, A., & Vlahov, D. (2007). What predicts psychological resilience after disaster? The role of demographics, resources, and life stress. *Journal of Consulting and Clinical Psychology, 75(5),* 671–682. (p. 432)

Bonanno, G. A., & Kaltman, S. (1999). Toward an integrative perspective on bereavement. *Psychological Bulletin, 125,* 760–777. (p. 101)

Bonanno, G. A., Kennedy, P., Galatzer-Levy, I. R., Lude, P., & Elfström, M. L. (2012). Trajectories of resilience, depression, and anxiety following spinal cord injury. *Rehabilitation Psychology, 57,* 236–247. (p. 432)

Bonanno, G. A., Westphal, M., & Mancini, A. D. (2011). Resilience to loss and potential trauma. *Annual Review of Clinical Psychology, 11,* 511–535. (p. 379)

Bond, C. F., Jr., & DePaulo, B. M. (2006). Accuracy of deception judgments. *Personality and Social Psychology Review, 10,* 214–234. (p. 275)

Bond, C. F., Jr., & DePaulo, B. M. (2008). Individual differences in detecting deception: Accuracy and bias. *Psychological Bulletin, 134,* 477–492. (p. 275)

Bond, M. H., Lun, V. M-C., Chan, J., Chan, W. W-Y., & Wong, D. (2012). Enacting modesty in Chinese culture: The joint contribution of personal characteristics and contextual features. *Asian Journal of Social Psychology, 15,* 14–25. (p. 333)

Bond, R., & Smith, P. B. (1996). Culture and conformity: A meta-analysis of studies using Asch's (1952b, 1956) line judgment task. *Psychological Bulletin, 119,* 111–137. (p. 343)

Bonetti, L., Campbell, M. A., & Gilmore, L. (2010). The relationship of loneliness and social anxiety with children's and adolescents' online communication. *Cyberpsychology, Behavior, and Social Networking, 13,* 279–285. (p. 267)

Bonezzi, A., Brendl, C. M., & DeAngelis, M. (2011). Stuck in the middle: The psychophysics of goal pursuit. *Psychological Science, 22,* 607–612. (p. B-3)

Bono, J. E., & Judge, T. A. (2004). Personality and transformational and transactional leadership: A meta-analysis. *Journal of Applied Psychology, 89,* 901–910. (p. B-6)

Boos, H. B. M., Aleman, A., Cahn, W., Hulshoff, H., & Kahn, R. S. (2007). Brain volumes in relatives of patients with schizophrenia. *Archives of General Psychiatry, 64,* 297–304. (p. 398)

Bornstein, M. H., Cote, L. R., Maital, S., Painter, K., Park, S-Y., Pascual, L., Pecheux, M-G., Ruel, J., Venute, P., & Vyt, A. (2004). Cross-linguistic analysis of vocabulary in young children: Spanish, Dutch, French, Hebrew, Italian, Korean, and American English. *Child Development, 75,* 1115–1139. (p. 231)

Bornstein, M. H., Tal, J., Rahn, C., Galperin, C. Z., Pecheux, M-G., Lamour, M., Toda, S., Azuma, H., Ogino, M., & Tamis-LeMonda, C. S. (1992a). Functional analysis of the contents of maternal speech to infants of 5 and 13 months in four cultures: Argentina, France, Japan, and the United States. *Developmental Psychology, 28,* 593–603. (p. 85)

Bornstein, M. H., Tamis-LeMonda, C. S., Tal, J., Ludemann, P., Toda, S., Rahn, C. W., Pecheux, M-G., Azuma, H., & Vardi, D. (1992b). Maternal responsiveness to infants in three societies: The United States, France, and Japan. *Child Development, 63,* 808–821. (p. 85)

Bornstein, R. F. (1989). Exposure and affect: Overview and meta-analysis of research, 1968–1987. *Psychological Bulletin, 106,* 265–289. (p. 359)

Bornstein, R. F. (1999). Source amnesia, misattribution, and the power of unconscious perceptions and memories. *Psychoanalytic Psychology, 16,* 155–178. (p. 359)

Bornstein, R. F., Galley, D. J., Leone, D. R., & Kale, A. R. (1991). The temporal stability of ratings of parents: Test-retest reliability and influence of parental contact. *Journal of Social Behavior and Personality, 6,* 641–649. (p. 205)

Boroditsky, L. (2009, June 12). How does our language shape the way we think? www.edge.org. (p. 230)

Boron, J. B., Willis, S. L., & Schaie, K. W. (2007). Cognitive training gain as a predictor of mental status. *Journal of Gerontology: Series B: Psychological Sciences and Social Sciences, 62B(1),* 45–52. (p. 97)

Bostwick, J. M., & Pankratz, V. S. (2000). Affective disorders and suicide risk: A re-examination. *American Journal of Psychiatry, 157,* 1925–1932. (p. 392)

Both, S., Everaerd, W., & Laan, E. (2005). Modulation of spinal reflexes by sexual films of increasing intensity. *Psychophysiology, 42,* 726–731. (p. 118)

Bothwell, R. K., Brigham, J. C., & Malpass, R. S. (1989). Cross-racial identification. *Personality and Social Psychology Bulletin, 15,* 19–25. (p. 353)

Bouchard, T. J., Jr. (2004). Genetic influence on human psychological traits. *Current Directions in Psychological Science, 13,* 148–151. (p. 72)

Bowden, E. M., & Beeman, M. J. (1998). Getting the right idea: Semantic activation in the right hemisphere may help solve insight problems. *Psychological Science, 9,* 435–440. (p. 50)

Bowen, S., Witkiewitz, K., Dillworth, T. M., Chawla, N., Simpson, T. L., Ostafin, B. D., Larimer, M. E., Blume, A. W., Parks, G. A., & Marlatt, G. A. (2006). Mindfulness meditation and substance use in an incarcerated population. *Psychology of Addictive Behaviors, 20,* 343–347. (p. 299)

Bower, B. (2009, February 14). The dating go round. *Science News,* pp. 22–25. (p. 359)

Bower, G. H. (1986). Prime time in cognitive psychology. In P. Eelen (Ed.), *Cognitive research and behavior therapy: Beyond the conditioning paradigm.* Amsterdam: North Holland Publishers. (p. 204)

Bower, G. H., & Morrow, D. G. (1990). Mental models in narrative comprehension. *Science, 247,* 44–48. (p. 198)

Bower, J. M., & Parsons, L. M. (2003, August). Rethinking the "lesser brain." *Scientific American,* pp. 50–57. (p. 40)

Bowers, J. S., Mattys, S. L., & Gage, S. H. (2009). Preserved implicit knowledge of a forgotten childhood language. *Psychological Science, 20,* 1064–1069. (p. 75)

Bowers, T. G., & Clum, G. A. (1988). Relative contribution of specific and nonspecific treatment effects: Meta-analysis of placebo-controlled behavior therapy research. *Psychological Bulletin, 103,* 315–323. (p. 422)

Bowler, M. C., & Woehr, D. J. (2006). A meta-analytic evaluation of the impact of dimension and exercise factors on assessment center ratings. *Journal of Applied Psychology, 91,* 1114–1124. (p. 328)

Boxer, P., Huesmann, L. R., Bushman, B. J., O'Brien, M., & Moceri, D. (2009). The role of violent media preference in cumulative developmental risk for violence and general aggression. *Journal of Youth and Adolescence, 38,* 417–428. (p. 188)

Boyatzis, C. J., Matillo, G. M., & Nesbitt, K. M. (1995). Effects of the "Mighty Morphin Power Rangers" on children's aggression with peers. *Child Study Journal, 25,* 45–55. (p. 188)

Braden, J. P. (1994). *Deafness, deprivation, and IQ.* New York: Plenum. (p. 248)

Bradley, D. R., Dumais, S. T., & Petry, H. M. (1976). Reply to Cavonius. *Nature, 261,* 78. (p. 145)

Bradley, R. B., & 15 others. (2008). Influence of child abuse on adult depression: Moderation by the corticotropin-releasing hormone receptor gene. *Archives of General Psychiatry, 65,* 190–200. (p. 83)

Brainerd, C. J. (1996). Piaget: A centennial celebration. *Psychological Science, 7,* 191–195. (p. 76)

Branas, C. C., Richmond, T. S., Culhane, D. P., Ten Have, Thomas, R., & Wiebe, D. J. (2009). Investigating the link between gun possession and gun assault. *American Journal of Public Health, 99,* 2034–2040. (p. 355)

Brandon, S., Boakes, J., Glaser, & Green, R. (1998). Recovered memories of childhood sexual abuse: Implications for clinical practice. *British Journal of Psychiatry, 172,* 294–307. (p. 213)

Brang, D., Edwards, L., Ramachandran, V. S., & Coulson, S. (2008). Is the sky 2? Contextual priming in grapheme-color synaesthesia. *Psychological Science, 19*, 421–428. (p. 161)

Brannon, L. A., & Brock, T. C. (1993). Comment on report of HIV infection in rural Florida: Failure of instructions to correct for gross underestimation of phantom sex partners in perception of AIDS risk. *New England Journal of Medicine, 328*, 1351–1352. (p. 117)

Bransford, J. D., & Johnson, M. K. (1972). Contextual prerequisites for understanding: Some investigations of comprehension and recall. *Journal of Verbal Learning and Verbal Behavior, 11*, 717–726. (p. 198)

Braun, S. (1996). New experiments underscore warnings on maternal drinking. *Science, 273*, 738–739. (p. 71)

Braun, S. (2001, Spring). Seeking insight by prescription. *Cerebrum*, pp. 10–21. (p. 386)

Braunstein, G. D., Sundwall, D. A., Katz, M., Shifren, J. L., Buster, J. E., Simon, J. A., Bachman, G., Aguirre, O. A., Lucas, J. D., Rodenberg, C., Buch, A., & Watts, N. B. (2005). Safety and efficacy of a testosterone patch for the treatment of hypoactive sexual desire disorder in surgically menopausal women: A randomized, placebo-controlled trial. *Archives of Internal Medicine, 165*, 1582–1589. (p. 115)

Bray, D. W., & Byham, W. C. (1991, Winter). Assessment centers and their derivatives. *Journal of Continuing Higher Education*, pp. 8–11. (p. 328)

Bray, D. W., & Byham, W. C., interviewed by Mayes, B. T. (1997). Insights into the history and future of assessment centers: An interview with Dr. Douglas W. Bray and Dr. William Byham. *Journal of Social Behavior and Personality, 12*, 3–12. (p. 328)

Brayne, C., Spiegelhalter, D. J., Dufouil, C., Chi, L-Y., Dening, T. R., Paykel, E. S., O'Connor, D. W., Ahmed, A., McGee, M. A., & Huppert, F.A. (1999). Estimating the true extent of cognitive decline in the old old. *Journal of the American Geriatrics Society, 47*, 1283–1288. (p. A-7)

Breedlove, S. M. (1997). Sex on the brain. *Nature, 389*, 801. (p. 123)

Breen, G., & 27 others. (2011, May). A genome-wide significant linkage for severe depression on chromosome 3: The depression network study. *American Journal of Psychiatry, 167*, 949–957. (p. 395)

Brehm, S., & Brehm, J. W. (1981). *Psychological reactance: A theory of freedom and control*. New York: Academic Press. (p. 346)

Breslin, C. W. & Safer, M. A. (2011). Effects of event valence on long-term memory for two baseball championship games. *Psychological Science, 22*, 1408–1412. (p. 201)

Brewer, J. A., Malik, S., Babuscio, T. A., Nich, C., Johnson, H. E., Deleone, C. M., Minnix-Cotton, C. A., Byrne, S. A., Kober, H., Weinstein, A. J., Carroll, K. M., & Rounsaville, B. J. (2011). Mindfulness training for smoking cessation: Results from a randomized controlled trial. *Drug and Alcohol Dependence, 119*, 72–80. (p. 299)

Brewer, W. F. (1977). Memory for the pragmatic implications of sentences. *Memory & Cognition, 5*, 673–678. (p. 198)

Brewin, C. R., Andrews, B., Rose, S., & Kirk, M. (1999). Acute stress disorder and posttraumatic stress disorder in victims of violent crime. *American Journal of Psychiatry, 156*, 360–366. (p. 379)

Brief, A. P., & Weiss, H. M. (2002). Organizational behavior: Affect in the workplace. *Annual Review of Psychology, 53*, 279–307. (p. B-4)

Briñol, P., Petty, R. E., & Barden, J. (2007). Happiness versus sadness as a determinant of thought confidence in persuasion: A self-validation analysis. *Journal of Personality and Social Psychology, 93*, 711–727. (p. 301)

Briscoe, D. (1997, February 16). Women lawmakers still not in charge. *Grand Rapids Press*, p. A23. (p. 113)

Brislin, R. W. (1988). Increasing awareness of class, ethnicity, culture, and race by expanding on students' own experiences. In I. Cohen (Ed.), *The G. Stanley Hall Lecture Series*. Washington, DC: American Psychological Association. (p. 84)

Broadbent, E., Kahokehr, A., Booth, R. J., Thomas, J., Windsor, J. A., Buchanan, C. M., Wheeler, B. R. L., Sammour, T., & Hill, A. G. (2012). A brief relaxation intervention reduces stress and improves surgical wound healing response: A randomized trial. *Brain, Behavior, and Immunity, 26*, 212–217. (p. 298)

Brody, J. E. (2002, November 26). When the eyelids snap shut at 65 miles an hour. *New York Times* (www.nytimes.com). (p. 57)

Brody, J. E. (2003, September). Addiction: A brain ailment, not a moral lapse. *New York Times* (www.nytimes.com). (p. 385)

Brody, S., & Tillmann, H. C. (2006). The post-orgasmic prolactin increase following intercourse is greater than following masturbation and suggests greater satiety. *Biological Psychology, 71*, 312–315. (p. 120)

Brodzinsky, D. M., & Schechter, M. D. (Eds.) (1990). *The psychology of adoption*. New York: Oxford University Press. (p. 91)

Bromet, E., & 21 others. (2011). Cross-national epidemiology of DSM-IV major depressive episode. *BMC Medicine, 9*, 91. (p. 393)

Brown, A. S. (2003). A review of the déjà vu experience. *Psychological Bulletin, 129*, 394–413. (p. 211)

Brown, A. S. (2004). *The déjà vu experience*. East Sussex, England: Psychology Press. (p. 211)

Brown, A. S., Begg, M. D., Gravenstein, S., Schaefer, C. A., Wyatt, R. J., Bresnahan, M., Babulas, V. P., & Susser, E. S. (2004). Serologic evidence of prenatal influenza in the etiology of schizophrenia. *Archives of General Psychiatry, 61*, 774–780. (p. 399)

Brown, A. S., Schaefer, C. A., Wyatt, R. J., Goetz, R., Begg, M. D., Gorman, J. M., & Susser, E. S. (2000). Maternal exposure to respiratory infections and adult schizophrenia spectrum disorders: A prospective birth cohort study. *Schizophrenia Bulletin, 26*, 287–295. (p. 399)

Brown, E. L., & Deffenbacher, K. (1979). *Perception and the senses*. New York: Oxford University Press. (p. 154)

Brown, J. A. (1958). Some tests of the decay theory of immediate memory. *Quarterly Journal of Experimental Psychology, 10*, 12–21. (p. 197)

Brown, J. D., Steele, J. R., & Walsh-Childers, K. (2002). *Sexual teens, sexual media: Investigating media's influence on adolescent sexuality*. Mahwah, NJ: Erlbaum. (p. 119)

Brown, K. W., Goodman, R. J., & Inzlicht, M. (2013). Dispositional mindfulness and the attenuation of neural responses to emotional stimuli. *Social Cognitive and Affective Neuroscience, 8*, 93–99. (p. 299)

Brown, S. L., Brown, R. M., House, J. S., & Smith, D. M. (2008). Coping with spousal loss: Potential buffering effects of self-reported helping behavior. *Personality and Social Psychology Bulletin, 34*, 849–861. (p. 101)

Brown, S. W., Garry, M., Loftus, E., Silver, B., DuBois, K., & DuBreuil, S. (1996). People's beliefs about memory: Why don't we have better memories? Paper presented at the American Psychological Society convention. (p. 209)

Browning, C. (1992). *Ordinary men: Reserve police battalion 101 and the final solution in Poland*. New York: HarperCollins. (p. 345)

Bruce-Keller, A. J., Keller, J. N., & Morrison, C. D. (2009). Obesity and vulnerability of the CNS. *Biochemica et Biophysica Acta, 1792*, 395–400. (p. 262)

Bruck, M., & Ceci, S. J. (1999). The suggestibility of children's memory. *Annual Review of Psychology, 50*, 419–439. (p. 212)

Bruck, M., & Ceci, S. J. (2004). Forensic developmental psychology: Unveiling four common misconceptions. *Current Directions in Psychological Science, 15,* 229–232. (p. 212)

Bruer, J. T. (1999). *The myth of the first three years: A new understanding of early brain development and lifelong learning.* New York: Free Press. (p. 245)

Brunwasser, S. M., Gillham, J. E., & Kim, E. S. (2009). A meta-analytic review of the Penn Resiliency Program's effect on depressive symptoms. *Journal of Consulting and Clinical Psychology, 77,* 1042–1054. (p. 418)

Buchanan, R. W., & 10 others. (2010). The 2009 schizophrenia PORT psychopharmacological treatment recommendations and summary statements. *Schizophrenia Bulletin, 36,* 71–93. (p. 425)

Buchanan, T. W. (2007). Retrieval of emotional memories. *Psychological Bulletin, 133,* 761–779. (p. 200)

Buckholtz, J. W., & 13 others. (2010). Mesolimbic dopamine reward system hypersensitivity in individuals with psychopathic traits. *Nature Neuroscience, 13,* 419–421. (p. 404)

Buckingham, M. (2007). *Go put your strengths to work: 6 powerful steps to achieve outstanding performance.* New York: Free Press. (p. B-2)

Buckingham, M., & Clifton, D. O. (2001). *Now, discover your strengths.* New York: Free Press. (p. B-2)

Buckley, C. (2007, January 3). Man is rescued by stranger on subway tracks. *New York Times* (www.nytimes.com). (p. 363)

Buckley, K. E., & Leary, M. R. (2001). Perceived acceptance as a predictor of social, emotional, and academic outcomes. Paper presented at the Society of Personality and Social Psychology annual convention. (p. 266)

Buday, S. K., Stake, J. E., & Peterson, Z. D. (2012). Gender and the choice of a science career: The impact of social support and possible selves. *Sex Roles, 66,* 197–209. (p. 328)

Buehler, R., Griffin, D., & Ross, M. (1994). Exploring the "planning fallacy": Why people underestimate their task completion times. *Journal of Personality and Social Psychology, 67,* 366–381. (p. 223)

Buehler, R., Griffin, D., & Ross, M. (2002). Inside the planning fallacy: The causes and consequences of optimistic time predictions. In T. Gilovich, D. Griffin, & D. Kahneman (Eds.), *Heuristics and biases: The psychology of intuitive judgment.* Cambridge: Cambridge University Press. (p. 223)

Buffardi, L. E., & Campbell, W. K. (2008). Narcissism and social networking web sites. *Personality and Social Psychology Bulletin, 34,* 1303–1314. (p. 268)

Bugelski, B. R., Kidd, E., & Segmen, J. (1968). Image as a mediator in one-trial paired-associate learning. *Journal of Experimental Psychology, 76,* 69–73. (p. 197)

Buka, S. L., Goldstein, J. M., Seidman, L. J., Zornberg, G., Donatelli, J-A. A., Denny, L. R., & Tsuang, M. T. (1999). Prenatal complications, genetic vulnerability, and schizophrenia: The New England longitudinal studies of schizophrenia. *Psychiatric Annals, 29,* 151–156. (pp. 398, 399)

Burcusa, S. L., & Iacono, W. G. (2007). Risk for recurrence in depression. *Clinical Psychology Review, 27,* 959–985. (p. 393)

Burger, J. M. (2009). Replicating Milgram: Would people still obey today? *American Psychologist, 64,* 1–11. (pp. 344, 345)

Burgess, M., Enzle, M. E., & Schmaltz, R. (2004). Defeating the potentially deleterious effects of externally imposed deadlines: Practitioners' rules-of-thumb. *Personality and Social Psychology Bulletin, 30,* 868–877. (p. B-6)

Buri, J. R., Louiselle, P. A., Misukanis, T. M., & Mueller, R. A. (1988). Effects of parental authoritarianism and authoritativeness on self-esteem. *Personality and Social Psychology Bulletin, 14,* 271–282. (p. 84)

Burish, T. G., & Carey, M. P. (1986). Conditioned aversive responses in cancer chemotherapy patients: Theoretical and developmental analysis. *Journal of Counseling and Clinical Psychology, 54,* 593–600. (p. 173)

Burke, D. M., & Shafto, M. A. (2004). Aging and language production. *Current Directions in Psychological Science, 13,* 21–24. (p. 96)

Burns, B. C. (2004). The effects of speed on skilled chess performance. *Psychological Science, 15,* 442–447. (p. 225)

Burns, J. M., & Swerdlow, R. H. (2003). Right orbitofrontal tumor with pedophilia symptom and constructional apraxia sign. *Archives of Neurology, 60,* 437–440. (p. 29)

Busby, D. M., Carroll, J. S., & Willoughby, B. J. (2010). Compatibility or restraint? The effects of sexual timing on marriage relationships. *Journal of Family Psychology, 24,* 766–774. (p. 120)

Bushman, B. J., Baumeister, R. F., Thomaes, S., Ryu, E., Begeer, S., & West, S. G. (2009). Looking again, and harder, for a link between low self-esteem and aggression. *Journal of Personality, 77,* 427–446. (p. 330)

Bushman, B. J., & Huesmann, L. R. (2010). Aggression. In S. T. Fiske, D. T. Gilbert, & G. Lindzey (Eds.), *Handbook of social psychology* (5th ed., Ch. 23, pp. 833–863). New York: John Wiley & Sons. (p. 108)

Bushman, B. J., Moeller, S. J., & Crocker, J. (2011). Sweets, sex, or self-esteem? Comparing the value of self-esteems boosts with other pleasant rewards. *Journal of Personality, 79,* 993–1012. (p. 329)

Bushman, B. J., Ridge, R. D., Das, E., Key, C. W., & Busath, G. L. (2007). When God sanctions killing: Effects of scriptural violence on aggression. *Psychological Science, 18,* 204–207. (p. 109)

Buss, A. H. (1989). Personality as traits. *American Psychologist, 44,* 1378–1388. (p. 326)

Buss, D. M. (1994). The strategies of human mating: People worldwide are attracted to the same qualities in the opposite sex. *American Scientist, 82,* 238–249. (p. 126)

Buss, D. M. (1995). Evolutionary psychology: A new paradigm for psychological science. *Psychological Inquiry, 6,* 1–30. (p. 126)

Buss, D. M. (2008). Female sexual psychology. World Question Center 2008 (edge.org). (p. 118)

Buster, J. E., Kingsberg, S. A., Aguirre, O., Brown, C., Breaux, J. G., Buch, A., Rodenberg, C. A., Wekselman, K., & Casson, P. (2005). Testosterone patch for low sexual desire in surgically menopausal women: A randomized trial. *Obstetrics and Gynecology, 105*(5), 944–952. (p. 115)

Butcher, L. M., Davis, O. S. P., Craig, I. W., & Plomin, R. (2008). Genome-wide quantitative trait locus association scan of general cognitive ability using pooled DNA and 500K single nucleotide polymorphism microarrays. *Genes, Brain and Behavior, 7,* 435–446. (p. 241)

Butler, A., Oruc, I., Fox, C. J., & Barton, J. J. S. (2008). Factors contributing to the adaptation aftereffects of facial expression. *Brain Research, 1191,* 116–126. (p. 137)

Butler, R. A. (1954, February). Curiosity in monkeys. *Scientific American,* pp. 70–75. (p. 256)

Byne, W., Tobet, S., Mattiace, L. A., Lasco, M. S., Kemether, E., Edgar, M. A., Morgello, S., Buchsbaum, M. S., & Jones, L. B. (2001). The interstitial nuclei of the human anterior hypothalamus: An investigation of variation with sex, sexual orientation, and HIV status. *Hormones and Behavior, 40,* 86–92. (p. 123)

Byrne, D. (1982). Predicting human sexual behavior. In A. G. Kraut (Ed.), *The G. Stanley Hall Lecture Series* (Vol. 2). Washington, DC: American Psychological Association. (pp. 116, 171)

Byrne, R. W. (1991, May/June). Brute intellect. *The Sciences,* pp. 42–47. (p. 234)

Byrne, R. W., Bates, L. A., & Moss, C. J. (2009). Elephant cognition in primate perspective. *Comparative Cognition & Behavior Reviews, 4,* 1–15. (p. 229)

Byron, K., & Khazanchi, S. (2011). A meta-analytic investigation of the relationship of state and trait anxiety to performance on figural and verbal creative tasks. *Personality and Social Psychology Bulletin, 37,* 269–283. (p. 227)

Cacioppo, J. T., & Hawkley, L. C. (2009). Perceived social isolation and cognition. *Trends in Cognitive Sciences, 13,* 447–454. (p. 266)

Cacioppo, J. T., & Patrick, C. (2008). *Loneliness.* New York: W. W. Norton. (p. 295)

Caddick, A., & Porter, L. E. (2012). Exploring a model of professionalism in multiple perpetrator violent crime in the UK. *Criminological & Criminal Justice: An International Journal, 12,* 61–82. (p. 109)

Cahill, L. (1994). (Beta)-adrenergic activation and memory for emotional events. *Nature, 371,* 702–704. (p. 201)

Cain, S. (2012). *Quiet: The power of introverts in a world that can't stop talking.* New York: Crown. (p. 323)

Cale, E. M., & Lilienfeld, S. O. (2002). Sex differences in psychopathy and antisocial personality disorder: A review and integration. *Clinical Psychology Review, 22,* 1179–1207. (p. 403)

Call, K. T., Riedel, A. A., Hein, K., McLoyd, V., Petersen, A., & Kipke, M. (2002). Adolescent health and well-being in the twenty-first century: A global perspective. *Journal of Research on Adolescence, 12,* 69–98. (p. 118)

Callaghan, T., Rochat, P., Lillard, A., Claux, M. L., Odden, H., Itakura, S., Tapanya, S., & Singh, S. (2005). Synchrony in the onset of mental-state reasoning. *Psychological Science, 16,* 378–384. (p. 78)

Calvin, C. M., Deary, I. J., Fenton, C., Roberts, B. A., Der, G., Leckenby, N., & Batty, G. D. (2011). Intelligence in youth and all-cause-mortality: Systematic review with meta-analysis. *International Journal of Epidemiology, 40,* 626–644. (p. 245)

Calvo-Merino, B., Glaser, D. E., Grèzes, J., Passingham, R. E., & Haggard, P. (2004). Action observation and acquired motor skills: An fMRI study with expert dancers. *Cerebral Cortex, 15,* 1243–1249. (p. 233)

Cameron, L., & Rutland, A. (2006). Extended contact through story reading in school: Reducing children's prejudice toward the disabled. *Journal of Social Issues, 62,* 469–488. (p. 366)

Campbell, D. T. (1975). On the conflicts between biological and social evolution and between psychology and moral tradition. *American Psychologist, 30,* 1103–1126. (p. 304)

Campbell, D. T., & Specht, J. C. (1985). Altruism: Biology, culture, and religion. *Journal of Social and Clinical Psychology, 3*(1), 33–42. (p. 321)

Campbell, L., & Marshall, T. (2011). Anxious attachment and relationship processes: An interactionist perspective. *Journal of Personality, 79,* 1219–1249. (p. 327)

Campbell, S. (1986). *The Loch Ness Monster: The evidence.* Willingborough, Northamptonshire, U.K.: Acquarian Press. (p. 138)

Campbell, W. K., Foster, C. A., & Finkel, E. J. (2002). Does self-love lead to love for others? A story of narcissistic game-playing. *Journal of Personality and Social Psychology, 83,* 340–354. (p. 330)

Camperio-Ciani, A., Corna, F., & Capiluppi, C. (2004). Evidence for maternally inherited factors favouring male homosexuality and promoting female fecundity. *Proceedings of the Royal Society of London B, 271,* 2217–2221. (p. 127)

Campitelli, G., & Gobet, F. (2011). Deliberate practice: Necessary but not sufficient. *Current Directions in Psychological Science, 20,* 280–285. (p. 238)

Campos, J. J., Bertenthal, B. I., & Kermoian, R. (1992). Early experience and emotional development: The emergence of wariness of heights. *Psychological Science, 3,* 61–64. (p. 146)

Canli, T., Desmond, J. E., Zhao, Z., & Gabrieli, J. D. E. (2002). Sex differences in the neural basis of emotional memories. *Proceedings of the National Academy of Sciences, 99,* 10789–10794. (p. 276)

Cannon, W. B. (1929). *Bodily changes in pain, hunger, fear, and rage.* New York: Branford. (p. 285)

Cannon, W. B., & Washburn, A. L. (1912). An explanation of hunger. *American Journal of Physiology, 29,* 441–454. (p. 258)

Cantor, N., & Kihlstrom, J. F. (1987). *Personality and social intelligence.* Englewood Cliffs, NJ: Prentice-Hall. (p. 238)

Caplan, N., Choy, M. H., & Whitmore, J. K. (1992, February). Indochinese refugee families and academic achievement. *Scientific American,* pp. 36–42. (p. 91)

Carey, B. (2007, September 4). Bipolar illness soars as a diagnosis for the young. *New York Times* (www.nytimes.com). (p. 392)

Carey, B. (2009, November 27). Surgery for mental ills offers both hope and risk. *New York Times* (www.nytimes.com). (p. 430)

Carey, B. (2011, February 14). Wariness on surgery of the mind. *New York Times* (www.nytimes.com). (p. 430)

Carey, G. (1990). Genes, fears, phobias, and phobic disorders. *Journal of Counseling and Development, 68,* 628–632. (p. 380)

Carlson, M. (1995, August 29). Quoted by S. Blakeslee, In brain's early growth, timetable may be crucial. *New York Times,* pp. C1, C3. (p. 83)

Carlson, M., Charlin, V., & Miller, N. (1988). Positive mood and helping behavior: A test of six hypotheses. *Journal of Personality and Social Psychology, 55,* 211–229. (p. 364)

Carnahan, T., & McFarland, S. (2007). Revisiting the Stanford Prison Experiment: Could participant self-selection have led to the cruelty? *Personality and Social Psychology Bulletin, 33,* 603–614. (p. 340)

Carpusor, A., & Loges, W. E. (2006). Rental discrimination and ethnicity in names. *Journal of Applied Social Psychology, 36,* 934–952. (p. 20)

Carroll, J. (2007, August 10). *Most Americans approve of interracial marriages.* Gallup News Services (www.gallup.com). (pp. 350, 351)

Carroll, J. M., & Russell, J. A. (1996). Do facial expressions signal specific emotions? Judging emotion from the face in context. *Journal of Personality and Social Psychology, 70,* 205–218. (p. 277)

Carstensen, L. I., & Mikels, J. A. (2005). At the intersection of emotion and cognition: Aging and the positivity effect. *Current Directions in Psychological Science, 14,* 117–121. (pp. 100, 246)

Carter, T. J., & Gilovich, T. (2010). The relative relativity of material and experiential purchases. *Journal of Personality and Social Psychology, 98,* 146–159. (p. 306)

Carver, C. S., Johnson, S. L., & Joormann, J. (2008). Serotonergic function, two-mode models of self-regulation, and vulnerability to depression: What depression has in common with impulsive aggression. *Psychological Bulletin, 134,* 912–943. (p. 395)

Carver, C. S., Scheier, M. F., & Segerstrom, S. C. (2010). Optimism. *Clinical Psychology Review, 30,* 879–889. (p. 294)

CASA. (2003). *The formative years: Pathways to substance abuse among girls and young women ages 8–22.* New York: National Center on Addiction and Substance Abuse, Columbia University. (pp. 383, 389)

CASA. (2004). *CASA 2004 teen survey.* National Center on Addiction and Substance Abuse, Columbia University (www.casacolumbia.org). (p. 117)

Casey, B. J., Getz, S., & Galvan, A. (2008). The adolescent brain. *Developmental Review, 28,* 62–77. (p. 86)

Cash, T., & Janda, L. H. (1984, December). The eye of the beholder. *Psychology Today,* pp. 46–52. (p. 360)

Caspi, A., McClay, J., Moffitt, T., Mill, J., Martin, J., Craig, I. W., Taylor, A., & Poulton, R. (2002). Role of genotype in the cycle of violence in maltreated children. *Science, 297,* 851–854. (p. 327)

Cassidy, J., & Shaver, P. R. (1999). *Handbook of attachment.* New York: Guilford. (p. 83)

Castillo, R. J. (1997). *Culture and mental illness: A client-centered approach.* Pacific Grove, CA: Brooks/Cole. (p. 374)

Cattell, R. B. (1963). Theory of fluid and crystallized intelligence: A critical experiment. *Journal of Educational Psychology, 54,* 1–22. (p. 246)

Cavalli-Sforza, L., Menozzi, P., & Piazza, A. (1994). *The history and geography of human genes.* Princeton, NJ: Princeton University Press. (p. 248)

Cavigelli, S. A., & McClintock, M. K. (2003). Fear of novelty in infant rats predicts adult corticosterone dynamics and an early death. *Proceedings of the National Academy of Sciences, 100,* 16131–16136. (p. 285)

Cawley, B. D., Keeping, L. M., & Levy, P. E. (1998). Participation in the performance appraisal process and employee reactions: A meta-analytic review of field investigations. *Journal of Applied Psychology, 83,* 615–633. (pp. B-7, B-8)

CDC. (2007, accessed May 31). Basic statistics. www.cdc.gov/hib/topics/surveillance/basic.htm:hivaidsage. (p. 117)

CDC. (2013). ADHD, data and statistics. U.S. Centers for Disease Control and Prevention (www.cdc.gov/NCBBDDD/adhd/data.html). (p. 373)

CDC. (2013, accessed June 8). Heart disease facts. Centers for Disease Control and Prevention (cdc.gov/heartdisease/facts.htm). (p. 289)

CDC. (2013, August 22). Who should get vaccinated against influenza? Centers for Disease Control and Prevention (http://www.cdc.gov/flu/protect/whoshouldvax.htm:should-vaccinate). (p. 399)

Ceci, S. J. (1993). Cognitive and social factors in children's testimony. Master lecture, American Psychological Association convention. (p. 212)

Ceci, S. J., & Bruck, M. (1993). Child witnesses: Translating research into policy. *Social Policy Report* (Society for Research in Child Development), 7(3), 1–30. (p. 212)

Ceci, S. J., & Bruck, M. (1995). *Jeopardy in the courtroom: A scientific analysis of children's testimony.* Washington, DC: American Psychological Association. (p. 212)

Ceci, S. J., Huffman, M. L. C., Smith, E., & Loftus, E. F. (1994). Repeatedly thinking about a non-event: Source misattributions among preschoolers. *Consciousness and Cognition, 3,* 388–407. (p. 212)

Cepeda, N. J., Pashler, H., Vul, E., Wixted, J. T., & Rohrer, D. (2006). Distributed practice in verbal recall tasks: A review and quantitative synthesis. *Psychological Bulletin, 132,* 354–380. (p. 198)

Cepeda, N. J., Vul, E., Rohrer, D., Wixted, J. T., & Pashler, H. (2008). Spacing effects in learning: A temporal ridgeline of optimal retention. *Psychological Science, 19,* 1095–1102. (p. 198)

Cerella, J. (1985). Information processing rates in the elderly. *Psychological Bulletin, 98,* 67–83. (p. 95)

CFI. (2003, July). International developments. Report. Amherst, NY: Center for Inquiry International. (p. 162)

Chabris, C. F., & Simons, D. (2010). *The invisible gorilla: And other ways our intuitions deceive us.* New York: Crown. (p. 52)

Chamove, A. S. (1980). Nongenetic induction of acquired levels of aggression. *Journal of Abnormal Psychology, 89,* 469–488. (p. 187)

Champagne, F. A. (2010). Early adversity and developmental outcomes: Interaction between genetics, epigenetics, and social experiences across the life span. *Perspectives on Psychological Science, 5,* 564–574. (p. 70)

Chance News. (1997, 25 November). More on the frequency of letters in texts. Dart.Chance@Dartmouth.edu. (p. 15)

Chandra, A., Mosher, W. D., & Copen, C. (2011, March). Sexual behavior, sexual attraction, and sexual identity in the United States: Data from the 2006–2008 National Survey of Family Growth. *National Health Statistics Reports,* Number 36 (Centers for Disease Control and Prevention). (p. 121)

Chang, E. C. (2001). Cultural influences on optimism and pessimism: Differences in Western and Eastern construals of the self. In E. C. Chang (Ed.), *Optimism and pessimism.* Washington, DC: APA Books. (p. 294)

Chang, P. P., Ford, D. E., Meoni, L. A., Wang, N-Y., & Klag, M. J. (2002). Anger in young men and subsequent premature cardiovascular disease: The precursors study. *Archives of Internal Medicine, 162,* 901–90. (p. 290)

Chang, Y-T., Chen, Y-C., Hayter, M., & Lin, M-L. (2009). Menstrual and menarche experience among pubescent female students in Taiwan: Implications for health education and promotion service. *Journal of Clinical Nursing, 18,* 2040–2048. (p. 111)

Chaplin, W. F., Phillips, J. B., Brown, J. D., Clanton, N. R., & Stein, J. L. (2000). Handshaking, gender, personality, and first impressions. *Journal of Personality and Social Psychology, 79,* 110–117. (p. 275)

Charness, N., & Boot, W. R. (2009). Aging and information technology use. *Current Directions in Psychological Science, 18,* 253–258. (p. 246)

Charpak, G., & Broch, H. (2004). *Debunked! ESP, telekinesis, and other pseudoscience.* Baltimore, MD: Johns Hopkins University Press. (p. 162)

Chartrand, T. L., & Bargh, J. A. (1999). The chameleon effect: The perception-behavior link and social interaction. *Journal of Personality and Social Psychology, 76,* 893–910. (p. 341)

Cheek, J. M., & Melchior, L. A. (1990). Shyness, self-esteem, and self-consciousness. In H. Leitenberg (Ed.), *Handbook of social and evaluation anxiety.* New York: Plenum. (p. 333)

Chen, A. W., Kazanjian, A., & Wong, H. (2009). Why do Chinese Canadians not consult mental health services: Health status, language or culture? *Transcultural Psychiatry, 46,* 623–640. (p. 423)

Chen, S-Y., & Fu, Y-C. (2008). Internet use and academic achievement: Gender differences in early adolescence. *Adolescence, 44,* 797–812. (p. 268)

Chen, X., Beydoun, M. A., & Wang, Y. (2008). Is sleep duration associated with childhood obesity? A systematic review and meta-analysis. *Obesity, 16,* 265–274. (p. 58)

Cherkas, L. F., Hunkin, J. L., Kato, B. S., Richards, J. B., Gardner, J. P., Surdulescu, G. L., Kimura, M., Lu, X., Spector, T. D., & Aviv, A. (2008). The association between physical activity in leisure time and leukocyte telomere length. *Archives of Internal Medicine, 168,* 154–158. (p. 95)

Chess, S., & Thomas, A. (1987). *Know your child: An authoritative guide for today's parents.* New York: Basic Books. (pp. 73, 82)

Cheung, B. Y., Chudek, M., & Heine, S. J. (2011). Evidence for a sensitive period for acculturation: Younger immigrants report acculturating at a faster rate. *Psychological Science, 22,* 147–152. (p. 232)

Chida, Y., & Hamer, M. (2008). Chronic psychosocial factors and acute physiological responses to laboratory-induced stress in healthy populations: A quantitative review of 30 years of investigations. *Psychological Bulletin, 134,* 829–885. (p. 290)

Chida, Y., & Steptoe, A. (2009). The association of anger and hostility with future coronary heart disease: A meta-analytic review of prospective evidence. *Journal of the American College of Cardiology, 17,* 936–946. (p. 290)

Chida, Y., Steptoe, A., & Powell, L. H. (2009). Religiosity/spirituality and mortality. *Psychotherapy and Psychosomatics, 78*, 81–90. (pp. 299, 301)

Chida, Y., & Vedhara, K. (2009). Adverse psychosocial factors predict poorer prognosis in HIV disease: A meta-analytic review of prospective investigations. *Brain, Behavior, and Immunity, 23*, 434–445. (p. 288)

Chisholm, K. (1998). A three-year follow-up of attachment and indiscriminate friendliness in children adopted from Romanian orphanages. *Child Development, 69*, 1092–1106. (p. 83)

Chivers, M. L. (2005). A brief review and discussion of sex differences in the specificity of sexual arousal. *Sexual and Relationship Therapy, 20*, 377–390. (p. 121)

Chivers, M. L., Rieger, G., Latty, E., & Bailey, J. M. (2004). A sex difference in the specificity of sexual arousal. *Psychological Science, 15*, 736–744. (p. 118)

Choi, I., & Choi, Y. (2002). Culture and self-concept flexibility. *Personality and Social Psychology Bulletin, 28*, 1508–1517. (p. 332)

Christakis, N. A., & Fowler, J. H. (2007). The spread of obesity in a large social network over 32 years. *New England Journal of Medicine, 357*, 370–379. (p. 262)

Christakis, N. A., & Fowler, J. H. (2009). *Connected: The surprising power of social networks and how they shape our lives.* New York: Little, Brown. (p. 296)

Christensen, A., & Jacobson, N. S. (1994). Who (or what) can do psychotherapy: The status and challenge of nonprofessional therapies. *Psychological Science, 5*, 8–14. (p. 423)

Christophersen, E. R., & Edwards, K. J. (1992). Treatment of elimination disorders: State of the art 1991. *Applied & Preventive Psychology, 1*, 15–22. (p. 414)

Chua, H. F., Boland, J. E., & Nisbett, R. E. (2005). Cultural variation in eye movements during scene perception. *Proceedings of the National Academy of Sciences, 102*, 12629–12633. (p. 338)

Chugani, H. T., & Phelps, M. E. (1986). Maturational changes in cerebral function in infants determined by 18FDG positron emission tomography. *Science, 231*, 840–843. (p. 74)

Church, T. S., Thomas, D. M., Tudor-Locke, C., Katzmarzyk, P. T., Earnest, C. P., Rodarte, R. Q., Martin, C. K., Blair, S. N., & Bouchard, C. (2011). Trends over 5 decades in U.S. occupation-related physical activity and their associations with obesity. *PLoS ONE, 6*(5), e19657. (p. 262)

CIA. (2010). *The World Fact Book:* Literacy. Washington, D.C.: CIA (https://www.cia.gov/library/publications/the-world-factbook/fields/2103.html). (p. 351)

Cialdini, R. B. (1993). *Influence: Science and practice* (3rd ed.). New York: HarperCollins. (p. 340)

Cialdini, R. B., & Richardson, K. D. (1980). Two indirect tactics of image management: Basking and blasting. *Journal of Personality and Social Psychology, 39*, 406–415. (p. 353)

Ciarrochi, J., Forgas, J. P., & Mayer, J. D. (2006). *Emotional intelligence in everyday life* (2nd ed.). New York: Psychology Press. (p. 238)

Cincotta, A. L., Gehrman, P., Gooneratne, N. S., & Baime, M. J. (2011). The effects of a mindfulness-based stress reduction programme on pre-sleep cognitive arousal and insomnia symptoms: A pilot study. *Stress and Health, 27*, e299–e305. (p. 299)

Clack, B., Dixon, J., & Tredoux, C. (2005). Eating together apart: Patterns of segregation in a multi-ethnic cafeteria. *Journal of Community and Applied Social Psychology, 15*, 1–16. (p. 366)

Clancy, S. A. (2005). *Abducted: How people come to believe they were kidnapped by aliens.* Cambridge, MA: Harvard University Press. (p. 54)

Clark, A., Seidler, A., & Miller, M. (2001). Inverse association between sense of humor and coronary heart disease. *International Journal of Cardiology, 80*, 87–88. (p. 294)

Clark, R. D., III, & Hatfield, E. (1989). Gender differences in receptivity to sexual offers. *Journal of Psychology & Human Sexuality, 2*, 39–55. (p. 127)

Cleary, A. M. (2008). Recognition memory, familiarity, and déjà vu experiences. *Current Directions in Psychological Science, 17*, 353–357. (p. 211)

Coan, J. A., Schaefer, H. S., & Davidson, R. J. (2006). Lending a hand: Social regulation of the neural response to threat. *Psychological Science, 17*, 1032–1039. (p. 295)

Coffey, C. E. (Ed.) (1993). *Clinical science of electroconvulsive therapy.* Washington, DC: American Psychiatric Press. (p. 427)

Cohen, D. (1995, June 17). Now we are one, or two, or three. *New Scientist,* pp. 14–15. (p. 402)

Cohen, P. (2010, June 11). Long road to adulthood is growing even longer. *New York Times* (www.nytimes.com). (p. 92)

Cohen, R. (2011, March 12). The happynomics of life. *New York Times* (www.nytimes.com). (p. 305)

Cohen, S. (2004). Social relationships and health. *American Psychologist, 59*, 676–684. (p. 296)

Cohen, S., Alper, C. M., Doyle, W. J., Treanor, J. J., & Turner, R. B. (2006b). Positive emotional style predicts resistance to illness after experimental exposure to rhinovirus or influenza A virus. *Psychosomatic Medicine, 68*, 809–815. (p. 287)

Cohen, S., Doyle, W. J., Alper, C. M., Janicki-Deverts, D., & Turner, R. B. (2009). Sleep habits and susceptibility to the common cold. *Archives of Internal Medicine, 169*, 62–67. (p. 57)

Cohen, S., Doyle, W. J., & Skoner, D. P. (1999). Psychological stress, cytokine production, and severity of upper respiratory illness. *Psychosomatic Medicine, 61*, 175–180. (pp. 287, 288)

Cohen, S., Doyle, W. J., Skoner, D. P., Rabin, B. S., & Gwaltney, J. M., Jr. (1997). Social ties and susceptibility to the common cold. *Journal of the American Medical Association, 277*, 1940–1944. (p. 296)

Cohen, S., Doyle, W. J., Turner, R., Alper, C. M., & Skoner, D. P. (2003). Sociability and susceptibility to the common cold. *Psychological Science, 14*, 389–395. (p. 287)

Cohen, S., Kaplan, J. R., Cunnick, J. E., Manuck, S. B., & Rabin, B. S. (1992). Chronic social stress, affiliation, and cellular immune response in nonhuman primates. *Psychological Science, 3*, 301–304. (p. 287)

Cohen, S., & Pressman, S. D. (2006a). Positive affect and health. *Current Directions in Psychological Science, 15*, 122–125. (p. 287)

Colapinto, J. (2000). *As nature made him: The boy who was raised as a girl.* New York: HarperCollins. (p. 112)

Colarelli, S. M., Spranger, J. L., & Hechanova, M. R. (2006). Women, power, and sex composition in small groups: An evolutionary perspective. *Journal of Organizational Behavior, 27*, 163–184. (p. 109)

Colcombe, S. J., Kramer, A. F., Erickson, K. I., Scalf, P., McAuley, E., Cohen, N. J., Webb, A., Jerome, G. J., Marquex, D. X., & Elavsky, S. (2004). Cardiovascular fitness, cortical plasticity, and aging. *Proceedings of the National Academy of Sciences, 101*, 3316–3321. (p. 95)

Collins, D. W., & Kimura, D. (1997). A large sex difference on a two-dimensional mental rotation task. *Behavioral Neuroscience, 111*, 845–849. (p. 247)

Collins, F. (2007, February 1). In the cathedral or the laboratory, it's the same God, National Prayer Breakfast told. www.newsweek.washingtonpost.com/onfaith. (p. 69)

Collins, G. (2009, March 9). The rant list. *New York Times* (nytimes.com). (p. 22)

Collins, R. L., Elliott, M. N., Berry, S. H., Danouse, D. E., Kunkel, D., Hunter, S. B., & Miu, A. (2004). Watching sex on television predicts adolescent initiation of sexual behavior. *Pediatrics, 114*, 280–289. (p. 16)

Collinson, S. L., MacKay, C. E., James, A. C., Quested, D. J., Phillips, T., Roberts, N., & Crow, T. J. (2003). Brain volume, asymmetry and intellectual impairment in relation to sex in early-onset schizophrenia. *British Journal of Psychiatry, 183*, 114–120. (p. 398)

Collishaw, S., Pickles, A., Natarajan, L., & Maughan, B. (2007, June). 20-year trends in depression and anxiety in England. Paper presented at the Thirteenth Scientific Meeting on The Brain and the Developing Child, London. (p. 394)

Confer, J. C., Easton, J. A., Fleischman, D. S., Goetz, C. D., Lewis, D. M. G., Perilloux, C., & Buss, D. M. (2010). Evolutionary psychology: Controversies, questions, prospects, and limitations. *American Psychologist, 65*, 110–126. (p. 128)

Conley, C. S., & Rudolph, K. D. (2009). The emerging sex difference in adolescent depression: Interacting contributions of puberty and peer stress. *Development and Psychopathology, 21*, 593–620. (p. 86)

Conley, K. M. & Lehman, B. J. (2012). Test anxiety and cardiovascular responses to daily academic stressors. *Stress and Health, 28*, 41–50. (p. 289)

Conley, T. D. (2011). Perceived proposer personality characteristics and gender differences in acceptance of casual sex offers. *Journal of Personality and Social Psychology, 100*, 309–329. (p. 127)

Connor, C. E. (2010). A new viewpoint on faces. *Science, 330*, 764–765. (p. 142)

Consumer Reports. (1995, November). Does therapy help? Pp. 734–739. (p. 420)

Conway, A. R. A., Skitka, L. J., Hemmerich, J. A., & Kershaw, T. C. (2009). Flashbulb memory for 11 September 2001. *Applied Cognitive Psychology, 23*, 605–623. (p. 201)

Conway, M. A., Wang, Q., Hanyu, K., & Haque, S. (2005). A cross-cultural investigation of autobiographical memory: On the universality and cultural variation of the reminiscence bump. *Journal of Cross-Cultural Psychology, 36*, 739–749. (p. 96)

Cooke, L. J., Wardle, J., & Gibson, E. L. (2003). Relationship between parental report of food neophobia and everyday food consumption in 2–6-year-old children. *Appetite, 41*, 205–206. (p. 157)

Cooper, M. (2010, October 18). From Obama, the tax cut nobody heard of. *New York Times* (www.nytimes.com). (p. 352)

Cooper, W. H., & Withey, M. J. (2009). The strong situation hypothesis. *Personality and Social Psychology Review, 13*, 62–72. (p. 326)

Coopersmith, S. (1967). *The antecedents of self-esteem.* San Francisco: Freeman. (p. 84)

Copeland, W., Shanahan, L., Miller, S., Costello, E. J., Angold, A., & Maughan, B. (2010). Outcomes of early pubertal timing in young women: A prospective population-based study. *American Journal of Psychiatry, 167*, 1218–1225. (p. 86)

Corcoran, D. W. J. (1964). The relation between introversion and salivation. *The American Journal of Psychology, 77*, 298–300. (p. 323)

Coren, S. (1996). *Sleep thieves: An eye-opening exploration into the science and mysteries of sleep.* New York: Free Press. (pp. 55, 57)

Corey, D. P., & 15 others. (2004). TRPA1 is a candidate for the mechano-sensitive transduction channel of vertebrate hair cells. *Nature* (advance online publication, October 13, at www.nature.com). (p. 153)

Corina, D. P. (1998). The processing of sign language: Evidence from aphasia. In B. Stemmer & H. A. Whittaker (Eds.), *Handbook of neurolinguistics.* San Diego: Academic Press. (p. 50)

Corina, D. P., Vaid, J., & Bellugi, U. (1992). The linguistic basis of left hemisphere specialization. *Science, 255*, 1258–1260. (p. 50)

Corkin, S., quoted by R. Adelson. (2005, September). Lessons from H. M. *Monitor on Psychology*, p. 59. (p. 193)

Correll, J., Park, B., Judd, C. M., & Wittenbrink, B. (2002). The police officer's dilemma: Using ethnicity to disambiguate potentially threatening individuals. *Journal of Personality and Social Psychology, 83*, 1314–1329. (p. 351)

Correll, J., Park, B., Judd, C. M., Wittenbrink, B., Sadler, M. S., & Keesee, T. (2007). Across the thin blue line: Police officers and racial bias in the decision to shoot. *Journal of Personality and Social Psychology, 92*, 1006–1023. (p. 351)

Costa, P. T., Jr., & McCrae, R. R. (2011). The five-factor model, five-factor theory, and interpersonal psychology. In L. M. Horowitz & S. Strack (Eds.), *Handbook of interpersonal psychology: Theory, research, assessment, and therapeutic interventions* (pp. 91–104). Hoboken, NJ: John Wiley & Sons. (p. 324)

Costa, P. T., Jr., Terracciano, A., & McCrae, R. R. (2001). Gender differences in personality traits across cultures: Robust and surprising findings. *Journal of Personality and Social Psychology, 81*, 322–331. (p. 275)

Costa, P. T., Jr., Zonderman, A. B., McCrae, R. R., Cornoni-Huntley, J., Locke, B. Z., & Barbano, H. E. (1987). Longitudinal analyses of psychological well-being in a national sample: Stability of mean levels. *Journal of Gerontology, 42*, 50–55. (p. 100)

Costello, E. J., Compton, S. N., Keeler, G., & Angold, A. (2003). Relationships between poverty and psychopathology: A natural experiment. *Journal of the American Medical Association, 290*, 2023–2029. (p. 16)

Courneya, K. S., & Carron, A. V. (1992). The home advantage in sports competitions: A literature review. *Journal of Sport and Exercise Psychology, 14*, 13–27. (p. 347)

Courtney, J. G., Longnecker, M. P., Theorell, T., & de Verdier, M. G. (1993). Stressful life events and the risk of colorectal cancer. *Epidemiology, 4*, 407–414. (p. 288)

Covin, R., Ouimet, A. J., Seeds, P. M., & Dozois, D. J. A. (2008). A meta-analysis of CBT for pathological worry among clients with GAD. *Journal of Anxiety Disorders, 22*, 108–116. (p. 419)

Cowan, N. (2010). The magical mystery four: How is working memory capacity limited, and why? *Current Directions in Psychological Science, 19*, 51–57. (p. 194)

Cowart, B. J. (1981). Development of taste perception in humans: Sensitivity and preference throughout the life span. *Psychological Bulletin, 90*, 43–73. (p. 158)

Cowart, B. J. (2005). Taste, our body's gustatory gatekeeper. *Cerebrum, 7*(2), 7–22. (p. 157)

Cox, J. J., & 18 others. (2006). An SCN9A channelopathy causes congenital inability to experience pain. *Nature, 444*, 894–898. (p. 155)

Coyne, J. C. (1976a). Toward an interactional description of depression. *Psychiatry, 39*, 28-40. (p. 327)

Coyne, J. C. (1976b). Depression and the response of others. *Journal of Abnormal Psychology, 85*, 186–193. (pp. 327, 417)

Crabbe, J. C. (2002). Genetic contributions to addiction. *Annual Review of Psychology, 53*, 435–462. (p. 388)

Crabtree, S. (2005, January 13). Engagement keeps the doctor away. *Gallup Management Journal* (gmj.gallup.com). (p. B-5)

Crabtree, S. (2010, July 14). Personal correspondence (Gallup Organization). (p. 99)

Crabtree, S. (2011, December 12). U.S. seniors maintain happiness highs with less social time. www.gallup.com. (p. 100)

Crary, D. (2009, May 9). 5 years on, gay marriage debate fades in Mass. AP article in *The Guardian* (guardian.co.uk). (p. 125)

Credé, M., & Kuncel, N. R. (2008). Study habits, skills, and attitudes: The third pillar supporting collegiate academic performance. *Perspectives on Psychological Science, 3,* 425–453. (p. 238)

Creswell, J. D., Way, B. M., Eisenberger, N. I., & Lieberman, M. D. (2007). Neural correlates of dispositional mindfulness during affect labeling. *Psychosomatic Medicine, 69,* 560–565. (p. 299)

Crews, F. T., He, J., & Hodge, C. (2007). Adolescent cortical development: A critical period of vulnerability for addiction. *Pharmacology, Biochemistry and Behavior, 86,* 189–199. (p. 383)

Crews, F. T., Mdzinarishvili, A., Kim, D., He, J., & Nixon, K. (2006). Neurogenesis in adolescent brain is potently inhibited by ethanol. *Neuroscience, 137,* 437–445. (p. 383)

Crocker, J., & Park, L. E. (2004). The costly pursuit of self-esteem. *Psychological Bulletin, 130,* 392–414. (p. 331)

Crocker, J., Thompson, L. L., McGraw, K. M., & Ingerman, C. (1987). Downward comparison, prejudice, and evaluation of others: Effects of self-esteem and threat. *Journal of Personality and Social Psychology, 52,* 907–916. (p. 353)

Croft, R. J., Klugman, A., Baldeweg, T., & Gruzelier, J. H. (2001). Electrophysiological evidence of serotonergic impairment in long-term MDMA ("Ecstasy") users. *American Journal of Psychiatry, 158,* 1687–1692. (p. 386)

Crook, T. H., & West, R. L. (1990). Name recall performance across the adult life-span. *British Journal of Psychology, 81,* 335–340. (p. 96)

Crosier, B. S., Webster, G. D., & Dillon, H. M. (2012). Wired to connect: Evolutionary psychology and social networks. *Review of General Psychology, 16,* 230–239. (p. 359)

Cross, S., & Markus, H. (1991). Possible selves across the life span. *Human Development, 34,* 230–255. (p. 328)

Cross-National Collaborative Group. (1992). The changing rate of major depression. *Journal of the American Medical Association, 268,* 3098–3105. (p. 394)

Crowell, J. A., & Waters, E. (1994). Bowlby's theory grown up: The role of attachment in adult love relationships. *Psychological Inquiry, 5,* 1–22. (p. 83)

Csikszentmihalyi, M. (1990). *Flow: The psychology of optimal experience.* New York: Harper & Row. (p. B-1)

Csikszentmihalyi, M. (1999). If we are so rich, why aren't we happy? *American Psychologist, 54,* 821–827. (p. B-1)

Csikszentmihalyi, M., & Hunter, J. (2003). Happiness in everyday life: The uses of experience sampling. *Journal of Happiness Studies, 4,* 185–199. (p. 90)

Cuijpers, P., van Straten, A., Schuurmans, J., van Oppen, P., Hollon, S. D., & Andersson, G. (2010). Psychotherapy for chronic major depression and dysthymia: A meta-analysis. *Clinical Psychology Review, 30,* 51–62. (p. 426)

Culbert, K. M., Burt, S. A., McGue, M., Iacono, W. G., & Klump, K. L. (2009). Puberty and the genetic diathesis of disordered eating attitudes and behaviors. *Journal of Abnormal Psychology, 118,* 788–796. (p. 401)

Cullum, J., & Harton, H. C. (2007). Cultural evolution: Interpersonal influence, issue importance, and the development of shared attitudes in college residence halls. *Personality and Social Psychology Bulletin, 33,* 1327–1339. (p. 342)

Cunningham, W. A., Johnson, M. K., Raye, C. L., Gatenby, J. C., Gore, J. C., & Banaji, M. R. (2004). Separable neural components in the processing of Black and White faces. *Psychological Science, 15,* 806–813. (p. 351)

Currie, T. E., & Little, A. C. (2009). The relative importance of the face and body in judgments of human physical attractiveness. *Evolution and Human Behavior, 30,* 409–416. (p. 361)

Curtis, R. C., & Miller, K. (1986). Believing another likes or dislikes you: Behaviors making the beliefs come true. *Journal of Personality and Social Psychology, 51,* 284–290. (p. 361)

Custers, R., & Aarts, H. (2010). The unconscious will: How the pursuit of goals operates outside of conscious awareness. *Science, 329,* 47–50. (p. 226)

Cyders, M. A., & Smith, G. T. (2008). Emotion-based dispositions to rash action: Positive and negative urgency. *Psychological Bulletin, 134,* 807–828. (p. 269)

Dabbs, J. M., Jr., Bernieri, F. J., Strong, R. K., Campo, R., & Milun, R. (2001). Going on stage: Testosterone in greetings and meetings. *Journal of Research in Personality, 35,* 27–40. (p. 354)

Dabbs, J. M., Jr., & Morris, R. (1990). Testosterone, social class, and antisocial behavior in a sample of 4,462 men. *Psychological Science, 1,* 209–211. (p. 354)

Dalenberg, C. J., Brand, B. L., Gleaves, D. H., Dorahy, M. J., Loewenstein, R. J., Cardeña, E., Frewen, P. A., Carlson, E. B., & Spiegel, D. (2012). Evaluation of the evidence for the trauma and fantasy models of dissociation. *Psychological Bulletin, 138,* 550–588. (p. 402)

Daley, J. (2011, July/August). What you don't know can kill you. *Discover* (www.discovermagazine.com). (p. 223)

Damasio, A. R. (2003). *Looking for Spinoza: Joy, sorrow, and the feeling brain.* New York: Harcourt. (p. 270)

Danner, D. D., Snowdon, D. A., & Friesen, W. V. (2001). Positive emotions in early life and longevity: Findings from the Nun Study. *Journal of Personality and Social Psychology, 80,* 804–813. (p. 294)

Danso, H., & Esses, V. (2001). Black experimenters and the intellectual test performance of white participants: The tables are turned. *Journal of Experimental Social Psychology, 37,* 158–165. (p. 250)

Darley, J. M., & Alter, A. (2011). Behavioral issues of punishment and deterrence. In E. Shafir (Ed.), *The behavioral foundations of policy.* Princeton, NJ: Princeton University Press and the Russell Sage Foundation. (p. 178)

Darley, J. M., & Latané, B. (1968a). Bystander intervention in emergencies: Diffusion of responsibility. *Journal of Personality and Social Psychology, 8,* 377–383. (p. 364)

Darley, J. M., & Latané, B. (1968b, December). When will people help in a crisis? *Psychology Today,* pp. 54–57, 70–71. (p. 363)

Darwin, C. (1872). *The expression of the emotions in man and animals.* London: John Murray, Albemarle Street. (p. 277)

Daskalakis, Z. J., Levinson, A. J., & Fitzgerald, P. B. (2008). Repetitive transcranial magnetic stimulation for major depressive disorder: A review. *Canadian Journal of Psychiatry, 53,* 555–564. (p. 429)

Daum, I., & Schugens, M. M. (1996). On the cerebellum and classical conditioning. *Psychological Science, 5,* 58–61. (p. 200)

Davey, G., & Rato, R. (2012). Subjective well-being in China: A review. *Journal of Happiness Studies, 13,* 333–346. (p. 304)

Davey, G. C. L. (1995). Preparedness and phobias: Specific evolved associations or a generalized expectancy bias? *Behavioral and Brain Sciences, 18,* 289–297. (p. 381)

Davidson, J. R. T., Connor, K. M., & Swartz, M. (2006). Mental illness in U.S. presidents between 1776 and 1974: A review of biographical sources. *Journal of Nervous and Mental Disease, 194,* 47–51. (p. 404)

Davidson, R. J., & Begley, S. (2012). *The emotional life of your brain: How its unique patterns affect the way you think, feel, and live—and how you can change them.* New York: Hudson Street Press. (p. 274)

Davidson, R. J., Kabat-Zinn, J., Schumacher, J., Rosenkranz, M., Muller, D., Santorelli, S. F., Urbanowski, F., Harrington, A., Bonus, K., & Sheridan, J. F. (2003). Alterations in brain and immune function produced by mindfulness meditation. *Psychosomatic Medicine, 65,* 564–570. (p. 299)

Davidson, R. J., Pizzagalli, D., Nitschke, J. B., & Putnam, K. (2002). Depression: Perspectives from affective neuroscience. *Annual Review of Psychology, 53,* 545–574. (p. 395)

Davidson, R. J., Putnam, K. M., & Larson, C. L. (2000). Dysfunction in the neural circuitry of emotion regulation—a possible prelude to violence. *Science, 289,* 591–594. (p. 355)

Davies, G., & 31 others. (2011). Genome-wide association studies establish that human intelligence is highly heritable and polygenic. *Molecular Psychiatry, 16,* 996–1005. (p. 241)

Davies, P. (1992). *The mind of God: The scientific basis for a rational world.* New York: Simon & Schuster. (p. 129)

Davies, P. (1999). *The fifth miracle: The search for the origin and meaning of life.* New York: Simon & Schuster. (p. 129)

Davies, P. (2004, April 14). Into the 21st century. *Metaviews* (www.metanexus.net). (p. 129)

Davis, B. E., Moon, R. Y., Sachs, H. C., & Ottolini, M. C. (1998). Effects of sleep position on infant motor development. *Pediatrics, 102,* 1135–1140. (p. 74)

Davis, J. O., & Phelps, J. A. (1995a). Twins with schizophrenia: Genes or germs? *Schizophrenia Bulletin, 21,* 13–18. (p. 400)

Davis, J. O., Phelps, J. A., & Bracha, H. S. (1995b). Prenatal development of monozygotic twins and concordance for schizophrenia. *Schizophrenia Bulletin, 21,* 357–366. (p. 400)

Davis, K., Christodoulou, J., Seider, S., & Gardner, H. (2011). The theory of multiple intelligences. In R. J. Sternberg & S. B. Kaufman (Eds.), *Cambridge Handbook of Intelligence* (pp. 485–503). Cambridge, UK; New York: Cambridge University Press. (p. 236)

Davison, S. L., & Davis, S. R. (2011). Androgenic hormones and aging—The link with female function. *Hormones and Behavior, 59,* 745–753. (p. 115)

Dawes, R. M. (1994). *House of cards: Psychology and psychotherapy built on myth.* New York: Free Press. (p. 329)

Dawkins, L., Shahzad, F-Z., Ahmed, S. S., & Edmonds, C. J. (2011). Expectation of having consumed caffeine can improve performance and moods. *Appetite, 57,* 597–600. (p. 18)

Deary, I. J. (2008). Why do intelligent people live longer? *Nature, 456,* 175–176. (p. 246)

Deary, I. J., Penke, L., & Johnson, W. (2009). The neuroscience of human intelligence differences. *Nature Reviews: Neuroscience, 11,* 201–211. (p. 246)

Deary, I. J., Thorpe, G., Wilson, V., Starr, J. M., & Whalley, L. J. (2003). Population sex differences in IQ at age 11: The Scottish mental survey 1932. *Intelligence, 31,* 533–541. (p. 246)

Deary, I. J., Weiss, A., & Batty, G. D. (2010) Intelligence and personality as predictors of illness and death: How researchers in differential psychology and chronic disease epidemiology are collaborating to understand and address health inequalities. *Psychological Science in the Public Interest, 11,* 53–79. (p. 245)

Deary, I. J., Whalley, L. J., & Starr, J. M. (2009). *A lifetime of intelligence: Follow-up studies of the Scottish Mental Surveys of 1932 and 1947.* Washington, DC: American Psychological Association. (pp. 241, 243, 245)

Deary, I. J., Whiteman, M. C., Starr, J. M., Whalley, L. J., & Fox, H. C. (2004). The impact of childhood intelligence on later life: Following up the Scottish mental surveys of 1932 and 1947. *Journal of Personality and Social Psychology, 86,* 130–147. (pp. 241, 245)

de Boysson-Bardies, B., Halle, P., Sagart, L., & Durand, C. (1989). A cross-linguistic investigation of vowel formats in babbling. *Journal of Child Language, 16,* 1–17. (p. 230)

Deci, E. L., & Ryan, R. M. (Eds.) (2002). *Handbook of self-determination research.* Rochester, NY: University of Rochester Press. (p. 264)

de Courten-Myers, G. M. (2005, February 4). Personal correspondence (estimating total brain neurons, extrapolating from her carefully estimated 20 to 23 billion cortical neurons). (p. 43)

de Dios, M. A., Herman, D. S., Britton, W. B., Hagerty, C. E., Anderson, B. J., & Stein, M. D. (2012). Motivational and mindfulness intervention for young adult female marijuana users. *Journal of Substance Abuse Treatment, 42,* 56–64. (p. 299)

De Dreu, C. K. W., Greer, L. L., Handgraaf, M. J. J., Shalvi, S., Van Kleef, G. A., Baas, M., Ten Velden, F. S., Van Dijk, E., & Feith, S. W. W. (2010). The neuropeptide oxytocin regulated parochial altruism in intergroup conflict among humans. *Science, 328,* 1409–1411. (p. 37)

de Gonzales, A. B., & 33 others. (2010). Body-mass index and mortality among 1.46 million white adults. *New England Journal of Medicine, 363,* 2211–2219. (p. 262)

Dehne, K. L., & Riedner, G. (2005). *Sexually transmitted infections among adolescents: The need for adequate health services.* Geneva: World Health Organization. (p. 117)

de Hoogh, A. H. B., den Hartog, D. N., Koopman, P. L., Thierry, H., van den Berg, P. T., van der Weide, J. G., & Wilderom, C. P. M. (2004). Charismatic leadership, environmental dynamism, and performance. *European Journal of Work and Organisational Psychology, 13,* 447–471. (p. B-6)

De Koninck, J. (2000). Waking experiences and dreaming. In M. Kryger, T. Roth, & W. Dement (Eds.), *Principles and practice of sleep medicine* (3rd ed.). Philadelphia: Saunders. (p. 60)

DeLamater, J. D. (2012). Sexual expression in later life: A review and synthesis. *Journal of Sex Research, 49,* 125–141. (p. 96)

DeLamater, J. D., & Sill, M. (2005). Sexual desire in later life. *Journal of Sex Research, 42,* 138–149. (p. 96)

Delaney, H. D., Miller, W. R., & Bisonó, A. M. (2007). Religiosity and spirituality among psychologists: A survey of clinician members of the American Psychological Association. *Professional Psychology: Research and Practice, 38,* 538–546. (p. 423)

de Lange, M., Debets, L., Ruitenberg, K., & Holland, R. (2012). Making less of a mess: Scent exposure as a tool for behavioral change. *Social Influence, 7,* 90–97. (p. 159)

Delaunay-El Allam, M., Soussignan, R., Patris, B., Marlier, L., & Schaal, B. (2010). Long-lasting memory for an odor acquired at the mother's breast. *Developmental Science, 13,* 849–863. (p. 73)

DeLoache, J. S., & Brown, A. L. (1987, October-December). Differences in the memory-based searching of delayed and normally developing young children. *Intelligence, 11*(4), 277–289. (p. 77)

DeLoache, J. S., Chiong, C., Sherman, K., Islam, N., Vanderborght, M., Troseth, G. L., Strouse, G. A., & O'Doherty, K. (2010). Do babies learn from baby media? *Psychological Science, 21,* 1570–1574. (p. 245)

DeLoache, J. S., Uttal, D. H., & Rosengren, K. S. (2004). Scale errors offer evidence for a perception-action dissociation early in life. *Science, 304,* 1027–1029. (p. 76)

Dement, W. C. (1978). *Some must watch while some must sleep.* New York: Norton. (pp. 53, 59)

Dement, W. C. (1999). *The promise of sleep.* New York: Delacorte Press. (pp. 55, 56, 59)

Dement, W. C., & Wolpert, E. A. (1958). The relation of eye movements, body mobility, and external stimuli to dream content. *Journal of Experimental Psychology, 55,* 543–553. (p. 60)

Demicheli, V., Rivetti, A., Debalini, M. G., & Di Pietrantonj, C. (2012, February 15). Vaccines for measles, mumps and rubella in children. *Cochrane Database of Systematic Reviews,* Issue 2, CD004407. (p. 78)

Demir, E., & Dickson, B. J. (2005). Fruitless splicing specifies male courtship behavior in *Drosophila. Cell, 121,* 785–794. (p. 123)

de Moraes, L. (2010, March 18). Reality show contestants willing to kill in French experiment. *Washington Post* (www.washingtonpost.com). (p. 344)

DeNeve, K. M., & Cooper, H. (1998). The happy personality: A meta-analysis of 137 personality traits and subjective well-being. *Psychological Bulletin, 124,* 197–229. (p. 305)

Denollet, J. (2005). DS14: Standard assessment of negative affectivity, social inhibition, and Type D personality. *Psychosomatic Medicine, 67,* 89–97. (p. 290)

Denollet, J., Sys, S. U., Stroobant, N., Rombouts, H. Gillebert, T. C., & Brutsaert, D. L. (1996). Personality as independent predictor of long-term mortality in patients with coronary heart disease. *Lancet, 347,* 417–421. (p. 290)

Denson, T. F. (2011). A social neuroscience perspective on the neurobiological bases of aggression. In P. R. Shaver & M. Mikulincer (Eds.), *Human aggression and violence: Causes, manifestations, and consequences.* Washington, DC: U. S. American Psychological Association. (p. 355)

Denson, T. F., von Hippel, W., Kemp, R. I., & Teo, L. S. (2010). Glucose consumption decreases impulsive aggression in response to provocation in aggressive individuals. *Journal of Experimental Social Psychology, 46,* 1023–1028. (p. 293)

Denton, K., & Krebs, D. (1990). From the scene to the crime: The effect of alcohol and social context on moral judgment. *Journal of Personality and Social Psychology, 59,* 242–248. (p. 383)

Depla, M. F. I. A., ten Have, M. L., van Balkom, A. J. L. M., & de Graaf, R. (2008). Specific fears and phobias in the general population: Results from the Netherlands Mental Health Survey and Incidence Study (NEMESIS). *Social Psychiatry and Psychiatric Epidemiology, 43,* 200–208. (p. 378)

Dermer, M., Cohen, S. J., Jacobsen, E., & Anderson, E. A. (1979). Evaluative judgments of aspects of life as a function of vicarious exposure to hedonic extremes. *Journal of Personality and Social Psychology, 37,* 247–260. (p. 305)

DeSteno, D., Petty, R. E., Wegener, D. T., & Rucker, D. D. (2000). Beyond valence in the perception of likelihood: The role of emotion specificity. *Journal of Personality and Social Psychology, 78,* 397–416. (p. 205)

Dettman, S. J., Pinder, D., Briggs, R. J. S., Dowell, R. C., & Leigh, J. R. (2007). Communication development in children who receive the cochlear implant younger than 12 months: Risk versus benefits. *Ear and Hearing, 28*(2), Supplement 11S–18S. (p. 153)

Deutsch, J. A. (1972, July). Brain reward: ESP and ecstasy. *Psychology Today,* 46–48. (p. 42)

DeValois, R. L., & DeValois, K. K. (1975). Neural coding of color. In E. C. Carterette & M. P. Friedman (Eds.), *Handbook of perception: Vol. V. Seeing.* New York: Academic Press. (p. 144)

Devilly, G. J., Gist, R., & Cotton, P. (2006). Ready! Fire! Aim! The status of psychological debriefing and therapeutic interventions: In the work place and after disasters. *Review of General Psychology, 10,* 318–345. (p. 379)

de Waal, F. (2011). Back cover quote for D. Blum, *Love at Goon Park: Harry Harlow and the science of affection.* New York: Basic Books. (p. 82)

DeWall, C. N., Baumeister, R. F., Stillman, T. F., & Gaillot, M. T. (2007). Violence restrained: Effects of self-regulation and its depletion on aggression. *Journal of Experimental Social Psychology, 43,* 62–76. (p. 293)

DeWall, C. N., & Bushman, B. J. (2009). Hot under the collar in a lukewarm environment: Words associated with hot temperature increase aggressive thoughts and hostile perceptions. *Journal of Experimental Social Psychology, 45,* 1045–1047. (p. 355)

DeWall, C. N., MacDonald, G., Webster, G. D., Masten, C. L., Baumeister, R. F., Powell, C., Combs, D., Schurtz, D. R., Stillman, T. F., Tice, D. M., & Eisenberger, N. I. (2010). Acetaminophen reduces social pain: Behavioral and neural evidence. *Psychological Science, 21,* 931–937. (p. 266)

de Wit, L., Luppino, F., van Straten, A., Penninx, B., Zitman, F., & Cuijpers, P. (2010). Depression and obesity: A meta-analysis of community-based studies. *Psychiatry Research, 178,* 230–235. (p. 261)

De Wolff, M. S., & van IJzendoorn, M. H. (1997). Sensitivity and attachment: A meta-analysis on parental antecedents of infant attachment. *Child Development, 68,* 571–591. (p. 82)

DeYoung, C. G., Hirsch, J. B., Shane, M. S., Papademetris, X., Rajeevan, N., & Gray, J. R. (2010). Testing predictions from personality neuroscience: Brain structure and the Big Five. *Psychological Science, 21,* 820–828. (p. 324)

Diaconis, P. (2002, August 11). Quoted by L. Belkin, The odds of that. *New York Times* (www.nytimes.com). (p. 11)

Diaconis, P., & Mosteller, F. (1989). Methods for studying coincidences. *Journal of the American Statistical Association, 84,* 853–861. (p. 11)

Diamond, L. (2008). *Sexual fluidity: Understanding women's love and desire.* Cambridge, MA: Harvard University Press. (p. 121)

Dickens, W. T., & Flynn, J. R. (2006). Black Americans reduce the racial IQ gap: Evidence from standardization samples. *Psychological Science, 17,* 913–920. (p. 248)

Dickler, J. (2007, January 18). *Best employers, great returns.* CNNMoney.com. (p. B-4)

Dickson, B. J. (2005, June 3). Quoted in E. Rosenthal, For fruit flies, gene shift tilts sex orientation. *New York Times* (www.nytimes.com). (p. 123)

Diekelmann, S., & Born, J. (2010). The memory function of sleep. *Nature Neuroscience, 11,* 114–126. (p. 208)

Diener, E. (2006). Guidelines of national indicators of subjective well-being and ill-being. *Journal of Happiness Studies, 7,* 397–404. (p. 305)

Diener, E., Emmons, R. A., & Sandvik, E. (1986). The dual nature of happiness: Independence of positive and negative moods. Unpublished manuscript, University of Illinois. (p. 100)

Diener, E., Ng, W., Harter, J., & Arora, R. (2009). Wealth and happiness across the world: Material prosperity predicts life evaluation, while psychosocial prosperity predicts positive feeling. Unpublished manuscript, University of Illinois and the Gallup Organization. (p. 305)

Diener, E., Nickerson, C., Lucas, R. E., & Sandvik, E. (2002). Dispositional affect and job outcomes. *Social Indicators Research, 59,* 229–259. (p. 301)

Diener, E., & Oishi, S. (2000). Money and happiness: Income and subjective well-being across nations. In E. Diener & E. M. Suh (Eds.), *Subjective well-being across cultures.* Cambridge, MA: MIT Press. (p. 304)

Diener, E., Oishi, S., & Lucas, R. E. (2003). Personality, culture, and subjective well-being: Emotional and cognitive evaluations of life. *Annual Review of Psychology, 54,* 403–425. (p. 305)

Diener, E., Tay, L., & Myers, D. G. (2011). The religion paradox: If religion makes people happy, why are so many dropping out? *Journal of Personality and Social Psychology, 101,* 1278–1290. (p. 15)

Diener, E., Wolsic, B., & Fujita, F. (1995). Physical attractiveness and subjective well-being. *Journal of Personality and Social Psychology, 69,* 120–129. (p. 360)

DiFranza, J. R. (2008, May). Hooked from the first cigarette. *Scientific American,* pp. 82–87. (p. 384)

DiLalla, D. L., Carey, G., Gottesman, I. I., & Bouchard, T. J., Jr. (1996). Heritability of MMPI personality indicators of psychopathology in twins reared apart. *Journal of Abnormal Psychology, 105,* 491–499. (p. 394)

Dimberg, U., Thunberg, M., & Elmehed, K. (2000). Unconscious facial reactions to emotional facial expressions. *Psychological Science, 11,* 86–89. (pp. 271, 278)

Dingfelder, S. F. (2010, November). A second chance for the Mexican wolf. *Monitor on Psychology,* pp. 20–21. (p. 182)

Dion, K. K., & Dion, K. L. (1993). Individualistic and collectivistic perspectives on gender and the cultural context of love and intimacy. *Journal of Social Issues, 49,* 53–69. (p. 332)

DiSalvo, D. (2010, January/February). Are social networks messing with your head? *Scientific American Mind,* pp. 48–55. (p. 267)

Di Tella, R., Haisken-De New, J., & MacCulloch, R. (2010). Happiness adaptation to income and to status in an individual panel. *Journal of Economic Behavior & Organization, 76,* 834–852. (p. 304)

Dixon, J., Durrheim, K., & Tredoux, C. (2007). Intergroup contact and attitudes toward the principle and practice of racial equality. *Psychological Science, 18,* 867–872. (p. 366)

Dobbs, D. (2009, April). The post-traumatic stress trap. *Scientific American,* pp. 64–69. (p. 379)

Dodman, N. H., Karlsson, E. K., Moon-Fanelli, A., Galdzicka, M., Perloski, M., Shuster, L., Lindblad-Toh, K., & Ginns, E. I. (2010). A canine chromosome 7 locus confers compulsive disorder susceptibility. *Molecular Psychiatry 15,* 8–10. (p. 380)

Dohrenwend, B. S., Pearlin, L., Clayton, P., Hamburg, B., Dohrenwend, B. P., Riley, M., & Rose, R. (1982). Report on stress and life events. In G. R. Elliott & C. Eisdorfer (Eds.), *Stress and human health: Analysis and implications of research* (A study by the Institute of Medicine/National Academy of Sciences). New York: Springer. (p. 284)

Dolezal, H. (1982). *Living in a world transformed.* New York: Academic Press. (p. 151)

Domhoff, G. W. (1996). *Finding meaning in dreams: A quantitative approach.* New York: Plenum. (p. 60)

Domhoff, G. W. (2000). Moving dream theory beyond Freud and Jung. Paper presented to the symposium, "Beyond Freud and Jung?" Graduate Theological Union, Berkeley, CA, 9/23/2000. (p. 61)

Domhoff, G. W. (2007). Realistic simulations and bizarreness in dream content: Past findings and suggestions for future research. In D. Barrett & P. McNamara (Eds.), *The new science of dreaming: Content, recall, and personality characteristics.* Westport, CT: Praeger. (p. 60)

Domhoff, G. W. (2010). *The case for a cognitive theory of dreams.* Unpublished manuscript: University of California at Santa Cruz (dreamresearch.net/Library/domhoff_2010.html). (p. 61)

Domhoff, G. W. (2011). The neural substrate for dreaming: Is it a subsystem of the default network? *Consciousness and Cognition, 20*(4), 1163–74. (p. 61)

Domjan, M. (1992). Adult learning and mate choice: Possibilities and experimental evidence. *American Zoologist, 32,* 48–61. (p. 171)

Domjan, M. (1994). Formulation of a behavior system for sexual conditioning. *Psychonomic Bulletin & Review, 1,* 421–428. (p. 171)

Domjan, M. (2005). Pavlovian conditioning: A functional perspective. *Annual Review of Psychology, 56.* (p. 171)

Donnellan, M. B., Trzesniewski, K. H., Robins, R. W., Moffitt, T. E., & Caspi, A. (2005). Low self-esteem is related to aggression, antisocial behavior, and delinquency. *Psychological Science, 16,* 328–335. (p. 331)

Donnerstein, E. (1998). Why do we have those new ratings on television? Invited address to the National Institute on the Teaching of Psychology. (pp. 187, 188)

Donnerstein, E. (2011). The media and aggression: From TV to the Internet. In J. Forgas, A. Kruglanski, & K. Williams (eds.), *The psychology of social conflict and aggression.* New York: Psychology Press. (p. 187)

Donohue, J., & Gebhard, P. (1995). The Kinsey Institute/Indiana University report on sexuality and spinal cord injury. *Sexuality and Disability, 13,* 7–85. (p. 118)

Donvan, J., & Zucker, C. (2010, October). Autism's first child. *The Atlantic* (www.theatlantic.com). (p. 79)

Douglas, K. S., Guy, L. S., & Hart, S. D. (2009). Psychosis as a risk factor for violence to others: A meta-analysis. *Psychological Bulletin, 135,* 679–706. (p. 376)

Douthat, R. (2010, November 28). The partisan mind. *New York Times* (www.nytimes.com). (p. 352)

Dovidio, J. F., & Gaertner, S. L. (1999). Reducing prejudice: Combating intergroup biases. *Current Directions in Psychological Science, 8,* 101–105. (p. 366)

Downs, E., & Smith, S. L. (2010). Keeping abreast of hypersexuality: A video game character content analysis. *Sex Roles, 62,* 721–733. (p. 119)

Doyle, R. (2005, March). Gay and lesbian census. *Scientific American,* p. 28. (p. 125)

Draguns, J. G. (1990a). Normal and abnormal behavior in cross-cultural perspective: Specifying the nature of their relationship. *Nebraska Symposium on Motivation 1989, 37,* 235–277. (p. 371)

Draguns, J. G. (1990b). Applications of cross-cultural psychology in the field of mental health. In R. W. Brislin (Ed.), *Applied cross-cultural psychology.* Newbury Park, CA: Sage. (p. 371)

Draguns, J. G. (1997). Abnormal behavior patterns across cultures: Implications for counseling and psychotherapy. *International Journal of Intercultural Relations, 21,* 213–248. (p. 371)

Driessen, E., Cuijpers, P., de Maat, S. C. M., Abbas, A. A., de Jonghe, F., & Dekker, J. J. M. (2010). The efficacy of short-term psychodynamic psychotherapy for depression: A meta-analysis. *Clinical Psychology Review, 30,* 25–36. (p. 422)

Druckman, D., & Bjork, R. A. (Eds.) (1994). *Learning, remembering, believing: Enhancing human performance.* Washington, DC: National Academy Press. (p. 156)

Drydakis, N. (2009). Sexual orientation discrimination in the labour market. *Labour Economics, 16,* 364–372. (p. 350)

Duckworth, A. L., Quinn, P. D., & Seligman, M. E. P. (2009). Positive predictors of teacher effectiveness. *Journal of Positive Psychology, 4,* 540–547. (p. B-3)

Duckworth, A. L., & Seligman, M. E. P. (2005). Discipline outdoes talent: Self-discipline predicts academic performance in adolescents. *Psychological Science, 12*, 939–944. (pp. 293, B-3)

Duckworth, A. L., & Seligman, M. E. P. (2006). Self-discipline gives girls the edge: Gender in self-discipline, grades, and achievement tests. *Journal of Educational Psychology, 98*, 198–208. (p. B-3)

Duclos, S. E., Laird, J. D., Sexter, M., Stern, L., & Van Lighten, O. (1989). Emotion-specific effects of facial expressions and postures on emotional experience. *Journal of Personality and Social Psychology, 57*, 100–108. (p. 278)

Duggan, J. P., & Booth, D. A. (1986). Obesity, overeating, and rapid gastric emptying in rats with ventromedial hypothalamic lesions. *Science, 231*, 609–611. (p. 259)

Dumont, K. A., Widom, C. S., & Czaja, S. J. (2007). Predictors of resilience in abused and neglected children grown-up: The role of individual and neighborhood characteristics. *Child Abuse & Neglect, 31*, 255–274. (p. 83)

Duncan, B. L. (1976). Differential social perception and attribution of intergroup violence: Testing the lower limits of stereotyping of blacks. *Journal of Personality and Social Psychology, 34*, 590–598. (p. 350)

Dunn, A. L., Trivedi, M. H., Kampert, J. B., Clark, C. G., & Chambliss, H. O. (2005). Exercise treatment for depression: Efficacy and dose response. *American Journal of Preventive Medicine, 28*, 1–8. (p. 297)

Dunn, E. W., Aknin, L. B., & Norton, M. I. (2008). Spending money on others promotes happiness. *Science, 319*, 1687–1688. (p. 364)

Dunn, M., & Searle, R. (2010). Effect of manipulated prestige-car ownership on both sex attractiveness ratings. *British Journal of Psychology, 101*, 69–80. (p. 126)

Dunson, D. B., Colombo, B., & Baird, D. D. (2002). Changes with age in the level and duration of fertility in the menstrual cycle. *Human Reproduction, 17*, 1399–1403. (p. 95)

Durante, K., Griskevicius, V., Hill, S. E., Perilloux, C., & Li, N. P. (2011). Ovulation, female competition, and product choice: Hormonal influences on consumer behavior. *Journal of Consumer Research, 37*, 921–934. (p. 115)

Dutton, D. G., & Aron, A. P. (1974). Some evidence for heightened sexual attraction under conditions of high anxiety. *Journal of Personality and Social Psychology, 30*, 510–517. (p. 362)

Dutton, D. G., & Aron, A. P. (1989). Romantic attraction and generalized liking for others who are sources of conflict-based arousal. *Canadian Journal of Behavioural Sciences, 21*, 246–257. (p. 362)

Dutton, K. (2012). *The wisdom of psychopaths: What saints, spies, and serial killers can teach us about success*. New York: Scientific American/Farrar, Straus and Giroux. (p. 403)

Dweck, C. S. (2012). In P. A. M. Van Lange, A. Kruglanski, & E. T. Higgins (Eds.), *Handbook of theories of social psychology* (Vol 2), pp. 43–61. Thousand Oaks, CA: Sage Publications Ltd. (p. 250)

Dye, M. W. G., Green, C. S., & Bavelier, D. (2009). Increasing speed of processing with action video games. *Current Directions in Psychological Science, 18*, 321–326. (p. 358)

Eagly, A. H. (2007). Female leadership advantage and disadvantage: Resolving the contradictions. *Psychology of Women Quarterly, 31*, 1–12. (p. B-6)

Eagly, A. H. (2009). The his and hers of prosocial behavior: An examination of the social psychology of gender. *American Psychologist, 64*, 644–658. (p. 110)

Eagly, A. H., Ashmore, R. D., Makhijani, M. G., & Kennedy, L. C. (1991). What is beautiful is good, but . . .: A meta-analytic review of research on the physical attractiveness stereotype. *Psychological Bulletin, 110*, 109–128. (p. 360)

Eagly, A. H., & Carli, L. (2007). *Through the labyrinth: The truth about how women become leaders*. Cambridge, MA: Harvard University Press. (p. 109)

Eagly, A. H., Eaton, A., Rose, S. M., Riger, S., & McHugh, M. C. (2012). Feminism and psychology: Analysis of a half-century of research on women and gender. *American Psychologist, 67*, 211–230. (p. 108)

Eagly, A. H., & Wood, W. (2013). The nature-nurture debates: 25 years of challenges in understanding the psychology of gender. *Perspectives on Psychological Science, 8*, 340–357. (p. 110)

Easterlin, R. A., Morgan, R., Switek, M., & Wang, F. (2012). China's life satisfaction, 1990–2010. *PNAS, 109*, 9670–9671. (p. 304)

Eastwick, P. W., & Finkel, E. J. (2008a). Speed-dating as a methodological innovation. *The Psychologist, 21*, 402–403. (p. 359)

Eastwick, P. W., & Finkel, E. J. (2008b). Sex differences in mate preferences revisited: Do people know what they initially desire in a romantic partner? *Journal of Personality and Social Psychology, 94*, 245–264. (p. 359)

Eberhardt, J. L. (2005). Imaging race. *American Psychologist, 60*, 181–190. (p. 351)

Eckensberger, L. H. (1994). Moral development and its measurement across cultures. In W. J. Lonner & R. Malpass (Eds.), *Psychology and culture*. Boston: Allyn & Bacon. (p. 88)

Eckert, E. D., Heston, L. L., & Bouchard, T. J., Jr. (1981). MZ twins reared apart: Preliminary findings of psychiatric disturbances and traits. In L. Gedda, P. Paris, & W. D. Nance (Eds.), *Twin research: Vol. 3. Pt. B. Intelligence, personality, and development*. New York: Alan Liss. (p. 380)

Economist. (2001, December 20). An anthropology of happiness. *The Economist* (www.economist.com/world/asia). (p. 265)

Edelman, S., & Kidman, A. D. (1997). Mind and cancer: Is there a relationship? A review of the evidence. *Australian Psychologist, 32*, 1–7. (p. 288)

Edwards, R. R., Campbell, C., Jamison, R. N., & Wiech, K. (2009). The neurobiological underpinnings of coping with pain. *Current Directions in Psychological Science, 18*, 237–241. (p. 155)

Ehrlichman, H., & Halpern, J. N. (1988). Affect and memory: Effects of pleasant and unpleasant odors on retrieval of happy and unhappy memories. *Journal of Personality and Social Psychology, 55*, 769–779. (p. 158)

Eisenberg, N., & Lennon, R. (1983). Sex differences in empathy and related capacities. *Psychological Bulletin, 94*, 100–131. (p. 276)

Eisenberger, N. I. (2012a). Broken hearts and broken bones: A neural perspective on the similarities between social and physical pain. *Psychological Science, 21*, 42–47. (p. 266)

Eisenberger, N. I. (2012b). The neural bases of social pain: Evidence for shared representations with physical pain. *Psychosomatic Medicine, 74*, 126–135. (p. 266)

Eisenberger, N. I., Master, S. L., Inagaki, T. K., Taylor, S. E., Shirinyan, D., Lieberman, M. D., & Nalifoff, B. D. (2011). Attachment figures activate a safety signal-related neural region and reduce pain experience. *Proceedings of the National Academy of Sciences, 108*, 11721–11726. (p. 266)

Eisenberger, R., & Rhoades, L. (2001). Incremental effects of reward on creativity. *Journal of Personality and Social Psychology, 81*, 728–741. (p. 184)

Ekman, P. (1994). Strong evidence for universals in facial expressions: A reply to Russell's mistaken critique. Psychological Bulletin, 115, 268–287. (p. 276)

Ekman, P., & Friesen, W. V. (1975). *Unmasking the face*. Englewood Cliffs, NJ: Prentice-Hall. (p. 276)

Ekman, P., Friesen, W. V., O'Sullivan, M., Chan, A., Diacoyanni-Tarlatzis, I., Heider, K., Krause, R., LeCompte, W. A., Pitcairn, T., Ricci-Bitti, P. E., Scherer, K., Tomita, M., & Tzavaras, A. (1987). Universals and cultural differences in the judgments of facial expressions of emotion. *Journal of Personality and Social Psychology, 53,* 712–717. (p. 276)

Elbogen, E. B., & Johnson, S. C. (2009). The intricate link between violence and mental disorder: Results from the National Epidemiologic Survey on Alcohol and Related Conditions. *Archives of General Psychiatry, 66,* 152–161. (p. 376)

Elfenbein, H. A., & Ambady, N. (1999). *Does it take one to know one? A meta-analysis of the universality and cultural specificity of emotion recognition.* Unpublished manuscript, Harvard University. (p. 276)

Elfenbein, H. A., & Ambady, N. (2002). On the universality and cultural specificity of emotion recognition: A meta-analysis. *Psychological Bulletin, 128,* 203–235. (p. 276)

Elfenbein, H. A., & Ambady, N. (2003a). When familiarity breeds accuracy: Cultural exposure and facial emotion recognition. *Journal of Personality and Social Psychology, 85,* 276–290. (p. 276)

Elfenbein, H. A., & Ambady, N. (2003b). Universals and cultural differences in recognizing emotions. *Current Directions in Psychological Science, 12,* 159–164. (p. 276)

Elkind, D. (1970). The origins of religion in the child. *Review of Religious Research, 12,* 35–42. (p. 87)

Elkind, D. (1978). *The child's reality: Three developmental themes.* Hillsdale, NJ: Erlbaum. (p. 87)

Ellenbogen, J. M., Hu, P. T., Payne, J. D., Titone, D., & Walker, M. P. (2007). Human relational memory requires time and sleep. *Proceedings of the National Academy of Sciences, 104,* 7723–7728. (p. 56)

Ellin, A. (2009, February 12). The recession. Isn't it romantic? *New York Times* (www.nytimes.com). (p. 359)

Elliot, A. J., & Niesta, D. (2008). Romantic red: Red enhances men's attraction to women. *Journal of Personality and Social Psychology, 95,* 1150–1164. (p. 183)

Elliot, A. J., Tracy, J. L., Pazda, A. D., & Beall, A. T. (2013). Red enhances women's attractiveness to men: First evidence suggesting universality. *Journal of Experimental Social Psychology, 49,* 165–168. (p. 182)

Ellis, A. (1980). Psychotherapy and atheistic values: A response to A. E. Bergin's "Psychotherapy and religious values." *Journal of Consulting and Clinical Psychology, 48,* 635–639. (p. 423)

Ellis, B. J., Bates, J. E., Dodge, K. A., Fergusson, D. M., John, H. L., Pettit, G. S., & Woodward, L. (2003). Does father absence place daughters at special risk for early sexual activity and teenage pregnancy? *Child Development, 74,* 801–821. (p. 119)

Ellis, B. J., & Boyce, W. T. (2008). Biological sensitivity to context. *Current Directions in Psychological Science, 17,* 183–187. (p. 380)

Ellis, L., & Ames, M. A. (1987). Neurohormonal functioning and sexual orientation: A theory of homosexuality-heterosexuality. *Psychological Bulletin, 101,* 233–258. (p. 123)

Else-Quest, N. M., Hyde, J. S., & Linn, M. C. (2010). Cross-national patterns of gender differences in mathematics: A meta-analysis. *Psychological Bulletin, 136,* 103–127. (p. 246)

Elzinga, B. M., Ardon, A. M., Heijnis, M. K., De Ruiter, M. B., Van Dyck, R., & Veltman, D. J. (2007). Neural correlates of enhanced working-memory performance in dissociative disorder: A functional MRI study. *Psychological Medicine, 37,* 235–245. (p. 402)

Emerging Trends. (1997, September). *Teens turn more to parents than friends on whether to attend church.* Princeton, NJ: Princeton Religion Research Center. (p. 91)

Emery, G., Jr. (2004). *Psychic predictions 2004.* Committee for the Scientific Investigation of Claims of the Paranormal (www.csicop.org). (p. 161)

Emery, G., Jr. (2006, January 17). Psychic predictions 2005. *Skeptical Inquirer* (www.csicop.org). (p. 161)

Emmons, R. A. (2007). *Thanks! How the new science of gratitude can make you happier.* Boston: Houghton Mifflin. (p. 306)

Emmons, S., Geisler, C., Kaplan, K. J., & Harrow, M. (1997). *Living with schizophrenia.* Muncie, IN: Taylor and Francis (Accelerated Development). (pp. 371, 397)

Endler, N. S. (1982). *Holiday of darkness: A psychologist's personal journey out of his depression.* New York: Wiley. (pp. 395, 428)

Engemann, K. M., & Owyang, M. T. (2005, April). So much for that merit raise: The link between wages and appearance. *Regional Economist* (www.stlouisfed.org). (p. 360)

Engen, T. (1987). Remembering odors and their names. *American Scientist, 75,* 497–503. (p. 158)

England, P. (2010). The gender revolution: Uneven and stalled. *Gender & Society, 24,* 149–166. (p. 107)

English, T., & Chen, S. (2011) Self-concept consistency and culture: The differential impact of two forms of consistency. *Personality and Social Psychology Bulletin, 37,* 838–849. (p. 333)

Entringer, S., Buss, C., Andersen, J., Chicz-DeMet, A., & Wadhwa, P. D. (2011). Ecological momentary assessment of maternal cortisol profiles over a multiple-day period predicts the length of human gestation. *Psychosomatic Medicine, 73,* 469–474. (p. 284)

Epel, E. S. (2009). Telomeres in a life-span perspective: A new "psychobiomarker"? *Current Directions in Psychological Science, 18,* 6–9. (p. 96)

Epley, N., Keysar, B., Van Boven, L., & Gilovich, T. (2004). Perspective taking as egocentric anchoring and adjustment. *Journal of Personality and Social Psychology, 87,* 327–339. (p. 78)

Epley, N., Savitsky, K., & Gilovich, T. (2002). Empathy neglect: Reconciling the spotlight effect and the correspondence bias. *Journal of Personality and Social Psychology, 83,* 300–312. (p. 329)

Epstein, J., Stern, E., & Silbersweig, D. (1998). Mesolimbic activity associated with psychosis in schizophrenia: Symptom-specific PET studies. In J. F. McGinty (Ed.), *Advancing from the ventral striatum to the extended amygdala: Implications for neuropsychiatry and drug use: In honor of Lennart Heimer. Annals of the New York Academy of Sciences, 877,* 562–574. (p. 398)

Epstein, K. (2006, Spring). Crisis mentality: Why sudden emergencies attract more funds than do chronic conditions, and how nonprofits can change that. *Stanford Social Innovation Review,* pp. 48–57. (p. 225)

Epstein, S. (1983a). Aggregation and beyond: Some basic issues on the prediction of behavior. *Journal of Personality, 51,* 360–392. (p. 325)

Epstein, S. (1983b). The stability of behavior across time and situations. In R. Zucker, J. Aronoff, & A. I. Rabin (Eds.), *Personality and the prediction of behavior.* San Diego: Academic Press. (p. 325)

Erdberg, P. (1990). Rorschach assessment. In G. Goldstein & M. Hersen (Eds.), *Handbook of psychological assessment* (2nd ed.). New York: Pergamon. (p. 317)

Erdelyi, M. H. (1985). *Psychoanalysis: Freud's cognitive psychology.* New York: Freeman. (p. 318)

Erdelyi, M. H. (1988). Repression, reconstruction, and defense: History and integration of the psychoanalytic and experimental frameworks. In J. Singer (Ed.), *Repression: Defense mechanism and cognitive style.* Chicago: University of Chicago Press. (p. 318)

Erdelyi, M. H. (2006). The unified theory of repression. *Behavioral and Brain Sciences, 29,* 499–551. (p. 318)

Erickson, K. I. (2009). Aerobic fitness is associated with hippocampal volume in elderly humans. *Hippocampus, 19,* 1030–1039. (p. 95)

Erickson, K. I., & 9 others. (2010). Physical activity predicts gray matter volume in late adulthood: The Cardiovascular Health Study. *Neurology, 75,* 1415–1422. (p. 95)

Erickson, M. F., & Aird, E. G. (2005). *The motherhood study: Fresh insights on mothers' attitudes and concerns.* New York: The Motherhood Project, Institute for American Values. (p. 99)

Ericsson, K. A. (2001). Attaining excellence through deliberate practice: Insights from the study of expert performance. In M. Ferrari (Ed.), *The pursuit of excellence in education.* Hillsdale, NJ: Erlbaum. (p. B-3)

Ericsson, K. A. (2002). Attaining excellence through deliberate practice: Insights from the study of expert performance. In C. Desforges & R. Fox (Eds.), *Teaching and learning: The essential readings.* Malden, MA: Blackwell Publishers. (p. 238)

Ericsson, K. A. (2006). The influence of experience and deliberate practice on the development of superior expert performance. In K. A. Ericsson, N. Charness, P. J. Feltovich, & R. R. Hoffman (Eds.), *The Cambridge handbook of expertise and expert performance.* Cambridge: Cambridge University Press. (p. B-3)

Ericsson, K. A. (2007). Deliberate practice and the modifiability of body and mind: Toward a science of the structure and acquisition of expert and elite performance. *International Journal of Sport Psychology, 38,* 4–34. (p. 238)

Ericsson, K. A., Roring, R. W., & Nandagopal, K. (2007). Giftedness and evidence for reproducibly superior performance: An account based on the expert performance framework. *High Ability Studies, 18,* 3–56. (pp. 250, B-3)

Erikson, E. H. (1963). *Childhood and society.* New York: Norton. (p. 89)

Erol, R. Y., & Orth, U. (2011). Self-esteem development from age 14 to 30 years: A longitudinal study. *Journal of Personality and Social Psychology, 101,* 607–619. (pp. 90, 329)

Ertmer, D. J., Young, N. M., & Nathani, S. (2007). Profiles of focal development in young cochlear implant recipients. *Journal of Speech, Language, and Hearing Research, 50,* 393–407. (p. 231)

Escobar-Chaves, S. L., Tortolero, S. R., Markham, C. M., Low, B. J., Eitel, P., & Thickstun, P. (2005). Impact of the media on adolescent sexual attitudes and behaviors. *Pediatrics, 116,* 303–326. (p. 119)

Esser, J. K., & Lindoerfer, J. S. (1989). Groupthink and the space shuttle *Challenger* accident: Toward a quantitative case analysis. *Journal of Behavioral Decision Making, 2,* 167–177. (p. 349)

Esterling, B. A., L'Abate, L., Murray, E. J., & Pennebaker, J. W. (1999). Empirical foundations for writing in prevention and psychotherapy: Mental and physical health outcomes. *Clinical Psychology Review, 19,* 79–96. (p. 296)

Esterson, A. (2001). The mythologizing of psychoanalytic history: Deception and self-deception in Freud's accounts of the seduction theory episode. *History of Psychiatry, 12,* 329–352. (p. 317)

Eurich, T. L., Krause, D. E., Cigularov, K., & Thornton, G. C., III. (2009). Assessment centers: Current practices in the United States. *Journal of Business Psychology, 24,* 387–407. (p. 328)

Evans, C. R., & Dion, K. L. (1991). Group cohesion and performance: A meta-analysis. *Small Group Research, 22,* 175–186. (p. B-7)

Evans, N., & Levinson, S. C. (2009). The myth of language universals: Language diversity and its importance for cognitive science. *Behavioral and Brain Sciences, 32,* 429–492. (p. 231)

Exline, J. J., Baumeister, R. F., Bushman, B. J., Campbell, W. K., & Finkel, E. J. (2004). Too proud to let go: Narcissistic entitlement as a barrier to forgiveness. *Journal of Personality and Social Psychology, 87,* 894–912. (p. 330)

Exner, J. E. (2003). *The Rorschach: A comprehensive system* (4th ed.). Hoboken, NJ: Wiley. (p. 317)

Eysenck, H. J. (1952). The effects of psychotherapy: An evaluation. *Journal of Consulting Psychology, 16,* 319–324. (p. 421)

Eysenck, H. J. (1990, April 30). An improvement on personality inventory. *Current Contents: Social and Behavioral Sciences, 22*(18), 20. (p. 323)

Eysenck, H. J. (1992). Four ways five factors are *not* basic. *Personality and Individual Differences, 13,* 667–673. (p. 323)

Eysenck, H. J., & Grossarth-Maticek, R. (1991). Creative novation behaviour therapy as a prophylactic treatment for cancer and coronary heart disease: Part II—Effects of treatment. *Behaviour Research and Therapy, 29,* 17–31. (p. 298)

Eysenck, H. J., Wakefield, J. A., Jr., & Friedman, A. F. (1983). Diagnosis and clinical assessment: The DSM-III. *Annual Review of Psychology, 34,* 167–193. (p. 375)

Eysenck, S. B. G., & Eysenck, H. J. (1963). The validity of questionnaire and rating assessments of extraversion and neuroticism, and their factorial stability. *British Journal of Psychology, 54,* 51–62. (p. 322)

Fabiano, G. A., Pelham, W. E., Jr., Coles, E. K., Gnagy, E. M., Chronis-Tuscano, A., & O'Connor, B. C. (2008). A meta-analysis of behavioral treatments for attention-deficit/hyperactivity disorder. *Clinical Psychology Review, 29,* 129–140. (p. 373)

Fagan, J. F., & Holland, C. R. (2007). Equal opportunity and racial differences in IQ. *Intelligence, 30,* 361–387. (p. 249)

Fairfield, H. (2012, February 4). Girls lead in science exam, but not in the United States. *New York Times* (www.nytimes.com). (p. 247)

Falk, R., Falk, R., & Ayton, P. (2009). Subjective patterns of randomness and choice: Some consequences of collective responses. *Journal of Experimental Psychology: Human Perception and Performance, 35,* 203–224. (p. 10)

Farah, M. J., Rabinowitz, C., Quinn, G. E., & Liu, G. T. (2000). Early commitment of neural substrates for face recognition. *Cognitive Neuropsychology, 17,* 117–124. (p. 47)

Farb, N. A. S., Anderson, A. K., Mayberg, H., Bean, J., McKeon, D., & Segal, Z. V. (2010). Minding one's emotions: Mindfulness training alters the neural expression of sadness. *Emotion, 10,* 25–33. (p. 299)

Farina, A. (1982). The stigma of mental disorders. In A. G. Miller (Ed.), *In the eye of the beholder.* New York: Praeger. (pp. 372, 375)

Farley, M., Baral, I., Kiremire, M., & Sezgin, U. (1998). Prostitution in five countries: Violence and post-traumatic stress disorder. *Feminism and Psychology, 8,* 405–426. (p. 379)

Farrington, D. P. (1991). Antisocial personality from childhood to adulthood. *The Psychologist: Bulletin of the British Psychological Society, 4,* 389–394. (p. 403)

Fazel, S., & Grann, M. (2006). The population impact of severe mental illness on violent crime. *American Journal of Psychiatry, 163,* 1397–1403. (p. 376)

Fazel, S., Langstrom, N., Hjern, A., Grann, M., & Lichtenstein, P. (2009). Schizophrenia, substance abuse, and violent crime. *JAMA, 301,* 2016–2023. (p. 376)

Fazel, S., Lichtenstein, P., Grann, M., Goodwin, G. M., & Långström, N. (2010). bipolar disorder and violent crime: new evidence from population-based longitudinal studies and systematic review. *Archives of General Psychiatry, 67,* 931–938. (p. 376)

Feeney, J. A. (2008). Adult romantic attachment: Developments in the study of couple relationships. In J. Cassidy & P. R. Shaver (Eds.), *Handbook* of attachment: Theory, research, and clinical applications (2nd ed., pp. 456–481). New York: Guilford. (p. 83)

Feingold, A. (1990). Gender differences in effects of physical attractiveness on romantic attraction: A comparison across five research paradigms. Journal of Personality and Social Psychology, 59, 981–993. (p. 360)

Feingold, A. (1992). Good-looking people are not what we think. Psychological Bulletin, 111, 304–341. (p. 360)

Feingold, A., & Mazzella, R. (1998). Gender differences in body image are increasing. Psychological Science, 9, 190–195. (p. 401)

Feinstein, J. S., Duff, M. C., & Tranel, D. (2010, April 27). Sustained experiences of emotion after loss of memory in patients with amnesia. Proceedings of the National Academy of Sciences, 107, 7674–7679. (pp. 41, 200)

Feng, J., Spence, I., & Pratt, J. (2007). Playing an action video game reduces gender differences in spatial cognition. Psychological Science, 18, 850–855. (p. 247)

Ferguson, C. J. (2009a). Media violence effects: Confirmed truth or just another X-file? Journal of Forensic Psychology Practice, 9, 103–126. (p. 188)

Ferguson, C. J. (2009b, June 14). Not every child is secretly a genius. The Chronicle Review (http://chronicle.com/article/Not-Every-Child-Is-Secretly/48001). (p. 237)

Ferguson, C. J. (2010). A meta-analysis of normal and disordered personality across the life span. Journal of Personality and Social Psychology, 98, 659–667. (p. 102)

Ferguson, C. J., & Kilburn, J. (2010). Much ado about nothing: The misestimation and overinterpretation of violent video game effects in Eastern and Western nations: Comment on Anderson et al. (2010). Psychological Bulletin, 136, 174–178. (p. 358)

Ferguson, C. J., San Miguel, C., Garza, A., & Jerabeck, J. M. (2011). A longitudinal test of video game violence influences on dating and aggression: A 3-year longitudinal study of adolescents. Journal of Psychiatric Research, 46, 141–146. (p. 358)

Ferguson, C. J., Winegard, B., & Winegard, B. M. (2011). Who is the fairest one of all? How evolution guides peer and media influences on female body dissatisfaction. Review of General Psychology, 15, 11–28. (p. 401)

Ferguson, M. J., & Zayas, V. (2009). Automatic evaluation. Current Directions in Psychological Science, 18, 362–366. (p. 136)

Fergusson, D. M., & Woodward, L. G. (2002). Mental health, educational, and social role outcomes of adolescents with depression. Archives of General Psychiatry, 59, 225–231. (p. 393)

Fernández-Dols, J-M., & Ruiz-Belda, M-A. (1995). Are smiles a sign of happiness? Gold medal winners at the Olympic Games. Journal of Personality and Social Psychology, 69, 1113–1119. (p. 277)

Fernyhough, C. (2008). Getting Vygotskian about theory of mind: Mediation, dialogue, and the development of social understanding. Developmental Review, 28, 225–262. (p. 80)

Ferriman, K., Lubinski, D., & Benbow, C. P. (2009). Work preferences, life values, and personal views of top math/science graduate students and the profoundly gifted: Developmental changes and gender differences during emerging adulthood and parenthood. Journal of Personality and Social Psychology, 97, 517–522. (p. 110)

Ferris, C. F. (1996, March). The rage of innocents. The Sciences, pp. 22–26. (p. 84)

Feynman, R. (1997). Quoted by E. Hutchings (Ed.), "Surely you're joking, Mr. Feynman." New York: Norton. (p. 9)

Fiedler, F. E. (1981). Leadership effectiveness. American Behavioral Scientist, 24, 619–632. (p. B-6)

Fiedler, F. E. (1987, September). When to lead, when to stand back. Psychology Today, pp. 26–27. (p. B-7)

Field, A. P. (2006). Is conditioning a useful framework for understanding the development and treatment of phobias? Clinical Psychology Review, 26, 857–875. (p. 379)

Field, T. (2010). Touch for socioemotional and physical well-being: A review. Developmental Review, 30, 367–383. (p. 74)

Fields, R. D. (2009). The other brain: From dementia to schizophrenia, how new discoveries about the brain are revolutionizing medicine and science. New York: Simon & Schuster. (p. 30)

Fikke, L. T., Melinder, A., & Landrø, N. I. (2011). Executive functions are impaired in adolescents engaging in non-suicidal self-injury. Psychological Medicine, 41, 601–610. (p. 392)

Fincham, F. D., & Bradbury, T. N. (1993). Marital satisfaction, depression, and attributions: A longitudinal analysis. Journal of Personality and Social Psychology, 64, 442–452. (p. 339)

Finchilescu, G., & Tredoux, C. (eds.) (2010). Intergroup relations in post apartheid South Africa: Change, and obstacles to change. Journal of Social Issues, 66, 223–236. (p. 366)

Fingelkurts, A. A., & Fingelkurts, A. A. (2009). Is our brain hardwired to produce God, or is our brain hardwired to perceive God? A systematic review on the role of the brain in mediating religious experience. Cognitive Processes, 10, 293–326. (p. 47)

Fingerman, K. L., & Charles, S. T. (2010). It takes two to tango: Why older people have the best relationships. Current Directions in Psychological Science, 19, 172–176. (p. 100)

Fink, M. (2009). Electroconvulsive therapy: A guide for professionals and their patients. New York: Oxford University Press. (p. 427)

Finkel, E. J., DeWall, C. N., Slotter, E. B., McNulty, J. K., Pond, R. S., Jr., & Atkins, D. C. (2012). Using I³ theory to clarify when dispositional aggressiveness predicts intimate partner violence perpetration. Journal of Personality and Social Psychology, 102, 533–549. (p. 293)

Finkel, E. J., & Eastwick, P. W. (2008). Speed-dating. Current Directions in Psychological Science, 17, 193–197. (p. 360)

Finkel, E. J., & Eastwick, P. W. (2009). Arbitrary social norms influence sex differences in romantic selectivity. Psychological Science 20, 1290–1295. (p. 359)

Finkel, E. J., Eastwick, P. W., Karney, B. R., Reis, H. T., & Sprecher, S. (2012a, September/October). Dating in a digital world. Scientific American Mind, pp. 26–33. (pp. 322, 359)

Finkel, E. J., Eastwick, P. W., Karney, B. R., Reis, H. T., & Sprecher, S. (2012b). Online dating: A critical analysis from the perspective of psychological science. Psychological Science in the Public Interest, 13, 3–66. (pp. 322, 359)

Fiore, M. C., & 23 others. (2008). Treating tobacco use and dependence: 2008 update. Clinical practice guideline. Rockville, MD: U.S. Department of Health and Human Services, Public Health Service. (p. 385)

Fischer, P., & Greitemeyer, T. (2006). Music and aggression: The impact of sexual-aggressive song lyrics on aggression-related thoughts, emotions, and behavior toward the same and the opposite sex. Personality and Social Psychology Bulletin, 32, 1165–1176. (p. 357)

Fischer, P., Greitemeyer, T., Kastenmüller, A., Vogrincic, C., & Sauer, A. (2011). The effects of risk-glorifying media exposure on risk-positive cognitions, emotions, and behaviors: A meta-analytic review. Psychological Bulletin, 137, 367–390. (pp. 188, 357)

Fischer, R., & Boer, D. (2011). What is more important for national well-being: Money or autonomy? A meta-analysis of well-being, burnout, and anxiety across 63 societies. Journal of Personality and Social Psychology, 101, 164–184. (p. 303)

Fischhoff, B. (1982). Debiasing. In D. Kahneman, P. Slovic, & A. Tversky (Eds.), *Judgment under uncertainty: Heuristics and biases.* New York: Cambridge University Press. (p. 223)

Fischhoff, B., Slovic, P., & Lichtenstein, S. (1977). Knowing with certainty: The appropriateness of extreme confidence. *Journal of Experimental Psychology: Human Perception and Performance, 3*, 552–564. (p. 223)

Fishbach, A., Dhar, R., & Zhang, Y. (2006). Subgoals as substitutes or complements: The role of goal accessibility. *Journal of Personality and Social Psychology, 91*, 232–242. (p. B-6)

Fisher, E. L., & Borgida, E. (2012). Intergroup disparities and implicit bias: A commentary. *Journal of Social Issues, 68*, 385–398. (p. 351)

Fisher, H. E. (1993, March/April). After all, maybe it's biology. *Psychology Today*, pp. 40–45. (p. 97)

Fisher, H. T. (1984). Little Albert and Little Peter. *Bulletin of the British Psychological Society, 37*, 269. (p. 414)

Fitzgerald, P. B., & Daskalakis, Z. J. (2008). The use of repetitive transcranial magnetic stimulation and vagal nerve stimulation in the treatment of depression. *Current Opinion in Psychiatry, 21*, 25–29. (p. 428)

Flack, W. F. (2006). Peripheral feedback effects of facial expressions, bodily postures, and vocal expressions on emotional feelings. *Cognition and Emotion, 20*, 177–195. (p. 278)

Flaherty, D. K. (2011). The vaccine-autism connection: a public health crisis caused by unethical medical practices and fraudulent science. *Annals of Pharmacotherapy, 45*, 1302–1304. (p. 78)

Flegal, K. M., Carroll, M. D., Kit, B. K., Ogden, C. L. (2012). Prevalence of obesity and trends in the distribution of body mass index among US adults, 1999–2010. *JAMA, 307*, 491–497. (p. 262)

Fleming, I., Baum, A., & Weiss, L. (1987). Social density and perceived control as mediator of crowding stress in high-density residential neighborhoods. *Journal of Personality and Social Psychology, 52*, 899–906. (p. 292)

Fleming, J. H. (2001, Winter/Spring). Introduction to the special issue on linkage analysis. *The Gallup Research Journal*, pp. i–vi. (p. B-5)

Fleming, J. H., & Scott, B. A. (1991). The costs of confession: The Persian Gulf War POW tapes in historical and theoretical perspective. *Contemporary Social Psychology, 15*, 127–138. (p. 276)

Fletcher, G. J. O., Fitness, J., & Blampied, N. M. (1990). The link between attributions and happiness in close relationships: The roles of depression and explanatory style. *Journal of Social and Clinical Psychology, 9*, 243–255. (p. 339)

Flora, S. R. (2004). *The power of reinforcement.* Albany, NJ: SUNY Press. (p. 180)

Flora, S. R., & Bobby, S. E. (2008, September/October). The bipolar bamboozle. *Skeptical Inquirer*, pp. 41–45. (p. 392)

Flynn, J. R. (2003). Movies about intelligence: The limitations of g. *Current Directions in Psychological Science, 12*, 95–99. (p. 244)

Flynn, J. R. (2007). *What is intelligence?* New York: Cambridge University Press. (pp. 244, 249)

Foa, E. B., & Kozak, M. J. (1986). Emotional processing of fear: Exposure to corrective information. *Psychological Bulletin, 99*, 20–35. (p. 415)

Food and Drug Administration. (2011). FDA Executive Summary. Prepared for the January 27–28, 2011 meeting of the Neurological Devices Panel (www.fda.gov). (p. 428)

Ford, E. S. (2002). Does exercise reduce inflammation? Physical activity and B-reactive protein among U.S. adults. *Epidemiology, 13*, 561–569. (p. 297)

Ford, M. T., Cerasoli, C. P., Higgins, J. A., & Deccesare, A. L. (2011). Relationships between psychological, physical, and behavioural health and work performance: A review and meta-analysis. *Work & Stress, 25*, 185–204. (p. B-5)

Foree, D. D., & LoLordo, V. M. (1973). Attention in the pigeon: Differential effects of food-getting versus shock-avoidance procedures. *Journal of Comparative and Physiological Psychology, 85*, 551–558. (p. 183)

Forgas, J. P. (2008). Affect and cognition. *Perspectives on Psychological Science, 3*, 94–101. (p. 301)

Forgas, J. P. (2009, November/December). Think negative! *Australian Science*, pp. 14–17. (p. 390)

Forgas, J. P., Bower, G. H., & Krantz, S. E. (1984). The influence of mood on perceptions of social interactions. *Journal of Experimental Social Psychology, 20*, 497–513. (p. 205)

Forhan, S. E., Gottlieb, S. L., Sternberg, M. R., Xu, F., Datta, D., Berman, S., & Markowitz, L. (2008). Prevalence of sexually transmitted infections and bacterial vaginosis among female adolescents in the United States: Data from the National Health and Nutrition Examination Survey (NHANES) 2003–2004. Paper presented to the 2008 National STD Prevention Conference, Chicago, Illinois. (p. 117)

Forsyth, D. R., Lawrence, N. K., Burnette, J. L., & Baumeister, R. F. (2007). Attempting to improve academic performance of struggling college students by bolstering their self-esteem: An intervention that backfired. *Journal of Social and Clinical Psychology, 26*, 447–459. (p. 330)

Foss, D. J., & Hakes, D. T. (1978). *Psycholinguistics: An introduction to the psychology of language.* Englewood Cliffs, NJ: Prentice-Hall. (p. 317)

Foster, R. G. (2004). Are we trying to banish biological time? *Cerebrum, 6*(2), 7–26. (p. 55)

Foubert, J. D., Brosi, M. W., & Bannon, R. S. (2011). Pornography viewing among fraternity men: Effects on bystander intervention, rape myth acceptance, and behavioral intent to commit sexual assault. *Sexual Addiction & Compulsivity, 18*, 212–231. (p. 118)

Foulkes, D. (1999). *Children's dreaming and the development of consciousness.* Cambridge, MA: Harvard University Press. (p. 61)

Fournier, J. C., DeRubeis, R. J., Hollon, S. D., Dimidjian, S., Amsterdam, J. D., Shelton, R. C., & Fawcett, J. (2010). Antidepressant drug effects and depression severity: A patient-level meta-analysis. *Journal of the American Medical Association, 303*, 47–53. (p. 427)

Fouts, R. S. (1992). Transmission of a human gestural language in a chimpanzee mother-infant relationship. *Friends of Washoe, 12/13*, pp. 2–8. (p. 235)

Fouts, R. S. (1997). *Next of kin: What chimpanzees have taught me about who we are.* New York: Morrow. (p. 235)

Fowles, D. C., & Dindo, L. (2009). Temperament and psychopathy: A dual-pathway model. *Current Directions in Psychological Science, 18*, 179–183. (p. 403)

Fox, B. H. (1998). Psychosocial factors in cancer incidence and prognosis. In P. M. Cinciripini & others (Eds.), *Psychological and behavioral factors in cancer risk.* New York: Oxford University Press. (p. 288)

Fox, E., Lester, V., Russo, R., Bowles, R. J., Pichler, A., & Dutton, K. (2000). Facial expression of emotion: Are angry faces detected more efficiently? *Cognition and Emotion, 14*, 61–92. (p. 275)

Fox, J. L. (1984). The brain's dynamic way of keeping in touch. *Science, 225*, 820–821. (p. 47)

Fox, M. L., Dwyer, D. J., & Ganster, D. C. (1993). Effects of stressful job demands and control on physiological and attitudinal outcomes in a hospital setting. *Academy of Management Journal, 36*, 289–318. (p. 291)

Fracassini, C. (2000, August 27). Holidaymakers led by the nose in sales quest. *Scotland on Sunday.* (p. 159)

Fraley, R. C., Roisman, G. I., Booth-LaForce, C., Owen, M. T., & Holland, A. S. (2013). Interpersonal and genetic origins of adult attachment styles: A longitudinal study from infancy to early adulthood. *Journal of Personality and Social Psychology, 104,* 817–838. (p. 83)

Fraley, R. C., Vicary, A. M., Brumbaugh, C. C., & Roisman, G. I. (2011). Patterns of stability in adult attachment: An empirical test of two models of continuity and change. *Journal of Personality and Social Psychology, 101,* 974–992. (p. 83)

Frances, A. J. (2012, December 2). DSM 5 is guide not Bible—Ignore its ten worst changes. www.psychologytoday.com/blog/dsm5-in-distress/201212/dsm-5-is-guide-not-bible-ignore-its-ten-worst-changes. (pp. 373, 375)

Frances, A. J. (2013). Saving normal: An insider's revolt against out-of-control psychiatric diagnosis, DSM-5, big pharma, and the medicalization of ordinary life. New York: HarperCollins. (p. 375)

Frank, J. D. (1982). Therapeutic components shared by all psychotherapies. In J. H. Harvey & M. M. Parks (Eds.), *The Master Lecture Series: Vol. 1. Psychotherapy research and behavior change.* Washington, DC: American Psychological Association. (pp. 422, 423)

Frankenburg, W., Dodds, J., Archer, P., Shapiro, H., & Bresnick, B. (1992). The Denver II: A major revision and restandardization of the Denver Developmental Screening Test. *Pediatrics, 89,* 91–97. (p. 74)

Frankl, V. E. (1962). *Man's search for meaning: An introduction to logotherapy.* Boston: Beacon Press. (p. 296)

Franklin, M., & Foa, E. B. (2011). Treatment of obsessive-compulsive disorder. *Annual Review of Clinical Psychology, 7,* 229–243. (p. 380)

Frasure-Smith, N., & Lesperance, F. (2005). Depression and coronary heart disease: Complex synergism of mind, body, and environment. *Current Directions in Psychological Science, 14,* 39–43. (p. 290)

Frattaroli, J. (2006). Experimental disclosure and its moderators: A meta-analysis. *Psychological Bulletin, 132,* 823–865. (p. 296)

Fredrickson, B. L. (2006). The broaden-and-build theory of positive emotions. In M. Csikszentmihalyi & I. S. Csikszentmihalyi (Eds.), *A life worth living: Contributions to positive psychology.* New York: Oxford University Press. (p. 301)

Freedman, D. H. (2011, February). How to fix the obesity crisis. *Scientific American,* pp. 40–47. (p. 264)

Freedman, D. J., Riesenhuber, M., Poggio, T., & Miller, E. K. (2001). Categorical representation of visual stimuli in the primate prefrontal cortex. *Science, 291,* 312–316. (p. 228)

Freedman, J. L. (1988). Television violence and aggression: What the evidence shows. In S. Oskamp (Ed.), *Television as a social issue.* Newbury Park, CA: Sage. (p. 188)

Freedman, J. L., & Perlick, D. (1979). Crowding, contagion, and laughter. *Journal of Experimental Social Psychology, 15,* 295–303. (p. 347)

Freedman, R., & 12 others. (2013). The initial field trials of DSM-5: New blooms and old thorns. *American Journal of Psychiatry, 170,* 1–5. (p. 375)

Freeman, E. C., & Twenge, J. M. (2010, January). Using MySpace increases the endorsement of narcissistic personality traits. Poster presented at the annual conference of the Society for Personality and Social Psychology, Las Vegas, NV. (p. 268)

Freeman, W. J. (1991, February). The physiology of perception. *Scientific American,* pp. 78–85. (p. 151)

Freud, S. (1935: reprinted 1960). *A general introduction to psychoanalysis.* New York: Washington Square Press. (p. 97)

Freyd, J. J., DePrince, A. P., & Gleaves, D. H. (2007). The state of betrayal trauma theory: Reply to McNally—Conceptual issues and future directions. *Memory, 15,* 295–311. (p. 213)

Freyd, J. J., Putnam, F. W., Lyon, T. D., Becker-Blease, K. A., Cheit, R. E., Siegel, N. B., & Pezdek, K. (2005). The science of child sexual abuse. *Science, 308,* 501. (p. 84)

Frick, L. R., Barreiro Arcos, M. L., Rapanelli, M., Zappia, M. P., Brocco, M., Mongini, C., Genaro, A. M., & Cremaschi, G. A. (2009). Chronic restraint stress impairs T-cell immunity and promotes tumor progression in mice. *Stress, 12,* 134–143. (p. 288)

Fridlund, A. J., Beck, H. P., Goldie, W. D., & Irons, G. (2012a). Little Albert: A neurologically impaired child. *History of Psychology, 15*(4), 302–327. (p. 173)

Fridlund, A. J., Beck, H. P., Goldie, W. D., & Irons, G. (2012b). Little Albert: Answering the criticism. *The Psychologist, 25,* 258. (p. 173)

Friedman, H. S., & Rosenman, R. (1974). *Type A behavior and your heart.* New York: Knopf. (p. 289)

Friedman, M., & Ulmer, D. (1984). *Treating Type A behavior—And your heart.* New York: Knopf. (pp. 289, 298)

Friedman, R., & James, J. W. (2008). The myth of the sages of dying, death and grief. *Skeptic, 14*(2), 37–41. (p. 101)

Friedman, R. A. (2012, December 17). In gun debate, a misguided focus on mental illness. *New York Times* (www.nytimes.com). (p. 376)

Friend, T. (2004). *Animal talk: Breaking the codes of animal language.* New York: Free Press. (p. 235)

Frisch, M., & Zdravkovic, S. (2010). Body size at birth and same-sex marriage in young adulthood. *Archives of Sexual Behavior, 39,* 117–123. (p. 124)

Frisell, T., Pawitan, Y., Långström, N., & Lichtenstein, P. (2012). Heritability, assortative mating and gender differences in violent crime: Results from a total population sample using twin, adoption, and sibling models. *Behavior Genetics, 42,* 3–18. (pp. 109, 403)

Frith, U., & Frith, C. (2001). The biological basis of social interaction. *Current Directions in Psychological Science, 10,* 151–155. (p. 78)

Fritz, T., Jentschke, S., Gosselin, N., Sammler, D., Peretz, I., Turner, R., Friederici, A., & Koelsch, S. (2009). Universal recognition of three basic emotions in music. *Current Biology, 19,* 573–576. (p. 277)

Fromkin, V., & Rodman, R. (1983). *An introduction to language* (3rd ed.). New York: Holt, Rinehart & Winston. (p. 231)

Fry, A. F., & Hale, S. (1996). Processing speed, working memory, and fluid intelligence: Evidence for a developmental cascade. *Psychological Science, 7,* 237–241. (p. 95)

Fry, R., & Cohn, D. (2010, January 19). Women, men and the new economics of marriage. Pew Research Center (pewresearch.org). (p. 113)

Fuhriman, A., & Burlingame, G. M. (1994). Group psychotherapy: Research and practice. In A. Fuhriman & G. M. Burlingame (Eds.), *Handbook of group psychotherapy.* New York: Wiley. (p. 419)

Fujita, F., & Diener, E. (2005). Life satisfaction set point: Stability and change. *Journal of Personality and Social Psychology, 88,* 158–164. (p. 305)

Fuller, M. J., & Downs, A. C. (1990). Spermarche is a salient biological marker in men's development. Poster presented at the American Psychological Society convention. (p. 112)

Fuller, T. D., Edwards, J. N., Sermsri, S., & Vorakitphokatorn, S. (1993). Housing, stress, and physical well-being: Evidence from Thailand. *Social Science & Medicine, 36,* 1417–1428. (p. 292)

Funder, D. C., & Block, J. (1989). The role of ego-control, ego-resiliency, and IQ in delay of gratification in adolescence. *Journal of Personality and Social Psychology, 57,* 1041–1050. (p. 88)

Furlow, F. B., & Thornhill, R. (1996, January/February). The orgasm wars. *Psychology Today,* pp. 42–46. (p. 116)

Furnham, A. (1982). Explanations for unemployment in Britain. *European Journal of Social Psychology, 12,* 335–352. (p. 339)

Furnham, A., & Baguma, P. (1994). Cross-cultural differences in the evaluation of male and female body shapes. *International Journal of Eating Disorders, 15,* 81–89. (p. 262)

Furnham, A., & Wu, J. (2008). Gender differences in estimates of one's own and parental intelligence in China. *Individual Differences Research, 6,* 1–12. (p. 351)

Furr, R. M., & Funder, D. C. (1998). A multimodal analysis of personal negativity. *Journal of Personality and Social Psychology, 74,* 1580–1591. (p. 396)

Gaillard, R., Dehaene, S., Adam, C., Clémenceau, S., Hasboun, D., Baulac, M., Cohen, L., & Naccache, L. (2009). Converging intracranial markers of conscious access. *PLoS Biology, 7*(e): e1000061. (p. 50)

Gailliot, M. T., Baumeister, R. F., DeWall, C. N., Maner, J. K., Plant, E. A., Tice, D. M., Brewer, L. E., & Schmeichel, B. J. (2007). Self-control relies on glucose as a limited energy source: Willpower is more than a metaphor. *Journal of Personality and Social Psychology, 92,* 325–336. (p. 293)

Gaissmaier, W., & Gigerenzer, G. (2012). 9/11, Act II: A fine-grained analysis of regional variations in traffic fatalities in the aftermath of the terrorist attacks. *Psychological Science, 23,* 1449–1454. (p. 224)

Galambos, N. L. (1992). Parent-adolescent relations. *Current Directions in Psychological Science, 1,* 146–149. (p. 90)

Galanter, E. (1962). Contemporary psychophysics. In R. Brown, E. Galanter, E. H. Hess, & G. Mandler (Eds.), *New directions in psychology.* New York: Holt Rinehart & Winston. (p. 135)

Gale, C. R., Batty, G. D., & Deary, I. J. (2008). Locus of control at age 10 years and health outcomes and behaviors at age 30 years: The 1970 British Cohort Study. *Psychosomatic Medicine, 70,* 397–403. (p. 293)

Gallese, V., Gernsbacher, M. A., Heyes, C., Hickok, G., & Iacoboni, M. (2011). Mirror neuron forum. *Perspectives on Psychological Science, 6,* 369–407. (p. 186)

Gallup. (2010, accessed June 28). Gallup daily: U.S. mood. Based on the Gallup-Healthways well-being index. www.gallup.com. (p. 15)

Gallup Brain. (2008, accessed February 20). Woman for president: Question qn2f, March, 2007 wave. Brain.Gallup.com. (p. 350)

Gallup Organization. (2004, August 16). 65% of Americans receive NO praise or recognition in the workplace. E-mail from Tom Rath: bucketbook Self-recognition. *Science, 167,* 86–87. (p. B-6)

Gallup, G. G., Jr., & Frederick, D. A. (2010). The science of sex appeal: An evolutionary perspective. *Review of General Psychology, 14,* 240–250. (pp. 360, 361)

Gallup, G. H. (1972). *The Gallup poll: Public opinion 1935–1971* (Vol. 3). New York: Random House. (p. 366)

Gangestad, S. W., & Simpson, J. A. (2000). The evolution of human mating: Trade-offs and strategic pluralism. *Behavioral and Brain Sciences, 23,* 573–587. (p. 126)

Gangestad, S. W., Thornhill, R., & Garver-Apgar, C. E. (2010). Men's facial masculinity predicts changes in their female partners' sexual interests across the ovulatory cycle, whereas men's intelligence does not. *Evolution and Human Behavior, 31,* 412–424. (p. 361)

Gangwisch, J. E., Babiss, L. A., Malaspina, D., Turner, J. B., Zammit, G. K., & Posner, K. (2010). Earlier parental set bedtimes as a protective factor against depression and suicidal ideation. *Sleep, 33,* 97–106. (p. 58)

Gao, Y., Raine, A., Venables, P. H., Dawson, M. E., & Mednick, S. A. (2010). Association of poor childhood fear conditioning and adult crime. *American Journal of Psychiatry, 167,* 56–60. (p. 403)

Garcia, J., & Gustavson, A. R. (1997, January). Carl R. Gustavson (1946–1996): Pioneering wildlife psychologist. *APS Observer,* pp. 34–35. (p. 182)

Garcia, J., & Koelling, R. A. (1966). Relation of cue to consequence in avoidance learning. *Psychonomic Science, 4,* 123–124. (p. 182)

Gardner, H. (1983). *Frames of mind: The theory of multiple intelligences.* New York: Basic Books. (p. 236)

Gardner, H. (1998, March 19). An intelligent way to progress. *The Independent* (London), p. E4. (p. 236)

Gardner, H. (1998, November 5). Do parents count? *New York Review of Books* (www.nybooks.com). (p. 91)

Gardner, H. (2006). *The development and education of the mind: The selected works of Howard Gardner.* New York: Routledge/Taylor & Francis. (pp. 213, 236)

Gardner, H. (2011). The theory of multiple intelligences: As psychology, as education, as social science. Address on the receipt of an honorary degree from José Cela University in Madrid and the Prince of Asturias Prize for Social Science. (p. 236)

Gardner, J., & Oswald, A. J. (2007). Money and mental well-being: A longitudinal study of medium–sized lottery wins. *Journal of Health Economics, 6,* 49–60. (p. 304)

Gardner, R. A., & Gardner, B. I. (1969). Teaching sign language to a chimpanzee. *Science, 165,* 664–672. (p. 234)

Garfield, C. (1986). *Peak performers: The new heroes of American business.* New York: Morrow. (p. 233)

Garon, N., Bryson, S. E., & Smith, I. M. (2008). Executive function in preschoolers: A review using an integrative framework. *Psychological Bulletin, 134,* 31–60. (p. 74)

Garrett, B. L. (2008). Judging innocence. *Columbia Law Review, 108,* 55–142. (p. 212)

Garry, M., Manning, C. G., Loftus, E. F., & Sherman, S. J. (1996). Imagination inflation: Imagining a childhood event inflates confidence that it occurred. *Psychonomic Bulletin & Review, 3,* 208–214. (p. 210)

Gartrell, N., & Bos, H. (2010). U.S. national longitudinal lesbian family study: Psychological adjustment of 17-year-old adolescents. *Pediatrics, 126,* 28–36. (p. 122)

Gatchel, R. J., Peng, Y. B., Peters, M. L., Fuchs, P. N., & Turk, D. C. (2007). The biopsychosocial approach to chronic pain: Scientific advances and future directions. *Psychological Bulletin, 133,* 581–624. (p. 155)

Gates, G. J., & Newport, F. (2012, October 18). Special report: 3.4% of U.S. adults identify as LGBT. www.gallup.com. (p. 121)

Gazzaniga, M. S. (1967, August). The split brain in man. *Scientific American,* pp. 24–29. (pp. 48, 49)

Gazzaniga, M. S. (1989). Organization of the human brain. *Science, 245,*947–952. (p. 49)

Gazzaniga, M. S. (2002, August 22). On "The brain: The final mystery." Broadcast on BBC2. (p. 48)

Ge, X., & Natsuaki, M. N. (2009). In search of explanations for early pubertal timing effects on developmental psychopathology. *Current Directions in Psychological Science, 18,* 327–441. (p. 86)

Geary, D. C. (1995). Sexual selection and sex differences in spatial cognition. *Learning and Individual Differences, 7,* 289–301. (p. 247)

Geary, D. C. (1996). Sexual selection and sex differences in mathematical abilities. *Behavioral and Brain Sciences, 19,* 229–247. (p. 247)

Geary, D. C. (2010). *Male, female: The evolution of human sex differences* (2nd ed.).Washington, DC: American Psychological Association. (p. 110)

Geary, D. C., Salthouse, T. A., Chen, G-P., & Fan, L. (1996). Are East Asian versus American differences in arithmetical ability a recent phenomenon? *Developmental Psychology, 32,* 254–262. (p. 249)

Geen, R. G., & Thomas, S. L. (1986). The immediate effects of media violence on behavior. *Journal of Social Issues, 42*(3), 7–28. (p. 188)

Gehring, W. J., Wimke, J., & Nisenson, L. G. (2000). Action monitoring dysfunction in obsessive-compulsive disorder. *Psychological Science, 11*(1), 1–6. (p. 381)

Geier, A. B., Rozin, P., & Doros, G. (2006). Unit bias: A new heuristic that helps explain the effects of portion size on food intake. *Psychological Science, 17,* 521–525. (p. 261)

Gentile, B., Grabe, S., Dolan-Pascoe, B., Wells, B. E., & Maitino, A. (2009). Gender differences in domain-specific self-esteem: A meta-analysis. *Journal of General Psychology, 13,* 34–45. (p. 357)

Gentile, D. A. (2009). Pathological video-game use among youth ages 8 to 18: A national study. *Psychological Science, 20,* 594–602. (p. 358)

Gentile, D. A., Lynch, P. J., Linder, J. R., & Walsh, D. A. (2004). The effects of violent video game habits on adolescent hostility, aggressive behaviors, and school performance. *Journal of Adolescence, 27,* 5–22. (p. 188)

George, L. K., Larson, D. B., Koenig, H. G., & McCullough, M. E. (2000). Spirituality and health: What we know, what we need to know. *Journal of Social and Clinical Psychology, 19,* 102–116. (p. 301)

George, M. S. (2003, September). Stimulating the brain. *Scientific American,* pp. 67–73. (p. 429)

George, M. S., & 12 others. (2010). Daily left prefrontal transcranial magnetic stimulation therapy for major depressive disorder: A sham-controlled randomized trial. *Archives of General Psychiatry, 67,* 507–516. (p. 429)

Geraerts, E., Bernstein, D. M., Merckelbach, H., Linders, C., Raymaekers, L., & Loftus, E. F. (2008). Lasting false beliefs and their behavioral consequences. *Psychological Science, 19,* 749–753. (p. 210)

Geraerts, E., Schooler, J. W., Merckelbach, H., Jelicic, M., Hauer, B. J. A., & Ambadar, Z. (2007). The reality of recovered memories: Corroborating continuous and discontinuous memories of childhood sexual abuse. *Psychological Science, 18,* 564–568. (p. 213)

Gerber, J., & Wheeler, L. (2009). On being rejected: A meta-analysis of experimental research on rejection. *Perspectives on Psychological Science, 4,* 468–488. (p. 266)

Gerbner, G. (1990). Stories that hurt: Tobacco, alcohol, and other drugs in the mass media. In H. Resnik (Ed.), *Youth and drugs: Society's mixed messages.* Rockville, MD: Office for Substance Abuse Prevention, U.S. Department of Health and Human Services. (p. 389)

Gerhart, K. A., Koziol-McLain, J., Lowenstein, S. R., & Whiteneck, G. G. (1994). Quality of life following spinal cord injury: Knowledge and attitudes of emergency care providers. *Annals of Emergency Medicine, 23,* 807–812. (p. 302)

Gerin, W., Chaplin, W., Schwartz, J. E., Holland, J., Alter, R., Wheeler, R., Duong, D., & Pickering, T. G. (2005). Sustained blood pressure increase after an acute stressor: The effects of the 11 September 2001 attack on New York City World Trade Center. *Journal of Hypertension, 23,* 279–284. (p. 289)

Gerrard, M., & Luus, C. A. E. (1995). Judgments of vulnerability to pregnancy: The role of risk factors and individual differences. *Personality and Social Psychology Bulletin, 21,* 160–171. (p. 119)

Gershoff, E. T. (2002). Parental corporal punishment and associated child behaviors and experiences: A meta-analytic and theoretical review. *Psychological Bulletin, 128,* 539–579. (p. 178)

Gershoff, E. T., Grogan-Kaylor, A., Lansford, J. E., Chang, L., Zelli, A., Deater-Deckard, K., & Dodge, K. A. (2010). Parent discipline practices in an international sample: Associations with child behaviors and moderation by perceived normativeness. *Child Development, 81,* 487–502. (p. 178)

Gertner, J. (2010, May 10). The rise and fall of the G.D.P. *New York Times* (www.nytimes.com). (p. 305)

Giancola, P. R. (2003). The moderating effects of dispositional empathy on alcohol-related aggression in men and women. *Journal of Abnormal Psychology, 112,* 275–281. (p. 109)

Gibbons, F. X. (1986). Social comparison and depression: Company's effect on misery. *Journal of Personality and Social Psychology, 51,* 140–148. (p. 305)

Gibson, E. J., & Walk, R. D. (1960, April). The "visual cliff." *Scientific American,* pp. 64–71. (p. 146)

Giesbrecht, T., Lynn, S. J., Lilienfeld, S. O., & Merckelbach, H. (2008). Cognitive processes in dissociation: An analysis of core theoretical assumptions. *Psychological Bulletin, 134,* 617–647. (p. 402)

Giesbrecht, T., Lynn, S. J., Lilienfeld, S. O., & Merckelbach, H. (2010). Cognitive processes, trauma, and dissociation—Misconceptions and misrepresentations: Reply to Bremmer (2010). *Psychological Bulletin, 136,* 7–11. (p. 402)

Gigantesco, A., Stazi, M. A., Alessandri, G., Medda, E., Tarolla, E., & Fagnani, C. (2011). Psychological well-being (PWB): A natural life outlook? An Italian twin study of heritability on PWB in young adults. *Psychological Medicine, 41,* 2637–2649. (p. 305)

Gigerenzer, G. (2004). Dread risk, September 11, and fatal traffic accidents. *Psychological Science, 15,* 286–287. (p. 224)

Gigerenzer, G. (2006). Out of the frying pan into the fire: Behavioral reactions to terrorist attacks. *Risk Analysis, 26,* 347–351. (p. 224)

Gigerenzer, G. (2010). *Rationality for mortals: How people cope with uncertainty.* New York: Oxford University Press. (p. A-1)

Gigerenzer, G., Gaissmaier, W., Kurz-Milcke, E., Schwartz, L. M., & Woloshin, S. (2008). Helping doctors and patients make sense of health statistics. *Psychological Science in the Public Interest, 8,* 53–96. (p. A-1)

Gigerenzer, G., Gaissmaier, W., Kurz-Milcke, E., Schwartz, L. M., & Woloshin, S. (2009, April/May). Knowing your chances. *Scientific American Mind,* pp. 44–51. (p. A-1)

Gilbert, D. T. (2006). *Stumbling on happiness.* New York: Knopf. (pp. 99, 209, 270, 330, 390)

Gildersleeve, K., DeBruine, L., Haselton, M. G., Frederick, D. A., Penton-Voak, I. S., Jones, B. C., & Perrett, D. L. (2013). Shifts in women's mate preferences across the ovulatory cycle: A critique of Harris (2011) and Harris (2012). *Sex Roles, 69*(9-10), 516–524. (p. 115)

Gilestro, G. F., Tononi, G., & Cirelli, C. (2009). Widespread changes in synaptic markers as a function of sleep and wakefulness in *Drosophila. Science, 324,* 109–112. (p. 56)

Gill, A. J., Oberlander, J., & Austin, E. (2006). Rating e-mail personality at zero acquaintance. *Personality and Individual Differences, 40,* 497–507. (p. 326)

Gillison, M. L., Broutian, T., Pickard, R. K. L., Tong, Z-Y., Xiao, W., Kahle, L., Graubard, B. I., & Chaturvedi, A. K. (2012). Prevalence of oral HPV infection in the United States, 2009–2010. *JAMA, 307*(7), 693–703. (p. 118)

Gilovich, T. D. (1996). The spotlight effect: Exaggerated impressions of the self as a social stimulus. Unpublished manuscript, Cornell University. (p. 328)

Gilovich, T. D., & Medvec, V. H. (1995). The experience of regret: What, when, and why. *Psychological Review, 102,* 379–395. (p. 99)

Gilovich, T. D., & Savitsky, K. (1999). The spotlight effect and the illusion of transparency: Egocentric assessments of how we are seen by others. *Current Directions in Psychological Science, 8,* 165–168. (p. 328)

Gilovich, T. D., Vallone, R., & Tversky, A. (1985). The hot hand in basketball: On the misperception of random sequences. *Cognitive Psychology, 17,* 295–314. (p. 11)

Giltay, E. J., Geleijnse, J. M., Zitman, F. G., Buijsse, B., & Kromhout, D. (2007). Lifestyle and dietary correlates of dispositional optimism in men: The Zutphen Elderly Study. *Journal of Psychosomatic Research, 63,* 483–490. (p. 294)

Giltay, E. J., Geleijnse, J. M., Zitman, F. G., Hoekstra, T., & Schouten, E. G. (2004). Dispositional optimism and all-cause and cardiovascular mortality in a prospective cohort of elderly Dutch men and women. *Archives of General Psychiatry, 61,* 1126–1135. (p. 294)

Gingerich, O. (1999, February 6). Is there a role for natural theology today? *The Real Issue* (www.origins.org/real/n9501/natural.html). (p. 129)

Gladue, B. A. (1990). Hormones and neuroendocrine factors in atypical human sexual behavior. In J. R. Feierman (Ed.), *Pedophilia: Biosocial dimensions.* New York: Springer-Verlag. (p. 123)

Glasman, L. R., & Albarracin, D. (2006). Forming attitudes that predict future behavior: A meta-analysis of the attitude-behavior relation. *Psychological Bulletin, 132,* 778–822. (p. 339)

Glass, R. I. (2004). Perceived threats and real killers. *Science, 304,* 927. (p. 225)

Glass, R. M. (2001). Electroconvulsive therapy: Time to bring it out of the shadows. *Journal of the American Medical Association, 285,* 1346–1348. (p. 427)

Gleaves, D. H. (1996). The sociocognitive model of dissociative identity disorder: A reexamination of the evidence. *Psychological Bulletin, 120,* 42–59. (p. 402)

Gluszek, A., & Dovidio, J. F. (2010). The way *they* speak: A social psychological perspective on the stigma of nonnative accents in communication. *Personality and Social Psychology Review, 14,* 214–237. (p. 352)

Godden, D. R., & Baddeley, A. D. (1975). Context-dependent memory in two natural environments: On land and underwater. *British Journal of Psychology, 66,* 325–331. (p. 204)

Goff, D. C., & Simms, C. A. (1993). Has multiple personality disorder remained consistent over time? *Journal of Nervous and Mental Disease, 181,* 595–600. (p. 402)

Gold, M., & Yanof, D. S. (1985). Mothers, daughters, and girlfriends. *Journal of Personality and Social Psychology, 49,* 654–659. (p. 90)

Gold, R. S. (2006). Unrealistic optimism about becoming infected with HIV: Different causes in different populations. *International Journal of STD & AIDS, 17,* 196–199. (p. 294)

Goldberg, J. (2007, accessed May 31). *Quivering bundles that let us hear.* Howard Hughes Medical Institute (www.hhmi.org/senses/c120.html). (p. 152)

Golder, S. A., & Macy, M. W. (2011). Diurnal and seasonal mood vary with work, sleep, and day-length across diverse cultures. *Science, 333,* 1878–1881. (p. 302)

Goldfried, M. R., Raue, P. J., & Castonguay, L. G. (1998). The therapeutic focus in significant sessions of master therapists: A comparison of cognitive-behavioral and psychodynamic-interpersonal interventions. *Journal of Consulting and Clinical Psychology, 66,* 803–810. (p. 422)

Goldman, A. L., Pezawas, L., Mattay, V. S., Fischl, B., Verchinski, B. A., Chen, Q., Weinberger, D. R., & Meyer-Lindenberg, A. (2009). Widespread reductions of cortical thickness in schizophrenia and spectrum disorders and evidence of heritability. *Archives of General Psychiatry, 66,* 467–477. (p. 398)

Goldstein, A. P., Glick, B., & Gibbs, J. C. (1998). *Aggression replacement training: A comprehensive intervention for aggressive youth* (rev. ed.). Champaign, IL: Research Press. (p. 356)

Goldstein, I. (2000, August). Male sexual circuitry. *Scientific American,* pp. 70–75. (p. 36)

Goldstein, I., Lue, T. F., Padma-Nathan, H., Rosen, R. C., Steers, W. D., & Wicker, P. A. (1998). Oral sildenafil in the treatment of erectile dysfunction. *New England Journal of Medicine, 338,* 1397–1404. (p. 19)

Goleman, D. (1980, February). 1,528 little geniuses and how they grew. *Psychology Today,* pp. 28–53. (p. B-3)

Goleman, D. (1995). *Emotional intelligence.* New York: Bantam. (p. 274)

Goleman, D. (2006). *Social intelligence.* New York: Bantam Books. (p. 238)

Gollwitzer, P. M., & Oettingen, G. (2012). Goal pursuit. In P. M. Gollwitzer & G. Oettingen (Eds.), *The Oxford handbook of human motivation,* pp. 208–231. New York: Oxford University Press. (p. 181)

Goodale, M. A., & Milner, D. A. (2004). *Sight unseen: An exploration of conscious and unconscious vision.* Oxford: Oxford University Press. (p. 8)

Goodale, M. A., & Milner, D. A. (2006). One brain—two visual systems. *The Psychologist, 19,* 660–663. (p. 8)

Goode, E. (1999, April 13). If things taste bad, 'phantoms' may be at work. *New York Times* (www.nytimes.com). (p. 155)

Goode, E. (2012, June 19). Senators start a review of solitary confinement. *New York Times* (www.nytimes.com). (p. 265)

Goodhart, D. E. (1986). The effects of positive and negative thinking on performance in an achievement situation. *Journal of Personality and Social Psychology, 51,* 117–124. (p. 294)

Goodman, G. S., Ghetti, S., Quas, J. A., Edelstein, R. S., Alexander, K. W., Redlich, A. D., Cordon, I. M., & Jones, D. P. H. (2003). A prospective study of memory for child sexual abuse: New findings relevant to the repressed-memory controversy. *Psychological Science, 14,* 113–118. (p. 213)

Goodman, G. S., & Quas, J. A. (2008). Repeated interviews and children's memory. *Current Directions in Psychological Science, 17,* 386–389. (p. 212)

Goodwin, P. Y., Mosher, W. D., & Chandra, A. (2010). Marriage and cohabitation in the United States: A statistical portrait based on Cycle 6 (2002) of the National Survey of Family Growth. National Center for Health Statistics. *Vital Health Statistics, 23*(28). (p. 98)

Goranson, R. E. (1978). *The hindsight effect in problem solving.* Unpublished manuscript, cited by G. Wood (1984), Research methodology: A decision-making perspective. In A. M. Rogers & C. J. Scheirer (Eds.), *The G. Stanley Hall Lecture Series* (Vol. 4). Washington, DC. (p. 10)

Gorchoff, S. M., John, O. P., & Helson, R. (2008). Contextualizing change in marital satisfaction during middle age. *Psychological Science, 19,* 1194–1200. (p. 99)

Gordon, A. M., & Chen, S. (2010). When you accept me for me: The relational benefits of intrinsic affirmations from one's relationship partner. *Personality and Social Psychology Bulletin, 36,* 1439–1453. (p. 321)

Gore-Felton, C., Koopman, C., Thoresen, C., Arnow, B., Bridges, E., & Spiegel, D. (2000). Psychologists' beliefs and clinical characteristics: Judging the veracity of childhood sexual abuse memories. *Professional Psychology: Research and Practice, 31,* 372–377. (p. 213)

Gorrese, A., & Ruggieri, R. (2012). Peer attachment: A meta-analytic review of gender and age differences and associations with parent attachment. *Journal of Youth and Adolescence, 41,* 650–672. (p. 83)

Gosling, S. D. (2008). *Snoop: What your stuff says about you.* New York: Basic Books. (p. 326)

Gosling, S. D., Kwan, V. S. Y., & John, O. P. (2003). A dog's got personality: A cross-species comparative approach to personality judgments in dogs and humans. *Journal of Personality and Social Psychology, 85*, 1161–1169. (p. 323)

Gotlib, I. H., & Hammen, C. L. (1992). *Psychological aspects of depression: Toward a cognitive-interpersonal integration*. New York: Wiley. (p. 396)

Gottesman, I. I. (1991). *Schizophrenia genesis: The origins of madness*. New York: Freeman. (p. 400)

Gottesman, I. I. (2001). Psychopathology through a life span—genetic prism. *American Psychologist, 56*, 867–881. (p. 400)

Gottfredson, L. S. (2002a). Where and why g matters: Not a mystery. *Human Performance, 15*, 25–46. (p. 238)

Gottfredson, L. S. (2002b). g: Highly general and highly practical. In R. J. Sternberg & E. L. Grigorenko (Eds.), *The general factor of intelligence: How general is it?* Mahwah, NJ: Erlbaum. (p. 238)

Gottfredson, L. S. (2003a). Dissecting practical intelligence theory: Its claims and evidence. *Intelligence, 31*, 343–397. (p. 238)

Gottfredson, L. S. (2003b). On Sternberg's "Reply to Gottfredson." *Intelligence, 31*, 415–424. (p. 238)

Gow, A. J., Johnson, W., Pattie, A., Brett, C. E., Roberts, B., Starr, J. M., & Deary, I. J. (2011). Stability and change in intelligence from age 11 to ages 70, 79, and 87: The Lothian birth cohorts of 1921 and 1936. *Psychology and Aging, 26*, 232–240. (p. 245)

Grady, C. L., McIntosh, A. R., Horwitz, B., Maisog, J. M., Ungeleider, L. G., Mentis, M. J., Pietrini, P., Schapiro, M. B., & Haxby, J. V. (1995). Age-related reductions in human recognition memory due to impaired encoding. *Science, 269*, 218–221. (p. 207)

Grande, G., Romppel, M., & Barth, J. (2012). Association between type D personality and prognosis in patients with cardiovascular diseases: A systematic review and meta-analysis. *Annals of Behavioral Medicine, 43*, 299–310. (p. 290)

Grant, A. M., Gino, F., & Hofmann, D. A. (2011). Reversing the extraverted leadership advantage: The role of employee proactivity. *Academy of Management Journal, 54*, 528–550. (p. 323)

Gray, P. (2010, July 7). ADHD and school: The problem of assessing normalcy in an abnormal environment. *Psychology Today Blog* (www.psychologytoday.com). (p. 373)

Gray-Little, B., & Burks, N. (1983). Power and satisfaction in marriage: A review and critique. *Psychological Bulletin, 93*, 513–538. (p. 362)

Green, C. S., Pouget, A., & Bavelier, D. (2010). Improved probabilistic inference as a general learning mechanism with action video games. *Current Biology, 20*, 1573–1579. (p. 358)

Green, J. D., Sedikides, C., & Gregg, A. P. (2008). Forgotten but not gone: The recall and recognition of self-threatening memories. *Journal of Experimental Social Psychology, 44*, 547–561. (p. 318)

Green, J. T., & Woodruff-Pak, D. S. (2000). Eyeblink classical conditioning: Hippocampal formation is for neutral stimulus associations as cerebellum is for association-response. *Psychological Bulletin, 126*, 138–158. (p. 200)

Green, M. F., & Horan, W. P. (2010). Social cognition in schizophrenia. *Current Directions in Psychological Science, 19*, 243–248. (p. 398)

Greenberg, J. (2008). Understanding the vital human quest for self-esteem. *Perspectives on Psychological Science, 3*, 48–55. (p. 329)

Greene, J. (2010). *Remarks to an Edge conference: The new science of morality*. www.edge.org. (p. 88)

Greene, J., Sommerville, R. B., Nystrom, L. E., Darley, J. M., & Cohen, J. D. (2001). An fMRI investigation of emotional engagement in moral judgment. *Science, 293*, 2105. (p. 88)

Greenwald, A. G. (1992). Subliminal semantic activation and subliminal snake oil. Paper presented to the American Psychological Association Convention, Washington, DC. (p. 136)

Greenwald, A. G., McGhee, D. E., & Schwartz, J. L. K. (1998). Measuring individual differences in implicit cognition: The implicit association test. *Journal of Personality and Social Psychology, 74*, 1464–1480. (p. 351)

Greenwald, A. G., Oakes, M. A., & Hoffman, H. (2003). Targets of discrimination: Effects of race on responses to weapons holders. *Journal of Experimental Social Psychology, 39*, 399. (p. 351)

Greenwald, A. G., Spangenberg, E. R., Pratkanis, A. R., & Eskenazi, J. (1991). Double-blind tests of subliminal self-help audiotapes. *Psychological Science, 2*, 119–122. (p. 136)

Greers, A. E. (2004). Speech, language, and reading skills after early cochlear implantation. *Archives of Otolaryngology—Head & Neck Surgery, 130*, 634–638. (p. 232)

Gregory, A. M., Rijksdijk, F. V., Lau, J. Y., Dahl, R. E., & Eley, T. C. (2009). The direction of longitudinal associations between sleep problems and depression symptoms: A study of twins aged 8 and 10 years. *Sleep, 32*, 189–199. (p. 430)

Gregory, R. L. (1978). *Eye and brain: The psychology of seeing* (3rd ed.). New York: McGraw-Hill. (p. 150)

Gregory, R. L., & Gombrich, E. H. (Eds.). (1973). *Illusion in nature and art*. New York: Charles Scribner's Sons. (p. 139)

Greif, E. B., & Ulman, K. J. (1982). The psychological impact of menarche on early adolescent females: A review of the literature. *Child Development, 53*, 1413–1430. (pp. 111, 112)

Greist, J. H., Jefferson, J. W., & Marks, I. M. (1986). *Anxiety and its treatment: Help is available*. Washington, DC: American Psychiatric Press. (p. 377)

Greitemeyer, T., & Osswald, S. (2010). Effects of prosocial video games on prosocial behavior. *Journal of Personality and Social Psychology, 98*, 211–221. (p. 357)

Grèzes, J., & Decety, J. (2001). Functional anatomy of execution, mental simulation, observation, and verb generation of actions: A meta-analysis. *Human Brain Mapping, 12*, 1–19. (p. 233)

Grilo, C. M., & Pogue-Geile, M. F. (1991). The nature of environmental influences on weight and obesity: A behavior genetic analysis. *Psychological Bulletin, 110*, 520–537. (p. 262)

Griskevicius, V., Tybur, J. M., Gangestad, S. W., Perea, E. F., Shapiro, J. R., & Kenrick, D. T. (2009). Aggress to impress: Hostility as an evolved context-dependent strategy. *Journal of Personality and Social Psychology, 96*, 980–994. (p. 126)

Groothuis, T. G. G., & Carere, C. (2005). Avian personalities: Characterization and epigenesis. *Neuroscience and Biobehavioral Reviews, 29*, 137–150. (p. 323)

Gross, A. E., & Crofton, C. (1977). What is good is beautiful. *Sociometry, 40*, 85–90. (p. 361)

Gruder, C. L. (1977). Choice of comparison persons in evaluating oneself. In J. M. Suls & R. L. Miller (Eds.), *Social comparison processes*. New York: Hemisphere. (p. 304)

Guéguen, N. (2011). Effects of solicitor sex and attractiveness on receptivity to sexual offers: A field study. *Archives of Sexual Behavior, 40*, 915–919. (p. 127)

Guerin, B. (1986). Mere presence effects in humans: A review. *Journal of Personality and Social Psychology, 22*, 38–77. (p. 347)

Guerin, B. (2003). Language use as social strategy: A review and an analytic framework for the social sciences. *Review of General Psychology, 7*, 251–298. (p. 229)

Guiso, L., Monte, F., Sapienza, P., & Zingales, L. (2008). Culture, gender, and math. *Science, 320*, 1164–1165. (p. 247)

Gunstad, J., Strain, G., Devlin, M. J., Wing, R., Cohen, R. A., Paul, R. H., Crosby, R. D., & Mitchell, J. E. (2011). Improved memory function 12 weeks after bariatric surgery. *Surgery for Obesity and Related Diseases, 7*, 465–472. (p. 262)

Guo, X., & 19 others. (2010). Effect of antipsychotic medication alone vs combined with psychosocial intervention on outcomes of early-stage schizophrenia. *Archives of General Psychiatry, 67*, 895–904. (p. 425)

Gustavson, C. R., Garcia, J., Hankins, W. G., & Rusiniak, K. W. (1974). Coyote predation control by aversive conditioning. *Science, 184*, 581–583. (p. 182)

Gustavson, C. R., Kelly, D. J., & Sweeney, M. (1976). Prey lithium aversions I: Coyotes and wolves. *Behavioral Biology, 17*, 61–72. (p. 182)

Guttmacher Institute. (1994). *Sex and America's teenagers.* New York: Alan Guttmacher Institute. (pp. 92, 117)

Guttmacher Institute. (2000). *Fulfilling the promise: Public policy and U.S. family planning clinics.* New York: Alan Guttmacher Institute. (p. 92)

Guttmacher Institute. (2012). Facts on American teens' sexual and reproductive health. Retrieved from http://www.guttmacher.org/pubs/FB-ATSRH.html. (p. 119)

H., Sally. (1979, August). *Videotape recording number T–3, Fortunoff Video Archive of Holocaust Testimonies.* New Haven, CT: Yale University Library. (p. 318)

Haase, C. M., Tomasik, M. J. H., & Silbereisen, R. K. (2008). Premature behavioral autonomy: Correlates in late adolescence and young adulthood. *European Psychologist, 13*, 255–266. (p. 84)

Habel, U., Koch, K., Kellerman, T., Reske, M., Frommann, N., Wolwer, W., Zilles, K., Shah, N. J., & Schneider, F. (2010). Training of affect recognition in schizophrenia: Neurobiological correlates. *Social Neuroscience, 5*, 92–104. (p. 430)

Hagger, M. S., Wood, C., Stiff, C., & Chatzisarantis, N. L. D. (2010). Ego depletion and the strength model of self-control: A meta-analysis. *Psychological Bulletin, 136*, 495–525. (p. 293)

Haidt, J. (2002). The moral emotions. In R. J. Davidson, K. Scherer, & H. H. Goldsmith (Eds.), *Handbook of affective sciences.* New York: Oxford University Press. (p. 88)

Haidt, J. (2006). *The happiness hypothesis: Finding modern truth in ancient wisdom.* New York: Basic Books. (p. 88)

Haidt, J. (2010). Moral psychology must not be based on faith and hope: Commentary on Narvaez. *Perspectives on Psychological Science, 5*, 182–184. (p. 88)

Hakuta, K., Bialystok, E., & Wiley, E. (2003). Critical evidence: A test of the critical-period hypothesis for second-language acquisition. *Psychological Science, 14*, 31–38. (p. 232)

Halberstadt, J., Sherman, S. J., & Sherman, J. W. (2011). Why Barack Obama is black. *Psychological Science, 22*, 29–33. (p. 353)

Halberstadt, J. B., Niedenthal, P. M., & Kushner, J. (1995). Resolution of lexical ambiguity by emotional state. *Psychological Science, 6*, 278–281. (p. 139)

Haldeman, D. C. (1994). The practice and ethics of sexual orientation conversion therapy. *Journal of Consulting and Clinical Psychology, 62*, 221–227. (p. 121)

Haldeman, D. C. (2002). Gay rights, patient rights: The implications of sexual orientation conversion therapy. *Professional Psychology: Research and Practice, 33*, 260–264. (p. 121)

Hall, C. S., Dornhoff, W., Blick, K. A., & Weesner, K. E. (1982). The dreams of college men and women in 1950 and 1980: A comparison of dream contents and sex differences. *Sleep, 5*, 188–194. (p. 60)

Hall, C. S., & Lindzey, G. (1978). *Theories of personality* (2nd ed.). New York: Wiley. (p. 317)

Hall, D. T., & Chandler, D. E. (2005). Psychological success: When the career is a calling. *Journal of Organizational Behavior, 26*, 155–176. (p. 319)

Hall, G. (1997). Context aversion, Pavlovian conditioning, and the psychological side effects of chemotherapy. *European Psychologist, 2*, 118–124. (p. 173)

Hall, J. A. (1984). *Nonverbal sex differences: Communication accuracy and expressive style.* Baltimore: Johns Hopkins University Press. (p. 275)

Hall, J. A. (1987). On explaining gender differences: The case of nonverbal communication. In P. Shaver & C. Hendrick (Eds.), *Review of Personality and Social Psychology, 7*, 177–200. (p. 275)

Hall, W. (2006). The mental health risks of adolescent cannabis use. *PloS Medicine, 3*(2), e39. (pp. 387, 388)

Halpern, D. F. (2000). *Sex-related ability differences: Changing perspectives, changing minds.* Mahwah, NJ: Erlbaum. (p. 247)

Halpern, D. F., Benbow, C. P., Geary, D. C., Gur, R. C., Hyde, J. S., & Gernsbacher, M. A. (2007). The science of sex differences in science and mathematics. *Psychological Science in the Public Interest, 8*, 1–51. (pp. 246, 247)

Halsey, A., III. (2010, January 26). U.S. bans truckers, bus drivers from texting while driving. *Washington Post* (www.washingtonpost.com). (p. 51)

Hamani, C., Mayberg, H., Snyder, B., Giacobbe, P., Kennedy, S., & Lozano, A. M. (2009). Deep brain stimulation of the subcallosal cingulated gyrus for depression: Anatomical location of active contacts in clinical responders and a suggested guideline for targeting. *Journal of Neurosurgery, 111*, 1209–1215. (p. 428)

Hammer, E. (2003). How lucky you are to be a psychology major. *Eye on Psi Chi, 4*–5. (p. C-5)

Hammersmith, S. K. (1982, August). Sexual preference: An empirical study from the Alfred C. Kinsey Institute for Sex Research. Paper presented at the meeting of the American Psychological Association, Washington, DC. (p. 122)

Hammond, D. C. (2008). Hypnosis as sole anesthesia for major surgeries: Historical and contemporary perspectives. *American Journal of Clinical Hypnosis, 51*, 101–121. (p. 156)

Hampson, R. (2000, April 10). In the end, people just need more room. *USA Today*, p. 19A. (p. 263)

Hankin, B. L., & Abramson, L. Y. (2001). Development of gender differences in depression: An elaborated cognitive vulnerability-transactional stress theory. *Psychological Bulletin, 127*, 773–796. (p. 395)

Hansen, C. H., & Hansen, R. D. (1988). Finding the face-in-the-crowd: An anger superiority effect. *Journal of Personality and Social Psychology, 54*, 917–924. (p. 275)

Harbaugh, W. T., Mayr, U., & Burghart, D. R. (2007). Neural responses to taxation and voluntary giving reveal motives for charitable donations. *Science, 316*, 1622–1625. (p. 364)

Hardt, O., Einarsson, E. O., & Nader, K. (2010). A bridge over troubled water: Reconsolidation as a link between cognitive and neuroscientific memory research traditions. *Annual Review of Psychology, 61*, 141–167. (p. 209)

Hare, R. D. (1975). Psychophysiological studies of psychopathy. In D. C. Fowles (Ed.), *Clinical applications of psychophysiology*. New York: Columbia University Press. (p. 403)

Harenski, C. L., Harenski, K. A., Shane, M. W., & Kiehl, K. A. (2010). Aberrant neural processing of moral violations in criminal psychopaths. *Journal of Abnormal Psychology, 119,* 863–874. (p. 404)

Harkins, S. G., & Szymanski, K. (1989). Social loafing and group evaluation. *Journal of Personality and Social Psychology, 56,* 934–941. (p. 347)

Harlow, H. F., Harlow, M. K., & Suomi, S. J. (1971). From thought to therapy: Lessons from a primate laboratory. *American Scientist, 59,* 538–549. (p. 81)

Harmon-Jones, E., Abramson, L. Y., Sigelman, J., Bohlig, A., Hogan, M. E., & Harmon-Jones, C. (2002). Proneness to hypomania/mania symptoms or depression symptoms and asymmetrical frontal cortical responses to an anger-evoking event. *Journal of Personality and Social Psychology, 82,* 610–618. (p. 273)

Harms, P. D., Roberts, B. W., & Winter, D. (2006). Becoming the Harvard man: Person-environment fit, personality development, and academic success. *Personality and Social Psychology Bulletin, 32,* 851–865. (p. 327)

Harper, C., & McLanahan, S. (2004). Father absence and youth incarceration. *Journal of Research on Adolescence, 14,* 369–397. (p. 356)

Harris Interactive. (2010). 2009 eHarmony® marriage metrics study: Methodological notes. www.eharmony.com/harrisinteractivepoll. (p. 359)

Harris, B. (1979). Whatever happened to Little Albert? *American Psychologist, 34,* 151–160. (p. 173)

Harris, J. R. (1998). *The nurture assumption.* New York: Free Press. (pp. 82, 90)

Harris, J. R. (2000). Beyond the nurture assumption: Testing hypotheses about the child's environment. In J. G. Borkowski & S. L. Ramey (Eds.), *Parenting and the child's world: Influences on academic, intellectual, and social-emotional development.* Washington, DC: APA Books. (p. 90)

Harris, J. R. (2007, August 8). Do pals matter more than parents? *The Times* (www.timesonline.co.uk). (p. 90)

Harris, R. J. (1994). The impact of sexually explicit media. In J. Brant & D. Zillmann (Eds.), *Media effects: Advances in theory and research.* Hillsdale, NJ: Erlbaum. (p. 357)

Harriston, K. A. (1993, December 24). 1 shakes, 1 snoozes: Both win $45 million. *Washington Post* release (in *Tacoma News Tribune,* pp. A1, A2). (p. 328)

Harter, J. K., Schmidt, F. L., Asplund, J. W., Killham, E. A., & Agrawal, S. (2010). Causal impact of employee work perceptions on the bottom line of organizations. *Perspectives on Psychological Science, 5,* 378–389. (p. B-5)

Harter, J. K., Schmidt, F. L., & Hayes, T. L. (2002). Business-unit-level relationship between employee satisfaction, employee engagement, and business outcomes: A meta-analysis. *Journal of Applied Psychology, 87,* 268–279. (p. 5)

Hartmann, E. (1981, April). The strangest sleep disorder. *Psychology Today,* pp. 14, 16, 18. (p. 59)

Hartwig, M., & Bond, C. F., Jr. (2011). Why do lie-catchers fail? A lens model meta-analysis of human lie judgments. *Psychological Bulletin, 137,* 643–659. (p. 275)

Harvey, A. G., & Tang, N. K. Y. (2012). (Mis)perception of sleep in insomnia: A puzzle and a resolution. *Psychological Bulletin, 138,* 77–101. (p. 58)

Haslam, S. A., & Reicher, S. (2007). Beyond the banality of evil: Three dynamics of an interactionist social psychology of tyranny. *Personality and Social Psychology Bulletin, 33,* 615–622. (p. 340)

Hassan, B., & Rahman, Q. (2007). Selective sexual orientation-related differences in object location memory. *Behavioral Neuroscience, 121,* 625–633. (p. 124)

Hatfield, E. (1988). Passionate and companionate love. In R. J. Sternberg & M. L. Barnes (Eds.), *The psychology of love.* New Haven, CT: Yale University Press. (pp. 361, 362)

Hatfield, E., & Sprecher, S. (1986). *Mirror, mirror . . . The importance of looks in everyday life.* Albany: State University of New York Press. (p. 360)

Havas, D. A., Glenberg, A. M., Gutowski, K. A., Lucarelli, M. J., & Davidson, R. J. (2010). Cosmetic use of botulinum toxin-A affects processing of emotional language. *Psychological Science, 21,* 895–900. (p. 278)

Haworth, C. M. A., & 17 others. (2009). A twin study of the genetics of high cognitive ability selected from 11,000 twin pairs in sex studies from four countries. *Behavior Genetics, 39,* 359–370. (p. 241)

Haxby, J. V. (2001, July 7). Quoted by B. Bower, Faces of perception. *Science News,* pp. 10–12. See also J. V. Haxby, M. I. Gobbini, M. L. Furey, A. Ishai, J. L. Schouten & P. Pietrini, Distributed and overlapping representations of faces and objects in ventral temporal cortex. *Science, 293,* 2425–2430. (p. 142)

Headey, B., Muffels, R., & Wagner, G. G. (2010). Long-running German panel survey shows that personal and economic choices, not just genes, matter for happiness. *PNAS, 107,* 17922–17926. (p. 305)

Heatherton, T. F., & Sargent, J. D. (2009). Does watching smoking in movies promote teenage smoking? *Current Directions in Psychological Science, 18,* 63–67. (p. 389)

Heckert, J. (2012, November 15). The hazards of growing up painlessly. *New York Times* (www.nytimes.com). (p. 154)

Heider, F. (1958). *The psychology of interpersonal relations.* New York: Wiley. (p. 338)

Heiman, J. R. (1975, April). The physiology of erotica: Women's sexual arousal. *Psychology Today,* pp. 90–94. (p. 118)

Heine, S. J., & Buchtel, E. E. (2009). Personality: The universal and the culturally specific. *Annual Review of Psychology, 60,* 369–394. (p. 333)

Heine, S. J., & Hamamura, T. (2007). In search of East Asian self-enhancement. *Personality and Social Psychology Review, 11,* 4–27. (p. 330)

Heine, S. J., Proulx, T., & Vohs, K. D. (2006). Meaning maintenance model: On the coherence of human motivations. *Personality and Social Psychology Review, 10,* 88–110. (p. 296)

Helfand, D. (2011, January 7). An assault on rationality. *New York Times* (www.nytimes.com). (p. 162)

Helmreich, W. B. (1992). *Against all odds: Holocaust survivors and the successful lives they made in America.* New York: Simon & Schuster. (p. 318)

Helmreich, W. B. (1994). Personal correspondence. Department of Sociology, City University of New York. (p. 318)

Helms, J. E., Jernigan, M., & Mascher, J. (2005). The meaning of race in psychology and how to change it: A methodological perspective. *American Psychologist, 60,* 27–36. (p. 248)

Helmuth, L. (2001). Boosting brain activity from the outside in. *Science, 292,* 1284–1286. (p. 429)

Hembree, R. (1988). Correlates, causes, effects, and treatment of test anxiety. *Review of Educational Research, 58,* 47–77. (p. 257)

Henderlong, J., & Lepper, M. R. (2002). The effects of praise on children's intrinsic motivation: A review and synthesis. *Psychological Bulletin, 128,* 774–795. (p. 184)

Henig, R. M. (2010, August 18). What is it about 20-somethings? *New York Times* (www.nytimes.com). (p. 92)

Henkel, L. A., Franklin, N., & Johnson, M. K. (2000, March). Cross-modal source monitoring confusions between perceived and imagined events. *Journal of Experimental Psychology: Learning, Memory, & Cognition, 26,* 321–335. (p. 211)

Hennenlotter, A., Dresel, C., Castrop, F., Ceballos Baumann, A., Wohschlager, A., & Haslinger, B. (2008). The link between facial feedback and neural activity within central circuitries of emotion: New insights from botulinum toxin-induced denervation of frown muscles. *Cerebral Cortex, 19,* 537–542. (p. 278)

Hennessey, B. A., & Amabile, T. M. (2010). Creativity. *Annual Review of Psychology, 61,* 569–598. (pp. 226, B-8)

Herbenick, D., Reece, M., Schick, V., Sanders, S. A., Dodge, B., & Fortenberry, J. D. (2010). Sexual behavior in the United States: Results from a national probability sample of men and women ages 14–94. *Journal of Sexual Medicine, 7*(suppl. 5), 255–265. (p. 121)

Herman, C. P., & Polivy, J. (1980). Restrained eating. In A. J. Stunkard (Ed.), *Obesity.* Philadelphia: Saunders. (p. 264)

Herman, C. P., & Polivy, J. (2008). External cues in the control of food intake in humans: the sensory-normative distinction. *Physiology and Behavior, 94,* 722–728. (p. 261)

Herman, C. P., Roth, D. A., & Polivy, J. (2003). Effects of the presence of others on food intake: A normative interpretation. *Psychological Bulletin, 129,* 873–886. (p. 261)

Herman-Giddens, M. E., Wang, L., & Koch, G. (2001). Secondary sexual characteristics in boys: Estimates from the National Health and Nutrition Examination Survey III, 1988–1994. *Archives of Pediatrics and Adolescent Medicine, 155,* 1022–1028. (p. 111)

Hernandez, A. E., & Li, P. (2007). Age of acquisition: Its neural and computational mechanisms. *Psychological Bulletin, 133,* 638–650. (p. 232)

Herrmann, E., Call, J., Hernández-Lloreda, M. V., Hare, B., & Tomasello, M. (2007). Humans have evolved specialized skills of social cognition: The cultural intelligence hypothesis. *Science, 317,* 1360–1365. (p. 186)

Herrnstein, R. J., & Loveland, D. H. (1964). Complex visual concept in the pigeon. *Science, 146,* 549–551. (p. 175)

Hertenstein, M. J., Hansel, C., Butts, S., Hile, S. (2009). Smile intensity in photographs predicts divorce later in life. *Motivation & Emotion, 33,* 99–105. (p. 101)

Hertenstein, M. J., Keltner, D., App, B. Bulleit, B., & Jaskolka, A. (2006). Touch communicates distinct emotions. *Emotion, 6,* 528–533. (p. 82)

Hertzog, C., Kramer, A. F., Wilson, R. S., & Lindenberger, U. (2008). Enrichment effects on adult cognitive development: Can the functional capacity of older adults be preserved and enhanced? *Psychological Science in the Public Interest, 9*(1), 1–65. (p. 97)

Herz, R. (2007). *The scent of desire: Discovering our enigmatic sense of smell.* New York: Morrow/HarperCollins. (p. 158)

Hess, E. H. (1956, July). Space perception in the chick. *Scientific American,* pp. 71–80. (p. 150)

Hess, U., & Thibault, P. (2009). Darwin and emotion expression. *American Psychologist, 64,* 120–128. (p. 277)

Hetherington, M. M., Anderson, A. S., Norton, G. N. M., & Newson, L. (2006). Situational effects on meal intake: A comparison of eating alone and eating with others. *Physiology and Behavior, 88,* 498–505. (p. 261)

Hettema, J. M., Neale, M. C., & Kendler, K. S. (2001). A review and meta-analysis of the genetic epidemiology of anxiety disorders. *American Journal of Psychiatry, 158,* 1568–1578. (p. 380)

Hickok, G., Bellugi, U., & Klima, E. S. (2001, June). Sign language in the brain. *Scientific American,* pp. 58–65. (p. 50)

Hilgard, E. R. (1986). *Divided consciousness: Multiple controls in human thought and action.* New York: Wiley. (p. 157)

Hilgard, E. R. (1992). Dissociation and theories of hypnosis. In E. Fromm & M. R. Nash (Eds.), *Contemporary hypnosis research.* New York: Guilford. (p. 157)

Hill, C. E., & Nakayama, E. Y. (2000). Client-centered therapy: Where has it been and where is it going? A comment on Hathaway. *Journal of Clinical Psychology, 56,* 961–875. (p. 413)

Hills, P. J., Werno, M. A., & Lewis, M. B. (2011). Sad people are more accurate at face recognition than happy people. *Consciousness and Cognition, 20,* 1502–1517. (p. 390)

Hines, M. (2004). *Brain gender.* New York: Oxford University Press. (p. 111)

Hingson, R. W., Heeren, T., & Winter M. R. (2006). Age at drinking onset and alcohol dependence. *Archives of Pediatrics & Adolescent Medicine, 160,* 739–746. (pp. 383, 390)

Hingson, R. W., Heeren, T., Zakocs, R. C., Kopstein, A., & Wechsler, H. (2002). Magnitude of alcohol-related mortality and morbidity among U.S. college students ages 18–24. *Journal of Studies on Alcohol, 63,* 136–144. (p. 382)

Hintzman, D. L. (1978). *The psychology of learning and memory.* San Francisco: Freeman. (p. 197)

Hinz, L. D., & Williamson, D. A. (1987). Bulimia and depression: A review of the affective variant hypothesis. *Psychological Bulletin, 102,* 150–158. (p. 401)

Hirsh, J. B., Galinsky, A. D., & Zhong, C-B. (2011). Drunk, powerful, and in the dark: How general processes of disinhibition produce both prosocial and antisocial behavior. *Perspectives on Psychological Science, 6,* 415–427. (p. 382)

Hirst, W., & 15 others (2009). Long-term memory for the terrorist attack of September 11: flashbulb memories, event memories, and the factors that influence their retention. *Journal of Experimental Psychology: General, 138,* 161–176. (p. 201)

HMHL. (2007, February). Electroconvulsive therapy. *Harvard Mental Health Letter,* Harvard Medical School, pp. 1–4. (p. 427)

Hobson, J. A. (2003). *Dreaming: An introduction to the science of sleep.* New York: Oxford. (p. 61)

Hobson, J. A. (2004). *13 dreams Freud never had: The new mind science.* New York: Pi Press. (p. 61)

Hobson, J. A. (2009). REM sleep and dreaming: Towards a theory of proto-consciousness. *Nature Reviews, 10,* 803–814. (p. 61)

Hochberg, L. R., Bacher, D., Jarosiewicz, B., Masse, N. Y., Simeral, J. D., Vogel, J., Haddadin, S., Liu, J., Cash, S. S., van der Smagt, P., & Donoghue, J. P. (2012). Reach and grasp by people with tetraplegia using a neutrally controlled robotic arm. *Nature, 485,* 375–375. (p. 44)

Hoebel, B. G., & Teitelbaum, P. (1966). Effects of forcefeeding and starvation on food intake and body weight in a rat with ventromedial hypothalamic lesions. *Journal of Comparative and Physiological Psychology, 61,* 189–193. (p. 259)

Hoffman, B. M., Babyak, M. A., Craighead, W. E., Sherwood, A., Doraiswamy, P. M., Coons, M. J., & Blumenthal, J. A. (2011). Exercise and pharmacotherapy in patients with major depression: One-year follow-up of the SMILE study. *Psychosomatic Medicine, 73,* 127–133. (p. 297)

Hoffman, C., & Hurst, N. (1990). Gender stereotypes: Perception or rationalization? *Journal of Personality and Social Psychology, 58,* 197–208. (p. 352)

Hoffman, D. D. (1998). *Visual intelligence: How we create what we see.* New York: Norton. (p. 143)

Hoffman, H. G. (2004, August). Virtual-reality therapy. *Scientific American,* pp. 58–65. (pp. 155, 415)

Hofmann, S. G., Sawyer, A. T., Witt, A. A., & Oh, D. (2010). The effect of mindfulness-based therapy on anxiety and depression: A meta-analytic review. *Journal of Consulting and Clinical Psychology, 78,* 169–183. (p. 299)

Hoge, C. W., & Castro, C. A. (2006). Post-traumatic stress disorder in UK and U.S. forces deployed to Iraq. *The Lancet, 368,* 837. (p. 378)

Hoge, C. W., Castro, C. A., Messer, S. C., McGurk, D., Cotting, D. I., & Koffman, R. L. (2004). Combat duty in Iraq and Afghanistan, mental health problems, and barriers to care. *New England Journal of Medicine, 351,* 13–22. (p. 378)

Hoge, C. W., Terhakopian, A., Castro, C. A., Messer, S. C., & Engel, C. C. (2007). Association of posttraumatic stress disorder with somatic symptoms, health care visits, and absenteeism among Iraq War veterans. *American Journal of Psychiatry, 164,* 150–153. (p. 378)

Hogg, M. A. (1996). Intragroup processes, group structure and social identity. In W. P. Robinson (Ed.), *Social groups and identities: Developing the legacy of Henri Tajfel.* Oxford: Butterworth Heinemann. (p. 352)

Hohmann, G. W. (1966). Some effects of spinal cord lesions on experienced emotional feelings. *Psychophysiology, 3,* 143–156. (p. 270)

Holahan, C. K., & Sears, R. R. (1995). *The gifted group in later maturity.* Stanford, CA: Stanford University Press. (p. 242)

Holden, C. (2008). Poles apart. *Science, 321,* 193–195. (p. 69)

Hollis, K. L. (1997). Contemporary research on Pavlovian conditioning: A "new" functional analysis. *American Psychologist, 52,* 956–965. (p. 171)

Hollon, S. D., Thase, M. E., & Markowitz, J. C. (2002). Treatment and prevention of depression. *Psychological Science in the Public Interest, 3,* 39–77. (p. 426)

Holstege, G., Georgiadis, J. R., Paans, A. M. J., Meiners, L. C., van der Graaf, F. H. C. E., & Reinders, A. A. T. S. (2003a). Brain activation during male ejaculation. *Journal of Neuroscience, 23,* 9185–9193. (p. 116)

Holstege, G., Reinders, A. A. T., Paans, A. M. J., Meiners, L. C., Pruim, J., & Georgiadis, J. R. (2003b). *Brain activation during female sexual orgasm.* Program No. 727.7. Washington, DC: Society for Neuroscience. (p. 116)

Holtgraves, T. (2011). Text messaging, personality, and the social context. *Journal of Research in Personality, 45,* 92–99. (p. 326)

Hooper, J., & Teresi, D. (1986). *The three-pound universe.* New York: Macmillan. (p. 42)

Hopkins, E. D., & Cantalupo, C. (2008). Theoretical speculations on the evolutionary origins of hemispheric specialization. *Current Directions in Psychological Science, 17,* 233–237. (p. 50)

Hopwood, C. J., Donnellan, M. B., Blonigen, D. M., Krueger, R. F., McGue, M., Iacono, W. G., & Burt, S. A. (2011). Genetic and environmental influences on personality trait stability and growth during the transition to adulthood: A three-wave longitudinal study. *Journal of Personality and Social Psychology, 100,* 545–556. (p. 102)

Hor, H., & Tafti, M. (2009). How much sleep do we need? *Science, 325,* 825–826. (p. 55)

Horn, J. L. (1982). The aging of human abilities. In J. Wolman (Ed.), *Handbook of developmental psychology.* Englewood Cliffs, NJ: Prentice-Hall. (p. 246)

Horner, V., Whiten, A., Flynn, E., & de Waal, F. B. M. (2006). Faithful replication of foraging techniques along cultural transmission chains by chimpanzees and children. *Proceedings of the National Academy of Sciences, 103,* 13878–13883. (p. 229)

Horrey, W. J., & Wickens, C. D. (2006). Examining the impact of cell phone conversations on driving using meta-analytic techniques. *Human Factors and Ergonomics Society, 48,* 196–205. (p. 51)

Horwood, L. J., & Fergusson, D. M. (1998). Breastfeeding and later cognitive and academic outcomes. *Pediatrics, 101*(1). (p. 16)

Hou, W-H., Chiang, P-T, Hsu, T-Y, Chiu, S-Y, & Yen, Y-C. (2010). Treatment effects of massage therapy in depressed people: A meta-analysis. *Journal of Clinical Psychiatry, 71,* 894–901. (p. 299)

House, R. J., & Singh, J. V. (1987). Organizational behavior: Some new directions for I/O psychology. *Annual Review of Psychology, 38,* 669–718. (p. B-6)

Houser-Marko, L., & Sheldon, K. M. (2008). Eyes on the prize or nose to the grindstone? The effects of level of goal evaluation on mood and motivation. *Personality and Social Psychology Bulletin, 34,* 1556–1569. (p. B-6)

Houts, A. C., Berman, J. S., & Abramson, H. (1994). Effectiveness of psychological and pharmacological treatments for nocturnal enuresis. *Journal of Consulting and Clinical Psychology, 62,* 737–745. (p. 414)

Houts, R. M., Caspi, A., Pianta, R. C., Arseneault, L., & Moffitt, T. E. (2010). The challenging pupil in the classroom: The effect of the child on the teacher. *Psychological Science, 21,* 1802–1810. (p. 101)

Hovatta, I., Tennant, R. S., Helton, R., Marr, R. A., Singer, O., Redwine, J. M., Ellison, J. A., Schadt, E. E., Verma, I. M., Lockhart, D. J., & Barlow, C. (2005). Glyoxalase 1 and glutathione reductase 1 regulate anxiety in mice. *Nature, 438,* 662–666. (p. 380)

Howell, A. J. (2009). Flourishing: Achievement-related correlates of students' well-being. *Journal of Positive Psychology, 4,* 1–13. (p. 250)

Hsee, C. K., Yang, A. X., & Wang, L. (2010). Idleness aversion and the need for justifiable busyness. *Psychological Science, 21,* 926–930. (p. B-2)

Hu, X-Z., Lipsky, R. H., Zhu, G., Akhtar, L. A., Taubman, J., Greenberg, B. D., Xu, K., Arnold, P. D., Richter, M. A., Kennedy, J. L., Murphy, D. L., & Goldman, D. (2006). Serotonin transporter promoter gain-of-function genotypes are linked to obsessive-compulsive disorder. *American Journal of Human Genetics, 78,* 815–826. (p. 380)

Huang, C. (2010). Mean-level change in self-esteem from childhood through adulthood: Meta-analysis of longitudinal studies. *Review of General Psychology, 14,* 251–260. (p. 99)

Huang, M-E., Wu, Z-Q., & Tang, G-Qi (2010). How does personality relate to mental health in service industry setting? The mediating effects of emotional labor strategies. *Acta Psychologica Sinica, 42,* 1175–1189. (p. 284)

Huang, X., Iun, J., Liu, A., & Gong, Y. (2010). Does participative leadership enhance work performance by inducing empowerment or trust? The differential effects on managerial and non-managerial subordinates. *Journal of Organizational Behavior, 31,* 122–143. (p. B-8)

Hubbard, E. M., Arman, A. C., Ramachandran, V. S., & Boynton, G. M. (2005). Individual differences among grapheme-color synesthetes: Brain-behavior correlations. *Neuron, 45,* 975–985. (p. 161)

Hubel, D. H., & Wiesel, T. N. (1979, September). Brian mechanisms of vision. *Scientific American,* pp. 150–162. (p. 142)

Hublin, C., Kaprio, J., Partinen, M., Heikkila, K., & Koskenvuo, M. (1997). Prevalence and genetics of sleepwalking: A population-based twin study. *Neurology, 48,* 177–181. (p. 59)

Hublin, C., Kaprio, J., Partinen, M., & Koskenvuo, M. (1998). Sleeptalking in twins: Epidemiology and psychiatric comorbidity. *Behavior Genetics, 28,* 289–298. (p. 59)

Hucker, S. J., & Bain, J. (1990). Androgenic hormones and sexual assault. In W. Marshall, R. Law, & H. Barbaree (Eds.), *The handbook on sexual assault.* New York: Plenum. (p. 116)

Hudson, J. I., Hiripi, E., Pope, H. G., & Kessler, R. C. (2007). The prevalence and correlates of eating disorders in the National Comorbidity Survey Replication. *Biological Psychiatry, 61,* 348–358. (p. 401)

Huey, E. D., Krueger, F., & Grafman, J. (2006). Representations in the human prefrontal cortex. *Current Directions in Psychological Science, 15,* 167–171. (p. 46)

Hughes, H. C. (1999). *Sensory exotica: A world beyond human experience.* Cambridge, MA: MIT Press. (p. 135)

Hughes, J. R., Peters, E. N., & Naud, S. (2008). Relapse to smoking after 1 year of abstinence: A meta-analysis. *Addictive Behaviors, 33,* 1516–1520. (p. 385)

Hugick, L. (1989, July). Women play the leading role in keeping modern families close. *Gallup Report, No. 286,* p. 27–34. (p. 110)

Hull, J. M. (1990). *Touching the rock: An experience of blindness.* New York: Vintage Books. (pp. 204, 360)

Hummer, R. A., Rogers, R. G., Nam, C. B., & Ellison, C. G. (1999). Religious involvement and U.S. adult mortality. *Demography, 36,* 273–285. (p. 299)

Humphrey, S. E., Nahrgang, J. D., & Morgeson, F. P. (2007). Integrating motivational, social, and contextual work design features: A meta-analytic summary and theoretical extension of the work design literature. *Journal of Applied Psychology, 92,* 1332–1356. (p. 292)

Hunsley, J., & Bailey, J. M. (1999). The clinical utility of the Rorschach: Unfulfilled promises and an uncertain future. *Psychological Assessment, 11,* 266–277. (p. 317)

Hunsley, J., & Di Giulio, G. (2002). Dodo bird, phoenix, or urban legend? The question of psychotherapy equivalence. *Scientific Review of Mental Health Practice, 1,* 11–22. (p. 422)

Hunt, C., Slade, T., & Andrews, G. (2004). Generalized anxiety disorder and major depressive disorder comorbidity in the National Survey of Mental Health and Well-Being. *Depression and Anxiety, 20,* 23–31. (p. 377)

Hunt, E., & Carlson, J. (2007). Considerations relating to the study of group differences in intelligence. *Perspectives on Psychological Science, 2,* 194–213. (p. 249)

Hunt, J. M. (1982). Toward equalizing the developmental opportunities of infants and preschool children. *Journal of Social Issues, 38*(4), 163–191. (p. 244)

Hunt, M. (1990). *The compassionate beast: What science is discovering about the humane side of humankind.* New York: William Morrow. (p. 5)

Hunt, M. (1993). *The story of psychology.* New York: Doubleday. (pp. 2, 173, 242)

Hutchinson, R. (2006). *Calum's road.* Edinburgh: Burlinn Limited. (p. B-4)

Hvistendahl, M. (2011). China's population growing slowly, changing fast. *Science, 332,* 650–651. (p. 351)

Hyde, J. S. (2005). The gender similarities hypothesis. *American Psychologist, 60,* 581–592. (p. 108)

Hyde, J. S., & Mertz, J. E. (2009). Gender, culture, and mathematics performance. *Proceedings of the National Academy of Sciences, 106,* 8801–8807. (p. 246)

Hyde, J. S., Mezulis, A. H., & Abramson, L. Y. (2008). The ABCs of depression: Integrating affective, biological, and cognitive models to explain the emergence of the gender difference in depression. *Psychological Review, 115,* 291–313. (p. 393)

Hyman, I. E., Jr., Boss, S. M., Wise, B. M., McKenzie, K. E., & Caggiano, J. M. (2010). Did you see the unicycling clown? Inattentional blindness while walking and talking on a cell phone. *Applied Cognitive Psychology, 24*(5), 597–607. (p. 51)

Iacoboni, M. (2009). Imitation, empathy, and mirror neurons. *Annual Review of Psychology, 60,* 653–670. (p. 186)

Ickes, W., Snyder, M., & Garcia, S. (1997). Personality influences on the choice of situations. In R. Hogan, J. Johnson, & S. Briggs (Eds.). *Handbook of Personality Psychology.* San Diego, CA: Academic Press. (p. 327)

Idson, L. C., & Mischel, W. (2001). The personality of familiar and significant people: The lay perceiver as a social-cognitive theorist. *Journal of Personality and Social Psychology, 80,* 585–596. (p. 338)

Iemmola, F., & Camperio Ciani, A. (2009). New evidence of genetic factors influencing sexual orientation in men: Female fecundity increase in the maternal line. *Archives of Sexual Behavior, 38,* 393–399. (p. 127)

Igarashi, T., Takai, J., & Yoshida, T. (2005). Gender differences in social network development via mobile phone text messages: A longitudinal study. *Journal of Social and Personal Relationships, 22,* 691–713. (p. 109)

IJzerman, H., & Semin, G. R. (2009). The thermometer of social relations: Mapping social proximity on temperature. *Psychological Science, 20,* 1214–1220. (p. 161)

Ikonomidou, C. C., Bittigau, P., Ishimaru, M. J., Wozniak, D. F., Koch, C., Genz, K., Price, M. T., Stefovska, V., Hoerster, F., Tenkova, T., Dikranian, K., & Olney, J. W. (2000). Ethanol-induced apoptotic neurodegeneration and fetal alcohol syndrome. *Science, 287,* 1056–1060. (p. 71)

Ilardi, S. S. (2009). *The depression cure: The six-step program to beat depression without drugs.* Cambridge, MA: Da Capo Lifelong Books. (pp. 395, 430)

Inbar, Y., Cone, J., & Gilovich, T. (2010). People's intuitions about intuitive insight and intuitive choice. *Journal of Personality and Social Psychology, 99,* 232–247. (p. 226)

Inbar, Y., Pizarro, D., & Bloom, P. (2011). Disgusting smells cause decreased liking of gay men. Unpublished manuscript, Tilburg University. (p. 159)

Ingham, A. G., Levinger, G., Graves, J., & Peckham, V. (1974). The Ringelmann effect: Studies of group size and group performance. *Journal of Experimental Social Psychology, 10,* 371–384. (p. 347)

Inglehart, R. (1990). *Culture shift in advanced industrial society.* Princeton, NJ: Princeton University Press. (pp. 99, 265)

Inglehart, R., Foa, R., Peterson, C., & Welzel, C. (2008). Development, freedom, and rising happiness: A global perspective (1981–2007). *Perspectives on Psychological Science, 3,* 264–285. (p. 292)

Insana, R. (2005, February 21). Coach says honey gets better results than vinegar (interview with Larry Brown). *USA Today,* p. 4B. (p. B-6)

Insel, T. R. (2010, April). Faulty circuits. *Scientific American,* pp. 44–51. (p. 381)

International Schizophrenia Consortium. (2009). Common polygenic variation contributes to risk of schizophrenia and bipolar disorder. *Nature, 460,* 748–752. (p. 400)

Inzlicht, M., & Ben-Zeev, T. (2000). A threatening intellectual environment: Why females are susceptible to experiencing problem-solving deficits in the presence of males. *Psychological Science, 11,* 365–371. (p. 250)

Inzlicht, M., & Gutsell, J. N. (2007). Running on empty: Neural signals for self-control failure. *Psychological Science, 18,* 933–937. (p. 293)

Inzlicht, M., & Kang, S. K. (2010). Stereotype threat spillover: How coping with threats to social identity affects aggression, eating, decision making, and attention. *Journal of Personality and Social Psychology, 99,* 467–481. (p. 249)

IPSOS. (2010a, June 29). Online Canadians report a large 35% decline in the amount of email received. www.ipsos-na.com. (p. 266)

IPSOS. (2010b, April 8). One in five (20%) global citizens believe that alien beings have come down to earth and walk amongst us in our communities disguised as humans. www.ipsos-na.com. (p. 15)

IPU. (2011). Women in national parliaments: Situation as of 31 November 2011. International Parliamentary Union (www.ipu.org). (p. 109)

Ireland, M. E., & Pennebaker, J. W. (2010). Language style matching in writing: Synchrony in essays, correspondence, and poetry. *Journal of Personality and Social Psychology, 99*, 549–571. (p. 186)

Ironson, G., Solomon, G. F., Balbin, E. G., O'Cleirigh, C., George, A., Kumar, M., Larson, D., & Woods, T. E. (2002). The Ironson-Woods spiritual/religiousness index is associated with long survival, health behaviors, less distress, and low cortisol in people with HIV/AIDS. *Annals of Behavioral Medicine, 24*, 34–48. (p. 300)

Irwin, M., Mascovich, A., Gillin, J. C., Willoughby, R., Pike, J., & Smith, T. L. (1994). Partial sleep deprivation reduces natural killer cell activity in humans. *Psychosomatic Medicine, 56*, 493–498. (p. 57)

Islam, S. S., & Johnson, C. (2003). Correlates of smoking behavior among Muslim Arab-American adolescents. *Ethnicity & Health, 8*, 319–337. (p. 300)

ITU. (2010). The world in 2009: ICT facts and figures. International Telecommunication Union (www.itu.int/ict). (p. 266)

Ives-Deliperi, V. L., Solms, M., & Meintjes, E. M. (2011). The neural substrates of mindfulness: An fMRI investigation. *Social Neuroscience, 6*, 231–242. (p. 299)

Iyengar, S. S., & Lepper, M. R. (2000). When choice is demotivating: Can one desire too much of a good thing? *Journal of Personality and Social Psychology, 79*, 995–1006. (p. 292)

Izard, C. E. (1977). *Human emotions.* New York: Plenum Press. (pp. 272, 276)

Izard, C. E. (1994). Innate and universal facial expressions: Evidence from developmental and cross-cultural research. *Psychological Bulletin, 114*, 288–299. (p. 276)

Jablensky, A. (1999). Schizophrenia: Epidemiology. *Current Opinion in Psychiatry, 12*, 19–28. (p. 399)

Jackson, G. (2009). Sexual response in cardiovascular disease. *Journal of Sex Research, 46*, 233–236. (p. 116)

Jackson, J. M., & Williams, K. D. (1988). Social loafing: A review and theoretical analysis. Unpublished manuscript, Fordham University. (p. 347)

Jackson, S. W. (1992). The listening healer in the history of psychological healing. *American Journal Psychiatry, 149*, 1623–1632. (p. 423)

Jacobs, B. L. (1994). Serotonin, motor activity, and depression-related disorders. *American Scientist, 82*, 456–463. (p. 395)

Jacobs, B. L. (2004). Depression: The brain finally gets into the act. *Current Directions in Psychological Science, 13*, 103–106. (p. 426)

Jacques, C., & Rossion, B. (2006). The speed of individual face categorization. *Psychological Science, 17*, 485–492. (p. 134)

Jaffe, E. (2004, October). Peace in the Middle East may be impossible: Lee D. Ross on naive realism and conflict resolution. *APS Observer*, pp. 9–11. (p. 139)

James, W. (1890). *The principles of psychology* (Vol. 2). New York: Holt. (pp. 214, 269, 277)

Jameson, D. (1985). Opponent-colors theory in light of physiological findings. In D. Ottoson & S. Zeki (Eds.), *Central and peripheral mechanisms of color vision.* New York: Macmillan. (p. 149)

Jamison, K. R. (1993). *Touched with fire: Manic-depressive illness and the artistic temperament.* New York: Free Press. (p. 392)

Jamison, K. R. (1995). *An unquiet mind.* New York: Knopf. (pp. 392, 409, 427)

Jang, K. L., Livesley, W. J., Ando, J., Yamagata, S., Suzuki, A., Angleitner, A., Ostendorf, F., Riemann, R., & Spinath, F. (2006). Behavioral genetics of the higher-order factors of the Big Five. *Personality and Individual Differences, 41*, 261–272. (p. 324)

Janis, I. L. (1982). *Groupthink: Psychological studies of policy decisions and fiascoes.* Boston: Houghton Mifflin. (p. 349)

Janis, I. L. (1986). Problems of international crisis management in the nuclear age. *Journal of Social Issues, 42*(2), 201–220. (p. 221)

Jaremka, L. M., Gabriel, S., & Carvallo, M. (2011). What makes us feel the best also makes us feel the worst: The emotional impact of independent and interdependent experiences. *Self and Identity, 10*, 44–63. (p. 265)

Jarrett, B., Bloch, G. J., Bennett, D., Bleazard, B., & Hedges, D. (2010). The influence of body mass index, age and gender on current illness: A cross-sectional study. *International Journal of Obesity, 34*, 429–436. (p. 262)

Jaynes, J. (1976) *The origin of consciousness in the breakdown of the bicameral mind.* Boston: Houghton-Mifflin. (p. 50)

Jedrychowski, W., Perera, F., Jankowski, J., Butscher, M., Mroz, E., Flak, E., Kaim, I., Lisowska-Miszczyk, I., Skarupa, A., & Sowa, A. (2012). Effect of exclusive breastfeeding on the development of children's cognitive function in the Krakow prospective birth cohort study. *European Journal of Pediatrics, 171*, 151–158. (p. 17)

Jenkins, J. G., & Dallenbach, K. M. (1924). Obliviscence during sleep and waking. *American Journal of Psychology, 35*, 605–612. (p. 208)

Jenkins, J. M., & Astington, J. W. (1996). Cognitive factors and family structure associated with theory of mind development in young children. *Developmental Psychology, 32*, 70–78. (p. 78)

Jensen, J. P., & Bergin, A. E. (1988). Mental health values of professional therapists: A national interdisciplinary survey. *Professional Psychology: Research and Practice, 19*, 290–297. (p. 423)

Jensen, M. P. (2008). The neurophysiology of pain perception and hypnotic analgesia: Implications for clinical practice. *American Journal of Clinical Hypnosis, 51*, 123–147. (p. 156)

Jepson, C., Krantz, D. H., & Nisbett, R. E. (1983). Inductive reasoning: Competence or skill. *The Behavioral and Brain Sciences, 3*, 494–501. (p. A-8)

Ji, D., & Wilson, M. A. (2007). Coordinated memory replay in the visual cortex and hippocampus during sleep. *Nature Neuroscience, 10*, 100–107. (p. 200)

Job, D. E., Whalley, H. C., McIntosh, A. M., Owens, D. G. C., Johnstone, E. C., & Lawrie, S. M. (2006). Grey matter changes can improve the prediction of schizophrenia in subjects at high risk. *BMC Medicine, 4*, 29. (p. 398)

Job, V., Dweck, C.S., & Walton, G.M. (2010). Ego depletion—Is it all in your head? Implicit theories about willpower affect self-regulation. *Psychological Science, 21*(11), 1686–1693. (p. 293)

John, O. P., & Srivastava, S. (1999). The Big Five trait taxonomy: History, measurement, and theoretical perspectives. In L. A. Pervin & O. P. John (Eds.), *Handbook of personality: Theory and research.* New York: Guilford. (p. 324)

John Paul II. (1995). Address of His Holiness Pope John Paul II to the Fiftieth General Assembly of the United Nations Organization. Available from http://www.vatican.va/holy_father/john_paul_ii/speeches/1995/october/documents/hf_jp-ii_spe_05101995_address-to-uno_en.html. (p. 350)

Johnson, D. L., Wiebe, J. S., Gold, S. M., Andreasen, N. C., Hichwa, R. D., Watkins, G. L., & Ponto, L. L. B. (1999). Cerebral blood flow and personality: A positron emission tomography study. *American Journal of Psychiatry, 156*, 252–257. (p. 323)

Johnson, E. J., & Goldstein, D. (2003). Do defaults save lives? *Science, 302*, 1338–1339. (p. 224)

Johnson, J. A. (2007, June 26). Not so situational. Commentary on the SPSP listserv (spsp-discuss@stolaf.edu). (p. 346)

Johnson, J. G., Cohen, P., Kotler, L., Kasen, S., & Brook, J. S. (2002). Psychiatric disorders associated with risk for the development of eating disorders during adolescence and early adulthood. *Journal of Consulting and Clinical Psychology, 70*, 1119–1128. (p. 401)

Johnson, J. S., & Newport, E. L. (1991). Critical period affects on universal properties of language: The status of subjacency in the acquisition of a second language. *Cognition, 39*, 215–258. (p. 232)

Johnson, M. H., & Morton, J. (1991). *Biology and cognitive development: The case of face recognition*. Oxford: Blackwell Publishing. (p. 73)

Johnson, M. P. (2008). *A typology of domestic violence: Intimate terrorism, violent resistance, and situational couple violence*. Boston: Northeastern University Press. (p. 108)

Johnson, R. E., Chang, C-H., & Lord, R. G. (2006). Moving from cognition to behavior: What the research says. *Psychological Bulletin, 132*, 381–415. (p. B-6)

Johnson, W. (2010). Understanding the genetics of intelligence: Can height help? Can corn oil? *Current Directions in Psychological Science, 19*, 177–182. (p. 241)

Johnson, W., Carothers, A., & Deary, I. J. (2008). Sex differences in variability in general intelligence: A new look at the old question. *Perspectives on Psychological Science, 3*, 518–531. (pp. 8, 238, 247)

Johnson, W., Carothers, A., & Deary, I. J. (2009). A role for the X chromosome in sex differences in variability in general intelligence? *Perspectives on Psychological Science, 4*, 598–611. (p. 72)

Johnson, W., Gow, A. J., Corley, J., Starr, J. M., & Deary, I. J. (2010). Location in cognitive and residential space at age 70 reflects a lifelong trait over parental and environmental circumstances: The Lothian Birth Cohort 1936. *Intelligence, 38*, 403–411. (p. 245)

Johnson, W., Turkheimer, E., Gottesman, I. I., & Bouchard, Jr., T. J. (2009). Beyond heritability: Twin studies in behavioral research. *Current Directions in Psychological Science, 18*, 217–220. (p. 244)

Johnston, L. D., O'Malley, P. M., Bachman, J. G., & Schulenberg, J. E. (2007). *Monitoring the Future: National results on adolescent drug use: Overview of key findings, 2006*. Bethesda, MD: National Institute on Drug Abuse. (p. 389)

Johnston, L. D., O'Malley, P. M., Bachman, J. G., & Schulenberg, J. E. (2013). *Monitoring the future: National results on drug use: 2012 overview, key findings on adolescent drug use*. Ann Arbor: Institute for Social Research, The University of Michigan. (p. 389)

Joiner, T. E., Jr. (2006). *Why people die by suicide*. Cambridge, MA: Harvard University Press. (p. 392)

Joiner, T. E., Jr. (2010). *Myths about suicide*. Cambridge, MA: Harvard University Press. (p. 392)

Jones, A. C., & Gosling, S. D. (2005). Temperament and personality in dogs (Canis familiaris): A review and evaluation of past research. *Applied Animal Behaviour Science, 95*, 1–53. (p. 323)

Jones, J. M. (2003, February 12). Fear of terrorism increases amidst latest warning. *Gallup News Service* (www.gallup.com/releases/pr030212.asp). (p. 377)

Jones, J. M. (2007, July 25). Latest Gallup update shows cigarette smoking near historical lows. *Gallup Poll News Service* (poll.gallup.com). (p. 385)

Jones, J. M., & Moore, D. W. (2003, June 17). Generational differences in support for a woman president. The Gallup Organization (www.gallup.com). (p. 350)

Jones, J. T., Pelham, B. W., Carvallo, M., & Mirenberg, M. C. (2004). How do I love thee? Let me count the Js: Implicit egotism and interpersonal attraction. *Journal of Personality and Social Psychology, 87*, 665–683. (p. 359)

Jones, M. C. (1924). A laboratory study of fear: The case of Peter. *Journal of Genetic Psychology, 31*, 308–315. (p. 414)

Jones, M. V., Paull, G. C., & Erskine, J. (2002). The impact of a team's aggressive reputation on the decisions of association football referees. *Journal of Sports Sciences, 20*, 991–1000. (p. 139)

Jones, S. S. (2007). Imitation in infancy: The development of mimicry. *Psychological Science, 18*, 593–599. (p. 186)

Jones, S. S., Collins, K., & Hong, H-W. (1991). An audience effect on smile production in 10–month-old infants. *Psychological Science, 2*, 45–49. (p. 277)

Jónsson, H., Hougaard, E., Bennedsen, B. E. (2011). Randomized comparative study of group versus individual cognitive behavioural therapy for obsessive compulsive disorder. *Acta Psychiatrica Scandinavica, 123*, 387–397. (p. 419)

Jorm, A. F., Reavley, N. J., & Ross, A. M. (2012). Belief in the dangerousness of people with mental disorders: A review. *Australian and new Zealand Journal of Psychiatry, 46*, 1029–1045. (p. 376)

Jose, A., O'Leary, D., & Moyer, A. (2010). Does premarital cohabitation predict subsequent marital stability and marital quality? A meta-analysis. *Journal of Marriage and Family, 72*, 105–116. (p. 98)

Jost, J. T., Kay, A. C., & Thorisdottir, H. (eds.) (2009). *Social and psychological bases of ideology and system justification*. New York: Oxford University Press. (p. 354)

Judge, T. A., Thoresen, C. J., Bono, J. E., & Patton, G. K. (2001). The job satisfaction/job performance relationship: A qualitative and quantitative review. *Psychological Bulletin, 127*, 376–407. (p. B-4)

Jung-Beeman, M., Bowden, E. M., Haberman, J., Frymiare, J. L., Arambel-Liu, S., Greenblatt, R., Reber, P. J., & Kounios, J. (2004). Neural activity when people solve verbal problems with insight. *PloS Biology 2(4)*, e111. (pp. 220, 221)

Kabat-Zinn, J. (2001). Mindfulness-based interventions in context: Past, present, and future. *Clinical Psychology: Science and Practice, 10*, 144–156. (p. 298)

Kagan, J. (1976). Emergent themes in human development. *American Scientist, 64*, 186–196. (p. 83)

Kagan, J. (1984). *The nature of the child*. New York: Basic Books. (p. 81)

Kagan, J. (1995). On attachment. *Harvard Review of Psychiatry, 3*, 104–106. (p. 82)

Kagan, J. (1998). *Three seductive ideas*. Cambridge, MA: Harvard University Press. (p. 102)

Kagan, J. (2010). *The temperamental thread: How genes, culture, time, and luck make us who we are*. Washington, DC: Dana Press. (p. 323)

Kagan, J., Lapidus, D. R., & Moore, M. (December, 1978). Infant antecedents of cognitive functioning: A longitudinal study. *Child Development, 49(4)*, 1005–1023. (p. 102)

Kagan, J., & Snidman, N. (2004). *The long shadow of temperament*. Cambridge, MA: Belknap Press. (p. 73)

Kahneman, D. (1985, June). Quoted by K. McKean, Decisions, decisions. *Discover*, pp. 22–31. (p. A-6)

Kahneman, D. (1999). Assessments of objective happiness: A bottom-up approach. In D. Kahneman, E. Diener, & N. Schwartz (Eds.), *Understanding well-being: Scientific perspectives on enjoyment and suffering*. New York: Russell Sage Foundation. (p. 156)

Kahneman, D. (2005, January 13). What were they thinking? Q&A with Daniel Kahneman. *Gallup Management Journal* (gmj.gallup.com). (p. 222)

Kahneman, D. (2005, February 10). Are you happy now? *Gallup Management Journal* interview (www.gmj.gallup.com). (p. 302)

Kahneman, D. (2011). *Thinking, fast and slow.* New York: Farrar, Straus, and Giroux. (p. 49)

Kahneman, D., Fredrickson, B. L., Schreiber, C. A., & Redelmeier, D. A. (1993). When more pain is preferred to less: Adding a better end. *Psychological Science, 4,* 401–405. (p. 155)

Kahneman, D., Krueger, A. B., Schkade, D. A., Schwarz, N., & Stone, A. A. (2004). A survey method for characterizing daily life experience: The day reconstruction method. *Science, 306,* 1776–1780. (p. 302)

Kail, R. (1991). Developmental change in speed of processing during childhood and adolescence. *Psychological Bulletin, 109,* 490–501. (p. 95)

Kail, R., & Hall, L. K. (2001). Distinguishing short-term memory from working memory. *Memory & Cognition, 29,* 1–9. (p. 194)

Kaiser Family Foundation. (2010, January). *Generation M²: Media in the lives of 8- to 18-year-olds* (by V. J. Rideout, U. G. Foeher, & D. F. Roberts). Menlo Park, CA: Henry J. Kaiser Family Foundation. (pp. 16, 268)

Kamarck, T., & Jennings, J. R. (1991). Biobehavioral factors in sudden cardiac death. *Psychological Bulletin, 109,* 42–75. (p. 290)

Kamel, N. S., & Gammack, J. K. (2006). Insomnia in the elderly: Cause, approach, and treatment. *American Journal of Medicine, 119,* 463–469. (p. 54)

Kaminski, J., Cali, J., & Fischer, J. (2004). Word learning in a domestic dog: Evidence for "fast mapping." *Science, 304,* 1682–1683. (p. 234)

Kandel, E R. (2012, March 5). Interview by Claudia Dreifus: A quest to understand how memory works. *New York Times* (www.nytimes.com). (p. 201)

Kandel, E. R., & Schwartz, J. H. (1982). Molecular biology of learning: Modulation of transmitter release. *Science, 218,* 433–443. (p. 201)

Kandler, C., Bleidorn, W., Riemann, R., Spinath, F. M., Thiel, W., & Angleitner, A. (2010). Sources of cumulative continuity in personality: A longitudinal multiple-rater twin study. *Journal of Personality and Social Psychology, 98,* 995–1008. (p. 102)

Kaplan, H. I., & Saddock, B. J. (Eds.). (1989). *Comprehensive textbook of psychiatry, V.* Baltimore, MD: Williams and Wilkins. (p. 425)

Kaplan, R. M., & Kronick, R. G. (2006). Marital status and longevity in the United States population. *Journal of Epidemiology and Community Health, 60,* 760–765. (p. 295)

Kaplan, S., Bradley, J. C., Luchman, J. N., & Haynes, D. (2009). On the role of positive and negative affectivity in job performance: A meta-analytic investigation. *Journal of Applied Psychology, 94,* 162–176. (p. B-4)

Kaplan, T., & Hakim, D. (2013, January 14). New York has gun deal, with focus on mental ills. *New York Times* (www.nytimes.com). (p. 376)

Kaprio, J., Koskenvuo, M., & Rita, H. (1987). Mortality after bereavement: A prospective study of 95,647 widowed persons. *American Journal of Public Health, 77,* 283–287. (p. 285)

Karacan, I., Goodenough, D. R., Shapiro, A., & Starker, S. (1966). Erection cycle during sleep in relation to dream anxiety. *Archives of General Psychiatry, 15,* 183–189. (p. 54)

Karau, S. J., & Williams, K. D. (1993). Social loafing: A meta-analytic review and theoretical integration. *Journal of Personality and Social Psychology, 65,* 681–706. (p. 347)

Kark, J. D., Shemi, G., Friedlander, Y., Martin, O., Manor, O., & Blondheim, S. H. (1996). Does religious observance promote health? Mortality in secular vs. religious kibbutzim in Israel. *American Journal of Public Health, 86,* 341–346. (p. 299)

Karo, A. (2012, February). Ruminations. *Funny Times,* p. 4. (p. 351)

Karpicke, J. D. (2012). Retrieval-based learning: Active retrieval promotes meaningful learning. *Current Directions in Psychological Science, 21,* 157–163. (p. 198)

Karpicke, J. D., & Roediger, H. L., III. (2008). The critical importance of retrieval for learning. *Science, 319,* 966–968. (p. 23)

Karremans, J. C., Frankenhis, W. E., & Arons, S. (2010). Blind men prefer a low waist-to-hip ratio. *Evolution and Human Behavior, 31,* 182–186. (pp. 127, 360)

Kasen, S., Chen, H., Sneed, J., Crawford, T., & Cohen, P. (2006). Social role and birth cohort influences on gender-linked personality traits in women: A 20-year longitudinal analysis. *Journal of Personality and Social Psychology, 91,* 944–958. (p. 110)

Kashdan, T. B. (2009). *Curious? Discover the missing ingredient to a fulfilling life.* New York: William Morrow. (p. 319)

Katz-Wise, S. L., & Hyde, J. S. (2012). Victimization experiences of lesbian, gay, and bisexual individuals: A meta-analysis. *Journal of Sex Research, 49,* 142–167. (p. 350)

Katz-Wise, S. L., Priess, H. A., & Hyde, J. S. (2010). Gender-role attitudes and behavior across the transition to parenthood. *Developmental Psychology, 46,* 18–28. (p. 110)

Kaufman, J. C., & Baer, J. (2002). I bask in dreams of suicide: Mental illness, poetry, and women. *Review of General Psychology, 6,* 271–286. (p. 392)

Kaufman, L., & Kaufman, J. H. (2000). Explaining the moon illusion. *Proceedings of the National Academy of Sciences, 97,* 500–505. (p. 149)

Kawakami, K., Dunn, E., Karmali, F., & Dovidio, J. F. (2009). Mispredicting affective and behavioral responses to racism. *Science, 323,* 276–278. (p. 350)

Kay, A. C., Baucher, D., Peach, J. M., Laurin, K., Friesen, J., Zanna, M. P., & Spencer, S. J. (2009). Inequality, discrimination, and the power of the status quo: Direct evidence for a motivation to see the way things are as the way they should be. *Journal of Personality and social Psychology, 97,* 421–434. (p. 354)

Kayser, C. (2007, April/May). Listening with your eyes. *Scientific American Mind,* pp. 24–29. (p. 160)

Kazantzis, N., & Dattilio, F. M. (2010b). Definitions of homework, types of homework and ratings of the importance of homework among psychologists with cognitive behavior therapy and psychoanalytic theoretical orientations. *Journal of Clinical Psychology, 66,* 758–773. (p. 418)

Kazantzis, N., Whittington, C., & Dattilio, F. M. (2010a). Meta-analysis of homework effects in cognitive and behavioral therapy: A replication and extension. *Clinical Psychology: Science and Practice, 17,* 144–156. (p. 418)

Kazdin, A. E., & Benjet, C. (2003). Spanking children: Evidence and issues. *Current Directions in Psychological Science, 12,* 99–103. (p. 178)

Keesey, R. E., & Corbett, S. W. (1983). Metabolic defense of the body weight set-point. In A. J. Stunkard & E. Stellar (Eds.), *Eating and its disorders.* New York: Raven Press. (p. 259)

Keith, S. W., & 19 others. (2006). Putative contributors to the secular increase in obesity: Exploring the roads less traveled. *International Journal of Obesity, 30,* 1585–1594. (p. 262)

Keller, J. (2007, March 9). As football players get bigger, more of them risk a dangerous sleep disorder. *Chronicle of Higher Education,* pp. A43–A44. (p. 59)

Keller, M. B., McCullough, J. P., Klein, D. N., Arnow, B., Dunner, D. L., Gelenberg, A. J., Markowitz, J. C., Nemeroff, C. B., Russell, J. M., Thase, M. E., Trivedi, M. H., & Zajecka J. (2000), A comparison of nefazodone, the cognitive behavioral-analysis system of psychotherapy, and their combination for the treatment of chronic depression. *New England Journal of Medicine, 342,* 1462–1470. (p. 426)

Kellerman, J., Lewis, J., & Laird, J. D. (1989). Looking and loving: The effects of mutual gaze on feelings of romantic love. *Journal of Research in Personality, 23,* 145–161. (p. 275)

Kellermann, A. L. (1997). Comment: Gunsmoke-changing public attitudes toward smoking and firearms. *American Journal of Public Health, 87*, 910–913. (p. 355)

Kellermann, A. L., Rivara, F. P., Rushforth, N. B., Banton, H. G., Feay, D. T., Francisco, J. T., Locci, A. B., Prodzinski, J., Hackman, B. B., & Somes, G. (1993). Gun ownership as a risk factor for homicide in the home. *New England Journal of Medicine, 329*, 1084–1091. (p. 355)

Kellermann, A. L., Somes, G. Rivara, F. P., Lee, R. K., & Banton, J. G. (1998). Injuries and deaths due to firearms in the home. *Journal of Trauma, 45*, 263-267. (p. 355)

Kelley, J., & De Graaf, N. D. (1997). National context, parental socialization, and religious belief: Results from 15 nations. *American Sociological Review, 62*, 639–659. (p. 91)

Kelling, S. T., & Halpern, B. P. (1983). Taste flashes: Reaction times, intensity, and quality. *Science, 219*, 412–414. (p. 157)

Kellner, C. H., & 15 others. (2005). Relief of expressed suicidal intent by ECT: A consortium for research in ECT study. *American Journal of Psychiatry, 162*, 977–982. (p. 427)

Kellner, C. H., & 16 others. (2006). Continuation electroconvulsive therapy vs. pharmacotherapy for relapse prevention in major depression: A multisite study from the Consortium for Research in Electroconvulsive Therapy (CORE). *Archives of General Psychiatry, 63*, 1337–1344. (p. 428)

Kelly, D. J., Quinn, P. C., Slater, A. M., Lee, K., Ge, L., & Pascalis, O. (2007). The other-race effect develops during infancy: Evidence of perceptual narrowing. *Psychological Science, 18*, 1084–1089. (p. 353)

Kelly, T. A. (1990). The role of values in psychotherapy: A critical review of process and outcome effects. *Clinical Psychology Review, 10*, 171–186. (p. 423)

Kendall-Tackett, K. A. (Ed.) (2004). *Health consequences of abuse in the family: A clinical guide for evidence-based practice.* Washington, DC: American Psychological Association. (p. 84)

Kendall-Tackett, K. A., Williams, L. M., & Finkelhor, D. (1993). Impact of sexual abuse on children: A review and synthesis of recent empirical studies. *Psychological Bulletin, 113*, 164–180. (pp. 84, 213)

Kendler, K. S. (1998, January). Major depression and the environment: A psychiatric genetic perspective. *Pharmacopsychiatry, 31*(1), 5–9. (p. 394)

Kendler, K. S. (2011). A statement from Kenneth S. Kendler, M.D., on the proposal to eliminate the grief exclusion criterion from major depression. www.dsm5.org. (p. 375)

Kendler, K. S., Jacobson, K. C., Myers, J., & Prescott, C. A. (2002a). Sex differences in genetic and environmental risk factors for irrational fears and phobias. *Psychological Medicine, 32*, 209–217. (p. 380)

Kendler, K. S., Myers, J., & Prescott, C. A. (2002b). The etiology of phobias: An evaluation of the stress-diathesis model. *Archives of General Psychiatry, 59*, 242–248. (p. 380)

Kendler, K. S., Neale, M. C., Thornton, L. M., Aggen, S. H., Gilman, S. E., & Kessler, R. C. (2002). Cannabis use in the last year in a U.S. national sample of twin and sibling pairs. *Psychological Medicine, 32*, 551–554. (p. 388)

Kendler, K. S., Thornton, L. M., & Gardner, C. O. (2001). Genetic risk, number of previous depressive episodes, and stressful life events in predicting onset of major depression. *American Journal of Psychiatry, 158*, 582–586. (p. 393)

Kennedy, S., & Over, R. (1990). Psychophysiological assessment of male sexual arousal following spinal cord injury. *Archives of Sexual Behavior, 19*, 15–27. (p. 36)

Kenrick, D. T., Nieuweboer, S., & Bunnk, A. P. (2009). Universal mechanisms and cultural diversity: Replacing the blank slate with a coloring book. In M. Schaller, S. Heine, A. Norenzayan, T. Yamagishi, & T. Kameda (Eds.), *Evolution, culture, and the human mind.* Mahwah, NJ: Erlbaum. (p. 74)

Kensinger, E. A. (2007). Negative emotion enhances memory accuracy: Behavioral and neuroimaging evidence. *Current Directions in Psychological Science, 16*, 213–218. (p. 200)

Keough, K. A., Zimbardo, P. G., & Boyd, J. N. (1999). Who's smoking, drinking, and using drugs? Time perspective as a predictor of substance use. *Basic and Applied Social Psychology, 2*, 149–164. (p. 313)

Kernis, M. H. (2003). Toward a conceptualization of optimal self-esteem. *Psychological Inquiry, 14*, 1–26. (p. 331)

Kerr, N. L., & Bruun, S. E. (1983). Dispensability of member effort and group motivation losses: Free-rider effects. *Journal of Personality and Social Psychology, 44*, 78–94. (p. 347)

Kessler, D., Lewis, G., Kaur, S., Wiles, N., King, M., Welch, S., Sharp, D. J., Araya, R., Hollinghurst, S., & Peters, T. J. (2009). Therapist-delivered Internet psychotherapy for depression primary care: A randomized controlled trial. *The Lancet, 374*, 628–634. (p. 419)

Kessler, M., & Albee, G. (1975). Primary prevention. *Annual Review of Psychology, 26*, 557–591. (p. 432)

Kessler, R. C. (2000). Posttraumatic stress disorder: The burden to the individual and to society. *Journal of Clinical Psychiatry, 61*(suppl. 5), 4–12. (p. 378)

Kessler, R. C. (2001). Epidemiology of women and depression. *Journal of Affective Disorders, 74*, 5–1. (p. 395)

Kessler, R. C., Foster, C., Joseph, J., Ostrow, D., Wortman, C., Phair, J., & Chmiel, J. (1991). Stressful life events and symptom onset in HIV infection. *American Journal of Psychiatry, 148*, 733–738. (p. 289)

Kessler, R. C., & 22 others. (2010). Age differences in the prevalence and co-morbidity of DSM-IV major depressive episodes: Results from the WHO World Mental Health Survey Initiative. *Depression and Anxiety, 27*, 351–364. (p. 394)

Keynes, M. (1980, December 20/27). Handel's illnesses. *The Lancet,* pp. 1354–1355. (p. 391)

Keys, A., Brozek, J., Henschel, A., Mickelsen, O., & Taylor, H. L. (1950). *The biology of human starvation.* Minneapolis: University of Minnesota Press. (p. 258)

Khera, M., Bhattacharya, R. K., Blick, G., Kushner, H., Nguyen, D., & Miner, M. M. (2011). Improved sexual function with testosterone replacement therapy in hypogonadal men: Real-world data from the Testim Registry in the United States (TRiUS). *Journal of Sexual Medicine, 8*, 3204–3213. (p. 116)

Kiecolt-Glaser, J. K. (2009). Psychoneuroimmunology: Psychology's gateway to the biomedical future. *Perspectives on Psychological Science, 4*, 367–369. (p. 286)

Kiecolt-Glaser, J. K., Page, G. G., Marucha, P. T., MacCallum, R. C., & Glaser, R. (1998). Psychological influences on surgical recovery: Perspectives from psychoneuroimmunology. *American Psychologist, 53*, 1209–1218. (p. 287)

Kiehl, K. A., & Buckholtz, J. W. (2010, September/October). Inside the mind of a psychopath. *Scientific American Mind,* pp. 22–29. (p. 404)

Kihlstrom, J. F. (1990). Awareness, the psychological unconscious, and the self. Address to the American Psychological Association convention. (p. 318)

Kihlstrom, J. F. (2005). Dissociative disorders. *Annual Review of Clinical Psychology, 1*, 227–253. (p. 403)

Kihlstrom, J. F. (2006). Repression: A unified theory of a will-o'-the-wisp. *Behavioral and Brain Sciences, 29*, 523. (p. 318)

Killingsworth, M. A., & Gilbert, D. T. (2010). A wandering mind is an unhappy mind. *Science, 330*, 932. (pp. 267, B-2)

Kilpatrick, L. A., Suyenobu, B. Y., Smith, S. R., Bueller, J. A., Goodman, T., Creswell, J. D., Tillisch, K., Mayer, E. A., & Naliboff, B. D. (2011). Impact of mindfulness-based stress reduction training on intrinsic brain activity. *Neuroimage, 56,* 290–298. (p. 299)

Kilpeläinen, T. O., & 116 others. (2012). Physical activity attenuates the influence of *FTO* variants on obesity risk: A meta-analysis of 218,166 adults and 19,268 children. *PLoS Medicine.* http://www.plosmedicine.org/article/info%3Adoi%2F10.1371%2Fjournal.pmed.1001116. (p. 297)

Kim, B. S. K., Ng, G. F., & Ahn, A. J. (2005). Effects of client expectation for counseling success, client-counselor worldview match, and client adherence to Asian and European American cultural values on counseling process with Asian Americans. *Journal of Counseling Psychology, 52,* 67–76. (p. 423)

Kim, G., & Tong, A. (2010, February 23). Airline passengers have grown, seats haven't. *Sacramento Bee* (reprinted by *Grand Rapids Press,* pp. B1, B3). (p. 263)

Kimata, H. (2001). Effect of humor on allergen-induced wheal reactions. *Journal of the American Medical Association, 285,* 737. (p. 294)

Kingston, D. W., Malamuth, N. M., Fedoroff, N. M., & Marshall, W. L. (2009). The importance of individual differences in pornography use: Theoretical perspectives and implications for treating sexual offenders. *Journal of Sex Research, 46,* 216–232. (p. 357)

Kinnier, R. T., & Metha, A. T. (1989). Regrets and priorities at three stages of life. *Counseling and Values, 33,* 182–193. (p. 99)

Kinzler, K. D., Shutts, K., Dejesus, J., & Spelke, E. S. (2009). Accent trumps race in guiding children's social preferences. *Social Cognition, 27,* 623–634. (p. 352)

Kirby, D. (2002). Effective approaches to reducing adolescent unprotected sex, pregnancy, and childbearing. *Journal of Sex Research, 39,* 51–57. (p. 119)

Kirsch, I. (2010). *The emperor's new drugs: Exploding the antidepressant myth.* New York: Basic Books. (pp. 18, 426)

Kirsch, I., Deacon, B. J., Huedo-Medina, T. B., Scoboria, A., Moore, T. J., & Johnson, B. T. (2008) Initial severity and antidepressant benefits: A meta-analysis of data submitted to the Food and Drug Administration. *Public Library of Science Medicine, 5,* e45. (p. 427)

Kirsch, I., Moore, T. J., Scoboria, A., & Nicholls, S. S. (2002, July 15). New study finds little difference between effects of antidepressants and placebo. *Prevention and Treatment* (journals.apa.org/prevention). (p. 426)

Kirsch, I., & Sapirstein, G. (1998). Listening to Prozac but hearing placebo: A meta-analysis of antidepressant medication. *Prevention and Treatment, 1,* posted June 26 at (journals.apa.org/prevention/volume1). (p. 426)

Kitayama, S., Chua, H. F., Tompson, S., & Han, S. (2013). Neural mechanisms of dissonance: An fMRI investigation of choice justification. *NeuroImage, 69,* 206–212. (p. 341)

Kitayama, S., Conway, L. G., III, Pietromonaci, P. R., Park, H., & Plaut, V. C. (2010). Ethos of independence across regions in the United States: The production-adoption model of cultural change. *American Psychologist, 65,* 559–574. (p. 332)

Klayman, J., & Ha, Y-W. (1987). Confirmation, disconfirmation, and information in hypothesis testing. *Psychological Review, 94,* 211–228. (p. 221)

Klein, D. N., & 16 others. (2003). Therapeutic alliance in depression treatment: Controlling for prior change and patient characteristics. *Journal of Consulting and Clinical Psychology, 71,* 997–1006. (p. 423)

Kleinke, C. L. (1986). Gaze and eye contact: A research review. *Psychological Bulletin, 1000,* 78–100. (p. 275)

Kleinmuntz, B., & Szucko, J. J. (1984). A field study of the fallibility of polygraph lie detection. *Nature, 308,* 449–450. (p. 274)

Kleitman, N. (1960, November). Patterns of dreaming. *Scientific American,* pp. 82–88. (p. 53)

Klemm, W. R. (1990). Historical and introductory perspectives on brainstem-mediated behaviors. In W. R. Klemm & R. P. Vertes (Eds.), *Brainstem mechanisms of behavior.* New York: Wiley. (p. 39)

Klimstra, T. A., Hale, W. W., III, Raaijmakers, Q. A. W., Branje, S. J. T., & Meeus, W. H. J. (2009). Maturation of personality in adolescence. *Journal of Personality and Social Psychology, 96,* 898–912. (p. 90)

Kline, D., & Schieber, F. (1985). Vision and aging. In J. E. Birren & K. W. Schaie (Eds.), *Handbook of the psychology of aging.* New York: Van Nostrand Reinhold. (p. 95)

Kline, N. S. (1974). *From sad to glad.* New York: Ballantine Books. (p. 396)

Klinke, R., Kral, A., Heid, S., Tillein, J., & Hartmann, R. (1999). Recruitment of the auditory cortex in congenitally deaf cats by long-term cochlear electrostimulation. *Science, 285,* 1729–1733. (p. 153)

Kluft, R. P. (1991). Multiple personality disorder. In A. Tasman & S. M. Goldfinger (Eds.), *Review of Psychiatry* (Vol. 10). Washington, DC: American Psychiatric Press. (p. 402)

Klump, K. L., Suisman, J. L., Burt, S. A., McGue, M., & Iacono, W. G. (2009). Genetic and environmental influences on disordered eating: An adoption study. *Journal of Abnormal Psychology, 118,* 797–805. (p. 401)

Klüver, H., & Bucy, P. C. (1939). Preliminary analysis of functions of the temporal lobes in monkeys. *Archives of Neurology and Psychiatry, 42,* 979–1000. (p. 41)

Knapp, S., & VandeCreek, L. (2000, August). Recovered memories of childhood abuse: Is there an underlying professional consensus? *Professional Psychology: Research and Practice, 31,* 365–371. (p. 213)

Knickmeyer, E. (2001, August 7). In Africa, big is definitely better. *Seattle Times,* p. A7. (p. 401)

Knight, R. T. (2007). Neural networks debunk phrenology. *Science, 316,* 1578–1579. (p. 47)

Knight, W. (2004, August 2). Animated face helps deaf with phone chat. NewScientist.com. (p. 160)

Knoblich, G., & Oellinger, M. (2006, October/November). The Eureka moment. *Scientific American Mind,* pp. 38–43. (p. 220)

Knutson, K. L., Spiegel, K., Penev, P., & Van Cauter, E. (2007). The metabolic consequences of sleep deprivation. *Sleep Medicine Reviews, 11,* 163–178. (p. 58)

Koch, C., & Greenfield, S. (2007, October). How does consciousness happen? *Scientific American,* pp. 76–83. (p. 50)

Koenen, K. C., Moffitt, T. E., Roberts, A. L., Martin, L. T., Kubzansky, L., Harrington, H., Poulton, R., & Caspi, A. (2009). Childhood IQ and adult mental disorders: A test of the cognitive reserve hypothesis. *American Journal of Psychiatry, 166,* 50–57. (p. 242)

Koenig, H. G., & Larson, D. B. (1998). Use of hospital services, religious attendance, and religious affiliation. *Southern Medical Journal, 91,* 925–932. (p. 300)

Koenig, L. B., McGue, M., Krueger, R. F., & Bouchard, T. J., Jr. (2005). Genetic and environmental influences on religiousness: Findings for retrospective and current religiousness ratings. *Journal of Personality, 73,* 471–488. (p. 91)

Koenig, L. B., & Vaillant, G. E. (2009). A prospective study of church attendance and health over the lifespan. *Health Psychology, 28,* 117–124. (p. 300)

Koenigs, M., Young, L., Adolphs, R., Tranel, D., Cushman, F., Hauser, M., & Damasio, A. (2007). Damage to the prefrontal cortex increases utilitarian moral judgements. *Nature, 446,* 908–911. (p. 46)

Koestner, R., Lekes, N., Powers, T. A., & Chicoine, E. (2002). Attaining personal goals: Self-concordance plus implementation intentions equals success. *Journal of Personality and Social Psychology, 83,* 231–244. (p. B-6)

Kohlberg, L. (1981). *The philosophy of moral development: Essays on moral development* (Vol. I). San Francisco: Harper & Row. (p. 87)

Kohlberg, L. (1984). *The psychology of moral development: Essays on moral development* (Vol. II). San Francisco: Harper & Row. (p. 87)

Kohler, C. G., Walker, J. B., Martin, E. A., Healey, K. M., & Moberg, P. J. (2010). Facial emotion perception in schizophrenia: A meta-analytic review. *Schizophrenia Bulletin, 36,* 1009–1019. (p. 398)

Kohler, I. (1962, May). Experiments with goggles. *Scientific American,* pp. 62–72. (p. 151)

Köhler, W. (1925; reprinted 1957). *The mentality of apes.* London: Pelican. (p. 228)

Kolata, G. (1987). Metabolic catch-22 of exercise regimens. *Science, 236,* 146–147. (p. 264)

Kolb, B. (1989). Brain development, plasticity, and behavior. *American Psychologist, 44,* 1203–1212. (p. 47)

Kolb, B., & Whishaw, I. Q. (1998). Brain plasticity and behavior. *Annual Review of Psychology, 49,* 43–64. (p. 74)

Kolker, K. (2002, December 8). Video violence disturbs some: Others scoff at influence. *Grand Rapids Press,* pp. A1, A12. (p. 357)

Koltko-Rivera, M. E. (2006). Rediscovering the later version of Maslow's hierarchy of needs: Self-transcendence and opportunities for theory, research, and unification. *Review of General Psychology, 10,* 302–317. (p. 257)

Konkle, T., Brady, T. F., Alvarez, G. A., & Oliva, A. (2010). Conceptual distinctiveness supports detailed visual long-term memory for real-world objects. *Journal of Experimental Psychology: General, 139,* 558–578. (p. 193)

Koopmans, J. R., Slutske, W. S., van Baal, G. C. M., & Boomsma, D. I. (1999). The influence of religion on alcohol use initiation: Evidence for a genotype x environment interaction. *Behavior Genetics, 29,* 445–453. (p. 300)

Kopta, S. M., Lueger, R. J., Saunders, S. M., & Howard, K. I. (1999). Individual psychotherapy outcome and process research: Challenges leading to greater turmoil or a positive transition? *Annual Review of Psychology, 30,* 441–469. (p. 421)

Kosslyn, S. M. (2005). Reflective thinking and mental imagery: A perspective on the development of posttraumatic stress disorder. *Development and Psychopathology, 17,* 851–863. (p. 379)

Kosslyn, S. M., & Koenig, O. (1992). *Wet mind: The new cognitive neuroscience.* New York: Free Press. (p. 35)

Kotchick, B. A., Shaffer, A., & Forehand, R. (2001). Adolescent sexual risk behavior: A multi-system perspective. *Clinical Psychology Review, 21,* 493–519. (p. 119)

Kotkin, M., Daviet, C., & Gurin, J. (1996). The *Consumer Reports* mental health survey. *American Psychologist, 51,* 1080–1082. (p. 420)

Kounios, J., & Beeman, M. (2009). The *Aha!* moment: The cognitive neuroscience of insight. *Current Directions in Psychological Science, 18,* 210–215. (p. 220)

Kraft, R. N. (2002). *Memory perceived: Recalling the Holocaust.* Westport, CT: Praeger. (p. 213)

Kramer, A. (2010). Personal correspondence. (p. 302)

Kramer, M. S., & 17 others. (2008). Breastfeeding and child cognitive development: New evidence from a large randomized trial. *Archives of General Psychiatry, 65,* 578–584. (p. 17)

Kramer, P. D. (2011, July 9). In defense of antidepressants. *New York Times* (www.nytimes.com). (p. 426)

Kranz, F., & Ishai, A. (2006). Face perception is modulated by sexual preference. *Current Biology, 16,* 63–68. (p. 123)

Kraut, R., Patterson, M., Lundmark, V., Kiesler, S., Mukopadhyay, T., & Scherlis, W. (1998). Internet paradox: A social technology that reduces social involvement and psychological well being? *American Psychologist, 53,* 1017–1031. (p. 267)

Kraut, R. E., & Johnston, R. E. (1979). Social and emotional messages of smiling: An ethological approach. *Journal of Personality and Social Psychology, 37,* 1539–1553. (p. 277)

KRC Research & Consulting. (2001, August 7). Memory isn't quite what it used to be (survey for General Nutrition Centers). *USA Today,* p. D1. (p. 96)

Krijn, M., Emmelkamp, P. M. G., Olafsson, R. P., & Biemond, R. (2004). Virtual reality exposure therapy of anxiety disorders: A review. *Clinical Psychology Review, 24,* 259–281. (p. 415)

Kring, A. M., & Caponigro, J. M. (2010). Emotion in schizophrenia: Where feeling meets thinking. *Current Directions in Psychological Science, 19,* 255–259. (p. 397)

Kring, A. M., & Gordon, A. H. (1998). Sex differences in emotion: Expression, experience, and physiology. *Journal of Personality and Social Psychology, 74,* 686–703. (p. 276)

Kristeller, J. L., Baer, R. A., & Quillian-Wolever, R. (2006). Mindfulness-based approaches to eating disorders. In R. A. Baer (Ed.), *Mindfulness-based treatment approaches: A clinician's guide to evidence base and applications.* San Diego, CA: Academic Press. (p. 299)

Kristensen, P., & Bjerkedal, T. (2007). Explaining the relation between birth order and intelligence. *Science, 316,* 1717. (p. A-8)

Krosnick, J. A., & Alwin, D. F. (1989). Aging and susceptibility to attitude change. *Journal of Personality and Social Psychology, 57,* 416–425. (p. 102)

Krosnick, J. A., Betz, A. L., Jussim, L. J., & Lynn, A. R. (1992). Subliminal conditioning of attitudes. *Personality and Social Psychology Bulletin, 18,* 152–162. (p. 136)

Kross, E., Berman, M. G., Mischel, W., Smith, E. E., & Wager, T. D. (2011). Social rejection shares somatosensory representations with physical pain. *PNAS, 108,* 6270–6275. (p. 266)

Krueger, A. B., & Malecková, J. (2009). Attitudes and action: Public opinion and the occurrence of international terrorism. *Science, 325,* 1534–1536. (p. 339)

Krueger, J., & Killham, E. (2005, December 8). At work, feeling good matters. *Gallup Management Journal* (www.gmj.gallup.com). (p. B-5)

Krueger, J., & Killham, E. (2006, March 9). Why Dilbert is right. Uncomfortable work environments make for disgruntled employees—just like the cartoon says. *Gallup Management Journal* (www.gmj.gallup.com). (p. 292)

Krueger, R. F., & Johnson, W. (2008). Behavioral genetics and personality: A new look at the integration of nature and nurture. In O. P. John, R. W. Robins, & L. A. Pervin (Eds.), *Handbook of personality: Theory and research* (3rd ed., pp. 287–310). New York, 324)

Kruger, J., Epley, N., Parker, J., & Ng, Z-W. (2005). Egocentrism over e-mail: Can we communicate as well as we think? *Journal of Personality and Social Psychology, 89,* 925–936. (p. 78)

Krumhansl, C. L. (2010). Plink: "Thin slices" of music. *Music Perception, 27,* 337–354. (p. 193)

Kübler, A., Winter, S., Ludolph, A. C., Hautzinger, M., & Birbaumer, N. (2005). Severity of depressive symptoms and quality of life in patients with amyotrophic lateral sclerosis. *Neurorehabilitation and Neural Repair, 19*(3), 182–193. (p. 302)

Kuhl, P. K., & Meltzoff, A. N. (1982). The bimodal perception of speech in infancy. *Science, 218,* 1138–1141. (p. 230)

Kunkel, D. (2001, February 4). *Sex on TV*. Menlo Park, CA: Henry J. Kaiser Family Foundation (www.kff.org). (p. 119)

Kupfer, D. J. (2012, June 1). Dr Kupfer defends DSM-5. www.medscape.com/viewarticle/764735. (p. 375)

Kuppens, P., Allen, N. B., & Sheeber, L. B. (2010). Emotional inertia and psychological maladjustment. *Psychological Science, 21*, 984–991. (p. 395)

Kvavilashvili, L., Mirani, J., Schlagman, S., Foley, K. & Kornbrot, D. E. (2009). Consistency of flashbulb memories of September 11 over long delays: Implications for consolidation and wrong time slice hypotheses. *Journal of Memory and Language, 61*,556–572. (p. 201)

Laan, E., Everaerd, W., & Evers, A. (1995a). Assessment of female sexual arousal: Response specificity and construct validity. *Psychophysiology, 32*, 476–485. (p. 118)

Laan, E., Everaerd, W., van der Velde, J., & Geer, J. H. (1995b). Determinants of subjective experience of sexual arousal in women: Feedback from genital arousal and erotic stimulus content. *Psychophysiology, 32*, 444–451. (p. 118)

Labonté, B., Suderman, M., Maussion, G., Navaro, L., Yerko, V., Mahar, I., Bureau, A., Mechawar, N., Szyf, M., Meaney, M. J., & Turecki, G. (2012). Genome-wide epigenetic regulation by early-life trauma. *Archives of General Psychiatry, 69*, 722–731. (p. 84)

Lacayo, R. (1995, June 12). Violent reaction. *Time Magazine*, pp. 25–39. (p. 15)

Lacey, H. P., Smith, D. M., & Ubel, P. A. (2006). Hope I die before I get old: Mispredicting happiness across the lifespan. *Journal of Happiness Studies, 7*, 167–182. (p. 99)

Lacey, M. (2010, December 11). He found bag of cash, but did the unexpected. *New York Times* (www.nytimes.com). (p. 365)

Lachman, M. E., Rocke, C., Rosnick, C., & Ryff, C. D. (2008, September). Realism and illusion in Americans' temporal views of their life satisfaction: Age differences in reconstructing the past and anticipating the future. *Psychological Science, 19*, 889–897. (p. 99)

Laird, J. D. (1974). Self-attribution of emotion: The effects of expressive behavior on the quality of emotional experience. *Journal of Personality and Social Psychology, 29*, 475–486. (p. 278)

Laird, J. D. (1984). The real role of facial response in the experience of emotion: A reply to Tourangeau and Ellsworth, and others. *Journal of Personality and Social Psychology, 47*, 909–917. (p. 278)

Laird, J. D., Cuniff, M., Sheehan, K., Shulman, D., & Strum, G. (1989). Emotion specific effects of facial expressions on memory for life events. *Journal of Social Behavior and Personality, 4*, 87–98. (p. 278)

Lally, P., Van Jaarsveld, C. H. M., Potts, H. W. W., & Wardle, J. (2010). How are habits formed: Modelling habit formation in the real world. *European Journal of Social Psychology, 40*, 998–1009. (p. 168)

Lalumière, M. L., Blanchard, R., & Zucker, K. J. (2000). Sexual orientation and handedness in men and women: A meta-analysis. *Psychological Bulletin, 126*, 575–592. (p. 124)

Lam, C. B., & McBride-Chang, C. A. (2007). Resilience in young adulthood: The moderating influences of gender-related personality traits and coping flexibility. *Sex Roles, 56*, 159–172. (p. 114)

Lambert, N. M., DeWall, C. N., Bushman, B. J., Tillman, T. F., Fincham, F. D., Pond, R. S. Jr., & Gwinn, A. M. (2011). Lashing out in lust: Effect of pornography on nonsexual, physical aggression against relationship partners. Paper presentation at the Society for Personality and Social Psychology convention. (p. 357)

Lambert, N. M., Negash, S., Stillman, T. F., Olmstead, S. B., & Fincham, F. D. (2012). A love that doesn't last: Pornography consumption and weakened commitment to a romantic partner. *Journal of Social and Clinical Psychology, 31*, 410–438. (pp. 18, 118)

Lambird, K. H., & Mann, T. (2006). When do ego threats lead to self-regulation failure? Negative consequences of defensive high self-esteem. *Personality and Social Psychology Bulletin, 32*, 1177–1187. (p. 331)

Landauer, T. K. (2001, September). Quoted by R. Herbert, You must remember this. *APS Observer*, p. 11. (p. 214)

Landauer, T. K., & Whiting, J. W. M. (1979). Correlates and consequences of stress in infancy. In R. Munroe, B. Munroe & B. Whiting (Eds.), *Handbook of Cross-Cultural Human Development*. New York: Garland. (p. 301)

Landberg, J., & Norström, T. (2011). Alcohol and homicide in Russia and the United States: A comparative analysis. *Journal of Studies on Alcohol and Drugs, 72*, 723–730. (p. 355)

Landry, M. J. (2002). MDMA: A review of epidemiologic data. *Journal of Psychoactive Drugs, 34*, 163–169. (p. 386)

Langer, E. J. (1983). *The psychology of control*. Beverly Hills, CA: Sage. (p. 292)

Langer, E. J., & Abelson, R. P. (1974). A patient by any other name . . .: Clinician group differences in labeling bias. *Journal of Consulting and Clinical Psychology, 42*, 4–9. (p. 375)

Langer, E. J., & Imber, L. (1980). The role of mindlessness in the perception of deviance. *Journal of Personality and Social Psychology, 39*, 360–367. (p. 375)

Langlois, J. H., Kalakanis, L., Rubenstein, A. J., Larson, A., Hallam, M., & Smoot, M. (2000). Maxims or myths of beauty? A meta-analytic and theoretical review. *Psychological Bulletin, 126*, 390–423. (p. 360)

Langlois, J. H., Roggman, L. A., Casey, R. J., Ritter, J. M., Rieser-Danner, L. A., & Jenkins, V. Y. (1987). Infant preferences for attractive faces: Rudiments of a stereotype? *Developmental Psychology, 23*, 363–369. (p. 360)

Langmeyer, A., Guglhör-Rudan, A., & Tarnai, C. (2012). What do music preferences reveal about personality? A cross-cultural replication using self-ratings and ratings of music samples. *Journal of Individual Differences, 33*, 119–130. (p. 326)

Langström, N. H., Rahman, Q., Carlström, E., & Lichtenstein, P. (2010). Genetic and environmental effects on same-sex sexual behavior: A population study of twins in Sweden. *Archives of Sexual Behavior, 39*, 75–80. (p. 123)

Lankford, A. (2009). Promoting aggression and violence at Abu Ghraib: The U.S. military's transformation of ordinary people into torturers. *Aggression and Violent Behavior, 14*, 388–395. (p. 346)

Larkin, K., Resko, J. A., Stormshak, F., Stellflug, J. N., & Roselli, C. E. (2002). Neuroanatomical correlates of sex and sexual partner preference in sheep. Paper presented at Society for Neuroscience convention. (p. 123)

Larrick, R. P., Timmerman, T. A., & Carton, A. M., & Abrevaya, J. (2011). Temper, temperature, and temptation: Heat-related retaliation in baseball. *Psychological Science, 22*, 423–428. (p. 356)

Larson, R. W., & Verma, S. (1999). How children and adolescents spend time across the world: Work, play, and developmental opportunities. *Psychological Bulletin, 125*, 701–736. (p. 249)

Larzelere, R. E. (2000). Child outcomes of non-abusive and customary physical punishment by parents: An updated literature review. *Clinical Child and Family Psychology Review, 3*, 199–221. (p. 178)

Larzelere, R. E., & Kuhn, B. R. (2005). Comparing child outcomes of physical punishment and alternative disciplinary tactics: A meta-analysis. *Clinical Child and Family Psychology Review, 8*, 1–37. (p. 179)

Larzelere, R. E., Kuhn, B. R., & Johnson, B. (2004). The intervention selection bias: An underrecognized confound in intervention research. *Psychological Bulletin, 130*, 289–303. (p. 178)

Lassiter, G. D., & Irvine, A. A. (1986). Video-taped confessions: The impact of camera point of view on judgments of coercion. *Journal of Personality and Social Psychology, 16,* 268–276. (p. 339)

Latané, B. (1981). The psychology of social impact. *American Psychologist, 36,* 343–356. (p. 347)

Latané, B., & Dabbs, J. M., Jr. (1975). Sex, group size and helping in three cities. *Sociometry, 38,* 180–194. (p. 364)

Latham, G. P., & Locke, E. A. (2007). New developments in and directions for goal-setting research. *European Psychologist, 12,* 290–300. (p. B-6)

Laumann, E. O., Gagnon, J. H., Michael, R. T., & Michaels, S. (1994). *The social organization of sexuality: Sexual practices in the United States.* Chicago: University of Chicago Press. (p. 126)

Laws, K. R., & Kokkalis, J. (2007). Ecstasy (MDMA) and memory function: A meta-analytic update. *Human Psychopharmacology: Clinical and Experimental, 22,* 381–388. (p. 386)

Lazarus, R. S. (1990). Theory-based stress measurement. *Psychological Inquiry, 1,* 3–13. (p. 285)

Lazarus, R. S. (1991). Progress on a cognitive-motivational-relational theory of emotion. *American Psychologist, 46,* 352–367. (p. 271)

Lazarus, R. S. (1998). *Fifty years of the research and theory of R. S. Lazarus: An analysis of historical and perennial issues.* Mahwah, NJ: Erlbaum. (pp. 271, 284)

Lea, S. E. G. (2000). Towards an ethical use of animals. *The Psychologist, 13,* 556–557. (p. 22)

Leaper, C., & Ayres, M. M. (2007). A meta-analytic review of gender variations in adults' language use: Talkativeness, affiliative speech, and assertive speech. *Personality and Social Psychology Review, 11,* 328–363. (p. 109)

Leary, M. R. (1999). The social and psychological importance of self-esteem. In R. M. Kowalski & M. R. Leary (Eds.), *The social psychology of emotional and behavioral problems.* Washington, DC: APA Books. (p. 329)

Leary, M. R., Haupt, A. L., Strausser, K. S., & Chokel, J. T. (1998). Calibrating the sociometer: The relationship between interpersonal appraisals and state self-esteem. *Journal of Personality and Social Psychology, 74,* 1290–1299. (p. 264)

LeDoux, J. E. (1996). *The emotional brain: The mysterious underpinnings of emotional life.* New York: Simon & Schuster. (p. 200)

LeDoux, J. E. (2002). *The synaptic self.* London: Macmillan. (p. 271)

LeDoux, J. E. (2009, July/August). Quoted by K. McGowan, Out of the past. *Discover,* pp. 28–37. (p. 209)

LeDoux, J. E., & Armony, J. (1999). Can neurobiology tell us anything about human feelings? In D. Kahneman, E. Diener, & N. Schwartz (Eds.), *Well-being: The foundations of hedonic psychology.* New York: Sage. (p. 271)

Lee, L., Frederick, S., & Ariely, D. (2006). Try it, you'll like it: The influence of expectation, consumption, and revelation on preferences for beer. *Psychological Science, 17,* 1054–1058. (p. 138)

Lee, P. S. N., Leung, L., Lo, V., Xiong, C., & Wu, T. (2011). Internet communication versus face-to-face interaction in quality of life. *Social Indicators Research, 100,* 375–389. (p. 267)

Lefcourt, H. M. (1982). *Locus of control: Current trends in theory and research.* Hillsdale, NJ: Erlbaum. (p. 293)

Legrand, L. N., Iacono, W. G., & McGue, M. (2005). Predicting addiction. *American Scientist, 93,* 140–147. (p. 389)

Lehman, A. F., Steinwachs, D. M., Dixon, L. B., Goldman, H. H., Osher, F., Postrado, L., Scott, J. E., Thompson, J. W., Fahey, M., Fischer, P., Kasper, J. A., Lyles, A., Skinner, E. A., Buchanan, R., Carpenter, W. T., Jr., Levine, J., McGlynn, E. A., Rosenheck, R., & Zito, J. (1998). Translating research into practice: The schizophrenic patient outcomes research team (PORT) treatment recommendations. *Schizophrenia Bulletin, 24,* 1–10. (p. 425)

Lehman, D. R., Wortman, C. B., & Williams, A. F. (1987). Long-term effects of losing a spouse or child in a motor vehicle crash. *Journal of Personality and Social Psychology, 52,* 218–231. (p. 101)

Leichsenring, F., & Rabung, S. (2008). Effectiveness of long-term psychodynamic psychotherapy: A meta-analysis. *JAMA, 300,* 1551–1565. (pp. 421, 422)

Leitenberg, H., & Henning, K. (1995). Sexual fantasy. *Psychological Bulletin, 117,* 469–496. (pp. 116, 118)

Lemonick, M. D. (2002, June 3). Lean and hungrier. *Time,* p. 54. (p. 259)

Lench, H. C., Flores, S. A., & Bench, S. W. (2011). Discrete emotions predict changes in cognition, judgment, experience, behavior, and physiology: A meta-analysis of experimental emotion elicitations. *Psychological Bulletin, 137,* 834–855. (p. 273)

Lenhart, A. (2010, April 20). Teens, cell phones and texting. Pew Internet and American Life Project. Pew Research Center (www.pewresearch.org). (p. 110)

Lenhart, A. (2012, March 19). Teens, smartphones & texting. Pew Internet & American Life Project (www.pewinternet.org). (p. 266)

Lenneberg, E. H. (1967). *Biological foundations of language.* New York: Wiley. (p. 232)

Lennox, B. R., Bert, S., Park, G., Jones, P. B., & Morris, P. G. (1999). Spatial and temporal mapping of neural activity associated with auditory hallucinations. *Lancet, 353,* 644. (p. 45)

Lenton, A. P., & Francesconi, M. (2010). How humans cognitively manage an abundance of mate options. *Psychological Science, 21,* 528–533. (p. 359)

Lenton, A. P., & Francesconi, M. (2012). Too much of a good thing? Variety is confusing in mate choice. *Biology Letters, 7,* 528–531. (p. 359)

Lenzenweger, M. F., Dworkin, R. H., & Wethington, E. (1989). Models of positive and negative symptoms in schizophrenia: An empirical evaluation of latent structures. *Journal of Abnormal Psychology, 98,* 62–70. (p. 425)

Leucht, S., Barnes, T. R. E., Kissling, W., Engel, R. R., Correll, C., & Kane, J. M. (2003). Relapse prevention in schizophrenia with new-generation antipsychotics: A systematic review and exploratory meta-analysis of randomized, controlled trials. *American Journal of Psychiatry, 160,* 1209–1222. (p. 425)

Leung, A. K-Y., Maddux, W. W., Galinsky, A. D., & Chiu, C-Y. (2008). Multicultural experience enhances creativity: The when and how. *American Psychologist, 63,* 169–181. (p. 228)

LeVay, S. (1991). A difference in hypothalamic structure between heterosexual and homosexual men. *Science, 253,* 1034–1037. (p. 122)

LeVay, S. (1994, March). Quoted in D. Nimmons, Sex and the brain. *Discover,* p. 64–71. (p. 122)

LeVay, S. (2011). *Gay, straight, and the reason why: The science of sexual orientation.* New York: Oxford University Press. (pp. 124, 127)

Levenson, R. W. (1992). Autonomic nervous system differences among emotions. *Psychological Science, 3,* 23–27. (p. 273)

Levine, J. A., Lanningham-Foster, L. M., McCrady, S. K., Krizan, A. C., Olson, L. R., Kane, P. H., Jensen, M. D., & Clark, M. M. (2005). Interindividual variation in posture allocation: Possible role in human obesity. *Science, 307,* 584–586. (p. 262)

Levine, R., Sato, S., Hashimoto, T., & Verma, J. (1995). Love and marriage in eleven cultures. *Journal of Cross-Cultural Psychology, 26,* 554–571. (p. 362)

Levinson, D. F., & 23 others. (2011). Copy number variants in schizophrenia: Confirmation of five previous findings and new evidence for 3q29 microdeletions and VIPR2 duplications. *American Journal of Psychiatry, 168,* 302–316. (p. 400)

Lewandowski, G. W., Jr., Aron, A., & Gee, J. (2007). Personality goes a long way: The malleability of opposite-sex physical attractiveness. *Personality Relationships, 14,* 571–585. (p. 361)

Lewinsohn, P. M., Hoberman, H., Teri, L., & Hautziner, M. (1985). An integrative theory of depression. In S. Reiss & R. Bootzin (Eds.), *Theoretical issues in behavior therapy.* Orlando, FL: Academic Press. (p. 393)

Lewinsohn, P. M., Petit, J., Joiner, T. E., Jr., & Seeley, J. R. (2003). The symptomatic expression of major depressive disorder in adolescents and young adults. *Journal of Abnormal Psychology, 112,* 244–252. (p. 393)

Lewinsohn, P. M., Rohde, P., & Seeley, J. R. (1998). Major depressive disorder in older adolescents: Prevalence, risk factors, and clinical implications. *Clinical Psychology Review, 18,* 765–794. (p. 393)

Lewinsohn, P. M., & Rosenbaum, M. (1987). Recall of parental behavior by acute depressives, remitted depressives, and nondepressives. *Journal of Personality and Social Psychology, 52,* 611–619. (p. 205)

Lewis, D. O., Yeager, C. A., Swica, Y., Pincus, J. H., & Lewis, M. (1997). Objective documentation of child abuse and dissociation in 12 murderers with dissociative identity disorder. *American Journal of Psychiatry, 154,* 1703–1710. (p. 402)

Lewis, M. (1992). Commentary. *Human Development, 35,* 44–51. (p. 205)

Lewontin, R. (1976). Race and intelligence. In N. J. Block & G. Dworkin (Eds.), *The IQ controversy: Critical readings.* New York: Pantheon. (p. 248)

Li, J., Laursen, T. M., Precht, D. H., Olsen, J., & Mortensen, P. B. (2005). Hospitalization for mental illness among parents after the death of a child. *New England Journal of Medicine, 352,* 1190–1196. (p. 101)

Liang, K. Y., Mintun, M. A., Fagan, A. M., Goate, A.M., Bugg, J. M., Holtzman, D. M., Morris, J. C., & Head, D. (2010). Exercise and Alzheimer's disease biomarkers in cognitively normal older adults. *Annals of Neurology, 68,* 311–318. (p. 95)

Liberman, V., Boehm, J. K., Lyubomirsky, S., & Ross, L. D. (2009). Happiness and memory: Affective significance of endowment and contrast. *Emotion, 9,* 666–680. (p. 301)

Lichtenstein, E., Zhu, S-H., & Tedeschi, G. J. (2010). Smoking cessation quitlines: An underrecognized intervention success story. *American Psychologist, 65,* 252–261. (p. 385)

Lieberman, M. D., Eisenberger, N. L., Crockett, M. J., Tom, S. M., Pfeifer, J. H., & Way, B. M. (2007). Putting feelings into words: Affect labeling disrupts amygdala activity in response to affective stimuli. *Psychological Science, 18,* 421–428. (p. 296)

Lilienfeld, S. O., Lynn, S. J., Kirsch, I., Chaves, J. F., Sarbin, T. R., Ganaway, G. K., & Powell, R. A. (1999). Dissociative identity disorder and the sociocognitive model: Recalling the lessons of the past. *Psychological Bulletin, 125,* 507–523. (p. 402)

Lilienfeld, S. O., Wood, J. M., & Garb, H. N. (2000). The scientific status of projective techniques. *Psychological Science in the Public Interest, 1,* 27–66. (p. 317)

Lim, J., & Dinges, D. F. (2010). A meta-analysis of the impact of short-term sleep deprivation on cognitive variables. *Psychological Bulletin, 136,* 375–389. (p. 57)

Lindau, S. T., Schumm, L. P., Laumann, E. O., Levinson, W., O'Muircheartaigh, C. A., & Waite, L. J. (2007). A study of sexuality and health among older adults in the United States. *New England Journal of Medicine, 357,* 762–774. (p. 115)

Lindberg, S. M., Hyde, J. S., Linn, M. C., & Petersen, J. L. (2010). New trends in gender and mathematics performance: A meta-analysis. *Psychological Bulletin, 136,* 1125–1135. (p. 246)

Lindner, I., Echterhoff, G., Davidson, P. S. R., & Brand, M. (2010). Observation inflation: Your actions become mine. *Psychological Science, 21,* 1291–1299. (p. 186)

Lindson, N., Aveyard, P., & Hughes, J. R. (2010). Reduction versus abrupt cessation in smokers who want to quit (review). *Cochrane Collaboration* (Cochrane Library, Issue 3; www.thecochranelibrary.com). (p. 385)

Lippa, R. A. (2005). *Gender, nature, and nurture* (2nd ed.). Mahwah, NJ: Erlbaum. (p. 110)

Lippa, R. A. (2006). The gender reality hypothesis. *American Psychologist, 61,* 639–640. (p. 110)

Lippa, R. A. (2007). The relation between sex drive and sexual attraction to men and women: A cross-national study of heterosexual, bisexual, and homosexual men and women. *Archives of Sexual Behavior, 36,* 209–222. (p. 360)

Lippa, R. A. (2008) Sex differences and sexual orientation differences in personality: Findings from the BBC Internet survey. *Archives of Sexual Behavior, Special Issue: Biological research on sex-dimorphic behavior and sexual orientation, 37*(1), 173–187. (p. 110)

Lipps, H. M. (1999). *A new psychology of women: Gender, culture, and ethnicity.* Mountain View, CA: Mayfield Publishing. (p. 351)

Lipsitt, L. P. (2003). Crib death: A biobehavioral phenomenon? *Current Directions in Psychological Science, 12,* 164–170. (p. 74)

Liu, Y., Balaraman, Y., Wang, G., Nephew, K. P., & Zhou, F. C. (2009). Alcohol exposure alters DNA methylation profiles in mouse embryos at early neurulation. *Epigentics, 4,* 500–511. (p. 71)

Livingstone, M., & Hubel, D. (1988). Segregation of form, color, movement, and depth: Anatomy, physiology, and perception. *Science, 240,* 740–749. (p. 143)

LoBue, V., & DeLoache, J. S. (2008). Detecting the snake in the grass: Attention to fear-relevant stimuli by adults and young children. *Psychological Science, 19,* 284–289. (p. 381)

Loehlin, J. C., & Nichols, R. C. (1976). *Heredity, environment, and personality.* Austin: University of Texas Press. (p. 72)

Loehlin, J. C., McCrae, R. R., & Costa, P. T., Jr. (1998). Heritabilities of common and measure-specific components of the Big Five personality factors. *Journal of Research in Personality, 32,* 431–453. (p. 324)

Loewenstein, G., & Furstenberg, F. (1991). Is teenage sexual behavior rational? *Journal of Applied Social Psychology, 21,* 957–986. (p. 176)

Loftus, E. F. (1979). The malleability of human memory. *American Scientist, 67,* 313–320. (p. 210)

Loftus, E. F. (1995, March/April). Remembering dangerously. *Skeptical Inquirer,* pp. 20–29. (p. 318)

Loftus, E. F. (2012, July). Manufacturing memories. Invited address to the International Congress of Psychology, Cape Town. (p. 210)

Loftus, E. F., & Ketcham, K. (1994). *The myth of repressed memory.* New York: St. Martin's Press. (p. 60)

Loftus, E. F., Levidow, B., & Duensing, S. (1992). Who remembers best? Individual differences in memory for events that occurred in a science museum. *Applied Cognitive Psychology, 6,* 93–107. (p. 210)

Loftus, E. F., & Loftus, G. R. (1980). On the permanence of stored information in the human brain. *American Psychologist, 35,* 409–420. (p. 199)

Loftus, E. F., & Palmer, J. C. (October, 1974). Reconstruction of automobile destruction: An example of the interaction between language and memory. *Journal of Verbal Learning & Verbal Behavior, 13*(5), 585–589. (p. 210)

Logan, T. K., Walker, R., Cole, J., & Leukefeld, C. (2002). Victimization and substance abuse among women: Contributing factors, interventions, and implications. *Review of General Psychology, 6,* 325–397. (p. 389)

Logue, A. W. (1998a). Laboratory research on self-control: Applications to administration. *Review of General Psychology, 2,* 221–238. (p. 176)

Logue, A. W. (1998b). Self-control. In W. T. O'Donohue (Ed.), *Learning and behavior therapy.* Boston, MA: Allyn & Bacon. (p. 176)

London, P. (1970). The rescuers: Motivational hypotheses about Christians who saved Jews from the Nazis. In J. Macaulay & L. Berkowitz (Eds.), *Altruism and helping behavior.* New York: Academic Press. (p. 186)

Lopes, P. N., Brackett, M. A., Nezlek, J. B., Schutz, A., Sellin, II, & Salovey, P. (2004). Emotional intelligence and social interaction. *Personality and Social Psychology Bulletin, 30,* 1018–1034. (p. 238)

López-Ibor, J. J., López-Ibor, M-I., & Pastrana, J. I. (2008). Transcranial magnetic stimulation. *Current Opinion in Psychiatry, 21,* 640–644. (p. 429)

Lord, C. G., Lepper, M. R., & Preston, E. (1984). Considering the opposite: A corrective strategy for social judgment. *Journal of Personality and Social Psychology, 47,* 1231–1247. (p. 223)

Lord, C. G., Ross, L., & Lepper, M. (1979). Biased assimilation and attitude polarization: The effects of prior theories on subsequently considered evidence. *Journal of Personality and Social Psychology, 37,* 2098–2109. (p. 223)

Louie, K., & Wilson, M. A. (2001). Temporally structured replay of awake hippocampal ensemble activity during rapid eye movement sleep. *Neuron, 29,* 145–156. (p. 61)

Lourenco, O., & Machado, A. (1996). In defense of Piaget's theory: A reply to 10 common criticisms. *Psychological Review, 103,* 143–164. (p. 80)

Lovaas, O. I. (1987). Behavioral treatment and normal educational and intellectual functioning in young autistic children. *Journal of Consulting and Clinical Psychology, 55,* 3–9. (p. 416)

Lowry, P. E. (1997). The assessment center process: New directions. *Journal of Social Behavior and Personality, 12,* 53–62. (p. 328)

Lozano, A., Mayberg, H., Giacobbe, P., Hami, C., Craddock, R., & Kennedy, S. (2008). Subcallosal cingulated gyrus deep brain stimulation for treatment-resistant depression. *Biological Psychiatry, 64,* 461–467. (p. 428)

Lubinski, D. (2009a). Cognitive epidemiology: with emphasis on untangling cognitive ability and socioeconomic status. *Intelligence, 37,* 625–633. (pp. 238, 242)

Lubinski, D. (2009b). Exceptional cognitive ability: The phenotype. *Behavioral Genetics, 39,* 350–358. (p. 242)

Luborsky, L., Rosenthal, R., Diguer, L., Andrusyna, T. P., Berman, J. S., Levitt, J. T., Seligman, D. A., & Krause, E. D. (2002). The dodo bird verdict is alive and well—mostly. *Clinical Psychology: Science and Practice, 9,* 2–34. (p. 421)

Lucas, A., Morley, R., Cole, T. J., Lister, G., & Leeson-Payne, C. (1992). Breast milk and subsequent intelligence quotient in children born preterm. *Lancet, 339,* 261–264. (p. 18)

Lucas, R. E. (2007a). Adaptation and the set-point model of subjective well-being. *Current Directions in Psychological Science, 16,* 75–79. (p. 302)

Lucas, R. E. (2007b). Long-term disability is associated with lasting changes in subjective well-being: Evidence from two nationally representative longitudinal studies. *Journal of Personality and Social Psychology, 92,* 717–730. (p. 302)

Lucas, R. E., Clark, A. E., Georgellis, Y., & Diener, E. (2003). Re-examining adaptation and the set point model of happiness: Reactions to changes in marital status. *Journal of Personality and Social Psychology, 84,* 527–539. (p. 100)

Lucas, R. E., Clark, A. E., Georgellis, Y., & Diener, E. (2004). Unemployment alters the set point for life satisfaction. *Psychological Science, 15,* 8–13. (p. 305)

Lucas, R. E., & Donnellan, M. B. (2011). Personality development across the life span: Longitudinal analyses with a national sample from Germany. *Journal of Personality and Social Psychology, 101,* 847–861. (pp. 90, 102, 324)

Ludwig, A. M. (1995). *The price of greatness: Resolving the creativity and madness controversy.* New York: Guilford Press. (p. 392)

Luigjes, J., van den Brink, W., Feenstra, M., van den Munckhof, P., Schuurman, P. R., Schippers, R., Mazaheri, A., De Vries, T. J., & Denys, D. (2012). Deep brain stimulation in addiction: A review of potential brain targets. *Molecular Psychiatry, 17,* 572–583. (p. 428)

Lumeng, J. C., Forrest, P., Appugliese, D. P., Kaciroti, N., Corwyn, R. F., Bradley, R. H. (2010). Weight status as a predictor of being bullied in third through sixth grades. *Pediatrics, 125,* e1301–1307. (p. 261)

Luo, F., Florence, C. S., Quispe-Agnoli, M., Ouyang, L., & Crosby, A. E. (2011). Impact of business cycles on US suicide rates, 1928–2007. *American Journal of Public Health, 101,* 1139–1146. (p. 392)

Luppino, F. S., de Wit, L. M., Bouvy, P. F., Stijnen, T., Cuijpers, P., Penninx, W. J. H., & Zitman, F. G. (2010). Overweight, obesity, and depression. *Archives of General Psychiatry, 67,* 220–229. (p. 261)

Luria, A. M. (1968). In L. Solotaroff (Trans.), *The mind of a mnemonist.* New York: Basic Books. (p. 193)

Lutfey, K. E., Link, C. L., Rosen, R. C., Wiegel, M., & McKinlay, J. B. (2009). Prevalence and correlates of sexual activity and function in women: Results from the Boston Area Community Health (BACH) survey. *Archives of Sexual Behavior, 38,* 514–527. (p. 117)

Lutgendorf, S. K., Russell, D., Ullrich, P., Harris, T. B., & Wallace, R. (2004). Religious participation, interleukin-6, and mortality in older adults. *Health Psychology, 23,* 465–475. (p. 300)

Lyall, S. (2005, November 29). What's the buzz? Rowdy teenagers don't want to hear it. *New York Times* (www.nytimes.com). (p. 96)

Lykken, D. T. (1991). Science, lies, and controversy: An epitaph for the polygraph. Invited address upon receipt of the Senior Career Award for Distinguished Contribution to Psychology in the Public Interest, American Psychological Association convention. (p. 274)

Lykken, D. T. (1995). *The antisocial personalities.* New York: Erlbaum. (p. 376)

Lykken, D. T. (1999). *Happiness: The nature and nurture of joy and contentment.* New York: Golden Books. (p. 241)

Lykken, D. T., & Tellegen, A. (1993). Is human mating adventitious or the result of lawful choice? A twin study of mate selection. *Journal of Personality and Social Psychology, 65,* 56–68. (p. 98)

Lykken, D. T., & Tellegen, A. (1996). Happiness is a stochastic phenomenon. *Psychological Science, 7,* 186–189. (p. 305)

Lynch, G. (2002). Memory enhancement: The search for mechanism-based drugs. *Nature Neuroscience, 5* (suppl.), 1035–1038. (p. 201)

Lynch, G., & Staubli, U. (1991). Possible contributions of long-term potentiation to the encoding and organization of memory. *Brain Research Reviews, 16,* 204–206. (p. 201)

Lynn, M. (1988). The effects of alcohol consumption on restaurant tipping. *Personality and Social Psychology Bulletin, 14,* 87–91. (p. 382)

Lynn, S. J., Lilienfeld, S. O., Merckelbach, H., Giesbrecht, T., & van der Kloet, D. (2012). Dissociation and dissociative disorders: Challenging conventional wisdom. *Current Directions in Psychological Science, 21,* 48–53. (p. 403)

Lynn, S. J., Rhue, J. W., & Weekes, J. R. (1990). Hypnotic involuntariness: A social cognitive analysis. *Psychological Review, 97,* 169–184. (p. 157)

Lynne, S. D., Graber, J. A., Nichols, T. R., Brooks-Gunn, J., & Botvin, G. J. (2007). Links between pubertal timing, peer influences, and externalizing behaviors among urban students followed through middle school. *Journal of Adolescent Health, 40,* 181.e7–181.e13. (p. 86)

Lyons, L. (2005, January 4). Teens stay true to parents' political perspectives. *Gallup Poll News Service* (www.gallup.com). (p. 91)

Lyubomirsky, S. (2001). Why are some people happier than others? The role of cognitive and motivational processes in well-being. *American Psychologist, 56,* 239–249. (p. 304)

Lyubomirsky, S. (2008). *The How of happiness.* New York: Penguin. (p. 301)

Maas, J. B., & Robbins, R. S. (2010). *Sleep for success: Everything you must know about sleep but are too tired to ask.* Bloomington, IN: Author House. (p. 56)

Maass, A., D'Ettole, C., & Cadinu, M. (2008). Checkmate? The role of gender stereotypes in the ultimate intellectual sport. *European Journal of Social Psychology, 38,* 231–245. (p. 250)

Macapagal, K. R., Janssen, E., Fridberg, D. J., Finn, P. R., & Heiman, J. R. (2011). The effects of impulsivity, sexual arousability, and abstract intellectual ability on men's and women's go/no-go task performance. *Archives of Sexual Behavior, 40,* 995–1006. (p. 119)

Maccoby, E. E. (1990). Gender and relationships: A developmental account. *American Psychologist, 45,* 513–520. (p. 109)

Maccoby, E. E. (1998). *The paradox of gender.* Cambridge, MA: Harvard University Press. (p. 110)

MacDonald, G., & Leary, M. R. (2005). Why does social exclusion hurt? The relationship between social and physical pain. *Psychological Bulletin, 131,* 202–223. (p. 266)

MacDonald, T. K., & Hynie, M. (2008). Ambivalence and unprotected sex: Failure to predict sexual activity and decreased condom use. *Journal of Applied Social Psychology, 38,* 1092–1107. (p. 119)

MacDonald, T. K., Zanna, M. P., & Fong, G. T. (1995). Decision making in altered states: Effects of alcohol on attitudes toward drinking and driving. *Journal of Personality and Social Psychology, 68,* 973–985. (p. 383)

MacFarlane, A. (1978, February). What a baby knows. *Human Nature,* pp. 74–81. (p. 73)

Machin, S., & Pekkarinen, T. (2008). Global sex differences in test score variability. *Science, 322,* 1331–1332. (p. 247)

Macmillan, M., & Lena, M. L. (2010). Rehabilitating Phineas Gage. *Neuropsychological Rehabilitation, 17,* 1–18. (p. 46)

MacNeilage, P. F., Rogers, L. J., & Vallortigara, G. (2009, July). Origins of the left and right brain. *Scientific American,* pp. 60–67. (p. 50)

Maddi, S. R., Harvey, R. H., Khoshaba, D. M., Fazel, M., & Resurreccion, N. (2009). Hardiness training facilitates performance in college. *Journal of Positive Psychology, 4,* 566–577. (p. B-4)

Maddux, W. W., Adam, H., & Galinsky, A. D. (2010). When in Rome . . . Learn why the Romans do what they do: How multicultural learning experiences facilitate creativity. *Personality and Social Psychology Bulletin, 36,* 731–741. (p. 228)

Maddux, W. W., & Galinsky, A. D. (2009). Cultural borders and mental barriers: The relationship between living abroad and creativity. *Journal of Personality and Social Psychology, 96,* 1047–1061. (p. 228)

Maes, H. H. M., Neale, M. C., & Eaves, L. J. (1997). Genetic and environmental factors in relative body weight and human adiposity. *Behavior Genetics, 27,* 325–351. (p. 262)

Maestripieri, D. (2003). Similarities in affiliation and aggression between cross-fostered rhesus macaque females and their biological mothers. *Developmental Psychobiology, 43,* 321–327. (p. 72)

Maglaty, J. (2011, April 8). When did girls start wearing pink? *Smithsonian.com.* (p. 108)

Magnusson, D. (1990). Personality research—challenges for the future. *European Journal of Personality, 4,* 1–17. (p. 404)

Maguire, E. A., Valentine, E. R., Wilding, J. M., & Kapur, N. (2003). Routes to remembering: The brains behind superior memory. *Nature Neuroscience, 6,* 90–95. (p. 197)

Maier, S. F., Watkins, L. R., & Fleshner, M. (1994). Psychoneuroimmunology: The interface between behavior, brain, and immunity. *American Psychologist, 49,* 1004–1017. (pp. 287, 288)

Major, B., Carrington, P. I., & Carnevale, P. J. D. (1984). Physical attractiveness and self-esteem: Attribution for praise from an other-sex evaluator. *Personality and Social Psychology Bulletin, 10,* 43–50. (p. 360)

Major, B., Schmidlin, A. M., & Williams, L. (1990). Gender patterns in social touch: The impact of setting and age. *Journal of Personality and Social Psychology, 58,* 634–643. (p. 109)

Malamuth, N. M., & Check, J. V. P. (1981). The effects of media exposure on acceptance of violence against women: A field experiment. *Journal of Research in Personality, 15,* 436–446. (p. 118)

Malkiel, B. (2007). *A random walk down Wall Street: The time-tested strategy for successful investing* (revised and updated). New York: Norton. (p. 11)

Malloy, E. A. (1994, June 7). Report of the Commission on Substance Abuse at Colleges and Universities, reported by Associated Press. (p. 383)

Malmquist, C. P. (1986). Children who witness parental murder: Posttraumatic aspects. *Journal of the American Academy of Child Psychiatry, 25,* 320–325. (p. 318)

Malnic, B., Hirono, J., Sato, T., & Buck, L. B. (1999). Combinatorial receptor codes for odors. *Cell, 96,* 713–723. (p. 158)

Maner, J. K., Kenrick, D. T., Neuberg, S. L., Becker, D. V., Robertson, T., Hofer, B., Delton, A., Butner, J., & Schaller, M. (2005). Functional projection: How fundamental social motives can bias interpersonal perception. *Journal of Personality and Social Psychology, 88,* 63–78. (p. 319)

Mann, T., Tomiyama, A. J., Westling, E., Lew, A-M., Samuels, B., & Chatman, J. (2007). Medicare's search for effective obesity treatments: Diets are not the answer. *American Psychologist, 62,* 220–233. (p. 263)

Manson, J. E. (2002). Walking compared with vigorous exercise for the prevention of cardiovascular events in women. *New England Journal of Medicine, 347,* 716–725. (p. 297)

Maquet, P. (2001). The role of sleep in learning and memory. *Science, 294,* 1048–1052. (p. 61)

Mar, R. A., & Oatley, K. (2008). The function of fiction is the abstraction and simulation of social experience. *Perspectives on Psychological Science, 3,* 173–192. (p. 186)

Marangell, L. B., Martinez, M., Jurdi, R. A., & Zboyan, H. (2007). Neurostimulation therapies in depression: A review of new modalities. *Acta Psychiatrica Scandinavica, 116,* 174–181. (p. 428)

Margolis, M. L. (2000). Brahms' lullaby revisited: Did the composer have obstructive sleep apnea? *Chest, 118*, 210–213. (p. 60)

Marinak, B. A., & Gambrell, L. B. (2008). Intrinsic motivation and rewards: What sustains young children's engagement with text? *Literacy Research and Instruction, 47*, 9–26. (p. 184)

Marks, I., & Cavanagh, K. (2009). Computer-aided psychological treatments: Evolving issues. *Annual Review of Clinical Psychology, 5*, 121–141. (p. 419)

Markus, H. R., & Kitayama, S. (1991). Culture and the self: Implications for cognition, emotion, and motivation. *Psychological Review, 98*, 224–253. (p. 423)

Markus, H. R., & Nurius, P. (1986). Possible selves. *American Psychologist, 41*, 954–969. (p. 328)

Marlatt, G. A. (1991). Substance abuse: Etiology, prevention, and treatment issues. Master lecture, American Psychological Association convention. (p. 383)

Marley, J., & Bulia, S. (2001). Crimes against people with mental illness: Types, perpetrators and influencing factors. *Social Work, 46*, 115–124. (p. 376)

Marshall, M. J. (2002). *Why spanking doesn't work.* Springville, UT: Bonneville Books. (p. 178)

Marshall, R. D., Bryant, R. A., Amsel, L., Suh, E. J., Cook, J. M., & Neria, Y. (2007). The psychology of ongoing threat: Relative risk appraisal, the September 11 attacks, and terrorism-related fears. *American Psychologist, 62*, 304–316. (p. 222)

Marteau, T. M. (1989). Framing of information: Its influences upon decisions of doctors and patients. *British Journal of Social Psychology, 28*, 89–94. (p. 224)

Marteau, T. M., Hollands, G. J., & Fletcher, P. C. (2012). Changing human behavior to prevent disease: The importance of targeting automatic processes. *Science, 337*, 1492–1495. (p. 261)

Martin, C. K., Anton, S. D., Walden, H., Arnett, C., Greenway, F. L., & Williamson, D. A. (2007). Slower eating rate reduces the food intake of men, but not women: Implications for behavioural weight control. *Behaviour Research and Therapy, 45*, 2349–2359. (p. 264)

Martin, C. L., & Ruble, D. (2004). Children's search for gender cues. *Current Directions in Psychological Science, 13*, 67–70. (p. 114)

Martin, C. L., Ruble, D. N., & Szkrybalo, J. (2002). Cognitive theories of early gender development. *Psychological Bulletin, 128*, 903–933. (p. 114)

Martin, R. J., White, B. D., & Hulsey, M. G. (1991). The regulation of body weight. *American Scientist, 79*, 528–541. (p. 260)

Martino, S. C., Collins, R. L., Kanouse, D. E., Elliott, M., & Berry, S. H. (2005). Social cognitive processes mediating the relationship between exposure to television's sexual content and adolescents' sexual behavior. *Journal of Personality and Social Psychology, 89*, 914–924. (p. 119)

Martins, Y., Preti, G., Crabtree, C. R., & Wysocki, C. J. (2005). Preference for human body odors is influenced by gender and sexual orientation. *Psychological Science, 16*, 694–701. (p. 123)

Marx, D. M., Ko, S. J., & Friedman, R. A. (2009). The "Obama effect": How a salient role model reduces race-based performance differences. *Journal of Experimental Social Psychology, 45*, 953–956. (p. 250)

Masicampo, E. J., & Baumeister, R. F. (2008). Toward a physiology of dual-process reasoning and judgment: Lemonade, willpower, and the expensive rule-based analysis. *Psychological Science, 19*, 255–260. (p. 293)

Maslow, A. H. (1970). *Motivation and personality* (2nd ed.). New York: Harper & Row. (pp. 257, 319)

Maslow, A. H. (1971). *The farther reaches of human nature.* New York: Viking Press. (p. 257)

Mason, C., & Kandel, E. R. (1991). Central visual pathways. In E. R. Kandel, J. H. Schwartz, & T. M. Jessell (Eds.), *Principles of neural science* (3rd ed.). New York: Elsevier. (p. 33)

Mason, H. (2003, September 2). Americans, Britons at odds on animal testing. *Gallup Poll News Service* (http://www.gallup.com). (p. 21)

Mason, M. F., Norton, M. I., Van Horn, J. D., Wegner, D. M., Grafton, S. T., & Macrae, C. N. (2007). Wandering minds: The default network and stimulus-independent thought. *Science, 315*, 393–395. (p. 318)

Mason, R. A., & Just, M. A. (2004). How the brain processes causal inferences in text. *Psychological Science, 15*, 1–7. (p. 50)

Mason, W. A., Hitch, J. E., Kosterman, R., McCarty, C. A., Herrenkohl, T. I., & Hawkins, J. D. (2010). Growth in adolescent delinquency and alcohol use in relation to young adult crime, alcohol use disorders, and risky sex: A comparison of youth from low versus middle-income backgrounds. *Journal of Child Psychology and Psychiatry, 51*, 1377–1385. (p. 119)

Masse, L. C., & Tremblay, R. E. (1997). Behavior of boys in kindergarten and the onset of substance use during adolescence. *Archives of General Psychiatry, 54*, 62–68. (p. 388)

Massimini, M., Ferrarelli, F., Huber, R., Esser, S. K., Singh, H., & Tononi, G. (2005). Breakdown of cortical effective connectivity during sleep. *Science, 309*, 2228–2232. (p. 53)

Master, S. L., Eisenberger, N. I., Taylor, S. E., Naliboff, B. D., Shirinyan, D., & Lieberman, M. D. (2009). A picture's worth: Partner photographs reduce experimentally induced pain. *Psychological Science, 20*, 1316–1318. (p. 296)

Masters, K. S. (2010). The role of religion in therapy: Time for psychologists to have a little faith? *Cognitive and Behavioral Practice, 17*, 393–400. (p. 423)

Masters, W. H., & Johnson, V. E. (1966). *Human sexual response.* Boston: Little, Brown. (p. 116)

Mastroianni, G. R. (2002). Milgram and the Holocaust: A reexamination. *Journal of Theoretical and Philosophical Psychology, 22*, 158–173. (p. 345)

Mastroianni, G. R., & Reed, G. (2006). Apples, barrels, and Abu Ghraib. *Sociological Focus, 39*, 239–250. (p. 340)

Masuda, T., & Kitayama, S. (2004). Perceiver-induced constraint and attitude attribution in Japan and the US: A case for the cultural dependence of the correspondence bias. *Journal of Experimental Social Psychology, 40*, 409–416. (p. 338)

Mataix-Cols, D., Rosario-Campos, M. C., & Leckman, J. F. (2005). A multi-dimensional model of obsessive-compulsive disorder. *American Journal of Psychiatry, 162*, 228–238. (p. 381)

Mataix-Cols, D., Wooderson, S., Lawrence, N., Brammer, M. J., Speckens, A., & Phillips, M. L. (2004). Distinct neural correlates of washing, checking, and hoarding symptom dimensions in obsessive-compulsive disorder. *Archives of General Psychiatry, 61*, 564–576. (p. 381)

Mather, M., & Sutherland, M. (2012, February). The selective effects of emotional arousal on memory. APA Science Brief (www.apa.org). (p. 201)

Matson, J. L., & Boisjoli, J. A. (2009). The token economy for children with intellectual disability and/or autism: A review. *Research on Developmental Disabilities, 30*, 240–248. (p. 416)

Matsumoto, D., & Ekman, P. (1989). American-Japanese cultural differences in intensity ratings of facial expressions of emotion. *Motivation and Emotion, 13*, 143–157. (p. 276)

Matsumoto, D., & Willingham, B. (2006). The thrill of victory and the agony of defeat: Spontaneous expressions of medal winners of the 2004

Athens Olympic Games. *Journal of Personality and Social Psychology, 91,* 568–581. (p. 277)

Matsumoto, D., & Willingham, B. (2009). Spontaneous facial expressions of emotion of congenitally and noncongenitally blind individuals. *Journal of Personality and Social Psychology, 96,* 1–10. (p. 277)

Matthews, R. N., Domjan, M., Ramsey, M., & Crews, D. (2007). Learning effects on sperm competition and reproductive fitness. *Psychological Science, 18,* 758–762. (p. 171)

Maurer, D., & Maurer, C. (1988). *The world of the newborn.* New York: Basic Books. (p. 73)

Mauss, I. B., Shallcross, A. J., Troy, A. S., John, O. P., Ferrer, E., Wilhelm, F. H., & Gross, J. J. (2011). Don't hide your happiness! Positive emotion dissociation, social connectedness, and psychological functioning. *Journal of Personality and Social Psychology, 100,* 738–748. (p. 301)

May, C., & Hasher, L. (1998). Synchrony effects in inhibitory control over thought and action. *Journal of Experimental Psychology: Human Perception and Performance, 24,* 363–380. (p. 52)

May, P. A., & Gossage, J. P. (2001). Estimating the prevalence of fetal alcohol syndrome: A summary. *Alcohol Research and Health, 25,* 159–167. (p. 71)

Mayberg, H. S., Lozano, A. M., Voon, V., McNeely, H. E., Seminowicz, D., Hamani, C., Schwalb, J. M., & Kennedy, S. H. (2005). Deep brain stimulation for treatment-resistant depression. *Neuron, 45,* 651–660. (p. 428)

Mayer, J. D., Salovey, P., & Caruso, D. R. (2002). *The Mayer-Salovey-Caruso emotional intelligence test (MSCEIT).* Toronto: Multi-Health Systems, Inc. (p. 238)

Mayer, J. D., Salovey, P., & Caruso, D. R. (2008). Emotional intelligence: New ability or eclectic traits? *American Psychologist, 63,* 503–517. (p. 238)

Mazure, C., Keita, G., & Blehar, M. (2002). *Summit on women and depression: Proceedings and recommendations.* Washington, DC: American Psychological Association (www.apa.org/pi/wpo/women&depression.pdf). (p. 395)

Mazzoni, G., & Memon, A. (2003). Imagination can create false autobiographical memories. *Psychological Science, 14,* 186–188. (p. 210)

Mazzoni, G., Scoboria, A., & Harvey, L. (2010). Nonbelieved memories. *Psychological Science, 21,* 1334–1340. (p. 210)

McAndrew, F. T. (2009). The interacting roles of testosterone and challenges to status in human male aggression. *Aggression and Violent Behavior, 14,* 330–335. (p. 354)

McAneny, L. (1996, September). Large majority think government conceals information about UFO's. *Gallup Poll Monthly,* pp. 23–26. (p. 211)

McBurney, D. H. (1996). *How to think like a psychologist: Critical thinking in psychology.* Upper Saddle River, NJ: Prentice-Hall. (p. 46)

McBurney, D. H., & Gent, J. F. (1979). On the nature of taste qualities. *Psychological Bulletin, 86,* 151–167. (p. 157)

McCain, N. L., Gray, D. P., Elswick, R. K., Jr., Robins, J. W., Tuck, I., Walter, J. M., Rausch, S. M., & Ketchum, J. M. (2008). A randomized clinical trial of alternative stress management interventions in persons with HIV infection. *Journal of Consulting and Clinical Psychology, 76,* 431–441. (p. 288)

McCann, I. L., & Holmes, D. S. (1984). Influence of aerobic exercise on depression. *Journal of Personality and Social Psychology, 46,* 1142–1147. (p. 297)

McCann, U. D., Eligulashvili, V., & Ricaurte, G. A. (2001). (+/−)3,4-Methylenedioxymethamphetamine ('Ecstasy')-induced serotonin neurotoxicity: Clinical studies. *Neuropsychobiology, 42,* 11–16. (p. 386)

McCarthy, P. (1986, July). Scent: The tie that binds? *Psychology Today,* pp. 6, 10. (p. 158)

McCauley, C. R. (2002). Psychological issues in understanding terrorism and the response to terrorism. In C. E. Stout (Ed.), *The psychology of terrorism* (Vol. 3). Westport, CT: Praeger/Greenwood. (p. 348)

McCauley, C. R., & Segal, M. E. (1987). Social psychology of terrorist groups. In C. Hendrick (Ed.), *Group processes and intergroup relations.* Beverly Hills, CA: Sage. (p. 348)

McClendon, B. T., & Prentice-Dunn, S. (2001). Reducing skin cancer risk: An intervention based on protection motivation theory. *Journal of Health Psychology, 6,* 321–328. (p. 339)

McClintock, M. K., & Herdt, G. (1996, December). Rethinking puberty: The development of sexual attraction. *Current Directions in Psychological Science, 5*(6), 178–183. (p. 111)

McClung, M., & Collins, D. (2007). "Because I know it will!": Placebo effects of an ergogenic aid on athletic performance. *Journal of Sport & Exercise Psychology, 29,* 382–394. (p. 18)

McConnell, R. A. (1991). National Academy of Sciences opinion on parapsychology. *Journal of the American Society for Psychical Research, 85,* 333–365. (p. 161)

McCool, G. (1999, October 26). Mirror-gazing Venezuelans top of vanity stakes. *Toronto Star* (via web.lexis-nexis.com). (p. 360)

McCrae, R. R., & Costa, P. T., Jr. (1986). Clinical assessment can benefit from recent advances in personality psychology. *American Psychologist, 41,* 1001–1003. (p. 324)

McCrae, R. R., & Costa, P. T., Jr. (2008). The Five-Factor Theory of personality. In O. P. John, R. W. Robins, & L. A. Pervin (eds.), *Handbook of personality: Theory and research* (3rd ed.). New York: Guilford. (p. 324)

McCrae, R. R., Costa, P. T., Jr., Ostendorf, F., Angleitner, A., Hrebickova, M., Avia, M. D., Sanz, J., Sanchez-Bernardos, M. L., Kusdil, M. E., Woodfield, R., Saunders, P. R., & Smith, P. B. (2000). Nature over nurture: Temperament, personality, and life span development. *Journal of Personality and Social Psychology, 78,* 173–186. (p. 73)

McCrae, R. R., Terracciano, A., & 78 others. (2005). Universal features of personality traits from the observer's perspective: Data from 50 cultures. *Journal of Personality and Social Psychology, 88,* 547–561. (p. 324)

McCrae, R. R., Terracciano, A., & Khoury, B. (2007). Dolce far niente: The positive psychology of personality stability and invariance. In A. D. Ong & M. H. Van Dulmen (Eds.), *Oxford handbook of methods in positive psychology.* New York: Oxford University Press. (p. 73)

McCullough, M. E., Hoyt, W. T., Larson, D. B., Koenig, H. G., & Thoresen, C. (2000). Religious involvement and mortality: A meta-analytic review. *Health Psychology, 19,* 211–222. (p. 299)

McCullough, M. E., & Laurenceau, J-P. (2005). Religiousness and the trajectory of self-rated health across adulthood. *Personality and Social Psychology Bulletin, 31,* 560–573. (p. 299)

McDaniel, M. A., Howard, D. C., & Einstein, G. O. (2009). The read-recite-review study strategy: Effective and portable. *Psychological Science, 20,* 516–522. (pp. 23, 25, 62, 102, 129, 163, 189, 198, 215, 250, 279, 307, 333, 367, 404, 433, A-8, B-8)

McDaniel, M. A. (2012). Put the SPRINT in knowledge training: Training with SPacing, Retrieval, and INTerleaving. In M. McDaniel (ed.), *Training cognition: Optimizing efficiency, durability, and generalizability,* pp. 267–286. New York: Psychology Press. (p. 198)

McDougall, C. (2011). *Born to run: A hidden tribe, superathletes, and the greatest race the world has never seen.* New York: Vintage. (p. 430)

McGaugh, J. L. (1994). Quoted by B. Bower, Stress hormones hike emotional memories. *Science News, 146,* 262. (p. 200)

McGaugh, J. L. (2003). *Memory and emotion: The making of lasting memories.* New York: Columbia University Press. (p. 200)

McGhee, P. E. (June, 1976). Children's appreciation of humor: A test of the cognitive congruency principle. *Child Development, 47*(2), 420–426. (p. 79)

McGrath, J. J., & Welham, J. L. (1999). Season of birth and schizophrenia: A systematic review and meta-analysis of data from the Southern hemisphere. *Schizophrenia Research, 35,* 237–242. (p. 399)

McGrath, J. J., Welham, J., & Pemberton, M. (1995). Month of birth, hemisphere of birth and schizophrenia. *British Journal of Psychiatry, 167,* 783–785. (p. 399)

McGue, M., & Bouchard, T. J., Jr. (1998). Genetic and environmental influences on human behavioral differences. *Annual Review of Neuroscience, 21,* 1–24. (p. 72)

McGue, M., Bouchard, T. J., Jr., Iacono, W. G., & Lykken, D. T. (1993). Behavioral genetics of cognitive ability: A life-span perspective. In R. Plomin & G. E. McClearn (Eds.), *Nature, nurture and psychology.* Washington, DC: American Psychological Association. (p. 243)

McGuire, W. J. (1986). The myth of massive media impact: Savings and salvagings. In G. Comstock (Ed.), *Public communication and behavior.* Orlando, FL: Academic Press. (p. 188)

McGurk, H., & MacDonald, J. (1976). Hearing lips and seeing voices. *Nature, 264,* 746–748. (p. 160)

McHugh, P. R. (1995a). Witches, multiple personalities, and other psychiatric artifacts. *Nature Medicine, 1*(2), 110–114. (p. 402)

McKenna, K. Y. A., & Bargh, J. A. (1998). Coming out in the age of the Internet: Identity "demarginalization" through virtual group participation. *Journal of Personality and Social Psychology, 75,* 681–694. (p. 359)

McKenna, K. Y. A., & Bargh, J. A. (2000). Plan 9 from cyberspace: The implications of the Internet for personality and social psychology. *Personality and Social Psychology Review, 4,* 57–75. (p. 359)

McKenna, K. Y. A., Green, A. S., & Gleason, M. E. J. (2002). What's the big attraction? Relationship formation on the Internet. *Journal of Social Issues, 58,* 9–31. (p. 359)

McLaughlin, M. (2010, October 2). JK Rowling: Depression, the 'terrible place that allowed me to come back stronger.' *The Scotsman* (www.scotsman.com). (p. 394)

McMurray, B. (2007). Defusing the childhood vocabulary explosion. *Science, 317,* 631. (p. 230)

McMurray, C. (2004, January 13). U.S., Canada, Britain: Who's getting in shape? *Gallup Poll Tuesday Briefing* (www.gallup.com). (p. 297)

McNally, R. J. (2003a). Progress and controversy in the study of posttraumatic stress disorder. *Annual Review of Psychology, 54,* 229–252. (p. 379)

McNally, R. J. (2003b). *Remembering trauma.* Cambridge, MA: Harvard University Press. (p. 213)

McNally, R. J. (2007). Betrayal trauma theory: A critical appraisal. *Memory, 15,* 280–294. (p. 213)

McNally, R. J. (2012). Are we winning the war against posttraumatic stress disorder? *Science, 336,* 872–874. (p. 379)

McNally, R. J., Bryant, R. A., & Ehlers, A. (2003). Does early psychological intervention promote recovery from post-traumatic stress? *Psychological Science in the Public Interest, 4,* 45–79. (p. 379)

McNally, R. J., & Geraerts, E. (2009). A new solution to the recovered memory debate. *Perspectives on Psychological Science, 4,* 126–134. (p. 213)

McNeil, B. J., Pauker, S. G., & Tversky, A. (1988). On the framing of medical decisions. In D. E. Bell, H. Raiffa, & A. Tversky (Eds.), *Decision making: Descriptive, normative, and prescriptive interactions.* New York: Cambridge University Press. (p. 224)

McWhorter, J. (2012, April 23). Talking with your fingers. *New York Times* (www.nytimes.com). (p. 266)

Meador, B. D., & Rogers, C. R. (1984). Person-centered therapy. In R. J. Corsini (Ed.), *Current psychotherapies* (3rd ed.). Itasca, IL: Peacock. (p. 413)

Medical Institute for Sexual Health. (1994, April). Condoms ineffective against human papilloma virus. *Sexual Health Update,* p. 2. (p. 117)

Mednick, S. A., Huttunen, M. O., & Machon, R. A. (1994). Prenatal influenza infections and adult schizophrenia. *Schizophrenia Bulletin, 20,* 263–267. (p. 399)

Medvec, V. H., Madey, S. F., & Gilovich, T. (1995). When less is more: Counterfactual thinking and satisfaction among Olympic medalists. *Journal of Personality and Social Psychology, 69,* 603–610. (p. 331)

Mehl, M. R., & Pennebaker, J. W. (2003). The sounds of social life: A psychometric analysis of students' daily social environments and natural conversations. *Journal of Personality and Social Psychology, 84,* 857–870. (p. 14)

Mehl, M. R., Vazire, S., Holleran, S. E., & Clark, C. S. (2010). Eavesdropping on happiness: Well-being is related to having less small talk and more substantive conversations. *Psychological Science, 21,* 539–541. (p. 306)

Mehta, M. R. (2007). Cortico-hippocampal interaction during up-down states and memory consolidation. *Nature Neuroscience, 10,* 13–15. (p. 200)

Meichenbaum, D. (1977). *Cognitive-behavior modification: An integrative approach.* New York: Plenum Press. (p. 418)

Meichenbaum, D. (1985). *Stress inoculation training.* New York: Pergamon. (p. 418)

Meltzoff, A. N., Kuhl, P. K., Movellan, J., & Sejnowski, T. J. (2009). Foundations for a new science of learning. *Science, 325,* 284–288. (pp. 186, 230)

Meltzoff, A. N., & Moore, M. K. (1997). Explaining facial imitation: A theoretical model. *Early Development and Parenting, 6,* 179–192. (p. 186)

Melzack, R. (1992, April). Phantom limbs. *Scientific American,* pp. 120–126. (p. 155)

Melzack, R. (1993). Distinguished contribution series. *Canadian Journal of Experimental Psychology, 47,* 615–629. (p. 155)

Melzack, R. (1998, February). Quoted in Phantom limbs. *Discover,* p. 20. (p. 155)

Mendes, E. (2009, May 26). In U.S., nearly half exercise less than three days a week. www.gallup.com. (p. 297)

Mendes, E. (2010, February 9). Six in 10 overweight or obese in U.S., more in '09 than in '08. www.gallup.com. (p. 261)

Mendes, E., & McGeeney, K. (2012, July 9). Women's health trails men's most in former Soviet Union. Gallup (www.gallup.com). (p. 393)

Mendle, J., Turkheimer, E., & Emery, R. E. (2007). Detrimental psychological outcomes associated with early pubertal timing in adolescent girls. *Developmental Review, 27,* 151–171. (p. 86)

Mendolia, M., & Kleck, R. E. (1993). Effects of talking about a stressful event on arousal: Does what we talk about make a difference? *Journal of Personality and Social Psychology, 64,* 283–292. (p. 296)

Merari, A. (2002). Explaining suicidal terrorism: Theories versus empirical evidence. Invited address to the American Psychological Association. (p. 348)

Merskey, H. (1992). The manufacture of personalities: The production of multiple personality disorder. *British Journal of Psychiatry, 160,* 327–340. (p. 402)

Merzenich, M. (2007). Quoted at Posit Science Brain Fitness Program (www.positscience.com). (p. 97)

Mesch, G. (2001). Social relationships and Internet use among adolescents in Israel. *Social Science Quarterly, 82,* 329–340. (p. 267)

Messias, E., Eaton, W. W., Grooms, A. N. (2011). Economic grand rounds: Income inequality and depression prevalence across the United States: An ecological study. *Psychiatric Services, 62,* 710–712. (p. 356)

Meston, C. M., & Buss, D. M. (2007). Why humans have sex. *Archives of Sexual Behavior, 36,* 477–507. (p. 118)

Metzler, D. (2011, Spring). Vocabulary growth in adult cross-fostered chimpanzees. *Friends of Washoe, 32*(3), 11–13. (p. 234)

Meyer-Bahlburg, H. F. L. (1995). Psychoneuroendocrinology and sexual pleasure: The aspect of sexual orientation. In P. R. Abramson & S. D. Pinkerton (Eds.), *Sexual nature/sexual culture.* Chicago: University of Chicago Press. (p. 124)

Meyerbröker, K., & Emmelkamp, P. M. (2010). Virtual reality exposure therapy in anxiety disorders: A systematic review of process-and-outcome studies. *Depression and Anxiety, 27,* 933–944. (p. 415)

Michael, R. B., Garry, M., & Kirsch, I. (2012). Suggestion, cognition, and behavior. *Current Directions in Psychological Science, 21,* 151–156. (p. 18)

Middlebrooks, J. C., & Green, D. M. (1991). Sound localization by human listeners. *Annual Review of Psychology, 42,* 135–159. (p. 154)

Miers, R. (2009, Spring). Calum's road. *Scottish Life,* pp. 36–39, 75. (p. B-4)

Mikulincer, M., & Shaver, P. R. (2001). Attachment theory and intergroup bias: Evidence that priming the secure base schema attenuates negative reactions to out-groups. *Journal of Personality and Social Psychology, 81,* 97–115. (p. 353)

Milan, R. J., Jr., & Kilmann, P. R. (1987). Interpersonal factors in premarital contraception. *Journal of Sex Research, 23,* 289–321. (p. 119)

Miles, D. R., & Carey, G. (1997). Genetic and environmental architecture of human aggression. *Journal of Personality and Social Psychology, 72,* 207–217. (p. 354)

Milgram, S. (1963). Behavioral study of obedience. *Journal of Abnormal & Social Psychology, 67*(4), 371–378. (p. 343)

Milgram, S. (1974). *Obedience to authority.* New York: Harper & Row. (pp. 343, 344, 346)

Miller, G. (2004). Axel, Buck share award for deciphering how the nose knows. *Science, 306,* 207. (p. 158)

Miller, G. (2005). The dark side of glia. *Science, 308,* 778–781. (p. 30)

Miller, G. (2010). Anything but child's play. *Science, 327,* 1192–1193. (p. 392)

Miller, G. (2012). Drone wars: Are remotely piloted aircraft changing the nature of war? *Science, 336,* 842–843. (p. 345)

Miller, G. (2012). The Smartphone psychology manifesto. *Perspectives on Psychological Science, 7,* 221–237. (p. 14)

Miller, G. A. (1956). The magical number seven, plus or minus two: Some limits on our capacity for processing information. *Psychological Review, 63,* 81–97. (p. 196)

Miller, H. C., Pattison, K. F., DeWall, C. N., Rayburn-Reeves, R., & Zentall, T. R. (2010). Self-control without a "self"? Common self-control processes in humans and dogs. *Psychological Science, 21,* 534–538. (p. 293)

Miller, J. G., & Bersoff, D. M. (1995). Development in the context of everyday family relationships: Culture, interpersonal morality and adaptation. In M. Killen & D. Hart (Eds.), *Morality in everyday life: A developmental perspective.* New York: Cambridge University Press. (p. 88)

Miller, L. K. (1999). The savant syndrome: Intellectual impairment and exceptional skill. *Psychological Bulletin, 125,* 31–46. (p. 236)

Miller, M., Azrael, D., & Hemenway, D. (2002). Household firearm ownership levels and suicide across U.S. regions and states, 1988–1997. *Epidemiology, 13,* 517–524. (p. 392)

Miller, P. (2012, January). A thing or two about twins. *National Geographic,* pp. 38–65. (p. 72)

Mineka, S. (1985). The frightful complexity of the origins of fears. In F. R. Brush & J. B. Overmier (Eds.), *Affect, conditioning and cognition: Essays on the determinants of behavior.* Hillsdale, NJ: Erlbaum. (p. 380)

Mineka, S. (2002). Animal models of clinical psychology. In N. Smelser & P. Baltes (Eds.), *International encyclopedia of the social and behavioral sciences.* Oxford, England: Elsevier Science. (p. 380)

Mineka, S., & Zinbarg, R. (1996). Conditioning and ethological models of anxiety disorders: Stress-in-dynamic-context anxiety models. In D. Hope (Ed.), *Perspectives on anxiety, panic, and fear* (Nebraska Symposium on Motivation). Lincoln: University of Nebraska Press. (pp. 381, 432)

Mineka, S., & Zinbarg, R. (2006). A contemporary learning theory perspective on the etiology of anxiety disorders: It's not what you thought it was. *American Psychologist, 61,* 10–26. (p. 379)

Minsky, M. (1986). *The society of mind.* New York: Simon & Schuster. (p. 37)

Mischel, W. (1968). *Personality and assessment.* New York: Wiley. (p. 325)

Mischel, W. (1981). Current issues and challenges in personality. In L. T. Benjamin, Jr. (Ed.), The G. Stanley Hall Lecture Series (Vol. 1). Washington, DC: American Psychological Association. (p. 328)

Mischel, W. (1984). Convergences and challenges in the search for consistency. *American Psychologist, 39,* 351–364. (p. 325)

Mischel, W. (2004). Toward an integrative science of the person. *Annual Review of Psychology, 55,* 1–22. (p. 325)

Mischel, W., & Shoda, Y. (1995). A cognitive-affective system theory of personality: Reconceptualizing situations, dispositions, dynamics, and invariance in personality structure. *Psychological Review, 102,* 246–268. (p. 325)

Mischel, W., Shoda, Y., & Peake, P. K. (1988). The nature of adolescent competencies predicted by preschool delay of gratification. *Journal of Personality and Social Psychology, 54,* 687–696. (pp. 88, 176)

Mischel, W., Shoda, Y., & Rodriguez, M. L. (1989). Delay of gratification in children. *Science, 244,* 933–938. (pp. 88, 176)

Mishkin, M. (1982). A memory system in the monkey. *Philosophical Transactions of the Royal Society of London: Biological Sciences, 298,* 83–95. (p. 200)

Mishkin, M., Suzuki, W. A., Gadian, D. G., & Vargha-Khadem, F. (1997). Hierarchical organization of cognitive memory. *Philosophical Transactions of the Royal Society of London: Biological Sciences, 352,* 1461–1467. (p. 200)

Mita, T. H., Dermer, M., & Knight, J. (1977). Reversed facial images and the mere-exposure hypothesis. *Journal of Personality and Social Psychology, 35,* 597–601. (p. 360)

Mitani, J. C., Watts, D. P., & Amsler, S. J. (2010). Lethal intergroup aggression leads to territorial expansion in wild chimpanzees. *Current Biology, 20,* R507–R509. (p. 229)

Mitchell, K. J., & Porteous, D. J. (2011). Rethinking the genetic architecture of schizophrenia. *Psychological Medicine, 41,* 19–32. (p. 400)

Mitte, K. (2008). Memory bias for threatening information in anxiety and anxiety disorders: A meta-analytic review. *Psychological Bulletin, 134,* 886–911. (p. 376)

Mobbs, D., Yu, R., Meyer, M., Passamonti, L., Seymour, B., Calder, A. J., Schweizer, S., Frith, C. D., & Dalgeish, T. (2009). A key role for similarity in vicarious reward. *Science, 324,* 900. (p. 185)

Moffitt, T. E., Caspi, A., Harrington, H., & Milne, B. J. (2002). Males on the life-course-persistent and adolescence-limited antisocial pathways: Follow-up at age 26 years. *Development and Psychopathology, 14,* 179–207. (p. 102)

Moffitt, T. E., Caspi, A., Harrington, H., Milne, B. J., Melchior, M., Goldberg, D., & Poulton, R. (2007a). Generalized anxiety disorder and depression: Childhood risk factors in a birth cohort followed to age 32. *Psychological Medicine, 37,* 441–452. (p. 377)

Moffitt, T. E., Harrington, H., Caspi, A., Kim-Cohen, J., Goldberg, D., Gregory, A. M., & Poulton, R. (2007b). Depression and generalized anxiety disorder: Cumulative and sequential comorbidity in a birth cohort followed prospectively to age 32 years. *Archives of General Psychiatry, 64,* 651–660. (p. 377)

Moffitt, T. E., & 12 others. (2011). A gradient of childhood self-control predicts health, wealth, and public safety. *Proceedings of the National Academy of Sciences, 108,* 2693–2698. (p. 293)

Moghaddam, F. M. (2005). The staircase to terrorism: A psychological exploration. *American Psychologist, 60,* 161–169. (p. 348)

Mondloch, C. J., Lewis, T. L., Budreau, D. R., Maurer, D., Dannemiller, J. L., Stephens, B. R., & Kleiner-Gathercoal, K. A. (1999). Face perception during early infancy. *Psychological Science, 10,* 419–422. (p. 73)

Money, J. (1987). Sin, sickness, or status? Homosexual gender identity and psychoneuroendocrinology. *American Psychologist, 42,* 384–399. (p. 124)

Money, J., Berlin, F. S., Falck, A., & Stein, M. (1983). *Antiandrogenic and counseling treatment of sex offenders.* Baltimore: Department of Psychiatry and Behavioral Sciences, The Johns Hopkins University School of Medicine. (p. 116)

Montag, C., Weber, B., Trautner, P., Newport, B., Markett, S., Walter, N. T., Felten, A., & Reuter, M. (2012). Does excessive play of violent first-person-shooter-video-games dampen brain activity in response to emotional stimuli? *Biological Psychology, 89,* 107–111. (p. 357)

Montoya, E. R., Terburg, D., Box, P. A., & van Honk, J. (2012). Testosterone, cortisol, and serotonin as key regulators of social aggression: A review and theoretical perspective. *Motivation and Emotion, 36,* 65–73. (p. 354)

Moody, R. (1976). *Life after life.* Harrisburg, PA: Stackpole Books. (p. 387)

Mook, D. G. (1983). In defense of external invalidity. *American Psychologist, 38,* 379–387. (p. 21)

Moore, D. W. (2004, December 17). Sweet dreams go with a good night's sleep. *Gallup News Service* (www.gallup.com). (p. 55)

Moore, D. W. (2005, June 16). Three in four Americans believe in paranormal. *Gallup New Service* (www.gallup.com). (p. 161)

Moore, D. W. (2006, March 10). Close to 6 in 10 Americans want to lose weight. *Gallup News Service* (poll.gallup.com). (p. 263)

Morales, L. (2011, May 27). U.S. adults estimate that 25% of Americans are gay or lesbian. www.gallup.com. (p. 121)

More, H. L., Hutchinson, J. R., Collins, D. F., Weber, D. J., Aung, S. K. H., & Donelan, J. M. (2010). Scaling of sensorimotor control in terrestrial mammals. *Proceedings of the Royal Society B, 277,* 3563–3568. (p. 30)

Moreines, J. L., McClintock, S. M., & Holtzheimer, P. E. (2011). Neuropsychologic effects of neuromodulation techniques for treatment-resistant depression: A review. *Brain Stimulation, 4,* 17–27. (p. 428)

Moreira, M. T., Smith, L. A., & Foxcroft, D. (2009). Social norms interventions to reduce alcohol misuse in university or college students. *Cochrane Database of Systematic Reviews.* 2009, Issue 3., Art. No. C06748. (p. 389)

Moreland, R. L., & Beach, S. R. (1992). Exposure effects in the classroom: The development of affinity among students. *Journal of Experimental Social Psychology, 28,* 255–276. (p. 359)

Moreland, R. L., & Zajonc, R. B. (1982). Exposure effects in person perception: Familiarity, similarity, and attraction. *Journal of Experimental Social Psychology, 18,* 395–415. (p. 359)

Morelli, G. A., Rogoff, B., Oppenheim, D., & Goldsmith, D. (1992). Cultural variation in infants' sleeping arrangements: Questions of independence. *Developmental Psychology, 26,* 604–613. (p. 85)

Moreno, C., Laje, G., Blanco, C., Jiang, H., Schmidt, A. B., & Olfson, M. (2007). National trends in the outpatient diagnosis and treatment of bipolar disorder in youth. *Archives of General Psychiatry, 64,* 1032–1039. (p. 392)

Morey, R. A., Inan, S., Mitchell, T. V., Perkins, D. O., Lieberman, J. A., & Belger, A. (2005). Imaging frontostriatal function in ultra-high-risk, early, and chronic schizophrenia during executive processing. *Archives of General Psychiatry, 62,* 254–262. (p. 398)

Morgan, A. B., & Lilienfeld, S. O. (2000). A meta-analytic review of the relation between antisocial behavior and neuropsychological measures of executive function. *Clinical Psychology Review, 20,* 113–136. (p. 404)

Mori, K., & Mori, H. (2009). Another test of the passive facial feedback hypothesis: When your face smiles, you feel happy. *Perceptual and Motor Skills, 109,* 1–3. (p. 279)

Morrison, A. R. (2003). The brain on night shift. *Cerebrum, 5*(3), 23–36. (p. 55)

Mortensen, P. B. (1999). Effects of family history and place and season of birth on the risk of schizophrenia. *New England Journal of Medicine, 340,* 603–608. (p. 399)

Moruzzi, G., & Magoun, H. W. (1949). Brain stem reticular formation and activation of the EEG. *Electroencephalography and Clinical Neurophysiology, 1,* 455–473. (p. 39)

Moscovici, S. (1985). Social influence and conformity. In G. Lindzey & E. Aronson (Eds.), *The handbook of social psychology* (3rd ed). Hillsdale, NJ: Erlbaum. (p. 346)

Moses, E. B., & Barlow, D. H. (2006). A new unified treatment approach for emotional disorders based on emotion science. *Current Directions in Psychological Science, 15,* 146–150. (p. 418)

Mosher, C. E., & Danoff-Burg, S. (2008). Agentic and communal personality traits: Relations to disordered eating behavior, body shape concern, and depressive symptoms. *Eating Behaviors, 9,* 497–500. (p. 114)

Mosher, D. L., & Anderson, R. D. (1986). Macho personality, sexual aggression, and reactions to guided imagery of realistic rape. *Journal of Research in Personality, 20,* 77–94. (p. 382)

Mosing, M. A., Zietsch, B. P., Shekar, S. N., Wright, M. J., & Martin, N. G. (2009). Genetic and environmental influences on optimism and its relationship to mental and self-rated health: A study of aging twins. *Behavior Genetics, 39,* 597–604. (p. 294)

Moss, H. A., & Susman, E. J. (1980). Longitudinal study of personality development. In O. G. Brim, Jr., & J. Kagan (Eds.), *Constancy and change in human development.* Cambridge, MA: Harvard University Press. (p. 102)

Moyer, K. E. (1983). The physiology of motivation: Aggression as a model. In C. J. Scheier & A. M. Rogers (Eds.), G. Stanley Hall Lecture Series (Vol. 3). Washington, DC: American Psychological Association. (p. 355)

Mroczek, D. K., & Spiro, A., III. (2003). Modeling intra-individual change in personality traits: Findings from the Normative Aging Study. *Journals of Gerontology: Series B. Psychological Sciences and Social Sciences, 58,* P153–P165. (p. 324)

Mroczek, D. K., & Spiro, A., III. (2005). Change in life satisfaction during adulthood: Findings from the Veterans Affairs normative aging study. *Journal of Personality and Social Psychology, 88,* 189–202. (p. 305)

Muller, J. E., Mittleman, M. A., Maclure, M., Sherwood, J. B., & Tofler, G. H. (1996). Triggering myocardial infarction by sexual activity. *Journal of the American Medical Association, 275,* 1405–1409. (p. 116)

Muller, J. E., & Verrier, R. L. (1996). Triggering of sudden death—Lessons from an earthquake. *New England Journal of Medicine, 334,* 461. (p. 285)

Mullin, C. R., & Linz, D. (1995). Desensitization and resensitization to violence against women: Effects of exposure to sexually violent films on judgments of domestic violence victims. *Journal of Personality and Social Psychology, 69*, 449–459. (p. 188)

Murray, H. A. (1938). *Explorations in personality.* New York: Oxford University Press. (p. B-3)

Murray, H. A., & Wheeler, D. R. (1937). A note on the possible clairvoyance of dreams. *Journal of Psychology, 3*, 309–313. (p. 162)

Murray, R., Jones, P., O'Callaghan, E., Takei, N., & Sham, P. (1992). Genes, viruses, and neurodevelopmental schizophrenia. *Journal of Psychiatric Research, 26*, 225–235. (p. 399)

Murray, R. M., Morrison, P. D., Henquet, C., & Di Forti, M. (2007). Cannabis, the mind and society: The hash realities. *Nature Reviews: Neuroscience, 8*, 885–895. (p. 388)

Murray, S. L., Bellavia, G. M., Rose, P., & Griffin, D. W. (2003). Once hurt, twice hurtful: How perceived regard regulates daily marital interactions. *Journal of Personality and Social Psychology, 84*, 126–147. (p. 139)

Musick, M. A., Herzog, A. R., & House, J. S. (1999). Volunteering and mortality among older adults: Findings from a national sample. *Journals of Gerontology, 54B*, 173–180. (p. 300)

Mustanski, B. S., & Bailey, J. M. (2003). A therapist's guide to the genetics of human sexual orientation. *Sexual and Relationship Therapy, 18*, 1468–1479. (p. 123)

Myers, D. G. (1993). *The pursuit of happiness.* New York: Harper. (pp. 305, 306)

Myers, D. G. (2000). *The American paradox: Spiritual hunger in an age of plenty.* New Haven, CT: Yale University Press. (p. 305)

Myers, D. G. (2001, December). Do we fear the right things? *American Psychological Society Observer,* p. 3. (p. 224)

Myers, D. G. (2002). *Intuition: Its powers and perils.* New Haven, CT: Yale University Press. (p. 11)

Myers, D. G. (2010). *Social psychology* (10th ed.). New York: McGraw-Hill. (p. 330)

Myers, D. G., & Bishop, G. D. (1970). Discussion effects on racial attitudes. *Science, 169*, 778–779. (p. 348)

Myers, D. G., & Diener, E. (1995). Who is happy? *Psychological Science, 6*, 10–19. (p. 305)

Myers, D. G., & Diener, E. (1996, May). The pursuit of happiness. *Scientific American.* (p. 305)

Myers, D. G., & Scanzoni, L. D. (2005). *What God has joined together?* San Francisco: HarperSanFrancisco. (p. 121)

Myers, T. A., & Crowther, J. H. (2009). Social comparison as a predictor of body dissatisfaction: A meta-analytic review. *Journal of Abnormal Psychology, 118*, 683–698. (p. 401)

Mykletun, A., Bjerkeset, O., Øverland, S., & Prince, M. (2009). Levels of anxiety and depression as predictors of mortality: The HUNT study. *British Journal of Psychiatry, 195*, 118–125. (p. 290)

Nagourney, A. (2002, September 25). For remarks on Iraq, Gore gets praise and scorn. *New York Times* (www.nytimes.com). (p. 339)

Nanni, V., Uher, R., & Danese, A. (2012). Childhood maltreatment predicts unfavorable course of illness and treatment outcome in depression: A meta-analysis. *American Journal of Psychiatry, 169*, 141–151. (p. 83)

Napolitan, D. A., & Goethals, G. R. (1979). The attribution of friendliness. *Journal of Experimental Social Psychology, 15*, 105–113. (p. 338)

Narvaez, D. (2010). Moral complexity: The fatal attraction of truthiness and the importance of mature moral functioning. *Perspectives on Psychological Science, 5*, 163–181. (p. 88)

National Academy of Sciences. (2001). *Exploring the biological contributions to human health: Does sex matter?* Washington, DC: Institute of Medicine, National Academy Press. (p. 112)

National Center for Health Statistics. (1990). *Health, United States, 1989.* Washington, DC: U.S. Department of Health and Human Services. (p. 96)

National Center for Health Statistics. (2004, December 15). Marital status and health: United States, 1999–2002 (by Charlotte A. Schoenborn). *Advance Data from Vital and Human Statistics, number 351.* Centers for Disease Control and Prevention. (p. 295)

National Institute of Mental Health. (2008). *The numbers count: Mental disorders in America.* (nimh.nih.gov). (p. 371)

National Institute of Mental Health. (2012, accessed October 30). The numbers count: Mental disorders in America (citing a 2005 analysis). www.nimh.nih.gov/health/publications/the-numbers-count-mental-disorders-in-america/index.shtml. (p. 371)

National Safety Council. (2010, January 12). *NSC estimates 1.6 million crashes caused by cell phone use and texting.* www.nsc.org. (p. 51)

National Sleep Foundation. (2009) *2009 sleep in America poll: Summary of findings.* Washington, DC: National Sleep Foundation (www.sleepfoundation.org). (p. 59)

Naumann, L. P., Vazire, S., Rentfrow, P. J., & Gosling, S. D. (2009). Personality judgments based on physical appearance. *Personality and Social Psychology Bulletin, 35*, 1661–1671. (p. 326)

Nayak, M. B., Byrne, C. A., Martin, M. K., & Abraham, A. G. (2003). Attitudes toward violence against women: A cross-nation study. *Sex Roles, 9*, 333–342. (p. 356)

Nazimek, J. (2009). Active body, healthy mind. *The Psychologist, 22*, 206–208. (p. 95)

Nedeltcheva, A. V., Kilkus, J. M., Imperial, J., Schoeller, D. A., & Penev, P. D. (2010). Insufficient sleep undermines dietary efforts to reduce adiposity. *Annals of Internal Medicine, 153*, 435–441. (p. 262)

NEEF. (2011; undated, accessed 17 June 2011). *Fact sheet: children's health and nature.* National Environmental Education Foundation (www.neefusa.org). (p. 430)

Neese, R. M. (1991, November/December). What good is feeling bad? The evolutionary benefits of psychic pain. *The Sciences*, pp. 30–37. (pp. 154, 182)

Neidorf, S., & Morin, R. (2007, May 23). Four-in-ten Americans have close friends or relatives who are gay. *Pew Research Center Publications* (pewresearch.org). (p. 366)

Neimeyer, R. A., & Currier, J. M. (2009). Grief therapy: Evidence of efficacy and emerging directions. *Current Directions in Psychological Science, 18*, 352–356. (p. 101)

Neisser, U. (1979). The control of information pickup in selective looking. In A. D. Pick (Ed.), *Perception and its development: A tribute to Eleanor J. Gibson.* Hillsdale, NJ: Erlbaum. (p. 51)

Neitz, J., Carroll, J., & Neitz, M. (2001). Color vision: Almost reason enough for having eyes. *Optics & Photonics News 12*, 26–33. (p. 144)

Nelson, C. A., III, Furtado, E. Z., Fox, N. A., & Zeanah, C. H., Jr. (2009). The deprived human brain. *American Scientist, 97*, 222–229. (p. 83)

Nelson, M. D., Saykin, A. J., Flashman, L. A., & Riordan, H. J. (1998). Hippocampal volume reduction in schizophrenia as assessed by magnetic resonance imaging. *Archives of General Psychiatry, 55*, 433–440. (p. 398)

Neria, Y., DiGrande, L., & Adams, B. G. (2011). Posttraumatic stress disorder following the September 11, 2001, terrorist attacks: A review of the literature among highly exposed populations. *American Psychologist, 66,* 429–446. (p. 379)

Nes, R. B. (2010). Happiness in behaviour genetics: Findings and implications. *Journal of Happiness Studies, 11,* 369–381. (p. 306)

Nesca, M., & Koulack, D. (1994). Recognition memory, sleep and circadian rhythms. *Canadian Journal of Experimental Psychology, 48,* 359–379. (p. 208)

Nestler, E. J. (2011, December). Hidden switches in the mind. *Scientific American,* pp. 77–83. (p. 395)

Nestoriuc, Y., Rief, W., & Martin, A. (2008). Meta-analysis of biofeedback for tension-type headache: Efficacy, specificity, and treatment moderators. *Journal of Consulting and Clinical Psychology, 76,* 379–396. (p. 298)

Neubauer, D. N. (1999). Sleep problems in the elderly. *American Family Physician, 59,* 2551–2558. (p. 54)

Neumann, R., & Strack, F. (2000). "Mood contagion": The automatic transfer of mood between persons. *Journal of Personality and Social Psychology, 79,* 211–223. (p. 278)

Nevicka, B., Ten Velden, F. S., De Hoogh, A. H. B., & Van Vianen, A. E. M. (2011). Reality at odds with perceptions: Narcissistic leaders and group performance. *Psychological Science, 22,* 1259–1264. (p. 330)

Newcomb, M. D., & Harlow, L. L. (1986). Life events and substance use among adolescents: Mediating effects of perceived loss of control and meaninglessness in life. *Journal of Personality and Social Psychology, 51,* 564–577. (p. 389)

Newport, F. (2001, February). Americans see women as emotional and affectionate, men as more aggressive. *The Gallup Poll Monthly,* pp. 34–38. (p. 275)

Newport, F. (2002, July 29). Bush job approval update. *Gallup News Service* (www.gallup.com/poll/releases/pr020729.asp). (p. 366)

Newport, F., Argrawal, S., & Witters, D. (2010, December 23). Very religious Americans lead healthier lives. *Gallup* (www.gallup.com). (p. 300)

Newport, F., Jones, J. M., Saad, L., & Carroll, J. (2007, April 27). Gallup poll review: 10 key points about public opinion on Iraq. *The Gallup Poll* (www.gallluppoll.com). (p. 109)

Newport, F., & Pelham, B. (2009, December 14). Don't worry, be 80: Worry and stress decline with age. www.gallup.com. (p. 284)

Ng, T. W. H., Sorensen, K. L., & Eby, L. T. (2006). Locus of control at work: A meta-analysis. *Journal of Organizational Behavior, 27,* 1057–1087. (p. 293)

Ng, T. W. H., Sorensen, K. L., & Yim, F. H. K. (2009). Does the job satisfaction–job performance relationship vary across cultures? *Journal of Cross-Cultural Psychology, 40,* 761–796. (p. B-4)

Nickell, J. (Ed.) (1994). *Psychic sleuths: ESP and sensational cases.* Buffalo, New York: Prometheus Books. (p. 162)

Nickell, J. (2005, July/August). The case of the psychic detectives. *Skeptical Inquirer* (skeptically.org/skepticism/id10.html). (p. 162)

Nickerson, R. S. (2002). The production and perception of randomness. *Psychological Review, 109,* 330–357. (p. 10)

Nickerson, R. S. (2005). Bertrand's chord, Buffon's needles, and the concept of randomness. *Thinking & Reasoning, 11,* 67–96. (p. 10)

NIDA. (2002). Methamphetamine abuse and addiction. *Research Report Series.* National Institute on Drug Abuse, NIH Publication Number 02–4210. (p. 384)

NIDA. (2005, May). Methamphetamine. *NIDA Info Facts.* National Institute on Drug Abuse. (p. 384)

NIDCD. (2011). Quick statistics. National Institute on Deafness and Other Communication Disorders (www.nidcd.nih.gov). (p. 153)

Nie, N. H. (2001). Sociability, interpersonal relations and the Internet: Reconciling conflicting findings. *American Behavioral Scientist, 45,* 420–435. (p. 267)

NIH. (2001, July 20). *Workshop summary: Scientific evidence on condom effectiveness for sexually transmitted disease (STD) prevention.* Bethesda: National Institute of Allergy and Infectious Diseases, National Institutes of Health. (p. 117)

NIH. (2006, December 4). NIDA researchers complete unprecedented scan of human genome that may help unlock the genetic contribution to tobacco addiction. *NIH News,* National Institutes of Health (www.nih.gov). (p. 388)

NIH. (2010). *Teacher's guide: Information about sleep.* National Institutes of Health (www.science.education.nih.gov). (p. 56)

Nikolas, M. A., & Burt, A. (2010). Genetic and environmental influences on ADHD symptom dimensions of inattention and hyperactivity: A meta-analysis. *Journal of Abnormal Psychology, 119,* 1–17. (p. 373)

Nisbett, R. E. (2003). *The geography of thought: How Asians and Westerners think differently...and why.* New York: Free Press. (p. 338)

Nixon, G. M., Thompson, J. M. D., Han, D. Y., Becroft, D. M., Clark, P. M., Robinson, E., Waldie, K E., Wild, C. J., Black, P. N., & Mitchell, E. A. (2008). Short sleep duration in middle childhood: Risk factors and consequences. *Sleep, 31,* 71–78. (p. 58)

Nizzi, M. C., Demertzi, A., Gosseries, O., Bruno, M. A., Jouen, F., & Laureys, S. (2012). From armchair to wheelchair: How patients with a locked-in syndrome integrate bodily changes in experienced identity. *Consciousness and Cognition, 21,* 431–437. (p. 302)

Nock, M. K. (2010). Self-injury. *Annual Review of Clinical Psychology, 6,* 339–363. (p. 392)

Nock, M. K., & Kessler, R. C. (2006). Prevalence of and risk factors for suicide attempts versus suicide gestures: Analysis of the National Comorbidity Survey. *Journal of Abnormal Psychology, 115,* 616–623. (p. 392)

Nolen-Hoeksema, S. (2001). Gender differences in depression. *Current Directions in Psychological Science, 10,* 173–176. (p. 395)

Nolen-Hoeksema, S. (2003). *Women who think too much: How to break free of overthinking and reclaim your life.* New York: Holt. (p. 395)

Nolen-Hoeksema, S., & Larson, J. (1999). *Coping with loss.* Mahwah, NJ: Erlbaum. (p. 101)

NORC. (2007). National Opinion Research Center (University of Chicago) General Social Survey data, 1972 through 2004, accessed via sda.berkeley.edu. (p. 265)

Norem, J. K. (2001). *The positive power of negative thinking: Using defensive pessimism to harness anxiety and perform at your peak.* New York: Basic Books. (p. 294)

Norton, M. I., & Ariely, D. (2011). Building a better America—One wealth quintile at a time. *Perspectives on Psychological Science, 6,* 9–12. (p. A-1)

Nowak, R. (1994). Nicotine scrutinized as FDA seeks to regulate cigarettes. *Science, 263,* 1555–1556. (p. 385)

NPR. (2009, July 11). Afraid to fly? Try living on a plane. www.npr.org. (p. 173)

Nurmikko, A. V., Donoghue, J. P., Hochberg, L. R., Patterson, W. R., Song, Y-K., Bull, C. W., Borton, D. A., Laiwalla, F., Park, S., Ming, Y., & Aceros, J. (2010). Listening to brain microcircuits for interfacing with external world—Progress in wireless implantable microelectronic neuroengineering devices. *Proceedings of the IEEE, 98,* 375–388. (p. 44)

Nurnberger, J. I., Jr., & Bierut, L. J. (2007, April). Seeking the connections: Alcoholism and our genes. *Scientific American,* pp. 46–53. (p. 388)

Nussinovitch, U., & Shoenfeld, Y. (2012). The role of gender and organ specific autoimmunity. *Autoimmunity Reviews, 11,* A377–A385. (p. 287)

Nuttin, J. M., Jr. (1987). Affective consequences of mere ownership: The name letter effect in twelve European languages. *European Journal of Social Psychology, 17,* 381–402. (p. 359)

Oaten, M., & Cheng, K. (2006a). Longitudinal gains in self-regulation from regular physical exercise. *British Journal of Health Psychology, 11,* 717–733. (p. 293)

Oaten, M., & Cheng, K. (2006b). Improved self-control: The benefits of a regular program of academic study. *Basic and Applied Social Psychology, 28,* 1–16. (p. 293)

Oberlander, J., & Gill, A. J. (2006). Language with character: A stratified corpus comparison of individual differences in e-mail communication. *Discourse Processes, 42,* 239–270. (p. 326)

O'Boyle, E. H., Jr., Humphrey, R. H., Pollack, J. M., Hawyer, T. H., & Story, P. A. (2011). The relation between emotional intelligence and job performance: A meta-analysis. *Journal of Organizational Behavior, 32,* 788–818. (p. 238)

O'Connor, P., & Brown, G. W. (1984). Supportive relationships: Fact or fancy? *Journal of Social and Personal Relationships, 1,* 159–175. (p. 423)

O'Donnell, L., Stueve, A., O'Donnell, C., Duran, R., San Doval, A., Wilson, R. F., Haber, D., Perry, E., & Pleck, J. H. (2002). Long-term reduction in sexual initiation and sexual activity among urban middle schoolers in the reach for health service learning program. *Journal of Adolescent Health, 31,* 93–100. (p. 119)

O'Donovan, A., Neylan, T. C., Metzler, T., & Cohen, B. E. (2012). Lifetime exposure to traumatic psychological stress is associated with elevated inflammation in the Heart and Soul Study. *Brain, Behavior, and Immunity, 26,* 642–649. (p. 289)

Offer, D., Ostrov, E., Howard, K. I., & Atkinson, R. (1988). *The teenage world: Adolescents' self-image in ten countries.* New York: Plenum. (p. 90)

Ogden, J. (2012, January 16). HM, the man with no memory. www.psychologytoday.com. (p. 193)

Öhman, A. (1986). Face the beast and fear the face: Animal and social fears as prototypes for evolutionary analyses of emotion. *Psychophysiology, 23,* 123–145. (p. 381)

Öhman, A., Lundqvist, D., & Esteves, F. (2001). The face in the crowd revisited: A threat advantage with schematic stimuli. *Journal of Personality and Social Psychology, 80,* 381–396. (p. 275)

Oishi, S., Diener, E. F., Lucas, R. E., & Suh, E. M. (1999). Cross-cultural variations in predictors of life satisfaction: Perspectives from needs and values. *Personality and Social Psychology Bulletin, 25,* 980–990. (p. 258)

Oishi, S., Kesebir, S., & Diener, E. (2011). Income inequality and happiness. *Psychological Science, 22,* 1095–1100. (p. 356)

Oishi, S., & Schimmack, U. (2010). Culture and well-being: A new inquiry into the psychological wealth of nations. *Perspectives in Psychological Science, 5,* 463–471. (p. 305)

Okimoto, T. G., & Brescoll, V. L. (2010). The price of power: Power seeking and backlash against female politicians. *Personality and Social Psychology Bulletin, 36,* 923–936. (p. 109)

Olds, J. (1975). Mapping the mind onto the brain. In F. G. Worden, J. P. Swazey, & G. Adelman (Eds.), *The neurosciences: Paths of discovery.* Cambridge, MA: MIT Press. (p. 41)

Olds, J., & Milner, P. (1954). Positive reinforcement produced by electrical stimulation of the septal area and other regions of rat brain. *Journal of Comparative and Physiological Psychology, 47,* 419–427. (p. 41)

Olff, M., Langeland, W., Draijer, N., & Gersons, B. P. R. (2007). Gender differences in posttraumatic stress disorder. *Psychological Bulletin, 135,* 183–204. (p. 379)

Olfson, M., & Marcus, S. C. (2009). National patterns in antidepressant medication treatment. *Archives of General Psychiatry, 66,* 848–856. (pp. 425, 427)

Oliner, S. P., & Oliner, P. M. (1988). *The altruistic personality: Rescuers of Jews in Nazi Europe.* New York: Free Press. (p. 186)

Olsson, A., Nearing, K. I., & Phelps, E. A. (2007). Learning fears by observing others: The neural systems of social fear transmission. *Social Cognitive and Affective Neuroscience, 2,* 3–11. (p. 380)

Olweus, D., Mattsson, A., Schalling, D., & Low, H. (1988). Circulating testosterone levels and aggression in adolescent males: A causal analysis. *Psychosomatic Medicine, 50,* 261–272. (p. 354)

Oman, D., Kurata, J. H., Strawbridge, W. J., & Cohen, R. D. (2002). Religious attendance and cause of death over 31 years. *International Journal of Psychiatry in Medicine, 32,* 69–89. (p. 300)

Oppenheimer, D. M., & Trail, T. E. (2010). Why leaning to the left makes you lean to the left: Effects of spatial orientation on political attitudes. *Social Cognition, 28,* 651–661. (p. 161)

Orth, U., Robins, R. W., & Roberts, B. W. (2008). Low self-esteem prospectively predicts depression in adolescence and young adulthood. *Journal of Personality and Social Psychology, 95,* 695–708. (p. 329)

Orth, U., Robins, R. W., Trzesniewski, K. H., Maes, J., & Schmitt, M. (2009). Low self-esteem is a risk factor for depressive symptoms from young adulthood to old age. *Journal of Abnormal Psychology, 118,* 472–478. (p. 329)

Osborne, L. (1999, October 27). A linguistic big bang. *New York Times Magazine* (www.nytimes.com). (p. 231)

Oskarsson, A. T., Van Voven, L., McClelland, G. H., & Hastie, R. (2009). What's next? Judging sequences of binary events. *Psychological Bulletin, 135,* 262–285. (p. 10)

Ost, L. G., & Hugdahl, K. (1981). Acquisition of phobias and anxiety response patterns in clinical patients. *Behaviour Research and Therapy, 16,* 439–447. (p. 380)

Ostfeld, A. M., Kasl, S. V., D'Atri, D. A., & Fitzgerald, E. F. (1987). *Stress, crowding, and blood pressure in prison.* Hillsdale, NJ: Erlbaum. (p. 292)

O'Sullivan, M., Frank, M. G., Hurley, C. M., & Tiwana, J. (2009). Police lie detection accuracy: The effect of lie scenario. *Law and Human Behavior, 33,* 530–538. (p. 275)

Osvath, M. (2009). Spontaneous planning for future stone throwing by a male chimpanzee. *Current Biology, 19,* R190–R191. (p. 229)

Ott, B. (2007, June 14). Investors, take note: Engagement boosts earnings. *Gallup Management Journal* (gmj.gallup.com). (p. B-5)

Ott, C. H., Lueger, R. J., Kelber, S. T., & Prigerson, H. G. (2007). Spousal bereavement in older adults: Common, resilient, and chronic grief with defining characteristics. *Journal of Nervous and Mental Disease, 195,* 332–341. (p. 101)

Ouellette, J. A., & Wood, W. (1998). Habit and intention in everyday life: The multiple processes by which past behavior predicts future behavior. *Psychological Bulletin, 124,* 54–74. (p. 328)

Owen, A. M., Coleman, M. R., Boly, M., Davis, M. H., Laureys, S., & Pickard, J. D. (2006). Detecting awareness in the vegetative state. *Science, 313,* 1402. (p. 37)

Owen, R. (1814). First essay in *New view of society, Or the formation of character.* Quoted in *The story of New Lanark Mills,* Lanark, Scotland: New Lanark Conservation Trust, 1993. (p. B-7)

Owens, J. A., Belon, K., & Moss, P. (2010). Impact of delaying school start time on adolescent sleep, mood, and behavior. *Archives of Pediatric Adolescent Medicine, 164*, 608–614. (p. 97)

Oxfam. (2005, March 26). *Three months on: New figures show tsunami may have killed up to four times as many women as men.* Oxfam Press Release (www.oxfam.org.uk). (p. 113)

Ozer, E. J., Best, S. R., Lipsey, T. L., & Weiss, D. S. (2003). Predictors of posttraumatic stress disorder and symptoms in adults: A meta-analysis. *Psychological Bulletin, 1*(9), 52–73. (p. 379)

Ozer, E. J., & Weiss, D. S. (2004). Who develops posttraumatic stress disorder? *Current Directions in Psychological Science, 13*, 169–172. (p. 379)

Pacifici, R., Zuccaro, P., Farre, M., Pichini, S., Di Carlo, S., Roset, P. N., Ortuno, J., Pujadas, M., Bacosi, A., Menoyo, E., Segura, J., & de la Torre, R. (2001). Effects of repeated doses of MDMA ("Ecstasy") on cell-mediated immune response in humans. *Life Sciences, 69*, 2931–2941. (p. 386)

Padgett, V. R. (1989). Predicting organizational violence: An application of 11 powerful principles of obedience. Paper presented to the American Psychological Association convention. (p. 345)

Pagani, L. S., Fitzpatrick, C., Barnett, T. A., & Dubow, E. (2010). Prospective associations between early childhood television exposure and academic, psychosocial, and physical well-being by middle childhood. *Archivers of Pediatric and Adolescent Medicine, 164*, 425–431. (p. 264)

Pallier, C., Colomé, A., & Sebastián-Gallés, N. (2001). The influence of native-language phonology on lexical access: Exemplar-based versus abstract lexical entries. *Psychological Science, 12*, 445–448. (p. 230)

Pandey, J., Sinha, Y., Prakash, A., & Tripathi, R. C. (1982). Right-left political ideologies and attribution of the causes of poverty. *European Journal of Social Psychology, 12*, 327–331. (p. 339)

Panksepp, J. (2007). Neurologizing the psychology of affects: How appraisal-based constructivism and basic emotion theory can coexist. *Perspectives on Psychological Science, 2*, 281–295. (p. 273)

Panzarella, C., Alloy, L. B., & Whitehouse, W. G. (2006). Expanded hopelessness theory of depression: On the mechanisms by which social support protects against depression. *Cognitive Theory and Research, 30*, 307–333. (p. 395)

Park, C. L., Riley, K. E., & Snyder, L. B. (2012). Meaning making coping, making sense, and post-traumatic growth following the 9/11 terrorist attacks. *The Journal of Positive Psychology, 7*, 198–207. (p. 432)

Park, D. C., Lautenschlager, G., Hedden, T., Davidson, N. S., Smith, A. D., & Smith, P. K. (2002). Models of visuospatial and verbal memory across the adult life span. *Psychology and Aging, 17*, 299–320. (p. 246)

Park, G., Lubinski, D., & Benbow, C. P. (2007). Contrasting intellectual patterns predict creativity in the arts and sciences. *Psychological Science, 18*, 948–952. (p. 242)

Park, G., Lubinski, D., & Benbow, C. P. (2008). Ability differences among people who have commensurate degrees matter for scientific creativity. *Psychological Science, 19*, 957–961. (p. 226)

Park, R. L. (1999). Liars never break a sweat. *New York Times*, July 12, 1999 (www.nytimes.com). (p. 274)

Parker, C. P., Baltes, B. B., Young, S. A., Huff, J. W., Altmann, R. A., LaCost, H. A., & Roberts, J. E. (2003). Relationships between psychological climate perceptions and work outcomes: A meta-analytic review. *Journal of Organizational Behavior, 24*, 389–416. (p. B-4)

Parker, E. S., Cahill, L., & McGaugh, J. L. (2006). A case of unusual autobiographical remembering. *Neurocase, 12*, 35–49. (p. 206)

Parsons, T. D., & Rizzo, A. A. (2008). Affective outcomes of virtual reality exposure therapy for anxiety and specific phobias: A meta-analysis. *Journal of Behavior Therapy and Experimental Psychiatry, 39*, 250–261. (p. 415)

Pascoe, E. A., & Richman, L. S. (2009). Perceived discrimination and health: A meta-analytic review. *Psychological Bulletin, 135*, 531–554. (p. 285)

Patel, S. R., Malhotra, A., White, D. P., Gottlieb, D. J., & Hu, F. B. (2006). Association between reduced sleep and weight gain in women. *American Journal of Epidemiology, 164*, 947–954. (p. 58)

Patrick, H., Knee, C. R., Canevello, A., & Lonsbary, C. (2007). The role of need fulfillment in relationship functioning and well-being: A self-determination theory perspective. *Journal of Personality and Social Psychology, 92*, 434–457. (p. 264)

Patterson, F. (1978, October). Conversations with a gorilla. *National Geographic*, pp. 438–465. (p. 234)

Patterson, G. R., Chamberlain, P., & Reid, J. B. (1982). A comparative evaluation of parent training procedures. *Behavior Therapy, 13*, 638–650. (pp. 179, 356)

Patterson, G. R., Reid, J. B., & Dishion, T. J. (1992). *Antisocial boys.* Eugene, OR: Castalia. (p. 356)

Patterson, M., Warr, P., & West, M. (2004). Organizational climate and company productivity: The role of employee affect and employee level. *Journal of Occupational and Organizational Psychology, 77*, 193–216. (p. B-4)

Patterson, P. H. (2007). Maternal effects on schizophrenia risk. *Science, 318*, 576–577. (p. 399)

Patton, G. C., Coffey, C., Carlin, J. B., Degenhardt, L., Lynskey, M., & Hall, W. (2002). Cannabis use and mental health of young people: Cohort study. *British Medical Journal, 325*, 1195–1198. (p. 388)

Pauker, K., Weisbuch, M., Ambady, N., Sommers, S. R., Adams, R. B., Jr., & Ivcevic, Z. (2009). Not so Black and White: Memory for ambiguous group members. *Journal of Personality and Social Psychology, 96*, 795–810. (p. 248)

Paus, T., Zijdenbos, A., Worsley, K., Collins, D. L., Blumenthal, J., Giedd, J. N., Rapoport, J. L., & Evans, A. C. (1999). Structural maturation of neural pathways in children and adolescents: In vivo study. *Science, 283*, 1908–1911. (p. 74)

Pavlov, I. (1927). *Conditioned reflexes: An investigation of the physiological activity of the cerebral cortex.* Oxford: Oxford University Press. (p. 169)

Payne, B. K., & Corrigan, E. (2007). Emotional constraints on intentional forgetting. *Journal of Experimental Social Psychology, 43*, 780–786. (p. 209)

Pazda, A. D., & Elliot, A. J. (2012). The color of attraction: How red influences physical appeal. In M. Paludi (Ed.), *The Psychology of Love.* Santa Barbara, CA: Praeger. (p. 182)

Peckham, A. D., McHugh, R. K., & Otto, M. W. (2010). A meta-analysis of the magnitude of biased attention in depression. *Depression and Anxiety, 27*, 1135–1142. (p. 393)

Peigneux, P., Laureys, S., Fuchs, S., Collette, F., Perrin, F., Reggers, J., Phillips, C., Degueldre, C., Del Fiore, G., Aerts, J., Luxen, A., & Maquet, P. (2004). Are spatial memories strengthened in the human hippocampus during slow wave sleep? *Neuron, 44*, 535–545. (p. 56)

Pelham, B., & Crabtree, S. (2008, October 8). Worldwide, highly religious more likely to help others. Gallup Poll (www.gallup.com). (p. 365)

Pelham, B. W. (1993). On the highly positive thoughts of the highly depressed. In R. F. Baumeister (Ed.), *Self-esteem: The puzzle of low self-regard.* New York: Plenum. (p. 330)

Pelham, B. W. (2009, October 22). About one in six Americans report history of depression. *Gallup* (www.gallup.com). (p. 393)

Pennebaker, J. W. (1990). *Opening up: The healing power of confiding in others.* New York: William Morrow. (p. 318)

Pennebaker, J. W. (2002, January 28). Personal communication. (p. 366)

Pennebaker, J. W., Barger, S. D., & Tiebout, J. (1989). Disclosure of traumas and health among Holocaust survivors. *Psychosomatic Medicine, 51,* 577–589. (p. 296)

Pennebaker, J. W., & O'Heeron, R. C. (1984). Confiding in others and illness rate among spouses of suicide and accidental death victims. *Journal of Abnormal Psychology, 93,* 473–476. (p. 296)

Pennebaker, J. W., & Stone, L. D. (2003). Words of wisdom: Language use over the life span. *Journal of Personality and Social Psychology, 85,* 291–301. (p. 100)

Peplau, L. A., & Fingerhut, A. W. (2007). The close relationships of lesbians and gay men. *Annual Review of Psychology, 58,* 405–424. (pp. 98, 125)

Peplau, L. A., & Garnets, L. D. (2000). A new paradigm for understanding women's sexuality and sexual orientation. *Journal of Social Issues, 56,* 329–350. (p. 121)

Peppard, P. E., Szklo-Coxe, M., Hla, K. M., & Young, T. (2006). Longitudinal association of sleep-related breathing disorder and depression. *Archives of Internal Medicine, 166,* 1709–1715. (p. 59)

Pepperberg, I. M. (2006). Grey parrot numerical competence: A review. *Animal Cognition, 9,* 377–391. (p. 228)

Pepperberg, I. M. (2009). *Alex & me: How a scientist and a parrot discovered a hidden world of animal intelligence—and formed a deep bond in the process.* New York: Harper. (p. 228)

Perani, D., & Abutalebi, J. (2005). The neural basis of first and second language processing. *Current Opinion in Neurobiology, 15,* 202–206. (p. 233)

Pereg, D., Gow, R., Mosseri, M., Lishner, M., Rieder, M., Van Uum, S., & Koren, G. (2011). Hair cortisol and the risk for acute myocardial infarction in adult men. *Stress, 14,* 73–81. (p. 289)

Pereira, A. C., Huddleston, D. E., Brickman, A. M., Sosunov, A. A., Hen, R., McKhann, G. M., Sloan, R., Gage, F. H., Brown, T. R., & Small, S. A. (2007). An *in vivo* correlate of exercise-induced neurogenesis in the adult dentate gyrus. *Proceedings of the National Academic of Sciences, 104,* 5638–5643. (pp. 95, 96)

Pereira, G. M., & Osburn, H. G. (2007). Effects of participation in decision making on performance and employee attitudes: A quality circles meta-analysis. *Journal of Business Psychology, 22,* 145–153. (p. B-7)

Pergadia, M. L., & 30 others. (2011). A 3p26-3p25 genetic linkage finding for DSM-IV major depression in heavy smoking families. *American Journal of Psychiatry. 168,* 848–852. (p. 395)

Perilloux, H. K., Webster, G. D., & Gaulin, S. J. (2010). Signals of genetic quality and maternal investment capacity: The dynamic effects of fluctuating asymmetry and waist-to-hip ratio on men's ratings of women's attractiveness. *Social Psychological and Personalty Science, 1,* 34–42. (pp. 127, 360)

Perkins, A., & Fitzgerald, J. A. (1997). Sexual orientation in domestic rams: Some biological and social correlates. In L. Ellis & L. Ebertz (Eds.), *Sexual orientation: Toward biological understanding.* Westport, CT: Praeger Publishers. (p. 122)

Person, C., Tracy, M., & Galea, S. (2006). Risk factors for depression after a disaster. *Journal of Nervous and Mental Disease, 194,* 659–666. (p. 432)

Pert, C. B., & Snyder, S. H. (1973). Opiate receptor: Demonstration in nervous tissue. *Science, 179,* 1011–1014. (p. 32)

Perugini, E. M., Kirsch, I., Allen, S. T., Coldwell, E., Meredith, J., Montgomery, G. H., & Sheehan, J. (1998). Surreptitious observation of responses to hypnotically suggested hallucinations: A test of the compliance hypothesis. *International Journal of Clinical and Experimental Hypnosis, 46,* 191–203. (p. 156)

Peschel, E. R., & Peschel, R. E. (1987). Medical insights into the castrati in opera. *American Scientist, 75,* 578–583. (p. 116)

Peters, M., Rhodes, G., & Simmons, L. W. (2007). Contributions of the face and body to overall attractiveness. *Animal Behaviour, 73,* 937–942. (p. 361)

Peters, T. J., & Waterman, R. H., Jr. (1982). *In search of excellence: Lessons from America's best-run companies.* New York: Harper & Row. (p. 180)

Petersen, J. L., & Hyde, J. S. (2011). Gender differences in sexual attitudes and behaviors: A review of meta-analytic results and large datasets. *Journal of Sex Research, 48,* 149–165. (p. 115)

Peterson, C., Peterson, J., & Skevington, S. (1986). Heated argument and adolescent development. *Journal of Social and Personal Relationships, 3,* 229–240. (p. 87)

Peterson, L. R., & Peterson, M. J. (1959). Short-term retention of individual verbal items. *Journal of Experimental Psychology, 58,* 193–198. (pp. 196, 197)

Petitto, L. A., & Marentette, P. F. (1991). Babbling in the manual mode: Evidence for the ontogeny of language. *Science, 251,* 1493–1496. (p. 230)

Pettegrew, J. W., Keshavan, M. S., & Minshew, N. J. (1993). 31P nuclear magnetic resonance spectroscopy: Neurodevelopment and schizophrenia. *Schizophrenia Bulletin, 19,* 35–53. (p. 398)

Petticrew, C., Bell, R., & Hunter, D. (2002). Influence of psychological coping on survival and recurrence in people with cancer: Systematic review. *British Medical Journal, 325,* 1066. (p. 288)

Petticrew, M., Fraser, J. M., & Regan, M. F. (1999). Adverse life events and risk of breast cancer: A meta-analysis. *British Journal of Health Psychology, 4,* 1–17. (p. 288)

Pettigrew, T. F., Christ, O., Wagner, U., & Stellmacher, J. (2007). Direct and indirect intergroup contact effects on prejudice: A normative interpretation. *International Journal of Intercultural Relations, 31,* 411–425. (p. 366)

Pettigrew, T. F., & Tropp, L. R. (2011). *When groups meet: The dynamics of intergroup contact.* New York: Psychology Press. (p. 366)

Pew Research Center. (2006, November 14). Attitudes toward homosexuality in African countries (pewresearch.org). (p. 121)

Pew Research Center. (2006). Remembering 9/11. Pew Research Center. (www.pewresearch.org). (p. 201)

Pew Research Center. (2007, July 18). Modern marriage: "I like hugs. I like kisses. But what I really love is help with the dishes." Pew Research Center (www.pewresearch.org). (p. 362)

Pew Research Center. (2009, November 4). Social isolation and new technology: How the Internet and mobile phones impact Americans' social networks. Pew Research Center (www.pewresearch.org). (p. 267)

Pew Research Center. (2010). Home broadband 2010. Pew Internet & American Life Project, Pew Research Center (www.pewinternet.org). (p. 246)

Pew Research Center. (2010, February 1). Almost all millennials accept interracial dating and marriage. Pew Research Center. (www.pewresearch.org). (p. 350)

Pew Research Center. (2010, July 1). Gender equality universally embraced, but inequalities acknowledged. Pew Research Center Publications (pewresearch.org). (p. 113)

Pew Research Center. (2012, March 19). Teens, smartphones & texting. Pew Research Center (pewresearch.org). (p. 90)

Pew Research Center. (2013). *The global divide on homosexuality: Greater acceptance in more secular and affluent countries.* [Data file]. Retrieved from http://www.pewglobal.org/files/2013/06/Pew-Global-Attitudes-Homosexuality-Report-FINAL-JUNE-4-2013.pdf. (p. 121)

Phelps, J. A., Davis J. O., & Schartz, K. M. (1997). Nature, nurture, and twin research strategies. *Current Directions in Psychological Science, 6,* 117–120. (p. 400)

Phillips, A. L. (2011). A walk in the woods. *American Scientist, 69,* 301–302. (p. 430)

Piaget, J. (1930). *The child's conception of physical causality.* London: Routledge & Kegan Paul. (p. 75)

Piaget, J. (1932). *The moral judgment of the child.* New York: Harcourt, Brace & World. (p. 87)

Picchioni, M. M., & Murray, R. M. (2007). Schizophrenia. *British Medical Journal, 335,* 91–95. (p. 398)

Piekarski, D. J., Routman, D. M., Schoomer, E. E., Driscoll, J. R., Park, J. H., Butler, M. P., & Zucker, I. (2009). Infrequent low dose testosterone treatment maintains male sexual behavior in Syrian hamsters. *Hormones and Behavior, 55,* 182–189. (p. 115)

Piliavin, J. A. (2003). Doing well by doing good: Benefits for the benefactor. In C. L. M. Keyes & J. Haidt (Eds.), *Flourishing: Positive psychology and the life well-lived.* Washington, DC: American Psychological Association. (p. 88)

Pillemer, D. B. (1998). *Momentous events, vivid memories.* Cambridge, MA: Harvard University Press. (p. 96)

Pilley, J. W., & Reid, A. K. (2011). Border collie comprehends object names as verbal referents. *Behavioural Processes, 86,* 184–195. (p. 234)

Pillsworth, E. G., & Haselton, M. G. (2006). Male sexual attractiveness predicts differential ovulatory shifts in female extra-pair attraction and male mate retention. *Evolution and Human Behavior, 27,* 247–258. (p. 115)

Pillsworth, E. G., Haselton, M. G., & Buss, D. M. (2004). Ovulatory shifts in female desire. *Journal of Sex Research, 41,* 55–65. (p. 115)

Pinker, S. (1995). The language instinct. *The General Psychologist, 31,* 63–65. (p. 235)

Pinker, S. (1998). Words and rules. *Lingua, 106,* 219–242. (p. 229)

Pinker, S. (2008). *The sexual paradox: Men, women, and the real gender gap.* New York: Scribner. (p. 110)

Pinker, S. (2010, June 10). Mind over mass media. *New York Times,* A31. (p. 268)

Pinker, S. (2011, September 27). A history of violence. *Edge* (www.edge.org). (p. 358)

Pipe, M-E., Lamb, M. E., Orbach, Y., & Esplin, P. W. (2004). Recent research on children's testimony about experienced and witnessed events. *Developmental Review, 24,* 440–468. (p. 212)

Pipher, M. (2002). *The middle of everywhere: The world's refugees come to our town.* New York: Harcourt Brace. (p. 265)

Place, S. S., Todd, P. M., Penke, L., & Asendorph, J. B. (2009). The ability to judge the romantic interest of others. *Psychological Science, 20,* 22–26. (pp. 275, 359)

Plassmann, H., O'Doherty, J., Shiv, B., & Rangel, A. (2008). Marketing actions can modulate neural representations of experienced pleasantness. *Proceedings of the National Academy of Sciences, 105,* 1050–1054. (p. 158)

Platek, S. M., & Singh, D. (2010) Optimal waist-to-hip ratios in women activate neural reward centers in men. *PLoS ONE 5(2):* e9042. doi:10.1371/journal.pone.0009042. (p. 360)

Plomin, R. (2011). Why are children in the same family so different? Nonshared environment three decades later. *International Journal of Epidemiology, 40,* 582–592. (p. 91)

Plomin, R., Corley, R., Caspi, A., Fulker, D. W., & DeFries, J. (1998). Adoption results for self-reported personality: Evidence for nonadditive genetic effects? *Journal of Personality and Social Psychology, 75,* 211–219. (p. 72)

Plomin, R., & Daniels, D. (1987). Why are children in the same family so different from one another? *Behavioral and Brain Sciences, 10,* 1–60. (p. 91)

Plomin, R., & DeFries, J. C. (1998, May). The genetics of cognitive abilities and disabilities. *Scientific American,* pp. 62–69. (p. 244)

Plomin, R., DeFries, J. C., McClearn, G. E., & Rutter, M. (1997). *Behavioral genetics.* New York: Freeman. (pp. 123, 262, 399)

Plomin, R., & McGuffin, P. (2003). Psychopathology in the postgenomic era. *Annual Review of Psychology, 54,* 205–228. (pp. 394, 395)

Plous, S., & Herzog, H. A. (2000). Poll shows researchers favor lab animal protection. *Science, 290,* 711. (p. 21)

Poelmans, G., Pauls, D. L., Buitelaar, J. K., & Franke, B. (2011). Integrated genome-wide association study findings: Identification of a neurodevelopmental network for attention deficit hyperactivity disorder. *American Journal of Psychiatry, 168,* 365–377. (p. 373)

Pogue-Geile, M. F., & Yokley, J. L. (2010). Current research on the genetic contributors to schizophrenia. *Current Directions in Psychological Science, 19,* 214–219. (p. 400)

Poldrack, R. A., Halchenko, Y. O., & Hanson, S. J. (2009). Decoding the large-scale structure of brain function by classifying mental states across individuals. *Psychological Science, 20,* 1364–1372. (p. 38)

Polivy, J., & Herman, C. P. (2002). Causes of eating disorders. *Annual Review of Psychology, 53,* 187–213. (p. 401)

Polivy, J., Herman, C. P., & Coelho, J. S. (2008). Caloric restriction in the presence of attractive food cues: External cues, eating, and weight. *Physiology and Behavior, 94,* 729–733. (p. 261)

Pollak, S., Cicchetti, D., & Klorman, R. (1998). Stress, memory, and emotion: Developmental considerations from the study of child maltreatment. *Developmental Psychopathology, 10,* 811–828. (p. 172)

Polusny, M. A., & Follette, V. M. (1995). Long-term correlates of child sexual abuse: Theory and review of the empirical literature. *Applied & Preventive Psychology, 4,* 143–166. (p. 84)

Poon, L. W. (1987). Myths and truisms: Beyond extant analyses of speed of behavior and age. Address to the Eastern Psychological Association convention. (p. 95)

Pope, H. G., & Yurgelun-Todd, D. (1996). The residual cognitive effects of heavy marijuana use in college students. *Journal of the American Medical Association, 275,* 521–527. (p. 388)

Popenoe, D. (1993). The evolution of marriage and the problem of stepfamilies: A biosocial perspective. Paper presented at the National Symposium on Stepfamilies, The Pennsylvania State University. (p. 332)

Porter, S., & Peace, K. A. (2007). The scars of memory: A prospective, longitudinal investigation of the consistency of traumatic and positive emotional memories in adulthood. *Psychological Science, 18,* 435–441. (p. 213)

Porter, S., & ten Brinke, L. (2008). Reading between the lies: Identifying concealed and falsified emotions in universal facial expressions. *Psychological Science, 19,* 508–514. (p. 275)

Posavac, H. D., Posavac, S. S., & Posavac, E. J. (1998). Exposure to media images of female attractiveness and concern with body weight among young women. *Sex Roles, 38,* 187–201. (p. 401)

Posner, M. I., & Carr, T. H. (1992). Lexical access and the brain: Anatomical constraints on cognitive models of word recognition. *American Journal of Psychology, 105,* 1–26. (p. 233)

Powell, K. E., Thompson, P. D., Caspersen, C. J., & Kendrick, J. S. (1987). Physical activity and the incidence of coronary heart disease. *Annual Review of Public Health, 8,* 253–287. (p. 297)

Powell, L. H., Schahabi, L., & Thoresen, C. E. (2003). Religion and spirituality: Linkages to physical health. *American Psychologist, 58,* 36–52. (p. 301)

Powell, R. A., & Boer, D. P. (1994). Did Freud mislead patients to confabulate memories of abuse? *Psychological Reports, 74,* 1283–1298. (p. 317)

Pratt, T. C., & & Cullen, F. T. (2000). The empirical status of Gottfredson and Hirschi's general theory of crime: A meta-analysis. *Criminology, 38,* 931–964. (p. 356)

Prentice, D. A., & Miller, D. T. (1993). Pluralistic ignorance and alcohol use on campus: Some consequences of misperceiving the social norm. *Journal of Personality and Social Psychology, 64,* 243–256. (p. 389)

Prince Charles. (2000). BBC Reith Lecture. (p. 9)

Prioleau, L., Murdock, M., & Brody, N. (1983). An analysis of psychotherapy versus placebo studies. *The Behavioral and Brain Sciences, 6,* 275–310. (p. 422)

Pritchard, R. M. (1961, June). Stabilized images on the retina. *Scientific American,* pp. 72–78. (p. 137)

Pronin, E. (2007). Perception and misperception of bias in human judgment. *Trends in Cognitive Sciences, 11,* 37–43. (p. 331)

Pronin, E., Berger, J., & Molouki, S. (2007). Alone in a crowd of sheep: Asymmetric perceptions of conformity and their roots in an introspection illusion. *Journal of Personality and Social Psychology, 92,* 585–595. (p. 343)

Pronin, E., & Ross, L. (2006). Temporal differences in trait self-ascription: When the self is seen as an other. *Journal of Personality and Social Psychology, 90,* 197–209. (p. 339)

Provine, R. R., Krosnowski, K. A., & Brocato, N. W. (2009). Tearing: Breakthrough in human emotional signaling. *Evolutionary Psychology, 7,* 52–56. (p. 278)

Pryor, J. H., Hurtado, S., DeAngelo, L., Blake, L. P., & Tran, S. (2010). *The American Freshman: National Norms Fall 2009, Expanded edition.* Los Angeles: Higher Education Research Institute, UCLA. (p. 247)

Pryor, J. H., Hurtado, S., DeAngelo, L., Blake, L. P., & Tran, S. (2011). *The American Freshman: National Norms Fall 2010.* Los Angeles: Higher Education Research Institute, UCLA. (pp. 110, 266)

Pryor, J. H., Hurtado, S., Saenz, V. B., Korn, J. S., Santos, J. L., & Korn, W. S. (2006). *The American freshman: National norms for fall 2006.* Los Angeles: Higher Education Research Institute, UCLA. (p. 395)

Pryor, J. H., Hurtado, S., Saenz, V. B., Lindholm, J. A., Korn, W. S., & Mahoney, K. M. (2005). *The American freshman: National norms for Fall 2005.* Los Angeles: Higher Education Research Institute, UCLA. (p. 126)

Przbylski, A. K., Rigby, C. S., & Ryan, R. M. (2010). A motivational model of video game engagement. *Review of General Psychology, 14,* 154–166. (p. 358)

Psychologist. (2003, April). Who's the greatest? *The Psychologist, 16,* p. 17. (p. 80)

Puetz, T. W., O'Connor, P. J., & Dishman, R. K. (2006). Effects of chronic exercise on feelings of energy and fatigue: A quantitative synthesis. *Psychological Bulletin, 132,* 866-876. (p. 297)

Putnam, F. W. (1991). Recent research on multiple personality disorder. *Psychiatric Clinics of North America, 14,* 489–502. (p. 402)

Pyszczynski, T. A., Rothschild, Z., & Abdollahi, A. (2008). Terrorism, violence, and hope for peace: A terror management perspective. *Current Directions in Psychological Science 17,* 318–322. (p. 353)

Pyszczynski, T. A., Solomon, S., & Greenberg, J. (2002). *In the wake of 9/11: The psychology of terror.* Washington, DC: American Psychological Association. (p. 353)

Qin, H-F., & Piao, T-J. (2011). Dispositional optimism and life satisfaction of Chinese and Japanese college students: Examining the mediating effects of affects and coping efficacy. *Chinese Journal of Clinical Psychology, 19,* 259–261. (p. 294)

Qirko, H. N. (2004) "Fictive kin" and suicide terrorism. *Science, 304,* 49–50. (p. 348)

Quinn, P. C., Bhatt, R. S., Brush, D., Grimes, A., & Sharpnack, H. (2002). Development of form similarity as a Gestalt grouping principle in infancy. *Psychological Science, 13,* 320–328. (p. 146)

Rabins, P., & 18 others. (2009). Scientific and ethical issues related to deep brain stimulation for disorders of mood, behavior, and thought. *Archives of General Psychiatry, 66,* 931–937. (p. 428)

Racsmány, M., Conway, M. A., & Demeter, G. (2010). Consolidation of episodic memories during sleep: Long-term effects of retrieval practice. *Psychological Science, 21,* 80–85. (p. 56)

Rahman, Q., & Koerting, J. (2008). Sexual orientation-related differences in allocentric spatial memory tasks. *Hippocampus, 18,* 55–63. (p. 124)

Rahman, Q., & Wilson, G. D. (2003). Born gay? The psychobiology of human sexual orientation. *Personality and Individual Differences, 34,* 1337–1382. (p. 123)

Rahman, Q., Wilson, G. D., & Abrahams, S. (2003). Biosocial factors, sexual orientation and neurocognitive functioning. *Psychoneuroendocrinology, 29,* 867–881. (p. 124)

Raine, A. (1999). Murderous minds: Can we see the mark of Cain? *Cerebrum: The Dana Forum on Brain Science 1*(1), 15–29. (pp. 355, 404)

Raine, A. (2005). The interaction of biological and social measures in the explanation of antisocial and violent behavior. In D. M. Stoff & E. J. Susman (Eds.) *Developmental psychobiology of aggression.* New York: Cambridge University Press. (pp. 355, 404)

Raine, A., Lencz, T., Bihrle, S., LaCasse, L., & Colletti, P. (2000). Reduced prefrontal gray matter volume and reduced autonomic activity in antisocial personality disorder. *Archives of General Psychiatry, 57,* 119–127. (p. 404)

Rainie, L., Purcell, K., Goulet, L. S., & Hampton, K. H. (2011, June 16). Social networking sites and our lives. *Pew Research Center* (pewresearch.org). (p. 267)

Rajendran, G., & Mitchell, P. (2007). Cognitive theories of autism. *Developmental Review, 27,* 224–260. (p. 78)

Ralston, A. (2004). Enough rope. Interview for ABC TV, Australia, by Andrew Denton. (www.abc.net.au/enoughrope/stories/s1227885.htm). (p. 255)

Ramachandran, V. S., & Blakeslee, S. (1998). *Phantoms in the brain: Probing the mysteries of the human mind.* New York: Morrow. (pp. 35, 155)

Randi, J. (1999, February 4). 2000 club mailing list e-mail letter. (p. 162)

Rapoport, J. L. (1989, March). The biology of obsessions and compulsions. *Scientific American,* pp. 83–89. (p. 381)

Räsänen, S., Pakaslahti, A., Syvalahti, E., Jones, P. B., & Isohanni, M. (2000). Sex differences in schizophrenia: A review. *Nordic Journal of Psychiatry, 54,* 37–45. (p. 398)

Rasch, B., & Born, J. (2008). Reactivation and consolidation of memory during sleep. *Current Directions in Psychological Science, 17,* 188–192. (p. 56)

Rasmussen, H. N., Scheier, M. F., & Greenhouse, J. B. (2010). Optimism and physical health: A meta-analytic review. *Annals of Behavioral Medicine, 37,* 239–256. (p. 294)

Raynor, H. A., & Epstein, L. H. (2001). Dietary variety, energy regulation, and obesity. *Psychological Bulletin, 127,* 325–341. (p. 260)

Read, J., & Bentall, R. (2010). The effectiveness of electroconvulsive therapy: A literature review. *Epidemiologica e Psichiatria Sociale, 19,* 333–347. (p. 428)

Reason, J. (1987). The Chernobyl errors. *Bulletin of the British Psychological Society, 40,* 201–206. (p. 349)

Reason, J., & Mycielska, K. (1982). *Absent-minded? The psychology of mental lapses and everyday errors.* Englewood Cliffs, NJ: Prentice-Hall. (p. 138)

Reed, P. (2000). Serial position effects in recognition memory for odors. *Journal of Experimental Psychology: Learning, Memory, and Cognition, 26,* 411–422. (p. 205)

Reichert, R. A., Robb, M. B., Fender, J. G., & Wartella, E. (2010). Word learning from baby videos. *Archives of Pediatrics & Adolescent Medicine, 164,* 432–437. (p. 245)

Reifman, A. S., Larrick, R. P., & Fein, S. (1991). Temper and temperature on the diamond: The heat-aggression relationship in major league baseball. *Personality and Social Psychology Bulletin, 17,* 580–585. (p. 355)

Reimann, F., & 24 others. (2010). Pain perception is altered by a nucleotide polymorphism in SCN9A. *PNAS, 107,* 5148–5153. (p. 155)

Reiner, W. G., & Gearhart, J. P. (2004). Discordant sexual identity in some genetic males with cloacal exstrophy assigned to female sex at birth. *New England Journal of Medicine, 350,* 333–341. (p. 112)

Reis, H. T., & Aron, A. (2008). Love: What is it, why does it matter, and how does it operate? *Perspectives on Psychological Science, 3,* 80–86. (p. 362)

Reisenzein, R. (1983). The Schachter theory of emotion: Two decades later. *Psychological Bulletin, 94,* 239–264. (p. 270)

Reiser, M. (1982). *Police psychology.* Los Angeles: LEHI. (p. 162)

Remick, A. K., Polivy, J., & Pliner, P. (2009). Internal and external moderators of the effect of variety on food intake. *Psychological Bulletin, 135,* 434–451. (p. 261)

Remington, A., Swettenham, J., Campbell, R., & Coleman, M. (2009). Selective attention and perceptual load in autism spectrum disorder. *Psychological Science, 20,* 1388–1393. (p. 78)

Remley, A. (1988, October). From obedience to independence. *Psychology Today,* pp. 56–59. (p. 84)

Renner, M. J., & Renner, C. H. (1993). Expert and novice intuitive judgments about animal behavior. *Bulletin of the Psychonomic Society, 31,* 551–552. (p. 74)

Renner, M. J., & Rosenzweig, M. R. (1987). *Enriched and impoverished environments: Effects on brain and behavior.* New York: Springer-Verlag. (p. 74)

Renninger, K. A., & Granott, N. (2005). The process of scaffolding in learning and development. *New Ideas in Psychology, 23*(3), 111–114. (p. 80)

Rentfrow, P. J., & Gosling, S. D. (2003). The Do Re Mi's of everyday life: The structure and personality correlates of music preferences. *Journal of Personality and Social Psychology, 84,* 1236–1256. (p. 326)

Resnick, M. D., Bearman, P. S., Blum, R. W., Bauman, K. E., Harris, K. M., Jones, J., Tabor, J., Beuhring, T., Sieving, R., Shew, M., Bearinger, L. H., & Udry, J. R. (1997). Protecting adolescents from harm: Findings from the National Longitudinal Study on Adolescent Health. *Journal of the American Medical Association, 278,* 823–832. (pp. 17, 52, 90)

Resnick, S. M. (1992). Positron emission tomography in psychiatric illness. *Current Directions in Psychological Science, 1,* 92–98. (p. 398)

Reuters. (2000, July 5). Many teens regret decision to have sex (National Campaign to Prevent Teen Pregnancy survey). www.washingtonpost.com. (p. 119)

Reyna, V. F., & Farley, F. (2006). Risk and rationality in adolescent decision making: Implications for theory, practice, and public policy. *Psychological Science in the Public Interest, 7*(1), 1–44. (p. 86)

Rhoades, G. K., Stanley, S. M., & Markman, H. J. (2009). The pre-engagement cohabitation effect: A replication and extension of previous findings. *Journal of Family Psychology, 23,* 107–111. (p. 98)

Rhodes, M. G., & Anastasi, J. S. (2012). The own-age bias in face recognition: A meta-analytic and theoretical review. *Psychological Bulletin, 138,* 146–174. (p. 353)

Rhodes, S. R. (1983). Age-related differences in work attitudes and behavior: A review and conceptual analysis. *Psychological Bulletin, 93,* 328–367. (p. 96)

Ribeiro, R., Gervasoni, D., Soares, E. S., Zhou, Y., Lin, S-C., Pantoja, J., Lavine, M., & Nicolelis, M. A. L. (2004). Long-lasting novelty-induced neuronal reverberation during slow-wave sleep in multiple forebrain areas. *PloS Biology, 2*(1), e37 (www.plosbiology.org). (p. 56)

Rice, M. E., & Grusec, J. E. (1975). Saying and doing: Effects on observer performance. *Journal of Personality and Social Psychology, 32,* 584–593. (p. 186)

Richards, D. (2011). Prevalence and clinical course of depression: A review. *Clinical Psychology Review, 31,* 1117–1125. (p. 393)

Richeson, J. A., & Shelton, J. N. (2007). Negotiating interracial interactions. *Current Directions in Psychological Science, 16,* 316–320. (p. 366)

Rieff, P. (1979). *Freud: The mind of a moralist* (3rd ed.). Chicago: University of Chicago Press. (p. 318)

Riis, J., Loewenstein, G., Baron, J., Jepson, C., Fagerlin, A., & Ubel, P. A. (2005). Ignorance of hedonic adaptation to hemodialysis: A study using ecological momentary assessment. *Journal of Experimental Psychology: General, 134,* 3–9. (p. 302)

Rindermann, H., & Ceci, S. J. (2009). Educational policy and country outcomes in international cognitive competence studies. *Perspectives on Psychological Science, 4,* 551–577. (p. 249)

Ring, K. (1980). *Life at death: A scientific investigation of the near-death experience.* New York: Coward, McCann & Geoghegan. (p. 387)

Ripke, S., & others (2011). Genome-wide association study identifies five new schizophrenia loci. *Nature Genetics, 43,* 969–976. (p. 400)

Rizzolatti, G., Fadiga, L., Fogassi, L., & Gallese, V. (2002). From mirror neurons to imitation: Facts and speculations. In A. N. Meltzoff & W. Prinz (Eds.), *The imitative mind: Development, evolution, and brain bases.* Cambridge: Cambridge University Press, 2002. (p. 186)

Rizzolatti, G., Fogassi, L., & Gallese, V. (2006, November). Mirrors in the mind. *Scientific American,* pp. 54–61. (p. 186)

Roberts, B. W., Caspi, A., & Moffitt, T. E. (2001). The kids are alright: Growth and stability in personality development from adolescence to adulthood. *Journal of Personality and Social Psychology, 81,* 670–683. (p. 102)

Roberts, B. W., Caspi, A., & Moffitt, T. E. (2003). Work experiences and personality development in young adulthood. *Journal of Personality and Social Psychology, 84,* 582–593. (p. 102)

Roberts, B. W., Walton, K. E., & Viechtbauer, W. (2006). Patterns of mean-level change in personality traits across the life course: A meta-analysis of longitudinal studies. *Psychological Bulletin, 132,* 1-25. (p. 102)

Roberts, L. (1988). Beyond Noah's ark: What do we need to know? *Science, 242,* 1247. (p. 291)

Roberts, T-A. (1991). Determinants of gender differences in responsiveness to others' evaluations. *Dissertation Abstracts International, 51*(8–B). (p. 109)

Robertson, K. F., Smeets, S., Lubinski, D., & Benbow, C. P. (2010). Beyond the threshold hypothesis: Even among the gifted and top math/science graduate students, cognitive abilities, vocational interests, and lifestyle preferences matter for career choice, performance, and persistence. *Current Directions in Psychological Science, 19,* 346–351. (p. 226)

Robins, R. W., & Trzesniewski, K. H. (2005). Self-esteem development across the lifespan. *Current Directions in Psychological Science, 14*(3), 158–162. (p. 99)

Robins, R. W., Trzesniewski, K. H., Tracy, J. L., Gosling, S. D., & Potter, J. (2002). Global self-esteem across the lifespan. *Psychology and Aging, 17*, 423–434. (p. 90)

Robinson, F. P. (1970). *Effective study.* New York: Harper & Row. (p. 23)

Robinson, J. P., & Martin, S. (2008). What do happy people do? *Social Indicators Research, 89*, 565–571. (p. B-2)

Robinson, J. P., & Martin, S. (2009). Changes in American daily life: 1965–2005. *Social Indicators Research, 93*, 47–56. (p. 187)

Robinson, T. N. (1999). Reducing children's television viewing to prevent obesity. *Journal of the American Medical Association, 282*, 1561–1567. (p. 264)

Robinson, T. N., Borzekowski, D. L. G., Matheson, D. M., & Kraemer, H. C. (2007). Effects of fast food branding on young children's taste preferences. *Archives of Pediatric and Adolescent Medicine, 161*, 792–797. (p. 138)

Robinson, V. M. (1983). Humor and health. In P. E. McGhee & J. H. Goldstein (Eds.), *Handbook of humor research: Vol. II. Applied studies.* New York: Springer-Verlag. (p. 294)

Rochat, F. (1993). How did they resist authority? Protecting refugees in Le Chambon during World War II. Paper presented at the American Psychological Association convention. (p. 345)

Rock, I., & Palmer, S. (1990, December). The legacy of Gestalt psychology. *Scientific American*, pp. 84–90. (p. 146)

Rodin, J. (1986). Aging and health: Effects of the sense of control. *Science, 233*, 1271–1276. (pp. 291, 292)

Roediger, H. L., III, & Finn, B. (2010, March/April). The pluses of getting it wrong. *Scientific American Mind*, pp. 39–41. (p. 23)

Roediger, H. L., III, & Karpicke, J. D. (2006). Test-enhanced learning: Taking memory tests improves long-term retention. *Psychological Science, 17*, 249–255. (pp. 23, 198)

Roediger, H. L., III, & McDermott, K. B. (1995). Creating false memories: Remembering words not presented in lists. *Journal of Experimental Psychology: Learning, Memory, and Cognition, 21*, 803–814. (p. 212)

Roediger, H. L., III, Wheeler, M. A., & Rajaram, S. (1993). Remembering, knowing, and reconstructing the past. In D. L. Medin (Ed.), *The psychology of learning and motivation: Advances in research and theory* (Vol. 30). Orlando, FL: Academic Press. (p. 212)

Roehling, M. V. (1999). Weight-based discrimination in employment: Psychological and legal aspects. *Personnel Psychology, 52*, 969–1016. (p. 261)

Roehling, P. V., Roehling, M. V., Johnston, A., Brennan, A., & Drew, A. (2010). Weighty decisions: The effect of weight bias on the selection and election of U.S. political candidates. Unpublished manuscript, Hope College. (p. 261)

Roehling, P. V., Roehling, M. V., & Moen, P. (2001). The relationship between work-life policies and practices and employee loyalty: A life course perspective. *Journal of Family and Economic Issues, 22*, 141–170. (p. B-7)

Roehling, P. V., Roehling, M. V., Vandlen, J. D., Blazek, J., & Guy, W. C. (2009). Weight discrimination and the glass ceiling effect among top US CEOs. *Equal Opportunities International, 28*, 179–196. (p. 261)

Roelofs, T. (2010, September 22). Somali refugee takes oath of U.S. citizenship year after his brother. *Grand Rapids Press* (www.mlive.com). (p. B-4)

Roenneberg, T., Kuehnle, T., Pramstaller, P. P., Ricken, J., Havel, M., Guth, A., Merrow, M. (2004). A marker for the end of adolescence. *Current Biology, 14*, R1038–R1039. (p. 52)

Roese, N. J., & Summerville, A. (2005). What we regret most . . . and why. *Personality and Social Psychology Bulletin, 31*, 1273-1285. (p. 99)

Roese, N. J., & Vohs, K. D. (2012). Hindsight bias. *Perspectives on Psychological Science, 7*, 411–426. (p. 10)

Roesser, R. (1998). What you should know about hearing conservation. *Better Hearing Institute* (www.betterhearing.org). (p. 153)

Rogers, C. R. (1961). *On becoming a person: A therapist's view of psychotherapy.* Boston: Houghton Mifflin. (p. 413)

Rogers, C. R. (1980). *A way of being.* Boston: Houghton Mifflin. (pp. 320, 413)

Rohan, M. J., & Zanna, M. P. (1996). Value transmission in families. In C. Seligman, J. M. Olson, & M. P. Zanna (Eds.), *The psychology of values: The Ontario Symposium* (Vol. 8). Mahwah, NJ: Erlbaum. (p. 91)

Rohner, R. P. (1986). *The warmth dimension: Foundations of parental acceptance-rejection theory.* Newbury Park, CA: Sage. (p. 85)

Roiser, J. P., Cook, L. J., Cooper, J. D., Rubinsztein, D. C., & Sahakian, B. J. (2005). Association of a functional polymorphism in the serotonin transporter gene with abnormal emotional processing in Ecstasy users. *American Journal of Psychiatry, 162*, 609–612. (p. 386)

Ronay, R., & von Hippel, W. (2010). The presence of an attractive woman elevates testosterone and physical risk taking in young men. *Social Psychology and Personality Science, 1*, 57–64. (p. 116)

Rosa-Alcázar, A. I., Sánchez-Meca, J., Gómez-Conesa, A., & Marín-Martínez, F. (2008). Psychological treatment of obsessive-compulsive disorder: A meta-analysis. *Clinical Psychology Review, 28*, 1310–1325. (p. 415)

Rosch, E. (1978). Principles of categorization. In E. Rosch & B. L. Lloyd (Eds.), *Cognition and categorization.* Hillsdale, NJ: Erlbaum. (p. 220)

Rose, A. J., & Rudolph, K. D. (2006). A review of sex differences in peer relationship processes: Potential trade-offs for the emotional and behavioral development of girls and boys. *Psychological Bulletin, 132*, 98–131. (p. 109)

Rose, J. S., Chassin, L., Presson, C. C., & Sherman, S. J. (1999). Peer influences on adolescent cigarette smoking: A prospective sibling analysis. *Merrill-Palmer Quarterly, 45*, 62–84. (p. 90)

Rose, R. J., Viken, R. J., Dick, D. M., Bates, J. E., Pulkkinen, L., & Kaprio, J. (2003). It *does* take a village: Nonfamiliar environments and children's behavior. *Psychological Science, 14*, 273–277. (p. 90)

Rose, S., Bisson, J., & Wessely, S. (2003). A systematic review of single-session psychological interventions ('debriefing') following trauma. *Psychotherapy and Psychosomatics, 72*, 176–184. (p. 379)

Roselli, C. E., Larkin, K., Schrunk, J. M., & Stormshak, F. (2004). Sexual partner preference, hypothalamic morphology and aromatase in rams. *Physiology and Behavior, 83*, 233–245. (p. 123)

Roselli, C. E., Resko, J. A., & Stormshak, F. (2002). Hormonal influences on sexual partner preference in rams. *Archives of Sexual Behavior, 31*, 43–49. (p. 123)

Rosenbaum, M. (1986). The repulsion hypothesis: On the nondevelopment of relationships. *Journal of Personality and Social Psychology, 51*, 1156–1166. (p. 361)

Rosenberg, N. A., Pritchard, J. K., Weber, J. L., Cann, H. M., Kidd, K. K., Zhivotosky, L. A., & Feldman, M. W. (2002). Genetic structure of human populations. *Science, 298*, 2381–2385. (p. 248)

Rosenberg, T. (2010, November 1). The opt-out solution. *New York Times* (www.nytimes.com). (p. 224)

Rosenhan, D. L. (1973). On being sane in insane places. *Science, 179*, 250–258. (p. 375)

Rosenthal, R., Hall, J. A., Archer, D., DiMatteo, M. R., & Rogers, P. L. (1979). The PONS test: Measuring sensitivity to nonverbal cues. In S. Weitz (Ed.), *Nonverbal communication* (2nd ed.). New York: Oxford University Press. (p. 275)

Rosenzweig, M. R. (1984). Experience, memory, and the brain. *American Psychologist, 39*, 365–376. (p. 74)

Roseth, C. J., Johnson, D. W., & Johnson, R. T. (2008). Promoting early adolescents' achievement and peer relationships: The effects of cooperative, competitive, and individualistic goal structures. *Psychological Bulletin, 134,* 223–246. (p. 367)

Rosin, H. (2010, July, August). The end of men. *The Atlantic* (www.theatlantic.com). (p. 113)

Rossi, P. J. (1968). Adaptation and negative aftereffect to lateral optical displacement in newly hatched chicks. *Science, 160,* 430–432. (p. 150)

Rothbart, M., Fulero, S., Jensen, C., Howard, J., & Birrell, P. (1978). From individual to group impressions: Availability heuristics in stereotype formation. *Journal of Experimental Social Psychology, 14,* 237–255. (p. 353)

Rothbart, M. K. (2007). Temperament, development, and personality. *Current Directions in Psychological Science, 16,* 207–212. (p. 73)

Rothblum, E. D. (2007). Same-sex couples in legalized relationships: I do, or do I? Unpublished manuscript, Women's Studies Department, San Diego State University. (p. 125)

Rothman, A. J., & Salovey, P. (1997). Shaping perceptions to motivate healthy behavior: The role of message framing. *Psychological Bulletin, 121,* 3–19. (p. 224)

Rovee-Collier, C. (1989). The joy of kicking: Memories, motives, and mobiles. In P. R. Solomon, G. R. Goethals, C. M. Kelley, & B. R. Stephens (Eds.), *Memory: Interdisciplinary approaches.* New York: Springer-Verlag. (p. 75)

Rovee-Collier, C. (1997). Dissociations in infant memory: Rethinking the development of implicit and explicit memory. *Psychological Review, 104,* 467–498. (p. 75)

Rovee-Collier, C. (1999). The development of infant memory. *Current Directions in Psychological Science, 8,* 80–85. (p. 75)

Rowe, D. C. (1990). As the twig is bent? The myth of child-rearing influences on personality development. *Journal of Counseling and Development, 68,* 606–611. (p. 72)

Rowe, D. C., Almeida, D. M., & Jacobson, K. C. (1999). School context and genetic influences on aggression in adolescence. *Psychological Science, 10,* 277–280. (p. 354)

Rowe, D. C., Jacobson, K. C., & Van den Oord, E. J. C. G. (1999). Genetic and environmental influences on vocabulary IQ: Parental education level as moderator. *Child Development, 70*(5), 1151–1162. (p. 244)

Rowe, D. C., Vazsonyi, A. T., & Flannery, D. J. (1994). No more than skin deep: Ethnic and racial similarity in developmental process. *Psychological Review, 101*(3), 396. (p. 86)

Royal College of Psychiatrists. (2009.) *Good psychiatric practice* (3rd ed.). London: Royal College of Psychiatrists. (p. 124)

Rozin, P., Dow, S., Mosovitch, M., & Rajaram, S. (1998). What causes humans to begin and end a meal? A role for memory for what has been eaten, as evidenced by a study of multiple meal eating in amnesic patients. *Psychological Science, 9,* 392–396. (p. 260)

Ruau, D., Liu, L. Y., Clark, J. D., Angst, M. S., & Butte, A. J. (2012). Sex differences in reported pain across 11,000 patients captured in electronic medical records. *Journal of Pain, 13,* 228–234. (p. 154)

Ruback, R. B., Carr, T. S., & Hopper, C. H. (1986). Perceived control in prison: Its relation to reported crowding, stress, and symptoms. *Journal of Applied Social Psychology, 16,* 375–386. (p. 292)

Rubenstein, J. S., Meyer, D. E., & Evans, J. E. (2001). Executive control of cognitive processes in task switching. *Journal of Experimental Psychology: Human Perception and Performance, 27,* 763–797. (p. 51)

Rubin, D. C., Rahhal, T. A., & Poon, L. W. (1998). Things learned in early adulthood are remembered best. *Memory and Cognition, 26,* 3–19. (p. 96)

Rubin, L. B. (1985). *Just friends: The role of friendship in our lives.* New York: Harper & Row. (p. 110)

Rubin, Z. (1970). Measurement of romantic love. *Journal of Personality and Social Psychology, 16,* 265–273. (p. 275)

Rubio, G., & López-Ibor, J. J. (2007). Generalized anxiety disorder: A 40-year follow-up study. *Acta Psychiatrica Scandinavica, 115,* 372–379. (p. 377)

Ruchlis, H. (1990). *Clear thinking: A practical introduction.* Buffalo, NY: Prometheus Books. (p. 220)

Rueckert, L., Doan, T., & Branch, B. (2010). Emotion and relationship effects on gender differences in empathy. Presented at the annual meeting of the Association for Psychological Science, Boston, MA, May, 2010. (p. 276)

Ruffin, C. L. (1993). Stress and health—little hassles vs. major life events. *Australian Psychologist, 28,* 201–208. (p. 285)

Rule, N. O., Ambady, N., & Hallett, K. C. (2009). Female sexual orientation is perceived accurately, rapidly, and automatically from the face and its features. *Journal of Experimental Social Psychology, 45,* 1245–1251. (p. 326)

Rumbaugh, D. M. (1977). *Language learning by a chimpanzee: The Lana project.* New York: Academic Press. (p. 234)

Rumbaugh, D. M., & Washburn, D. A. (2003). *Intelligence of apes and other rational beings.* New Haven, CT: Yale University Press. (p. 235)

Rushton, J. P. (1975). Generosity in children: Immediate and long-term effects of modeling, preaching, and moral judgment. *Journal of Personality and Social Psychology, 31,* 459–466. (p. 186)

Ryan, R. M., & Deci, E. L. (2004). Avoiding death or engaging life as accounts of meaning and culture: Comment on Pyszczynski et al. (2004). *Psychological Bulletin, 130,* 473–477. (p. 331)

Rydell, R. J., Rydell, M. T., & Boucher, K. L. (2010). The effect of negative performance stereotypes on learning. *Journal of Personality and Social Psychology, 99,* 883–896. (p. 249)

Saad, L. (2002, November 21). Most smokers wish they could quit. *Gallup News Service* (www.gallup.com). (p. 385)

Sabbagh, M. A., Xu, F., Carlson, S. M., Moses, L. J., & Lee, K. (2006). The development of executive functioning and theory of mind: A comparison of Chinese and U.S. preschoolers. *Psychological Science, 17,* 74–81. (p. 78)

Sabini, J. (1986). Stanley Milgram (1933–1984). *American Psychologist, 41,* 1378–1379. (p. 343)

Sachdev, P., & Sachdev, J. (1997). Sixty years of psychosurgery: Its present status and its future. *Australian and New Zealand Journal of Psychiatry, 31,* 457–464. (p. 430)

Sachs, J. (2012). Introduction. In J. Helliwell, R. Layard, & J. Sachs (Eds.), *World happiness report.* New York: The Earth Institute, Columbia University. (p. 305)

Sacks, O. (1985). *The man who mistook his wife for a hat.* New York: Summit Books. (pp. 159, 206)

Sadler, M. S., Correll, J., Park, B., & Judd, C. M. (2012). The world is not Black and White: Racial bias in the decision to shoot in a multiethnic context. *Journal of Social Issues, 68,* 286–313. (p. 351)

Safron, A., Barch, B., Bailey, J. M., Gitelman, D. R., Parrish, T. B., & Reber, P. J. (2007). Neural correlates of sexual arousal in homosexual and heterosexual men. *Behavioral Neuroscience, 121,* 237–248. (p. 123)

Saks, E. (2007, August 27). A memoir of schizophrenia. *Time.* http://content.time.com/time/arts/article/0,8599,1656592,00.html. (p. 425)

Salimpoor, V. N., Benovoy, M., Larcher, K., Dagher, A., & Zatorre, R. J. (2011). Anatomically distinct dopamine release during anticipation and experience of peak emotion to music. *Nature Neuroscience, 14,* 257–262. (p. 42)

Salmon, P. (2001). Effects of physical exercise on anxiety, depression, and sensitivity to stress: A unifying theory. *Clinical Psychology Review, 21,* 33–61. (p. 430)

Salomon, J. A., Wong, H., Freeman, M. K., Vos, T., Flaxman, A. D., Lopez, A. D., & Murray, C. J. L. (2012). Healthy life expectancy for 187 countries, 1990–2010: A systematic analysis for the Global Burden Disease Study 2010. *The Lancet, 380,* 2144–2162. (p. 95)

Salovey, P. (1990, January/February). Interview. *American Scientist,* pp. 25–29. (p. 301)

Salthouse, T. A. (2004). What and when of cognitive aging. *Current Directions in Psychological Science, 13,* 140–144. (p. 246)

Salthouse, T. A. (2009). When does age-related cognitive decline begin? *Neurobiology of Aging, 30,* 507–514. (p. 246)

Salthouse, T. A. (2010). Selective review of cognitive aging. *Journal of the International Neuropsychological Socie6y, 16,* 754–760. (pp. 97, 246)

Sampson, E. E. (2000). Reinterpreting individualism and collectivism: Their religious roots and monologic versus dialogic person–other relationship. *American Psychologist, 55,* 1425–1432. (p. 332)

Samuels, S., & McCabe, G. (1989). Quoted by P. Diaconis & F. Mosteller, Methods for studying coincidences. *Journal of the American Statistical Association, 84,* 853–861. (p. 11)

Sandfort, T. G. M., de Graaf, R., Bijl, R., & Schnabel, P. (2001). Same-sex sexual behavior and psychiatric disorders. *Archives of General Psychiatry, 58,* 85–91. (p. 121)

Sandkühler, S., & Bhattacharya, J. (2008). Deconstructing insight: EEG correlates of insightful problem solving. *PloS ONE, 3,* e1459 (www.plosone.org). (p. 220)

Sandler, W., Meir, I., Padden, C., & Aronoff, M. (2005). The emergence of grammar: Systematic structure in a new language. *Proceedings of the National Academy of Sciences, 102,* 2261–2265. (p. 231)

Sanz, C., Morgan, D., & Gulick, S. (2004). New insights into chimpanzees, tools, and termites from the Congo Basin. *American Naturalist, 164,* 567–581. (p. 229)

Sapadin, L. A. (1988). Friendship and gender: Perspectives of professional men and women. *Journal of Social and Personal Relationships, 5,* 387–403. (p. 110)

Saphire-Bernstein, S., Way, B. M., Kim, H. S, Sherman, D. K., & Taylor, S. E. (2011). Oxytocin receptor gene (OXTR) is related to psychological resources. *Proceedings of the National Academy of Sciences, 108,* 15118–15122. (p. 294)

Sapolsky, B. S., & Tabarlet, J. O. (1991). Sex in primetime television: 1979 versus 1989. *Journal of Broadcasting and Electronic Media, 35,* 505–516. (p. 119)

Sapolsky, R. (2005). The influence of social hierarchy on primate health. *Science, 308,* 648–652. (p. 291)

Saulny, S. (2006, June 21). A legacy of the storm: Depression and suicide. *New York Times* (www.nytimes.com). (p. 284)

Savage-Rumbaugh, E. S., Murphy, J., Sevcik, R. A., Brakke, K. E., Williams, S. L., & Rumbaugh, D. M., with commentary by Bates, E. (1993). Language comprehension in ape and child. *Monographs of the Society for Research in Child Development, 58* (233), 1–254. (p. 235)

Savage-Rumbaugh, E. S., Rumbaugh, D., & Fields, W. M. (2009). Empirical Kanzi: The ape language controversy revisited. *Skeptic, 15,* 25–33. (p. 235)

Savani, K., & Rattan, A. (2012). A choice mind-set increases the acceptance and maintenance of wealth inequality. *Psychological Science, 23,* 796–804. (p. 339)

Savic, I., Berglund, H., & Lindstrom, P. (2005). Brain response to putative pheromones in homosexual men. *Proceedings of the National Academy of Sciences, 102,* 7356–7361. (p. 123)

Savitsky, K., Epley, N., & Gilovich, T. (2001). Do others judge us as harshly as we think? Overestimating the impact of our failures, shortcomings, and mishaps. *Journal of Personality and Social Psychology, 81,* 44–56. (p. 328)

Savitsky, K., & Gilovich, T. (2003). The illusion of transparency and the alleviation of speech anxiety. *Journal of Experimental Social Psychology, 39,* 618–625. (p. 329)

Savoy, C., & Beitel, P. (1996). Mental imagery for basketball. *International Journal of Sport Psychology, 27,* 454–462. (p. 233)

Sayal, K., Heron, J., Golding, J., Alati, R., Smith, G. D., Gray, R., & Emond, A. (2009). Binge pattern of alcohol consumption during pregnancy and childhood mental health outcomes: Longitudinal population-based study. *Pediatrics, 123,* e289. (p. 71)

Sbarra, D. A., Law, R. W., & Portley, R. M. (2011). Divorce and death: A meta-analysis and research agenda for clinical, social, and health psychology. *Perspectives on Psychological Science, 6,* 454–474. (pp. 265, 295)

Scarr, S. (1984, May). What's a parent to do? A conversation with E. Hall. *Psychology Today,* pp. 58–63. (p. 245)

Scarr, S. (1989). Protecting general intelligence: Constructs and consequences for interventions. In R. J. Linn (Ed.), *Intelligence: Measurement, theory, and public policy.* Champaign: University of Illinois Press. (p. 237)

Scarr, S. (1993, May/June). Quoted by *Psychology Today,* Nature's thumbprint: So long, superparents, p. 16. (p. 91)

Schab, F. R. (1991). Odor memory: Taking stock. *Psychological Bulletin, 109,* 242–251. (p. 158)

Schachter, S., & Singer, J. E. (1962). Cognitive, social and physiological determinants of emotional state. *Psychological Review, 69,* 379–399. (p. 270)

Schacter, D. L. (1992). Understanding implicit memory: A cognitive neuroscience approach. *American Psychologist, 47,* 559–569. (p. 206)

Schacter, D. L. (1996). *Searching for memory: The brain, the mind, and the past.* New York: Basic Books. (pp. 95, 206, 211, 318)

Schaie, K. W., & Geiwitz, J. (1982). *Adult development and aging.* Boston: Little, Brown. (p. A-7)

Scheibe, S., & Carstensen, L. L. (2010). Emotional aging: Recent findings and future trends. *Journal of Gerontology: Psychological Sciences, 65B,* 135–144. (p. 100)

Scheier, M. F., & Carver, C. S. (1992). Effects of optimism on psychological and physical well-being: Theoretical overview and empirical update. *Cognitive Therapy and Research, 16,* 201–228. (p. 293)

Schein, E. H. (1956). The Chinese indoctrination program for prisoners of war: A study of attempted brainwashing. *Psychiatry, 19,* 149–172. (p. 340)

Scherer, K. R., Banse, R., & Wallbott, H. G. (2001). Emotion inferences from vocal expression correlate across languages and cultures. *Journal of Cross-Cultural Psychology, 32,* 76–92. (p. 275)

Schick, V., Herbenick, D., Reece, M., Sanders, S. A., Dodge, B., Middlestadt, S. E., & Fortenberry, J. D. (2010). Sexual behaviors, condom use, and sexual health of Americans over 50: Implications for sexual health promotion for older adults. *Journal of Sexual Medicine, 7*(suppl 5), 315–329. (p. 96)

Schiffenbauer, A., & Schiavo, R. S. (1976). Physical distance and attraction: An intensification effect. *Journal of Experimental Social Psychology, 12,* 274–282. (p. 347)

Schilt, T., de Win, M. M. L, Koeter, M., Jager, G., Korf, D. J., van den Brink, W., & Schmand, B. (2007). Cognition in novice ecstasy users with minimal exposure to other drugs. *Archives of General Psychiatry, 64,* 728–736. (p. 386)

Schkade, D., Sunstein, C. R., & Hastie, R. (2006). *What happened on deliberation day?* (University of Chicago Law and Economics, Olin Working Paper No. 298). (p. 348)

Schlegel, R. J., Hicks, J. A., King, L. A., & Arndt, J. (2011). Feeling like you know who you are: Perceived true self-knowledge and meaning in life. *Personality and Social Psychology Bulletin, 37,* 745–756. (p. 329)

Schlomer, G. L., Del Giudice, M., & Ellis, B. J. (2011). Parent-offspring conflict theory: An evolutionary framework for understanding conflict within human families. *Psychological Review, 118,* 496–521. (p. 90)

Schmader, T. (2010). Stereotype threat deconstructed. *Current Directions in Psychological Science, 19,* 14–18. (p. 249)

Schmidt, F. L., & Hunter, J. E. (1998). The validity and utility of selection methods in personnel psychology: Practical and theoretical implications of 85 years of research findings. *Psychological Bulletin, 124,* 262–274. (p. 328)

Schmitt, D. P. (2007). Sexual strategies across sexual orientations: How personality traits and culture relate to sociosexuality among gays, lesbians, bisexuals, and heterosexuals. *Journal of Psychology and Human Sexuality, 18,* 183–214. (p. 125)

Schmitt, D. P., & Allik, J. (2005). Simultaneous administration of the Rosenberg Self-esteem Scale in 53 nations: Exploring the universal and culture-specific features of global self-esteem. *Journal of Personality and Social Psychology, 89,* 623–642. (p. 330)

Schmitt, D. P., Allik, J., McCrae, R. R., & Benet-Martínez, V., with many others. (2007). The geographic distribution of Big Five personality traits: Patterns and profiles of human self-description across 56 nations. *Journal of Cross-Cultural Psychology, 38,* 173–212. (p. 324)

Schnall, E., Wassertheil-Smoller, S., Swencionis, C., Zemon, V., Tinker, L., O'Sullivan, M. J., Van Horn, L., & Goodwin, M. (2010). The relationship between religion and cardiovascular outcomes and all-cause mortality in the Women's Health Initiative Observational Study. *Psychology and Health, 25,* 249–263. (p. 299)

Schnall, S., Haidt, J., Clore, G. L., & Jordan, A. (2008). Disgust as embodied moral judgment. *Personality and Social Psychology Bulletin, 34,* 1096–1109. (p. 159)

Schnaper, N. (1980). Comments germane to the paper entitled "The reality of death experiences" by Ernst Rodin. *Journal of Nervous and Mental Disease, 168,* 268–270. (p. 387)

Schneider, S. L. (2001). In search of realistic optimism: Meaning, knowledge, and warm fuzziness. *American Psychologist, 56,* 250–263. (p. 294)

Schneiderman, N. (1999). Behavioral medicine and the management of HIV/AIDS. *International Journal of Behavioral Medicine, 6,* 3–12. (p. 288)

Schneier, B. (2007, May 17). Virginia Tech lesson: Rare risks breed irrational responses. *Wired* (www.wired.com). (p. 225)

Schoenborn, C. A., & Adams, P. F. (2008). *Sleep duration as a correlate of smoking, alcohol use, leisure-time physical inactivity, and obesity among adults: United States, 2004–2006.* Centers for Disease Control and Prevention (www.cdc.gov/nchs). (p. 58)

Schoeneman, T. J. (1994). Individualism. In V. S. Ramachandran (Ed.), *Encyclopedia of human behavior.* San Diego: Academic Press. (p. 332)

Schofield, J. W. (1986). Black-White contact in desegregated schools. In M. Hewstone & R. Brown (Eds.), *Contact and conflict in intergroup encounters.* Oxford: Basil Blackwell. (p. 366)

Schonfield, D., & Robertson, B. A. (1966). Memory storage and aging. *Canadian Journal of Psychology, 20,* 228–236. (p. 97)

Schooler, J. W., Gerhard, D., & Loftus, E. F. (1986). Qualities of the unreal. *Journal of Experimental Psychology: Learning, Memory, and Cognition, 12,* 171–181. (p. 212)

Schorr, E. A., Fox, N.A., van Wassenhove, V., & Knudsen, E.I. (2005). Auditory-visual fusion in speech perception in children with cochlear implants. *Proceedings of the National Academy of Sciences, 102,* 18748–18750. (p. 153)

Schuman, H., & Scott, J. (June, 1989). Generations and collective memories. *American Sociological Review, 54*(3), 359–381. (p. 96)

Schumann, K., & Ross, M. (2010). Why women apologize more than men: Gender differences in thresholds for perceiving offensive behavior. *Psychological Science, 21,* 1649–1655. (p. 109)

Schurger, A., Pereira, F., Treisman, A., Cohen, J. D. (2010, Jan.). Reproducibility distinguishes conscious from nonconscious neural representations. *Science, 327,* 97–99. (p. 50)

Schwartz, B. (1984). *Psychology of learning and behavior* (2nd ed.). New York: Norton. (pp. 172, 379)

Schwartz, B. (2000). Self-determination: The tyranny of freedom. *American Psychologist, 55,* 79–88. (p. 292)

Schwartz, B. (2004). *The paradox of choice: Why more is less.* New York: Ecco/HarperCollins. (p. 292)

Schwartz, J., & Estrin, J. (2004, November 7). Living for today, locked in a paralyzed body. *New York Times* (www.nytimes.com). (p. 302)

Schwartz, J. M., Stoessel, P. W., Baxter, L. R., Jr., Martin, K. M., & Phelps, M. E. (1996). Systematic changes in cerebral glucose metabolic rate after successful behavior modification treatment of obsessive-compulsive disorder. *Archives of General Psychiatry, 53,* 109–113. (pp. 418, 430)

Schwartz, S. H., & Rugel-Lifschitz, T. (2009). Cross-national variation in the size of sex differences in values: Effects of gender equality. *Journal of Personality and Social Psychology, 97,* 171–185. (p. 109)

Schwartzman-Morris, J., & Putterman, C. (2012). Gender differences in the pathogenesis and outcome of lupus and of lupus nephritis. *Clinical and Developmental Immunology, 2012,* 604892. doi: 10.1155/2012/604892. (p. 287)

Schwarz, A. (2012, June 9). Risky rise of the good-grade pill. *New York Times* (www.nytimes.com). (p. 373)

Schwarz, A., & Cohen, S. (2013, March 31). A.D.H.D. seen in 11% of U.S. children as diagnoses rise. *New York Times* (www.nytimes.com). (p. 373)

Schwarz, N., Strack, F., Kommer, D., & Wagner, D. (1987). Soccer, rooms, and the quality of your life: Mood effects on judgments of satisfaction with life in general and with specific domains. *European Journal of Social Psychology, 17,* 69–79. (p. 205)

Sclafani, A. (1995). How food preferences are learned: Laboratory animal models. *Proceedings of the Nutrition Society, 54,* 419–427. (p. 261)

Scott, D. J., & others. (2004, November 9). U-M team reports evidence that smoking affects human brain's natural "feel good" chemical system (press release by Kara Gavin). *University of Michigan Medical School.* (www.med.umich.edu). (p. 385)

Scott, K. M., & 18 others. (2010). Gender and the relationship between marital status and first onset of mood, anxiety and substance use disorders. *Psychological Medicine, 40,* 1495–1505. (p. 98)

Scott, W. A., Scott, R., & McCabe, M. (1991). Family relationships and children's personality: A cross-cultural, cross-source comparison. *British Journal of Social Psychology, 30,* 1–20. (p. 85)

Scott-Sheldon, L. A. J., Terry, D. L., Carey, K. B., Garey, L., & Carey, M. P. (2012). Efficacy of expectancy challenge interventions to reduce college student drinking: A meta-analytic review. *Psychology of Addictive Behaviors, 26,* 393–405. (pp. 381, 383)

Scullin, M. K., & McDaniel, M. A. (2010). Remembering to execute a goal: Sleep on it! *Psychological Science, 21,* 1028–1035. (p. 208)

Sdorow, L. M. (2005). The people behind psychology. In B. Perlman, L. McCann, & W. Buskist (Eds.), *Voices of experience: Memorable talks from the National Institute on the Teaching of Psychology.* Washington, DC: American Psychological Society. (p. 316)

Seal, K. H., Bertenthal, D., Miner, C. R., Sen, S., & Marmar, C. (2007). Bringing the war back home: Mental health disorders among 103,788 U.S. veterans returning from Iraq and Afghanistan seen at Department of Veterans Affairs facilities. *Archives of Internal Medicine, 167,* 467–482. (p. 378)

Sechrest, L., Stickle, T. R., & Stewart, M. (1998). The role of assessment in clinical psychology. In A. Bellack, M. Hersen (series eds.), & C. R. Reynolds (vol. ed.), *Comprehensive clinical psychology: Vol. 4. Assessment.* New York: Pergamon. (p. 317)

Seeman, P. (2007). Dopamine and schizophrenia. *Scholarpedia, 2*(10), 3634 (www.scholarpedia.org). (p. 398)

Seeman, P., Guan, H-C., & Van Tol, H. H. M. (1993). Dopamine D4 receptors elevated in schizophrenia. *Nature, 365,* 441–445. (p. 398)

Seery, M. D. (2011). Resilience: A silver lining to experiencing adverse life events. *Current Directions in Psychological Science, 20,* 390–394. (p. 84)

Segall, M. H., Dasen, P. R., Berry, J. W., & Poortinga, Y. H. (1990). *Human behavior in global perspective: An introduction to cross-cultural psychology.* New York: Pergamon. (pp. 80, 113)

Segerstrom, S. C., Hardy, J. K., Evans, D. R., & Greenberg, R. N. (2012). Vulnerability, distress, and immune response to vaccination in older adults. *Brain, Behavior, and Immunity, 26,* 747–753. (p. 288)

Segerstrom, S. C., Taylor, S. E., Kemeny, M. E., & Fahey, J. L. (1998). Optimism is associated with mood, coping, and immune change in response to stress. *Journal of Personality and Social Psychology, 74,* 1646–1655. (p. 294)

Seibert, S. E., Wang, G., & Courtright, S. H. (2011). Antecedents and consequences of psychological and team empowerment in organizations: A meta-analytic review. *Journal of Applied Psychology, 96,* 981–1003. (p. B-5)

Self, C. E. (1994). *Moral culture and victimization in residence halls.* Dissertation: Thesis (M.A.). Bowling Green University. (p. 389)

Seligman, M. E. P. (1975). *Helplessness: On depression, development and death.* San Francisco: Freeman. (p. 291)

Seligman, M. E. P. (1991). *Learned optimism.* New York: Knopf. (p. 395)

Seligman, M. E. P. (1994). *What you can change and what you can't.* New York: Knopf. (pp. 296, 329)

Seligman, M. E. P. (1995). The effectiveness of psychotherapy: The *Consumer Reports* study. *American Psychologist, 50,* 965–974. (pp. 420, 421)

Seligman, M. E. P. (2002). *Authentic happiness: Using the new positive psychology to realize your potential for lasting fulfillment.* New York: Free Press. (pp. 8, 329)

Seligman, M. E. P. (2011). *Flourish: A visionary new understanding of happiness and well-being.* New York: Free Press. (p. 8)

Seligman, M. E. P., & Maier, S. F. (1967). Failure to escape traumatic shock. *Journal of Experimental Psychology, 74,* 1–9. (p. 291)

Seligman, M. E. P., Steen, T. A., Park, N., & Peterson, C. (2005). Positive psychology progress: Empirical validation of interventions. *American Psychologist, 60,* 410–421. (pp. 8, 306)

Seligman, M. E. P., & Yellen, A. (1987). What is a dream? *Behavior Research and Therapy, 25,* 1–24. (p. 53)

Sellers, H. (2010). *You don't look like anyone I know.* New York: Riverhead Books. (p. 133)

Selye, H. (1936). A syndrome produced by diverse nocuous agents. *Nature, 138,* 32. (p. 285)

Selye, H. (1976). *The stress of life.* New York: McGraw-Hill. (p. 285)

Senate Select Committee on Intelligence. (2004, July 9). *Report of the select committee on intelligence on the U.S. intelligence community's prewar intelligence assessments on Iraq.* Washington, DC: Author. (pp. 221, 349)

Senghas, A., & Coppola, M. (2001). Children creating language: How Nicaraguan Sign Language acquired a spatial grammar. *Psychological Science, 12,* 323–328. (p. 231)

Sengupta, S. (2001, October 10). Sept. 11 attack narrows the racial divide. *New York Times* (www.nytimes.com). (p. 366)

Senju, A., Southgate, V., White, S., & Frith, U. (2009). Mindblind eyes: An absence of spontaneous theory of mind in Asperger syndrome. *Science, 325,* 883–885. (p. 78)

Service, R. F. (1994). Will a new type of drug make memory-making easier? *Science, 266,* 218–219. (p. 201)

Shadish, W. R., & Baldwin, S. A. (2005). Effects of behavioral marital therapy: A meta-analysis of randomized controlled trials. *Journal of Consulting and Clinical Psychology, 73,* 6–14. (p. 422)

Shadish, W. R., Matt, G. E., Navarro, A. M., & Phillips, G. (2000). The effects of psychological therapies under clinically representative conditions: A meta-analysis. *Psychological Bulletin, 126,* 512–529. (p. 421)

Shafir, E., & LeBoeuf, R. A. (2002). Rationality. *Annual Review of Psychology, 53,* 491–517. (p. 225)

Shamir, B., House, R. J., & Arthur, M. B. (1993). The motivational effects of charismatic leadership: A self-concept based theory. *Organizational Science, 4*(4), 577–594. (p. B-6)

Shamosh, N. A., & Gray, J. R. (2008). Delay discounting and intelligence: A meta-analysis. *Intelligence, 36,* 289–305. (p. 119)

Shan, W., Shengua, J., Davis, H., Hunter, M., Peng, K., Shao, X., Wu, Y., Liu, S., Lu, J., Yang, J., Zhang, W., Qiao, M., Wang, J., & Wang, Y. (2012). Mating strategies in Chinese culture: Female risk-avoiding vs. male risk-taking. *Evolution and Human Behavior, 33,* 182–192. (p. 126)

Shanahan, L., McHale, S. M., Osgood, D. W., & Crouter, A. C. (2007). Conflict frequency with mothers and fathers from middle childhood to late adolescence: Within- and between-families comparisons. *Developmental Psychology, 43,* 539–550. (p. 90)

Shapiro, D. (1999). *Psychotherapy of neurotic character.* New York: Basic Books. (p. 412)

Shapiro, K. A., Moo, L. R., & Caramazza, A. (2006). Cortical signatures of noun and verb production. *Proceedings of the National Academic of Sciences, 103,* 1644–1649. (p. 233)

Sharma, A. R., McGue, M. K., & Benson, P. L. (1998). The psychological adjustment of United States adopted adolescents and their nonadopted siblings. *Child Development, 69,* 791–802. (p. 91)

Shaver, P. R., & Mikulincer, M. (2007). Adult attachment strategies and the regulation of emotion. In J. J. Gross (Ed.), *Handbook of emotion regulation.* New York: Guilford Press. (p. 83)

Shaver, P. R., Morgan, H. J., & Wu, S. (1996). Is love a basic emotion? *Personal Relationships, 3,* 81–96. (p. 272)

Shaw, B. A., Liang, J., & Krause, N. (2010). Age and race differences in the trajectories of self-esteem. *Psychology and Aging, 25,* 84–94. (p. 102)

Shedler, J. (2009, March 23). That was then, this is now: Psychoanalytic psychotherapy for the rest of us. Unpublished manuscript, Department of Psychiatry, University of Colorado Health Sciences Center. (p. 412)

Shedler, J. (2010a, November/December). Getting to know me. *Scientific American Mind*, pp. 53–57. (p. 412)

Shedler, J. (2010b). The efficacy of psychodynamic psychotherapy. *American Psychologist, 65*, 98–109. (p. 422)

Sheehan, S. (1982). *Is there no place on earth for me?* Boston: Houghton Mifflin. (p. 397)

Sheldon, K. M., Abad, N., & Hinsch, C. (2011). A two-process view of Facebook use and relatedness need-satisfaction: Disconnection drives use, and connection rewards it. *Journal of Personality and Social Psychology, 100*, 766–775. (p. 267)

Sheldon, K. M., & Niemiec, C. P. (2006). It's not just the amount that counts: Balanced need satisfaction also affects well-being. *Journal of Personality and Social Psychology, 91*, 331–341. (p. 264)

Shenton, M. E. (1992). Abnormalities of the left temporal lobe and thought disorder in schizophrenia: A quantitative magnetic resonance imaging study. *New England Journal of Medicine, 327*, 604–612. (p. 398)

Shepard, R. N. (1990). *Mind sights*. New York: Freeman. (p. 22)

Shepherd, C. (1999, June). News of the weird. *Funny Times*, p. 21. (p. 263)

Shergill, S. S., Bays, P. M., Frith, C. D., & Wolpert, D. M. (2003). Two eyes for an eye: The neuroscience of force escalation. *Science, 301*, 187. (p. 365)

Sherif, M. (1966). *In common predicament: Social psychology of intergroup conflict and cooperation*. Boston: Houghton Mifflin. (p. 366)

Sherman, P. W., & Flaxman, S. M. (2001). Protecting ourselves from food. *American Scientist, 89*, 142–151. (p. 261)

Sherry, S. B., & Hall, P. A. (2009). The perfectionism model of binge eating: Tests of an integrative model. *Journal of Personality and Social Psychology, 96*, 690–709. (p. 401)

Shettleworth, S. J. (1973). Food reinforcement and the organization of behavior in golden hamsters. In R. A. Hinde & J. Stevenson-Hinde (Eds.), *Constraints on learning*. London: Academic Press. (p. 183)

Shifren, J. L., Monz, B. U., Russo, P. A., Segreti, A., Johannes, C. B. (2008). Sexual problems and distress in United States women: Prevalence and correlates. *Obstetrics & Gynecology, 112*, 970–978. (p. 117)

Shockley, K. M., Ispas, D., Rossi, M. E., & Levine, E. L. (2012). A meta-analytic investigation of the relationship between state affect, discrete emotions, and organizational performance. *Human Performance, 25*, 377–411. (p. B-5)

Showers, C. (1992). The motivational and emotional consequences of considering positive or negative possibilities for an upcoming event. *Journal of Personality and Social Psychology, 63*, 474–484. (p. 294)

Shrestha, A., Nohr, E. A., Bech, B. H., Ramlau-Hansen, C. H., & Olsen, J. (2011). Smoking and alcohol during pregnancy and age of menarche in daughters. *Human Reproduction, 26*, 259–265. (p. 111)

Siegel, J. M. (1990). Stressful life events and use of physician services among the elderly: The moderating role of pet ownership. *Journal of Personality and Social Psychology, 58*, 1081–1086. (p. 296)

Siegel, J. M. (2003, November). Why we sleep. *Scientific American*, pp. 92–97. (p. 56)

Siegel, R. K. (1977, October). Hallucinations. *Scientific American*, pp. 132–140. (p. 387)

Siegel, R. K. (1980). The psychology of life after death. *American Psychologist, 35*, 911–931. (p. 387)

Siegel, R. K. (1982, October). Quoted by J. Hooper, Mind tripping. *Omni*, pp. 72–82, 159–160. (p. 387)

Siegel, R. K. (1984, March 15). Personal communication. (p. 387)

Siegel, R. K. (1990). *Intoxication*. New York: Pocket Books. (pp. 386, 387)

Siegel, S. (2005). Drug tolerance, drug addiction, and drug anticipation. *Current Directions in Psychological Science, 14*, 296–300. (p. 173)

Siegler, R. S., & Ellis, S. (1996). Piaget on childhood. *Psychological Science, 7*, 211–215. (p. 76)

Silber, M. H., & 11 others. (2008). The visual scoring of sleep in adults. *Journal of Clinical Sleep Medicine, 3*, 121–131. (p. 54)

Silbersweig, D. A., Stern, E., Frith, C., Cahill, C., Holmes, A., Grootoonk, S., Seaward, J., McKenna, P., Chua, S. E., Schnorr, L., Jones, T., & Frackowiak, R. S. J. (1995). A functional neuroanatomy of hallucinations in schizophrenia. *Nature, 378*, 176–179. (p. 398)

Silva, A. J., Stevens, C. F., Tonegawa, S., & Wang, Y. (1992). Deficient hippocampal long-term potentiation in alpha-calcium-calmodulin kinase II mutant mice. *Science, 257*, 201–206. (p. 201)

Silva, C. E., & Kirsch, I. (1992). Interpretive sets, expectancy, fantasy proneness, and dissociation as predictors of hypnotic response. *Journal of Personality and Social Psychology, 63*, 847–856. (p. 156)

Silver, M., & Geller, D. (1978). On the irrelevance of evil: The organization and individual action. *Journal of Social Issues, 34*, 125–136. (p. 346)

Silver, N. (2009, December 27). The odds of airborne terror. www.fivethirtyeight.com. (p. 225)

Silver, R. C., Holman, E. A., McIntosh, D. N., Poulin, M., & Gil-Rivas, V. (2002). Nationwide longitudinal study of psychological responses to September 11. *Journal of the American Medical Association, 288*, 1235–1244. (p. 284)

Silverman, J. (2008, September 8). Quoted by A. Zaharov-Reutt, Skype: The "wow" started 5 years ago. www.itwire.com. (p. 263)

Silverman, K., Evans, S. M., Strain, E. C., & Griffiths, R. R. (1992). Withdrawal syndrome after the double-blind cessation of caffeine consumption. *New England Journal of Medicine, 327*, 1109–1114. (p. 384)

Simon, H. A., & Chase, W. G. (1973) Skill in chess. *American Scientist, 61*, 394-403. (p. 238)

Simon, V., Czobor, P., Bálint, S., Mésáros, A., & Bitter, I. (2009). Prevalence and correlates of adult attention-deficit hyperactivity disorder: Meta-analysis. *British Journal of Psychiatry, 194*, 204–211. (p. 373)

Simons, D. J., & Chabris, C. F. (1999). Gorillas in our midst: Sustained inattentional blindness for dynamic events. *Perception, 28*, 1059–1074. (p. 51)

Simonton, D. K. (1988). Age and outstanding achievement: What do we know after a century of research? *Psychological Bulletin, 104*, 251–267. (p. 246)

Simonton, D. K. (1990). Creativity in the later years: Optimistic prospects for achievement. *The Gerontologist, 30*, 626–631. (p. 246)

Simonton, D. K. (1992). The social context of career success and course for 2,026 scientists and inventors. *Personality and Social Psychology Bulletin, 18*, 452–463. (p. 227)

Sin, N. L., & Lyubomirsky, S. (2009). Enhancing well-being and alleviating depressive symptoms with positive psychology interventions: A practice-friendly meta-analysis. *Journal of Clinical Psychology: In session, 65*, 467–487. (pp. 305, 306)

Sinclair, R. C., Hoffman, C., Mark, M. M., Martin, L. L., & Pickering, T. L. (1994). Construct accessibility and the misattribution of arousal: Schachter and Singer revisited. *Psychological Science, 5*, 15–18. (p. 270)

Singer, T., Seymour, B., O'Doherty, J., Kaube, H., Dolan, R. J., & Frith, C. (2004). Empathy for pain involves the affective but not sensory components of pain. *Science, 303*, 1157–1162. (p. 186)

Singh, D. (1995). Female health, attractiveness, and desirability for relationships: Role of breast asymmetry and waist-to-hip ratio. *Ethology and Sociobiology, 16,* 465–481. (p. 126)

Singh, S. (1997). *Fermat's enigma: The epic quest to solve the world's greatest mathematical problem.* New York: Bantam Books. (p. 226)

Singh, S., & Riber, K. A. (1997, November). Fermat's last stand. *Scientific American,* pp. 68–73. (p. 227)

Sio, U. N., & Ormerod, T. C. (2009). Does incubation enhance problem solving? A meta-analytic review. *Psychological Bulletin, 135,* 94–120. (p. 226)

Sipski, M. L., Alexander, C. J., & Rosen, R. C. (1999). Sexual response in women with spinal cord injuries: Implications for our understanding of the able bodied. *Journal of Sexual & Marital Therapy, 25,* 11–22. (pp. 36, 118)

Sireteanu, R. (1999). Switching on the infant brain. *Science, 286,* 59, 61. (p. 153)

Skeem, J. L., & Cooke, D. J. (2010). Is criminal behavior a central component of psychopathy? Conceptual directions for resolving the debate. *Psychological Assessment, 22,* 433–445. (p. 403)

Skinner, B. F. (1953). *Science and human behavior.* New York: Macmillan. (p. 177)

Skinner, B. F. (1956). A case history in scientific method. *American Psychologist, 11,* 221–233. (p. 178)

Skinner, B. F. (1961, November). Teaching machines. *Scientific American,* pp. 91–102. (p. 177)

Skinner, B. F. (1983, September). Origins of a behaviorist. *Psychology Today,* pp. 22–33. (p. 179)

Skov, R. B., & Sherman, S. J. (1986). Information-gathering processes: Diagnosticity, hypothesis-confirmatory strategies, and perceived hypothesis confirmation. *Journal of Experimental Social Psychology, 22,* 93–121. (p. 221)

Slovic, P. (2010, Winter). The more who die, the less we care: Confronting psychic numbing. *Trauma Psychology* (APA Division 56 Newsletter), pp. 4–8. (p. 223)

Slutske, W. S. (2005). Alcohol use disorders among U.S. college students and their non-college-attending peers. *Archives of General Psychiatry, 62,* 321–327. (p. 383)

Slutske, W. S., Moffitt, T. E., Poulton, R., & Caspi A. (2012). Undercontrolled temperament at age 3 predicts disordered gambling at age 32: A longitudinal study of a complete birth cohort. *Psychological Science, 23,* 510–516. (p. 101)

Small, D. A., Loewenstein, G., & Slovic, P. (2007). Sympathy and callousness: The impact of deliberative thought on donations to identifiable and statistical victims. *Organizational Behavior and Human Decision Processes, 102,* 143–153. (p. 223)

Small, M. F. (1997). Making connections. *American Scientist, 85,* 502–504. (p. 85)

Smedley, A., & Smedley, B. D. (2005). Race as biology is fiction, racism as a social problem is real: Anthropological and historical perspectives on the social construction of race. *American Psychologist, 60,* 16–26. (p. 248)

Smelser, N. J., & Mitchell, F. (Eds.). (2002). *Terrorism: Perspectives from the behavioral and social sciences.* Washington, DC: National Research Council, National Academies Press. (p. 354)

Smilek, D., Carriere, J. S. A., & Cheyne, J. A. (2010). Out of mind, out of sight: Eye blinking as indicator and embodiment of mind wandering. *Psychological Science, 21,* 786–789. (p. 51)

Smith, A. (1983). Personal correspondence. (p. 398)

Smith, B. C. (2011, January 16). The senses and the multi-sensory. *World Question Center* (www.edge.org). (p. 160)

Smith, D. M., Loewenstein, G., Jankovic, A., & Ubel, P. A. (2009). Happily hopeless: Adaptation to a permanent, but not to a temporary, disability. *Health Psychology, 28,* 787–791. (p. 302)

Smith, E., & Delargy, M. (2005). Clinical review: Locked-in Syndrome. *British Medical Journal, 330,* 406–409. (p. 302)

Smith, M. B. (1978). Psychology and values. *Journal of Social Issues, 34,* 181–199. (p. 321)

Smith, M. L., & Glass, G. V. (1977). Meta-analysis of psychotherapy outcome studies. *American Psychologist, 32,* 752–760. (p. 421)

Smith, M. L., Glass, G. V., & Miller, R. L. (1980). *The benefits of psychotherapy.* Baltimore: Johns Hopkins Press. (p. 421)

Smith, P. B., & Tayeb, M. (1989). Organizational structure and processes. In M. Bond (Ed.), *The cross-cultural challenge to social psychology.* Newbury Park, CA: Sage. (p. B-7)

Smith, P. F. (1995). Cannabis and the brain. *New Zealand Journal of Psychology, 24,* 5–12. (p. 388)

Smith, S. J., Axelton, A. M., & Saucier, D. A. (2009). The effects of contact on sexual prejudice: A meta-analysis. *Sex Roles, 61,* 178–191. (p. 366)

Smith, T. B., Bartz, J., & Richards, P. S. (2007). Outcomes of religious and spiritual adaptations to psychotherapy: A meta-analytic review. *Psychotherapy Research, 17,* 643–655. (p. 423)

Smith, T. W. (1998, December). *American sexual behavior: Trends, sociodemographic differences, and risk behavior.* (National Opinion Research Center GSS Topical Report No. 25). (p. 122)

Smith, T. W. (2006). Personality as risk and resilience in physical health. *Current Directions in Psychological Science, 15,* 227–231. (p. 290)

Smits, I. A. M., Dolan, C. V., Vorst, H. C. M., Wicherts, J. M., & Timmerman, M. E. (2011). Cohort differences in big five personality traits over a period of 25 years. *Journal of Personality and Social Psychology, 100,* 1124–1138. (pp. 297, 324)

Snedeker, J., Geren, J., & Shafto, C. L. (2007). Starting over: International adoption as a natural experiment in language development. *Psychological Science, 18,* 79–86. (p. 231)

Snodgrass, S. E., Higgins, J. G., & Todisco, L. (1986). The effects of walking behavior on mood. Paper presented at the American Psychological Association convention. (p. 278)

Snowdon, D. A., Kemper, S. J., Mortimer, J. A., Greiner, L. H., Wekstein, D. R., & Markesbery, W. R. (1996). Linguistic ability in early life and cognitive function and Alzheimer's disease in late life: Finds from the Nun Study. *Journal of the American Medical Association, 275,* 528–532. (p. 245)

Snyder, S. H. (1984). Neurosciences: An integrative discipline. *Science, 225,* 1255–1257. (pp. 30, 375)

Snyder, S. H. (1986). *Drugs and the brain.* New York: Scientific American Library. (p. 427)

Social Watch. (2006, March 8). No country in the world treats its women as well as its men (www.socialwatch.org). (p. 113)

Solomon, D. A., Keitner, G. I., Miller, I. W., Shea, M. T., & Keller, M. B. (1995). Course of illness and maintenance treatments for patients with bipolar disorder. *Journal of Clinical Psychiatry, 56,* 5–13. (p. 427)

Solomon, J. (1996, May 20). Breaking the silence. *Newsweek,* pp. 20–22. (p. 375)

Solomon, M. (1987, December). Standard issue. *Psychology Today,* pp. 30–31. (p. 360)

Song, S. (2006, March 27). Mind over medicine. *Time*, p. 47. (p. 156)

Soto, C. J., John, O. P., Gosling, S. D., & Potter, J. (2011). Age differences in personality traits from 10 to 65: Big five domains and facets in a large cross-sectional sample. *Journal of Personality and Social Psychology, 100*, 330–348. (p. 324)

Spanos, N. P., & Coe, W. C. (1992). A social-psychological approach to hypnosis. In E. Fromm & M. R. Nash (Eds.), *Contemporary hypnosis research*. New York: Guilford. (p. 157)

Sparrow, B., Liu, J., & Wegner, D. M. (2011). Google effects on memory: Cognitive consequences of having information at our fingertips. *Science, 333*, 776–778. (p. 194)

Speer, N. K., Reynolds, J. R., Swallow, K. M., & Zacks, J. M. (2009). Reading stories activates neural representations of visual and motor experiences. *Psychological Science, 20*, 989–999. (pp. 186, 233)

Spence, I., & Feng, J. (2010). Video games and spatial cognition. *Review of General Psychology, 14*, 92–104. (p. 150)

Spencer, S. J., Steele, C. M., & Quinn, D. M. (1997). Stereotype threat and women's math performance. Unpublished manuscript, Hope College. (p. 249)

Sperling, G. (1960). The information available in brief visual presentations. *Psychological Monographs, 74* (Whole No. 498). (p. 196)

Sperry, R. W. (1964). Problems outstanding in the evolution of brain function. James Arthur Lecture, American Museum of Natural History, New York. Cited by R. Ornstein (1977), *The psychology of consciousness* (2nd ed.). New York: Harcourt Brace Jovanovich. (p. 49)

Spiegel, D. (2007). The mind prepared: Hypnosis in surgery. *Journal of the National Cancer Institute, 99*, 1280–1281. (p. 156)

Spiegel, K., Leproult, R., L'Hermite-Balériaux, M., Copinschi, G., Penev, P. D., & Van Cauter, E. (2004). Leptin levels are dependent on sleep duration: Relationships with sympathovagal balance, carbohydrate regulation, cortisol, and thyrotropin. *Journal of Clinical Endocrinology and Metabolism, 89*, 5762–5771. (p. 58)

Spielberger, C., & London, P. (1982). Rage boomerangs. *American Health, 1*, 52–56. (p. 290)

Sprecher, S. (1989). The importance to males and females of physical attractiveness, earning potential, and expressiveness in initial attraction. *Sex Roles, 21*, 591–607. (p. 360)

Spring, B., Pingitore, R., Bourgeois, M., Kessler, K. H., & Bruckner, E. (1992). The effects and non-effects of skipping breakfast: Results of three studies. Paper presented at the American Psychological Association convention. (p. 264)

Srivastava, S., John, O. P., Gosling, S. D., & Potter, J. (2003). Development of personality in early and middle adulthood: Set like plaster or persistent change? *Journal of Personality & Social Psychology, 84*, 1041–1053. (p. 102)

Srivastava, S., McGonigal, K. M., Richards, J. M., Butler, E. A., & Gross, J. J. (2006). Optimism in close relationships: How seeing things in a positive light makes them so. *Journal of Personality and Social Psychology, 91*, 143–153. (p. 294)

St. Clair, D., Xu, M., Wang, P., Yu, Y., Fang, Y., Zhang, F., Zheng, X., Gu, N., Feng, G., Sham, P., & He, L. (2005). Rates of adult schizophrenia following prenatal exposure to the Chinese famine of 1959–1961. *Journal of the American Medical Association, 294*, 557–562. (p. 399)

Stager, C. L., & Werker, J. F. (1997). Infants listen for more phonetic detail in speech perception than in word-learning tasks. *Nature, 388*, 381–382. (p. 230)

Stanford University Center for Narcolepsy. (2002). Narcolepsy is a serious medical disorder and a key to understanding other sleep disorders (www.med.stanford.edu/school/Psychiatry/narcolepsy). (p. 59)

Stanley, J. C. (1997). Varieties of intellectual talent. *Journal of Creative Behavior, 31*, 93–119. (p. 242)

Stanovich, K. E. (1996). *How to think straight about psychology*. New York: HarperCollins. (p. 312)

Stanovich, K. E., & West, R. F. (2008). On the relative independence of thinking biases and cognitive ability. *Journal of Personality and Social Psychology, 94*, 672–695. (p. 225)

Starr, J. M., Deary, I. J., Lemmon, H., & Whalley, L. J. (2000). Mental ability age 11 years and health status age 77 years. *Age and Ageing, 29*, 523–528. (p. 245)

State, M. W., & Sestan, N. (2012). The emerging biology of autism spectrum disorders. *Science, 337*, 1301–1304. (pp. 78, 79)

Staub, E. (1989). *The roots of evil: The psychological and cultural sources of genocide*. New York: Cambridge University Press. (p. 340)

Staub, E., & Vollhardt, J. (2008). Altruism born of suffering: The roots of caring and helping after experiences of personal and political victimization. *American Journal of Orthopsychiatry, 78*, 276–280. (p. 432)

Steel, P., Schmidt, J., & Schultz, J. (2008). Refining the relationship between personality and subject well-being. *Psychological Bulletin, 134*, 138–161. (p. 305)

Steele, C. M. (1990, May). A conversation with Claude Steele. *APS Observer*, pp. 11–17. (p. 248)

Steele, C. M., Spencer, S. J., & Aronson, J. (2002). Contending with group image: The psychology of stereotype and social identity threat. *Advances in Experimental Social Psychology, 34*, 379–440. (p. 250)

Stein, S. (2009, August 20). New poll: 77 percent support "choice" of public option. *Huffington Post* (huffingtonpost.com). (p. 15)

Steinberg, L., Cauffman, E., Woolard, J., Graham, S., & Banich, M. (2009). Are adolescents less mature than adults? Minors' access to abortion, the juvenile death penalty, and the alleged APA "flip-flop." *American Psychologist, 64*, 583–594. (p. 87)

Steinberg, L., & Morris, A. S. (2001). Adolescent development. *Annual Review of Psychology, 52*, 83–110. (pp. 90, 91)

Steinberg, L., & Scott, E. S. (2003). Less guilty by reason of adolescence: Developmental immaturity, diminished responsibility, and the juvenile death penalty. *American Psychologist, 58*, 1009–1018. (p. 87)

Steinberg, L. (1987, September). Bound to bicker. *Psychology Today*, pp. 36–39. (p. 90)

Steinberg, L. (2010, March). Analyzing adolescence. Interview with Sara Martin. *Monitor on Psychology*, pp. 26–29. (p. 86)

Steinberg, N. (1993, February). Astonishing love stories (from an earlier United Press International report). *Games*, p. 47. (p. 359)

Stepanikova, I., Nie, N. H., & He, X. (2010). Time on the Internet at home, loneliness, and life satisfaction: Evidence from panel time-diary data. *Computers in Human Behavior, 26*, 329–338. (p. 267)

Sternberg, R. J. (1985). *Beyond IQ: A triarchic theory of human intelligence*. New York: Cambridge University Press. (p. 237)

Sternberg, R. J. (1988). Applying cognitive theory to the testing and teaching of intelligence. *Applied Cognitive Psychology, 2*, 231–255. (p. 226)

Sternberg, R. J. (1999). The theory of successful intelligence. *Review of General Psychology, 3*, 292–316. (p. 237)

Sternberg, R. J. (2003). Our research program validating the triarchic theory of successful intelligence: Reply to Gottfredson. *Intelligence, 31*, 399–413. (pp. 226, 237)

Sternberg, R. J. (2006). The Rainbow Project: Enhance the SAT through assessments of analytical, practical, and creative skills. *Intelligence, 34*, 321–350. (p. 227)

Sternberg, R. J., & Grajek, S. (1984). The nature of love. *Journal of Personality and Social Psychology, 47*, 312–329. (p. 362)

Sternberg, R. J., & Kaufman, J. C. (1998). Human abilities. *Annual Review of Psychology, 49*, 479–502. (p. 235)

Sternberg, R. J., & Lubart, T. I. (1991). An investment theory of creativity and its development. *Human Development, 1*–31. (p. 226)

Sternberg, R. J., & Lubart, T. I. (1992). Buy low and sell high: An investment approach to creativity. *Psychological Science, 1*, 1–5. (p. 226)

Stetter, F., & Kupper, S. (2002). Autogenic training: A meta-analysis of clinical outcome studies. *Applied Psychophysiology and Biofeedback, 27*, 45–98. (p. 298)

Stevenson, H. W. (1992, December). Learning from Asian schools. *Scientific American*, pp. 70–76. (p. 249)

Stice, E., & Shaw, H. E. (1994). Adverse effects of the media portrayed thin-ideal on women and linkages to bulimic symptomatology. *Journal of Social and Clinical Psychology, 13*, 288–308. (p. 401)

Stice, E., Shaw, H., Bohon, C., Marti, C. N., & Rohde, P. (2009). A meta-analytic review of depression prevention programs for children and adolescents: Factors that predict magnitude of intervention effects. *Journal of Consulting and Clinical Psychology, 77*, 486–503. (p. 418)

Stice, E., Spangler, D., & Agras, W. S. (2001). Exposure to media-portrayed thin-ideal images adversely affects vulnerable girls: A longitudinal experiment. *Journal of Social and Clinical Psychology, 20*, 270–288. (p. 401)

Stickgold, R. (2000, March 7). Quoted by S. Blakeslee, For better learning, researchers endorse, "sleep on it" adage. *New York Times*, p. F2. (p. 61)

Stickgold, R., & Ellenbogen, J. M. (2008, August/September). Quiet! Sleeping brain at work. *Scientific American Mind*, pp. 23–29. (p. 56)

Stickgold, R., Hobson, J. A., Fosse, R., & Fosse, M. (2001). Sleep, learning, and dreams: Off-line memory processing. *Science, 294*, 1052–1057. (p. 61)

Stiglitz, J. (2009, September 13). Towards a better measure of well-being. *Financial Times* (www.ft.com). (p. 305)

Stillman, T. F., Baumeister, R. F., Vohs, K. D., Lambert, N. M., Fincham, F. D., & Brewer, L. E. (2010). Personal philosophy and personnel achievement: Belief in free will predicts better job performance. *Social Psychological and Personality Science, 1*, 43–50. (p. 293)

Stillman, T. F., Lambet, N. M., Fincham, F. D., & Baumeister, R. F. (2011). Meaning as magnetic force: Evidence that meaning in life promotes interpersonal appeal. *Social Psychological and Personality Science, 2*, 13–20. (p. 432)

Stith, S. M., Rosen, K. H., Middleton, K. A., Busch, A. L., Lunderberg, K., & Carlton, R. P. (2000). The intergenerational transmission of spouse abuse: A meta-analysis. *Journal of Marriage and the Family, 62*, 640–654. (p. 187)

Stix, G. (2011, March). The neuroscience of true grit. *Scientific American, 304*, 28–33. (p. 379)

Stockton, M. C., & Murnen, S. K. (1992). Gender and sexual arousal in response to sexual stimuli: A meta-analytic review. Paper presented at the American Psychological Society convention. (p. 118)

Stone, A. A., & Neale, J. M. (1984). Effects of severe daily events on mood. *Journal of Personality and Social Psychology, 46*, 137–144. (p. 302)

Stone, A. A., Schwartz, J. E., Broderick, J. E., & Deaton, A. (2010). A snapshot of the age distribution of psychological well-being in the United States. *PNAS, 107*, 9985–9990. (p. 100)

Storbeck, J., Robinson, M. D., & McCourt, M. E. (2006). Semantic processing precedes affect retrieval: The neurological case for cognitive primary in visual processing. *Review of General Psychology, 10*, 41–55. (p. 271)

Storms, M. D. (1973). Videotape and the attribution process: Reversing actors' and observers' points of view. *Journal of Personality and Social Psychology, 27*, 165–175. (p. 339)

Storms, M. D. (1983). *Development of sexual orientation*. Washington, DC: Office of Social and Ethical Responsibility, American Psychological Association. (p. 122)

Storms, M. D., & Thomas, G. C. (1977). Reactions to physical closeness. *Journal of Personality and Social Psychology, 35*, 412–418. (p. 347)

Stowell, J. R., Oldham, T., & Bennett, D. (2010). Using student response systems ("clickers") to combat conformity and shyness. *Teaching of Psychology, 37*, 135–140. (p. 342)

Strack, F., Martin, L., & Stepper, S. (1988). Inhibiting and facilitating conditions of the human smile: A nonobtrusive test of the facial feedback hypothesis. *Journal of Personality and Social Psychology, 54*, 768–777. (p. 278)

Strand, S., Deary, I. J., & Smith, P. (2006). Sex differences in cognitive abilities test scores: A UK national picture. *British Journal of Educational Psychology, 76*, 463–480. (p. 247)

Strange, B. A., & Dolan, R. J. (2004). b-Adrenergic modulation of emotional memory-evoked human amygdala and hippocampal responses. *Proceedings of the National Academy of Sciences, 101*, 11454–11458. (p. 200)

Strange, D., Hayne, H., & Garry, M. (2008). A photo, a suggestion, a false memory. *Applied Cognitive Psychology, 22*, 587–603. (p. 210)

Strasburger, V. C., Jordan, A. B., & Donnerstein, E. (2010). Health effects of media on children and adolescents. *Pediatrics, 125*, 756–767. (p. 187)

Stratton, G. M. (1896). Some preliminary experiments on vision without inversion of the retinal image. *Psychological Review, 3*, 611–617. (p. 150)

Straub, R. O., Seidenberg, M. S., Bever, T. G., & Terrace, H. S. (1979). Serial learning in the pigeon. *Journal of the Experimental Analysis of Behavior, 32*, 137–148. (p. 234)

Straus, M. A., Sugarman, D. B., & Giles-Sims, J. (1997). Spanking by parents and subsequent antisocial behavior of children. *Archives of Pediatric Adolescent Medicine, 151*, 761–767. (p. 178)

Strawbridge, W. J. (1999). Mortality and religious involvement: A review and critique of the results, the methods, and the measures. Paper presented at a Harvard University conference on religion and health, sponsored by the National Institute for Health Research and the John Templeton Foundation. (p. 300)

Strawbridge, W. J., Cohen, R. D., & Shema, S. J. (1997). Frequent attendance at religious services and mortality over 28 years. *American Journal of Public Health, 87*, 957–961. (p. 300)

Strayer, D. L., & Watson, J. M. (2012, March/April). Supertaskers and the multitasking brain. *Scientific American Mind*, pp. 22–29. (p. 51)

Strick, M., Dijksterhuis, A., Bos, M. W., Sjoersdma, A., & van Baaren, R. B. (2011). A meta-analysis on unconscious thought effects. *Social Cognition, 29*, 738–762. (p. 226)

Strick, M., Dijksterhuis, A., & van Baaren, R. B. (2010). Unconscious-thought effects take place off-line, not on-line. *Psychological Science, 21*, 484–488. (p. 226)

Stroebe, W., Schut, H., & Stroebe, M. S. (2005). Grief work, disclosure and counseling: Do they help the bereaved? *Clinical Psychology Review, 25*, 395–414. (p. 101)

Stross, R. (2011, July 9). The therapist will see you now, via the web. *New York Times* (www.nytimes.com). (p. 419)

Strully, K. W. (2009). Job loss and health in the U.S. labor market. *Demography, 46*, 221–246. (p. 284)

Štulhofer, A., Šoh, D., Jelaska, N., Ba_ak, V., & Landripet, I. (2011). Religiosity and sexual risk behavior among Croatian college students, 1998–2008. *Journal of Sex Research, 48,* 360–371. (p. 119)

Stunkard, A. J., Harris, J. R., Pedersen, N. L., & McClearn, G. E. (1990). A separated twin study of the body mass index. *New England Journal of Medicine, 322,* 1483–1487. (p. 262)

Stutzer, A., & Frey, B. S. (2006). Does marriage make people happy, or do happy people get married? *Journal of Socio-Economics, 35,* 326–347. (p. 301)

Su, R., Rounds, J., & Armstrong, P. I. (2009). Men and things, women and people: A meta-analysis of sex differences in interests. *Psychological Bulletin, 135,* 859–884. (p. 110)

Subrahmanyam, K., & Greenfield, P. (2008). Online communication and adolescent relationships. *The Future of Children, 18,* 119–146. (p. 90)

Suddath, R. L., Christison, G. W., Torrey, E. F., Casanova, M. F., & Weinberger, D. R. (1990). Anatomical abnormalities in the brains of monozygotic twins discordant for schizophrenia. *New England Journal of Medicine, 322,* 789–794. (p. 399)

Sue, S. (2006). Research to address racial and ethnic disparities in mental health: Some lessons learned. In S. I. Donaldson, D. E. Berger, & K. Pezdek (Eds.), *Applied psychology: New frontiers and rewarding careers.* Mahwah, NJ: Erlbaum. (p. 423)

Suedfeld, P. (1998). Homo invictus: The indomitable species. *Canadian Psychology, 38,* 164–173. (p. 432)

Suedfeld, P. (2000). Reverberations of the Holocaust fifty years later: Psychology's contributions to understanding persecution and genocide. *Canadian Psychology, 41,* 1–9. (p. 432)

Suedfeld, P., & Mocellin, J. S. P. (1987). The "sensed presence" in unusual environments. *Environment and Behavior, 19,* 33–52. (p. 387)

Sullivan, P. F., Neale, M. C., & Kendler, K. S. (2000). Genetic epidemiology of major depression: Review and meta-analysis. *American Journal of Psychiatry, 157,* 1552–1562. (p. 394)

Sullivan/Anderson, A. (2009, March 30). How to end the war over sex ed. *Time,* pp. 40–43. (p. 118)

Suls, J. M., & Tesch, F. (1978). Students' preferences for information about their test performance: A social comparison study. *Journal of Experimental Social Psychology, 8,* 189–197. (p. 304)

Summers, M. (1996, December 9). Mister Clean. *People Weekly,* pp. 139–142. (p. 371)

Sun, Q. I., Townsend, M. K., Okereke, O., Franco, O. H., Hu, F. B., & Grodstein, F. (2009). Adiposity and weight change in mid-life in relation to healthy survival after age 70 in women: Prospective cohort study. *British Medical Journal, 339,* b3796. (p. 262)

Sundie, J. M., Kenrick, D. T., Griskevicius, V., Tybur, J. M., Vohs, K. D., & Beal, D. J. (2011). Peacocks, Porsches, and Thorsten Veblen: Conspicuous consumption as a sexual signaling system. *Journal of Personality and Social Psychology, 100,* 664–680. (p. 126)

Sundstrom, E., De Meuse, K. P., & Futrell, D. (1990). Work teams: Applications and effectiveness. *American Psychologist, 45,* 120–133. (p. B-8)

Sunstein, C. R. (2007). On the divergent American reactions to terrorism and climate change. *Columbia Law Review, 107,* 503–557. (p. 222)

Suomi, S. J. (1986). Anxiety-like disorders in young nonhuman primates. In R. Gettleman (Ed.), *Anxiety disorders of childhood.* New York: Guilford Press. (p. 380)

Suomi, S. J., Collins, M. L., Harlow, H. F., & Ruppenthal, G. C. (1976). Effects of maternal and peer separations on young monkeys. *Journal of Child Psychology and Psychiatry, 17,* 101–112. (p. 154)

Surgeon General. (1986). *The Surgeon General's workshop on pornography and public health,* June 22–24. Report prepared by E. P. Mulvey & J. L. Haugaard and released by Office of the Surgeon General on August 4, 1986. (p. 357)

Surgeon General. (1999). *Mental health: A report of the surgeon general.* Rockville, MD: U.S. Department of Health and Human Services. (p. 376)

Susser, E., Neugenbauer, R., Hoek, H. W., Brown, A. S., Lin, S., Labovitz, D., & Gorman, J. M. (1996). Schizophrenia after prenatal famine. *Archives of General Psychiatry, 53*(1), 25–31. (p. 399)

Sutherland, A. (2006a). *Bitten and scratched: Life and lessons at the premier school for exotic animal trainers.* New York: Viking. (p. 167)

Sutherland, A. (2006b, June 25). What Shamu taught me about a happy marriage. *New York Times* (www.nytimes.com). (p. 167)

Swami, V., & 60 others. (2010). The attractive female body weight and female body dissatisfaction in 26 countries across 10 world regions: Results of the international body project I. *Personality and Social Psychology Bulletin, 36,* 309–325. (p. 401)

Swann, W. B., Jr., Chang-Schneider, C., & McClarty, K. L. (2007). Do people's self-views matter? Self-concept and self-esteem in everyday life. *American Psychologist, 62,* 84–94. (p. 329)

Sweat, J. A., & Durm, M. W. (1993). Psychics: Do police departments really use them? *Skeptical Inquirer, 17,* 148–158. (p. 162)

Swerdlow, N. R., & Koob, G. F. (1987). Dopamine, schizophrenia, mania, and depression: Toward a unified hypothesis of cortico-stiato-pallido-thalamic function (with commentary). *Behavioral and Brain Sciences, 10,* 197–246. (p. 398)

Swinburn, B. A., Sacks, G., Hall, K. D., McPherson, K., Finegood, D. T., Moodie, M. L., & Gortmaker, S. L. (2011). The global obesity pandemic: Shaped by global drivers and local environments. *The Lancet, 378,* 804–814. (p. 262)

Taheri, S. (2004a, 20 December). Does the lack of sleep make you fat? *University of Bristol Research News* (www.bristol.ac.uk). (p. 262)

Taheri, S., Lin, L., Austin, D., Young, T., & Mignot, E. (2004b). Short sleep duration is associated with reduced leptin, elevated ghrelin, and increased body mass index. *PloS Medicine, 1*(3), e62. (p. 262)

Tajfel, H. (Ed.). (1982). *Social identity and intergroup relations.* New York: Cambridge University Press. (p. 352)

Tamres, L. K., Janicki, D., & Helgeson, V. S. (2002). Sex differences in coping behavior: A meta-analytic review and an examination of relative coping. *Personality and Social Psychology Review, 6,* 2–30. (p. 110)

Tangney, J. P., Baumeister, R. F., & Boone, A. L. (2004). High self-control predicts good adjustment, less pathology, better grades, and interpersonal success. *Journal of Personality, 72,* 271–324. (p. 293)

Tannen, D. (1990). *You just don't understand: Women and men in conversation.* New York: Morrow. (p. 110)

Tannenbaum, P. (2002, February). Quoted by R. Kubey & M. Csikszentmihalyi, Television addiction is no mere metaphor. *Scientific American,* pp. 74–80. (p. 137)

Tanner, J. M. (1978). *Fetus into man: Physical growth from conception to maturity.* Cambridge, MA: Harvard University Press. (pp. 86, 111)

Tardif, T., Fletcher, P., Liang, W., Zhang, Z., Kaciroti, N., & Marchman, V. A. (2008). Baby's first 10 words. *Developmental Psychology, 44,* 929–938. (p. 231)

Taubes, G. (2001). The soft science of dietary fat. *Science, 291,* 2536–2545. (p. 264)

Taubes, G. (2002, July 7). What if it's all been a big fat lie? *New York Times.* (www.nytimes.com). (p. 264)

Tavernise, S. (2013, February 13). To reduce suicide rates, new focus turns to guns. *New York Times* (www.nytimes.com). (p. 392)

Taylor, C. A., Manganello, J. A., Lee, S. J., & Rice, J. C. (2010). Mothers' spanking of 3-year-old children and subsequent risk of children's aggressive behavior. *Pediatrics, 125,* 1057–1065. (p. 179)

Taylor, P. J., Gooding, P., Wood, A. M., & Tarrier, N. (2011). The role of defeat and entrapment in depression, anxiety, and suicide. *Psychological Bulletin, 137,* 391–420. (p. 392)

Taylor, S. (2011). Etiology of obsessions and compulsions: A meta-analysis and narrative review of twin studies. *Clinical Psychology Review, 31,* 1361–1372. (p. 380)

Taylor, S., Kuch, K., Koch, W. J., Crockett, D. J., & Passey, G. (1998). The structure of posttraumatic stress symptoms. *Journal of Abnormal Psychology, 107,* 154–160. (p. 379)

Taylor, S. E. (1983). Adjustment to threatening events: A theory of cognitive adaptation. *American Psychologist, 38,* 1161–1173. (p. 296)

Taylor, S. E. (1989). *Positive illusions.* New York: Basic Books. (p. 223)

Taylor, S. E. (2002). *The tending instinct: How nurturing is essential to who we are and how we live.* New York: Times Books. (p. 110)

Taylor, S. E. (2006). Tend and befriend: Biobehavioral bases of affiliation under stress. *Current Directions in Psychological Science, 15,* 273–277. (p. 286)

Taylor, S. E., Cousino, L. K., Lewis, B. P., Gruenewald, T. L., Gurung, R. A. R., & Updegraff, J. A. (2000). Biobehavioral responses to stress in females: Tend-and-befriend, not fight-or-flight. *Psychological Review, 107,* 411–430. (p. 286)

Taylor, S. E., Pham, L. B., Rivkin, I. D., & Armor, D. A. (1998). Harnessing the imagination: Mental simulation, self-regulation, and coping. *American Psychologist, 53,* 429–439. (p. 233)

Taylor, S. E., Saphire-Bernstein, S., & Seeman, T. E. (2010). Are plasma oxytocin in women and plasma vasopressin in men biomarkers of distressed pair-bond relationships? *Psychological Science, 21,* 3–7. (p. 286)

Tedeschi, R. G., & Calhoun, L. G. (2004). Posttraumatic growth: Conceptual foundations and empirical evidence. *Psychological Inquiry, 15,* 1–18. (p. 432)

Teghtsoonian, R. (1971). On the exponents in Stevens' law and the constant in Ekinan's law. *Psychological Review, 78,* 71–80. (p. 136)

Teller. (2009, April 20). Quoted by J. Lehrer, Magic and the brain: Teller reveals the neuroscience of illusion. *Wired* (www.wired.com). (p. 51)

Tenenbaum, H. R., & Leaper, C. (2002). Are parents' gender schemas related to their children's gender-related cognitions? A meta-analysis. *Developmental Psychology, 38,* 615–630. (p. 114)

Teran-Santos, J., Jimenez-Gomez, A., & Cordero-Guevara, J. (1999). The association between sleep apnea and the risk of traffic accidents. *New England Journal of Medicine, 340,* 847–851. (p. 59)

Terrace, H. S. (1979, November). How Nim Chimpsky changed my mind. *Psychology Today,* pp. 65–76. (p. 234)

Terre, L., & Stoddart, R. (2000). Cutting edge specialties for graduate study in psychology. *Eye on Psi Chi, 23*–26. (p. C-1)

Tesser, A., Forehand, R., Brody, G., & Long, N. (1989). Conflict: The role of calm and angry parent-child discussion in adolescent development. *Journal of Social and Clinical Psychology, 8,* 317–330. (p. 90)

Tew, J. D., Mulsant, B. H., Haskett, R. F., Joan, P., Begley, A. E., Sackeim, H. A. (2007). Relapse during continuation pharmacotherapy after acute response to ECT: A comparison of usual care versus protocolized treatment. *Annals of Clinical Psychiatry, 19,* 1–4. (p. 428)

Thaler, R. H., & Sunstein, C. R. (2008). *Nudge: Improving decisions about health, wealth, and happiness.* New Haven, CT: Yale University Press. (p. 224)

Thatcher, R. W., Walker, R. A., & Giudice, S. (1987). Human cerebral hemispheres develop at different rates and ages. *Science, 236,* 1110–1113. (pp. 74, 94)

Thiel, A., Hadedank, B., Herholz, K., Kessler, J., Winhuisen, L., Haupt, W. F., & Heiss, W-D. (2006). From the left to the right: How the brain compensates progressive loss of language function. *Brain and Language, 98,* 57–65. (p. 47)

Thomas, A., & Chess, S. (1986). The New York Longitudinal Study: From infancy to early adult life. In R. Plomin & J. Dunn (Eds.), *The study of temperament: Changes, continuities, and challenges.* Hillsdale, NJ: Erlbaum. (p. 102)

Thomas, L. (1992). *The fragile species.* New York: Scribner's. (pp. 231, 421)

Thompson, G. (2010). The $1 million dollar challenge. *Skeptic, 15,* 8–9. (p. 162)

Thompson, J. K., Jarvie, G. J., Lahey, B. B., & Cureton, K. J. (1982). Exercise and obesity: Etiology, physiology, and intervention. *Psychological Bulletin, 91,* 55–79. (p. 264)

Thompson, P. M., Giedd, J. N., Woods, R. P., MacDonald, D., Evans, A. C., & Toga, A. W. (2000). Growth patterns in the developing brain detected by using continuum mechanical tensor maps. *Nature, 404,* 190–193. (p. 74)

Thompson, R., Emmorey, K., & Gollan, T. H. (2005). "Tip of the fingers" experiences by Deaf signers. *Psychological Science, 16,* 856–860. (p. 208)

Thompson-Schill, S. L., Ramscar, M., & Chrysikou, E. G. (2009). Cognition without control: When a little frontal lobe goes a long way. *Current Directions in Psychological Science, 18,* 259–263. (p. 74)

Thorndike, E. L. (1898). Animal intelligence: An experimental study of the associative processes in animals. *Psychological Review Monograph Supplement 2,* 4–160. (p. 174)

Thorne, J., with Larry Rothstein. (1993). *You are not alone: Words of experience and hope for the journey through depression.* New York: HarperPerennial. (p. 371)

Thornton, B., & Moore, S. (1993). Physical attractiveness contrast effect: Implications for self-esteem and evaluations of the social self. *Personality and Social Psychology Bulletin, 19,* 474–480. (p. 360)

Thorpe, W. H. (1974). *Animal nature and human nature.* London: Metheun. (p. 235)

Tiihonen, J., Lönnqvist, J., Wahlbeck, K., Klaukka, T., Niskanen, L., Tanskanen, A., Haukka, J. (2009). 11-year follow-up of mortality in patients with schizophrenia: A population-based cohort study (FIN11 study). *Lancet, 374,* 260–267. (p. 425)

Time. (2009, Oct. 14). The state of the American woman. pp. 32–33. (p. 110)

Timmerman, T. A. (2007) "It was a thought pitch": Personal, situational, and target influences on hit-by-pitch events across time. *Journal of Applied Psychology, 92,* 876–884. (p. 355)

Tirrell, M. E. (1990). Personal communication. (p. 171)

Tobin, D. D., Menon, M., Menon, M., Spatta, B. C., Hodges, E. V. E., & Perry, D. G. (2010). The intrapsychics of gender: A model of self-socialization. *Psychological Review, 117,* 601–622. (p. 114)

Toews, P. (2004, December 30). Dirk Willems: A heart undivided. *Mennonite Brethren Historical Commission.* (www.nbhistory.org/profiles/dirk.en.html). (p. 337)

Tolman, E. C., & Honzik, C. H. (1930). Introduction and removal of reward, and maze performance in rats. *University of California Publications in Psychology, 4,* 257–275. (p. 184)

Tondo, L., Jamison, K. R., & Baldessarini, R. J. (1997). Effect of lithium maintenance on suicidal behavior in major mood disorders. In D. M. Stoff & J. J. Mann (Eds.), *The neurobiology of suicide: From the bench to the clinic*. New York: New York Academy of Sciences. (p. 427)

Topolinski, S., & Reber, R. (2010). Gaining insight into the "aha" experience. *Current Directions in Psychological Science, 19*, 401–405. (p. 220)

Torrey, E. F. (1986). *Witchdoctors and psychiatrists*. New York: Harper & Row. (p. 423)

Torrey, E. F., & Miller, J. (2002). *The invisible plague: The rise of mental illness from 1750 to the present*. New Brunswick, NJ: Rutgers University Press. (p. 399)

Torrey, E. F., Miller, J., Rawlings, R., & Yolken, R. H. (1997). Seasonality of births in schizophrenia and bipolar disorder: A review of the literature. *Schizophrenia Research, 28*, 1–38. (p. 399)

Totterdell, P., Kellett, S., Briner, R. B., & Teuchmann, K. (1998). Evidence of mood linkage in work groups. *Journal of Personality and Social Psychology, 74*, 1504–1515. (p. 341)

Tovee, M. J., Mason, S. M., Emery, J. L., McCluskey, S. E., & Cohen-Tovee, E. M. (1997). Supermodels: Stick insects or hourglasses? *The Lancet, 350*, 1474–1475. (p. 401)

Tracey, J. L., & Robins, R. W. (2004). Show your pride: Evidence for a discrete emotion expression. *Psychological Science, 15*, 194–197. (p. 272)

Treffert, D. A., & Christensen, D. D. (2005, December). Inside the mind of a savant. *Scientific American*, pp. 108–113. (p. 236)

Treffert, D. A., & Wallace, G. L. (2002). Island of genius—The artistic brilliance and dazzling memory that sometimes accompany autism and other disorders hint at how all brains work. *Scientific American, 286*, 76–86. (p. 236)

Treisman, A. (1987). Properties, parts, and objects. In K. R. Boff, L. Kaufman, & J. P. Thomas (Eds.), *Handbook of perception and human performance*. New York: Wiley. (p. 146)

Triandis, H. C. (1994). *Culture and social behavior*. New York: McGraw-Hill. (pp. 332, 356)

Triandis, H. C., Bontempo, R., Villareal, M. J., Asai, M., & Lucca, N. (1988). Individualism and collectivism: Cross-cultural perspectives on self-ingroup relationships. *Journal of Personality and Social Psychology, 54*, 323–338. (p. 332)

Trickett, P. K., & McBride-Chang, C. (1995). The developmental impact of different forms of child abuse and neglect. *Developmental Review, 15*, 311–337. (p. 84)

Trillin, C. (2006, March 27). Alice off the page. *The New Yorker*, p. 44. (p. 320)

Trimble, J. E. (1994). Cultural variations in the use of alcohol and drugs. In W. J. Lonner & R. Malpass (Eds.), *Psychology and culture*. Boston: Allyn & Bacon. (p. 389)

Triplett, N. (1898). The dynamogenic factors in pacemaking and competition. *American Journal of Psychology, 9*, 507–533. (p. 346)

Tsang, Y. C. (1938). Hunger motivation in gastrectomized rats. *Journal of Comparative Psychology, 26*, 1–17. (p. 258)

Tse, D., Langston, R. F., Kakeyama, M., Bethus, I., Spooner P. A., Wood, E. R., Witter, M. P., & Morris, R. G. M. (2007). Schemas and memory consolidation. *Science, 316*, 76–82. (p. 200)

Tsuang, M. T., & Faraone, S. V. (1990). *The genetics of mood disorders*. Baltimore, MD: Johns Hopkins University Press. (p. 394)

Tuber, D. S., Miller, D. D., Caris, K. A., Halter, R., Linden, F., & Hennessy, M. B. (1999). Dogs in animal shelters: Problems, suggestions, and needed expertise. *Psychological Science, 10*, 379–386. (p. 22)

Tucker, K. A. (2002). I believe you can fly. *Gallup Management Journal*. (www.gallupjournal.com/CA/st/20020520.asp). (p. B-5)

Turner, J. C. (1987). *Rediscovering the social group: A self-categorization theory*. New York: Basil Blackwell. (p. 352)

Turner, N., Barling, J., & Zacharatos, A. (2002). Positive psychology at work. In C. R. Snyder & S. J. Lopez (Eds.), *The handbook of positive psychology*. New York: Oxford University Press. (p. B-6)

Tuvblad, C., Narusyte, J., Grann, M., Sarnecki, J., & Lichtenstein, P. (2011). The genetic and environmental etiology of antisocial behavior from childhood to emerging adulthood. *Behavior Genetics, 41*, 629–640. (p. 403)

Tversky, A. (1985, June). Quoted in K. McKean, Decisions, decisions. *Discover*, pp. 22–31. (p. 222)

Tversky, A., & Kahneman, D. (1974). Judgment under uncertainty: Heuristics and biases. *Science, 185*, 1124–1131. (pp. 222, A-6)

Twenge, J. M. (2000). The age of anxiety? Birth cohort change in anxiety and neuroticism, 1952–1993. *Journal of Personality and Social Psychology, 79*, 1007–1021. (p. 381)

Twenge, J. M. (2001). Birth cohort changes in extraversion: A cross-temporal meta-analysis, 1966–1993. *Personality and Individual Differences, 30*, 735–748. (p. 324)

Twenge, J. M., Abebe, E. M., & Campbell, W. K. (2010). Fitting in or standing out: Trends in American parents' choices for children's names, 1880–2007. *Social Psychology and Personality Science, 1*, 19–25. (p. 332)

Twenge, J. M., Baumeister, R. F., DeWall, C. N., Ciarocco, N. J., & Bartels, J. M. (2007). Social exclusion decreases prosocial behavior. *Journal of Personality and Social Psychology, 92*, 56–66. (p. 266)

Twenge, J. M., Baumeister, R. F., Tice, D. M., & Stucke, T. S. (2001). If you can't join them, beat them: Effects of social exclusion on aggressive behavior. *Journal of Personality and Social Psychology, 81*, 1058–1069. (p. 266)

Twenge, J. M., & Campbell, W. K. (2008). Increases in positive self-views among high school students: Birth-cohort changes in anticipated performance, self-satisfaction, self-liking, and self-competence. *Psychological Science, 19*, 1082–1086. (p. 321)

Twenge, J. M., Campbell, W. K., & Freeman, E. C. (2012). Generational differences in young adults' life goals, concern for others, and civic orientation, 1966-2009. *Journal of Personality and Social Psychology, 102*, 1045–1062. (p. 332)

Twenge, J. M., Catanese, K. R., & Baumeister, R. F. (2002). Social exclusion causes self-defeating behavior. *Journal of Personality and Social Psychology, 83*, 606–615. (p. 266)

Twenge, J. M., Gentile, B., DeWall, C. D., Ma, D., & Lacefield, K. (2008). *A growing disturbance: Increasing psychopathology in young people 1938–2007 in a meta-analysis of the MMPI*. Unpublished manuscript, San Diego State University. (p. 394)

Twenge, J. M., Gentile, B., DeWall, C. N., Ma, D., Lacefield, K., & Schurtz, D. R. (2010). Birth cohort increases in psychopathology among young Americans, 1938–2007: A cross-temporal meta-analysis of the MMPI. *Clinical Psychology Review, 30*, 145–154. (p. 293)

Twenge, J. M., & Nolen-Hoeksema, S. (2002). Age, gender, race, socioeconomic status, and birth cohort differences on the children's depression inventory: A meta-analysis. *Journal of Abnormal Psychology, 111*, 578–588. (p. 90)

Twenge, J. M., Zhang, L., & Im, C. (2004). It's beyond my control: A cross-temporal meta-analysis of increasing externality in locus of control, 1960-2002. *Personality and Social Psychology Review, 8*, 308-319. (p. 293)

Twiss, C., Tabb, S., & Crosby, F. (1989). Affirmative action and aggregate data: The importance of patterns in the perception of discrimination.

In F. Blanchard & F. Crosby (Eds.), *Affirmative action: Social psychological perspectives*. New York: Springer-Verlag. (p. A-4)

Tyler, K. A. (2002). Social and emotional outcomes of childhood sexual abuse: A review of recent research. *Aggression and Violent Behavior, 7,* 567–589. (p. 84)

Uchida, Y., & Kitayama, S. (2009). Happiness and unhappiness in East and West: Themes and variations. *Emotion, 9,* 441–456. (p. 305)

Uchino, B. N. (2009). Understanding the links between social support and physical health. *Perspectives on Psychological Science, 4,* 236–255. (p. 295)

Uchino, B. N., Cacioppo, J. T., & Kiecolt-Glaser, J. K. (1996). The relationship between social support and physiological processes: A review with emphasis on underlying mechanisms and implications for health. *Psychological Bulletin, 119,* 488–531. (p. 295)

Uchino, B. N., Uno, D., & Holt-Lunstad, J. (1999). Social support, physiological processes, and health. *Current Directions in Psychological Science, 8,* 145–148. (p. 295)

Udry, J. R. (2000). Biological limits of gender construction. *American Sociological Review, 65,* 443–457. (p. 111)

UK ECT Review Group. (2003). Efficacy and safety of electroconvulsive therapy in depressive disorders: A systematic review and meta-analysis. *Lancet, 361,* 799–808. (p. 427)

UNAIDS. (2013, accessed May 17). Data and analysis. www.unaids.org/en/dataanalysis. (p. 117)

United Nations. (2011, November 17). Discriminatory laws and practices and acts of violence against individuals based on their sexual orientation and gender identity. Report of the United Nations High Commissioner for Human Rights. (p. 350)

Urry, H. L., & Gross, J. J. (2010). Emotion regulation in older age. *Current Directions in Psychological Science, 19,* 352–357. (p. 100)

Urry, H. L., Nitschke, J. B., Dolski, I., Jackson, D. C., Dalton, K. M., Mueller, C. J., Rosenkranz, M. A., Ryff, C. D., Singer, B. H., & Davidson, R. J. (2004). Making a life worth living: Neural correlates of well-being. *Psychological Science, 15,* 367–372. (p. 274)

Vacic, V., & 29 others. (2011). Duplications of the neuropeptide receptor gene VIPR2 confer significant risk for schizophrenia. *Nature, 471,* 499–503. (p. 400)

Vaillant, G. E. (2002). *Aging well: Surprising guideposts to a happier life from the landmark Harvard study of adult development*. Boston: Little, Brown. (p. 295)

Vaillant, G. E. (2009). Quoted by J. W. Shenk, What makes us happy? *The Atlantic* (www.theatlantic.com). (p. 266)

Valenstein, E. S. (1986). *Great and desperate cures: The rise and decline of psychosurgery*. New York: Basic Books. (p. 430)

Valkenburg, P. M., & Peter, J. (2009). Social consequences of the Internet for adolescents: A decade of research. *Current Directions in Psychological Science, 18,* 1–5. (pp. 90, 267)

Vallone, R. P., Griffin, D. W., Lin, S., & Ross, L. (1990). Overconfident prediction of future actions and outcomes by self and others. *Journal of Personality and Social Psychology, 58,* 582–592. (p. 10)

van Anders, S. M., & Dunn, E. J. (2009). Are gonadal steroids linked with orgasm perceptions and sexual assertiveness in women and men? *Journal of Sexual Medicine, 6,* 739–751. (p. 115)

Van Cauter, E., Holmback, U., Knutson, K., Leproult, R., Miller, A., Nedeltcheva, A., Pannain, S., Penev, P., Tasali, E., & Spiegel, K. (2007). Impact of sleep and sleep loss on neuroendocrine and metabolic function. *Hormone Research, 67*(1), Supp. 1: 2–9. (p. 58)

vanDellen, M. R., Campbell, W. K., Hoyle, R. H., & Bradfield, E. K. (2011). Compensating, resisting, and breaking: A meta-analytic examination of reactions to self-esteem threat. *Personality and Social Psychological Review, 15,* 51–74. (p. 330)

Vandenberg, S. G., & Kuse, A. R. (1978). Mental rotations: A group test of three-dimensional spatial visualization. *Perceptual and Motor Skills, 47,* 599–604. (p. 247)

van den Boom, D. C. (1990). Preventive intervention and the quality of mother-infant interaction and infant exploration in irritable infants. In W. Koops, H. J. G. Soppe, J. L. van der Linden, P. C. M. Molenaar, & J. J. F. Schroots (Eds.), *Developmental psychology research in The Netherlands*. The Netherlands: Uitgeverij Eburon. Cited by C. Hazan & P. R. Shaver (1994). Deeper into attachment theory. *Psychological Inquiry, 5,* 68–79. (p. 82)

van den Boom, D. C. (1995). Do first-year intervention effects endure? Follow-up during toddlerhood of a sample of Dutch irritable infants. *Child Development, 66,* 1798–1816. (p. 82)

van den Bos, K., & Spruijt, N. (2002). Appropriateness of decisions as a moderator of the psychology of voice. *European Journal of Social Psychology, 32,* 57–72. (p. B-8)

Van Dijk, W. W., Van Koningsbruggen, G. M., Ouwerkerk, J. W., & Wesseling, Y. M. (2011). Self-esteem, self-affirmation, and schadenfreude. *Emotion, 11,* 1445–1449. (p. 330)

Van Dyke, C., & Byck, R. (1982, March). Cocaine. *Scientific American*, pp. 128–141. (p. 386)

van Engen, M. L., & Willemsen, T. M. (2004). Sex and leadership styles: A meta-analysis of research published in the 1990s. *Psychological Reports, 94,* 3–18. (p. 109)

van Goozen, S. H. M., Fairchild, G., Snoek, H., & Harold, G. T. (2007). The evidence for a neurobiological model of childhood antisocial behavior. *Psychological Bulletin, 133,* 149–182. (p. 403)

van Honk, J., Schutter, D. J., Bos, P. A., Kruijt, A-W., Lentje, E. G. & Baron-Cohen, S. (2011). Testosterone administration impairs cognitive empathy in women depending on second-to-fourth digit ratio. *Proceedings of the National Academy of Sciences, 108,* 3448–3452. (p. 79)

Van Horn, J., Irimia, A., Torgerson, C., Chambers, M., Kikinis, R., & Toga, A. (2012). Mapping connectivity damage in the case of Phineas Gage. *PLoS ONE, 7,* e37454. (p. 46)

van IJzendoorn, M. H., & Juffer, F. (2005). Adoption is a successful natural intervention enhancing adopted children's IQ and school performance. *Current Directions in Psychological Science, 14,* 326–330. (p. 241)

van IJzendoorn, M. H., & Juffer, F. (2006). The Emanual Miller Memorial Lecture 2006: Adoption as intervention. Meta-analytic evidence for massive catch-up and plasticity in physical, socio-emotional, and cognitive development. *Journal of Child Psychology and Psychiatry, 47,* 1228–1245. (p. 241)

van IJzendoorn, M. H., & Kroonenberg, P. M. (1988). Cross-cultural patterns of attachment: A meta-analysis of the strange situation. *Child Development, 59,* 147–156. (p. 82)

van IJzendoorn, M. H., Luijk, M. P. C. M., & Juffer, F. (2008). IQ of children growing up in children's homes: A meta-analysis on IQ delays in orphanages. *Merrill-Palmer Quarterly, 54,* 341–366. (p. 244)

Van Ittersum, K., & Wansink, B. (2012). Plate size and color suggestibility: The Delboeuf illusion's bias on serving and eating behavior. *Journal of Consumer Research, 39,* 215–228. (p. 261)

Van Kestern, P. J. M., Asscheman, H., Megens, J. A. J., & Gooren, J. G. (1997). Mortality and morbidity in transsexual subjects treated with cross-sex hormones. *Clinical Endocrinology, 47,* 337–342. (p. 114)

Van Leeuwen, M. S. (1978). A cross-cultural examination of psychological differentiation in males and females. *International Journal of Psychology, 13,* 87–122. (p. 113)

Vanman, E. J., Saltz, J. L., Nathan, L. R., & Warren, J. A. (2004). Racial discrimination by low-prejudiced Whites. *Psychological Science, 15,* 711–714. (p. 351)

Van Yperen, N. W., & Buunk, B. P. (1990). A longitudinal study of equity and satisfaction in intimate relationships. *European Journal of Social Psychology, 20,* 287–309. (p. 362)

Van Zeijl, J., Mesman, J., van IJzendoorn, M. H., Bakermans-Kranenburg, M. J., Juffer, F., Stolk, M. N., Koot, H. M., & Alink, L. R. A. (2006). Attachment-based intervention for enhancing sensitive discipline in mothers of 1- to 3-year-old children at risk for externalizing behavior problems: A randomized controlled trial. *Journal of Consulting and Clinical Psychology, 74,* 994–1005. (p. 83)

Varnum, M. E. W., & Kitayama, S. (2011). What's in a name? Popular names are less common on frontiers. *Psychological Science, 22,* 176–183. (p. 332)

Vaughn, K. B., & Lanzetta, J. T. (1981). The effect of modification of expressive displays on vicarious emotional arousal. *Journal of Experimental Social Psychology, 17,* 16–30. (p. 278)

Verbeek, M. E. M., Drent, P. J., & Wiepkema, P. R. (1994). Consistent individual differences in early exploratory behaviour of male great tits. *Animal Behaviour, 48,* 1113–1121. (p. 323)

Verhaeghen, P., & Salthouse, T. A. (1997). Meta-analyses of age-cognition relations in adulthood: Estimates of linear and nonlinear age effects and structural models. *Psychological Bulletin, 122,* 231–249. (p. 95)

Verosky, S. C., & Todorov, A. (2010). Generalization of affective learning about faces to perceptually similar faces. *Psychological Science, 21,* 779–785. (p. 172)

Vigil, J. M. (2009). A socio-relational framework of sex differences in the expression of emotion. *Behavioral and Brain Sciences, 32,* 375–428. (pp. 275, 276)

Vigil, J. M., Geary, D. C., & Byrd-Craven, J. (2005). A life history assessment of early childhood sexual abuse in women. *Developmental Psychology, 41,* 553–561. (p. 111)

Vigliocco, G., & Hartsuiker, R. J. (2002). The interplay of meaning, sound, and syntax in sentence production. *Psychological Bulletin, 128,* 442–472. (p. 230)

Vinkhuyzen, A. A. E., van der Sluis, S., Posthuma, D., & Boomsma, D. I. (2009). The heritability of aptitude and exceptional talent across different domains in adolescents and young adults. *Behavior Genetics, 39,* 380–392. (p. 241)

Visich, P. S., & Fletcher, E. (2009). Myocardial infarction. In J. K. Ehrman P. M. Gordon, P. S. Visich, & S. J. Keleyian (Eds.). *Clinical exercise physiology* (2nd ed.). Champaign, IL: Human Kinetics. (p. 297)

Vitello, P. (2006, June 12). A ring tone meant to fall on deaf ears. *New York Times* (www.nytimes.com). (p. 96)

Vitello, P. (2012, August 1). George A. Miller, a pioneer in cognitive psychology, is dead at 92. *New York Times* (www.nytimes.com). (p. 196)

Vittengl, J. R., Clark, L. A., Dunn, T. W., & Jarrett, R. B. (2007). Reducing relapse and recurrence in unipolar depression: A comparative meta-analysis of cognitive-behavioral therapy's effects. *Journal of Consulting and Clinical Psychology, 75,* 475–488. (p. 426)

Vogel, G. (2010). Long-fought compromise reached on European animal rules. *Science, 329,* 1588–1589. (p. 22)

Vohs, K. D., & Baumeister, R. F. (eds.) (2011). *Handbook of self-regulation,* (2nd ed.). New York: Guilford. (pp. 293, 356)

Volkow, N. D., & 12 others. (2009). Evaluating dopamine reward pathway in ADHD: Clinical implications. *JAMA, 302,* 1084–1091. (p. 373)

von Hippel, W. (2007). Aging, executive functioning, and social control. *Current Directions in Psychological Science, 16,* 240–244. (p. 95)

von Hippel, W., & Trivers, R. (2011). The evolution and psychology of self-deception. *Behavioral and Brain Sciences, 34,* 1–56. (p. 330)

von Senden, M. (1932). *The perception of space and shape in the congenitally blind before and after operation.* Glencoe, IL: Free Press. (p. 150)

von Stumm, S., Hell, B., & Chamorro-Premuzic, T. (2011). The hungry mind: Intellectual curiosity is the third pillar of academic performance. *Perspectives on Psychological Science, 6,* 574–588. (p. 238)

Vorona, R. D., Szklo-Coxe, M., Wu, A., Dubik, M., Zhao, Y., & Ware, J. C. (2011). Dissimilar teen crash rates in two neighboring Southeastern Virginia cities with different high school start times. *Journal of Clinical Sleep Medicine, 7,* 145–151. (p. 57)

Vroom, V. H., & Jago, A. G. (2007). The role of the situation in leadership. *American Psychologist, 62,* 17–24. (p. B-6)

VTTI. (2009, September). Driver distraction in commercial vehicle operations. Virginia Tech Transportation Institute and U.S. Department of Transportation. (p. 51)

Waber, R. L., Shiv, B., Carmon, Z., & Ariely, D. (2008). Commercial features of placebo and therapeutic efficacy. *Journal of the American Medical Association, 299,* 1016–1017. (p. 18)

Wade, K. A., Garry, M., Read, J. D., & Lindsay, D. S. (2002). A picture is worth a thousand lies: Using false photographs to create false childhood memories. *Psychonomic Bulletin & Review, 9,* 597–603. (p. 210)

Wade, N. G., Worthington, E. L., Jr., & Vogel, D. L. (2006). Effectiveness of religiously tailored interventions in Christian therapy. *Psychotherapy Research, 17,* 91–105. (p. 423)

Wagenmakers, E-J., Wetzels, R., Borsboom, D., & van der Maas, H. (2011). Why psychologists must change the way they analyze their data: The case of psi. *Journal of Personality and Social Psychology, 100,* 1–12. (p. 162)

Wagner, D. T., Barnes, C. M., Lim, V. K. G., & Ferris, D. L. (2012). Lost sleep and cyberloafing: Evidence from the laboratory and a daylight saving time quasi-experiment. *Journal of Applied Psychology, 97,* 1068–1076. (p. 57)

Wagner, U., Gais, S., Haider, H., Verleger, R., & Born, J. (2004). Sleep inspires insight. *Nature, 427,* 352–355. (p. 56)

Wagstaff, G. (1982). Attitudes to rape: The "just world" strikes again? *Bulletin of the British Psychological Society, 13,* 275–283. (p. 339)

Wai, J., Cacchio, M., Putallaz, M., & Makel, M. C. (2010). Sex differences in the right tail of cognitive abilities: A 30-year examination. *Intelligence, 38,* 412–423. (p. 247)

Wai, J., Lubinski, D., & Benbow, C. P. (2005). Creativity and occupational accomplishments among intellectually precocious youths: An age 13 to age 33 longitudinal study. *Journal of Educational Psychology, 97,* 484–492. (p. 242)

Wakefield, J. C., & Spitzer, R. L. (2002). Lowered estimates—but of what? *Archives of General Psychiatry, 59,* 129–130. (p. 379)

Walker, E., Shapiro, D., Esterberg, M., & Trotman, H. (2010). Neurodevelopment and schizophrenia: Broadening the focus. *Current Directions in Psychological Science, 19,* 204–208. (p. 400)

Walker, M. P., & van der Helm, E. (2009). Overnight therapy? The role of sleep in emotional brain processing. *Psychological Bulletin, 135,* 731–748. (pp. 58, 430)

Walker, W. R., Skowronski, J. J., & Thompson, C. P. (2003). Life is pleasant—and memory helps to keep it that way! *Review of General Psychology, 7,* 203–210. (p. 100)

Walkup, J. T., & 12 others. (2008). Cognitive behavioral therapy, sertraline, or a combination in childhood anxiety. *New England Journal of Medicine, 359,* 2753–2766. (p. 426)

Wallach, M. A., & Wallach, L. (1983). *Psychology's sanction for selfishness: The error of egoism in theory and therapy.* New York: Freeman. (p. 321)

Wallach, M. A., & Wallach, L. (1985, February). How psychology sanctions the cult of the self. *Washington Monthly,* pp. 46–56. (p. 321)

Walster (Hatfield), E., Aronson, V., Abrahams, D., & Rottman, L. (1966). Importance of physical attractiveness in dating behavior. *Journal of Personality and Social Psychology, 4,* 508–516. (p. 359)

Walton, G. M., & Spencer, S. J. (2009). Latent ability: Grades and test scores systematically underestimate the intellectual ability of negatively stereotyped students. *Psychological Science, 20,* 1132–1139. (p. 250)

Wampold, B. E. (2001). *The great psychotherapy debate: Models, methods, and findings.* Mahwah, NJ: Erlbaum. (p. 423)

Wampold, B. E. (2007). Psychotherapy: The humanistic (and effective) treatment. *American Psychologist, 62,* 857–873. (p. 421)

Wang, F., DesMeules, M., Luo, W., Dai, S., Lagace, C. & Morrison, H. (2011). Leisure-time physical activity and marital status in relation to depression between men and women: A prospective study. *Health Psychology, 30,* 204–211. (p. 296)

Wang, X. T., & Dvorak, R. D. (2010). Sweet future: Fluctuating blood glucose levels affect future discounting. *Psychological Science, 21,* 183–188. (p. 293)

Wansink, B. (2007). *Mindless eating: Why we eat more than we think.* New York: Bantam Dell. (p. 261)

Warburton, W. A., Williams, K. D., & Cairns, D. R. (2006). When ostracism leads to aggression: The moderating effects of control deprivation. *Journal of Experimental Social Psychology, 42,* 213–220. (p. 292)

Ward, A., & Mann, T. (2000). Don't mind if I do: Disinhibited eating under cognitive load. *Journal of Personality and Social Psychology, 78,* 753–763. (p. 264)

Ward, C. (1994). Culture and altered states of consciousness. In W. J. Lonner & R. Malpass (Eds.), *Psychology and culture.* Boston: Allyn & Bacon. (p. 381)

Ward, C. A. (2000). Models and measurements of psychological androgyny: A cross-cultural extension of theory and research. *Sex Roles, 43,* 529–552. (p. 114)

Ward, J. (2003). State of the art synaesthesia. *The Psychologist, 16,* 196–199. (p. 161)

Ward, K. D., Klesges, R. C., & Halpern, M. T. (1997). Predictors of smoking cessation and state-of-the-art smoking interventions. *Journal of Social Issues, 53,* 129–145. (p. 385)

Ward, L. M., & Friedman, K. (2006). Using TV as a guide: Associations between television viewing and adolescents' sexual attitudes and behavior. *Journal of Research on Adolescence, 16,* 133–156. (p. 119)

Wardle, J., Cooke, L. J., Gibson, L., Sapochnik, M., Sheiham, A., & Lawson, M. (2003). Increasing children's acceptance of vegetables: A randomized trial of parent-led exposure. *Appetite, 40,* 155–162. (p. 157)

Warner, J., McKeown, E., Johnson, K., Ramsay, A., Cort, C., & King, M. (2004). Rates and predictors of mental illness in gay men, lesbians and bisexual men and women. *British Journal of Psychiatry, 185,* 479–485. (p. 121)

Wason, P. C. (1960). On the failure to eliminate hypotheses in a conceptual task. *Quarterly Journal of Experimental Psychology, 12,* 129–140. (p. 221)

Wasserman, E. A. (1993). Comparative cognition: Toward a general understanding of cognition in behavior. *Psychological Science, 4,* 156–161. (p. 175)

Wasserman, E. A. (1995). The conceptual abilities of pigeons. *American Scientist, 83,* 246–255. (p. 228)

Waterhouse, R. (1993, July 19). Income for 62 percent is below average pay. *The Independent,* p. 4. (p. A-2)

Watson, D. (2000). *Mood and temperament.* New York: Guilford Press. (p. 302)

Watson, J. B. (1913). Psychology as the behaviorist views it. *Psychological Review, 20,* 158–177. (p. 173, 183)

Watson, J. B. (1924). The unverbalized in human behavior. *Psychological Review, 31,* 339–347. (p. 183)

Watson, J. B., & Rayner, R. (1920). Conditioned emotional reactions. *Journal of Experimental Psychology, 3,* 1–14. (p. 173)

Watson, R. I., Jr. (1973). Investigation into deindividuation using a cross-cultural survey technique. *Journal of Personality and Social Psychology, 25,* 342–345. (p. 348)

Watson, S. J., Benson, J. A., Jr., & Joy, J. E. (2000). Marijuana and medicine: Assessing the science base: A summary of the 1999 Institute of Medicine report. *Archives of General Psychiatry, 57,* 547–553. (p. 388)

Watters, E. (2010). *Crazy like us: The globalization of the American psyche.* New York: Free Press. (p. 374)

Way, B. M., Creswell, J. D., Eisenberger, N. I., & Lieberman, M. D. (2010). Dispositional mindfulness and depressive symptomatology: Correlations with limbic and self-referential neural activity during rest. *Emotion, 10,* 12–24. (p. 299)

Wayment, H. A., & Peplau, L. A. (1995). Social support and well-being among lesbian and heterosexual women: A structural modeling approach. *Personality and Social Psychology Bulletin, 21,* 1189–1199. (p. 98)

Webb, W. B. (1992). *Sleep: The gentle tyrant.* Bolton, MA: Anker. (p. 58)

Webb, W. B., & Campbell, S. S. (1983). Relationships in sleep characteristics of identical and fraternal twins. *Archives of General Psychiatry, 40,* 1093–1095. (p. 55)

Wechsler, H., Davenport, A., Dowdall, G., Moeykens, B., & Castillo, S. (1994). Health and behavioral consequences of binge drinking in college. *Journal of the American Medical Association, 272,* 1672–1677. (p. 383)

Wechsler, H., Lee, J. E., Kuo, M., Seibring, M., Nelson, T. F., & Lee, H. (2002). Trends in college binge drinking during a period of increased prevention efforts. *Journal of American College Health, 50,* 203–217. (p. 383)

Weingarten, G. (2002, March 10). Below the beltway. *Washington Post,* p. W03. (p. B-1)

Weinstein, N., Ryan, W. S., DeHaan, C. R., Przybylski, A. K., Legate, N., & Ryan, R. M. (2012). Parental autonomy support and discrepancies between implicit and explicit sexual identities: Dynamics of self-acceptance and defense. *Journal of Personality and Social Psychology, 102,* 815–832. (p. 318)

Weinstein, N. D. (1980). Unrealistic optimism about future life events. *Journal of Personality and Social Psychology, 39,* 806–820. (p. 294)

Weinstein, N. D. (1982). Unrealistic optimism about susceptibility to health problems. *Journal of Behavioral Medicine, 5,* 441–460. (p. 294)

Weinstein, N. D. (1996, October 4). 1996 optimistic bias bibliography. (weinstein_c@aesop.rutgers.edu). (p. 294)

Weisbuch, M., Ivcevic, Z., & Ambady, N. (2009). On being liked on the web and in the "real world": Consistency in first impressions across personal webpages and spontaneous behavior. *Journal of Experimental Social Psychology, 45,* 573–576. (p. 268)

Weiss, A., King, J. E., & Perkins, L. (2006). Personality and subjective well-being in orangutans (*Pongo pygmaeus* and *Pongo abelii*). *Journal of Personality and Social Psychology, 90,* 501–511. (p. 323)

Welch, W. W. (2005, February 28). Trauma of Iraq war haunting thousands returning home. *USA Today* (www.usatoday.com). (p. 378)

Weller, S., & Davis-Beaty, K. (2002). The effectiveness of male condoms in prevention of sexually transmitted diseases (protocol). *Cochrane Database of Systematic Reviews*, Issue 4, Art. No. CD004090. (p. 117)

Wellman, H. M., & Gelman, S. A. (1992). Cognitive development: Foundational theories of core domains. *Annual Review of Psychology, 43,* 337–375. (p. 77)

Wells, G. L. (1981). Lay analyses of causal forces on behavior. In J. Harvey (Ed.), *Cognition, social behavior and the environment.* Hillsdale, NJ: Erlbaum. (p. 168)

Wells, J. E., McGee, M. A., & Beautrais, A. L. (2011). Multiple aspects of sexual orientation: Prevalence and sociodemographic correlates in a New Zealand national survey. *Archives of Sexual Behavior, 40,* 155–168. (p. 121)

Westen, D. (1996). Is Freud really dead? Teaching psychodynamic theory to introductory psychology. Presentation to the Annual Institute on the Teaching of Psychology, St. Petersburg Beach, FL. (p. 316)

Westen, D. (1998). The scientific legacy of Sigmund Freud: Toward a psychodynamically informed psychological science. *Psychological Bulletin,* 124, 333–371. (p. 317)

Westen, D. (2007). *The political brain: The role of emotion in deciding the fate of the nation.* New York: PublicAffairs. (p. 272)

Westerhoff, N. (2007). Fantasy therapy. *Scientific American Mind,* 71–75. (p. 415)

Whalley, L. J., Starr, J. M., Athawes, R., Hunter, D., Pattie, A., & Deary, I. J. (2000). Childhood mental ability and dementia. *Neurology, 55,* 1455–1459. (p. 245)

White, H. R., Brick, J., & Hansell, S. (1993). A longitudinal investigation of alcohol use and aggression in adolescence. *Journal of Studies on Alcohol,* Supplement No. 11, 62–77. (p. 354)

White, L., & Edwards, J. (1990). Emptying the nest and parental well-being: An analysis of national panel data. *American Sociological Review, 55,* 235–242. (p. 99)

White, P. H., Kjelgaard, M. M., & Harkins, S. G. (1995). Testing the contribution of self-evaluation to goal-setting effects. *Journal of Personality and Social Psychology, 69,* 69–79. (p. B-6)

Whitehead, B. D., & Popenoe, D. (2001). *The state of our unions 2001: The social health of marriage in America.* Rutgers University: The National Marriage Project. (p. 98)

Whiten, A., & Boesch, C. (2001, January). Cultures of chimpanzees. *Scientific American,* pp. 60–67. (p. 229)

Whiting, B. B., & Edwards, C. P. (1988). *Children of different worlds: The formation of social behavior.* Cambridge, MA: Harvard University Press. (p. 85)

Whitlock, J. R., Heynen, A. L., Shuler, M. G., & Bear, M. F. (2006). Learning induces long-term potentiation in the hippocampus. *Science, 313,* 1093–1097. (p. 201)

Whitmer, R. A., Gustafson, D. R., Barrett-Connor, E. B., Haan, M. N., Gunderson, E. P., & Yaffe, K. (2008). Central obesity and increased risk of dementia more than three decades later. *Neurology, 71,* 1057–1064. (p. 262)

WHO. (1979). *Schizophrenia: An international followup study.* Chichester, England: Wiley. (p. 398)

WHO. (2000). *Effectiveness of male latex condoms in protecting against pregnancy and sexually transmitted infections.* World Health Organization (www.who.int). (p. 117)

WHO. (2002). *The global burden of disease.* Geneva: World Health Organization (www.who.int/msa/mnh/ems/dalys/intro.htm). (p. 390)

WHO. (2003). *The male latex condom: Specification and guidelines for condom procurement.* Department of Reproductive Health and Research, Family and Community Health, World Health Organization. (p. 117)

WHO. (2004). *Women, girls, HIV, and AIDS.* World Health Organization, Western Pacific Regional Office. (p. 117)

WHO. (2011). Country reports and charts available. Geneva: World Health Organization (int/mental_health/prevention/suicide/country_reports/en/index.html). (p. 398)

WHO. (2010, September). Mental health: strengthening our response. Geneva: World Health Organization (www.who.int/mediacentre/factsheets/fs220/en/). (p. 371)

WHO. (2012, May). Tobacco: Fact sheet N339. Geneva: World Health Organization (www.who.int). (p. 385)

WHO. (2012, August). How can suicide be prevented? Geneva: World Health Organization (www.who.int/features/qa/24/en/index.html). (p. 392)

Wicherts, J. M., Dolan, C. V., Carlson, J. S., & van der Maas, H. L. J. (2010). Raven's test performance of sub-Saharan Africans: Mean level, psychometric properties, and the Flynn Effect. *Learning and Individual Differences,* 20, 135–151. (p. 249)

Wickelgren, W. A. (1977). *Learning and memory.* Englewood Cliffs, NJ: Prentice-Hall. (p. 198)

Widom, C. S. (1989a). Does violence beget violence? A critical examination of the literature. *Psychological Bulletin, 106,* 3–28. (p. 83)

Widom, C. S. (1989b). The cycle of violence. *Science, 244,* 160–166. (p. 83)

Wiens, A. N., & Menustik, C. E. (1983). Treatment outcome and patient characteristics in an aversion therapy program for alcoholism. *American Psychologist, 38,* 1089–1096. (p. 416)

Wierson, M., & Forehand, R. (1994). Parent behavioral training for child noncompliance: Rationale, concepts, and effectiveness. *Current Directions in Psychological Science, 3,* 146–149. (p. 180)

Wierzbicki, M. (1993). Psychological adjustment of adoptees: A meta-analysis. *Journal of Clinical Child Psychology, 22,* 447–454. (p. 91)

Wiesel, T. N. (1982). Postnatal development of the visual cortex and the influence of environment. *Nature, 299,* 583–591. (p. 150)

Wigdor, A. K., & Garner, W. R. (1982). *Ability testing: Uses, consequences, and controversies.* Washington, DC: National Academy Press. (p. 249)

Wilcox, A. J., Baird, D. D., Dunson, D. B., McConnaughey, D. R., Kesner, J. S., & Weinberg, C. R. (2004). On the frequency of intercourse around ovulation: Evidence for biological influences. *Human Reproduction, 19,* 1539–1543. (p. 115)

Wilder, D. A. (1981). Perceiving persons as a group: Categorization and intergroup relations. In D. L. Hamilton (Ed.), *Cognitive processes in stereotyping and intergroup behavior.* Hillsdale, NJ: Erlbaum. (p. 352)

Wilkinson, P., & Goodyer, I. (2011). Non-suicidal self-injury. *European Child & Adolescent Psychiatry, 20,* 103–108. (p. 393)

Wilkinson, R., & Pickett, K. (2009). *The spirit level: Why greater equality makes societies stronger.* London: Bloomsbury Press. (p. 356)

Wilkowski, B. M., Robinson, M. D., & Troop-Gordon, W. (2011). How does cognitive control reduce anger and aggression? The role of conflict monitoring and forgiveness processes. *Journal of Personality and Social Psychology, 98,* 830–840. (p. 355)

Williams, J. E., & Best, D. L. (1990). *Measuring sex stereotypes: A multination study.* Newbury Park, CA: Sage. (p. 109)

Williams, J. E., Paton, C. C., Siegler, I. C., Eigenbrodt, M. L., Nieto, F. J., & Tyroler, H. A. (2000). Anger proneness predicts coronary heart disease risk: Prospective analysis from the artherosclerosis risk in communities (ARIC) study. *Circulation, 101*(17), 2034–2040. (p. 290)

Williams, K. D. (2007). Ostracism. *Annual Review of Psychology, 58*, 425–452. (p. 265)

Williams, K. D. (2009). Ostracism: A temporal need-threat model. *Advances in Experimental Social Psychology, 41*, 275–313. (p. 265)

Williams, K. D., & Zadro, L. (2001). Ostracism: On being ignored, excluded and rejected. In M. Leary (Ed.), *Rejection*. New York: Oxford University Press. (p. 265)

Williams, L. E., & Bargh, J. A. (2008). Experiencing physical warmth promotes interpersonal warmth. *Science, 322*, 606–607. (p. 161)

Williams, N. M., & 13 others. (2010). Rare chromosomal deletions and duplications in attention-deficit hyperactivity disorder: A genome-wide analysis. *Lancet, 376*, 1401–1408. (p. 373)

Williams, R. (1993). *Anger kills*. New York: Times Books. (p. 290)

Williams, S. L. (1987). Self-efficacy and mastery-oriented treatment for severe phobias. Paper presented to the American Psychological Association convention. (p. 415)

Willingham, D. T. (2010, Summer). Have technology and multitasking rewired how students learn? *American Educator, 42*, 23-28. (pp. 197, 268)

Willis, J., & Todorov, A. (2006). First impressions: Making up your mind after a 100-ms. exposure to a face. *Psychological Science, 17*, 592–598. (p. 97)

Willmuth, M. E. (1987). Sexuality after spinal cord injury: A critical review. *Clinical Psychology Review, 7*, 389–412. (p. 118)

Wilson, A. E., & Ross, M. (2001). From chump to champ: People's appraisals of their earlier and present selves. *Journal of Personality and Social Psychology, 80*, 572–584. (p. 331)

Wilson, C. M., & Oswald, A. J. (2002). How does marriage affect physical and psychological health? A survey of the longitudinal evidence. Working paper, University of York and Warwick University. (p. 295)

Wilson, G. D., & Rahman, Q. (2005). *Born gay: The biology of sex orientation*. London: Peter Owen Publishers. (p. 124)

Wilson, R. S. (1979). Analysis of longitudinal twin data: Basic model and applications to physical growth measures. *Acta Geneticae Medicae et Gemellologiae, 28*, 93–105. (p. 74)

Wilson, R. S., Beck, T. L., Bienias, J. L., & Bennett, D. A. (2007). Terminal cognitive decline: Accelerated loss of cognition in the last years of life. *Psychosomatic Medicine, 69*, 131–137. (p. 97)

Wilson, T. D. (2006). The power of social psychological interventions. *Science, 313*, 1251–1252. (p. 250)

Windholz, G. (1989, April-June). The discovery of the principles of reinforcement, extinction, generalization, and differentiation of conditional reflexes in Pavlov's laboratories. *Pavlovian Journal of Biological Science, 26*, 64–74. (p. 172)

Windholz, G. (1997). Ivan P. Pavlov: An overview of his life and psychological work. *American Psychologist, 52*, 941–946. (p. 170)

Winner, E. (2000). The origins and ends of giftedness. *American Psychologist, 55*, 159–169. (p. 242)

Winter, W. C., Hammond, W. R., Green, N. H., Zhang, Z., & Bilwise, D. L. (2009). Measuring circadian advantage in major league baseball: A 10-year retrospective study. *Internal Journal of Sports Physiology and Performance, 4*, 394–401. (p. 56)

Wiseman, R., & Greening, E. (2002). The Mind Machine: A mass participation experiment into the possible existence of extra-sensory perception. *British Journal of Psychology, 93*, 487–499. (p. 162)

Witek-Janusek, L., Albuquerque, K., Chroniak, K. R., Chroniak, C., Durazo, R., & Mathews, H. L. (2008). Effect of mindfulness based stress reduction on immune function, quality of life and coping in women newly diagnosed with early stage breast cancer. *Brain Behavior and Immunity, 22*(6), 969–981. (p. 299)

Witters, D., & Ander, S. (2013, January 4). Depression increases in areas Superstorm Sandy hit hardest. www.gallup.com. (p. 394)

Witvliet, C. V. O., & Vrana, S. R. (1995). Psychophysiological responses as indices of affective dimensions. *Psychophysiology, 32*, 436–443. (p. 273)

Wixted, J. T., & Ebbesen, E. B. (1991). On the form of forgetting. *Psychological Science, 2*, 409–415. (p. 207)

Wolfson, A. R., & Carskadon, M. A. (1998). Sleep schedules and daytime functioning in adolescents. *Child Development, 69*, 875–887. (p. 61)

Wolitzky-Taylor, K. B., Horowitz, J. D., Powers, M. B., & Telch, M. J. (2008). Psychological approaches in the treatment of specific phobias: A meta-analysis. *Clinical Psychology Review, 28*, 1021–1037. (p. 415)

Woll, S. (1986). So many to choose from: Decision strategies in videodating. *Journal of Social and Personal Relationships, 3*, 43–52. (p. 360)

Wollmer, M. A., & 18 others. (2012). Facing depression with botulinum toxin: A randomized controlled trial. *Journal of Psychiatric Research, 46*, 574–581. (p. 278)

Wolpe, J. (1958). *Psychotherapy by reciprocal inhibition*. Stanford, CA: Stanford University Press. (p. 414)

Wolpe, J., & Plaud, J. J. (1997). Pavlov's contributions to behavior therapy: The obvious and the not so obvious. *American Psychologist, 52*, 966–972. (p. 414)

Wong, D. F., Wagner, H. N., Tune, L. E., Dannals, R. F., et al. (1986). Positron emission tomography reveals elevated D_2 dopamine receptors in drug-naive schizophrenics. *Science, 234*, 1588–1593. (p. 398)

Wood, J. M. (2003, May 19). Quoted by R. Mestel, Rorschach tested: Blot out the famous method? Some experts say it has no place in psychiatry. *Los Angeles Times* (www.latimes.com). (p. 317)

Wood, J. M., Bootzin, R. R., Kihlstrom, J. F., & Schacter, D. L. (1992). Implicit and explicit memory for verbal information presented during sleep. *Psychological Science, 3*, 236–239. (p. 208)

Wood, J. M., Nezworski, M. T., Garb, H. N., & Lilienfeld, S. O. (2006). The controversy over the Exner Comprehensive System and the Society for Personality Assessment's white paper on the Rorschach. *Independent Practitioner, 26*. (p. 317)

Wood, W. (1987). Meta-analytic review of sex differences in group performance. *Psychological Bulletin, 102*, 53–71. (p. 109)

Wood, W., & Eagly, A. H. (2002). A cross-cultural analysis of the behavior of women and men: Implications for the origins of sex differences. *Psychological Bulletin, 128*, 699–727. (p. 109)

Wood, W., & Eagly, A. H. (2007). Social structural origins of sex differences in human mating. In S. W. Gagestad & J. A. Simpson (Eds.), *The evolution of mind: Fundamental questions and controversies*. New York: Guilford Press. (p. 109)

Wood, W., Kressel, L., Joshi, P., & Louie, B. (2012). *Meta-analytic review of menstrual cycle effects on mate preferences*. Manuscript submitted for publication. (p. 115)

Wood, W., Lundgren, S., Ouellette, J. A., Busceme, S., & Blackstone, T. (1994). Minority influence: A meta-analytic review of social influence processes. *Psychological Bulletin, 115*, 323–345. (p. 346)

Wood, W., & Neal, D. T. (2007, October). A new look at habits and the habit-goal interface. *Psychological Review, 114*, 843–863. (p. 168)

Woods, N. F., Dery, G. K., & Most, A. (1983). Recollections of menarche, current menstrual attitudes, and premenstrual symptoms. In S. Golub (Ed.), *Menarche: The transition from girl to woman*. Lexington, MA: Lexington Books. (p. 112)

Woolett, K., & Maguire, E. A. (2011). Acquiring "the knowledge" of London's layout drives structural brain changes. *Current Biology, 21*, 2109–2114. (p. 201)

Woolley, A. W., Chabris, C. F., Pentland, A., Hasmi, N., & Malone, T. W. (2010). Evidence for a collective intelligence factor in the performance of human groups. *Science, 330*, 686–688. (p. B-7)

World Federation for Mental Health. (2005). ADHD: The hope behind the hype (www.wfmh.org). (p. 373)

Wortham, J. (2010, May 13). Cellphones now used more for data than for calls. *New York Times* (www.nytimes.com). (p. 266)

Worthington, E. L., Jr. (1989). Religious faith across the life span: Implications for counseling and research. *The Counseling Psychologist, 17*, 555–612. (p. 87)

Worthington, E. L., Jr., Kurusu, T. A., McCullogh, M. E., & Sandage, S. J. (1996). Empirical research on religion and psychotherapeutic processes and outcomes: A 10-year review and research prospectus. *Psychological Bulletin, 119*, 448–487. (p. 424)

Wortman, C. B., & Silver, R. C. (1989). The myths of coping with loss. *Journal of Consulting and Clinical Psychology, 57*, 349–357. (p. 101)

Wren, C. S. (1999, April 8). Drug survey of children finds middle school a pivotal time. *New York Times* (www.nytimes.com). (p. 389)

Wrenn, J. M. (2012). NBA rookie Royce White battles anxiety disorder and fear of flying. CNN (www.cnn.com). (p. 377)

Wright, I. C., Rabe-Hesketh, S., Woodruff, P. W. R., David, A. S., Murray, R. M., & Bullmore, E. T. (2000). Meta-analysis of regional brain volumes in schizophrenia. *American Journal of Psychiatry, 157*, 16–25. (p. 398)

Wright, P., Takei, N., Rifkin, L., & Murray, R. M. (1995). Maternal influenza, obstetric complications, and schizophrenia. *American Journal of Psychiatry, 152*, 1714–1720. (p. 399)

Wright, P. H. (1989). Gender differences in adults' same- and cross-gender friendships. In R. G. Adams & R. Blieszner (Eds.), *Older adult friendships: Structure and process*. Newbury Park, CA: Sage. (p. 110)

Wrosch, C., & Miller, G. E. (2009). Depressive symptoms can be useful: Self-regulatory and emotional benefits of dysphoric mood in adolescence. *Journal of Personality and Social Psychology, 96*, 1181–1190. (p. 390)

Wrzesniewski, A., & Dutton, J. E. (2001). Crafting a job: Revisioning employees as active crafters of their work. *Academy of Management Review, 26*, 179–201. (p. B-1)

Wrzesniewski, A., McCauley, C. R., Rozin, P., & Schwartz, B. (1997). Jobs, careers, and callings: People's relations to their work. *Journal of Research in Personality, 31*, 21–33. (p. B-1)

Wuethrich, B. (2001, March). Getting stupid: Surprising new neurological behavioral research reveals that teenagers who drink too much may permanently damage their brains and seriously compromise their ability to learn. *Discover, 56*, 56–64. (p. 383)

Wulsin, L. R., Vaillant, G. E., & Wells, V. E. (1999). A systematic review of the mortality of depression. *Psychosomatic Medicine, 61*, 6–17. (p. 290)

Wyatt, J. K., & Bootzin, R. R. (1994). Cognitive processing and sleep: Implications for enhancing job performance. *Human Performance, 7*, 119–139. (p. 208)

Wynne, C. D. L. (2004). *Do animals think?* Princeton, NJ: Princeton University Press. (p. 234)

Wynne, C. D. L. (2008). Aping language: A skeptical analysis of the evidence for nonhuman primate language. *Skeptic, 13*(4), 10–13. (p. 234)

Xu, Y., & Corkin, S. (2001). H. M. revisits the Tower of Hanoi puzzle. *Neuropsychology, 15*, 69–79. (p. 206)

Yamagata, S., & 11 others. (2006). Is the genetic structure of human personality universal? A cross-cultural twin study from North America, Europe, and Asia. *Journal of Personality and Social Psychology, 90*, 987–998. (p. 324)

Yang, S., Markoczy, L., & Qi, M. (2006). Unrealistic optimism in consumer credit card adoption. *Journal of Economic Psychology, 28*, 170–185. (p. 294)

Yarkoni, T. (2010). Personality in 100,000 words: A large-scale analysis of personality and word use among bloggers. *Journal of Research in Personality, 44*, 363–373. (p. 324)

Yarnell, P. R., & Lynch, S. (1970, April 25). Retrograde memory immediately after concussion. *Lancet*, 863–865. (p. 202)

Yatham, L. N., Liddle, P. F., Lam, R. W., Zis, A. P., Stoessel, A. J., Sossi, V., Adam, M. J., & Ruth, T. J. (2010). Effect of electroconvulsive therapy on brain 5-HT2 receptors in major depression. *British Journal of Psychiatry, 196*, 474–479. (p. 427)

Ybarra, O. (1999). Misanthropic person memory when the need to self-enhance is absent. *Personality and Social Psychology Bulletin, 25*, 261–269. (p. 330)

YOU Magazine. (2009, September 10). Wow, look at Caster now! http://you.co.za/. (p. 112)

Young, S. G., Hugenberg, K., Bernstein, M. J., & Sacco, D. F. (2012). Perception and motivation in face recognition: A critical review of theories of the cross-race effect. *Personality and Social Psychology Review, 16*, 116–142. (p. 353)

Younger, J., Aron, A., Parke, S., Chatterjee, N., & Mackey, S. (2010). Viewing pictures of a romantic partner reduces experimental pain: Involvement of neural reward systems. *PLoS ONE 5*(10), e13309. doi:10.1371/journal.pone.0013309. (p. 266)

Zabin, L. S., Emerson, M. R., & Rowland, D. L. (2005). Child sexual abuse and early menarche: The direction of their relationship and its implications. *Journal of Adolescent Health, 36*, 393–400. (p. 111)

Zaccaro, S. J. (2007). Trait-based perspectives of leadership. *American Psychologist, 62*, 6–16. (p. B-6)

Zagorsky, J. L. (2007). Do you have to be smart to be rich? The impact of IQ on wealth, income and financial distress. *Intelligence, 35*, 489–501. (p. 238)

Zajonc, R. B. (1965). Social facilitation. *Science, 149*, 269–274. (p. 347)

Zajonc, R. B. (1980). Feeling and thinking: Preferences need no inferences. *American Psychologist, 35*, 151–175. (p. 270)

Zajonc, R. B. (1984). On the primacy of affect. *American Psychologist, 39*, 117–123. (p. 270)

Zajonc, R. B. (2001). Mere exposure: A gateway to the subliminal. *Current Directions in Psychological Science, 10*, 224–228. (p. 359)

Zajonc, R. B., & Markus, G. B. (1975). Birth order and intellectual development. *Psychological Review, 82*, 74–88. (p. A-8)

Zauberman, G., & Lynch, J. G., Jr. (2005). Resource slack and propensity to discount delayed investments of time versus money. *Journal of Experimental Psychology: General, 134*, 23–37. (p. 223)

Zeeuws, D., De Rycker, K., De Raedt, R., De Beyne, M., Baeken, C., Vanderbruggen, N. (2011). Intensive high-frequency repetitive transcranial magnetic stimulation treatment in an electroconvulsive shock therapy-resistant bipolar I patient with mixed episode. *Brain Stimulation, 4,* 46–49. (p. 429)

Zeidner, M. (1990). Perceptions of ethnic group modal intelligence: Reflections of cultural stereotypes or intelligence test scores? *Journal of Cross-Cultural Psychology, 21,* 214–231. (p. 248)

Zell, E., & Alicke, M. D. (2010). The local dominance effect in self-evaluation: Evidence and explanations. *Personality and Social Psychology Review, 14,* 368–384. (p. 304)

Zhong, C-B., & Leonardelli, G. J. (2008). Cold and lonely: Does social exclusion literally feel cold? *Psychological Science, 19,* 838–842. (pp. 161, 228)

Zilbergeld, B. (1983). *The shrinking of America: Myths of psychological change.* Boston: Little, Brown. (p. 420)

Zillmann, D. (1986). Effects of prolonged consumption of pornography. Background paper for *The surgeon general's workshop on pornography and public health,* June 22–24. Report prepared by E. P. Mulvey & J. L. Haugaard and released by Office of the Surgeon General on August 4, 1986. (p. 270)

Zillmann, D. (1989). Effects of prolonged consumption of pornography. In D. Zillmann & J. Bryant (Eds.), *Pornography: Research advances and policy considerations.* Hillsdale, NJ: Erlbaum. (pp. 118, 357)

Zillmann, D., & Bryant, J. (1984). Effects of massive exposure to pornography. In N. Malamuth & E. Donnerstein (Eds.), *Pornography and sexual aggression.* Orlando, FL: Academic Press. (p. 357)

Zimbardo, P. G. (1970). The human choice: Individuation, reason, and order versus deindividuation, impulse, and chaos. In W. J. Arnold & D. Levine (Eds.), *Nebraska Symposium on Motivation, 1969.* Lincoln, NE: University of Nebraska Press. (p. 348)

Zimbardo, P. G. (1972, April). Pathology of imprisonment. *Transaction/Society,* pp. 4–8. (p. 340)

Zimbardo, P. G. (2001, September 16). Fighting terrorism by understanding man's capacity for evil. Op-ed essay distributed by spsp-discuss@stolaf.edu. (p. 352)

Zimbardo, P. G. (2004, May 25). Journalist interview re: Abu Ghraib prison abuses: Eleven answers to eleven questions. Unpublished manuscript, Stanford University. (p. 340)

Zimbardo, P. G. (2007, September). Person x situation x system dynamics. *The Observer* (Association for Psychological Science), p. 43. (p. 340)

Zimmer-Gembeck, M. J., & Helfand, M. (2008). Ten years of longitudinal research on U.S. adolescent sexual behavior: Developmental correlates of sexual intercourse, and the importance of age, gender and ethnic background. *Developmental Review, 28,* 153–224. (p. 119)

Zogby, J. (2006, March). Survey of teens and adults about the use of personal electronic devices and headphones. *Zogby International.* (p. 153)

Zornberg, G. L., Buka, S. L., & Tsuang, M. T. (2000). At issue: The problem of obstetrical complications and schizophrenia. *Schizophrenia Bulletin, 26,* 249–256. (p. 399)

Zou, Z., & Buck, L. B. (2006, March). Combinatorial effects of odorant mixes in olfactory cortex. *Science, 311,* 1477-1481. (p. 158)

Zubieta, J-K., Heitzeg, M. M., Smith, Y. R., Bueller, J. A., Xu, K., Xu, Y., Koeppe, R. A., Stohler, C. S., & Goldman, D. (2003). COMT val158met genotype affects μ-opioid neurotransmitter responses to a pain stressor. *Science, 299,* 1240–1243. (p. 155)

Zucker, G. S., & Weiner, B. (1993). Conservatism and perceptions of poverty: An attributional analysis. *Journal of Applied Social Psychology, 23,* 925–943. (p. 339)

Zuckerman, M. (1979). *Sensation seeking: Beyond the optimal level of arousal.* Hillsdale, NJ: Erlbaum. (p. 256)

Zvolensky, M. J., & Bernstein, A. (2005). Cigarette smoking and panic psychopathology. *Current Directions in Psychological Science, 14,* 301–305. (p. 377)

Name Index

Subject Index

(continued from inside front cover)

How Does Psychology Apply to YOUR Everyday Life? Why are smells so closely associated with important memories? (pp. 158–159) Why is it that social exclusion may literally feel cold, and physical warmth (as in holding a coffee cup) may promote social warmth? (pp. 160–161) How long does it take to learn a good habit? (p. 168) How could you use operant conditioning principles to shape new behaviors in your pet (or partner)? (pp. 167, 174–175) How can you use operant conditioning techniques to make a change, such as stopping smoking, eating less, or studying or exercising more? (p. 181) What is the relationship between viewing media violence and violent behavior? (p. 188) How is our memory affected by the context or mental state we're in? (pp. 204–205) What causes us to forget? (pp. 207–209) What causes those frustrating tip of the tongue memory problems? (p. 208) Why is it so hard to recognize false memories? (pp. 211–212) What are some specific tips for improving your memory in your studies? (p. 214) How do social and emotional intelligence affect success in career, marriage, and parenting roles? (p. 238)

How can those memorable exceptions (the uncle who smoked two packs a day and lived to be 89) mislead us? (p. 14) ◉ How can you use the *testing effect* to improve retention and get better grades? (pp. 23-25) ◉ How could a brain tumor cause a person to become a child molester? (p. 29) ◉ Why do we find kissing so pleasurable? (p. 45) ◉ How can music therapy, sleep, exercise, and stimulating environments help the brain repair itself? (p. 47) ◉ How does sleep affect memory? mood? weight gain? (pp. 57-58) ◉ How can we get a better night's sleep? (p. 59) ◉ What and why do we dream? (pp. 60-62) ◉ Why can't we remember anything from those first few years of life? (p. 75) ◉ Do our early attachments form the foundation for adult relationships? (p. 83) ◉ What are the long-term effects of attachment deprivation and of abuse? (pp. 83-84) ◉ How do parenting-style differences affect children? (p. 84) ◉ What is the effect of living together before marriage on divorce risk later? (p. 98) ◉ How does viewing pornography affect men's attitude toward women, including their own partners? (p. 118)